Frommer's®

Florida

SO-AAZ-782

Here's what the critics say about Frommer's:

"The best series for travelers who want one easy-to-use guidebook."

—*U.S. Air Magazine*

♦

"Amazingly easy to use. Very portable, very complete."

—*Booklist*

♦

"The only mainstream guide to list specific prices. The Walter Cronkite of guidebooks—with all that implies."

—*Travel & Leisure*

♦

"Complete, concise, and filled with useful information."

—*New York Daily News*

Other Great Guides for Your Trip:

Frommer's Florida from $60 a Day

Frommer's Walt Disney World & Orlando

The Unofficial Guide to Walt Disney World

The Unofficial Disney Companion

The Complete Idiot's Travel Guide to Walt Disney World & Orlando

Mini Mickey
(The Pocket-Sized Unofficial Guide to Walt Disney World)

Frommer's Best Driving Tours in Florida

Frommer's Miami & The Keys

Frommer's Irreverent Guide to Miami

The Unofficial Guide to Miami & The Keys

Frommer's Portable Guide to Tampa & St. Petersburg

Frommer's®

Florida

by Bill Goodwin, Victoria Pesce Elliott
& Mary Meehan

MACMILLAN • USA

ABOUT THE AUTHORS

Bill Goodwin began his career as an award-winning newspaper reporter before becoming legal counsel and speechwriter for two U.S. senators. Now based in Virginia, he is also the author of *Frommer's South Pacific* and *Frommer's Virginia,* and he compiles and edits *Frommer's USA.*

Victoria Pesce Elliott is a freelance jounalist and native of Miami. She returned there after nearly a decade in New York City, where she graduated from Barnard College and the Columbia Graduate School of Journalism. She is also the author of *Frommer's Miami & the Keys.*

From opening day at Universal Studios to that first plunge down the Tower of Terror, **Mary Meehan** has an insider's view of the best things to see and do in Central Florida. She is an Orlando-based writer whose work has appeared in regional and national publications.

MACMILLAN TRAVEL

A Simon & Schuster Macmillan Company
1633 Broadway
New York, NY 10019

Find us online at **www.frommers.com**

ISBN 0-02862255-3
ISSN 1044-2391

Editor: Bob O'Sullivan
Production Editor: Kristi Hart
Design by Michele Laseau
Digital Cartography by Peter Bogaty, John DeCamillis and Ortelius Design

SPECIAL SALES

Bulk purchases (10+ copies) of Frommer's and selected Macmillan travel guides are available to corporations, organizations, mail-order catalogs, institutions, and charities at special discounts, and can be customized to suit individual needs. For more information write to Special Sales, Macmillan General Reference, 1633 Broadway, New York, NY 10019.

Contents

13 Northwest Florida: The Panhandle 526

by Bill Goodwin

14 Northeast Florida 592

by Bill Goodwin

Index 648

List of Maps

AN INVITATION TO THE READER

In researching this book, we discovered many wonderful places—hotels, restaurants, shops, and more. We're sure you'll find others. Please tell us about them, so we can share the information with your fellow travelers in upcoming editions. If you were disappointed with a recommendation, we'd love to know that, too. Please write to:

Frommer's Florida
Macmillan Travel
1633 Broadway
New York, NY 10019

AN ADDITIONAL NOTE

Please be advised that travel information is subject to change at any time—and this is especially true of prices. We therefore suggest that you write or call ahead for confirmation when making your travel plans. The authors, editors, and publisher cannot be held responsible for the experiences of readers while traveling. Your safety is important to us, however, so we encourage you to stay alert and be aware of your surroundings. Keep a close eye on cameras, purses, and wallets, all favorite targets of thieves and pickpockets.

WHAT THE SYMBOLS MEAN

✪ Frommer's Favorites

Our favorite places and experiences—outstanding for quality, value, or both.

The following abbreviations are used for credit cards:

AE American Express	EURO EuroCard
CB Carte Blanche	JCB Japan Credit Bank
DC Diners Club	MC MasterCard
DISC Discover	V Visa

FIND FROMMER'S ONLINE

Arthur Frommer's Outspoken Encyclopedia of Travel (www.frommers.com) offers more than 6,000 pages of up-to-the-minute travel information—including the latest bargains and candid, personal articles updated daily by Arthur Frommer himself. No other Web site offers such comprehensive and timely coverage of the world of travel.

The Best of Florida

Every year, millions of visitors escape bleak northern winters to bask in Florida's warmth, lured to the Sunshine State by the promise of clear skies and 800 miles of spectacular sandy beaches. A host of kid-pleasers, from Busch Gardens to Walt Disney World, make this the country's most popular year-round family vacation destination.

Here you can choose from a wide array of accommodations, from deluxe resorts to mom-and-pop motels. You can visit remote little towns like Apalachicola or a megalopolis like Miami. Devour fresh seafood, from amberjack to oysters—and work off those calories in such outdoor pursuits as bicycling, golf, or kayaking. Despite over-development in many parts of the state, Floridians have maintained thousands of acres of wilderness areas, from the little respite of Clam Pass County Park in downtown Naples to the magnificent Everglades National Park, which stretches across the state's southern tip.

Choosing the "best" of all this is a daunting task, and the selections in this chapter are only a rundown on some of the highlights. You'll find numerous other outstanding resorts, hotels, destinations, activities, and attractions—all described in the pages of this book. With a bit of serendipity you'll come up with some bests of your own.

1 The Best Beaches

- **Bill Baggs Cape Florida State Recreation Area** (Key Biscayne): At the very tip of Key Biscayne, this secluded bend of beach juts out into the Atlantic Ocean, surrounded by sand dunes, sea oats, towering palms, and palmettos. Its centerpiece is a recently restored lighthouse and small museum. Next door is an outfit that rents boating equipment and lounge chairs. And, in the newly built Lighthouse Cafe (El Farito), you get good, cheap Cuban specialties. See chapter 5.
- **Crandon Park Beach** (Key Biscayne): A well-equipped, active beach, Crandon Park has 3 miles of oceanfront and nearly 500 acres of grassy grounds that sport barbecue grills, soccer and softball fields, and a public 18-hole championship golf course. Families and young soccer players scatter throughout the area on weekends, while more relaxed visitors walk along nature trails and take in the view of Miami Beach across Biscayne Bay. See chapter 5.
- **Lummus Park Beach** (South Beach, Miami): This *is* South Beach. Against the backdrop of Ocean Drive's fanciful art deco buildings

and bustling cafe scene is a wide beach crowded with the beautiful people. See chapter 5.

- **Sebastian Inlet** (North Hutchinson Island): At the tip of North Hutchinson Island, Sebastian Inlet is the beach where surfers find the biggest swells. Nonsurfers will come for the flat sandy beaches and miles of shaded walkways; facilities include kayak, paddleboat, and canoe rentals; picnic tables; and a snack shop. See chapter 9.

- **Cayo Costa State Park** (off Captiva Island): These days, deserted tropical islands with great beaches are scarce in Florida, but this 2,132-acre barrier strip of sand, pine forests, mangrove swamps, oak hammocks, and grasslands provides a genuine get-away-from-it-all experience. The only nonnative residents are wild pigs and a lone park ranger; access is only by boat from nearby Gasparilla, Pine, and Captiva islands. See chapter 10.

- **Clam Pass County Park** (Naples): Although Clam Pass sits in a developed part of Naples, a free tram takes you along a 3,000-foot boardwalk winding through mangrove swamps and across a back bay to this fine white-sand beach. It's a strange sight, what with high-rise condos standing beyond the mangrove-bordered backwaters, but this miniature wilderness actually boasts some 6 miles of canoe and kayak trails, a multitude of birds, and the occasional alligator. See chapter 10.

- **Naples Beach** (Naples): Many Florida cities and towns have beaches, but few are as lovely as the gorgeous strip that runs in front of Naples's famous Millionaires' Row. You don't have to be rich to wander its length, peer at the mansions, and stroll on historic Naples Pier to catch a sunset over the gulf. See chapter 10.

- **Caladesi Island State Park** (Clearwater): Even though it's in the heavily developed Tampa Bay area, 3½-mile Caladesi Island has a lovely, relatively secluded beach with soft sand edged in sea grass and palmettos. Dolphins cavort in offshore waters. In the park itself, there's a nature trail, and you might see one of the rattlesnakes, black racers, raccoons, armadillos, or rabbits that live here. The park is accessible only by ferry from Honeymoon Island State Recreation Area off Dunedin. See chapter 11.

- **Fort Desoto Park** (St. Pete Beach): At the very mouth of Tampa Bay, this group of five connected barrier islands is a 900-acre bird, animal, and plant sanctuary. Watch dolphins play in the gulf off of one of the nation's best white-sand beaches, and there's a Spanish-American War–era fort, fishing piers, a large playground for kids, and trails for in-line skaters, bicyclists, and joggers. See chapter 11.

- **Typhoon Lagoon** (Orlando): All the benefits of the beach, without the travel to the coast. Located within Walt Disney World, it lacks the natural beauty of the real thing, but Typhoon Lagoon is certainly the best beach in landlocked Orlando. Besides, what other beach offers a water slide, as well as a 50-foot geyser that goes off every 30 minutes? See chapter 12.

- **Gulf Islands National Seashore** (Pensacola): You could argue that all of Northwest Florida's gulf shore is one of America's great beaches—an almost uninterrupted stretch of pure white sand that runs the entire length of the Panhandle, from Perdido Key to St. George Island. The Gulf Islands National Seashore preserves much of this natural wonder in its undeveloped state. Countless terns, snowy plover, black skimmers, and other birds nest along the dunes topped with sea oats. East of the national seashore and equally as beautiful are Grayton Beach State Recreation Area near Destin, and St. Joseph Peninsula and St. George Island state parks near Apalachicola. See chapter 13.

- **St. Andrews State Recreation Area** (Panama City Beach): With more than 1,000 acres of dazzling white sand and dunes, this preserved wilderness demonstrates what Panama City Beach looked like before motels and condominiums lined its shore.

Lacy, golden sea oats sway in gulf breezes, and fragrant rosemary grows wild. The area is home to foxes, coyotes, and a herd of deer. See chapter 13.

- **Canaveral National Seashore** (Cape Canaveral): Midway between the crowded attractions at Daytona Beach and the Kennedy Space Center is a protected stretch of coastline 24 miles long, backed by cabbage palms, sea grapes, and palmettos. Their neighbor is the 140,000-acre Merritt Island National Wildlife Refuge, home to hundreds of Florida birds, reptiles, alligators, and mammals. Wooden boardwalks lead from a free parking lot to the huge expanse of soft brown sand and a few well-spaced picnic tables. See chapter 14.

- **Main Street Pier** (Daytona Beach): This city is known for its cars—and the traffic doesn't just cruise on roads and speedways. For a small fee, you can drive directly on the wide 500-foot beaches. The beach at the Main Street Pier is the hub of local activity, putting you close to concessions, a boardwalk, and a small amusement park. It's popular with families and also with bikers and surfers. See chapter 14.

- **Jacksonville Beach** (Jacksonville): You can fish, snorkel, sail, surf, sunbathe, or stroll on Jacksonville Beach, a lively stretch of sand and dunes with nearby concessions, rental shops, a fishing pier, and further north—toward Atlantic Beach—busy nightlife and excellent restaurants. See chapter 14.

- **Fort Clinch State Park** (Amelia Island): One of the best and most remote in the state, this gray-sand beach is wide and deserted. Boardwalks lead from the parking area through lush dunes to the beach. A jetty and a pier at its north end are popular with fishermen. See chapter 14.

2 The Best Snorkeling

- **John Pennekamp Coral Reef State Park** (Key Largo): This 188-square-mile park is the nation's first undersea preserve, established to protect the only living coral reef in the continental United States. The water throughout much of the park is shallow, so it's an especially great place for snorkelers to see tree-sized elkhorn coral, giant brain coral, colorful sea fans, hundreds of rainbow-colored fish, and a sunken statue, Christ of the Deep. See chapter 6.

- **Looe Key National Marine Sanctuary** (off Big Pine Key): Voted the number one dive spot in North America by *Skin Diver* magazine, Looe Key has some of the most beautiful underwater scenery in the country, including more than 150 varieties of hard and soft coral—some centuries old. Nearly every type of tropical fish, including the gold and blue parrot fish, moray eels, barracudas, French angels, and tarpon, calls this dense and diverse reef home. See chapter 6.

3 The Best Fishing

- **Dry Tortugas:** These waters off Key West can be rough in winter, but fishing is excellent year-round. Good "eating fish" like snapper and grouper are plentiful, as are other boaters looking to get a big catch. See chapter 6.

- **The Keys:** The Keys boast some world-class deep-sea fishing; the prize is such big-game fish as marlin, sailfish, and tuna. There's reef fishing as well, for "eating fish" like snapper and grouper, and backcountry fishing for bonefish, tarpon, and other "stalking" fish.

Dozens of charter-fishing boats operate from Key West marinas and less-popular Keys. Islamorada, in the Upper Keys, is the sportfishing capital of the world. Anglers, including former President Bush, compete for trophy sailfish, marlin, wahoo, and kingfish at many annual big-money tournaments. Seven-Mile Bridge, linking the Middle and Lower Keys, is known as "the longest fishing bridge in the world"; it's a favorite spot for local fishers who wait for barracuda, yellowtail, and dolphin to bite. See chapter 6.

- **Lake Okeechobee:** The second-largest freshwater lake in the country, Okeechobee covers nearly half a million acres and claims to be the "Speckled Perch Capital of the World." It's also famous for its largemouth bass and bream. Fishing tournaments go on year-round. See chapter 9.
- **Stuart:** Known as the "Sailfish Capital of the World," Stuart is an angler's haven. They bite all year, but peak months are December through March and June and July. Sailfishing is an art of its own—beginners need to learn to feel that exact moment to let the reel drag so the fish run with the lure. See chapter 9.
- **Boca Grande:** The deep, shadowy holes of Boca Grande Pass, between Gasparilla and Cayo Costa islands off Fort Myers, harbor the mighty tarpon, the "silver king of the seas." Teddy Roosevelt and his rich buddies used to bag tarpon in these waters, and anglers from around the globe still compete every July in the World's Richest Tarpon Tournament. See chapter 10.
- **Fort Myers Beach:** Another town with a large fishing and shrimping fleet, Fort Myers Beach is known for its large number of party boats that take groups out on the gulf. You'll have company, but the rates are reasonable, they supply the gear and bait, and you don't have to bother with a fishing license. See chapter 10.
- **Disney's Grand Floridian Beach Resort:** This grand resort offers fishing excursions that prove the Disney magic extends to catching bass. Many of the Disney parks and resorts are buffeted by lakes and connected by canals. Reel in the big ones on these artificial waterways. See chapter 12.
- **Destin:** Florida's largest charter-boat fleet, with more than 140 vessels, is based in this Panhandle town, the "World's Luckiest Fishing Village." They've landed championship catches of grouper, amberjack, snapper, mackerel, cobia, sailfish, wahoo, tuna, and blue marlin. See chapter 13.

4 The Best Golf Courses

- **Biltmore Hotel** (Miami): This rolling 18-hole course on the grounds of Miami's most historic and elegant resort was designed by Donald Ross and renovated in 1992. Despite the fancy Coral Gables backdrop, this course is open to the public and is popular with the likes of President Clinton and other world figures. See chapter 4.
- **Doral Golf Resort and Spa:** There are four championship courses here, including the famous Blue Monster, which is the site of the annual Doral-Ryder Open. The Gold Course, recently restored by golf great Raymond Floyd, has water on every hole. See chapter 4.
- **Turnberry Isle Resort and Club** (Aventura, North Miami): Unfortunately, these two Robert Trent Jones championship courses are open only to resort guests. If you like a serious challenge and want to enjoy a host of other amenities, this is a worthwhile destination. See chapter 4.
- **Crandon Park Golf Course** (Key Biscayne): Formerly known as the Links of Key Biscayne, this stunning and famous course is a stop on the Senior Men's PGA Tour. Located on a posh residential island, it's one of the few courses remaining in South Florida not surrounded by development. Golfers enjoy pristine vistas of hammocks and stretches of water, with a glimpse of Miami's dramatic skyline to the north. See chapter 5.

- **Emerald Dunes Golf Course** (West Palm Beach): This beautiful Tom Fazio championship course features 60 acres of water, including a waterfall, and great views of the Atlantic. It's pricey, but it is one of the only great courses open to the public in this area of ritzy resorts. See chapter 8.

- **PGA National Resort & Spa** (Palm Beach Gardens): The headquarters of the Professional Golfers Association of America, PGA National is the granddaddy of Florida golf venues. The five tournament courses were designed by George and Tom Fazio, Arnold Palmer, and Karl Litten. The Fazio-designed Champion was redesigned by Jack Nicklaus in 1990; his 15th, 16th, and 17th holes are called "The Bear Trap" to honor their 1992 induction into the "Ten Toughest Holes on the Seniors Tour." See chapter 8.

- **Mangrove Bay Golf Course** (St. Petersburg): One of the nation's top 50 municipal courses, the Mangrove Bay course hugs the inlets of Old Tampa Bay and offers 18-hole, par-72 play. Facilities include a driving range; lessons and golf-club rental are also available. See chapter 11.

- **The Westin Innisbrook Resort** (Tarpon Springs): *Golfweek* has called Innisbrook's Copperhead Course, home of the annual JC Penney Classic, number one in Florida. One thousand students a year go through Innisbrook's Golf Institute, and golfers from around the world come to play the 600 acres of courses. Saturday morning youth clinics are complimentary. See chapter 11.

- **Saddlebrook Resort** (Wesley Chapel): Northeast of Tampa, this is world headquarters of the Arnold Palmer Golf Academy, with a five-to-one student/teacher ratio and two fine Palmer courses. It's one of Florida's top golf schools for teens. See chapter 11.

- **Bay Hill** (Orlando): Among the famous local courses is the legendary Arnold Palmer's Bay Hill Club, site of the Bay Hill Invitational. Its 18th hole, nicknamed the Devil's Bathtub, is supposed to be the toughest par-4 on the PGA tour. Open to the public. See chapter 12.

- **Hyatt Regency Grand Cypress Resort** (Orlando): Dedicated duffers will find the cost of staying at this luxury hotel worth a shot at playing on this renowned course. The 45-hole, par-72 course was designed by the Golden Bear, Jack Nicklaus, and is for guests and their guests only. The Hyatt also features a 9-hole pitch-and-putt course. See chapter 12.

- **Walt Disney World Resorts** (Orlando): Stride the same greens as some of the country's top PGA tour players at this home of the Walt Disney World Oldsmobile Golf Classic. Three courses designed by Joe Lee host the PGA players in October. The rest of the year, even amateurs whose game is not up to par can get into the swing of things. Day rates are available for those not staying in Disney hotels. See chapter 12.

- **Marriott's Bay Point Resort Village** (Panama City Beach): Thirty-six holes of championship golf at this Marriott include the Lagoon Legends course, one of the country's most difficult. Nearby is The Hombre, an 18-holer where O. J. Simpson played a round right after his acquittal. See chapter 13.

- **Hilaman Park Municipal Golf Course** (Tallahassee): Another outstanding municipal course, Hilaman Park has 18 rolling, par-72 holes, a driving range, racquetball, squash courts, and a swimming pool. The park also includes the Jake Gaither Municipal Golf Course, with a 9-hole, par-35 fairway, and a pro shop. Compared to the greens fees at most Florida courses, these are a steal. See chapter 13.

- **Ladies Professional Golf Association/LPGA** (Daytona Beach): This "women-friendly" course has multiple tee settings, unrestricted tee times, a great pro shop, and state-of-the-art facilities. Designed by Rees-Jones, the older of the two courses here was chosen as one of the "Top Ten You Can Play" by *Golf Magazine* and number one of "America's Most Women-Friendly Courses" by *Golf for Women*. See chapter 14.

- **Marriott at Sawgrass Resort** (Ponte Vedra Beach, near Jacksonville): With 99 holes, there's something for the scratch golfer as well as the weekend duffer. *Money* magazine has called it the number one golf-resort value in America. Pete Dye's TPC Stadium Course makes top-10 lists everywhere. The 17th hole, on a tricky island, is one of the most photographed holes in the world. See chapter 14.

- **Amelia Island Plantation** (Amelia Island): This exclusive resort has two of the state's best courses. Long Point Club, designed by Tom Fazio, is the most beautiful and challenging (27 holes). Pete Dye's Amelia Links (18 holes) is another ocean-front course. Both are open only to resort guests. See chapter 14.

5 The Best Bird Watching

- **Dry Tortugas** (about 70 miles west of Key West): Fort Jefferson offers extra-ordinary views of migratory birds of all types. Spring and fall are the best times for viewing. See chapter 6.

- **The Lower Keys:** A stopping point for migratory birds on the eastern flyway, the Lower Keys are populated with many West Indian bird species, especially during spring and fall. The small vegetated islands of the Keys are the only nesting sites in the United States for the great white heron and the white-crowned pigeon. The entire gulf side of the lower half of the Keys is designated the Great White Heron National Refuge. See chapter 6.

- **Everglades National Park:** More than 350 species of birds make their homes in the Everglades. Tropical birds from the Caribbean and temperate species from North America can be found here, along with exotics that have blown in from more dis-tant regions. The park service hands out free checklists to keep track of them. Adja-cent Big Cypress National Preserve offers close-up views of great blue herons, snowy egrets, and white pelicans, among others. See chapter 7.

- **Jonathan Dickinson State Park** (Hobe Sound): This huge, low-maintenance park is a great spot to see ospreys, woodpeckers, ibises, herons, anhingas, egrets, and even some bald eagles. See chapter 9.

- **J. N. (Ding) Darling National Wildlife Refuge** (Sanibel Island): Preserving most of the mangrove forests and winding waterways on Sanibel Island's north side, this famous 5,000-acre refuge is rich in such barrier-island wildlife as roseate spoonbill, osprey, shorebirds, white pelican, ducks, loon, and mangrove cuckoo. Visitors can hike, bike, or canoe on their own or be escorted by experts such as former Sanibel Mayor Mark "Bird" Westall. See chapter 10.

- **Cayo Costa Island** (off Captiva Island): A huge variety of sea- and shorebirds con-gregate on this state preserve, which encompasses one of the northernmost of Southwest Florida's Ten Thousand Islands. This uninhabited island is only acces-sible via boat. See chapter 10.

- **Corkscrew Swamp Sanctuary** (Naples): Maintained by the National Audubon Society, this 11,000-acre bald cypress wilderness is a favorite wood-stork nesting ground. It's also home to herons, bald eagles, and a host of other birds and wildlife, plus ferns and colorful orchids. Some of North America's oldest trees are here. See chapter 10.

- **St. George Island State Park** (Apalachicola): Countless terns, snowy plovers, black skimmers, and other birds nest along the dunes and 9 miles of beaches in a state park on this island's eastern end. You'll see wildlife from a hiking trail and an observation platform. See chapter 13.

- **St. Marks National Wildlife Refuge** (Tallahassee): On the gulf due south of Tallahassee, this 65,000-acre preserve is home to more species of birds than anyplace else in Florida except the Everglades. Built of limestone blocks 4 feet thick at the base, the 80-foot-tall St. Marks Lighthouse has marked the harbor entrance since 1842. The nearby Apalachicola National Forest is another good spot. See chapter 13.

6 The Best Canoeing

- **Everglades National Park:** Within the millions of acres of federally protected lands, canoers will see manatee, dolphin, the endangered key deer, alligators, reptiles, and hundreds of species of birds. To the north are the Big Cypress National Preserve and the Big Cypress Swamp. Based in Everglades City, near the park's western entrance, North American Canoe Tours (☎ **941/695-4666** from November to April, or 860/739-0791 May to October) will furnish canoes, camping equipment, and a personal guide; they even conduct fully outfitted tours. See chapter 7.
- **Jonathan Dickinson State Park** (Hobe Sound): You can rent a canoe and explore a scenic route that winds through a variety of botanical habitats. You may see a gator, a variety of reptiles, and even an occasional manatee. See chapter 9.
- **J. N. (Ding) Darling National Wildlife Refuge** (Sanibel Island): The winding waterways here are great for both canoeing and kayaking. The refuge's concessionaire, Tarpon Bay Recreation (☎ **941/472-8900**) has guided canoe and kayak trips, as does Mark "Bird" Westall (☎ **941/472-5218**), a naturalist, avid conservationist, and former Sanibel Island mayor. See chapter 10.
- **Briggs Nature Center** (Marco Island): Operated by The Conservancy and part of the Rookery Bay National Estuarine Research Reserve, this refuge is a pristine example of Florida's disappearing scrublands, home to the threatened scrub jays and gopher tortoises. There's a self-guided canoe trail and canoes for rent during winter. You can also canoe through The Conservancy's smaller Naples Nature Center in Naples. See chapter 10.
- **Blackwater River State Park** (Milton, near Pensacola): The little town of Milton is the official "Canoe Capital of Florida" (by act of the state legislature, no less). It's a well-earned title, for the nearby Blackwater River, Coldwater River, Sweetwater Creek, and Juniper Creek are all perfect for canoeing, kayaking, tubing, rafting, and paddleboating. The Blackwater is considered one of the world's purest sand-bottom rivers and has retained its primordial, backwoods beauty. See chapter 13.

7 The Best Family Attractions

- **Miami Metrozoo** (Miami): This completely cageless zoo offers such star attractions as a monorail "safari" and a petting zoo. Kids love the elephant rides. See chapter 5.
- **Miami Seaquarium** (Key Biscayne, Miami): Trained dolphins, killer whales, and frolicking sea lions are on display in this Old Florida animal park that's been popular with locals and tourists for nearly 50 years. See chapter 5.
- **Edison and Ford Winter Estates** (Fort Myers): Inventor Thomas Alva Edison and his friend, automobile magnate Henry Ford, built side-by-side winter homes on the banks of the Caloosahatchee River in Fort Myers. Today these Victorian cottages serve as memorials to the two men, and especially to Edison. The museum will

show the kids how we got the lightbulb, the phonograph, and hundreds of other Edison inventions. See chapter 10.

- **Teddy Bear Museum** (Naples): More than 3,000 examples of stuffed teddy bears from around the world are cleverly displayed descending from the rafters in hot-air balloons, attending board meetings, sipping afternoon tea, celebrating a wedding, reading in the "Li-bear-y," even doing bear things like hibernating. Kids can even buy their own bear to take home. See chapter 10.

- **Busch Gardens Tampa Bay** (Tampa): Although the thrill rides, live entertainment, shops, restaurants, and games get most of the ink at this 335-acre family theme park, Busch Gardens ranks among the top zoos in the country, with several thousand animals living in naturalistic environments. If you can get them off the roller coasters, the kids can find out what all those wild beasts they've seen on the Discovery Channel look like in person. See chapter 11.

- **Museum of Science and Industry (MOSI)** (Tampa): One of the largest educational science centers in the Southeast, MOSI has more than 450 interactive exhibits in which the kids can experience hurricane-force winds, defy the laws of gravity, cruise the mysterious world of microbes, explore the human body, and much more. They can also watch stunning movies in MOSIMAX, Florida's first IMAX dome theater. See chapter 11.

- **Orlando Science Center** (Orlando): Lift a Volkswagen to understand how pulleys work, gaze at the stars, or explore the everyday uses of math in this hands-on interactive center. A $44 million expansion completed in 1997 made the Orlando Science Center the largest center of its kind in the Southeast. Fun for inquisitive kids of all ages. Families can easily spend most of a day touring the 10 exhibit halls. See chapter 12.

- **RainForest Cafe** (Orlando): With an (almost) equal mixture of entertainment and education, the RainForest Cafe, with its indoor menagerie and wild decor, is a place where monkey business is encouraged. Located at the Disney Village Marketplace just outside Walt Disney World in Orlando, it's a themed respite from the real jungle of the theme parks. See chapter 12.

- **Universal Studios Florida** (Orlando): The "other" Orlando theme park takes itself a bit less seriously than Mickey & Co. Rides dazzle with special effects inspired by familiar Hollywood blockbusters—*Jaws, E.T.,* and *King Kong,* to name just a few— and what budding Olivier wouldn't love to be discovered during an honest-to-goodness screen test? Kids can tour the Nickelodeon studios, where, if caught unawares, they could end up getting "slimed." See chapter 12.

- **Walt Disney World, Epcot Center, and MGM Studios** (Orlando): The granddaddies of 'em all. It's all here—the lifelike animation, the rides both thrilling and hokey, and yes, that song you'll *never* get out of your head ("It's a Small World"). But look past the polished Disney image and you may be surprised—by the quiet grandeur of Epcot's Temple of Heaven, in the China pavilion, for example, or the sly humor lurking in the Magic Kingdom's Haunted Mansion. So expect a crowd, take the little ones to meet Mickey, Donald, and the gang, and make sure you ride scary Space Mountain at least once. See chapter 12.

- **Medieval Times** (Kissimmee): A longtime favorite for Orlando visitors, the Kissimmee-based show is billed as "dinner and tournament." Jousting contests, armored clashes, and 80 Andalusian stallions performing with military precision are just some of the performances on display. It's all put on for you and 1,000 of the "special" guests of the castle, who eat off heavy metal plates while watching the tournament contestants tumble about before them. The food is so-so, but it's fabulous family fun. See chapter 12.

- **ZooWorld Zoological & Botanical Park** (Panama City Beach): "Mr. Bubba," the largest captive alligator in Florida, lives in a re-created pine forest habitat at this educational and entertaining zoo, an active participant in the Species Survival Plan, which helps protect endangered species with specific breeding and housing programs. Other guests include rare and endangered animals as well as orangutans and other primates, big cats, and more reptiles. Also included are a walk-through aviary, a bat exhibit, and a petting zoo. See chapter 13.
- **Kennedy Space Center** (Cape Canaveral): There is plenty to keep kids and parents busy for at least a full day at the nation's spaceport, including interactive computer games, IMAX films, dozens of informative displays on the space program, and multitudes of real rockets. Try to schedule a visit during the dozen or so launches each year. See chapter 14.
- **Daytona USA** (Daytona Beach): Opened in late 1996 on Daytona International Speedway grounds, this huge state-of-the-art interactive attraction is an exciting and fast-paced stop even for nonrace fans. Kids can see real stock cars, go-carts, and motorcycles, and even participate in a pit stop on a NASCAR Winston Cup race car. See chapter 14.

8 The Best Offbeat Travel Experiences

- **Sleeping Beneath the Seas at Jules' Undersea Lodge** (Key Largo): Ever spend the night under water? Well, this has to be the most unusual accommodation in the state. This single-room hotel offers a comfortable suite 30 feet down and is especially popular with hard-core diving honeymooners. See chapter 6.
- **Swimming with the Dolphins at the Dolphin Research Center** (Marathon): Of the four such centers in the continental United States, the Dolphin Research Center is the most organized and informative. With advanced reservations you can swim and play with dolphins in their natural lagoon homes. There is no better way to get a feel for Florida's smartest and most loved animal. See chapter 6.
- **Houseboating** (Everglades National Park): Cruising the shallow waterways of the Everglades on your own is an exciting way to explore the region by day and by night. Available through the **Flamingo Lodge** (☎ **800/600-3813** or 941/695-3101), these spacious motorized houseboats let you get lost for days (or just overnight). You'll fall asleep to the sounds of frogs, crickets, and the lapping waves. See chapter 7.
- **Babcock Wilderness Adventures** (Fort Myers): Experienced naturalists lead "swamp buggy" tours through the Babcock Ranch, including the mysterious Telegraph Swamp where alligators lounge in the sun. Although the Babcock Ranch is the largest cattle operation east of the Mississippi (with bison and quarter horses, too), it is a major wildlife preserve inhabited by countless birds and other creatures. See chapter 10.
- **Swimming with the Manatees** (Homosassa Springs, north of Clearwater): Some 300 manatees spend the winter in the Crystal River, and you can swim, snorkel, or scuba with them in the warm-water natural spring of Kings Bay, about 7 miles north of Homosassa Springs. It's not uncommon to be surrounded in the 72-degree water by 30 to 40 "sea cows," which nudge and caress you as you swim with them. See chapter 11.
- **Disney Weddings** (Orlando): Divorce court notwithstanding, this is a once-in-a-lifetime trip. Thousands of people every year forgo Elvis and Vegas in favor of Mickey and Disney, tying the knot on Disney's not-quite-hallowed ground. A special Disney department handles all arrangements; special honeymoon vacation

packages are offered. From rented coachmen to topiaries in the shape of Pluto, you're limited only by your imagination and budget. They'll serve up whatever Disney reference or character you desire, even if it is Goofy. See chapter 12.

- **Sea World—Swim with the Dolphins** (Orlando): If you long to frolic with Flipper, Sea World Orlando offers a chance to get up close and personal with a porpoise. Of course, it's not cheap—a couple of hundred dollars. Limited to a few folks each day, visitors climb into the water and interact under the watchful eye of the Sea World trainers. See chapter 12.
- **Learning to Surf the Big Curls at Cocoa Beach Surfing School** (Cocoa Beach): Even if you don't know how to hang 10, this school will get you riding the waves with the best of them. They offer all equipment and lessons for beginners or pros at these world-famous beaches. See chapter 14.

9 The Best Small Towns

- **Boca Grande** (Southwest Florida): Founded in the 1880s by the du Pont family, this little village on Gasparilla Island retains the flavor of those Victorian times. Luxurious mansions coexist with simple homes of fishers who guide the rich folks in search of tarpon just as their ancestors did a century ago. The du Ponts, Mellons, and Astors once arrived for wintertime's "social season" at the town's railway depot, which has been restored and now houses shops and the Loose Caboose Restaurant and Ice Cream Parlor. See chapter 10.
- **Olde Naples** (Naples): Despite being founded as a real-estate development in 1886, the original part of Naples retains much of Old Florida's charm, with tree-lined streets dividing many of the original clapboard homes. With the houses on Millionaires' Row virtually hidden by dense foliage and no high-rises in sight, Naples Beach seems far removed from today's modern city. See chapter 10.
- **Tarpon Springs** (Tampa Bay Area): Tarpon Springs calls itself the "Sponge Capital of the World" because immigrants from Greece settled here in the late 1800s to harvest the sponges that grew in abundance offshore. Their descendants make Tarpon Springs a fascinating center of transplanted Greek culture. Sponges still arrive at the historic Sponge Docks, where a lively, carnival-like atmosphere and Greek cuisine prevail. Restored Victorian homes facing Spring Bayou also make this one of the most picturesque towns in the state. See chapter 11.
- **Winter Park:** This lakeside town north of downtown Orlando is a lovely place to spend the afternoon. Ladies who lunch head for the shops and restaurants that line posh Park Avenue. The city park, with its fountains, carefully tended trees, and Amtrak station, evokes some of the city's old Southern charm. The Charles Hosmer Morse Museum of American Art has an impressive collection of large-scale works in Tiffany glass. See chapter 12.
- **Apalachicola** (Northwest Florida): Located at the mouth of the Apalachicola River, this gulf-shore town was a major cotton port before the Civil War; and a later timber boom resulted in the fine Victorian homes that still grace Apalachicola's uncurbed streets. It was here that Dr. John Gorrie invented the forerunner of the air conditioner, which revolutionized Florida's tourism industry. Today, the major industry is seafood, with famous Apalachicola oysters eaten fresh off the boats (see "Aphrodisiacs from Apalachicola," below). See chapter 13.
- **Pensacola** (Northwest Florida): One of America's oldest communities, Pensacola has preserved its Spanish, French, and English heritage in the Seville Historic District and Historic Pensacola Village. Spanish-named streets are bordered both by

French-style wrought-iron balconies reminiscent of New Orleans and English colonial churches like those in Williamsburg, Virginia. See chapter 13.

- **Fernandina Beach** (Amelia Island): You can stay at two of Florida's ritziest resorts on Amelia Island, but the real charm for many visitors is in the quaint town of Fernandina Beach, where a 50-block area of Victorian and Queen Anne homes is listed on the National Register of Historic Places. See chapter 14.

10 The Best Florida Kitsch

- **Art Deco District** (South Beach, Miami): The fantastic and colorful shapes that have come to define Miami Beach architecture are as flashy and silly as when they were first erected (from the late 1920s through the 1940s). Tour the historic district for some classic examples of Florida kitsch—namely, hotels and condos shaped like cruise ships, space rockets, and Mediterranean villas. See chapter 5.
- **Coral Castle** (Homestead): There's no way to explain the massive stone structures that have been around for more than 75 years. This prehistoric-looking, roofless "castle" was allegedly built by a crazed Latvian with a bad case of unrequited love. See chapter 5.
- **Frozen Treat** (Fort Myers Beach): Skyrocketing real-estate prices are quickly doing away with buildings like the Frozen Treat, whose roof swirls skyward like the soft ice-cream cones it sells. You can't miss this 1950s relic on Estero Boulevard, the main drag in Fort Myers Beach.
- **Weeki Wachee Spring** (Spring Hill): "Mermaids" have been putting on acrobatic swimming shows behind 4-inch-thick windows every day since 1947, at one of Florida's original tourist attractions. The show's been gussied up in recent years, but it's still a sight to see them dance in waters that come from one of America's most prolific freshwater springs. See chapter 11.
- **Gatorland** (near Kissimmee): You've got to love any place that you enter through a large, yawning gator mouth. Created in 1949, this reptilian homage features thousands of real-live gators and crocodiles on its 70-acre spread. Don't miss the alligator jumping (hard to describe, but you'll know it when you see it). It's cheesy fun, though probably not for the animal-rights crowd. See chapter 12.
- **Langford Resort Hotel** (Winter Park): The guest roster of this Winter Park hotel once routinely listed people like Eleanor Roosevelt, Mamie Eisenhower, Lillian Gish, and Vincent Price. You have to wonder if they stayed in the jungle room, or one of the other theme rooms in this bastion of the "so-tacky-it's-cool" school. Check out the poolside bathrooms, complete with elaborate paintings of mermaids and mermen. See chapter 12.
- **St. Augustine Alligator Farm** (St. Augustine): An amazing collection of alligators, crocodiles, caiman, gharial, geckos, prehensile-tailed skinks, lizards, snakes, tortoises, spider monkeys, and exotic birds is on display for curious tourists. Catch one of the hokey shows for real Florida kitsch. See chapter 14.

11 The Best Places to Avoid the Crowds

- **Pigeon Key** (Upper Keys): At the curve of the old Seven-Mile Bridge is a tiny island that was once the camp for the crew who built "Flagler's Folly" in the early part of this century. No cars are allowed, but bikers and walkers can see for miles with sights that include bridges, many old wooden cottages, and a truly tranquil stretch of lush foliage and water. See chapter 6.

- **Cayo Costa State Park** (off Captiva Island): You can't get any more deserted than this state park, which occupies a 2,132-acre, completely unspoiled barrier island. Go for the miles of white-sand beaches, pine forests, mangrove swamps, oak-palm hammocks, and grasslands. See chapter 10.
- **Lover's Key** (Fort Myers Beach): Just south of Fort Myers Beach, the Carl E. Johnson–Lover's Key State Recreation Area provides respite from the hustle and bustle of its busy neighbor. A highway runs the length of the island, but otherwise Lover's Key is totally undeveloped. Access through a mangrove forest to a truly fine beach is by foot or by a tractor-pulled tram driven by park rangers, who take a dim view of anyone leaving trash behind. See chapter 10.
- **Useppa Island** (off Captiva Island): Pres. Theodore Roosevelt and his tarpon-loving industrialist friends used to hang out on this ancient Calusa Indian shell midden. New York advertising magnate Barron G. Collier bought the island in 1906 and built a lovely wooden home overlooking Pine Island Sound. His mansion is now the Collier Inn, where day-trippers and overnight guests can enjoy lunches and seafood dinners. See chapter 10.
- **Cypress Gardens** (Winter Haven): Founded in 1936, this is one of Florida's original tourist attractions. What began as a 16-acre public park surrounding a lake now spreads over 200 acres. The whole point of Cypress Gardens is to get away from the crowds, taking a leisurely stroll among the flora. See chapter 12.
- **Amelia Island:** This remote, exclusive island offers all the amenities and none of the hustle of a city. Check out Fort Clinch Beach for real solitude. See chapter 14.
- **Canaveral National Seashore:** See "The Best Beaches," in section 1.

12 The Best Swimming Pools

- **Albion Hotel** (South Beach, Miami): An architectural masterpiece originally designed in 1939, the huge pool and artificial "beach" are fun and whimsical examples of art deco details. You can see guests swimming in the bright blue water through the portholes that line the garden walkway. See chapter 4.
- **Biltmore Hotel** (Coral Gables, Miami): This 21,000-square-foot swimming pool lays claim to the title of largest hotel pool in the country. Surrounded by dramatic, stone archways and classical sculptures, it is beautiful, too. See chapter 4.
- **The Delano** (South Beach, Miami): The large outdoor pool behind the famous Delano is designed to spill over with water like a fountain. Most of the pool is shallow, making it more appealing for waders than for swimmers. And diners can even enjoy the cool waters at the wrought-iron tables and chairs placed in the very shallowest edge. See chapter 4.
- **Venetian Pool** (Coral Gables, Miami): Built in 1924, Miami's most unusual swimming pool holds 800,000 gallons of water and is shaded by towering Spanish porticos and old stucco walls. The huge pool with dramatic fountains and waterfalls is open to the public and is a great place to spend an afternoon. See chapter 5.
- **Disney's Vero Beach Resort** (Vero Beach): This lagoonlike pool has a two-story-high winding slide that elicits squeals of delight from kids and adults alike. For younger kids, a pirate ship that squirts water is also a fun way to cool off. See chapter 9.
- **Casa Ybel Resort** (Sanibel Island):This modern condo resort is built around Thistle Lodge, a turn-of-the-century inn whose clapboard sides and steeplelike roof are dramatically mirrored in a large, beachside swimming pool. See chapter 10.
- **Disney's Wilderness Lodge** (Orlando): In true Disney form, the "imagineers" pulled out all the stops to create this faux mountain retreat. The pool meanders

through several layers and is surrounded by boulders and edged in river rock. The best part? Float amid the pool's calm, crystal waters while watching Disney's version of Old Faithful gush about 100 yards away. See chapter 12.

- **Disney's Beach Club Resort** (Orlando): From the palm-fringed entranceway and manicured gardens to its plush sun-dappled lobby, this Disney resort property resembles the luxury of Victorian Cape Cod. The biggest draw is Stormalong Bay, a vast free-form swimming pool/water park sprawling over 3 acres. See chapter 12.
- **Hyatt Regency Grand Cypress Resort** (Orlando): A rope bridge spans this half-acre swimming pool, which flows through rock grottoes and includes 12 waterfalls, two steep water slides, three whirlpools, and a white-sand beach. See chapter 12.
- **Ramada Plaza Beach Resort** (Fort Walton Beach): Once you get past the gaudy, Vegas-style gold facade of the resort, you come to one of the most beautiful swimming pool/patio areas anywhere. Waterfalls cascading over lofty rocks and thick tropical foliage surround a romantic grotto bar. There's even a shack that serves Southern-style barbecue. Unfortunately, it's cut off from the beach by a six-story block of hotel rooms. See chapter 13.

13 The Best Spas

- **Doral Golf Resort and Spa** (Miami); ☎ **800/22-DORAL,** 800/71-DORAL, or 305/592-2000: Voted among the top spas by Zagat and *Condé Nast Traveler,* this 650-acre resort has something for every family member. The ambience is pure luxury—marble, crystal, formal gardens, and soft-spoken white-clad therapists. The healing muds and minerals come from ancient volcanic pools. Besides the great golf, tennis, swimming, and spa services, you'll find gourmet food and newly refurbished guest rooms. Day programs are available for those wanting just a taste of the luxury. See chapter 4.
- **The Spa at Turnberry Isle Resort and Club** (Aventura, North Miami); ☎ **800/327-7028** or 305/932-6200: Turkish steam rooms, authentic Finnish sauna, shiatsu pressure treatments, private exercise classes, oxygenation treatments, slimming baths containing botanical extracts, and a full complement of herbal, thalassotherapy, and holistic health counseling—this spa is serious, and equally recognized for its golf, tennis, and yachting facilities. Turnberry offers a nice selection of day and half-day packages. See chapter 4.
- **PGA National Resort & Spa** (Palm Beach Gardens); ☎ **800/633-9150** or 561/627-2000: Known primarily as a golf destination, this sprawling resort also has a top-rated Mediterranean-style spa with unique offerings for pregnant guests—specialized exercise and nutrition classes, custom-designed massage tables, and more. In addition, the resort has nine pools and a private lake where you can ski or sail, as well as six restaurants and lounges (including one with a surprisingly delicious spa menu). See chapter 8.
- **Wyndham Resort and Spa** (Fort Lauderdale); ☎ **800/996-3426** or 954/389-3300: A $10 million renovation in 1997 has turned the former Bonaventure Resort & Spa into one of the area's premier resorts. With all the sports facilities like tennis, golf, and lots of pools, this spa joins the ranks of Florida's other highly recommended destinations. See chapter 8.
- **Sanibel Harbour Resort & Spa** (Fort Myers); ☎ **800/767-7777** or 941/466-2166: Many call this high-rise resort overlooking Sanibel Island the best spa value in the country. The spa obliges your every whim. Try the amazing Betar Bed, a suspended "bed of music" that floats you to a level where stresses disappear. There are also mud, algae, seaweed, and mineral wraps; Swiss showers; paraffin facials; and

more. Day packages, makeovers, and men's sports packages are popular. The fitness center is state-of-the-art. See chapter 10.

- **Safety Harbor Resort and Spa** (Tampa Bay Area); ☎ **800/237-0155** or 813/726-1161: Tucked away off the beaten track amid moss-draped oaks and cobblestone streets, Safety Harbor is the oldest continually running spa in the United States, and Florida's only spa built around natural healing springs. The feeling is very European. They've recently added some spiffy, youthful programs, including the Fitness Attitude Adjustment Weekend. The Phil Green Tennis School is also on the grounds, and many tennis programs are available. See chapter 11.
- **Buena Vista Palace Resort and Spa** (Orlando); ☎ **407/827-3200:** The spa at this Disney property is a treat from head to toe. From massage and body wraps to manicures, pedicures, and hairstyling, you can come out feeling like a new person. Half- and full-day rates are offered for nonguests. See chapter 12.

14 The Best Luxury Resorts

- **Biltmore Hotel** (Coral Gables, Miami); ☎ **800/727-1926** or 305/445-1926: For more than 70 years, this glorious landmark has been a centerpiece of the city. Restored to its original Mediterranean splendor, it's now one of the Miami area's most romantic and luxurious resorts. A super golf course, huge lagoon-pool, and first-class service make it a place worth going back to. See chapter 4.
- **Grand Bay Hotel** (Coconut Grove, Miami); ☎ **800/327-2788** or 305/858-9600: This sleek, modern tower overlooking Biscayne Bay is especially popular with European and South American guests who appreciate the ultra-elegant details like towering vases of exotic flowers, halls of gleaming marble, and extra-courteous service that make this one of Miami's most desirable properties. See chapter 4.
- **Sonesta Beach Resort Hotel** (Key Biscayne, Miami); ☎ **800/SONESTA** or 305/361-2021: This large, luxurious beachfront resort is at the tip of an exclusive residential island and offers every imaginable amenity, from tennis to jet-skiing. A great place to bring the kids—fully supervised programs keep the children as busy and happy as their parents. See chapter 4.
- **Boca Raton Resort and Club** (Boca Raton); ☎ **800/327-0101** or 561/395-3000: An architectural masterpiece that has kept pace with the times, this ultra-elegant resort has beaches, golf courses, tennis, and every imaginable amenity. The grounds reek of old money, but the atmosphere is casual and laid-back. See chapter 8.
- **The Breakers** (Palm Beach); ☎ **800/833-3141** or 561/655-6611: The biggest and grandest of all of Florida's resorts, this five-star historic beauty epitomizes tony Palm Beach. From the expansive manicured lawns to the elegant marble lobby, The Breakers is the place to be. Rooms may not be as huge as at some of the newer resorts, but constant retrofitting has made it as popular today as when it was first constructed, in 1926. It also boasts Florida's oldest 18-hole golf course. See chapter 8.
- **Four Seasons Resort Palm Beach** (Palm Beach); ☎ **800/332-3442** or 561/582-2800: With the most convenient location and modern amenities, this Four Seasons is a welcome addition to the already superior choices on the island. First-class dining and a super-hospitable staff make it a top pick. See chapter 8.
- **Ritz-Carlton Palm Beach** (Manalpan); ☎ **800/241-3333** or 561/533-6000: As is to be expected from any member of this upscale chain, the Palm Beach Ritz-Carlton is super-luxurious. Located farther than its other five-star neighbors from Palm Beach's shopping and dining area, this resort has elegant rooms overlooking a

spectacular private beach, and an incredible ambience and attention to detail. See chapter 8.

- **Naples Beach Hotel & Golf Club** (Naples); ☎ **800/237-7600** or 941/261-2222: A beachside setting on Millionaires' Row couldn't be better for carrying on the hallowed but relaxed Old Florida traditions at this family-operated hotel. The least expensive units here, in fact, are in the Old Florida wing, a two-story relic from 1948 but recently spiffed up during a $10 million overhaul. The beachside "chickee" (covered wooden platforms on stilts) hut bar is one of Florida's best sunset venues, and the dining room serves an exceptional, reasonably priced breakfast buffet. See chapter 10.
- **Ritz-Carlton Naples** (Naples); ☎ **800/241-3333** or 941/598-3300: This opulent 14-story Mediterranean-style hotel at Vanderbilt Beach is a favorite of affluent guests who like standard Ritz-Carlton amenities such as imported marble floors, antique art, Oriental rugs, Waterford crystal chandeliers, and afternoon British-style high tea. Guests relax in high-backed rockers on the verandas or unwind by the heated swimming pool set in a landscaped terrace, but they must walk through a narrow mangrove forest to reach the beach. See chapter 10.
- **South Seas Plantation Resort & Yacht Harbour** (Captiva Island); ☎ **800/237-3102** or 941/472-5111: Built on what was a 330-acre copra plantation, this exclusive spot is one of the best choices in southern Florida for serious tennis buffs (22 courts with pro). Its gulf-side golf course is one of the most picturesque nineholers anywhere. There are no high-rise buildings, just an assortment of luxury homes and condos, some with private pools and their own tennis courts. With three bedrooms or more, some units are ideal for families or couples who want to share the cost of a vacation. See chapter 10.
- **Colony Beach & Tennis Resort** (Longboat Key, Sarasota); ☎ **800/4-COLONY** or 941/383-6464: This beachside facility is consistently rated one of the nation's finest tennis resorts. Luxurious one- and two-bedroom villa suites are built around 21 lighted courts staffed by 10 pros. The beachside Colony Restaurant and swimming pool date from 1952 when this was a beach club. Next door are three private gulf-side cottages right on the superb beach. See chapter 11.
- **Don CeSar Beach Resort and Spa** (St. Pete Beach); ☎ **800/637-7200**, 800/282-1116, or 727/360-1881: Dating from 1928 and listed on the National Register of Historic Places, this "Pink Palace" tropical getaway is so romantic you may bump into six or seven honeymooning couples in one weekend. The lobby has classic high windows and archways, crystal chandeliers, marble floors, and original artworks. Most rooms have high ceilings and offer views of the gulf or Boca Ciega Bay. See chapter 11.
- **Renaissance Vinoy Resort** (St. Petersburg); ☎ **800/HOTELS-1** or 727/894-1000: Built as the grand Vinoy Park in 1925, this elegant Spanish-style establishment reopened in 1992 after a total and meticulous $93 million restoration and refurbishment that has made it even more luxurious than ever. Dominating the northern part of downtown, it overlooks Tampa Bay and is within walking distance of St. Petersburg's major attractions. Guest rooms offer the utmost in comfort and luxury. See chapter 11.
- **Disney's Grand Floridian Beach Resort** (Lake Buena Vista); ☎ **407/W-DISNEY** or 407/824-3000: The Grand Floridian is magnificent, from the moment you step into its opulent five-story lobby (complete with a Chinese Chippendale aviary) under triple-domed stained-glass skylights. A pianist entertains during afternoon tea, and an orchestra plays big-band music every evening. See chapter 12.

- **Hyatt Regency Grand Cypress Resort** (Orlando); ☎ **407/239-1234:** This hotel stands out among all of the many Orlando offerings. Let the numbers speak for themselves: one-half-acre pool with 12 waterfalls and 3 whirlpools; 12 tennis courts; a 45-hole, 72-par Jack Nicklaus–designed golf course; and a 45-acre Audubon nature walk. It all adds up to luxury. See chapter 12.
- **Amelia Island Plantation** (Amelia Island); ☎ **800/874-6878** or 904/261-6161: Set amid magnolias, oak trees, and the Atlantic Ocean, this gracious resort is straight out of the Deep South. It's more rustic than the nearby Ritz, but has excellent hiking and biking paths, tennis, swimming, horseback riding, and boating. Golfers especially enjoy exclusive use of two of the top courses in Florida. See "The Best Golf Courses," in section 4. See chapter 14.
- **Ritz-Carlton Amelia Island;** ☎ **800/241-3333** or 904/277-1100: Set on 13 acres of stunning beachfront, the Ritz-Carlton is more glitzy and modern than its older neighbor, the Amelia Island Plantation. You'll find all the first-class amenities, as well as remarkable service. The Grill, the hotel's finest restaurant, is one of the island's best. See chapter 14.

15 The Best Romantic Hideaways

- **Little Palm Island** (Little Torch Key); ☎ **800/343-8567** or 305/872-2524: This former fishing camp on its own private 5-acre island is accessible only by boat and offers the ultimate escape only miles from the real world. There are no phones, faxes, or TVs in the romantic thatched-roof cottages, only lots of romantic touches and tons of luxury. See chapter 6.
- **Marquesa Hotel** (Key West); ☎ **800/869-4631** or 305/292-1919: With all the charm of a B&B but with the amenities of a large resort, the Marquesa is a well-kept secret—perfect for those who want plush, private accommodations with a fun town just out the door. See chapter 6.
- **Cabbage Key Inn** (off Captiva Island); ☎ **941/283-2278:** Sitting out in Pine Island Sound east of Fort Myers, this speck of land appears much as it did when the son of novelist Mary Roberts Rhinehart built a house on it in 1938. Today, the home serves as a casual restaurant popular with the likes of singer Jimmy Buffet. When the famous sail away at sunset, you'll have this funky Old Florida relic all to yourselves. See chapter 10.
- **South Seas Plantation Resort & Yacht Harbour** (Captiva Island); ☎ **800/237-3102** or 941/472-5111: Most of the beachfront cottages and condominiums at this luxury resort are spaced far enough apart—and surrounded by enough tropical foliage—to provide plenty of privacy. Some units even have sliding glass walls between the master bedrooms and private Jacuzzis. Sun-filled days can be topped off at romantic restaurants. See chapter 10.
- **Harrington House** (Holmes Beach, Anna Maria Island); ☎ **941/778-5444:** Flowers, a private beach, and Old Florida ambience await at this B&B, built in 1925 on Anna Maria Island. Some of the eight bedrooms have four-poster or brass beds and French doors leading to balconies overlooking the gulf. Some rooms are in the adjacent Beach House, a remodeled 1920s captain's home. See chapter 11.
- **Disney's Wilderness Lodge** (Lake Buena Vista); ☎ **407/W-DISNEY** or 407/824-3200: Modeled after a turn-of-the-century national park lodge, the 56-acre resort is surrounded by towering oak and pine forests; many rooms overlook 340-acre Crystal Bay. There is a secluded feeling, even though the lodge is on Disney property. A first-rate restaurant, Artist's Point, means you never have to leave this unique romantic hideaway. See chapter 12.

- **Disney's Port Orleans Resort** (Lake Buena Vista); ☎ **407/W-DISNEY** or 407/934-5000: One of Walt Disney World's more modestly priced resorts encompasses pastel buildings with shuttered windows and wrought-iron balconies that create a cozy atmosphere. The flower gardens and fountained courtyards are ideal for moonlight strolls. Bonfamille's Café offers hot Creole creations for dinner. See chapter 12.
- **Peabody Orlando** (Orlando); ☎ **407/345-4550:** Known for the five white ducks that serve as goodwill ambassadors, this 27-story resort offers plenty to quack about. On International Drive, this luxurious hotel steeped in sophistication feels miles away from the tourist bustle. For a romantic dinner, try Dux, the hotel's elegant signature restaurant, which has a warm, candlelit ambience. See chapter 12.
- **Henderson Park Inn** (Destin); ☎ **800/336-4853** or 904/837-4853: This shingle-sided, Cape Hatteras–style building right next to Henderson Beach State Recreation Area is a grown-ups' escape (no children are accepted). Individually decorated in a Victorian theme, the inn rooms have high ceilings, fireplaces, and Queen Anne furniture, and gulf views from private balconies. Some have canopied beds. The main building sports a beachside veranda complete with old-fashioned rocking chairs to sit in and admire the glorious sunsets. See chapter 13.
- **Seaside** (near Destin); ☎ **800/277-8696** or 904/231-1320: Ask residents of Northwest Florida where they go for romantic getaways, and they invariably will answer, "The cottages at Seaside." Built in the 1980s but evoking the 1880s, the Victorian-style village of Seaside (a short drive east of Destin) has several cozy beachfront cottages designed especially for honeymooners. See chapter 13.
- **Fairbanks House** (Fernandina Beach, Amelia Island); ☎ **800/261-4838** or 904/277-0500: This meticulously restored 1885 Italianate home is one of the most romantic inns in the Northeast. The cottages (and some suites) have their own entrances, so guests can choose to see only each other. Without seeming obtrusive, servants provide individual attention, gourmet breakfasts, and all-around luxurious service. See chapter 14.

16 The Best Moderately Priced Accommodations

- **Bay Harbor Inn** (Bay Harbor Island, Miami); ☎ **305/868-4141:** On an exclusive island in Miami Beach, this gem offers charm and value in an area that has precious little of either. See chapter 4.
- **Indian Creek Hotel** (Miami Beach); ☎ **800/207-2727** or 305/531-2727: It's modest but full of character, and so close to South Beach. Modest rooms are brightly outfitted in period furnishings, and many overlook the pretty pool and garden. For the price, there's no competition. See chapter 4.
- **The Kent** (South Beach, Miami); ☎ **800/OUTPOST** or 305/531-6771: One of the taller buildings on South Beach, this moderately priced hotel is one of the Island Outpost group's art deco hotels. Although it isn't right on the ocean, it couldn't be more convenient to the South Beach action. See chapter 4.
- **Conch Key Cottages** (Marathon); ☎ **800/330-1577** or 305/289-1377: Right on the ocean, this little hideaway offers rustic but clean and well-outfitted cottages that are especially popular with families. Each has a hammock, barbecue grill, and kitchen. See chapter 6.
- **Beachcomber Apartment Motel** (Palm Beach); ☎ **800/833-7122** or 561/585-4646: This simple pink motel sits right on the ocean just a few miles from the super-high-priced accommodations that make Palm Beach, well, Palm Beach. No fancy frills here, but rooms are pleasant and clean. See chapter 8.

- **Harborfront Inn Bed & Breakfast** (Stuart); ☎ **800/294-1703** or 561/288-7289: Located on the riverfront and within walking distance of the restaurants and shops of downtown Stuart, this handsome, highly recommended B&B offers private rooms with their own entrances. See chapter 9.

- **Best Western Pink Shell Beach Resort** (Fort Myers Beach); ☎ **800/237-5786** or 941/463-6161: This popular, family-oriented spot fronting both the gulf and the bay has hotel rooms, suites, one- and two-bedroom apartments, and beach cottages. The pink-sided cottages make up for a lack of luxury with lots of 1950s-style charm. Units in two midrise, gulf-front buildings have lovely views of Sanibel Island from their screened balconies. See chapter 10.

- **Tides Inn of Naples** (Naples); ☎ **800/438-8763** or 941/262-6196: One of Florida's most remarkable values, this immaculate two-story motel is right on the beach and on the edge of Millionaires' Row and Olde Naples. Comfortable suites and efficiencies, all tropically furnished and decorated, have screened balconies or patios angled to face the beach across a courtyard with coconut palms and heated swimming pool. See chapter 10.

- **Island's End Resort** (St. Pete Beach); ☎ **727/360-5023:** A wonderful respite from the maddening crowd, and a great bargain to boot, this little all-cottage hideaway sits right on the southern tip of St. Pete Beach, smack-dab on Pass-a-Grille, where the Gulf of Mexico meets Tampa Bay. You can step from the six contemporary cottages right onto the beach. See chapter 11.

- **Disney's Caribbean Beach Resort** (Lake Buena Vista); ☎ **407/W-DISNEY** or 407/934-3400: Five distinct Caribbean "villages" are grouped around a large, duck-filled lake. Each village has its own lake, and the 200-acre resort includes a jogging trail, a short nature trail, and picnic area. A good value for families. See chapter 12.

- **Courtyard by Marriott** (Lake Buena Vista); ☎ **800/223-9930** or 407/828-8888: The rooms are attractive with a full-service restaurant offering American fare, a cocktail lounge, poolside bar, and on-site deli. Located near the shopping mecca of Disney Village Marketplace. See chapter 12.

- **Holiday Inn Sunspree Resort** (Lake Buena Vista); ☎ **800/FON-KIDS** or 407/239-4500: In addition to the standard amenities that make Holiday Inn a dependable choice across the country, this location has special Kids Suites. Decorated as Western fortresses or polar igloos, the suites offer separate kid-sized rooms, affording parents privacy and kids their personal space. See chapter 12.

- **Gibson Inn** (Apalachicola); ☎ **904/653-2191:** Built in 1907 as a seaman's hotel and gorgeously restored in 1985, this cupola-topped inn is such a brilliant example of Victorian architecture that it's listed on the National Register of Historic Inns. No two guest rooms are alike (some still have the original sinks in the sleeping area), but all are richly furnished with period reproductions. Grab a drink from the bar and relax in one of the high-back rockers on the old-fashioned veranda. See chapter 13.

- **Daytona Beach Hilton Oceanfront Resort** (Daytona Beach); ☎ **800/525-7350** or 904/767-7350: Perhaps the best choice in Daytona Beach, the Hilton has all the amenities of a pricey resort, including a very good restaurant and lounge, but prices like those of a mom-and-pop hotel. It's slightly south of the insane spring-break action, making it more peaceful than some of the area's more expensive choices. See chapter 14.

- **Kenwood Inn** (St. Augustine); ☎ **904/824-2116:** Somewhere between a B&B and a cozy inn, the Kenwood is one of Old Town's best choices. Rooms are larger and more private than in most other B&Bs and are brimming with antiques. The large patio and outdoor swimming pool are rarities in historic downtown St. Augustine. See chapter 14.

- **Radisson Ponce de León Golf & Conference Resort** (St. Augustine); ☎ **800/333-3333** or 904/824-2821: The only resort in St. Augustine, this scenic 400-acre compound also has one of the area's only golf courses. Just 5 minutes from historic Old Town, this lushly landscaped Radisson is the area's most gracious spot. See chapter 14.

17 The Best Places for Sunset Cocktails

Any beachside restaurant, swimming pool bar, or pub on Florida's west coast will supply cocktails as the sun sets brilliantly over the Gulf of Mexico. All you have to do is go west. Here are a few places that stand out.

- **Louie's Backyard** (Key West); ☎ **305/294-1061:** Nestled amid blooming bougainvillea on a lush slice of the gulf, this spot—a rear deck that juts out over the water—personifies romance. See chapter 6.
- **Mallory Square on Duval Street** (Key West): Join the circus that is Mallory Square at dusk. If the spectacular colors of the sun dropping into the sea aren't dramatic enough for you, take in the cat show, the street performers, and the crowd of tourists from all over the world. See chapter 6.
- **Anthony's on the Gulf and the Junkanoo Beach Bar** (Fort Myers Beach); ☎ **941/463-2600:** The party never ends in the Junkanoo Beach Bar, underneath Anthony's on the Gulf Italian restaurant. The Junkanoo's bar and Anthony's large windows and appropriately named Sunset Terrace are two of the better places on Estero Island for sundowners. A casual, unpretentious tropical ambience prevails. See chapter 10.
- **Mucky Duck** (Captiva Island); ☎ **941/472-3434:** The one place on Captiva with beachside dining, this lively, British-style pub has picnic tables on the sand. Order a drink from the bar inside and bring it out before the "green flash" occurs as the sun slips below the horizon. See chapter 10.
- **Naples Beach Hotel & Golf Club** (Naples); ☎ **800/237-7600** or 941/261-2222: Since this charming, Old Florida–style resort predates the strict historic district zoning laws, it has the only restaurants and bars directly on the beach in Olde Naples. Wedged between the beach and an Olympic-size pool, the Sunset Beach Bar is one of the region's most famous beachside "chickee" bars and is always crammed as the sun sets over the gulf. It's hopping on Sunday afternoons during the winter season, when live bands perform. See chapter 10.
- **South Beach** (Boca Grande); ☎ **941/964-0765:** The only place in ritzy Boca Grande where you can dine or have a sunset cocktail by the gulf, this casual establishment has a covered patio with plastic chairs and tables right by the white sand. The "help" likes to hang out here, lending a relaxed, don't-give-a-hoot atmosphere. See chapter 10.
- **Sandbar** (Anna Maria Island, off Bradenton); ☎ **941/778-0444:** Sitting on the site of the former Pavilion, built in 1913 when people from Tampa and St. Pete took the ferry here, this popular restaurant is right on the beach overlooking the gulf. The action is under the umbrellas on the lively beachside deck, with a snack menu and live music weeknights and on weekend afternoons. See chapter 11.
- **TradeWinds Resort** (St. Pete Beach); ☎ **800/237-0707** or 813/367-6461: The Flying Bridge, a Florida cracker-house-style beachside bar, actually floats on one of the lily ponds at this large resort. You can take your drink out to the sands as the "sun goes to bed," as the French say. See chapter 11.

- **Artist Point** (Orlando): The fading sun reflects the muted palette of dusk off of the 340 acres of Crystal Bay while you enjoy the rustic, romantic surroundings of this restaurant. Reminiscent of a turn-of-the-century hunting cabin, this Wilderness Lodge restaurant feels secluded, though the theme parks are just minutes away. See chapter 12.

18 The Best Seafood Restaurants

- **Fishbone Grille** (downtown Miami); ☎ 305/530-1915: It isn't scenic and it isn't where the tourists go, but this stellar little fish restaurant has some of the area's best seafood. In addition to an excellent ceviche, the stews, crab cakes, and starters are all superb. If you like Caribbean flavor, try the daily special with jerk seasoning. See chapter 4.
- **Monty's Bayshore Restaurant** (Coconut Grove and South Beach, Miami); ☎ 305/858-1431: Forget Joe's; this multifaceted seafood restaurant serves all-you-can-eat stone crabs in season, with prices way below those of their South Beach neighbor. Other seafood specialties are available. See chapter 4.
- **Atlantic's Edge** (Islamorada); ☎ 305/664-4651: An innovative and varied menu includes some of the best fresh fish, steak, and chicken you'll find. The crab cakes are among the most delicious in the Keys; the Thai spiced fresh baby snapper is likewise spectacular. See chapter 6.
- **Marker 88** (Islamorada); ☎ 305/852-9315: A legend in the Keys, this dark, romantic restaurant has standard fare as well as a winning version of nouvelle cuisine. You'll find the area's largest selection of seafood, including lobster from the Keys, conch from The Bahamas, frog legs from the Everglades, stone crabs from the Florida Bay, and shrimp from the West Coast, among other dishes. See chapter 6.
- **Capt. Charlie's Reef Grill** (Juno Beach); ☎ 561/624-9924: The cooking is imaginative and mouthwatering. A wide range of ever-changing selections include a Caribbean chili, a sizable tuna spring roll, and an enormous Cuban crab cake. Ask for suggestions, and enjoy this, one of the area's best-kept secrets, hidden behind a tiny strip mall. See chapter 8.
- **Channel Mark** (Fort Myers Beach); ☎ 941/463-9127: Every table looks out on a maze of channel markers on Hurricane Bay, and a dock with palms growing through it makes this a relaxing place for a waterside lunch. The atmosphere changes dramatically at night, when the relaxed tropical ambience is ideal for kindling romance. Congenial owners Mike McGuigan and Andy Welsh put a creative spin on their seafood dishes, and their delicately seasoned crab cakes are tops. See chapter 10.
- **Mad Hatter** (Sanibel Island); ☎ 941/472-0033: Brian and Jayne Baker's little gulf-front restaurant has only 12 tables, but each has a glorious water view that's best at sunset. They offer a fantasy of New American cuisines with some exotic accents. The menu changes frequently, with no dish repeated (so as not to bore their loyal local following). Whatever they serve, you'll enjoy. See chapter 10.
- **Lobster Pot** (Redington Shores, near St. Pete Beach); ☎ 727/391-8592: Owner Eugen Fuhrmann supplies the finest seafood dishes on the St. Pete and Clearwater beaches. Among his amazing variety of lobster dishes is one flambéed in brandy with garlic, and the bouillabaisse—as authentic as any you'll find in the south of France. See chapter 11.
- **Bahama Breeze** (Orlando); ☎ 407/248-2499: Traditional Caribbean foods are used to create unusual items such as "fish in a bag"—strips of mahimahi in a

Aphrodisiacs from Apalachicola

Seafood is a major culinary draw all across Florida. Some waterfront restaurants even operate their own fishing boats, so you're guaranteed super-fresh offerings. You'll dine on snapper, swordfish, amberjack, triggerfish, pompano, grouper, clams, gulf shrimp, blue crab, and sweet deep-sea scallops.

Some seafood specialties may be new to your palate. The clawless tropical **lobsters** are smaller and sweeter than the cold-water Maine variety, with all of their meat concentrated in the tail. You should also try **conch,** a chewy shellfish that's often served in deep-fried fritters, in chowder, or in a spicy salad marinated in lime juice. You're sure to fall in love with the taste of Florida's succulent **stone crab claws** (the crustacean is thrown back into the sea to grow another hand), and you won't soon forget the sweet, slightly briny taste of **Apalachicola oysters** (which reputedly have aphrodisiac properties).

parchment pillow flavored with carrots, sweet peppers, mushrooms, celery, and spices. Also featured are more traditional favorites such as paella. See chapter 12.

- **Disney's Beach Club Resort** (Lake Buena Vista); ☎ **407/W-DISNEY** or 407/934-8000: The 19th-century-style clambake buffet at the Cape May Café in Disney's Beach Club Resort is a feast—seafood stews, clams, mussels, and lobster cooked in a rockwood steamer pit. It's all offered for a price that won't leave you feeling soaked. See chapter 12.
- **Staff's Seafood Restaurant** (Fort Walton Beach); ☎ **904/243-3526:** Staff's started as a hotel in 1913 and moved to this barnlike building in 1931. Among the display of memorabilia are an old-fashioned phonograph lamp and a 1914 cash register. All main courses are served with heaping baskets of hot, home-baked wheat bread from a secret 70-year-old recipe. The tangy seafood gumbo also has gained fame for this casual, historic restaurant. See chapter 13.
- **Back Porch** (Destin); ☎ **904/837-2022:** The food isn't gourmet at this cedar-shingled shack, whose long porch offers glorious beach and gulf views, but this is where charcoal-grilled amberjack originated. Today, you'll see it on menus throughout Florida. Other fish and seafood, as well as chicken and juicy hamburgers, also come from the coals. See chapter 13.
- **Marina Cafe** (Destin); ☎ **904/837-7960:** Destin's best restaurant provides a classy atmosphere with soft candlelight, subdued music, and formally attired waiters. The outdoor balconied deck overlooks Destin Harbor. The creative chef prepares pizzas and pastas with a special emphasis on light, spicy fare. See chapter 13.
- **Chef Eddie's Magnolia Grill** (Apalachicola); ☎ **850/653-8000:** Chef Eddie Cass's cozy restaurant occupies a small bungalow built in the 1880s, and is still in possession of the original black cypress paneling in its central hallway. Nightly specials emphasize fresh local seafood and New Orleans–style sauces. He received more than 2,000 orders for his spicy seafood gumbo at a recent Florida Seafood Festival. See chapter 13.

19 The Best Local Dining Experiences

- **Bayside Seafood Restaurant and Hidden Cove Bar** (Key Biscayne); ☎ **305/361-0808:** Visiting boaters and Key Biscayners call it simply "the Hut." But even those from over the bridge don't know about this laid-back bar and tiki-covered restaurant that serves good, cheap fish platters on paper plates. It's often plagued by mosquitoes, so bring protection and enjoy the rustic ambience that has become so rare in Miami. See chapter 4.

- **Caribbean Delite** (downtown Miami); ☎ **305/381-9254:** Jamaicans who live in Miami frequent this little dive for authentic specialties like curried goat and oxtail stew and, for breakfast, the hard-to-find ackee and saltfish (the national dish of Jamaica). See chapter 4.
- **Versailles** (Little Havana, Miami); ☎ **305/444-0240:** A tacky diner dressed up with mirrors, imitation crystal, and murals of the French countryside, this old Cuban hangout serves hearty dishes from the home country. This is the place to discover the many rich flavors of Cuban food, or at least try a *café con leche*. See chapter 4.
- **Coco's Kitchen** (Big Pine Key); ☎ **305/872-4495:** This tiny storefront is downright cheap and has been pleasing area Cuban food fans for years. You can't go wrong with the daily special, especially if it's roasted pork or any fresh fish. It's all served with a huge portion of rice and beans or salad and crispy fries. See chapter 6.
- **Blue Heaven** (Key West); ☎ **305/296-8666:** By now everyone knows about this once-secret hideaway in Bahama Village, an area tourists are often warned not to visit (it's depressed but hardly dangerous). It's popular with bohemians and those who crave fresh, homemade food, especially for breakfast. See chapter 6.
- **Islamorada Fish Company** (Islamorada); ☎ **800/258-2559** or 305/664-9271: They've been doing it since 1948, and apparently they've been doing it right. To accommodate the crowds, a second restaurant and an outdoor deck have opened, where tourists and locals enjoy the view and the super-rich fish sandwiches. See chapter 6.
- **Robert Is Here** (Homestead/near Everglades National Park); ☎ **305/246-1592:** Stop in for a snack or a fresh tropical fruit shake. Exotic fruits, bottled jellies, hot sauces, and salad dressings are stacked in bins throughout this local landmark farm stand. See chapter 7.
- **John G's** (Lake Worth, Palm Beach County); ☎ **561/585-9860:** This greasy spoon, right on the beach, is best known for its terrific fish-and-chips. They also serve great big breakfasts and good soups. See chapter 8.
- **Old South Barbecue Ranch** (Clewiston); ☎ **941/983-7756:** This landmark on Lake Okeechobee serves the best smoke sauce around. You can get rich and smoky barbecued pork, meat, and chicken. Try a taste of fried alligator or catfish. See chapter 9.
- **Farmers Market Restaurant** (Fort Myers); ☎ **941/334-1687:** The retail Farmers Market next door may be tiny, but the best of the cabbage, okra, green beans, and tomatoes end up here at this simple eatery, frequented by everyone from business executives to truck drivers. The specialties of the house are Southern favorites like smoked ham hocks with a bowl of black-eyed peas. See chapter 10.
- **Mel's Hot Dogs** (Tampa); ☎ **813/985-8000:** Just outside Busch Gardens, Tampa Bay, this red-and-white cottage offers everything from "bagel-dogs" and corn dogs to a bacon/Cheddar Reuben. Even the decor is dedicated to wieners: The walls and windows are lined with hot-dog memorabilia. See chapter 11.
- **Columbia** (Tampa); ☎ **813/248-4961:** Dating from 1905, this historic building occupies an entire city block in the heart of Ybor City, Tampa's dining and nightlife mecca. Visitors and locals alike flock here to clap along during fire-belching Spanish floor shows in the main dining room. You'll come back for the famous Spanish bean

soup and original "1905" salad. The decor throughout is graced with hand-painted tiles, wrought-iron chandeliers, dark woods, rich red fabrics, and stained-glass windows. You can breathe your own fumes in the Cigar Bar. See chapter 11.

- **Fourth Street Shrimp Store** (St. Petersburg); ☎ **727/822-0325:** The outside of this place looks like it's covered with graffiti, but it's actually a gigantic drawing of people eating. Inside, murals on two walls seem to look out on an early-19th-century seaport (one painted sailor permanently peers in to see what you're eating). This is the best and certainly the most interesting bargain in St. Petersburg. See chapter 11.
- **Hopkins' Boarding House** (Pensacola); ☎ **850/438-3979:** There's a delicious peek into the past at this Victorian boardinghouse, surrounded by ancient trees and a wraparound porch with old-fashioned rocking chairs. Everyone eats family style—at your elbow could be the mayor or a mechanic, for everyone in town dines here. Platters are piled high with seasonal Southern-style vegetables from nearby farms. In true boardinghouse fashion, guests bus their own dishes. See chapter 13.
- **Shuckums Oyster Pub & Seafood Grill** (Panama City Beach); ☎ **850/235-3214:** "We shuck 'em, you suck 'em" is the motto of this extremely informal pub, which became famous when comedian Martin Short tried unsuccessfully to shuck oysters here during the making of an MTV spring-break special. The original bar is virtually papered over with dollar bills signed by patrons who have been flocking here since 1967. See chapter 13.
- **The Boss Oyster** (Apalachicola); ☎ **850/653-9364:** This rustic, dockside eatery is a good place to see if what they say about the aphrodisiac properties of Apalachicola oysters is true. The bivalves are served raw, steamed, or under a dozen toppings ranging from capers to crabmeat. They'll even steam three dozen of them and let you do the shucking. Dine inside or at picnic tables on a screened dockside porch. Everyone in town eats here, from bankers to watermen. See chapter 13.
- **Dunn Toys & Hobbies** (Daytona Beach); ☎ **904/253-3644:** This old-time toy store with one of the biggest selections in the state also maintains an old-fashioned soda fountain and coffee shop with a surprisingly good selection of sandwiches, bagels, hot dogs, soups, salads, and pastries, and, of course, ice cream. See chapter 14.
- **Singleton's Seafood Shack** (Mayport/Jacksonville); ☎ **904/246-9440:** A rustic fish house in Florida that has kept up with the times by offering fresh fish in more ways than just battered and fried. Yet, they have retained the charming casualness of a riverside fish camp. Even if you don't want seafood, this spot is worth stopping in just for a feel of Old Florida. See chapter 14.

20 The Best Bars & Nightspots

- **Cafe Nostalgia** (Little Havana, Miami); ☎ **305/541-2631:** They start with films from the old country and follow up with the hot sounds of Afro-Cuban jazz. It's become popular with a few gringos and lots of sentimental exiles. See chapter 5.
- **The Clevelander** (South Beach, Miami); ☎ **305/531-3485:** On one of Ocean Drive's busiest corners, there's always a mixed crowd gathered around the large outdoor pool area drinking brightly colored concoctions from plastic cups. See chapter 5.
- **The Forge** (Miami Beach); ☎ **305/538-8533:** Step back in time at this ultra-elegant restaurant and bar where Wednesday night is the time to hang with singles in Armani and Versace. See chapter 5.

- **Tobacco Road** (downtown Miami); ☎ **305/374-1198:** Open every day of the year since 1912, Tobacco Road is a Miami institution. No matter who is playing, this two-story dive bar is worth a visit. From homegrown blues to nationally known jazz acts to poetry readings, you'll find the best music and atmosphere at "The Road." See chapter 5.
- **Yuca** (South Beach, Miami); ☎ **305/532-9822:** One of South Beach's best restaurants also operates an expensive upstairs club on the weekends. No matter who is playing, you will appreciate the high-energy scene at this upscale Latin hot spot. See chapter 5.
- **Duval Street** (Key West): The partying-est strip this side of Bourbon Street, home to literally dozens of bars and dance spots. Explore them for yourself. See chapter 6.
- **Epoch** (Key West); ☎ **305/296-8521:** Formerly known as The Copa, this warehouse-style dance club made famous by its colorful gay patrons is right on Duval Street. They play everything from techno to house to disco and welcome anyone. See chapter 6.
- **Woody's Saloon and Restaurant** (Islamorada); ☎ **305/664-4335:** This raunchy bar has live bands almost every night, but it is the house band you want to see. Big Dick and the Extenders is headed by a 300-pound Native American who does a lewd, rude, and crude routine of jokes and songs guaranteed to offend everyone in the house. See chapter 6.
- **Clematis Street** (West Palm Beach): This newly gentrified area has some of the area's best (and only) nightlife. Just over the bridge from stodgy Palm Beach, this 5-block area, from Flagler Drive to Rosemary Avenue, has everything from late-night bookshops and wine bars to dance clubs and outdoor cafes. See chapter 8.
- **Las Olas Boulevard** (Ft. Lauderdale): This wide, scenic street, dotted with good clubs and late-night shopping, is especially popular with a more mature local crowd and European visitors. See chapter 8.
- **Dock at Crayton Cove** (Naples); ☎ **941/263-9940:** Right on the City Dock, this lively pub is a perfect place for an open-air meal or a libation while watching the action on Naples Bay. See chapter 10.
- **Junkanoo Beach Bar** (Fort Myers Beach); ☎ **941/463-2600:** Away from the crowds of Fort Myers Beach's busy Times Square, the Junkanoo attracts a more affluent crowd for its constant bohemian-style beach parties with live reggae and other island music. A concessionaire rents beach cabanas and water-sports toys, making it a good place for a lively day at the beach. See chapter 10.
- **Shooters Waterfront Café USA** (Fort Myers); ☎ **941/334-2727:** A setting right on the river makes this Fort Myers's most popular watering hole. There's live music every night, and the place is absolutely packed after work on Friday and Saturday. See chapter 10.
- **Frankie's Patio Bar & Grill** (Tampa); ☎ **813/249-3337:** All you have to do is stroll along 7th Avenue East, between 15th and 20th streets, in Tampa's Ybor City to find a club or bar to your liking. Frankie's stands out for its exposed industrial pipes—a stark contrast to the Spanish-style architecture prevalent here. There's seating indoors, on a large outdoor patio, or on an open-air balcony overlooking the action on the street. Pick up a calendar at the reception desk: There's that much live jazz, blues, reggae, and rock here. See chapter 11.
- **Pleasure Island** (near Disney Village, Orlando): You can two-step to Charlie Pride or groove to Charlie Parker; this all-in-one complex runs the entertainment gamut

from country to jazz to modern rock to dance music. Special appearances by big-name artists on two stages are an occasional nighttime option. A nightly fireworks display ensures every evening ends with a bang. See chapter 12.

- **Church Street Station** (downtown Orlando): Between Garland and Orange avenues, this renovated train depot is an architectural treat and a genuine good time. There are 20 shows nightly in this collection of bars, restaurants, and shops. Enjoy live music and bustling dance floors, or sip a cocktail while sitting along the cobblestone streets. See chapter 12.

- **CityWalk** (Orlando): The 12-acre entertainment complex, next to Universal Studios, could easily be renamed theme-restaurant heaven. Not only is it home to the world's largest Hard Rock Cafe—the grande dame of them all—but also the Nascar Cafe, the Motown Cafe, and Marvel Mania, a theme homage to villains and superheroes. Along with places to dine there are places to dance to jazz, reggae, hip-hop, and pop. If you're cinematically deprived, head for the state-of-the-art Cineplex Odeon Megaplex. See chapter 12.

- **Hathaway's Landing** (Panama City Beach); ☎ **850/230-0409:** There's live entertainment nightly and on Saturday and Sunday afternoons from March to September under one of the largest thatch pavilions in Florida. The emphasis is on Jimmy Buffet–style music, reggae, and some country and western. While the young crowd hoots the night away over by the gulf, Hathaway's draws lots of customers on the far side of 30. See chapter 13.

- **Seville Quarter** (Pensacola); ☎ **850/434-6211:** In Pensacola's Seville Historic District, this restored antique-brick complex with New Orleans–style wrought-iron balconies contains pubs and restaurants whose names capture the ambience: Rosie O'Grady's Goodtime Emporium; Lili Marlene's Aviator's Pub; Apple Annie's Courtyard; End o' the Alley Bar; Phineas Phogg's Balloon Works (a dance hall, not a balloon shop); and Fast Eddie's Billiard Parlor (which has electronic games for kids, too). Live entertainment ranges from Dixieland jazz to country and western. See chapter 13.

- **Flora-Bama Lounge** (Perdido Key, near Pensacola); ☎ **850/492-0611:** This slapped-together gulf-side pub is a shrine to country music, with jam sessions from noon until way past midnight on Saturday and Sunday. Flora-Bama is the prime sponsor and a key venue for the Frank Brown International Songwriters' Festival during the first week of November. Take in the great gulf views from the Deck Bar. See chapter 13.

2

Planning a Trip to Florida

by Bill Goodwin

Bill Goodwin began his career as an award-winning newspaper reporter before becoming legal counsel and speechwriter for two U.S. senators. He also is the author of *Frommer's South Pacific* and *Frommer's Virginia*, and is the editor of *Frommer's USA*.

1 Visitor Information

For general information about the state, contact **Visit Florida,** P.O. Box 1100, Tallahassee, FL 32399-1100 (☎ **800/7-FLA-USA;** www.flausa.com), which will send you its *Florida Vacation Guide* and an official state highway map.

Visit Florida also has offices in:

Canada: 121 Bloor St. E., Suite 1003, Toronto M4W 3M5 (☎ **416/928-3139;** fax 416/928-6841).

United Kingdom: Roebuck House, Palace Street, London SW1E 5BA (☎ **171/630-6602;** fax 171/630-7703).

Germany: Schillerstrasse 10, 60313 Frankfurt/Main (☎ **69/ 131-0092;** fax 69/131-0647).

Japan: Belevedere Kudan Building., no. 204, 2-15-5, Fujimi, Chiyoda-Ku, Tokyo 102 (☎ **35276-0260;** fax 35276-0264).

Visit Florida also has **welcome centers** on I-10 west of Pensacola, I-75 north of Jennings, I-95 north of Yulee, and U.S. 231 at Campbellton. There's also a walk-in information office in the west foyer of the New Capitol Building in Tallahassee (see chapter 13).

Once you've chosen a specific destination in Florida, you can get much more detailed information from the **local visitor information offices.** They're listed under "Orientation" or "Essentials" in the following chapters.

2 When to Go

To a large extent, the timing of your visit will determine how much you'll spend—and how much company you'll have—once you get here. That's because room rates can more than double during the high seasons, when countless visitors migrate to Florida.

The weather determines the high seasons (see "Climate," below). In subtropical southern Florida, it's during the winter, from mid-December to mid-April. On the other hand, you'll be rewarded with incredible bargains if you can stand the heat and humidity of a South Florida summer between June and early September. In northern Florida, the reverse is true: Tourists flock here during the summer, from Memorial Day to Labor Day.

Presidents' Day weekend in February, Easter week, Memorial Day weekend at the end of May, the Fourth of July, Labor Day weekend at the start of September, Thanksgiving, Christmas, and New Year's are busy throughout the state, and especially at Walt Disney World and the other Orlando area attractions, which can be packed anytime school's out (see chapter 12).

Both northern and southern Florida share the same "shoulder seasons": April and May and from September to November, when the weather is pleasant throughout Florida and hotel rates are considerably less than during the high seasons. If price is a consideration, then these months of pleasant temperatures and fewer tourists are the best times to visit.

See the accommodations sections in the chapters that follow for specifics about the local high, shoulder, and off-seasons.

CLIMATE   Northern Florida has a temperate climate, and even in the warmer southern third of the state, it's subtropical, not tropical. Accordingly, Florida sees more extremes of temperatures than, say, the Caribbean islands.

Spring sees warm temperatures throughout Florida, but it also brings tropical showers, and May contributes the first waves of summertime humidity.

Summer runs from May to September in Florida, when it's hot and *very* humid throughout the state. If you're in an inland city during these months, you may not want to do anything too taxing when the sun is at its peak. Coastal areas, however, reap the benefits of sea breezes. Severe afternoon thunderstorms are prevalent during the summer heat (there aren't professional sports teams here named Lightening and Thunder for nothing), so schedule your activities for earlier in the day, and take precautions to avoid being hit by lightening during the storms.

Fall is a great time to visit—the really hottest days are gone, and the crowds have thinned out a bit. August through November, however, is hurricane season—you may remember Hurricanes Andrew and Opal in 1992 and 1995, respectively, which caused billions of dollars' worth of damage to South Florida and to the Panhandle. Fortunately, the National Weather Service closely tracks hurricanes and gives ample warning if there's any need to evacuate coastal areas.

Winter can get a bit nippy throughout the state, and sometimes downright cold in northern Florida. Although snow is rare, a flake or two has been known to fall as far south as Miami. The "cold snaps" usually last only a few days in the southern half of the state, however, and daytime temperatures quickly return to the 70s.

For up-to-the-minute weather info, tune in to cable TVs **Weather Channel,** or click on its Web site: www.weather.com.

Average Temperatures in Selected Florida Cities (°F)

	Jan	Feb	Mar	Apr	May	June	July	Aug	Sept	Oct	Nov	Dec
Key West	69	72	74	77	80	82	85	85	84	80	74	72
Miami	69	70	71	74	78	81	82	84	81	78	73	70
Tampa	60	61	66	72	77	81	82	82	81	75	67	62
Orlando	60	63	66	71	78	82	82	82	81	75	67	61
Tallahassee	53	56	63	68	72	78	81	81	77	74	66	59

Florida

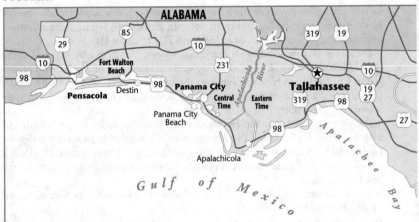

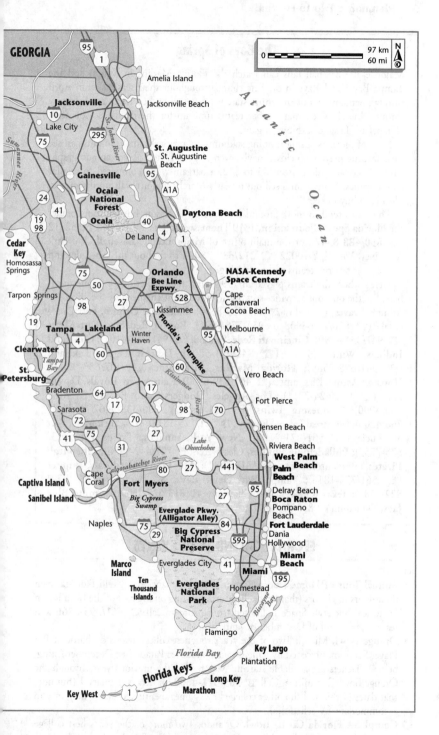

The Boys of Spring

Major-league baseball fans can watch the Florida Marlins in Miami and the Tampa Bay Devil Rays in St. Petersburg throughout their seasons from April through September, but the entire state is a baseball hotbed from late February through March when many other teams tune up for the regular season with "Grapefruit League" exhibition games.

Most of Florida's spring training stadiums are relatively small, so fans can see their favorite players up close, maybe even to get a handshake or an autograph. Also, tickets are priced from $5 to $12, a bargain when compared to regular season games. Many games sell out by early March, so don't wait until you're in Florida to buy tickets.

The teams tend to move around from season to season, but you can contact the **Florida Sports Foundation,** 1319 Thomaswood Dr., Tallahassee, FL 32312 (☎ **850/488-8347**), or the main office of **Major League Baseball,** 350 Park Ave., New York, NY 10022 (☎ **212/339-7800**), to find out the schedules and where your favorite teams will be playing.

Here's where the teams played in 1998, with their ticket office phone numbers. See the outdoor activities sections in subsequent chapters for specifics. **Atlanta Braves,** Orlando (☎ 407/939-8600); **Baltimore Orioles,** Fort Lauderdale (☎ 800/236-8908 or 954/776-1921); **Boston Red Sox,** Fort Myers (☎ 941/334-4799); **Cincinnati Reds,** Sarasota (☎ 941/954-4101); **Cleveland Indians,** Winter Haven (☎ 941/291-5803); **Detroit Tigers,** Lakeland (☎ 941/688-9589); **Florida Marlins,** Melbourne (☎ 407/633-9200); **Houston Astros,** Kissimmee (☎ 407/839-6500); **Kansas City Royals,** Davenport (☎ 941/424-7211); **Los Angeles Dodgers,** Vero Beach (☎ 407/569-4900); **Minnesota Twins,** Fort Myers (☎ 800/338-9467 or 941/768-4200); **Montreal Expos,** Jupiter (☎ 561/775-1818); **New York Mets,** Port St. Lucie (☎ 561/871-2100); **New York Yankees,** Tampa (☎ 813/875-7753); **Philadelphia Phillies,** Clearwater (☎ 727/442-8496); **Pittsburgh Pirates,** Bradenton (☎ 941/747-3031); **St. Louis Cardinals,** Jupiter (☎ 561/775-1818); **Tampa Bay Devil Rays,** St. Petersburg (☎ 727/822-3384); **Texas Rangers,** Port Charlotte (☎ 813/625-9500); **Toronto Blue Jays,** Dunedin (☎ 813/733-9302).

FLORIDA CALENDAR OF EVENTS

January

- **Annual Tour of Homes,** Boca Raton. Exclusive mansions in Old Floresta open their doors to visitors (thanks to a little arm twisting on the part of the Boca Raton Historical Society). Space is limited, so be sure to call ☎ **561/395-6766** and reserve early. End of December or January.
- **Orange Bowl,** Miami. Two of the year's toughest college teams do battle at Pro Player Stadium, preceded by King Orange Jamboree Parade (see December listing, below). Tickets are available starting March 1 of the previous year through the Orange Bowl Committee. Call ☎ **305/371-4600** for details. January 1 (but note that dates of this and the other college bowl games mentioned below may vary to accommodate TV schedules).
- ✪ **CompUSA Florida Citrus Bowl,** Orlando. Two more of the year's best college teams duke it out on the gridiron. Downtown parade a few days before the game

features dozens of marching bands, parade units, and a few floats. New Year's Eve extravaganza at Sea World (see December listing, below). Game tickets go on sale in late October or early November. Call ☎ **407/423-2476** for information; 407/839-3900 for tickets. January 1.

- **Gator Bowl,** Jacksonville. Yet two more of the country's better college football teams battle it out in Alltel Stadium. Call ☎ **904/798-1700** for information on tickets and postgame festivities. January 1.

- **Outback Bowl,** Tampa. Two top college teams kick off at Houlihan's Stadium, preceded by weeklong series events. Call ☎ **813/874-2695** for schedule and tickets. January 1.

- **Art Miami,** Miami. This fine-arts fair features more than a hundred galleries from all over the world. International, modern, and contemporary works are featured at this annual event, attracting thousands of visitors and buyers to the Coconut Grove Convention Center. For information and ticket prices, call ☎ **561/220-2690.** Early January.

- **Three Kings Parade, Miami.** Since Cuban President Fidel Castro outlawed this religious celebration more than 25 years ago, Cuban Americans in Little Havana have put on a bacchanalian parade winding through Calle Ocho from 4th Avenue to 27th Avenue, with horse-drawn carriages, native costumes, and marching bands. Call WQBA at ☎ **305/447-1140** for the exact date during the first week of January.

- **Epiphany Celebration,** Tarpon Springs. After morning services at St. Nicholas Cathedral, young folks dive for the Epiphany cross in Spring Bayou. For information, call ☎ **727/937-3540.** First Saturday in January.

- ✪ **Art Deco Weekend,** South Beach, Miami. Held along the beach between 5th and 15th streets, this festival—with bands, food stands, antique vendors, artists, tours, and other festivities—celebrates the whimsical architecture that has made South Beach one of America's most unique neighborhoods. Call ☎ **305/672-2014** for details. Usually held on Martin Luther King Jr. weekend.

- **Martin Luther King Jr. Day Parade,** Miami. This parade along NW 62nd Avenue, north of downtown, honors Dr. King, Jr.. For information, call ☎ **305/636-1924.** Second weekend in January.

- **International Circus Festival and Parade,** Sarasota. Circus acts, clowns, and rides for kids honor the city's rich circus heritage. Call ☎ **941/351-8888** for schedule. Day after Christmas through January.

- ✪ **Royal Caribbean Classic,** Key Biscayne. World-renowned golfers compete for more than $1 million in prize money at Crandon Park Golf Course, formerly known as The Links. Lee Trevino is a two-time winner of this championship tournament. Call ☎ **305/374-6180** for more information. Late January.

- **Palm Beach Antique Show,** Palm Beach. Dealers from around the world attract collectors and regular shoppers alike to this international art and antique show which features museum quality art, antique furniture, jewelry, tapestries, books, porcelain and much more. Call ☎ **561/220-2690.** Late January to early February.

- ✪ **Walt Disney World Marathon,** Orlando. This 26.2-mile marathon winding through the resort and theme-park areas is open to all, including the physically challenged. The $50 entry fee is included in room price with some Disney resort packages. Preregistration is required. Call ☎ **407/824-4321** for details.

- ✪ **Zora Neale Hurston Festival,** Eatonville. This 4-day celebration in Eatonville, the first incorporated African American town in America, highlights the life and works of author Zora Neale Hurston. Eatonville is about 25 miles north of the theme parks. Call ☎ **800/352-3865** for details. Usually last weekend in January.

- **Taste of the Grove Food and Music Festival,** Miami. This fund-raiser in the Grove's Peacock Park is an excellent chance for visitors to sample menu items from some of the city's top restaurants and sounds from international and local performers. Call ☎ **305/444-7270** for details. Mid-January.

- **The Key Biscayne Art Festival,** Key Biscayne. Really one of the finest in the country, this art festival, held in Cape Florida State Park, brings hundreds of artists, some crafts makers, and lots of great international food together for a high-quality, juried fine art show-all for charity. Call ☎ **305/361-0049** for details. Last weekend in January.

- **Goodland Mullet Festival,** Marco Island. Stan Gober's Idle Hour Seafood Restaurant in Goodland is mobbed during a massive party featuring the Buzzard Lope dance and the Best Men's Legs Contest. Call ☎ **941/394-3041** for details. Sunday before Super Bowl.

- **Winter Antique Show,** Miami Beach. Antique glasswork, coins, jewelry, furniture and more fill 800 booths and two halls at the mammoth Miami Beach Convention Center. Call ☎ **305/673-7311** for details. Late January to early February.

February

- ✪ **Edison Pageant of Light,** Fort Myers. The spectacular Parade of Lights tops off arts-and-crafts shows, pageants, and a 5K race. Call ☎ **800/237-6444** or 941/334-2550. First 2 weeks in February.

- ✪ **Everglades Seafood Festival,** Florida City. As many as 75,000 people show up each year for this 2-day eating festival in the quaint old town of Florida City. Florida delicacies like stone crab and gator tails are dished up from shacks and food booths on the outskirts of town. Friday night is family night where a carnival and craft fair attracts the youngsters. No admission charge. Call ☎ **941/695-4100** for more details. First full weekend in February.

- **Winter Gayla,** Ft. Lauderdale. More than 10,000 gay men and women turn out for this 10-day pride festival with parties, games, vendors, and displays. Call ☎ **954/561-2020** for details. Early February.

- ✪ **Gasparilla Pirate Fest,** Tampa. Hundreds of boats and rowdy "pirates" invade the city, then parade along Bayshore Boulevard, showering crowds with beads and coins. For information, call ☎ **813/273-6495.** Early February.

- **Artigras,** Palm Beach Gardens. This 3-day event featuring local and national artists was named 15th best art show in the nation. It boasts local and regional musicians and entertainers, activities for kids and seniors, and international foods. Call ☎ **561/748-8844** for details. Presidents' Day weekend.

- ✪ **Speedweeks,** Daytona. Nineteen days of events with a series of races that draw the top names in NASCAR stock-car racing, all culminating in the **Daytona 500.** All events take place at the Daytona International Speedway. Especially for the Daytona 500, tickets must be purchased even a year in advance. They go on sale January 1 of the prior year. Call ☎ **904/253-7223** for ticket information. First 3 weeks of February.

- ✪ **Miami Film Festival.** This 10-day festival has made an impact as an important screening opportunity for Latin American cinema and American independents. It's relatively small, well priced, and easily accessible to the general public. Contact the Film Society of Miami at ☎ **305/377-FILM.** Early February.

- ✪ **Coconut Grove Art Festival,** Miami. The state's largest art festival and the favorite annual event of many locals. More than 300 artists are selected from thousands of entries to show their works at this prestigious and bacchanalian event. Almost every medium is represented during this outside festival, including the culinary arts. Call ☎ 305/447-0401 for details. Presidents' Day weekend.

- **Florida State Fair,** Tampa. Despite all its development, Florida still is a major agricultural state, which status it celebrates at this huge annual exposition. Judged competitions, botanical gardens, crafts building, carny rides, nationally known entertainers. Call ☎ 800/345-FAIR for details. Mid-February.
- **Mardi Gras at Universal Studios,** Orlando. Started in the mid-1990s, this evening event has become more elaborate each year. Authentic parade floats from New Orleans, stilt walkers, and doubloons and beads thrown to the crowd add to the fun. Special entertainment is also part of the fun. Included in the price of admission to the park. For information call ☎ 407/363-8000 for details. Mid-February.
- ❂ **Miami International Boat Show,** Miami. This show draws almost a quarter of a million boat enthusiasts to the Miami Beach Convention Center and surrounding locations to see the megayachts, sailboats, dinghies, and accessories. It's the biggest anywhere. Call ☎ 305/531-8410 for more information and ticket prices. Mid-February.
- **Palm Beach Seafood Festival,** West Palm Beach. This festival at Currie Park features arts and crafts, kiddie rides, and of course, stone crabs, lobster, and more. Call ☎ 561/832-6397 for the word on the day's catch. Mid-February.
- ❂ **Silver Spurs Rodeo,** Kissimmee. The rodeo featuring real cowboys in contests of calf roping, bull and bronco riding, barrel racing, and more is a celebration of the area's rural, pre-Disney roots. It's held at the Silver Spurs Arena, 1875 E. Irlo Bronson Memorial Hwy. (U.S. 192) in Kissimmee. Call ☎ 407/847-5000 for details. Tickets $15. Third weekend in February
- **St. Lucie County Fair,** Fort Pierce. Agricultural youth and livestock fair that features an impressive country music lineup. Stars like Loretta Lynn, Brenda Lee, Mark Chestnut, and Johnny and June Carter Cash have performed in recent years. Call ☎ 561/464-2910 for more details. End of February.
- **Doral-Ryder Golf Open.** One of the county's most prestigious annual tournaments. Call ☎ 305/477-GOLF for more information. Late February to early March.
- **Medieval Fair,** Sarasota. Knights in shining armor and fair maidens in flowing gowns on the grounds of the Ringling Museum. For information, call ☎ 941/351-8497. Late February to early March.

March

- **Bike Week,** Daytona Beach. An international gathering of motorcycle enthusiasts draws a crowd of more than 200,000. In addition to major races held at Daytona International Speedway (featuring the world's best road racers, motocrossers, and dirt trackers), there are motorcycle shows, beach parties, and the Annual Motorcycle Parade, with thousands of riders. Call ☎ 800/854-1234 or 904/255-0981, or online at www.officialbikeweek.com. First week in March.
- **The Central Florida Fair.** This 11-day fair, held at the Central Florida Fairgrounds, 4603 W. Colonial Dr., features rides, entertainers, 4-H and livestock exhibits, a petting zoo, and food booths. Adults pay $6, children 6 to 10 are charged $3, and children 5 and under enter free. Call ☎ 407/295-3247 for details. Early March (some years beginning late February).
- **Winter Party,** Miami. The Dade Human Rights Foundation hosts this gay and lesbian weekend-long party that features several activities at clubs around town and culminates in a huge all-day dance fest on the beach on Sunday. For more information on specific events and ticket prices, call ☎ 305/538-5908 or check out their Web site at www.winterparty.com. Early March.

- **Florida Strawberry Festival,** Plant City. Country music's brightest stars entertain and overdose on strawberry shortcake in the "Winter Strawberry Capital of the World." Call ☎ **813/752-9194.** First weekend in March.
- **Kissimmee Bluegrass Festival,** Kissimmee. Major bluegrass and gospel entertainers from all over the country perform at this 4-day festival at the Silver Spurs Arena, 1875 E. Irlo Bronson Memorial Hwy. Tickets are $12 to $20; multiday packages are available. Call ☎ **800/473-7773** for details. Begins first weekend in March.
- **Renaissance Festival,** Largo. Knights jousting for honor, arts and crafts, entertainment, rides, plus medieval food and drink. Call ☎ **813/586-5423.** Weekends March to mid-April.
- ✪ **Sanibel Shell Fair,** Sanibel and Captiva islands. A show of shells from around the world and the sale of unusual shell art. Call ☎ **941/472-2155.** Begins first Thursday in March.
- **Grand Prix of Miami.** An auto race that rivals the big ones in Daytona. This high-purse, high-profile event attracts the top Indy car drivers and large crowds. For information and tickets, contact Homestead Motorsports Complex at ☎ **305/230-5200.** First week of March.
- **Winter Party,** Miami. The Dade Human Rights Foundation hosts this gay and lesbian weekend-long party which features several activities at clubs around town and culminates in a huge all-day dancefest on the beach on Sunday. For more information on specific events and ticket prices, call ☎ **305/538-5908** or check out their Web site at www.winterparty.com. Early March.
- ✪ **Calle Ocho Festival,** Miami. A salsa-filled blowout that marks the end of a 10-day extravaganza called Carnival Miami. One of the world's biggest block parties held along 23 blocks of Little Havana's Southwest 8th Street between 4th and 27th avenues. Call ☎ **305/644-8888** for more information. Early to mid-March.
- **The Italian Renaissance Festival,** Miami. Stage plays, music, and period costumes complement Villa Vizcaya's neo-Italian architectural style. Call ☎ **305/250-9133** for more information. Mid-March.
- **Miami Gay & Lesbian Film Festival,** Miami. A 10-day festival of short and feature-length films and videos by gay filmmakers at South Beach's Colony Theater on Lincoln Road and other smaller venues. For details, call Robert Rosenberg ☎ **305/532-7256.** Mid-March.
- ✪ **Bay Hill Invitational,** Orlando. Hosted by Arnold Palmer, and featuring some Orlando-based golfers like Tiger Woods, this PGA Tour event is held at the Bay Hill Club, 9000 Bay Hill Blvd. Daily admission is Tuesday and Wednesday $18; Thursday to Sunday $28; weeklong admission, $50 for grounds-only access; $70 for clubhouse access. Call ☎ **407/876-2888** for details. Mid-March.
- **Indian River County's Firefighter's Fair,** Vero Beach. To really get the local flavor of the Treasure Coast, spend a day watching the cattle judging and steer auction. Call ☎ **561/562-2974** to find out more about the fair, which features down-home cooking and carnival rides, too. Third Friday of March.
- **Artsfest,** Stuart. Arts and crafts share the spotlight with real blues, jazz, and classical music as well as food from the best local restaurants. Call the **Council on Arts** at ☎ **561/287-6676** for more information. Mid- to late March.
- **Spring Break,** Daytona Beach, Miami Beach, Panama City Beach, Key West, and other beaches. College students from all over the United States and Canada flock to Florida for endless partying, wet T-shirt and bikini contests, free concerts, volleyball tournaments, and more. Tune into MTV if you can't be here. Call the local visitor information offices. Three weeks in March.

- **Lipton Championships,** Miami. One of the world's largest tennis events hosted at the lush Tennis Center at Crandon Park on Key Biscayne. Call ☎ **305/446-2200** for details. Mid- to late March.
- **Blues Festival,** Miami. Mozart Stub restaurateur Harald Neuweg hosts this all-day street fest featuring down-home blues tunes as well as great food and lots of beer. Call ☎ **305/446-1600** for more details or see "Oktoberfest" listing, below. Third weekend in March.
- ✪ **Bay Hill Invitational,** Orlando. Hosted by Arnold Palmer, this PGA Tour event is held in mid-March at the Bay Hill Club, 9000 Bay Hill Blvd. Daily admission is $28; weeklong admission, $50. Call ☎ **407/876-2888** for details.
- **Sidewalk Art Festival,** Winter Park. Central Park exhibition draws artists from all over North America during the third full weekend in March. The festival is consistently named one of the best in the nation by the national magazine *Sunshine Artist.* Call ☎ **407/623-3234** or 407/644-8281 for details. Admission is free, although you may have to pay for parking.
- **Players Championship,** Ponte Vedra Beach. A major golf event held at the Tournament Player's Club, the toughest course on the PGA tour. Call ☎ **904/285-7888** for details. Late March.
- **Spring Speedway Spectacular,** Daytona. A car show and swap meet at the Daytona International Speedway featuring a wide variety of collector vehicles. Admission is charged. Call ☎ **904/255-7355** for details. Late March or early April.
- **The Spring Flower Festival,** Cypress Gardens. More than 30,000 brightly colored bedding plants and flowers create beautiful topiaries shaped as butterflies, birds, and animals. You have to pay admission to the park to get into the festival: adults $29.50, children 6 to 12, $19.50, seniors $24.50. Call ☎ **941/324-2111** for details. March to May.

April

- **Springtime Tallahassee,** Tallahassee. One of the South's largest celebrations welcomes abundant azaleas, camellias, and other blossoms. Call ☎ **850/224-1373.** Runs 4 weeks from late March.
- **Festival of States,** St. Petersburg. Since 1921 one of the South's largest civic celebrations sees national band competition, three parades, concerts, sports, and more. Call ☎ **727/898-3654.** First full week in April.
- **Highland Games and Festival,** Dunedin. Scottish band contests and Highland dancing, piping, and drumming celebrate Dunedin's Scottish heritage. Call ☎ **813/733-6240.** First full week in April.
- **Miller Lite Professional Men's Beach Volleyball Tournament,** Clearwater Beach. One of the largest pro beach volleyball events is nationally televised. Call ☎ **727/461-0011.** Second weekend in April.
- **PGA Seniors Golf Championship,** Palm Beach Gardens. Held at the PGA National Resort & Spa, it's the oldest and most prestigious of the senior tournaments. Call ☎ **561/624-8400** for the lineup. Mid-April.
- **Black College Reunion**, Daytona Beach. Some 75,000 students from 115 historically black universities bring an end to the spring break season. Call ☎ **800/854-1234** or 904/255-0415. Mid-April.
- **World Cup Polo Tournament,** Palm Beach. Join royalty at the Palm Beach Polo and Country Club to see the best in international polo circles as the season closes. Call ☎ **561/793-1440** for details. Mid-April.
- ✪ **Fringe Festival,** Orlando. Over 100 diverse acts from around the world participate in this eclectic event, held for 10 days at various stages in downtown Orlando.

Everything from sword swallowers to actors doing a 7-minute version of Hamlet perform on outdoor stages available to Fringe goers for free after they purchase a festival button for under $5. Ticket prices vary, but individual performances are generally under $12. Call ☎ **407/648-1333** for details.

- **Easter Sunday,** Orlando. Mickey and friends celebrate with an old-fashioned parade and early opening/late closing throughout Easter week. Call ☎ **407/ 824-4321** for details. Also, an interdenominational service, with music, is presented at the Atlantis Theatre at Sea World, 7007 Sea World Dr. It is hosted by a well-known person each year, most recently Elizabeth Dole. Admission is free. Call ☎ **407/351-3600** for details.
- **Easter Surfing Festival,** Cocoa Beach. More than 250 surfers ride the waves at the "Surf Capital of the East Coast," while Brazen Bikini Contests liven things up ashore. Call ☎ **800/936-2326** for details. Easter weekend.
- **World's Largest Easter Egg Hunt,** Bradenton. The city tries to break into the *Guinness Book of World Records* by burying 200,000 eggs in the sand of Coquina Beach. Call ☎ **941/746-7117.** Easter week.
- **Underwater Easter Egg Hunt,** Destin. Certified divers scour East Pass for colored golf balls and $10,000 in prizes. Call ☎ **800/322-3319** for details. Easter weekend.
- **Beach Goes Pops,** St. Pete Beach. The Florida Orchestra and Florida Opera perform on the gulf shore, with restaurateurs serving dinner at tables on the sand. Call ☎ **727/360-6957.** Last Saturday in April.
- **Sunfest,** West Palm Beach. A huge party happens on Flagler Drive in the downtown area with four stages of continuous music, a craft marketplace, a juried art show, a youth park, and fireworks. Call ☎ **561/659-5992** for details. Late April to early May.

May

- **Epcot International Flower and Garden Festival,** Orlando. A monthlong event with theme gardens, topiary characters, special floral displays, speakers, and seminars.
- **Arabian Nights Festival,** Opa-Locka. This yearly event commemorates the distinctive Moorish architecture in the heart of Opa-Locka. Historical tours, street festivals, live music, and food booths are part of the fun. For details, call ☎ **305/688-4611.** Early May.
- **Turtle Time Festival,** Juno Beach. Swing by the Marine Center at Loggerhead Park and help the locals celebrate the beginning of sea-turtle nesting season. Kids can learn about the marine environment with arts and crafts and children's activities including stage shows. Call ☎ **561/627-8280** for more information. A Saturday in early to mid-May (Mother's Day weekend).
- **Texaco/Hemingway Key West Classic.** Hailed as the top fishing tournament in Florida, this catch-and-release competition offers $50,000 in prizes to be divided between the top anglers in three divisions: sailfish, marlin, and light tackle. Call ☎ **305/294-4440** for more information. Mid-May.
- **Coconuts Dolphin Tournament,** Key Largo. The largest fishing tournament in the Keys, offering $5,000 and a Dodge Ram pickup truck to the person who breaks the record for the largest fish caught. The competition is fierce! Call ☎ **305/451-4107** for details. Mid-May.
- **Cajun/Zydeco Crawfish Festival,** Fort Lauderdale. Spend 3 days at Mills Pond Park dancing to Cajun music—if you don't know how, sign up for free lessons. Can you peel? If so, enter the crawfish-eating contest. Call the Crazee Crawfish 24-hour hotline at ☎ **954/761-5934.** Early May.

- **Shell Air and Sea Show,** Fort Lauderdale. A spectacular display of aeronautics featuring the Blue Angels and aquatic demonstrations by the navy guaranteed to evoke oohs and aahs. Call ☎ 954/527-5600 for details. Early May.
- **Grayton Beach Fine Arts Festival,** South Walton County. With artists from the artsy community of Seaside participating, this is one of the state's finest fine arts festivals. Music and good food, too. Call ☎ 850/267-3511. Early May.
- **Mayfest,** Destin. Upscale arts and crafts festival attracts more than 20,000 people to look, buy, and sample fine cuisine at the Panhandle's ritziest resort. Call ☎ 850/837-6241. Third full weekend in May.
- **The Great Sunrise Balloon Race & Festival,** Homestead. Dozens of multicolored balloons rise up over Homestead Air Reserve Base as sky divers fall from the sky. The race is celebrated on the ground with a variety of food, music, arts, and crafts. For information, call ☎ 305/275-3317. Memorial Day weekend.

June

- **Walt Disney World All-American College Orchestra and College Band.** The best collegiate musical talent in the country performs at Epcot and the Magic Kingdom throughout the summer. Call ☎ 407/824-4321 for details.
- **Fiesta of Five Flags,** Pensacola. Extravaganza commemorates the Spanish conquistador Tristan de Luna's arrival in 1559. Call ☎ 850/433-6512 for information. First week in June.
- **Billy Bowlegs Festival,** Fort Walton Beach. A fleet of modern-day pirates captures the Emerald Coast in a rollicking, weeklong bash honoring notorious buccaneer William Augustus Bowles. Treasure hunt, parade, and carnival, too. Call ☎ 800/322-3319. First week of June.
- **Gay Weekend,** Orlando. The first weekend in June has become known for attracting tens of thousands of gay and lesbian travelers to Central Florida. In 1997, Universal City Travel offered a "Gay Weekend" tour package including tickets to Universal Studios, Sea World, and Church Street Station. This has all grown out of "Gay Day," which has been held unofficially at Walt Disney World for about 5 years, drawing upward of 40,000 folks. Special events throughout the weekend cater to gay and lesbian travelers throughout Central Florida. **Universal City Travel** offers special packages (☎ 800/224-3838 for information). Also get information on the Web at www.gayday.com.
- **Walt Disney World Wine Festival,** Orlando. More than 60 wineries from all over the United States participate. Events include wine tastings, seminars, food, and celebrity-chef cooking demonstrations at Disney's Yacht and Beach Club Convention Center. Call ☎ 407/827-7200 or 407/824-4321 for details.
- **Super Boat Racing Series,** Key West. A day of food, fun, and powerboat racing in downtown Key West. Call ☎ 305/296-8963 for details. Early June.
- ✪ **Coconut Grove Goombay Festival,** Miami. Bahamian bacchanalia with dancing in the streets of Coconut Grove and music from the Royal Bahamian Police marching band. This bash is one of the country's largest black-heritage festivals. The food and music draw thousands to an all-day celebration of Miami's Caribbean connection. It's lots of fun if the weather isn't scorching. Call ☎ 305/372-9966 for festival details. Early June.
- **Spanish Night Watch Ceremony,** St. Augustine. Actors in period dress lead a torchlight procession through historic St. Augustine and reenact the closing of the city gates with music and pageantry. Call ☎ 800/OLD-CITY for details. Third Saturday in June.

- **International Hemingway Festival,** Key West. Literary conferences have replaced beery Ernest-look-alike contests as highlights of this high-brow festival organized by the author's family. Call ☎ 800/533-4753. Third weekend in June.
- **Soulfest,** West Palm Beach. Celebrate African American culture with cuisine, arts and crafts, and entertainment, as well as children's activities. Call the Suncoast Chamber of Commerce at ☎ 561/842-7146 for details.

July

- **Dodger Home Stadium Fireworks Display,** Vero Beach. A day of all-American fun centered around some hometown baseball as well as a barbecue and fireworks. Call ☎ 561/569-4900 for more information. July 3.
- **Independence Day,** Orlando. Walt Disney World's Star-Spangled Spectacular brings bands, singers, dancers, and unbelievable fireworks displays to all the Disney parks, which stay open late. Call ☎ 407/824-4321 for details. Sea World also features a dazzling laser/fireworks spectacular; call ☎ 407/351-3600 for details. There is also a free fireworks display in downtown Orlando at Lake Eola Park. For information call ☎ 407/246-2827.
- **Independence Day,** Miami. Celebrate July 4th on the beach, where parties, barbecues, and fireworks flare all day and night. For a weekend's worth of events on Key Biscayne, call ☎ 305/361-5207. You can also find one of the wildest parties around complete with fireworks and top-notch festivities at Bayfront Park, 301 N. Biscayne Blvd. For more on this free event call ☎ 305/358-7550.
- **Miccosukee Everglades Music and Crafts Festival,** Miami. Native American rock, razz (reservation jazz), and folk bands perform down south while visitors gorge themselves on exotic treats like pumpkin bread and fritters. Watch the hulking old gators wrestle with Native Americans. Call ☎ 305/223-8380 for prices and details. Late July.
- ✪ **Lower Keys Underwater Music Fest,** Looe Key. At this outrageous celebration, boaters go out to the underwater reef of Looe Key Marine Sanctuary off Big Pine Key, drop speakers into the water, and pipe in music. It's entertainment for the fish and swimmers alike! A snorkeling Elvis can usually be spotted. Call ☎ 800/872-3722 for details. Second Saturday of July.
- **Space Week Celebration,** Cape Canaveral. Kennedy Space Center celebrates humans landing on the moon. Science fairs, space art, and a space station design competition are featured. Call ☎ 407/452-2121 for details. Mid-July.
- ✪ **Fourth of July Festivities,** Delray Beach. You can attend a celebration featuring art and jazz on Atlantic Avenue and Fla. A1A and enter a sand-sculpting contest, fly a kite, and sample fare from Delray's neighborhood restaurants. Call ☎ 561/278-0424 for more information. July 4.
- **Pepsi 400,** Daytona. A race marking the halfway point in the NASCAR Winston Cup Series for stock cars. Held at the Daytona International Speedway at 11am. Call ☎ 904/253-7223 for details. July 4.
- **World's Richest Tarpon Tournament,** Boca Grande. Some $175,000 is at stake in the great tarpon waters off Southwest Florida. Call the event hotline at ☎ 800/237-6444 or 941/964-2995. Second Wednesday and Thursday in July.
- **Blue Angels Air Show,** Pensacola. World-famous navy pilots do their aerial acrobatics just 100 yards off the beach. Call ☎ 800/874-1234 for schedule.
- **Wine and All That Jazz,** Boca Raton. A great way to quench your thirst on a sweltering summer day. It's one of the largest wine-tasting parties in the state; sample your choice from more than 100 wines and vintages while listening to a little live

jazz. For details, call ☎ **561/395-4433.** Friday night at the end of July or beginning of August.

August

- **Boca Festival Days,** Boca Raton. A monthlong, city-wide event for the summer-weary featuring everything from baby contests to swim meets. One of the best events is the food and wine tasting thrown by the Hospice-by-the-Sea. Dozens of Palm Beach county's best chefs turn out succulent dishes for the black-tie-optional affair. Add to that booth upon booth of the world's most renowned vintners serving sips of fine wine and a silent auction, and this could be one of the year's finest and most accessible benefits. Call ☎ **561/395-4433** for details.
- **Miami Reggae Festival,** Miami. Jamaica's best dance-hall and reggae artists turn out for this 2-day festival. Burning Spear, Steel Pulse, Spragga Benz, and Jigsy King participated recently. Call Jamaica Awareness at ☎ **305/891-2944** for more details. Early August.

September

- **Labor Day Pro-Am Surfing Festival,** Cocoa Beach. One of the largest surfing events on East Coast draws pros and amateurs from around the country. Rock-and-roll bands, swimsuit contests. Call ☎ **800/936-2326** for details. Labor Day weekend.
- **Festival Miami.** A 4-week program of performing arts featuring local and invited musical guests. Centered in the University of Miami School of Music and Maurice Gusman Concert Hall. For a schedule of events, call ☎ **305/284-4940.** Mid-September to mid-October.
- **Night of Joy,** Orlando. One weekend in September, the Magic Kingdom hosts a festival of contemporary Christian music featuring top artists. This is a very popular event; obtain tickets early. Each year performers make a personal appearance at Long's Christian Bookstore in nearby College Park, about 20 minutes north of Disney. Admission to the concert is about $25 to $30 per night. Exclusive use of Magic Kingdom attractions is included. Call ☎ **407/824-4321** for details about the concert. For information about the free appearance at Long's, call ☎ **407/ 422-0293.**

October

- **Destin Seafood Festival,** Destin. The "World's Luckiest Fishing Village" cooks its bountiful catch in every style of cuisine imaginable. Also offered are arts, crafts, and music. Comes right after **Destin Fishing Rodeo,** with 450 angler awards, giant dock parties. Call ☎ **850/837-6241.** First full weekend in October.
- ✪ **Columbus Day Regatta,** Miami. Find anything that can float—from an inner tube to a 100-foot yacht—and you'll fit right in. Yes, there actually is a race, but who can keep track when you're partying with a bunch of seminaked psychos in the middle of Biscayne Bay? It's free and it's wild. Rent a boat, jet ski, or sailboard to get up close. Be sure to secure a vessel early, though—everyone wants to be there. Check local newspapers for exact date and time. Columbus Day weekend.
- **Biketoberfest,** Daytona. Road-racing stars compete at the CCS Motorcycle Championship at Daytona International Speedway, plus parties, parades, concerts, and more. Call ☎ **904/253-7223** for race ticket information, ☎ **800/854-1235** for other activities. Mid-October.
- ✪ **Walt Disney World Oldsmobile Golf Classic.** Top PGA tour players compete for a total purse of $1 million at WDW golf courses in October's major golf event. Transplanted local golf phenom Tiger Woods is usually among the players. Daily

ticket prices range from $8 to $15. The event is preceded by the world's largest golf tournament, the admission-free **Oldsmobile Scramble.** Call ☎ **407/824-4321** for details.

- **Walt Disney World Village Boat Show.** Central Florida's largest in-the-water boat show, featuring the best of new watercraft. At the Village Marketplace, over a 3-day weekend. Call ☎ **407/824-4321** for details. Early October.

- **Oktoberfest,** Miami. They close the streets for this German beer and food festival thrown by the Mozart Stub Restaurant in Coral Gables. You'll find loads of great music and dancing at this wild party. Call owner, Harald Neuweg at ☎ **305/446-1600** to find out where and when. See www.mozartstub.com for more details.

- ✪ **Fantasy Fest,** Key West. It might feel as if the rest of the world is joining you if you're in Key West for this inane, world-famous Halloween festival, Florida's version of Mardi Gras. Crazy costumes, wild parades, and even more colorful revelers gather for an opportunity to do things Mom said not to do. Definitely leave the kids at home! Call ☎ **305/296-1817.** Last week of October.

- ✪ **Goombay Festival,** Key West. Sample Caribbean dishes and purchase art and ethnic clothing in this celebration with a Jamaican flair that coincides with Fantasy Fest (see above).

- ✪ **Fort Lauderdale International Boat Show.** Your chance to meet fellow boating enthusiasts and look over more than 1,400 boats and every imaginable variety of marine paraphernalia. Call ☎ **800/940-7642** for details. Late October to early November.

- **Clearwater Jazz Holiday,** Clearwater. Top jazz musicians play for 4 days and nights at bay-front Coachman Park in this free musical extravaganza. Call ☎ **727/363-7866** for schedule. Mid-October.

- ✪ **Halloween Horror Nights,** Orlando. Universal Studios Florida transforms its studios and attractions for several weeks before and after Halloween—with haunted attractions, live bands, a psychopath's maze, special shows, and hundreds of ghouls and goblins roaming the studio streets. The studio essentially closes at dusk, reopening in a new macabre form a few hours later. Special admission is charged. Call ☎ **407/363-8000** for details.

- **Guavaween,** Tampa. Ybor City's Latin-style Halloween celebration begins with the "Mama Guava Stumble," a wacky costume parade. All-night concerts from rock to reggae. For information, call ☎ **813/248-3712.** October 31.

- **Amelia Heritage Festival,** Amelia Island. Civil War reenactments, tours of Fernandina Beach historic district, more. Call ☎ **800/2-AMELIA.** Late October.

- ✪ **John's Pass Seafood Festival,** Madeira Beach. Tons of fish, shrimp, crab, and other seafood go down the hatch at one of Florida's largest seafood festivals. Call ☎ **813/391-7373.** Last weekend in October.

- ✪ **Jacksonville Jazz Festival.** This free weeklong, nonstop music event in Metropolitan Park features major artists. Call ☎ **904/353-7770** for details. Late October or early November.

November

- **Frank Brown International Songwriters' Festival,** Pensacola. Composers gather at the infamous Flora-Bama Lounge and other beach venues to perform their country-music hits. Call ☎ **850/492-4660** for information. First week in November.

- ✪ **Florida Seafood Festival,** Apalachicola. Book a room at the Gibson Inn 5 years in advance of this huge chow-down in Florida's oystering capital. Call ☎ **850/653-9419** for details. First Saturday in November.

- **Mum Festival,** Cypress Gardens. November's monthlong flower festival at Cypress Gardens features millions of mums, their colorful flowers displayed in beds, "blooming" gazebos, poodle baskets, and bonsai. Call ☎ **941/324-2111** for details.

- **Walt Disney World Festival of the Masters,** Orlando. One of the largest art shows in the South takes place at Disney's Village Marketplace for 3 days, including the second weekend in November. The exhibition features top artists, photographers, and craftspeople—winners of juried shows throughout the country. Free admission. Call ☎ **407/824-4321** for details.

- **Mercury Outboards Cheeca/Redbone Celebrity Tournament,** Islamorada, in the Upper Keys. Curt Gowdy from *American Sportsman* hosts this tournament, whose proceeds go to finding a cure for cystic fibrosis. The likes of Wade Boggs, actor James B. Sikking, and Gen. Norman Schwarzkopf compete almost yearly. Call ☎ **305/664-2002** for details. This event is followed by the George Bush Cheeca Lodge Bonefish Tournament. Call ☎ **305/743-7000** for more information. Second and third weekends of November.

- **The Jiffy Lube Miami 300 weekend of NASCAR,** Miami. Here's more world-class racing at the recently constructed 344-acre motor-sports complex. For information and tickets contact Homestead Motorsports Complex, One Speedway Blvd., Homestead, ☎ **305/230-5200.** Mid-November.

- **Chili Cook-Off,** Miami. Sample some of the nation's best chili as the area's "hottest" restaurants compete for the glory of being the best. For details, call ☎ **305/441-6677.** Mid-November.

- **Blues Festival at Riverwalk,** Fort Lauderdale. Receive a blues infusion during this weekend-long festival which features several live music stages scattered throughout area clubs. You can buy individual event tickets but a 3-day pass is definitely worthwhile. Call ☎ **954/489-3256** for more details. Mid-November.

- **White Party Week,** Miami. This weeklong AIDS fund-raiser begins with a series of events in Miami Beach nightclubs and leads up to the Sunday night gala, where Miami's gay community comes out to celebrate at the Renaissance mansion, Vizcaya. Since this gala always sells out, make sure to buy your tickets as soon as they go on sale October 1. Call ☎ **305/759-6181** for details. Thanksgiving weekend.

- **Walt Disney World Doll and Teddy Bear Convention,** Orlando. The top doll and teddy-bear designers from around the world travel to WDW for this major November event. Call ☎ **407/824-4321** for details.

- **Fort Lauderdale International Film Festival.** Showcases 3 weeks worth of international, independent, and student film-competition winners. Also, don't forget about the star-studded parties hosted by the festival. Call ☎ **954/563-0500** for details. Mid-November.

- **Miami Book Fair International.** An event that draws hundreds of thousands of visitors, including foreign and domestic publishers and authors from around the world, with great lectures and readings by world-renowned authors. Call ☎ **305/237-3258.** Mid-November.

- **The Ramble,** Miami. Old-time Floridians love this yearly event at the Fairchild Tropical Gardens. Here you can buy antiques, exotic orchids, or vintage clothes. If you're not shopping, it's still worth strolling around the lush park where you can learn about various botanical miracles. For more information, call ☎ **305/667-1651.** Mid-November.

- **Daytona Beach Fall Speedway Spectacular.** Featuring the Annual Turkey Rod Run, this is the Southeast's largest combined car show and swap meet, with thousands of street rods and classic vehicles on display and for sale. It takes place at the International Speedway. Call ☎ **904/255-7355** for details. Thanksgiving weekend.
- **Blue Angels Homecoming Air Show,** Pensacola. World-famous navy pilots do their aerial acrobatics just 100 yards off the beach. Call ☎ **800/874-1234** or 850/452-2583 for information. Second weekend in November.
- **Sarasota French Film Festival,** Sarasota. Acclaimed French films, directors, and celebrities come for premiere screenings. For information, call ☎ **941/351-9010.** Second weekend in November.
- **Fort Myers Beach Sand Sculpting Contest,** Fort Myers Beach. Some 50,000 gather to sculpt or see the world's finest sand castles. Call ☎ **800/782-9283** or 941/463-6451. First weekend in November.
- **Poinsettia Festival,** Cypress Gardens. A spectacular floral showcase of more than 40,000 red, white, and pink poinsettia blooms (including topiary reindeer) highlight this flower festival. This is actually one of the best ways to view the park. Call ☎ **941/324-2111** for details. Late November to mid-January.
- **Jolly Holidays Dinner Shows,** Orlando. From late November to mid-December these all-you-can-eat events are offered at the Contemporary Resort's Fantasia Ballroom. A cast of more than 100 Disney characters, singers, and dancers performs in an old-fashioned Christmas extravaganza. Call ☎ **407/W-DISNEY** for details and ticket prices.

December

- **Edison/Ford Winter Homes Holiday House,** Fort Myers. Thousands of lights and Christmas music hail the holiday season. At the same time, candles create a spectacular Luminary Trail along the full length of Sanibel Island's Periwinkle Way. Call ☎ **941/275-1088** for information. First week of December.
- **Captiva Sea Kayak Classic,** Captiva Island. Sea kayaker and surf skiers from around the nation depart from beach in front of 'Tween Waters Inn for a series of races. Call ☎ **941/472-5161.** First weekend in December.
- **JC Penney Mixed Team Golf Classic,** Tarpon Springs. Westin Innisbrook Resort hosts mixed-gender teams of top pro golfers. Call ☎ **727/942-2000,** ext. 5393. First week in December.
- **Burger King Classic Half-Marathon and Hooter's 5K Run,** Orlando. This annual race, early in December, takes place in downtown Orlando, beginning at 8am at Church Street Market, 200 S. Orange Ave. Anyone can participate. An entry fee is charged. The event kicks off the Citrus Bowl season. Call ☎ **407/ 423-2476** for information.
- **Winterfest Boat Parade,** Fort Lauderdale. A hundred boats decorated with lights cruise up the Intracoastal Waterway from Port Everglades to Lake Santa Barbara. There's no better way to get into the Christmas spirit. Call ☎ **954/767-0686** for details. Second weekend in December.
- **City Link Music Fest,** Fort Lauderdale. The largest 1-night music fest in the state of Florida. More than 100 local bands play jazz, blues, and rock at different nightclubs throughout Fort Lauderdale. Call ☎ **954/356-4943** for details. Mid-December.
- **Grand Illumination Ceremony,** St. Augustine. A torchlight procession from Government House through the Spanish Quarter. Kicks off a month of Christmas festivities: reenactments of British colonial customs, encampments, 18th-century music, crafts demonstrations, cannon firings, caroling, an 18th-century bazaar, a

performance of Handel's *Messiah,* parade, and more. Call ☎ **800/OLD-CITY** for details. First Saturday in December.

○ **Christmas at Walt Disney World,** Orlando. Main Street is lavishly decked out with lights, holly, 80-foot tree, and carolers who greet visitors. Resorts offer special embellishments and entertainment, including Mickey's Very Merry Christmas Party, an after-dark ticketed event ($25). Magic Kingdom has traditional Christmas parade and breathtaking fireworks display. Candlelight procession at Epcot features hundreds of candle-holding carolers, a celebrity narrator telling the Christmas story, and a 450-voice choir. Osborne Family Christmas Lights. Call ☎ **407/824-4321** for events, 407/934-7639 to inquire about hotel/events packages. Most of December.

• **Christmas at Sea World,** Orlando. Sea World features a special Shamu show and a luau show called *Christmas in Hawaii.* The 400-foot sky tower is lit like a Christmas tree nightly. Call ☎ **407/351-3600** for details.

• **World Karting Association Enduro World Championships,** Daytona. The biggest go-carting event in the country takes place between Christmas and New Year's at the Daytona International Speedway. Call ☎ **904/253-7223** for details.

• **Annual Tour of Homes,** Boca Raton. Exclusive mansions in Old Floresta open their doors to visitors (thanks to a little arm twisting on the part of the Boca Raton Historical Society). Space is limited, so be sure to call ☎ **561/395-6766** and reserve early. End of December or January.

• **King Mango Strut,** Coconut Grove, Miami. This fun-filled march encourages everyone to wear wacky costumes and join the floats in a spoof of the King Orange Jamboree Parade, held the following night. Runs from Commodore Plaza to Peacock Park in Coconut Grove. Comedians and musical entertainment follow in the park. Call ☎ **305/444-7270** for details. December 30.

• **Walt Disney World New Year's Eve Celebration,** Orlando. For 1 night the Magic Kingdom is open until 2am for a massive fireworks exhibition. Other New Year's festivities in the WDW parks include a big bash at Pleasure Island featuring music headliners, a special *Hoop-Dee-Doo Musical Revue* show, and guest performances by well-known musical groups at Disney–MGM Studios and Epcot. Call ☎ **407/824-4321** for details.

○ **Citrus Bowl Parade,** Orlando. On an annually selected date in late December, the parade features lavish floats and high school bands for a nationally televised event. Reserved seats in the bleachers are $12. Call ☎ **407/423-2476** for details.

• **CompUSA Florida Citrus Bowl New Year's,** Orlando. The official New Year's Eve celebration of the CompUSA Florida Citrus Bowl takes place at Sea World. Events include headliner concerts, a laser and fireworks spectacular, a countdown to midnight, and special shows throughout the park. Admission is charged. Call ☎ **407/423-2476** for details.

○ **King Orange Jamboree Parade,** Miami. The world's largest nighttime parade is followed by a long night of festivities leading up to the Orange Bowl football game (see January listing, above). Runs along Biscayne Boulevard. For information and tickets (which cost $7.50 to $13), contact the Greater Miami Convention and Visitors Bureau at ☎ **305/539-3063.** Usually December 31.

3 Health & Insurance

STAYING HEALTHY   Florida doesn't present any unusual health hazards for most people. Folks with certain medical conditions such as liver disease, diabetes, and stomach ailments, however, should avoid eating raw **oysters,** which can carry a natural bacterium linked to severe diarrhea, vomiting, and even fatal blood poisoning. Cooking kills the bacteria, so if in doubt, order your oysters steamed, broiled, or fried.

Florida has millions of **mosquitoes** and invisible biting **sand flies** (known as "no-see-ums"), especially in the coastal and marshy areas. Fortunately, neither insect carries malaria or other diseases. Keep these pests at bay with a good insect repellent.

It's especially important to protect yourself against **sunburn.** Don't underestimate the strength of the sun's rays down there, even in the middle of winter. Limit the amount of time you spend in the sun, especially during the first couple of days of your trip and always from 11am to 2pm. Use a sunscreen with a high protection factor and apply it liberally. And children need more protection from the sun than adults do.

Pack any **prescription medications** you need to take in your carry-on luggage. Also bring along copies of your prescriptions in case you lose your pills or run out.

If you have a serious condition or allergy, consider wearing a Medic Alert identification bracelet; contact the **Medic Alert Foundation,** P.O. Box 1009, Turlock, CA 95381-1009 (☎ **800/432-5378**). If you have dental problems, a nationwide referral service known as **1-800-DENTIST** (☎ **800/336-8478**) will give you the name of a nearby dentist or clinic.

INSURANCE   Many travelers buy insurance policies providing health and accident, trip-cancellation and -interruption, and lost-luggage protection. The coverage you should consider will depend on how you're getting to Florida and how much protection is already contained in your existing health insurance or other policies. Some credit- and charge-card companies may insure you against travel accidents if you buy plane, train, or bus tickets with their cards. Before purchasing additional insurance, read your policies and agreements over carefully. Call your insurers or credit/charge-card companies if you have any questions.

Here are some American firms offering travel insurance:

Worldwide Assistance (☎ **800/821-2828** or 202/347-2025); **Travel Guard International** (☎ **800/782-5151** or 715/345-0505); **Access America** (☎ **800/ 284-8300** or 804/285-3300); or **Mutual of Omaha** (☎ **800/228-9792**). The **Divers Alert Network (DAN)** (☎ **800/446-2671** or 919/684-2948) insures scuba divers.

4 Tips for Travelers with Special Needs

FOR TRAVELERS WITH DISABILITIES   **Walt Disney World** and **Universal Studios** do everything possible to assist guests with disabilities. Disney's many services are detailed in their *Guidebook for Guests with Disabilities.* For a free copy, contact Guest Letters, P.O. Box 10,040, Lake Buena Vista, FL 32830-0040 (☎ **407/ 824-4321**). For information about Universal Studios, CityWalk, and Islands of Adventure, contact Universal Studios Florida, 1000 Universal Studios Dr., Orlando, FL 32816 (☎ **407/393-8080**).

A free copy of the *Florida Planning Companion for People with Disabilities* is available from the **Florida Governor's Alliance,** 345 S. Magnolia Dr., Suite D-11, Tallahassee, FL 32301 (☎ **850/487-2223** or 850/487-2222 TTD).

Nationwide resources include **Mobility International USA** (☎ **503/343-1284**), which offers its members travel-accessibility information and has many interesting travel programs for the disabled; the **Travel Information Service** (☎ **215/ 456-9600**); **AccessAbility Travel** (☎ **800/645-0001** or 617/661-9200); and the **Society for the Advancement of Travel for the Handicapped** (☎ **212/447-7284**).

In addition, **Twin Peaks Press,** P.O. Box 129, Vancouver, WA 98666 (☎ **360/694-2462**), publishes travel-related books for people with disabilities.

Companies offering tours for those with physical or mental disabilities include **Accessible Journeys** (☎ **800/TINGLES** or 610/521-0339); **Flying Wheels Travel** (☎ **800/535-6790** or 507/451-5005); **The Guided Tour, Inc.** (☎ **215/782-1370**); and **Wilderness Inquiry** (☎ **800/728-0719** or 612/379-3858).

In addition, both **Amtrak** (☎ **800/USA-RAIL;** www.amtrak.com) and **Greyhound** (☎ **800/752-4841;** www.greyhound.com) offer special fares and services for the disabled. Call at least a week in advance of your trip for details.

The **National Park Service** issues free "Golden Access Passports," which waives admission fees into national parks, forests, and wildlife refuges for a disabled person and a companion. Get them at park entrances.

FOR SENIORS   With one of the largest retired populations of any state, Florida offers a wide array of activities and benefits for senior citizens. Don't be shy about asking for discounts, but always carry some kind of identification, such as a driver's license, that shows your date of birth.

Also, mention the fact that you're a senior citizen when you first make your travel reservations. For example, both **Amtrak** (☎ **800/USA-RAIL;** www.amtrak.com) and **Greyhound** (☎ **800/752-4841;** www.greyhound.com) offer discounts to persons over 62. And many hotels offer seniors discounts, including the **Choice Hotels** (Clarion Hotels, Quality Inns, Comfort Inns, Sleep Inns, Econo Lodges, Friendship Inns, and Rodeway Inns), which give 30% off their published rates to anyone over 50, provided you book your room through their nationwide toll-free reservations numbers (that is, not directly with the hotels or through a travel agent).

Members of the **American Association of Retired Persons (AARP),** 601 E St. NW, Washington, DC 22049 (☎ **800/424-3410** or 202/434-2277), get discounts not only on hotels but on airfares and car rentals, too.

Other helpful organizations include the nonprofit **National Council of Senior Citizens,** 1331 F St. NW, Washington, DC 20004 (☎ **202/347-8800**), part of whose magazine is devoted to travel tips. **Mature Outlook,** 6001 N. Clark St., Chicago, IL 60660 (☎ **800/336-6330**), offers discounts at ITC-member hotels and savings on selected auto rentals and restaurants. **Golden Companions,** P.O. Box 5249, Reno, NV 89513 (☎ **702/324-2227**), helps travelers 45-plus find compatible companions through a personal voice-mail service. Contact them for more information.

Companies specializing in seniors' travel include **Grand Circle Travel,** 347 Congress St., Suite 3A, Boston, MA 02210 (☎ **800/221-2610** or 617/350-7500); and **SAGA International Holidays,** 222 Berkeley St., Boston, MA 02115 (☎ **800/343-0273**).

FOR FAMILIES   Florida is a great family destination, with most of its hotels and restaurants willing and eager to cater to families traveling with children. Many hotels and motels let children 17 and under stay free in their parents' room (be sure to ask when you reserve).

At the beaches, it's the exception rather than the rule for a resort not to have a children's activities program (some will even mind the youngsters while the parents enjoy a night off!). Even if they don't have a children's program of their own, most will arrange baby-sitting services.

If you call ahead before dining out, you'll see that most restaurants have some facilities for children, such as booster chairs and low-priced kids' menus.

FOR STUDENTS   It's worthwhile to bring along your valid high school or college identification. Presenting it can mean discounted admission to museums and other

● **Did You Know?**

- Ponce de León, the Spanish conquistador who discovered Florida in 1513, had earlier sailed with Columbus.
- Movie star Burt Reynolds played defensive back for Florida State University's Seminoles football team.
- Pres. Teddy Roosevelt once fought all day to land a 30-foot manta ray at Sanibel Island. It took some 50 steel-jacketed bullets to kill the huge "devilfish."
- Now a luxury resort, Clarence Chadwick's Captiva Island plantation once supplied 90% of the nation's key limes.
- Ed Watson, reputed killer of notorious female outlaw Belle Star, was himself gunned down near Everglades City.
- Although it looks like a marsh, the Everglades is actually a river 40 miles wide and 6 inches deep.
- The 800 buildings in Miami Beach's Art Deco District were the first 20th-century structures to be included in the National Register of Historic Places.
- The Tampa Bay Hotel, located on the campus of the University of Tampa, is considered the finest example of Moorish architecture in the Western Hemisphere.
- The old Tarzan movies starring Johnny Weissmuller were filmed at Wakulla Springs near Tallahassee.
- Now surviving only in Florida, manatees were once common from the Carolinas to Texas.

attractions. And remember, alcoholic beverages cannot be sold in Florida to anyone who is under 21, so if you're eligible and intend to imbibe, bring your driver's license or another valid photo identification showing your date of birth.

FOR GAY & LESBIAN TRAVELERS   According to the editors of *Out and About*, a gay and lesbian newsletter, Miami's **South Beach** is the "hippest, hottest, most happening gay travel destination in the world." For many years that could also be said of **Key West,** which still is one of the country's most popular destinations for gays. And Fort Lauderdale—where gays own some 21 motels, 40 bars, and numerous other businesses—is definitely on the gay-friendly map.

The popularity of **Orlando** with gay and lesbian travelers is highlighted with Gay Weekend in early June, which draws as many as 40,000 participants and includes events at Disney World, Universal Studios, and Sea World. **Universal City Travel** (☎ 800/224-3838), offers a "Gay Weekend" tour package including tickets to Universal Studios, Sea World, and Church Street Station. For information about events for that weekend, or throughout the year, contact the **Gay & Lesbian Community Services of Central Florida,** 714 E. Colonial Dr., Orlando, FL 32804 (☎ 407/425-4527). You can get information on the World Wide Web at www.gayday.com.

Florida is not without its intolerant contingent, but there are active gay and lesbian contingents in most other cities here.

The **International Gay Travel Association (IGTA),** P.O. Box 4974, Key West, FL 33041 (☎ **800/448-8550,** or 305/292-0217 for voice mailbox), links travelers up with the appropriate gay-friendly service organization or tour specialist. Contact the IGTA for a list of its member agencies, who will be tied into IGTA's information resources.

In addition to its editor's choices, *Out and About,* 8 W. 19th St., Suite 401, New York, NY 10011 (☎ **800/929-2268**), profiles the best gay or gay-friendly hotels, gyms, clubs, and other places and destinations throughout the world. *Our World,* 1104 N. Nova Rd., Suite 251, Daytona Beach, FL 32117 (☎ **904/441-5367**), is a magazine devoted to options and bargains for gay and lesbian travel worldwide.

5 Getting There

BY PLANE

Many major domestic airlines fly to and from Florida, including **American** (☎ **800/433-7300**), **Continental** (☎ **800/525-0280**), **Delta** (☎ **800/221-1212**), **Northwest** (☎ **800/225-2525**), **TWA** (☎ **800/221-2000**), **United** (☎ **800/ 241-6522**), and **US Airways** (☎ **800/428-4322**).

Several so-called no-frills airlines—low fares but no meals or other amenities—fly to Florida. The biggest, best, and most reliable is ✪ **Southwest Airlines** (☎ **800/ 435-9792**), which has flights from many U.S. cities to Fort Lauderdale, Jacksonville, Orlando, and Tampa. An arm of the popular cruise line, **Carnival Air** (☎ **800/ 824-7386**) flies from New York and Washington, D.C., to Fort Lauderdale. **AirTran** (☎ **800/AIR-TRAN**) flies from several Northeast, Midwest, and southern cities to its hub in Orlando and several other Florida cities.

Others flying to Florida include **Delta Express,** a branch of Delta Airlines (☎ **800/ 325-5205**); **Eastwind** (☎ **800/644-3592**); **Kiwi International** (☎ **800/538-5494**); **MetroJet,** an arm of US Airways (☎ **800/428-4322**); **Midway** (☎ **800/ 44-MIDWAY**); **Midwest Express** (☎ **800/452-2022**); **Spirit** (☎ **800/ 722-7117**); **SunJet** (☎ **800/478-6538**); **Tower Air** (☎ **800/348-6937**); and **Vanguard** (☎ **800/826-4827**).

There's no shortage of **discounted and promotional fares** to Florida. November, December, and January often see fare wars that can result in savings of 50% or more. Watch for advertisements in your local newspaper and on TV, or call the airlines.

Ask the airlines for their lowest fares, and ask if it's cheaper to book in advance, fly in midweek, or stay over a Saturday night. Don't stop at the 7-day advance purchase; ask how much the 14- and 30-day plans cost. Decide when you want to go before you call, since many of the best deals are nonrefundable.

Many **charter flights** go to Florida, especially during the winter season. They cost less than regularly scheduled flights, but they are very complicated. It's best to go to a good travel agent and ask him or her to find one for you and to explain the problems as well as the advantages.

You might also get a low fare by calling a "consolidator" such as **TFI Tours International** (☎ **800/745-8000** or 212/736-1140), which serves as a clearinghouse for unused seats, or a "rebator" such as **Travel Avenue** (☎ **800/333-3335** or 312/876-1116) and the **Smart Traveller** (☎ **800/448-3338** in the U.S., or 305/448-3338), which rebate part of their commissions to you. A travel agent can tell you more about consolidators and shop among them to find their best deals. Look in your local newspaper's Sunday travel section for rebators' usually tiny advertisements.

Another possibility is travel clubs such as **Moment's Notice** (☎ **718/234-6295**) and **Sears Discount Travel Club** (☎ **800/433-9383**, or 800/255-1487 to join), which supply unsold tickets at discounted prices. You pay an annual membership fee to get the club's hotline number. Of course, you're limited to what's available, so you have to be flexible.

If you live overseas, see "Getting to & Around the U.S.," in chapter 3.

BY CAR

Florida is reached by **I-95** along the east coast, **I-75** from the central states, and **I-10** from the west. **The Florida Turnpike,** a toll road, links Orlando, West Palm Beach, Fort Lauderdale, and Miami (it's a shortcut from Wildwood on I-75 north of Orlando to Miami). **I-4** cuts across the state from Cape Canaveral through Orlando to Tampa.

See "Getting Around," below, for more information about driving in Florida and the car-rental firms operating here.

If you're a member, your local branch of the **American Automobile Association (AAA)** will provide a free trip-routing plan. AAA also has nationwide emergency road service (☎ **800/AAA-HELP**).

BY TRAIN

Amtrak (☎ **800/USA-RAIL;** www.amtrak.com) offers train service to Florida from both the East and West coasts. It takes some 26 hours from New York to Miami, 68 hours from Los Angeles to Miami, and Amtrak's fares aren't much less than many deals offered by the airlines.

Amtrak's *Silver Meteor* and *Silver Star* each run twice daily between New York and either Miami or Tampa, with intermediate stops along the East Coast and in Florida. Amtrak's Thruway Bus Connections are available from the Fort Lauderdale Amtrak station and Miami International Airport to Key West, and from Tampa to St. Petersburg, Treasure Island, Clearwater, Bradenton, Sarasota, and Fort Myers. Depending on date of travel, the round-trip fare between New York and Miami for midweek travel ranges from about $150 to $400. The highest fares are between mid-June and mid-August.

From the West Coast, the *Sunset Limited* runs three times weekly between Los Angeles and Orlando. It stops in Pensacola, Crestview (Fort Walton Beach and Destin), Chipley (Panama City Beach), and Tallahassee. Round-trip coach fares between Los Angeles and Miami range from about $300 in low season to $550 in summer. Sleeping accommodations are available for an extra charge.

If you intend to stop off along the way, you can save money with Amtrak's **Explore America** (or All Aboard America) fares, which are based on three regions of the country. At press time, you could stop three times in the eastern states for about $318 in summer, $258 during the off-season.

Amtrak's **Auto Train** runs daily from Lorton, Virginia (12 miles south of Washington, D.C.), to Sanford, Florida (just northeast of Orlando). You ride in a coach while your car is secured in an enclosed vehicle carrier. Round-trip fares at press time ranged from $110 to $170 for each passenger, plus $220 for your car. You should make your train reservations as far in advance as possible.

6 Package Deals

Travel agents offer hundreds of package tour options to the Sunshine State. Quite often a package tour will result in savings not just on airfares but on hotels and other activities as well. You pay one price for a package that varies from one tour operator to the next. Airfare, transfers, and accommodations are always covered, and sometimes meals and specific activities are thrown in. The specifics vary a great deal, so consult your travel agent to find out the best deals at the time you want to travel.

There are some drawbacks: The least expensive tours may put you up at a bottom-end hotel. And since the lower costs depend on volume, some more expensive tours could send you to a large, impersonal property. And since the tour prices are based on double occupancy, the single traveler is almost invariably penalized.

Ask your travel agent to find the best package tours to Florida. Many are offered by subsidiaries of the major airlines, including American, Continental, Delta, Northwest, and TWA. **American Express** (☎ **800/241-1700**) also has several tours available.

In Orlando, the **Walt Disney World Central Reservations Office** (☎ **407/ W-DISNEY**) and **Universal City Travel Co.** (☎ **800/224-3838**) both have numerous packages including air, hotel, and discounted admissions.

Premier Cruise Lines (☎ **800/726-5678**) and **Disney Cruise Line** (☎ **407/ 939-7787**) offer 3- and 4-night luxury ocean cruises to The Bahamas in conjunction with 3- or 4-day Orlando theme-park package vacations. Cruises depart from and return to Port Canaveral, 45 minutes east of Walt Disney World.

In addition to these all-inclusive tours, many Florida hotels and resorts and even some motels offer **golf and tennis packages,** which bundle the cost of room, greens and court fees, and sometimes equipment into one price. These deals usually don't include airfare, but they do represent savings over paying for the room and golf or tennis separately. See the accommodations sections in the following chapters for hostelries offering special packages to their guests.

7 Getting Around

Having a car is the best and easiest way to see Florida's sights, or just to get to and from the beach. Public transportation is available only in the larger metropolitan areas, and even there it may provide infrequent or even inadequate service. When it comes to getting from one city to another, cars and planes are the ways to go.

BY CAR   Jacksonville is about 350 miles north of Miami and 500 miles north of Key West, so don't underestimate how long it will take you to drive all the way down the state. The speed limit is either 65 m.p.h. or 70 m.p.h. on the rural interstate highways, so you can make good time between cities. Not so on U.S. 1, U.S. 17, U.S. 19, U.S. 41, and U.S. 301; although most have four lanes, these older highways tend to be heavily congested, especially in built-up areas.

Every major car-rental company is represented here, including **Alamo** (☎ **800/327-9633**), **Avis** (☎ **800/331-1212**), **Budget** (☎ **800/527-0700**), **Dollar** (☎ **800/800-4000**), **Enterprise** (☎ **800/325-8007**), **Hertz** (☎ **800/654-3131**), **National** (☎ **800/227-7368**), **Thrifty** (☎ **800/367-2277**), and **Value** (☎ **800/GO-VALUE**).

If you decide to rent a car, shop around and ask a lot of questions; the rental firms certainly aren't going to tell you how to save money. You may have to try different dates, different pickup and drop-off points, and different discount offers yourself to find the best deal. It changes constantly. Also, if you're a member of any organization (AARP or AAA, for example), check to see if you're entitled to discounts.

Be prepared to have local taxes of 10% or more added to your rental bill, plus $1.05 per day for state-use taxes.

Most of the companies pad their profits by selling Loss/Damage Waiver (LDW) insurance. You may already be covered by your insurance carrier and credit- or charge-card companies, so check with them before succumbing to the hard sell. Also, the rental companies will offer to refill your gas tank at "competitive" prices when you return, but fuel usually is less expensive in town.

Most also require a minimum age, ranging from 19 to 25, and some also set maximum ages. Others deny cars to anyone with a bad driving record. Ask about rental requirements and restrictions when you book to avoid problems later. You must have a valid credit card to rent a vehicle.

Many packages are available that include airfare, accommodations, and a rental car with unlimited mileage. Compare these prices with the cost of booking airline tickets and renting a car separately to see if these offers are good deals.

BY PLANE   Most major Florida cities are connected by both the major commuter airlines (see "Getting There," above) and smaller intrastate airlines such as **Gulf Stream International** (☎ **800/992-8532**) which has an in-state network; **Cape Air** (☎ **800/352-0714**), which flies between Key West, Fort Myers, and Naples; and **Sky America** (☎ **800/368-2307**), which links Key West to St. Petersburg and Sarasota. Fares for these short hops tend to be reasonable.

BY TRAIN   You'll find that train travel from destination to destination isn't terribly feasible in Florida, and it's not a great deal less expensive than flying. See "Getting There," above, for Florida towns served by **Amtrak** (☎ **800/USA-RAIL;** www.amtrak.com).

The **Florida Fun Train** (☎ **888/FUN-TRACK** or 954/920-0606) operates daily between Orlando and Hollywood, on the Gold Coast north of Miami. It's more of an excursion than a means of transportation, with music, dancing, wine and espresso bars, and a diner, plus electronic games and videos to keep the children busy. Call for schedules and fares.

8 The Active Vacation Planner

Florida will keep active vacationers very busy. Bird watching, boating and sailing, camping, canoeing and kayaking, fishing, golfing, tennis—you name it, the Sunshine State has it. In fact, you'll find them almost everywhere you go. Of course, beach lovers and water-sports enthusiasts can indulge their passions almost anywhere along the state's lengthy coastlines. Merely head east or west, and you'll easily find plenty to do— or viewed another way, Florida's multitudinous water-sports operators will find you.

These and other activities are described in the outdoor activities sections of the following chapters, but here's a brief overview of some of best places to move your muscles, with tips on how to get more detailed information.

The **Florida Sports Foundation,** 1319 Thomaswood Dr., Tallahassee, FL 32312 (☎ **850/488-8347**), publishes free brochures, calendars, schedules, and guides to outdoor pursuits and spectator sports throughout Florida. I've noted some of its specific publications in the sections below.

For excellent color maps of state parks, campgrounds, canoe trails, aquatic preserves, caverns, and more, contact the **Florida Department of Environmental Protection,** Office of Communications, 3900 Commonwealth Blvd., Tallahassee, FL 32399 (☎ **850/488-6327**). Some of the department's publications are mentioned below.

ACTIVITIES A TO Z
BICYCLING & IN-LINE SKATING   Florida's relatively flat terrain makes it ideal for riding bikes and skating on blades. You can bike right into the **Everglades National Park** along the 38-mile Main Park Road, for example, and bike or skate from St. Petersburg to Tarpon Springs on the 47-mile converted railroad bed known as the **Pinellas Trail.** Many towns and cities have designated routes for cyclists, skaters, joggers, and walkers, such as the paved pathways running the length of **Sanibel Island,** the lovely Bayshore Boulevard in **Tampa,** and the bike lanes from

downtown **Sarasota** out to St. Armands, Lido, and Longboat keys. We've detailed all the many options in the following chapters.

Florida Outback Bike & Boat Tours (☎ **888/269-1169** or 407/518-9311) has biking and kayaking excursions to the Everglades. The national companies **Vermont Bicycle Touring** (☎ **800/537-3850** or 802/453-4811) and **Backroads Bicycle Touring** (☎ **800/462-2848** or 510/527-1555; www.backroads.com) sometimes offer Florida bike tours for cyclists of all fitness levels.

BIRD WATCHING   With hundreds of both land- and sea-based species, Florida is one of America's best places for bird watching. We've picked the best places in chapter 1, but birds are everywhere in Florida—if you're not careful, pelicans will even steal your picnic lunch on the historic **Naples Pier.** The **J. N. "Ding" Darling National Wildlife Refuge** is great for watching, and it shares Sanibel Island with luxury resorts and fine restaurants.

The Florida Audubon Society manages four exceptional sites: **Corkscrew Swamp Sanctuary** near Naples, **Madalyn Baldwin Center for Birds of Prey** in Maitland, **Turkey Creek Wildlife Sanctuary** in Palm Bay, and **Sabal Point Wildlife Sanctuary** on the Wekiva River in Central Florida.

Many of the state's wildlife preserves have gift shops that carry books about Florida's birds, including the *Florida Wildlife Viewing Guide,* in which authors Susan Cerulean and Ann Morrow profile 96 great parks, refuges, and preserves throughout the state.

BOATING & SAILING   With some 1,350 miles of shoreline, it's not surprising that Florida is a boating and sailing mecca. In fact, you won't be anyplace near the water very long before you see flyers and other advertisements for rental boats and for cruises on sailboats. Many of them are mentioned in the following chapters.

The Moorings, the worldwide sailboat charter company, has its headquarters in Clearwater and its Florida yacht base nearby in St. Petersburg (☎ **800/437-7880** or 813/530-5424; www.moorings.com). From St. Pete, experienced sailors can take its bareboats as far as the Keys and the Dry Tortugas, out in the Gulf of Mexico.

Key West keeps gaining prominence as a world sailing capital. Yachting magazine sponsors the largest winter regatta in America here each January, and smaller events take place regularly.

Even if you've never hauled on a halyard, you can learn the art of sailing at **Steve and Doris Colgate's Offshore Sailing School** headquartered at the South Seas Plantation Resort & Yacht Harbour on Captiva Island, and at the prestigious **Annapolis Sailing School,** which has bases in St. Petersburg and on Marathon in the Keys.

If you don't want to do any real work on the water, you can rent a houseboat along the St. John's River in the northeastern part of the state; contact the **Hontoon Landing Marina,** 2317 River Ridge Rd., Deland (☎ **904/734-2474**). In the Everglades, houseboat rentals are available through the **Flamingo Lodge** (☎ **800/ 600-3813,** 813/695-3101, or 305/253-2241). You might also try **Houseboat Vacations of the Florida Keys,** MM 85.9, Islamorada (☎ **305/664-4009**). Book everything well in advance.

The free *Florida Boater's Guide* has tips about safe boating in the state, available from the **Florida Marine Patrol,** 3900 Commonwealth Blvd., Tallahassee, FL 32399-3000 (☎ **850/488-5600**). The annual *Florida Cruising Directory* is a treasure trove of charts and tables, coast guard customs and regulations, locations of marinas, hotels, and resorts, marine products and services, and more, in magazine format. It's sold in bookstores and marinas all over the state.

CAMPING   Florida is literally dotted with RV parks (if you own such a vehicle, it's the least expensive way to spend your winters here). But for the best tent camping, look to Florida's national preserves and 110 state parks and recreation areas. Options range from luxury sites with hot-water showers and cable TV hookups to primitive island and beach camping with no facilities whatsoever.

Primitive camping in **St. Joseph Peninsula State Park** near Apalachicola, in fact, is a bird watcher's dream, and you'll be on one of the nation's most magnificent beaches. Equally great are the sands at **St. Andrews State Recreation Area** in Panama City Beach (with sites right beside the bay). Other top spots are **Caladesi Island State Park** off Clearwater, the remarkably preserved **Cayo Costa Island State Park** between Boca Grande and Captiva Island in Southwest Florida, **Canaveral National Seashore** near the Kennedy Space Center, **Anastasia State Recreation Area** in St. Augustine, at **Fort Clinch State Park** on Amelia Island, and **Bill Baggs Cape Florida Recreation Area** on Key Biscayne in Miami. Down in the Keys, the ocean-side sites in **Long Key State Recreation Area** are about as nice it gets.

Many sites are accessible only by boat, such as the chickee huts (round, square, or rectangular thatch or tin roofs supported by poles, with open sides) on stilts in Everglades National Park and the backcountry sites in Caladesi Island State Park off Clearwater and **Collier Seminole State Park** near Marco Island.

These are all popular campgrounds, so reservations are essential, especially in the high seasons. All of Florida's state parks take bookings up to 11 months in advance.

The **Florida Department of Environmental Protection,** Division of Recreation and Parks, Mail Station 535, 3900 Commonwealth Blvd., Tallahassee, FL 32399-3000 (☎ **850/488-9872**), publishes an annual guide of tent and RV sites in Florida's state parks and recreation areas. For private campgrounds, the **Florida Association of RV Parks & Campgrounds,** 1340 Vickers Dr., Tallahassee, FL 32303 (☎ **850/ 562-7151;** fax 850/562-7179), issues an annual *Florida Camping Directory* with locator maps and details about its member establishments throughout the state.

CANOEING & KAYAKING   From picturesque rivers to sandy coastlines to gigantic Lake Okeechobee, from the marshes of northern and Central Florida to the mangroves of the southwest, canoers and kayakers have almost limitless options here. We've picked the best in chapter 1, which generally are exceptional trails through parks and wildlife preserves, including **Everglades National Park,** the **J. N. "Ding" Darling National Wildlife Refuge** on Sanibel Island, and **Collier Seminole State Park** and the **Briggs Nature Center,** both on the edge of the Everglades near Marco Island.

Another local favorite is **Myakka River State Park** near Sarasota, Florida's largest state park with approximately 28,000 acres of pure backcountry.

According to the Florida state legislature, however, the state's official "Canoe Capital" is the Panhandle town of **Milton,** on U.S. 90 near Pensacola. Up there, the Blackwater River, Coldwater River, Sweetwater Creek, and Juniper Creek are perfect for tubing, rafting, and paddleboating as well as canoeing and kayaking.

Many conservation groups throughout the state offer half-day, day, and overnight canoe trips. For example, **The Conservancy of Naples** (☎ **941/262-0304**) has a popular series of moonlight canoe trips through the mangroves, among other programs.

Based during the winter at Everglades City, on the park's western border, **North American Canoe Tours, Inc.** (☎ **941/695-4666** November through April, or 860/739-0791 May through October), offers 1-day, 4-day and weeklong guided canoe expeditions through the Everglades. **Florida Outback Bike & Boat Tours** (☎ **888/269-1169** or 407/518-9311) also has kayaking excursions to the Everglades.

Thirty-six creek and river trails, covering 950 miles altogether, are itemized in the excellent free *Canoe Trails* **booklet** published by the Florida Department of

Environmental Protection, Office of Communications, 3900 Commonwealth Blvd., Tallahassee, FL 32399 (☎ 850/488-6327).

Specialized guidebooks include *A Canoeing and Kayaking Guide to the Streams of Florida:* Volume 1, *North Central Florida and Panhandle,* by Elizabeth F. Carter and John L. Eearch, and Volume II, *Central and Southern Peninsula,* by Lou Glaros and Dough Sphar. Both are published by Menasha Ridge Press.

FISHING   In addition to the amberjack, bonito, grouper, mackerel, mahimahi, marlin, pompano, redfish, sailfish, snapper, snook, tarpon, tuna, and wahoo running offshore and in its inlets, Florida has countless miles of rivers and streams, plus about 30,000 lakes and springs stocked with more than 100 species of freshwater fish. Indeed, Floridians seem to fish everywhere: off canal banks and old bridges, from fishing piers and fishing fleets. You'll even see them standing alongside the Tamiami Trail (U.S. 41) that cuts across the Everglades—one eye on their line, the other watching for alligators.

We listed our favorite places to fish in chapter 1, but nearly every marina in Florida harbors charter boats. You don't have to pay them a small fortune to try your luck, for most ports also have "party" boats that take groups out to sea. You'll have lots of company, but their rates are reasonable, they provide the gear and bait, and you won't need a fishing license.

Anglers age 16 and older need fishing licenses for any other kind of saltwater or freshwater fishing, including lobstering and spearfishing. Licenses are sold at bait and tackle shops.

The **Florida Department of Environmental Protection,** 3900 Commonwealth Blvd., Tallahassee, FL 32399-3000 (☎ 850/488-7326), publishes the annual *Fishing Lines,* a free magazine with a wealth of information about fishing in Florida, including regulations and licensing requirements. It also distributes free brochures with annual freshwater and saltwater limits. And the **Florida Sports Foundation** (see the introduction to this section) publishes *Florida Fishing,* another treasure trove of information.

HIKING   There are thousands of beautiful hiking trails in Florida. The ideal hiking months are October through April, when the weather is cool and dry and mosquitoes are less prominent. Like anywhere else, you'll find trails that are gentle and short and others that are challenging—some trails in the Everglades require you to wade waist-deep in water!

If you're venturing into the backcountry, watch out for gators, and don't ever try to feed them (or any wild animal). You risk getting bitten (they can't tell the difference between the food and your hand). You're also upsetting the balance of nature, since animals fed by humans lose their ability to find their own food. Most Florida snakes are harmless, but a few have deadly bites, so it's a good idea to avoid them all.

The **Florida Trail Association,** P.O. Box 13708, Gainesville, FL 32604 (☎ 800/343-1882 or 352/378-8823), maintains a large percentage of the public trails in the state and puts out an excellent book packed with maps, details, and color photos.

For a copy of *Florida Trails,* which outlines the many options, contact Visit Florida (see "Visitor Information," above). Another resource is *A Guide to Your National Scenic Trails,* Office of Greenways and Trails, Department of Environmental Protection, 3900 Commonwealth Blvd., Tallahassee, FL 32399 (☎ 850/487-4784). You can also contact the office of **National Forests in Florida,** Woodcrest Office Park, 325 John Knox Rd., Suite F-100, Tallahassee, FL 32303 (☎ 850/942-9300). And *Hiking Florida,* by M. Timothy O'Keefe (Falcon Press), details 132 hikes throughout the state, with maps and photos.

The **Florida Conservation Foundation, Inc.,** 1191 Orange Ave., Winter Park, FL 32789 (☎ **407/644-5377**), publishes information about the state's ecology, including **"Common Florida Natural Areas,"** an illustrated brochure explaining what you'll find in each ecosystem.

GOLF   Florida has more golf courses than any other state. We picked the best in chapter 1, but suffice it to say that you can tee off almost anytime and anywhere. The highest concentrations of excellent courses are in Southwest Florida around Naples and Fort Myers (some 1,000 holes!), the Orlando area (Disney alone has 99 holes open to the public), and in the Panhandle around Destin and Panama City Beach. And it's a rare town in Florida that doesn't have a municipal golf course—even Key West has 18 great holes.

Greens fees are usually much lower at the municipal courses than at privately owned clubs. Whether public or private, greens fees tend to vary greatly depending on the time of year. You could pay $100 or more at a private course during the high season, but only half that when the tourists are gone. The fee structures vary so much that it's best to call ahead and ask, and always reserve a tee time as far in advance as possible.

You can learn the game or hone your strokes at one of several excellent golf schools in the state. David Ledbetter has teaching facilities in Orlando and Naples, Fred Griffin is in charge of the Grand Cypress Academy of Golf at Grand Cypress Resort in Orlando, and you'll find Jimmy Ballard's school at the Ocean Reef Club on Key Largo. The Westin Innisbrook Resort at Tarpon Springs has its Innisbrook Golf Institute, Amelia Island near Jacksonville is home to Amelia Island Plantation Golf School, and Saddlebrook Resort north of Tampa hosts the Arnold Palmer Golf Academy.

You can get information about most Florida courses, including current greens fees, and reserve tee times through **Tee Times USA,** P.O. Box 641, Flagler Beach, FL 32136 (☎ **800/374-8633,** 888/465-3567, or 904/439-0001; fax 904/439-0099). This company also publishes a vacation guide which includes many stay-and-play golf packages.

Fairways in the Sunshine, published by the **Florida Sports Foundation** (see the introduction to this section), lists every course in Florida. *Golfer's Guide* magazine publishes monthly editions covering most regions of Florida; it is available free at all the local visitors centers and hotel lobbies, or you can contact the magazine at P.O. Box 5926, Hilton Head, SC 29938 (☎ **800/864-6101** or 803/842-7878; fax 803/842-5743; www.homes.com). Northwest Florida is covered by *Gulf Coast Tee Time,* published by Tee Time LLC, 3 W. Garden St., Pensacola, FL 32501 (☎ **888/520-4300** or 850/435-4858; fax 850/435-7383; www.teetimeweb.com).

You also can get more information from the **Professional Golfers' Association (PGA),** 100 Avenue of the Champions, Palm Beach Gardens, FL 33418 (☎ 407/624-8400); or the **Ladies Professional Golf Association (LPGA),** 2570 Volusia Ave., Suite B, Daytona Beach, FL 32114 (☎ **904/254-8800**).

SCUBA DIVING & SNORKELING   Divers love the Keys, where you can see magnificent formations of tree-sized elk horn coral and giant brain coral, as well as colorful sea fans and dozens of other varieties, sharing space with 300 or more species of rainbow-hued fish. Reef diving is good all the way from Key Largo to Key West, with plenty of tour operators, outfitters, and dive shops along the way. Particularly worthy are **John Pennekamp Coral Reef State Park** in Key Largo and **Looe Key National Marine Sanctuary** off Big Pine Key. *Skin Diver* magazine picked Looe Key as the number one dive spot in North America. Also, the clearest waters in which to view some of the 4,000 sunken ships along Florida's coast are in the Middle Keys and the waters between Key West and the Dry Tortugas. Snorkeling in the Keys is particularly fine between Islamorada and Marathon.

In Northwest Florida, the 100-fathom curve draws closer to the white, sandy Panhandle beaches than to any other spot on the Gulf of Mexico. It's too far north here for coral, but you can see brilliant-colored sponges, fish, and Timber Hole, an undersea "petrified forest" of sunken planes, ships, and even a railroad car. And the battleship USS *Massachusetts* lies in 30 feet of water just 3 miles off Pensacola. Every beach town in Northwest Florida has dive shops to outfit, tour, or certify visitors.

In the Crystal River area, north of the St. Petersburg and Clearwater beaches, you can dive with the manatees as they bask in the warm spring waters of Kings Bay.

The "cave-diving capital of the world" can be found between High Springs and Branford in northern Florida. The two most renowned spots are in crystal-clear Ginnie Springs, on the Santa Fe River, and in Ichetucknee Springs State Park, a few miles farther north. The **Ginnie Springs Resort,** 7300 NE Ginnie Springs Rd., High Springs (☎ **800/874-8571** or 904/454-2202), is a 200-acre campsite park along the Santa Fe River with dive packages and canoe rentals. Underwater explorers have found artifacts from the native tribes that once inhabited the region around Ichetucknee, and topside explorers often sight limpkin, wood duck, otter, and beaver. This 2,241-acre state park also offers camping, nature trails, canoeing, and tubing. **The Steamboat Dive Inn,** U.S. 27 at U.S. 129, Branford, FL 32008 (☎ **904/935-DIVE**), on the Suwannee River, has its own on-site, full-service diving center with certified instructors for every level. Also in Branford, the **Branford Dive Center,** U.S. 27 and the Suwannee River, Branford, FL 32008 (☎ **904/935-1141**), offers guides, air, rentals, accessories, and instruction.

If you want to keep up with what's going on statewide, you can subscribe to *Florida Scuba News,* a monthly magazine published in Jacksonville (☎ **904/783-1610;** www.scubanews.com). You might also want to pick up a specialized guidebook. Some good ones include *Coral Reefs of Florida,* by Gilbert L. Voss (Pineapple Press), and *The Diver's Guide to Florida and the Florida Keys,* by Jim Stachowicz (Windward Publishing).

TENNIS Year-round sunshine makes Florida a tennis paradise. There are some 7,700 places to play, from municipal courts to exclusive resorts. Even some of the municipal facilities—Cambier Park Tennis Center in Naples leaps to mind—are equal to those at expensive resorts, and they're either free or close to it.

If you can afford it, you can learn from the best in Florida. **Nick Bollettieri** has sports academies in Bradenton and at the Westin Innisbrook Resort in Tarpon Springs. The Saddlebrook Resort in Wesley Chapel north of Tampa is home to the **Phil Green Tennis Program.** Amateurs can hobnob with the superstars at **ATP Tour International Headquarters** in Ponte Vedra Beach, near Jacksonville. **Peter Burwash International** has a tennis program at Doral Golf Resort & Spa in Miami. And **Chris Evert, Robert Seguso,** and **Carling Basset** have their own center in Boca Raton.

Other top places to learn and play are **Amelia Island Plantation** on Amelia Island; **Colony Beach and Tennis Resort** on Longboat Key off Sarasota (which *Tennis* magazine picked as the number two tennis resort in the nation); **Sanibel Harbour Resort & Spa** in Fort Myers, whose 5,500-seat stadium has hosted Davis Cup matches; **South Seas Plantation Resort & Yacht Harbour** on Captiva Island; **The Registry Resort** in Naples (it will have changed names by 1999); and **World Tennis Center Resort & Club** in Naples, where the World Tennis Academy is headed by renowned tennis psychologist and coach Roland Carlstedt.

ECO-TOURS If you don't want to do it yourself, some organizations offer excursions to observe Florida's flora and fauna and have a little adventure while you're at it.

The Florida chapter of the **Nature Conservancy** has protected 578,000 acres of natural lands in Florida and presently owns and manages 36 preserves. For a small fee, you can join one of its field trips or work parties that take place periodically throughout the year; fees vary from year to year, event to event, so call for more information. Participants get a chance to learn about and even participate in the preservation of the ecosystem. For details of all the preserves and adventures, contact the Nature Conservancy, Florida Chapter, 222 S. Westmonte Dr., Suite 300, Altamonte Springs, FL 32714 (☎ **407/682-3664**).

The **Sierra Club,** America's oldest and largest grassroots environmental organization, offers exceptional eco-adventures through its Florida chapters. You can go canoeing or kayaking through the Everglades, hiking the Florida Trail in America's southernmost national forest, camping on a barrier island, or exploring the sinkhole phenomenon in north central Florida. You do have to be a Sierra Club member, but you can join at the time of the trip. Contact the national office at Department J-319, P.O. Box 7959, San Francisco, CA 94120 (☎ **415/923-5653**), for a current outings magazine and local chapter contacts.

Soft eco-adventure experiences are available at **Silver Springs,** a 350-acre nature theme park near Ocala (☎ **800/234-7458** or 352/236-2121). It has been conducting ecotours since before the term was invented. You can take a sunrise breakfast cruise to photograph great blue herons, white-tail deer, and other wildlife; or you can take a "Jungle Cruise" or "Jeep Safari" to get a feeling of the ecosystem without getting your feet dirty.

9 Tips on Accommodations

Florida has a vast array of accommodations, from rock-bottom roadside motels to some of the nation's finest resorts. Whether you'll spend a pittance or a bundle depends on your budget and your tastes. But, to repeat a well-worn phrase, you can enjoy "champagne on a beer budget"—if you plan carefully.

The **Florida Hotel & Motel Association,** P.O. Box 1529, Tallahassee, FL 32302 (☎ **850/224-2888**), publishes a directory listing all of its member establishments. This is a handy booklet to have if you're taking your animal along, since it tells which properties **accept pets.** For a copy, send a check for $2 if you live in the U.S., $4 if you live elsewhere. The association also has a free **reservation service** (☎ **800/ 847-4835**) covering the entire state.

Inn Route, P.O. Box 6187, Palm Harbor, FL 34684 (☎ **800/524-1880;** fax 281/403-9335; www.florida-inns.com; e-mail: innroute@worldnet.att.net), publishes the *Inns of Florida,* which lists inns and bed-and-breakfasts throughout the state. Inn Route inspects each property, thus ensuring quality and cleanliness of its members.

At the inexpensive end, **Hostelling International/American Youth Hostels,** 733 15th St. NW, Suite 840, Washington, DC 20005 (☎ **800/444-6111** or 202/ 783-6161), offers low-cost accommodations in Miami Beach, Key West, Fort Lauderdale, and Orlando.

MONEY-SAVING TIPS

The rates quoted in this book are "rack" or "published" rates; that is, the highest regular rates charged by a hotel or motel. Not long ago the rack rate was what you paid, unless you were part of a tour group or had purchased a vacation package. Today most hotels give discounts to corporate travelers, government employees, senior citizens, automobile club members, active duty military personnel, and others.

Most hotels usually don't advertise these discounted rates or even volunteer them at the front desk, but you can take advantage of them by asking politely if there's a special rate which applies to you. One company that does advertise a major discount is **Choice Hotels** (see "For Seniors" under "Tips for Travelers with Special Needs," above).

Computerized reservations systems also have permitted many larger properties to adjust their rates on an almost daily basis, depending on how much business they anticipate having. Even if they don't officially reduce their rates, they may drop them rather than having beds go empty. Don't hesitate to ask if a less-expensive rate is available on the days you plan on being there.

Most rack rates include commissions of 10% to 25% or more for travel agents, which many hotels will knock off if you make your own reservations and bargain a little.

Downtown hotels catering to business travelers during the week usually have big discounts on Friday and Saturday nights. If you're staying over a weekend in an off-beach city such as Tampa, always ask about a special rate or package deal. Weekend rates don't apply in the resort areas, nor in college towns like Tallahassee, but you should ask about weekday or weeklong vacation packages.

Many Florida hotels and motels offer weekly rates, which as a general rule will knock off the price of one night if you stay for seven.

Most also have free self-parking, but fees can run up the cost at some downtown and beachfront hotels. We've indicated in the listings if a hotel or resort charges for parking; if no charge is given, parking is free. And many hotels jack up the price of long-distance phone calls made from your room. Accordingly, always inquire about the costs of parking, and use a pay phone if the hotel tacks a hefty surcharge on calls.

CONDOS, HOMES & COTTAGES

It may seem at first impression that many Florida beaches are lined with great walls of high-rise condominium buildings. That's not much of an overstatement, for the state literally has thousands upon thousands of condo units. People actually live in many of them year-round, but others are for rent on a daily, weekly, or monthly basis. In addition, there are many private homes and cottages for rent throughout Florida.

Some of the resorts listed in this book actually are condo complexes operated as full-service hotels, but usually you'll have to do without such hotel amenities as on-site restaurants, room service, and even daily maid service. On the other hand, almost every condo, home, and cottage has a fully equipped kitchen, and many have washers, dryers, and other such niceties of home, which means they can represent significant savings, especially if you're traveling with children or are sharing with another couple or family.

We have pointed out a few of the best condo complexes in the "Where to Stay" sections of the following chapters, and we have named some of the reputable **real estate agencies** which have inventories of condos, private homes, and cottages to rent.

If you think a condo will meet your needs, your best bet is to contact the rental agencies well in advance and request a brochure describing all the properties they represent, and their rates.

FAST FACTS: Florida

American Express   There are a number of American Express offices in Florida. Call Cardmember Services (☎ 800/528-4800) for the location nearest you.

Banks   Banks are usually open Monday to Friday from 9am to 3 or 4pm, and most have automated teller machines (ATMs) for 24-hour banking. You won't have a problem finding a Cirrus or PLUS machine. Of the national banks, **First Union Bank** and **NationsBank** have offices throughout Florida. **Barnett** and **Sun** are the largest in-state banks.

Car Rentals   See "Getting Around," earlier in this chapter.

Climate   See "When to Go," earlier in this chapter.

Currency Exchange   See "Money" under "Preparing for Your Trip," in chapter 3.

Emergencies   Call ☎ **911** anywhere in the state to summon the police, the fire department, or an ambulance.

Liquor Laws   You must be 21 to purchase or consume alcohol in Florida. This law is strictly enforced, so if you look young, carry some photo identification that gives your date of birth. Minors can usually enter bars where food is served.

Newspapers/Magazines   Most cities of any size have a local daily paper, but the well-respected *Miami Herald* is generally available all over the state, with regional editions available in many areas.

Safety   Whenever you're traveling in an unfamiliar city, stay alert. Be aware of your immediate surroundings. Always lock your car doors and the trunk when your vehicle is unattended, and don't leave any valuables in sight. See "Safety" under "Preparing for Your Trip," in chapter 3, for more information.

Taxes   The Florida state sales tax is 6%. Many municipalities add 1% or more to that, and most levy a special tax on hotel and restaurant bills. See "Where to Stay," in the following chapters, for details.

Time   The Florida peninsula observes eastern standard time, but most of the Panhandle west of the Apalachicola River is on central standard time, 1 hour behind the rest of the state.

Tourist Information   See "Visitor Information," earlier in this chapter, for the tourist office serving the entire state. For local offices, which will have more detailed information on your particular destination, see "Orientation" or "Essentials" in the following chapters.

For Foreign Visitors   3

by Bill Goodwin

American fads, fashions, and television may have spread across the world so much that the United States may seem like familiar territory, but there are still many peculiarities and uniquely American situations that you likely will encounter while here. This chapter points out many of the perhaps unexpected differences from what you are used to at home, and explains some of the more confusing aspects of daily life in the United States.

1 Preparing for Your Trip

ENTRY REQUIREMENTS

DOCUMENT REGULATIONS   Immigration laws have been a hot political issue in the United States in recent years, so it's wise to check at any U.S. embassy or consulate for current information and requirements. You can also plug into the U.S. State Department's Internet site at www.state.gov.

Canadians may enter the United States without passports or visas; you need only proof of residence.

The U.S. State Department has a **Visa Waiver Program** allowing citizens of the United Kingdom, Australia, New Zealand, Japan, and most western European countries to enter the United States without a visa for stays of up to 90 days. If you're from one of these countries, you will need only a valid passport and a round-trip air or cruise ticket in your possession upon arrival. Once here, you may then visit Mexico, Canada, Bermuda, and/or the Caribbean islands and return to the United States without needing a visa. Further information is available from any U.S. embassy or consulate.

If you're from any other country, you must have (1) a valid **passport** with an expiration date at least 6 months later than the scheduled end of your visit to the United States; and (2) a **tourist visa,** which may be obtained without charge from the nearest U.S. consulate.

To obtain a visa, submit a completed application form with a 1½-inch-square photo and demonstrate binding ties to your residence abroad. If you cannot go in person, contact the nearest U.S. embassy or consulate for directions on applying by mail. Your travel agent or airline office may also be able to provide you with the visa application forms and instructions. The U.S. embassy or consulate where you apply will determine whether you receive a multiple- or single-entry visa and any restrictions regarding the length of your stay. This may take a few days or even weeks, so apply well in advance.

Foreign **driver's licenses** are recognized in Florida, but you may want to get an international driver's license if your home license is not written in English.

MEDICAL REQUIREMENTS   No inoculations are needed to enter the United States unless you are coming from, or have stopped over in, areas known to be suffering from epidemics, particularly cholera or yellow fever.

CUSTOMS REQUIREMENTS   Every adult visitor may bring in free of duty: 1 liter of wine or hard liquor; 200 cigarettes *or* 100 cigars (but no cigars made in Cuba) *or* 3 pounds of smoking tobacco; and $100 worth of gifts. You must spend at least 72 hours in the United States and must not have claimed the exemptions within the preceding 6 months. It is altogether forbidden to bring into the country foodstuffs (particularly cheese, fruit, cooked meats, and canned goods) and plants (vegetables, seeds, tropical plants, and so on). Foreign tourists may bring in or take out up to $10,000 in U.S. or foreign currency with no formalities; larger sums must be declared to Customs upon entering or leaving.

Penalties are severe for smuggling illegal narcotics into the United States, so if you have a disease requiring treatment with medications containing narcotics or drugs (especially those administered by syringe), carry a valid signed prescription from your physician to allay any suspicions that you are smuggling drugs.

INSURANCE   There is no national health-care system in the United States, and the cost of medical care here is extremely high; therefore, we strongly advise that you secure health insurance coverage before setting out. You may want to take out a comprehensive travel policy that covers sickness or injury costs (medical, surgical, and hospital), as well as loss or theft of your baggage, trip-cancellation costs, guarantee of bail in case you are arrested, and costs of accident, repatriation, or death. See "Health & Insurance" in chapter 2 for more information. Packages such as Europ Assistance in Europe are sold by automobile clubs and travel agencies at attractive rates. **Worldwide Assistance Services, Inc.** (☎ **800/821-2828** or 202/347-2025) is the agent for Europ Assistance in the United States.

Canadians should check with their provincial health plan offices or call **Health-Canada** (☎ **613/957-3025**) to find out the extent of their coverage and what documentation and receipts they must take home in case they are treated in the United States.

MONEY

The U.S. monetary system has a decimal base: one American dollar ($1) = 100 cents (100¢). Notes come in $1 ("a buck"), $5, $10, $20, $50, and $100 denominations (the last two are not welcome when paying for small purchases and are not accepted in taxis or at subway ticket booths). There are also $2 bills, but you are unlikely to see one since Americans consider them to be unlucky. There are six denominations of coins: 1¢ (one cent, known here as "a penny"), 5¢ (five cents or "a nickel"), 10¢ (ten cents or "a dime"), 25¢ (twenty-five cents or "a quarter"), 50¢ (fifty cents or "a half dollar"), and the rare $1 piece.

Changing foreign currency in the United States is a hassle, so leave any currency other than U.S. dollars at home—it will prove more of a nuisance than it's worth. Even banks here may not want to change your home currency into U.S. dollars. The exceptions are the currency exchange desks in the Miami, Orlando, Tampa, and Fort Myers airports, and **Thomas Cook Foreign Exchange,** which changes foreign currency and sells commission-free foreign and U.S. traveler's checks, drafts, and wire

---

Walt Disney World Services for International Visitors

Walt Disney World, which welcomes thousands of foreign visitors each year, has numerous services designed to meet their needs. Unless otherwise indicated, call ☎ **407/W-DISNEY** for details. Services include:

- A special phone number (☎ **407/824-7900**) to speak with someone in French, Spanish, German, and other languages.
- Personal translator units (in French, German, and Spanish) to translate narration at some shows and attractions.
- Detailed guidebooks to the three major parks in Spanish, French, German, Portuguese, and Japanese (available at any guest relations location).
- Currency exchange (see below).
- World Key Terminals at Epcot that offer basic park information and assistance with dining reservations in Spanish.
- Resort phones equipped with software that expedites international calls by allowing guests to dial direct to foreign destinations.

---

transfers. Thomas Cook has offices in Miami, Fort Lauderdale, Orlando, and Fort Myers. Call ☎ **800/287-7362** for its branch locations and hours.

Traveler's checks denominated in U.S. dollars are readily accepted at most hotels, motels, restaurants, and large stores. Do not bring traveler's checks denominated in other currencies. Sometimes a passport or other photo identification is necessary.

Credit and charge cards are the most widely used form of payment in the United States: Visa (BarclayCard in Britain), MasterCard (EuroCard in Europe, Access in Britain, Chargex in Canada), American Express, Diners Club, Discover, and Carte Blanche. You must have a credit or charge card to rent a car. Widespread in Florida, some automated teller machines (ATMs) will allow you to draw U.S. currency against your bank and credit cards. Check with your bank before leaving home, and remember that you will need your personal identification number (PIN) to do so.

SAFETY

GENERAL   While tourist areas are generally safe, crime is on the increase everywhere, and U.S. urban areas tend to be less safe than those in Europe or Japan. You should always stay alert. This is particularly true of large U.S. cities. It is wise to ask your hotel front desk staff or the city's or area's tourist office if you're in doubt about which neighborhoods are safe.

Remember also that hotels are open to the public, and in a large hotel, security may not be able to screen everyone entering. Always lock your room door—don't assume that once inside your hotel you are automatically safe and no longer need be aware of your surroundings.

DRIVING   Recently more and more crime has involved vehicles, so safety while driving is particularly important. Question your rental agency about personal safety, or ask for a brochure of traveler safety tips when you pick up your car. Obtain written directions, or a map with the route clearly marked, from the agency showing how to get to your destination. And, if possible, arrive and depart during daylight hours.

If you drive off a highway into a doubtful neighborhood, leave the area as quickly as possible. If you have an accident, even on the highway, stay in your car with the doors locked until you assess the situation or until the police arrive. If you are bumped from behind on the street or are involved in a minor accident with no injuries and the situation appears to be suspicious, motion to the other driver to follow you. *Never* get out of your car in such situations. You can also keep a premade sign in your car which reads: PLEASE FOLLOW THIS VEHICLE TO REPORT THE ACCIDENT. Show the sign to the other driver and go directly to the nearest police precinct, well-lighted service station, or all-night store.

If you see someone on the road who indicates a need for help, do *not* stop. Take note of the location, drive on to a well-lighted area, and telephone the police by dialing ☎ **911.**

Park in well-lighted, well-traveled areas if possible. Always keep your car doors locked, whether attended or unattended. Look around you before you get out of your car, and never leave any packages or valuables in sight. If someone attempts to rob you or steal your car, do *not* try to resist the thief/carjacker—report the incident to the police department immediately.

Also, make sure that you have enough gasoline in your tank to reach your intended destination, so that you're not forced to look for a service station in an unfamiliar and possibly unsafe neighborhood, especially at night.

2 Getting to & Around the U.S.

GETTING TO THE U.S.

A number of U.S. airlines offer service from Europe and Latin America to Florida, including American, Delta, Northwest, and United. Many of the major international airlines, such as **British Airways, KLM Royal Dutch Airlines,** and **Lufthansa** also have direct flights from Europe to various Florida cities, either in their own planes or in conjunction with an American "partner" airline (KLM and Northwest, to name one partnership). Call the airlines' local offices or contact your travel agent, and be sure to ask about promotional fares and discounts.

Attractive values are offered by **Virgin Atlantic Airways** (☎ **800/662-8621** in the U.S., or 01/293-74-77-47 in the U.K.), which has cut-rate fares on its flights from London and Manchester to Miami and Orlando. The same is true with **Laker Airways** (☎ **888/525-3724** in the U.S., or 011-44-129-377-2020 in the U.K.), which flies from London to Fort Lauderdale, and with the Belgian airline **CityBird** (☎ **888/637-4985** in the U.S.), which flies from Brussels to Miami and Orlando. **LTU International** (☎ **800/888-0200** in the U.S.) frequently has reduced fares from Frankfurt, Munich, and Düsseldorf in Germany to Miami, Orlando, and Fort Myers.

You should always ask about **advance purchase excursion (APEX) fares,** which represent substantial savings over regular fares. Most require tickets to be bought 21 days prior to departure. **British Airways** has a 90-day advance purchase plan with fares about $100 lower than its 21-day APEX program.

Canadians should check with **Air Canada** (☎ **800/776-3000**), which offers service from Toronto and Montréal to Miami, Tampa, West Palm Beach, Fort Lauderdale, and Fort Myers. Also ask your travel agent about **Canada 3000** (☎ **800/993-4378**), which has wintertime charter flights to several Florida destinations.

On the World Wide Web, the European Travel Network (ETN) operates a site at **www.discount-tickets.com,** which offers cut-rate prices on international airfares to the United States, accommodations, car rentals, and tours. Another site to click for current discount fares worldwide is **www.etn.nl/discount.htm#disco**.

No matter at which airport you land, getting through immigration control may take as long as 2 hours on some days, especially summer weekends. Accordingly, you should make very generous allowances for delay in planning connections between international and domestic flights.

In contrast, travelers arriving by car or by rail from Canada will find border-crossing formalities streamlined to the vanishing point. And air travelers from Canada, Bermuda, and some places in the Caribbean can sometimes go through Customs and Immigration at the point of departure, which is much quicker.

For further information, see "Getting There," in chapter 2.

GETTING AROUND THE U.S.

BY AIR   The United States is one of the world's largest countries, with vast distances separating many of its key sights. From New York to Miami, for example, is more than 1,350 miles (2,173km) by road or train. Accordingly, flying is the quickest and most comfortable way to get around the country.

Ask your travel agent or local airline office about a **Visit USA** discount ticket sold by some large American airlines (for example, American, Delta, Northwest, TWA, and United) to travelers on their transatlantic or transpacific flights. It allows travel between many U.S. destinations at minimum rates. They must be purchased before you leave your foreign point of departure. The conditions attached to these discount tickets can be changed without warning.

BY TRAIN   Long-distance trains in the United States are operated by **Amtrak** (☎ 800/USA-RAIL; www.amtrak.com), the national passenger rail corporation. Be aware, however, that with a few notable exceptions (for instance, the Northeast Corridor line between Boston and Washington, D.C.), intercity service is not up to European standards. Delays are common, routes are limited and often infrequently served, and fares are seldom significantly lower than discount airfares. Thus cross-country train travel should be approached with caution.

International visitors can buy a **USA Railpass,** good for 15 or 30 days of unlimited travel on Amtrak. The pass is available through many foreign travel agents, and with a foreign passport, you can also buy them at some Amtrak offices in the United States, including Boston, Chicago, Los Angeles, Miami, New York, San Francisco, and Washington, D.C. The prices are based on a zone system: eastern, central, and western United States. At press time, a 15-day pass good in the eastern third of the country ranged from $205 to $250, depending on the time of travel, while 30-day passes ranged from about $255 to $310. The highest prices are in summer and at holidays. Reservations are generally required and should be made for each part of your trip as early as possible.

If you'll be traveling in both the United States and Canada, Amtrak and VIA, the Canadian railway system, offer a joint **North American Rail Pass,** good for unlimited travel over 30 consecutive days anywhere the two systems go. One key restriction: you must travel by rail in both the United States and Canada. At press time, these cost $645 from June to mid-October, $450 the rest of the year.

See "Getting There," in chapter 2, for more information about Amtrak's services to and within Florida.

BY BUS   Although it's the least expensive way to get around the country, long-distance bus service here can be both slow and uncomfortable, so it's not for everyone. The only national bus company is **Greyhound** (☎ 800/231-2222 in the United States; www.greyhound.com), which offers an **Ameripass** for unlimited travel anywhere on its system. In 1998, prices for a 7-day pass started at $199; 15 days at $299; 30 days at $409; and 60 days at $599. Senior citizens get a discount ranging from $20 to $60.

BY CAR   Traveling by car gives you the freedom to make (and alter) your itinerary to suit your own needs and interests. And especially in Florida, it offers the possibility of visiting some of the off-the-beaten-path locations, places that cannot be reached easily by public transportation. For information on renting cars in the United States, see "Getting Around," in chapter 2, and "Automobile Organizations" and "Automobile Rentals" in "Fast Facts: For the Foreign Traveler," below.

Please note that in the United States we drive on the **right side of the road** as in Europe, not on the left side as in the United Kingdom, Australia, and New Zealand.

4 Shopping Tips

The U.S. government charges very low duties when compared to the rest of the world, so you could get some excellent deals here on imported electronic goods, cameras, and clothing. Of course, it all depends on the value of your home currency versus the dollar, and how much duty you'll have to pay on your purchases when you get home.

The national "discount" chain stores consistently offer some of our best shopping deals. For televisions, VCRs, radios, camcorders, computers, and other electronic goods, go to **Best Buy, Circuit City,** and **Radio Shack.** Best Buy also has a wide selection of music. **CompUSA, Computer City,** and **Micro Center** specialize in computer hardware, accessories, and software. **Service Merchandise** is one of our best chains for cameras, and it also has electronics, jewelry, and many other items.

Many computers and other electronic equipment sold here use only 110- to 120-volt AC (60-cycle) electricity. You will need a transformer to use them at home if your power is 220 to 240 volts AC (50 cycles). Be sure to ask the salesperson if an item has a universal power adapter.

Our major department store chains are **Sears, Macy's, Saks Fifth Avenue, Lord & Taylor,** and **JC Penney.** In Florida, you'll also find **Burdines, Jordan Marsh,** and **Dillard's** anchoring many shopping malls. You get real deals in department stores only during sales, when selected merchandise is marked down 25% or more. The **Marshall's** and **TJ Maxx** chains carry name-brand clothing at department-store sale prices, but their stock tends to vary greatly.

Outlet malls are another source, in which manufacturers operate their own shops, selling directly to the consumer. Sometimes you can get very good buys at the outlets, especially when sales are going on. Most lingerie and china outlets have good prices when compared to department stores, but that's not necessarily the case with designer clothing. In addition, some manufacturers produce items of lesser quality so they can charge less at their outlets, so inspect the quality of all merchandise carefully. The main advantage to outlet malls is that if you are looking for a specific brand—Levi's jeans, for example—the company's outlet will have it.

You'll find national chain stores, department stores, and outlet malls throughout Florida; many are listed under "Shopping" in the following chapters. You can also look under their names in the White Pages of the local telephone directory for addresses and phone numbers, or under subjects such as computer dealers, television and radio dealers, stereo and hi-fi dealers, department stores, and discount stores in the Yellow Pages directory.

FAST FACTS: For the Foreign Traveler

Automobile Organizations   Auto clubs will supply maps, suggested routes, guidebooks, accident and bail-bond insurance, and emergency road service. The

American Automobile Association (AAA) is the major auto club in the United States. If you belong to an auto club in your home country, inquire about AAA reciprocity before you leave. You may be able to join AAA even if you're not a member of a reciprocal club; to inquire, call AAA (☎ **800/222-4357**). AAA is actually an organization of regional auto clubs; in Florida, look under "AAA Automobile Club South" in the White Pages of the telephone directory. AAA has a nationwide emergency road service telephone number (☎ **800/AAA-HELP**).

Automobile Rentals   See "Getting Around," in chapter 2.

Business Hours   See "Fast Facts: Florida," in chapter 2.

Currency & Currency Exchange   See "Entry Requirements" and "Money" under "Preparing for Your Trip," above.

Electricity   Like Canada, the United States uses 110 to 120 volts AC (60 cycles), compared to 220 to 240 volts AC (50 cycles) in most of Europe, Australia, and New Zealand. If your small appliances use 220 to 240 volts, you'll need a 110-volt transformer and a plug adapter with two flat parallel pins to operate them here. Downward converters that change 220 to 240 volts to 110 to 120 volts are difficult to find in the United States, so bring one with you.

Embassies & Consulates   All embassies are located in the national capital, Washington, D.C. Some consulates are located in major U.S. cities, and most nations have a mission to the United Nations in New York City.

The embassy of **Australia** is at 1601 Massachusetts Ave. NW, Washington, DC 20036 (☎ **202/797-3000**). There are consulates in New York, Honolulu, Houston, Los Angeles, and San Francisco.

The embassy of **Canada** is at 501 Pennsylvania Ave. NW, Washington, DC 20001 (☎ **202/682-1740**). There's a Canadian consulate in Florida at 200 S. Biscayne Blvd., Suite 1600, Miami, FL 33131 (☎ **305/579-1600**). Other Canadian consulates are in Atlanta, Buffalo (N.Y.), Chicago, Cleveland, Dallas, Detroit, Los Angeles, Minneapolis, New York, and Seattle.

The embassy of the **Republic of Ireland** is at 2234 Massachusetts Ave. NW, Washington, DC 20008 (☎ **202/462-3939**). Irish consulates are in Boston, Chicago, New York, and San Francisco.

The embassy of **New Zealand** is at 37 Observatory Circle NW, Washington, DC 20008 (☎ **202/328-4800**). New Zealand consulates are in Los Angeles, Salt Lake City, San Francisco, and Seattle.

The embassy of the **United Kingdom** is at 3100 Massachusetts Ave. NW, Washington, DC 20008 (☎ **202/462-1340**). In Florida, there's a full-service British consulate in Miami at Suite 2110, Brickell Bay Office Tower, 1001 S. Bayshore Dr. (☎ **305/374-1522**), and a vice consulate for emergency situations in Orlando at the Sun Trust Center, Suite 2110, 200 S. Orange Ave. (☎ **407/426-7855**). Other British consulates are in Atlanta, Boston, Chicago, Cleveland, Dallas, Houston, Los Angeles, and New York.

Emergencies   Call ☎ **911** to report a fire, call the police, or get an ambulance anywhere in the United States. This is a toll-free call (no coins are required at public telephones).

If you encounter traveler's problems, check the local telephone directory to find an office of the **Traveler's Aid Society,** a nationwide, nonprofit, social-service organization geared to helping travelers in difficult straits. Their services might include reuniting families separated while traveling, providing food and/or shelter to people stranded without cash, or even emotional counseling. If you're in trouble, seek them out.

Gasoline (Petrol) Petrol is known as gasoline (or simply "gas") in the United States, and petrol stations are known as both gas stations and service stations. Gasoline costs about half as much here as it does in Europe (about $1.05 per gallon at press time). One U.S. gallon equals 3.8 liters or .85 Imperial gallons. A majority of gas stations in Florida are now actually convenience grocery stores with gas pumps outside; they do not service automobiles. All but a very few stations have self-service gas pumps.

Holidays Banks, government offices, post offices, and many stores, restaurants, and museums are closed on the following legal national holidays: January 1 (New Year's Day), the third Monday in January (Martin Luther King, Jr. Day), the third Monday in February (Presidents' Day, Washington's Birthday), the last Monday in May (Memorial Day), July 4 (Independence Day), the first Monday in September (Labor Day), the second Monday in October (Columbus Day), November 11 (Veterans' Day/Armistice Day), the last Thursday in November (Thanksgiving Day), and December 25 (Christmas). Also, the Tuesday following the first Monday in November is Election Day and is a federal government holiday in presidential-election years (1996 was the most recent, 2000 is the next).

Legal Aid The foreign tourist will probably never become involved with the American legal system. If you are "pulled over" for a minor infraction (for example, of the highway code, such as speeding), never attempt to pay the fine directly to a police officer; this could be construed as attempted bribery, a much more serious crime. Pay fines by mail, or directly into the hands of the clerk of the court. If accused of a more serious offense, say and do nothing before consulting a lawyer, since here the burden is on the state to prove a person's guilt beyond a reasonable doubt, and everyone has the right to remain silent, whether he or she is suspected of a crime or actually arrested. Once arrested, a person can make one telephone call to a party of his or her choice. Call your embassy or consulate.

Mail If you aren't sure what your address will be in the United States, mail can be sent to you, in your name, **c/o General Delivery** at the main post office of the city or region where you expect to be. You must pick it up in person and must produce proof of identity (driver's license, passport, etc.).

Generally to be found at intersections, **mailboxes** are blue with a red-and-white stripe and carry the inscription U.S. MAIL. If your mail is addressed to a U.S. destination, don't forget to add the five-digit postal code, or ZIP code, after the two-letter abbreviation of the state to which the mail is addressed (FL for Florida).

Our postal service is expected to raise its rates in 1999, but at press time domestic **postage rates** were 20¢ for a postcard and 32¢ for a letter. Airmail postcards to Canada cost 30¢, while letters were 46¢. Airmail letters to other countries were 60¢ for the first half ounce.

Newspapers/Magazines All over Florida, you'll be able to purchase the *Miami Herald,* one of the most highly respected dailies in the country. Every city has its own daily paper.

Safety See "Safety" in "Preparing for Your Trip," above, and in "Fast Facts: Florida," in chapter 2.

Taxes In the United States there is no value-added tax (VAT) or other indirect tax at the national level. Every state, county, and city has the right to levy its own local tax on all purchases, including hotel and restaurant checks, airline tickets, and so on. For Florida's sales taxes, see "Fast Facts: Florida," in chapter 2. Florida's hotel tax varies from county to county; we give the rates in the accommodation sections of the chapters that follow.

Telephone, Telegraph, Telex & Fax The telephone system in the United States is run by private corporations, so rates, especially for long-distance service and operator-assisted calls, can vary widely. Generally, hotel surcharges on long-distance and local calls are astronomical, so you're usually better off using a **public pay telephone,** which you'll find clearly marked in most public buildings and private establishments as well as on the street. Convenience grocery stores and gas stations always have them. Many convenience groceries and packaging services sell prepaid calling cards in denominations up to $50; these can be the least expensive way to call home. Many public phones at airports now accept American Express, MasterCard, and Visa credit cards. Local calls made from public pay phones in most locales in Florida cost 35¢.

Most **long-distance and international calls** can be dialed directly from any phone. For calls within the United States and to Canada, dial 1 followed by the area code and the seven-digit number. For other international calls, dial 011 followed by the country code, city code, and the telephone number of the person you are calling.

Calls to area codes 800 and 888 are toll-free. However, calls to numbers in area codes 700 and 900 (chat lines, bulletin boards, "dating" services, and so on) can be very expensive—usually a charge of 95¢ to $3 or more per minute, and they sometimes have minimum charges that can run as high as $15 or more.

For **reversed-charge** or **collect calls,** and for **person-to-person calls,** dial 0 (zero, *not* the letter O) followed by the area code and number you want; an operator will then come on the line, and you should specify that you are calling collect, or person-to-person, or both. If your operator-assisted call is international, ask for the overseas operator.

For local **directory assistance** ("information"), dial 411; for long-distance information, dial 1, then the appropriate area code and 555-1212.

Telegraph and telex services are provided primarily by Western Union. You can bring your telegram into the nearest Western Union office (there are hundreds across the country) or dictate it over the phone (☎ **800/325-6000**). You can also telegraph money or have it telegraphed to you, very quickly over the Western Union system, but this service can cost as much as 15% to 25% of the amount sent.

Most hotels have **fax** machines available for guest use (be sure to ask about the charge to use it), and many hotel rooms are even wired for guests' fax machines. A less expensive way to send and receive faxes may be at stores such as **Mail Boxes Etc.,** a national chain of packing service shops (look in the Yellow Pages directory under "Packing Services").

There are two kinds of telephone directories in the United States. The so-called **White Pages** list private and business subscribers in alphabetical order. The inside front cover lists emergency numbers for police, fire, ambulance, the coast guard, poison-control center, crime-victims hotline, and so on. The first few pages will tell you how to make long-distance and international calls, complete with country codes and area codes. Government numbers usually are on pages printed on blue paper. Printed on yellow paper, the so-called **Yellow Pages** list all local services, businesses, industries, and churches and synagogues by type of activity, with an index at the front or back. The Yellow Pages also include city plans or detailed area maps, often showing postal ZIP codes and public transportation routes.

Time   The continental United States is divided into four **time zones:** eastern standard time (EST), central standard time (CST), mountain standard time (MST), and Pacific standard time (PST). Alaska and Hawaii have their own zones. For example, noon in New York City (EST) is 11am in Chicago (CST), 10am in Denver (MST), 9am in Los Angeles (PST), 8am in Anchorage (AST), and 7am in Honolulu (HST). Most of Florida observes eastern standard time, though the Panhandle west of the Apalachicola River is on central standard time (1 hour earlier than Tallahassee, Orlando, and Miami).

Daylight saving time is in effect from 1am on the first Sunday in April through 1am the last Sunday in October. Daylight saving time moves the clock 1 hour ahead of standard time.

Tipping   Tipping is so ingrained in the American way of life that the annual income tax of tip-earning service personnel is based on how much they should have received in light of their employers' gross revenues. Accordingly, they may have to pay tax on a tip you didn't actually give them.

Here are some rules of thumb: bartenders, 10% to 15% of the check; bellhops, at least 50¢ per bag, or $2 to $3 for a lot of luggage; cab drivers, 10% of the fare; chambermaids, $1 per day; checkroom attendants, $1 per garment; hairdressers and barbers, 15% to 20% of the bill; waiters and waitresses, 15% to 20% of the check; valet parking attendants, $1 per vehicle; rest room attendants, 25¢. We do not tip theater ushers, gas station attendants, or the staff at cafeterias and fast-food restaurants.

Toilets   You won't find public toilets (euphemistically referred to here as "rest rooms") on the streets in most U.S. cities, but they can be found in hotel lobbies, bars, restaurants, museums, department stores, railway and bus stations, or service stations. Note, however, that restaurants and bars in resorts or heavily visited areas may reserve their rest rooms for the use of their patrons.

Settling into Miami 4

by Victoria Pesce Elliott

As gritty as it is glamorous, sprawling Miami is not your typical American city. From the bustling airport to the palm-lined beachfront you'll hear Creole, French, Italian, Portuguese, Yiddish, Patois, and, of course, Spanish spoken all around you. The city's diversity is its very essence—a virtual bouillabaisse of colors, sounds, and scents.

This is Miami. Really the area commonly referred to as Miami is a huge metropolis made up of more than 30 cities and countless neighborhoods within or near Dade county. In November 1997, the county was renamed Miami-Dade County in an effort to cut down on the confusion. The actual city called Miami is home to only 350,000 residents out of Dade County's more than 2 million. And though this young city, which celebrated its 100th birthday in 1996, has become a major commerce center and trendy resort destination, it has had more than its share of growing pains.

Of course, there was the spate of tourist murders in the early 1990s contributing to Miami's status as the nation's murder capital, and the wave of immigration, especially from Cuba, that continues today. Citizens even introduced a referendum to abolish the city of Miami in 1997 after a series of corruption scandals and a huge fiscal deficit made the papers.

On the other extreme, the trendy resort area, South Beach, often shows up in glossy magazines and the style pages for its glitzy nightlife, exuberant architecture, and celebrity sightings. It is the colorful backdrop for hundreds of fashion shoots and major movies, too.

Through its many incarnations, two Miami characteristics have remained constant: its predictable year-round warmth and its location, a lush peninsula surrounded by deep clear waters pointing emphatically toward the Caribbean and the rest of the Americas. These traits have attracted waves of eager people seeking a new life since the Spanish first colonized the area in the 16th century.

They continue to come from all over the world for leisure, for business (primarily banking and shipping), for the excellent cuisine, and for the varied cultural offerings.

1 Orientation

ARRIVING
BY PLANE

Miami International Airport (MIA) (☎ **305/876-7000**) has emerged as one of the busiest airports in the world. More than 34 million passengers passed through this huge structure in 1997. Unfortunately, it's undergoing major reconstruction to expand its capacity, and it can feel like a maze with inadequate signage and surly employees, many of whom speak limited English.

The airport is located about 6 miles west of downtown and about 12 miles from the beaches. You can usually get from the plane to your hotel room anywhere in Miami-Dade County in well under an hour. If you're arriving from an international destination, however, you'll have to go through Customs and Immigration, a process that can double your time in the airport.

You can change money or use your Honor or PLUS System ATM card at Barnett Bank of South Florida with two locations. One is located on the fourth level in Concourse B and another is on the second level in Concourse C. Tourist information booths are located on the lower levels of Concourses B, D, E, and G.

Virtually every major car-rental company has a desk at Miami airport. However, no matter which one you are renting from (see "Getting Around," in chapter 2), you'll have to take one of the free shuttles to the rental site. Buses and vans, clearly marked with rental-car logos, circle the airport every few minutes.

GETTING INTO THE CITY   At the airport's exit, bright-orange sunbursts point the way to tourist-friendly zones, but getting into the city can still be confusing. You'll find Miami's signage, especially at or near I-95, utterly inadequate. Make sure you get a free map and clear directions to your destination before you leave the car-rental desk. or better yet, take a taxi or shuttle to your hotel and then arrange to rent a car nearer to your lodging. It is safer since the area surrounding the airport is plagued with thieves preying on lost tourists.

Taxis line up in front of a dispatcher's desk outside the airport's arrival terminals. Some companies offer flat rates to tourist zones; others charge by the meter. In either case, prices should be around $14 to Coral Gables, $24 to Miami Beach, $26 to South Beach, and $30 to Key Biscayne. Tip 10% to 15%, plus a few dollars extra if the driver helps with your bags.

A less-expensive alternative, especially if you are traveling solo, is a multipassenger van you can hail outside the first-floor baggage claim. The best and biggest is **Super-Shuttle** (☎ **305/871-2000**). You'll pay a flat fee ranging from $12 to $28 per person for door-to-door service in any part of the county. A uniformed dispatcher can summon a van if you don't see one with your destination displayed above the front windshield of the ubiquitous blue and yellow vehicles. They operate 24 hours a day and accept major credit cards.

Public transportation, though notoriously inefficient, is available. Buses heading downtown leave the airport only once every half hour or 40 minutes from the arrivals level. Bus no. 7 to downtown departs every 40 minutes Monday to Friday from 5:30am to 8:30pm and Saturday and Sunday from 7am to 7pm. Bus J heads south to Coral Gables every 30 minutes from about 6am to 7:30pm, and east to Miami Beach every 30 minutes from about 4:30am to 11:30pm. Bus no. 42 goes to Coconut Grove hourly from 5:30am to 7:15pm. All city buses cost $1.25 for adults and 60¢ for seniors and children who are taller than the bus fare box. For detailed schedule information or a map, call ☎ **305/638-6700** weekdays from 6am to 10pm, or weekends from 9am to 5pm.

BY CAR

No matter where you start your journey, chances are you'll reach Miami by way of I-95. This north-south interstate is the city's lifeline and an integral part of the region connecting the city's larger neighborhoods on the mainland and leading to all other major roads that go to the beaches and airport. Unfortunately, many of Miami's road signs are completely confusing and notably absent when you need them. Take time out to study a map before getting on the highway. You'll notice the far left lane of the interstate is labeled HOV (high-occupancy vehicles). Solo drivers are prohibited from driving in the "fast" lane at designated times corresponding to rush hours. Exceeding the speed limit by 10 to 15 miles an hour usually won't draw the attention of highway troopers; however, driving in the restricted lane will almost certainly get you an expensive ticket and points on your license.

Seat-belt laws are also enforced but only if you are pulled over for another infraction. Anyone in the front seat of a moving car must be buckled in. Children under the age of four must be in a car seat, whether they are seated in the front or back seat.

For a more detailed description of the city's main arteries and streets, see "City Layout," below.

BY TRAIN

If you're traveling to Miami by train, you'll pull into **Amtrak's** Miami terminal at 8303 NW 37th Ave. (off 79th Street; ☎ 305/835-1206). Unfortunately, none of the major car-rental companies have an office at the train station; you'll have to go to one near the airport (see "Getting Around," below). **Hertz** (☎ 800/654-3131) will reimburse your cab fare up to $10—or 7 miles from the train station—if you rent from them.

Taxis meet each Amtrak arrival. Depending on traffic, the fare to downtown should run about $23; to South Beach, about $35. Either trip should take less than 30 minutes.

SAFETY

Florida suffers from one of the highest crime rates in the nation. You can, however, take specific steps to lessen your chances of being victimized. When driving around Miami, always have a good map and know where you're going. Don't walk alone at night, and be extra wary when walking or driving through areas in and around downtown. There has also been an increase in muggings, car break-ins, and pickpocketing in the bustling center of Coconut Grove. You are better off paying higher parking fees to a valet or guarded lot than parking at meters a few blocks away from your destination.

When arriving in Miami late in the evening, consider shuttling to your hotel by taxi or shared van and then renting a car the next day when you have the time to get your bearings. Many rental agencies will deliver a vehicle directly to your hotel. Plus, many have offices throughout Miami, especially in the beach areas.

VISITOR INFORMATION

The **Greater Miami Convention and Visitors Bureau,** 701 Brickell Ave. (downtown), Suite 2700, Miami, FL 33131 (☎ 800/283-2707 or 305/539-3063; e-mail: gmcvb@miamiandbeaches.com; www.miamiandbeaches.com), is the best source of information for tourists intending to travel to any of the many regions that are collectively known as Miami. Even if you don't have a specific question, you may want to phone ahead for the free magazine, *Greater Miami and the Beaches Visitor's Guide,* which includes several good, clear maps and details on sports, attractions, and events. The office is open Monday to Friday from 8:30am to 5pm.

Greater Miami's various chambers of commerce also can send maps and details about their particular regions. These include the **Coconut Grove Chamber of Commerce,** 2820 McFarlane Rd., Miami, FL 33133 (☎ 305/444-7270; fax 305/ 444-2498); the **Coral Gables Chamber of Commerce,** 50 Aragon Ave., Coral Gables, FL 33134 (☎ 305/446-1657; fax 305/446-9900); the **Key Biscayne Chamber of Commerce,** 328 Crandon Blvd., Suite 217, Key Biscayne, FL 33149 (☎ 305/361-5207; fax 305/361-9411); the **Florida Gold Coast Chamber of**

Local Calls Get New Digits

After July 1, 1998, all new telephone numbers assigned within Miami-Dade County will have the area code 786 (SUN). After that time, to reach any local number (even one with a 305 area code), you will have to dial 10 digits, meaning 1 plus the area code and then the number. For example, to call for a reservation at that Italian place around the corner, you will dial 305-538-7850. Previously you would simply dial the seven-digit number. If you are calling the new little bistro on the corner that opened in time for the Fourth of July, you will call 1-786 plus the seven-digit number.

Commerce, 1100 Kane Concourse (Bay Harbor Islands), Miami, FL 33154 (☎ **305/ 866-6020**), which represents Bal Harbour, Sunny Isles, Surfside, and other North Dade waterfront communities; the **Greater Miami Chamber of Commerce,** Omni International, 1601 Biscayne Blvd., Miami, FL 33132 (☎ **800/283-2707** or 305/350-7700; fax 305/374-6902); and the **Miami Beach Chamber of Commerce,** 1920 Meridian Ave., Miami Beach, FL 33139 (☎ **305/672-1270;** fax 305/538-4336; www.sobe.com/miamibeachchamber), which represents South Beach. This chamber operates a conveniently located information center at Meridian Avenue and Dade Boulevard, just a few blocks from Lincoln Road and across the street from the Holocaust Memorial. It is staffed from 9am to 5pm weekdays and from 10am to 4pm on Saturday.

CITY LAYOUT

The area commonly called Miami is actually made up of dozens of cities and many more distinctive neighborhoods in and surrounding Dade County, which was renamed Miami-Dade County in 1997 in an attempt to allay the confusion. Geographically, it is divided into two main sections: the mainland and the adjacent barrier islands to the east (the largest is Miami Beach and includes South Beach at its tip). These two parts are connected by a series of causeways that hopscotch their way across the many islands dotting Biscayne Bay. Miami's international airport and towering city center are located on the mainland. Coconut Grove and Coral Gables, two of the city's most popular neighborhoods, sit more or less adjacent to one another a short drive south of the center. The working-class streets of Little Havana are immediately west of downtown, and Little Haiti is immediately north.

The main barrier island is divided crosswise into the communities of South Beach, Miami Beach, Surfside, Bal Harbour, and Sunny Isles—areas that, collectively, are simply referred to as Miami Beach.

FINDING AN ADDRESS   Finding a street on the mainland is infinitely easier once you learn how the city's numbering system works. The City of Miami is divided into quadrants—NE, NW, SE, and SW—by the intersection of Flagler Street and North Miami Avenue. These two otherwise unremarkable roads meet in the city center, and are colored dark red on most city maps. Along with places, courts, terraces, and lanes, street and avenue numbers increase from this intersection. The streets of Hialeah, a middle-class residential suburb northwest of the city center, are exceptions to this pattern, and are listed separately in map indexes.

In most cases you can determine the cross street of an address by lopping off the last two digits. For example, 12301 Biscayne Blvd. is located at 123rd Street. It's also helpful to remember that avenues generally run north-south, while streets go east-west.

The City of Miami Beach consists of 16 narrow islands. The largest is only 7 miles long and 1½ miles wide and is the main area referred to throughout the book, Here, street numbering starts with 1st Street, near Miami Beach's southern tip (South Pointe), and increases to 192nd Street, in the northern part of Sunny Isles. Named streets intersect and are usually clearly marked. Collins Avenue (Fla. A1A) makes the entire journey from head to toe.

You should know that the numbered streets in Miami Beach are not the geographical equivalents of those on the mainland, but they are close. For example, the 79th Street Causeway leads into 71st Street on Miami Beach, and the 125th Street exit on I-95 brings you to 96th Street on the beach.

MAPS   A reliable map is essential. If you aren't planning on exploring extensively, the maps located inside the tourist board's free publication *Greater Miami and the Beaches Visitor's Guide* are adequate. If you really want to get to know the city, invest in one of the small, accordion-fold maps available at most gas stations and bookstores. Rand McNally's Easy Finder is a colorful accordion that gives great details of most of Miami-Dade County with the exception of some of West and South Miami.

NEIGHBORHOODS IN BRIEF

A region that has long attracted sun-seekers, retirees, immigrants, international businesses, and drifters, Miami is home to a great number of diverse and interesting communities.

South Beach/The Art Deco District   The revitalization that began in the early 1980s and made South Beach famous continues today. The beautiful skyline is dotted with cranes scaffolding. Really just a 15-block strip at the southern tip of Miami Beach, South Beach happens to have more art deco architecture than any other place in the world. The colorful, whimsical shapes that define this 1920s style are evident on almost every building in the neighborhood. Once known as "God's waiting room," because of the legions of retirees who settled here, South Beach is now home to models, photographers, musicians, world-renowned writers, and a large gay contingency that fell in love with the climate and the excitement inherent in a burgeoning community.

By the way, never refer to this area as "SoBe." Only tourists and public relations people use this abbreviation.

Miami Beach   This is the area used to describe the central and northern parts of Miami Beach situated north of South Beach—generally considered to begin at 24th Street. To tourists in the 1950s, Miami Beach was Miami. Extravagant resort hotels offered northerners everything under one roof and hosted major performers like Frank Sinatra and Jackie Gleason. In the 1960s and 1970s many failing hotels converted to condominiums, resulting in the nickname "Condo Canyon." In the late 1980s, the mammoth hotels that survived the slow years renovated their properties to accommodate the huge number of tourists returning to the area, and Miami Beach proper is once again a destination in its own right.

Surfside, Bal Harbour, and Sunny Isles lie in the northern part of Miami Beach. Collins Avenue (Fla. A1A), Miami Beach's most active thoroughfare, links these neighborhoods together seamlessly.

Surfside, packed with moderately priced "resort" motels, is very popular with European and ultra-conservative Jewish tourists, who return year after year. Bal Harbour, a shopping mecca, is the highest net worth zip code in South Florida. Elegant bay-front homes are clustered on small islands that are part of the city. Sunny Isles, at the far north end of the beach, is for budgeteers. With some outstanding exceptions, the farther north you go on Miami Beach, the cheaper lodging and eating becomes.

Key Biscayne   Located south of Miami Beach, off the shores of Coconut Grove, Key Biscayne is protected from the troubles of the mainland by the long Rickenbacker Causeway and a $1 toll (which the city has debated raising). For the most part, the island is an exclusive residential community with million-dollar homes enjoying priceless views. For tourists, this key offers great beaches, a spectacular golf course, a top resort hotel, and a couple of good restaurants.

Downtown   Downtown's high-tech buildings perched on the water's edge and neon-lighted monorail system make the area visually stunning, but are better enjoyed from afar. Some great shopping and a few excellent restaurants cater primarily to the nine-to-five crowd and cruise-boat passengers who usually don't get farther than the Bayside marketplace. Plans are in the works to revitalize the area with a new waterside arena, entertainment complex, and retail shops. Also showing signs of life is the area known as the Design District, in the northern part of downtown. Suddenly little cafes, galleries, and clubs are popping up just west of Biscayne Boulevard starting at about 36th Street.

Little Havana   Miami's original Cuban center is still the city's most vibrant ethnic enclave. Referred to locally as "Calle Ocho," Southwest 8th Street, a one-way street lined with car-repair shops, tailors, electronics stores, cafeterias, and bodegas is the region's main thoroughfare. Old men in guayaberas suck on stogies over their daily games of dominoes. Despite some shabby-looking buildings, the neighborhood is unusually safe for visitors at any hour.

Little Haiti   During a brief period in the late 1970s and early 1980s almost 35,000 Haitians arrived in Miami. The influx continues today. Most of the new refugees settle in a decaying 200-square-block area north of downtown. Extending from 41st to 79th streets and bordered by I-95 and Biscayne Boulevard, Little Haiti, as it is known, is a relatively depressed neighborhood with at least 60,000 residents, more than half of whom were born in Haiti. Unfortunately, gangs and petty theft make this area unsafe even in the daytime.

Coconut Grove   There was a time when the heart of Coconut Grove was populated by artists and intellectuals, hippies and radicals. But these days, gentrification has pushed most alternative types out, leaving in their place a multitude of cafes, boutiques, and nightspots. The Grove's hub is the intersection of Grand Avenue, Main Highway, and McFarlane Road. Around this center are dozens of shops and eateries that attract businesspeople, students, and loads of foreign tourists—especially at night, when the Grove becomes a colorful parade of people.

Don't wander far from your destination. Unfortunately, much of the property surrounding the Grove's active center is an impoverished residential area plagued by drugs and crime.

Coral Gables   Built in the early 1920s, the Gables was one of the country's first planned developments and one of Dade County's oldest neighborhoods. Modest and beautiful houses here were built in a Mediterranean style along lush tree-lined streets that open onto fountained plazas. Many businesses, especially Latin American companies and some foreign embassies, are based in the large modern office buildings that have been integrated into the unique cityscape. Coral Gables offers visitors some of the city's best restaurants, shopping, and top hotels, within 5 minutes of the airport—but no ocean or beach.

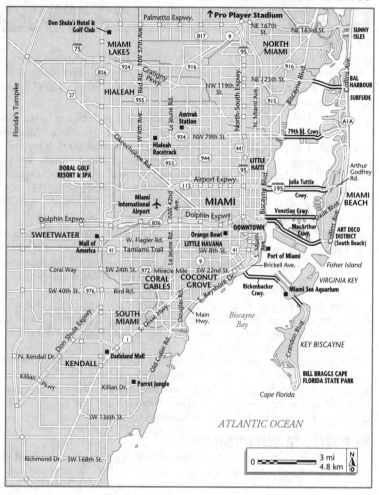

South Miami To locals, South Miami is both a specific area, southwest of Coral Gables, and a general region that encompasses all of southern Dade County and includes Kendall, Perrine, Cutler Ridge, and Homestead. For the purpose of clarity, this book has grouped all these southern suburbs under the rubric "South Miami." Similar attributes unite the communities: They're heavily residential, and all are packed with strip malls as well as rapidly diminishing acres of farmland. Few tourists stay in these parts as there is no beach and few cultural offerings. But South Miami does contain some worthwhile attractions, making it likely that you'll spend some time here during your stay.

North Dade This suburban area across the Biscayne Bay from Miami Beach has a number of excellent restaurants and good shopping, but very little else to interest most visitors. With the exception of the Turnberry Resort, there are no major hotels here. The areas include Aventura, North Miami, and North Miami Beach (a misleadingly named residential area on the mainland near the Dade-Broward county line).

2 Getting Around

BY CAR

Unless you're going to spend your entire vacation at a self-contained resort, on pedestrian-friendly South Beach, or are traveling directly to the Port of Miami for a cruise, a car is a necessity in this sprawling metropolis. See "Safety," under "Orientation," earlier in this chapter, for special driving tips.

RENTALS Every major car-rental company has at least one office in Miami. Consequently, the city is one of the cheapest places in the world to rent a car. Many firms regularly advertise prices in the neighborhood of $180 per week for their bottom-of-the-line tin can, and it can often be had even cheaper. Rates vary seasonally. See "Getting Around," in chapter 2, for a list of national car-rental companies. One growing and recommendable company is **Enterprise** (☎ **800/325-8007** or 305/534-9037), which rents cars from dozens of well-placed locations throughout the city and offers extremely competitive rates.

PARKING Especially in South Beach and Coconut Grove, parking is a hassle. On beach-perfect weekends parking is close to impossible, especially on Ocean Drive. It's good to know about the parking lot on 13th Street, between Collins Avenue and Ocean Drive, and the new one on 6th Street, between Collins Avenue and Ocean Drive. The charge is usually $1 per hour and $5 per day.

If you do find a vacant metered spot, remember to bring plenty of quarters. Depending on the area, they are enforced daily, including Sunday and holidays, usually from 9am to 9pm—and sometimes until midnight. A quarter buys you as little as 15 minutes or as much as an hour.

Valet services at restaurants and nightclubs are commonplace. Expect to wait for your car and to pay $5 to $15 in Coconut Grove and on South Beach's Ocean Drive on busy weekend nights. Don't leave any valuables in your car since they are usually left unattended on the street. Also, valets have been known to look in glove compartments and change-holders for a little extra compensation.

BY PUBLIC TRANSPORTATION

Notoriously inefficient, Greater Miami's mass transit system is operated by the **Metro-Dade Transit Agency,** 360 NE 185th St., Miami, FL 33179 (☎ **305/654-6586,** or 305/638-6700 for route information). Free schedules, maps, and a "First-Time Rider's Kit" are available at Government Center Station, 111 NW 1st St. (1 block from Flagler Street), in downtown Miami, or by mail from the address above.

BY RAIL Two rail lines, operated by the Metro-Dade Transit Agency (☎ **305/ 638-6700**), run in concert with each other. **Metrorail,** the city's modern high-speed commuter train, is a 21-mile elevated line that connects Miami's northern and southern suburbs to downtown and each other. If you're staying in Coral Gables or Coconut Grove, you can park your car at a nearby station and ride the rail downtown. Unfortunately for visitors, the line's usefulness is limited. The trains simply don't go most places that tourists go. Metrorail operates daily from 6am to midnight; trains run every 7½ minutes during rush hours and every 15 minutes at other times. The fare is $1.25.

Metromover, a 4½-mile elevated line, circles the city center in two big loops, and connects with Metrorail at Government Center and Brickell Station. Riding on rubber tires, the single-train car winds past 21 stations and through some of the city's most important business and retail locations, including the Omni International Mall and the Brickell Financial District. At 25¢ a ride, the Disneyesque Metromover is one of Miami's best sightseeing bargains. Service runs daily from 6am to midnight about every 5 minutes. Transfers to Metrorail are $1.

BY BUS Miami's suburban layout is not conducive to getting around by bus. Metrobus provides service with widely varying frequency. Stops are marked by green-and-blue signs that are usually accompanied by route information. Standard bus fare is $1.25, though some express routes charge $2.75, and exact change is required. Transfers cost 25¢. Most buses are wheelchair accessible. Disabled passengers, students, and those over 65 pay only 60¢ (10¢ per transfer).

BY TAXI

If you're not planning to travel any great distance, an occasional taxi is a good alternative to renting a car. Especially if you plan to spend most of your vacation in South Beach's Art Deco District, you'd be wise to avoid the parking hassles and expense that come with a car. Consider renting a car only for the days you choose to venture onto the mainland.

The meter starts at $1.10 for the first one-seventh of a mile and increases at the rate of $1.75 for each additional mile. Major cab companies include **Metro** (☎ 305/888-8888) and **Yellow** (☎ 305/444-4444). On Miami Beach, the reigning cab company is **Central** (☎ 305/532-5555). A flat-rate schedule is in place only for rides to the airport and prices range from $22 to $46.

BY BICYCLE

The sprawling nature of Miami makes distance bicycling both difficult and dangerous, but if you're staying in South Beach or Coral Gables, cycling to neighborhood spots makes sense. See "More Places to Play, Both Indoors & Out," in chapter 5, for details.

ON FOOT

With the exception of a few areas in Coconut Grove and South Beach, Miami is not a walker's city. Most attractions are too far apart from each other to make walking feasible. Like the citizens of Los Angeles, most Miamians get into their cars even when going just a few blocks.

FAST FACTS: Miami

American Express For travel arrangements, traveler's checks, currency exchange, and other member services, Miami offices include 330 Biscayne Blvd., downtown (☎ 305/358-7350); 9700 Collins Ave., Bal Harbour (☎ 305/865-5959); and 32 Miracle Mile, Coral Gables (☎ 305/446-3381). Offices are open Monday to Friday from 9am to 5pm and Saturday from 10am to 4pm. Bal Harbour also keeps hours on Sunday from noon to 5pm.

To report lost or stolen traveler's checks, call ☎ 800/221-7282.

Camera Repair The following are shops known for reliable repair work: **Dan's Camera Clinic,** 5142 Biscayne Blvd., downtown (☎ 305/759-2541); **World Wide Photo,** with various locations in Miami, including 219 7th St., South Beach (☎ 305/672-5188); and **Aberbach's of Miami Beach,** 441 41st St., Miami Beach (☎ 305/532-5446).

Car Rentals See "Getting Around," earlier in this chapter, and in chapter 2.

Convention Center A high-tech "new-deco" facade fronts over a million square feet of exhibition space at the **Miami Beach Convention Center,** 1901 Convention Center Dr., Miami Beach, FL 33139 (☎ 305/673-7311), the venue for many annual huge shows, including the world's largest boat show (see "Florida Calendar of Events," in chapter 2).

Curfew   The city of Miami sporadically enforces a curfew of 11pm for unchaperoned teenagers 18 or younger on weekdays and midnight on weekends.

Doctors   In an emergency, call an ambulance by dialing ☎ **911** from any phone. No coins are required.

The Dade County Medical Association sponsors a **Physician Referral Service** (☎ **305/324-8717**), open Monday to Friday from 9am to 4:30pm.

Health South Doctors' Hospital, 5000 University Dr., Coral Gables (☎ **305/666-2111**), is a 285-bed acute-care hospital with a 24-hour physician-staffed emergency department.

Emergencies   To reach the **police, ambulance,** or **fire department,** dial ☎ **911** from any phone. No coins are needed.

Emergency hotlines include **Crisis Intervention** (☎ **305/358-4357** or 305/358-HELP); **Poison Information Center** (☎ **800/282-3171**); and **Rape Hotline** (☎ **305/585-5185**).

Gratuities   Many area restaurants and bars automatically add a 15% gratuity to bar and food checks without telling customers. Read the check carefully and make it a habit to ask your server if a tip has already been included before paying any bill. Some unscrupulous servers count on being double tipped by unwary customers.

Information   Always check local newspapers for special things to do during your visit. See "Newspapers/Magazines," below. For a complete list of tourist boards and other information sources, see "Visitor Information," under "Orientation," earlier in this chapter.

Liquor Laws   Only adults 21 or older may legally purchase or consume alcohol in the state of Florida. Minors are usually permitted in bars that serve food. Liquor laws are strictly enforced; if you look young, carry identification. Beer and wine are also sold in most supermarkets and convenience stores. Liquor stores in the City of Miami Beach and most of Miami are open 7 days a week, but can't sell alcohol until after noon on Sunday.

Luggage Storage/Lockers   In addition to the baggage check at Miami International Airport (see "Arriving," under "Orientation," earlier in this chapter), most hotels offer luggage-storage facilities. If you're taking a cruise from the Port of Miami (see chapter 5), bags can be stored in your ship's departure terminal.

Newspapers/Magazines   The well-respected *Miami Herald* is the city's only English-language daily. It's especially known for its Latin American coverage and its excellent Friday "Weekend" entertainment guide. The most useful alternative weekly is the well-respected tabloid *New Times. South Florida,* on sale at newsstands, is the area's trendy glossy with articles and listings to keep local readers up on events. *TWN* is a gay publication distributed free in Miami in purple boxes.

Pharmacies   **Walgreens Pharmacies** are all over town, including 8550 Coral Way, Coral Gables (☎ **305/221-9271**); 1845 Alton Rd., South Beach (☎ **305/531-8868**); and 6700 Collins Ave., Miami Beach (☎ **305/861-6742**). The branch at 5731 Bird Rd., at Southwest 40th Street (☎ **305/666-0757**), is open 24 hours, and the **Eckerd Drugs** at 1825 Miami Gardens Dr. (at Northeast 185th Street), North Miami Beach (☎ **305/932-5740**), is open until midnight.

Police   For emergencies, dial ☎ **911** from any phone. No coins are needed. For other matters, call ☎ **305/595-6263** to find the precinct nearest you.

Post Office   The main post office, 2200 NW 72nd Ave. (☎ **305/470-0222**), is located west of Miami International Airport. Conveniently located post offices include 1300 Washington Ave., South Beach (☎ **305/599-1787**), and 3191 Grand Ave., Coconut Grove (☎ **305/599-1750**).

Safety   Miami has been plagued by a spate of bad press, and for good reason. In general, however, visitors are safe in the beach areas and in the daylight hours. For more specifics, see "Safety," under "Orientation," earlier in this chapter.

Taxes   A 6% state sales tax plus 0.5% local tax, for a total of 6.5%, is added on at the register for all goods and services purchased. In addition, most municipalities levy special taxes on restaurants and hotels. In Surfside, hotel taxes total 10.5%; in Bal Harbour, 9.5%; in Miami Beach (including South Beach), 11.5%; and in the rest of Miami-Dade County, 12.5%. Combined, these taxes can add 16% to 19% to your hotel bill—a hefty sum to keep in mind.

In Miami Beach, Surfside, and Bal Harbour, the resort (hotel) tax also applies to hotel restaurants and restaurants with liquor licenses.

Taxis   See "Getting Around," earlier in this chapter.

Transit Information   For **Metrorail** or **Metromover** schedule information, phone ☎ **305/638-6700.** See "Getting Around," earlier in this chapter, for more information.

Weather   For an up-to-date recording of current weather conditions and forecast reports, dial ☎ **305/229-4522.**

3 Where to Stay

Many of the old hotels from the 1930s, 1940s, and 1950s (when most Miami resorts were constructed) have been totally overhauled; others have survived with occasional coats of paint and new carpeting, which some owners like to call renovation. Be sure to ask about what work has been done since; especially on the ocean, sea air and years of tourist wear can result in musty, paint-peeled rooms. Also, be sure to find out if the hotel you're booking is undergoing reconstruction while you're there. There's nothing worse than the sounds of jackhammers over breakfast. I've omitted the more worn hotels and tried to list only those that have been fully upgraded recently. Exceptions are noted.

If you can't get a room after inquiring at the hotels listed in this guide (an extremely unlikely prospect), look along Miami Beach's Collins Avenue. There are dozens of hotels and motels on this strip, in all price categories, so there's bound to be a vacancy.

SEASONS & RATES   South Florida's tourist season is well defined, beginning in mid-November and lasting until Easter. Hotel prices escalate until about March, after which they begin to decline. During the off-season, hotel rates are typically 30% to 50% lower than their winter highs.

But timing isn't everything. In many cases, rates will also depend on your hotel's proximity to the beach and how much ocean you can see from your window. Small motels a block or two from the water can be up to 40% cheaper than similar hostelries right on the sand. When a hotel is right on the beach, its oceanfront rooms will usually be significantly more expensive than similar accommodations in the rear.

I've selected several good chain hotels in each area—all the big ones are here—and included contact information in the introduction to each section.

For the sake of simplicity, the rates have been broken down into broad categories: **winter** (usually between November and March or April) and **off-season** (usually May to August). The months in between, the shoulder season, should fall somewhere in between the highs and lows. These listings should be read as a guideline, not as a guarantee.

The prices listed below are based on 1998 rates and don't include state and city taxes, which, in some parts of Miami, are as high as 12.5%. Some hotels, especially in South Beach, tack on an additional service charge.

PRICE CATEGORIES   The hotels below are divided first by area, then by price, using the following guidelines: **very expensive,** over $250; **expensive,** over $180; **moderate,** $90 to $180; and **inexpensive,** below $90. Prices are based on published rates (or rack rates) for a standard double room during the high season. Check with the reservations agent since many rooms are also available above and below the category ranges listed. And always ask about packages, since it's almost always possible to get a better deal than these "official" rates.

LONG-TERM STAYS   If you plan to visit Miami for a month, a season, or more, think about renting a room in a long-term hotel or condominium apartment. Long-term accommodations exist in every price category from budget to deluxe and in general are extremely reasonable, especially during the off-season. A short note to the chamber of commerce in the area in which you're interested will be answered with a list of available accommodations. Also check with the reservation services below. In addition, many area real estate agents also handle short-term rentals (meaning less than a year).

RESERVATION SERVICES   **Central Reservations** (☎ **800/950-0232** or 305/274-6832; www.//reservation-services.com; e-mail: rooms@america.com) works with many of Miami's hotels and can often secure discounts of up to 40% off for otherwise unyielding hotels and offer advice on the specific locales, especially in Miami Beach and downtown; the **South Florida Hotel Network** lists more than 300 hotels throughout Palm Beach to Miami and the Keys (☎ **800/538-3616** or 305/538-3616).

SOUTH BEACH

South Beach's hotels were mostly built in the late 1930s, just after the Depression, in an area originally planned as an affordable destination for middle-class northeasterners. Therefore, none of the hotels were really luxurious—they just happened to be situated on one of the most beautiful strips of beach in the country. Large resorts like the Fontainebleau were built later, 20 or so blocks north of South Beach, to cater to celebrities and jet-setters.

But after many years of transition, South Beach gained national recognition for its unique art deco architecture. The area is now South Florida's number one tourist destination and home to many of the city's best restaurants and nightclubs.

The most expensive rooms are on Ocean Drive or Collins Avenue, just across the street from the beach. Thankfully, for at least most of South Beach, new buildings cannot be built directly on the sand and cannot exceed three stories. Remember, with a few notable exceptions, the art deco hotels generally are small and have tiny bathrooms and few services and facilities.

Unless noted otherwise, most offer no-smoking rooms. Inquire before booking.

Some very well located chain hotel options include the **Days Inn** (☎ **800/325-2525** or 305/538-6631) at 100 21st St. (off Collins Avenue) or **Holiday Inn**

(☎ **800/327-5476** or 305/534-1511) at 2201 Collins Ave. Both are at the north edge of the historic district and are within walking distance to the scene. Both hotels play up the tropical look and offer standard chain-hotel-style rooms. Also, each has its own pool, sundeck, and pool bar and is directly on the ocean. The Holiday Inn has lushly landscaped grounds hidden behind an Eckerd's drugstore and lots of amenities, including a private beach, water-sports equipment rentals, and car-rental desk. Both offer rooms for under $90 even in season.

VERY EXPENSIVE

Casa Grande Suite Hotel. 834 Ocean Dr., South Beach, FL 33139. ☎ **800/OUTPOST** or 305/672-7003. Fax 305/673-3669. 33 units. A/C MINIBAR TV TEL. Winter $245 junior suite; $280–$400 one-bedroom suite; $495 two-bedroom suite; $1,125 three-bedroom suite. Off-season $160 junior suite; $225–$265 one-bedroom suite; $345 two-bedroom suite; $750 three-bedroom suite. Extra person $15. Children 11 and under stay free in parents' room. AE, CB, DC, DISC, MC, V. Valet parking $14.

Europeans and vacationing celebs looking for privacy enjoy the casual elegance and thoughtful service of this hotel right on "Deco Drive." You'll feel as if you're staying in a very stylish apartment, not in a cookie-cutter hotel room, at the Casa Grande. Every room is outfitted in a slightly different style with fully equipped kitchenettes, beautifully tiled baths, reed rugs, mahogany beds, handmade batik prints, and antiques from all over the world, especially Indonesia. Although there is no pool on the property, considering the fact that you can see the ocean, stock your own fridge, and veg out with a good stereo and VCR, this is one of the most desirable hotels on South Beach. Some rooms facing the ocean can be loud, especially on a weekend night.

Amenities: Room service, overnight dry cleaning and laundry, complimentary newspaper and evening turndown with chocolates, twice-daily maid service, express checkout, baby-sitting arrangements. VCRs and videos are available to rent. Full kitchens, CD/cassette stereo, conference rooms, car rental, activities desk, access to a nearby health club.

✪ The Delano. 1685 Collins Ave., South Beach, FL 33139. ☎ **800/555-5001** or 305/672-2000. Fax 305/532-0099. 201 units, 8 bungalows. A/C MINIBAR TV TEL. Winter $310–$415 double; $475 loft; $700 suite; $1,850 two-bedroom; $2,200 penthouse; $800 bungalow. Off-season $180–$265 double (weekend rates for double same as winter rates); all other unit rates same as winter rates. Extra person $35. Children 17 and under stay free in parents' room. AE, DC, DISC, MC, V. Valet parking $16.

When The Delano (pronounced like FDR's middle name) opened in 1995, it made the front page of nearly every architecture and style magazine in the country for its whimsical and elegant design. Look for a huge hedge with a simple blue arched door in its center, or look up for a rocketlike fin (an original 1947 detail) sprouting from the top of the all-white building. New York's Ian Shrager, of Studio 54 fame, brought in designer Philippe Starck, who went wild with an impossible decor of 40-foot sheer white curtains hanging outside, mirrors everywhere, white billowing curtains, Adirondack chairs, and fur-covered beds. The guest rooms are all white; a perfectly crisp green Granny Smith apple is the only dose of color. It may sound antiseptic, but it's not: It's sexy and sophisticated. The poolside cabanas are the most desirable rooms because of their huge size, but they can be noisy since they are on an active poolside walkway. Unfortunately, the model-gorgeous staff is often aloof or simply unavailable. But the location is ideal; it's just north of the Art Deco District strip of bars and restaurants, away from the noisy street traffic but close enough to walk to hopping Lincoln Road Mall. And of course, it is right on the ocean.

Dining/Diversions: An elegant bar attracts curious beautiful people nightly. The Blue Door (owned in part by Madonna) is known more as a place to be seen than for its great cuisine. Food and service are inconsistent. The thatched Beach Bar restaurant serves fantastic sandwiches and salads. A cozy kitchen table is loaded alternately with homemade pastries, stone crabs, or champagne and caviar.

Amenities: Concierge, room service, same-day dry cleaning and laundry, newspaper delivery, evening turndown, in-room massage, executive business services, express checkout. VCRs, video rentals, children's movie theater and child activity programs, large outdoor pool, wide guarded beach, 24-hour state-of-the-art David Barton gym with sauna, business center, conference rooms, rooftop solarium, extensive watersports recreation, funky gift shop; Aqua Spa, $10 for hotel guests, open for women 9am to 7pm, men 7:30 to 11pm, closed Tuesday night, offering facials, a plethora of massages, and water treatments.

Hotel Astor. 956 Washington Ave., South Beach, FL 33139. ☎ **800/270-4981** or 305/531-8081. Fax 305/531-3193. 40 units. A/C MINIBAR TV TEL. Winter $145–$200 double; $275–$320 suite. Off-season $115–$190 double; $245–$290 suite. Astor suite $420–$600. Extra person $30. AE, MC, V. Valet parking $14.

An elegant and modern hotel, the Astor is a small property that attracts many loyal, return guests. Originally built in 1936, the renovation in 1995 greatly improved on the original design of this simple three-story gem. There is a small lap pool and a beautiful waterfall outside the sleek lobby bar area. And, all the details are pure luxury, like swivel stands for the large-screen TVs, ministereo systems, Belgian linens and towels, and funky custom lighting with dimmer switches. The hotel staff is known for bending over backwards in a town where most fall flat. For the price (about half the Delano), this is a great option for those who like intimate but terribly hip accommodations. This is definitely a place for those in the know. Unfortunately, the few moderately priced standard rooms are usually booked months in advance.

Dining: Astor Place is one of Miami's best restaurants. The Florida-style menu is diverse and delicious (see listing under "Where to Dine"). Sunday brunch is one of the best in town.

Amenities: 24-hour concierge service, room service, dry cleaning, laundry, newspaper delivery, in-room massage, twice-daily maid service, baby-sitting, secretarial service, express checkout. VCRs available on request, video-rental, outdoor pool with jet-streams, access to nearby health club, two phones in suites.

The Tides. 1220 Ocean Dr., South Beach, FL 33139. ☎ **800/OUTPOST** or 305/604-5000. Fax 305/672-6288. www.islandlife.com. E-mail: outpost800@aol.com. 45 units. A/C MINIBAR TV TEL. Winter $275 superior; $350–$425 suite; $900–$2,000 penthouse suite. Off-season $150 superior; $200–$275 suite; $600–$1,100 penthouse suite. Extra person $20. Rates include continental breakfast. AE, DC, CB, DISC, MC, V. Valet parking $15.

Opened in late 1997 to rave reviews, this 12-story art deco masterpiece is one of the tallest buildings on the strip of Ocean Drive. It is owned by Chris Blackwell and his Island Outpost group, which includes the Cavalier, The Kent, and Casa Grande (reviewed in this section), and others. Rooms are Delano-esqe, meaning they are starkly white but luxurious. The advantage here is the warm staff and more central location. Also, all rooms are large and have ocean views. Amenities include terraces, exercise facilities, a lobby lounge with live entertainment, a freshwater pool on the rear mezzanine, and two alfresco restaurants featuring Mediterranean cuisine and fresh local seafood. As in most of Outpost's hotels, there are VCRs and CD/cassette stereos as well as an eclectic collection of CDs in each room.

South Beach Accommodations & Dining

Accommodations:
Albion Hotel 7
Astor Hotel 19
The Avalon Hotel 22
Banana Bungalow 1
Brigham Gardens 12
Casa Grande 21
The Cavalier 14
Clay Hotel & Youth Hostel 11
The Delano 8
Essex House 18
Hotel Leon 20
Hotel Continental Riande 2
The Kent 16
Loews Miami Beach 9
Marseilles Deco Beach Hotel 6
The Park Washington Hotel 17
The Tides 15

Dining:
Joe's Stone Crab Restaurant 26
La Sandwicherie 13
Mrs. Mendoza 27
Nemo's 25
Nirvana 23
Norma's 5
Osteria del Teatro 10
Sport Cafe 24
World Resources 3
Yuca 4

1-0674

Dining: Twelve Twenty is the hotel's fine restaurant and serves dinner nightly 6pm to midnight, while The Terrace, a gorgeous marble floored outdoor cafe overlooking the ocean, does a fine job of breakfast and lunch.

Amenities: Concierge, 24-hour room service, dry cleaning, laundry service, newspaper delivery, in-room massage, twice daily maid service, baby-sitting, secretarial services, express checkout. Stereos with cassette and CD, VCRs, video rentals, heated outdoor pool, across the street from the most popular beach, small health club, discount at nearby Club Bodytech, one conference room.

EXPENSIVE

✪ **Albion Hotel.** 1650 James Ave. (at Lincoln Rd.). ☎ **888/665-0008** or 305/913-1000. Fax 305/674-0507. 100 units. A/C MINIBAR TV TEL. Winter $205–$215 double; $375–$700 suite. Off-season $125–$145 double; $195–$550 suite. AE, DC, DISC, MC, V. Valet parking $15.

An architectural masterpiece originally designed in 1939, this large streamline moderne building looks like a cruise ship with portholes, smokestack, and sleek curved lines. It was totally renovated in 1997, under the guidance of the hip, New York family, the Rubells. Although you would have to walk a few blocks to find beach access, you may not want to. A huge pool and artificial beach are original features at this unusual and recommendable resort. Rooms are furnished with drop-dead modern furnishings custom designed for the space.

Dining/Diversions: A poolside restaurant serves snacks and light meals. The Fallabella bar is a popular hangout.

Amenities: Concierge, room service, dry cleaning and laundry, evening turndown, in-room massage, newspaper delivery, twice-daily maid service, baby-sitting, executive business services, valet parking, airport limo service available, VCRs, large outdoor heated pool with adjacent artificial sand beach, small fitness room and access to nearby health club, business center, conference and production rooms, stereos with CD and cassette, state-of-the-art phones with data port and voice mail.

Loews Miami Beach Hotel. 1601 Collins Ave., South Beach, FL 33139. ☎ **800/23-LOEWS** or 305/604-1601. 857 units. A/C MINIBAR TV TEL. Winter from $300 double. Off-season from $250 double. AE, DISC, DC, MC, V.

Not yet completed at press time, this 857-unit hotel is the first new hotel to be built in South Beach for the last 30 years. It is also the largest. A good thing, since the beach was sorely in need of a large hotel to accommodate business travelers who come to the nearby convention center. Accordingly, it will feature plenty of meeting rooms, ballrooms, a large health club, and seven restaurants and lounges. Like the Fountainbleau and Eden Roc 30 blocks north, it will be a full-service, beachfront resort. However, it has the advantage of being brand new and being situated right in the heart of the bustling Art Deco District scene.

MODERATE

Avalon Hotel. 700 Ocean Dr., South Beach, FL 33139. ☎ **800/933-3306** or 305/538-0133. Fax 305/534-0258. 106 units. A/C TV TEL. Winter $120–$180 double. Off-season $65–$145 double. Rates include continental breakfast, full breakfast off-season. Extra person $10. Children 11 and under stay free in parents' room. 10% discount for stays of 7 days or more. AE, CB, DC, DISC, MC, V. Valet parking $14.

Classic art deco digs right on the beach, occupying a pretty parcel of land that wraps around the corner of 7th Street, the hotel is striking both inside and out. The rooms are well decorated in traditional 1930s style. The modest lobby is occupied by a casual restaurant, best for lunch either inside or on the breezy outdoor patio. The experienced management, known for its excellent inns in Newport, Rhode Island, runs this hotel with an even hand.

If the Avalon is full, don't hesitate to accept a room in its other hostelry, the Majestic, located across the street. Room service, free coffee, refreshments, and breakfast are also available.

Cavalier. 1320 Ocean Dr., South Beach, FL 33139. ☎ **800/OUTPOST** or 305/604-5000. Fax 305/531-5543. 45 units. A/C MINIBAR TV TEL. Winter $125–$195 double; $275–$350 suite. Off-season $95–$155 double; $230–$250 suite. Extra person $15. Children 11 and under stay free in parents' room. AE, DC, DISC, MC, V. Valet parking $14, self-parking $6.

The Cavalier, a hip, well-priced hotel, is kept in shape by yearly refurbishments. You can't beat this oceanfront location, which is adjacent to shops and restaurants. Palm trees brush the ceilings of the modest lobby, where young trendy guests make their way to their rooms. Funky prints cover the walls, which are the colors of a tequila sunrise. A young, competent staff waits on guests and offers lots of good advice about local clubs, restaurants, and shopping. Rooms come equipped with CD players and discs. You can also use a VCR and rent videos. Considering it is on Ocean Drive, most rooms are relatively quiet.

Essex House. 1001 Collins Ave., South Beach, FL 33139. ☎ **800/55-ESSEX** or 305/ 534-2700. Fax 305/532-3827. 79 units. A/C TV TEL. Winter $155–$195 double; $255–$300 suite. Off-season $99–$139 double; $199–$245 suite. Rates include deluxe continental breakfast. Minimum stay 2 nights on weekends in season, 3 nights on holidays. Extra person $10. AE, DC, CB, DISC, MC, V. Valet parking $14. Nearby parking available for $4 weekdays, $6 weekends and holidays.

This art deco landmark is one of South Beach's gems, especially since the $3 million renovation in 1997. The pretty Essex House is the result of a painstaking restoration and is a textbook example of streamline moderne style, complete with large porthole windows, original etched glasswork, ziggurat arches, and detailed crown moldings. The solid-oak bedroom furnishings are also original and, like many other details in this special hotel, were carefully restored. Suites feature minibars, coffeemakers, and VCRs. Ask for a room with a refrigerator, since more than a dozen standard rooms do have them. The Essex also features 24-hour reception, a high-tech piano in the lobby/lounge, and a state-of-the-art security system. Located 1 block from the ocean, this hotel is spick-and-span, almost too much like a chain. But the staff is extremely pleasant and helpful.

A new, very small pool is just one of the many new additions here. Coming soon— a new martini bar and piano lounge.

Hotel Continental Riande. 1825 Collins Ave., South Beach, FL 33139. ☎ **800/RIANDE-1** or 305/531-3503. Fax 305/531-2803. 251 units. A/C MINIBAR TV TEL. Winter $135–$160 double. Off-season $105–$135 double. Extra person $10. Children 11 and under stay free in parents' room. Frommer's readers get a 20% discount. AE, DC, DISC, MC, V. Valet parking $8.

Catering to a largely Latin and European clientele, the Riande has become quite well known with its simple formula for success. The rooms and lobby areas are clean and well kept, but not too fussy. The hotel overlooks the ocean and is just 2 blocks from the best of South Beach. Also, there's a large outdoor pool and sundeck just out back. There's a restaurant/coffeeshop with both buffet and menu service. Room service is available daily for breakfast and dinner. The Riande is just the ticket if you want value and convenience right on South Beach.

Hotel Leon. 841 Collins Ave., South Beach, FL 33139. ☎ **305/673-3767.** Fax 305/ 673-5866. E-mail: hotel-leon@travelbase.com. 18 units. A/C TV TEL. Winter $125 double;

$165–$215 suite; $375 penthouse. Off-season $100 double; $135–$185 suite; $315 penthouse. $10 for an extra bed. AE, DC, MC, V. Valet parking $14.

A true value, this stylish sliver of a property has won the loyalty of fashion industrialists and romantics alike. The very central location, 1 block from the sea and in the heart of shopping and dining, means a car isn't necessary. Unfortunately, there is no pool. The spacious, well-renovated rooms are sparkling clean and warmly appointed. Gleaming wood floors and simple pale furnishings are appreciated in a neighborhood where many others overdo the art deco motif. Each room has two phones, sunken oval tubs, robes, and CD players and CDs. A meeting room and business center make this a fine choice for business trips. In the standard rooms there are no minibars or fridges, but you can order room service anytime. In the morning enjoy a moderately priced breakfast ($8.50) of croissants, fresh rolls, ham, cheese, and eggs cooked to order. Young German owners Eric and Angela Gabriel have made a commitment to providing excellent service with a distinctly personal touch, and they have succeeded.

✪ **The Kent.** 1131 Collins Ave., South Beach, FL 33139. ☎ **800/OUTPOST** or 305/604-5000. Fax 305/531-0720. www.islandlife.com. E-mail: outpost800@aol.com. 54 units. A/C MINIBAR TV TEL. Winter $125–$195 double; $275 suite. Off-season $95–$155 double; $230 suite. Extra person $15. Children 11 and under stay free in parents' room. AE, DC, DISC, MC, V. Valet parking $14, self-parking $6.

When the other Island Outpost hotels are full, you are likely to find a spot at this property. The prices are the same as at their beachside hotels, the Cavalier and the Leslie, but the rooms tend to be less noisy. The staff includes an eager-to-please group of Caribbeans, and they cater to a clientele largely made up of the fashion industry. Frequent movie and photo shoots are coordinated in the lobby and conference room, where full office services are available. Thanks to a vacant lot in the backyard (for now), some rooms in the rear offer nice views of the ocean. The decor is modest but tasteful, with bright, whimsical furnishings and standard CD players. VCRs are available, and video rentals can be delivered. For the price, this is an excellent value right in South Beach's center. There is no pool or sundeck, but you're only 1 block from the beach.

Inexpensive

Banana Bungalow. 2360 Collins Ave., Miami Beach, FL 33139. ☎ **800/7-HOSTEL** or 305/538-1951. Fax 305/531-3217. E-mail: MIAMIres@bananabungalow.com. 60 private units, 30 shared units. A/C TV TEL. Winter $13–$16 per person in shared unit; $54–$60 single; $64–$70 double. Off-season $12–$14 per person in shared unit; $40–$46 single; $50–$56 double. MC, V. Free parking.

Opened in late 1996, this youth hostel-like hotel is the most recent and recommendable addition to the South Beach budget scene. Situated across the street from a popular beach and only 6 or 7 blocks from the best shops, clubs, and restaurants, this redone 1950s two-story newcomer surrounds a pool and deck complete with shuffleboard, a small alfresco restaurant, and a tiki bar where young European travelers hang out.

The best rooms face a narrow canal where motorboats and kayaks are available to rent for a small charge. In general, rooms are clean and well kept despite a few rusty faucets and chipped Formica furnishings. Guests in shared rooms need to bring their own towels.

It's unusual for a hostel, but all rooms have telephones, televisions, and air conditioners. It's also one of the only hotels in this price range with a private pool. In addition, guests can enjoy free nightly movies, sightseeing tours, discounts at local clubs, and a great community spirit.

Brigham Gardens. 1411 Collins Ave., South Beach, FL 33139. ☎ **305/531-1331.** Fax 305/538-9898. 19 units and suites. A/C TV TEL. Winter $85–$130 double. Off-season $60–$110 double. Extra person $5. Pets stay for $6 a night, and young children stay free in parents' room. 10% discount on all stays of 1 week or longer. AE, MC, V.

When you enter the tropically landscaped garden, you'll hear macaws and parrots chirping and see cats and lizards running through the bougainvillea. The tiny but lush grounds are framed by the quaint Mediterranean buildings that are pleasant though in need of some sprucing up. Thanks to the fact that many of the rooms have kitchens, you'll find many people staying for longer than a weekend. You may, too. You can make your own coffee and do your own laundry on the premises. This happy spot is run by a mother and daughter who go out of their way to see that their guests and their pets are well cared for. There is no pool or other niceties, but you'll find the funky setting a homey and affordable place in the midst of crazy pricing and overcommercialization. Also, the location is prime. Like most other small properties on South Beach, parking can be a pain. Consider ditching the car.

✪ **Clay Hotel & Hostelling International.** 438 Washington Ave. (at Española), South Beach, FL 33139. ☎ **305/534-2988.** Fax 305/673-0346. 350 beds in singles, doubles, and dorm units. A/C. $40–$50 single; $45–$65 double; $14–$16 dorm bed. Sheets $2 extra. Pay for 6 nights in advance and get seventh night free. JCB, MC, V.

A member of the International Youth Hostel Federation, the Clay occupies a beautiful 1920s-style Spanish Mediterranean building at the corner of historic Española Way. Like other IYHF members, this hostel is open to all ages and is a great place to meet like-minded travelers. The usual smattering of Australians, Europeans, and other budget travelers makes this place Miami's best clearinghouse of "insider" travel information. Even if you don't stay here, you might want to check out the ride board or mingle with fellow travelers over a beer at the sidewalk cafe.

Although a thorough renovation in 1996 made this hostel an incredible value and a step above any others in town, don't expect nightly turndown service or chocolates. You will find a self-serve Laundromat, occasional movie nights, and a tour desk with car rental available. Reservations are essential for private rooms year-round and recommended in season. Private rooms have TVs and telephones, plus there's a TV room for those in the dorms. Don't bother with a car in this congested area.

Park Washington Hotel. 1020 Washington Ave., South Beach, FL 33139. ☎ **305/532-1930.** Fax 305/672-6706. 36 units. A/C TV TEL. Winter $79–$99 double; $129 suite. Off-season $59–$69 double; $99 suite. Rates include self-serve coffee and Danish. Extra person $20. Children stay free in parents' room. AE, MC, V.

The Park Washington is a large, refurbished hotel that offers some of the best values in South Beach. Located 2 blocks from the ocean, this hotel has made a name for itself by offering good-quality accommodations at incredible prices. Designed in the 1930s by Henry Hohauser, one of the beach's most famous architects, the Park Washington reopened in 1989. Most of the rooms have original furnishings and well-kept interiors, and some have kitchenettes.

You'll also enjoy a decent-sized outdoor heated pool with a sundeck, bikes for rent, and access to a nearby health club.

The same owners run the adjacent Taft House and Kenmore hotels. All three attract a large gay clientele, and all offer privacy, lush landscaping, a great pool and sundeck, consistent quality, and a value-oriented philosophy. No parking on the premises but there is a public garage at 7th Street, less than 3 blocks away.

MIAMI BEACH

The area just north of South Beach encompasses Surfside, Bal Harbour, and Sunny Isles. Unrestricted by zoning codes throughout the 1950s, 1960s, and especially the 1970s, area developers went nuts, building ever-bigger and more brazen structures, especially north of 41st Street, which is now known as "Condo Canyon." Subsequently, there's now a glut of medium-quality condos, with a few scattered holdouts of older hotels and motels that front the ocean casting shadows over the sand by afternoon.

Miami Beach, as described here, runs from 24th Street to 192nd Street, a long strip that varies slightly from end to end. The southern section, from 24th to 42nd streets, is really an extension of South Beach and can be a great deal if you want to pay slightly lower rates for your lodging while enjoying the scene in South Beach. Bal Harbour and Bay Harbor are at its center and retain their exclusivity and character. The neighborhoods north and south of here, like Surfside and Sunny Isles, have nice beaches and some shops, but seem a little worn around the edges.

Just north of South Beach is the **Days Inn** (☎ **800/325-2525** or 305/673-1513) at 42nd Street and Collins Avenue. It is right on the ocean and is very well kept. The **Howard Johnson** (☎ **800/446-4656** or 305/532-4411) at 4000 Alton Rd., just off the Julia Tuttle Causeway (I-95), is a generic eight-story building on a strip of land near a busy road. But it is convenient to the beach, by car or bike. Rooms, renovated in 1995, are clean and spacious, and some have pretty views of the city and the Intracoastal Waterway. Farther north in Miami Beach, in an uncrowded section of beach, there is an oceanfront **Ramada Inn** (☎ **800/272-6232** or 305/865-8511) at 6701 Collins Ave. and a **Howard Johnson** (☎ **800/446-4656** or 305/868-1200) at 6261 Collins Ave.

VERY EXPENSIVE

Alexander All-Suite Luxury Hotel. 5225 Collins Ave., Miami Beach, FL 33140. ☎ **800/327-6121** or 305/865-6500. Fax 305/341-6553. Telex 808172. 150 suites. A/C TV TEL. Winter $325 one-bedroom suite; $470 two-bedroom suite. Off-season $250 one-bedroom suite; $370 two-bedroom suite. Extra person $35. Children 17 and under stay free in parents' room. Packages available. AE, CB, DC, DISC, MC, V. Valet parking $12.50.

This stunning hotel is a good choice if you want to be off the beaten path but stay in the lap of luxury. The Alexander is an all-suite hotel featuring spacious one- and two-bedroom mini-apartments. Each suite contains a living room, a fully equipped kitchen, two baths, and a balcony. The hotel itself is well decorated with sculptures, paintings, antiques, and tapestries, most of which were garnered from the Cornelius Vanderbilt mansion. The pretty hotel's two oceanfront pools are surrounded by lush vegetation; one of the "lagoons" is also fed by a cascading waterfall. You'll feel truly pampered—you'll pay a lot for the service and attention, but it's worth it. The rooms are elegant without being pretentious and have every convenience you could want, including full kitchens, hair dryers, coffeemakers, balconies, VCRs upon request, and cable TVs.

Dining/Diversions: A pricey steak house opened in 1998 by former Dolphins football coach, Don Shula occupies a beautiful seaside spot. A more casual garden restaurant, a piano lounge, and a pool bar are also available.

Amenities: Concierge, 24-hour room service, dry cleaning and laundry service, newspaper delivery, evening turndown upon request, in-room massage upon request, twice-daily maid service, secretarial services, express checkout. Kitchens, Spectravision movie channels, two large outdoor pools, beach, small state-of-the-art health club, four Jacuzzis, sauna, adequate business center and conference rooms, car rental through concierge, sundeck, water-sports equipment, beauty salon.

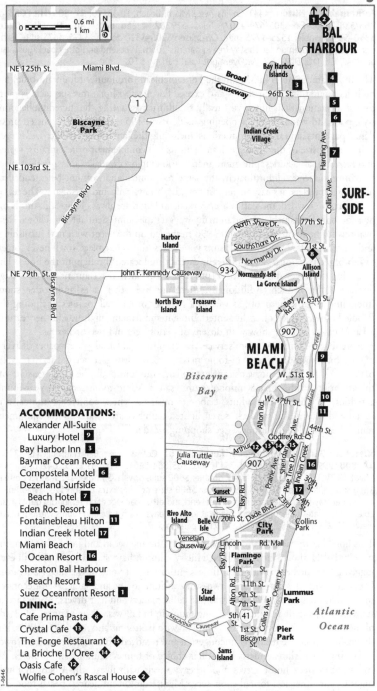

ACCOMMODATIONS:
Alexander All-Suite
 Luxury Hotel **9**
Bay Harbor Inn **3**
Baymar Ocean Resort **5**
Compostela Motel **6**
Dezerland Surfside
 Beach Hotel **7**
Eden Roc Resort **10**
Fontainebleau Hilton **11**
Indian Creek Hotel **17**
Miami Beach
 Ocean Resort **16**
Sheraton Bal Harbour
 Beach Resort **4**
Suez Oceanfront Resort **1**
DINING:
Cafe Prima Pasta **8**
Crystal Cafe **13**
The Forge Restaurant **15**
La Brioche D'Oree **14**
Oasis Cafe **12**
Wolfie Cohen's Rascal House **2**

1-0646

Fontainebleau Hilton. 4441 Collins Ave., Miami Beach, FL 33140. ☎ **800/HILTONS** or 305/538-2000. Fax 305/674-4607. Telex 519362. 1,266 units. A/C TV TEL. Winter $310–$340 double; $525–$725 suite. Off-season $205–$310 double; $475–$675 suite. Extra person $30. Children under 18 stay free in parents' room. Weekend and other packages available. AE, CB, DC, DISC, MC, V. Overnight valet parking $10.

The most famous hotel in Miami, the Fontainebleau (pronounced fountain-blue) has built its reputation on garishness and excess. For most visitors, this spectacle is more tourist attraction than hotel; you really shouldn't miss seeing the incredible lagoon-style pool and waterfall. Since opening its doors in 1954, the hotel has hosted presidents, pageants, and movie productions, including the James Bond thriller *Goldfinger*.

The sheer size of the Fontainebleau, with its full complement of restaurants, stores, and recreational facilities, plus more than 1,100 employees, makes this a perfect place for conventioneers. Unfortunately, the same recommendation cannot be extended to individual travelers. It's easy to get lost here, both physically and personally. The lobby is terminally crowded, the staff is overworked, and lines are always long. Still, this is the one and only Fontainebleau, and in many ways it's the quintessential Miami hotel. Renovations to the rooms in 1995 and 1996 freshened up the decor with new furnishings and pastel accents. No matter if it suits your tastes, this is one place you'll never forget.

Dining/Diversions: Seven different eateries are located throughout the hotel. The Steak House serves dinner until 11pm and a continental restaurant serves a huge Sunday buffet brunch. Additionally, there are five other cafes and coffee shops (including two by the pool), as well as a number of cocktail lounges, including the Poodle Lounge, which offers live entertainment and dancing nightly. Another features a Las Vegas–style floor show with dozens of performers and two orchestras.

Amenities: Concierge, room service, dry cleaning and laundry, newspaper delivery, nightly turndown on request, in-room massage, baby-sitting, secretarial services, valet parking. VCRs, video movie channels, two large outdoor pools, beach, large state-of-the-art health club, three whirlpool baths, sauna, game rooms, special year-round activities for children and adults, elaborate business center, conference rooms, car-rental and tour desks, sundeck, seven lighted tennis courts, water-sports equipment rental, beauty salon, boutique, large shopping arcade.

Sheraton Bal Harbour Beach Resort. 9701 Collins Ave., Bal Harbour, FL 33154. ☎ **800/999-9898** or 305/865-7511. Fax 305/864-2601. Telex 519355. 642 units. A/C MINIBAR TV TEL. Winter $319–$409 double; $600 suite or villa. Summer $225–$315 double; $600 suite. Off-season $279–$379 double; $600 suite or villa. Extra person $25. Children 17 and under stay free in parents' room. Weekend and other packages and senior discounts available. Lowest rates reflect bookings made at least 14 days in advance and rooms without ocean views. AE, CB, DC, DISC, JCB, MC, V. Valet parking $12.

This hotel has the best location in Bal Harbour, on the ocean and just across from the swanky Bal Harbour Shops. Bill and Hillary Clinton have stayed here, and Bill even jogged along the beach with local fitness enthusiasts. It's one of the nicest Sheratons I've seen, with a glass-enclosed two-story atrium lobby and large, well-decorated rooms that include convenient extras like coffeemakers and hair dryers. A spectacular staircase wraps itself around a cascading fountain full of wished-on pennies. One side of the hotel caters to corporations, complete with ballrooms and meeting facilities, but the main sections are relatively uncongested and removed from the convention crowd.

Dining/Diversions: Guests have their choice of four restaurants and lounges. An Argentinean steak house serves good, heavy meals with live Latin American music nightly. The other less formal spots serve Mediterranean-influenced beach food and pizzas and gourmet coffees. A lounge serves good tropical drinks.

Amenities: Concierge, 24-hour room service, laundry and dry cleaning, valet, newspaper delivery, nightly turndown, in-room massage, twice-daily maid service on request, baby-sitting, secretarial services, express checkout, valet parking, free coffee and refreshments in the lobby. Spectravision movie channels, VCRs in some rooms, a full complement of aquatic playthings can be rented on the beach (including sailboats and jet-skis), outdoor heated pool, sundeck, large state-of-the-art fitness center and spa (with aerobics, Jacuzzi, sauna, and sundeck), two outdoor tennis courts, jogging track, game room, children's programs, large business center, conference rooms, tour desk, gift shop and shopping arcade, nearby golf course.

EXPENSIVE

Eden Roc Resort and Spa. 4525 Collins Ave., Miami Beach, FL 33140. ☎ **800/327-8337** or 305/531-0000. Fax 305/531-6955. 350 units. A/C TV TEL. Winter $195–$350 double; $275–$1,500 suite. Off-season $120–$250 double; $175–$1,000 suite. Extra person $15. Children 16 and under stay free in parents' room. Weekend, spa, and honeymoon packages available. AE, CB, DC, DISC, MC, V. Valet parking $8.50.

Originally opened in 1956 and located just next door to the mammoth Fontainebleau Hilton, this flamboyant and large hotel seems almost intimate by comparison. The accommodations here are a bit gaudy, but this is Miami Beach after all. The amenities by far make up for the ostentation. The huge, modern spa has excellent facilities and exercise classes, including yoga. The popular pool deck overlooking the ocean is a great place to spend the afternoon.

The big, open, and airy lobby is dressed in solid tropical colors and diamond-pattern carpeting and fleur-de-lis wallpaper and are often full of name-tagged conventioneers. The rooms, uniformly outfitted with purple and aquatic-colored interiors and retouched 1930s furnishings, are unusually spacious. Because of the hotel's size, you should be able to negotiate a good rate unless there's a big event going on.

Dining/Diversions: A Mediterranean restaurant serves exceptionally good food, from carved meats to a full selection of tapas. From a seat at the poolside sports bar, patrons can watch swimmers through an underwater "porthole" window. A casual deli is open for breakfast, lunch, and dinner and features pizza from a wood-burning oven.

Amenities: Concierge, room service, dry cleaning and laundry, newspaper delivery, in-room massage, nightly turndown, baby-sitting, secretarial services, express checkout, valet parking. Kitchenettes in suites and penthouses, VCRs for rent, Spectravision movie channels, two outdoor pools, beach, full-service spa and health club with sauna, business center and conference rooms, car-rental desk, sundeck, squash, racquetball and basketball courts as well as a rock-climbing arena, water-sports equipment, tour desk, beauty salon, sundries shop.

Miami Beach Ocean Resort. 3025 Collins Ave., Miami Beach, FL 33140. ☎ **800/550-0505** or 305/534-0505. Fax 305/534-0515. 243 units. A/C TV TEL. Winter $170–$200, one to four people; $220–$600 suite. Off-season $140–$170, one to four people; $200–$550 suite. AE, DC, MC, V.

Popular with tour groups and Europeans, this oceanfront resort reopened in 1995 and is a great choice for those who want a quiet place on the ocean in close proximity to South Beach and the mainland. The elegant and vast lobby is done up in Mexican tile, wood fretwork, and tasteful furnishings. Rooms are basic but very tastefully decorated with new wicker and rattan furnishings. A giant outdoor area is landscaped with palms and hibiscus and has a large heated pool as its centerpiece. It faces the large beach where water-sports equipment is available. The resort is a giant step above a good Holiday Inn at comparable prices.

Dining/Diversions: The recommendable restaurant serves a breakfast and dinner buffet of simple but good Caribbean and international cuisine to many who choose modified American plan (MAP) programs. Á la carte offerings and lunch are also available. A patio garden offers cake and coffee and a pool bar serves snacks and drinks. A colorful indoor/outdoor lounge features cocktails and live music most nights.

Amenities: Concierge, room service, valet parking, laundry and dry-cleaning services, baby-sitting. Spectravision movie channels, outdoor heated pool, beach, sundeck, bicycle rental, game room, self-service Laundromat, currency exchange, tour desk, conference rooms, car-rental desk, beauty salon, boutique.

MODERATE

✪ **Bay Harbor Inn.** 9601 E. Bay Harbor Dr., Bay Harbor Island, FL 33154. ☎ **305/ 868-4141.** Fax 305/867-9094. 24 units. A/C TV TEL. Winter $139 double; $149 suite; $169 penthouse suite. Off-season $60 double; $70 suite; $90 penthouse suite. Extra person $25. Children 12 and under stay free in parents' room. Rates include continental breakfast. AE, MC, V. Free parking.

This quaint little inn looks as if it ought to be in Vermont or somewhere woodsy and remote, but it's just moments from the beach, fine restaurants, and some of the city's best shopping. Actually the inn comes in two parts. The more modern section sits squarely on a little river, or "the creek" as it's called, and overlooks a heated outdoor pool and a boat named Celeste where guests eat breakfast. On the other side of the street is the cozier, antique-filled portion, where glass-covered bookshelves hold good beach reading. The rooms have a hodgepodge of wood furnishings, like oak-framed mirrors, canopied beds, Victorian chairs, and modern vanities. Some of the rooms are slightly larger (like nos. 301, 305, 308, and 311) and boast an extra half bath at no extra cost. You do at times smell the aroma of cooking from the restaurant below, but you might find that this only adds to the charm of this homey inn.

Adjacent to the hotel is The Palm, a clubby steak-and-lobster house. Students from a nearby culinary institute run a restaurant and bar in the creekside building across the street, and a deluxe continental breakfast is served on a yacht.

Baymar Ocean Resort. 9401 Collins Ave., Miami Beach, FL 33154. ☎ **800/8-BAYMAR** or 305/866-5446. Fax 305/866-8053. 96 units. A/C TV TEL. Winter $115–$125 double; $125–$135 efficiency; $150–$235 suite. Off-season $85–$95 double; $95–$105 efficiency; $125–$185 suite. Extra person $10. Children 11 and under stay free in parents' room. AE, DISC, MC, V. Parking $5.

Last year's renovation did wonders for this little hotel on the strip, just south of Bal Harbour, and it is extremely popular with conservative religious groups and budget-conscious travelers.

Depending on what you're looking for, this could be one of the beach's best buys, assuming prices hold at their current level. The hotel is right on the ocean, with a low-key beach that attracts few other tourists, and offers all the modern conveniences, including some kitchenettes and large closets. You won't flip over the decor, but it's pleasant enough and all brand new. There isn't much within walking distance from this spot (much of the rest of the area is run-down or has been converted into condos), but you aren't far from anything you could possibly want to drive to. It may not be worth it to pay more for the oceanfront rooms since they tend to be smaller than the others. Rooms overlooking the large pool and sundeck area could get loud on busy days. You do get nice shared balcony space on the first-floor ocean-view rooms.

A small restaurant serving basic American fare and a tiki bar are popular with guests.

Dezerland Surfside Beach Hotel. 8701 Collins Ave., Miami Beach, FL 33154. ☎ **800/331-9346** in the U.S., 800/331-9347 in Canada, or 305/865-6661. Fax 305/866-2630. 225 units. A/C TV TEL. Winter $85–$115 double. Off-season $60–$75 double. Extra person $8. Children 18 and under stay free in parents' room. Special packages and group rates available. AE, CB, DC, DISC, MC, V. Self parking.

Designed by car enthusiast Michael Dezer, the Dezerland is a unique place—part hotel and part 1950s automobile wonderland. Visitors, who include many German tourists, are welcomed by a 1959 Cadillac stationed by the front door, one of a dozen mint-condition classics around the grounds and lobby.

While it isn't pristine, the place is clean and constant renovations improve it every year. Some rooms contain fully equipped kitchenettes. Dezerland is located directly on the beach and features a mosaic of a pink Cadillac at the bottom of its surfside pool.

Other amenities include a Jacuzzi, adjacent tennis courts and jogging track, Windsurfer and jet-ski rental, game room, launderette, car-rental and tour services desk, and an antique shop featuring 1950s memorabilia.

There is also a restaurant and a lobby lounge with all-you-can-eat buffets and nightly entertainment.

✪ **Indian Creek Hotel.** 2727 Indian Creek Dr., Miami Beach, FL 33140. ☎ **800/491-2772** or 305/531-2727. Fax 305/531-5651. 61 units. A/C TV TEL. Winter $130 double; $220 suite. Off-season $90 double; $150 suite. Extra person $10. Group packages available. 18% gratuity added to room service, 15% added to restaurant check. AE, CB, DC, DISC, MC, V. Limited parking available on street.

Slightly north of South Beach is this small hotel where every detail of the 1936 building has been meticulously restored, from one of the beach's first operating elevators to the period steamer trunk in the lobby. The modest rooms are outfitted in art deco furnishings with pretty tropical prints and all the modern amenities. Just 1 short block from a good stretch of sand, the hotel is perfectly situated away from the hectic scene on South Beach, yet close enough to walk to most activities there. A landscaped pool area is a great place to lounge in the sun. The hotel also offers a small fitness center and conference facilities.

A tiny, cozy pan-Caribbean restaurant and bar serves wonderfully innovative food for breakfast, lunch, and dinner.

INEXPENSIVE

Compostela Motel. 9040 Collins Ave., Miami Beach, FL 33154. ☎ **305/861-3083.** Fax 305/861-2996. 20 units. A/C TV TEL. Winter from $75 suite; from $65 one-bedroom apt; $55 efficiency. Off-season from $65 suite; $55 one-bedroom apt; $45 efficiency. Extra person $10. Children 17 and under stay free in parents' room. AE, MC, V. Free parking.

The owners of the Compostela have recently set to renovating their three buildings, all within walking distance of the exclusive Bal Harbour Shops and many good shopping and dining areas. Although the buildings were run-down efficiencies for many years, the new interiors are really quite nice. All are carpeted and most have full kitchenettes, a bonus when you're on a budget. There's no fancy lobby, no doorman to greet you as you enter, and no amenities to speak of save an outdoor pool and laundry facilities. But the area is safe and the staff courteous, although at some hours only Spanish speakers are available. Best of all, you're across the street from a great beach. You get a lot of space and a great location for a low price.

Suez Oceanfront Resort. 18215 Collins Ave., Sunny Isles, FL 33160. ☎ **800/327-5278,** 800/327-5279 reservations from 9am to 5pm only, or 305/932-0661. Fax 305/937-0058. 150 units. A/C TV TEL. Winter $67–$110 double; $175 suite. Off-season $39–$67 double; $125 suite. Kitchenettes $10–$15 extra. Extra person $15. AE, DC, MC, V. Free parking.

Guarded by a replica of Egypt's famed Sphinx, this motel, with its orange-and-yellow motif, is more reminiscent of a fast-food restaurant than anything in ancient Egypt. It offers decent rooms on the beach, where most of the other hotels have gone condo. The thatch umbrellas over beach lounges and the Spanish Mediterranean–style fountains in the courtyard add to the confused decor. But it's on the ocean and technically in Miami Beach, though its location in Sunny Isles is closer to Hallandale in Broward County than to South Beach.

There's an outdoor heated pool and a free launderette—perfect for long stays. A kitschy but pleasant lounge offers good prices and a palm-lined area reminds you that you're indeed in a tropical paradise.

KEY BISCAYNE

There are only a few hotels here, although the super-luxurious Grand Bay should be up and running by sometime in the year 2000. All are on the beach, and room rates are uniformly high. There are no budget listings here, but if you can afford it, Key Biscayne is a great place to stay. The island is far enough from the mainland to make it feel like a secluded tropical paradise yet close enough to downtown to take advantage of everything Miami has to offer.

Silver Sands Oceanfront. 301 Ocean Dr., Key Biscayne, FL 33149. ☎ **305/361-5441.** Fax 305/361-5477. 52 units, 4 cottages. A/C TV TEL. Winter $149–$179 minisuite; $300 cottage; $385 oceanfront suite. Off-season $109–$129 minisuite; $200 cottage; $385 oceanfront suite. Extra person $30. Children 14 and under stay free in parents' room. Weekly rates available. AE, DC, MC, V. Free parking.

If Key Biscayne is where you want to be and you don't want to pay the prices of the next-door Sonesta, consider this quaint, one-story motel where everything is crisp and clean and a pleasant staff will help with anything you may need, including baby-sitting. The well-appointed rooms are very beachy, sporting a tropical motif and simple furnishings; extras include microwaves, refrigerators, and coffeemakers. Oceanfront suites have the added convenience of full kitchens with stoves and pantries. You'll sit poolside with an unpretentious set of Latin American families and Europeans who have come for a long and simple vacation—and get it.

Dining/Diversions: The Sandbar, a casual beachfront restaurant/bar and a favorite local hangout, was destroyed during Hurricane Andrew, and as of late 1997, was still not restored. Plans are in the works.

Amenities: Secretarial services, twice-daily maid service. VCRs in some rooms, medium-sized outdoor pool, beach, kitchenettes, coin laundry.

✪ **Sonesta Beach Resort Key Biscayne.** 350 Ocean Dr., Key Biscayne, FL 33149. ☎ **800/SONESTA** or 305/361-2021. Fax 305/361-3096. 303 units. A/C MINIBAR TV TEL. Winter $255–$395 double; $750–$1,650 suite; $600–$900 villa. Off-season $165–$315 double; $525–$1,325 suite; $500–$800 villa. Up to two children 17 and under stay free in parents' room. 15% gratuity added to food and beverage bills. Special packages available. AE, CB, DC, DISC, EURO, JCB, MC, V. Valet parking $12.

One of South Florida's most private and luxurious resorts, the Sonesta is an ideal retreat. From the moment the valets, clad in tropical prints, take your car, you'll know you've entered a world of no concern. If you like sports, you can be sure that you've got everything, from tennis to jet-skiing, at your feet. When you want to relax, VCRs are available (you can rent from a neighboring shop), and TVs have 30-channel Spectravision selections. The vacation homes have fully equipped kitchenettes.

Although you may not want to leave the lush grounds, Bill Baggs State Recreation Area and the area's best beaches are right at hand, and if you choose to venture out, you're only about 15 minutes from Miami Beach and even closer to the mainland and Coconut Grove.

Dining/Diversions: The hotel has four restaurants, including Two Dragons with fine Chinese cuisine, an excellent seafood restaurant with a terrace, and several lounges and bars. The restaurants regularly draw locals, who have few dining options on "The Key."

Amenities: Concierge, 24-hour room service, dry cleaning and laundry, newspaper delivery, nightly turndown, baby-sitting, secretarial services, express checkout, complimentary transportation to and from Miami's shopping districts; children are well cared for with day and night field trips and activities. Spectravision movie channels, Olympic-size pool, beach, large state-of-the-art fitness center, Jacuzzi, sauna, nearby jogging track, bicycle rental, access to nearby championship golf course, game rooms, children's programs, elaborate business center, conference rooms, car-rental and tour desks, sundeck, nine tennis courts (three lighted), water-sports equipment rental, beauty salon, boutiques.

DOWNTOWN

Most downtown hotels cater primarily to business travelers, but tourists with a reason to stay downtown can get well-located, good-quality accommodations, too.

Although business hotels are expensive and seasonal markdowns are hard to find, quality and service are also of a high standard. Look for weekend discounts and packages, when offices are closed and rooms often go empty. After dark there's virtually nothing outside of the hotels; the streets are often deserted and crime can be a problem.

In downtown Miami, with rates from $95 to $175, the **Wyndham** (☎ **800/ 332-0232** or 305/374-0000), at 1601 Biscayne Blvd. located above the Omni Mall, is a perfect option for the thrifty business traveler. It offers a full business center as well as a heated rooftop pool. Also, it is just a few minutes away from Bayside and Miami Beach.

I also recommend the **Miami River Inn Bed & Breakfast,** at 118 SW South River Dr. (☎ **305/325-0045;** fax 305/325-9227; e-mail: miami100@ix.netcom.com). With rates from $70 to $110, this cozy yet unusual inn is a great deal for those who want to be in a central location, close to the highway, public transportation, downtown eateries, and museums. Extras include a small outdoor pool, Jacuzzi, and complimentary coffee and wine in the lobby. Although many predict that the riverfront area will soon undergo a renaissance, for now the area is still a bit seedy.

VERY EXPENSIVE

Hotel Inter-Continental Miami. 100 Chopin Plaza, Miami, FL 33131. ☎ **800/327-3005** or 305/577-1000. Fax 305/577-0384. Telex 153127. 644 units. A/C MINIBAR TV TEL. Winter $209–$289 double; $325–$450 suite. Off-season $159–$259 double; $325–$450 suite. Extra person $20. Weekend and other packages available. AE, CB, DC, DISC, MC, V. Valet parking $12.

Especially since the $5 million renovation of all its guest rooms and some common areas, the Inter-Continental is downtown's swankiest hotel. It boasts more marble than a mausoleum (both inside and out), but it's warmed by colorful, homey touches. The five-story lobby features a marble centerpiece sculpture by Henry Moore and is topped by a pleasing skylight. Plenty of plants, palm trees, and brightly colored wicker chairs also add charm and enliven the otherwise stark space. Brilliant downtown and bay views add luster to already posh rooms that are outfitted with every convenience known to hoteldom, including VCRs and eight-channel Spectravision selection. Some suites have fully equipped kitchenettes.

Dining/Diversions: Three restaurants cover all price ranges and are complemented by two full-service lounges.

Amenities: Concierge, room service, dry cleaning and laundry, newspaper delivery, twice-daily maid service, express checkout, free refreshments in lobby, baby-sitting. Olympic-size heated outdoor pool, health spa, sundeck, jogging track, large business center, 15 conference rooms, self-service Laundromat, car-rental desk, travel-agency/tour desk, beauty salon and barbershop, shopping arcade, access to nearby golf course.

MODERATE

Riande Continental Bayside. 146 Biscayne Blvd., Miami, FL 33132. ☎ **800/RIANDE-1** or 305/358-4555. Fax 305/371-5253. 250 units. A/C MINIBAR TV TEL. Winter $115–$175 double. Off-season $85–$155 double. Frommer's readers get a 20% discount. Children stay free in parents' room. AE, DC, MC, V. Parking $7.50.

Like its sister hotel in South Beach, this Riande caters to a Latin American crowd that descends on downtown in droves to shop for clothes and electronics. The location is ideal, only steps away from Bayside Shopping Center, many great ethnic restaurants, and a Metrorail stop. The rooms come with extras such as 10-channel Spectravision. The reasonable prices and helpful staff are reason enough to consider staying here if you want to be right in downtown Miami.

COCONUT GROVE

This intimate enclave hugs the shores of Biscayne Bay just south of U.S. 1 and about 10 minutes from the beaches. The Grove is a great place to stay, offering ample nightlife, excellent restaurants, and beautiful surroundings. Unfortunately all the hotels are very expensive and there are no chains here.

VERY EXPENSIVE

✪ **Grand Bay Hotel.** 2669 S. Bayshore Dr., Coconut Grove, FL 33133. ☎ **800/327-2788** or 305/858-9600. Fax 305/859-2026. E-mail: grandbay@von.net. 178 units. A/C MINIBAR TV TEL. Winter from $295 double. Off-season $255 double. Year-round $350–$1,400 suite. Extra person $20. Packages available. AE, CB, DC, MC, V. Valet parking $15.

The Grand Bay opened in 1983 and immediately won praise as one of the most elegant hotels in the world. Outfitted with the highest-quality interiors, this stunning pyramid-shaped hotel is a masterpiece both inside and out. The rooms are luxurious, each featuring high-quality linens, comfortable overstuffed love seats and chairs, a large writing desk, and all the amenities you'd expect in deluxe accommodations, including VCRs, movie channels, and video rentals. They have recently added ironing boards, irons, and voice mail to all rooms as well. Original art and armfuls of fresh flowers are generously displayed throughout.

The Grand Bay consistently attracts wealthy, high-profile people, and it basks in its image as a rendezvous for royalty, socialites, and superstars. Guests come here to be pampered and to see and be seen.

Dining/Diversions: The hotel's Grand Café is one of the top-rated restaurants in Miami. Drinks are served in the Ciga Bar and the Lobby Lounge, where a traditional afternoon tea is served.

Amenities: Concierge, 24-hour room service, same-day laundry and dry cleaning, newspaper delivery, evening turndown, masseuse on call, twice-daily maid service, baby-sitting, secretarial services, express checkout, courtesy limousine service to Cocowalk, free refreshments in the lobby. Heated indoor pool, small health club,

Coral Gables, Coconut Grove, Downtown Miami & Key Biscayne

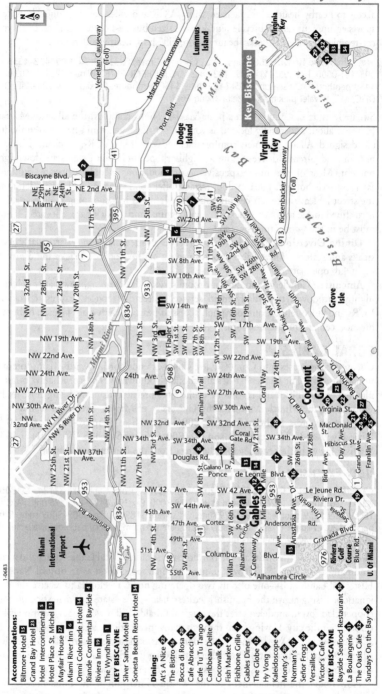

Accommodations:
Biltmore Hotel 15
Grand Bay Hotel 23
Hotel Intercontinental 5
Hotel Place St. Michel 13
Mayfair House 27
Miami River Inn 6
Omni Colonnade Hotel 14
Riande Continental Bayside 4
Riviera Inn 19
The Wyndham 1
KEY BISCAYNE
Silver Sands Motel 33
Sonesta Beach Resort Hotel 34

Dining:
At's A Nice 22
The Bistro 17
Bocca di Rosa 20
Cafe Abracci 21
Cafe Tu Tu Tango 26
Caribbean Delite 3
Cocowalk 7
Fish Market 4
Fishbone Grille 10
Gables Diner 9
The Globe 24
Hy Vong 6
Kaleidoscope 25
Monty's 28
Norman's 16
Señor Frogs 24
Versailles 12
Victor's Cafe 18
KEY BISCAYNE
Bayside Seafood Restaurant 30
La Boulangerie 31
The Oasis Cafe 32
Sundays On the Bay 29

97

access to nearby health club, Jacuzzi, sauna, VCR and video rentals, sundeck, water-sports equipment rental, bicycle rental, good-sized business center, conference rooms, car-rental and activities desks, beauty salon, gift shop, nearby golf course.

Mayfair House Hotel. 3000 Florida Ave., Coconut Grove, FL 33133. ☎ **800/433-4555** or 305/441-0000. Fax 305/441-1647. 182 units. A/C MINIBAR TV TEL. Winter $235–$450 suite; $450 penthouse. Off-season $205–$440 suite; $450 penthouse. Packages available. AE, DC, DISC, MC, V. Valet parking $15, self-parking $6.

Situated inside Coconut Grove's posh Mayfair Shops complex, the all-suite Mayfair House is about as centrally located as you can get. Each guest unit has been individually designed. All are extremely comfortable, with extras like VCRs, 16-channel Lodgenet, and video-rental delivery from a neighborhood shop. Some suites are downright opulent. Most of the more expensive accommodations include a private, outdoor, Japanese-style hot tub. The top-floor terraces offer good views, and all are hidden from the street by leaves and latticework. Since the lobby is in a shopping mall, recreation is confined to the roof, where a small pool, a sauna, and a snack bar are located. If you must be in the Grove, this is a good choice.

Dining/Diversions: The Mayfair Grill serves a varied menu with particularly good steaks and seafood. There's also a rooftop snack bar for poolside snacks and a private nightclub open late.

Amenities: Concierge and 24-hour room service, dry cleaning, newspaper delivery, nightly turndown, twice-daily maid service, secretarial services, express checkout. VCRs and video rentals, outdoor pool, access to nearby health club, Jacuzzi, elaborate business center, conference rooms.

CORAL GABLES

Coconut Grove eases into Coral Gables, which extends north toward Miami International Airport. "The Gables," as it's affectionately known, was one of Miami's original planned communities and is still one of the city's prettiest. It means being close to the shops along the Miracle Mile and the University of Miami. Two popular and well-priced chains are a **Holiday Inn** (☎ 800/327-5476 or 305/667-5611) at 1350 S. Dixie Hwy., and a **Howard Johnson** (☎ 800/446-4656 or 305/665-7501) at 1430 S. Dixie Hwy., both located across the street from the University of Miami.

VERY EXPENSIVE

✪ **Biltmore Hotel Coral Gables.** 1200 Anastasia Ave., Coral Gables, FL 33134. ☎ **800/727-1926**, 305/445-1926, or Westin at 800/228-3000. Fax 305/442-9496. 275 units. A/C TV TEL. Winter $259 double; $379–$479 suite. Off-season $189 double; $309–$409 suite. Extra person $20. Children 17 and under stay free in parents' room. Special packages available. AE, CB, DC, DISC, MC, V. Valet parking $9.

Not far from its 75th birthday, the Biltmore is the oldest Coral Gables hotel and a city landmark. In fact, in 1996 it was granted national recognition as an official National Historical Landmark—one of only two operating hotels in Florida to receive the designation. Rising above the Spanish Mediterranean–style estate is a majestic 300-foot copper-clad tower, modeled after the original Giralda bell tower in Seville and visible throughout the city. Having been through many incarnations, including being used as a VA hospital after World War II, the Biltmore is back to its original 1926 splendor. Always a popular destination for golfers, including President Clinton, it is situated on a lush rolling 18-hole course that is as challenging as it is beautiful.

Now under the management of the Westin Hotel group, the hotel boasts large rooms decorated with tasteful period reproductions as well as high-tech amenities like

VCRs (on request) and movie channels. The enormous lobby, with its 45-foot ceilings, serves as an entry point for hundreds of weddings and business meetings each year.

Just 5 minutes from the airport and excellent dining and shopping selections, and about 20 minutes from Miami Beach, this hotel is a wonderful option for those seeking a luxurious getaway.

Dining/Diversions: An elegant European restaurant serves excellent French/Italian cuisine nightly and champagne brunch on Sunday. An impressive wine cellar and cigar room make the hotel popular with local connoisseurs. The more casual Courtyard Café and Poolside Grille both serve three meals daily. There's also a lounge and piano bar where drinks are accompanied by live music nightly.

Amenities: Concierge, 24-hour room service, laundry and dry cleaning, newspaper delivery, nightly turndown upon request, twice-daily maid service, baby-sitting, secretarial services, express checkout. Kitchenettes in tower suite, VCR and video rentals, Spectravision movie channels, 21,000-square-foot swimming pool surrounded by arched walkways and classical sculptures, state-of-the-art health club, full-service spa, sauna, rolling 18-hole golf course, elaborate business center, conference rooms, car rental through concierge, sundeck, 10 lighted tennis courts, beauty salon, boutiques.

EXPENSIVE

✪ **Hotel Place St. Michel.** 162 Alcazar Ave., Coral Gables, FL 33134. ☎ **800/848-HOTEL** or 305/444-1666. Fax 305/529-0074. 27 units. A/C TV TEL. Winter (including continental breakfast) $165 single or double; $200 suite. Off-season $125 double; $160 suite. Extra person $10. Children 11 and under stay free in parents' room. AE, DC, MC, V. Parking $7.

This unusual little hotel in the heart of Coral Gables is one of the city's most romantic options. The accommodations and hospitality are straight out of old-world Europe, complete with dark wood–paneled walls, cozy beds, beautiful antiques, and a quiet elegance that seems startlingly out of place in trendy Miami. Everything here is charming, from the parquet floors to the paddle fans, and one-of-a-kind furnishings make each guest room special. Guests are treated to fresh fruit baskets upon arrival and enjoy every imaginable service throughout their stay.

Dining/Diversions: The Restaurant St. Michel is a very romantic and elegant dining choice. A lounge and deli complete the hotel options.

Amenities: Concierge, room service, laundry and dry cleaning, newspaper delivery, evening turndown, in-room massage, twice-daily maid service, complimentary continental breakfast.

The Omni Colonnade Hotel. 180 Aragon Ave. (at Ponce de León and Miracle Mile), Coral Gables, FL 33134. ☎ **800/THE OMNI** or 305/441-2600. Fax 305/445-3929. 157 units. A/C MINIBAR TV TEL. Winter $195–$265 double; $405 suite. Off-season $125–$225 double; $365 suite. Packages available. AE, CB, DC, DISC, MC, V. Valet parking $10.

The Colonnade occupies part of a large historic building, originally built by Coral Gables' founder George Merrick in 1926. Faithful to its original style, the hotel is a successful amalgam of new and old, with emphasis on modern conveniences. The structure stands 14 elegant stories high although guest rooms occupy only four floors.

The oversized guest rooms feature sitting areas, historic photographs, marble counters, gold-finished faucets, and solid wood furnishings worthy of the hotel's rates. Many business travelers enjoy the thoughtful extras like complimentary shoe shines and champagne upon arrival.

Dining/Diversions: Doc Dammers Saloon is probably the best happy hour for the 30-something crowd. There is live entertainment on weekends.

Amenities: 24-hour concierge and room service, same-day laundry and dry-cleaning service, newspaper delivery, evening turndown upon request, in-room massage, twice-daily maid service upon request, baby-sitting, express checkout, valet parking, free morning coffee and tea in the lobby. Spectravision, heated outdoor pool on rooftop, small up-to-date rooftop fitness center, Jacuzzi, sundeck, large conference centers and meeting rooms, Laundromat, car-rental and tour desks, gift shop, and shopping arcade.

INEXPENSIVE

Riviera Inn. 5100 Riviera Dr. (on U.S. 1), Coral Gables, FL 33146. ☎ **800/368-8602** or 305/665-3528. 20 units. A/C TV TEL. Winter $68 double; $78 efficiency. Off-season from $55 double; $78 efficiency. 10% discount for seniors and AAA members. AE, CB, DC, DISC, MC, V.

Besides the newly renovated Holiday Inn down the road, this family owned motel is the best discount option in this otherwise pricey area. Built in 1954, this comfortable and clean two-story property has a small pool and is set back from the road so that the rooms are all relatively quiet. Vending machines are your only choice for refreshments, but you are near many great dining spots. Or, you may choose to stay in an efficiency, all of which have fully stocked kitchens.

WEST MIAMI/AIRPORT AREA

As Miami continues to grow at its rapid pace, expansion has begun in earnest westward, where land is plentiful. Several resorts have taken advantage of the space to build world-class tennis and golf courses. While there's no sea to swim in, a plethora of facilities makes up for the lack of an ocean view.

Don Shula's Hotel and Golf Club. Main St., Miami Lakes, FL 33014. ☎ **800/24-SHULA** or 305/821-1150. Fax 305/820-8190. 330 units. A/C TV TEL. Winter from $230 double; $279 suite. Off-season $139–$159 double; $189–$209 suite. Extra person $10. Children stay free in parents' room. Business packages available. AE, CB, DC, MC, V.

Guests come to Shula's mostly for the golf, but there's plenty here to keep nongolfers busy, too. Opened in 1992 to much fanfare from the sports and business community, Shula's resort is an all-encompassing oasis in the middle of a highly planned residential neighborhood complete with Main Street and nearby shopping facilities—a good thing since the site is more than a 20-minute drive on the highways from anything. The guest rooms, located in the main building or surrounding the golf course, are plain but pretty, and come with VCRs (on request) and 10-channel Spectravision.

Dining: The award-winning Shula's Steak House and the newer Steak House II rank in the top 10 nationwide. They serve huge, tasty steaks and seafood. Another restaurant on the premises serves health food.

Amenities: Concierge, room service, newspaper delivery, express checkout, valet parking, free morning coffee in the lobby. Large outdoor swimming pool, Don Shula's state-of-the-art athletic club (with aerobics, Cybex equipment, and trainers who assist all exercisers), Jacuzzi, sauna, sundeck, 16 outdoor tennis courts, racquetball courts, two golf courses (one a championship course), 22 conference and banquet rooms, beauty salon, and shopping arcade.

✪ **Doral Golf Resort and Spa.** 4400 NW 87th Ave., Miami, FL 33178. ☎ **800/ 22-DORAL**, 800/71-DORAL, or 305/592-2000. Fax 305/594-4682. 678 units. A/C MINIBAR TV TEL. Winter $225–$315 double; $315–$945 suite; $350–$1,280 spa suite. Off-season $95–$275 double; $175–$380 golf suite; $350–$825 spa suite. Extra person $35. One or two children 15 and under stay free in parents' room. 18% service charge added. Golf and spa packages available. AE, CB, DC, DISC, MC, V. Valet parking $8.50.

The Doral epitomizes the luxury resort in Florida. While the pampering in the spa attracts worldwide attention, the next-door golf resort hosts world-class tournaments and is home to the Blue Monster Course, rated one of the top 25 in the country. The season is booked well in advance by those who have been here before or have just read about the fantastic offerings on this 650-acre resort. The area is surrounded only by warehouses and office buildings, just moments from the Miami airport.

The spacious lobbies and dining areas shimmer with polished marble, mirrors, and gold. The rooms, too, are luxuriously large and tastefully decorated; large windows allow views of the tropical gardens or golf courses below.

Dining/Diversions: The Spa restaurant serves delicious low-fat cuisine, including reduced-calorie desserts. Various other options include a cafe with super Italian sandwiches, salads, and pasta. A sports bar at the golf club has excellent club fare.

Amenities: Concierge, room service, laundry and dry cleaning, newspaper delivery, evening turndown, in-room massage in spa suites only by appointment, baby-sitting, secretarial services, express checkout, courtesy car or limo, shuttle to the Doral Ocean Resort. Olympic-size outdoor heated pool, access to the spa ($25), small exercise room, steam room and sauna, jogging track, bicycle rentals, extensive golf facilities, game rooms, children's programs during the holidays, business center, conference wing, car-rental desk, sundeck, 15 outdoor tennis courts, tour and activities desks, beauty salon, boutiques.

Miami International Airport Hotel. P.O. Box 997510. NW 20th St. and LeJeune Rd., Airport Terminal Concourse E, Miami, FL 33299-7510. ☎ **800/327-1276** or 305/871-4100. Fax 305/871-0800. 260 units. A/C TV TEL. Winter $135–$185 double; $250–$650 suite. Off-season $150–$170 double; $250–$265 suite. Extra person $10. Up to two children under 12 stay free in parents' room. AE, CB, DC, EURO, JCB, MC, V. Parking $9.

I don't know of a nicer airport hotel, and this one couldn't be more convenient—it's actually in the airport at Concourse E. The hotel also has every amenity of a first-class tourist destination, including a large rooftop pool, health club, Jacuzzi, sauna, sundeck, racquetball courts, jogging track, small business center, conference room, a beauty salon, eight-channel Spectravision, Laundromat, tour desk, boutiques, and several cocktail lounges and restaurants. You'd think you'd be deaf from the roar of the planes, but all of the rooms have been soundproofed and allow in very little noise. In addition, the hotel is extremely safe with modern security systems.

The rooms are modern and spacious with industrial-grade carpeting and nondescript furnishings, but clean and tasteful. If you need to be at the airport and want excellent service this is your best bet.

NORTHERN MIAMI-DADE

✪ **Turnberry Isle Resort and Club.** 19999 W. Country Club Dr., Aventura, FL 33180. ☎ **800/327-7028** or 305/932-6200. Fax 305/933-6550. 340 units. A/C MINIBAR TV TEL. Winter $375–$495 resort rm or suite; $295–$335 yacht club rm or suite. Off-season $195–$300 resort rm or suite; $150–$175 yacht club rm or suite. AE, DC, DISC, MC, V. Valet parking $8, free self-parking.

A top-rated destination resort, this gorgeous 300-acre compound has every possible facility for active guests, especially golfers. The main attractions are two newly renovated Trent Jones courses available only to members and guests of the hotel. The impeccable service from check-in to checkout brings loyal fans back for more.

Unless you're into boating, the higher priced resort rooms are where you'll want to stay. Here you're steps from perfect spa facilities and the renowned Veranda restaurant. The well-proportioned rooms are gorgeously tiled to match the Mediterranean-style architecture. The bathrooms even have a color TV mounted in reach of the whirlpool bathtubs, and video rental is available.

The location is convenient to Fort Lauderdale and Miami, about halfway between the two. But right in North Miami Beach, the area surrounding the hotel, you'll find excellent shopping and some of the best dining in Miami. You'll pay a lot to stay at this luxurious resort, but it's worth it.

Dining/Diversions: There are six restaurants, including the Veranda, which serves healthful and tropical "New World" cuisine in an elegant dining room. The several bars and lounges, including a popular disco, also have enough entertainment and local flavor to keep anyone busy for weeks.

Amenities: Concierge, 24-hour room service, same-day laundry service, newspaper delivery, in-room massage, nightly turndown, twice-daily maid service, baby-sitting services, express checkout. Four large swimming pools; complete state-of-the-art health spa with Turkish steam rooms, authentic Finnish sauna, shiatsu pressure treatments, private exercise classes, oxygenation treatments, slimming baths containing botanical extracts, and a full complement of herbal, thalassotherapy, and holistic health counseling; beach; Jacuzzi; sauna; two 36-hole golf courses; nature trails; sundeck; 24 outdoor tennis courts (including 16 lighted for night play); squash/racquetball courts; water-sports equipment; 3-mile jogging course; bicycle rental; game room; children's center and programs; large business center; four large meeting and conference centers; tour desk; boutiques; limousine and car-rental desks; helipad; beauty salon.

4 Where to Dine

Regional cuisine in Miami is hard to define. It encompasses the varied tastes of the Caribbean, especially Cuba, as well as an old-time rural Florida influence. The chefs who pioneered what's been dubbed "Floribbean" have fused the many influences into an ever-changing style that's limited only by the imagination of those preparing or eating the food.

It's a blend of Caribbean and American fare accented with dashes of Latin American, Spanish, Asian, and Western Europe. In general, the result is spectacular, although it can be overambitious and pretentious at times. Think of mango-infused oils dotted on tuna tartar with jicama slaw served in a cracked coconut. Welcome to the new world. It's not for the xenophobic or the meat-and-potatoes crowd.

And you can always find exotic foods—from Cuban to Haitian to Jamaican to Vietnamese. I've included a good cross section of these.

Also, a number of chains that originated here are worth trying when you want a quick and inexpensive bite. Try **Pollo Tropical,** a Cuban fast-food chain serving delicious moist chicken, rice and beans, and garlic-drenched yucca (a potato-like root vegetable). Locations include 18710 S. Dixie Hwy. (at 186th Street), South Miami (☎ 305/225-7858); 1454 Alton Rd., Miami Beach (☎ 305/672-8888); and 11806 Biscayne Blvd., North Miami (☎ 305/895-0274). Check the phone book for others. **Miami Subs Grill** is also popular since it serves the basic fast-food favorites like burgers and fries, but also offers a selection of salads, grilled chicken, beer and wine, as well as key lime pie and frozen yogurt. Locations include 351 Lincoln Rd. (off Washington Avenue), South Beach (☎ 305/538-9044), and 3030 Grand Ave., Coconut Grove (☎ 305/567-0041).

To help you choose where to eat, the restaurants below are divided first by neighborhood, then by price.

SOUTH BEACH

With the largest concentration of restaurants in South Florida, South Beach offers something for every palate and pocketbook. Unfortunately, service can often be rude and inefficient.

Be aware that many South Beach restaurants automatically add a service charge to each bill. When this is the case, the restaurant's policy should be written on the menu. Check and ask. Many unscrupulous waiters "forget" to mention this, however, and will deliver your credit- or charge-card receipt with the tip space left open. Don't tip twice unless you mean to.

There is a pizza joint or Cuban diner on nearly every block of South Beach. Take your pick.

VERY EXPENSIVE

Joe's Stone Crab Restaurant. 227 Biscayne St. (at the corner of Washington Ave.). ☎ **305/673-0365.** Reservations not accepted. No shorts allowed. Market price for stone crabs varies but averages $10–$18 per claw. Other main courses $6–$26. AE, CB, DC, DISC, MC, V. Sun–Mon 5–10pm, Tues–Thurs 11:30am–2pm and 5–10pm, Fri–Sat 11:30am–2pm and 5–11pm. Closed mid-May to mid-October. SEAFOOD.

Open since 1913 and steeped in tradition, this restaurant is famous in Florida and beyond, as evidenced by the long lines of people waiting to get in. A full menu is available, but to order anything but stone crabs is unthinkable—the restaurant only serves stone crabs when they're in season—and the snobby waiters will let you know it. Service is brusque and pushy. Even after the $5 million renovation, which more than doubled the size of the place, the lines are ridiculously long—sometimes more than 3 hours. If you have to say you were there, brave it and enjoy drinks in the newly renovated oak bar. Otherwise, try the take-out bar next door for the same price and less hassle. The claws here are pricier than at other local restaurants, but you're paying for history.

Yuca. 501 Lincoln Rd. (corner of Drexel Ave.). ☎ **305/532-9822.** Reservations required. Main courses $19–$32. AE, CB, DC, MC, V. Daily 11:30am–4pm and 6–11pm or midnight. NOUVELLE CUBAN.

Don't give yourself away as a gringo by calling it Yucka. It's pronounced *yoo*-ka and besides being the name of a staple root vegetable, it's an acronym for Young Upscale Cuban-Americans. It is known for its superb reinvention of Cuban comfort food. To enjoy your meal, you'll have to demand to be seated in the front of the restaurant, facing Lincoln Road; otherwise you will be in the hectic path of the kitchen. On weekends, try to get a reservation between 7 and 8pm so you can catch the excellent show upstairs afterward (see "Miami After Dark," in chapter 5).

All of the large and exotic appetizers are tempting and beautifully displayed. Try the lobster medallions with sautéed spinach and a portobello mushroom stuffed with vegetarian paella. The pieces of lobster tail are expertly grilled and served over wilted greens. The mushroom is deliciously rich, though the paella can be a bit pasty. For a main course, the pork tenderloin will steal the show. It must be marinated for days and can be cut with a butter knife. The addition of a hearty congri, a mash of red beans and rice, and a mango salsa is a perfect balance. The menu is badly translated, so don't be shy about asking for a waiter who is proficient in English if you don't speak Spanish.

EXPENSIVE

✪ **Astor Place in the Astor Hotel.** 956 Washington Ave. ☎ **305/672-7217.** Reservations recommended. Main courses $15–$30. AE, DC, MC, V. Daily 7am– 2:30pm and 7–11pm weekdays, 6pm–midnight weekends. NEW FLORIDA BARBECUE.

The Astor Hotel not only has a great bar, but perhaps the very best restaurant on the beach. Known as the Caribbean Cowboy, chef Johnny Vinczencz has created an elegant but unstuffy menu using local ingredients and a lot of imagination. From his signature corn-crusted yellowtail snapper with lemon boniato (a sweet root vegetable similar to potato or yuca) mash and roasted corn sauce to his sushi salad, a concoction of curry, fresh tuna, ginger shrimp, caviar, wasabi, and smoked salmon dressed in an orange sesame vinaigrette, all his dishes are dramatic and delicious. A stack of portobello mushrooms is served pancake style with balsamic syrup and sun-dried tomato butter. Nightly specials sell out every single night and are always worth a try. Also, a hot seller is the decadent lobster pot pie with shrimp and vegetables. If it's available, order it. The sleek dining room with low level lighting, a glass-enclosed atrium, and marble floors is romantic in an ultra-modern way. Well-dressed hipsters flock to the restaurant especially on weekend nights while a sophisticated family crowd shows up for the Sunday jazz brunch.

Nemo's. 100 Collins Ave. (at 1st St.). ☎ **305/532-4550.** Reservations recommended for weekends. Main courses $18–$20; sandwiches and platters $6–$12; Sun brunch $19. Mon–Fri noon–3pm and 7pm–midnight, Sat 6pm–midnight, Sun noon–4pm and 6–11pm. MULTICULTURAL.

This dark, super-stylish hot spot is an oasis in a newly hip area of South Beach, below 5th Street. Here models and celebrities rub elbows (literally, since the tables are so close together). The din in the main dining room is unbearable. Ask to be seated in the back or on the patio. Nemo's may have managed to find the only really professional serving staff on the beach; you'll find them personable, intelligent, and efficient. Amazing! They're full of helpful suggestions regarding the daily specials or the regular menu, which offers many fish dishes. One of the most popular is the charred salmon with a crisp sprout salad, toasted pumpkin seeds, and a soy vinaigrette; flash-cooking the fish in a wok gives a unique, slightly blackened flavor to the outside while leaving the inside tender and sweet. If you want something light, try the grilled portobello mushroom appetizer, served with creamy garlic polenta—modern comfort food. The spicy Vietnamese beef salad is indeed spicy and is served with a crisp assortment of vegetables; my only complaint is that it's too small.

✪ **Norma's.** 646 Lincoln Rd. ☎ **305/532-2809.** Reservations recommended. Main courses $12–$24. AE, DC, DISC, MC, V. Tues–Thurs noon–11pm, Fri–Sat noon–midnight, Sun noon–10:30pm. Closed for lunch in summer. JAMAICAN/NEW WORLD CARIBBEAN.

This tiny jewel on Lincoln Road sparkles with an eclectic mix of classical and Caribbean cooking. The multilingual staff is polite, if sometimes slightly flustered. An extensive list of daily specials is always good, but you may want to call in advance to reserve whatever sounds best—they sell out quickly. For starters, definitely go for the smoked marlin platter with cucumbers, capers, onions, spicy pepper salsa, and a creamy dipping sauce. The tender marlin is flown in weekly from Montego Bay, where the original Norma's enjoys the reputation of "Julia Child of the Caribbean." At lunch, a surprisingly tasty jerk tofu salad is served on callaloo (a slightly sweeter cousin to spinach) with tomatoes and onions. The seared jerk tuna has a kick (like all the jerk-seasoned dishes) and is one of the beach's best. If you'd like something milder, the rasta chicken is a casserole of chicken breast, roasted red and yellow peppers, cream cheese, and callaloo layered to evoke the Rastafarian red, green, and gold flag. A delicate white-wine sauce melds the distinct flavors into a rich and satisfying main course. Be sure not to drive after you've had the Appleton rum cake and rum whipped cream. Share a piece and then wander along Lincoln Road to reflect on this most exciting restaurant.

Steak Houses in Miami Are No Longer So Rare

Miami's always had more than its ration of pricey fish houses and surf-and-turf spots, too. This is a tourist city, after all. And don't forget the huddle of trendy spots serving "New World" cuisine, the pasta joints, Cuban cafeterias, and fast-food drive-throughs. In this multicultural metropolis you could always find cuisine from Delhi, Honduras, or Beijing. But a good old-fashioned steak? It wasn't always so easy.

The old standbys like **Christy's** in Coral Gables (☎ **305/446-1400**), **Ruth's Chris** in North Miami Beach (☎ **305/949-0100**) and **The Palm** in Bay Harbor Islands (☎ **305/531-1338**) had been the lonely mainstays over the years. When Don Shula's took over the old **Legends** steakhouse in Miami Lakes in 1989 (☎ **305/820-8102**) it became so popular—even in its remote location—that over the years it has opened five branches around the country. One of the latest **Shula's** (☎ **305/341-6565**) opened in the luxurious Alexander Hotel on Miami Beach, which in 1998 took the place of a very well respected French restaurant, Dominique's.

Of course, who could forget **The Forge** in Miami Beach (☎ **305/604-9798**), one of the premier dining spots in town, which serves an extraordinary steak. In fact, it was voted the number one steak in America by *Wine Spectator* magazine in 1996. But that was before the stampede of new restaurants came to town to capitalize on a renewed desire for flesh. The National Cattlemen's Association reported a 41.6% increase of restaurant traffic at casual and upscale steakhouses between 1993 and 1996.

Following that trend, Miami has seen a glut of new steakhouses opening up over the years. From the Argentinean **La Fusta** in Sunny Isles (☎ **305/949-0888**) to downtown's Brazilian **Porcao** (☎ **305/373-2777**) and the more upscale **Capital Grille** (☎ **305/374-4500**), it seems that every month a new one jumps in the fire. In late 1997, New York's **Smith & Wollensky** expanded with its first restaurant outside of Manhattan. The clubby and elegant haven for beef lovers now occupies a scenic spot in South Pointe Park on South Beach (☎ **305/673-2800**). The venerable **Morton's** of Chicago turned up the heat in December 1997 with a luxurious spot in downtown Miami (☎ **305/400-9990**). Another superb newcomer is the French brasserie **Les Halles** in Coral Gables (☎ **305/461-1099**). So far it seems each of the establishments has found its niche and is serving up its own kind of beef in all price ranges.

Less-expensive spots around town include **Houston's** in North Miami (☎ **305/947-2000**) and three **Outback Steak Houses** in Kendall (☎ **305/596-6771**), Miami Beach (☎ **305/531-1338**), and Sunny Isles (☎ **305/944-4329**). Don Shula's also has a more casual spot in Miami Lakes called **Shula's Steak 2** (☎ **305/820-8047**).

✪ **Osteria del Teatro.** 1443 Washington Ave. (at Española Way). ☎ **305/538-7850.** Reservations recommended. Main courses $21–$25. AE, CB, DC, MC, V. Sun–Mon and Wed–Thurs 6–11pm, Fri–Sat 6pm–midnight. Closed Tues. NORTHERN ITALIAN.

The curved entryway of this well-established enclave of reliable, if slightly overpriced, Italian cuisine is abuzz nightly as locals and tourists wait to get a seat at one of the small tables. Start with any of the grilled vegetables, most notably the portobello mushrooms with Fontina or the garlic-infused peppers. Many of the pastas are handmade and are done to perfection. The risotto al'Aragosta is a creamy rice dish with a decadent lobster-and-shrimp sauce full of tasty morsels of seafood. Of the five or so entrees offered nightly, usually at least three are seafood. They are all great.

MODERATE/EXPENSIVE

La Sandwicherie. 229 14th St. (east of Washington Ave., behind the Amoco Station). ☎ **305/532-8934.** Sandwiches and salads $4.50–$7. No credit cards. Sun–Mon 10am–5pm. Delivery Sun–Mon 10am–6pm. FRENCH SNACK BAR.

If you want the most incredible gourmet sandwich you've ever tasted, stop by the green-and-white awning that hides this fabulously French lunch and snack counter. Choose pâté saucisson, salami, prosciutto, turkey, tuna, ham, roast beef, or any of the perfect cheeses (Swiss, mozzarella, cheddar, or provolone). You could make a meal of the optional sandwich toppings (black olives, cornichons, cucumbers, lettuce, onions, green or hot peppers, tomatoes) that are included in the sandwich price. The fresh French bread has a golden crust and is just thick enough to hold all you'll want to have stuffed into it.

Mrs. Mendoza's Tacos al Carbon. 1040 Alton Rd. ☎ **305/535-0808.** Main courses $3–$5; side dishes 80¢–$3. No credit cards. Mon–Thurs 11am–10pm, Fri–Sat 11am–11pm, Sun noon–10pm. FAST FOOD/MEXICAN.

Popular with locals and those who work in the area, this hard-to-spot storefront eatery is a godsend. It's the only fresh California-style Mexican joint in town where the steak and chicken are grilled as you wait and then stuffed into homemade flour or corn wrappings. You order at the tile counter and pick up your dish on a plastic tray in minutes. One of my favorites is the chicken burrito, which includes rice, black beans, cheese, lettuce, and guacamole doused in tomato salsa. They offer three types of salsa, from mild to superhot. The chips are hand-cut and flavorful but a bit too coarse. Skip them and enjoy an order of the rich and chunky guacamole with a fork.

Another branch is located at Doral Plaza, 9739 NW 41st St. (☎ 305/477-5119).

✪ **Nirvana.** 630 6th St. (off Washington Ave.) ☎ **305/534-3700.** Reservations accepted. Main courses $8–$16. AE, DC, DISC, MC, V. Sun–Thurs 6–11pm, Fri–Sat 6pm–midnight. NORTHERN INDIAN.

Offering a wide selection of both vegetarian and meat, chicken, seafood, and lamb dishes, this reasonably priced trendy hot spot qualifies as the best Indian in Miami. Expert chef-owner Raghu Raturr has created a simple and elegant menu with all the favorites like Saag paneer and chicken vindaloo, a variety of curries, and a few unusual specialties like baigan bharta, a creamy concoction of mashed eggplant, is a rich and hearty main dish served, like all other entrees, with a large helping of fragrant pulao rice. A rich chicken curry, though not listed on the menu, is one of the restaurant's finest offerings. The gentle mustard-colored sauce is savory yet not overly thick, spicy but not sharp. Despite the budget prices, the atmosphere is romantic and elegant enough for a Saturday night date. So far, it's popular mostly with young locals and a few East Indians in the know. It seems to me that very few Miamians are into Indian food. Good—that just means there's more for us.

✪ **Sport Cafe.** 538 Washington Ave. ☎ **305/674-9700.** Reservations accepted only for parties of four or more. Main courses $7–$10; sandwiches and pizzas $4.50–$7. AE, MC, V. Daily 11am–1am (sometimes open earlier for coffee). RUSTIC ITALIAN.

Inside the decor is dark and smoky, with a beautiful wooden bar and a large-screen TV that dominates the small dining room. But don't expect to see the latest football or baseball aired here; soccer and bicycle races are more popular with the European crowd. The Sport Cafe is owned by brothers Tonino and Paolo Doino from Rome, and the food is really made by their mother, Rosa. Prices are so low that you often have to wait for a seat, especially at the sidewalk tables.

The simple menu lists only three entrees and a few pizzas. Ask for the day's specials and go for one of them. Always good is the penne with salmon served with a pink sauce. Rosa also makes the very best eggplant parmigiana I've had (except for my mother's). The vegetable discs are lightly sautéed without any heavy breading and then layered in a rich tomato sauce with lots of sweet mozzarella. Though not on the menu, this dish is available almost every day. Ordering from the newly arrived Italian waiters can be a challenge.

Also try its sister restaurant, Rosinella, at 525 Lincoln Rd. (☎ 305/672-6777).

World Resources. 719 Lincoln Rd. ☎ **305/535-8987.** Main courses $6–$8; sushi hand rolls $3–$4. AE, DC, MC, V. Daily noon–11:30pm. JAPANESE/THAI.

World Resources is a popular little cafe and sushi bar masquerading as an Indonesian furniture and bric-a-brac store. Local hippie types and Euros frequent this downright cheap hangout instead of cooking at home. Offerings include some of the freshest and most innovative sushi and many Thai specialties. The portions are generous and the cooking simple. The basil chicken, for example, is a tasty combination of white meat sautéed in a coconut sauce with subtle hints of basil and garlic. The Thai salad is heaped with fresh vegetables including cauliflower, sprouts, and cucumbers. Although you can get better Thai food at a number of spots on the beach, you can't beat the atmosphere. Dozens of outside tables surround a tiny pond and stage where musicians perform a variety of styles, from African drumming to Indian sitar playing.

MIAMI BEACH

The dining scene in Miami Beach runs the gamut. Many old steak and seafood shops and bagel joints are popular with locals and seasonal condo-dwellers. Some of the most formal restaurants on the beach are here. A growing number of low-priced Italian places have sprouted up in recent years, too.

VERY EXPENSIVE

The Forge Restaurant. 432 Arthur Godfrey Rd. (at 41st St.). ☎ **305/538-8533.** Reservations required. Main courses $18–$35. AE, DC, MC, V. Sun–Thurs 4pm–midnight, Fri–Sat 5pm–3am. STEAK/AMERICAN.

English oak paneling and Tiffany glass suggest high prices and haute cuisine, and that's exactly what you get at The Forge. Each elegant dining room possesses its own character and features high ceilings, ornate chandeliers, and high-quality European artwork. The Forge's huge American menu has a northern Italian bias, evidenced by a long list of creamy pasta appetizers. Equal attention is given to fish, veal, poultry, and beef dishes, many prepared on the kitchen's all-important oak grill. Look for appetizers like oak-grilled tomatoes with mozzarella. The Forge has one of Miami's biggest wine lists. Ask the very knowledgeable and affable head wine steward, Gino Santangelo, for a tour of the cellar. No matter what your budget, stop in for a drink at least to see the magnificent interior and some of the most stylish Miamians. Also, see "Miami After Dark," in chapter 5, for details on this now hip hangout and the cigar bar next door.

EXPENSIVE

✪ **Crystal Cafe.** 726 41st St. ☎ **305/673-8266.** Reservations recommended Sat–Sun. Main courses $13–$22. AE, MC, V. Tues–Sun 5–11pm. CONTINENTAL/NOUVELLE.

The decor is black and white, with Lucite salt-and-pepper grinders and a bottle of wine as the only centerpiece on each of the 15 or so tables. Chef Klime (pronounced *Klee*-me), with the help of his affable wife and a superb service staff, has created a neighborhood bistro that attracts stars and locals alike. With nearly 30 entrees and a dozen side dishes from which to choose, it's amazing that each comes out perfectly, with some unexpected addition that was not mentioned in the unpretentious menu. The shrimp cake appetizer, for example, is the size of a bread plate and rests on top of a small mound of lightly sautéed watercress and mushrooms. Surrounding the delicately breaded disk are concentric circles of beautiful sauces—tomato and a basil mayonnaise. The osso buco is gaining renown among Miami foodies, and with good reason. The tender, almost buttery meat is steeped in chicken broth and is piled high with an assortment of vegetables. Desserts are tempting but hard to commit to after such generous portions. If you're able, consider the crepe stuffed with warm berry compote with a nutty topping.

MODERATE

Cafe Prima Pasta. 414 71st St. (just west of Collins Ave.). ☎ **305/867-0106.** Main courses $12–$14; pastas $7–$9. No credit cards. Mon–Fri noon–3pm; Mon–Thurs 6–11pm, Fri 6pm–midnight, Sat–Sun 1pm–midnight. ITALIAN.

Another tiny pasta joint that serves phenomenal homemade noodles with good old Italian sauces like carbonara, Bolognese, puttanesca, and pomodoro. With only 30 seats, the restaurant feels a bit cramped, but it's not usually a problem squeezing in with this young, laid-back crowd. The stuffed agnolotti—with pesto, spinach, and ricotta or tomato—are incredibly delicate and flavorful. Try the apple tart with golden caramel sauce; you might ask for it à la mode.

INEXPENSIVE

✪ **La Brioche D'Oree.** 4017 Prairie Ave. (just off of 41st St.), Miami Beach. ☎ **305/ 538-4770.** Sandwiches and salads $6–$8. No credit cards. Mon–Fri 7:30am–5pm, closed Sat, Sun 7:30am–2pm. FRENCH BAKERY.

You won't find better croissants anywhere but Paris—maybe. Sandwiches and salads are good, too, since they are served on deliciously crusty French bread or, of course, the aforementioned killer croissants. Sit at one of the four outdoor tables or cram inside the tiny storefront to enjoy a real French treat for breakfast or lunch.

The Oasis Cafe. 976 41st St. (Arthur Godfrey Rd.), Miami Beach. ☎ **305/674-7676.** salads and sandwiches $5–$7; main courses $7–$14. AE, MC, V. Mon–Thurs 11am–10pm, Fri–Sat 11am–11pm, Sun 5–10pm. MEDITERRANEAN/JUICE BAR.

A welcome addition on the street where The Forge, Crystal Cafe, and a dozen kosher eateries compete for attention is truly an Oasis. This cozy and casual corner cafe has dozens of salads and a range of entrees from burgers to grilled vegetable and tofu platters. Especially good are their grilled fishes and generous salads. The patrons range from granola-eating hipsters to scrub-clad doctors from the nearby hospitals. All appreciate the diverse and reasonably priced menu with lots of healthy options. Unfortunately, the waitresses sometimes seem to be better at checking their hair than checking on their customers. Still, this neighborhood hot spot is well worth a visit.

Wolfie Cohen's Rascal House. 17190 Collins Ave., Sunny Isles. ☎ **305/947-4581.** Omelettes and sandwiches $4–$6; other dishes $5–$14. AE, MC, V. Daily 24 hours. JEWISH/BAKERY/DELICATESSEN.

Opened in 1954 and still going strong, this culinary extravaganza is a Miami Beach institution. Simple tables and booths, packed with plenty of patrons, fill the airy 425-seat dining room. The menu is as huge as the portions; try the corned beef, schmaltz herring, brisket, kreplach, chicken soup, or other authentic Jewish staples. Some dishes are overpriced, but this is a favorite for those seeking authentic New York–style deli food. Takeout and delivery is available.

KEY BISCAYNE

There are surprisingly few great restaurants on "the Key," considering how many wealthy visitors vacation in this pristine enclave each year. For good takeout, try **La Boulangerie**, 328 Crandon Blvd., in the Eckerd's shopping mall (☎ **305/361-0281**). You'll find luscious sandwiches and salads vegetarian omelettes, and dangerous desserts. Also good is **The Oasis** at 19 Harbor Dr. on the corner of Crandon Boulevard. (☎ **305/361-5709**), a rugged little shack where everyone, from the city's mayor to the local handypersons, meet for Cuban coffees, delicious paella, or good Cuban sandwiches. It's a little dingy, but the food is good and cheap.

EXPENSIVE

Sundays on the Bay. 5420 Crandon Blvd. ☎ **305/361-6777.** Reservations accepted; recommended for Sun brunch. Main courses $15–$24; Sun brunch $18.95. AE, CB, DC, MC, V. Mon–Sat 11:30am–11:30pm, Sun 10:30am–11:30pm. AMERICAN.

Although the food is fine, Sundays is really a fun tropical bar that features an unbeatable view of downtown, Coconut Grove, and the Sundays marina. The menu features local favorites—grouper, tuna, snapper, and good shellfish when in season. Competent renditions of such classics as oysters Rockefeller, shrimp scampi, and lobster fra diablo are also recommendable. Sunday brunches are particularly popular, when a buffet the size of Bimini attracts the city's late-rising in-crowd.

The lively bar stays open all week until 2:30am, with a deejay spinning Thursday to Sunday from 9pm. Some legal trouble put the owners in hot water in 1995, leaving the future of this reggae scene up in the air. For more information, see "Miami After Dark," in chapter 5.

INEXPENSIVE

✪ **Bayside Seafood Restaurant and Hidden Cove Bar.** 3501 Rickenbacker Causeway. ☎ **305/361-0808.** Reservations accepted only for parties of more than 15. Salads and sandwiches $4.50–$6; platters $7–$13. AE, MC, V. Sun–Thurs 11:30am–11pm (later on weekends). SEAFOOD.

Known by locals as "the Hut," this ramshackle restaurant and bar is a laid-back outdoor tiki hut and terrace that serves pretty good sandwiches and fish platters on paper plates. A chalkboard lists the latest catches, which can be ordered blackened, fried, broiled, or in a garlic sauce. I prefer blackened, which is super-crusty and spicy. The fish dip is wonderfully smoky and moist, if a little heavy on mayonnaise.

Weekdays you'll find a great happy hour. On weekends the Hut features live reggae or disco until as late as 4am. They sometimes charge a cover of $5. Bring bug spray or ask the waitresses for some (they usually keep packets behind the bar) because this place is always plagued by mosquitoes. Local anglers and yacht owners share this rustic outpost with equal enthusiasm and loyalty.

DOWNTOWN

A number of inexpensive and fantastic ethnic options are available throughout the densely packed streets of downtown Miami, including great Cuban, Brazilian, and Peruvian lunch counters and sit-down restaurants. Check out the food court in the **Galeria International Mall,** hidden at East Flagler Street between Northeast 2nd Avenue and Northeast 1st Court; or at **Bayside's** second-floor food court, you'll find lots of great and inexpensive choices. You many want to try **Las Tapas** (☎ **305/ 372-2737**), at the entrance, for delicious Spanish samplings. Also nearby are a tourist-friendly **Hard Rock Cafe** (☎ **305/377-3110**) and a number of more elegant restaurants overlooking the bay.

EXPENSIVE

The Fish Market. In the Wyndham Hotel, 1601 Biscayne Blvd. (at the corner of 16th St.). ☎ **305/374-0000,** ext. 475. Reservations recommended. Main courses $17–$22. AE, CB, DC, MC, V. Mon–Sat 5:30–11pm. SEAFOOD.

One of Miami's most celebrated seafood restaurants is this understated, elegant dining room right in the heart of the city. Located in an unassuming corner, just off the fourth-floor lobby, the restaurant is both spacious and comfortable, featuring high ceilings, marble floors, reasonable prices, and a sumptuous dessert-table centerpiece. Don't overlook the appetizers, which include meaty Mediterranean-style seafood soup and delicate yellowfin tuna carpaccio. Local fish prepared and presented simply is always the menu's main feature.

MODERATE

✪ **Fishbone Grille.** 650 S. Miami Ave. (at SW 7th Ave., next to Tobacco Rd.). ☎ **305/ 530-1915.** Reservations recommended Fri–Sat. Main courses $7–$16. AE, DC, MC, V. Mon–Thurs 11:30am–10pm, Fri 11:30am–11pm, Sat 5:30–11pm. SEAFOOD.

Located in a small strip center it shares with Tobacco Road, this sensational and casual fishery prepares dozens of outstanding specials daily. The atmosphere is nothing to speak of, though there's a cool table where you can stare into a lively fish tank. This is by far Miami's best and most reasonably priced seafood restaurant. Try the excellent ceviche; there's just enough spice to give it a zing but not enough to overwhelm the superfresh fish flavor. The stews, crab cakes, and all the starters are superb. If you like Caribbean flavor, try the jerk corvina or one of the excellent dolphin (the fish, not the mammal) specialties.

INEXPENSIVE

✪ **Caribbean Delite.** 236 NE 1st Ave. (across the street from Miami Dade Community College). ☎ **305/381-9254.** Full meals $5.50–$9. AE, MC, V. Daily 8:30am–7:30pm. Closed some Sun. JAMAICAN.

You'd never see this tiny storefront diner from the one-way street on which it stands, though you might smell it from the sidewalk. The aroma of succulent jerk chicken and pork beckons regulars from all over. Try Jamaican specialties like the curried goat, tender and tasty pieces of meat on the bone in a spicy yellow sauce, or oxtail stew. The kitchen can be stingy with the spectacular sauces, so consider asking for an extra helping on the side. They're happy to oblige. For breakfast, ask for the national dish of Jamaica, ackee, and saltfish, a rare and delicious find in the United States.

LITTLE HAVANA

If you don't speak Spanish, you'll want to pick up a Spanish dictionary to help you get along in Little Havana. More and more restaurants, however, have started providing English-language menus. If not, you may have to find a young patron or employee to help translate. The following is but a tiny sampling of the area's best eateries and include an aberration, one of the city's only Vietnamese restaurants.

EXPENSIVE

Victor's Cafe. 2340 SW 32nd Ave. (1 block south of Coral Way). ☎ **305/445-1313.** Reservations recommended. Main courses $9.50–$32. AE, CB, DC, MC, V. Daily noon–midnight. Cabaret until 2am on weekends. CUBAN.

Offering average food in an upscale setting, Victor's is a place for celebrations and tourists. The cooking takes liberties with Cuban classics, but with generally good results. Some of the best dishes are the fish and shrimp plates, all of which are served with rice and beans. My favorite appetizer is the snapper ceviche marinated in Cachucha pepper and lime juice. The beef dishes also win favor among meat fans. The bistec alo Victor con tamal en balsa is a tender oak-grilled top sirloin served with Cuban-style polenta. Strolling guitarists add an air of romance to this kitschy Old Havana–style restaurant, while in adjacent rooms the lively salsa music wafts through the regal dining room where attentive waiters look after most details. Stick around for the wild cabaret featuring live Afro-Cuban music most nights after 11.

INEXPENSIVE

✪ **Hy-Vong.** 3458 SW 8th St. (between 34th and 35th aves.). ☎ **305/446-3674.** Reservations not accepted. Main courses $8–$12. No credit cards. Tues–Sun 6–11pm. Closed 2 weeks in Aug. VIETNAMESE.

Expect to wait for hours for a table and don't even think of mumbling a complaint. The owner/chef/waitress will be sure to forget to stop by your small wooden table to refill your glass or take an order if you do. Enjoy the wait with a traditional Vietnamese beer and lots of company. Outside this tiny storefront restaurant you'll meet interesting students, musicians, and foodies who come for the large and delicious portions, not for the plain wood-paneled room or painfully slow service. It's worth it. The Vietnamese food at Hy-Vong is elegantly simple and super-spicy. Appetizers include small, tightly packed Vietnamese spring rolls and kimchee, a spicy, fermented cabbage. Star entrees include pastry-enclosed chicken with watercress/cream-cheese sauce and fish in tangy mango sauce.

✪ **Versailles.** 3555 SW 8th St. ☎ **305/444-0240.** Main courses $5–$8. DC, MC, V. Mon–Thurs 8am–1:30am, Fri–Sat 8am–3:30am, Sun 9am–1:30am. CUBAN.

Versailles is the place where Miami's Cuban power brokers meet daily over *café con leche.* A glorified diner, the place sparkles with glass, chandeliers, murals, and mirrors meant to evoke its French namesake. There's nothing fancy here—nothing French either, just straightforward food from the home country. The menu is a veritable survey of Cuban cooking and includes specialties like *Moros y Cristians* (flavorful black beans with white rice), *ropa vieja* (a Cuban beef stew), and fried whole fish.

COCONUT GROVE

The Grove's biggest tourist draw is Cocowalk, a cluster of shops, theaters, restaurants, bars, and cafes that provide all the entertainment and dining options for any taste or budget. Especially recommendable here is **The Cheesecake Factory** (☎ **305/447-9898**), a newish franchise that is flourishing because of its varied and sophisticated menu. Expect a wait. **Cafe Tu Tu Tango** (☎ **305/529-5222**) is another great option. This artsy cafe serves appetizer-sized portions from an extensive and ethnically varied menu. Just up the block at Mayfair House is **Planet Hollywood** (☎ **305/445-7277**) or on Grand Avenue is **Johnny Rocket's** (☎ **305/444-1000**) for burgers and fries.

EXPENSIVE

Bocca di Rosa. 2833 Bird Ave. (between SW 27th Ave. and Virginia St.), Coconut Grove. ☎ **305/444-4222.** Reservations suggested. Main courses $16–$24; pastas $11–$17. AE, DC, DISC, MC, V. Daily 6–11pm, until midnight on weekends. ITALIAN.

This elegant restaurant is nestled in a cozy corner of the Grove. But from the smells and tastes you encounter here you might as well be in Roma or Sicilia. With dishes like coniglio all contadina (rabbit stew with white beans and polenta) and penne cons salsa di sarde (a sardine and fennel pasta), the menu touches all points on the boot.

On any day, there may be as many as 15 specials. The remarkably fresh seafood is especially recommended. My favorite is a savory bowl of steamed mussels in a white wine broth and a delicately seared swordfish. Frankly, whatever Chef Girogio is cooking up is bound to be good.

MODERATE

At's a Nice. 2779 Bird Ave. (off SW 27th Ave.). ☎ **305/441-9119.** Pizza pies $6–$16; entrees $9–$16. AE, MC, V. Tues–Sun 4–11pm. ITALIAN.

A welcome addition to the Coconut Grove dining scene, this Italian eatery has won immediate fans for their superb pizza and good pastas, too. The setting is as casual as you can get, with a wood deck and plastic patio furniture the setting for the half a dozen tables overlooking a busy street.

Kaleidoscope. 3112 Commodore Plaza (1 block from Main Hwy.). ☎ **305/446-5010.** Reservations recommended. Main courses $14–$20; pastas $12–$15. AE, CB, DC, DISC, MC, V. Mon 6–11pm; Tues–Sun 11:30am–3pm and 6–11pm; Fri–Sat 6pm–midnight; Sun 5:30–10pm. NEW AMERICAN.

Kaleidoscope is an unusually low-key and elegant restaurant in the heart of Coconut Grove. It's conveniently located slightly off the main drag and perched on a second-floor terrace assuring privacy and a good view. The dishes are well prepared, and the pastas, topped with sauces like seafood and fresh basil or pesto with grilled yellowfin tuna, are especially tasty. The linguine with salmon and fresh dill is perfection. Although there's no specially priced before-theater dinner, many locals stop in at this always reliable and reasonable spot for dinner before a show at the Coconut Grove Playhouse a few blocks away.

✪ Monty's Bayshore Restaurant. 2560 S. Bayshore Dr. ☎ **305/858-1431.** Reservations recommended upstairs Sat–Sun. Main courses $19–$35; sandwiches $6–$8; platters $7–$12. AE, CB, DC, MC, V. Daily 11:30am–midnight. Call for hours of each of the three restaurants; some are open later. SEAFOOD.

This place comes in three parts: a lounge, a raw bar, and a restaurant. Among them, Monty's serves everything from steak and seafood to munchies like nachos, potato skins, and Buffalo chicken wings. This is a fun kind of place, usually with more revelers and drinkers than diners. At the outdoor dockside bar there's live music nightly and all day on weekends (see "Miami After Dark," in chapter 5). Upstairs is an upscale dining room that serves one of the city's best Caesar salads and respectable stone crab claws in season. However, do not order the claws from May to October, since the local product is out of season; they'll serve you imported ones that simply don't compare. In season, however, splurge on the all-you-can-eat jumbo claws for $40 to $50. That's about the same price as three or four claws at Joe's.

INEXPENSIVE

Cafe Tu Tu Tango. 3015 Grand Ave. (on the second floor of Cocowalk), Coconut Grove. ☎ **305/529-2222.** Reservations not accepted. Tapas $4–$8. AE, MC, V. Sun–Wed 11:30am–midnight, Thurs 11:30am–1am, Fri–Sat 11:30am–2am. SPANISH/INTERNATIONAL.

In the bustling microcosm of Cocowalk, this second-floor restaurant is designed to look something like a disheveled artist's loft. Dozens of original paintings—some only half finished—hang on the walls and studio easels. Seating at sturdy wooden tables and chairs is either inside, on wooden floors among the clutter, or outdoors, overlooking the Grove's main drag. Flamenco and other Latin-inspired tunes complement a menu of small tasting plates. Hummus spread on rosemary flat bread and baked goat cheese in marinara sauce are delicious. Also good are the luscious little pizzas dressed with every imaginable topping from pine nuts to spinach. Try the sweet and potent sangria and enjoy the warm and lively atmosphere from a seat with a view.

Señor Frogs. 3480 Main Hwy. (across from the Barnacle), Coconut Grove. ☎ **305/ 448-0999.** Reservations recommended on weekends. Full meals $9–$15. AE, CB, DC, DISC, MC, V. Mon–Sat 11:30am–2am, Sun 11:30am–1am. MEXICAN.

Filled with a college-student crowd, this restaurant is known for a raucous good time, its mariachi band, and especially its powerful margaritas. The food at this rocking cantina is a bit overly cheesy, but tasty, if not exactly authentic. The mole enchiladas, with 14 different kinds of mild chiles mixed with chocolate, is as flavorful as any I've tasted. Almost everything is served with rice and beans in quantities so large that few diners are able to finish. Consider one of the generous appetizers like the Quesadilla Tia Esther, a sandwich of tortillas piled with shredded beef and lots of cheese. It comes with guacamole and beans, too.

CORAL GABLES & ENVIRONS
VERY EXPENSIVE

Norman's. 21 Almeria Ave. (3 blocks south of Miracle Mile between Douglas and Ponce de León Blvd.). ☎ **305/446-6767.** Reservations highly recommended. Main courses $25–$32. AE, DC, MC, V. Mon–Fri noon–2pm and 6–10:15pm, Sat 6–10:45pm. NEW WORLD CUISINE/ REGIONAL.

Master chef and one of the originators of what has become known as New World cuisine after various stints in and around the Miami circuit, Norman Van Aken opened what he calls his culmination in 1995. The result is an open kitchen where a handful of silent and industrious chefs prepare Asian- and Caribbean-inspired dishes for the well-dressed patrons. The atmosphere is comfortable and subdued with hand-painted walls, marble floors, and an upstairs gallery. Eating here is an experience where the food is the main focus of attention. It's difficult not to let the exotic-sounding list of ingredients on the menu be the topic of conversation. Some think it's pretentious and overwrought. I think there's plenty to enjoy, like the pizzas and pastas with a good glass of wine.

The staff is adoring and professional, and the atmosphere is tasteful without being too formal. You'll want to try some of the wacky desserts like mango ice cream served with Asian pears and crushed red pepper (the pepper really just adds color to the plate); like the restaurant, it's hot but very approachable.

EXPENSIVE/MODERATE

The Bistro. 2611 Ponce de León Blvd. ☎ **305/442-9671.** Reservations recommended. Main courses $16–$26. AE, CB, DC, DISC, MC, V. Tues–Fri 11:30am–2pm and 6–10:30pm, Sat 6–11pm. FRENCH.

The Bistro's intimate atmosphere is heightened by soft lighting, 19th-century European antiques and prints, and an abundance of flowers atop crisp white tablecloths. Co-owners Ulrich Sigrist and André Barnier keep a watchful eye over their experienced kitchen staff, which serves up artful French dishes with an international accent. Look for the terrine maison, a country-style veal-and-pork appetizer that's the house specialty. Common French bistro fare like escargots au Pernod and coquilles St-Jacques are prepared with uncommon spices and accompaniments, livening a rather typical continental menu. Especially recommended are the roast duck with honey-mustard sauce and the chicken breast in mild curry sauce, each served with fried bananas and pineapple.

○ **Caffé Abbracci.** 318 Aragon Ave. (between Le Jeune Rd. and Miracle Mile). ☎ **305/441-0700.** Reservations recommended for dinner. Main courses $16–$24; pasta $13–$20. AE, CB, DC, MC, V. Mon–Fri 11:30am–3pm and 6pm–midnight. NORTHERN ITALIAN.

You'll be greeted with a hug by owner and maître d' Nino, who oversees this wonderful spot as only an Italian could. The food is remarkable, and the place is packed on weekends by those in the know. It's hard to get beyond the appetizers here, all of which are so good that you could order a few and be satisfied. My favorite is the shrimp with a bright pesto sauce that has just enough garlic to give it a kick, but not so much you won't get a kiss later. The risottos are excellent and can be served in half portions so that you'll have room for the indescribable fish dishes. You're guaranteed perfect service in a pretty wood-and-marble setting—the only drawback is the unfortunately loud dining room.

Gables Diner. 2320 Galiano Dr. (between Ponce de León and 37th Ave.). ☎ **305/ 567-0330.** Main courses $9–$16; pastas $10–$12; burgers and sandwiches $7–$9; salads $8–$10. AE, DC, DISC, MC, V. Daily 8am–10pm. AMERICAN.

This upscale diner serves an eclectic mix of comfort food and nouvelle health food. From meat loaf to Chinese chicken salad, there is some moderately priced option for everyone. My favorite is the chicken pot pie, a homemade flaky crusted pie filled with large chunks of white meat, pearl onions, peas, and mushrooms. Also good are the large burgers with every imaginable condiment. Vegetarians can find a few good choices including pastas, bean soups, pizzas, a vegetable stir-fry, and some hearty salads. All the ingredients are fresh and crisp. No need to dress up here, though you will find a clean and almost romantic setting that is as appropriate for families as it is for first dates.

INEXPENSIVE

The Globe. 377 Alhambra Circle (just off Le Jeune Rd.), Coral Gables. ☎ **305/445-3555.** Reservations only for more than six. Salads $4–$10; pizzas and sandwiches $7–$11. AE, DISC, MC, V. Mon–Fri 11:30am–midnight; Sat 6:30pm–2am. INTERNATIONAL/CASUAL.

This funky coffee shop/travel agency is an odd addition to a neighborhood dominated by fancy eateries and hotels. Take advantage of the hip surroundings and enjoy the quite recommendable food. Especially good are the pizzas and salads. In addition to an extensive list of wines and specialty beers, there are many interesting nonalcoholic choices. Sample some of the excellent live music every weekend.

NORTH DADE

The area is mostly residential, with lots of condos filled with seasonal visitors. And though there are no real attractions here, except the Spanish Monastery (see chapter 5 for details), this cluster of neighborhoods has some of Miami's very best restaurants and shopping.

VERY EXPENSIVE

○ **Chef Allen's.** 19088 NE 29th Ave. (at 190th St.), North Miami Beach. ☎ **305/ 935-2900.** Reservations suggested. Main courses $20–$27. AE, MC, V. Sun–Thurs 6–10:30pm, Fri–Sat 6–11pm. MIAMI REGIONAL.

Head here for one of South Florida's finest dining experiences. Owner/chef Allen Susser, one of Miami's so-called Mango gang has built a classy yet relaxed restaurant with art deco furnishings, a glass-enclosed kitchen, and a hot-pink swirl of neon surrounding the dining room's ceiling.

The delicious homemade breadsticks are enough to hold you, but don't let them tempt you away from an appetizer—say, lobster and crab cakes served with strawberry-ginger chutney or baked Brie with spinach, sun-dried tomatoes, and pine nuts. Served by an energetic, young staff, favorite main dishes include crisp roast duck with cranberry sauce and mesquite-grilled Norwegian salmon with champagne grapes, green onions, and basil spaetzle. Local fish dishes, in various delectable guises, and homemade pastas are always on the menu. The extensive wine list is well chosen and features several good buys. Handmade desserts are works of art and sinfully delicious.

MODERATE/INEXPENSIVE

The Gourmet Diner. 13951 Biscayne Blvd. (between NE 139th and 140th sts.), North Miami Beach. ☎ **305/947-2255.** Reservations not accepted. Main courses $10–$17. No credit cards. Mon–Fri 11am–11pm, Sat 8am–11:30pm, Sun 8am–10:30pm. BELGIAN/FRENCH.

This retro 1950s-style diner serves plain old French fare without pretensions. The atmosphere is a bit brash and the lines are often out the door. You'll want to get here early anyway to taste some of the house specialties (beef burgundy, trout amandine, and frogs' legs Provençal), which tend to sell out quickly. Check the chalkboard (which, depending on where you're seated, can be hard to see) for the salads and soups all prepared to order. Even a simple hearts-of-palm salad becomes a gourmet treat under the tangy vinaigrette. A well-rounded wine list with reasonable prices makes this place a standout and a great deal. The homemade daily pastries are also delicious.

Here Comes the Sun. 2188 NE 123rd St. (west of the Broad Causeway), North Miami. ☎ **305/893-5711.** Reservations recommended in season. Main courses $10–$14; early bird special 4–6:30pm, $7.95; sandwiches and salads $5–$7.50. AE, DC, DISC, MC, V. Mon–Sat 11am–8:30pm. AMERICAN/HEALTH FOOD.

One of Miami's early health-food spots, this bustling grocery-store-turned-diner serves hundreds of plates a night, mostly to blue-haired locals. It's noisy and hectic, but worth it. In season, all types pack the place for a $7.95 special, served between 4 and 6:30pm, which includes one of more than 20 choices of entrees, soup or salad, coffee or tea, and a small frozen yogurt. Fresh grilled fish and chicken entrees are reliable and served with a nice array of vegetables. The miso burgers with "sun sauce" are a vegetarian's dream.

SOUTH MIAMI

This mostly residential area has a few good dining spots and every possible chain restaurant you can imagine, most scattered along U.S. 1. The fast-food Cuban chain, Pollo Tropical (see above), is a good quick stop if you are heading to one of South Miami's attractions. One of the old favorites that must be mentioned is listed below.

Shorty's. 9200 S. Dixie Hwy. (between U.S. 1 and Dadeland Blvd.), South Miami. ☎ **305/670-7732.** Main courses $5–$9. MC, V. Daily 11am–11pm (later on weekends). BARBECUE.

A tradition in Miami since 1951, this hokey log cabin is still serving some of the best ribs and chicken in South Florida. People line up for the smoky slow-cooked meat, so tender it wants to jump off the bone into your mouth. The secret, however, is to ask for your order with sweet sauce—the regular stuff tastes bland and bottled. All the side dishes, including coleslaw, corn on the cob, and baked beans, look commercial, but you really need to try them to complete the experience. This is barbecue with a neon *B*.

A second Shorty's is located in Davie at 5989 S. University Dr. (☎ 305/944-0348).

The Tea Room. 12310 SW 224th St. (at Cauley Square), South Miami. ☎ **305/258-0044.** Sandwiches and salads $6–$7; soups $3–$4. AE, MC, V. Mon–Sat 11am–4pm. ENGLISH TEA.

Do stop in for a spot of tea at this recently rebuilt tea room in historic Cauley Square off of U.S. 1. The little lace-curtained room is an unusual site in this heavily industrial area better known for its warehouses than its doilies. Sample some simple sandwiches like the turkey club with potato salad and a small lettuce garnish or an onion soup that is full of rich brown broth and stringy cheese. Daily specials, like spinach-and-mushroom quiche, and delectable desserts are a must before beginning your explorations of the old antique and art shops in this little enclave of civility down south.

What to See & Do in Miami 5

by Victoria Pesce Elliott

More and more visitors are coming to Miami each year—around 10 million in 1997—to get a taste of the incredibly diverse offerings scattered throughout this sprawling metropolis.

Unlike the theme-park landscape of Central Florida, Miami is more attractive for its natural resources than for its mega-entertainment complexes. Head for the treasures that nature put here, like the sea and sand, or check out the places that locals built for their own enjoyment, like Villa Vizcaya or Coral Castle. And definitely sample the Caribbean cuisine that dominates the area's menus.

But don't discount the human-made attractions altogether. The city was, and is still, designed to court visitors (and their dollars) from around the world, and many of these efforts make for fantastic entertainment. Some of the city's older animal attractions, for example, like Monkey Jungle, Parrot Jungle, and the Seaquarium, make for great diversions and are popular with locals and visitors alike. With professional hockey, baseball, football, and basketball teams based here, you are sure to find a game to watch. In addition, you'll find a new wave of world-class exhibitions, theater, dance, a plethora of sports- and water-related activities, the country's largest cruise-ship port, incredible shopping, and an unbelievably varied and wild nightlife, especially in hip South Beach.

1 Beaches

There are more than 35 miles of beachfront in Miami-Dade County; most is open to the public. The character of each of Miami's many beaches is as varied as the city's population. Some are shaded by towering palm trees, while others are darkened by the shadows of formidable condominium complexes. Some attract families or old-timers; some, an active singles scene; while still others are crowded with topless Europeans and models. In short, there are two distinct beach alternatives: Miami Beach and Key Biscayne. It's all explained below. You can bring picnics, but no alcohol or glass bottles, to most beaches. Most beaches also forbid dogs. Have fun, but also be sure to check warning signs posted at beaches to avoid powerful rip currents and rough seas.

MIAMI BEACH   This long barrier island, which includes the much-photographed South Beach area at its tip has something for everyone.

Collins Avenue and Ocean Drive front nearly a dozen miles of gray-sand beach and blue-green waters from 1st to 192nd streets. Although most of this stretch is lined with a solid wall of hotels and condos, beach access is plentiful, and you're free to frolic along the entire strip. Granted, finding a parking spot can be a challenge. There are lots of amenities on the public beaches here, including lifeguards, toilet facilities, concession stands, and metered parking (bring lots of quarters). Miami Beach's beaches are generally wide and well maintained. Except for a thin strip close to the water, most of the sand here is hard-packed, the result of a $10 million Army Corps of Engineers Beach Rebuilding Project meant to protect buildings from the effects of eroding sand.

You'll find the beaches on this barrier island become less crowded the farther north you go. A wooden boardwalk runs along the hotel side of the beach from 21st to 47th streets (about 1½ miles), offering a terrific sun-and-surf experience without getting sand in your shoes. Aside from the "Best Beaches" listed below, Miami Beach's lifeguard-protected public beaches include Lummus Park, between 6th and 14th streets, where whimsical lifeguard stands don't look like anything you've ever seen on *Baywatch*. Instead, you'll see stands in the shape of a bed, a rocket ship, a Japanese Shinto-style temple, and other fanciful shapes. Lifeguard stands are located at the following streets: 1, 3, 6, 8, 10, 12, 13, 14, 17, 21, 29, 35, 46, 53, 64, 72, 74, 79, 81, and 83. Also for safe swimming (usually no undertow or breaking waves), try 21st Street, at the beginning of the boardwalk; 35th Street, popular with an older crowd; 46th Street, near the popular Jimmy Johnson's Sports Bar in the Eden Roc Hotel and the Fontainebleau Hilton; 53rd Street, a narrower, more sedate beach; 64th Street, one of the quietest strips around; and 72nd Street, a local old-timers' spot.

KEY BISCAYNE If Miami Beach isn't private enough for you, Key Biscayne might be what you have in mind. Crossing Rickenbacker Causeway ($1 toll) is almost like crossing into The Bahamas. The 5 miles of public beach here (especially at the island's tip) are blessed with softer sand and are less developed and more laid-back than the hotel-laden strips to the north.

THE BEST BEACHES

Here are my picks for the best beaches for the following activities and audiences:

- **Best Surfing Beach:** Just north of Miami Beach at about 108th Street, **Haulover Beach/Harbor House** seems to get Miami's biggest swells. Go early and avoid the rush of young locals who wish they were on Maui.
- **Best Party Beach:** On Key Biscayne, **Crandon Park Beach,** on Crandon Boulevard, has 3 miles of oceanfront beach, 493 acres of park, 75 grills, three parking lots, several soccer and softball fields, and a public 18-hole championship golf course. The beach is particularly wide and the water is usually so clear you can see to the bottom. Admission is $2 per vehicle. It's open daily from 8am to sunset.
- **Best People Watching:** The ultra-chic **Lummus Park Beach,** which runs along Ocean Drive from about 6th to 14th streets in South Beach, is the best place to go if you're seeking entertainment as well as a great tan. On any day of the week you might spy models primping for a photo shoot or topless sunbathers wearing sunglasses larger than their bikini bottoms.
- **Best Swimming Beach:** The **85th Street Beach,** along Collins Avenue, is the best place to swim away from the crowds. It's one of Miami's only stretches of sand with no condos or hotels looming over sunbathers. A shady green park with a fitness track and a small playground offers a refuge from the sun. Lifeguards patrol the area throughout the day.

In case you want to see the world.

At American Express, we're here to make your journey a smooth one. So we have over 1,700 travel service locations in over 120 countries ready to help. What else would you expect from the world's largest travel agency?

do more

Travel

http://www.americanexpress.com/travel

In case you want to be welcomed there.

We're here to see that you're always welcomed at establishments everywhere. That's why millions of people carry the American Express® Card—for peace of mind, confidence, and security, around the world or just around the corner.

do more ®

Cards

In case you're running low.

We're here to help with more than 118,000 Express Cash

locations around the world. In order to enroll, just call

American Express before you start your vacation.

do more

Express Cash

And just in case.

We're here with American Express® Travelers Cheques and Cheques *for Two*.® They're the safest way to carry money on your vacation and the surest way to get a refund, practically anywhere, anytime.

Another way we help you...

do more

Travelers Cheques

- **Best Shell-Hunting Beach:** You'll find plenty of colorful shells at **Bal Harbour Beach,** Collins Avenue at 96th Street, just a few yards north of Surfside Beach. There's also an exercise course and good shade, but no lifeguards.
- **Best All-Around Tanning Beach:** Although the state has been trying to pass ordinances to outlaw nudity, there is a small secluded beach in the **southern portion of Haulover Beach,** just north of the Bal Harbour border at about 106th Street, which attracts nudists from around the world and has created something of a boom for area businesses that cater to them.

2 The Art Deco District

Located in South Beach, the Art Deco District is a whole community made up of outrageous and fanciful 1920s and 1930s architecture. The Art Deco District is roughly bounded by the Atlantic Ocean on the east, Alton Road on the west, 6th Street on the South, and Dade Boulevard (along the Collins Canal) on the north. This approximately 1-square-mile area is listed on the National Register of Historic Places. Most of the finest examples of this whimsical style are concentrated along three parallel streets—Ocean Drive, Collins Avenue, and Washington Avenue—from about 6th to 23rd streets.

After years of neglect and calls for the wholesale demolition of its buildings, South Beach got a new lease on life in 1979. Under the leadership of Barbara Baer Capitman, a dedicated crusader for the art deco region and the Miami Design Preservation League, an area made up of an estimated 800 buildings, was granted a listing on the National Register of Historic Places.

Long-lost architectural details were highlighted with soft sherbets of peach, periwinkle, turquoise, and purple. Developers soon moved in, and the full-scale refurbishment of the area's hotels was under way.

Today, dozens of new hotels, restaurants, and nightclubs are undergoing renovation, and South Beach is on the cutting edge of Miami's cultural and nightlife scene.

If you're exploring on your own, start at the **Art Deco Welcome Center,** 1001 Ocean Dr. (☎ **305/531-3484**), which has several informative giveaways, including maps and art deco architecture information. Art deco books (including an informative compendium, *The Art Deco Guide,* of all buildings here), T-shirts, postcards, mugs, and other similarly styled items are sold. It's open Monday to Saturday from 9am to 6pm, sometimes later.

Among the highlights to seek out are the **Essex House,** 1001 Collins Ave., at 10th Street, an excellent example of nautical moderne, complete with porthole windows and sleek "racing stripes" along its sides. Along Ocean Drive, between 6th and 8th streets there's the **Park Central** and the **Imperial, Majestic,** and **Colony hotels.** At 1020 Ocean Dr., the **Clevelander Hotel** is one of the few in the area with an original swimming pool and a deco-style sundeck area that now hosts a popular bar scene (see "Miami After Dark," below.)

Other particularly memorable areas for strolling include **Lincoln Road**, which is lined with galleries, cafes, and funky art and antique stores. The **Community Church,** at the corner of Lincoln Road and Drexel Avenue, is the neighborhood's first church and, built in 1921, one of the oldest surviving buildings.

Also on Lincoln Road, 1 block east of Washington Avenue, you'll find the **Albion Hotel,** a spectacular building in streamline moderne style that dates from 1939; it just underwent a $10 million renovation. Just around the corner on Collins Avenue, **The Delano** is the hottest hotel in town. Although most of the original 1947 details disappeared with the overhaul in 1995, the outrageous new decor and old exterior are worth checking out (see "Where to Stay," in chapter 4).

For informative walking and biking tours of the area, see "Sightseeing Cruises & Organized Tours," below.

3 Animal Parks

Kids of all ages will enjoy Miami's animal parks, which feature everything from dolphins to lions to parrots to alligators. And what's a trip to Florida without seeing a gator?

✪ **Miami Metrozoo.** SW 152nd St. and SW 124th Ave. ☎ **305/251-0403.** Admission $8 adults, $4 children 3–12. Daily 9:30am–5:30pm (ticket booth closes at 4pm). From U.S. 1 south, turn right on SW 152nd St. and follow signs about 3 miles to the entrance.

It's about a 35 minute drive from the beaches to this huge 290-acre complex which is completely cageless—animals are kept at bay by cleverly designed moats. Especially if you are with children, it's worth it. Mufasa and Simba (of Disney fame) were modeled on Metrozoo's lions, still in residence. Plus, there are two rare white Bengal tigers, a Komodo dragon, rare koala bears, a monorail "safari," and a petting zoo. You can even ride an elephant.

✪ **Miami Seaquarium.** 4400 Rickenbacker Causeway (south side), Key Biscayne. ☎ **305/361-5705.** Admission $18.95 adults, $13.95 seniors over 55, $16.95 children 3–9. Daily 9:30am–6pm (ticket booth closes at 4:30pm). I-95 south to the Rickenbacker Causeway.

You'll want to arrive early to experience all of this fun and educational attraction. It takes about 4 hours to tour the 35-acre oceanarium and see all four daily shows starring the world's most impressive ocean mammals. Trained dolphins, killer whales, and frolicking sea lions play with trainers and visitors. If you want, you can even volunteer for one of their big wet fishy kisses!

Monkey Jungle. 14805 SW 216th St., South Miami. ☎ **305/235-4253.** Admission $11.50 adults, $9.50 seniors and active-duty military, $6 children 4–12. Daily 9:30am–5pm (tickets sold until 4pm). Take U.S. 1 south to SW 216th St. or from Florida Turnpike Exit 11.

See rare Brazilian golden lion tamarins. Watch the "skin-diving" Asian macaques. Yes, it's primate paradise! There are no cages to restrain the antics of the monkeys as they swing, chatter, and play their way into your heart. Screened-in trails wind through acres of "jungle," and daily shows feature the talents of the park's most progressive pupils. You've got to love primates to get over the heavy smell of the jungle; it's been here for more than 60 years.

Parrot Jungle and Gardens. 11000 SW 57th Ave., South Miami-Dade County. ☎ **305/666-7834.** Admission $12.95 adults, $11.95 seniors, $8.95 children 3–10. Daily 9:30am–6pm. Cafe opens at 8am. Take U.S. 1 south, turn left at SW 57th Ave. or exit Kendall Dr. from Turnpike and turn right on U.S. 1.

It's loud and it's silly, but fun. Not just parrots, but hundreds of magnificent macaws, peacocks, cockatoos, and flamingos occupy this 22-acre park. Continuous shows in the Parrot Bowl Theater star roller-skating cockatoos, card-playing macaws, and more stunt-happy parrots than you ever thought possible. Alligators, tortoises, and iguanas are also on exhibit. Other attractions include a wildlife show focusing on indigenous Florida animals, an area called "Primate Experience," a children's playground, and a petting zoo.

Parrot Jungle, which has been at this location for more than 50 years, is planning to move to its own island midway between downtown Miami and the beaches; the move is scheduled for 1999.

Attractions in South Miami–Dade County

Coral Castle **7**
Fairchild Tropical Gardens **2**
Miami Metrozoo **4**
Monkey Jungle **5**
Parrot Jungle **1**
Preston B. Bird and Mary Heinlein
    Fruit and Spice Park **6**
Week's Air Museum **3**

4 Miami's Museum & Art Scene

Miami's museum scene has always been quirky, interesting, and inconsistent at best. Though several exhibition spaces have made forays into collecting nationally acclaimed work, limited support and political infighting have made it a difficult proposition. Recently, with the reinvention of the Wolfsonian, the reincarnation of MOCA, and the increased daringness of the Miami Art Museum, the scene has improved dramatically. It's now safe to say that world-class exhibitions start here. Listed below is an excellent cross section of the valuable treasures that have become a part of the city's cultural heritage, and as such, are as diverse as the city itself.

For gallery lovers, see "Organized Tours," below, for scheduled gallery walks, and "Shopping" for a highlight of a few of the best.

IN SOUTH BEACH

Bass Museum of Art. 2121 Park Ave. (just west of Collins Ave.), South Beach. ☎ **305/ 673-7530.** Admission $5 adults, $3 students with ID and senior citizens, free for children 6 and under; second and fourth Wed of the month by donation from 5–9pm. Tues–Sat 10am–5pm, Sun 1–5pm (every second and fourth Wed open 1–9pm). Closed major holidays.

An important and growing visual arts museum in Miami Beach, Bass displays European paintings, sculptures, and tapestries from the Renaissance, baroque, rococo, and modern periods as part of their small permanent collection. Temporary exhibitions alternate between traveling shows and rotations of the Bass's stock, with themes ranging from 17th-century Dutch art to contemporary architecture.

Built from coral rock in 1930, the Bass sits in the middle of six tree-topped, landscaped acres. Wander the grounds to enjoy the changing outdoor sculpture exhibits before the heavy construction starts—a 12-acre expansion is due to be completed in 1998.

The Wolfsonian. 1001 Washington Ave., South Beach. ☎ **305/531-1001.** Admission $5 adults; $3.50 senior citizens, students, and children 6–12; $5 tour-group members; free Thurs eve. Children under 6 and members free. Tues–Sat 11am–6pm, Sun noon–5pm, and Thurs 6–9pm.

Mitchell Wolfson, Jr., an eccentric collector of late 19th- and 20th-century art and other paraphernalia, was spending so much money storing his booty he decided to buy the warehouse that held the more than 70,000 items, including glass, ceramics, sculptures, paintings, and photographs. Now this incredibly diverse and controversial collection is on display, in the former storage facility retrofitted with such painstaking detail that it's the envy of curators around the world. In 1997, he gifted the collection to a local college, so the future of the exhibitions remains in question.

Holocaust Memorial. 1933 Meridian Ave. (at Dade Blvd.), South Beach. ☎ **305/538-1663.** Free admission. Daily 9am–9pm.

This heart-wrenching memorial of the genocide that took place in 1940s Europe is hard to miss and would be a shame to overlook. The powerful centerpiece is a bronze statue by Kenneth Treister that depicts millions of people crawling into an open hand to freedom. You can walk through an open hallway lined with photographs and the names of concentration camps and their victims. From the street, you'll see the outstretched arm, but do stop and tour the sculpture at ground level. What's hidden behind the beautiful stone facade is extremely moving.

IN & NEAR DOWNTOWN

The Cuban Museum of the Americas. 1300 SW 12th Ave., Little Havana. ☎ **305/858-8006.** Donations, $3 adults, $1 students and children. Tues–Fri noon–6pm and weekends by appointment. Closed major holidays. Hours vary drastically. Call first.

This politically charged museum created by Cuban exiles has been open on and off since 1974. They display all mediums from ceramics to photography and sculpture to painting by artists throughout Latin and South America. Exhibits change frequently. Call for details.

Florida Museum of Hispanic and Latin American Art. 4006 Aurora St. (between Bird Rd. and Ponce de León Blvd.) ☎ **305/444-7060.** Free admission. Tues–Fri 11am–5pm, Sat 11am–4pm. Closed Aug and major holidays.

In addition to the permanent collection of contemporary artists from Spain and Latin America, this museum, with more than 3,500 square feet, hosts monthly exhibitions of works from Latin America and the Caribbean Basin. Usually the group shows focus on a theme, such as international women or surrealism. It's not a major attraction, but for art lovers it is worth a stop. On the same block, you will find a few other Latin American galleries.

Miami Art Museum at the Miami-Dade Cultural Center. 101 W. Flagler St., Miami. ☎ **305/375-1700** or 305/375-3000. Admission $5 adults, $2.50 senior citizens and students with ID, free for children 11 and under, Tues is contribution day. Tues–Wed and Fri 10am–5pm; Thurs 10am–9pm; Sat–Sun noon–5pm. Closed major holidays. From I-95 south, exit at Orange Bowl–NW 8th St. and continue south to NW 2nd St.; turn left at NW 2nd St. and go 1½ blocks to NW 2nd Ave., turn right, and park at the Metro-Dade Garage. Bring the parking ticket to the lobby for validation.

The recently renamed Miami Art Museum (it was called the Center for the Fine Arts until 1996) features an eclectic mix of modern and contemporary works by such artists as Eric Fischl, Max Beckman, Jim Dine, and Stuart Davis. Rotating exhibitions span the ages and styles and often focus on Latin American or Caribbean artists. The shows are almost always superbly curated and installed, and sometimes subject to controversy from the ultra-political Cuban community.

The Miami-Dade Cultural Center, where the museum is housed, is an oasis for those seeking cultural enrichment during their trip to Miami. In addition to the world-acclaimed Miami Art Museum, the center houses the main branch of the Miami-Dade Public Library, which sometimes features art and cultural exhibits, and the Historical Museum of Southern Florida, which highlights the fascinating history of Florida and, in particular, the state's southern region.

Weeks Air Museum. 14710 SW 28th St. (at the Kendall-Tamiami Airport west of the Turnpike and south of 120th St.), Miami. ☎ **305/233-5197.** www.weeksairmuseum.com. Admission $6.95 adults, $5.95 seniors, $4.95 children under 12. Daily 10am–5pm.

This well-maintained museum is a must-see for aeronautic buffs who will delight in hanging out with the thoroughly dedicated staff are eager to answer questions from fellow enthusiasts. Exhibitions include a dramatic portrait of the Tuskegee Airmen who tell of their experiences on video. Also on display are dozens of airplanes dating from the turn of the century and an intriguing display of planes damaged by hurricane Andrew in 1992. Other highlights include a collection of propellers throughout the ages; a J47 jet engine; an aerobatic plane, the "Little Stinker" Soviet bombers, and lots of war memorabilia.

American Police Hall of Fame and Museum. 3801 Biscayne Blvd., Miami. ☎ **305/573-0070.** Admission $6 adults, $4 seniors over 61, $3 children 11 and under, free for police officers worldwide. 50% off coupons often available from hotel racks. Daily 10am–5:30pm. Drive north on U.S. 1 from downtown until you see the building with the real police car affixed to its side.

This strange museum appeals mostly to those fascinated with police and their gadgetry. Inside the block building from which protrudes a police car is a combination of reality and fantasy that's part thoughtful tribute, part Hollywood-style drama. Just past the car featured in the motion picture *Blade Runner* is a mock prison cell, in which visitors can take pictures of themselves pretending they're doing 5 to 10. Also displayed are execution devices, including a guillotine and an electric chair. In the entry is a touching memorial to the more than 3,000 police officers who have lost their lives in the line of duty.

The Rubell Family Collection. Call for address, just north of Miami Design Center, downtown Miami. ☎ **305/573-6090.** Open by appointment only, Fri.-Sat., 11am–5pm.

Part of the Rubell Family Collection is open for art lovers or students only by appointment. More than a hundred works are displayed in a dilapidated warehouse that was once used by the Drug Enforcement Agency. The pieces, many of which are too big or too daring for your average museum, reveal the Rubell's taste for the strange, humorous, and irreverent. Included in this diverse and shocking menagerie are works by some of the most well known artists of the last half century: Keith Haring, Jean-Michel Basquiat, Charles Ray, Cindy Sherman, Paul McCarthy and Beverly Semme. If you don't know these names, or are traveling with kids, skip this stop.

Miami Area Attractions & Beaches

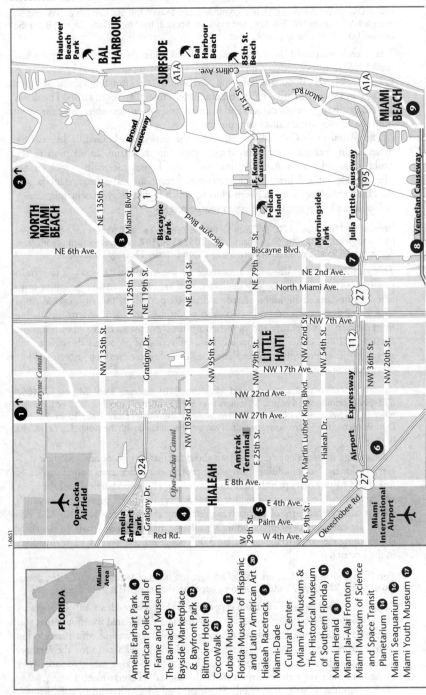

Amelia Earhart Park ④
American Police Hall of
  Fame and Museum ⑦
The Barnacle ㉒
Bayside Marketplace
  & Bayfront Park ⑫
Biltmore Hotel ⑱
CocoWalk ㉓
Cuban Museum ⑬
Florida Museum of Hispanic
  and Latin American Art ⑳
Hialeah Racetrack ⑤
Miami-Dade
  Cultural Center
  (Miami Art Museum &
  The Historical Museum
  of Southern Florida) ⑪
Miami Herald ⑧
Miami Jai-Alai Fronton ⑥
Miami Museum of Science
  and Space Transit
  Planetarium ⑭
Miami Seaquarium ⑯
Miami Youth Museum ⑰

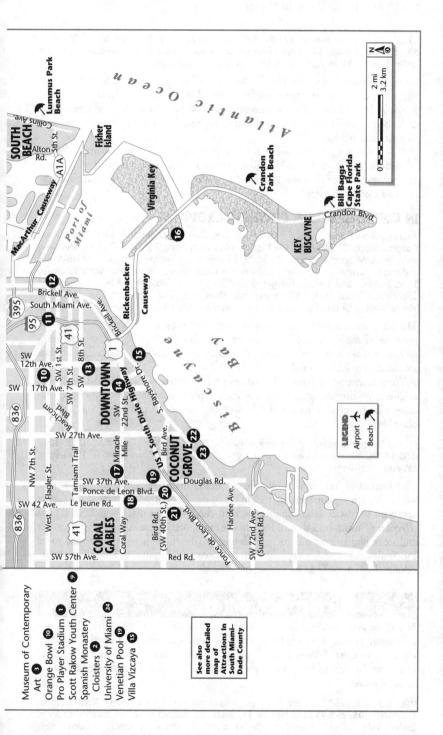

Museum of Contemporary Art **3**
Orange Bowl **10**
Pro Player Stadium **1**
Scott Rakow Youth Center **9**
Spanish Monastery Cloisters **2**
University of Miami **24**
Venetian Pool **19**
Villa Vizcaya **15**

See also more detailed map of Attractions in South Miami-Dade County

LEGEND
✈ Airport
⛱ Beach

N

2 mi
3.2 km
0

Atlantic Ocean

SOUTH BEACH
Lummus Park Beach
Collins Ave.
Alton Rd.
5th St.
A1A

Fisher Island

Virginia Key

16

Crandon Park Beach

Bill Baggs Cape Florida State Park
Crandon Blvd.

KEY BISCAYNE

MacArthur Causeway
Port of Miami

Rickenbacker Causeway

Brickell Ave.
South Miami Ave.
12

395
95
11
41

SW 12th Ave.
SW 17th Ave.
10
SW
SW

836

NW 7th St.
Flagler St.
SW 42 Ave.
West

Beacom Blvd.
SW 7th Ave.
SW 27th Ave.

SW 1st St.
SW 8th St.
13
Tamiami Trail
41

DOWNTOWN
14
SW 22nd St.

Brickell Ave.

1
15

Biscayne Bay

S. Bayshore Dr.

Miracle Mile
17
19
20
18

US 1 South Dixie Highway
Bird Ave.

COCONUT GROVE
22
23

CORAL GABLES
Ponce de Leon Blvd.
Le Jeune Rd.
Coral Way
Bird Rd. (SW 40th St.)
21
Red Rd.
SW 57th Ave.

Douglas Rd.
Hardee Ave.
Ponce de Leon Blvd.
SW 72nd Ave. (Sunset Rd.)

125

✪ **Museum of Contemporary Art (MOCA).** 770 NE 125th St., North Miami. ☎ **305/ 893-6211.** Admission $4 adults, $2 seniors and students with ID, free for children 12 and under. Tues–Sat 11am–5pm, Sun noon–5pm. Closed major holidays.

MOCA recently acquired a new 23,000-square-foot space in which to display its impressive collection of internationally acclaimed art with a local flavor. You can see works by Jasper Johns, Roy Lichtenstein, Larry Rivers, Duane Michaels, and Claes Oldenberg. Guided tours are offered in English, Spanish, French, Creole, Portuguese, German, and Italian.

A new screening facility allows for film presentations that will complement the exhibitions. Although the $3.75 million project was built in an area that otherwise is an uncharted tourist destination, MOCA is worth a drive to view important contemporary art in South Florida.

IN CORAL GABLES & COCONUT GROVE

Miami Museum of Science and Space Transit Planetarium. 3280 S. Miami Ave., Coconut Grove. ☎ **305/854-4247** for general information, 305/854-2222 for planetarium show times. Museum of Science $6 adults, $4 seniors and children 3–12, free for children 2 and under. Planetarium $5 adults, $2.50 children and seniors. Combination ticket $9 adults, $5.50 children and seniors. Twilight price 4:30–6pm weekdays is half-price. Museum of Science daily 10am–6pm; call for planetarium show times. Closed major holidays. Metrorail: Vizcaya station. Or take I-95 south to Exit 1 and follow the signs.

The Museum of Science features more than 140 hands-on exhibits that explore the mysteries of the universe. Live demonstrations and collections of rare natural history specimens make a visit here fun and informative. Two or three major traveling exhibits are usually on display as well.

The adjacent Space Transit Planetarium projects astronomy and laser shows as well as interactive demonstrations of upcoming computer technology and cyberspace features. Plan to spend at least 3 or 4 hours exploring the fascinating exhibits and displays here.

Miami Youth Museum. On Level B of Paseos, 3301 Coral Way, Coral Gables. ☎ **305/ 446-4-FUN.** Admission $4 anyone over 1 year old. Mon–Thurs 10am–5pm, Fri 10am–9pm, Sat–Sun 11am–6pm.

This interactive "museum" is more like a theater than a museum, since it's a place where kids can explore their interests in the "grown-up world." If you're in the Gables and want to placate (and educate) the kids, check out this place, which has a great selection of hands-on exhibits, including a minigrocery store complete with cashier and stock boy assignments for role-playing. Maybe the kids want to pretend to be Dr. Smiles, the dentist, or publish their own newspaper from the "Hot off the Press" exhibit. Tours are offered in English and Spanish.

5 Fantastic Feats of Architecture

Not all the great buildings in Miami are in South Beach's Art Deco District. You'll also find many exciting enclaves filled with Mediterranean gems and eclectic wonders, especially in Coral Gables. Even if you aren't staying there, check out the Biltmore Hotel (see "Where to Stay," in chapter 4) and the stunning Congregational Church across the street.

Villa Vizcaya. 3251 S. Miami Ave. (just south of Rickenbacker Causeway), North Coconut Grove. ☎ **305/250-9133.** Admission $10 adults, $5 children 6–12, free for children 5 and under. Villa daily 9:30am–5pm (ticket booth closes at 4:30pm); gardens daily 9:30am–5:30pm. Closed Christmas. Take I-95 south to Exit 1 and follow the signs.

Sometimes referred to as the "Hearst Castle of the East," this magnificent villa is the setting for many society weddings and galas. It was built in 1916 as a winter retreat for James Deering, co-founder and former vice president of International Harvester. The industrialist was fascinated by 16th-century art and architecture, and his ornate mansion, which took 1,000 artisans 5 years to build, became a celebration of these designs. Most of the original furnishings, including dishes and paintings, are still intact.

The spectacularly opulent villa wraps itself around a central courtyard. Outside, lush formal gardens, accented with statuary, balustrades, and decorative urns, front an enormous swath of Biscayne Bay, neighboring the homes of Sylvester Stallone and Madonna.

The Barnacle State Historic Site. 3485 Main Hwy. (1 block south of Commodore Plaza), Coconut Grove. ☎ **305/448-9445.** Admission $1. Tours Fri–Sun at 10am, 11:30am, 1pm, and 2:30pm from the main house porch. Group tours Mon–Thurs with 2-week advance reservation. From downtown Miami, take U.S. 1 south to 27th Ave., make a left turn, and continue to S. Bayshore Dr., where you make a right, follow it to the intersection of Main Hwy., and turn left.

The former home of naval architect and early settler Ralph Middleton Munroe is now a museum in the heart of Coconut Grove. The house's quiet surroundings, wide porches, and period furnishings illustrate how Miami's privileged class lived in the days before skyscrapers and luxury hotels. Enthusiastic and knowledgeable state park employees offer a wealth of historical information to those interested in quiet, low-tech attractions like this one.

✪ **Coral Castle.** 28655 S. Dixie Hwy., Homestead. ☎ **305/248-6344.** Admission $7.75 adults, $6.50 seniors, $5 children 7–12. Daily 9am–6pm. Closed Christmas. Take U.S. 1 south to SW 286th St.

There's plenty of competition, but Coral Castle is probably the strangest attraction in Florida. In 1923, the story goes, a crazed Latvian, suffering from unrequited love, immigrated to South Miami and spent the next 25 years of his life carving huge boulders into a prehistoric-looking, roofless "castle." It seems impossible that one rather short man could have done all this, but there are scores of affidavits on display from neighbors who swear it happened. Apparently experts have studied this phenomenon to help figure out how the Great Pyramids and Stonehenge were built.

Listen to the audio tour to learn about this bizarre spot, now on the National Register of Historic Places. The commentary lasts about 25 minutes and is available in four languages. Although Coral Castle is a bit overpriced and undermaintained, it is worth a visit when in the area.

Spanish Monastery Cloisters. 16711 W. Dixie Hwy. (at NE 167th St.), North Miami Beach. ☎ **305/945-1461.** Admission $4.50 adults, $2.50 seniors, $1 children 11 and under. Mon–Sat 10am–4pm, Sun noon–4pm.

Did you know that the oldest building in the western hemisphere dates from A.D. 1141 and is located in Miami? The Spanish Monastery Cloisters were first erected in Segovia, Spain, and centuries later, newspaper magnate William Randolph Hearst purchased and brought the Cloisters to America in pieces. The carefully numbered stones were quarantined for years until they were finally reassembled on the present site in 1954. Visitors are free to explore; you'll want to spend about an hour touring the cold, ancient structure, the beautiful grounds, and the gift shop.

✪ **Venetian Pool.** 2701 DeSoto Blvd. (at Toledo St.), Coral Gables. ☎ **305/460-5356.** Admission $5 adults, $4 teens, $2 children 3–12 and under (children under 36 months not allowed in the water). June–Aug, Mon–Fri 11am–7:30pm, Sat–Sun 10am–4:30pm; Apr–May and Sept–Oct Tues–Fri 11am–5:30pm, Sat–Sun 10am–4:30pm; Nov–Mar Tues–Fri 10am–4:30pm, Sat–Sun 10am–4:30pm.

Miami's most beautiful and unusual swimming pool, dating from 1924, is hidden behind pastel stucco walls and is honored with a listing on the National Register of Historic Places. Underground artesian wells feed the free-form lagoon, which is shaded by three-story Spanish porticos and features both fountains and waterfalls. It can be cold in the winter months. During summer, the pool's 800,000 gallons of water are drained and refilled nightly, ensuring a cool, clean swim. Visitors are free to swim and sunbathe here, just as Esther Williams and Johnny Weissmuller did decades ago. For a modest fee, you or your children can learn to swim during special summer programs.

6 Nature Preserves, Parks & Gardens

The Miami area is a great place for outdoors-minded visitors, with beaches, parks, and gardens galore. Plus, South Florida is the country's only area with two national parks; see chapter 7 for coverage of the Everglades and Biscayne National Park.

BOTANICAL GARDENS & A SPICE PARK

In Miami, the **Fairchild Tropical Gardens,** 10901 Old Cutler Rd. (☎ 305/ 667-1651), features a veritable rain forest of both rare and exotic plants on 83 acres. Palmettos, vine pergola, palm glades, and other unique species create a scenic, lush environment. It's well worth taking the free hourly tram to learn what you always wanted to know about the various flowers and trees on a 30-minute narrated tour.

Admission is $8 for adults, free for children 12 and under accompanied by an adult. Open daily from 9:30am to 5pm. Take I-95 south to U.S. 1, turn left onto Le Jeune Road, and follow it straight to the traffic circle; there, take Old Cutler Road 2 miles to the park.

A testament to Miami's unusual climate, the **Preston B. Bird and Mary Heinlein Fruit and Spice Park,** 24801 SW 187th Ave., Homestead (☎ 305/247-5727), harbors rare fruit trees that cannot survive elsewhere in the country.

Definitely ask for a guide. If a volunteer is available, you'll learn some fascinating things about this 30-acre living plant museum where the most exotic varieties of fruits and spices, including ackee, mango, ugly fruits, carambola, and breadfruit, grow on strange-looking trees with unpronounceable names.

The best part? You're free to take anything that falls to the ground. You'll also find samples of interesting fruits and jellies made from the park's bounty in the gift store. Cooks who like to experiment must visit the park store, which carries exotic ingredients and cookbooks.

Admission to the spice park is $2 for adults and 50¢ for children under 12. Open daily from 10am to 5pm. Closed major holidays. Tours are $1.50 for adults and $1 for children on Saturday and Sunday at 1 and 3pm. Take U.S. 1 south, turn right on SW 248th Street, and go straight for 5 miles to SW 187th Avenue.

MORE MIAMI PARKS

Amelia Earhart Park, 401 E. 65th St., Hialeah (☎ 305/685-8389), has five lakes stocked with bass, and sunfish for fishing; playgrounds; picnic facilities; and a big red barn that houses cows, sheep, and goats for petting and ponies for riding. There's also a country store and dozens of old-time farm activities like horseshoeing, sugarcane processing, and more. On weekdays parking is free and on weekends $3.50 per car. Open daily from 9am to sunset. To drive here, take I-95 north to the NW 103rd Street exit, go west to East 4th Avenue, and then turn right. Parking is 1½ miles down the street.

At the very tip of Key Biscayne, the historic ✪ **Bill Baggs Cape Florida State Recreation Area,** 1200 Crandon Blvd. (☎ **305/361-5811**), features a recently reopened lighthouse. You can explore the unfettered wilds and enjoy some of the most secluded beaches in Miami. A rental shack rents bikes, hydrobikes, kayaks, and many more water toys. It's a great place to picnic, and a newly constructed restaurant serves homemade Latin food, including great fish soups and sandwiches. Just be careful that the raccoons don't get your lunch, because the furry black-eyed beasts are everywhere. Admission is $4 per car with up to eight people. Open daily from 8am to sunset. A tour of the recently renovated lighthouse, lightkeeper's quarters, and kitchen costs $1 to $2.

Tropical Park, 7900 SW 40th St. (☎ **305/226-0796**), has it all. Enjoy a game of tennis and racquetball for a minimal fee or swim and sun yourself on the secluded little lake. You can use the fishing pond for free, and they'll even supply you with the rods and bait. If you catch anything, however, you're on your own. Open daily from sunrise to sunset.

7 Especially for Kids

The Scott Rakow Youth Center, 2700 Sheridan Ave. (☎ **305/673-7767**), is a hidden treasure on Miami Beach. This two-story facility boasts an ice-skating rink, bowling alleys, a basketball court, gymnasium equipment, and full-time supervision for kids. Call for a complete schedule of organized events. The only drag is that it's not open to adults (except on Sunday). Admission is $1.50 per day for visiting children 9 to 17. Open daily from 2 to 8:30pm.

Following is a roundup of other attractions kids will especially enjoy. Details on each one can be found earlier in the chapter.

AMELIA EARHART PARK   This is the best park in Miami for kids. They'll like the petting zoos, pony rides, and a private island with hidden tunnels.

MIAMI METROZOO   This completely cageless zoo offers such star attractions as a monorail "safari" and a petting zoo. Kids love the elephant rides.

✪ **MIAMI MUSEUM OF SCIENCE AND SPACE TRANSIT PLANETARIUM** At the Planetarium, kids can learn about space and science by watching entertaining films and cosmic shows. The space museum also offers child-friendly explanations for natural occurrences.

✪ **MIAMI SEAQUARIUM**   Kids can get a kiss from a dolphin and watch exciting performances.

MIAMI YOUTH MUSEUM   Here children can dabble in fantasy land, playing at what they're interested in. It's one huge game of "what do you want to be when you grow up?"

8 Sightseeing Cruises & Organized Tours

Always call ahead to check prices and times. Reservations are usually suggested.

BOAT & CRUISE-SHIP TOURS

Gondola Adventures. Docked at Bayside Marina, at the Biscayne Market Place, 401 Biscayne Blvd., Miami. ☎ **305/358-6400.** Rates from $5 and up.

A real gondola in Miami? Well, it may not be the canals of Venice, but with a little imagination, the Bayside Marina will do. You can go on a simple ride around Bayside for $5, or splurge on your own private and cozy sunrise cruise to an island.

Heritage Miami II Topsail Schooner. Bayside Marketplace Marina, 401 Biscayne Blvd., downtown. ☎ **305/442-9697.** Tickets $12 adults, $7 children 12 and under. Sept–May only. The 2-hour tours leave daily at 1:30, 4, and 6:30pm, and on weekends also at 9, 10, and 11pm.

More adventure than tour, this relaxing ride aboard Miami's only tall ship is a fun way to see the city. The 2-hour cruises pass by Villa Vizcaya, Coconut Grove, and Key Biscayne and put you in sight of Miami's spectacular skyline. Call to make sure the ship is running on schedule.

Lady Lucille. 4441 Collins Ave. (docked across from the Fontainebleau Hotel), Miami Beach. ☎ **305/534-7000.** Tickets $15 adults, $6 children. The 3-hour cruise leaves daily at 11am and 2pm.

Set your sights and sails on Miami's human-made beauty: Millionaires' Row. You can cruise along Biscayne Bay and check out Gloria Estefan's or Fitipaldi's mansion all in the comfort of an air-conditioned 150-passenger boat, complete with snacks and two full bars.

AIR TOURS

Action Helicopter. 1901 Brickell Ave., B602, Miami. ☎ **305/358-4723.** Tickets $65 for 15 miles, $109 for 25 miles, $149 for 45 miles; $650 hourly rate for air taxi. Daily 9am–6pm. Helipad located at 950 MacArthur Causeway.

If you want to experience Miami from a bird's-eye view, try it from a helicopter. A short, exhilarating ride around the city and the beach will show you the Seaquarium, Bayside, and stars' homes from a decidedly different perspective.

Ultralight Adventures! 3401 Rickenbacker Causeway at the marina, Key Biscayne. ☎ **305/361-3909,** or 305/478-9055 for a pager. Tickets $65 for 20 minutes, $100 for an hour. Flights Wed–Sun 8am–6pm, weather permitting.

For the brave soul, there's an air tour over Miami and Key Biscayne on an ultralight. For those who've never seen it, an ultralight is a small open plane of sorts with a small motor. There's no better way to see all of Miami. Fun Flight does live up to its name and can even certify you to fly one of their planes and join their ranks.

SIGHTSEEING TOURS

Miami Nice Excursion, Inc., Travel and Service. 18430 Collins Ave., Miami Beach. ☎ **305/949-9180.** Admission $29–$55 adults, $25 children. Daily 7am–10pm. Call ahead for directions to various pickup areas.

Pick your destination. The Miami Nice tours will take you to the Everglades, Fort Lauderdale, the Seaquarium, Key West, Cape Canaveral, or even The Bahamas. Included in most Miami trips is a fairly comprehensive city tour narrated by knowledgeable guides. The company is one of the oldest in town.

SPECIALIZED TOURS

Miami Design Preservation League. The Art Deco Welcome Center, 1001 Ocean Dr., South Beach. ☎ **305/672-2014.** Walking tours $10 per person. Self-guided audio tours also available 7 days a week for $5. Call ahead for updated schedules.

On Thursday evenings and Saturday mornings the league sponsors walking tours that offer a fascinating inside look at the city's historic Art Deco District. Tour-goers meet for a 1½-hour walk through some of America's most exuberantly "architectured" buildings. The Design Preservation League led the fight to designate this area a National Historic District and is proud to share the splendid results with visitors on Saturday at 10:30am and on Thursday at 6:30pm.

Art Deco Cycling Tour. 601 5th St., South Beach. ☎ **305/674-0150.** $10 per person, plus another $5 if you rent a bike. Tours depart every other Sun at 10am from the Miami Beach Bicycle Center.

Since the bicycle seems to be the most efficient mode of transportation through the streets of South Beach, what better way to view the historic Art Deco District than perched on the seat of a bike? Call to reserve a spot. If you'd rather bike or in-line skate than walk around the area, catch this fun and interesting Sunday-morning tour.

Biltmore Hotel Tour. 1200 Anastasia Ave., Coral Gables. ☎ **305/445-1926.** Free admission. Tours depart Sun at 1:30, 2:30, and 3:30pm. Call to reserve.

Take advantage of these free walking tours offered on Sunday to enjoy the hotel's beautiful grounds. The Biltmore is chock-full of history and mystery, including a few ghosts; go out there and uncover it.

Coral Gables Art and Gallery Tour. Various locations in Coral Gables. Free. For more information, call Richard Arregui (☎ **305/447-3973**) or stop by any of the galleries in the area. First Fri of month 7am–10pm.

Vans shuttle art lovers to more than 20 galleries that participate in Gables Night in the gallery section of Coral Gables. Viewers can sip wine as they view American folk art; African, Native American, and Latin art; and photography. Most galleries are on Ponce de León Boulevard, between SW 40th and SW 24th streets. The vans run every 15 minutes from 7 to 10pm.

Lincoln Road Gallery Walk. On Lincoln Rd. between Washington Ave. and Alton Rd. ☎ **305/674-8278.** Free. Second Sat every month.

Though in a state of flux, the gallery walks, which were suspended for a while, have resumed and will show eager art lovers the vast and varied landscape of art on hip South Beach. Still, definitely call for updated schedules.

9 Water Sports

BOATING & SAILING   You can rent sailboats and catamarans through the beachfront concessions desk of several top resorts, such as the Doral Ocean Beach Resort, Sheraton Bal Harbour Beach Resort, and Dezerland Surfside Beach Hotel (see "Where to Stay," in chapter 4).

Private rental outfits include **Beach Boat Rentals,** 2400 Collins Ave., Miami Beach (☎ **305/534-4307**), where 50-horsepower, 18-foot powerboats rent for some of the best prices on the beach. Rates are $61.25 for an hour, $165.13 for 4 hours, and $225.70 for 8 hours. All rates include taxes and gas. A $250 cash or credit-card deposit is required. Cruising is exclusively in and around Biscayne Bay—ocean access is prohibited. Renters must be over 21. The rental office is at 23rd Street, on the inland waterway in Miami Beach, and it's open from 9am to 6pm (weather permitting) during the high season and 9am to 8pm during the summer.

Club Nautico of Coconut Grove, 2560 S. Bayshore Dr., Coconut Grove (☎ **305/858-6258**), rents high-quality powerboats for fishing, waterskiing, diving, and cruising in the bay or ocean. All boats are coast guard–equipped with VHF radios and safety gear. Rates range from $199 for 4 hours and $299 for 8 hours to as much as $419 on weekends. Club Nautico is open daily from 9am to 5pm (weather permitting). Other locations include the Crandon Park Marina, 4000 Crandon Blvd., Key Biscayne (☎ 305/361-9217), with the same rates as the Coconut Grove location; and the Miami Beach Marina, Pier E, 300 Alton Rd., South Beach (☎ 305/673-2502), where rates are $229 for 4 hours and $299 for 8 hours to rent a 20-foot boat. A 24-footer will run you $259 for half a day and $359 for a full day. Nautico on Miami Beach is open daily from 9am to 5pm.

If speedboats aren't your style, **Sailboats of Key Biscayne Rentals and Sailing School,** in the Crandon Marina (next to Sundays on the Bay), 4000 Crandon Blvd., Key Biscayne (☎ **305/361-0328** days, or 305/279-7424 evenings), offers a slightly more subdued ride. A 22-foot sailboat can be rented for $27 an hour, or $81 for a half day. A Cat-25 or J24 is available for $35 an hour or $110 for a half day. If you've always had a dream to win the America's Cup but can't sail, Sailboats will get you started. It offers a 10-hour course over 5 days for $250 for one person or $350 for you and a buddy; $50 for each additional person.

Shake a Leg, 2600 Bayshore Dr., Coconut Grove (☎ **305/858-5550**), is a unique sailing program for disabled and able-bodied people alike. The program pairs up sailors for day and evening cruises and offers sailing lessons as well. Consider a moonlight cruise (offered monthly) or a race clinic. Shake a Leg members also welcome able-bodied volunteers for activities on and off the water. It costs $60 for nonmembers to rent a boat for 3 hours; free for volunteers. Open on Wednesday through Sunday from 9am to 5pm.

JET-SKIS/WAVERUNNERS Many beachfront concessionaires rent a variety of these popular water scooters. The latest models are fast and smooth. Don't miss a chance to tour the islands on the back of your own little watercraft. Try **Tony's Jet Ski Rentals,** 3601 Rickenbacker Causeway, Key Biscayne (☎ **305/361-8280**), one of the city's largest rental shops, located on a private beach in the Miami Marine Stadium lagoon. Jet-skis rent for about $38 for a half hour and $64 for an hour. WaveRunners rent for $45 for a half hour and $70 for an hour. Tony's is open daily from 10:30am to 6:30pm.

KAYAKS The laid-back **Urban Trails Kayak Company** rents boats from 10800 Collins Ave., Haulover Park (☎ **305/947-1302**). It offers scenic routes through rivers with mangroves and islands as your destination. Most of the kayaks are sit-on-tops, which is what it sounds like. Most boats are plastic, though there are some fiberglass ones available, too. Rates are $8 an hour, $20 for up to 4 hours ($25 for over 4 hours). Tandems are $12 an hour, $30 for up to 4 hours, $35 for the day. Open daily from 9am to 5pm.

The outfitters give interested explorers a map to take with them and quick instructions on how to work the paddles and boats. If you want a guided tour, you'll need at least four people and will pay $35 per person for half a day. This is a fun way to experience some of Miami's unspoiled wildlife, including the mangrove forests of Uleta Park, and it is good exercise, too.

SCUBA DIVING In 1981 the U.S. government began a wide-scale project designed to increase the number of habitats available to marine organisms. One of the program's major accomplishments has been the creation of nearby artificial reefs, which have attracted all kinds of tropical plants, fish, and animals. In addition, Biscayne National Park (see chapter 7) offers a protected marine environment just south of downtown.

Several dive shops around the city offer organized weekend outings, either to the reefs or to one of more than a dozen old shipwrecks around Miami's shores. Check "Divers" in the Yellow Pages for rental equipment and for a full list of undersea tour operators.

Divers Paradise of Key Biscayne, 4000 Crandon Blvd. (☎ **305/361-3483**), offers two dive expeditions daily to the more than 30 wrecks and artificial reefs off the coast of Miami Beach and Key Biscayne. Take a 3-day certification course for $399, which includes all the dives and gear. If you already have your C-card, a dive trip costs about $90 for those with no equipment and only $35 if you show up with your own gear.

It's open Monday to Friday from 10am to 6pm and Saturday and Sunday from 8am to 6pm. Call ahead for times and locations of dives. This is the best way to see Miami.

WINDSURFING   Many hotels rent Windsurfers to their guests. But if yours doesn't have a water-sports concession stand, head for Key Biscayne, the area's best spot for windsurfing.

Sailboards Miami, Rickenbacker Causeway, Key Biscayne (☎ **305/361-SAIL**), operates out of big yellow trucks on Hobie Beach, the most popular windsurfing spot in the city. For those who've never ridden a board but want to try their hand at it, for $39 Sailboards Miami offers a 2-hour lesson that's guaranteed to turn you into a wave warrior or you get your money back. After that, you can rent a windsurf board for $20 an hour, or $37 for 2 hours. If you want to make a day of it, a 10-hour card costs $130. Open daily from 10am to 5:30pm. Make your first right after the toll booth to find the outfitters.

10 More Places to Play, Both Indoors & Out

BIKING & SCOOTERS   The cement promenade on the southern tip of the island is a great place to ride. Biking up the beach is great for surf, sun, sand, exercise, and people-watching. You may not want to subject your bicycle to the salt and sand, but there are plenty of oceanfront rental places here. Most of the big beach hotels rent bicycles, as does the **Miami Beach Bicycle Center,** 601 5th St., South Beach (☎ **305/674-0150**). This shop rents bicycles for $5 per hour or $14 per day. It's open Monday to Saturday from 10am to 7pm and Sunday from 10am to 5pm.

Bikers can also enjoy more than 130 miles of paved paths throughout Miami. The beautiful and quiet streets of Coral Gables and Coconut Grove beg for the attention of bicyclists. Old trees form canopies over wide, flat roads lined with grand homes and quaint street markers. Several bicycle trails are spread throughout these neighborhoods.

In Key Biscayne the terrain is perfect for biking, especially along the park and beach roads. If you don't mind the sound of cars whooshing by, Rickenbacker Causeway is also fantastic since it is one of the only bikeable inclines in Miami from which you get fantastic elevated views of the city and waterways.

Key Cycling, 61 Harbor Dr., Key Biscayne (☎ **305/361-0061**), rents mountain bikes for $5 an hour or $15 for the day. They're open Monday through Friday from 10am to 7pm, Saturday from 10am to 6pm, and Sunday from 11am to 4pm.

If you want to avoid the traffic altogether, head out to **Shark Valley** in the Everglades National Park, one of South Florida's most scenic bicycle trails and a favorite haunt of city-weary locals. See chapter 7 for more details.

FISHING   Bridge fishing is popular in Miami; you'll see people with poles over most every waterway.

Some of the best surf casting in the city can be had at Haulover Beach Park, at Collins Avenue and 105th Street, where there's a bait-and-tackle shop right on the pier. South Pointe Park, at the southern tip of Miami Beach, is another popular fishing spot and features a long pier, comfortable benches, and a great view of the ships passing through Government Cut.

You can also choose to do some deep-sea fishing. One bargain outfitter, the **Kelley Fishing Fleet,** at the Haulover Marina, 10800 Collins Ave. (at 108th Street), Miami Beach (☎ **305/945-3801**), has half-day, full-day, and night fishing aboard diesel-powered "party boats." The fleet's emphasis on drifting is geared toward trolling and bottom fishing for snapper, sailfish, and mackerel; but it also schedules 2- and 3-day trips to The Bahamas. Half-day and night fishing trips are $21 for adults and $14.50

for children; full-day trips are $33 for adults and $26.50 for children; rod and reel rental is $5. Daily departures are scheduled at 9am, 1:45pm, and 8pm; reservations are recommended.

Also at the **Haulover Marina** is the charter boat *Helen C,* 10800 Collins Ave., Haulover (☎ **305/947-4081**). Although there's no shortage of private charter boats here, Capt. Dawn Mergelsberg is a good pick, since she puts individuals together to get a full boat. Her *Helen C* is a twin-engine 55-footer, equipped for big-game "monster" fish like marlin, tuna, dolphin, shark, and sailfish. The cost is $70 per person, and sailings are scheduled for 8am to noon and 1 to 5pm daily; call for reservations. Private charters and transportation are also available. Children are welcome.

Key Biscayne offers deep-sea fishing to those willing to get their hands dirty and pay a lot. The competition among the boats is fierce, but the prices are basically the same no matter which boat you choose. The going rate is about $400 to $450 for a half day and $600 to $700 for a full day of fishing. These rates are usually for a party of up to six, and the boats supply you with rods and bait as well as instruction for first-timers. Some will take you out to Key Biscayne and even out to the Upper Keys if the fish aren't biting in Miami.

You might consider the following boats, all of which sail out of the Key Biscayne marina; call for reservations: *Sunny Boy III* (☎ **305/361-2217**); *Queen B* (☎ **305/361-2528**); and *L&H* (☎ **305/361-9318**).

GAMBLING Although it is technically illegal to gamble in Miami, plenty of loopholes allow for casinos off-shore, bingo, dominoes, jai alai, card rooms, horse races, and dog races.

Especially popular is the huge outpost west of Miami, **Miccosukee Indian Gaming,** 500 SW 177th Ave. (☎ **800/741-4600** or 305/222-4600). This glitzy casino isn't Vegas, but you can play slots, all kinds of bingo, and even poker (with a $10 maximum pot).

One of many gambling "cruises to nowhere" is the **Sea Kruz.** It departs daily and most evenings from 1280 5th St., South Beach (☎ **800/688-PLAY** or 305/538-8300). Tickets are $15 . For an extra $5 on the lunch cruise there's an all-you-can-eat soup-and-salad bar, and for an additional $9 on the dinner cruise there's an all-you-can-eat dinner with a carving station. The food isn't gourmet, but there is plenty of it. Throw in a little dancing to a live band and the trip is complete. Ask for free chips or discount coupons, usually offered for the asking.

Casino Miami (☎ **305/577-7775**) sails every day but Monday and most evenings from the Dupont Plaza Hotel in downtown Miami. Admission is usually the same as Sea Kruz ($15), but this boat is slightly newer and the crowd a little more subdued.

Dominoes is also popular here and is played at **Flagler Dog Track,** 401 NW 38th Ct. (☎ **305/649-3000**) and at **Miami Jai Alai Fronton** (see below). Poker rooms are also available here.

GOLF There are more than 50 private and public golf courses in the Greater Miami area. Contact the **Greater Miami Convention and Visitors Bureau** (☎ **800/283-2707** or 305/539-3063) for a complete list of courses and costs. Some of the area's best and most expensive are at the big resorts, many of which allow nonguests to play—the Doral Blue Course at the Doral Resort and Spa in West Miami; Don Shula's Hotel and Golf Club also in West Miami; and the Biltmore in Coral Gables. See "Where to Stay," in chapter 4, for more details.

Otherwise, the following represent some of the area's best public courses. ✪ **Crandon Park Golf Course,** formerly known as The Links, 6700 Crandon Blvd., Key Biscayne (☎ **305/361-9129**), is the number one–ranked municipal course in the state and one of the top five in the country. The park is situated on 200 bay-front acres and offers a pro shop, rentals, lessons, carts, and a lighted driving range. The course is open daily from dawn to dusk; greens fees (including cart) are $86 per person during the winter and $45 per person during the summer. Special twilight rates available.

Known as one of the best in Miami, the **Golf Club of Miami,** 6801 Miami Gardens Dr., at NW 68th Avenue (☎ 305/829-8456), has three 18-hole courses of varying degrees of difficulty. You'll encounter lush fairways, rolling greens, and some history. The west course, designed in 1961 by Robert Trent Jones and updated in the 1990s by the PGA, was where Jack Nicklaus played his first professional tournament and Lee Trevino won his first professional championship. The course is open daily from 6:30am to sunset. Cart and greens fees are $45 to $75 per person during the winter, $20 to $34 per person during the summer. Special twilight rates are available.

Amateurs practicing their game or golfers on a budget looking for some cheap practice time will appreciate **Haulover Park,** 10800 Collins Ave., Miami Beach (☎ 305/940-6719). The longest hole on this par-27 course is 125 yards in a pretty bay-side location. The course is open daily from 7:30am to 5:30pm during the winter, until 7:30pm during the summer. Greens fees are $5 per person during the winter, $4 per person during the summer. Hand carts cost $1.40.

HEALTH CLUBS Although many of Miami's full-service hotels have fitness centers, you can't count on them in less upscale establishments or in the small Art Deco District hotels. Several health clubs around the city will take in nonmembers on a daily basis. If you're already a member at the mega-health club chain **Bally's Total Fitness,** dial ☎ 800/777-1117 to find the clubs in the area. There are no outlets on the beaches; most are in South Miami.

There are many other clubs that welcome walk-in guests, including **Crunch Fitness,** 1253 Washington Ave., South Beach (☎ 305/674-8222), where you might work out with Cindy Crawford, Madonna, or any of a number of supermodels when they're in town. Trendy Club Body Tech offers star appeal and top-of-the-line equipment. Use of the facility is $16 daily or $149 monthly with discounts for guests of most area hotels. Open Monday to Friday from 6am to midnight, Saturday from 8am to 9pm, and Sunday from 9am to 8pm.

IN-LINE SKATING Miami's consistently flat terrain should make in-line skating easy. The heavy traffic and construction however, make it tough to find long routes. Remember to keep a pair of sandals or sneakers with you since many area shops won't allow you inside with skates on. The following rental outfits can help chart an interesting course for you and provide you with all the necessary gear.

In Coral Gables, **Extreme Skate & Sport,** 7876 SW 40th St. (☎ 305/261-6699), is one of South Florida's largest in-line skate dealers. Even if you know nothing about this trendy new sport, a knowledgeable sales staff and a large selection to choose from ensure that you can't go wrong.

In South Beach, **Fritz's Skate Shop,** 726 Lincoln Rd. Mall (☎ 305/532-1954), rents top-quality skates, including safety pads, for $7.50 per hour, $22.50 per day, and $14 overnight. If you're an in-line skate virgin, an instructor will hold your hand for $25 an hour. The shop also stocks lots of gear and clothing.

Also in South Beach, **Skate 2000,** at 1200 Ocean Dr. (☎ 305/538-8282) and 650 Lincoln Rd. (☎ 305/538-9491), will help you keep up with the beach crowd by renting in-line skates and safety accessories. Rates are $8 an hour and $24 a day plus $100 deposit, credit card or cash. Skate 2000 also offers free lessons by a certified instructor on South Beach's boardwalk every Sunday at 10am. You can either rent or bring your own skates.

SWIMMING There is no shortage of water here, including the vast and mild Atlantic Ocean. See "Best Beaches" and also the Venetian Pool under "Fantastic Feats of Architecture," above, for descriptions of good swimming options.

TENNIS Hundreds of tennis courts in South Florida are open to the public for a minimal fee. Most courts operate on a first-come, first-served basis, and most are open from sunrise to sunset. For information and directions to the one nearest where you're staying, call one of these government offices: the **City of Miami Beach Recreation, Culture, and Parks Department** (☎ 305/673-7730); or the **City of Miami Parks and Recreation Department** (☎ 305/575-5256).

The three hard courts and seven clay courts at the **Key Biscayne Tennis Association at the Links,** located at 6702 Crandon Blvd. (☎ 305/361-5263), get crowded on weekends since they're some of Miami's most beautiful courts. You'll play on the same courts as Lendl, Graf, Evert, McEnroe, and other greats; this the venue for one of the world's biggest annual tennis events, the Lipton Championship (see "Florida Calendar of Events," in chapter 2). There's a pleasant, if limited, pro shop, plus many good pros. Only four courts are lit at night, but if you reserve at least 48 hours in advance, you can usually take your pick. It costs $4 to $5 per person per hour. The courts are open daily from 8am to 9pm.

11 Spectator Sports

Check the *Miami Herald*'s sports section for a daily listing of local events and the paper's Friday "Weekend" section for comprehensive coverage and in-depth reports. For last-minute tickets, call the stadium directly since many season ticket holders sell singles and return unused tickets. Expensive tickets are available from brokers or individuals, listed in the classified sections of the local papers. Some tickets are also available through **Ticketmaster** (☎ 305/358-5885 or 305/350-5050).

BASEBALL Especially since winning the World Series in 1997, the young Florida Marlins have been attracting a loyal following. For the time being home games are at the **Pro Player Stadium,** 2267 NW 199th St., North Miami Beach (☎ 305/626-7426). The team currently holds spring training in Melbourne, Florida. Tickets are $4 to $30. Box office hours are Monday to Friday from 8:30am to 6pm, Saturday from 8:30am to 4pm, and prior to games; tickets are also available through Ticketmaster.

BASKETBALL The Miami Heat, now coached by celebrity Pat Riley, made its NBA debut in November 1988. Predictably, it's also one of Miami's hottest tickets. The season of approximately 41 home games lasts from November to April, with most games beginning at 7:30pm at the **Miami Arena,** 721 NW 1st Ave. (☎ 305/577-HEAT). Plans are in the works to build a new arena on the waterfront. Tickets are $14 to $44. Box office hours are Monday to Friday from 10am to 4pm (until 8pm on game nights); tickets are also available through Ticketmaster (see above for phone number).

FOOTBALL Miami's golden boys are the Miami Dolphins, the city's most recognizable team, followed by thousands of "dolfans." Coached by Jimmy Johnson, the team plays at least eight home games during the season, between September and December, at the **Pro Player Stadium,** 2267 NW 199th St., North Miami Beach (☎ 305/626-7426 or 305/623-6100). Tickets cost about $30 and are predictably tough to come by. The box office is open Monday to Friday from 10am to 6pm; tickets are also available through **Ticketmaster** (see above for phone number).

HORSE RACING Wrapped around an artificial lake, **Gulfstream Park,** at U.S. 1 and Hallandale Beach Boulevard, Hallandale (☎ 305/931-7223), is both pretty and popular. Large purses and important races are commonplace at this suburban course, and the track is often crowded. Call for schedules. Admission is $3 to the grandstand, $3 to the clubhouse. Free parking. January 3 to March 15, post times are Wednesday to Monday at 1pm.

You've seen the pink flamingos at **Hialeah Park,** 2200 E. 4th Ave., Hialeah (☎ **305/885-8000**), on Miami Vice, and indeed, this famous colony is the largest of its kind. This track, listed on the National Register of Historic Places, is one of the most beautiful in the world, featuring old-fashioned stands and acres of immaculately manicured grounds. Admission is $1 to the grandstand and $2 to the clubhouse weekdays; and weekends $2 and $4, respectively. Children 17 and under enter free with an adult. Parking starts at $2. Races are held mid-March to mid-May, but the course is open year-round for sightseeing Monday to Saturday from 9am to 5pm. Call for post times.

ICE HOCKEY   The young **Florida Panthers** (☎ **954/768-1900**) have already made history. In the 1994–95 season they won the Eastern Championships and played in the Stanley Cup finals. And the fans love them—most home games sell out. Even if you don't have tickets in hand yet, there is still a chance to see them skate, so long as you don't mind sitting in the nosebleed section. Just before each game, approximately 900 tickets go on sale for $12, and many scalpers hang out in the area. For now, games are played at the **Miami Arena,** 721 NW 1st Ave. in downtown Miami (☎ **305/530-4400**). Miami Arena box office hours are Monday to Friday from 10am. Games are now played in Sunrise at the new 19,000-seat **Broward County Arena,** 2555 NW 137th Way (off Rt. 595 North). Tickets are also available through Ticketmaster.

JAI ALAI   Sort of a Spanish-style indoor lacrosse, jai alai was introduced to Miami in 1924 and is regularly played in two Miami-area frontons (arenas). Although the sport has roots stemming from ancient Egypt, the game as it's now played was invented by Basque peasants in the Pyrenees mountains during the 17th century.

Players use woven baskets, called cestas, to hurl balls, pelotas, at speeds that sometimes exceed 170 miles per hour. Spectators, who are protected behind a wall of glass, place bets on the evening's players.

The **Miami Jai Alai Fronton,** 3500 NW 37th Ave., at NW 35th Street (☎ 305/633-6400), is America's oldest jai alai fronton, dating from 1926. It schedules 13 games per night. Admission is $1 to the grandstand, $5 to the clubhouse. It's open year-round. There are games Monday and Wednesday to Saturday at 7pm, with matinees on Monday, Wednesday, and Saturday at noon. A second area fronton is located in nearby Dania (see chapter 8).

12 Shopping

A mecca for hard-core shoppers from Latin America, the Caribbean, and the rest of the state, Miami has everything you could ever want and things you never dreamed of. This shopping capital has strip malls, boutiques, and enclosed malls in every conceivable nook and cranny of the city, which makes for lots of competition among retailers and good bargains for those who like to hunt.

THE SHOPPING SCENE
THE MALLS

The **Aventura Mall,** 19501 Biscayne Blvd. (☎ **305/935-4222**), is an enclosed mall with more than 200 shops, a varied food court, an enormous Bloomingdale's and a Macy's. The high-end **Bal Harbour Shops,** 9700 Collins Ave. (☎ **305/866-0311**), has the big names: Bvlgari, Chanel, Hermès, Versace, Tiffany & Co., Neiman Marcus, Polo/Ralph Lauren, Saks Fifth Avenue, Fendi, Rodier, Gucci, Brooks Brothers, Cartier, Tourneau, and a well-dressed shopping crowd. The **Bayside Marketplace,** 401 Biscayne Blvd., downtown (☎ **305/577-3344**), consists of 16 beautiful waterfront acres along Biscayne Bay with lively and exciting shops and carts selling everything from plastic fruit to high-tech electronics. The **Dadeland Mall,** 7535 N. Kendall Dr., Kendall (☎ **305/665-6226**), is the granddaddy of Miami's suburban mall scene, featuring more than 175 specialty shops, anchored by five large department stores. **The Falls,** 8888 Howard Dr., Kendall area (☎ **305/255-4570**), is an outdoor shopping center set among tropical waterfalls, with dozens of upscale shops, including Bloomingdale's. The newly renovated **Streets of Mayfair,** 2911 Grand Ave., Coconut Grove (☎ **305/448-1700**), is a small open-air complex, just across the street from Cocowalk, with several top-quality shops, restaurants, art galleries, and nightclubs. Finally, **Sawgrass Mills,** 12801 W. Sunrise Blvd., Sunrise (☎ **954/846-2300**), which is actually located in Broward County, west of Ft. Lauderdale, is a phenomenon worth mentioning—it's a behemoth with more than 270 shops and kiosks in nearly 2½ million square feet covering 50 acres (see "Shopping & Browsing," in chapter 8, for more details). Call **Classic Lines Bus Service** (☎ **800/533-7755** or 305/887-6223) to ride to the mall for only $10 round-trip. Buses depart daily from locations at the beach and downtown.

GREAT SHOPPING AREAS

COCONUT GROVE   Downtown Coconut Grove is one of Miami's few pedestrian-friendly zones. Centered on Main Highway and Grand Avenue and branching onto the adjoining streets, the Grove's wide, cafe- and boutique-lined sidewalks provide hours of browsing pleasure. Look for dozens of avant-garde clothing stores, funky import shops, and excellent sidewalk cafes.

CORAL GABLES/MIRACLE MILE   Actually only half a mile, this central shopping street was an integral part of George Merrick's original city plan. Today the strip still enjoys popularity for its old-fashioned ladies' shops, haberdashers, bridal stores, shoe stores, and gift shops. Lined primarily with small 1970s storefronts, the Miracle Mile, which terminates at the Mediterranean-style City Hall rotunda, also features several good and unusual restaurants and is worth a stop on your tour of Coral Gables.

✪ SOUTH BEACH/LINCOLN ROAD   This luxurious pedestrian mall recently underwent a multimillion-dollar renovation that added new lighting, more than 500 palm trees, and necessary repairs to the infrastructure. Here shoppers can find an array of clothing and art and a collection of South Beach's finest restaurants. Enjoy an afternoon of gallery hopping and be sure to look into the open studios of the Miami City Ballet. Monthly gallery tours, periodic jazz concerts, and a weekly farmer's market are just a few of the offerings on "The Road."

DOWNTOWN MIAMI   This is the place for discounts on all types of goods—from watches and jewelry to luggage and leather. But watch out for a handful of unscrupulous businesses trying to rip you off. Look around Flagler Street and Miami Avenue for all kinds of cluttered bargain stores. Most of the signs around here are printed in both English and Spanish, for the benefit of locals and tourists alike.

HOURS & TAXES

Most stores around the city maintain shopping hours Monday to Saturday from 10am to 6pm and Sunday from noon to 5pm. Many stay open late (usually until 9pm) one night of the week (usually Thursday). Shops in trendy Coconut Grove are open until

9pm Sunday through Thursday and even later on Friday and Saturday nights. Department stores and shopping malls keep longer hours, staying open from 10am to 9 or 10pm Monday to Saturday and noon to 6pm on Sunday.

The 6.5% state and local sales tax is added to the price of all nonfood purchases.

SHOPPING A TO Z
ART & ANTIQUES

The best hunting grounds are scattered in small pockets around Miami. Some of these areas are located in North Miami, along West Dixie Highway.

Several top galleries have moved into trendy Lincoln Road on South Beach. But the majority of the art and antique dealers are in Coral Gables, mostly along Ponce de León Boulevard, extending from U.S. 1 to Bird Road. See "Sightseeing Cruises & Organized Tours," above, for details on walking tours of these areas. Or pick up the *Coral Gable's Gallery Guide* at the Greater Miami Visitor's Bureau, the Coral Gables Chamber of Commerce, or any of the more than 20 galleries in the area. One of the largest is the **Engman Gallery,** at 2111 Ponce de León Blvd., across from the Hotel Place St. Michel, near Alcazar Avenue (☎ **305/445-5125**).

Also, many funky galleries are sprouting up in and around NE 40th Street in downtown's Design District.

BEACHWEAR/SURFING GEAR

As you'd expect, there's a plethora of beachwear stores in Miami. However, if you want to get away from the cookie-cutter styles available at any local mall and in the resort areas, here are a few notable stores that will surely make you stand out while you're basking on the beach or out giving the waves a workout.

Alice's Day Off. 5900 SW 72nd St., South Miami. ☎ **305/284-0301.**

Alice's comes out season after season with pretty and flattering patterns. If an itsy-bitsy bikini is not your style, Alice's has a range of more modest cuts that won't make you look like one of the local retirees.

Bird's Surf Shop. 250 Sunny Isles Blvd., North Miami Beach. ☎ **305/940-0929.**

If you're a hard-core surfer, head to Bird's Surf Shop. Although Miami doesn't regularly get huge swells, if you're here during the winter and one should happen to hit, you'll be ready. The shop carries more than 150 boards.

Call their surf line (☎ 305/947-7170) before going out, to find the best conditions, from South Beach to Cape Hatteras and even The Bahamas and Florida's west coast.

Up Wind Watersports. 238 Biscayne Blvd., downtown Miami. ☎ **305/374-5321.**

This pleasant spot across the street from Bayside is run by a young set of very helpful water fanatics who cater to surfers. If they haven't got it, they will find it. From a full selection of sunglasses and wet suits to boards and bikinis.

X-Isle Surf Shop. 437 Washington Ave., South Beach. ☎ **305/534-7873.**

Prices are slightly high at this beach location, but the young staff is knowledgeable.

BOOKS

Books & Books. 933 Lincoln Rd., South Beach. ☎ **305/532-3222,** and 296 Aragon Ave., Coral Gables (☎ 305/442-4408).

Need a good beach book? How about the latest art or photo collection? An obscure biography? The history of the Deco District? Stop in for a wide selection of trash or culture and check out the schedule of free readings. There's an active cafe filled with buff bookworms inside and on the sidewalk of the South Beach store. Dial ☎ 305/444-POEM to hear a new poem every day.

Borders Book Stop. 2905 S. Dixie Hwy., Kendall. ☎ **305/665-8800.**

Although all three Borders (see below) have cafes on the premises, only the Coconut Grove and North Miami Beach locations have extensive music sections. You can browse through your selection while eating a bagel at the cafe and listening to the live music Borders offers to its customers. Borders also schedules lots of readings, discussions, and other events. Call for schedules.

Other locations in Miami include Borders Books and Music Cafe at 19925 Biscayne Blvd., North Miami Beach (☎ 305/935-0027), and 3390 Mary St., Coconut Grove (☎ 305/447-1655).

Cuba Art and Books. 2317 Le Jeune Rd., Coral Gables. ☎ **305/567-1640.**

This shop specializes in old Cuban books about that island nation and some prints and paintings by Cuban artists. Most titles are in Spanish and focus on art and politics.

Grove Antiquarian. 3318 Virginia St., Coconut Grove. ☎ **305/444-5362.**

One of very few out-of-print bookstores in Miami, the Grove Antiquarian specializes in Florida and the Caribbean, but also boasts a large selection of out-of-print cookbooks, sci-fi, and first editions.

Kafka's Used Book Store. 1460 Washington Ave., South Beach. ☎ **305/673-9669.**

This stunning wood-and-glass corner shop is well organized and well stocked. There is a little bit of everything here all at very reasonable prices.

CIGARS/SMOKE SHOPS

Although it's illegal to bring Cuban cigars into this country, somehow Cohibas show up at every dinner party and nightclub in town. Not that I condone it, but if you hang around the cigar smokers in town, no doubt one will be able to tell you where you can get some of the highly prized contraband. Be careful, however, of counterfeits.

Some of the following stores sell excellent hand-rolled cigars made with domestic and foreign-grown tobacco, as well. Many of the *viejos* (old men) got their training in Cuba working for the government-owned factories in the heyday of Cuban cigars.

Ba-balú. 500 Española Way (at Drexel Ave.), South Beach. ☎ **305/538-0679.**

Including an extensive collection of Cuban memorabilia from pre-1959 Cuba, Ba-balú offers a taste of Cuba, selling not only their hand-rolled cigars (they do about a thousand a week) but also T-shirts, baseball caps, Cuban coins, bills, postcards, stamps, and coffee. Enjoy live bongo music nightly and ask Herbie Sosa, the owner, for a free shot of Cuban coffee.

La Gloria Cubana. 1106 SW 8th St., Little Havana. ☎ **305/858-4162.**

This tiny storefront shop employs about 45 veteran Cuban rollers who sit all day rolling the very popular torpedoes and other critically acclaimed blends. They've got back orders until next Christmas, but it's worth stopping in. They will sell you a box and show you around.

Mike's Cigars. 1030 Kane Concourse (at 96th St.), Bay Harbor Island. ☎ **305/866-2277.**

Recently moved to this location, Mike's is perhaps one of the oldest in Miami. Since 1950 Mike's has been selling the best of Honduras, the Dominican Republic, and

Jamaica as well as the very hot local brand, La Gloria Cubana. Most say they've got the best prices, too.

South Beach News and Tobacco. 1710 Washington Ave., South Beach. ☎ **305/ 673-3002.**

A walk-in humidor stocks cigars from the Dominican Republic, Honduras, and Jamaica, and a hand-roller comes in as he pleases to roll for the tourists. You'll also find a large selection of wines, coffees, and cigar paraphernalia in this pleasant little shop.

ELECTRONICS

Many people travel to Miami from South America and other parts of the world to buy playthings and gadgets. Although there are many electronics stores around, a trip to downtown Miami is both amazing and overwhelming when you're shopping around for a good Walkman or television. The streets of downtown are littered with bargain electronics stores. Bargain! But beware—make sure any equipment comes with a warranty. It would be wise to charge instead of paying cash.

Sound Advice. 1220 SW 88th St., Kendall. ☎ **305/273-1225.**

An audio junkie's candy store, Sound Advice features the latest in high-end stereo equipment, as well as TVs, VCRs, and telephone equipment. Techno-minded, but sometimes pushy salespeople, are on hand to educate.

Other locations in Miami include 17641 Biscayne Blvd. (☎ 305/933-4434), and 1222 S. Dixie Hwy., Coral Gables (☎ 305/665-4434).

FASHIONS FOR MEN, WOMEN & CHILDREN

In addition to the many clothing stores in the malls and shopping areas listed above, more than 100 retail outlets are clustered in Miami's mile-square Fashion District just north of downtown. Surrounding Fashion Avenue (NW 5th Avenue) and known primarily for swimwear, sportswear, children's clothing, and glittery women's dresses, Miami's fashion center is second in size only to New York's. The district features European- and Latin-influenced designs with tropical hues and subdued pastels. Most stores offer medium-quality clothing at a 25% to 70% discount, as well as on-site alterations. Most stores are open only weekdays from 9am to 5:30pm. Another discount favorite is **Loehmann's** at 18703 Biscayne Blvd. (Fashion Island), North Miami Beach (☎ **305/932-4207**). If you don't mind fighting other zealous shoppers and communal dressing rooms, you'll find some great deals here on everything from bathing suits to evening wear.

In addition to the many designer shops in Bal Harbour, you'll find that other boutiques are scattered throughout town especially on trendy South Beach's Lincoln Road and around 8th Street. The best shoe stores are in Coconut Grove around Cocowalk and Mayfair.

FRUIT BASKETS

There was a time when it seemed as though almost every other store was shipping fruit home for tourists. Today such stores are a dying breed. Some, like **Todd's Fruit Shippers** (☎ 305/448-5215), still send the best quality fruit anywhere in the country. Boxes are sold by the bushel or fractions thereof and start at about $20. You can order by phone only. Ask for their catalog.

GOURMET GROCERS

There are a number of ethnic grocery stores in and around Miami. You can find Indian selections at **Bombay Bazaar,** 2008 NE 164th St., North Miami Beach

(☎ 305/ 948-7258), Caribbean at **Kingston Miami Trading Company,** 280 NE 2nd St., downtown (☎ **305/372-9547**), and Italian at **Laurenzo's Italian Supermarket and Farmer's Market,** 16385 and 16445 W. Dixie Hwy., North Miami Beach (☎ **305/945-6381** or 305/944-5052). Many Cuban, Nicaraguan, and Peruvian outposts are also in the area. Check the phone book for those in your neighborhood. And check out these gourmet markets listed below for a variety of food specialties.

Epicure. 1656 Alton Rd., South Beach. ☎ **305/672-1861.**

There's not only fancy produce, like portobello mushrooms the size of a yarmulke, but pineapples, cherries, and salad greens like you can't imagine. You can get all the usual prepared foods as well, including great chicken soup and smoked fish at this landmark Jewish deli and gourmet shop combined into one.

Gardner's Market. 7301 Red Rd., South Miami. ☎ **305/271-3211.**

This place is a tradition in South Miami, with anything a gourmet or novice cook could desire—the freshest and best from fish to cheese.

Scotty's Grocery. 3117 Bird Ave., Coconut Grove. ☎ **305/443-5257.** A vast selection of wines, fresh fish, meats, and superb prepared goods, Scotty's will tempt any food lover. From racks of fresh endive to fantastic salads, you will find it all here.

GOLF

Alf's Golf Shop. 524 Arthur Godfrey Rd., Miami Beach. ☎ **305/673-6568.**

The best pro shop on the beach, Alf's can sell you balls, clubs, gloves, and instructional videos—plus, the neighboring golf course offers discounts to Alf's clients.

Another Miami location is 15369 S. Dixie Hwy., Miami (☎ 305/378-6086).

Edwin Watts Golf Shops. 15100 N. Biscayne Blvd., North Miami Beach. ☎ **305/ 944-2925.**

This full-service golf retail shop has it all, including clothing, pro-line equipment, gloves, bags, balls, videos, and books. Ask the pros for advice, and ask for coupons for discounted greens fees for various courses.

Nevada Bob's. 7930 NW 36th St., at NW 79th Ave., Miami (near the airport). ☎ **305/ 593-2999.**

With more than 6,000 square feet of store, this place has everything for golfers—discounted Greg Norman and Antigua clothing, pro-line equipment, steel-shafted conventional clubs and high-tech Yonex clubs. Practice your swing at an indoor driving range with a radar gun. No commission salespeople here—they're a laid-back crew and very up on the latest of soft and hard equipment.

JAMES BOND GADGETS

Spy Shops International, Inc. 280 NE 4th St. (at Biscayne Blvd.), downtown. ☎ **305/374-4779.**

Where else could you find electronic surveillance equipment, day and night optical devices, stun guns, minisafes, doorknob alarms, and other anticrime gadgets?

JEWELRY

The International Jeweler's Exchange. 18861 Biscayne Blvd. (in the Fashion Island), North Miami Beach. ☎ **305/931-7032.**

At least 50 jewelers hustle their wares from individual counters at one of the city's most active jewelry centers. Haggle your brains out for excellent prices on timeless antiques from Tiffany's, Cartier, or Bulgari, or unique designs you can create yourself. Closed Sunday and early on Friday.

The Seybold Building. 36 NE 1st St., downtown. ☎ **305/377-0122.**

Jewelers of every assortment gather here daily to sell their diamonds and gold. The glare is blinding as you enter this multilevel retail marketplace. You'll see handsome and up-to-date designs, but there aren't too many bargains to be had here.

MUSIC

Blue Note Records. 16401 NE 15th Ave., North Miami Beach. ☎ **305/940-3394.**

New and used and discounted CDs and old vinyl, too—this place has hard-to-find progressive and underground music and a good bunch of music aficionados who can tell you a thing or two.

They are also in the midst of opening a new Blue Note Jazz Cafe, offering live shows and coffee.

Casino Records, Inc. 1208 SW 8th St., Little Havana. ☎ **305/856-6888.**

Here you'll find the largest selection of Latin music in Miami, including pop icons like Willy Chirino, Gloria Estefan, Albita, and local boy Nil Lara. Its slogan translates as "If we don't have it, forget it." Believe me, they've got it.

CD Warehouse. 13150 Biscayne Blvd., North Miami. ☎ **305/892-1048.**

Buy, sell, or trade your old CDs at this eclectic music hut.

Specs Music. 501 Collins Ave., South Beach. ☎ **305/534-3667.**

Call to find out who is playing at this mega-music mall. In addition to a great collection of multicultural sounds, you'll find a lively scene most weekends. Also, there is a coffee bar with donuts and pastries and live performances. There's another store at 1655 Washington Ave. (532-6455)

SEAFOOD

Miami's most famous restaurant is **Joe's Stone Crab,** 227 Biscayne St., South Beach (☎ **800/780-CRAB** or 305/673-0365). Joe's makes overnight air shipments of stone crabs to anywhere in the country from October to May. It will cost you.

East Coast Fisheries. 330 W. Flagler St., downtown. ☎ **305/577-3000.**

This retail market and restaurant has shipped millions of pounds of seafood worldwide from its own fishing fleet. It's equipped to wrap and send 5- or 10-pound packages of stone crab claws, Florida lobsters, Florida Bay pompano, fresh Key West shrimp, and a variety of other local delicacies to your door via overnight mail.

13 Miami After Dark

Miami's nightlife is as varied as its population. On any night, you'll find world-class opera or dance as well as grinding rock and seductive salsa. Restaurants and bars are open late, and many clubs, especially on South Beach, stay open past dawn.

For up-to-date entertainment listings, check the *Miami Herald*'s "Weekend" section, which runs on Friday, or the comprehensive *New Times,* Miami's free alternative weekly. Available in red boxes around the city each Wednesday, this award-winning paper prints articles, previews, and advertisements on upcoming local events.

Tickets for most performances can be purchased by phone through **Ticketmaster** (☎ **305/358-5885** or 305/350-5050). The company accepts all major credit and charge cards and has phone lines open 24 hours daily. If you want to pick up your tickets from a Ticketmaster outlet, call for the location nearest you. Outlets are open Monday to Saturday from 10am to 9pm and Sunday from noon to 5pm. There's a service charge for each ticket.

For sold-out events, you're at the mercy of ticket brokers who charge a premium, especially for big-name concerts. One well-known broker is **Ultimate Travel & Entertainment,** 3001 Salzedo St., Coral Gables (☎ **305/444-8499**). It's open Monday to Friday from 9am to 6pm and Saturday from 10am to 4pm.

THE PERFORMING ARTS
THEATER

Miami has an active and varied selection of dramas and musicals throughout the year. Thanks to the support of many loyal theater aficionados, season subscriptions are common and allow the theaters to survive. Some traveling Broadway shows make it to town, as do revivals. In South Beach, many are shown at the **Jackie Gleason Theater of the Performing Arts,** 1700 Washington Ave. (☎ **305/673-7300**), or the **Colony Theater** on Lincoln Road (☎ **305/674-1026**).

Some theaters are dark in the summer or show a limited schedule. Call the following especially recommendable venues to see what's coming up.

The **Actors' Playhouse,** at the newly restored Miracle Mile Theater in Coral Gables (☎ **305/444-9293**), is a grand 1948 art deco movie palace with a 600-seat main theater as well as a smaller theater/rehearsal hall.

The **Coconut Grove Playhouse,** 3500 Main Hwy. in Coconut Grove (☎ **305/442-4000**), was also a former movie house, built in 1927 in an ornate Spanish rococo style. Today this respected venue is known for its original and innovative staging. The more intimate Encore Room is well suited to alternative and experimental productions.

The **Florida Shakespeare Theatre,** at the Biltmore Hotel, on Anastasia Avenue in Coral Gables (☎ **305/446-1116**), stages at least one Shakespeare play, one classic, and one contemporary piece a year. In addition, this well-regarded theater usually tries to get the rights to a national or local premiere. Tickets cost $20 and $22, $12 and $17 for students and seniors.

New Theater, 65 Almeria Ave., Coral Gables (☎ **305/443-5909**), prides itself on showing world-renowned works from America and Europe. As the name implies, you'll find mostly contemporary plays, with a few classics thrown in for variety. Performances are staged Wednesday to Sunday year-round. Tickets are $20 weekdays, $25 weekends. They don't widely advertise it, but on most weekdays you can get a second ticket for half price. Students always pay half price.

CLASSICAL MUSIC & OPERA

Although it looked as though classical music was in trouble for a while in Miami, the influx of international music lovers to the area has revitalized the classical scene. Most companies still suffer from economic problems, and the musicians tend to be underpaid, but there are many offerings, especially in the fall and winter.

In addition to a number of local orchestras and operas, which regularly offer high-quality music and world-renowned guest artists, each year brings a slew of special events and touring artists. One of the most important and longest-running series is produced by the **Concert Association of Florida (CAF),** 555 17th St., South Beach (☎ **305/532-3491**). Known for almost a quarter of a century for its high-caliber, star-packed schedules, CAF regularly arranges the best "serious" music concerts for the city.

Season after season the schedules are punctuated by world-renowned dance companies and seasoned virtuosi like Itzhak Perlman, Andre Watts, and Kathleen Battle. Performances are usually scheduled in either the Dade County Auditorium or the Jackie Gleason Theater of the Performing Arts. The season lasts from October to April, and ticket prices range from $20 to $60.

Florida Grand Opera, 1200 Coral Way, Coral Gables (☎ **800/741-1010** or 305/854-1643), is South Florida's oldest arts organization. It has been featuring singers from America's and Europe's top houses for nearly 60 years. All productions are sung in their original language and staged with projected English supertitles. Tickets become scarce when Placido Domingo or Luciano Pavarotti (who made his American debut here in 1965) comes to town. The opera's season runs roughly from November to April, with five performances each week.

The **New World Symphony,** at Lincoln Road in South Beach (☎ **305/673-3331;** e-mail: ticketsenws.org), is a stepping stone for gifted young musicians seeking professional careers. Accepting artists on the basis of a 3-year fellowship and led by artistic advisor Michael Tilson Thomas, the orchestra specializes in ambitious, innovative, energetic performances and often features guest soloists and renowned conductors. The symphony's season lasts from October to May. Tickets cost $10 to $40, and student and senior discounts are available.

The **Florida Philharmonic Orchestra,** 169 E. Flagler St., Miami (☎ **800/ 226-1812** or 305/930-1812), is South Florida's premier symphony orchestra, under the direction of James Judd. It presents a full season of classical and pops programs interspersed with several children's and contemporary popular music dates. The Philharmonic performs downtown in the Gusman Center for the Performing Arts or the Jackie Gleason Theater of the Performing Arts, and puts on children's concerts at the Dade County Auditorium.

An inexpensive alternative to the high-priced classical venues is the **Miami Chamber Symphony,** 5690 N. Kendall Dr., Kendall (☎ **305/858-3500**). Renowned international soloists regularly perform with this professional orchestra. The symphony performs October to May, and most concerts are held in the Gusman Concert Hall, on the University of Miami campus. Tickets are $12 to $30.

DANCE

Several local dance companies train and perform in the Greater Miami area. In addition, top traveling troupes regularly pass through the city, stopping at the venues listed above. Keep your eyes open for special performances, like those by **Ballet Flamenco La Rosa** (☎ **305/672-0552**), a local Flamenco and Afro-Caribbean dance troupe that really puts the heat in Latin dance.

Miami City Ballet. (Office and rehearsal studios) Lincoln Road Mall at Jefferson, South Beach. ☎ **305/532-4880,** box office 305/532-7713. Tickets $17 (repertory single tickets) to $54 (orchestra center seats on weekend nights).

Headquartered in a storefront in the middle of the Art Deco District's popular pedestrian mall, this Miami company has quickly emerged as a top troupe, performing both classical and contemporary works. The artistically acclaimed and innovative company, directed by Edward Villella, has premiered more than 30 ballets, and has a repertoire of more than 75 works, many by George Balanchine. Stop by most afternoons to watch rehearsals through the large storefront window. Plans are in the works to move to a bigger studio by 2000. The City Ballet season runs from September to April, with performances in South Beach at the Jackie Gleason Theater of the Performing Arts and other venues around the state.

LIVE MUSIC/JAZZ

Despite the spotty success of local music, South Florida's jazz scene is very much alive with traditional and contemporary performers. Additionally, many area hotels feature live music of every assortment. Schedules are listed in the newspaper entertainment sections.

The Globe. 377 Alhambra Circle (at LeJeune), Coral Gables. ☎ **305/445-3555.** No cover.

This odd little cafe is attached to a travel agency. On weekends, a red curtain transforms a corner into a stage where you'll find decent jazz.

✪ **Tobacco Road.** 626 S. Miami Ave. (over the Miami Ave. Bridge near Brickell Ave.), downtown. ☎ **305/374-1198.** Cover none–$8.

Offering blues, zydeco, brass, jazz, and more, this place has been around since 1912. These days you'll find a good bar menu along with the best live music anywhere usually until 5am. Some regulars include the Dirty Dozen Brass Band from New Orleans, who play a mean mix of zydeco and blues with an actual dozen brass players; and Bill Warton and the Ingredients, who make a pot of gumbo while on stage. Friday and Saturday the music is upstairs, where people dance like crazy, though it's packed and there's no real dance floor. Monday, of course, is reserved for the blues. Escape the smoke and sweat in the backyard patio. The downright-cheap dinner specials, like a $10 lobster dinner, are quite good and served until 2am. This is a Miami institution and a must-see.

Van Dyke Cafe. 846 Lincoln Rd., South Beach. ☎ **305/534-3600.** No cover.

Live jazz 7 nights a week until midnight and it's free! In an elegant little upstairs lounge, the likes of Eddie Higgins, Mike Renzi, and some locals play strictly jazz for a well-dressed crowd. You can have a drink or two at the pristine oak bar or enjoy some snacks from the bustling patio seats below.

BARS & DANCE CLUBS

A new trend in Miami's club scene is the popularity of "one-off" nights—events organized by a promoter and held in established venues on irregular schedules. Word of mouth, local advertising, and listings in the free weekly *New Times* are the best ways to find out about these hot events.

BARS

Kids from Kendall and couples from the Gables head to South Beach in droves for the super late-night scene—it's the hub of most of the area's nightlife. I've given the highlights below and included many spots around town for those staying in other parts of the city.

There are dozens of late-night bars in South Beach clustered along Washington Avenue between 6th and 8th streets. If you want to rack a few, head to Brandt's Break, where the seven tables fill up quickly, especially after midnight. Check out the others for yourself since many of the neon signs over their doors flicker and die before the first batch of fliers have been handed out.

China Grill. 404 Washington Ave., South Beach. ☎ **305/534-2211.** No cover.

Don't bother with the food, but do stop in for an overpriced drink and some superb spectating. The dinner and bar crowd arrive decked out as if going to a disco, and from the look-over you get on the way in, you get the idea that the front-door staff would like to hang a velvet rope and do some picking at the door.

✪ **The Clevelander Hotel.** 1021 Ocean Dr., South Beach. ☎ **305/531-3485.** No cover.

This old standby is always a sure bet. On one of Ocean Drive's busiest and most spacious corners, you'll find a crowd gathered around the large outdoor pool area up until 5am. Cheap drinks in plastic cups complete the beachy atmosphere in this casual spring-breaky bar.

Dan Marino's American Sports Bar & Grill. 3015 Grand Ave. (on the third level of Cocowalk), Coconut Grove. ☎ **305/567-0013.** No cover.

Packed every day and night with a mix of young sports fans and drinking fans, this large multifaceted bar has a varied menu that's also popular with families since kids eat free Monday through Friday with one adult entree from 4 to 8pm. There is plenty to keep guests busy here—including video games, pool tables, motorcycle and ski games, plus three bars and a terrace bar for great people-watching. An added bonus is a large and lively no-smoking section.

The Delano. 1685 Collins Ave., South Beach. ☎ **305/672-2000.** No cover.

I'm surprised they haven't started charging admission to this spectacular attraction. In the lobby is the Rose Bar, one of the best spots in South Beach to see beautiful people decked out in trendy splendor. Lounge on a cushy sofa or in any of the plump beds that are casually arranged throughout the lobby and backyard, and grab an expensive drink. This is a good place to start the evening before heading out to the more lively clubs in the area. *Note:* Don't valet park your car here. Not only will you pay about $15 for the privilege, you will also wait forever for the handsome valets to retrieve your car.

✪ **The Forge.** 432 41st St., Miami Beach. ☎ **305/538-8533.** No cover.

Step back in time at this ultra-elegant restaurant and bar where Wednesday night is the night to hang with dolled up Euro-singles and New Yorkers. Call well in advance if you want to watch the parade of characters from your dinner table (see "Where to Dine," in chapter 4). A deejay plays Latin and dance music until 2am, when the crowd is at its peak.

Howl at the Moon Saloon. 3015 Grand Ave. (on the second level of Cocowalk), Coconut Grove. ☎ **305/442-8300.** Cover $5–$10.

Thursday night is college night and the only night when anyone over 19 is welcome. If you are over 21 and have a college ID, you can skip the cover and enjoy cheap buckets of beer. Drink specials are a regular fixture on Sunday, when beers are $1.75 a pop, and on other nights throughout the week, except Monday, when the Moon is dark.

Mac's Club Deuce. 222 14th St., South Beach. ☎ **305/673-9537.** No cover. Open daily 8am–5am.

Housed in a squat, neon-covered deco building, this old dive bar is popular with bikers and barflies and pool players who love the dark and smoky scene. A real local's favorite for those who like to slum it, here you'll no doubt catch a great conversation, some old tunes on the juke box, or a good scene out the front picture window that faces a busy all-night tattoo parlor.

Molly Malone's. 166 Sunny Isles Blvd., North Miami. ☎ **305/948-3512.** No cover.

Open all day and into the next, Molly's is a divey Irish pub that is popular with young and old drinkers and folk lovers. There's a pool table and darts and occasional Irish rock or acoustic music from all over and, of course, a selection of good ales and lagers.

Murphy's Law Irish Pub. 2977 McFarlane Dr., Coconut Grove. ☎ **305/446-9956.** No cover.

Another good Irish pub, this relatively new outpost is for those who want to escape the more antiseptic night scene at Cocowalk down the road. A big-screen TV shows sports events, and otherwise it's you and a pint sharing the bar with old-timers, grungers, and young professionals.

Wet Willies. 760 Ocean Dr., South Beach. ☎ **305/532-5650.** No cover.

The upstairs deck right on the main drag is one of the prime spots for watching the hectic parade that defines Ocean Drive. From up here, you can see the ocean and the spectacle of folks who walk the strip night and day. After just one Wet Willie frozen concoction, you may not be able to see much of anything. Watch out: They taste like soda pop but bite like a mad dog.

DANCE CLUBS

Just for the record: No, Madonna, the original Material Girl, does not own a night-club in South Beach. The club that uses her name on its oversized billboard on Washington Avenue is a strip joint, one of a handful in South Beach that cater to the area's many tourists and traveling businessmen. There are, however, dozens of great dance clubs in the area open until the sun rises, especially in South Beach. See also "The Latin Scene," below.

Bash. 655 Washington Ave., South Beach. ☎ **305/538-2274.** Cover $10 weeknights and $15 weekends.

Worth a mention of its own since this place has been around longer than most and is always predictably hot. Open every night but Monday, Bash features different events each night. Tuesday is European underground dance; Wednesday is fashion-show night; Thursday is sponsored theme night; Friday and Saturday are European dance; Sunday is disco and funk. No matter what the event, you'll probably have to wait out-side a rope to be picked by a group of stoic bouncers who have heard it all.

Bermuda Bar. 3509 NE 163rd St. (in the Intracoastal Mall), North Miami. ☎ **305/945-0196.** Cover none–$10. No cover before 9pm.

This huge suburban "danceteria" specializes in ladies' nights (Wednesday and Thursday when there is no cover for women). Plus, it hosts cash-prize dance contests and contests for women who dare to wear the skimpiest outfits. Still, everybody loves the high-energy music that packs the dance floor every night but Monday and Tuesday. Thursday is Latin night and Friday is happy hour from 5 to 8pm. Saturday is the biggest night when all the goings-on are broadcast live on a local radio station. This place usually stays open until the sun comes up.

Groove Jet. 323 23rd St. (next to the Fina gas station), South Beach. ☎ **305/532-2002.** No cover before midnight and $10 after.

This fantastic hidden spot north of the South Beach scene has been through many incarnations. Its most recent, Groove Jet, has three distinct areas playing totally dif-ferent music. Whatever name it's going by, do drive by this spot to see what's hap-pening—usually out back it's rock and roll, and in the main room you'll hear deep house and trance. A very hip young crowd hangs in this out-of-the-way scene, which gets going late, Thursday to Sunday 11pm to 5am.

Liquid. 1439 Washington Ave., South Beach. ☎ **305/532-9154.** Cover $10–$15.

Reminiscent of the '80s New York club scene, Liquid is a place where you can expect to wait at the ropes until a disdainful bouncer chooses you. Don't come dressed in the usual South Beach attire; they're looking for casual chic. Once inside, you'll find a cavernous space with up-to-the-minute dance music and two beautiful bars, VIP seating in a cozy back area, a hip-hop side room, and soon, a downstairs lounge playing jazz and funk. Sunday night is gay. The action starts late, after 11pm, although it really doesn't get really torqued until 2am.

Marsbar. 8505 Mills Dr. (in the Kendall Town & Country Mall on the corner of 88th and 117th sts.), Miami. ☎ **305/271-6909.** Cover $5.

This alternative/dance/retro club is packed with young ravers who come from neighboring South Miami and Kendall. Disco is the rage on Friday. Some nights, local bands play.

THE LATIN SCENE

With a large Hispanic population and a huge influx of visitors from the Caribbean and Central and South America, there are, of course, some great Latin nightclubs here. In recent years, many new clubs have attracted a mix of curious Anglos and Europeans as well. The meteoric rise of Miami's international music scene has brought many international stars to town to do business with MTV Latino, Sony International, and the multitude of Latin TV studios based here. You'll find a good club scene, especially on weekends.

✪ **Cafe Nostalgia.** 2212 SW 8th St. (Calle Ocho), Little Havana, Miami. ☎ **305/541-2631.** Cover $10 Fri–Sat.

As the name implies, Cafe Nostalgia is dedicated to reminiscing about Old Cuba. After watching a film with Celia Cruz, you can dance to the hot sounds of Afro-Cuban jazz. With pictures of old and young Cuban stars smiling down on you and a live band celebrating Cuban heritage, it's hard not to get excited about the island's former glory days. Be prepared: It's packed after midnight, and dance space is mostly between the tables. Films are shown from 10pm to midnight Wednesday to Sunday, followed by live music until 3am. The club is closed Monday and Tuesday. *Note:* At press time, another Cafe Nostalgia was expected to open adjacent to the Forge in Miami Beach.

Casa Panza. 1620 SW 8th St. (Calle Ocho), Miami. ☎ **305/643-5343.** No cover.

Clap your hands or your castanets if you have them. Every Tuesday and Thursday night, Casa Panza in the heart of Little Havana becomes the House of Flamenco, with shows at 8 and 11pm. Patrons of the restaurant can enjoy a flamenco show or don their own dancing shoes and participate in the celebration. Enjoy a fantastic dinner before the show or have a few drinks before you do some stomping.

Mango's. 900 Ocean Dr., South Beach. ☎ **305/673-4422.** Cover $3–$15, depending on the performer.

If you want to dance to a funky, loud Brazilian beat until you drop, check out Mango's on the beach. They feature nightly live Brazilian and Latin music on a little patio bar. When you need refreshment, you can choose from a schizophrenic menu of Caribbean, Mexican, vegetarian, and Cuban specialties. Open daily from 11am to 5:30am.

✪ **Yuca.** 501 Lincoln Rd., South Beach. ☎ **305/532-9822.** Cover $25, plus two-drink minimum for the Albita Performance Fri–Sat at 11pm.

One of the city's best restaurants (see "Where to Dine," in chapter 4) also serves up hot music in an upstairs club. If Albita is playing, don't miss her. The bill will be high and you'll be squeezed into a table no bigger than a cocktail napkin, but it is worth it for some of the highest-energy dance music, including traditional sol, salsa, and son from

Learn to Salsa in Six Easy Lessons

If you're feeling shy about hitting a Latin club because you have two left feet, it might be a good idea to take a few lessons before tripping the light fantastic. Several dance companies and dance teachers around the city offer individual and group lessons to Anglos or bad dancers of any origin willing to learn. The following folks make it their mission to teach merengue, flamenco, and more to gringo wannabes or Latin left-foots.

Ballet Flamenco La Rosa, at the PAN, Performing Arts Network building, 555 17th St., South Beach (☎ 305/672-0552), wants to teach you how to flamenco, salsa, or merengue with the best of them. This is the only professional flamenco company in the area, and you'll hear those castanets going. Private lessons are $50 if you're feeling shy, or $10 an hour will allow you to learn the art of the dance with a group of other beginners.

Nobody salsas like **Luz Pinto** (☎ 305/868-9418), and she can help you master the basics with patience and humor. She charges between $45 and $50 for a private lesson for up to four people and $10 per person for a group lesson. A good introduction is her multilevel group class, at 7pm Sunday evening at the PAN building. Though she teaches everything from ballroom to merengue, her specialty is Casino-style salsa, popularized in the 1950s in Cuba, Luz's homeland. A mix between disco and country square dancing, Casino-style salsa is all the rage in Latin clubs in town. If you are a very good student, you may be able to talk Luz into chaperoning a trip to a nightclub to show off your moves. She'll work out a fee based on the number of participants and their ability.

Angel Arroya has been teaching salsa to the clueless out of his home at 16464 NE 27th Ave., North Miami Beach (☎ 305/949-7799), for the past 10 years. Just $10 will buy you an hour's time in his "school." He traditionally teaches Monday and Wednesday nights, but call ahead to check for any schedule changes.

the old country. No matter who is playing, you are bound to have fun at this super authentic Latin hot spot. If you don't speak Spanish, sign language works here, too.

THE GAY & LESBIAN SCENE

821. 821 Lincoln Rd., South Beach. ☎ **305/531-1188.** No cover.

821 is something between a neighborhood bar and a nightclub with a deejay or live performance every night. Thursday and Saturday are for ladies only, and the other nights they're welcome, too. Offering good music and limited attitude in a basic black box, this hot spot is a staple on Lincoln Road. Open daily 3pm until 3 or 5am.

Twist. 1057 Washington Ave., South Beach. ☎ **305/53-TWIST.** No cover.

Open from mid-afternoon until 5am every day, Twist is one of the beach's first and still most popular cruise-bars; its dark friendly spot attracts mostly male customers but welcomes anyone.

Warsaw Ballroom. 1450 Collins Ave., South Beach. ☎ **305/531-4555.** Cover $10–$15.

One of Miami's oldest and most fun nightclubs, Warsaw hosts various theme nights and some of the best dance music in town. After all these years, regulars still line up down the sidewalk, waiting to get in and dance until 5am. New owners may be slipping a bit, but check it out.

LATE-NIGHT BITES

If you want a quick bite after clubbing and you find that it's 4am, don't fret! There are a vast number of pizza places lining Washington Avenue in South Beach that are open past 6am. Especially good is **Pucci's** with several locations including one at 651 Washington Avenue. **La Sandwicherie,** 229 14th St. (behind the Amoco station; ☎ 305/532-8934), serves up a great late-night sandwich until 5am. Another place of note for night owls is the **News Cafe,** 800 Ocean Dr. (☎ 305/538-6397), with one in Coconut Grove at 2901 Florida Ave. behind Mayfair (☎ 305/774-6397), a trendy and well-priced cafe with an enormous menu offering great all-day breakfasts, Middle Eastern platters, fruit bowls, or steak and potatoes.

If you've just left a Latin club, stop in at **Versailles,** 3555 SW 8th St. (☎ 305/444-0240). What else but a Cuban medianoche (midnight sandwich) will do? They may not be open all night, but their hours extend until about 2am, catering to gangs of revelers young and old.

14 Cruises & Quick Flights to the Caribbean & Other Islands

Most of the Caribbean-bound ships sailing out of the Port of Miami are relatively inexpensive, can be booked without advance notice, and make for excellent excursions.

Home to more than 20 cruise ships from all around the world, the Port of Miami is the world's busiest, with a passenger load of close to three million people annually. All the cruises are well equipped for gambling, and casinos open as soon as the ship clears U.S. waters—typically 45 minutes after leaving port. Usually, four full-size meals are served daily, with portions so huge they're impossible to finish. Games, movies, and other onboard activities ensure that you're always busy. Passengers can board up to 2 hours before departure for meals, games, and cocktails.

There are dozens of cruise options—from a 1-day excursion to a trip around the world. Pick up the *Passport to Adventure,* an up-to-date list of cruises sailing from the port, from the **Metro-Dade Seaport Department,** 1015 N. America Way, in Miami (☎ 305/371-7678), open Monday to Friday from 8am to 5pm. It's just off NE 5th Street and Biscayne Boulevard, near the Bayside Marketplace. Also, see "More Places to Play, Both Indoors & Out," above, for details on gambling "cruises to nowhere."

Most of the big lines listed below offer 3- and 4-day excursions to The Bahamas, Key West, and other islands in the Atlantic. Cruise ships usually depart Miami on Friday night and return on Monday morning. If you want more brochures or other information, contact **The Bahamas Tourist Office,** 19495 Biscayne Blvd., Suite 809, in Aventura (☎ 800/422-4262 or 305/932-0051). All passengers must travel with a passport or proof of citizenship for reentry into the United States.

Carnival Cruise Lines, 35201 Blue Lagoon Dr., Miami (☎ 800/327-9501 or 305/599-2200), sails the *Ecstasy* on 3- to 4-night cruises to Nassau, usually departing on Friday at 4pm and returning on Monday at 7am. The cost starts at $519, but discounts are available if you book well in advance. Carnival also sails one of the largest cruise ships in the world, the *Destiny.* It made its debut in November 1996 with lots of publicity. Several swimming pools, game rooms, and lounges surround a spectacular multistory foyer that has quickly made the *Destiny* the centerpiece of Carnival's fast-growing fleet. The 101,000-ton ship can accommodate up to 3,400 passengers.

Norwegian Cruise Line, 95 Merrick Way, Coral Gables (☎ 800/327-7030 or 305/436-0866), offers 3- and 4-day trips. Departures are on Friday and Monday at 5pm. Bookings start at $349 ($639 including airfare). A more intimate ship, the 950-passenger *Leeward,* spends a full day in Nassau or Key West and Cozumel. As on other

Caribbean-bound ships, you can choose to disembark at any destination, or you can stay on board for food, drinks, and games.

Royal Caribbean Cruise Line, 1050 Caribbean Way, Miami (☎ **800/327-6700** or 305/539-6000), now sails its old *Sovereign of the Seas* on 3- and 4-night cruises to Nassau, Key West, and Coco Cay (the cruise line's private island), departing on Friday and Monday at 5pm, with fares that start at around $600, including airfare from most major U.S. cities. Beautifully renovated in 1996, this stylized ship offers a huge youth center for kids and treats its 2,000-plus passengers to some pampering. For brochures, call ☎ **800/ALL-HERE.**

Note that port charges are additional and can be more than $70 per person, depending on the destination. Ask before booking.

If you want a quick getaway to the Caribbean without the experience of cruising, many airlines and hotels team up to offer extremely affordable weekend packages.

Competitively priced packages are available from **American Flyaway Vacations,** operated by American Airlines (☎ **800/321-2121**); **Bahamas Air** (☎ **800/222-4262**); **Pan Am Bridge** (☎ **305/359-7980**); the slightly run-down **Princess Casino** in Freeport (☎ **305/359-9898**); and **US Airways Vacations** (☎ **800/455-0123**). Call for rates, since they vary dramatically throughout the year and depend on the type of accommodations you choose.

Finally, for more in-depth information on cruises to the Caribbean, consult *Frommer's Caribbean Cruises and Ports of Call.*

The Keys 6

by Victoria Pesce Elliott

As if the very tip of Florida's peninsula had shattered into hundreds of wayward fragments, the islands of the Keys are scattered across the sea like the loose beads of an exotic coral necklace. Each of the more than 400 islands that make up this 150-mile chain has a distinctive character. While some are crammed with strip malls and tourist traps, most are dense with unusual species of tropical plants, birds, and reptiles. Surrounded by calm blue waters and graced by year-round warmth, all offer a fascinating experience for travelers.

Despite the intriguing landscape, the stark and rocky coast hardly looks inviting from the bow of a ship. When Spanish explorers Juan Ponce de León and Antonio de Herrera sailed amidst these craggy and dangerous rocks in 1513 they and their men dubbed the string of islands "Los Martires" (The Martyrs), because they thought the rocks looked like men suffering in the surf. It wasn't until the early 1800s that the larger islands were settled by pirates who amassed great wealth by salvaging cargo from ships that wrecked at sea—wrecks often caused by the "salvagers" who occasionally moved and removed vital markers in the sea.

Wars, fires, hurricanes, mosquitoes, and the Depression took their toll on these resilient islands in the early part of this century, causing wild swings between fortune and poverty. In 1938, the spectacular Overseas Highway (U.S. 1) was finally completed atop the ruins of Henry Flagler's railroad, opening the region to tourists who had never been able to drive to this sea-bound destination.

These days, the highway connects more than 30 of the populated islands in the Keys. The hundreds of small, undeveloped islands that surround these "mainline" keys are known locally as the "backcountry" and are home to dozens of exotic animals and plants. To get to them, you must take to the water—a vital part of any trip to the Keys. Whether you fish, snorkel, dive, or just cruise, include some time on a boat in your itinerary; otherwise, you really haven't seen the Keys.

The sea and the myriad life beneath it are the main attractions here. Warm, shallow waters nurture living coral that supports a complex and delicate ecosystem of plants and animals—sponges, anemones, jellyfish, crabs, rays, sharks, turtles, snails, lobsters, and thousands of types of fish. This vibrant underwater habitat thrives on one of only two living tropical reefs in the entire North American continent (the other is off the coast of Belize). As a result, anglers, divers, snorkelers, and water-sports enthusiasts of all descriptions come to explore. The heavy traffic has taken its toll on this fragile eco-scape and efforts are underway to protect this unique resource.

Although the atmosphere throughout the Keys is that of a low-key beach town, don't expect to find many impressive beaches here. With the exception of a few private beachfront resorts, small, sandy beaches in Bahia Honda State Park and in Key West (see below), there are no wide natural beaches to speak of once you head south of Miami. To appease beach-hungry visitors, some hoteliers ship in Caribbean sand to create tiny stretches of sand near the sea.

I have divided this chapter into three sections. The Upper and Middle Keys are closest to the Florida mainland and therefore are popular with weekend warriors who come by boat or car to fish, drink, or relax in towns like Key Largo, Islamorada, and Marathon. Next, you'll find the Lower Keys, a small unspoiled swath of islands teeming with wildlife. It is in the protected regions of the Lower Keys that you are most likely to catch sight of the area's many endangered animals. With patience you may spot the rare eagle, egret, or Key deer. Also, keep an eye out for alligators, turtles, rabbits, and a huge variety of birds.

Key West, literally at the end of the road, is the most popular destination in the Florida Keys, and has its own section that highlights the best of this "Conch Republic." Made famous by the Nobel Prize–winning rogue Ernest Hemingway, this tiny island has been overrun with cruise-ship passengers, day-trippers, franchises, and T-shirt shops. Still, you'll find here a tightly knit community of permanent residents who cling fiercely to their live-and-let-live attitude—an atmosphere that has made Key West famously popular with gay travelers.

1 Exploring the Keys by Car

Once you have gotten off the turnpike and landed on U.S. 1 (see "Getting There," below), you'll have no trouble negotiating these narrow islands.

U.S. 1, also known as the Overseas Highway, is the only main road connecting the Keys. Although some find the long, straight drive from Miami to Key West tedious, it can be enjoyable if you linger and explore the diverse towns and islands along the way. If you have the time, I recommend allowing at least 3 days to work your way down to Key West.

Most of U.S. 1 is a narrow, two-lane highway, with some wider passing zones along the way. The speed limit is usually 55 m.p.h. (35 to 45 m.p.h. on Big Pine Key and in some commercial areas). Despite the protestations of island residents, there has been talk of expanding the highway, but by publication date plans had not been finalized. Even on the narrow road, you can usually get from downtown Miami to Islamorada within an hour. If you're determined to drive straight through to Key West, allow at least 3½ hours. No matter what, avoid driving anywhere in the Keys on Friday afternoons or Sunday evenings, when the roads are jammed with weekenders from the mainland.

To find an address in the Keys, don't bother looking for building numbers; most addresses (except in Key West and parts of Marathon) are delineated by mile markers (MM), small green signs on the bay side of the road that announce the distance from Key West. The markers start at number 127, just south of the Florida mainland. The zero marker is in Key West, at the corner of Whitehead and Fleming streets. Addresses in this chapter are accompanied by a mile marker (MM) designation when appropriate.

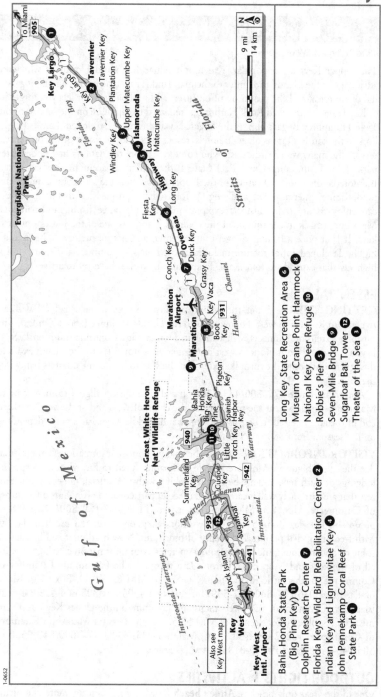

The Florida Keys

Bahia Honda State Park (Big Pine Key) 11
Dolphin Research Center 7
Florida Keys Wild Bird Rehabilitation Center 2
Indian Key and Lignumvitae Key 4
John Pennekamp Coral Reef State Park 1

Long Key State Recreation Area 6
Museum of Crane Point Hammock 8
National Key Deer Refuge 10
Robbie's Pier 5
Seven-Mile Bridge 9
Sugarloaf Bat Tower 12
Theater of the Sea 3

2 The Upper & Middle Keys: Key Largo to Marathon

48 to 105 miles SW of Miami

The Upper Keys are a popular, year-round refuge for South Floridians who take advantage of the islands' proximity to the mainland. This is the fishing and diving capital of America, and the profusion of outfitters and billboards never lets you forget it.

Key Largo, once called Rock Harbor but renamed to capitalize on the success of the 1948 Humphrey Bogart film, is the largest key and is more developed than its neighbors to the south. Dozens of chain hotels, restaurants, and tourist information centers service the many water enthusiasts who come to explore the nation's first underwater park, John Pennekamp Coral Reef State Park, and its adjacent marine sanctuary. Islamorada, the unofficial capital of the Upper Keys, offers the area's best atmosphere, food, fishing, entertainment, and lodging. It is in these "purple isles" that nature-lovers can enjoy nature trails, historic explorations, and big-purse fishing tournaments. Marathon, smack in the middle of the chain of islands, is one of the most populated keys. It is at once a fishing village, tourist center, and nature preserve. This island's highly developed infrastructure includes resort hotels, a commercial airport, and a highway that expands to four lanes. Thankfully, high-rises have yet to arrive.

ESSENTIALS

GETTING THERE   From the Miami airport, take Le Jeune Road (NW 42nd Avenue) to Route 836 west. Follow signs to the Florida Turnpike (about 7 miles). The turnpike extension connects with U.S. 1 in Florida City. Continue south on U.S. 1. If you're coming from Florida's west coast, take Alligator Alley to the Miami exit and then turn south onto the turnpike extension. Be sure to have some quarters handy for the tolls.

American Eagle (☎ 800/433-7300) has daily nonstop flights from Miami to Marathon, which is near the midpoint of the chain of Keys and at the very southern end of the area referred to here as the Upper and Middle Keys. Fares range depending on the season, from $88 to $336 round-trip.

VISITOR INFORMATION   Avoid the many "Tourist Information Centers" that dot the main highway. Most are private companies hired to lure visitors to specific lodgings or outfitters. You are better off sticking with the official, not-for-profit centers that are extremely well located and staffed. In particular, the **Key Largo Chamber of Commerce,** U.S. 1 at MM 106, Key Largo, FL 33037 (☎ 800/822-1088 or 305/451-1414; fax 305/451-4726; www.floridakeys.org), runs an excellent facility with free direct-dial phones and plenty of brochures. Now headquartered in a handsome clapboard house, the chamber now operates as an information clearinghouse for all of the keys and is open daily from 9am to 6pm. The **Islamorada Chamber of Commerce,** in the Little Red Caboose, U.S. 1 at MM 82.5 (P.O. Box 915), Islamorada, FL 33036 (☎ 800/322-5397 or 305/664-4503; fax 305/664-4289; e-mail: islacc@ix.netcom.com), also offers maps and literature on the Upper Keys. You can't miss the big blue visitor's center at MM 53.5. It is the **Greater Marathon Chamber of Commerce,** 12222 Overseas Hwy., Marathon, FL 33050 (☎ 800/842-9580 or 305/743-5417; fax 305/289-0183; www.flakeys.com).

OUTDOOR SIGHTS & ACTIVITIES

One of the area's only beaches, **Anne's beach** (at MM 73.5) is really more of a picnic spot than a full-fledged beach. Still, die-hard suntanners congregate on this tiny strip of coarse sand. Others, enjoy the wide wooden boardwalk which connects a dozen or so chickee huts or venture off the walkways into the mangroves. This minipark was dedicated to Anne Eaton, a local naturist. Parking is free and there are clean, safe bathrooms at the park's northern end.

Indian Key and Lignumvitae Key. Off Indian Key Fill, Overseas Hwy., MM 79. ☎ **305/664-4815.**

If you are interested in seeing the Keys in their natural state, before modern development, you must venture off the highway and take to the water. Two backcountry islands that offer visitors a glimpse of the "real" Keys are Indian Key and Lignumvitae Key.

Named for the lignum vitae ("wood of life") trees found there, Lignumvitae Key supports a virgin tropical forest, the kind that once thrived on most of the Upper Keys. Over the years, human settlers have imported "exotic" plants and animals to the Keys, irrevocably changing the botanical makeup of many backcountry islands and threatening much of the indigenous wildlife. Over the past 25 years, the Department of Natural Resources has successfully removed most of the exotic vegetation, leaving this 280-acre site much as it existed in the 18th century.

Indian Key, a much smaller island on the Atlantic side of Islamorada, was occupied by Native Americans for thousands of years before European settlers arrived. The 10-acre historic site was also the original seat of Dade County before the Civil War. You can see the ruins of the prior settlement and tour the lush grounds on well-marked trails.

If you want to see both islands, plan to spend half a day relaxing and enjoying the lush hammocks and colorful birds that call these islands home. To get there, you can rent your own boat at Robbie's Rent-A-Boat (U.S. 1 at MM 77.5 on the bay side). Rates range from $60 for a 14-foot boat for half a day, to $155 for an 18-foot boat for a full day. It's then a $1 admission fee to each island, which includes an informative hour-long guided tour by park rangers. This is a good option if you are a confident boater. However, I recommend taking Robbie's ferry service for $15, which includes the $1 park admission. Trips to both islands cost $25 per person. Not only is the ferry more economical, but it is easier to enjoy the natural beauty of the islands when you are not negotiating the shallow reefs along the way. If you are only planning to visit one island, make it Lignumvitae, which has a historic house built in 1919 and has survived numerous storms and major hurricanes. The runabouts, which carry up to six people, depart from Robbie's Pier Thursday to Monday at 9am and 1pm for Indian Key, and at 10am and 2pm for Lignumvitae Key. In the busy season, you may need to book as early as 2 days before departure. Call ☎ **305/664-4815** for information from the park service or ☎ 305/664-9814 for Robbie's.

✪ **Museum of Crane Point Hammock.** 5550 Overseas Hwy. (MM 50), Marathon. ☎ **305/743-9100.** Admission $7.50 adults, $6 seniors over 64, $4 students, children under 6 free. Mon–Sat 9am–5pm, Sun noon–5pm.

Crane Point Hammock is a little-known but very worthwhile stop, especially for those interested in the rich botanical and archaeological history of the Keys. This privately owned 64-acre nature area is considered one of the most important historical sites in the Keys. Although Crane Point Hammock is surrounded by shopping centers and condominiums, it contains what is probably the last virgin thatch palm hammock in North America. Also, an archaeological dig site contains evidence of pre-Colombian and prehistoric Bahamian artifacts.

Now headquarters for the Florida Keys Land and Sea Trust, the hammock's small nature museum has simple and informative displays of the Keys's wildlife, including a walk-through replica of a coral-reef cave and life-size dioramas with tropical birds and

Key deer. A single-room children's museum is very popular with kids who can play with a miniature railway station, walk though a Native American thatched hut, and touch a variety of sea creatures in a small saltwater touch tank.

Outside, visitors are encouraged to wander through the museum's quarter-mile nature trail amidst species of exotic plants that grow nowhere else in the country.

Seven-Mile Bridge. Between MM 40 and 47 on U.S. 1. ☎ **305/289-0025.**

A stop at the Seven-Mile Bridge is a rewarding and relaxing break from the drive south. Built alongside the ruins of oil magnate Henry Flagler's incredible Overseas Railroad, the new Seven-Mile Bridge (between MM 40 and 47) is still considered an architectural feat. Completed in 1982, at a cost of more than $45 million, the wide arched span is impressive, its apex being the highest point in all of the Keys. The new bridge and especially its now defunct neighbor provide an excellent vantage point from which to view the stunning waters of the Keys. Take a few minutes or spend a few hours to appreciate this free attraction. The old "ghost bridge" is the perfect place to watch the sunset, especially if you have had enough of the bars. In the daytime, you may want to jog, walk, or bike along the scenic 4-mile stretch, or join local anglers, who use shrimp as bait to catch barracuda, yellowtail, and dolphin on what is known as "the longest fishing pier in the world." To get there, from the southbound lane of the Overseas Highway, slow down just before the bridge and turn right, off the road, into the unpaved parking lot at the foot of the bridge.

Recently opened to the public, ✪ **Pigeon Key,** at the curve of the old bridge, is an intriguing historical site that has been under renovation since late 1995. It was once the camp for the crew that built "Flagler's Folly" in the early part of the century. From here your vista includes both bridges, many old wooden cottages, and a truly tranquil stretch of lush foliage and sea. The key is open every day except Monday from 9am to 5pm. Admission is $2 and free for children under 8. Shuttle service is provided for visitors who don't want to walk or bike the 2-mile trail to the 5-mile island. Cars cannot drive on the old bridge. Parking is available at the Knight's Key end of the bridge, at MM 48, or at the visitor's center at the old train car across the highway.

VISITING WITH THE ANIMALS

✪ **Dolphin Research Center.** U.S. 1 at MM 59 (on the bay side), Marathon. ☎ **305/ 289-1121.** Swim with the dolphins, $90 per person. Call on the first day of the month to book for the following month. Educational walking tours five times every day: 10am, 11am, 12:30pm, 2pm, and 3:30pm. Admission $9.50 adults, $7.50 seniors, $6 children 4–12, free for children 3 and under. (Prices are scheduled to increase in 1998.) MC, V. Daily 9:30am–4pm. Look for the 30-foot statue of a dolphin.

Try not to miss this experience. If you've always wanted to touch, swim, or play with dolphins, this is the most respected place to do it. Of the three such centers in the continental United States (all located in the Keys), the Dolphin Research Center is the most organized and informative. The group's main goal is to protect the mammals and educate the public about these unusually smart beasts.

Although some people argue that training dolphins is cruel and selfish, the knowledgeable trainers at the Dolphin Research Center will tell you that the dolphins need stimulation and enjoy human contact. They certainly seem to. They nuzzle and seem to smile and kiss the lucky few who get to swim with them in the daily program. The "family" of 15 dolphins swims in a 90,000-square-foot, coral, natural saltwater pool carved out of the shoreline.

The procedure for making reservations is quite unbending. If you can't book your choice of dates, don't despair. You can still take a walking tour or a half-day class in how to do hand signals and feed the dolphins from docks. Kids must be at least 12 years old.

Florida Keys Wild Bird Rehabilitation Center. U.S. 1 at MM 94, Tavernier. ☎ **305/ 852-4486.** Fax 305/852-3186. Donations suggested. Daily 8:30am–6pm. Heading south on U.S. 1, look right for the wooden bird sculptures to point the way.

Wander through lush canopies of mangroves on narrow wooden walkways to see some of the Keys's most famous residents—the large variety of native birds, including broad-wing hawks, great blue and white herons, roseate spoonbills, white ibis, cattle egrets, and a variety of pelicans. This not-for-profit center operates as a hospital for the many birds who have been injured. If you have the stomach for it, ask to see naturalist Laura Quinn at work removing a fish hook from a bird's throat or untangling fishing line from a broken wing. Or come at feeding time, usually about 2pm, when you can watch the dedicated staff feed the hundreds of hungry beaks. Keep alert. The big-billed pelicans often poke their heads down from the low structures just to check out who is visiting.

✪ **Robbie's Pier.** U.S. 1 at MM 77.5, Islamorada. ☎ **305/664-9814.** Admission $1. Bucket of fish $2. Daily 8am–5pm. Look for the Hungry Tarpon restaurant sign on the right after the Indian Key channel.

One of the best and definitely one of the cheapest attractions in the Upper Keys is the famed Robbie's Pier. Here, steely tarpons, a fierce fighting fish and a prized catch for backcountry anglers, have been gathering for the last 20 years. You may recognize these prehistoric-looking giants that grow up to 200 pounds. Many are displayed as trophies and mounted on some local restaurant walls. To see them live, head to Robbie's Pier, where tens and sometimes hundreds of these behemoths circle the shallow waters waiting for you to feed them. New kayak tours promise an even closer glimpse.

Theater of the Sea. U.S. 1 at MM 84.5, Islamorada. ☎ **305/664-2431.** Fax 305/ 664-8162. Admission $15.25 adults, $8.75 children 3–12; Swim with the Dolphins and Trainer for a Day program by reservation, $85 and $75 per person, respectively. Daily 9:30am–4pm.

Established in 1946, the Theater of the Sea is one of the world's oldest marine zoos. Although the facilities could use some sprucing up, the dolphin and sea lion shows are entertaining and informative, especially for children who can also see sharks, sea turtles, and tropical fish. The price is a bit steep for the rather limited resources here. Still, if you want to swim with the dolphins and you haven't booked well in advance, this is the place you may be able to get in with just a few hours' or days' notice as opposed to the more rigid Dolphin Research Center in Marathon (see above). After an hour's orientation session where you'll learn everything you'd ever want to know about these incredible swimming mammals—from their food preferences to their mating habits— you can climb into one of the three lagoons to touch and frolic with the playful beasts. Though the water is murky and individual time with the animals is short, for those who have dreamed of swimming beside these clever creatures, this is a great experience. Cat lovers will be thrilled to learn that the facility also serves as a haven for dozens of stray cats that have free run of the entire grounds and gift shop. Those who are allergic or sensitive to cat fur and smells should skip this stop.

TWO EXCEPTIONAL STATE PARKS

One of the best places to discover the diverse ecosystem of the Upper Keys is in its most famous park, ✪ **John Pennekamp Coral Reef State Park,** located on U.S. 1 at MM 102.5, in Key Largo (☎ **305/451-1202**). Named for a former *Miami Herald* editor and conservationist, the 188-square-mile park is the nation's first undersea preserve. It's a sanctuary for part of the only living coral reef in the continental United States. The original plans for Everglades National Park included this part of the reef within its boundaries, but opposition from local homeowners made its inclusion politically impossible.

Because the water is extremely shallow, the 40 species of coral and more than 650 species of fish are particularly accessible to divers, snorkelers, and glass-bottom-boat passengers. Unfortunately, the reef is a little too accessible, and the ecosystem is showing signs of stress from a steady stream of divers and boaters.

You can't see the reef from shore. To experience this park, visitors must get in the water. Your first stop should be the visitor's center, which is full of demonstrative fish tanks and a mammoth 30,000-gallon saltwater aquarium that re-creates a reef ecosystem. At the adjacent dive shop, visitors can rent snorkeling and diving equipment and join one of the boat trips that depart for the reef throughout the day. They also rent motorboats, sailboats, Windsurfers, and canoes. The 2-hour glass-bottom-boat tour is the best way to see the coral reefs if you refuse to get wet.

Canoeing around the park's narrow mangrove channels and tidal creeks is also popular. You can go on your own in a rented canoe, or in winter sign up for a tour led by a local naturalist. Hikers have two short trails to choose from: a boardwalk through the mangroves and a dirt trail through a tropical hardwood hammock. Ranger-led walks are usually scheduled daily from the end of November to April. Phone for schedule information and reservations.

Park admission is $2.50 per vehicle for one occupant; for two or more, it is $4 per vehicle, plus 50¢ per passenger; $1.50 per pedestrian or bicyclist. Call ☎ 305/451-1621 for information. On your way into the park, ask the ranger for a map. Glass-bottom-boat tours cost $13 for adults and $8.50 for children 11 and under. Snorkeling tours are $23.95 for adults and $18.95 for children 17 and under, including equipment. Sailing and snorkeling tours are $28.95 for adults, $23.95 for children 17 and under, including equipment but not tax. Canoes rent for $8 per hour, or $28 for 4 hours. Reef boats (powerboats) rent for $25 to $45 per hour; call ☎ 305/ 451-6325. Open daily from 8am to 5pm; phone for tour and dive times. Also, see below for more options on diving, fishing, and snorkeling these reefs.

Long Key State Recreation Area, U.S. 1 at MM 68, Long Key (☎ **305/664-4815**), situated atop the remains of ancient coral reef, the 965-acre park is one of the best places in the Middle Keys for hiking, camping, and canoeing. At the entrance gate, ask for a free flyer describing the local trails and wildlife.

Railroad builder Henry Flagler created the Long Key Fishing Club here in 1906, and the waters surrounding the park are still popular with game fishers. In summer, sea turtles lumber onto the protected coast to lay their eggs.

You can hike along two nature trails. The **Golden Orb Trail** is a 1-mile loop around a lagoon that attracts a large variety of birds. Rich in West Indian vegetation, the trail leads to an observation tower that offers good views of the mangroves. **Layton Trail,** the only part of the park that doesn't require an admission fee, is a quarter-mile shaded loop that goes through tropical hammock before opening onto Florida Bay. The trail is well marked with interpretive signs; you can easily walk it in about 20 minutes.

The park's excellent 1½-mile canoe trail is also short and sweet, allowing visitors to loop around the mangroves in about an hour—it couldn't be easier. You can rent canoes at the trailhead for about $4 per hour. Long Key is also a great spot to stop for a picnic if you get hungry on your way to Key West.

Admission is $3.25 per car plus 50¢ per person (except for the Layton Trail, which is free). Open daily from 8am to sunset.

WATER SPORTS A TO Z

There are literally hundreds of outfitters in the Keys who will set up all kinds of water activities from cave dives to parasailing. If those recommended below are booked up or unreachable, ask the local chamber of commerce for a list of qualified members.

BOATING   In addition to the rental shops in the state parks, you will find dozens of outfitters along U.S. 1 offering a range of runabouts and skiffs for boaters of any experience level. **Captain Pip's,** U.S. 1 at MM 47.5, Marathon (☎ **800/707-1692** or 305/743-4403), rents 18.5- to 24-foot motorboats with 90- to 225-horsepower engines for $110 to $170 per day.

Robbie's Rent-a-Boat, U.S. 1 at MM 77.5, Islamorada (☎ **305/664-9814**), rents 14- to 27-foot motorboats with engines ranging from 15 to 200 horsepower. Boats cost $60 to $205 for a half day and $80 to $295 for a whole day.

CANOEING/KAYAKING   I can think of no better way to explore the uninhabited, shallow backcountry than by kayak or canoe. You can reach places big boats just can't get to because of their large draft. Sometimes manatees will cuddle up to the boats, thinking them another friendly species.

For a more enjoyable time, ask for a sit-inside boat—you'll stay drier. Also, a fiber-glass (as opposed to plastic) boat with a rudder is generally more stable and easier to maneuver. Many area hotels rent kayaks and canoes to guests, as do the outfitters listed here. **Florida Bay Outfitters,** U.S. 1 at MM 104, Key Largo (☎ **305/451-3018**), rents canoes and sea kayaks for use in and around John Pennekamp Coral Reef State Park for $20 to $30 for a half day and $35 to $50 for a whole day. Canoes cost $25 for a half day and $35 for a whole day. At **Coral Reef Park Co.,** on U.S. 1 at MM 102.5, Key Largo (☎ **305/451-1621**), you can rent canoes and kayaks for $8 per hour, $28 for a half day—most canoes are sit-on-tops.

DIVING & SNORKELING   The **Florida Keys Dive Center,** on U.S. 1 at MM 90.5, Tavernier (☎ **305/852-4599;** fax 305/852-1293), takes snorkelers and divers to the reefs of John Pennekamp Coral Reef State Park and environs every day. PADI training courses are also available for the uninitiated. Tours leave at 8am and 12:30pm and cost $25 per person to snorkel (including mask, snorkel, and fins) and $40 per person to dive, plus an extra $30 if you need to rent all the gear.

At **Hall's Dive Center & Career Institute,** U.S. 1 at MM 48.5, Marathon (☎ **305/743-5929;** fax 305/743-8168), snorkelers and divers can choose to dive at Looe Key, Sombrero Reef, Delta Shoal, Content Key, and Coffins Patch. Tours are scheduled daily at 9am and 1pm. If you mention this guide, you will get a special dis-counted rate of $30 per person to snorkel (including equipment) and $40 per person to dive. Choose from a wide and impressive array of equipment. Rental is extra.

With **Snuba Tours of Key Largo** (☎ **305/451-6391**), you can dive down to 20 feet attached to a comfortable breathing apparatus that really gives you the feeling of scuba diving without having to be certified. You can tour shallow coral reefs teeming with hundreds of colorful fish and plant life, from sea turtles to moray eels. Reserva-tions are required; call to find out where and when to meet—usually in the late after-noon from the Westin or the Cheeca Lodge. A 2- to 3-hour underwater tour costs $70, including all equipment. If you have never dived before, you may require a 1-hour lesson in the pool, which costs an additional $40. The best part is you can bring the kids—as long as they're at least 8 years old.

FISHING   **Robbie's Partyboats & Charters,** on U.S. 1 at MM 84.5, Islamorada (☎ **305/664-8070** or 305/664-4196), located at the south end of the Holiday Isle Resort docks (see "Where to Stay," below), offers day and night deep-sea and reef fishing trips aboard a 65-foot party boat. Big game fishing charters are also available, and "splits" are arranged for solo fishers. Party-boat fishing costs $25 for a half day, $40 for a full day, and $30 at night. Charters run $400 for a half day, $600 for a full day; splits begin at $65 per person. Phone for information and reservations.

Bud n' Mary's Fishing Marina, on U.S. 1 at MM 79.8, Islamorada (☎ **800/ 742-7945** or 305/664-2461; fax 305/664-5592), one of the largest marinas between Miami and Key West, is packed with sailors offering guided backcountry fishing charters. This is the place to go if you want to stalk tarpon, bonefish, and snapper. If the seas are not too rough, deep-sea and coral fishing trips can be arranged. Charters cost $400 to $500 for a half day, $600 to $800 for a full day, and splits begin at $125 per person.

The Bounty Hunter, 15th Street, Marathon (☎ **305/743-2446**), offers full- and half-day outings. For years, Capt. Brock Hook's huge sign has boasted no fish, no pay. You're guaranteed to catch something. Choose your prey from shark, barracuda, sailfish, or whatever else is running. Prices are $350 for a half day, $375 for three quarters of a day, and $450 for a full day. Rates are for groups of no more than six people.

SHOPPING

The Upper and Middle Keys have no shortage of tacky tourist shops that sell shells, T-shirts, and hokey souvenirs. But for real Keys-style shopping, check out the **weekend flea markets.** One of the best is held every Saturday and Sunday, bay side at MM 103.5 (☎ **305/ 451-0677**). From 9am to 4 or 5pm, dozens of vendors open their stalls and sell antiques, T-shirts, plants, shoes, books, toys and games, and some good old-fashioned junk.

A shopping mecca for fishing and sports enthusiasts is **The World Wide Sportsman** (☎ **305/664-4615**). Opened in late 1997 at MM 81.5, it's not only the largest fishing store in the Keys (more than 25,000 square feet), but also a meeting place for anglers from all over the world. Every possible gizmo and gadget, plus hundreds of T-shirts, hats, books, and gift items. The salespeople are knowledgeable and eager to help, and there are travel specialists on premises that can arrange charter trips and backcountry tours for you. The store is open daily from 7am to 8:30pm. The staff is also happy to relay weather and travel data over the phone (ask for the tackle department, where the weather station operates).

WHERE TO STAY

U.S. 1 is lined with chain hotels in all price ranges. In the Upper Keys the best moderately priced options are the **Holiday Inn Key Largo Resort & Marina,** U.S. 1 at MM 99.7 (☎ **800/THE KEYS** or 305/451-2121), and right next door, at MM 100, the **Ramada Limited Resort & Casino** (☎ **800/THE-KEYS** or 305/451-3939). Both hotels share three pools and a casino boat; however, the Ramada is cozier and offers slightly cheaper rates. Also, the **Best Western Suites at Key Largo,** 201 Ocean Dr., MM 100 (☎ **800/462-6079** or 305/451-5081), is just 3 miles from John Pennekamp Coral Reef State Park. Another good option in the Upper Keys is **Islamorada Days Inn,** U.S. 1 at MM 82.5 (☎ **800/DAYS-INN** or 305/664-3681). In the Middle Keys, the **Howard Johnson** at 13351 Overseas Hwy., MM 54 in Marathon (☎ **800/ 321-3496** or 305/743-8550), also offers reasonably priced ocean-side rooms.

Since the real beauty of the Keys lies mostly beyond the highways, there is no better way to see this area than by boat. So why not stay in a floating hotel? Especially if traveling with a group, houseboats can be economical, and usually accommodate up to six people. To rent a houseboat, call Ruth and Michael Sullivan at **Smilin' Island Houseboat Rentals** (MM 99.5), Key Largo, FL (☎ **305/451-1930**). Rates are from $750 to $1,350 for 3 nights.

For land options, consider the following recommendations, grouped first by price, and then geographically from north to south. See chapter 4 for an explanation of price breakdowns.

VERY EXPENSIVE

✪ **Cheeca Lodge.** U.S. 1 at MM 82 (P.O. Box 527), Islamorada, FL 33036. ☎ **800/327-2888** or 305/664-4651. Fax 305/664-2893. 267 units. A/C MINIBAR TV TEL. Winter $240–$610 double; $315 suite. Off-season $160–$425 double; $275 suite. AE, CB, DC, DISC, MC, V.

One of the better places to stay in the Upper Keys, Cheeca has been hosting celebrities, royalty, and politicians since its opening in 1949. This lodge offers all the amenities of a world-class resort in a very laid-back setting. You may not feel compelled to leave the sprawling grounds, but it's good to know the hotel is conveniently situated near the best restaurants and nightlife. Located on 27 acres of beachfront property, this rambling resort is known for its excellent sports facilities, including diving and snorkeling programs and one of the only golf courses in the Upper Keys.

Although rooms are not particularly plush, all are spacious and have small balconies. The nicer ones overlook the ocean and have large marble bathrooms. Privacy is valued here; almost all rooms have entrances accessible from open-air hallways, and guests can park their cars in private spots near their rooms. The staff is always available, but thankfully not overly visible.

Dining/Diversions: The Atlantic's Edge restaurant is one of the best in the Upper Keys (see "Where to Dine," below). A pool bar and comfortable lounge offer more casual options throughout the day and evening.

Amenities: Concierge, room service, dry-cleaning and laundry services, in-room massage, newspaper delivery, baby-sitting, express checkout, valet parking, free coffee and refreshments in lobby. Kitchenettes, VCRs and video rentals, three outdoor heated pools, kids' pool, five hot tubs, beach, access to nearby health club, Jacuzzi, bicycle rental, 9-hole, par-3 golf course, children's nature programs, conference rooms, car-rental desk, sundeck, six lighted tennis courts, water-sports equipment rental, tour desk, nature trail, boutiques.

✪ **Hawk's Cay Resort.** U.S. 1 at MM 61, Duck Key, FL 33050. ☎ **800/432-2242** or 305/743-7000. Fax 305/743-5215. 176 units. A/C TV TEL. Winter $220–$350 double; $400–$850 suite. Off-season $160–$250 double; $300–$750 suite. AE, DC, DISC, MC, V.

Located on its own 60-acre island just outside of Marathon in the Middle Keys, Hawk's Cay is a sprawling and impressive resort encompassing a marina as well as a saltwater lagoon that's home to a half dozen dolphins. It's especially popular with families who appreciate the many activities and reasonably priced diversions. It's also more casual than other resorts, like Cheeca Lodge, which offers many of the same amenities. The manicured grounds are dotted with handsome two- and three-story flamingo-colored buildings. The guest rooms within are all quite similar—views account for the differences in price. All are large and have Caribbean-style bamboo furnishings padded with colorful fabrics, walk-in closets, small refrigerators, and a sliding glass door that opens onto a private balcony. If you want to splurge, the top-floor suites have separate seating areas with pull-out sofas and large wraparound terraces with spectacular views.

Dining/Diversions: Three good restaurants and a lounge have a wide range of food, from Italian to seafood. A well-stocked ship's store has snacks and basic groceries. A lively lounge features live music every evening and most weekend afternoons.

Amenities: Concierge, room service, overnight laundry, in-room massage, express checkout, transportation to airport and golf course, free refreshments in lobby.

Spectravision movie channels, outdoor heated pool, a new adults-only private pool, beach, small fitness room, Jacuzzi, nearby golf course, sundeck, eight (two lighted) tennis courts, water-sports equipment, bicycle rental, game room, children's center or programs, self-service laundry, marina store and gift shop, conference rooms, car-rental desk.

Westin Beach Resort, Key Largo. U.S. 1 at MM 97, Key Largo, FL 33037. ☎ **800/ 728-2738**, 800/325-3535, or 305/852-5553. Fax 305/852-8669. 210 units. A/C MINIBAR TV TEL. Winter $239–$289 double; from $389 Jacuzzi suite. Off-season $210–$260 double; from $389 Jacuzzi suite. AE, DC, DISC, MC, V.

Under new ownership since 1996, this resort has benefited from an extensive $3 million renovation. In addition to an overall rehab, the resort distinguishes itself by its secluded yet convenient location. It is set back on 12 private acres of gumbo-limbo and hardwood trees, making it invisible from the busy highway. Despite its hideaway location, the sprawling pink-and-blue four-story complex is surprisingly large. A three-story atrium lobby is flanked by two wings that face 1,200 feet of the Florida Bay. The large guest rooms have tasteful tropical decor and private balconies. The suites are twice the size of standard rooms and have better-quality wicker furnishings and double-size balconies. Ten suites feature private spa tubs and particularly luxurious bathrooms with adjustable showerheads, bidets, and lots of room for toiletries.

Dining/Diversions: The hotel restaurant offers terrific views of the bay and surf-and-turf dinners nightly. A casual cafe serves breakfast, lunch, and dinner both inside and outdoors. A poolside snack bar serves sandwiches, salads, and refreshments. The top-floor lounge has a dance floor and a pool table.

Amenities: Concierge, 24-hour room service, newspaper delivery, dry cleaning and laundry service, in-room massage, twice-daily maid service, baby-sitting, secretarial services, express checkout, free morning coffee in lobby, valet parking. Two outdoor heated swimming pools, beach, small but modern fitness room with Universal equipment, Jacuzzi, nature trails, two lighted tennis courts, water-sports equipment rental, children's programs, conference rooms, hair salon.

EXPENSIVE

✪ **Jules' Undersea Lodge.** 51 Shoreland Dr. (P.O. Box 3330), Key Largo, FL 33037. ☎ **305/451-2353.** Fax 305/451-4789. 1 unit. A/C TV TEL. Year-round $195–$295 per person. Rates include breakfast and dinner as well as all equipment and unlimited scuba diving in the lagoon. AE, DISC, MC, V. From U.S. 1 south, at MM 103.2, turn left onto Transylvania Ave., across from the Central Plaza shopping mall.

Originally built as a research lab in the 1970s, this small underwater compartment now operates as a single-room hotel. As expensive as it is unusual, Jules' is most popular with diving honeymooners. The lodge rests on pillars on the ocean floor. To get inside, guests swim under the structure and pop up into the unit through a 4-by-6-foot "moon pool" that gurgles soothingly all night long. The 30-foot-deep underwater suite consists of a bedroom and galley, and sleeps up to six. There is a television and VCR. Also, room service will bring breakfast, lunch, and daily newspapers in waterproof containers at no extra charge. Needless to say, this novelty is not for everyone.

Marriott Key Largo Bay Beach Resort. 103800 Overseas Hwy. (MM 103.8), Key Largo FL 33037. ☎ **800/932-9332** or 305/453-0000. Fax 305/453-0093. E-mail: baybeach@reefnet. com. 150 units. A/C MINIBAR TV TEL. Winter $209–$269; $500 suite. Off-season $139–$179; $250 suite. AE, DC, DISC, MC, V.

When this mammoth chain resort was built in 1993 many thought the sleepy little island town would be forever spoiled. On the contrary, this pristine, two-story Marriott created some major competition for the area's older resorts and the run-down 1950s motels resulting in an overall upgrade of the neighboring accommodations. And while it is hardly quaint, this amenities-laden complex built on 17 acres has everything an active or resting traveler could want. There's a large outdoor pool, sundeck, Jacuzzi, an up-to-date fitness center, and extensive dive shop offering every imaginable water sport. There is a moderately priced restaurant and tiki bar on site as well as a decent sized beach. All guests are welcome to sail for free on a gambling cruise ship that anchors in international waters from 2pm until 2am daily. Rooms are decorated in a pleasant (if generic) tropical style and include extras like coffeemakers, hair dryers, and safes. Most rooms (all but 22) also offer balconies overlooking the stunning Florida Bay. For real pampering, consider the enormous suites which can easily sleep a family of five. All have large wraparound terraces and large sitting areas. And with rates that are slightly cheaper than the nearby Westin and Cheeca Lodge, you'll find it a good value. Many conference groups and conventioneers also favor this spot since it is one of the most convenient to Miami (about an hour's drive). Reserve early; winter weekends usually book up months in advance.

Dining/Diversions: A casual bay-side grill offers casually elegant dining and an outdoor tiki bar has snacks and cocktails throughout the afternoon and evening.

Amenities: Concierge, room service, dry-cleaning and laundry services, in-room massage, newspaper delivery, baby-sitting, express checkout. Large outdoor pool, Jacuzzi, three small beach areas, VCRs upon request, gym, bicycle rental, conference rooms, sundeck, access to nearby tennis and racquetball courts, water-sports equipment rental, business center, tour desk, children's programs, game room, nature trail, boutiques.

○ **The Moorings.** 123 Beach Rd. (near MM 81.5 on the ocean side), Islamorada, FL 33036. ☎ **305/664-4708.** Fax 305/664-4242. 17 units. A/C TV TEL. Year-round $165–$200 smaller 1-bedroom cottages; $350 large 1-bedroom cottages. $2,450–$6,300 weekly, 2- and 3-bedroom cottages. 3-night minimum for smaller house; 1-week minimum for larger houses. MC, V.

Staying at the Moorings is more like staying at your second home than at a hotel. You'll never see another soul on this 18-acre resort if you choose not to. There isn't even maid service unless you request it. The romantic whitewashed houses are spacious and modestly decorated with funky island prints, bamboo, and tropical motifs. All have full kitchens and most have washers and dryers. Some have CD players and VCRs, so ask when you book. The real reason to come to this cool resort is to relax on the more than 1,000-foot beach (one of the only real beaches around) and to soak up some old-fashioned Keys simplicity. There is a simple hard tennis court, a few kayaks and Windsurfers, but absolutely no motorized water vehicles. There is no room service or restaurant (though Morada Bay across the street is excellent). This is a place for people who like each other a lot. If you want to be pampered, pamper each other. Picture yourself in a wide rope hammock under a palm tree watching the sunset with a glass of wine and a good book by your side. Leave the kids at home unless they are extremely well-behaved and not easily bored.

Amenities: Laundry and dryers, full kitchens, some VCRs, large sandy beach, sundeck, large pool, one hard tennis court, washing machines and dryers, boats, jogging trails.

MODERATE/INEXPENSIVE

Banana Bay Resort & Marina. U.S. 1 at MM 49.5, Marathon, FL 33050. ☎ **800/ BANANA-1** or 305/743-3500. Fax 305/743-2670. 60 units. A/C TV TEL. Winter $95–$175 double. Off-season $75–$125 double. Rates include breakfast. Children 4 and under stay free in parents' room. Weekend and 3- and 7-night packages available. AE, DC, DISC, MC, V.

It doesn't look like much from the sign-cluttered Overseas Highway, but once you enter the lush grounds of Banana Bay you will realize that you're in for one of the most bucolic and best-run properties in the Upper Keys. Built in the early 1950s as a fishing camp, the resort is a puzzle of pink-and-white two-story buildings hidden among banyans and palms. Guest rooms are very similar, but those with better views are more expensive. The rooms are moderately sized, and many have private balconies where you can enjoy complimentary coffee and newspapers every morning.

The restaurant serves breakfast, lunch, and dinner by the pool or in a kitschy old dining room. A waterfront tiki bar offers great sunset views. Head down to the marina to sign up for charter fishing, sailing, and diving. Kids will enjoy the small game room and free use of bicycles.

✪ **Conch Key Cottages.** Near U.S. 1 at MM 62.3 (RR 1, Box 424), Marathon, FL 33050. ☎ **800/330-1577** or 305/289-1377. Fax 305/743-8207. 12 units. A/C TV. Winter $100 efficiency; $126 1-bedroom apt; $147 1-bedroom cottage; $194–$249 2-bedroom cottage. Off-season $72 efficiency; $115 1-bedroom apt; $132 1-bedroom cottage; $147–$215 2-bedroom cottage. DISC, MC, V.

Occupying its own private micro-island just off U.S. 1, Conch Key Cottages is a unique and comfortable hideaway run by live-in owners Ron Wilson and Wayne Byrnes, who are constantly fixing and adding to their unique property. Request one of the new two-bedroom cottages, completed in 1997, especially if you are traveling with the family. These are the most spacious and well designed, practically tailor-made for couples or families. This is a place to get away from it all; the cottages aren't close to much, except maybe one or two interesting eateries. The cabins, which were built at different times over the last 40 years, overlook their own stretch of natural, but very small, private beach and have screened-in porches and cozy bedrooms and baths. Each has a hammock and barbecue grill. On the other side of the pool are a handful of efficiency apartments that are similarly outfitted, but enjoy no beach frontage. All have fully equipped kitchens. There's also a small heated freshwater pool.

Faro Blanco Marine Resort. 1996 Overseas Hwy., U.S. 1 at MM 48.5, Marathon, FL 33050. ☎ **800/759-3276** or 305/743-9018. 100 units, 23 condos, 31 houseboats with 4 units each. A/C TV TEL. Winter $65–$150 cottage; $99–$200 houseboat; $185 lighthouse; $240 condo. Off-season $55–$125 cottage; $79–$150 houseboat; $150 lighthouse; $210 condo. AE, DISC, MC, V.

Spanning both sides of the Overseas Highway and all on waterfront property, this huge, two-shore marina and hotel complex offers something for every taste. Free-standing, camp-style cottages with a small bedroom are the resort's least-expensive accommodations, but are in dire need of rehabilitation. Old appliances and a musty odor also make these the least desirable units on the property. There are some larger apartments with modern furniture and cleaner bathrooms and kitchens.

The houseboats are the best choice and value. Permanently tethered in a tranquil marina, these white rectangular boats look like floating mobile homes and are uniformly clean, fresh, and recommendable. They have colonial American-style furnishings, fully equipped kitchenettes, front and back porches, and water, water everywhere. The boats are so tightly moored, you hardly move at all, even in the roughest weather.

Finally, there are two unusual rental units located in a lighthouse on the pier; circular staircases, unusually shaped rooms and showers, and nautical decor make this quite a unique place to stay, but some guests might find it claustrophobic. Guests in any of the accommodations can enjoy the Olympic-size pool, any of the four casual restaurants, a fully equipped dive shop, barbecue/picnic areas, and a playground.

Holiday Isle Resort. U.S. 1 at MM 84, Islamorada, FL 33036. ☎ **800/327-7070** or 305/664-2321. Fax 305/664-2703. 199 units. Winter $85–$425. Off-season $65–$350. AE, CB, DISC, MC, V.

A huge resort complex encompassing five restaurants, lounges, and shops, and four distinct (if not distinctive) hotels, the Holiday Isle is one of the biggest resorts in the Keys and attracts a spring-break kind of crowd year-round. Their Tiki Bar claims the invention of the rum runner drink (151-proof rum, blackberry brandy, banana liquor, grenadine, and lime juice), and there's no reason to doubt it. Hordes of partiers are attracted to the resort's nonstop merrymaking, live music, and beachfront bars. As a result, some of the accommodations can be noisy.

Rooms can be bare-bones-budget to oceanfront luxury, as the broad range of prices reflect. Even the nicest rooms could use a good cleaning. El Captain and Harbor Lights, two of the least-expensive hotels on the property, are both austere and basic. Like the other hotels here, rooms could use a thorough rehab. Howard Johnson's, another Holiday Isle property, is a little farther from the action and a shred more civilized. If you plan to be there for a few days, choose an efficiency or suite; both have kitchenettes. Guests can choose between two outdoor heated pools and a kids' pool. They also offer water-sports equipment rental, gift boutiques, and a shopping arcade.

✪ **Kona Kai Resort & Gallery.** 97802 Overseas Hwy., U.S. 1 at MM 97.8, Key Largo, FL 33037. ☎ **800/365-7829** or 305/852-7200. Fax 305/852-4629. E-mail: KonaKai@aol.com. 11 units. Winter $141–$165 unit; $175–$400 suite. Off-season $94–$145 unit; $117–$205 suite. 3- to 4-night minimum stay usually required. AE, DISC, MC, V.

No one seems to get quite as thrilled over the Florida Keys's low-key beauty as a transplanted city boy. The garrulous proprietor of Kona Kai, Joe Harris, is the quintessential New Yorker and an enthusiastic tour guide who will bend over backwards to accommodate your every need. Former executives with NBC-television, he and his partner, Ronnie Farina, have created this peaceful haven in the overcommericalized Upper Keys, set amid 2 acres of tropical fruit trees. The rooms, all very private and simply furnished, are spaced out and protected by low walls of tropical trees. The lack of phones within and the 4-day minimum stay during winter make relaxing imperative. A small tennis court, pool, Jacuzzi, Ping-Pong, volleyball, and all kinds of water sports are available. For the adventurous, Joe and Ronnie will organize excursions to the Everglades or the backcountry.

Lime Tree Bay Resort Motel. U.S. 1 at MM 68.5 in Layton, Long Key, FL 33001. ☎ **800/723-4519** or 305/664-4740. Fax 305/664-0750. www.limetreebayresort.com. 30 units. A/C TV TEL. $75–$110 motel room or efficiency; $105–$125 deluxe motel room; $150–$180 one-bedroom suite, $155–$230 two-bedroom suite; $115–$150 cottage. AE, DC, DISC, MC, V.

The Lime Tree Bay Resort is the only hotel in the tiny town of Layton (pop. 183). Midway between Islamorada and Marathon, the hotel is only steps from Long Key State Recreation Area. Motel rooms and efficiencies have tiny bathrooms with standing showers, but are clean and well maintained. The best deal is the two-bedroom bay-view apartment. The large living area with new fixtures and furnishings leads out to a large private deck where you can enjoy a view of the gulf from your hammock. A full kitchen and two full baths make this a comfortable space for six people.

This affordable little hideaway has all the amenities you could want, including shuffleboard, tennis, a small pool, water sports, and a little cafe with a small but decent menu. It's situated on a very pretty piece of waterfront graced with hundreds of mature palm trees and lots of other tropical foliage.

INEXPENSIVE

Bay Harbor Lodge. U.S. 1 at MM 97.7 (off the southbound lane of U.S. 1), Key Largo, FL 33037. ☎ **305/852-5695.** 16 units. A/C TV TEL. Year-round $58–$78 double; $78–$98 efficiency; $85–$125 cottage. MC, V.

A small, simple retreat that's big on charm, the Bay Harbor Lodge is an extraordinarily welcoming place. The lodge is far from fancy, and the wide range of accommodations are not all created equal. The motel rooms are small in size and ordinary in decor, but even the least-expensive is recommendable. The efficiencies are larger motel rooms with fully equipped kitchenettes. The oceanfront cottages are larger still, have full kitchens, and represent one of the best values in the Keys. The vinyl-covered furnishings and old-fashioned wallpapers won't win any design awards, but elegance isn't what the "real" Keys are about. The 1½ lush acres of grounds are planted with banana trees and have an outdoor heated pool and several small barbecue grills. Guests are free to use the rowboats, paddleboats, canoes, kayaks, and snorkeling equipment. Bring your own beach towels.

CAMPING

John Pennekamp Coral Reef State Park. U.S. 1 at MM 102.5 (P.O. Box 487), Key Largo, FL 33037. ☎ **305/451-1202.** 47 campsites. Phone or in-person camping reservations only. $24–$26 per site. MC, V.

One of Florida's best parks (see above), Pennekamp offers 47 well-separated campsites, half available by advance reservation, the rest distributed on a first-come, first-served basis. The car-camping sites are small but well equipped with bathrooms and showers. A little lagoon nearby attracts many large wading birds. Reservations are held until 5pm, and the park must be notified of late arrival by phone on the check-in date. Pennekamp opens at 8am and closes around sundown. No pets.

Long Key State Recreation Area. U.S. 1 at MM 67.5 (P.O. Box 776), Long Key, FL 33001. ☎ **305/664-4815.** 60 campsites. $24–$26 per site for one to four people. MC, V.

The Upper Keys's other main state park is more secluded than its northern neighbor and more popular. All sites are located ocean-side and are surrounded by narrow rows of trees and nearby toilet and bath facilities. Reserve well in advance, especially in winter.

WHERE TO DINE

Although not known as a culinary hot spot, the Upper and Middle Keys do offer some excellent restaurants, many of which specialize in seafood. Often visitors (especially those who fish) take advantage of accommodations that have kitchen facilities and cook their own meals. Also, most restaurants will clean and cook your catch for a nominal charge.

VERY EXPENSIVE

✪ **Atlantic's Edge.** In the Cheeca Lodge, U.S. 1 at MM 82, Islamorada. ☎ **305/664-4651.** Reservations recommended. Main courses $20–$36. AE, CB, DC, DISC, MC, V. Daily 5:30–10pm. SEAFOOD/REGIONAL.

Ask for a table by the oceanfront window to feel really privileged at this, the most elegant restaurant in the Keys. Although the service and food are first-class, don't get dressed up—a sport coat will be fine, but isn't necessary. Choose from an innovative and varied menu, which offers several choices of fresh fish, steak, chicken, and pastas. Their crab cakes, made with stone crab when it's in season, are the very best in the Keys; served on a warm salad of baby greens with a mild sauce of red peppers, this is the stuff cravings are made from. Other excellent dishes include a Thai-spiced fresh baby snapper and the vegetarian angel-hair pasta with mushrooms, asparagus, and peppers in a rich broth. Service can sometimes be less than efficient but is always courteous and professional.

EXPENSIVE

Barracuda Grill. U.S. 1 at MM 49.5 (bay side), Marathon. ☎ **305/743-3314.** Reservations not accepted. Main courses $11–$25. AE, DISC, MC, V. Mon–Sat 6–10pm. BISTRO/SEAFOOD.

Owned by Lance Hill and his wife, Jan (who used to be a sous chef at Little Palm Island), this casual spot serves excellent seafood and traditional bistro fare. It's too bad they are only open for dinner. Some of the favorite dishes are old-fashioned meat loaf, classic beef Stroganoff, rack of lamb, and seafood stew. The pork tenderloin roasted with red onions and figs is one of the menu's best selections. In addition, this small barracuda-themed restaurant features a well-priced American wine list with a vast sampling of California vintages.

✪ **Marker 88.** U.S. 1 at MM 88 (bay side), Islamorada. ☎ **305/852-9315.** Reservations not usually required. Main courses $14–$29. AE, DC, DISC, MC, V. Tues–Sun 5–11pm. SEAFOOD/REGIONAL

An institution in the Upper Keys, Marker 88 has been pleasing locals, visitors, and critics since it opened in the early 1970s. Chef-owner Andre Mueller has created a "gourmet" restaurant in a tropical-fish house setting that serves a wide range of standard fare that's tinged with his take on nouvelle cuisine. Taking full advantage of his island location, Andre offers dozens of seafood selections, including Keys lobster, Bahamas conch, Everglades frog's legs, Florida Bay stone crabs, Gulf Coast shrimp, and an impressive variety of fish from around the country. Once you've figured out what kind of fish to have, you can choose from a dozen styles of preparation. The Keys's standard is meunière, which is a subtle and tasty sauce of lemon and parsley. I love the more dramatic rangoon, with currant jelly, cinnamon, and fresh tropical fruits, including bananas and mangos. Though everything looks tempting, don't overorder—portions are huge. The waitresses, who are pleasant enough, require a bit of patience, but the food is worth it.

✪ **Morada Bay.** U.S. 1 at MM 81.6, Islamorada. ☎ **305/664-0604.** Reservations recommended for large groups. Main courses $16–$22. Sandwiches $7–$8. AE, MC, V. Mon–Thurs 11:30am–10pm, Fri–Sun 11am–11pm. CARIBBEAN/AMERICAN.

This lovely bay-side bistro provides a great setting for its superfresh and innovative seafood as well as some more basic offerings like chicken fajitas, hamburgers, and salads. Salads like the Sunshine Salad are large and generously lavished with slices of avocado, mango, and tomato. When in season raw oysters are imported from Long Island and are delicious. Fish dishes are always fresh. I like mine jerked with a peppery coating and nearly black finish. For those who can't decide, share a few items from the tapas menu: jumbo shrimp cocktails, fried calamari, conch fritters, smoked fish dip, or a charcuterie of sausages and hams on country bread.

MODERATE

Lazy Days Oceanfront Bar and Seafood Grill. U.S. 1 at MM 79.9, Islamorada. ☎ **305/664-5256.** Main courses $11–$20. AE, DISC, MC, V. Tues–Sun 11:30am–10pm. SEAFOOD/AMERICAN.

Opened in 1992, the Lazy Days quickly became one of the most popular restaurants around, mostly because of the large portions and lively atmosphere. Meals are pricier than the casual dining room would suggest, but the food is good enough and the menu varied. Steamed clams with garlic and bell peppers make a tempting appetizer. The menu focuses on—what else?—seafood, but you can find Italian dishes. Most main courses come with baked potato, vegetables, a tossed salad, and French bread, making appetizers redundant.

✪ **Lorelei Restaurant and Cabana Bar.** U.S. 1 at MM 82, Islamorada. ☎ **305/ 664-4656.** Reservations not usually required. Main courses $9–$22. AE, DC, DISC, MC, V. Daily 7am–10pm. Outside bar serves lunch menu 11am–9pm. Bar closes at midnight. SEAFOOD/BAR FOOD.

Don't resist the siren call of the enormous, sparkling, roadside mermaid—you won't be dashed into the rocks. This big old fish house and bar is a great place for a snack, a meal, or a beer. Inside, a good-value menu focuses mainly on seafood. When in season, lobsters are the way to go. For $20 you can get a good-sized tail—at least a 1-pounder—prepared any way you like. Other fare includes the standard clam chowder, fried shrimp, and doughy conch fritters. Salads and soups are hearty and satisfying. For those tired of fish, the menu does offer a few beef selections. The outside bar has live music every evening, and you can order snacks and light meals from a limited menu that is satisfying and well priced. Enjoy the live entertainment every night.

INEXPENSIVE

✪ **Henry's Bakery and Gourmet Pizza Shop.** U.S. 1 at MM 82.5 (adjacent to Days Inn), Islamorada. ☎ **305/664-4030.** Pastas $7–$9.50; pizzas $8–$18; sandwiches and salads $4.50–$8. No credit cards. Mon–Sat 6am–10pm (sometimes later on weekends). BAKERY/PIZZERIA.

It's easy to miss this tiny storefront bakery that serves the best pizzas and sandwiches in town, so keep an eye out for it. My favorite sandwich here is freshly sliced turkey on homemade warm French bread, with a splash of superbly tangy vinaigrette. Most days Henry bakes fresh multigrain, semolina, and Italian bread, too. Stop by early for delicious pastries and croissants. If you want pizza, consider the decadent Sublime Pie with lobster tail, roasted bell peppers, and sun-dried tomatoes. The crust has the perfect texture—just chewy enough without being too doughy. The shop has only one table inside, so order to go, or call for delivery in the evenings after 5pm.

✪ **Islamorada Fish Company.** U.S. 1 at MM 81.5 (up the street from Cheeca Lodge), Islamorada. ☎ **800/258-2559** or 305/664-9271. Main courses $8–$20. DISC, MC, V. Mon–Sat 8am–9pm, Sun 9am–9pm. SEAFOOD. Also, just up the block, Islamorada Fish Company Restaurant & Bakery, MM 81.6; ☎ 305/664-8363; Thurs–Tues 6am–9pm, Wed 6am–2pm. DISC, MC, V.

The original Islamorada Fish Company has been selling seafood out of its roadside shack since 1948. It's still the best place to pick up a cooler of stone crab claws in season (October through early April). Enjoy spectacular views from picnic tables on the store's bay-side dock while munching on their famous (and fattening) Islamorada fish sandwich, served with melted American cheese, fried onions, and coleslaw. A few hundred yards up the road is the newer establishment, which looks like an average diner, but has a fantastic selection of seafood and pastas. It's also the place to eat breakfast—locals gather for politics and gossip as well as delicious grits, oatmeal, omelettes, and homemade pastries (the fresh donuts are great dunked in coffee).

Key Largo's Crack'd Conch. U.S. 1 at MM 105.5 (ocean side). ☎ **305/451-0732.** Main courses $9–$13; sandwiches $5–$7. AE, MC, V. Thurs–Tues noon–10pm. SEAFOOD.

This colorful little shack looks appealing from the road and actually isn't a bad place to stop, especially if you like beer. Over a hundred imported and domestic lagers, porters, stouts, and ales are available. Food choices, on the other hand, are not as varied or as predictable. The Crack'd Conch will deliver decent baskets of fried clams, shrimp, chicken, and, of course, conch. The soups are okay, but they're certainly not made from scratch. The zesty conch salad and the messy po' boy sandwiches are your best options. Prices are higher than they ought to be, considering the quality and atmosphere, but it won't break you.

THE UPPER & MIDDLE KEYS AFTER DARK

Nightlife in the Upper Keys tends to start before the sun goes down, since most people—visitors and locals alike—are on vacation. Partying starts at noon. Also, many anglers and sports-minded folk go to bed early. It's not that they're a puritanical lot; it's just many have been drinking all day and need to crash by midnight in order to be able to get up and do it again.

Opened in the early '90s by some young locals who were tired of tourist traps, **Hog Heaven**, at MM 85.3 just off the main road on the ocean side in Islamorada (☎ **305/664-9669**), is a welcome respite from the neon-colored cocktail circuit. This whitewashed biker bar offers a waterside view and diversions that include big-screen TVs and video games. The food isn't bad either. The atmosphere is cliquish since most patrons are regulars, so start up a game of pool or skeet to break the ice.

No trip is complete without a stop at the **Tiki Bar** at the Holiday Isle Resort, U.S. 1 at MM 84, Islamorada (☎ **800/327-7070** or 305/664-2321). Hundreds of revelers stop at this ocean-side spot for drinks and dancing any time of day, but the live rock music starts at 8:30pm.

In the afternoon and early evening (when everyone is either sunburned, drunk, or just happy to be alive and dancing to live reggae), head for **Kokomo's,** just next door to the thatched-roof Tiki Bar. Kokomo's closes at 7:30pm on weekends, so get there early.

Locals and tourists mingle at the outdoor cabana bar at **Lorelei Restaurant and Cabana Bar** (see "Where to Dine," above). Most evenings after 5, you'll find local bands playing on a thatched-roof stage—mainly rock and roll, Caribbean, and sometimes blues.

✪ **Woody's Saloon and Restaurant,** on U.S. 1 at MM 82, Islamorada (☎ **305/ 664-4335**), is a lively, wacky, raunchy place serving up mediocre pizzas and live bands almost every night. The house band, Big Dick and the Extenders, showcases a 300-pound Native American who does a lewd, rude, and crude routine of jokes and songs starting at 9pm, Tuesday through Sunday. He is a legend. There is a small cover charge most nights. By the way, don't think you're lucky if you are offered the front table: It's the target seat for Big Dick's haranguing. Avoid the lame karaoke performance on Sunday and Monday evenings. Drink specials, contests, and the legendary Big Dick keep this place packed until 4am almost every night.

For a more subdued atmosphere, try the handsome wood bar at **Zane Grey's** (on the second floor of WorldWide Sportsman at MM 81.5). Outside, enjoy a view of the calm waters of the bay or inside soak up the history of some real old anglers. Original manuscripts and photographs are displayed in mahogany cases. You feel like a real aristocrat in this stained-glass, clubby atmosphere. It is open from 11am to 11pm and later on weekends. But call to find out who is playing on weekends (☎ **305/664-4244**) when there is live entertainment and no cover charge.

3 The Lower Keys: Big Pine Key to Coppitt Key

110 to 140 miles SW of Miami

Big Pine, Sugarloaf, Summerland, and the other Lower Keys are less developed and more tranquil than the Upper Keys. If you're looking for haute cuisine and a happening nightlife, look elsewhere. If you're looking to commune with nature or adventure in solitude, you've come to the right place. Unlike their neighbors to the north and south, the Lower Keys are devoid of rowdy spring-break crowds, boast few T-shirt and trinket shops, and have almost no late-night bars. What they do offer are the very best opportunities to enjoy the vast natural resources, on land and on water, that make the area so rich. Stay overnight in the Lower Keys, rent a boat, and explore the reefs—it might be the most memorable part of your trip.

ESSENTIALS

GETTING THERE   See "Essentials" for the Upper and Middle Keys. Continue south on U.S. 1. The Lower Keys start at the end of the Seven-Mile Bridge.

VISITOR INFORMATION   The **Lower Keys Chamber of Commerce,** ocean side of U.S. 1 at MM 31 (P.O. Box 430511), Big Pine Key, FL 33043 (☎ **800/872-3722** or 305/872-2411; fax 305/872-0752; e-mail: lkchamber@aol.com), is open Monday through Friday from 9am to 5pm and Saturday from 9am to 3pm. The pleasant staff will help with anything a traveler may need. Call, write, or stop in for a comprehensive and detailed information packet.

ENJOYING THE OUTDOORS

The centerpiece of the Lower Keys and its greatest asset is ✪ **Bahia Honda State Park,** U.S. 1 at MM 37.5, Big Pine Key (☎ **305/872-2353**), which has one of the most beautiful coastlines in South Florida and one of the only natural beaches in the Keys. Bahia Honda is a great place for hiking, bird watching, swimming, snorkeling, and fishing. The 524-acre park encompasses a wide variety of ecosystems, including coastal mangroves, beach dunes, and tropical hammocks. There are miles of trails packed with unusual plants and animals and a small white beach. Although the beach is never wider than 5 feet even at low tide, this is one of the Keys's best beach areas. Shaded seaside picnic areas are fitted with tables and grills.

True to its name (Spanish for "deep bay"), the park has relatively deep waters close to shore that are perfect for snorkeling and diving. Head to the stunning reefs at Looe Key where the coral and fish are more vibrant than anywhere in the United States. Snorkeling trips depart daily from March through September and cost $22 for adults, $18 for youths 6 to 14, and free for children 5 and under. Call ☎ **305/872-3210** for a schedule.

Admission to the park is $4 per vehicle (and 50¢ per person), $1.50 per pedestrian or bicyclist, free for children 5 and under. Open daily from 8am to sunset.

NATIONAL KEY DEER REFUGE

The most famous residents of the Lower Keys are the tiny Key deer. Of the estimated 300 existing in the world, two-thirds live on Big Pine Key's National Key Deer Refuge. To get your bearings, stop by the ranger's office, at the Winn-Dixie Shopping Plaza near MM 30.5 off U.S. 1. They'll give you an informative brochure and map of the area. It is open Monday through Friday from 8am to 5pm.

If the office is closed, head out to the Blue Hole, a former rock quarry that's now filled with the fresh water that's vital to the deers' survival. To get there, turn right at Big Pine Key's only traffic light onto Key Deer Boulevard (take the left fork immediately after the turn), and continue 1½ miles to the observation site parking lot, on your left. The half-mile Watson Hammock Trail, located about one-third of a mile past the Blue Hole, is the refuge's only marked footpath. Try coming out here in the early morning or late evening to catch a glimpse of these gentle, dog-sized deer. Refuge lands are open daily from half an hour before sunrise to half an hour after sunset.

Whatever you do, do not feed them—it will threaten their survival. Call the park office (☎ 305/872-2239) to find out about the infrequent, free tours of the refuge, scheduled at different times throughout the year.

OUTDOOR ACTIVITIES A TO Z

BICYCLING   If you have your own bike, or your lodging offers rental (many do), the Lower Keys is a great place to get off busy U.S. 1 to explore the beautiful back roads. On Big Pine Key, cruise along Key Deer Boulevard (at MM 30)—those with fat tires can ride into the National Key Deer Refuge.

BIRD WATCHING   Bring your birding books. A stopping point for migratory birds on the Eastern Flyway, the Lower Keys are populated with many West Indian bird species, especially during spring and fall. The small vegetated islands of the Keys are the only nesting sites in the United States for the great white heron and the white-crowned pigeon. It's also one of a very few breeding places for the reddish egret, the roseate spoonbill, the mangrove cuckoo, and the black-whiskered vireo. Look for them on Bahia Honda and the many uninhabited islands nearby.

BOATING   Dozens of shops rent powerboats for fishing and reef exploring. Most also rent tackle, sell bait, and have charter captains available. **Bud Boats,** at the Old Wooden Bride Fishing Camp and Marina, MM 30 in Big Pine Key (☎ **305/ 872-9165**), has a wide selection of well-maintained boats. Depending on the size, rentals will cost between $70 and $250 for a day; between $50 and $130 for a half day. Another good option is **Jaybird's Powerboats,** U.S. 1 at MM 33, Big Pine Key (☎ **305/872-8500**). They rent only for full days. Prices start at $127 for a 19-footer.

CANOEING & KAYAKING   The Overseas Highway (U.S. 1) only touches on a few dozen of the many hundreds of islands that make up the Keys. To really see the Lower Keys, rent a kayak or canoe—perfect for these shallow and exciting waters. **Reflections Kayak Nature Tours,** operating out of Parmer's Place Resort Motel, on U.S. 1 at MM 28.5, Little Torch Key (☎ **305/872-2896**), offers fully outfitted back-country wildlife tours, either on your own or with an expert. A former U.S. Forest Service guide, Mike Wedeking, keeps up an engaging discussion describing the area's fish, sponges, coral, osprey, hawks, eagles, alligators, raccoons, and deer. The 3-hour tours cost $45 per person and include spring water, fresh fruit, granola bars, and use of binoculars. Bring a towel and sea sandals or sneakers.

FISHING   A day spent fishing, either in the shallow backcountry or in the deep sea, is a great way to assure yourself a fresh fish dinner. Or release your catch and appreciate the challenge. **Larry Threlkeld's Strike Zone Charters,** U.S. 1 at MM 29.5, Big Pine Key (☎ **305/872-9863**), is one of the area's best chartered boats in either the deep sea or the backcountry. Prices start at $250 to $400 for a half day. Especially if you have enough anglers to share the price, it isn't too steep. They may be able to match you with other interested visitors. Call a day or two in advance to see. Reef fishing trips are also offered by **Scandia-Tomi,** U.S. 1 at MM 25, Summerland Key (☎ **305/745-8633;** fax 305/872-0520). There's a six-passenger maximum.

HIKING   You can hike throughout the flat and marshy Keys, on both marked trails and meandering coastlines. The best places to trek through nature are **Bahia Honda State Park** (at MM 29.5) and **National Key Deer Refuge** (at MM 30). Bahia Honda Park has a free brochure describing an excellent self-guided tour along the Silver Palm Nature Trail. You'll traverse hammocks, mangroves, sand dunes, and cross a lagoon. You can do the walk (which is less than a mile) in less than half an hour, and can explore a great cross section of the natural habitat in the Lower Keys. See "Enjoying the Outdoors," above.

SNORKELING/DIVING   Snorkelers and divers should not miss the Keys's most dramatic reefs at the ✪ **Looe Key National Marine Sanctuary.** Between 2 and 30 feet underwater you'll see more than 150 varieties of hard and soft coral, some centuries old. Also, every type of tropical fish, including the gold and blue parrot fish, moray eels, barracudas, French angels, and tarpon, call this dense and diverse reef home. **Looe Key Dive Center,** U.S. 1 at MM 27.5, Ramrod Key (☎ **305/872-2215**), offers a mind-blowing 2½-hour tour aboard a 45-foot catamaran with two shallow 1-hour dives for snorkelers and scuba divers. Snorkelers pay $30, and divers with their own equipment pay $65. Good-quality rentals are available. (See "Enjoying the Outdoors," above, for other diving options.)

THE ONLY HUMAN-MADE ATTRACTION IN THE LOWER KEYS

Sugarloaf Bat Tower. Off U.S. 1 at MM 17 (next to Sugarloaf Airport on the bay side). Free admission.

In a vain effort to battle the ubiquitous and troublesome mosquitoes in the Lower Keys, developer Clyde Perkey built this odd structure to lure bug-eating bats. Despite his alluring design and a pungent bat aphrodisiac, his guests never showed. Since 1929, this wooden, flat-topped pyramid has stood empty and deserted, except for the occasional tourist who stops to wonder what it is. There is no sign or marker to commemorate this odd remnant of ingenuity. It's worth a 5-minute detour to see the odd 45-foot-high tower. To reach the tower, turn right at the Sugarloaf Airport sign, then right again, onto the dirt road that begins just before the airport gate; the tower is about 100 yards ahead.

SHOPPING

Certainly not known for great shopping, the Lower Keys do happen to be home to many good visual artists, particularly those who specialize in depicting their natural surroundings. The **Artists in Paradise Gallery,** on Big Pine Key in the Winn-Dixie Shopping Plaza, near MM 30.5 1 block north of U.S. 1 at the traffic light (☎ **305/872-1828**), displays an ever-changing selection of watercolors, oils, photos, and sculptures. This cooperative gallery displays the work of more than a dozen artists who share the task of watching the store. Usually hours are daily from 10am to 6pm. Even more impressive is the ✪ **Gallery at Kona Kai Resort** (see "Where to Stay," above), which shows dramatic black-and-white photos, oils and watercolors, and more.

WHERE TO STAY

There are a number of cheap fish shacks along the highway for those who want bare-bones accommodations. However, so far, there are no national hotel chains in the Lower Keys.

VERY EXPENSIVE

✪ **Little Palm Island.** Launch is at the ocean side of U.S. 1 at MM 28.5, Little Torch Key, FL 33042. ☎ **800/343-8567** or 305/872-2524. Fax 305/872-4843. 28 bungalows, 2 houseboat suites. A/C MINIBAR. Winter $495–$625 suite. Off-season $400–$425 suite. No children under 16. AE, CB, DC, DISC, MC, V.

Under new ownership since 1997, Little Palm Island received a much needed renovation which included new roofs, a new dining room and a thorough update of the guest rooms. This exclusive resort, host to presidents and royalty, is not just a place to stay while in the Lower Keys; it is a resort destination all its own. Formerly a fishing camp for the country's elite, it is built on a private 5-acre island that's accessible only by boat. Guests stay in thatched-roof villas amid lush foliage and flowering tropical plants.

Many have ocean views and private sundecks fitted with rope hammocks. Inside, the romantic suites have all the comforts and conveniences of a luxurious contemporary beach cottage, but without telephones, TVs, or alarm clocks. Note that on the breeze-less south side of the island, you may get invaded by mosquitoes, even in the winter. Bring bug repellent and lightweight long-sleeved clothing. Known for its innovative and pricey food, little Palm also hosts guests just for dinner or lunch. If you are staying on the island, opt for the full American plan, which includes three meals a day for about $100 per person. If you pay à la carte, you could spend that much just on dinner. At these prices, Little Palm appeals to those who aren't keeping count. Note that children are not welcome.

Dining/Diversions: The Little Palm Restaurant offers fine dining either indoors or alfresco at inflated prices, and a pool bar offers refreshments and light snacks all day.

Amenities: Concierge, room service, dry cleaning, laundry, newspaper delivery, twice-daily maid service, in-room massage, courtesy van from Key West or Marathon airport. Outdoor pool with small waterfall, wide beach, in-room Jacuzzi tubs, sauna, sundeck, water-sports equipment, jogging trail, boutique.

MODERATE

Barnacle Bed & Breakfast. 1557 Long Beach Dr. (P.O. Box 780), Big Pine Key, FL 33043. ☎ **800/465-9100** or 305/872-3298. Fax 305/872-3863. 4 units. A/C TV TEL. Winter $95–$125 double. Off-season $85–$125 double. Rates include breakfast. No children under 16 accepted. DISC, MC, V. From U.S. 1 south, turn left at the Spanish Harbor Bridge (MM 33) onto Long Beach Rd. Look left for the stone wall and signs to the house on the left.

Joan Cornell, the Barnacle's owner, was once an innkeeper in Vermont; she knows what amenities travelers are looking for and goes out of her way to accommodate. Her Big Pine Key home has only four bedrooms, each with its own character. Two are located upstairs in the main house—their doors open into the home's living room, which contains a small Jacuzzi-style tub. For privacy, the remaining two rooms are best; each has its own entrance and is out of earshot of the common areas. The Cottage Room, a free-standing, peak-topped bedroom, is best, outfitted with a kitchenette and pretty furnishings. The accommodations are standard, not luxurious. All rooms have small refrigerators and private baths. The property has its own private sandy beach where you can float all day on the inn's rafts, rubber boat, or kayak. Beach towels, chairs, bicycles, and coolers are available at no charge. Neither children nor pets are welcome.

Deer Run Bed and Breakfast. Long Beach Dr. (P.O. Box 431), Big Pine Key, FL 33043. ☎ **305/872-2015.** Fax 305/872-2842. E-mail: deerrunbb@aol.com. 3 units. Winter from $110 double. Off-season from $95 double. Rates include full American breakfast. No children under 16 accepted. No credit cards. From U.S. 1 south, turn left at the Big Pine Fishing Lodge (MM 33); continue for about 2 miles.

Located directly on the beach, Sue Abbott's small, homey, smoke-free B&B is a real find. One upstairs and two downstairs guest rooms are comfortably furnished with queen-size beds, good closets, and touch-sensitive lamps. Rattan and 1970s-style chairs and couches furnish the living room, along with 13 birds and three cats. Breakfast, which is served on a pretty, fenced-in porch, is cooked to order by Sue herself. The wooded area around the property is full of deer, often spotted on the beach as well. Ask to use one of the bikes to explore nearby nature trails. The owner prefers adults and mature children only.

INEXPENSIVE

✪ **Parmer's Place Cottages.** Barry Ave. (P.O. Box 430665), near MM 28.5, Little Torch Key, FL 33043. ☎ **305/872-2157.** Fax 305/872-2014. 41 units. In winter and during festivals from $77 double; from $93.50 efficiency. Off-season $55–$65 double; from $75 efficiency. AE, DISC, MC, V. Turn right onto Barry Ave. Resort is ½ mile down on the right.

This downscale resort offers modest but comfortable cottages. Every unit is different: Some face the water, while others are a few steps away; some have small kitchenettes, and others are just a bedroom. Room 26, a one-bedroom efficiency, is especially nice, with a small sitting area that faces the water. Room 6, a small efficiency, has a little kitchenette and an especially large bathroom. The rooms have linoleum floors, dated 1970s-style painted rattan furnishings, fake flowers, and thrift-store art. They're very clean, and many can be combined to accommodate large families. Facilities include a horseshoes court and boat ramp, plus a heated swimming pool. Parmer's, a fixture here for more than 20 years, is well known for its charming hospitality and helpful staff.

Also, see "Camping," below, for inexpensive options in fully equipped cabins or rented trailers.

CAMPING

Bahia Honda State Park offers some of the best camping in the Keys. See "Enjoying the Great Outdoors," above, or call ☎ **305/872-2353.** It is as loaded with facilities and activities as it is with campers. However, don't be discouraged by its popularity—this park encompasses more than 500 acres of land. There are 80 campsites and six spacious and comfortable cabin units. If you're lucky enough to get one, the park's cabins represent a very good value. Each holds up to eight guests and comes complete with linens, kitchenettes, and utensils. Ask for a cabin overlooking the bay, which offers the best views and most privacy. You'll enjoy the wraparound terrace, barbecue pit, and rocking chairs.

Camping costs about $25 per site for one to four people without electricity and $26 with electricity. Depending on the season, cabin prices change: From December 15 to September 14 it's about $125 per cabin for one to four people; from September 15 to December 14 it's $97.28 per cabin. Additional people (over four) cost $6. MasterCard and Visa are accepted.

Another excellent value can be found at the **KOA Sugarloaf Key Resort,** near mile marker 20. This ocean-side facility has 200 fully equipped sites that rent for about $53 a night ($36 with no hookups). Or pitch a tent on the 5 acres of lush waterfront property. They also rent out travel trailers. The 22-foot dutchman sleeps six and is equipped with eating and cooking utensils The cost is about $100 a day. More luxurious trailers go for $160 a day. They take all major credit cards. For details contact KOA at P.O. Box 420469, Summerland Key, FL 33042 (☎ **800/562-7731** or 305/745-3549; fax 305/745-9889; e-mail: sugarloaf@koa.net).

WHERE TO DINE

There aren't many fine-dining options in the Lower Keys. There's decent food for the motorists passing through, but nothing too fancy. The following are worth a stop.

MODERATE

✪ **Mangrove Mama's Restaurant.** U.S. 1 at MM 20, Sugarloaf Key. ☎ **305/745-3030.** Main courses $13–$19; lunch $2–$9; brunch $5–$7. MC, V. Daily 11:30am–10pm (11am in season). SEAFOOD/CARIBBEAN.

As dedicated locals who come daily for happy hour will tell you, Mangrove Mama's is a true Lower Keys institution and a dive in the best sense of the word. The restaurant is a shack that used to have a gas pump as well as a grill. Now, guests share the property with some miniature horses (out back) and stray cats. A handful of simple tables, inside and out, are shaded by banana trees and palm fronds. Fish is, not surprisingly, the menu's mainstay, though soups, salads, sandwiches, and omelettes are also good. Grilled teriyaki chicken and club sandwiches are tasty alternatives to fish, as are meatless chef's salad and spicy barbecued baby back ribs.

✪ **Monte's.** U.S. 1 at MM 25, Summerland Key. ☎ **305/745-3731.** Main courses $10–$14; lunch $3–$8. No credit cards. Mon–Sat 9:30am–10pm, Sun 10am–9pm. SEAFOOD.

Nobody goes to this restaurant/fish market for its atmosphere: Plastic place settings rest on plastic-covered picnic-style tables in a screen-enclosed dining patio. Monte's has survived for more than 20 years because the food is very good and incredibly fresh. The day's catch may include shark, tuna, lobster, stone crabs, or shrimp.

INEXPENSIVE

✪ **Coco's Kitchen.** 283 Key Deer Blvd. (in the Winn-Dixie Shopping Center), Big Pine Key. ☎ **305/872-4495.** Main courses $5–$12; lunch $2–$5; breakfast $1–$4.50. No credit cards. Mon–Sat 7am–7:30pm. Turn right at traffic light near MM 30.5. Stay in the left lane. CUBAN/NICARAGUAN.

This tiny storefront has been dishing out black beans and rice and shredded beef to Cuban food fans for more than 10 years. The owners, who are actually from Nicaragua, cook not only superior Cuban food but also some local specialties, Italian food, and Caribbean food. The best bet is the daily special, which may be roasted pork or fresh grouper, served with rice and beans or salad and crispy fries. Top off the huge, cheap meal with a rich caramel-soaked flan.

No Name Pub. ¼ mile south of No Name Bridge on N. Watson Blvd., Big Pine Key. ☎ **305/872-9115.** Pizzas $8–$18; subs $5. MC, V. 11am–11pm. Turn right at Big Pine's only traffic light (near MM30.5) onto Key Deer Blvd. Turn right on Watson Blvd. At stop sign, turn left. Look for a small wooden sign on the left marking the spot. PUB FOOD/PIZZA.

This funky old bar out in the boonies serves snacks and sandwiches until 11pm on most nights and drinks until midnight. The pizzas are tasty—thick crusted and super cheesy. Try one topped with local shrimps. Or, consider a bowl of chili with all the fixins. It's hearty and cheap. Also decent is the smoked fish dip. Everything is served on paper plates. Locals hang out at the rustic bar, one of the Florida Keys's oldest, drinking beer and listening to a jukebox that's heavy with '80s selections. The decor—if you can call it that—is basic. Walls and ceilings are plastered with thousands of autographed dollar bills. Ask the waitress for a stapler to affix yours. At sunset, look outside and you may see one of the famed Key deer.

THE LOWER KEYS AFTER DARK

The mellow islands of the Lower Keys aren't exactly known as a haven for wild nightlife; however, there are a number of friendly bars and restaurants where locals and tourists gather to hang out and drink.

One of the most scenic is **Sandbar** (☎ 305/872-9989), a wide-open, breezy wooden house built on slender stilts and overlooking a wide channel on Barry Avenue (near MM 28.5). It attracts an odd mix of bikers and blue-hairs daily from 11am until 11pm. Pool tables are the main attraction but there is also live music some nights. The drinks are reasonably priced and the food isn't too bad either.

For a fun bar scene, see No Name Pub, above.

4 Key West

The local salts and the developers have been at odds for years. The once low-key island has been thoroughly commercialized. There is no denying it now that there is a Hard

Rock Cafe smack in the middle of Duval Street, Sloppy Joe's has opened franchises around the country, and thousands of cruise-ship passengers descend on Mallory Square each day. This is definitely not the seedy town Hemingway and his cronies once called their own.

Laid-back Key West still exists, but it's now found in the backyard of a popular guest house, in an art gallery, in a secret garden, in the hip hangouts of Bahama Village, and, of course, on the sea.

The heart of town offers a more wild time. There are some good restaurants, lively bars, live music, rickshaw rides, and lots of shopping. Don't bother with a watch or tie. This is the home of the perennial vacation.

ESSENTIALS

GETTING THERE   See "Essentials" for the Upper and Middle Keys. Continue south on U.S. 1. When entering Key West, stay in the far-right lane onto North Roosevelt Boulevard, which becomes Truman Avenue in Old Town. Continue for a few blocks and you will find yourself on Duval Street, in the heart of the city. If you stay to the left, you'll also reach the city center after passing the airport and historic houseboat row, where a motley collection of boats make up one of Key West's most interesting neighborhoods.

GETTING AROUND   With limited parking, narrow streets, and congested traffic, the best way to get around Key West is by bicycle. The island is small and as flat as a board, which makes it easy to negotiate, especially away from the crowded downtown. More tourists choose to cruise by moped, an option that can make navigating the streets risky, especially since there are no helmet laws in Key West. Spend the extra money and rent a helmet; there are hundreds of serious accidents each year.

Rates for simple one-speed cruisers start at about $6 per day (from $30 per week). Tacky, pink mopeds start at about $25 per day and $100 per week. The best rental shops include **The Bike Shop,** 1110 Truman Ave. (☎ **305/294-1073**); the **Moped Hospital,** 601 Truman Ave. (☎ **305/296-3344**); and **Tropical Bicycles & Scooter Rentals,** 1300 Duval St. (☎ **305/294-8136**).

Several regional airlines fly nonstop from Miami to Key West; fares are about $120 to $300 round-trip. **American Eagle** (☎ **800/443-7300**) and **US Airways Express** (☎ **800/428-4322**) land at **Key West International Airport,** South Roosevelt Boulevard (☎ **305/296-5439**), on the southeastern corner of the island.

VISITOR INFORMATION   The **Florida Keys and Key West Visitors Bureau,** P.O. Box 1147, Key West, FL 33041 (☎ **800/FLA-KEYS**), offers a free vacation kit that's packed with visitor information. The **Key West Chamber of Commerce,** 402 Wall St., Key West, FL 33040 (☎ **800/527-8539** or 305/294-2587), also offers general as well as specialized information. The lobby is open daily from 8:30am to 6pm; phones are answered 8am to 8pm. The **Key West Visitor's Center** also provides information on accommodations, goings-on, and restaurants; the number is ☎ **800/ LAST-KEY.** They're open weekdays from 8am to 5:30pm and weekends from 8:30am to 5pm.

ORIENTATION   A mere 2-by-4-mile island, Key West is simple to navigate, even though there is no real order to the arrangement of named streets and avenues. As you enter town on U.S. 1 (also called Roosevelt Boulevard), you will see most of the moderately priced chain hotels and fast-food restaurants. The better restaurants, shops, and outfitters are crammed onto Old Town's main thoroughfare, Duval Street. On surrounding streets are the many inns and lodges in picturesque Victorian/Bahamian homes. On the southern side of the island is the coral beach area and some of the larger resort hotels.

SEEING THE SIGHTS

✪ **Audubon House & Tropical Gardens.** 205 Whitehead St. (between Greene and Caroline sts.). ☎ **305/294-2116.** Admission $7.50 adults, $3.50 children 6–12. Daily 9:30am–5pm (last admission at 4:45pm) Discounts for students, and AAA and AARP members.

This well-preserved home dating from the early 19th century stands as a prime example of early Key West architecture and life. Named after the renowned painter and bird expert, John James Audubon, who was said to have visited the house in 1832, the graceful two-story home is a peaceful retreat from the bustle of nearby Duval Street and Mallory Square. Included in the price of admission is a self-guided audiotape tour that lasts just under half an hour. With voices of several characters from the house's past, the tour never gets boring—though it is at times a bit hokey. See rare Audubon prints, gorgeous antiques, historical photos and lush tropical gardens and, while you are at it, learn a little about the island's colorful history. Even if you don't want to spend the time and money to explore the grounds and home, check out the impressive gift shop which sells a variety of fine mementos at reasonable prices.

Ernest Hemingway Home and Museum. 907 Whitehead St. (between Truman Ave. and Olivia St.). ☎ **305/294-1575** or 305/294-1136. Admission $6.50 adults, $4 children. Daily 9am–5pm.

One-time Key West resident Ernest Hemingway has become somewhat of a touristic icon down here; the novelist's gruff image is emblazoned on T-shirts and mugs and is used to sell everything from beer to suntan lotion. Hemingway's particularly handsome stone Spanish Colonial house was built in 1851 and was one of the first on the island to be fitted with indoor plumbing and a built-in fireplace. The author lived here from 1928 until 1940 along with about 50 six-toed cats, whose descendants still roam the premises. It was during those years that the Nobel Prize winner wrote some of his most famous works, including *For Whom the Bell Tolls, A Farewell to Arms,* and *The Snows of Kilimanjaro.* Fans may want to take the optional half-hour tour. It's interesting and included in the price of admission.

Key West Cemetery. Entrance at Margaret and Angela sts. Free admission. Daily dawn to dusk. Tours can be arranged by calling ☎ **305/294-WALK.**

Epitomizing the quirky Key West image, this funky and picturesque cemetery is as irreverent as it is humorous. Many tombs are stacked several high, condominium style—the rocky soil made digging 6 feet under nearly impossible for early settlers. And pets are often buried beside their owners. Many of the memorials are emblazoned with nicknames—a common Key West informality that's literally taken to the grave. Look for headstones labeled "The Tailor," "Bean," "Shorty," and "Bunny." Other headstones also reflect residents' lighthearted attitudes toward life and death. "I Told You I Was Sick" is one of the more famous epitaphs, as is the tongue-in-cheek widow's inscription, "At Least I Know Where He's Sleeping Tonight."

East Martello Museum and Gallery. 3501 S. Roosevelt Blvd. ☎ **305/296-3913.** Admission $6 adults, $2 children 8–12, free for children 7 and under. Daily 9:30am–5pm (last admission is at 4pm).

Adjacent to the airport, the East Martello Museum is located in a Civil War–era brick fort that itself is worth a visit. The museum contains a bizarre variety of exhibits that, collectively, do a thorough job interpreting the city's intriguing past. Historical artifacts include ship models, a deep-sea diver's wooden air pump, a crude raft from a

Cuban "boat lift," a supposedly haunted doll, a Key West–style children's playhouse from 1918, and a horse-drawn hearse. Exhibits illustrate the Keys's history of wrecking, sponging, and cigar making. And if all that's not enough, the museum also exhibits modern works by local artists. After seeing the galleries, climb a steep spiral staircase to the top of a lookout tower for good views over the island and ocean.

✪ **Key West Aquarium.** 1 Whitehead St. (at Mallory Sq.). ☎ **305/296-2051.** Admission $8 adults, $4 children 4–12. Free for children under 4. Tickets are good for 2 consecutive days (a bonus for kids with short attention spans). Look for discount coupons from local hotels, Duval St. kiosks, and from trolley and train tours. Daily 10am–6pm.

The oldest attraction on the island, the Key West Aquarium is a modest but fascinating exhibit. A long hallway of eye-level displays showcase dozens of variety of fish and crustaceans. See delicate sea horses swaying in the backlit tanks. Kids can touch sea cucumbers and sea anemones in a shallow touch tank in the entryway. If you can, catch one of the free guided tours offered daily at 11am, 1, 3, and 4pm. Then you'll witness the dramatic feeding frenzy of the sharks, tarpon, barracudas, stingrays, and turtles.

Key West Lighthouse Museum. 938 Whitehead St. ☎ **305/294-0012.** Admission $6 adults, $2 children 7–12, free for children 6 and under. Daily 9:30am–5pm (last admission at 4:30pm).

When the Key West Lighthouse was opened in 1848, many locals mourned. Its bright warning to ships signaled the end of a profitable era for wreckers, pirate salvagers who looted reef-stricken ships. The story of this, and other Keys's lighthouses, is illustrated in a small museum that was formerly the keeper's quarters. When radar and sonar made the lighthouse obsolete, it was opened to visitors as a tourist attraction. It's worth mustering the energy to climb the 88 claustrophobic steps to the top, where you'll be rewarded with magnificent panoramic views of Key West and the ocean.

✪ **Mel Fisher Maritime Heritage Museum.** 200 Greene St. ☎ **305/294-2633.** Admission $6.50 adults, $2 children 6–12, free for children 5 and under. Open daily 9:30am–5pm.

This museum honors local hero Mel Fisher, who, along with a crew of other salvagers, found a multimillion-dollar treasure trove in 1985 aboard the wreck of the Spanish galleon Nuestra Señora de Atocha. The admission price is steep, but if you're into diving, pirates, and the mystery of sunken treasures, check out this small and informative museum, full of doubloons, pieces of eight, emeralds, and solid-gold bars. A dated but informative film provides a good background of Fisher's incredible story. The museum also features a new exhibit entitled "Battleship," about the USS *Maine*.

ORGANIZED TOURS

TROLLEY-BUS TOURS   Yes, it's more than a bit hokey to sit in these red cars, but worth the embarrassment. The city's whole story is packed into a neat, 90-minute package on the Conch Tour Train, which covers the island and all its rich, raunchy history. The "train's" engine is a propane-powered Jeep disguised as a locomotive. Tours depart from both Mallory Square and the Welcome Center, near the intersection of U.S. 1 and North Roosevelt Boulevard, on the other side of the island. For more information, contact the **Conch Train** at 1 Key Lime Sq., Key West (☎ **305/294-5161;** fax 305/292-8993). The cost is $15 for adults, $7 for children 4 to 12, and free for children 3 and under. Daily departures are every half hour from 9am to 4:30pm.

The other option to get a good perspective on this history-packed island is the **Old Town Trolley.** Drivers maintain a running commentary as the open-air tram loops around the island's streets past all the major sights. The main advantage of this 90-minute tour is that riders can get off at any of 14 stops, explore a museum or visit a

Attractions

Aquarium 18
Audubon House & Tropical Gardens 23
Cemetery 9
Chamber of Commerce 21
East Martello Museum and Gallery 2
Ernest Hemingway Home and Museum 25
Fort Zachary Beach 29
Higgs Beach 6
Lighthouse Museum 26
Mallory Square 19
Mel Fisher Maritime Heritage Museum 22
Smathers Beach 3

Accommodations

Big Ruby's 24
The Brass Key 4
Island City House Hotel 7
Blue Lagoon Resort 1
Chelsea House 12
The Grand 5
Key West Hilton Resort & Marina 20
Key West International Hostel 13
La Pensione 10
Marquesa Hotel 11
Marriott's Beach Resort 15
Oasis 8
Ocean Key House 17
Pier House Resort & Caribbean Spa 16
Rainbow House 14
South Beach Oceanfront Motel 28
Southernmost Point Guest House 27

restaurant, and then reboard later at will. Trolleys depart from Mallory Square and other points around the island. For details, contact them at 1910 N. Roosevelt Blvd. (☎ **305/296-6688**). Tours are $16 for adults, $7 for children 4 to 12, and free for children 3 and under. Departures are daily from 9am to 4pm.

AIRPLANE TOURS   Proclaimed by the mayor as "the official air force of the Conch Republic," **Island Airplane Tours,** at Key West Airport, 3469 S. Roosevelt Blvd. (☎ **305/294-8687** for reservations), offers windy rides in its open-cockpit 1940 Waco biplanes over the reefs and around the islands. Thrill seekers—and they only—will enjoy a spin in the company's S2-B aerobatics airplane that does loops, rolls, and sideways figure eights. Company owner Fred Cabanas was "decorated" in 1991, after he spotted a Cuban airman defecting to the United States in a Russian-built MiG fighter. Sightseeing flights cost $50 to $200, depending on the duration.

BOAT TOURS   ✪ *The Pride of Key West/Fireball,* at 2 Duval St. (☎ **305/ 296-6293;** fax 305/294-8704), is a 58-foot glass-bottom catamaran that goes on both day and evening coral-reef tours and sunset cruises by evening. Reef trips cost $20 per person; sunset cruises are $25 per person and include snacks, sodas, and a glass of champagne.

The Wolf, at Schooner Wharf, Key West Seaport (☎ **305/296-9653;** fax 305/294-8388), is a 44-passenger topsail schooner that sets sail daily for daytime and sunset cruises around the Keys, equipped with a cannon. Key West Seaport is located at the end of Greene Street. Day tours cost $25 per person; sunset sails cost $30 per person and include champagne, wine, beer, or soda, and live music.

OTHER TOURS   For a lively tour of Key West, try a 2-hour tour of Key West's five most famous pubs daily at 2:30pm. The tour takes 1½ hours, costs $21, and includes four drinks. Another fun and interesting tour for those into the paranormal is the nightly ghost tour. Cost is $18 for adults and $10 for children. Guests report sightings periodically. Both are offered by Key West Tour Association. New in 1998 is a cemetery tour at 10:30am (☎ **305/294-WALK**).

SPORTS & OUTDOOR ACTIVITIES

BICYCLING & MOPEDING   A popular mode of transportation for locals and visitors, bikes and mopeds are available at many rental outlets in the city (see "Getting Around," above). Escape the hectic downtown scene and explore the island's scenic side streets. Head away from Duval Street to South Roosevelt Boulevard and the beach-side enclaves along the way.

BEACHES   At the end of the chain of keys are finally a few beaches, though they do not compare to the state's natural and wide wonders up the coast. If you want to go to the beach, here are your options: **Smathers Beach,** off South Roosevelt Boulevard west of the airport; **Higgs Beach,** along Atlantic Boulevard between White Street and Reynolds Road; and **Fort Zachary Beach,** located off the western end of Southard Boulevard.

Although there is an entrance fee ($3.75 per car, plus more for each passenger), Fort Zachary is the most recommendable of the beaches, since it also includes a great historical fort, a Civil War museum, and a large picnic area with tables, barbecue grills, bathrooms, and showers.

DIVING   One of the area's largest scuba schools, **Dive Key West Inc.,** 3128 N. Roosevelt Blvd. (☎ **800/426-0707** or 305/296-3823; fax 305/296-0609; www.divekeywest.com; e-mail: divekeywest@flakeysol.com), offers instruction on all levels. Dive boats take participants to scuba and snorkel sites on nearby reefs.

Wreck dives and night dives are two of the special offerings of **Lost Reef Adventures,** 261 Margaret St. (☎ **800/952-2749** or 305/296-9737). Regularly scheduled runs and private charters can be arranged. Phone for departure information.

FISHING   Dozens of charter-fishing boats operate from Key West marinas. You can negotiate good deals at Charter Boat Row located at 1801 N. Roosevelt Ave. (across from the Shell station). There are more than 30 charter fishing and party boats. Just show up to arrange your cruise, or call **Garrison Bite Marina** (☎ **305/292-8167**) for details. One especially good deal is the *Gulfstream II* (☎ **305/296-8494**). This all-day charter goes out daily from 9:30am until 4pm. You'll pay $30, plus $3 for a rod and reel. This 65-foot party-boat usually has at least 30 other anglers. Bring your own cooler or buy snacks on the boat. Beer and wine is allowed. Others include Capt. Jim Brienza's 27-foot *Sea Breeze,* docked at 25 Arbutus Dr. (☎ **305/294-6027**), and Capt. Henry Otto's 44-foot *Sunday,* docked at the Hyatt in Key West (☎ **305/294-7052**).

GOLF   One of the area's only courses is **Key West Golf Club,** an 18-hole course located just north of the island of Key West at MM 4.5 (turn onto College Road to the course entrance; ☎ **305/294-5232**). Designed by Rees Jones, the course has plenty of mangroves and water hazards on its 6,526 yards. It's open to the public, and there's a new pro shop. Call ahead for tee-time reservations.

SHOPPING

Like any tourist destination, Key West has an abundance of tacky tourist shops. They also happen to have a wide variety of fantastic antique stores, designer boutiques, art galleries, and bookstores.

On Duval Street, T-shirt shops outnumber almost any other business. If you must get a wearable memento, be careful of unscrupulous salespeople. Despite efforts to curtail the practice, many shops have been known to rip off unwitting shoppers. A few too many Rum Runners sometimes result in some very expensive souvenirs. It pays to check the prices and the exchange rate before signing any sales slips. You are entitled to a written estimate of any T-shirt work before you pay for it.

At Mallory Square is the Clinton Street Market, an over-air-conditioned mall of kiosks and stalls designed for the many cruise ship passengers who never venture beyond this super-commercial zone. Amid the dreck are some delicious coffee and candy shops and some high-priced hats and shoes. There is also a free and clean rest room.

Once the main industry of Key West, cigar making is enjoying renewed success at the handful of factories that survived the slow years. Stroll through "Cigar Alley," between Front and Greene streets, where you will find *viejitos* (little old men) rolling fat stogies just as they used to do in their homeland across the Florida Straits. Stop at the **Key West Cigar Factory,** at 308 Front St. (☎ **305/294-3470**), for an excellent selection of imported and locally rolled smokes, including the famous El Hemingway. Remember, buying or selling Cuban-made cigars is illegal. Shops advertising "Cuban Cigars" are usually referring to domestic cigars made from tobacco grown from seeds that were brought from Cuba decades ago.

If you are looking for local or Caribbean art, you will find nearly a dozen galleries and shops clustered on Duval Street between Catherine and Fleming streets. You'll also find some excellent shops scattered on the side streets. One worth seeking out is the ✪ **Haitian Art Co.,** 600 Frances St. (☎ **305/296-8932**), where you can browse through room upon room of original paintings from well-known and obscure Haitian artists in a range of prices from a few dollars to a few thousand. Also, check out **Cuba, Cuba!** at 814 Duval St. (☎ **305/295-9442**). Here you will find paintings, sculpture, and photos by Cuban artists.

A favorite stop in the Keys is the deliciously fragrant **Key West Aloe.** Since 1971, this shop has been selling a simple line of bath products, including lotions, shampoos, and soothing balms for those who have spent too much time in the hot tropical sun. Sweet aromas waft from the several outlets in town. At the main shop (open until 8pm) you can find great gift baskets, tropical perfumes, and candies and cookies, too. In addition to frangipani, vanilla, and hibiscus scents, sample Key West for Men, a unique and alluringly musky best-seller. Stop by 524 Front St. (between Simonton and Duval streets), or call for a catalog (☎ **305/294-5592**).

Literature buffs will appreciate the many book shops and record stores on the island. **Flaming Maggie's** at 800 Caroline St. carries a wide selection of gay books (☎ **305/294-3931**). **Key West Island Bookstore,** at 513 Fleming St. (☎ **305/ 294-2904**), carries new, used, and rare books and specializes in fiction by Keys's residents, including Hemingway, Tennessee Williams, Shel Silverstein, Ann Beattie, Richard Wilbur, and John Hersey. Both are open daily.

For anything else, from bed linens to candlesticks to clothing, go to downtown's oldest and most renowned department store, **Fast Buck Freddie's,** 500 Duval St. (☎ **305/ 294-2007**); it's open daily from 10am to 6pm in season, 11am to 7pm in the summer, and until 10pm most Saturdays and some evenings in season. For the same merchandise at more reduced prices, try ✪ **Half Buck Freddie's,** 726 Caroline St. (☎ **305/ 294-6799**). Here you can shop for out-of-season bargains and "rejects" from the main store. Half Buck is open on Thursday, Friday, Saturday, and Sunday only, from 11am to 5pm.

WHERE TO STAY

You'll find a wide variety of places to stay in Key West, from resorts with all the amenities to seaside motels, quaint bed-and-breakfasts, and clothing-optional guest houses. Unless you're in town during Key West's most popular holidays: Fantasy Fest (around Halloween), Hemingway Days (in July), Christmas and New Year's Eve, or for a big fishing tournament, you can almost always find a place to stay at the last minute. However, you may want to book early, especially in the winter, when prime properties fill up and many require 2- or 3-night minimums. Try **Reservation Hotline of Key West,** one of the most pleasant reservation services in town, to help you sort out the many small lodgings that couldn't all be reviewed here or to find a private home or condo. Rita Logan can help you find the perfect place; call ☎ **800/546-5397** or 305/745-9977 between 9am and 6pm, Monday through Saturday. During high season this service is open on Sunday, too. The **Key West Innkeepers Association,** P.O. Box 6172, Key West, FL 33041 (☎ **800/492-1911** or 305/292-3600), can also help find lodging in any price range from its dozens of members and affiliates.

Most major hotel chains have at least one location in Key West; many are clustered on North Roosevelt Boulevard (U.S. 1). Moderately priced options include **Howard Johnson,** 3031 N. Roosevelt Blvd. (☎ **800/942-0913** or 305/296-6595); the **Ramada Inn,** 3420 N. Roosevelt Blvd. (☎ **800/330-5541** or 305/294-5541); the **Econo Lodge,** 3820 N. Roosevelt Blvd. (☎ **800/553-2666** or 305/294-5511); the **Holiday Inn Beachside,** 3841 N. Roosevelt Blvd. (☎ **800/292-7706** or 305/ 294-2571); and the **Quality Inn,** 3850 N. Roosevelt Blvd. (☎ **800/228-5151** or 305/294-6681). The Howard Johnson and the Holiday Inn are the only hotels with gulf-view rooms; the other hotels listed are just across the street. You can drive or taxi to Duval Street in less than 5 minutes.

However, if you want to be closer to Key West's historic section and you like the idea of staying at a national chain, you might want to try **Holiday Inn La Concha Hotel,** at 430 Duval St. (☎ **800/745-2191**). It is centrally located but room rates are high for a mediocre room (from $160 in season). Like much of Key West, service here can be brusque. Avoid the Best Western Hibiscus Hotel, located at 1313 Simonton St. The property is in bad shape, management is rude, and prices are high.

Note that parking in Old Town is severely limited. There is a well-placed municipal parking lot at Simonton and Angela streets just behind the firehouse and police station. You may want to stash your car there while you enjoy the very walkable downtown section of Key West.

Gay travelers will want to call the **Key West Business Guild** (☎ **305/294-4603**), which represents more than 50 guest houses and B&Bs in town as well as many other gay-owned businesses. Ask for its 52-page color brochure.

Or, try **Good Times Travel** (☎ **305/294-0980**), which will set up package tours on the island.

One of the most elegant and popular gay guest houses is **Big Ruby's** (☎ 800/ 477-7829 or 305/296-2323), at 409 Applerouth Lane (a little alley just off Duval Street). A low cluster of buildings surrounds a lushly landscaped courtyard where a hearty breakfast is served each morning and wine poured at dusk. The mostly male guests hang out by a good-sized pool tanning in the buff. Also popular is **Oasis**, at 823 Fleming St. (☎ **305/296-2131**). It's super clean and friendly. Guests can enjoy a central location and a 14-seat hot tub.

Another luxurious property is **The Brass Key,** at 412 Frances St. (☎ **305/ 296-4719**), which is more romantic and traditionally decorated and welcomes many lesbian travelers as well. *Out and About* gave it a five-star rating. For women only, the **Rainbow House** at 525 United St. (☎ **800-74-WOMYN** or 305/292-1450) is a large, gorgeous guest house with lots of amenities including two pools and two hot tubs. If you're uncomfortable with nudity, be sure to ask if your accommodation is like most gay guest houses, which have a clothing-optional policy.

VERY EXPENSIVE

✪ **Key West Hilton Resort and Marina.** 245 Front St., Key West, FL 33040. ☎ **800/ 221-2424** or 305/294-4000. Fax 305/294-4086. 211 units. A/C MINIBAR TV TEL. Winter $259–$475 double; $325–$750 suite. Off-season $169–$375 double; $250–$750 suite. Sunset Key Cottages: winter $870–$1395; off-season $670–$925. AE, DC, DISC, MC, V.

Completed in fall 1996, this Hilton is a truly luxurious addition to downtown's hotel scene. This rambling two-building hotel is at the very end of Duval Street in the middle of all of Old Town's action. The sparkling new rooms are large and well appointed with tropical decor and all the modern conveniences. Choose a suite in the main building if you want a large Jacuzzi in your living room. Otherwise, the marina building has great views. This giant will no doubt be very popular with corporate and convention visitors.

Amenities: Concierge, room service, laundry and dry-cleaning services, newspaper delivery, in-room massage, nightly turndown, twice-daily maid service, express checkout, valet parking, complimentary in-room coffee, secretarial services. Spectravision movie channels, outdoor heated pool, offshore secluded beach, health club, Jacuzzi, sundeck, water-sports equipment, full-service marina, bicycle rental, game room, business center, self-service laundry, conference rooms, gift shops and boutiques.

✪ **Marriott's Reach Resort.** 1435 Simonton St., Key West, FL 33040. ☎ **800/874-4118** or 305/296-5000. Fax 305/296-2830. 149 units. A/C MINIBAR TV TEL. Winter $309–$419 double. Off-season $170–$310 double. AE, CB, DC, DISC, MC, V. Valet parking $9 per day.

With nicer rooms than its other property, the Marriott Casa Marina, the Reach is one of the few hotels on the island with its own strip of sandy beach. Supported by stilts that leave the entire ground floor for car parking, the hotel offers four floors of rooms designed around atriums. The guest rooms are large and feature tile floors, sturdy wicker furnishings, and tropical colors. Each contains a small service bar with a sink, fridge, and tea/coffeemaker, and has a vanity area that's separate from the bathroom. The rooms are so nice you can easily forgive the small closets and diminutive dressers. All rooms have sliding glass doors that open onto balconies; some have ocean views.

Ample palm-planted grounds surround a small pool area with plenty of colorfully striped lounge chairs and a private pier for fishing and suntanning. The protected waters are tame and shallow. The drawback here is the location; the hotel is a 15-minute walk away from the center of the Duval Street action.

Amenities: Concierge, room service, dry cleaning, newspaper delivery, in-room massage, baby-sitting, express checkout. Movie channels, outdoor heated swimming pool, beach, health spa, Jacuzzi, sauna, bicycle rental, business center, tour desk, conference rooms, sailboats, Windsurfers, beauty salon.

✪ **Pier House Resort and Caribbean Spa.** 1 Duval St., Key West, FL 33040. ☎ **800/327-8340** or 305/296-4600. Fax 305/296-9085. 154 units. A/C MINIBAR TV TEL. Winter $275–$450 double; $450–$795 suite. Off-season $195–$350 double; $325–$645 suite. Children under 16 stay free in parents' room. AE, CB, DC, DISC, MC, V.

Pier House is one of the area's best resort choices, especially since the renovation of its best waterfront suites and rooms. Its excellent location—at the foot of Duval Street and just steps from Mallory Docks—is the envy of every hotel on the island. Set back from the busy street, on a short strip of beach, the hotel is a welcome oasis of calm, offering luxurious rooms, top-notch service, and even a full-service spa. The accommodations here vary tremendously, from relatively simple business-style rooms to romantic guest quarters complete with integrated stereo systems and whirlpool tubs. Though every accommodation has either a balcony or a patio, not all overlook the water. My favorites, in the two-story spa building, don't have any view at all. But what they lack in scenery, they make up for in opulence; each well-appointed Spa Room has a sitting area and a huge Jacuzzi bathroom.

Dining/Diversions: The restaurant serves very respectable meals in a dark dining room or on an umbrella-covered patio overlooking the docks. Old Havana Docks is a good waterfront bar, especially at sunset.

Amenities: Concierge, room service, laundry services, newspaper delivery, in-room massage, express checkout. Heated swimming pool, beach, health club, spa treatments, two Jacuzzis, sauna, sundeck, water-sports equipment rentals, bicycle rental, tour desk, conference rooms, beauty salon.

EXPENSIVE

Island City House Hotel. 411 William St., Key West, FL 33040. ☎ **800/634-8230** or 305/294-5702. Fax 305/294-1289. 24 units. A/C TV TEL. Winter $165 studio; $195–$225 one-bedroom suite; $255–$285 two-bedroom suite. Off-season $95 studio; $125–$155 one-bedroom suite; $165–$190 two-bedroom suite. Rates include breakfast. AE, CB, DC, DISC, MC, V.

A little resort unto itself, the Island City House consists of three separate and unique buildings that share a common junglelike patio and pool. The Island City House shares its property name with one of the buildings on it, making descriptions more complicated. The Island City House building is a historic three-story wooden structure with wraparound verandas that allow guests to walk around the entire edifice on any floor. The warmly dressed old-fashioned interiors include wood floors and many antique furnishings. Many rooms have full-size kitchens, queen-size beds, and sumptuous floral window treatments. The tile bathrooms could use more counter space, and the room lighting isn't always perfect, but eccentricities are part of this hotel's charm. The unpainted wooden Cigar House's particularly large bedrooms are similar in ambience to those in the Island City House. Most rooms are furnished with wicker chairs and king-size beds and enjoy big bathrooms that also suffer from a lack of counter space. As with the Island City House, rooms facing the property's interior courtyard are best. The hotel's Arch House is the least appealing of the three buildings, but still very recommendable. Built of Dade County pine, the Arch House's cozy bedrooms are furnished in wicker and rattan and come with small kitchens and baths.

Amenities: Concierge providing arrangements for dry cleaning, laundry service, in-room massage, baby-sitting; newspaper delivery, free coffee in lobby. Kitchenettes, VCR rental and complimentary videos, outdoor heated pool, Jacuzzi, bicycle rental, sundeck, self-service Laundromat.

✪ **Marquesa Hotel.** 600 Fleming St. (at Simonton St.), Key West, FL 33040. ☎ **800/869-4631** or 305/292-1919. Fax 305/294-2121. 40 units. A/C MINIBAR TV TEL. Winter $215–$265 double; from $325 suite. Off-season $135–$165 double; from $235 suite. No children under 12 allowed. AE, DC, MC, V.

One of my very favorite properties, the Marquesa offers all the charm of a small historic hotel with the amenities of a large resort. The Marquesa encompasses four different buildings, two adjacent swimming pools, and a three-stage waterfall that cascades into a lily pond. Two of the hotel's houses are luxuriously restored Victorian homes with rooms outfitted with extra-plush antiques and oversize contemporary furniture. The rooms in the two newly constructed buildings are even richer, some of which include four-poster wrought-iron beds with bright floral spreads. The green-marble baths are lush and spacious. The decor is simple, elegant, and spotless. It is the only hotel room I have ever seen that I would like my home to resemble.

Amenities: Concierge, valet, newspaper delivery, twice-daily maid service, valet parking. Two outdoor swimming pools (one is heated), access to nearby health club.

Ocean Key House. Zero Duval St., Key West, FL 33040. ☎ **800/328-9815** or 305/296-7701. Fax 305/292-7685. www.oceankeyhouse.com. 96 units. A/C MINIBAR TV TEL. Winter from $160 double; $340–$525 one-bedroom suite; $420–$700 two-bedroom suite. Off-season $135 double; $225–$495 one-bedroom suite; $320–$600 two-bedroom suite. Children 17 and under stay free in parents' room. AE, CB, DC, DISC, MC, V.

You can't get much more central than this modern hotel, located across from the Pier House at the foot of Duval Street. Most of the guest rooms here are suites, ample-sized accommodations fitted with built-in couches. Many rooms have sliding glass doors that open onto small balconies, some of which enjoy unobstructed water views. All suites have Jacuzzi tubs in either the master bedroom or living room. For the same price as the best rooms, you may do better at one of the more intimate accommodations like the Marquesa or the Pier House. The standard guest rooms are much less desirable. These are small and dark and have no views.

Dining: A casual dockside grill serves lunch and dinner. Breakfast is served at an indoor/outdoor cafe.

Amenities: Concierge, room service, dry-cleaning and laundry services. VCRs and video rentals, outdoor heated pool, access to nearby health club, Jacuzzi in every suite, conference rooms, sundeck, water-sports concession, tour desk.

MODERATE

Chelsea House. 707 Truman Ave., Key West, FL 33040. ☎ **800/845-8859** or 305/296-2211. Fax 305/296-4822. 20 units. A/C TV TEL. Winter $120–$180 double; $360 apt. Off-season $75–$125 double; $250 apt. Rates include breakfast. Pets $10 extra. AE, CB, DC, DISC, MC, V.

Despite its decidedly English name, the Chelsea House is "all American," a term that in Key West isn't code for "conservative." Chelsea House caters to a mixed gay/straight clientele with a liberal philosophy that exhibits itself most demonstratively on the clothing-optional sundeck.

One of only a few guest houses in Key West that offers TVs, VCRs, private baths, and kitchenettes in each room, Chelsea House has a large number of repeat visitors. The apartments come with full kitchens and a separate living area, as well as a palm-shaded balcony in back. The baths and closets could be bigger, but both are adequate and serviceable.

When weather permits, which is almost always, breakfast is served outside by the pool. There is private parking. However, note that children 14 and under are not accepted.

✪ **La Pensione.** 809 Truman Ave. (between Windsor and Margaret sts.), Key West, FL 33040. ☎ **800/893-1193** or 305/292-9923. Fax 305/296-6509. 9 units. A/C TEL. Winter from $158 double with Frommer's discount. Off-season from $98 double with Frommer's discount. Rates include breakfast and represent a 10% discount for readers who mention this guide. AE, DC, DISC, JCB, MC, V. Children not accepted.

This classic bed-and-breakfast in the 1891 home of a former cigar executive distinguishes itself from other similar inns by its extreme attention to details. The friendly and knowledgeable staff treats the stunning home and the guests with extraordinary care. Rooms, which are comfortable, all have air-conditioning, ceiling fans, king-size beds, and private bathrooms. Many have French doors opening onto spacious verandas. Although the rooms have no phones or televisions, you'll find the distractions of Duval Street, only steps away, keep you adequately occupied during your visit. Breakfast, which includes made-to-order Belgian waffles, fresh fruit, and a variety of breads or muffins, can be taken on the wraparound porch or at the communal dining table.

South Beach Oceanfront Motel. 508 South St. (at the Atlantic Ocean), Key West, FL 33040. ☎ **800/354-4455** or 305/296-5611. Fax 305/294-8272. 47 units, 3 kitchenettes. A/C TV TEL. Winter $105–$199 double. Off-season $69–$140 double. AE, MC, V.

This standard two-story motel is located directly on the ocean, within walking distance of Duval Street. Because it is built perpendicular to the water, however, most of the rooms overlook a pretty Olympic-size swimming pool rather than a wide swath of beach. The best and by far most expensive rooms are those lucky two on the end (nos. 115 and 215) that are beachfront.

All rooms share similar aging decor and include standard furnishings. The smallish bathrooms could also use a makeover, and include showers but no tubs. There's a private pier, an on-site water-sports concession, and a laundry room available for guest use. When booking, ask for a room that's as close to the beach (and as far from the road) as possible. If you'll be there a while, ask for one of the rooms with a kitchenette; there is no restaurant on the premises.

Southernmost Point Guest House. 1327 Duval St., Key West, FL 33040. ☎ **305/294-0715.** Fax 305/296-0641. 6 units. A/C TV TEL. Winter $95–$175 double; $150 suite. Off-season $55–$125 double; $95 suite. Rates include breakfast. AE, MC, V.

One of the only inns that actually welcomes children and pets, this romantic and historic inn is a real find. Kids will enjoy the swings in the backyard and the pet rabbits. The B&B's antiseptically clean rooms are not as fancy as the house's ornate 1885 exterior. Each room has basic beds and couches and a hodgepodge of furnishings, including futon couches, high-back wicker chairs, and plenty of mismatched throw rugs. Each room is different. Room 5 is best; situated upstairs, it has a private porch and an ocean view, and windows that let in lots of light. Every room has a refrigerator and a full decanter of sherry. Mona Santiago, the hotel's kind and laid-back owner, provides chairs and towels that can be brought to the beach, which is just a block away. Plus, guests can help themselves to wine as they soak in the new 14-seat hot tub.

INEXPENSIVE

Blue Lagoon Resort. 3101 N. Roosevelt Blvd., Key West, FL 33040-4118. ☎ **305/296-1043.** Fax 305/296-6499. 72 units. A/C TV TEL. Winter $80–$240 double. Off-season $50–$110 double. MC, V.

More than half of the rooms at this funky ocean-side resort rent for less than $100 year-round—an all-too-unusual occurrence in Key West, especially for full-service resorts. The pricier waterfront rooms aren't really worth the extra money (although some include a jet-ski ride). The rooms, furnished in heavy cedar wood, are basic and a bit run-down but still decent—along the lines of a Howard Johnson or other budget accommodation. Second-floor rooms are generally quieter. Guests tend to be young college-aged kids out for a wild time. Although pretty far from Old Town, the resort is convenient by scooter and car. And it is literally surrounded by wave runners, boats, parasailing and diving fun. Some room rates actually include the price of a water-bike ride.

✪ **The Grand.** 1116 Grinnell St. (between Virginia and Catherine sts.), Key West, FL 33040. ☎ **888/947-2630** or 305/294-0590. E-mail: thegrand@conch.net. 10 units. A/C TV TEL. Winter $68–$98 double; $118 suite. AE, DISC, MC, V.

Don't expect cabbies or locals to know about this gem. Opened in 1997, this little-known guest house wasn't even in the phone book its first or second year. Lucky for you! It's got everything you could want including a very moderate price tag. All rooms have private baths, air-conditioning, telephones, and private entrances. The floors are painted in bright colors and beds are dressed in light tropical prints. It's run by another one of those happy-to-be-alive northeastern transplants, Elizabeth Rose, who goes out of her way to provide any and all services for her appreciative guests. Room no. 2 on the back side of the house is the best deal. And although it is small it also has a porch and the most privacy. Suites are a real steal, too. The large two-room units come with a complete kitchen, which are outfitted with dishes and utensils. The house is in a modest residential section of Old Town, only about 7 blocks from Duval Street. With the exception of the youth hostel/motel, other accommodations in this price range tend to be in Caribbean Village, a more seedy part of Key West. This is without a doubt the best bargain in town.

Key West International Hostel. 718 South St., Key West, FL 33040. ☎ **800/51-HOSTEL** or 305/296-5719. Fax 305/296-0672. 86 beds and 14 private motel units. A/C TV. Winter dorm bed $17 for IYHF members, $20 for nonmembers; $75–$105 motel unit. Off-season dorm bed from $15 for IYHF members, from $18 for nonmembers; $50–$85 motel unit. DISC, MC, V.

This well-run hostel is a 3-minute walk to the beach and to Old Town. It's not the Ritz, but it's cheap. Very busy with European backpackers, this is a fine place to spend a few nights and a great place to meet people. The dorm rooms are dark and sparse but clean enough. The higher priced motel rooms are a good deal, especially those that are equipped with full kitchens. Facilities include a pool table under a tiki-hut roof and bicycle rentals for $6 per day. There is also cheap food available for breakfast, lunch, and dinner. As in all community living arrangements, you'll want to watch your valuables. There are minisafes in each room.

WHERE TO DINE

Key West offers a vast and tempting array of food. You'll find most every ethnicity represented, from Thai to Cuban, plus the usual drive-through franchises (mostly up on Roosevelt Boulevard). There is even a Hard Rock Cafe on Duval Street. Wander Old Town and browse menus after you have exhausted the list below. Or, if you don't feel like venturing out, you can call **We Deliver** (☎ **305/293-0078**), a service that for a small fee (between $3 and $6) will bring you anything you want from any area restaurants or stores. We Deliver operates between 3 and 11pm. **Fausto's Food Palace,** operated since 1926, will deliver groceries, beer, wine, or snacks to stock your fridge (✪ **305/294-5221** or 305/296-5663). Fausto's has a $25 minimum.

The Truth About Keys Cuisine

There are few world-class chefs in the Florida Keys. But that isn't to say the food isn't great. You'll find restaurants that are bursting with atmosphere serving very fresh fish and a few local specialties—most notably conch fritters and chowder, key lime pie, plus stone crab claws and lobster when they're in season.

Although a commercial net-fishing ban has diminished the stock of once abundant fish in these parts, even the humblest of restaurants can be counted on to take full advantage of the gastronomic treasures of their own backyard. The Keys have everything a cook could want: the Atlantic and the Gulf of Mexico for impeccably fresh seafood; a tropical climate for year-round farm-stand produce, with great tomatoes, beans, berries, and citrus fruit; and a freshwater swamp for rustic delicacies like alligator, frog's legs, and hearts of palm.

Conch fritters and chowder are mainstays on most tourist-oriented menus. But since the queen conch was listed as an endangered species by the U.S. government in 1985, the conch in your dish was most likely shipped fresh-frozen from The Bahamas or the Caribbean.

Key lime pie, *the* dessert in the Keys, consists of the juice of tiny yellow key limes, a fruit unique to South Florida, with condensed milk, in a graham cracker crust. Experts debate whether the veritable key lime pie should have a whipped cream or a meringue topping, but all agree that the filling should be yellow—never green.

If you are around at the right time of year—generally, October to March for stone crabs and August to March for lobster—then every meal is sure to be fantastic. It's tough to make these fresh crustaceans any way but delicious.

Florida lobster is an entirely different species from the more common Maine variety, and has a sweeter meat. You'll see only the tails on the menu because the Florida lobster has no claws. And it's that very lack of claws that makes the Florida lobster vulnerable to its one and only real predator, people.

Stone crabs are my all-time favorite. They've been written about and talked about by kings, presidents, and poets. Although you'll find them on nearly every menu in season, consider buying a few pounds of jumbos at the fish store to take to the beach in a cooler. Don't forget to ask them to crack them for you and to get a cup of creamy mustard sauce. You'll be glad to know that after the claws are harvested, the crabs grow new claws, thus ensuring a long-lasting supply of these unique delicacies.

VERY EXPENSIVE

Café des Artistes. 1007 Simonton St. (near Truman Ave.). ☎ **305/294-7100.** Reservations recommended. Main courses $23–$39. AE, MC, V. Daily 6–11pm. FRENCH.

Open more than a dozen years, the Café des Artistes's impressive longevity is the result of its winning combination of food and atmosphere. Traditional French meals benefit from a subtle tropical twist and are served with sincerity by uniformed waiters who are well versed on the virtues of fine food.

Start with the duck-liver pâté made with fresh truffles and old cognac, or Maryland crabmeat served with an artichoke heart and herbed tomato confit. Nouvelle and traditional French entrees include lobster flambé with mango and basil, and wine-basted lamb chops rubbed with rosemary and ginger.

✪ **Louie's Backyard.** 700 Waddell Ave. ☎ **305/294-1061.** Reservations highly recommended. Main courses $25–$30; lunch $8–$15. AE, CB, DC, MC, V. Daily 11:30am–3pm and 6–10:30pm. CARIBBEAN CONTEMPORARY.

Louie's, once known as Key West's most elegant restaurant, has lost its luster. Still nestled amid blooming bougainvillea on a lush slice of the gulf, the spot remains one of the most romantic on earth. Unfortunately, the gorgeous real estate doesn't improve the uneven food, sluggish service, and snooty attitude. Part of the problem seems to be that the kitchen doors seem to be constantly swinging. Depending on who is cooking, you may or may not have an interesting or tasty meal. Try the weekend brunches, which tend to be more reliable than dinners. Or, to be assured of a good time, you may just want to sit at the dockside bar and enjoy a cocktail at sunset.

EXPENSIVE

Antonia's. 615 Duval St., Key West. ☎ **305/294-6565.** Reservations suggested. Main courses $17–$24; pastas $12–$15. Daily 6–11pm. AE, DC, MC, V. NORTHERN ITALIAN.

The food is great but the atmosphere a bit fussy for Key West. If you don't have a reservation in season, don't bother. The management is less than accommodating, Still, if you are organized and don't mind paying high prices for dishes that elsewhere go for much less, try this old standby. From the perfectly seasoned homemade focaccia to an exemplary crème brûlée, this elegant little standout is amazingly consistent. The menu, a small selection of classics like zuppa di pesce, rack of lamb in a rosemary sauce, and veal marsala never disappoint. But the way to go is with the nightly specials. If offered, try the flaky and tender mutton snapper served with a light anchovy cream sauce (or your choice). The presentation is simple but elegant; the sauce, perfectly subtle. You can't go wrong with either fresh pastas or beef dishes.

✪ **Bagatelle.** 115 Duval St. ☎ **305/296-6609.** Reservations recommended. Main courses $16–$24; lunch $5–$12. AE, DC, DISC, MC, V. Daily 11:30am–3pm and 5:30–10pm. SEAFOOD/TROPICAL.

Reserve a seat at the elegant second-floor veranda overlooking Duval Street's mayhem. From the calm above enjoy any of the selections from this large menu. You may want to start your meal with the excellent herb-and-garlic stuffed whole artichoke or the sashimi-like seared tuna rolled in black peppercorns. One of the best pastas is a lightly creamy garlic-herb pasta topped with gulf shrimp, Florida lobster, and mushrooms. The best chicken and beef dishes are given a tropical treatment: grilled with papaya, ginger, and soy.

✪ **Mangoes.** 700 Duval St. (at Angela St.). ☎ **305/292-4606.** Reservations recommended for parties of six or more. Main courses $12–$24; pizzas $10–$12; lunch $7–$14. AE, CB, DC, DISC, MC, V. Daily 11am–midnight, pizza until 1am. Upstairs bar, Limbo, 7pm–4am. AMERICAN/REGIONAL.

The restaurant's large brick patio draped with greenery, directly on Duval, is so seductive to passersby that it's packed most every night of the week. The food and service are some of the best in the Keys. Mangoes enjoys a good buzz among locals, and even competitors envy the restaurant's servers, who are some of the best on Duval. Appetizers include conch chowder laced with sherry, lobster dumplings with tangy key lime sauce, and grilled shrimp cocktail with spicy mango chutney. Spicy sausage with black beans and rice, crispy curried chicken, and local snapper with passion fruit sauce are typical among the entrees, but Mangoes' outstanding individual-size designer pizzas are the best menu items by far. They're baked in a Neapolitan-style oven that's fired by buttonwood.

MODERATE

○ **Blue Heaven.** 729 Thomas St. (at the corner of Petronia St., in Bahama Village). ☎ **305/ 296-8666.** Main courses $9–$23; lunch $5.25–$12; breakfast $3–$8.50. DISC, MC, V. Mon– Sat 8am–3:30pm and 6–10:30pm, Sun 8am–1pm and 6–10:30pm. SEAFOOD/AMERICAN/ NATURAL.

You'll wait in line forever at this little hippie-run gallery and restaurant, which has become the place to be in Key West—and with good reason. This ramshackle Mediterranean-revival house serves up some of the best food in town, especially for breakfast. In this former bordello, where Hemingway was said to hang out watching cockfights, you can enjoy homemade granolas, huge tropical fruit pancakes, and seafood Benedict. Dinners are just as good and run the gamut from just-caught fish dishes to Jamaican-style jerk chicken, curried soups, and vegetarian stews. But if you are a neat freak, don't bother. Some people are put off by the dirt floors and roaming cats and birds. A bakery/coffeehouse has opened next door and has proved a big hit.

Mangia, Mangia. 900 Southard St. (at Margaret St.). ☎ **305/294-2469.** Reservations not accepted. Main courses $9–$14.50. AE, MC, V. Daily 5:30–10pm. ITALIAN/AMERICAN.

A low-key Italian trattoria, Mangia, Mangia is one of Key West's best values. Locals appreciate that they can get inexpensive and good food here in a town of so many tourist traps. Off the beaten track, in a little corner storefront, you'll find this great Chicago-style pasta place serving some of the best Italian food in the Keys. The family run restaurant offers superb homemade pastas of every description, including one of the tastiest marinaras around. The simple grilled chicken breast that's brushed with olive oil and sprinkled with pepper is a tasty dish, too. You wouldn't know it from the glossy glass front room, but there's a fantastic little outdoor patio dotted with twinkling pepper lights and lots of plants. There's often a wait for one of the tables outside when the weather permits, so relax out back with a glass of one of their excellent wines or homemade beer while you wait.

○ **Pepe's.** 806 Caroline St., (between Margaret and Williams sts.). ☎ **305/294-7192.** Main courses $11–$20; lunch $5–$9; breakfast $2–$9. DISC, MC, V. Daily 6:30am–10:30pm. AMERICAN.

This old dive has been serving good, basic food for nearly a century. Steaks and Apalachicola Bay oysters are the big draw for regulars who appreciate the rustic bar-room setting and historic photos on the walls. See original scenes of Key West in 1909, when Pepe's first opened. If the weather is nice, choose a seat on the patio under a stunning mahogany tree. Burgers, fish sandwiches, and standard chili satisfy hearty eaters. Buttery sautéed mushrooms and rich mashed potatoes are the best comfort food in Key West. Stop by early for breakfast when you can get old-fashioned chipped beef on toast and all the usual egg dishes. In the evening enjoy reasonably priced cocktails on the deck.

INEXPENSIVE

○ **El Siboney Restaurant.** 900 Catherine St. (at Margaret St.). ☎ **305/296-4184.** Main courses $5–$13. No credit cards. Mon–Sat 11am–9pm. CUBAN.

For good, cheap Cuban food, stop at this corner dive that looks more like a gas station than a diner. Be prepared however, to wait like the locals for succulent roast pork, Cuban sandwiches, grilled chicken, and *ropa vieja* (literally "old clothes," this is a delicious stew made of finely shredded beef), all served with heaps of rice and beans. This tiny storefront is a worthwhile and very affordable choice in a town with lots of glossy tourist traps.

The Ten Keymandments

The Keys has long attracted independent spirits, from Ernest Hemingway and Tennessee Williams to Jimmy Buffett and Mel Fisher and Zane Grey. The writers, artists, and free-thinkers have drifted down to get away from society's rigid demands. And standards do seem to be different here. In 1982, for example, when drug-enforcement agents blocked off the main highway leading into Key West, residents decided to do what they do best—throw a party. The festivities marked the "independence" of the newly formed "Conch Republic." The distinctive flag with its conch insignia now flies throughout "the Republic."

While you'll still find a very laid-back and tolerant code of behavior in the Keys, some rules do exist. Be sure to respect the Ten Keymandments while you are here, or suffer the consequences as proscribed below:

- Don't anchor on a reef. (Reefs are Alive. Alive. A-L-I-V-E.)
- Don't feed the animals. (They'll want to follow you home, and you can't keep them.)
- Don't trash our place. (Or we'll send Bubba to trash yours.)
- Don't touch the coral. (After all, you don't even know them.)
- Don't speed. (Especially on Big Pine Key where deer reside and tar-and-feathering is still practiced.)
- Don't catch more fish than you can eat. (Better yet, let them go. Some of them support schools.)
- Don't collect conch. (This species is protected. By Bubba.)
- Don't disturb the bird nests. (They find it very annoying.)
- Don't damage the seagrass. (And don't even think about making a skirt out of it.)
- Don't drink and drive on land or sea. (There's absolutely nothing funny about it.)

PT's Late Night. 920 Caroline St. (at the corner of Margaret St.). ☎ **305/296-4245.** Main courses $5–$14; lunch $5–$12. DISC, MC, V. Daily 11am–4am. AMERICAN.

This place is worth knowing about not only because it's one of the only places in town serving food past 10pm, but it also happens to serve good food at extremely reasonable prices. The sports-bar atmosphere might make you wonder, but I've never been disappointed. Service can be a bit slow and brusque, but let's say it's 1am, you're starving, and you've just parked your bike outside: You'll be ecstatic when your heaping plate of nachos arrives. Fajitas are served sizzling hot with a huge platter of fixings, including beans, rice, lettuce, jalapeños, and tomatoes. Superfresh salads are so big they can be a meal in themselves. There are nightly specials, like corned beef and cabbage on Monday and roast turkey with all the trimmings on Thursday. This place is worth knowing about at any time of day.

KEY WEST AFTER DARK

Duval Street is the Bourbon Street of Florida. Amid the T-shirt shops and clothing boutiques you'll find bar after bar serving stiff drinks to revelers who bounce from one to another. Bands and crowds vary from night to night and season to season. Your best bet is to start at Truman Avenue and head up Duval to check them out for yourself. Cover charges are mostly unheard of, so stop in to a dozen and see which you like.

Hanging Out in the Keys

The primary activity in Key West is relaxing. Most visitors, whether they have come from Düsseldorf or Ft. Lauderdale, look forward to a trip to Key West to escape the hectic pace of "real" life. The island does not disappoint.

With a multitude of first-class resorts, inns, and guest houses, many folks never venture farther than their lodging's poolside. In fact, many accommodations host evening happy hours to encourage guests to stay put. But with hundreds of outdoor cafes and bars in and around the city center, there are wonderful spots to hang out in Key West. Like New Orlean's Bourbon Street, Duval Street is the hub.

A tradition in Key West, the ✪ **Mallory Square Sunset Celebration** can be relaxing or overwhelming, depending on your vantage point. Every evening, locals and visitors gather at the docks behind Mallory Square (at the westernmost end of Duval Street) to celebrate the day gone by. Get a spot on the docks to experience the carnival of portrait artists, acrobats, food vendors, and animal acts. Better yet, get a seat at the **Hilton's Sunset Deck** (☎ **305/294-4000**), a luxurious bar on top of its restaurant at the intersection of Front and Greene streets. From the civilized calm of a casual bar, you can look down on the mayhem with a drink in hand.

If you want to get away from crowds altogether, head to the beaches at the southern end of the island. At **Indigenous Park,** at Atlantic Avenue and White Street, you can catch an assortment of locals playing bocce on many weekday evenings. These aren't your stereotypical set of old Italian cronies either. "Organized" teams compete for a championship title between late August and December and from January through May. Stop by after 6pm to watch a few sets. At other times, bring a picnic or a good book and enjoy the quiet ocean views.

Perhaps the most perfect retreat for any weary traveler is **Nancy's Secret Garden,** a peaceful shade garden nestled amid Key West's busy downtown. Nancy Forrester opened her haven to the public in 1994 in an effort to raise money to keep up the maintenance on this 1-acre miracle. She calls the site, which includes a small gallery and gift shop, a work of "installation art." There are no explanatory signs or recorded descriptions. This is a place for people who aren't looking to be educated, entertained, or enlightened. With the help of dedicated volunteers, she keeps the place open from 10am until 5pm every day. For a fee of $6, picnickers, nature lovers, or tourist-weary travelers can escape to the serene spot. To get there, walk down Duval Street, away from Mallory Square. Turn left on Fleming, and after 1 long block, turn right onto Simonton Street (just behind the Marquesa Hotel). On your left there will be a tiny alley named Free School Lane. The garden is just beyond the swinging wooden gates. There may or may not be a sign—Nancy can't decide.

One of Duval's largest entertainment complexes, **Durty Harry's,** 208 Duval St. (☎ **305/296-4890**), features live rock bands almost every night. You can wander to one of the many outdoor bars or head up to **Upstairs at Rick's,** an indoor/outdoor dance club that gets going late. For the more racy singles or couples, there is the Red Garter, a pocket-size strip club popular with bachelor and divorce parties. The hawker outside reminds couples, "The family that strips together sticks together."

You'll have to stop in to **Sloppy Joe's,** at 201 Duval St. (☎ **305/294-5717**), just to say you did. Scholars and drunks debate whether this is the same Sloppy Joe's that

Hemingway wrote about, but there's no argument that this classic bar's turn-of-the-century wooden ceiling and cracked tile floors are Key West originals. The popular and raucous bar is crowded with tourists almost 24 hours a day, and there's almost always live music.

Named after another Key West legend, **Jimmy Buffett's Margaritaville Cafe,** at 500 Duval St. (☎ 305/292-1435), is another worthwhile stop. Although Mr. Buffett moved to glitzy Palm Beach years ago, his name is still attracting large crowds. This kitschy restaurant/bar/gift shop features live bands every night—from rock to blues to reggae and everything in between. The touristy cafe is furnished with plenty of Buffett memorabilia, including gold records, photos, and drawings. The margaritas are tasty, but the cheeseburgers aren't really worth singing about.

Just around the corner from Duval's beaten path is **Captain Tony's,** 428 Greene St. (☎ 305/294-1838), which is about as authentic as you'll find. The smoky old wooden bar comes complete with old-time regulars who remember the island before cruise ships docked here; they say Hemingway drank, caroused, and even wrote here. Owner Capt. Tony Tarracino, a former and controversial Key West mayor, has recently capitalized on the success of this once-quaint tavern by franchising the place.

Limbo, a secret little hideaway above the well-known restaurant Mangoes (see "Where to Dine," above), is a great bar with all kinds of music ranging from house/techno to calypso, rock and roll, jazz, blues, and classical guitar; they boast, "We've had it all." Cozy individual booths allow patrons to talk while catching a great view of the crowd that sometimes dances in the small space near the outside deck.

THE GAY & LESBIAN SCENE

In Key West, the best music and dancing can be found at the predominantly gay clubs. While many of the area's other hot spots are geared toward tourists who like to imbibe, the gay clubs are for those who want to rave—mostly locals (or at least, recent transplants). None of the spots described here discriminate—anyone open-minded and fun is welcome.

The gay nightlife was once dominated by The Copa. However, an arsonist put an end to the former legend in 1995. Back and better than ever in its place at 623 Duval St. is a bigger, more modern club called ✪ **Epoch** (☎ 305/296-8521). The music is still an eclectic mix, with everything from techno to house to disco. But with a bigger dance floor, a huge outside deck overlooking Duval Street, and a new state-of-the-art sound system, this a better choice than ever for people of any orientation who appreciate a good dance club. Another popular late-night spot is **One Saloon,** 524 Duval St. (☎ 305/296-8118), featuring great drag and lots more disco. A mostly male clientele frequents this hot spot from 9pm until 4am. Escape to the outdoor garden bar if it gets too steamy inside.

Sunday nights are fun at two local spots. **Tea by the Sea,** on the pier at the Atlantic Shores Motel, 510 South St. (☎ 305/296-2491), attracts a faithful following of regulars and visitors alike. Show up after 7:30pm. Better known around town as La-Te-Da, **La Terraza,** at 1125 Duval St. (☎ 305/296-6706), is a great spot to gather poolside for the best martini in town—but don't bother with the food.

5 The Dry Tortugas

70 miles W of Key West

As long as you have come this far, you might as well take a trip to the Dry Tortugas, especially if you are into bird watching, which is the primary draw of these seven small islands. Because of their remoteness, few people realize that Florida's Keys don't end at Key West.

Ponce de León, who discovered this far-flung cluster of coral keys in 1513, named them "las Tortugas" because of the many sea turtles, which still flock to the area during the nesting season in the warm summer months. Oceanic charts later carried the preface "dry" to warn mariners that fresh water was unavailable here.

Modern intervention has made drinking water available, but little else. Now, rustic campers come for the very lack of amenities that these islands offer.

Popular with serious bird watchers, these islands are nesting grounds and roosting sites for thousands of tropical and subtropical oceanic birds.

A stopping point for migratory birds on the Eastern Flyway, these keys are populated with many West Indian bird species, especially during spring and fall. The small vegetated islands of the Keys are the only nesting sites in the United States for the great white heron and the white-crowned pigeon. The islands are also one of a very few breeding places for the reddish egret, the roseate spoonbill, the mangrove cuckoo, and the black-whiskered vireo.

These underdeveloped islands make a great day trip for any travelers interested in seeing the truly natural anomalies of the Florida Keys. You'll find a historical fort, snorkeling, good fishing, and terrific snorkeling around shallow reefs.

GETTING THERE

The Yankee Fleet, based in Key West (☎ **800/634-0939** or 305/294-7009), offers day trips from Key West for sightseeing, snorkeling, or both. Cruises leave daily from the Land's End Marina, at Margaret Street, 7:30am, and breakfast is served on board. The journey takes 3 hours. Once on the island, you can join a guided tour or explore Garden Key on your own. Boats return to Key West by 7pm. Tours cost $85 per person, including breakfast; or $50 for children 16 and under; $75 for seniors, students, and military personnel. Snorkeling equipment rental is free. Phone for reservations.

The best option for air service from Key West to the Dry Tortugas is **Seaplanes of Key West,** based at Key West Airport (☎ **800/950-2-FLY** or 305/294-0709). Flights, departing at 8am, 10am, noon, and 2pm are almost twice as fast as the competitors. The 40-minute flight at about 500 feet offers a great introduction to these little-known islets. Fares for adults start at $159 for half-day trips and $275 for full-day excursions that include snorkeling equipment and a cooler for use on the island. Rates for kids under 12 are discounted by about 30%. Call for detailed rate schedules and flight plans.

EXPLORING THE DRY TORTUGAS

Fort Jefferson, a huge six-sided 19th-century fortress, is built almost to the water's edge of Garden Key, giving the appearance that it floats in the middle of the sea. The monumental structure is surrounded by formidable 8-foot-thick walls that rise up from the sand to nearly 50 feet. Impressive archways, stonework, and parapets make this 150-year-old monument a grand sight. With the invention of the rifled cannon, the fort's masonry construction became obsolete, and the building was never completed. For 10 years, from 1863 to 1873, Fort Jefferson served as a prison, a kind of "Alcatraz East." Among its prisoners were four of the "Lincoln Conspirators," including Samuel A. Mudd, the doctor who set the broken leg of fugitive assassin John Wilkes Booth. In 1935 Fort Jefferson became a national monument administered by the National Park Service.

BIRD WATCHING   Bring your binoculars and your bird books. This is the reason to visit this little cluster of tropical islands that are tagged onto the southernmost tip of the United States. The islands, uniquely situated in the middle of the migration flyway between North and South America, serve as an important rest stop for the more than 200 winged varieties that pass through here annually. The season peaks from mid-March to mid-May, when thousands of birds—including thrushes, orioles, boobies, swallows, noddy, and snooty terns—show up. In season, a continuous procession of migrant birds fly over or rest at the islands. About 10,000 terns nest here each spring, and many other species from the West Indies can be found here year-round.

DIVING & SNORKELING   The warm, clear, and shallow waters of the Dry Tortugas combine to produce optimum conditions for snorkeling and scuba diving. Four endangered species of sea turtles—the green, leatherback, Atlantic ridley, and hawksbill—can be found here, along with myriad marine life. The region just outside the seawall of Garden Key's Fort Jefferson is excellent for underwater touring; an abundant variety of fish, corals, and more live in just 3 or 4 feet of water.

FISHING   Snapper, tarpon, grouper, and other fish are common, and fishing is popular. A saltwater fishing permit is mandatory and costs $7 for 3 days and $17 for 7 days. No bait or boating services are available in the Tortugas, but there are day docks on Garden Key as well as a cleaning table. Waters are roughest during winter, but the fishing is excellent year-round. Outfitters from Key West can arrange day charters to the islands (see "Sports & Outdoor Activities," above). Or contact **Florida Fish Finder,** 8262 NW 58th St., Miami, FL 33166 (☎ **305/513-9955;** fax 305/513-9955), specializing in 2- and 3-day fishing trips to the Dry Tortugas. The rugged 115-foot fishing boat leaves from Stock Island, MM 5 (about 5 miles north of Key West). Two-day trips leave Friday night, return Sunday afternoon, and cost $200 per person. The price includes sleeping accommodations in bunk beds, bait, and tackle, but not food. For an extra fee, you can purchase breakfast, lunch, and dinner, or bring your own cooler of food and snacks. Three-day trips leave the last Friday morning of every month, return the following Sunday afternoon, and cost $240 per person. Phone for reservations. Bring a towel, your camera, a cooler, and a bathing suit. This is real ocean adventure.

CAMPING

The rustic beauty of tiny Garden Key is a camper's dream. You won't be sharing your site with noisy RVs or motor homes; they can't get here. This is the most isolated spot in Florida. The abundance of birds doesn't make it quiet, but camping here—literally a stone's throw from the water—is as picturesque as it gets. Campers are allowed to pitch tents only on Garden Key. Picnic tables, cooking grills, and toilets are provided, but there are no showers. All supplies must be packed in and out. Sites are free and are available on a first-come, first-served basis. No stoves are permitted. For more information about Fort Jefferson and the Dry Tortugas, call the **National Park Service** (☎ **305/242-7700**).

7

South Florida's National Parks: The Everglades & Beyond

by Victoria Pesce Elliott

Described poetically as the "river of grass" by conservationist Marjory Stoneman Douglas, the Everglades is actually a shallow, 40-mile-wide, slow-moving river. Rarely more than knee-deep, the water is the lifeblood of this wilderness. Subtle shifts in water level dictate the life cycle of plants and animals. Most folks viewed it as a worthless swamp until Ms. Douglas, who died in 1998 at the age of 107, focused attention on the area with her moving and insightful book *The Everglades: River of Grass,* published in 1947.

It was that same year that 1.5 million acres—less than 20% of Everglades wilderness—were established as Everglades National Park. At that time few lawmakers understood how neighboring ecosystems relate to each other: You can't just chop off a chunk of a much larger wilderness and expect it to survive. The land is intertwined with its surroundings, at the butt end of every environmental insult that occurs upstream.

Environmental activists have succeeded in persuading politicians to enact some legislation to clean up the pollution that has threatened this unusual ecosystem ever since the days when heavy industry, most notably the sugar industry, first moved into the area. There has been a marked decrease in the indigenous wildlife here, but it remains one of the few places where you can see dozens of endangered species in their natural habitat, including the swallowtail butterfly, American crocodile, leatherback turtle, southern bald eagle, West Indian manatee, and Florida panther.

Impressions

There are no other Everglades in the world. They are, they have always been, one of the unique regions of the earth, remote, never wholly known. Nothing anywhere else is like them: their vast glittering openness, wider than the enormous visible round of the horizon, the racing free saltiness and sweetness of their massive winds, under the dazzling blue heights of space.

—Marjory Stoneman Douglas,
The Everglades: River of Grass, 1947

It takes 1 gallon of water 1 month to move through the park. A similar pace is recommended to visitors who want to fully experience the Everglades' grandeur. Take your time on the trails, and a hypnotic beauty begins to unfold. Follow the rustling of a bush, and you might see a small green tree frog or tiny brown anole lizard, with its bright-red spotted throat. Crane your head around a bend and discover a delicate, brightly painted mule-ear orchid.

The slow and subtle splendor of this exotic land may not be immediately appealing to kids raised on video games and rapid-fire commercials, but they'll certainly remember the experience and no doubt thank you for it later. Meanwhile, you'll find plenty of dramatic fun around the park, like airboat rides, alligator wrestling, and biking to keep the kids satisfied for at least a day. For most families—and others who aren't especially intrigued with nature—an afternoon is probably plenty of time to spend in and around the park.

1 Everglades National Park

35 miles SW of Miami

In the 1800s, before the southern Everglades were designated a national park, the only inhabited piece of this wilderness was a quiet fishing village called Flamingo. Accessible only by boat and leveled every few years by hurricanes, the mosquito-infested town never grew very popular. When the 38-mile road from Florida City was completed in 1922, many of those who did live here fled to someplace either more or less remote. Today, Flamingo is a center for visitor activities and the main jumping-off point for backcountry camping and exploration. Flamingo is now home to National Park Service and concessionaire employees and their families.

Everglades National Park's northern Shark Valley entrance and the eastern approaches described in this section are the most accessible from Miami and the rest of Florida's east coast. You'll find great amenities along the way, like Indian villages, alligator farms, and boat rides. An excellent tram tour goes deep into the park along a trail that's also terrific for biking. This is also the best way to reach the park's only accommodation (and full-service outfitter), the Flamingo Lodge.

There are hiking trails also from Everglades City, the "western gateway" to Everglades National Park. This entrance provides access to a maze of islands and swamps that can be reached only by boat and is home to a number of recommendable boat tours of the area. For more information on the town of Everglades City, including lodging and dining options there, see section 2 of this chapter.

JUST THE FACTS

GETTING THERE & ACCESS POINTS   Everglades National Park has four entrances. The following three are the most popular and the ones most convenient to visitors from Florida's east coast, including Miami. No matter which part of Miami you are starting in, the drive should take no longer than an hour. Unless of course you are traveling during rush hour: between 8 and 9:30am or from 4 until 6pm. Then, the roads, especially S.R. 836, will be backed up, and your driving time could be doubled.

If you're coming from Florida's west coast, use the fourth entrance in Everglades City. See section 2 of this chapter for details.

The main entrance, in Homestead on the park's east side, is located 10 miles southwest of Florida City. From Miami, take S.R. 836 west to the Florida Turnpike south until it ends in Florida City. Signs will point you southwest onto the road that leads into the park, S.R. 9336. The main entrance's Park Ranger Station is open 24 hours.

Everglades National Park

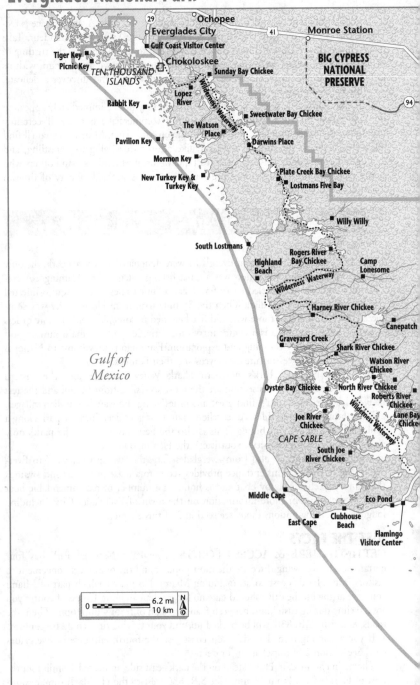

Ochopee

29

Everglades City

Gulf Coast Visitor Center

41 Monroe Station

Tiger Key

Picnic Key

TEN THOUSAND
ISLANDS

Chokoloskee

Sunday Bay Chickee

BIG CYPRESS
NATIONAL
PRESERVE

94

Rabbit Key

Lopez
River

Wilderness Waterway

Sweetwater Bay Chickee

The Watson
Place

Pavilion Key

Darwins Place

Mormon Key

Plate Creek Bay Chickee

New Turkey Key &
Turkey Key

Lostmans Five Bay

Willy Willy

South Lostmans

Rogers River
Bay Chickee

Camp
Lonesome

Highland
Beach

Wilderness Waterway

Harney River Chickee

Canepatch

Graveyard Creek

Shark River Chickee

Gulf of
Mexico

Watson River
Chickee

Oyster Bay Chickee

North River Chickee

Roberts River
Chickee

Joe River
Chickee

Wilderness Waterway

Lane Bay
Chickee

CAPE SABLE

South Joe
River Chickee

Middle Cape

Eco Pond

East Cape

Clubhouse
Beach

Flamingo
Visitor Center

0 6.2 mi
10 km

N

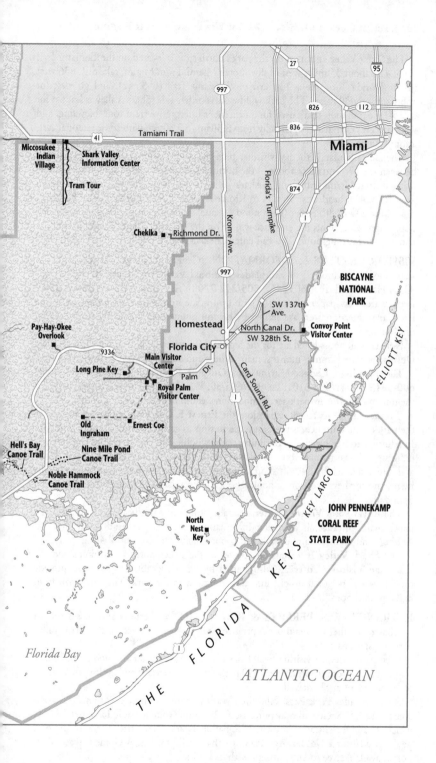

Miccosukee
Indian
Village

Shark Valley
Information Center

Tram Tour

Tamiami Trail

41

997

27

826

112

95

836

874

Florida's Turnpike

Miami

1

Chekika

Richmond Dr.

Krome Ave.

997

SW 137th
Ave.

BISCAYNE
NATIONAL
PARK

Pay-Hay-Okee
Overlook

9336

Homestead

North Canal Dr.
SW 328th St.

Convoy Point
Visitor Center

ELLIOTT KEY

Long Pine Key

Main Visitor
Center

Florida City

Palm   Dr.

Card Sound Rd.

1

Royal Palm
Visitor Center

Old
Ingraham

Ernest Coe

Hell's Bay
Canoe Trail

Nine Mile Pond
Canoe Trail

Noble Hammock
Canoe Trail

North
Nest
Key

KEY LARGO

JOHN PENNEKAMP
CORAL REEF
STATE PARK

THE   FLORIDA   KEYS

1

Florida Bay

ATLANTIC OCEAN

The Shark Valley entrance, on the park's north side, is located on the Tamiami Trail (U.S. 41), about 35 miles west of downtown Miami. From Miami, take S.R. 836 west to the Florida Turnpike south; exit on Tamiami Trail (U.S. 41), and go west for approximately 30 miles. The park will be on your left side. Shark Valley is known for its 15-mile trail loop that's used for an excellent interpretive tram tour, bicycling, and walking. This entrance is open daily from 8:30am to 5:30pm, with some seasonal variation. Call ahead.

Chekika, popular with day visitors, picnickers, and campers, is located halfway between the two entrances above in the northeast section of the park. Chekika can be reached from Miami as if going to Shark Valley (see above). After exiting on Tamiami Trail (U.S. 41), head west 5 miles to Krome Avenue (177th Avenue); turn left, then proceed to SW 168th Street (Richmond Avenue) and head west (left) until you reach a stop sign. Turn right; the entrance will be on the left side. There are picnic facilities and a 20-site campground. You can enter Chekika from 8:30am until sundown.

VISITOR CENTERS & INFORMATION   General inquiries and specific questions should be directed to **Everglades National Park Headquarters,** 40001 S.R. 9336, Homestead, FL 33034 (☎ **305/242-7700**). Ask for a copy of *Parks and Preserves,* a free newspaper that's filled with up-to-date information on goings-on in the Everglades. Headquarters are staffed by helpful phone operators daily from 8:30am until 4:30pm.

Note that all hours listed are for the high season, generally November through May. During the slow summer months, many offices and outfitters keep abbreviated hours.

The **Flamingo Lodge, Marina and Outpost Resort,** in Flamingo (☎ **800/ 600-3813** or 941/695-3101; fax 941/695-3921), is the one-stop clearinghouse, and the only option, for in-park accommodations, equipment rentals, and tours.

Especially since its recent expansion, the **Ernest F. Coe Visitor Center,** located at the park's main entrance, is the best place to stop to gather information for your trip. In addition to free brochures outlining trails, wildlife and activities, and information on tours and boat rentals, you will also find state-of-the-art educational displays, films, and interactive exhibits. A gift shop sells postcards, film, insect repellent, unusual gift items, and the best selection of books about the Everglades. It is open from 8am until 5pm daily.

The **Royal Palm Visitor Center,** a small nature museum located 3 miles past the park's main entrance, is a smaller information center at the head of the popular Anhinga and Gumbo-Limbo trails and is open daily from 8am until 4pm.

The **Shark Valley Information Center** at the park's northern entrance and the **Flamingo Visitor Center** are also staffed by knowledgeable rangers who provide brochures and personal insight into the goings-on in the park. They are open from 8:30am until 5pm.

ENTRANCE FEES, PERMITS & REGULATIONS   Permits and passes can be purchased at either the main park entrance, the Chekika entrance, or the Shark Valley entrance stations only.

Even if you are just visiting Everglades National Park for an afternoon, you'll need to buy a 7-day permit, which costs $10 per vehicle. Pedestrians and cyclists are charged $5 each and $4 at Shark Valley.

An **Everglades Park Pass,** valid for a year's worth of unlimited entrances, is available for $20. U.S. citizens may purchase a 12-month **Golden Eagle Passport** for $50, which is valid for entrance into any U.S. national park. U.S. citizens ages 62 and over pay only $10 for a **Golden Age Passport** that's valid for life. A Golden Access Passport is available free to U.S. citizens with disabilities.

Permits are required for campers wanting to stay overnight either in the back-country or in primitive campsites. See "Camping & Houseboating in the Everglades," in "Where to Stay," below.

Those who want to fish without a charter captain must obtain a standard State of Florida saltwater fishing license. These are available in the park at Flamingo Lodge or any tackle shop or sporting-goods store nearby. Nonresidents will pay $17 for a 7-day license and $7 for 3 days. Florida residents can get a fishing license good for the whole year for $14. Snook and crawfish licenses must be purchased separately at a cost of $2.

Charter captains carry vessel licenses that cover all paying passengers. Ask to be sure. Freshwater fishing licenses are available at various bait and tackle shops outside the park at the same rates. A good one close by is **Don's Bait & Tackle** located at 30710 S. Federal Hwy. in Homestead right on U.S. 1 (☎ **305/247-6616**). Most of the area's freshwater fishing, limited to murky canals and artificial lakes near housing developments, is hardly worth the trouble when so much good saltwater fishing is available.

Firearms are not allowed anywhere in the park.

SEASONS   There are two distinct seasons in the Everglades: high season and mosquito season. High season is also dry season, lasting approximately from late November to May. This is the best time to visit, as low water levels attract the largest variety of wading birds and their predators. As the dry season wanes, wildlife follows the receding water, and by the end of May, the only living things you are sure to spot will cause you to itch.

Many establishments and operators in the area either close or curtail offerings in the summer, so always call ahead to check schedules.

RANGER PROGRAMS   More than 50 ranger programs, free with admission, are offered each month during high season and give visitors an opportunity to gain an expert's perspective. Some programs occur regularly, such as **Glade Glimpses,** a walking tour during which rangers point out flora and fauna and discuss issues affecting the Everglade's survival. These tours are scheduled at 10:15am, noon, and 3:30pm daily. The **Anhinga Ambles,** a similar program that takes place on the Anhinga Trail, starts at 10:30am, 1:30pm, and 4pm.

A more interesting program, the **Slough Slog,** is offered occasionally. On this journey, participants wade into the park and through the muck, stopping at an alligator hole, which is a particularly interesting and vital ecological community unto itself. Lace-up shoes and long pants (preferably ones you don't care about) are required on this walking trip. On Saturday and Sunday rangers can choose programs they want to offer in some time slots.

Park rangers tend to be helpful, well informed, good-humored, and happy to answer questions. Since times, programs, and locations vary from month to month, check a schedule, available at any of the visitor centers (see above).

SAFETY   There are dangers inherent in this vast wilderness area. Always let someone know your itinerary before you set out on an extended hike. It's mandatory that you file an itinerary when camping overnight in the backcountry. When on the water, watch for weather changes; severe thunderstorms and high winds often develop very rapidly. Swimming is not recommended because of the presence of alligators, sharks, and barracudas. Watch out for the region's four indigenous poisonous snakes: diamondback and pygmy rattlesnakes, coral snakes (identifiable by their colorful rings), and water moccasins (which swim on the surface of the water). And bring insect repellent to ward off mosquitoes and biting flies.

First aid is available from park rangers. The nearest hospital is in Homestead, 10 miles from the park's main entrance.

SEEING THE HIGHLIGHTS

Shark Valley provides a fine introduction to the wonder of the Everglades, but visitors shouldn't expect to spend more than a few hours there. Bicycling or taking a guided tram tour can be a satisfying experience, but neither fully captures the wonders of the park. Likewise, boaters who choose to explore via the Everglades City entrance to the park are likely to see a lot of mangroves and not much else.

If you want to see a greater array of plant and animal life, make sure that you venture into the park through the main entrance, pick up a trail map, and dedicate at least a day to exploring from there.

Stop first along the **Anhinga and Gumbo-Limbo trails,** which start right next to one another, 3 miles from the park's main entrance. These trails provide a thorough introduction to Everglades flora and fauna and are highly recommended to first-time visitors. There's more water and wildlife here than in most parts of the Everglades, especially during dry season. Alligators, turtles, river otters, herons, egrets, and other animals abound, making this one of the best trails for seeing wildlife. Arrive early to spot the widest selection of exotic birds; like the Anhinga Trail's namesake, a large black fishing bird that is so used to humans, many of these birds build their nests in plain view. Others travel deeper into the park during daylight hours. Take your time— at least an hour is recommended. If you treat the trails and modern boardwalk as pathways to get through quickly, rather than destinations to experience and savor slowly, you'll miss out on the still beauty and hidden treasures that await.

Those who love to mountain bike, and who prefer solitude, might check out the infrequently traveled **Old Ingraham Highway.** This dirt road delves deeper into the Glades and isn't used by most visitors. Since this pathway is sometimes closed, check at the visitor center when you arrive.

Also, it's worth climbing the observation tower at the end of the quarter-mile-long **Pa-hay-okee Trail.** The panoramic view of undulating grass and seemingly endless vistas gives the impression of a semiaquatic Serengeti. Flocks of tropical and semitropical birds traverse the landscape, alligators and fish stir the surface of the water, small grottoes of trees thrust up from the sea of grass marking higher ground, and the vastness of the hidden world you've entered seems unparalleled.

If you want to get closer to nature, a few hours in a canoe along any of the trails allows paddlers the chance to sense the park's fluid motion, and to become a part of the ecosphere. Visitors who choose this option end up feeling more like explorers than merely observers. (See "Sports & Outdoor Activities," below.)

No matter which option you choose (and there are many), I strongly recommend staying for the 7pm program, available during high season at the **Long Pine Key Amphitheater.** This talk by one of the park's rangers, along with the accompanying slide show, gives a detailed overview of the park's history, natural resources, wildlife, and threats to its survival.

SPORTS & OUTDOOR ACTIVITIES

BIKING The relatively flat 38-mile paved **Main Park Road** is excellent for bicycling, as are many park trails, including **Long Pine Key.** Cyclers should expect to spend 2 to 3 hours along the path.

If the park isn't flooded from excess rain (which it often is especially in spring), **Shark Valley** in Everglades National Park is South Florida's most scenic bicycle trail. Many locals haul their bikes out to the Glades for a relaxing day of wilderness-trail riding. You can ride the 17-mile loop with no other traffic in sight. Instead, you'll share the flat paved road only with other bikers and a menagerie of wildlife. Don't be surprised to see a gator lounging in the sun or a deer munching on some grass. Otters, turtles, alligators, and snakes are common companions in the Shark Valley area.

You can rent bikes at the **Flamingo Lodge, Marina and Outpost Resort** (see "Where to Stay," below) for $14 per full day, $8.50 per half day (any 4-hour period), and $3 per hour. Bicycles are also available from **Shark Valley Tram Tours,** at the park's Shark Valley entrance (☎ **305/221-8455**), for $3.25 per hour; rentals can be picked up any time after 8:30am and must be returned by 4pm.

BIRDING   More than 350 species of birds make their homes in the Everglades. Tropical birds from the Caribbean and temperate species from North America can be found here, along with exotics that have blown in from more distant regions. Eco and Mrazek ponds, located near Flamingo, are two of the best places for birding, especially in early morning or late afternoon in the dry winter months. Pick up a free birding checklist from a visitor center (see "Just the Facts," above), and ask a park ranger what's been spotted in recent days.

BOATING   Motorboating around the Everglades seems like a great way to see plants and animals in remote habitats. However, environmentalists are taking stock of the damage motorboats (especially airboats) inflict on the delicate ecosystem. (See "Airboat tours," below.) If you choose to motor, remember that most of the areas near land are "no wake" zones, and for the protection of nesting birds, landing is prohibited on most of the little mangrove islands. There's a long list of restrictions and restricted areas, so get a copy of the park's boating rules from National Park Headquarters before setting out (see "Just the Facts," above).

The Everglades' only marina—accommodating about 50 boats with electric and water hookups—is the Flamingo Lodge, Marina and Outpost Resort, located in Flamingo. The well-marked channel to Flamingo is accessible to boats with a maximum 4-foot draft and is open year-round. Reservations can be made through the **marina store** (☎ **941/695-3101**, ext. 304). Skiffs with 15-horsepower motors are available for rent. These low-power boats cost $90 per day, $65 per half day (any 5-hour period), and $22 per hour. A $50 deposit is required.

CANOEING   The most intimate view of the Everglades comes from the humble perspective of a simple low boat. From a canoe, you'll get a closer look into the park's shallow estuaries where water birds, sea turtles, and endangered manatees make their homes.

Everglades National Park's longest "trails" are designed for boat and canoe travel, and many are marked as clearly as walking trails. The **Noble Hammock Trail,** a 2-mile loop, takes 1 to 2 hours, and is recommended for beginning canoers. The **Hell's Bay Trail,** a 3- to 6-mile course for hardier paddlers, takes 2 to 6 hours, depending on how far you choose to go. Park rangers can recommend other trails that best suit your abilities, time limitations, and interests.

You can rent a canoe at the Flamingo Lodge, Marina and Outpost Resort (see "Where to Stay," below) for $40 for 24 hours, $32 per full day, $22 per half day (any 4-hour period), and $8 per hour. They also have family canoes that rent for $12, $30, $40, and $50, respectively. A $50 deposit is required. Skiffs, kayaks, and tandem kayaks are also available. The concessionaire will shuttle your party to the trailhead of your choice and pick you up afterward. Rental facilities are open daily from 6am to 8pm.

FISHING   About one-third of Everglades National Park is open water. Freshwater fishing is popular in brackish **Nine-Mile Pond** (25 miles from the main entrance) and other spots along the **Main Park Road,** but because of the high mercury levels found in the Everglades, freshwater fishers are warned not to eat what they catch. Before

casting, check in at a visitor center, as many of the park's lakes are preserved for observation only. Fishing licenses are required (see "Just the Facts," above).

Saltwater anglers will find that snapper and sea trout are plentiful throughout the
area. Charter boats and guides are available at Flamingo Lodge, Marina and Outpost
Resort (see "Where to Stay," below). Phone ahead for information and reservations.

ORGANIZED TOURS

AIRBOAT TOURS   Shallow-draft, fan-powered airboats were invented in the Everglades by frog hunters who were tired of polling through the rushes. And though it is
the most efficient way to get around, airboats are not permitted in the park. Just outside the boundaries are many outfitters offering rides. These shallow-bottom runabouts tend to inflict severe damage on the animals and plants there. If you choose to
ride on one, you may consider bringing earplugs; these high-speed boats are loud. Airboat rides are offered at the **Miccosukee Indian Village,** just west of the Shark Valley
entrance on U.S. 41, the Tamiami Trail (☎ **305/223-8340**). Native American guides
will take you through the reserve's rushes at high speed and stop along the way to point
out alligators, native plants, and exotic birds. Prices are just $7.

Also, the **Everglades Alligator Farm,** 4 miles south of Palm Drive (S.R. 9336)
(☎ **305/247-2628**), offers half-hour guided airboat tours from 9am until 6pm daily.
The price, which includes admission to the park, is $12 for adults, $6 for children.

MOTORBOAT TOURS   Both Florida Bay and backcountry tours are offered at the
Flamingo Lodge, Marina and Outpost Resort (see "Where to Stay," below). Both
are available in 1½- and 2-hour versions that cost an average of $16 adults, $8 children, under 6 free. There are also charter-fishing and sightseeing boats that can be
booked through the main reservation number (☎ **941/695-3101**). Florida Bay tours
cruise nearby estuaries and sandbars, while six-passenger backcountry boats visit
smaller sloughs. Tours depart throughout the day, and reservations are recommended.

TRAM TOURS   At the park's Shark Valley entrance, open-air tram buses take visitors on 2-hour naturalist-led tours that delve 7½ miles into the wilderness. At the
trail's midsection, passengers can disembark and climb a 65-foot observation tower
that offers good views of the Glades. The tour offers visitors considerable views that
include plenty of wildlife and endless acres of sawgrass. Tours run November to April
only, daily from 9am to 4pm, and are sometimes stalled by flooding or particularly
heavy mosquito infestation. Reservations are recommended from December to
March. The cost is $8 for adults, $4 for children 12 and under, and $7 for seniors. For
further information, contact the **Shark Valley Tram Tours** at ☎ **305/221-8455.**

SHOPPING

You won't find big malls or lots of boutiques in this area, although there is an outlet
center, the **Keys Factory Shops** (☎ **305/248-4727**), at 250 E. Palm Dr. (where the
Florida Turnpike meets U.S. 1), in Florida City, with more than 60 stores including
Nike Factory Store, Bass Co., Levi's, Osh Kosh, and Izod. Travelers can pick up a free
coupon booklet from the Customer Service Center called the Come Back Pack. In it
are coupons good for discounts in the outlet. It's open every day until 9pm. except for
Sunday when the stores close at 6pm.

A necessary stop and good place for a refreshment is one of Florida's best-known
fruit stands, ✪ **Robert Is Here** (☎ **305/246-1592**). Robert has been selling homegrown treats for nearly 40 years at the corner of SW 344th Street (Palm Drive) and
SW 192nd Avenue. You'll find the freshest and biggest pineapples, bananas, papayas,
mangos, and melons anywhere as well as his famous shakes in unusual flavors like key

lime, coconut, orange, and cantaloupe. Exotic fruits, bottled jellies, hot sauces, and salad dressings are also available. This is a great place to pick up culinary souvenirs and sample otherwise unavailable goodies. Open daily 8am until 7pm.

Along Tamiami Trail there are several roadside shops hawking Indian handicrafts, including one at the **Miccosukee Indian Village** (☎ 305/223-8380), just west of the Shark Valley entrance. At nearly every one you'll find the same stock of feathered dream-catchers, stuffed alligator heads and claws, turquoise jewelry, and other trinkets. However, do note the unique and colorful handmade cloth Miccosukee dolls.

WHERE TO STAY

In addition to the rooms, cottages, houseboats, and campsites described below, the town of Everglades City at the western edge of the park has several lodging options, including the historic Rod & Gun Lodge. See section 2 of this chapter for more information.

IN EVERGLADES NATIONAL PARK

Flamingo Lodge, Marina and Outpost Resort. 1 Flamingo Lodge Hwy., Flamingo, FL 33034. ☎ **800/600-3813** or 941/695-3101. Fax 941/695-3921. 103 units, 24 cottages. A/C TV (in some) TEL. Winter $75–$89 double; $99–$125 cottage; $110–$130 suite. Off-season from $65 double; from $79 cottage; from $85 suite. Rates for cottages and the suite are for up to four people. AE, DC, DISC, MC, V.

The Flamingo Lodge is the only lodging actually located within the boundaries of Everglades National Park. This woodsy sprawling complex offers rooms overlooking the Florida Bay in either a two-story simple motel or the lodge. Situated right in the center of the action, it can sometimes feel like summer camp.

VCRs and videos are available for guests in the regular rooms or in the suite, but not in more primitively outfitted cottages. Still, the cottages are an especially good choice if you plan to stay more than a night or two since they come with small kitchens, equipped with dishes and flatware, but no television. They are also larger, more private, and almost romantic.

Facilities include a very good restaurant (see "Where to Dine," below) and bar, freshwater swimming pool, gift shop, and coin-op laundry (available from 8am to 10pm). Binoculars, bikes, canoes, and kayaks can be rented at the front desk, which is open daily from 6am to 11pm, and fishing poles and ice chests are available at the marina. The hotel is open year-round, and reservations are accepted daily from 8am to 5pm. Guests are treated to free coffee in the lobby. And of course, you have the vast resources of the Everglades just outside your door.

CAMPING & HOUSEBOATING IN THE EVERGLADES

Campgrounds are available in Flamingo and Long Pine Key, where there are more than 300 campsites designed for tents and RVs. They have level parking pads, tables, and charcoal grills. There are no electrical hookups, and showers are cold water. Private ground fires are not permitted, but supervised campfire programs are conducted during winter months. Campsites are $14 per night with a 14-day consecutive stay limit, 30 days a year maximum.

Camping is also available in the backcountry year-round on a first-come first-served basis and is only accessible by boat, foot, or bicycle. Campers must register in person or by telephone no more than 24 hours prior to the start of their trip. Permits, which cost $10 per group of up to 6 people, must be obtained at ranger stations in either Flamingo or Everglades City. Campers can use only designated campsites, which are plentiful and well marked on visitor maps.

Many backcountry sites are chickees—covered wooden platforms on stilts. They're accessible only by canoe. Ground sites are located along interior bays and rivers, and beach camping is also popular. In summer especially, mosquito repellent is necessary gear.

Houseboat rentals are one of the park's best-kept secrets. Available through the Flamingo Lodge, Marina and Outpost Resort, motorized houseboats make it possible to explore some of the park's more remote regions without having to worry about being back by nightfall. You can choose from two different types of houseboats. The first, a 40-foot pontoon boat, sleeps six to eight people in a single large room that's separated by a central head (bathroom) and shower. There's a small galley (kitchen) that contains a stove, oven, and charcoal grill. Prices aren't cheap unless you are with a good sized group. It rents for between $340 and $475 for 2 nights (there's a 2-night minimum in high season).

The newer, sleeker Gibson fiberglass boats sleep six, have a head and shower, air-conditioning, and electric stove. There's also a full rooftop sundeck. These rent for $575 for two nights (with a 2-night minimum). With either boat, the 7th night is free when renting for a full week.

Boating experience is helpful, but not mandatory, as the boats only cruise up to 6 miles per hour and are surprisingly easy to use. Reservations should be made far in advance; call **Flamingo Lodge, Marina and Outpost Resort (☎ 800/600-3813** or 941/695-3101).

NEARBY IN HOMESTEAD & FLORIDA CITY

Homestead and Florida City, two adjacent towns that were almost blown off the map by Hurricane Andrew, have come back better than before. Located about 10 miles from the park's main entrance, along U.S. 1, 35 miles south of Miami, these somewhat rural towns offer several budget options, including a handful of chain hotels such as a **Days Inn (☎ 305/245-1260)** in Homestead and a **Hampton Inn (☎ 800/426-7866** or 305/247-8833) right off the turnpike in Florida City. The best option is the **Best Western Gateway to the Keys,** 1 Strano Blvd. (U.S. 1), Florida City, FL 33034 (☎ **800/528-1234** or 305/246-5100), with rates in high season starting at about $85. This two-story, pink-and-white hotel was opened in late 1994 and offers contemporary style and comfort. The suites and some larger rooms offer convenient extras like a microwave, coffeemaker, extra sink, and small fridge. There's also a swimming pool, Jacuzzi, and self-service Laundromat.

WHERE TO DINE

For dining options at the western edge of the park, see section 2 of this chapter.

IN FLAMINGO

If you aren't cooking up your own catch or eating a picnic under the shade of the hammocks, the only restaurant in the park is a very civilized alternative, **Flamingo Restaurant (☎ 941/695-3101)**, in the Flamingo Lodge (see "Where to Stay," above). Besides the spectacular view of Florida Bay and numerous Keys from the large, airy dining room, you'll also find fresh fish, including my very favorite, mahimahi. All fish is prepared grilled, blackened, or deep-fried; and dinner entrees come with salad or conch chowder, and steamed vegetables, black beans and rice, or baked potato. More adventurous offerings include a fantastic Caribbean steak marinated in jerk seasonings and citrus chicken marinated in fruit juices. The large menu has something for everyone, including basic and very tasty sandwiches, pastas, burgers, and salads. You may need reservations for dinner, especially in season. Prices are surprisingly moderate, with full meals starting at about $11 and going no higher than $20.

IN NEARBY HOMESTEAD & FLORIDA CITY

You won't find fancy nouvelle cuisine in this suburbanized farm country, but there are plenty of fast-food chains along U.S. 1 and a few old favorites worth checking out.

Housed in a squat, one-story, windowless stone building that looks something like a medieval fort, the **Capri Restaurant,** 935 N. Krome Ave., Florida City (☎ **305/ 247-1542**), has been serving hearty Italian American fare since 1958. Great pastas and salads complement a full menu of meat and fish dishes. Portions are big. They serve lunch and dinner every day (except Sunday) until 11pm.

Another landmark is **Potlikker's,** 591 Washington Ave. (at the corner of NE 6th Street), in Homestead (☎ **305/248-0835**), featuring fried fish and shrimp baskets, along with barbecued chicken and ribs, roast pork, grilled fish, and lots of local veggies. It's good, unadulterated Southern feed at popular prices. Main courses range from $6 to $13. The kitchen is open every day from 7am until 9pm.

The **Miccosukee Restaurant** (☎ **305/223-8380**), just west of the Shark Valley entrance on the Tamiami Trail (U.S. 41), serves authentic pumpkin bread, fry bread, fish, and not-so-authentic Native American interpretations of tacos and fried chicken. This interesting and affordable spot is worth a stop for lunch or dinner, served daily from 8am until 3pm. Meals cost from $5 to $14.

2 Everglades City: Western Gateway to the Everglades

The brainchild of advertising magnate Barron Collier, who funded the completion of the Tamiami Trail from Miami to Naples, Everglades City was conceived as a major center of activity on Florida's west coast.

While building the highway in the 1920s, Collier dredged a channel through the Ten Thousand Islands and created a new island with the spoil, upon which he laid out Everglades City. Although it became a popular hunting and fishing destination for the rich and famous, Everglades City never became the metropolis he hoped for. In 1947, Everglades National Park took in most of the land and bays around the town.

Everglades City, only 2 miles long by ¹/₂ mile wide, is an isolated little town with one school, a post office, and a bank as well as a dozen or so seafood restaurants, some motels and B&Bs, and a few tourist shops. It lies in the Ten Thousand Islands area, and the Wilderness Waterway twists and turns 99 miles from here all the way to Flamingo at the southwestern edge of the Everglades. This makes the town a perfect starting point for canoe or boat explorations of the area.

ESSENTIALS

GETTING THERE   Take I-75 or U.S. 41 east to S.R. 29 and turn south to Everglades City. S.R. 29 runs through town and then over a causeway along beautiful Chokoloskee Bay to Chokoloskee Island, an old Calusa shell mound that's the highest point in the Everglades.

VISITOR CENTER & INFORMATION   The **National Park's Gulf Coast Visitor Center,** on S.R. 29 at the south end of Everglades City (☎ **941/695-3311;** fax 941/695-3621), offers information and advice to visitors during the high season from 8:30am to 4:30pm, and intermittently in the summer.

The **Everglades City Area Chamber of Commerce,** P.O. Box 130, Everglades City, FL 34139 (☎ **941/695-3941;** fax 941/695-3919), provides information on tours and outfitters operating near the park's northwestern entrance at the intersection of U.S. 41 and S.R. 29. See section 1 of this chapter for information sources within the national park. They are there every day from 9am until 5pm.

SPORTS & OUTDOOR ACTIVITIES

BIKING   In Everglades City, a 4-mile paved bike path runs from town across a picturesque causeway to Chokoloskee Island. The **Ivey House Bed & Breakfast,** 107 Camellia St., 1 block behind the Circle K store (☎ **941/695-3299**), rents bikes during the winter months for $3 per hour or $15 for the day November to May. It's open from 8:30am to 4:30pm.

BIRDING   Pick up a free brochure on area birds at the visitor center. (Also, see "Boat Tours," below.)

CANOEING   Canoes are one of the best ways to cruise through these shallow waters which contain gators, manatees, and dolphins. They are available at Everglades City, near the Park Ranger Station at the Everglades' western entrance, from **North American Canoe Tours,** 107 Camelia St., Everglades City (☎ **941/695-4666**), November to April, or ☎ 860/739-0791 May to October; fax 941/695-4155 November to April. The 17-foot aluminum canoes can be rented with or without camping equipment, a personal guide, or fully outfitted tour. Canoes cost $20 per day. Canoes with camping supplies cost $50 per person per day.

For information about boat tours, hiking, canoeing, boating, fishing, and other outdoor activities in the park, see section 1 of this chapter.

SEEING THE SIGHTS BY WATER

You can wander a few trails and relax in this pristine park and visit the simple attractions below, but most of the sights in this region are accessible only after you leave land. Try at least one of the tours below for a look at the beautiful natural wilderness.

AIRBOAT TOURS   Flat-bottom, airplane-propeller-driven airboats can take from two people to large groups speeding across the waterways. They operate on privately owned property, since they're not allowed in the national park or other nearby federal preserves.

The most advertised and touristy operator is **Wooten's Everglades Adventure,** on U.S. 41, 2 miles east of S.R. 29 (☎ **800/282-2781** or 941/695-2781). This large operation has airboat and swamp-buggy rides, an alligator farm, gift shop, and snack bar. Buggy and boat rides cost $13.25 each. Admission to the alligator farm is $6.36 (free for children 6 and under). Combined tickets for both rides and a visit to the farm are about $30. Wooten's is open daily from 8:30am to 5pm. Discount coupons are available from the visitor center.

In town on S.R. 29, **Jungle Erv's Airboat World** (☎ **800/432-3367** or 941/695-2805) has a large airboat tour charging $12.50 for adults and $8 for children. Private rides in small boats cost $30 per person. A jungle tour by pontoon boat costs $12.50. **Eden's Jungle Boat Tours** (☎ **800/543-3367** or 941/695-2800) has a nature tour by large pontoon boat as well as private airboat rides for the same prices.

BOAT TOURS   Tours from Everglades City are offered by **Everglades National Park Boat Tours** (☎ **800/445-7724** in Florida, or 941/695-2591). The Mangrove Wilderness Tour explores the Glades' inland rivers and creeks at high tide. White ibis, cuckoos, egrets, herons, and other animals can often be seen through the thick mangroves. The Ten Thousand Islands Cruise navigates through the mangrove estuaries of the Gulf Coast. The endangered manatee can often be spotted, along with dozens of species of birds, including the southern bald eagle. Tours depart daily, every half hour from 9am to 5pm (less frequently off-season), last about 90 minutes, and cost $11 for adults, $5.50 for children 6 to 12. Reservations are not accepted. Tours depart from the Park Docks, on Chokoloskee Causeway (Fla. 29), half a mile south of the traffic circle by the ranger station.

Everyone raves about the narrated tours given by naturalists Frank and Georgia Garrett of **Majestic Everglades Excursions** (☎ **941/695-2777**). They take up to six passengers on 4-hour excursions through the islands on their covered-deck boat and explain the bird, marine, animal, and plant life. The trips cost $65 for adults, $35 for children 11 and under. Reservations are required; pickup is at the Seas Store and Deli in Everglades City.

If you are up for an intriguing all-day tour, **Everglades Excursions** (☎ **800/ 592-0848** or 941/598-1050) offers full-day guided trips to Everglades City from both Naples and Marco Island, which include a nature cruise, an airboat ride, and a visit to Ted Smallwood's store (described below). The trips cost $79 for adults and $64 for children; they also stop for an Old Florida–style lunch of seafood and other fare at a neighborhood restaurant (the cost is included in the price of the trip).

One-hour boat tours leave from the dock of Ted Smallwood's Store, at the south end of Mamie Street on Chokoloskee Island. (See "Seeing the Sights on Land," below.) You'll see where Ed Watson, reputed murderer of the notorious female outlaw Belle Star, was gunned down. Boat tours cost $15 per person.

CANOE TOURS   David Harraden and sons Jason and Jeremy of **North American Canoe Tours** (☎ **941/695-4666** November to April; 860/739-0791 May to October; fax 941/695-4155 November to April) have been leading canoe expeditions into the Everglades every winter since 1978, offering trips ranging from a day to a week. The 1-day trips cost $40 per person.

SEEING THE SIGHTS ON LAND

For an overview of this watery region, climb the E. J. Hamilton Observation Tower, opposite the visitor center. It is not part of the national park, but for $1 you can rise above the trees and see for miles across the islands and sawgrass plains.

Plan to take at least a half-hour break at **Smallwood's Store Museum** (☎ **941/ 695-2989**), at the south end of Mamie Street on Chokoloskee Island. Looking almost exactly as it did in pioneering days, this former trading post dates from 1906 and operated continuously as a store, post office, and voting place until 1982. Some 90% of the stock still on its shelves was there when it closed. That stuff is not for sale but there is a well-stocked gift shop selling books, gator heads, T-shirts, and Native American dolls. The museum is open daily from 10am to 5pm during winter; hours vary the rest of the year. Admission is $2.50 for adults, $2 for seniors, and free for children 11 and under. See "Seeing the Sights by Water," above, for details on the boat tour from Smallwood's.

Midway between Everglades City and the Shark Valley entrance to the park is **Big Cypress Gallery** (☎ **941/695-2428**) at 52388 Tamiami Trail, where the renowned local photographer Clyde Butcher displays his monumental depictions of the area landscape. See "Big Cypress National Preserve," below.

WHERE TO STAY

Captain's Table Lodge & Villas. 102 E. Broadway (P.O. Box 530), Everglades City, FL 34139. ☎ **800/741-6430** or 941/695-4211. Fax 941/695-2633. www.everglades.com. 32 units, 24 villas. A/C TV TEL. Winter $75–$95 double. Off-season $55–$70 double. DISC, MC, V. Take I-75 to Exit 14A, which is S.R. 29, to Everglades City. Follow S.R. 29 to the front door.

Stone Crab City, or Where to Find "the Filet Mignon of the Ocean"

If you haven't tasted them, don't bother making comparisons. No, they aren't like blue crabs, snow crabs, soft-shelled crabs, Alaskan kings, or even lobster. These meaty limbs are whiter, juicier, and sweeter than any other crustacean I've ever known. It was these tender morsels that James Bond devoured in *Goldfinger,* the same delicacy that drew the normally reclusive duke and duchess of Windsor out for their only public meal in Miami when they visited in 1941.

Made famous in the 1920s by a Miami Beach institution called Joe's (see "Where to Dine," in chapter 4), this delicacy took off in popularity and has since been the object of cravings for locals and visitors alike.

Demand is so high, in fact, that most stone crabs never make their way across the state border. Fish stores and restaurants report a brisk business in overnight shipping, but with Joe's alone serving nearly 500,000 pounds of the stuff each year, there is hardly enough to export commercially. Thousands more are consumed at the Everglades City Seafood Festival each February (see "When to Go," in chapter 2, for details).

Thankfully, there is no real threat to the survival of the stone crabs. Unlike most commercially harvested crustaceans, these sweeties are cultivated only for their luscious claws, which actually regenerate in little over a year.

It's estimated that more than two-thirds of Florida's claws come from the waters surrounding Everglades City, making it the number one source for the claws. So, swing into town any evening from mid-October through early May and watch the trappers returning from their daily hunts, hauling their catch, and you'll witness a tradition that has kept these fishing families profitable and popular for decades.

Most every local restaurant serves the tender flesh in season, but you can save some money by buying direct from the fish markets. They're sold precooked and ready to crack and dunk in some mustard sauce (see recipe below).

There are several reputable vendors in town. Make a stop at **Everglades Fish Corp** at 208 Cammelia St.) (☎ **941/695-3241**). They are open every day and

Located in the heart of town on S.R. 29, this collection of rooms, suites, and villas actually is a condo development, so the units are furnished and decorated in each owner's tastes, some with kitchens. The rooms and suites are in a main building, while the villas are built on stilts and have a cottagelike feel to them. A swimming pool sits by canal-like Lake Placid along the property's eastern flank. Bicycle rental is also available here.

Ivey House Bed & Breakfast. 107 Camellia St. (P.O. Box 5038), Everglades City, FL 34139. ☎ **941/695-3299**, or 860/739-0791 May–Oct. Fax 941/695-4155. www.iveyhouse.com. E-mail: sandee@iveyhouse.com. 10 units with shared bath; 1 cottage. A/C. $50 double ($70 double during Seafood Festival, with a 2-night minimum); $85 double in cottage ($120 cottage during Seafood Festival). Rates include continental breakfast. MC, V. Closed May–Oct.

This wooden structure was operated by Mrs. Ivey as a boardinghouse for men working on the Tamiami Trail in the 1920s. Today, it's run during the winter by canoe specialist David Harraden and clan. A center hallway separates the simple rooms. Guests share separate men's and women's bathrooms. There are two decks and a large living room for relaxation. A cottage next door has two bedrooms with baths, a screened porch, and antiques. Breakfasts and dinners are served in a spacious kitchen at the rear of the main sell the very freshest claws as well as some excellent fresh smoked fish. They also take most major credit cards. **Triad Fish Co.** (☎ 941/695-2662) at 410 School Dr. sells claws at reasonable prices (as well as Mrs. Hilton's famous mustard sauce). Perhaps the area's oldest purveyor is **Ernest Hamiltons'** on Chokoloskee Island at 100 Hamilton Lane (☎ 941/695-2771). To get there, take S.R. 29 to Chokoloskee; after the post office turn right just across the street from JT's grocery store; go straight and see the bright yellow building.

Bargain hunters may be lured roadside with promises of cheap claws. If prices are less than $9 or $10 a pound, you can be sure these are the castaways from the more reputable traders. The seconds are waterlogged and less meaty than their super-fresh counterparts. You can tell the difference by feeling the weight in the palm of your hand. "They're light as a hawk's feather," said one local trapper. A good fresh claw of any size should feel solid and hefty. Any visible meat should not look shriveled or as if it is shrinking away from its shell.

And no matter what anyone tells you, size counts! Claws are usually graded in four categories: medium, large, jumbo, and colossal. A pound of mediums usually contains between six and eight claws; colossals can weigh nearly three quarters of a pound each. Get the biggest claws you can afford. And ask them to crack them for you. Digging into those hard shells is tough work, but someone's got to do it.

Mustard Sauce from Joe's Stone Crab Restaurant, Miami Beach

3½ teaspoons Coleman's dry English mustard
1 cup mayonnaise
2 teaspoons Lea & Perrin's sauce
1 teaspoon A-1 sauce
⅛ cup light cream
⅛ teaspoon salt

Combine mustard and mayonnaise and beat for one minute. Add remaining ingredients and beat until the mixture reaches a creamy consistency. Chill. Serves 4.

---

house (dinners cost $10 to $15 per person, and outsiders are welcome by reservation). Guests have free use of bicycles but have to pay to use the coin laundry. They can smoke and drink on the decks, but not in the house. All of their bed-and-breakfast rooms have numerous 1900–1920 antiques—a wood washing machine and 1918 Hoosier apple-green-speckled enamelware, for example. In the plans for next year is an additional building with private baths and a hot tub. Full-day and half-day guided adventures and kayak rentals are available.

Rod & Gun Lodge. Riverside Dr. and Broadway (P.O. Box 190), Everglades City, FL 33929. ☎ **941/695-2101.** 17 units. A/C TV. Winter $85 double. Off-season $65 double. No credit cards.

For those who can do without modern conveniences, this charming old white clapboard house has plenty of history and all kinds of activities for sports enthusiasts, including a swimming pool, bicycle rental, tennis center, tennis courts, nearby boat rentals, and private fishing guides. This famous outpost on the banks of the sleepy Barron River was originally built as a private residence nearly 170 years ago, but Barron Collier turned it into a cozy hunting lodge in the 1920s. Pres. Herbert Hoover vacationed here after his 1928 election victory, and Pres. Harry S Truman flew in to sign Everglades National Park into existence in 1947. Other guests have included Richard Nixon, Burt Reynolds, and Mick Jagger. The public rooms are beautifully paneled and hung with tarpon, wild boar, deer antlers, and other trophies. Out by the swimming pool and riverbank, a screened veranda with ceiling fans offers a pleasant place for a libation. The dining room serves breakfast, lunch, and dinner.

WHERE TO DINE

Everglades City has no gourmet restaurants, but you can get your fill of fresh seafood at several local eateries. Since the town produces about two-thirds of Florida's crab catch, all have fresh-off-the-boat claws from mid-October through mid-May. If you are in town on a weekend, swing by the Shell station at S.R. 29 and U.S. 41 to sample a local delicacy, boiled peanuts. "Goobers," as the old-timers call them, are sold in paper bags from a colorful trailer. These soggy, spicy nuts are a real treat for some. I don't really get it, but hey, they have been around a lot longer than I have.

Despite being in the old Spanish-style railroad depot at Collier Avenue and Broadway, the ✪ **Captain's Table Restaurant** (☎ **941/695-2727**) looks like the lower decks of a 16th-century galleon. It offers a wide selection of seafood, with main courses ranging from $11 to $27. It's Everglades City's swankiest eatery, and its bar is one of the town's favorite watering holes. Open daily from 11am to 10pm.

The Oyster House, on S.R. 29 opposite the national park visitor center (☎ **941/695-2073**), also specializes in seafood. Main courses range from $12 to $17; sandwiches are $4.50 to $9.50. A narrow, screened front porch here is a fine place to sip a drink while watching the sunset over the Everglades. Open daily from 11am to 9pm. On some weekends you may find live music and dancing, too.

The down-home **Oar House Restaurant,** 305 Collier Ave. (Fla. 29), in town (☎ **941 695-3535**), offers "cooters, legs, and tails" (turtles, frog's legs, and alligator tails) as specialties. Main courses range from $8 to $16, and sandwiches and seafood baskets run $2 to $8. Open daily from 6am to 9pm.

3 Big Cypress National Preserve

50 miles W of Miami, 22 miles E of Naples

In Big Cypress, northwest of the Florida Everglades, "big" refers not to the size of the trees, but to the vastness of the stands. More than half a million acres of parkland were acquired by the National Park Service in 1974, and the Big Cypress National Preserve Addition Act of 1988 is gradually adding 146,000 additional acres.

The preserve is intentionally lean on visitor facilities and contains few marked trails of any kind. As a result, Big Cypress feels plenty big and remote. If you are looking for a true wilderness experience, you'll want to spend an afternoon exploring here. Just be sure you have a full tank of gas before entering—there are no gas stations or food services in the preserve.

Camping is available throughout the preserve. It's free, but there are no facilities: no fresh water, no toilets, no picnic tables, no grills.

To see one artist's incredible renderings of the area, stop at **Big Cypress Gallery** (☎ 941/695-2428) at 52388 Tamiami Trail (less than 1 mile east of the Oasis Visitor Center). This museum/gallery showcases Clyde Butcher's award-winning black-and-white photographs of his backyard—the vast expanse that is the Everglades. Many have been featured in television specials and magazines throughout the world. His landscape prints are huge—some spread 4 by 7 feet across—allowing you to focus into the quiet beauty of the Everglades. It's worth a drive. The gallery is open daily 9:30am to 5pm.

JUST THE FACTS

Entrance is free to Big Cypress National Preserve. Contact **Big Cypress National Preserve Headquarters,** P.O. Box 110, Ochopee, FL 33943 (☎ **941/695-4111** or 941/695-2000), for a map and specialized information on the preserve.

On-site information is dispensed at the **Oasis Visitor Center,** at the preserve's main entrance, on the Tamiami Trail (U.S. 41) in Ochopee, 37 miles west of Florida City and 22 miles east of Naples. During the winter months, information is also available at Preserve Headquarters, on the Tamiami Trail, about 18 miles west of Oasis. The visitor centers are staffed daily from about 8:30am to 4:30pm.

EXPLORING THE PRESERVE

The preserve is a sprawling expanse that was designated as a national preserve primarily to help protect the ecosystem of the Everglades. There's little to attract tourists except for die-hard walkers sure to enjoy more than 30 miles of flat trails. Pick up a free trail map from the visitor center before heading out. Otherwise, there is nothing you will see here that you won't find in the main park area.

If you want to explore, start on the Florida Trail, the preserve's main hiking trail, that stretches northwest (with significant gaps) all the way into the Florida Panhandle. The part of the trail that's inside Big Cypress is about 30 miles long and runs north from the Oasis Visitor Center. Hikers should be prepared for wet areas ankle- to waist-deep in the rainy season. There are two primitive campsites but no potable water on the trail.

4 Biscayne National Park

35 miles S of Miami

Many people who arrive at Biscayne National Park's main entrance at Convoy Point take one look around and exclaim, "Are we there?" You see, the park is very large—181,500 acres to be exact—but some visitors don't realize that 95% of it is underwater. In 1968, Pres. Lyndon Johnson signed a bill to conserve the barrier islands off South Florida's east coast as a national monument, a protected status that's one rung below national park. After being twice enlarged, once in 1974 and again in 1980, the waters surrounding the northernmost coral reef in North America became a full-fledged national park.

To be fully appreciated, it should be thought of more as a preserve than a destination. I suggest using your time here to explore underwater life—but most of all, to relax.

There's not much for landlubbers here. The park's small mainland mangrove shoreline and 44 islands are best explored by boat. Its extensive reef system is extremely popular with divers and snorkelers. The concessionaire at Convoy Point rents canoes, runs dive trips, and offers popular glass-bottom-boat tours.

Elliott Key, one of the park's 44 little mangrove-fringed islands and the recently restored Boca Chita, contain visitors centers, hiking trails, and campgrounds. Located about 9 miles from Convoy Point, Elliott Key and Boca Chita are accessible only by boat.

JUST THE FACTS

GETTING THERE & ACCESS POINTS   The park's mainland entrance is Convoy Point, located 9 miles east of Homestead. To reach the park from Miami, take the Florida Turnpike to the Speedway Boulevard (Exit 6). Turn left, heading south 4½ miles, then left again at North Canal Drive (SW 328th Street), and follow signs to the park. If you're coming from U.S. 1, whether you're heading north or south, turn east at North Canal Drive (SW 328th Street). The entrance is approximately 9 miles away.

Biscayne National Park is especially accessible to boaters. Mooring buoys abound, since it's illegal to anchor on coral. When no buoys are available, boaters must anchor on sand. Even the most experienced boaters should carry NOAA nautical chart no. 11451, which is available at Convoy Point. The waters are often murky, making the abundant reefs and sandbars difficult to detect—and there are more interesting ways to spend a day than waiting for the tide to rise. There's a boat launch at adjacent Homestead Bayfront Park, and there is dock space on Elliott Key and Boca Chita, available free on a first-come, first-served basis.

VISITOR CENTERS & INFORMATION   For information on park activities and tours, contact **Biscayne National Underwater Park Inc.,** P.O. Box 1270, Homestead, FL 33030 (☎ **305/230-1100;** fax 305/230-1120). The center is open daily from 9am to 5pm.

The **Convoy Point Visitor Center,** 9700 SW 328th St., at the park's main entrance (☎ **305/230-7275;** fax 305/230-1190), is the natural starting point for any venture into the park. In addition to providing comprehensive information on the park, rangers will show you a short video on request. Open Monday to Friday from 8:30am to 4:30pm and Saturday and Sunday from 8:30am to 5pm. The permanent visitor center opened in early 1997, and museum exhibits were installed during the summer of 1997.

ENTRANCE FEES & PERMITS   Entrance is free to Biscayne National Park. Back-country permits are also free and available at the visitor center.

SEEING THE HIGHLIGHTS

Since Biscayne National Park is primarily underwater, the only way to truly experience it is with snorkel or scuba gear. And you'll need a boat. Beneath the surface, the aquatic universe pulses with multicolored life: Bright parrot and angelfish, gently rocking sea fans, and coral labyrinths abound. Before entering the water, be sure to apply waterproof sunblock or wear a T-shirt. Once you begin to explore, it's easy to lose track of time, and the Florida sun is brutal, even during winter.

Afterward, take a picnic out to Elliott Key or Boca Chita and taste the crisp salt air blowing off the Atlantic. Transportation is available from the concession stand for $21 round-trip per person. Call ☎ **305/230-1100**

SPORTS & OUTDOOR ACTIVITIES

CANOEING   Biscayne National Park offers excellent canoeing, either along the coast or across open water to nearby mangrove islands. Since tides can be strong, only experienced canoeists should attempt to paddle far from shore. If you plan to go far, first obtain a tide table from the visitor center (see "Just the Facts," above) and paddle with the current. Free ranger-led canoe tours are scheduled for most weekend mornings; phone for information. You can rent a canoe at the park; rates are $7 an hour or $20 for a half day.

FISHING   Ocean fishing is excellent year-round; many people cast their lines right from the breakwater jetty at Convoy Point. A fishing license is required (see "Entrance Fees, Permits & Regulations" under "Just the Facts," in section 1, for complete information). Bait is not available in Biscayne, but is sold in adjacent Homestead Bayfront Park. Stone crabs and Florida lobsters can be found here, but you're only allowed to catch these on the ocean side when they're in season. There are strict limitations on size, season, number, and method of take (including spear fishing) for both fresh- and saltwater fishing. The latest regulations are available at most marinas, bait and tackle shops, and at the park's visitor centers. Or you can contact the **Florida Game and Fresh Water Fish Commission,** Bryant Building, 620 S. Meridian St., Tallahassee, FL 32399-1600 (☎ **904/488-1960**).

HIKING   Since the majority of this park is underwater, hiking is not great, but there are some short trails. At Convoy Point, you can walk along the 370-foot boardwalk, and along the half-mile jetty that serves as a breakwater for the park's harbor. From there, you can usually see brown pelicans, little blue herons, snowy egrets, and a few exotic fish.

Elliott Key is accessible only by boat, but once you're there, you have two good trail options. True to its name, the Loop Trail makes a 1½-mile circle from the bay-side visitor center, through a hardwood hammock and mangroves, to an elevated ocean-side boardwalk. It's likely that you'll see purple and orange land crabs scurrying around the mangrove roots.

The Old Road is a 7-mile tropical hammock trail that runs the length of Elliott Key. Because the visitor center is located about a third of the way along the trail, you can walk (or bike) only about 2½ miles north or 4½ miles south before turning around. This trail is one of the few places left in the world to see the highly endangered Schaus's swallowtail butterfly, recognizable by its black wings with diagonal yellow bands. They're usually out from late April to July.

SNORKELING & SCUBA DIVING   The clear, warm waters of Biscayne National Park are packed with colorful tropical fish that swim in the offshore reefs. Snorkeling and scuba gear is rented and sold at Convoy Point. Or bring your own.

Biscayne National Underwater Park Inc. (☎ **305/230-1100**) operates daily snorkel trips that last about 4 hours and cost $27.95 per person. They also run two-tank dives for certified divers and provide instruction for beginners. The price is $34.50 per person. It's open daily from 8am to 5:30pm. Two-tank dives depart on Wednesday, Saturday, and Sunday at 8:30am. Reservations are essential.

SWIMMING   You can swim at the protected beaches of Elliott Key and adjacent Homestead Bayfront Park, but neither of these beaches match other South Florida beaches for width, softness, or surf.

ORGANIZED TOURS

Biscayne National Underwater Park offers regularly scheduled glass-bottom-boat trips. These tours offer a fish's-eye view of some of the country's most accessible coral reefs. Boats depart year-round, daily from Convoy Point, every half hour from 10am to 1pm. Tours cost $19.95 for adults, $17.95 for seniors, and $9.95 for children 12 and under. Reservations are required. The company also offers guided scuba and snorkeling reef trips led by underwater naturalists. See "Snorkeling & Scuba Diving," above.

CAMPING

Although you won't find hotels or lodges in Biscayne National Park, there are some of the state's most pristine campsites. Since they are completely inaccessible by motor vehicle, you'll be sure to avoid the mass of RVs so prevalent in so many of the state's other campgrounds. Sites are on Elliott Key and Boca Chita, and can be reached only by boat. If you don't have your own, call ☎ **305/230-1100** to arrange a drop-off. Transportation to and from the visitor center costs $21 per person. The best facilities are on the northeast side of newly reopened Boca Chita where there are brand new showers, solar powered rest rooms, and drinking fountains, as well as barbecue grills and picnic tables. With a backcountry permit, available from the ranger station, you can pitch your tent somewhere even more private. Ask for a map at the visitor center. And be sure to bring plenty of bug spray.

8

The Gold Coast

by Victoria Pesce Elliott

Especially over the last decade, the cities along Florida's southeast coast have been growing at an explosive rate. Many newcomers have relocated from neighboring Miami where a number of circumstances—a huge influx of immigrants from the Caribbean, a drastic increase in violent crimes, and a devastating hurricane in 1992—caused many old-timers to settle in the cities of Broward and Palm Beach counties.

As a result, there has been a boom in building in the existing cities and westward into the swampy areas of the Everglades. Another by-product is the successful revitalization of Hollywood, Ft. Lauderdale, and West Palm Beach's downtown areas. The areas have been spruced up and now attract more young travelers and families than ever before. The dozens of gorgeous beaches, of course, have always drawn a steady stream of sun worshippers and water-sports enthusiasts.

Beyond the sands, the Gold Coast offers fantastic shopping, entertainment, clubbing, boating, golfing, tennis, and plain old relaxing.

Active travelers in particular enjoy the array of facilities available year-round in this beautiful region. With some of the country's most famous golf courses and even more tennis courts, this area attracts big-name tournaments in both sports (see "Florida Calendar of Events," in chapter 2).

Unfortunately, like its neighbors to the south, the Gold Coast can be prohibitively hot and buggy in the summer. The good news is that bargains are plentiful in the slow months (between May and October), when many locals take advantage of discounts and uncrowded resorts.

EXPLORING THE GOLD COAST BY CAR

Like most of the rest of South Florida, the Gold Coast consists of a mainland and an adjacent strip of barrier islands. You'll have to check the maps to keep track of the many bridges that allow access to the islands where most of the tourist activity is centered. Interstate 95, which runs north-south, is the area's main highway. Farther west is the Florida Turnpike, a toll road that can be worth the expense since the speed limit is higher and it is often less congested than I-95. Also on the mainland is U.S. 1, which generally runs parallel to I-95 (to the east) and is a narrower thoroughfare mostly crowded with strip malls and seedy hotels.

I recommend taking Fla. A1A, a slow ocean-side road that connects the long, thin islands of Florida's whole east coast. Though the road is narrow, it is the most scenic and forces you into the ultra-relaxed atmosphere of these resort towns.

1 Broward County: Hallandale & Hollywood to Fort Lauderdale

23 miles N of Miami

With more than 23 miles of beachfront and 300 miles of navigable waterways, Broward County is a great destination for outdoor lovers. Scattered amid the tacky shopping malls, gaudy condos, and glitzy tourist areas are some impressive natural wonders, including hundreds of parks, golf courses, and tennis courts, too. With year-round temperatures averaging 77° and a growing industrial base, the area attracts more than 6 million visitors each year. Some 1.3 million residents call the more than 28 cities and dozens of towns that make up Broward County home.

Like many other small American towns, the quaint city of Hollywood has been working on redeveloping its downtown area for years. Finally, in the late 1990s, the effort paid off. A spate of redevelopment has made the pedestrian-friendly center—along Hollywood Boulevard and Harrison Street east of Dixie Highway—a popular destination for travelers and locals alike. Some predict Hollywood will be South Florida's next big destination—South Beach without the attitude, traffic jams, and parking nightmares. Prices are a fraction of other tourist areas, and a true artsy image is apparent in the galleries, clubs, and restaurants that dot the new "strip." Its gritty undercurrent, however, still makes it more popular with bohemians and backpackers than society-page regulars.

Fort Lauderdale and its well-known strip of beaches, restaurants, bars, and souvenir shops has also undergone a major transformation. Once especially famous (or infamous) for the annual mayhem it hosted each spring when hedonism-bent college students descended from all over the country, this area is now attracting a more upscale and mainstream crowd.

In addition to beautiful wide beaches, the city includes more than 300 miles of navigable waterways and innumerable canals that permit thousands of residents to anchor boats in their backyards. Boating is not just a hobby here; it's a lifestyle. It's the reason many choose to live in this area known as the "yachting capital of the world," along with a string of other evocative names. Visitors can easily get on the water, too, by renting a boat, or simply by hailing a moderately priced water taxi.

Huge cruise ships also take advantage of Florida's deepest harbor, Port Everglades. It is the second-busiest cruise-ship base in Florida (after Miami) and one of the top five in the world. If you are interested in cruising, see chapter 2 for more information on particular lines and packages, or consult *Frommer's Caribbean Cruises and Ports of Call.*

ESSENTIALS

GETTING THERE If you're driving up or down the Florida coast, you'll probably reach Hollywood and Fort Lauderdale on I-95. Visitors on their way to or from Orlando should take the Florida Turnpike to Exit 53, 54, 58, or 62, depending on the location of your accommodations.

The Fort Lauderdale/Hollywood International Airport is small, easy to negotiate, and located just 15 minutes from both of the downtown areas it services.

Amtrak (☎ **800/USA-RAIL**) stations are at 200 SW 21st Terrace (Broward Boulevard and I-95), Fort Lauderdale (☎ 954/587-6692), and 3001 Hollywood Blvd., Hollywood (☎ 954/921-4517).

VISITOR INFORMATION   The **Greater Fort Lauderdale Convention & Visitors Bureau,** 1850 Eller Dr., Suite 303 (off I-95 and I-595 east), Fort Lauderdale, FL 33316 (☎ **954/765-4466;** fax 954/765-4467; e-mail: gflcvb@co.broward.fl.us; www.sunny.org), is an excellent resource in Spanish, French, or English. Call them for a free comprehensive guide with just about everything you could want to know about events, accommodations, and sightseeing in Broward County. In addition, once you are in town, you can call an **information line** (☎ **954/527-5600**) to get easy-to-follow directions, travel advice, and assistance from multilingual operators who staff a round-the-clock help line.

The **Greater Hollywood Chamber of Commerce,** 330 N. Federal Hwy. (on the corner of U.S. 1 and Taylor Street), Hollywood, FL 33020 (☎ **954/923-4000;** fax 954/923-8737), is open Monday through Friday from 8:30am to 5pm.

HITTING THE BEACH

The southern part of the Gold Coast, Broward County, has the region's most popular and amenities-laden beaches. Most do not charge for access, though all are well maintained. Here's a rundown on the county's best from south to north.

Hollywood Beach, stretching from Sheridan Street to Georgia Street, is a real carnival with an odd assortment of young hipsters, big families, and sunburned French Canadians dodging bicyclers and skaters along the rows of tacky souvenir shops, game rooms, snack bars, beer stands, hotels, and even miniature golf courses. The 3-mile-long Hollywood Beach Boardwalk is notable as one of the area's only beach paths where the diversions are right on the beach—separated from the sand and sea by only a thin paved strip instead of a busy highway and tall buildings. Popular with runners, skaters, and cruisers, the Boardwalk is also renowned as a hangout for thousands of retirement-age snowbirds, especially from Canada, who get together for frequent dances and shows at a faded outdoor amphitheater. Despite efforts to clear out a seedy element, the area remains a haven for drunks and scammers. Keep alert.

If you tire of the hectic diversity that defines Hollywood's Boardwalk, enjoy the natural beauty of the beach itself, which is wide and clean. There are lifeguards, showers, bathroom facilities, and public areas for picnics and parties.

The Fort Lauderdale Beach Promenade has just undergone a $26 million renovation, and it looks fantastic. However, note that this beach is hardly pristine; it is across the street from an uninterrupted stretch of low- and high-rise hotels, bars, and retail outlets. Also, on the scene is a mega-retail and dining complex, Beach Place, on Fla. A1A, midway between Las Olas and Sunrise boulevards (see "Shopping & Browsing," below).

Just across the road, on the sand, most days you will find hard-core volleyballers, who always welcome anyone with a good spike, and a calm ocean welcoming swimmers of any level. The unusually clear waters are under the careful watch of some of Florida's best-looking lifeguards. Freshen up afterward in any of the clean showers and rest rooms conveniently located along the strip.

Especially on weekends, parking along the ocean-side meters is nearly impossible to find. Try biking, skating, or hitching a ride on the water taxi instead. The strip is located on Fla. A1A, between SE 17th Street and Sunrise Boulevard.

Still known as the HoJo's Beach since it used to sit behind a Howard Johnson Hotel, this little-known hideaway is a perennial favorite with locals. Now the hotel has changed names and is called Lauderdale by the Sea, but the crowd is the same. High school and college students throwing Frisbees and hackey-sacks share this area with an older crowd of tourists staying at the oceanfront resort. A jetty bounds the beach on the south side, making it rather private; the water here gets a little choppy—a bonus

Fort Lauderdale Area Attractions & Accommodations

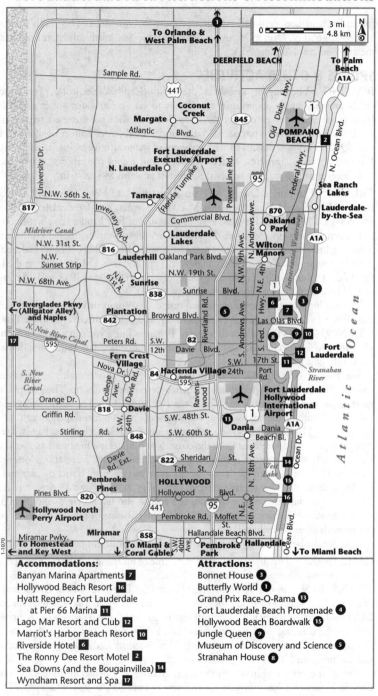

Accommodations:

Banyan Marina Apartments **7**
Hollywood Beach Resort **16**
Hyatt Regency Fort Lauderdale
    at Pier 66 Marina **11**
Lago Mar Resort and Club **12**
Marriot's Harbor Beach Resort **10**
Riverside Hotel **6**
The Ronny Dee Resort Motel **2**
Sea Downs (and the Bougainvillea) **14**
Wyndham Resort and Spa **17**

Attractions:

Bonnet House **3**
Butterfly World **1**
Grand Prix Race-O-Rama **13**
Fort Lauderdale Beach Promenade **4**
Hollywood Beach Boardwalk **15**
Jungle Queen **9**
Museum of Discovery and Science **5**
Stranahan House **8**

for surfers and boogey boarders, but not great for swimmers. This locals' spot is located at 4660 N. Ocean Dr., in Lauderdale-by-the-Sea, a half-mile north of Commercial Boulevard, on Fla. A1A.

SPORTS & OTHER ACTIVITIES

BOATING   A boating city known as "the yachting capital of the world," Fort Lauderdale provides ample opportunity for visitors to get on the water, either along the Intracoastal Waterway or out on the open ocean. If your hotel doesn't rent boats, try **Bill's Sunrise Watersports,** 2025 E. Sunrise Blvd., Fort Lauderdale (☎ 954/462-8962). They will outfit you with a variety of watercraft, including jet-skis, Wave Runners, 13-foot Cigarettes, 15-foot jet boats, and 8-foot powerboats, year-round. Bill's is open daily from 9am to 6pm. Rates start at about $45 an hour.

CRUISES   The **Jungle Queen,** 801 Sea Breeze Blvd. (3 blocks south of Las Olas Boulevard on Fla. A1A), in the Bahia Mar Yacht Center, Fort Lauderdale (☎ 954/462-5596), a Mississippi River–style steamer, is one of Fort Lauderdale's best-known attractions cruising up and down the New River. All-you-can-eat dinner cruises and 3-hour sightseeing tours take visitors past Millionaires' Row, Old Fort Lauderdale, and the new downtown. Cruises depart nightly at 7pm and cost $24 for adults and $12 for children 12 and under. Sightseeing tours are scheduled daily at 10am and 2pm and cost $11 for adults and $8 for children 10 and under.

If you're interested in gambling, several casino boat companies operate day cruises out of Port Everglades and offer blackjack, slots, and poker. **Discovery Cruise Lines** (☎ 800/937-4477) has daily cruises to The Bahamas where you can gamble, eat, and party for 5 to 6 hours for about $120. The price includes breakfast, lunch, and dinner, but drinks cost extra.

Sea Escape (☎ 800/327-2005 or 954/453-3333) also launches daily casino cruises. But theirs don't travel more than a few miles offshore. These trips "to nowhere" depart every day except Monday at 10am until 4pm. The party cruises offer buffet meals and full casinos for about $30 a person. I'd recommend spending an additional $10 to $15 for a cabin so you can stretch out and relax in between hands. Even though the cruises don't go far from the coast, 5 or 6 hours is a long time to spend at sea, especially if the weather is rough. Evening cruises, which leave at 7:30pm and return at 12:30 or 1:30am, cost a few dollars more and offer full buffet dinners and a Las Vegas show. Port charges are included, although you must pay a $3 departure tax. This is one of the best deals you'll find. Sea Escape also has a new 2- and 3- night cruise option, where visitors can go to Nassau, The Bahamas, for as little as $199 per person with all meals included.

Also, see the box "More Than a Boat Tour," below, for details on the water taxi.

GAME PARKS   This area seems to be the home of more mega-entertainment complexes than any other region in Southeast Florida. The **Grand Prix Race-O-Rama,** at 1500 NW 1st St., east of I-95 between Griffin and Sterling road exits, in Dania, is one of the originals and still the best for kids. With a massive video arcade, which is open 24 hours, five challenging miniature golf greens, go-carts for those over 4 feet 6 inches, and NASCAR racing for those over 5 feet tall, batting cages, and a huge sky coaster, this place is as exciting as it is exhausting. Plan to spend all day or night—or both. Call for prices and hours (☎ 954/921-1411).

One of the newest additions to the scene is **Dave & Busters** at 3000 Oakwood Blvd. in Hollywood, just off the Sheridan Street exit of I-95 (☎ 954/923-5505). This 50,000-square-foot complex caters primarily to adults; it features a full liquor bar and sit-down restaurant, as well as a more casual spot with table service as well. On weekends this place is packed with young adults on dates and rowdy groups of guys of all ages. An admission of $5 is charged only on Friday and Saturday after 10pm. D&B's opens weekdays at 11am and at 11:30am on weekends and usually closes by 1am.

GOLF   Most of the area's best courses are farther north in the very expensive resorts and many private country clubs; however, don't despair—dozens of great courses are open to the public. Some of the best include **Emerald Hills** at 4100 North Hills Dr., Hollywood, just west of I-95 between Sterling Road and Sheridan Street. This beauty consistently lands on "best of" lists of golf writers throughout the country. The last and 18th hole on a two-tier green is the challenging course's signature; it's surrounded by water and is more than a bit rough. Greens fees start at $80. Call ☎ **954/961-4000** for tee times. For one of Broward's best municipal challenges, try the 18-holer at the **Orangebrook Golf Course** at 400 Entrada Dr. in Hollywood (☎ **954/967-GOLF**). Built in 1937, this is one of the state's oldest courses and one of the area's best bargains. Morning and noon rates range from $17 to $32. After 2pm, you can play for less than $23, including a cart.

SCUBA DIVING   In Broward County, the best wreck dive is the *Mercedes I,* a 197-foot freighter that washed up in the backyard of a Palm Beach socialite in 1984 and was sunk for divers the following year off Pompano Beach. The artificial reef, filled with colorful sponges, spiny lobsters, and barracudas, is located 97 feet below the surface, a mile offshore between Oakland Park and Sunrise boulevards. Dozens of reputable dive shops line the beach. Ask at your hotel for a nearby recommendation or contact **Lauderdale Undersea Adventures,** 2150 SE 17th St., Fort Lauderdale (☎ **954/527-0187**).

SPECTATOR SPORTS   Baseball fans can get their fix at the **Fort Lauderdale Stadium,** 5301 NW 12th Ave. (☎ **954/938-4980**). The Baltimore Orioles now play exhibition games starting in late February; call ☎ **954/776-1921** for tickets. They cost $6 for a spot in the grandstand, $9 for reserved seats, and $12 for box seats. During the season, the spectacular Florida Marlins (World Series winners in 1997) play just south of Hallandale at the **Pro Player Stadium** near the Dade-Broward County line. Call **Ticketmaster** for tickets (☎ **305/358-5885**), which range from $2 to $40.

The **Pompano Harness Track,** 1800 SW 3rd St., Pompano Beach (☎ **954/972-2000**), Florida's only harness track, features horse racing and betting from October to early August. Grandstand admission is free; clubhouse admission is $2. They, like many other pari-mutuel outlets in the area, opened poker rooms in 1997.

The home of the Florida Derby, **Gulfstream Park,** 901 S. Federal Hwy., Hallandale (☎ **954/454-7000**), recently underwent a revamp that has made it one of the state's biggest and best-known tracks. It has a popular clubhouse and is open January to mid-March from Wednesday to Monday starting at 11am.

A sort of Spanish-style indoor lacrosse, jai-alai was introduced to Florida in 1924 and still draws big crowds who bet on the fast-paced action. Broward's only fronton, **Dania Jai-Alai,** 301 E. Dania Beach Blvd. at the intersection of Fla. A1A and U.S. 1; (☎ **954/920-1511** or 954/426-4330), is a great place to spend an afternoon or evening.

TENNIS   There are literally hundreds of courts in Broward County and plenty are accessible to the public. Many are at resorts and hotels. If not at yours, try one of these.

Famous as the spot where Chris Evert got in her early serves, **Holiday Park,** 701 NE 12th Ave. (off Sunrise Boulevard), Fort Lauderdale (☎ **954/761-5378**), has 18 clay and 3 hard courts (15 lighted). Her coach and father, James Evert, still teaches

More Than a Boat Tour

Plan to spend at least an afternoon or evening cruising Fort Lauderdale's 300 miles of waterways the only way you can—by boat. The **Water Taxi of Fort Lauderdale** (☎ **954/467-6677**) is one of the greatest innovations for water lovers since those cool Velcro sandals. A trusty fleet of old-port boats serves the dual purpose of transporting and entertaining visitors as they cruise through "The Venice of the Americas."

Each taxi operates on demand—and also along a fairly regular route—and carries up to 48 passengers. Choose a hotel on the route so that you can take advantage of this convenient and inexpensive system. You can be picked up at your hotel, usually within 15 minutes of calling, and then be shuttled to any of the dozens of restaurants, bars, and attractions on or near the waterfront. If you aren't sure where you want to go, ask one of the personable captains who can point out historic and fun spots along the way.

For a day cruise with the kids, pack lunch, bathing suits, sunscreen, and sunglasses and hail or call the taxi for pickup from any safe dock or seawall. Your afternoon of cruising might start with a tour of Millionaires' Row, where Lauderdale's largest yachts are dwarfed only by the homes at which they are docked. Make a stop at the Museum of Discovery and Science where you can catch an IMAX film or just enjoy the current educational exhibits. Then, if you are up for a walk, head across the 3-mile Riverwalk, a scenic palm-lined walkway along the New River where you can enjoy your picnic lunch, or try one of the restaurants dotting the way to Las Olas Boulevard. When you are ready for some shopping or a sit-down meal, reboard and head to Beach Place at Las Olas Boulevard and Cortez Street in the heart of Fort Lauderdale's most famous "strip." Stop for a refreshment at Casablanca Cafe and then hit the beach.

In the evening, the water taxi is ideal for bar-hopping—no worrying about parking or choosing a designated driver. Make your first stop at Shooters where professionals, boaters, and tourists share the large lively patio for a popular happy hour from 5 to 7pm on weekdays. Right next door is Bootlegger's, featuring more than 70 beers at an outside bar. You can eat at either spot or keep your eyes on the waterway for your ride (or call for a quicker pickup).

For a hard-to-beat meal, head over to Beach Place to Splash, a gourmet's delight on the second floor, featuring a mix of coastal specialties, including sushi. Or a few short blocks away, try Casablanca, a more romantic option, with piano music.

For those who want good jazz, you might want to take the taxi to the downtown section of Las Olas Boulevard. O'Hara's (see "Where to Dine") can always be relied on for a great mix of live jazz and blues.

Starting daily from 10am, boats usually run until midnight, and until 2am on weekends, depending on the weather. The cost is $7 per person per trip, $12 round-trip, and $15 for a full day. Children under 12 ride for half price and free on Sunday. Opt for the all-day pass—it's worth it.

All establishments described above (listed under the appropriate headings elsewhere in this chapter) are used to calling the taxi for guests. Still, you may want to keep a few quarters and the phone number on hand, just in case. And, if you find yourself inland without a paddle, call **Yellow Cab** (☎ **954/565-5400**).

young players here, although he is very picky about who he'll accept. Non–Fort Lauderdale residents pay $3 to $4 per hour. Reservations are accepted on weeknights, but cost an extra $3. Lights are also an extra $3 per hour and are only available for the clay courts.

At the **Marina Bay Resort,** 2175 S.R. 84, west of I-95 and just behind the Ramada Inn, Fort Lauderdale (☎ **954/791-7600**), visitors can play free on any one of nine hard courts on a first-come, first-served basis. Three are lighted at night.

SEEING THE SIGHTS

For an overview of Fort Lauderdale you may want to take an informative spin around the downtown area with **South Florida Trolley Tours** (☎ **954/429-3100**). Drivers narrate the history of the area as they loop around the city's streets past all the major (and many minor) sights. The charge for the 90-minute tour is $12 for adults, free for children 11 and under. The trolleys pick up passengers from most major hotels for six tours daily, starting at 9am. Call for current schedule.

For a tour by water, see the box above.

Museum of Discovery & Science. 401 SW 2nd St., Fort Lauderdale. ☎ **954/467-6637.** Museum admission $9 adults, $8 seniors, $7 children 3–12, free for children 2 and under; combo prices $12.50 adults, $11.50 seniors, $10.50 children. Mon–Sat 10am–5pm, Sun noon–6pm. From I-95, exit on Broward Blvd. E.; continue to SW 5th Ave.; turn right, garage on right.

Children and teenagers especially love this interactive science museum that is a model of high-tech "infotainment." During the week, school groups meander through the cavernous two-story modern building. However, most weekend nights you'll find a diverse crowd ranging from hip high school kids to 30-somethings enjoying a rock film in the Blockbuster IMAX 3D theater, which also shows short, science-related, super-size films daily. Out front, see a 52-foot-tall "Great Gravity Clock," located in the museum's atrium, the largest kinetic-energy sculpture in the state. Exhibits vary, so call for the latest details.

Bonnet House. 900 N. Birch Rd. (1 block west of the ocean, south of Sunrise Blvd.), Fort Lauderdale. ☎ **954/563-5393.** Admission $9 adults, $8 seniors, $7 students under 18, free for children 6 and under. Tours Wed–Fri 10am–1pm, Sat–Sun noon–3pm; arrive 15 minutes before the tour.

This historic 35-acre plantation home and estate survives in the middle of an otherwise highly developed beachfront condominium area and is only open by guided tour.

Built in 1921, the sprawling two-story waterfront home surrounded with formal tropical gardens is really the backdrop of a love story, which the very chatty volunteer guides will share with you if you ask. Some have actually lunched with the former resident of the house, Evelyn Bartlett, the wife of world-acclaimed artist Frederic Clay Bartlett. If you like quirky people, whimsical artwork, lush grounds, and very interesting details of design, you'll love this tour, which takes about 1½ hours.

Butterfly World. Tradewinds Park South, 3600 W. Sample Rd., Coconut Creek (west of the Florida Turnpike and I-95). ☎ **954/977-4400.** Admission $10.95 adults, $6 children 4–12, free for children 3 and under. Mon–Sat 9am–5pm, Sun 1–5pm; last admission at 4pm.

One of the world's largest butterfly breeders, Butterfly World cultivates more than 150 species of these colorful and delicate insects. In the park's walk-through, screened-in aviary, visitors can see thousands of caterpillars and watch newborn butterflies emerge from their cocoons and flutter around as they learn to fly. Depending on how interested you are in these winged beauties, you may want to allow from 1 to 2 hours to tour the gardens and the well-stocked gift shop. Look for a new lorikeet aviary to open in the near future, where guests will be able to hand feed these birds.

Florida Fun Train. From Sheridan Street Station (just west of I-95) in Hollywood. ☎ **888/ 386-8722.** $69.95 one way. Adults $120 round-trip. Children under 12 $49.95. Free for children 2 and under. Food and beverages not included. Mon–Thurs at 10:15am.

Note: This service started up in late 1997 to a rocky beginning. If it is still in business when you are reading this, the prices may have changed.

If you aren't up for the 4-hour car trip from Hollywood to Disney World and the other attractions in and around Orlando, consider a relatively new way to get there from Broward County. It isn't any quicker, but there are plenty of activities to pass the time. The brightly painted cars feature clowns, magicians, video games, a play area as well as a wine bar and pub, a tiki bar with a live band, and a game room. Full meals are served in a '50s-style diner, or any of the lounges. Those who want a more peaceful ride can escape to the quiet cars or card rooms. If you are with restless kids, this relatively costly adventure may be the ticket. If not, take **Greyhound** (☎ **800/231-2222**) for about 30% less and save the extra money for the pricey parks.

Stranahan House. 335 SE 6th Ave. (Las Olas Blvd. at the New River Tunnel), Fort Lauderdale. ☎ **954/524-4736.** Admission $5 adults, $2 students and children. Wed–Sat 10am–4pm, Sun 1–4pm; last tour begins at 3:30pm. Also accessible by water taxi.

In a town whose history isn't even as old as many of its residents, visitors may want to take a minute to see Fort Lauderdale's very oldest standing structure and a prime example of classic "Florida Frontier" architecture. Built in 1901 by "the father of Fort Lauderdale," this house once served as a trading post for Seminole trappers who came here to sell pelts. It's been a post office, town hall, and general store and now is a worthwhile little museum of South Florida pioneer life, containing turn-of-the-century furnishings and historical photos of the area, It is also the site of occasional concerts and social functions. Call for details.

SHOPPING & BROWSING

Broward County has some of Florida's best malls and some fantastic boutique areas, too.

Dania is known for its many antique shops clustered along Dixie Highway. Known as "Antique Row," this area has some of South Florida's best old treasures. Although many of the more upscale shops are overpriced, some of the smaller dealers offer great bargains to hagglers.

Also for bargain mavens is a strip of "fashion" stores on Hallandale Beach Boulevard's "Schmatta Row," east of Dixie Highway and the railroad tracks, where off-brand shoes, bags, and jewelry are sold at deep discounts. Funky Hollywood Boulevard also offers some wild shops with everything from Indonesian artifacts to used and rare books to leather bustiers to handmade hats. Dozens of shops line the pedestrian-friendly strip just west of Young Circle. The art galleries are clustered along Harrison Street just east of Dixie Highway.

The area's only beachfront mall, Beach Place, is in Ft. Lauderdale on Fla. A1A just north of Las Olas Boulevard. Completed in 1997 at a cost of $23 million, this 100,000-square-foot giant sports the usual chains like Sunglass Hut, Limited Express, Banana Republic, and The Gap as well as lots of popular bars and restaurants.

Other more traditional malls include the upscale Galleria at Sunrise Boulevard near the Fort Lauderdale Beach, and Broward Mall, west of I-95 on Broward Boulevard, in Plantation.

If you are looking for unusual boutiques, especially art galleries, head to trendy ✪ **Las Olas Boulevard,** where there are literally hundreds of shops with alluring window decorations and intriguing merchandise. You may find kitchen utensils posing as modern art sculptures or mural-size oil paintings.

The well-known department store **Lord & Taylor** has a little-known clearance center where discounts on new clothing for women, kids, and men can be as big as 75%. If you can handle open dressing rooms, overstuffed racks, and surly sales help, it's a great find at 6820 N. University Dr. in Tamarac. You may want to call (☎ **954/720-1915**) to find out about specials.

The **Fort Lauderdale Swap Shop,** 3291 W. Sunrise Blvd. (☎ **954/791-SWAP**), is one of the world's largest flea markets. In addition to endless acres of vendors, there's a miniamusement park, a 13-screen drive-in movie theater, weekend concerts, and even a free circus complete with elephants, horse shows, high-wire acts, and clowns.

The monster of all outlet malls is **Sawgrass Mills,** 12801 W. Sunrise Blvd., Sunrise (☎ **800-FL-MILLS** or 954/846-2350). Since the most recent expansion, which added more than 30 new designer outlet stores, this behemoth (shaped like a Florida alligator) now holds more than 275 shops and kiosks in nearly 2.3 million square feet covering 50 acres. Wear your most comfortable shoes or buy an extra pair while you are there. Stores include Donna Karan Company Store, Levi's Outlet, Sunglass Hut, Ann Taylor Loft, Barney's New York, all selling goods at between 20% and 80% below retail. Label-conscious shoppers are especially impressed with Off Fifth, the Saks Fifth Avenue outlet store and Last Call, the Neiman-Marcus clearance center. Take I-95 north to I-595 west to the Flamingo Road exit, turn right, and drive 2 miles to Sunrise Boulevard; you will see the large complex on the left. From the Florida Turnpike, exit Sunrise Boulevard west. Parking is free, but don't forget where you parked; the lot is huge. You may want to invest in a coupon booklet ($5), which entitles you to even greater discounts at many of the malls stores and restaurants as well as area attractions. Books are good for up to a year and can be turned in for updated books at no charge.

WHERE TO STAY

The Fort Lauderdale beach has a hotel or motel on nearly every block, and they range from the rundown to the luxurious. Both the **Howard Johnson** (☎ **800/327-8578** or 954/563-2451), at 700 N. Atlantic Blvd. (on Fla. A1A, south of Sunrise Blvd.), and the **Days Inn** (☎ **800/866-6501** or 954/462-0444), at 435 N. Atlantic Blvd. (Fla. A1A), offer clean ocean-side rooms.

In Hollywood, where prices are generally cheaper, the **Holiday Inn** at 101 N. Ocean Blvd. (☎ **954/921-0990**) operates a full-service hotel right on the ocean. With prices starting at around $110 in season and discounts for AAA, it's a great deal. **Howard Johnson** (☎ **800/423-9867** or 954/925-1411) has a great location right on the beach at 2501 N. Ocean Dr. (I-95 to Sheridan Street east to Fla. A1A south).

If you are looking for something more private or for longer than a few days, you may want to call a reservations service for help. Especially for rentals for a few weeks or months, call **Florida Sunbreak** (☎ **888-SUNBREAK**). Or call the **South Florida Hotel Network** (☎ **800/538-3616**) for help finding small inns and lodges in any price range. Also, check out the annual list of small lodgings compiled by the **Ft. Lauderdale Convention & Visitors Bureau** (☎ **954/765-4466**). It is especially helpful for those looking for privately owned, charming, and affordable lodgings.

VERY EXPENSIVE

Hyatt Regency Fort Lauderdale at Pier 66 Marina. 2301 SE 17th St. Causeway, Fort Lauderdale, FL 33316. ☎ **800/233-1234** or 954/525-6666. Fax 954/728-3541. 396 units. A/C MINIBAR TV TEL. Winter $209 double. Off-season $169 double. Year-round from $1,000 suite. AE, DC, DISC, MC, V.

The Pier 66 hotel and 142-slip marina has been hosting guests, especially boaters, since 1954. The luxurious resort attracts mega-yachts from all over the world, in addition to large groups and business travelers. Despite the emphasis on groups, for services and amenities this Hyatt is hard to beat.

The hotel's atrium-style lobby impresses with high ceilings and marble floors. The lushly landscaped grounds add to the exotic feel of this super convenient locale, situated across from the beach, and within walking distance to the best shopping and dining. Every room has a balcony; the priciest have expansive panoramas of the marina, the beach across the street, and all of Fort Lauderdale beyond. The best part is that it is serviced by the convenient water taxi (see box, above).

Dining/Diversions: Best known for its revolving rooftop lounge, the hotel also offers an American grill and a very popular waterfront cafe for dinner and lunch.

Amenities: Concierge, room service (24 hours), dry-cleaning and laundry services, newspaper delivery, twice-daily maid service, baby-sitting, secretarial services, express checkout, valet parking $8, courtesy car or limo. Spectravision movie channels, two swimming pools, beach, a fully equipped spa, Jacuzzi, sauna, 40-person whirlpool, jogging track, children's center or programs, business center, conference rooms, self-service Laundromat, sundeck, two lighted clay tennis courts, water-sports equipment and boat rentals, 142-slip marina, tour desk, beauty salon, boutiques, shopping arcade.

Marriott's Harbor Beach Resort. 3030 Holiday Dr., Fort Lauderdale, FL 33316. ☎ **800/ 222-6543** or 954/525-4000. Fax 954/766-6165. 659 units. A/C TV TEL. Winter $299–$339 double. Off-season $139–$179 double. Year-round from $600 suite. AE, CB, DC, DISC, MC, V. From I-95, exit on I-595 east to U.S. 1 north; proceed to SE 17th St.; make a right and go over the intracoastal bridge past three traffic lights to Holiday Dr.; turn right.

Situated on 16 oceanfront acres just south of Fort Lauderdale's "strip" is the popular and predictable Marriott. From the spacious rooms and suites to the 8,000-square-foot swimming pool, everything in this very well run hotel is huge. All rooms open onto private balconies overlooking either the ocean or the Intracoastal Waterway. Return guests include many convention groups and families who enjoy the space to spread out. Service is more efficient than personal.

Dining: A formal restaurant serves one of Fort Lauderdale's most elegant dinners and a less formal Japanese restaurant serves hibachi dinners that are prepared at your table. Three other casual restaurants serve breakfast, lunch, dinner, and late-night drinks.

Amenities: Concierge, room service, in-room massage, laundry services, newspaper delivery, baby-sitting, twice-daily maid service, express checkout, secretarial services, valet parking, courtesy car for shopping and golf, free coffee in lobby. Outdoor heated pool, beach, health club, Jacuzzi, sauna, sundeck, five clay tennis courts, water-sports equipment, bicycle rental, game room, children's center and programs, business center, self-service Laundromat, tour desk, boutiques, conference rooms, car-rental desk, beauty salon.

✪ **Wyndham Resort and Spa.** 250 Racquet Club Rd., Fort Lauderdale, FL 33326. ☎ **800/ 996-3426** or 954/389-3300. Fax 954/384-1416. 500 units. A/C TV TEL. Winter from $245 double. Off-season from $175 double. Golf and spa packages (with or without meals) $115–$305 per person based on double occupancy. AE, CB, DC, DISC, MC, V. From I-95, exit at I-595 west to I-75; exit on Arvida Pkwy.; continue west to Weston Blvd.; turn right and proceed to Saddle Club Rd.; turn left to Bonaventure Blvd. Make a right to Racquet Club Rd. From Florida Turnpike, take I-595 West, take Exit 1, SW 136th Ave., S.R. 84, and proceed to Bonaventure Blvd.

Having changed hands frequently, this unusual spa and golf resort is a bit difficult to peg down. Built in 1981 on 23 acres, this active resort quickly earned a great reputation for its world-class facilities. Unfortunately, years of mismanagement resulted in its deterioration. A $10 million renovation begun in 1996 improved things, but then the resort was sold again to Wyndham resorts, which has big plans. Though it lacks any real charm, so far the overhaul looks fantastic.

The rooms, scattered throughout nine four-story buildings, have also been thoroughly gutted and reoutfitted in a bright tropical style, with conveniences like telephone voice mail and data ports, irons, ironing boards, coffeemakers, clock radios, and hair dryers. Also, suites and deluxe rooms offer wet bars and small refrigerators.

Although it is a lengthy trek to the nearest beach, this first-class property has plenty of opportunities to sun and swim—with five pools, including separate lap pools for men and women, and a private lake.

Dining/Diversions: With four restaurants, including one serving superb Tuscan food in a formal setting and another with real spa cuisine, you'll find plenty of delicious choices. You may even want to request recipes to take home. Also on the premises are four lounges for afternoon and evening entertainment and cocktails.

Amenities: Concierge, 24-hour room service, dry-cleaning and laundry service, newspaper delivery, in-room massage, twice-daily maid service, express checkout, secretarial services, valet parking, shopping transportation. Limited kitchenettes in some suites, Spectravision movie channels, five swimming pools, full-service spa, Jacuzzi, sauna, two championship golf courses, sundeck, 15 night-lit tennis courts, children's programs, business center, tour desk, boutiques, conference rooms, car-rental desk, beauty salon, boutique and gift shop.

EXPENSIVE

✪ **Lago Mar Resort and Club.** 1700 S. Ocean Lane, Fort Lauderdale, FL 33316. ☎ **800/255-5246** or 954/523-6511. Fax 954/524-6627. E-mail: reservations@lagomar.com. 170 units. A/C TV TEL. Winter $195 double; from $265 suite. Off-season $90–$100 double; from $125 suite. AE, DC, MC, V. From Federal Hwy. (U.S. 1), turn east onto SE 17th St. Causeway; turn right onto Mayan Dr.; turn right again onto S. Ocean Dr.; turn left onto Grace Dr.; then left again onto S. Ocean Lane to the hotel.

After extensive renovations, this sprawling family owned resort is even better than before. Lago Mar, a casually elegant resort, occupies its own little island between Lake Mayan and the Atlantic and is very family oriented, with lots of facilities and supervised activities for children, especially during spring break and Christmas vacations. It's also good for business travelers looking for value. Unfortunately, the word has gotten out and it has become difficult to get reservations during the season.

Most accommodations here are suites, available in a variety of configurations. The smallest suites, called "executive," are decorated in contemporary prints and are simple and comfortable. The executive suites are very large, with a king-size bed, separate dressing area, pull-out sofa, and separate tub and shower in an extra-large bathroom. Each has a private balcony and full kitchen, or at least a microwave and a refrigerator. Ask for one of the newer units since they are generally larger and have more closet space. Definitely take advantage of the hotel's waterfront location to use the convenient water taxi (see box above).

Dining/Diversions: Three excellent restaurants and two lounges may tempt you to never leave this top-rated resort.

Amenities: Room service, dry-cleaning and laundry service, secretarial services, valet parking. Kitchenettes in most suites, outdoor pool and lagoon, beach, small fitness center, game rooms, children's playground, supervised children's programs during holiday periods, business center, conference rooms, sundeck, four tennis courts, miniature golf course, volleyball courts, shuffleboard, water-sports concession, men's and women's apparel shops, Laundromat, tour desk.

Riverside Hotel. 620 E. Las Olas Blvd., Fort Lauderdale, FL 33301. ☎ **800/325-3280** or 954/467-0671. Fax 954/462-2148. www.riversidehotel.com. 116 units. A/C TV TEL. Winter $179–$189 double; from $249 suite. Off-season $99–$129 double; from $139 suite. AE, DC, MC, V. From I-95, exit onto Broward Blvd.; turn right onto Federal Hwy. (U.S. 1), then left onto Las Olas Blvd.

Right in the thick of Ft. Lauderdale's hottest downtown area, the six-story Riverside Hotel is one of the oldest in South Florida. Built in 1936, it looks like a Wild West movie set, complete with a second-floor wooden terrace and an enormous mural on the front facade. You are in the middle of trendy Las Olas Boulevard and on the route of the popular water taxi. On weekends the hotel is often packed with wedding guests attending ceremonies that are held outside by the small heated swimming pool. A bit nicer than the public areas which are outfitted in Mexican tile and wicker furnishings, the guest rooms upstairs are spacious and well maintained. Details like intricately tiled bathrooms and old-style furniture enhance the charm of the otherwise stark building. The best rooms face the New River, but it's hard to see the water past the parking lot and trees. The hotel does not have an abundance of services or facilities but the central downtown location makes almost anything you could desire just steps away.

Dining/Diversions: Do sample Indigo, a fantastic Asian/Indonesian restaurant in the hotel lobby (see "Where to Dine," below). Also on the premises is a more standard grill restaurant and a lounge.

Amenities: Room service, dry-cleaning and laundry service, secretarial services, valet parking, gift shop. Refrigerators, outdoor pool, nearby health club, conference rooms, sundeck.

MODERATE

✪ **Banyan Marina Apartments.** 111 Isle of Venice, Fort Lauderdale, FL 33301. ☎ **954/524-4430.** Fax 954/764-4870. www.banyanmarinaapts.com. E-mail: banyan-laud@travelbase.com. 10 apts. A/C TV TEL. Winter $80–$175 apt. Off-season $50–$120 apt. Weekly and monthly rates available. MC, V. To get there from I-95, exit Broward Blvd. E.; cross U.S. 1 and turn right on SE 15th Ave.; at the first traffic light (Las Olas Blvd.), turn left. Turn left at the third island (Isle of Venice).

You'll feel as if your best friends left you their keys to their well-kept waterfront apartment at Peter and Dagmar Neufeldt's Banyan Marina. One of the best accommodation values in South Florida, this hidden treasure is built around a dramatic 75-year-old banyan tree and is located directly on an active waterway, halfway between Fort Lauderdale's downtown and the beach. The accommodations, one- and two-bedroom apartments, are all decorated differently. All are comfortable and spacious with full kitchens and living rooms. The best part of staying here, besides your gracious and knowledgeable hosts, is that the water taxi will find you here and take you anywhere you want to be day or night. There is also a small outdoor heated pool and a marina for those with boats.

✪ **Hollywood Beach Resort.** 101 N. Ocean Dr. (at Fla. A1A and Hollywood Blvd.), Hollywood, FL 33019. ☎ **954/921-0990.** Fax 954/920-9480. 400 units (approximately 200 on rental program). A/C TV TEL. Winter from $109. Off-season from $68. AE, DC, DISC, MC, V.

There is nothing cozy or quaint about this sprawling 1920s beachfront hotel, but it couldn't be better located or better priced. The two best features are that all the rooms have full kitchens and the hotel is directly on the ocean. This eight-story building actually operates as a privately held condominium where owners can elect to put their units on a rental program. So there is no telling how rooms may be furnished or outfitted (management does maintain certain standards). All the units I have seen are clean and modest. Larger units and those with views are significantly more expensive than studios. If the weather is bad, consider shopping at the adjacent Ocean Walk Mall or hit a movie at the on-site multiplex movie theater. Also on the premises is a large outdoor pool and Jacuzzi. The many conveniences of this well situated property make it especially popular with tour groups from Europe, South America, and Canada.

INEXPENSIVE

Ronny Dee Resort Motel. 717 S. Ocean Blvd., Pompano Beach, FL 33062. ☎ **954/943-3020.** Fax 954/783-5112. 35 units. A/C TV. Winter from $62 double; from $469 efficiency. Off-season from $32 double; from $225 efficiency. AE, MC, V. From I-95, exit Atlantic Blvd. E. to Fla. A1A N.

The bad news is that this family owned motel is located on busy Fla. A1A; the good news is that it's just 100 yards from the beach and amazingly inexpensive. Popular with European guests, this two-story yellow motel, wrapped around a central swimming pool, contains almost three dozen suburban-style wood-paneled guest rooms filled with an eclectic mix of furniture. All contain a small refrigerator, but none have a telephone; pay phones are located in a public area, near a large game room that contains a pool table, VCR, books, and other games. Ping-Pong and shuffleboard are also available.

Sea Downs (and the Bougainvillea). 2900 N. Surf Rd., Hollywood, FL 33019. ☎ **954/923-4968.** Fax 954/923-8747. 14 units. A/C TV TEL. Winter $67–$82 efficiency; $93–$108 one-bedroom apt; $118 penthouse. Off-season $44–$59 efficiency; $57–$80 one-bedroom apt; $85–$88 penthouse. Special weekly and monthly rates also available. No credit cards accepted. From I-95, exit Sheridan St. E. to Fla. A1A south; drive $1/2$ mile to Coolidge St.; turn left.

This bargain accommodation is often booked months in advance by returning guests who want to be directly on the beach without paying a fortune. The hosts of this superclean '50s motel, Claudia and Karl Herzog, live on the premises and keep things running smoothly. Renovations completed in 1997 have replaced bathroom fixtures, and many rooms have been redecorated here and at the Herzogs' other even less expensive property next door, the Bougainvillea. Guests at either spot can use the heated pool, barbecue grills, picnic area, laundry facilities, and sundeck.

A HOSTEL

Floyd's Youth Hostel/Crew House. Please call for address and directions in Fort Lauderdale. ☎ **954/462-0631.** Fax 954/462-6881. E-mail: FECreamer@aol.com. 20-plus beds. $12.20–$13.50 per person for a dorm bed. No credit cards. Free daytime pickup.

Although there are a number of cheap hostels operating near Fort Lauderdale's renowned strip, the best place to crash is Floyd's. While it is a few miles inland from the beach, this well-kept lodging offers what every backpacker and international traveler wants—safety and good, warm fellow travelers. Floyd himself takes care of the guests, many of whom have come looking for work on the area's yachts. In fact, we have agreed not to list the address since Floyd insists on interviewing each prospective guest by phone before booking. Rest assured, you've found one of the area's best and safest hostels with extras like a cupboard full of complimentary staples—milk, cereal, and generic-brand macaroni and cheese.

WHERE TO DINE

Having hosted visitors for so long, Fort Lauderdale, and to some extent Hollywood as well, have some of South Florida's finest restaurants. Increasingly, ethnic options are joining the legions of surf-and-turf options that dominated the area for so long. Las Olas Boulevard has dozens of eateries (so many in fact that the city has disallowed any new restaurants to open on the overcrowded 2-mile street). In addition to those reviewed below, consider **Jackson's 450,** 450 E. Las Olas Blvd. (☎ **954/522-4450**), and **ZAN(Z)BAR,** a romantic South African restaurant decked out in zebra and leopard skin at 602 E. Las Olas Blvd. (☎ **954/767-3377**).

VERY EXPENSIVE

Cafe Arugula. 3110 N. Federal Hwy., Lighthouse Point. ☎ **954/785-7732.** Reservations recommended. Main courses $18–$32. AE, CB, DC, DISC, MC, V. Sun–Thurs 5:30–10pm, Fri–Sat 5:30–10:30pm. From I-95, take Sample Rd. E. to U.S. 1; make a right. AMERICAN CONTEMPORARY.

Although it is a bit out of the way, loyal customers come from neighboring counties to experience one of Broward's first nouvelle restaurants. Chef/owner Dick Cingolani oversees every aspect of this elegant eatery on the very northern edge of Broward County.

The main dining room with an open kitchen and oak-burning oven as its center-piece is elegant but not overly stuffy. Food is the main focus here. From the sautéed jumbo lump crab cakes to the handcrafted chocolate cakes, everything that comes out of the kitchen is superb. Salads and appetizers are large and beautifully displayed. One of the best is the spicy Thai shrimp "taco" served with slightly sweet and lightly spiced coconut and lemongrass sauce. For vegetable lovers, the grilled portobello mushrooms over baby greens with a crumble of herbed feta cheese also stands out. The veal chop, grilled with rosemary, is tender and aromatic and is served with a creamy mound of mashed potatoes flavored with a hint of garlic as well as a delicate stir-fry of fresh vegetables. Like all meals here, the side dishes are perfectly paired with the flavors of the main attraction.

✪ **Cafe Maxx.** 2601 E. Atlantic Blvd., Pompano Beach. ☎ **954/782-0606.** Reservations recommended. Main courses $18–$32. AE, CB, DC, DISC, MC, V. Mon–Thurs 5:30–10:30pm, Fri–Sat 5:30–11pm, Sun 5:30–10pm. From I-95, exit at Atlantic Blvd. E. The restaurant is three lights east of Federal Hwy. INTERNATIONAL.

Every one of chef/owner Oliver Saucy's restaurants has received accolades from all who bestow them in the culinary arena. This is his best. An oak-burning grill fills the contemporary and casually formal space with enticing aromas from around the globe. The pricey à la carte offerings borrow from Italian, Asian, Creole, Cuban, and Caribbean kitchens to create exotic and delicious mixes like potato-encrusted soft-shell crab, barbecued chicken quesadilla, and pistachio-fried oysters, as well as a host of other exciting but not overwrought dishes. Reserve early on weekends when the most coveted seats, the cozy booths, book well in advance.

EXPENSIVE

East City Grill. 505 N. Atlantic Blvd. (Fla. A1A between Las Olas and Sunrise blvds.), Fort Lauderdale. ☎ **954/565-5569.** Reservations recommended well in advance. Main courses $13–$27. AE, DC, DISC, MC, V. Mon–Fri 9am–3pm and 5:30–11pm, Sat 8am–3pm and 5:30pm–midnight, Sun 8am–3pm and 5:30–10pm. ASIAN AMERICAN/SEAFOOD.

This happening spot on the beach offers an ocean-side location and a killer nouvelle-style menu; it's yet another hit by the mega-Maxx group (see the Cafe Maxx, above). For starters consider steamed crab and goat-cheese dumplings, lots of innovative sushi dishes, or Jamaican beer-steamed prawns. A steamer bar allows you to create your own dinner with a choice of steaming broths, sauces, and sides. You must be creative to dine here. If you are, and you love fresh, interesting seafood, you won't mind the wait at the stunning oak bar where you can look into the open kitchen. Otherwise, stick to the old-fashioned steak and fish houses in town.

Revolution 2029. 2029 Harrison St., Hollywood. ☎ **954/920-4748.** Reservations suggested. Main courses $13–$24. AE, DC, DISC, MC, V. Tues–Fri 11:30am–3pm, Sun–Thurs 5–10pm, Fri–Sat 5pm–midnight. MULTICULTURAL.

One of the first froufrou eateries in otherwise dowdy Hollywood, Revolution attracts upscale hipsters looking for a dining "experience." While nearby South Beach has plenty of this kind of thing, Hollywood is just catching on. The menu is as modern as the sleek decor. With the best of everything from around the world, the menu varies both nightly and seasonally. You may want to start with gorgeous green New Zealand mussels gently flavored with coriander, coconut curry broth, and chunks of crisp apple or a rich roasted corn chowder with sweet potato and spinach corn custard. For vegetarians, there are many great options like oven-roasted portabello mushrooms, crispy vegetable egg rolls, and almond-crusted goat cheese. Innovative dishes like tamarind grilled swordfish and port marinated pork chops are interesting but not overly fussy. Except on busy weekends, service is efficient and friendly.

MODERATE

Aruba Beach Cafe. 1 E. Commercial Blvd., Lauderdale-by-the-Sea. ☎ **954/776-0001.** Reservations accepted only for parties of 10 or more. Main courses $9–$16. AE, DC, DISC, MC, V. Daily 11am–11pm (bar stays open later). SEAFOOD/AMERICAN.

More recommendable as a spot to drink than to eat, Aruba is popular at all hours, especially because of its very central location, directly on the beach at the end of Commercial Boulevard. The extensive menu offers salads, sandwiches, and the requisite seafood offerings. The food is fine, but uninspired. Choose a few good appetizers like the creamy smoked fish dip served with seasoned flat bread, the fried calamari, or a selection from the raw bar.

✪ **Casablanca Cafe.** On the ocean at the corner of Fla. A1A and Alahambra St., Fort Lauderdale. ☎ **954/764-3500.** Reservations not accepted. Main courses $8–$18. AE, DISC, DC, MC, V. Daily 11:30am–11pm. CONTINENTAL/AMERICAN.

Although it may seem odd to sit next to a roaring fire while listening to live music in the warm South Florida climate, at Casablanca it's a perfect complement to the stunning architecture and stupendous cooking. Everything from the warm macadamia nut–encrusted goat-cheese salad to a filet mignon in a cognac-and-mushroom sauce served with perfectly al dente pasta is immaculately prepared and served by a friendly staff. Six or seven specials are included daily on the menu; the best are seafood creations with superfresh local fish or lobster.

Conca'D'Oro. 1833 Tyler St. (on Young Circle), Hollywood. ☎ **954/927-6704.** Reservations not accepted. Pizzas $7–$12.50. Main courses $12–$18. MC, V. Mon–Thurs 11am–11pm, Fri–Sat 11am–midnight, Sun 4–11pm. ITALIAN.

This bustling Italian eatery is always busy. It's not that the food is so extraordinary, but that the portions are large, service is quick, and the attitude is straight from Brooklyn. The pizzas, served Neapolitan (thin crust) or Sicilian style, are large and topped with lots of cheese and a good tangy tomato sauce. Don't expect more than iceberg lettuce in the salads but do take advantage of the huge heroes and tasty house wines. If you are with a group, order one or two entrees to share. You will have leftovers. Although they are not always on the menu, ask for fresh mussels if they are in season. While other appetizers are battered and fried, the young black mussels are done to perfection in a red or white sauce. Also good is the hearty lasagna that is full of chunks of garlicky meatballs and mild sausage.

✪ **Indigo.** In the Riverside Hotel, 620 E. Las Olas Blvd. ☎ **954/467-0671.** Reservations only for groups of six or more. Main courses $11–$19. AE, DC, MC, V. Daily 7am–11pm; weekends until midnight or later. SOUTHEAST ASIAN/ECLECTIC.

This not-so-traditional Southeast Asian meal begins with a basket of pappadoms, naan, and shrimp puff bread. All are delicious and easy to fill up on, especially when spread with the tangy pineapple chutney or cucumber pickle. An impressive appetizer is a lightly peppered dusted seared tuna served in crispy basket of udon noodles. Look underneath for a hidden dab of sweet apricot puree. It's fantastically rich and a good complement to the spicy fish. A macadamia-encrusted brie is astounding, served over baby lettuce and mixed with a citrusy basil dressing. Extra crispy crostini are scattered over the hearty dish for extra dipping advantage. Entrees run the gamut from a lean though somewhat dry Balinese lamb to a musky smoked duckling to a rosemary skewered shrimp. As to be expected in Asian cuisine, vegetarians have plenty of choices, too. In addition to a super rich grilled vegetable cassoulet au gratin and a fried rice dish with shallots, corn, and asparagus, there are pizzas baked on top of puffy naan bread covered with such toppings as onions, shiitake mushrooms, goat cheese, spinach, eggplant, garlic, curried tomato, and pine nuts. Particularly good is a meaty soy and portobello mushroom combination wrapped in fluffy puff pastry served with a delicate broccoli sauce. Most dishes are as tasty as they are interesting. Ask servers for suggestions, though. Even if they are a bit harried on weekends, they tend to be knowledgeable and honest.

✪ **Sugar Reef.** 600 N. Surf Rd. (on the Broadwalk just north of Hollywood Blvd.), Hollywood. ☎ **954/922-1119.** Reservations only for groups over six. Main courses $12–$20; sandwiches and salads $5–$8.50. AE, DISC, MC, V. Mon 4–10:30pm, Tues–Thurs 11am–10:30pm, Fri–Sun 11am–11pm (sometimes later in winter). TROPICAL FRENCH.

A welcome addition to a strip of greasy fish joints, hot-dog stands, and bars, Sugar Reef has captured the attention of visitors and locals who appreciate superior and imaginative meals served for very reasonable prices. Chef/owner Patrick Farnault left a successful and formal restaurant in Fort Lauderdale to open this ocean-side bistro. Simple offerings might include a salmon BLT with dill mayonnaise or Jamaican-style pork loin or a burger and fries. Portions are generous but not huge. Escargot in a green curry sauce with lemongrass is a delicious twist on an old favorite, evoking memories of subtle and spicy Vietnamese dishes. More than half a dozen salads, some with cheese, chicken, or fish, are a perfect meal for beach-goers looking for something light and healthful as they enjoy the view. As is fitting for a beachside eatery, service is laidback but still professional.

Sushi Blues Cafe. 1836 S. Young Circle (east on Hollywood Blvd.), Hollywood. ☎ **954/929-9560.** Reservations recommended on weekends. Main courses $11–$20; nigiri sushi $1.50–$2.75 per piece. AE, MC, V. Mon–Thurs 6pm–midnight, Fri–Sat 6pm–1:30am. JAPANESE.

Live loud blues and jazz combine with pretty good sushi to make an unusual pair at this small storefront eatery located on Hollywood's largest traffic circle. There are only about 12 tables and a dozen counter stools in this relatively straightforward and unadorned sushi room. In addition to raw fish, the cafe offers some inventive specials like salmon carpaccio with caper sauce, fried soft-shell crab drizzled with a spicy sesame sauce, miso-broiled eggplant, and grilled smoked sausage with Japanese mustard. The restaurant is popular with a 20-something crowd and is packed when there's live music, Friday and Saturday nights.

INEXPENSIVE

East Coast Burrito Factory. 261 E. Commercial Blvd., Fort Lauderdale. ☎ **954/ 772-8007.** Tacos and burritos $3–$6; salads $4–$6. AE, CB, DC, DISC, MC, V. Mon–Sat 11am–9:45pm, Sun noon–7:45pm. FLORIDA/MEXICAN.

Just off of I-95 is an oasis. A dozen wooden benches line the counter at this super Mexican diner, which serves made-to-order soft tacos, burritos, hot dogs, and salads. For a healthier spin on a burrito, try the Florito, made with black beans instead of refried beans—a uniquely Florida invention. My favorite is the "Super Veggie," stuffed with corn, salsa, mushrooms, black olives, carrots, peppers, and hearts of palm, then doused with the restaurant's own super-hot chile pepper sauce. The guacamole and various huge salads are also fantastic, especially on a sunny day on the back patio. To finish it off, try a Latin flan or an honest slice of key lime pie.

Thai Spice. 1514 E. Commercial Blvd. (east of I-95), Fort Lauderdale. ☎ **954/771-4535.** Main courses $9–$26. AE, DC, DISC, MC, V. Mon–Thurs and Sun 11am–3pm and 5–10pm, Fri–Sat 5–11pm. THAI.

The tacky and typical decor of Thai Spice belies the authentic and delicious food turned out here. Soft-shell crab in a light and subtle chile sauce and tender shrimp cakes are fantastic and frequent specials. Regular menu items include a slightly sweet and almost buttery pad Thai with a generous serving of shrimp, chicken chunks, and scallion. Lunch specials are obscenely cheap and include all the favorites.

Topanga! 5001 N. Federal Hwy. (at Commercial Blvd.), Ft. Lauderdale. ☎ **954/771-8555.** Reservations for five or more suggested. Main courses $9–$13, pastas $7–$10. AE, CB, DISC, MC, V. Mon–Thurs 11:30am–10pm, Fri 11:30am–11pm, Sat noon–11pm, Sun noon–10pm. CALIFORNIA-STYLE GRILL AND PIZZA BISTRO.

This bright and bustling restaurant is a perfect choice for a quick healthy lunch or dinner. Local businesspeople favor it in the afternoons since they can get in and out within 45 minutes or linger for hours in the pleasant sun-drenched eatery. There is even an outside terrace for those who don't mind the busy highway as a backdrop. With a large but not overwhelming menu featuring Italian favorites like chicken marsala, pizzas, and more than a dozen pastas, this is a place that appeals to everyone (including the kids). Salads are large (like most other entrees) and can easily be shared by three. Or, ask for a half portion, which is plenty big for one or two. My favorite is a mix of fresh baby greens with large slabs of moist and spicy dolphin (mahimahi) and chunks of feta cheese, briny Greek olives, and a slightly sweet champagne vinaigrette dressing. Pizzas, too, are fresh and filling. Try the goat cheese and basil or the unusual Acapulco chicken with tequila, lime, herbs, and a side of guacamole and salsa. The daily specials like beef and veal meat loaf, seafood quesadilla, or lemon and dill salmon are usually a good bet. An impressive selection of wines and beers plus lots of decadent desserts makes this place a super value and a great find in the middle of fast-food glutted highway.

THE HOLLYWOOD & FORT LAUDERDALE AREA AFTER DARK

The newly hip downtown area of Hollywood is centered around Harrison Street and Young Circle (east of Dixie Highway at Hollywood Boulevard). A funky menagerie of bookstores, coffee shops, galleries, and a couple of live music joints are worth exploring. One of the latest and most welcome additions is **O'Hara's Pub and Jazz Cafe** at 1905 Hollywood Blvd. (☎ **954-925-2555**). Kitty Ryan, who operates another club with the same name in Ft. Lauderdale, has duplicated her successes here with a smoking jazz club which attracts superior acts from all over.

A funkier set hangs out at **Warehaus 57** just across the street (☎ **954-926-6633**), where long-hairs converse over killer frozen coffee drinks or glasses of jug wine. This used bookstore, clothing store, and acoustic music venue is an inviting and happening little spot. During the week, come for a game of backgammon or a cup of joe. Folky local bands play on weekends to the delight of an eclectic crowd that comes at the generous invitation of owner Lauren Tellman (who also designs the racy and strappy leather clothing in the back). During the week she closes at 6pm. But Fridays and Saturdays she's there until at least midnight.

Sushi Blues was one of the first spots to offer live music in this neighborhood (see "Where to Dine," above). Live bands play jazz, blues, or world music on Friday and Saturday, and if you have dinner there you can skip the cover (usually $10).

Also in Hollywood, just west of Young Circle at Federal Highway, is **Club M** (☎ 954/925-8396), a small local blues showcase with a bit of good jazz and electric thrown in. On busy Friday and Saturday nights when live bands perform, you'll pay a small cover.

Fort Lauderdale has hundreds of bars and clubs for every taste. There are essentially four main areas that have clusters of happening scenes you can check out for yourself. To get you started, I have highlighted the best in each neighborhood. Plus, I have listed a few out-of-the-way spots for the more adventurous.

The waterfront bars and restaurants on the Intracoastal just south of Oakland Park Boulevard are especially recommendable for their outdoor patio bar scenes at all hours. Accessible by boat or car, **Bootlegger's,** at 3003 NE 32nd Ave. (☎ **954/563-4337**), features more than 70 kinds of beers, with a featured draft of the day going for only $1. Here and next door at **Shooters,** 3033 NE 32nd Ave. (☎ **954/566-2855**), you'll find nautical types, families, and young professionals mixed in with a good dose of sunburned tourists enjoying the live reggae, jazz, or Jimmy Buffett–style tunes with the gorgeous backdrop of the bay and marinas all around. If you don't have your own boat, take the water taxi to really get the feel (see box above). Both are open until 2am.

The once famous "Strip" on the waterfront just north of Las Olas was overrun with spring-breakers. Now it's been replaced with a mellower (and unfortunately more generic) scene. A newish shopping and entertainment complex called Beach Place is a sort of outdoor mega-mall modeled after Miami's hugely successful Bayside and Cocowalk. This block-long monster is the new home to a number of franchised bars and restaurants, like Sloppy Joe's (of Key West fame), Howl at the Moon, and Hooters, amid the requisite Gap and Banana Republic. The view, overlooking the ocean, makes it worth a stop for a drink.

Some of the college kids' old standbys remain in the neighborhood, including the **Elbo Room** at 241 S. Atlantic Blvd., on the corner of Las Olas Boulevard and Fla. A1A (☎ **954/463-4615**). It's maintained its rowdy and divey reputation by serving up frequent drink specials and live bands. A dedicated beer-drinking, football-watching crowd mingles with young tourists. This area is also accessible by water taxi.

An older crowd hangs out after dark on Las Olas Boulevard where there are blocks and blocks of good restaurants and music clubs. One of the most happening is **O'Hara's Pub and Jazz Cafe,** at 722 E. Las Olas Blvd. (☎ **954/524-1764**). They pack 'em in until they spill onto the sidewalk of this smoky little club. Best known for presenting original jazz performers, O'Hara's also has blues and big-band music some Sunday afternoons. Call their jazz hotline (☎ **954/524-2801**) to hear the lineup for this and the newer Hollywood Cafe.

Most of the alternative music scene is centered in the downtown area of Fort Lauderdale. One good choice is the **Chili Pepper** (☎ **954/525-0094**) at 200 W. Broward Blvd., east of I-95. With big-name concerts as well as local band showcases, this place captures the heart and soul of the young and super-charged Wednesday through Sunday.

To find the heart of Fort Lauderdale's relatively small gay scene, head to **The Copa,** at 2800 S. Federal Hwy., east on I-595, near the airport (☎ **954/463-1507**). This big '80s-style black box has been the cornerstone of Fort Lauderdale's gay scene forever. Popular and updated shows are common on the many elevated stages surrounding a large and loud dance floor.

THE PERFORMING ARTS

Pick up *City Link,* a free weekly in newsstands around the city, the *Sun-Sentinel,* or the *Miami Herald* for current offerings of music, dance, and theater staged in Fort Lauderdale's impressive **Broward Center for the Performing Arts,** 201 SW 5th Ave. (☎ **954/462-0222**). This stunning $55 million complex contains both a 2,700-seat auditorium and a smaller 590-seat theater. The center attracts top opera, symphony, dance, and Broadway productions, as well as more modest-size shows. Or, call the *Sun-Sentinel*'s **source line,** from Fort Lauderdale (☎ **954/523-5463**), from Boca/Delray (☎ **561/496-5463**), and from Boynton Beach (☎ **561/625-5463**), for a recording of the area's happenings.

2 Boca Raton & Delray Beach

26 miles S of Palm Beach, 40 miles N of Miami

With its many mansions and waterfront condominiums, it is the winter home to many of society's wealthy industrialists and retirees. Increasingly, the area is also attracting young families from other areas in the state who have tired of crime, corruption, and overcrowding. This planned city, known simply as "Boca," is a bit overmanicured and glitzy for my taste, although there are certainly some great restaurants and resorts worth exploring.

Delray, named after a suburb of Detroit, grew up completely separate from its southern neighbor. This community was founded in 1894 by a midwestern postmaster who sold off 5-acre lots through Michigan newspaper ads. Because of their close proximity, Boca and Delray can easily be explored together. Budget-conscious travelers would do well to eat and sleep in Delray and dip into Boca for sightseeing and beaching only.

ESSENTIALS

Before your trip, call or write the **Palm Beach County Convention and Visitors Bureau,** 1555 Palm Beach Lakes Blvd., Suite 204, West Palm Beach, FL 33401 (☎ **800/554-PALM** or 561/471-3995; fax 561/471-3990). On weekdays from 8:30am until at least 4pm, stop by the **Boca Raton Chamber of Commerce** at 1800 N. Dixie Hwy., 4 blocks north of Glades Road (☎ **561/395-4433;** fax 561/ 392-3780; www.bocaraton.com), Boca Raton, FL 33432, for information on attractions, accommodations, and events in the area. Also, try the **Delray Beach Chamber of Commerce** (☎ **561/278-0424;** fax 561/278-0555; e-mail: chamber@delraybeach. com), at 64 SE 5th Ave., half a block south of Atlantic Avenue on U.S. 1, Delray Beach, FL 33483.

WHERE TO PLAY, ON & OFF THE BEACH

BEACHES   Thankfully, Florida had the foresight to set aside some of its most beautiful coastal areas for the public's enjoyment. Many of the area's best beaches are located in state parks and are free to pedestrians and bikers. Most do charge for parking.

The Delray Beach Public Beach, on Ocean Boulevard at the east end of Atlantic Avenue, is one of the area's most popular hangouts. Weekends especially attract a young and good-looking crowd of active locals and tourists. Regular volleyball, Frisbee, and paddleball games make for good entertainment. For refreshments, a number of snack shops, bars, and restaurants are just across the street. Families enjoy the protection of lifeguards on the clean, wide beach. Gentle waters make it a good swimming beach, too. There's limited parking at meters along Ocean Boulevard.

Spanish River Park, on North Ocean Boulevard (Fla. A1A), 2 miles north of Palmetto Park Road in Boca Raton, is a huge oceanfront park with a large grassy area, making it one of the best choices for picnicking. Facilities include picnic tables, grills, rest rooms, and a bilevel 40-foot observation tower. You can walk through tunnels under the highway to nature trails that wind through fertile grasslands. Volleyball nets are ocean-side and always have at least one serious game going on. The park is open from 8am until 8pm. Also, read below about Red Reef Park.

GOLF   This area has plenty of good courses. Unfortunately, most of the best are private or are in the very expensive resorts. However, from May to October or November, about a dozen private courses open their greens to visitors staying in Palm Beach County hotels. This "Golf-A-Round" program is free or severely discounted (carts are additional), and reservations can be made through most major hotels. Ask at your hotel, or contact the **Palm Beach County Convention and Visitors Bureau** (☎ **561/471-3995**) for information on which clubs are available for play.

The semiprivate, 18-hole, par-61 course at the Boca Raton Executive Country Club, 7601 E. Country Club Blvd. (☎ **561/997-9410**), is usually open to the public. A driving range is also on the property as well as a pro shop and a restaurant. A PGA professional gives lessons, and rental clubs are available. From Yamato Road East, turn left onto Old Dixie Highway; after about a mile, turn left onto Hidden Valley Boulevard and continue straight to the club. Greens fees are $14 to $26.

The **Boca Raton Municipal Golf Course,** 8111 Golf Course Rd. (☎ **561/483-6100**), is located just north of Glades Road, half a mile west of the Florida Turnpike. This public 18-hole, par-72 course covers approximately 6,200 yards. There's a snack bar and a pro shop where clubs can be rented. Greens fees are $11 to $14 for 9 holes and $19 to $25 for 18 holes. Ask for special summer discount fees.

SCUBA DIVING & SNORKELING   Moray Bend, a 58-foot dive spot located about three-quarters of a mile off Boca Inlet, is the area's most popular. It's home to three moray eels that are used to being fed by scuba divers. The reef is accessible by boat from **Force E Dive Center,** 877 E. Palmetto Park Rd., Boca Raton (☎ **561/368-0555**). Phone for dive times. Dives cost $38 to $45 per person.

Red Reef Park, 1400 N. Fla. A1A (☎ **561/393-7974**), a fully developed 67-acre oceanfront park in Boca Raton, has year-round lifeguard protection. There's good snorkeling for beginners around the rocks and reefs that lie just off the beach in 2 to 6 feet of water. There's also good swimming and a small picnic area with grills, tables, and rest rooms. The park, located a half mile north of Palmetto Park Road, is open daily from 8am to 10pm. You only pay if you drive in. It's $8 per car during the week or $10 on weekends.

TENNIS   The snazzy **Delray Beach Tennis Center,** 201 W. Atlantic Ave. (☎ **561/243-7360**), has 14 lighted clay courts and 5 hard courts available by the hour. Phone for rates and reservations.

The 17 public lighted hard courts at **Patch Reef Park,** 2000 NW 51st St. (☎ **561/997-0881**), are available by reservation. The fee for nonresidents is $5.75 per person per hour. Courts are available Monday to Saturday from 7:30am to 10pm and Sunday from 7:30am to dusk; you can phone ahead to see if a court is available. To reach the park from I-95, exit at Yamato Road West and continue past Military Trail to the park.

SEEING THE SIGHTS

Boca Raton Museum of Art. 801 W. Palmetto Park Rd. (1 mile east of I-95), Boca Raton. ☎ **561/392-2500.** Admission $3 adults, $2 seniors, $1 students. Tues, Thurs, and Fri 10am–4pm, Sat–Sun noon–4pm, Wed 10am–9pm. Free admission Wed.

In addition to a relatively small but well-chosen permanent collection that's strongest in 19th-century European oils, the museum stages a wide variety of temporary exhibitions by local and international artists. Lectures and films are offered on a fairly regular basis; phone for details.

Gumbo Limbo Environmental Complex. 1801 N. Ocean Blvd. (on Fla. A1A between Spanish River Blvd. and Palmetto Park), Boca Raton. ☎ **561/338-1473.** Free admission. Mon–Sat 9am–4pm, Sun noon–4pm.

Named for an indigenous hardwood tree with continuously shedding bronze bark, the 20-acre complex protects one of the few surviving coastal hammocks, or forest islands, in South Florida. Visitors can walk through the hammock, on a one-third-of-a-mile-long elevated boardwalk that ends at a 40-foot observation tower, from which you can see the Atlantic Ocean, the Intracoastal Waterway, and much of Boca Raton. From mid-April to September, sea turtles come ashore here to lay their eggs. During this time, the center conducts turtle-watching tours and sea-turtle lectures. If you haven't seen turtles doing their thing, definitely stop in for a memorable experience.

In the museum is an impressive array of local flora and fauna, including live snakes, fish, crabs, sea turtles, and scorpions. Even city kids seem to like touching all the strange creatures here.

International Museum of Cartoon Art. 201 Plaza Real at Mizner Park, Boca Raton. ☎ **561/391-2200.** www.cartoon.org. Admission $6 adults, $5 seniors, $4 students, $3 children 6–12 years old, under 5 free as well as members.

Reborn and hugely expanded after nearly 20 years of life in New York City, this extensive collection of cartoon art spans the decades and styles in its glitzy home in Mizner Park. In a gorgeous 52,000-square-foot gallery space, cartoon fans can see prints, frames, moving pictures, and books by some of the world's greatest cartoonists, including many by the museum's founder, Mort Walker (of *Beetle Bailey* fame). A fantastic gift shop offers posters, books, and lots of memorabilia.

✪ Morikami Museum and Japanese Gardens. 16869 Jog Rd., Delray Beach. ☎ **561/495-0233.** Museum $4.25 adults, $3.75 seniors, $2 children 6–18, free for children 5 and under, free for everyone Sun 10am–noon; gardens free. Museum Tues–Sun 10am–5pm; gardens Tues–Sat 10am–5pm. Closed major holidays.

Slip off your shoes and into a serene Japanese garden community that dates from 1905, when an entrepreneurial farmer, Jo Sakai, came to Boca Raton to build a tropical agricultural community. The Yamato Colony, as it was known, was short-lived; by the 1920s only one tenacious colonist remained: George Sukeji Morikami. But Morikami was quite successful, eventually holding one of the largest pineapple plantations in the area. The 200-acre Morikami Museum and Japanese Gardens, which opened to the public in 1977, was Morikami's gift to Palm Beach County and the State of Florida. The park section, dedicated to the preservation of Japanese culture, is constructed to appeal to all the senses. An artificial waterfall that cascades into a koi-and carp-filled moat, a small rock garden for meditation, and a large bonsai collection that includes miniature maple, buttonwood, juniper, and Australian pine trees are all worth contemplation—and it's free. There is also a great Asian restaurant on the premises worth checking out for lunch.

SHOPPING & BROWSING

Famous in New York City for its upscale antiques and gorgeous rugs, **ABC Carpet & Home** also has an outlet store in Delray Beach just off I-95 at 777 S. Congress (between Linton and Atlantic). Look for deep discounts (usually at least 30%) on very high-priced furnishings and flooring.

Mizner Park, on Federal Highway (between Palmetto Park and Glades roads) in Boca Raton (☎ 561/362-0606), is the town square of this tiny enclave, complete with clothing shops, shoe stores, restaurants, live performances, and lots of beautiful landscaping. It's really an outdoor mall, with 45 specialty shops, seven good restaurants, and a multiscreen movie house. Each shop front faces a grassy island with blue and green gazebos, potted plants, and garden benches. It's extremely popular with folks who come here just to stroll, often until late in the evening.

Town Center Mall of Boca Raton has six huge department stores including Bloomingdale's, Burdines, Lord & Taylor, and Saks Fifth Avenue. Add to that hundreds of specialty shops, an extensive food court, and a range of other restaurants, and you have got the area's most comprehensive and beautiful shopping opportunity. The mall is located on the south side of Glades Road just west of I-95.

Another great area for a stroll is in the more artsy community of **Delray Beach,** known by many as Pineapple Grove. Here, along Atlantic Avenue, especially east of Swinton Avenue, you'll find a fantastic array of antique shops, clothing stores, and art galleries shaded by palm trees and colorful awnings. A lively cafe culture and many celebrations take place on this quaint old-style main street. Pick up the "Downtown Delray Beach" map and guide at almost any of the stores on this strip, or call ☎ **561/278-0424** for more information.

WHERE TO STAY

If you choose to stay in Boca or the surrounding areas, you will find some very luxurious lodgings, epitomized by the famous and often photographed pink Boca Raton Hotel and Country Club, where deluxe suites have gone for up to $6,000 per night. But don't worry: There are plenty of other choices on and near the beach.

A number of national chain hotels worth considering include a moderately priced **Holiday Inn Highland Beach Oceanside** at 2809 S. Ocean Blvd., on Fla. A1A southeast of Linton Boulevard (☎ **800/234-6835** or 561/278-6241). The **Radisson Bridge Resort** at 999 E. Camino Real (☎ **800/333-3333** or 561/368-9500), operates a particularly popular and affordable resort on the Intracoastal Waterway just a few blocks from the Boca Raton Resort. It books up well in advance.

Although you won't find the rows and rows of cheap hotels as in Fort Lauderdale and Hollywood, a handful of mom-and-pop motels have survived along Fla. A1A in between the towering condos of Delray Beach. Look along the beach just south of Atlantic Boulevard. Especially noteworthy is a pleasant little two-story, shingle-roofed **Bermuda Inn** at 64 S. Ocean Blvd. (☎ **561/276-5288**).

Even more economical options can be found in Deerfield Beach, Boca's neighbor, south of the county line. A number of beachfront efficiencies offer great deals, even in the winter months. Try the **Panther Motel and Apartments,** at 715 S. Fla. A1A (☎ **954/427-0700**). This clean and convenient motel has rates starting as low as $40. Al-though in season, you may find you have to book for a week at a time. Weekly rates in season start at $445.

If you are looking for something more private or for longer than just a few days, you may want to call a reservations service for help. Especially for rentals for a few weeks or months, call **Palm Beach Accommodations** (☎ 800/543-SWIM).

VERY EXPENSIVE

✪ **Boca Raton Resort and Club.** 501 E. Camino Real Dr. (P.O. Box 5025), Boca Raton, FL 33431. ☎ **800/327-0101** or 561/395-3000. Fax 561/447-3183. 1,000 units, 70 golf villa apts. A/C MINIBAR TV TEL. Winter $200–$450 double; $450 golf villa apt; $420–$6,000 suite. Off-season $95–$250 double; $210 golf villa apt; $195–$450 suite. Very reasonable seasonal packages available. AE, DC, DISC, MC, V. From I-95 N., exit onto Palmetto Park Rd. E.; turn right onto Federal Hwy. (U.S. 1), and then left onto Camino Real to the resort.

Boca's most historical and romantic resort straddles both sides of the Intracoastal Waterway and encompasses more than 350 acres of land, with extensive and outstanding facilities for tennis, golf, and anything else an active family or individual could want, including three fitness centers with brand-new equipment, more than 30 tennis courts, and two respected 18-hole golf courses. Since 1926, this palatial hotel has been hosting the most discriminating international guests. Now with a sizable population of local sports enthusiasts who have joined the country club, and lots of conferences going on, the place is still pleasing demanding visitors. Don't worry: The huge proportions of the Spanish-Moorish architecture and the sprawling grounds will ensure that you will never feel crowded or processed. And yearly renovations guarantee that you won't feel as if you are staying in a musty museum.

Compared to other destination resorts on Florida's east coast, this superior facility is a great value with all the amenities and elegance but none of the stuffiness. Everything is easy once you have decided which type of room you'll stay in. There are several options. Those in the original Cloisters building have exquisite architectural details, like arched doorways, high-beamed ceilings, a mix of reproduction antiques, and the most charm. The best part is that, although they are more modest in size than newer rooms, they are also the least expensive. The Boca Beach Club building, just a 5-minute drive and accessible by free shuttle or your own car, offers spacious cabana-style rooms on the ocean with sliding glass doors that open to beach breezes. Dressed with dark woods and rich colors, the rooms in the modern 27-story tower adjacent to the Cloisters are the most formal and enjoy sweeping views of this idyllic coast. Golf villas overlook the perfectly manicured greens. All are outfitted with two phones, large bathrooms, fluffy robes, and first-class furnishings.

Dining/Diversions: There are nine restaurants and three lounges to satisfy all tastes and budget. A formal Italian restaurant on the top floor of the main building offers extraordinary views over Boca Raton. A seafood restaurant at the Boca Beach Club is known for its excellent and diverse menu. A coffee bar in the Cloister building is particularly popular in mornings and afternoons.

Amenities: Concierge, room service (24 hours), fitness classes, evening turndown, laundry, overnight shoe shine. An impressive array of children's programs. Three fitness centers, 5 swimming pools, 2 golf courses, 34 tennis courts (9 lighted), watersports and bicycle rentals, snorkeling and scuba instruction, croquet, volleyball, basketball court, 2-mile jogging course, business center, well-priced boutiques and gift shops, racquetball.

MODERATE

Colony Hotel & Cabana Club. 525 E. Atlantic Ave. (P.O. Box 970), Delray Beach, FL 33483. ☎ **800/552-2363** or 561/276-4123. Fax 561/276-0123. www.thecolonyhotel.com/florida/. E-mail: info-fla@thecolonyhotel.com. 66 units. A/C TV TEL. Winter $145–$165 double. Off-season $90–$110 double. AE, MC, V.

This lovely three-story hotel is located right on Delray's main commercial thoroughfare about a mile from the hotel's private beach and club. The Colony benefited from a 1996 refurbishment that brought back some of its original 1926 details, including hardwood floors and authentic furnishings. Still, the rooms are modest in size and style but comfortable and clean. The hotel is popular with families who appreciate the many planned activities at the hotel's beachfront club 1 mile away, which offers a heated saltwater swimming pool, a private beach, as well as putting and shuffleboard tournaments. All facilities are free for guests.

Seagate Hotel & Beach Club. 400 S. Ocean Blvd., Delray Beach, FL 33483. ☎ **800/233-3581** or 561/276-2421. Fax 561/243-4714. 77units. A/C TV TEL. Winter $160–$290 suite; $335–$370 two-bedroom suite. Off-season $74–$105 suite; $136–$152 two-bedroom suite. AE, CB, DC, DISC, MC, V. From I-95, exit onto Atlantic Ave. E., turn right onto Ocean Blvd. (Fla. A1A), and continue ¹/₂ mile to the hotel.

This modest well-located hotel features generously sized rooms located in two buildings directly across the street from the beach. To make your stay more affordable and convenient, the hotel furnishes coffeemakers, fully stocked kitchens or kitchenettes, irons, large closets, and safes in each room. A recent redecorating replaced the quaint Old Florida furnishings with industrial Formica, plain blond wood, and commercial-grade carpeting. Also regretful are the tiny bathrooms with little to no counter space.

The Beach Club is located across the street, directly on the sand, where you can relax on a chaise longue or dip into one of the heated pools. A moderately priced restaurant and bar will deliver snacks and cocktails to the beach. There's 400 feet of private beach, and special children's programs are offered during the high season. Overall, the resort is pleasant and extremely practical, especially for families. Little extras like newspapers and refreshments in the lobby make this an especially appealing option.

Spanish River Resort. 111 E. Atlantic Ave., Delray Beach, Fl 33483. ☎ **800/543-SWIM** or 561-243-7946. Fax 561/276-9634. 75 units. A/C TV TEL. Winter $150–$250 studio or 1-bedroom; $315–$350 2-bedroom. Off-season from $85 studio or 1-bedroom; from $250 2-bedroom. AE, DISC, MC, V. Free 6th and 7th night with weekly booking.

An especially good value for those staying for longer than a few days, this pleasant family oriented property offers fully furnished condominiums half a block from a popular beach and walking distance to Delray's best shops, restaurants, and galleries. The 11-story Mediterranean-style building has free lighted tennis courts, a large outdoor pool, and lovely ocean-view balconies. Apartments are spacious and outfitted with fully equipped kitchens. All units also have pullout queen-size sofa beds. The best part is there is no additional charge for extra guests. A one-bedroom unit can comfortably fit four or five people; a two-bedroom unit can easily accommodate six. Cots and roll-away beds are available at a minimum charge. Compared with many of the run-down 1950s motels in the area, this moderately priced, well-maintained tower is a real find.

INEXPENSIVE

Ocean Lodge. 531 N. Ocean Blvd. (just north of Palmetto Park Rd. on Fla. A1A), Boca Raton, FL 33432. ☎ **800/STAY-BOCA** or 561/395-7772. Fax 561/395-0554. 18 units. A/C TV TEL. Winter $65–$80 double; $75–$95 efficiency. Off-season $45–$80 double; $55–$95 efficiency. AE, MC, V.

Situated around a small heated pool and sundeck, this two-story little motel is a particularly well-kept accommodation in an area of run-down or overpriced options. The large rooms offer furnishings and decor that are clean but a bit impersonal. A recent do-over that added modern Formica and floral wallpaper makes this a notch above a

Palm Beach & Boca Raton

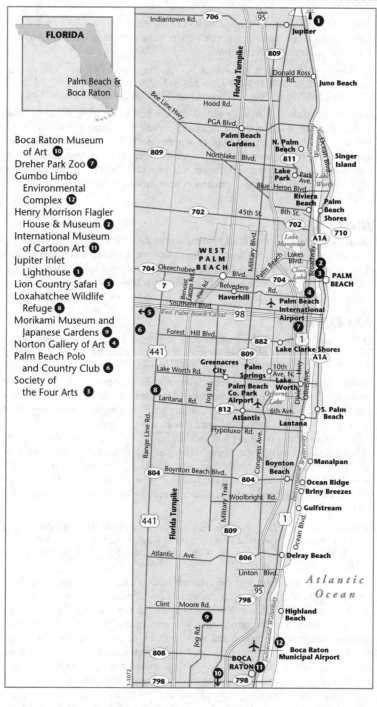

FLORIDA

Palm Beach &
Boca Raton

Boca Raton Museum
of Art **10**
Dreher Park Zoo **7**
Gumbo Limbo
Environmental
Complex **12**
Henry Morrison Flagler
House & Museum **2**
International Museum
of Cartoon Art **11**
Jupiter Inlet
Lighthouse **1**
Lion Country Safari **5**
Loxahatchee Wildlife
Refuge **8**
Morikami Museum and
Japanese Gardens **9**
Norton Gallery of Art **4**
Palm Beach Polo
and Country Club **6**
Society of
the Four Arts **3**

Indiantown Rd. **706**
Jupiter
95
809
Donald Ross
Rd.
Juno Beach
Florida Turnpike
Bee Line Hwy
Hood Rd.
PGA Blvd.
Palm Beach
Gardens
N. Palm
Beach
811
Singer
Island
809
Northlake Blvd.
Lake
Park
Park
Ave.
Blue Heron Blvd.
Riviera
Beach
Palm
Beach
Shores
702
45th St.
8th St.
702
710
A1A
WEST
PALM
BEACH
Military Blvd.
Lake
Mangonia
Broadway
Lakes Blvd.
2
Clear
Lake
3 PALM
BEACH
704 Okeechobee
Blvd.
Palm Beach Blvd.
7
Benoist Farms Rd.
Pike Rd.
Belvedere
Rd.
704
4
Haverhill
Palm Beach
International
Airport
Southern Blvd.
98
5
West Palm Beach Canal
7
6
Forest Hill Blvd.
882
Lake Clarke Shores
1
441
809
A1A
Greenacres
City
Palm
Springs
10th
Ave. N.
Lake
Worth
Lake Worth Rd.
Lake
Worth
Dixie Hwy
Olive Ave.
8
Jog Rd.
Palm Beach
Co. Park
Airport
Osborne
Lake
Lantana Rd.
6th Ave.
S. Palm
Beach
812
Atlantis
Lantana
Range Line Rd.
Hypoluxo Rd.
Congress Ave.
Boynton
Beach
Manalpan
804 Boynton Beach Blvd.
804
Ocean Ridge
Briny Breezes
Military Trail
Woolbright Rd.
1
Gulfstream
441
Florida Turnpike
809
Ocean Blvd.
Atlantic Ave.
806
Delray Beach
Linton Blvd.
*Atlantic
Ocean*
95
Clint Moore Rd.
798
Intracoastal Waterway
9
Highland
Beach
Jog Rd.
808
12 Boca Raton
Municipal Airport
10
BOCA
RATON **11**
798
798

1-1072

243

basic motel. Ask for a room in the back since the street noise can be a bit loud especially in season. The bonus is that you are across the street from the ocean and in one of Florida's most upscale resort towns.

Shore Edge Motel. 425 N. Ocean Blvd. (on Fla. A1A, north of Palmetto Park Rd.), Boca Raton, FL 33432. ☎ **561/395-4491.** Fax 561/347-8759. 16 units. A/C TV TEL. Winter $60–$75 double; $80–$95 efficiency. Off-season from $45 double; from $55 efficiency. MC, V.

Another relic of the '50s recently spiffed up with new landscaping and some redecorating, this motel is a good choice, especially because of its location—across the street from a public beach, just north of downtown Boca Raton. It's the quintessential South Florida motel: a small, pink, single-story structure surrounding a modest swimming pool and courtyard. Although the rooms are a bit on the small side, they're very neat and clean. The higher-priced accommodations are larger and come with full kitchens.

WHERE TO DINE

The Boca Raton and Delray areas have more than their fair share of expensive fish and steak houses. Thankfully, too, there are more and more innovative and health-conscious places moving in. Mizner Park has nearly a dozen eateries including a fantastic oyster bar, serving microbrew beers, called **Gigi's** (☎ **561/368-4488**). The area's other great options are highlighted below.

VERY EXPENSIVE

✪ **Damiano's at the Tarrimore House.** 52 N. Swinton Ave. (just north of Atlantic Ave.), Delray Beach. ☎ **561/272-4706.** Reservations suggested. Main courses $19–$28. AE, MC, V. Wed–Sun, seatings between 6 and 9pm. TRANSCONTINENTAL/FLORASIAN.

Anthony and Lisa Damiano are the quintessential hosts. Refugees from the New York restaurant scene, where their careers included long stints at the Russian Tea Room, the pair have retained some of their Eastern European training while venturing off into many other wonderful regions. In their charming little restaurant, a former home to Delray's mayor and a one-time bed-and-breakfast, they have created the ultimate in intimate dining. Gracious but young waiters are happy to explain the varied menu, which spans the continents. To start, you should try the ostrich carpaccio if it's offered—it's so rich and flavorful you'll wish it were a main course. The pan-seared yellowtail with ginger and scallions is addictive, as are the delicious Italian pastas and risottos.

La Vieille Maison. 770 E. Palmetto Park Rd., Boca Raton. ☎ **561/391-6701** or 561/737-5677. Reservations required. Main courses $17–$40; fixed-price dinners $40 and $59. AE, CB, DC, DISC, MC, V. Daily 11:30am–2pm and 6–9:30pm (call for seating times). FRENCH.

Find an excuse to celebrate and treat yourself to this elegant dining experience that has won the loyalty of critics from far and wide. The luxurious setting, a Mediterranean-inspired home filled with a variety of antique French furnishings and paintings, gives you the feeling of walking into a friend's country manor. Begin with lobster bisque, gratin of escargots with fennel and pistachio nuts, or pan-seared foie gras—each is equally delectable. It's difficult to choose from the many enticing entrees, which range from red snapper in black- and green-olive potato crust to medallions of beef, lamb, and venison over three sauces. You'll surely have to try at least a few of the gorgeous cheeses the server offers after your main course—the most extensive selection I've ever seen in this country. The lemon crepe soufflé with raspberry sauce is the dessert of choice—remember to order it early.

New York Prime. 2350 Executive Center Dr. (west of I-95, exit Glades Rd.), Boca Raton. ☎ **561/998-3881.** Reservations suggested. Main courses $20–$60. AE, CB, DC, DISC, MC, V. Daily 5–11pm. STEAK HOUSE.

This ultra-formal steak house is rivaled only by New York's famous few for its excellent meat, fish, and lobster dinners—and for the price. A professional staff of uniformed waiters knows the small but selective menu intimately and can recommend the appropriate cut of steak, the restaurant's signature dish. The sparkling atmosphere of the dining room allows for great people-watching and quiet conversation. If anything, they may want to turn the lights a bit lower to make this very expensive dining experience a bit more romantic. Ask for a seat in the cozy booths. Unless you are a smoker, avoid the bar area. Cigar and cigarette smoking are encouraged in this den of excess. The expensive filtering system does a decent job of clearing stale smoke, but the aroma of freshly lighted cigars does waft far.

EXPENSIVE

Fifth Avenue Grill. 821 S. Federal Hwy., Delray Beach. ☎ **561/265-0122.** Additional location 4650 N. Federal Hwy., Lighthouse Point. ☎ 954/782-4433. Reservations accepted only for large parties. Main courses $16–$26. AE, DC, MC, V. Sun–Mon 11:30am–4pm and 5–11pm. STEAK HOUSE.

The old-world Fifth Avenue Grill is very popular with well-dressed seniors who come for the superb steaks, reliable service, and classic selections—onion soup, shrimp scampi, London broil, Caesar salad, and broiled local fish. This is the kind of place where they still remember to offer a touch of sherry for your conch chowder. Every main course includes unlimited house salad and is accompanied by a cheese-stuffed baked potato, fried shoestrings, or brown rice. Add to that a huge and varied wine list, and you've got a perfect night out in Delray. Everything on the predictable menu is well prepared and presented by professional servers in a dark and woodsy dining room.

Max's Grille. 404 Plaza Real, in Mizner Park, Boca Raton. ☎ **561/368-0080.** Reservations accepted only for six or more. Main courses $14–$26; pastas $10.95–$16.95. AE, CB, DC, MC, V. Daily 11:30am–3pm, Mon–Thurs 5–10:30pm, Fri–Sat 5–11pm, Sun 5–10pm. AMERICAN.

One of the most popular choices in restaurant-crowded Mizner Park, Max's Grille is part of the growing chain of Unique Restaurants that have been wowing critics and diners for years. With a large exhibition kitchen that occupies the entire back wall of the restaurant, patrons can watch as their yellowfin tuna steak or filet mignon is seared on a flaming oak grill. A large selection of chicken, meat loaf, pastas, and main-course salads provide healthful and delicious choices for sophisticated palates. A stunning bar serves trendy martinis in more than 15 varieties. For a more economical option, try Max's coffee shop next door at 402 Plaza Real for good old-fashioned comfort food in a real diner atmosphere.

MODERATE

Splendid Blendeds. 432 E. Atlantic Ave., Delray. ☎ **561/265-1035.** Reservations recommended. Main courses $10–$17; sandwiches and salads $3–$8. AE, MC, V. Dinner Mon–Sat 5:30–10pm; lunch Mon–Fri 11:30am–2:30pm. Closed Sun. ECLECTIC.

Loyal regulars would like to keep this storefront bistro a secret so that the lines won't get even longer on weekends. The draw here is fresh, uncomplicated seafood and pastas that are interesting without being overly ambitious. The Southwestern-inspired chicken Santa Cruz is tender and juicy, served with a black-bean sauce and tangy pico de gallo. Many seafood specialties, like tuna, snapper, and shrimp dishes, are slight departures from classic recipes and seem to work most of the time. The drawback of this otherwise superb spot is the staff; they're well-meaning but easily flustered.

INEXPENSIVE

The Tin Muffin Café. 364 E. Palmetto Park Rd. (between Federal Hwy. and the Intercoastal Bridge). ☎ 561/392-9446. Sandwiches and salads $5.50–$7.50. No credit cards. Mon–Fri 11am–5pm, Sat 11am–4pm. BAKERY/SANDWICH SHOP.

Popular with the downtown lunch crowd, this excellent storefront bakery keeps them lining up for big fresh sandwiches on fresh bread, muffins, quiches, and good home-made soups like split pea or lentil. The curried chicken sandwich is stuffed with over-sized chunks of only white meat doused in a creamy curry dressing and fruit. There are a few cafe tables inside and even one outside on a tiny patio. Be warned, however, that service is forgivably slow and parking is a nightmare. Try parking a few blocks away at a meter on the street.

Tom's Place. 7251 N. Federal Hwy., Boca Raton. ☎ **561/997-0920.** Reservations not accepted. Main courses $8–$15; sandwiches $5–$6; early bird special $6.95. MC, V. Tues–Fri 11:30am–10pm, Sat noon–10pm. Closed Mon. BARBECUE.

There are two important factors in a successful barbecue: the cooking and the sauce. Tom and Helen Wright's no-nonsense cook shack wins on both counts, offering flaw-lessly grilled meats paired with well-spiced sauces. Beef, chicken, pork, and fish are served soul-food style, with your choice of two sides like rice with gravy, collard greens, black-eyed peas, coleslaw, or mashed potatoes. Decoration is limited to signed celebrity photographs and plastic tablecloths.

BOCA RATON & DELRAY AFTER DARK
THE BAR, CLUB & MUSIC SCENE

The best variety of entertainment is offered in Delray Beach where a younger and funkier set makes its home. Atlantic Avenue now boasts several venues for live music, including **The Back Room,** 16 E. Atlantic Ave. near the corner of Swinton Avenue (☎ 561/243-9110). A reasonable cover, usually between $2 and $6, depends on who is playing. A funky decor, eclectic crowd, and excellent music almost every night make this old standby another good option for live music from jazz to big band to classic rock. Only beer and wine are served (in plastic glasses). It's open Tuesday to Saturday until 3am.

    Boston's on the Beach, at 40 S. Ocean Blvd. (☎ 561/278-3364), is always a good choice for happy hour, Monday to Friday from 4 to 8pm, or for live reggae on Monday. A lively bar scene and good seafood on a deck overlooking the beach keep this place packed almost every night.

    Plenty of locals and visitors make a night of strolling the luxurious grounds of Mizner Park (see "Shopping & Browsing," above). After a meal, diners can shop or listen to musicians or watch performers who often are scheduled to entertain the public.

    Boca Raton's most famous dance spot, **Club Boca** at 7000 W. Palmetto Park Rd. (☎ 561/368-3333), which you'll hear advertised on obnoxious radio commercials, is a big, noisy warehouse out west of the highway that attracts a range of big-haired girls and macho guys. It's a fun diversion in otherwise sterile Boca and is open Thursday to Sunday until 5am.

    True to her word, Gloria Gaynor has survived, and she is in Boca at **Polly Esther's,** 99 SE 1st Ave. (☎ 561/447-8955). She and other disco divas can be heard blasting from the enormous sound system as the mixed young and 30-something set dances like it's Saturday night and they have the fever. Open Wednesday to Saturday. Take Palmetto Park Road East to Federal Highway; turn left onto SE 1st Avenue, where you'll see the club on the left.

THE PERFORMING ARTS

For details on upcoming events, check the *Boca News, Sun-Sentinel,* or call the **Palm Beach County Cultural Council information line** at ☎ **800/882-ARTS.** During business hours, a staffer can give details on current performances. After hours, a recorded message describes the week's events. The *Sun-Sentinel* also hosts a comprehensive "Source Line" for information on everything from weather to garage sales. Detailed arts information is included.

Although the larger and more renowned venues are farther north in Palm Beach and West Palm Beach, the southern part of Palm Beach County has its fair share of performing arts. The **Florida Symphonic Pops,** a 70-piece professional orchestra, performs jazz, swing, rock, big band, and classical music throughout Boca Raton. For nearly 50 years this ever-growing musical force has entertained audiences of every age. Call ☎ **561/393-7677** for a schedule of concerts.

Boca's best theater company is the **Caldwell Theatre,** and it's worth checking out. Located in a strip shopping center at 7873 N. Federal Hwy., this equity showcase does well-known dramas, comedies, classics, off-Broadway hits, and new works throughout the year. Prices are reasonable (usually between $29 and $38). Full-time students will be especially interested in the little-advertised "Student Rush." Bring a valid ID and arrive at least an hour before show time to get in line. If available, tickets are sold for $5 to those who arrived earliest. Call the box office (☎ **561/241-7432**) for details.

3 Palm Beach & West Palm Beach

65 miles N of Miami, 193 miles E of Tampa

Palm Beach County encompasses cities including Boca Raton in the south to Jupiter and Tequesta in the north. But it is Palm Beach, the small island town across the Intracoastal Waterway, that has been the traditional winter home of America's superrich— the Kennedys, the Rockefellers, the Pulitzers, the Trumps (more recently), and plenty of CEOs. Gawking at their palatial homes is the number one tourist activity, and a stroll along Palm Beach's tony Worth Avenue is a must even for nonshoppers.

The island holds the distinction of being the only continental destination with three resorts that have earned the prestigious AAA Five-Diamonds rating.

And beyond the upscale resorts and chic boutiques, it holds some surprises too, from a world-class art museum to one of the top bird-watching areas in the state.

By contrast, West Palm Beach is a grittier workaday city. Recent renovations have made the metropolitan area a lively and affordable place to dine, shop, and hang out.

In addition to good beaching, boating, and diving, you'll find great golf and tennis throughout the county.

ESSENTIALS

GETTING THERE   If you're driving up or down the Florida coast, you'll probably reach the Palm Beach area by I-95. Exit at Belvedere Road or Okeechobee Boulevard and head east to reach the most central part of Palm Beach.

Visitors on their way to or from Orlando or Miami should take the Florida Turnpike, a toll road with a speed limit of 65 m.p.h. If you are watching your budget, avoid the Turnpike—tolls are high. You may pay upward of $9 from Orlando and $4 from Miami. Finally, if you're coming from Florida's west coast, you can take either S.R. 70, which runs north of Lake Okeechobee to Fort Pierce, or S.R. 80, which runs south of the lake to Palm Beach.

GETTING AROUND Although a car is almost a necessity in this area, a recently revamped public transportation system is extremely convenient for getting to some attractions. Palm Tran underwent a major expansion in late 1996, increasing service to 32 routes and more than 140 buses. The fare is $1 for adults, 50¢ for children ages 3 to 18, as well as for the elderly and disabled. Free route maps are available by calling ☎ **561/ 233-4BUS**. Information operators are available from 6am to 7pm, except Sunday.

In downtown West Palm free shuttles operates Monday through Friday from 9am until 4pm with plans to expand operations to evenings and weekends too. Look for the bubble-gum-pink minibuses throughout downtown. Call ☎ 561-833-8873 for more details.

For a more nostalgic route, consider the stately wicker chariots that run in the downtown area especially on weekends and during special events. Rates vary according to the time of day but average $1 to $2 per block, plus a per person charge of $1. Call ☎ **561/835-8922** for pickup or information.

Among the airlines serving **Palm Beach International Airport,** at Congress Avenue and Belvedere Road (☎ **561/471-7400**), are **American** (☎ **800/433-7300**), **Continental** (☎ **800/525-0280**), **Delta** (☎ **800/221-1212**), **Kiwi** (☎ **800/ 538-5494**), **Northwest** (☎ **800/225-2525**), **TWA** (☎ **800/221-2000**), **United** (☎ **800/241-6522**), and **US Airways** (☎ **800/428-4322**).

Amtrak (☎ **800/USA-RAIL**) has a terminal in West Palm Beach, at 201 S. Tamarind Ave. (☎ **561/832-6169**).

VISITOR INFORMATION The **Palm Beach County Convention and Visitors Bureau,** 1555 Palm Beach Lakes Blvd., Suite 204, West Palm Beach, FL 33401 (☎ **800/554-PALM** or 561/471-3995), distributes an informative brochure and will answer questions about visiting the Palm Beaches. Ask for a map as well as a copy of its *Arts and Attractions Calendar,* a day-to-day guide to art, music, stage, and other events in the county.

SPORTS & OUTDOOR ACTIVITIES

In West Palm Beach, stop by the **Seaside Activities Station** at 400A Flagler Dr. (on the waterfront at the corner of Banyan St.) or call **561/659-4005** to arrange historic tours and sailboat, jet-ski, bicycle, kayak, water ski, and parasail rentals.

BEACHES Public beaches are a rare commodity here in Palm Beach. Most of the island's best beaches are fronted by private estates and inaccessible to the general public. However, there are a few notable exceptions, including the newly renourished Midtown Beach on Ocean Boulevard, between Royal Palm Way and Gulfstream Road, which boasts more than 100 feet of beach that is still undeveloped and uncrowded. There are no rest rooms or concessions here, although a lifeguard is on duty until sundown. This newly widened sandy coast is now a centerpiece and a natural oasis in a town dominated by commercial glitz. Also, about 1½ miles north near Dunbar Street is a popular hangout for locals who enjoy the relaxed atmosphere. Parking is available at meters along Fla. A1A. To the south is a less popular but better equipped beach at Phipps Ocean Park. On Ocean Boulevard, between the Southern Boulevard and Lake Avenue causeways, is a large and lively public beach encompassing over 1,300 feet of groomed and guarded oceanfront. With picnic and recreation areas as well as plenty of parking, the area is especially good for families.

BICYCLING Rent anything from an English single-speed to a full-tilt mountain bike at the **Palm Beach Bicycle Trail Shop,** 223 Sunrise Ave. (☎ **561/659-4583**).

The Sport of Kings

The annual ritual of "the ponies" is played out each season at the posh Palm Beach Polo and Country Club. It is one of the world's premier polo grounds and hosts some of the sport's top-rated players.

Even if you're not a sports fan, you absolutely must attend a match. Although the field is actually on the mainland in an area called Wellington, rest assured, the spectators, and many of the players, are pure Palm Beach. After all, a day at the pony grounds is one of the only good reasons to leave Palm Beach proper.

Don't worry, though—you need not be a Vanderbilt or a Kennedy to attend. Matches are open to the public and are surprisingly affordable.

Even if you haven't a clue how the game is played, you can spend your time people-watching. Star-gazers have spotted Prince Charles, the duchess of York, Sylvester Stallone, and Ivana Trump in recent years, among others. Dozens of lesser-known royalty, and just plain old characters, keep box seats or chalets right on the grounds.

The general admission seats will land you a spot on metal bleachers across the field from the boxes, where celebrity spotting during a match is a bit difficult. If you want to mingle with the elite, splurge on the more expensive boxes for a chance to overhear great tidbits, like the one I caught recently—"Oh, I know I should be rooting for the Coca-Cola team. That's how I made all my money," whined one flamboyant heiress dressed all in gold as she cheered for the opposing team. "Still, I just can't help cheering for my friends."

Good eavesdropping is possible even with a ticket from the bleachers, since you can wander the grounds and see the whole show. Between chukkers, head to the Polo Club, a covered tent where you can enjoy snacks like popcorn, hot dogs, ice cream, pretzels, and a cocktail from the full bar while listening to live music. Or on a Sunday afternoon, enjoy brunch in the Polo House or Players Club restaurant on the north end of field no. 1.

Incidentally, the point of polo is to keep the other team from getting the ball through your goal. The fast-paced game is divided into six chukkers—like an inning in baseball—each 7 minutes long. There are 3-minute breaks between chukkers except at half-time, which lasts 10 minutes. The whole thing is narrated by a British chap who sounds as though he has walked off a Monty Python set.

Oh dear, whatever will you wear? Unless, it is an opening game or some other special event, dress is casual. A navy or tweed blazer over jeans or khakis is a standard for men, while neat-looking jeans or a pantsuit is the norm for ladies. On warmer days, shorts and, of course, a polo shirt are fine, too.

General admission is $6 to $10; box seats cost $18 to $26. Matches are held throughout the week. Schedules vary, but the big names usually compete on Sunday at 3:30pm from January to April.

The fields are located at 11809 Polo Club Rd., Wellington, 10 miles west of the Forest Hill Boulevard exit of I-95. Call ☎ **561/798-7000** for a detailed schedule of events.

The rates—$7 an hour, $18 a half day (9am to 5pm), or $24 for 24 hours—include a basket and lock (not that it's necessary in this fortress of a town). The most scenic route is called the Lake Trail, running the length of the island along the Intracoastal Waterway. On it you'll see some of the most magnificent mansions and grounds. Enjoy the views of downtown West Palm Beach and some great wildlife.

CRUISES   The *Star of Palm Beach,* 900 E. Blue Heron Blvd., Singer Island (☎ 561/848-7827), runs regularly scheduled tours along the Intracoastal Waterway, offering visitors unobstructed views of the area's grand mansions. Daily sightseeing as well as lunch, dinner, and theme cruises are offered, some with live entertainment. They cost $10 to $30. Phone for more information and reservations.

The *Palm Beach Princess* (☎ **800/841-7447** or 561/845-7447), a small cruise ship (421 feet), offers reasonably priced casino gambling cruises out of the Port of Palm Beach (U.S. 1 between 45th Street and Blue Heron Boulevard) every day and evening. Evening cruises usually leave at 7pm and cost $20 to $25; they include a large buffet with average food like spaghetti and meatballs, chicken, shrimp, Greek salad, and vegetables. Best is the prime rib at the carving board. Day trips cost the same and offer slightly less food. Sunday brunch trips cost $25. A popular monthly Bahamas voyage costs $95. Call during business hours for details. Choose from craps, roulette, poker, blackjack, and slots.

GOLF   There's good golfing here, but many of the private club courses are maintained exclusively for the use of their members. Ask at your hotel, or contact the **Palm Beach County Convention and Visitors Bureau** (☎ 561/471-3995) for information on which clubs are currently available for play. In the off-season, some private courses open their greens to visitors staying in a Palm Beach County hotel. This "Golf-A-Round" program offers free greens fees (carts are additional); reservations can be made through most major hotels.

One of the state's best courses that is open to the public is ✪ **Emerald Dunes Golf Course,** 2100 Emerald Dunes Dr. in West Palm Beach (☎ **561/687-1700**). Designed by Tom Fazio, this dramatic 7,006-yard, par-72 course was voted "One of the Best 10 You Can Play" by *Golf* magazine. It is located just off the Florida Turnpike at Okeechobee Boulevard. Bookings are taken up to 30 days ahead. Fees start at $125.

The Palm Beach Public Golf Course, 2345 S. Ocean Blvd. (☎ **561/547-0598**), a popular public 18-hole course, is a par-54 and is open at 8am; the course is run on a first-come, first-served basis. Club rentals are available. Greens fees start at $18 per person.

POLO   What's Palm Beach without polo? See box above for details.

SCUBA DIVING   Year-round warm waters, barrier reefs, and plenty of wrecks make South Florida one of the world's most popular places for diving. One of the best-known artificial reefs in this area is a vintage Rolls-Royce Silver Shadow, which was sunk offshore in 1985. Mother Nature has taken her toll, however, and divers can no longer sit in the car ravaged by time and salt water. The offshore reef is located three-quarters of a mile east of the Florida Power and Light smokestacks, just south of the Palm Beach Inlet.

Call any of the following outfitters for gear and excursions: **The Aqua Shop,** 505 Northlake Blvd., North Palm Beach (☎ **561/848-9042**); **Dixie Divers,** 1401 S. Military Trail, West Palm Beach (☎ **561/969-6688**); and **Ocean Sports Scuba Center,** 1736 S. Congress Ave., West Palm Beach (☎ **561/641-1144**).

TENNIS   There are literally hundreds of tennis courts in Palm Beach County. Wherever you are staying, you are bound to be within walking distance of one. In addition to the many hotel tennis courts (see "Where to Stay," below), you can play at **Currie Park,** 2400 N. Flagler Dr., West Palm Beach (☎ **561/835-7025**), a public park with three lighted hard courts. They are free and available on a first-come, first-served basis.

A WATER PLAYGROUND   On a sunny day don't miss a chance to play with the locals at the Centennial Fountain on the eastern end of Clematis Street, near

Narcissus, where dozens of little kids (and a few full-grown ones) jump and play in the vertical streams of water that shoot from the ground. A computer guarantees that the jets will spout unpredictably, and a fountain guard on busy weekends assures kids are well looked after. The fountain, built to commemorate Palm Beach's hundred-year anniversary in 1994, is free and operates around the clock. It's especially fun on hot summer nights when the dramatic lights make the shiny wet playground one of the best attractions in town.

SEEING THE SIGHTS

Henry Morrison Flagler Museum. 1 Whitehall Way (at Cocoanut Row), Palm Beach. ☎ 561/655-2833. www.flagler.org. Admission $7 adults, $3 children. Tues–Sat 10am–5pm, Sun noon–5pm.

Known as the "Taj Mahal of North America," this luxurious mansion was commissioned as a gift to his third wife by the renowned Henry Flagler, a cofounder of the Standard Oil Company and builder of the Florida East Coast Railroad. The classically columned Edwardian-style mansion contains 55 rooms that include a Louis XIV music room and art gallery, a Louis XV ballroom, and 14 guest suites outfitted with original antique European furnishings. Out back, climb aboard "The Rambler," Mr. Flagler's recently revamped railroad car. Allow at least 1½ hours to tour the stunning grounds and interior.

Norton Museum of Art. 1451 S. Olive Ave., West Palm Beach. ☎ 561/832-5196. Admission $5 adults, $2 students, free for children 12 and under. Tues–Sat 10am–5pm, Sun 1–5pm. From I-95, take Belvedere Rd. (Exit 51) east to the end; then turn left onto S. Olive Ave. to the museum.

Since a 1997 expansion doubled the Norton's space, the museum has gained even more prominence in the art world. It is world famous for its prestigious permanent collection and top temporary exhibitions. The museum's major collections are divided geographically. The American galleries contain major works by Edward Hopper, Georgia O' Keeffe, and Jackson Pollack. The French collection contains Impressionist and post-Impressionist paintings by Cézanne, Degas, Gauguin, Matisse, Monet, Picasso, Pissarro, and Renoir. And the Chinese collection contains more then 200 bronzes, jades, and ceramics as well as a collection of monumental Buddhist sculptures.

Society for the Four Arts. 2 Four Arts Plaza (off Royal Palm Way), Palm Beach. ☎ 561/655-7226. Admission varies depending on program. Gardens, library, Sunday-afternoon films, art exhibitions, and gallery talks free to the public. Movies, concerts, and lectures $3–$25. Call for schedule.

Especially good for children who may be bored with the beach, this Palm Beach institution is a great place just to hang out or to enrich yourself. More than 60 years ago, the society was founded to encourage appreciation of art, music, drama, and literature, and it does a stellar job with at least three of the four (there hasn't been much drama lately), with frequent concerts, year-round art exhibitions, and weekly lectures by big names like John Updike, Gregory Hines, David Frost, and Colin Powell. Explore the well-manicured flower and sculpture gardens. Also, stop by a tremendous and little-known children's library, which includes an enormous collection of books, videos, and games for the little ones.

NATURE PRESERVES & ATTRACTIONS

Lion Country Safari. Southern Blvd. W. at S. R. 80, West Palm Beach. ☎ 561/793-1084, or 561/793-9797 for camping reservations. Admission $14.95 adults, $9.95 seniors and children 3–16, free for children under 3. Daily 9:30am–5:30pm (last vehicle admitted at 4:30pm). From I-95, exit on Southern Blvd. W. Travel 18 miles and follow signs to the attraction.

Even if you've been on an African safari, you probably haven't seen the variety of animals you'll see at this 500-acre wildlife preserve. More than 1,300 animals are divided into their indigenous regions, from the East African preserve of the Serengeti to the American West. You'll see elephants, wildebeest, ostriches, American bison, buffalo, watusi, pink flamingos, and many other more unusual species. Even the lions and elephants roam the huge grassy landscape without a cage in sight. In fact, you're the one who's confined, in your own car without an escort (no convertibles allowed). You're given a detailed informational pamphlet with photos and descriptions and are instructed to obey the 15-m.p.h. speed limit—unless you see the rhinos charge, in which case you're encouraged to floor it. To drive the loop takes just over an hour, though you could make a day of just watching the chimpanzees play on their secluded islands. Included in the admission price is Safari World, an amusement park with paddleboats, a carousel, and a nursery for baby animals born in the preserve. Picnics are encouraged and camping is available (call for reservations). Don't miss this incredible experience. Rental cars are also available for $6 per hour.

Dreher Park Zoo. 1301 Summit Blvd. (east of I-95 between Southern and Forest Hill blvds.) ☎ **561/547-WILD.** Admission $6, $5 senior citizens, $4 children 3–12, children under 3 free. Daily 9am–5pm.

Unlike big city zoos, this intimate 23-acre park is more like a stroll in the park than an all-day excursion. It features about 500 animals representing more than 100 different species. A special monkey exhibit and petting zoo are favorites with kids. Stroller and wagon rental available.

SHOPPING & BROWSING

People may complain of the lack of nightlife or beaches, but no one would dare question Palm Beach's shopping opportunities. From thrift to jewels, Palm Beach has it all.

Known as the Rodeo Drive of the south, Worth Avenue is a window-shopper's dream. No matter what your budget, don't miss the Worth Avenue experience, and don't be put off. These days shopkeepers have learned that sometimes the most affluent shoppers wear ripped jeans or cowboy hats. Still, to fit in you might want to dress as if you were going to an elegant luncheon, not to the mall down the street. The 4 blocks between South Ocean Boulevard and Cocoanut Row—a stretch of more than 200 boutiques, posh shops, art galleries, and upscale restaurants—are home to the stores of Armani, Louis Vuitton, Cartier, Polo Ralph Lauren, and Chanel, among like company.

Victoria's Secret, Limited Express, and several other less-impressive chains have snuck in here too, but so have a good number of unique boutiques. Stop into **Paper Treasures,** at 217 Worth Ave.; it's an autograph gallery with a priceless collection of John Hancocks like those of Joe DiMaggio, Mickey Mantle, Andrew Jackson, Abe Lincoln, Howard Hughes, and hundreds more, all displayed in beautiful frames. At **Myer's Luggage,** 313 Worth Ave., Richard Myers is happy to demonstrate his impressive assortment of toys and gifts, including a vast collection of amusing alarm clocks, spy equipment, gorilla masks, and gag gifts, along with pricey leather bags and English picnic baskets. Just off Worth Avenue, at 374 S. County Rd., is the **Church Mouse** (☎ 561/659-2154), a great consignment/thrift shop with antique furnishings and tableware. Lots of good castaway clothing and shoes are reasonably priced. This shop usually closes for 2 months during the summer. Call to be sure.

The **Palm Beach Mall,** on Palm Beach Lakes Boulevard just east of I-95 (☎ 561/686-3513), is a huge and pleasantly designed mall with tropical fountains, plants, and skylights. You will find several department stores, including JC Penney, Sears, Burdines, and Lord & Taylor, as well as hundreds of specialty boutiques and restaurants.

The **Palm Beach Outlet Center,** at 5700 Okeechobee Blvd. (3 miles west of I-95), West Palm Beach, is the most elegant outlet mall I have ever seen. Upscale clothing, luggage, and shoes at bargain prices are offered in lushly decorated surroundings. The fully enclosed mall also sports a food court.

Downtown West Palm Beach has a number of interesting boutiques along Clematis Street. In addition to a large and well-organized bookstore, **Clematis Street Books,** at 206 Clematis (☎ **561/832-2302**), there are used-record stores, clothing shops, and a few interesting art galleries. Many new and more upscale shops are opening soon. On Saturday mornings, a fantastic green market sets up stalls along Narcissus, which runs perpendicular to Clematis between Flagler and Banyan streets.

WHERE TO STAY

The island of Palm Beach is perhaps the most exclusive in the country. Royalty comes to winter here, and there are plenty of royally priced options to accommodate them. It is no accident that the only three hotels in the state to receive five stars from AAA are all located in Palm Beach County. Happily, there exist a few special little inns that offer reasonably priced rooms in elegant settings. Surrounding the island are many more modest places to lay your straw hat.

A few of the larger hotel chains operating in Palm Beach include the **Howard Johnson Palm Beach,** at 2870 S. Ocean Blvd., (☎ **800/654-2000** or 561/582-2581), which is across the street from the beach. Also beachside is the pricey **Palm Beach Hilton,** at 2842 S. Ocean Blvd. (☎ **800/433-1718** or 561/586-6542).

An excellent and affordable alternative right in the middle of Palm Beach's commercial section is a condo that operates as a hotel, too: the **Palm Beach Hotel,** at 235 Sunrise Ave. (between County Road and Bradley Place, across the street from Publix) (☎ **561/659-7794**). With winter prices starting at about $105, this clean and comfortable accommodation is a great option for those looking for the rarely available bargain in Palm Beach.

In West Palm Beach the chain hotels are mostly located on the main arteries close to the highways and a short drive to the activities in downtown. They include a **Best Western,** 1800 Palm Beach Lakes Blvd. (☎ **800/331-9569** or 561/683-8810), and, just down the road, a **Comfort Inn,** 1901 Palm Lakes Blvd, (☎ **800/221-2222** or 561/689-6100). Further south is the **Parkview Motor Lodge,** 4710 S. Dixie Hwy. (☎ **561/833-4644**). This 28-room, single-story motel is the best of the many motels along Dixie Highway (U.S. 1). With rates starting at $50 for a room with television, air-conditioning, and telephone, you can't ask for more. This family run and very clean motel is located south of I-95's Exit 50 (Southern Boulevard) on South Dixie Highway.

If you're looking for something more private or for longer than just a few days, you may want to call a reservations service for help. Especially for rentals for a few weeks or months, call **Palm Beach Accommodations** (☎ **800/543-SWIM**).

VERY EXPENSIVE

✪ **The Breakers.** 1 S. County Rd., Palm Beach, FL 33480. ☎ **800/833-3141,** 888/ BREAKERS, or 561/655-6611. Fax 561/659-8403. 574 units. A/C MINIBAR TV TEL. Winter $340–$575 double; $510 club double; from $785 suite. Off-season $160–$345 double; $275 club double; from $500 suite. Special packages available. AE, CB, DC, DISC, MC, V. From I-95, exit onto Okeechobee Blvd. E., and turn left onto S. County Rd.; the hotel is just ahead on your right.

The biggest and grandest of all of this area's resorts, this five-star historic beauty epitomizes Palm Beach luxury. It's one of only two Florida properties to win five stars from the Mobil guide and five diamonds from AAA. From the expansive manicured lawns to the elegant marble lobby, The Breakers is the place to be in Palm Beach if you want to be walking distance from all the area's most exclusive shopping and dining and be right on the beach. The lush 130-acre grounds also sport one of the island's only 18-hole golf courses.

An attentive staff is as accustomed to handling steamer trunks and fur wraps as they are to sending faxes and programming VCRs. Though this 1926 palace was built for the world's most elite, it now handles more corporate clients and families with ease. While the Gatsby-esque grounds of Palm Beach's first hotel reveal a sense of history, the newly reconstructed rooms are equipped with all the modern conveniences. A $75 million renovation completed in time for the behemoth's 100th birthday has increased the size of the smaller rooms and spruced up the fading common areas.

There are more than a dozen categories of rooms from which to choose, with the traditional and superior being the smallest and least expensive. Even these relatively miniature rooms are luxuriously appointed and include all the amenities you could desire. Ask for one of the few corner rooms, which tend to be larger and have more windows for the same price. The exclusive Flagler club rooms entitle guests to round-the-clock concierge services, continental breakfast, afternoon tea, before-dinner hors d'oeuvres, evening cocktails, and late-night desserts that are served in an elegant and private lounge. Oceanfront suites offer huge sitting areas, closets, and sleeping quarters.

The Breakers is great for families, though the formality of the lobbies and restaurants may put some off. Jackets are suggested in the formal restaurants and lounge.

Dining/Diversions: Five restaurants and three bars offer a delicious range of meals and snacks from an elegant European dining room to a beach bar with burgers and fries. A romantic oceanfront bar (Palm Beach's only) is reserved for hotel guests.

Amenities: Concierge, 24-hour room service, dry-cleaning and laundry service, overnight shoe shine, newspaper delivery, in-room massage, evening turndown, twice-daily maid service, baby-sitting, secretarial services, express checkout, valet parking $10. VCR and video rentals, outdoor pool, private beach, health club, bicycle rental, two golf courses (one, the Ocean Course, ca. 1897, is Florida's oldest 18-hole course), putting green, game rooms, supervised children's activities, children's playground, business center, car-rental desk, 14 tennis courts (11 of which are lighted), water-sports concession (including scuba and sailing), croquet, shuffleboard, beach volleyball courts, beauty salon, boutiques and shopping arcade. Three new pools, a full-service spa/fitness center and a grand ballroom are planned for construction in 1999.

✪ **Four Seasons Resort Palm Beach.** 2800 S. Ocean Blvd., Palm Beach, FL 33480. ☎ **800/332-3442** or 561/582-2800. Fax 561/547-1557. 210 units. A/C MINIBAR TV TEL. Winter $340–$575 double; from $875 suite. Off-season $255–$475 double; $775 suite. AE, CB, DC, DISC, MC, V. From I-95, take 6th Ave. exit east and turn left onto Dixie Hwy.; then turn east onto Lake Ave. and north onto S. Ocean Blvd., and the hotel is just ahead on your right.

For over-the-top pampering in a perfect location, this Four Seasons is a favorite in an area with many other fantastic resorts. Built in 1989 at the edge of Palm Beach's downtown district, this elegant resort has quickly gained accolades from around the world. An incredibly hospitable staff works hard to be sure this beachfront gem lives up to its reputation. The elegant marble lobby is replete with hand-carved European furnishings, grand oil paintings, tapestries, and dramatic flower arrangements.

The ambience of the common areas extends to the guest rooms as well. All are exceptionally spacious and thoughtfully appointed with extras like a small color TV in the bathroom. Club-floor rooms include access to a special lounge where continental breakfast, afternoon refreshments, and evening cocktails are served gratis. One-bedroom suites include an additional sitting room, a CD/stereo, oversize balconies, and two bathrooms.

Dining/Diversions: The main dining room for dinner serves one of the best meals in Palm Beach. An impeccable menu of Southeastern regional cuisine includes daily fish, meat, and pasta specials served in white-glove elegance. Two other less formal restaurants, including a pool bar and grill, round out the dining options. The lobby lounge is one of the best places in town for an intimate cocktail. Weekend evenings promise excellent live jazz.

Amenities: Concierge, room service (24 hours), evening turndown, dry-cleaning and laundry services, overnight shoe shine, complimentary newspaper delivery, in-room massage, twice-daily maid service, baby-sitting and a wide range of other baby and child amenities, pet amenities (including special water, biscuits, and dog walking), secretarial services, express checkout, valet parking. VCRs and complimentary video rental, movie channels and video games, outdoor heated pool, beach, whirlpool, jogging track, bicycle rentals, supervised activities for children 3 to 12, conference rooms, weekly cooking classes, sundeck, three tennis courts, water-sports rentals, beauty salon, gift shop, spa shop. The 6,000-square-foot spa contains cardiovascular equipment, free weights, and saunas and offers classes, massages, and body wraps.

✪ **Ritz-Carlton Palm Beach.** 100 S. Ocean Blvd., Manalpan, FL 33462. ☎ **800/ 241-3333** or 561/533-6000. Fax 561/540-4999. 326 units. A/C MINIBAR TV TEL. Winter $345–$625 double; $655–$775 club-level double; from $995–$3,000 suite. Off-season $245–$425 double; $475–$525 club-level double; from $595–$3,000 suite. AE, CB, DC, DISC, MC, V. From I-95, take Exit 45 (Hypoluxo Rd.) east; after a mile, turn left onto Federal Hwy. (U.S. 1), continue north for about a mile, and turn right onto Ocean Ave.; cross the Intracoastal Waterway, turn right onto Fla. A1A, and the hotel is on your left.

As is to be expected from any member of this upscale chain, the Palm Beach Ritz-Carlton is superluxurious. In this case, it is on a beautiful beach in a tiny town about 8 miles from Palm Beach's shopping and dining area—a plus for those who want privacy and a drawback for those interested in the activity of "town."

The hotel's elegant and dramatic lobby is dominated by a huge, double-sided pink-marble fireplace, and French 18th- and 19th-century antique furnishings give no hint that the property is not yet 10 years old. The ambience and attention to detail here is rivaled by no other hotel in the area.

Each room has a private balcony and at least a glimpse of the ocean below. All are spacious and decorated in lush contemporary design. Thoughtful details include plush bathrobes and telephones in the large marble bathrooms. Club-level accommodations come with dedicated concierge service and a private lounge where complimentary continental breakfasts, afternoon snacks, and evening cordials are served.

Dining/Diversions: The elegant dining room serves continental-style dinners in ornate surroundings. Other restaurants on the property include a grill, for dinner only; a casual restaurant, which serves all day; and a poolside cafe and bar. Cocktails are also served in the lobby lounge, where you can often find live entertainment. Afternoon tea is served daily but is best Wednesday to Saturday when a jazz trio entertains.

Amenities: Concierge, 24-hour room service, dry-cleaning and laundry services, overnight shoe shine, newspaper delivery, in-room massage, evening turndown, twice-daily maid service, baby-sitting, secretarial services, express checkout, valet parking, airport transportation, free coffee or refreshments in lobby. VCR rentals, Spectravision movie channels, outdoor pool, beach, health club, Jacuzzi, sauna, bicycle rental, children's center and programs, business center, conference rooms, car-rental desk, seven night-lit tennis courts, scuba and snorkeling concessions, beauty salon, gift shop.

EXPENSIVE

Chesterfield Hotel. 363 Cocoanut Row, Palm Beach, FL 33480. ☎ **800/243-7871** or 561/659-5800. Fax 561/659-6707. 65 units. A/C TV TEL. Winter $269–$349 double; from $529 suite. Off-season $89–$169 double; from $219 suite. Rollaway bed $15 extra. AE, DC, DISC, MC, V. From I-95, exit onto Okeechobee Blvd. E., cross the Intracoastal Waterway, and turn right onto Cocoanut Row; the hotel is ahead on your left, just past Australian Ave.

With more charm than its more expensive rivals, the intimate Chesterfield, located just 1 block from Worth Avenue, has been popular with visitors in the know since the 1920s. Behind its light stucco facade, arched windows, and colorful flags is an overly designed interior with Laura Ashley prints battling Ralph Lauren. It all creates a wonderfully authentic country-manor feel.

Guest rooms also have formal chintz and taffeta prints. Heavy wooden furniture and plush carpets give each room a warm but dark feel. Although most rooms have no view to speak of, they are comfortable and attractive. A stunning lobby library provides a quiet nook for those who may want to read at the large oak desk or borrow a book for the beach. Afternoon tea completes the illusion of being in a well-run country inn across the Atlantic.

Dining/Diversions: The Leopard Room serves fantastic English, French, and continental favorites all day; reservations are essential for dinner and Sunday brunch. The Leopard Lounge is an area hangout in the evenings when there is usually live music and no cover charge (see "The Palm Beaches After Dark," below).

Amenities: Concierge, room service, newspaper delivery, in-room massage, dry cleaning, twice-daily maid service, baby-sitting, valet parking, secretarial services, express checkout. Swimming pool, access to nearby health club, Jacuzzi, nature trails, bicycle rental, video rentals, conference rooms, business center, car-rental desk, tour desk.

Plaza Inn. 215 Brazilian Ave., Palm Beach, FL 33480. ☎ **800/233-2632** or 561/832-8666. Fax 561/835-8776. 49 units. A/C TV TEL. Winter $160–$235 double; $255 suite. Off-season $95–$145 double; $135 suite. Rates include breakfast. AE, MC, V. From I-95, exit onto Okeechobee Blvd. E., cross the Intracoastal Waterway, turn right onto Cocoanut Row, then left onto Brazilian Ave.; the hotel is just ahead on your left.

This ever-improving bed-and-breakfast-style inn is as understated and luxurious as the handsome guests it hosts. Nothing is flashy here. From the simple and elegant flower arrangements in the marble lobby to the well-worn period antiques haphazardly strewn throughout, the Plaza Inn has the look of studied nonchalance. A small staff, including owner Ajit Asrani, is remarkably hospitable and knowledgeable about the island's inner workings.

Each uniquely decorated room is dressed with quality furnishings, several with carved four-poster beds, hand-crocheted spreads, and lace curtains. The bathrooms are lovely if quite small, and the wall-mounted air conditioners can be noisy when they are needed in the warm months. Choose a corner room or one overlooking the small pool deck for the best light.

In any room, you are sure to appreciate the convenient location: less than 2 blocks from the ocean and all of the best shopping. For those who appreciate the fine hospitality of a small lodging without the sometimes invasive feel of a bed-and-breakfast, this is the island's number one choice.

Dining/Diversions: A full cooked-to-order breakfast that includes fresh fruit, breakfast breads, and hot main dishes is served each morning in a charming, English country–style dining room. The cozy Stray Fox Pub, a comfortable little bar with mahogany tables, serves cocktails throughout the evening and sometimes has live piano music on the weekends.

Amenities: Concierge, dry-cleaning and laundry services, newspaper delivery, in-room massage, baby-sitting, secretarial services. VCRs, heated outdoor pool, Jacuzzi and small workout room, access to nearby health club.

MODERATE

Heart of Palm Beach Hotel. 160 Royal Palm Way, Palm Beach, FL 33480. ☎ **800/ 523-5377** or 561/655-5600. Fax 561/832-1201. 90 units. A/C TV TEL. Winter $149–$219 double; $275 suite. Off-season $69–$139 double; $175 suite. AE, CB, DC, MC, V. From I-95, exit onto Okeechobee Blvd. E. and continue over the Royal Park Bridge onto Royal Palm Way; the hotel is ahead on your right, past S. County Rd.

The centrally located Heart of Palm Beach Hotel is within walking distance of Worth Avenue's shops and just half a block from the beach. Ongoing renovations since the 1990s have improved the patio space as well as the rooms in the hotel's two buildings. Most are decorated with modest but new furnishings and fittings in a colorful contemporary style. The tiled bathrooms are small, clean, and functional. Besides the great location, another plus here is that each accommodation comes with a private balcony or patio. Choose a room on a higher floor, as those on the ground floor tend to be a bit dark. The staff is particularly outgoing and will help guests plan outings and itineraries.

There's a heated swimming pool and complimentary covered parking. A clubby restaurant serves a selection of salads, sandwiches, pastas, and cocktails. Breakfast is served in a bright dining room overlooking the gardens.

Palm Beach Historic Inn. 365 S. County Rd., Palm Beach, FL 33480. ☎ **561/832-4009.** Fax 561/832-6255. 13 units. A/C TV TEL. Winter $125–$150 double; from $175 suite. Off-season $75–$95 double; from $100 suite. Rates include continental breakfast. Children 9 and under stay free in parents' room. AE, CB, DC, DISC, MC, V.

Despite a rather abandoned look, this bed-and-breakfast is a cozy and comfortable place to stay in Palm Beach. Built in 1923, the Palm Beach Historic Inn is an area landmark located within walking distance of Worth Avenue, the beach, and several good restaurants. The small lobby is filled with antiques, books, magazines, and an old-fashioned umbrella stand, all of which add to the homey feel of this intimate bed-and-breakfast. All the rooms are on the second floor, and each is uniquely decorated and full of frills. Floral prints, sheer curtains, and the plethora of lace can sometimes be overwhelming, masking rather than complementing beautiful antique writing desks and dressers. Happily, there are also fluffy bathrobes, an abundance of towels, and plenty of good-smelling toiletries.

INEXPENSIVE

✪ **Beachcomber Apartment Motel.** 3024 S. Ocean Blvd., Palm Beach, FL 33480. ☎ **800/833-7122** or 561/585-4646. Fax 561/547-9438. 45 units. A/C TV TEL. Winter $85–$155 motel rm; from $105–$210 apt. Off-season $42–$80 motel rm; from $55–$120 apt. Apr 17–Oct 31, $42–$80 motel rm; from $55 apt. Fall $55–$100 motel rm; from $85–$165 apt. AE, DISC, MC, V. From I-95, exit 10th Ave. N., head east to Federal Hwy., and turn right. Continue to Lake Worth Ave. and turn left. Go over bridge and turn right at first traffic light (S. Ocean Dr.); the hotel is 1½ blocks on the left.

It's not just the bright-pink building that makes this two-story motel stand out. For more than 35 years the Beachcomber has been bringing sanity to pricey Palm Beach by offering a good standard of accommodation at reasonable prices. Squeezed between beachfront high-rises, the motel is located oceanfront, adjacent to Lake Worth Beach and a short drive from Worth Avenue shops and local attractions. Every room has two double beds, large closets, and distinctive green-and-white tropical-style furnishings; some have kitchenettes. The most expensive have balconies overlooking the ocean. The bathrooms are basic, and amenities are limited to towels and soap. Facilities at the motel include a coin-operated laundry, shuffleboard, a large pool, and a sundeck overlooking the Atlantic.

Hibiscus House. 501 30th St., West Palm Beach, FL 33407. ☎ **800/203-4927** or 561/ 863-5633. Fax 561/863-5633. www.hibiscushouse.com. 8 units. A/C TV TEL. Winter $95–$175 double. Off-season $65–$130 double. Rates include breakfast. AE, DC, MC, V. From I-95, exit onto Palm Beach Lakes Blvd. E. and continue 4 miles; turn left onto Flagler Dr., continue for about 20 blocks, then turn left onto 30th St.; the inn is 2 blocks ahead on your right.

Inexpensive bed-and-breakfasts are rare in Southeast Florida, making the Hibiscus House one of the area's firsts, a true find. Located a few miles from the coast in a quiet residential neighborhood, this 1920s-era B&B is filled with handsome antiques and tapestried in luxurious fabrics. Every room has its own private terrace or balcony. The backyard, a peaceful retreat, has been transformed into a tropical garden with a heated swimming pool and lounge chairs. Also there are plenty of pretty areas for guests to enjoy inside; one little sitting room is wrapped in glass and is stocked with playing cards and board games. *Beware:* Breakfast portions are enormous. The gourmet creations are as filling as they are beautiful. Ask for any special requests in advance; owners Raleigh Hill and Colin Rayer will be happy to oblige.

WHERE TO DINE

Palm Beach has some of the area's finest restaurants, with many classical and elegant options as well as a few more innovative choices. Dress here is slightly more formal than in most other areas of Florida: Men wear blazers, and women generally put on modest dresses when they dine out—even in the dead of summer.

EXPENSIVE

Amici. 288 S. County Rd. (at Royal Palm Way), Palm Beach. ☎ **561/832-0201.** Fax 561/ 659-3540. Reservations strongly recommended on weekends. Main courses $18–$29; pastas and pizzas $8–$19. AE, DC, MC, V. Mon–Thurs 11:30am–3pm and 5:30–10:30pm, Fri–Sat 11:30am–3pm and 5:30–11pm, Sun 5:30–10:30pm. ITALIAN.

You'd think that there would be a dozen good Italian restaurants in Palm Beach. There are plenty of decent ones, but Amici tops them all. With homemade pastas, a vast array of innovative antipasti, and a variety of lighter fare, Amici is certainly making friends fast. They come dressed in blazers and ties at lunch, though the atmosphere here is fairly casual, with simple decor and lots of window space to let in light. The food is nothing unusual—grilled sandwiches, pastas with rustic sauces, pizzas, grilled shrimp and fish—but the execution is flawless. You could argue that the prices don't match the simple food, but where else in Palm Beach can you get broccoli di rabe, fresh roasted peppers loaded with garlic, and pizzas with escarole, homemade sausage, and pine nuts?

Cafe l'Europe. 331 S. County Rd. (at the corner of Brazilian Ave.), Palm Beach. ☎ **561/ 655-4020.** Reservations recommended. Main courses $18–$32. AE, CB, DC, DISC, MC, V. Tues–Sat noon–2:30pm and 5:45–10:30pm, Fri–Sat open until 1am. Sun 6–10:30pm. FRENCH/CONTINENTAL.

One of Palm Beach's very finest, this award-winning formal restaurant is located on the upper level of the Esplanade, a Spanish-style shopping arcade. The interior is made romantic and luxurious by the tapestried cafe chairs and linen-topped tables set with crystal and china. The enticing appetizers served by a superb staff might include Chinese spring rolls, baked goat-cheese salad with raspberry-walnut dressing, poached salmon, or chilled gazpacho with avocado. Main courses run the gamut from sautéed potato-crusted Florida snapper to lamb chops to roast Cornish game hen. Seafood dishes and steaks in sumptuous but light sauces are always exceptional.

For even more atmosphere, you may want to check out the Caviar Bar, located adjacent to the dining room. The intimate rooms feature a large marble bar and small European-style cafe tables. Here you can choose from half a dozen different roes with all the accoutrements. Or have your coffee and desserts here for more privacy.

Chuck & Harold's Cafe. 207 Royal Poinciana Way (corner of S. County Rd.), Palm Beach. ☎ 561/659-1440. Reservations recommended. Main courses $14–$28. AE, DC, DISC, MC, V. Mon–Thurs 7:30am–midnight, Fri–Sat 7:30am–1am, Sun 8am–11pm. SEAFOOD/ AMERICAN.

For standard and predictable American fare, this old standby delivers. Chuck & Harold's serves good food at inflated prices. Remember, you are paying for one of the area's best people-watching perches. Sit outside and enjoy the view. Main dishes include fresh grilled or broiled fish, boiled lobster, and a small variety of straightforward homemade pasta and chicken dishes. If you happen to visit during stone crab season, order them here. The crab claws are steamed or chilled and served with a traditional honey-mustard sauce. *One final hint:* You might skip ordering dessert, as complimentary cookies are served at the end of each meal.

Zazu. 313 Clematis St., West Palm Beach (between Olive and Dixie Hwy.). ☎ **561/832-1919.** Reservations suggested. Main courses $15–$23, pastas $11–$22. AE, DISC, DC, MC, V. Mon–Fri 11:30am–2:30pm and 5:30–10pm. Thurs–Sat, dinner until 11pm and nightclub until 3am. MULTICULTURAL.

This star along trendy Clematis Street has earned the loyalty of locals and visitors for its fantastically innovative cuisine and also for its lively nightlife. Most weekends feature a DJ late night and live music a few nights too. The menu is eclectic, featuring such recommendable appetizers as wild mushroom gnocchi roasted and served on top of slightly wilted greens with sweet browned caramelized onions and a classic Caesar salad with tiny rounds of Parmesan-laden pizza-bread. A varied menu of fish, chicken, beef, and veal prepared with an Italian, Southern, or Asian flare tend to work well— though a few are overwrought. Upstairs is Daddy O's where a young attractive crowd has a raucous time, singing and dancing to whatever is going on. Arrive early (before 8pm) if you plan to get up there. Overall, the art deco decor, funky food, and lively vibe makes it a fun night out for anyone looking for a good time.

MODERATE

✪ **Aquaterra.** 230 Sunrise Ave. (between Sunrise and Park aves.), Palm Beach. ☎ **561/ 366-4000.** Reservations recommended, especially on weekends. Main courses $15–$18.50. Fixed-price menu 5–6pm $19. AE, MC, V. Tues–Sun 9:30am–2:30pm and 5–11pm. Mon 5–11pm. INNOVATIVE AMERICAN.

New York's Charlie Palmer, James Beard winner for best chef in 1997, has taken his spatula south and opened a stunning new lunch and dinner spot in Palm Beach. Slightly off the beaten track on Sunrise Avenue (across the street from the Palm Beach Hotel) but still centrally located, this fantastic restaurant is bound to please even the pickiest eaters. With nearly 20 options for bar snacks and appetizers including crispy fried oysters, beef skewers with peanut sauce, vegetable spring rolls, eggplant fritters, luscious rock shrimp pillows, and lobster salad in cold tomato consommé, the menu is simple yet diverse. A more limited selection of entrees, as the name suggests, is from the sea or land. The best choices are waterborne. Depending on the season there is mahimahi (dolphin), salmon, swordfish, snapper or tuna, all of which can be prepared to your liking: grilled, roasted, or sautéed with a complimentary array of herbs and seasonings. I favor the clean-tasting snapper grilled with caramelized lemon, olive oil and fresh parsley. Also, an exceptional sea bass is braised tableside with a subtly licorice and basil broth. Likewise, you can choose how you'd like your meats or chicken cooked. A delicate filet mignon sautéed with wild mushroom ragout is memorable. So too are the divine side dishes like a cheesy risotto (Italian rice) with a hint of pepper and olive, mashed potatoes with a splash of pungent roasted garlic and the heavenly potato and onion tart topped with an ever-so-light dusting of bacon. Don't skip the architecturally striking and delicious desserts. Especially good is the double caramelized banana parfait and the bittersweet chocolate torte with homemade mint ice cream.

Rhythm Cafe. 3800 S. Dixie Hwy., West Palm Beach. ☎ **561/833-3406.** Reservations recommended on weekends. Main courses $10–24. AE, DISC, MC, V. Tues–Fri 11am–3pm and 6–10pm; Sat–Sun 8am–2pm and 6–10pm. Sometimes earlier on Sunday. From I-95, exit east on Southern Blvd., 1 block north of Southern Blvd., on the right. ECLECTIC AMERICAN.

This hole-in-the-wall is where those in the know come to eat some of West Palm Beach's most laid-back gourmet food. On the handwritten, photocopied menu, you will always find a fish specialty with a hefty dose of greens and garnishes. Also reliably outstanding is the sautéed medallion of beef tenderloin served on a bed of arugula with a tangy rosemary vinaigrette. Salads and soups are a great bargain since the portions are relatively large and the display usually spectacular. The kitschy decor of this tiny cafe comes complete with vinyl tablecloths and paintings by local amateurs. Young handsome waiters are attentive but not solicitous. The old drugstore where the restaurant recently relocated features an original '50s lunch counter and stools.

Taboo. 221 Worth Ave., Palm Beach. ☎ **561/835-3500.** Reservations recommended. Main courses $14–$22. AE, DC, MC, V. Sun–Thurs 11:30am–11pm, Fri–Sat 11:30am–1am. AMERICAN BISTRO.

Taboo is a snazzy Worth Avenue eatery that successfully combines the classic and the trendy. Lots of greenery, a fireplace, and a contemporary Southwestern charm make it comfortable and inviting. Variety is always the chef's special, with extensive lunch and dinner offerings that are often calorie- and cholesterol-conscious. For lunch, the kitchen creates California-style individual-size pizzas topped with delicacies like barbecued chicken, goat and mozzarella cheeses, and sweet roasted red peppers. Other choices include a delicious sandwich of sweet peppers and goat cheese. The best dinner starter is fresh tuna marinated in ginger and lime. Dinner choices change nightly and may include grilled swordfish topped with olive-caper sauce or grilled veal served on the bone.

INEXPENSIVE

Green's Pharmacy. 151 N. County Rd., Palm Beach. ☎ **561/832-0304.** Breakfast $2–$5; burgers and sandwiches $3–$6. AE, MC, V. Mon–Sat 7am–6pm, Sun 7am–5pm. AMERICAN.

This neighborhood corner pharmacy offers one of the best meal deals in Palm Beach. Both breakfast and lunch are served coffee-shop style at either a Formica bar or plain tables above a black-and-white checkerboard floor. Breakfast specials include eggs and omelettes served with home fries and bacon, sausage, or corned-beef hash. At lunch the grill serves burgers and sandwiches, as well as ice-cream sodas and milkshakes, to a loyal crowd of pastel-clad Palm Beachers.

✪ **John G's.** 10 S. Ocean Blvd., Lake Worth. ☎ **561/585-9860.** Reservations not accepted. Breakfast $3–$8.50; lunch $5–$14. No credit cards. Daily 7am–3pm. Off Florida Turnpike, take the Lake Worth exit and head toward the ocean. AMERICAN.

This coffee shop is the most popular in the county. For decades, John G's has been attracting huge breakfast crowds; lines run out the door, or, on weekends, all the way down the block. They come for good, greasy-spoon-style food served in heaping portions right on the beachfront. This place is known for fresh and tasty fish-and-chips and its selection of creative omelettes and grill specials.

TooJay's. 313 Royal Poinciana Plaza (3 miles east of I-95 off Exit 52A), Palm Beach. ☎ **561/659-7232.** Reservations not accepted. Main courses $7–$12. CB, DC, MC, V. Daily 8am–9pm. DELICATESSEN.

This simple and predictable restaurant and take-out deli is a favorite with locals and out-of-towners who want good old-fashioned deli food. So popular, in fact, that TooJay's now has more than a dozen outlets. For good cover while people-watching, choose a booth surrounded by a jungle of potted plants. The food is excellent and could hardly be fresher. All the classic sandwiches are available: hot pastrami, roast beef, turkey, chicken, chopped liver, egg salad, and more. Comfort food in the form of huge portions of stuffed cabbage, chicken pot pie, beef brisket, and sautéed onions and chicken livers is sure to satisfy.

THE PALM BEACHES AFTER DARK
THE BAR, CAFE & MUSIC SCENE: DOWNTOWN WEST PALM BEACH

A decade-old project to revitalize downtown West Palm Beach has finally become a reality, with ✪ **Clematis Street** at the heart. Artist lofts, sidewalk cafes, bars, restaurants, consignment shops, and galleries dot the street from Flagler Drive to Rosemary Avenue, creating a hot spot for a night out, especially on weekends when young professionals mingle with suit-clad Europeans and disheveled artists. Every Thursday night is a popular night out called Clematis by Night. Each week features a different rock, blues, or reggae band plus an art show. Vendors sell food and drinks and the street's bars and restaurants are packed. It is a bit raucous at times, but fun. Note that minors unaccompanied by their guardians are not permitted in the downtown area around Clematis Street after 10pm on week nights and after 11pm on weekend nights.

Some highlights of the Strip include **Napa Valley Wine Bar** in the front of the Clematis Street Bookstore, 206 Clematis St. (☎ 561/832-5398), which serves a good selection of wines by the glass, coffees, and light snacks in a comfortable, slightly bohemian setting. Quiet artsy types whisper politely at small tables while listening to live jazz on weekends. Service is bumbling but the atmosphere is comfortable. **Sforza,** at 223 Clematis St., is the only Italian restaurant I've ever been to that needs a bouncer at the door. On weekends this place draws crowds of yuppies and well-dressed Euros who wait to be picked to get in the elegant dining room to dance and sip expensive martinis (☎ 561/832-8819).

If you are looking for a more casual scene, stop by **Ray's,** at 519 Clematis St. (☎ 561/835-1577), on a Thursday, Friday, or Saturday for free blues and mediocre drinks. This dusty little bar hosts homegrown blues bands who give it all up for the few patrons who appreciate the rough stuff.

Across the street is a longtime favorite, **Respectable Street Café,** at 518 Clematis St. (☎ 561/832-9999). The cafe's plain storefront exterior belies its funky high-ceilinged interior decorated with large black booths, psychedelic wall murals, and a large checkerboard-tile dance floor where young hipsters dance to both live and recorded alternative music.

Just around the corner at 109 N. Olive Ave. is **Enigma** (☎ **561/832-5040**), a huge "danceteria" in the style of '80s New York clubs. Music varies, and the crowd represents the most outrageous Palm Beach County has to offer.

Over the bridge in Palm Beach is **E.R. Bradley's Saloon,** at 111 Bradley Place, between Royal Poinciana Way and Sunset Avenue (☎ **561/833-3520**). Bradley's, as it is known, is about as wild as the "island" allows. Most nights a rowdy crowd of young professionals share the old wooden tavern with hard-drinking regulars in blue blazers. Random hooting and a conga line around the block usually ends with at least a couple of wannabe go-go dancers up on the bar enjoying the applause of a tipsy crowd. Check out the happy-hour buffets in the late afternoon.

A more sophisticated crowd gathers nightly at the Leopard Lounge in the Chesterfield Hotel (see "Where to Stay," above). Live piano music, good conversation, and a comfortable sofa make this a perfect place to spend an evening.

The Performing Arts

With a number of dedicated patrons and enthusiastic supporters of the arts, this area happily boasts many good venues for those craving culture. Check the *Palm Beach Post* or the *Palm Beach Daily News,* known as "the shiny sheet," for up-to-date listings and reviews. Call ☎ **800/882-ARTS** for a recorded announcement of the week's events.

The **Raymond F. Kravis Center for the Performing Arts,** 701 Okeechobee Blvd., West Palm Beach (☎ **561/832-7469**), is the area's largest and most active performance space. With a huge curved-glass facade and more than 2,500 seats in two lushly decorated indoor spaces, and a new outdoor amphitheater, The Kravis, as it is known, stages more than 300 performances each year. Phone for a current schedule of Palm Beach's best music, dance, and theater.

If you are in town when the **Miami City Ballet** is performing, consider yourself lucky. With a performance schedule that takes them around the state from late September to April, this critically acclaimed young company is worth catching. Call ☎ **561/833-4492.**

4 Jupiter & Northern Palm Beach County

20 miles N of Palm Beach, 81 miles N of Miami

Northern Palm Beach County and its main town, Jupiter, are known primarily for pristine beaches and expansive tracts of land. The surrounding towns of Tequesta, Jupiter, Juno Beach, North Palm Beach, Palm Beach Gardens, and Singer Island are inviting for tourists who want to enjoy the many outdoor activities that make this area so popular with retirees, snowbirds, and families. Beaches and parks are clean, large, and easily accessible to the public.

ESSENTIALS

GETTING THERE   The quickest route from West Palm Beach to Jupiter is by the sometimes congested I-95. You can also take a slower but more scenic coastal route, U.S. 1 or Fla. A1A.

Since Jupiter is so close to Palm Beach, it's easy to fly into the **Palm Beach International Airport** (☎ **561/471-7420**) and rent a car there. The drive should take less than half an hour.

VISITOR INFORMATION   For free maps, an arts-and-attractions calendar, and detailed trip planning guide, contact the **Palm Beach County Convention and Visitors Bureau,** 1555 Palm Beach Lakes Blvd., Suite 204, West Palm Beach, FL 33401

(☎ **800/554-PALM** or 561/471-3995). Also open is a brand-new Visitor Information Center, located between I-95 and the Florida Turnpike at 8020 Indiantown Rd. in Jupiter. This center is open from 9am to 6pm daily.

BEACHES & OUTDOOR PURSUITS

BASEBALL The newly built **Roger Dean Stadium,** 4751 Main St. (☎ **561/ 775-1818**), hosts spring training for both the St. Louis Cardinals and the Montreal Expos, along with minor-league action from Florida's state league, The Hammerheads. Tickets range in price from $5 to $15. Baseball aficionados should call for schedules and specific ticket information.

BEACHES The farther north you head from populated Palm Beach, the more peaceful and pristine the coast becomes. Just a few miles north of the bustle, castles and condominiums give way to wide open space and public parkland. There are dozens of recommendable spots. Following are a few of the best.

John D. MacArthur Beach, a state park, dominates a large portion of Singer Island, the barrier island just north of Palm Beach. Straddling the island from shore to shore, the park has lengthy frontage on both the Atlantic Ocean and Lake Worth Cove. The beach is great for hiking, swimming, and sunning. To reach the park from the mainland, cross the Intracoastal Waterway on Blue Heron Boulevard and turn north on Ocean Boulevard.

Jupiter Inlet meets the ocean at **Dubois Park,** a 29-acre beach that is popular with families. The shallow waters and sandy shore are perfect for kids, while adults can play in the rougher swells of the lifeguarded inlet. A footbridge leads to Ocean Beach, an area popular with windsurfers and surfers. There's a short fishing pier, and plenty of trees shading barbecue grills and picnic tables. Visitors can also explore the Dubois Pioneer Home, a small house situated atop a shell mound built by the Jaega Indians. The park entrance is on Dubois Road, about a mile south of the junction of U.S. 1 and Fla. A1A.

BICYCLING Bring your own, get one from your hotel, or rent one from **Raleigh Bicycles of Jupiter** (☎ **561/746-0585**). Bicycle enthusiasts will enjoy exploring this flat and uncluttered area. North Palm Beach has hundreds of miles of smooth paved roads. Loggerhead Park in Juno Beach or Fla. A1A along the ocean has great trails for starters. You'll find many more scenic routes over the bridges and west of the highway.

BOATING & CANOEING You can rent a boat at several outlets throughout northern Palm Beach County, including **Classic Adventures,** at 2385 PGA Blvd. (at the base of the Intracoastal Bridge), Palm Beach Gardens (☎ **561/626-6771**). This friendly outpost rents a variety of bow-riders that hold up to eight people for rates starting at $199 for a half day and $299 for a full day. Also fun are the WaveRunners starting at $60 an hour.

Canoe Outfitters, 9060 Indiantown Rd. (west of I-95), North Jupiter (☎ **561/ 746-7053**), provides access to one of the area's most beautiful natural waterways. Canoers start at Riverbend Park along an 8-mile stretch of Intracoastal Waterway where the lush foliage supports dozens of exotic birds and reptiles. Keep your eyes open for gators who love to sunbathe on the shallow shores of the river. You'll end up tired and thoroughly wide-eyed at Jonathan Dickinson Park about 5 or 6 hours later. Eric Bailey, a local who runs the concession, will sell the environmentally minded a pamphlet for $1 that describes local flora and fauna. Trips run Wednesday to Sunday and cost $16 per person, including park charges.

CRUISES Several sightseeing cruises offer scenic tours of the magnificent waterways that make up northern Palm Beach County. Several water taxis conduct daily narrated tours through the scenic waters. One interesting excursion departs from **Panama Hatties** at PGA Boulevard and the Intracoastal Waterway. Prices are $15 per person for the 1½-hour ride. Call ☎ 561/775-2628. The *Manatee Queen,* 18487 U.S. 1 (2 miles north of Jupiter Lighthouse), Blowing Rocks Marina, Jupiter (☎ 561/744-2191), a 40-foot catamaran with bench seating for up to 49 people, offers 2-hour tours of Jupiter Island departing daily at 2:30pm that pass Burt Reynolds's and Perry Como's mansions, among other historical and natural spots of interest. Reservations are highly recommended, especially in season; call for the current schedule of offerings. The cruise is wheelchair-accessible. Prices start at $12.50 for adults and $10 for children and can range up to $15 for special tours. Bring your own lunch or purchase chips and sodas at the minisnack bar.

FISHING   Before you leave, send for an information-packed fishing kit with details on fish camps, charters, tournament and tide schedules, distributed by the **West Palm Beach Fishing Club,** c/o Fish Finder, P.O. Box 468, West Palm Beach, FL 33402. The cost is $10 and is well worth it. Allow at least 4 weeks for delivery.

Once in town, several outfitters along U.S. 1 and Fla. A1A have vessels and equipment for rent if your hotel doesn't. One of the most complete facilities is the **Sailfish Marina & Resort,** 98 Lake Dr. (off Blue Heron Boulevard), Palm Beach Shores (☎ 561/ 844-1724). Call for equipment, bait, guided trips, or boat rentals.

GOLF   Even if you're not lucky enough to be staying at the PGA National Resort, you may still be able to play on their award-winning courses. If you or someone in your group is a member of another golf or country club, have the head pro write a note on club letterhead to Jackie Rogers at PGA (see "Where to Stay," below) or send a fax to ☎ 561/627-015 to request a play date. Be sure the pro includes his PGA number and contact information. Allow at least 2 weeks for a response. Also, ask about the Golf-A-Round program, where selected private clubs open to nonmembers for free or discounted rates. Contact the **Palm Beach County Convention and Visitors Bureau** (☎ 561/471-3995) for details.

Plenty of other great courses dot the area, including the **Indian Creek Golf Club,** 1800 Central Blvd., Jupiter (☎ 561/747-6262). A well-respected 18-hole, par-70 course is situated on over 6,200 yards featuring narrow fairways and fast greens. Fees are $27 to $55, depending on the season, and include a mandatory cart. The course borders I-95.

HIKING   In an area that's not particularly known for extraordinary natural diversity, **Blowing Rocks Preserve** wows with a terrific hiking trail along a dramatic limestone outcropping. You won't find hills or scenic vistas, but you will see Florida's unique and varied tropical ecosystem. The well-marked mile-long trail passes oceanfront dunes, coastal strands, mangrove wetlands, and a coastal hammock. The preserve, owned and managed by the Nature Conservancy, also protects an important habitat for West Indian manatees and loggerhead turtles.

Formed over millions of years by an accumulation of marine sediments, the cliffs are a dramatic sight. At high tide, seawater crashes through the huge fissures and sends spectacular plumes high into the air. There are no beach facilities, and swimming is a bit dangerous, but I've often seen people dive and snorkel here. Fishing is also popular. Food, beverages, and pets are not permitted, and visitors must remain on designated trails. The preserve is located along South Beach Drive (Fla. A1A), north of the Jupiter inlet, about a 10-minute drive from Jupiter. From U.S. 1, head east on S.R. 707 and cross the Intracoastal Waterway to the park. Admission is free, but a $3 per person donation is requested. For more information, contact the Preserve Manager, Blowing Rocks Preserve, P.O. Box 3795, Tequesta, FL 33469 (☎ **561/575-2297**).

Discovering a Remarkable Natural World

North Palm is well known for the giant sea turtles that lay their eggs on the county's beaches from May to August. These endangered marine animals return here annually, from as far as South America, to lay their clutch of about 115 eggs each. Nurtured by the warm sand, but preyed upon by birds and other predators, only about one or two babies from each nest survive to maturity.

Many environmentalists recommend that visitors take part in an organized turtle-watching program (rather than going on their own) to minimize disturbance to the turtles. The Jupiter Beach Resort (see "Where to Stay," below) and the Marinelife Center of Juno Beach (see below) both sponsor free guided expeditions to the egg-laying sites from May to August. Phone for times and reservations.

Just south of Jupiter, in Juno Beach, is the **Marinelife Center of Juno Beach,** in Loggerhead Park, 14200 U.S. 1, Juno Beach (☎ **561/627-8280**). A small combination science museum and nature trail, the Marinelife Center is dedicated to the coastal ecology of northern Palm Beach County. Hands-on exhibits teach visitors about wetlands and beach areas, as well as offshore coral reefs and the local sea life. Visitors are encouraged to walk the center's sand dune nature trails, all of which are marked with interpretive signs. This is one place that you're guaranteed to see live sea turtles year-round, and during high breeding season (June and July) the center conducts narrative walks along a nearby beach. Reservations are a must. The book opens on May 1 and is usually full by mid-month. Admission to the center is free, though donations are accepted. Open Tuesday to Saturday from 10am to 4pm and Sunday from noon to 3pm.

SCUBA DIVING & SNORKELING Year-round, warm, clear waters make northern Palm Beach County great for both diving and snorkeling. The closest coral reef is located a quarter-mile from shore and can easily be reached by boat. Three popular wrecks are clustered near each other less than a mile off shore of the Lake Worth Inlet at about 90 feet. If your hotel doesn't offer dive trips, call **Gulf Stream Diver II,** 1030 U.S. 1, Suite 101, North Palm Beach (☎ **800/771-DIVE** or 561/627-9558); **Seafari Dive and Surfing,** 75 E. Indiantown Rd., Suite 603, Jupiter (☎ **561/ 747-6115**).

TENNIS In addition to the many hotel tennis courts (see "Where to Stay," below), you can swing a racquet at a number of local clubs. The **Jupiter Bay Tennis Club,** 353 U.S. 1, Jupiter (☎ **561/744-9424**), has seven clay courts (three lighted) and charges $12 per person per day. Reservations are highly recommended.

More economical options are available at relatively well-maintained municipal courts. Call for locations and hours (☎ **561/966-6600**). Many are available free on a first-come, first-served basis.

A HISTORIC LIGHTHOUSE

Jupiter Inlet Lighthouse. U.S. 1 and Alt. Fla. A1A, Jupiter. ☎ **561/747-8380.** Admission $5. Sun–Wed 10am–4pm (last tour departs at 3:15pm). Children must be 4 feet or taller to climb.

Completed in 1860, this redbrick structure is the oldest extant building in Palm Beach County. Still owned and maintained by the U.S. Coast Guard, the lighthouse is now home to a small historical museum, located at its base. The Florida History Museum sponsors tours of the lighthouse, enabling visitors to explore the cramped interior, which is filled with artifacts and photographs illustrating the rich history of the area. First a 15-minute video explains the various shipwrecks, Indian wars, and other events that helped shape this region. Helpful volunteers are eager to tell colorful stories to highlight the 1-hour tour.

SHOPPING

Northern Palm Beach County may not have the glitzy boutiques of Worth Avenue, but it does have an impressive indoor mall, the **Gardens of the Palm Beaches,** at 3101 PGA Blvd., where you can find large department stores including Bloomingdale's, Burdines, Macy's, and Saks Fifth Avenue, as well as more than 100 specialty shops with everything from handmade chocolates to sports equipment. A large and diverse food court and fine sit-down restaurants in this 1.3 million-square-foot facility make this shopping excursion an all-day affair. Call ☎ **561/775-7750** for store information.

WHERE TO STAY

The northern part of Palm Beach County is much more laid-back and less touristy than the rest of the Gold Coast. Here there are relatively few fancy hotels or attractions. Singer Island has the largest concentration of beachfront chains including the **Days Inn Oceanfront Resort** (☎ **800/325-2525** or 561/848-8661), 2700 N. Ocean Dr.; the **Holiday Inn SunSpree Resort** (☎ **800/443-4077** or 561/848-3888), 3700 N. Ocean Dr.; and the **Quality Resort of the Palm Beaches** (☎ **800/765-5502** or 561/848-5502), 3800 N. Ocean Dr.

Also notable is the very reasonably priced and recently renovated **Wellesley Inn,** at 34 Fisherman's Wharf (I-95, exit east on Indian Town Road; turn left before the bridge), in Jupiter (☎ **800/444-8888**). Suites include sofa beds, refrigerators, and microwave ovens. Though not within walking distance of the beach, the inn is located near shops and restaurants and Fla. A1A.

VERY EXPENSIVE

Jupiter Beach Resort. 5 N. Fla. A1A, Jupiter, FL 33477. ☎ **800 228-8810** or 561/746-2511. Fax 561/747-3304. 176 units. A/C MINIBAR TV TEL. Winter $200–$340 double; $310–$450 suite; $750–$1,000 penthouse. Off-season $115–$205 double; $135–$205 suite; $400–$600 penthouse. AE, CB, DC, DISC, MC, V. From I-95, take Exit 59A east to the end of Indiantown Rd. and then head north to Jupiter Beach Rd. The resort is on the right.

The only resort located directly on Jupiter's beach, this unpretentious retreat is a world away from the more luxurious resorts just a few miles to the south. The lobby and public areas have a formal Caribbean motif, accented with green marble, arched doorways, and chandeliers. The simple and elegant guest rooms are furnished in a comfortable island style, and every room has a private balcony with ocean or sunset views looking out over the uncluttered beachfront. A thorough refurbishing in the mid-1990s has made this resort very popular with conventions and large groups. In fact, it is so popular that it is being gradually converted into a time-share property. Excursions are available to top-rated golf courses in the area.

Dining: A popular and well-run lobby restaurant serves an eclectic mix of continental, Southwestern, and Caribbean cuisine. Three other pool and beach bars serve snacks and refreshments throughout the day. The lounge features live music several nights a week.

Amenities: Concierge, room service, dry-cleaning and laundry services, overnight shoe shine, newspaper delivery, daily maid service, baby-sitting, express checkout, valet parking, free coffee in lobby. Kitchenettes and VCRs in suites, VCR rentals, Spectravision movie channels, outdoor heated swimming pool, beach, exercise room, bicycle rental, supervised children's programs, conference rooms, self-service Laundromat, car-rental desk, night-lit tennis court, water-sports equipment rentals, boutique, dive shop, summer turtle-watch program.

✪ **PGA National Resort & Spa.** 400 Avenue of the Champions, Palm Beach Gardens, FL 33418. ☎ **800/633-9150** or 561/627-2000. Fax 561/622-0261. 399 units. A/C MINIBAR TV TEL. Winter $305–$335 double; from $450 suite. Off-season $119–$139 double; from $195 suite. Children 16 and under stay free in parents' room. Special packages regularly available. AE, DC, DISC, MC, V. From I-95, take Exit 57B (PGA Blvd.) west and continue for approximately 2 miles to the resort entrance on the left.

This rambling resort, built in 1981, is known primarily as a golf destination. With five 18-hole courses on more than 2,300 acres, golfers and other sports-minded travelers will find plenty to keep them occupied—croquet, tennis, sailing, a health and fitness center, and a top-rated Mediterranean-style spa. Constant updating has kept the grounds and buildings in like-new condition. The par-72 Champion Course, redesigned in 1990 by Jack Nicklaus, is the resort's most valuable asset. More than 100 sand bunkers and plenty of water on 6,400-square-foot greens keep golfers of all levels alert. Watch out for hole 16.

When you are ready to rest, you will enjoy the comfortable and spacious accommodations and good food. Ample-size guest rooms are furnished with tasteful modern furnishings and tropical prints. Bathrooms are large and thoughtfully outfitted with cushy robes, good light, and magnifying mirrors. Although you are miles from the beach, the resort has nine pools and a private lake where you can ski or sail. As for views, the best you will get is the golf course or gardens.

Dining: Six restaurants and lounges include one offering superb northern Italian cuisine, a poolside grill, and another with a surprisingly delicious spa menu.

Amenities: Concierge, room service, evening turndown, overnight shoe shine, laundry, baby-sitting. This is the national headquarters of the PGA, so it's no surprise that there are five 18-hole tournament courses, plus the PGA National's Academy of Golf. There are also 19 clay tennis courts (12 lighted), nine swimming pools, a private beach on a 26-acre lake, water-sports equipment rentals, five tournament croquet lawns, five indoor racquetball courts, a full-service Mediterranean spa, aerobics studio, salon, and car rental.

INEXPENSIVE

Baron's Landing Hotel. 18125 Ocean Blvd. (Fla. A1A at the corner of Love St.), Jupiter, FL 33477. ☎ **561/746-8757.** 8 units. A/C TV. Winter from $90 double. Off-season from $50 double. No credit cards.

This charming family run inn is a perfect little beach getaway. It's not elegant, but it's cozy. A single-story motel fronting the Intracoastal Waterway is often full in winter with snowbirds, who dock their boats at the hotel's marina for weeks or months at a time. Nearly all rooms, which are situated around a small pool, have small kitchenettes. Each unit has a hodgepodge of used furniture, and some have pull-out sofas. Considering that you're a few blocks from some of the most expensive real estate in the country, this is a good deal.

Cologne Motel. 220 U.S. 1, Tequesta/Jupiter, FL 33469. ☎ **561/746-0616.** 9 units. A/C TV. Winter $50–$60 double. Off-season $45 double. Weekly rates available. MC, V.

The pleasant Hungarian couple that runs this modest roadside motel is always busy. After they finish the landscaping and pool, they hope to add more rooms to this nine-room, one-story little gem. The small rooms have just been updated with modest but bright bedspreads and curtains, and the newly retiled bathrooms are small but clean.

The area is safe if not scenic and only about a 5-minute drive to the beach. A more direct route by foot gets you there in about 15 minutes.

WHERE TO DINE

In addition to all the national fast-food joints that line Indiantown Road and U.S. 1, you'll find a number of touristy fish restaurants serving battered and fried everything. There are only a few really exceptional eateries in North Palm Beach and Jupiter. Try these listed below for guaranteed good food at reasonable prices.

Athenian Cafe. In the Chasewood Shopping Center, 6350 Indiantown Rd., Suite 7, Jupiter. ☎ **561/744-8327.** Main courses $5–$16. AE, MC, V. Mon–Sat 11am–9pm. Sun 4–9pm during season. GREEK.

Peter Papadelis and his family have been running this pleasant storefront cafe for nearly 10 years. Tucked in the corner of a strip mall, this place is a favorite with businesspeople, who stop in for a heaping portion of rich and meaty moussaka or a flaky spinach pie made fresh by Peter himself. You could make a meal of the thick and lemony Greek soup and the large fresh antipasto. In a town replete with tourist-priced fish joints, this is a welcome alternative. Early bird specials, served until 7pm, include many Greek favorites and broiled local fish with soup or salad, rice, vegetables, pita, dessert, and coffee or tea.

✪ **Capt. Charlie's Reef Grill.** 12846 U.S. 1 (behind O'Brian's and French Connection), Juno Beach. ☎ **561/624-9924.** Reservations not accepted. Main courses $9–$18. MC, V. Mon–Thurs 5–9:30pm, Fri–Sat 5–10pm. Tapas/dessert Mon–Thurs 3–11pm, Fri–Sat 3–midnight. SEAFOOD/CARIBBEAN.

For seafood with more integrity and taste than any other in the county, come to Capt. Charlie's. The trick here is to arrive early, ahead of the crowd of local foodies. Here you'll find more than a dozen daily local-catch specials prepared any way you like. Do sample the imaginative appetizers, which include Caribbean chili, a rich chunky stew filled with fresh seafood; or a tuna spring roll big enough for two. The enormous Cuban crab cake is moist and perfectly browned without tasting fried and is served with homemade mango chutney and black beans and rice. A newly opened tapas and dessert bar features both traditional as well as tropical tapas. Sit at the bar to watch the hectic kitchen turn out perfect dishes on the 14-burner stove. Somehow the pleasant waitresses keep their cool even when the place is packed. Service is not white glove, and the ambience is early 1970s nautical. Concentrate instead on the terrific seafood and the extensive, affordable wine and beer selection—more than 30 of each from around the world.

Nick's Tomato Pie. 1697 W. Indiantown Rd. (1 mile east of I-95, Exit 59A), Jupiter. ☎ **561/744-8935.** Reservations accepted only for parties of 6 or more. Main courses $11–$19; pastas $9–$14. AE, DC, DISC, MC, V. Mon–Thurs 5–10pm, Fri–Sat 4:30–11pm, Sun 4:30–10pm. ITALIAN.

A Bennigan's-style family restaurant, Nick's is a popular attraction in otherwise food-poor Jupiter. With a huge menu of pastas, pizzas, fish, chicken, and beef, this cheery (and noisy) spot has something for everyone. On Saturday night you'll see lots of couples on dates and some families leaving with take-out bags left over from the impossibly generous portions. The homemade sausage is a delicious treat, served with sautéed onions and peppers. The pollo marsala, too, is good and authentic.

No Anchovies! 2650 PGA Blvd., Palm Beach Gardens. ☎ **561/622-7855.** Pizza and pasta $7–$13; main courses $10–$17. AE, DC, MC, V. Mon–Thurs 11:30am–2:30pm and 4:30–10:30pm, Fri–Sat 11:30am–2:30pm and 4:30–11pm, Sun 4:30–10:30pm. ITALIAN.

This large and colorful restaurant is popular with families who appreciate the large portions and reasonably priced children's specials. An equally colorful menu offers a large variety of pastas, pizzas, salads, and a variety of meat and fish specials. Mix and match your pasta with half a dozen sauces. My favorite is the thick and simple fillete de tomato over fusilli. You may also want to try some of the delicious chicken or meats prepared on the oak-burning grill.

JUPITER & NORTHERN PALM BEACH COUNTY AFTER DARK

If you have tired of your hotel lounge, you'll want to do what most residents and visitors to this area do—drive south to West Palm Beach's downtown scene where live music, cafes, dance clubs, and bars offer something for everyone (see "The Palm Beaches After Dark," above).

With one notable exception, there just isn't much going on here after dark. **Club Safari,** 4000 PGA Blvd. (just east of I-95), in Palm Beach Garden's Marriott Hotel (☎ **561/622-7024**), is more hip than any hotel dance club I have ever seen, although the safari theme is a bit much. The huge, sunken dance floor is surrounded by vines and lanky, potted trees. Nearby, a large Buddha statue blows steam and smoke while waving its burly arms in front of a young gyrating crowd. There is deejay music, a large video screen, and a modest cover charge on the weekends.

9

The Treasure Coast

by Victoria Pesce Elliott

Over the past few years, the Treasure Coast has been attracting unprecedented numbers of new residents. Yet, this area retains its small-town feel. The growth is happening at a reasonable pace, and the influx has brought with it a renewed interest in renovating the once abandoned downtown areas. The result is a batch of freshly spruced up accommodations, shops, and restaurants from Stuart to Sebastian. Interspersed along the way are miles and miles of wild rivers, state parks, and of course beaches.

In addition to a number of welcoming small communities and vast array of wildlife, the Treasure Coast also has a history rich and colorful as its provocative nickname.

For hundreds of years, Florida's east coast was a popular stopover for European explorers, many of whom arrived from Spain to fill coffers with gold and silver. Rough weather and poor navigation often took a toll on their ships; but in 1715, a violent hurricane stunned the northeast coast and sank an entire fleet of Spanish ships laden with gold. Though Spanish salvagers worked for years to collect the lost treasure, much of it remained buried beneath the shifting sand. Then, builders hired to excavate the area in the 1950s and 1960s discovered centuries-old coins under their tractors.

Today, on these same beaches you'll find an occasional treasure hunter trolling the sand with a metal detector, and swimmers and sunbathers who come to enjoy the stretches of beach that extend into the horizon. The sea, especially around Sebastian Inlet, is a mecca for surfers who find some of the largest swells in the state.

The Treasure Coast, for the purposes of this chapter, runs roughly from Hobe Sound in the south to the Sebastian Inlet in the north, encompassing some of Martin, St. Lucie, and Indian River counties and all of Hutchinson Island.

Florida's largest inland lake, Lake Okeechobee, a favorite destination for anglers, lies just west of this coastal area and is covered at the end of this chapter.

ESSENTIALS
GETTING TO THE TREASURE COAST

Since virtually every town described in this chapter runs along a straight route, along the Atlantic Ocean, I've given all directions below.

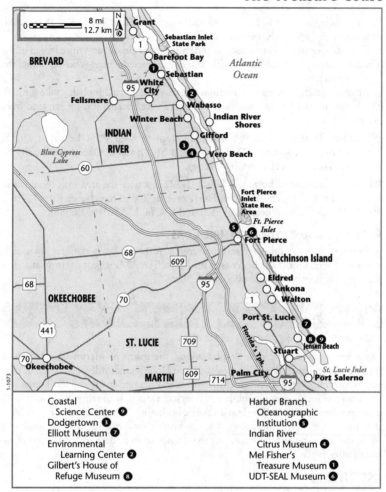

Coastal
    Science Center **9**
Dodgertown **3**
Elliott Museum **7**
Environmental
    Learning Center **2**
Gilbert's House of
    Refuge Museum **8**

Harbor Branch
    Oceanographic
    Institution **5**
Indian River
    Citrus Museum **4**
Mel Fisher's
    Treasure Museum **1**
UDT-SEAL Museum **6**

BY PLANE   The **Palm Beach International Airport** (☎ **561/471-7420**), located about 35 miles south of Stuart, is the closest gateway to this region if you're flying. See the "Getting Around" section on Palm Beach in chapter 8 for complete information. If you are traveling to the northern part of the Treasure Coast, **Melbourne International Airport,** off U.S. 1 in Melbourne (☎ **407/723-6227**), is less than 25 miles north of Sebastian and about 35 miles north of Vero Beach.

BY CAR   If you're driving up or down the Florida coast, you'll probably reach the Treasure Coast via I-95. If you are heading to Stuart or Jensen Beach, take Exit 61 (Route 76/Tanner Highway) or 62 (Route 714); to Port St. Lucie or Fort Pierce, take Exit 63 or 64 (Okeechobee Road); to Vero Beach, take Exit 68 (S.R. 60); to Sebastian, take Exit 69 (County Road).

You can also take the Florida Turnpike; this toll road is the fastest (but not the most scenic) route, especially if you're coming from Orlando. If you are heading to Stuart or Jensen Beach, take Exit 133; to Fort Pierce, take Exit 152 (Okeechobee Road); to

Port St. Lucie, take Exit 142 or 152; to Vero Beach, take Exit 193 (S.R. 60); to Sebastian, take Exit 193 to S.R. 60 east and connect to I-95 north.

If you are staying in Hutchinson Island, which runs almost the entire length of the Treasure Coast, you should check with your hotel, or see the listings below, to find the best route to take.

Finally, if you're coming directly from the west coast, you'll probably take S.R. 70, which runs north of Lake Okeechobee to Fort Pierce, located just up the road from Stuart.

BY RAIL   Amtrak (☎ **800/USA-RAIL**) stops in West Palm Beach, at 201 S. Tamarind Ave. (☎ **800/872-7245** or 561/832-6169); and in Okeechobee at 801 N. Parrot Ave., off U.S. 441 north (no phone).

BY BUS   Greyhound buses (☎ **800/231-2222**) service the area with terminals in Stuart, at 1308 S. Federal Hwy.; in Fort Pierce, at 7005 Okeechobee Rd. (☎ 561/461-3299); and in Vero Beach, at U.S. 1 and S.R. 60 (☎ 561/562-6588).

GETTING AROUND THE TREASURE COAST

A car is a necessity in this large and rural region. Although heavy traffic is not usually a problem here, on the smaller coastal roads, like Fla. A1A, expect to travel at a slow pace, usually between 25 and 40 miles an hour.

1 Hobe Sound, Stuart & Jensen Beach

130 miles SE of Orlando, 98 miles N of Miami

Once just a stretch of pineapple plantations, the towns of Martin County, which include Stuart, Jensen Beach, Port Salerno, and Hobe Sound, still retain much of their rural character. Dotted between citrus groves and mangroves are modest homes and an occasional high-rise condominium. Though the area is definitely still seasonal (with a distinct rise in street and pedestrian traffic beginning after the Christmas holidays), the atmosphere is pure small town. Even in historic downtown Stuart, the result of a successful, ongoing restoration, expect the storefronts to be dark and the streets abandoned after 10pm.

ESSENTIALS

The **Stuart/Martin County Chamber of Commerce,** 1650 S. Kanner Hwy., Stuart, FL 34994 (☎ **800/524-9704** in Florida, or 561/287-1088; fax 561/220-3437), is the region's main source for information. The **Jensen Beach Chamber of Commerce,** 1901 NE Jensen Beach Blvd., Jensen Beach, FL 34957 (☎ **561/334-3444**), also offers visitors information about its simple beachfront town.

OUTDOOR ACTIVITIES: THE BEACHES & BEYOND

BEACHES   Beaches are easily accessible throughout Hutchinson Island, the long, thin barrier island that stretches north and south from Stuart. Look for "coastal access" signs pointing the way to the public beach areas.

The best of them is **Bathtub Beach,** on North Hutchinson Island. Here, the calm waters are protected by coral reefs and visitors can explore the region on dune and river trails. Pick a secluded spot on the wide stretch of beach or enjoy marked nature trails across the street. Facilities include showers and toilets open during the day. To reach the park, head east on Ocean Boulevard (Stuart Causeway) and turn right onto MacArthur Boulevard. The beach is about a mile ahead on your left, just north of the Indian River Plantation. Parking is plentiful.

Wildlife Exploration: From Gators to Manatees to Turtles

One of the most scenic areas on this stretch of the coast is ✪ **Jonathan Dickinson State Park,** at 16450 S. Federal Hwy. (U.S. 1), Hobe Sound (☎ **561/ 546-2771**). The park is intentionally low managed so that it will resemble the habitat of hundreds of years ago, before Europeans started chopping, dredging, and "improving" the area. Dozens of species of Florida's unique wildlife, including alligators and manatees, live on more than 11,300 acres. Bird watchers will want to bring their books and binoculars to spot the many ospreys, woodpeckers, ibises, herons, anhingas, egrets, and even some bald eagles. Deer, reptiles, tortoises, and snakes also call this area home. There are concession areas for daytime snacks and four different scenic nature and bike trails through the scrublands and flatwoods. You can also rent canoes from the concession stand to explore the Loxahatchee River on your own. Admission is $3.25 per car of up to eight adults. Day hikers, bikers, and walkers pay $1 each. The park is open from 8am until sundown. See "Where to Stay," below, for details on camping.

Nearby is **Hobe Sound Wildlife Refuge,** on North Beach Road off S.R. 708, at the north end of Jupiter Island (☎ **561/546-6141**). This is one of the best places to see sea turtles that nest on the shore in the summer months, especially in June and July. Because it's home to a large variety of other plant and animal species, the park is worth visiting at other times of year as well. Admission is $4 per car, and the preserve is open daily from sunrise to sunset. Exact times are posted at each entrance and change seasonally.

CANOEING **Jonathan Dickinson State Park** (see the "Wildlife Exploration" box, above) is the area's most popular for canoeing. The route winds through a variety of botanical habitats. You'll see lots of birds, and, of course, the occasional manatee. Canoes cost $6 per hour. The concession is open Monday to Friday from 9am to 5pm and Saturday and Sunday from 8am to 5pm.

FISHING Several independent charter captains operate on Hutchinson Island and Jensen Beach. One of the largest operators is the **Sailfish Marina,** 3565 SE St. Lucie Blvd., in Stuart (☎ **561/221-9456**), which maintains half a dozen charter boats for fishing excursions year-round. Also on site is a bait and tackle shop and a knowledgeable, helpful staff.

GOLF The pricey **Indian River Plantation Beach Resort** is a terrific destination for golfers, but unless you're a guest at the resort or are playing with a member, you cannot play these courses. Instead, try the **Champions Club at Summerfield,** on U.S. 1, south of Cove Road in Stuart (☎ **561/283-1500**), a somewhat challenging championship course designed by Tom Fazio. This rural course, the best in the area, was built in 1994 and offers great glimpses of wildlife amid the wetlands. In winter, greens fees are around $60, and carts are mandatory. Reservations are a must and are taken 4 days in advance.

SCUBA DIVING & SNORKELING Three popular artificial reefs off Hutchinson Island provide excellent scenery for both novice and experienced divers. The **USS Rankin,** sunk in 120 feet of water in 1988, lies 7 miles east-northeast of the St. Lucie Inlet. The 58-foot-deep **Donaldson Reef** consists of a cluster of plumbing fixtures sunk in 58 feet of water. It's located due east of the Gilbert's House of Refuge Museum. The **Ernst Reef,** made from old tires, is a 60-foot dive located 4½ miles east-southeast of the St. Lucie inlet.

Deep Divers Unlimited, 6083 SE Federal Hwy. (corner of Cove Road and U.S. 1), Stuart (☎ **561/286-0078**), arranges two-tank dive trips to these sites and others starting at about $37 a person. A full set of gear will cost you another $25 for the day. They can also rent gear to those wanting to explore the area's best snorkeling at Bathtub Beach (see "Beaches," above). There's a natural coral reef within swimming distance of shore.

SEEING THE SIGHTS

✪ **Coastal Science Center.** 890 NE Ocean Blvd. (across the street from the Elliott Museum), Hutchinson Island, Stuart. ☎ **561/225-0505.** Admission $3.50 adults, $2 children 3–12, free for children under 3. Mon–Sat 10am–5pm.

Opened by the South Florida Oceanographic Society in late 1994, this 44-acre site surrounded by coastal hammock and mangroves is its own little ecosystem and serves as an outdoor classroom, teaching visitors about the region's flora and fauna. The modest building houses saltwater tanks and wet and dry "discovery tables" with small indigenous animals. The incredibly eager staff of volunteers encourage visitors to wander the lush, well-marked nature trails.

✪ **Elliott Museum.** 825 NE Ocean Blvd. (north of Indian River Plantation Resort), Hutchinson Island, Stuart. ☎ **561/225-1961.** Admission $6 adults, $2 children 6–13, free for children 5 and under. Daily 10am–4pm.

A treasure trove of early Americana, the Elliott Museum is a rich tribute to inventors, sports heroes, and collectors. A series of life-size dioramas depicts an apothecary, a barbershop, a blacksmith forge, a clock and watch shop, and other old-fashioned commercial enterprises.

Sports lovers will appreciate the baseball memorabilia—a half-million dollars' worth—including an autographed item from every player in the Baseball Hall of Fame.

A gallery of patents and models of machines, invented by the museum's founder, Harmon Parker Elliott, and his son, provides an intriguing glimpse into the business of tinkering. Their collection of restored antique cars is also pretty impressive. Expect to spend at least an hour seeing the highlights.

Gilbert's House of Refuge Museum. 301 SE MacArthur Blvd. (south of Indian River Plantation resort), Hutchinson Island, Stuart. ☎ **561/225-1875.** Admission $4 adults, $2 children 6–13, free for children 5 and under. Daily 10am–4pm.

Gilbert's, the oldest structure in Martin County, dates from 1875, when it functioned as one of 10 such rescue centers for shipwrecked sailors. Restored to its original condition along the rocky shores, the house now displays marine artifacts and turn-of-the-century lifesaving equipment and photographs and is worth a quick visit to get a feel for the area's early days.

A BOAT TOUR

✪ The *Loxahatchee Queen*, a 35-foot pontoon boat (☎ 800/746-1466 or 561/746-1466) in Jonathan Dickinson State Park in Hobe Sound, makes daily tours of the area's otherwise inaccessible backwater where curious alligators, manatees, eagles, and tortoises often peek out to see who's in their yard. Try to catch the 2-hour tour, given Wednesday to Sunday as tide permits, when it includes a stop at Trapper Nelson's home. Known as the "Wildman of Loxahatchee," Nelson lived in primitive conditions—on a remote stretch of the water in a log cabin fashioned from his own hand—which are preserved for visitors to see. Tours leave four times daily at 9am, 11am, 1pm, and 3pm and cost $10 for adults, $5 for children 6 to 12, and free for children 5 and under. See the "Wildlife Excursions" box, above, for more information on the park.

SHOPPING

Downtown Stuart's historic district, along Flagler Avenue between Confusion Corner and St. Lucie Avenue, offers shoppers diversity and quality in a small old-town setting. Shops offer a range of goods: antique bric-a-brac, old lamps and fixtures, books, gourmet foods, furnishings, and souvenirs.

B&A Farmer's Market at 2885 SE Federal Hwy. (in front of B&A Flea market), Stuart (☎ **561/223-1570**), sells all types of locally grown produce, includ-ing the famous Indian River grapefruit and oranges, watermelons, berries, bananas, and other tropical fruits. You can arrange to have fruits and baskets shipped.

WHERE TO STAY

Although the area boasts some beautiful beaches, the bulk of the hotel scene is down-town, where the nicer (and more reasonably priced) accommodations can be found among the shops and restaurants. There are, however, a few excellent beachfront hotels and inns. One of the bigger hotel chains in the area is the **Holiday Inn.** Its recently renovated, stunning beachfront property is at 3793 NE Ocean Blvd., Jensen Beach (☎ **800/992-4747** or 561/225-3000). Holiday Inn also has a downtown location at 1209 S. Federal Hwy. (☎ 561/287-6200). This simple two-story building on a busy main road is kept in very good shape and is convenient to Stuart's downtown historic district.

VERY EXPENSIVE

✪ **Indian River Plantation Marriott Resort.** 555 NE Ocean Blvd., Hutchinson Island, Stuart, FL 34996. ☎ **800/775-5936** or 561/225-3700. Fax 561/225-0003. 306 units. A/C TV TEL. Winter $239–$279 double; from $329 suite. Off-season $119–$149 double; from $199 suite. AE, CB, DC, DISC, MC, V. From downtown Stuart, take E. Ocean Blvd. over two bridges to NE Ocean Blvd.; turn right.

This sprawling 190-acre compound offers so many diversions for active (or not-so-active) vacationers, you won't want to leave. Undergoing $6 million in renovations during the first months of 1998, Indian River is Hutchinson Island's best resort, occu-pying the lush grounds of a former pineapple plantation. Family oriented activities include tennis, golfing, and boating. Sportfishing (especially for sailfish) is a big draw here, as are scuba diving and other water sports.

The grand, white lattice-and-wicker lobby is filled with a jungle of plants, and large windows overlook the hotel's swimming pool and tiki bar. Generously sized rooms, some with fully equipped kitchens, are decorated with colorful spreads and draperies. Some rooms could use a thorough renovation, since old fixtures have suffered from years of exposure to sea air and salt.

Be sure to sign up for a "turtle watch" in the summer months to watch the large tur-tles crawl onto the sand to lay their eggs.

Dining/Diversions: Scalawags, a seafood restaurant, is the resort's top dining room and is popular with locals. A less-formal restaurant serves continental breakfast, lunch, and all-day snacks. There's live music nightly in two bars.

Amenities: Room service, laundry and dry-cleaning services, newspaper delivery, baby-sitting, express checkout, on-property transportation, free juice in lobby. Four outdoor pools, beach, health club, Jacuzzi, 18-hole golf course, nature trails, some kitchenettes, sundeck, 13 tennis court (5 night-lit), nearby racquetball courts, water-sports equipment, jogging track, bicycle rental, game room, children's program,

Spectravision movie channels, self-service Laundromat, conference rooms, car-rental desk, boutiques.

MODERATE

⭕ **Harborfront Inn Bed & Breakfast.** 310 Atlanta Ave., Stuart, FL 34994. ☎ **800/ 294-1703** or 561/288-7289. Fax 561/221-0474. www.harborfrontinn.com. 6 units. A/C TV. $80–$100 double; from $125 suite, $145 suite with whirlpool and outdoor spa. Off-season specials. Rates include breakfast. No smoking and no children. AE, DISC, MC, V. From I-95 take Exit 61 east to U.S. 1 north; turn left on W. Ocean Blvd. and then make the first right (Atlanta Ave.).

The Harborfront Inn has the advantage of being right on the river where you can sail and ski. It consists of a series of little blue-trimmed shingled cottages within walking distance of the restaurants of downtown Stuart. Each room in this highly recommended B&B has its own private entrance making it more like a rambling inn. Also, every accommodation has a sitting area and private bathroom. The two best rooms are the bright Garden Suite, which has a queen-size bed, rattan furnishings, and a deck with river and garden views; and the Guest House, which has an extra-large bathroom with two sinks and can be rented with an adjoining full kitchen.

Dining: The inn's cozy public areas are surrounded by an enclosed porch where breakfast is served. The morning meal usually includes fresh fruit from the trees that grow on the property.

Amenities: Kitchenettes in cottages, VCRs in suites, a Jacuzzi and sundeck, watersports equipment rentals.

⭕ **The Home Place.** 501 Akron Ave., Stuart, FL 34994. ☎ **561/220-9148.** Fax 561/ 221-3265. 4 units, all with bathroom (1 with private bathroom down a hall). Year-round $85–$110. Off-season and weekday specials. Rates include full breakfast. No smoking and no children under 12. MC, V. From I-95 take Exit 61 east on S.R. 76 about 7 miles to U.S. 1. Turn left. Continue ½ mile to W. Ocean Blvd.; turn left. Turn right on Akron.

Perfect for those who like the feel of a classic B&B, Home Place is as charming as one can get. Suzanne and Michael Pescetelli are the gracious owners of this historic home, and they're just the kind of innkeepers you want in a classic little bed-and-breakfast. They offer taste, style, good conversation, superb homemade sweets, wine, an always-open fridge, and a perfectly maintained inn, which is a favorite locale for weddings. They live in the adjacent building, just a few steps from the 1913 guest house and beautifully landscaped pool and Jacuzzi area. You'll be comfortable in any of the Victorian-trimmed rooms chock-full of warm details like lace curtains, old steamer trunks, and crystal decanters. The large captain's room is a favorite for its size and big fluffy bed. While you're a few miles inland from the beach, you're only a few blocks from the quaint and rejuvenated downtown area. There isn't much in the way of grounds or amenities, but there is a medium-sized pool and sundeck with lounge chairs and cushy towels.

Hutchinson Inn. 9750 S. Ocean Dr. (Fla. A1A), Jensen Beach, FL 34957. ☎ **561/ 229-2000.** 21 units. A/C TV TEL. Winter from $90 double; $150–$225 efficiency or suite. Off-season $65 double; from $95–$150 efficiency or suite. Rates include continental breakfast. MC, V. From I-95 take Exit 61 east to Indian St.; turn right to St. Lucie Blvd.; turn left and continue to the bridge where you will turn right onto E. Ocean Blvd. The inn is approximately 8 miles ahead.

It doesn't look like much from the road—only the tennis court is visible—but you'll soon happen upon striking white gazebos dotting thick green lawns. Located directly on the beach, the Hutchinson Inn is a quiet and charming two-story hideaway. Unfortunately, so many people know about it that it's usually booked a year in advance in high season.

The newly refurbished rooms have rattan furnishings; sofas convert into pull-out beds, and several rooms can be joined to accommodate large families.

Amenities: A good swimming beach, a large outdoor pool, one outdoor night-lit tennis court, water-sports equipment, bicycle rentals, a self-service Laundromat. Freshly baked cookies are offered each evening before bedtime.

CAMPNG

There are comfortable campsites in **Jonathan Dickinson State Park** in Hobe Sound (see the "Wildlife Exploration" box, above). You can stay overnight in rustic cabins or in your tent or camper in two different sections of the park. The River Camp area offers the benefit of the nearby Loxahatchee River, while the Pine Grove site has beautiful shade trees. There are concession areas for daytime snacks and 135 campsites with showers, clean rest rooms, water, optional electricity, and an open-fire pit for cooking. Overnight rates in the winter are $18 without electricity, $20 with electricity. In the summer, rates are about $14, for four people.

For a more cushy camping experience, reserve a wood-sided cabin with a furnished kitchen, a bathroom with shower, heat and air-conditioning, and an outside grill. Bring your own linens. Cabins rent for $65 and up a night and sleep four people comfortably, six if your group is really into togetherness. Call ☎ **800/746-1466** or 561/546-2771 Monday to Friday from 9am to 5pm well in advance to reserve a spot. A $50 key deposit is required.

WHERE TO DINE
EXPENSIVE

Eleven Maple Street. 11 Maple St., Jensen Beach. ☎ **561/334-7714.** Reservations recommended. Main courses $15–$25. MC, V. Wed–Sun 6–10pm. Head east on Jensen Beach Blvd. and turn right after the railroad tracks. AMERICAN.

The most highly rated restaurant in Jensen Beach, Eleven Maple Street occupies a lovely little house with a white picket fence, French doors, lace curtains, and pink-clothed tables. Dining is both indoors and out, in any one of a series of cozy dining rooms or on a covered patio surrounded by gardens. Straightforward meat and fish dishes run the gamut from local seafood to game and poultry like venison and duck. Maine lobster, filet mignon, and pastas are also available, and most everything is spiced with fresh-picked herbs from the restaurant's own organic garden.

✪ **Flagler Grill.** 47 SW Flagler Ave. (just before the Roosevelt Bridge), downtown Stuart. ☎ **561/221-9517.** Reservations strongly suggested in season. Main courses $17–$23. AE, MC, V. Winter daily 5:30–10pm. Off-season Thurs–Sat 5:30–9:30pm. Lounge open to 11:30pm. CONTEMPORARY AMERICAN.

In the heart of historic downtown, this Manhattan-style bistro serves up classics with a twist. The dishes are not so unusual as to alienate the conservative pink-shirted golfers who frequent the place, yet they're fresh and light enough to quench the appetites of the more adventurous—for example, the saffron and mushroom pasta with Cajun shrimp and roasted tomatoes. The menu changes every few weeks, so see what your server recommends (ask for Victoria; she's friendly and knowledgeable). It's hard to go wrong with any of the many salads, pastas, fishes, or delectable beef choices. The desserts, too, are worth the calories.

MODERATE

Black Marlin. 53 W. Osceola St., downtown Stuart. ☎ **561/286-3126.** Reservations not accepted. Salads and sandwiches $4–$8; full meals $9–$24. AE, MC, V. Mon–Thurs 5–10pm, Fri–Sat 5–11pm (the bar is open later). FLORIDA REGIONAL.

Although it sports the look and feel of an English pub, the Black Marlin offers regional flavor. The salmon BLT is typical of the dishes here—grilled salmon on a toasted bun topped with bacon, lettuce, tomato, and coleslaw. Designer pizzas are topped with shrimp, roasted red peppers, and the like; and main dishes, all of which are served with vegetables and potatoes, include lobster tail with a honey-mustard sauce, and a charcoal-grilled chicken breast served on radicchio with caramelized onions.

Conchy Joe's Seafood. 3945 NE Indian River Dr. (½ mile from the Jensen Beach Causeway), Jensen Beach. ☎ **561/334-1130.** Main courses $12–$20. AE, DISC, MC, V. Daily 11:30am–2:30pm and 5–10pm (happy hour 3–6pm). SEAFOOD.

Known for fresh seafood and Old Florida hospitality, Conchy Joe's enjoys an excellent reputation that's far bigger than the restaurant itself. Dining is either indoors, at red-and-white cloth-covered tables, or on a covered patio overlooking the St. Lucie River. The restaurant features a wide variety of freshly shucked shellfish and daily-catch selections that are baked, broiled, or fried. Beer is the drink of choice here, though other beverages and a full bar are available. Conchy Joe's has been the most active place in Jensen Beach since it opened in 1983. The large bar is especially popular at night and during weekday happy hours.

INEXPENSIVE

✪ **Bubba's Fish Camp.** 421 S. Federal Hwy. (at base Roosevelt Bridge), Stuart. ☎ **561/220-3747.** Full meals $8–$10; seafood specials $8–$12. AE, MC, V. Daily 11am–10pm and later on weekends. Call for details on weekend breakfasts. SEAFOOD/SOUTHERN

Owned by the same family who created the lovely B&B Home Place and just a stone's throw from there is an ultra-casual spot designed to resemble an old-Florida fish camp. Don't miss the great crawfish gumbo, corn bread, catfish, creamy spinach, hush puppies (fried cornmeal), and fried green tomatoes, too. After 4pm, you'll find bargain deals on hearty Southern classics like meat loaf, baked Virginia ham with red-eye gravy, fried chicken, or pork chops. Each includes a choice of delicious side dishes. Fresh and crispy onion rings are actually served on tiny bathroom plunger handles. Locals and highway travelers line up outside the screen porch to get into this rustic eatery just at the base of the new Roosevelt Bridge.

✪ **Nature's Way Cafe.** 25 SW Osceola St., in the Post Office Arcade, Stuart. ☎ **561/220-7306.** Sandwiches and salads $4–$7; juices and shakes $1–$3. No credit cards. Mon–Fri 10am–4pm, Sat 11am–3pm. HEALTH FOOD.

This lovely clean and green dining room has dozens of little tables, a few bar stools, and some sidewalk seating, too. A sort of health-food deli, Nature's Way excels in putting out quick and nutritious meals like huge salads, vegetarian sandwiches, and frozen yogurts. Try some of the homemade baked goods. Sit outside on quaint Osceola Street or ask them to pack your lunch for you to take to the beach.

STUART & JENSEN BEACH AFTER DARK

Local restaurants serve as the nightlife centers of Stuart and Jensen Beach. And "night" ends pretty early here, even on the weekends. The bar at the Black Marlin (see "Where to Dine," above) is popular with local professionals and tourists alike.

No list of Jensen nightlife would be complete without mention of Conchy Joe's Seafood (see "Where to Dine," above), one of the region's most active spots. Inside, locals chug beer and watch a large-screen TV, while outside on the waterfront patio live bands perform a few nights a week for a raucous crowd of dancers. Happy hours, weekdays from 3 to 6pm, draw large crowds with low-priced drinks and snacks. No cover.

In a strip mall just outside of downtown you'll find pickup trucks as far as the eye can see parked outside **The Rock'in Horse,** 1580 S. Federal Hwy. (U.S. 1), Stuart (☎ **561/286-1281**). It's a real locals' country-and-western spot that rocks, especially on Tuesday night, when women drink all night for $5. Bring your hat and boots for line dancing, beer drinking, and a good time in one of the only real late-night spots in town. Cover varies.

The centerpiece of Stuart's slowly expanding cultural offerings is the newly restored **Lyric Theater,** at 59 SW Flagler Ave. (☎ **561/220-1942**). This beautiful 1920s-era, 600-seat theater hosts a variety of shows and films throughout the year. Programs run the gamut from amateur plays to top-name theatrical shows, poetry readings, and concerts.

2 Port St. Lucie, Fort Pierce & North Hutchinson Island

7 miles N of Stuart

Port St. Lucie and Fort Pierce, two Old Florida towns, thrive on sportfishing. A seemingly endless row of piers jut out along the Intracoastal Waterway and the Fort Pierce Inlet for both river and ocean runs. Here visitors can also dive, snorkel, beachcomb, and sunbathe in an area that hasn't been visited by the overdevelopment that's altered its neighbors to the south and north.

Most sightseeing takes place along the main beach road. Driving along Fla. A1A on Hutchinson Island, you'll discover several secluded beach clubs interspersed with 1950s-style homes, a few small inns, grungy raw bars, and a few high-rise condominiums. Much of this island is government owned and kept undeveloped for the public's enjoyment.

ESSENTIALS

The **St. Lucie County Chamber of Commerce,** 2200 Virginia Ave., Fort Pierce 34982 (☎ **561/595-9999**), is the region's main source of information. Another location is at 1626 SE Port St. Lucie Blvd., in Port St. Lucie. These are open Monday through Friday from 9am to 5pm.

BEACHES & NATURE PRESERVES

North Hutchinson Island's beaches are the most pristine in this area. You won't find restaurants, hotels, or shopping; instead, spend your time swimming, surfing, fishing, and diving. Most of the beaches are private along this stretch of the Atlantic Ocean. Thankfully, the state has set aside some of the best areas for the public.

Fort Pierce Inlet State Recreation Area (☎ **561/468-3985**) is a stunning 340-acre park with almost 4,000 feet of sandy shores that was once the training ground for the original navy frogmen. A short nature trail leads through a canopy of live oaks, cabbage palms, sea grapes, and strangler figs. The western side of the area has swamps of red mangroves that are home to fiddler crabs, osprey, and a multitude of wading birds. Jack Island State Preserve, in the State Recreation Area, is popular with bird watchers and offers hiking and nature trails. Jutting out into the Indian River, the mangrove-covered peninsula contains several marked trails, varying in distance from a half mile to over 4 miles. The trails go through mangrove forests and lead to a short observation tower.

The best beach here is called Jetty Park, in the northern part of the park. Families enjoy the large picnic areas and barbecue grills. There are rest rooms and outdoor showers, and swimmers are looked after by lifeguards.

The park is located at 905 Shorewinds Dr., north of Fort Pierce Inlet. To get there from I-95, take Exit 66 east (Route 68) and turn left onto U.S. 1 north; in about 2 miles, you will see signs to Fla. A1A and the North Bridge Causeway. Turn right on A1A and cross over to North Hutchinson Island. Admission is $3.25 per vehicle, and it's open daily from 8am to sunset.

SPORTS & OUTDOOR ACTIVITIES

BASEBALL The **New York Mets** hold spring training in Port St. Lucie from late February through March at the **Thomas J. White Stadium,** 525 NW Peacock Blvd. (☎ 561/871-2115). Tickets cost $9 to $12. During the summer, their farm team, the Port St. Lucie Mets, plays home games in the stadium.

FISHING The **Fort Pierce City Marina,** 1 Avenue A, Fort Pierce (☎ 561/464-1245), has more than a dozen charter captains who keep their motors running for anglers anxious to catch a few. The price starts at $150 per person for half-day tours, depending on the season. Charters are organized on an as-desired basis. In general, plan to arrive very early in the morning (by 6am) before all the other early birds have gotten the worms.

GOLF The most notable courses in Port Saint Lucie are at the **PGA Golf Club at the Reserve** (☎ 561/467-1300) at 1916 Perfect Dr. PGA's first public golf course opened in January 1996 and was designed by Tom Fazio. The club will soon complete its fourth 18-hole course. The South Course, a classic Old Florida–style course, is set on wetlands and offers views of native wildlife. It is the most popular. Greens fees are under $60.

SEEING THE SIGHTS

Harbor Branch Oceanographic Institution. 5600 U.S. 1 N., Fort Pierce. ☎ **800/333-4264** or 561/465-2400. www.hboi.edu.tours@hboi.edu. Admission $6 adults, $4 children 3–13, free for children 5 and under. Mon–Sat 10am–4pm (tours scheduled at 10am, noon, and 2pm), Sun noon–5pm (tours scheduled at noon and 2pm). Arrive at least 20 minutes before tour.

Harbor Branch is a working nonprofit scientific institute that studies oceanic resources and welcomes visitors on regularly scheduled tours. The first stop is the J. Seward Johnson Marine Education Center, which houses institute-built submersibles that are used to conduct marine research at depths of up to 3,000 feet. A video details current research projects, and several large aquariums simulate the environments of the Indian River Lagoon and a saltwater reef. Tour-goers are then shuttled by minibus to the Aqua-Culture Farming Center, a research facility containing shallow tanks growing seaweed and other oceanic plants. The new Lagoon Explorer Cruise, examining the Indian River Lagoon, departs at 10am, noon, and 2pm; price is $15 adults, $12 children 3 to 13.

UDT-SEAL Museum. 3300 N. Fla. A1A, Fort Pierce. ☎ **561/595-5845.** Admission $3.25 adults, $1.25 children, free for children 6 and under. Mon–Sat 10am–4pm, Sun noon–4pm. Closed Mon in off-season.

Florida is full of unique museums, but none are more curious than the UDT-SEAL Museum, a most peculiar tribute to the secret forces of the U.S. Navy frogmen and their successors, the SEAL teams. Chronological displays trace the history of these clandestine divers and detail their most important achievements. The best exhibits are those of the intricately detailed equipment used by the navy's most elite members.

A BOAT TOUR

The Spirit of St. Joseph Cruise Line, 424 Seaway Dr., Fort Pierce (☎ **561/ 467-BOAT**), takes up to 200 passengers on guided tours of the Indian River. Most of the regularly scheduled cruises include a meal and/or entertainment, which is good because scenery in this sleepy region is relatively monotonous. Phone for fluctuating prices and tour times.

WHERE TO STAY

The Port St. Lucie mainland is pretty run-down, but there are a number of inexpensive hotel options on scenic Hutchinson Island that are both charming and well priced. Probably the best option is the **Hampton Inn** (☎ **800/426-7866** or 561/ 460-9855), 2831 Reynolds Dr., which is relatively new and beautifully maintained. However, if you want to be closer to the water, try the **Days Inn Hutchinson Island,** 1920 Seaway Dr. (☎ **800/325-2525** or 561/461-8737), a small motel that sits along the intracoastal inlet and is simple but very well kept.

Budget travelers will be glad to know about the **Edgewater Motel and Apartments,** 1160 Seaway Dr. (next door to and under the same ownership as the Harbor Light Inn), Fort Pierce (☎ **800/433-0004** or 561/468-3555). Motel rooms start at less than $50 in high season and efficiencies are also available from $80. Guests can enjoy a private pool, shuffleboard courts, and nearby fishing pier.

EXPENSIVE

Club Med—Sandpiper. 3500 SE Morningside Blvd., Port St. Lucie, FL 34952. ☎ **800/ CLUB-MED** or 561/335-4400. Fax 561/398-5101. www.clubmed.com. 331 units. A/C TV TEL. $165–$270 per person, based on double occupancy. Off-season $150–$255 per person, based on double occupancy. Rates include three meals per day. AE, MC, V. From U.S. 1 south, turn left onto Westmoreland Blvd.; turn left onto Pine Valley Rd.; the resort entrance is straight ahead.

The Sandpiper is not one of the French-owned company's flagship properties. It's a decent resort housed in buildings that could use some major renovation. A former Hilton Hotel, the 400-acre resort was purchased by Club Med in 1985 and marketed to Europeans looking for a Florida getaway. They come in droves with all the kids and nannies for a sunny, active vacation with meals for a reasonable prepaid price. The drawback is that guests are 20 minutes to the nearest beach. On the grounds there is plenty of diversion, like golf and tennis and waterskiing, sailing, and boating on the Indian River. There's even a circus school.

Like most other Club Meds, the rooms are sparse and small, but pleasant enough. All come with in-room safes, large closets, tiled bathrooms, and minirefrigerators.

Dining/Diversions: All-you-can-eat buffets are served in the main dining room three times a day. In addition, La Fontana serves late breakfasts and Italian cuisine at dinner, and a French restaurant is open for dinner. Excellent live entertainment is provided in bars and a showroom nightly. Another bonus is free wine and beer at lunch and dinner.

Amenities: Laundry services, massage, baby-sitting. Five outdoor heated pools, kids' pool, fitness center, 3 golf courses (36-hole, 18-hole, and 9-hole), 19 tennis courts (9 of which are lighted), circus workshops, Ping-Pong and billiards, children's center and programs, water-sports equipment, self-service Laundromat, tour desk, boutique, conference rooms, car-rental desk, waterskiing, volleyball courts, basketball, softball, soccer, bocce, exercise classes, in-line skating.

MODERATE

Dockside–Harbor Light Inn. 1160 Seaway Dr., Fort Pierce, Hutchinson Island, FL 34949. ☎ **800/433**-**0004** or 561/468-3555. 21 units. A/C MINIBAR TV TEL. Winter $78–$95 guest rooms, $67–$95 efficiencies. Off-season $59–$79 guest rooms and efficiencies. AE, CB, DC, DISC, MC, V. From I-95, exit at 66B east to U.S. 1 north to Seaway Dr.

Fronting the Intracoastal Waterway, the Harbor Light is a good choice for boating and fishing enthusiasts, offering 15 boat slips and two private fishing piers. The hotel itself carries on the nautical theme with pierlike wooden stairs and rope railings. While not exactly captain's quarters, the rooms, simply decorated with pastel colors and small wall prints, are adequate. Higher-priced rooms have either waterfront balconies or small kitchenettes that contain a coffeemaker, refrigerator, oven, and toaster. Facilities include an outdoor heated pool with a large sundeck and a self-service Laundromat.

Mellon Patch Inn. 3601 N. Fla. A1A, North Hutchinson Island, FL 34949. ☎ **800/MLN-PTCH** or 561/461-5231. Fax 561/464-6463. www.sunet.net/mlnptch. 4 units. A/C TV TEL. $70–$120 double. Rates include breakfast. No smoking and no children. AE, DISC, MC, V.

Opened in mid-1994 by innkeepers Andrea and Arthur Mellon, the Mellon Patch offers just four bright rooms in what looks like a single-family house, each with a large bathroom and sturdy soundproof walls.

The public living room is nicer than any of the small guest rooms. It's designed with a two-story vaulted ceiling, a fireplace, and lots of windows that overlook the Indian River. A gourmet breakfast that might include waffles topped with strawberries and pecans, chocolate-chip pancakes, or spinach soufflé is served here each morning. The best part is there's a public beach and free tennis courts across the street.

✪ **Villa Nina Island Beach Bed & Breakfast.** 3851 North Fla. A1A, North Hutchinson Island, FL 34949. ☎ and fax **561/467-8673.** www.gate.net/~villanin@gate.net. 3 units. Winter $115–$150. Off-season $105–$140. DISC, MC, V.

A more private option just down the road from the Mellon Patch is the newest B&B in the area in another simple but brand-new home on the river's edge. Innkeepers Nina and Glenn live in the main house and have built rooms along the back, each with a private entrance and either a fully equipped kitchen or kitchenette. Enjoy breakfast in your room or near the outdoor heated pool. Guests are free to use the laundry facilities and the canoes and rowboats for river rides. The new casino cruise ship called the "Midnight Gambler" is also available to guests for $15, which includes a 5-hour tour with food and drink.

The honeymoon suite in the back is the largest and brightest of all the pleasant rooms. Night-lit tennis and basketball courts, a public beach, and nature trails are just across the street.

WHERE TO DINE

There are a number of good seafood restaurants in the Fort Pierce and St. Lucie area, but it's also easy to drive to Stuart for more diverse dining options. See section 1 of this chapter for recommendations in Stuart.

MODERATE

✪ **Harbortown Fish House.** 1930 Harbortown Dr., Fort Pierce. ☎ **561/466-8732.** Reservations accepted. Main courses $14–$20. AE, DISC, MC, V. Sun–Thurs 11:30am–9pm, Fri–Sat 5–10pm. SEAFOOD.

You have to drive to the end of the harbor to reach this open-air waterfront fish house. It's a rustic place with outdoor tables overlooking the port, and you might be surprised to learn that it serves the area's best and freshest seafood. The menu is posted on white boards throughout the dining room and might include jumbo shrimp cocktail or New England clam chowder. The list of main courses is long and contains both fish and meat dishes. There's angel-hair pasta with scallop- and anchovy-stuffed mushrooms, roast Muscovy duck with wild-mushroom risotto, and charcoal-grilled pepper-crusted tuna served over sautéed escarole.

✪ **P.V. Martin's.** 5150 N. Fla. A1A (North Hutchinson Island), Fort Pierce. ☎ **561/569-0700.** Reservations recommended. Main courses $9–$20. AE, MC, V. Mon–Sat 11am–3:30pm and 5–9pm, Sun 10:30am–2:30pm and 5–8:30pm. SEAFOOD/AMERICAN.

This relatively elegant eatery with an eclectic American menu is tops in Fort Pierce. The wood floors, beamed ceilings, tiled-top tables, and rattan chairs would be nice anywhere, but here they look out, through floor-to-ceiling windows, onto sweeping ocean vistas. At night, the room is warmed by a huge central stone fireplace, and on weekends there's live entertainment in the adjacent bar.

Surf-and-turf dinners run the gamut from crab-stuffed shrimp and grouper baked with bananas and almonds to Brie- and asparagus-stuffed chicken breast and barbe-cued baby back ribs. An excellent selection of appetizers includes escargots in mush-room caps and a succulent fried soft-shell crab (available in season).

Theo Thudpucker's Raw Bar and Seafood Restaurant. 2025 Seaway Dr., Fort Pierce. ☎ **561/465-1078.** Reservations not accepted. Main courses $8–$24. MC, V. Mon–Thurs 11:30am–9:30pm, Fri–Sat 11:30am–11pm, Sun 1–9:30pm. SEAFOOD.

Located in a little building by the beach, wallpapered with maps and newspapers, Thudpucker's is a straightforward chowder bar. There's not much more to the dining room than one long bar and a few simple tables. Prominently placed signs attest to the food's purity: Both clams and oysters are packed with ice and are not opened until you place your order. Please be patient. Chowder and stews, often made with sherry and half-and-half, make excellent starters or light meals. The most recommendable (and filling) dinner dishes are sautéed scallops, deviled crabs, and deep-fried Okeechobee catfish.

PORT ST. LUCIE/FORT PIERCE AFTER DARK

Besides a few heavy-drinking bars, waterside restaurants (see P.V. Martin's, above), and hotel lounges, the nightlife of Port St. Lucie and Fort Pierce takes place in the neigh-boring towns north and south of here. See sections 1 and 3 of this chapter for nightspots in Stuart, Jensen Beach, Vero Beach, and Sebastian.

3 Vero Beach & Sebastian

85 miles SE of Orlando, 130 miles N of Miami

Vero Beach and Sebastian are located at the northern tip of the Treasure Coast region in Indian River County. These two beach towns are populated with folks who knew Miami and Fort Lauderdale in the days before massive high-rises and overcrowding. They appreciate the area's small-town feel, and that's exactly the area's appeal for visi-tors as well: a laid-back, relaxed atmosphere, friendly people, and friendlier prices.

A crowd of well-tanned surfers from all over the state descends on the region, espe-cially the Sebastian Inlet, to catch some of the state's biggest waves. Water-sports enthusiasts enjoy the area's fine diving, surfing, and windsurfing. Anglers are in heaven here. In spring, baseball buffs can catch some action from the L.A. Dodgers as they train in exhibition games.

ESSENTIALS

The **Indian River County Tourist Council,** 1216 21st St., Vero Beach, FL 32961 (☎ **561/567-3491;** fax 561/778-3181; www.vero-beach.fl.us/chamber), will send visitors an incredibly detailed information packet on the entire county, which includes Vero Beach and Sebastian and Fellsmere. You'll find a detailed full-color map of the area, a comprehensive listing of upcoming events, a hotel guide, and more.

BEACHES & OUTDOOR ACTIVITIES

BEACHES   Most of Vero's beachfront is open to the public and is almost never crowded. The best spots are described here, but there are many others.

South Beach Park, on South Ocean Drive, at the end of Marigold Lane, is a busy, developed, lifeguarded beach with picnic tables, restrooms, and showers. It's known as one of the best swimming beaches and also attracts a young crowd that plays volleyball and Frisbee. A well-laid-out nature walk takes you into beautiful secluded trails.

At the very north tip of the island, ✪ **Sebastian Inlet** has flat sandy beaches with lots of facilities including kayak, paddleboat, and canoe rentals, a well-stocked surf shop, picnic tables, and a snack shop. The winds seem to stir up the surf with no jetty to stop their swells, to the delight of surfers and boarders, who get here early to catch the big waves. Campers enjoy fully equipped sites in a woody area. Admission to the **Sebastian Inlet State Recreation Area,** 9700 S. A1A, Melbourne, is $3.25 per car and $1 for those who walk or bike in.

FISHING   Capt. Jack Jackson works 7 days a week out of **Vero's Tackle and Sportshop,** 57–59 Royal Palm Point (☎ **561/567-6550**), taking anglers out on his 25-foot boat for private river excursions. Captain Jackson provides all the equipment. Half-day jaunts on the Indian River cost $175 for two people (the minimum required for a charter).

You can also head up to Sebastian, where **Capt. Hiram's,** 1606 Indian River Rd. (☎ **800/797-1582** or 561/589-5433), offers private sailboat charters on the Indian River. In addition, it runs a party boat, the *Capt. Kidd II,* which heads out daily for a full day of bottom fishing for grouper, snapper, and more (it's usually only a half day on Monday). The cost is $35 per person ($40 per person will get you your rod, reel, and bait). You can bring your own lunch and beer on board, and someone will be available to clean your fish for you. Call ahead to reserve your place.

Many other charters, guides, party boats, and tackle shops operate in this area. Ask at your hotel for suggestions, or call the chamber of commerce for a list of local operators.

GOLF   Hard-core golfers insist that of the dozens of courses in the area, only a handful are worth their plot of grass.

Set on rolling hills with uncluttered views of sand dunes and sky, the **Sandridge Golf Club** (☎ **561/770-5000**), at 5300 73rd St., Vero Beach, offers two par-72 18-holers. The Dunes is a long course with rolling fairways, and the newer Lakes course has lots of water. Both charge less than $50 including a cart. There is a small snack bar selling beer and sandwiches. Reservations are recommended and are taken 2 days in advance.

Though less challenging, the **Sebastian Municipal Golf Course** (☎ **561/ 589-6800**), at 1010 E. Airport Dr., is a good 18-hole par-72. It's scenic, well-maintained, and a great bargain. Greens fees are $33 with a cart and about half that if you want to play 9 holes after 1:30pm.

Also, see Dodgertown in "Seeing the Sights," below.

SPECTATOR SPORTS   See Dodgertown in "Seeing the Sights," below.

SURFING   See Sebastian Inlet details under "Beaches," above. Also, consider the beach north of the Barber Bridge (S.R. 70), where waves are slightly gentler and the scene less competitive, and Wabasso Beach, Fla. A1A and County Road 510, a secluded area near Disney's resort where lots of teenage locals congregate, especially when the weather gets rough.

TENNIS   There are dozens of tennis courts around Vero Beach and Sebastian, many of which are at hotels and resorts. Check the phone book, or try **Riverside Park,** 350 Dahlia Lane, at Royal Palm Boulevard at the east end of Barber Bridge in Vero Beach (☎ 561/231-4787). This popular park has 10 hard courts (6 lighted) that can be rented for $3 per person per hour, and two racquetball courts with reasonable rates as well. Reservations are accepted up to 24 hours in advance. On the premises, you'll also find nature trails and other facilities.

SEEING THE SIGHTS

Environmental Learning Center. 255 Live Oak Dr. (just off the 510 Causeway), Wabasso Island. ☎ 561/589-5050. Free admission. Mon–Fri 9am–5pm, Sat 9am–noon, Sun 1–4pm.

The Indian River is not really a river at all, but a large brackish lagoon that's home to a greater variety of species than any other estuary in North America. The privately funded Environmental Learning Center was created to protect the local habitat and educate visitors about their environment. Situated on 51 island acres, the center features dozens of hands-on exhibits that are geared to both children and adults. There are live touch tanks, exhibits, and microscopes for viewing the smallest sea life close up. The best thing to do here is join one of the center's interpretive canoe trips, offered by reservation only. The cost for these is $10 for adults, $5 for children. Phone for details.

Indian River Citrus Museum. 2140 14th Ave., Vero Beach. ☎ 561/770-2263. Admission $1 donation. Tues–Fri 10am–4pm.

The tiny Indian River Citrus Museum exhibits artifacts relating to the history of the citrus industry, from its initial boom in the late 1800s to the present. Also, a small grove has taped information on the varieties of fruits there. The gift shop sells unique citrus-themed gift items, along with, of course, ready-to-ship fruit.

Mel Fisher's Treasure Museum. 1322 U.S. 1, Sebastian. ☎ 561/589-9874. Admission $5 adults, $4 seniors over 55, $1.50 children 6–12, free for children 5 and under. Mon–Sat 10am–5pm, Sun noon–5pm.

Here's where you can see the treasures from the fateful fleet that went down in 1715. Though not as extensive as the museum in Key West, this exhibit includes gold coins, bars, and Spanish artifacts that are worth a look. Also, the preservation lab shows how the goods are extricated, cleaned, and preserved.

DODGERTOWN

✪ **Vero** is the winter home of the Los Angeles Dodgers, and the town hosts the team in grand style. The 450-acre compound at 3901 26th St. (☎ 561/569-4900) encompasses two golf courses, a conference center, country club, movie theater, and recreation room. You can watch afternoon exhibition games during the winter (usually between mid-February and the end of March) in the comfortable 6,474-seat outdoor stadium. Even if the game sells out, you can catch the action from a seat on the grassy field with a $5 standing-room ticket. The stadium has never turned away an eager fan.

Even when spring training is over, you can still catch a game; the Dodgers' farm team, the Vero Beach Dodgers, has a full season of minor-league baseball in summer.

Admission to the complex is free; tickets to games are $5 to $9. The complex is open daily from 9am to 5pm; game time is usually 1pm. From I-95 take Exit S.R. 60 east to 43rd Avenue; turn left; continue to 26th Street, and turn right.

SHOPPING

Ocean Boulevard and Cardinal Drive are Vero's two main shopping streets. Both are near the beach and lined with specialty boutiques, including antique and home decorating shops.

If you want to send fruit back home, the local source is **Hale Indian River Groves,** 615 Beachland Blvd. (☎ **561/231-1752**), a shipper of local citrus and jams since 1947. Note that it is closed 2 to 3 months a year, usually late summer or early fall, depending on the year's crop.

The **Horizon Outlet Center,** at S.R. 60 and I-95, Vero Beach (☎ **800/866-5900** or 561/770-6171), contains more than 80 discount stores selling shoes, kitchenware, books, clothing, and other items. The mall, which added a food court and new stores in 1996, is open Monday to Saturday from 9am to 8pm and Sunday from 11am to 6pm.

The **Indian River Mall** (☎ **561/770-6255**), 6200 20th St. (S.R. 60 about 5 miles east of I-95), which opened its doors in November 1996, is a big deal in Vero Beach. This monster mall has all the big national chains, like The Gap, Structure, and Victoria's Secret, as well as several large department stores, and is open Monday through Saturday from 10am to 9pm and Sunday from noon to 6pm.

WHERE TO STAY

Ocean Drive is dotted with a number of old dilapidated hotels in dire need of renovations. Although the area is being fixed up, it's slow going. A few of the well-maintained hotels are listed below. In Vero, both the **Days Resort** (☎ **800/329-7466** or 561/231-2800), at 3244 Ocean Dr., and the **Holiday Inn Oceanside** (☎ **800/465-4329** or 561/231-2300), at 3384 Ocean Dr., offer oceanfront rooms and suites at comparable prices. However, the Holiday Inn is probably a better choice since it was fully remodeled in '95, and its restaurant and lounge directly face the ocean. Also, a great spot to know, especially if you are planning to fish, is **Capt. Hiram's** (see "Fishing," above, and also "Vero Beach & Sebastian After Dark," below), where there are four clean and cozy rooms available adjacent to the restaurant and overlooking the water. Rates are between $80 and $110.

EXPENSIVE

✪ **Disney's Vero Beach Resort.** 9250 Island Grove Terrace, Vero Beach, FL 32963. ☎ **800/359-8000** or 561/234-2000. Fax 561/234-2030. 112 units, 60 cottages. A/C TV TEL. Rates from $140 inn-garden view; from $160 inn-ocean view/studio; from $210 one-bedroom villa; from $280 two-bedroom villa; from $590 three-bedroom beach cottage. AE, MC, V. From I-95 take Exit 69 (512 east); turn right onto County Rd. 510 east; turn right onto S. Fla. A1A. The resort is immediately visible on the left.

Disney's mega-resort opened in 1995 with much fanfare on the otherwise sleepy shores of Florida's Treasure Coast. They call it a membership-based club; as far as I can figure, it's simply a time-share. For now, nonowners are welcome. Take advantage of it—your kids will love it.

The sprawling complex is designed to resemble a turn-of-the-century Florida beach community, complete with sandwashed buildings and faux-worn furniture. The beachside cottages are huge and tasteful. The villas have fully equipped kitchens with dishwashers and microwaves.

Situated on the tip of one of the most pristine beaches on the coast, the resort takes advantage of its setting by offering truly exciting children's programs like canoe adventures, poolside miniature golf, stories around a campfire, a trip to a working cattle ranch, and stargazing from a powerful telescope. The best part is a large lagoonlike pool with a huge winding slide that elicits squeals of delight from kids and adults alike. And also, for younger kids, a pirate ship that squirts water is a fun way to cool off.

Promoters say that this is a return to "the Old Florida," but I can't imagine that it was ever quite like this—this clean, this quaint, this fun, and this convenient. This is Disney, without the rides or lines. Sign me up.

Dining/Diversions: The resort offers some of the best food in the region. An elegant steak house, Sonya's, serves dinner from an eclectic, Florida-inspired menu with superb steaks, pecan-crusted salmon, and salads. In addition, a casual restaurant for lunch and dinner serves interesting pizzas, sandwiches, salads, roasted vegetables, and pastas. A picturesque lounge, which overlooks the ocean and hosts live music most nights, is popular with guests and sometimes even locals. A poolside snack bar rounds out this resort's food and drink options.

Amenities: Concierge, room service, laundry services for inn rooms, dry-cleaning, newspapers in lobby, express checkout, secretarial services during business hours, baby-sitting, free morning coffee in lobby. Large theme-based pool with two-story pool slide as well as a treasure ship pool deck, beach, health club, Jacuzzi, sauna, sundeck, nature trails, kitchenettes, VCRs, video rentals, shuffleboard, croquet lawn, two night-lit tennis courts, water-sports equipment, jogging track, tee times available at local courses, nine-hole miniature golf, basketball half-court, volleyball, tetherball, game room, extensive children's programs, conference rooms, business center, self-service Laundromat, tour desk/guest services, gift shop, general store.

Doubletree Guest Suites. 3500 Ocean Dr., Vero Beach, FL 32963. ☎ **800/841-5666** or 561/231-5666. Fax 561/234-4866. 55 units. A/C TV TEL. Winter $210–$245 1-bedroom suite; $265–$295 2-bedroom suite. Off-season $110–$150 one-bedroom suite; $165 two-bedroom suite. AE, CB, DC, DISC, MC, V.

Vero's best all-suite hotel, part of the Doubletree chain, is located directly on the beach and is close to local restaurants and shops. First-class accommodations are located in a modern four-story building. The guest rooms, which were renovated in late 1996, are unremarkable, but clean and attractive. What the nearly identical suites lack in character they make up for in content. The rooms are equipped with small refrigerators and coffeemakers, two phones, and modern baths that include hair dryers.

Dining/Diversions: The Lanai Room is open for breakfast only, daily from 7am to 10pm. The Seabreeze pool bar is open daily for lunch, dinner, and cocktails.

Amenities: Room service, dry cleaning, laundry service, newspaper delivery, express checkout. VCRs and video rentals for additional charge, outdoor heated swimming pool and kids' pool, beach, access to nearby health club, Jacuzzi, self-service Laundromat, conference rooms, sundeck.

MODERATE

Driftwood Resort. 3150 Ocean Dr., Vero Beach, FL 32963. ☎ **561/231-0550.** Fax 561/234-1981. 100 units. A/C TV TEL. Winter $90–$210 double; from $170–$230 2-bedroom suite. Off-season $55–$125 double; from $130 2-bedroom suite. AE, MC, V.

Originally planned in the 1930s as a private estate by local legend Waldo Sexton, the Driftwood was opened to the public after several travelers stopped to inquire about renting a room here. Today the hotel's rooms and public areas are filled with nautical knickknacks collected by Sexton on his travels all over the world.

All the guest rooms are different. Some feature terra-cotta-tiled floors and lighter furniture while others have a more rustic feel with hardwoods and antiques. Each accommodation has its own bath and few frills. The resort, which was recently listed on the National Register of Historic Places, offers two outdoor heated pools, a some-times narrow beach, bicycle trail, dry-cleaning services, as well as VCR and video rentals.

○ **Islander Motel.** 3101 Ocean Dr., Vero Beach, FL 32963. ☎ **800/952-5886** or 561/231-4431. 16 units. A/C TV TEL. Winter $89 double. Off-season $49–$59 double. Efficiencies cost $10 extra. AE, MC, V.

Resident owner Tom Collins runs one of the most comfortable and welcoming inns in the area. Well located in downtown Vero Beach, this motel is just a short walk to the beach, restaurants, and shops. Every guest room has a small refrigerator and either a king-size bed or two double beds. The accommodations are designed in a Caribbean motif with bright fabrics and white rattan furniture. There's a pool and a barbecue area in the handsomely landscaped central courtyard, along with a small walk-up cafe.

INEXPENSIVE

Davis House Inn. 607 Davis St., Sebastian, FL 32958. ☎ **561/589-4114.** Fax 561/589-3108. 12 units. Winter $69–$89 double. Off-season $54–$79 double. Rates include continental breakfast. Weekly and monthly rates available. AE, DISC, MC, V. From I-95, take Exit 69 east to Indian River Dr., turn left, go 1¼ miles to Davis St., turn left on Davis St; the inn is on the left.

Each of the dozen rooms in this contemporary, three-story, blue-and-white bed-and-breakfast on the mainland has a private entrance and doorfront parking. The rooms are large and clean, although somewhat plain, and each has a king-size bed, a pull-out sofa, and a small kitchenette, making them popular with long-term guests. The bathrooms are equally ample and have plenty of counter space. There's a large wooden deck for sunbathing, a sunny second-floor breakfast room, and a self-service Laundromat.

CAMPING

This area is popular with campers, who can choose from nearly a dozen sites throughout Vero and Sebastian. If you aren't camping at the scenic and very popular Sebastian Inlet (see "Beaches," above), then try the **Vero Beach KOA RV Park,** 8850 U.S. 1, Wabasso (☎ **561/589-5665**). This 120-site campground is 2 miles from the ocean and the Intracoastal Waterway and one quarter of a mile from the Indian River, a big draw for the crowd of regular fishing fanatics. There's running water and electricity as well as showers, a shop, and hookups for RVs. Rates range from $20 to $24 per site, and $19 for tents. To get there, take I-95 to Exit 69 east; at U.S. 1 turn left.

WHERE TO DINE
EXPENSIVE

○ **Chez Yannick.** 1605 S. Ocean Dr., Vero Beach. ☎ **561/234-4115.** Reservations recommended. Main courses $15–$28; fixed-price dinner $18.95 off-season. AE, MC, V. Mon–Sat open at 6pm; closing time may vary based on last reservation. FRENCH/CONTINENTAL.

Fine French cooking complements the crystal and gilded decor. The nightly fixed-price dinner includes soup or salad, entree, and dessert, and is a truly outstanding value. Excellent starters include a succulent sliced duckling breast, cream of lobster soup, and hearts-of-palm salad with a slightly spicy vinaigrette. Some items, like lobster and shrimp in a cognac-dill sauce, are available as either an appetizer or an entree. Other main courses include beef tenderloin stuffed with Gorgonzola cheese and sautéed soft-shell crabs. Desserts might include profiteroles with ice cream and chocolate or raspberry sauce, crème caramel, chocolate-mousse pie, or raspberry sorbet.

MODERATE

✪ Black Pearl. 2855 Ocean Dr., Vero Beach. ☎ **561/234-4426.** Reservations recommended. Main courses $12–$21. AE, CB, DC, DISC, MC, V. Mon–Fri 11:30am–2:30pm and 5:30–10pm, Sat–Sun 5:30–10pm. CONTINENTAL.

It's unusual that such a small, moderately priced, and unassuming restaurant should make absolutely everything from scratch. But that's exactly what they do, and you'll be wooed by seductive smells even before you walk through the front door. There's just a single, art deco–accented dining room featuring bright prints on clean pastel walls.

The restaurant's small list of appetizers may include feta cheese and spinach fritters, chilled leek-and-watercress soup, or oysters baked with crabmeat and butter. Equally creative main courses recently included Cajun pasta (topped with shrimp, scallops, and sausage), sautéed crabmeat-stuffed veal covered with hollandaise sauce, and blackened rib eye steak.

Ocean Grill. 1050 Sexton Plaza (by the ocean at the end of S.R. 60), Vero Beach. ☎ **561/231-5409.** Reservations accepted only for large parties. Main courses $11–$18. AE, DC, DISC, MC, V. Mon–Fri 11:30am–2:30pm and 5:45–10pm, Sat–Sun 5:45–10pm. AMERICAN.

Founded in 1941, the Ocean Grill is an institution that attracts tourists and locals alike with its simple but rich cooking and stunning locale, right on the ocean's edge. For a dramatic experience, ask for a table along the wall of newly enlarged windows that open onto the sea. Dinners are uniformly good. Try stone crab claws when they are in season or any of the big servings of pasta or meats.

Pearl's Bistro. 56 Royal Palm Point, Vero Beach. ☎ **561/778-2950.** Reservations recommended. Main courses $9–$17. AE, MC, V. Mon–Fri 11:30am–2:30pm and 5:30–closing, Sat 6–10pm. Take U.S. 1 south to 20th St.; turn left; at Indian River Blvd. turn left again; then turn right onto Royal Palm Blvd. CARIBBEAN.

This small bistro serves one of the tastiest and best-value meals in town. The single narrow dining room is brightened with a colorful tropical mural and soothing lime walls. White chicken chili and the grilled swordfish club sandwich are two top lunch recommendations. The dinner menu includes an excellent open-face grilled-chicken burrito, steak fajita salad, and a shrimp enchilada with rice and beans.

Waldo's. In the Driftwood Resort, 3150 Ocean Dr., Vero Beach. ☎ **561/231-7091.** Main courses $10–$13. AE, MC, V. Thurs–Sun 8am–10pm, Fri–Sat 8am–11pm. SEAFOOD/AMERICAN.

Everyone who hears that you went to Vero Beach will ask you if you went to Waldo's. The restaurant isn't famous for its food, which is good but not great. Waldo's is known for its unusual setting: Outdoor picnic tables are set as close to the ocean as you can get without getting wet. Breakfast and lunch snacks are the best bet. Sandwiches like turkey clubs, broiled chicken, or burgers served on paper plates are satisfying and hearty. Dinners are just slightly more elaborate and include Danish-style barbecued ribs and Cajun seafood kebabs.

VERO BEACH & SEBASTIAN AFTER DARK

Even on weekends, this town retires relatively early, but there are a few popular spots, in addition to the many hotel lounges, that have live music and a good bar scene, especially in high season.

A mostly 30-something and younger crowd goes to Vero's **Bombay Louie's,** at 398 21st St. (☎ **561/978-0209**), where a deejay spins dance music after 9pm from Wednesday to Saturday.

In Sebastian, you'll find live music every weekend (and daily in season) at **Capt. Hiram's,** 1606 N. Indian River Dr. (☎ **561/589-4345**), a salty outdoor restaurant and bar on the Intracoastal Waterway. The feel is tacky Key West, complete with a sand floor and thatched-roof bar that locals and tourists love at all hours of the day and night.

North of the inlet, head for the tried-and-true **Sebastian Beach Inn** (or SBI to locals), 7035 S. Fla. A1A (☎ **407/728-4311**). Jazz, blues, or sometimes rock and roll starts at 9pm on Friday and Saturday. On Sunday, it's old-style reggae after 2pm.

4 A Side Trip Inland: Fishing at Lake Okeechobee

60 miles SW of West Palm Beach

Many visitors to the Treasure Coast come to fish, and they certainly get their fill off the miles of Atlantic shore and on the inland rivers. But if you want to fish freshwater and nothing else, head for "The Lake"— ✪ **Lake Okeechobee,** that is. The state's largest, it's chock-full of good eating fish. Only about a 1½-hour drive from the coast, it makes a great day or weekend excursion.

Two things happen in the area surrounding Lake Okeechobee: sugar production and fishing. The area, which actually encompasses five counties, is known as the bass fishing and winter vegetable capital of the state.

Okeechobee comes from the Seminole Indian word for "big water"—and big it is. The lake covers more than 467,000 acres; that's more than 730 square miles. At one time, the lake supported an enormous commercial fishing industry. Due to a commercial fishing-net ban, much of that industry has died off, leaving the sportfishers all the rich bounty of the lake.

As you approach the lake area, you'll notice a large levy surrounding its circumference. This was built after two major hurricanes, including one in 1947 that killed hundreds of area residents and cattle. In an effort to control future flooding, the Army Corps of Engineers, which had already built a cross-state waterway, constructed a series of locks and dams. The region is now safe from the threat of floods, but the ecological results of the flood control have not been as positive. The bird and wildlife population suffered dramatically, as did the southern portion of the Everglades, which relied on the downflow of water from the lake to replenish and clean the entire ecosystem.

Another threat to the region is posed by the area's largest employer, U.S. Sugar, which owns most of the land around Belle Glade and Clewiston, "America's Sweetest Town."

Still, the area retains its rural charm and boasts the best bass fishing in the state.

ESSENTIALS

GETTING THERE   The best route is to take I-95 south to Southern Boulevard (U.S. 98 west) in West Palm Beach, which merges with S.R. 80 and S.R. 441. Follow signs for S.R. 80 west through Belle Glade to South Bay. In South Bay, turn right onto U.S. 27 north, which leads directly to Clewiston.

VISITOR INFORMATION   Contact the **Clewiston Chamber of Commerce,** 544 W. Sugarland Hwy., Clewiston, FL 33440 (☎ **941/983-7979**), for maps, business directories, and the names of numerous fishing guides throughout the area. In addition, you might contact the **Pahokee Chamber of Commerce,** 115 E. Main St., Pahokee, FL 33476 (☎ **561/924-5579;** fax 561/924-8116); they'll send a complete package of magazines, guides, and accommodations listings.

Going After the Big One

Fishing on the lake is a year-round affair, though the fish tend to bite a little better in the winter, perhaps for benefit of the many snowbirds who flock here, especially in February and March. RV camps are mobbed with fish-frenzied anglers who come down for weeks at a time for a decent catch.

You'll need a fishing license to go out with a rod and reel. It's a simple matter to apply. The chamber of commerce and most fishing shops can sign you up on the spot. The cost for non-Florida residents for 7 days is $16.50, $31.50 for the year.

You can rent, charter, or bring your own boat to Clewiston; just be sure to schedule your trip in advance. You don't want to show up during one of the frequent fishing tournaments, only to find you can't get a room, campsite, or fishing boat because hundreds of the country's most intense bass fishermen are vying for the $100,000 prizes in the Redman Competition, which happens four times a year in the spring and winter.

There are, of course, more than a few marinas where you can rent or charter boats. If it's your first time on the lake, I suggest chartering a boat with a guide who can show you the lake's most fertile spots and handle your tackle while you drink a beer and get some sun. **Roland Martin,** 920 E. Del Monte (☎ **941/ 983-3151**), is the one-stop spot where you can find a guide, boat, tackle, rods, bait, coolers, picnic supplies, and a choice of boats. Rates start at $40 for a half day (about 4 hours). If you've never fished these waters, consider hiring a guide. Rates, including the boat start at $165 for a half day. A full day costs $225 and includes all necessary equipment except bait. You'll need a license for this, too, which Roland Martin also sells. They also have boat rentals: A 16-foot john boat is $40 for half a day, $60 for a full day with a $40 deposit. A 26-foot pontoon is $125 for a full day and $85 for half a day with a $50 deposit.

Another reputable boat-rental spot is **Angler's Marina,** 910 Okeechobee Blvd. (☎ **800/741-3141** or 941/983-BASS). Rentals for a 14-footer start at $40 for a half day, with a maximum of four people. A full day is $60. I'd opt for the 22-foot pontoon, which comes with a 50-horsepower engine and fits a max of 10 people and some more space for supplies and fish. If you want a guide, rates start at $150 (for two people) for a half day, though in the summer (June to October), when it's slow, you can usually get a cheaper deal.

For an excellent map and brief history of the area, contact the **U.S. Army Corps of Engineers, Natural Resources Office,** 525 Ridgelawn Rd., Clewiston, FL 33440 (☎ **941/983-8101;** fax 941/983-8579). It is open weekdays from 8am to 4:30pm.

OUTDOOR ACTIVITIES

BOAT TOURS   Captain JP's Boat Charters (☎ **800/845-7411** or 561/924-2100) go out every day on a number of tour and dinner cruises on his 350-passenger *Viking Starliner* throughout the southern region of Lake Okeechobee. Most cruises leave from Pahokee or Moore Haven marina, though schedules change daily. Most cruises depart at 10am during the season and include breakfast and an all-you-can-eat buffet of salads, cheeses, and hot entrees. Prices start at $30. Call for seasonal schedules.

FISHING   See box "Going After the Big One," above.

SKYDIVING   Besides fishing, the biggest sport in Clewiston is jumping out of planes. Because of the limited air traffic and vast areas of flat undeveloped land, this area attracts novice and expert skydivers. **Air Adventures** (☎ **800/533-6151** or 941/983-6151) operates a year-round program from the Airglades Airport. If you've never jumped before, you can go on a tandem dive, which means, as the name implies, you'll be attached to a "jumpmaster." For the first 60 seconds, the two of you free-fall, from about 12,500 feet. Then a quick pull of the chute turns your rapid descent into a gentle, balletic cruise to the ground with time to see the whole majestic lake from a privileged perspective. Dive packages start at $150 on weekdays and $165 on weekends. Group rates are available.

WHERE TO STAY

If you aren't camping, book a room at the ✪ **Clewiston Inn,** 108 Royal Palm Ave., Clewiston (☎ **800/749-4466** or 941/983-8151). Built in 1938 by U.S. Sugar to house executives and visitors, this Southern plantation–inspired hotel is the oldest in the Lake Okeechobee region. It still hosts sugar executives and visiting sportfishers in its 52 simply decorated, nondescript, Holiday Inn–style rooms. The lounge area sports a 1945 mural depicting the animals of the region. Double rooms rent for $79 a night; bungalows, for $99. All have air-conditioning, TVs, and telephones.

Another choice, especially if you're here to fish, is **Roland Martin,** 920 E. Del Monte (☎ **800/473-6766** or 941/983-3151), the "Disney of Clewiston." This RV park offers modest motel rooms, efficiencies, condominiums, apartments, or campsites, with two heated pools, gift and marina shops, and a restaurant. The modern complex, dotted with pre-fab buildings painted in sparse white and gray, is clean and well manicured. Rooms rent for $55 to $65 and efficiencies for $70 to $85. Condos are about $130 a night with a 3-night minimum. RV sites are about $23 with TV and cable hookup.

CAMPING

During the winter, campers own the Clewiston area. Campsites are jammed with regulars who come year after year for the simple pleasures of the lake and, of course, the warm weather. Every manner of RV, from simple pop-top Volkswagens to Winnebagos to fully decked-out mobile homes, find their way to the many campsites along the lake. Also, see Roland Martin, above.

Okeechobee Landings, U.S. 27 east (☎ **941/983-4144**), is one of the best; it has every conceivable amenity included in the price of a site. More than 250 sites are situated around a small lake, clubhouse, snack bar, pool, Jacuzzi, horseshoe pit, shuffleboard court, and tennis court. Full hookup includes sewer, which is not the case throughout the county. RV spots are sold to regulars. But there are usually some spots available for rental to one-time visitors. Rates are $23 a day or $350 a month, including hookup. Year-round rates for trailer rentals, which sleep two people, are $32 from Sunday to Thursday and $37 on Friday and Saturday.

WHERE TO DINE

If you aren't frying up your own catch for dinner, you can find a number of good eating spots in town. At the **Clewiston Inn** (see "Where to Stay," above), you can get catfish, beef Stroganoff, ham hocks, fried chicken, and liver and onions in a setting as Southern as the food. The dining room is open daily from 6am to 2pm and 5 to 9pm, and entrees cost $9 to $18.

At **Julian's** (formerly Donnelly's), 842 E. Sugarland Hwy., Clewistown (☎ **941/ 983-8119**), in addition to the full menu of steaks and superfresh seafood, you can order alligator tail, quail, or a choice of barbecued specialties. Dinners range from $10 to $18 and include salad and vegetables. You can bring your own catch, which they'll cook however you like it, served with hush puppies, french fries, and coleslaw for just $5.95. Breakfast starts early so that the birds can get out by 5am to catch some worms. Donnelly's closes when "the fishermen are done drinking," usually Monday to Thursday by 10pm and Friday and Saturday by 11pm.

Not to be missed is the ✪ **Old South Barbecue Ranch,** 602 E. Sugarland Hwy. (☎ **941/983-7756**). You'll see signs from miles around imploring you to come to this Lake Okeechobee landmark. Go ahead; they're known for their barbecued pork, meat, and chicken, but the catfish isn't bad either. You can also get good fried gator. The place looks like a movie set from an old Western. It's open Sunday through Thursday from 11am to 9pm and Friday and Saturday from 11am to 10pm.

10

Southwest Florida

by Bill Goodwin

Residents of Sanibel form a "McSpoil" committee and prevent McDonald's from getting a fast-food toehold on their remarkably beautiful island. Neapolitans successfully force a referendum on development that would change the nature of their charming Olde Naples historic district. The town council in Fort Myers Beach designates a new and growing part of Estero Island as a safe haven for wildlife. And the federal government tells airboat operators to keep their noisy machines out of the pristine Everglades National Park.

If you think these recent efforts to protect both the past and the present environment make Southwest Florida one of the best parts of the state for enjoying the great outdoors and discovering remnants of Old Florida, you're right.

The region traces its nature-loving roots to inventor and amateur botanist Thomas A. Edison, who was so enamored of Southwest Florida that he spent his winters in Fort Myers from 1885 until 1931. His friend Henry Ford built his own winter home next door. The world's best tarpon fishing lured Pres. Teddy Roosevelt and his buddies to Useppa, one of literally 10,000 islands along this coast. Some of the planet's best shelling helped entice the du Ponts of Delaware to Gasparilla Island, where they founded the Nantucket-like village of Boca Grande. The unspoiled beauty of Sanibel and Captiva so entranced Pulitzer Prize–winning political cartoonist J. N. "Ding" Darling that he campaigned to preserve much of those islands in their natural states. And the millionaires who settled in Naples enacted tough zoning laws that to this day make their city one of the most alluring in Florida.

Southwest Florida International Airport, on the eastern outskirts of Fort Myers, is this region's major airport (see "Essentials" in section 1, below). From here it's only 20 miles to Sanibel Island, 35 miles to Naples, or 46 miles to Marco Island. If you have a car, you can see the area's sights and participate in most of its activities easily from one base of operations.

EXCURSIONS TO THE EVERGLADES & KEY WEST You won't be in Southwest Florida for long before you see advertisements for excursions to the Everglades. Naples is only 36 miles from Everglades City, the "back door" to wild and wonderful Everglades National Park, so it's easy to combine a visit to the national park with your stay in Southwest Florida. See chapter 7 for full details about the Everglades.

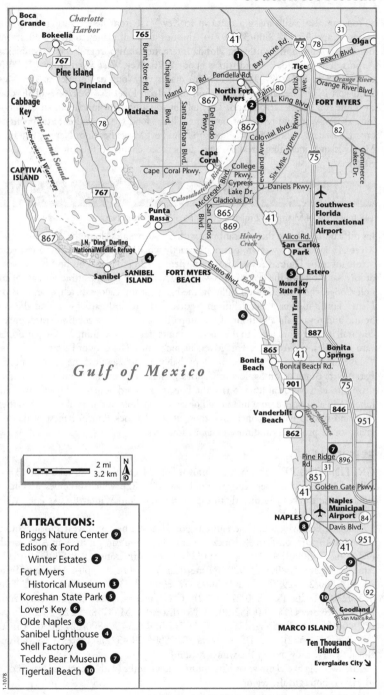

Southwest Florida

Boca Grande

Charlotte Harbor

Bokeelia

765

767

Pine Island

Pineland

Cabbage Key

Burnt Store Rd.

Chiquita Island Blvd.

Pine Island Rd.

78

Matlacha

78

CAPTIVA ISLAND

Santa Barbara Blvd.

Pine Island Sound

Intracoastal Waterway

767

Del Prado Pkwy.

867

Pondella Rd.

North Fort Myers

41

1

Bay Shore Rd.

75

78

31

Olga

Tice

Orange River

Orange River Blvd.

Beach Blvd.

Palm. **80** Ortiz Ave.

M.L. King Blvd.

FORT MYERS

2

867

3

Cape Coral

Cape Coral Pkwy.

McGregor Blvd.

Cleveland Avenue

Colonial Blvd.

Six Mile Cypress Pkwy.

82

Commerce Lakes Dr.

75

College Pkwy.

Cypress Lake Dr.

Gladiolus Dr.

865

869

Daniels Pkwy.

41

Southwest Florida International Airport

Caloosahatchee River

San Carlos Blvd.

Punta Rassa

867

Hendry Creek

Alico Rd.

San Carlos Park

J.N. 'Ding' Darling National Wildlife Refuge

4

Estero Blvd.

Estero Bay

5 Estero

Mound Key State Park

Sanibel **SANIBEL ISLAND**

FORT MYERS BEACH

6

Tamiami Trail

887

865

41

Bonita Springs

Gulf of Mexico

Bonita Beach

Bonita Beach Rd.

901

75

Vanderbilt Beach

Cocohatchee River

846

951

862

7

Pine Ridge Rd.

896

851

31

Golden Gate Pkwy.

	2 mi
0	3.2 km

N

41

Naples Municipal Airport

NAPLES

84

8

Davis Blvd.

951

41

9

ATTRACTIONS:

Briggs Nature Center **9**

Edison & Ford
  Winter Estates **2**

Fort Myers
  Historical Museum **3**

Koreshan State Park **5**

Lover's Key **6**

Olde Naples **8**

Sanibel Lighthouse **4**

Shell Factory **1**

Teddy Bear Museum **7**

Tigertail Beach **10**

10

Goodland

San Marco Rd.

92

MARCO ISLAND

Ten Thousand Islands

Everglades City ↘

1-1078

You can also easily make a day trip to Key West from here. During the winter season, **Cape Air** (☎ **800/352-0714**) shuttles its small planes to Key West several times a day from both Southwest Florida International Airport and Naples Municipal Airport. The same-day round-trip is about $170. **Key West Excursions** (☎ **800/650-KEYS** or 941/262-3900 in Florida) makes very long day cruises to Key West from Fort Myers Beach and Naples, and the **Falcon Fleet** (☎ **941/642-1166**) does the same run from Marco Island. They all put you ashore for lunch and an afternoon look at Key West and return late at night. There's food service and entertainment on board. The cost is about $100 per person from Fort Myers Beach or Naples, $80 from Marco Island, including breakfast and dinner. See chapter 6 for information about Key West.

1 Fort Myers

148 miles NW of Miami, 142 miles S of Tampa, 42 miles N of Naples

It's difficult to picture this pleasant city with broad avenues along the Caloosahatchee River as a raucous cow town, but that's exactly what Fort Myers was just a few years before inventor Thomas Alva Edison came here in 1885 to regain his health after years of incessant toil and the death of his wife. Today, the city's prime attractions are Seminole Lodge, the home Edison built on the banks of the Caloosahatchee, and his pal Henry Ford's digs next door. Edison planted lush tropical gardens around the two homes and royal palms in front of the properties along McGregor Boulevard, once a cow trail leading from town to the docks at Punta Rassa. Now lining McGregor Boulevard for miles, the trees give Fort Myers its nickname: The City of Palms.

Like most visitors to the area, you'll probably opt to stay near the sands at nearby Fort Myers Beach or on Sanibel or Captiva islands (see sections 2 and 3, below), but drive into Fort Myers at least to visit the Edison and Ford homes and have a riverside lunch. You also can venture inland and observe incredible numbers of wildlife in their river and swamp habitats, including those at the Babcock Ranch, largest of the surviving cattle producers and now a major game preserve.

ESSENTIALS

GETTING THERE   To reach downtown Fort Myers from I-75, take Exit 23 and follow Dr. Martin Luther King Jr. Boulevard (Fla. 82), which becomes McGregor Boulevard and takes you directly to the Edison and Ford Winter Estates (see "What to See & Do," below).

Not just Fort Myers but the entire region is served by **Southwest Florida International Airport,** on Daniels Parkway east of I-75. You can get here on **Air Canada** (☎ 800/776-3000), **AirTran** (☎ 800/247-8726), **Air Transat** (☎ 800/470-1011), **America West** (☎ 800/235-9292), **American** (☎ 800/433-7300), **American Trans Air** (☎ 800/225-2995), **Canada 3000** (☎ 800/993-4378), **Continental** (☎ 800/525-0280), **Delta** (☎ 800/221-1212), **LTU International** (☎ 800/888-0200), **Midwest Express** (☎ 800/452-2022), **Northwest/KLM** (☎ 800/225-2525), **Royal** (☎ 800/667-7692), **Spirit** (☎ 800/772-7117), **TWA** (☎ 800/221-2000), **United** (☎ 800/241-6522), and **US Airways** (☎ 800/428-4322). (Note: American and Royal fly here only during the winter season.)

The two baggage-claim areas have information booths (with maps) and free phones to various hotels in the region.

All major car-rental agencies are at the airport.

Vans and taxis are available at a booth across the street from the baggage claim. The maximum fares for one to three passengers are $24 to downtown Fort Myers, $35 to

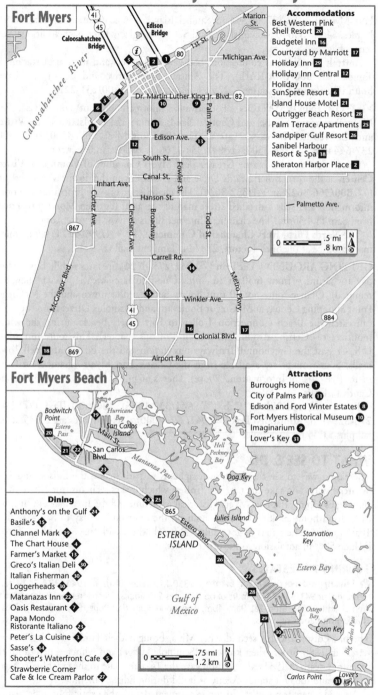

Fort Myers & Fort Myers Beach

Fort Myers

Marion St.
Caloosahatchee Bridge
Edison Bridge
Caloosahatchee River
1st St.
Michigan Ave.
Dr. Martin Luther King Jr. Blvd.
Palm Ave.
Edison Ave.
South St.
Canal St.
Inhart Ave.
Hanson St.
Palmetto Ave.
Cortez Ave.
Cleveland Ave.
Broadway
Fowler St.
Todd St.
McGregor Blvd.
Carrell Rd.
Metro Pkwy.
Winkler Ave.
Colonial Blvd.
Airport Rd.

0   .5 mi
0   .8 km
N

Accommodations
Best Western Pink Shell Resort **20**
Budgetel Inn **16**
Courtyard by Marriott **17**
Holiday Inn **29**
Holiday Inn Central **12**
Holiday Inn SunSpree Resort **6**
Island House Motel **21**
Outrigger Beach Resort **28**
Palm Terrace Apartments **25**
Sandpiper Gulf Resort **26**
Sanibel Harbour Resort & Spa **18**
Sheraton Harbor Place **2**

Fort Myers Beach

Bodwitch Point
Estero Pass
Bodwitch Bay
Hurricane Bay
San Carlos Island
Main St.
San Carlos Blvd.
Mantanza Pass
Hell Peckney Bay
Dog Key
Julies Island
ESTERO ISLAND
Estero Blvd.
865
Gulf of Mexico
Starvation Key
Estero Bay
Ostego Bay
Coon Key
Big Carlos Pass
Carlos Point
Lover's Key

0   .75 mi
0   1.2 km
N

Attractions
Burroughs Home **1**
City of Palms Park **11**
Edison and Ford Winter Estates **8**
Fort Myers Historical Museum **10**
Imaginarium **9**
Lover's Key **31**

Dining
Anthony's on the Gulf **24**
Basile's **15**
Channel Mark **19**
The Chart House **4**
Farmer's Market **13**
Greco's Italian Deli **30**
Italian Fisherman **30**
Loggerheads **30**
Matanazas Inn **22**
Oasis Restaurant **7**
Papa Mondo Ristorante Italiano **23**
Peter's La Cuisine **3**
Sasse's **14**
Shooter's Waterfront Cafe **5**
Strawberrie Corner Cafe & Ice Cream Parlor **27**

Fort Myers Beach, $37 to $44 to Sanibel Island, $56 to Captiva Island, $100 to Naples, $46 to $56 to Marco Island, and $70 to Everglades City. Each additional passenger pays $8.

Amtrak provides bus connections between Fort Myers and its nearest station, in Tampa (☎ **800/USA-RAIL**). The Amtrak buses arrive and depart the **Greyhound/Trailways** bus station, 2275 Cleveland Ave. (☎ **800/231-2222**).

VISITOR INFORMATION   For advance information about Fort Myers, Fort Myers Beach, and Sanibel and Captiva islands, contact the **Lee Island Coast Visitor and Convention Bureau,** 2180 W. First St., Fort Myers, FL 33901 (☎ **800/ 237-6444** or 941/338-3500; fax 941/334-1106; www.leeislandcoast.com).

Once in town, drop by the **Greater Fort Myers Chamber of Commerce Visitor Center,** at the corner of Edwards Drive and Lee Street on the downtown waterfront (☎ **800/366-3622** or 941/332-3624). The chamber gives away brochures and other information and sells a detailed street map of the area. It's open Monday to Friday from 8am to 4:30pm. The chamber's Internet site is at www.fortmyers.org.

The **North Fort Myers Chamber of Commerce** (☎ **941/997-9111**) has an information office at the Shell Factory, 2787 N. Tamiami Trail (U.S. 41).

GETTING AROUND   **LeeTran** (☎ **941/275-8726**) operates public buses Monday to Saturday from 6:30am to 8pm. One-ride fares are $1 (exact change is required). Orange route no. 50 runs hourly between downtown and the McGregor Point Shopping Center, at McGregor Boulevard and Gladiolus Drive; from there you can catch the Beach Connection Trolley to Fort Myers Beach during the winter months (see "Getting Around" in section 2 of this chapter). This route runs along U.S. 41 past the Greyhound/Trailways bus station and the Edison and Bell Tower malls. System maps are available from the Greater Fort Myers Chamber of Commerce (see "Visitor Information," above). There's no public bus service to Sanibel and Captiva islands.

For a taxi, call **Yellow Cab** (☎ **941/332-1055**), **Bluebird Taxi** (☎ **941/ 275-8294**), or **Admiralty Taxi** (☎ **941/275-7000**). Metered fares are $1.35 at flag fall plus $1.35 for each mile.

WHAT TO SEE & DO

The easiest way to see the downtown sights is to park free at the Edison and Ford Winter Estates and take the narrated **trolley,** which makes a circuit from there to the Burroughs Home, the Fort Myers Historical Museum, and the Imaginarium. It leaves the Edison home parking lot every hour on the hour on Tuesday to Saturday from 10am to 4pm. The fare is $5 for adults, $2 for children, with free reboarding. Tickets include 50¢ off admission to the other attractions.

TOURING THE ESTATES

✪ **Edison and Ford Winter Estates.** 2350 McGregor Blvd. ☎ **941/334-3614** for a recording, or 941/334-7419. Tours of both estates $10 adults, $5 children 6–12, free for children 5 and under. Mon–Sat 9am–4pm, Sun noon–4pm (last tour daily 3:30pm). Closed Thanksgiving and Christmas.

Thomas Edison and his second wife, Mina, brought their family to this Victorian retreat in 1886 (it was then known as Seminole Lodge) and wintered here until the inventor's death in 1931. Mrs. Edison gave the 14-acre estate to the city of Fort Myers in 1947, and today it stands exactly as it did during Edison's lifetime.

An avid amateur botanist, Edison experimented with the exotic foliage he planted in the lush tropical gardens surrounding the mansion (he turned goldenrod into rubber and used bamboo for lightbulb filaments). Some of his lightbulbs dating from the 1920s still burn in the laboratory where he and his staff worked on some of his 1,093 inventions. The monstrous banyan tree that shades the laboratory was 4 feet tall when Harvey S. Firestone presented it to Edison in 1925; today it's the largest banyan in Florida.

A museum displays some of Edison's inventions, as well as his unique Model T Ford, a gift from friend Henry Ford. In 1916, Ford and his wife, Clara, built **Mangoes,** their bungalow-style house next door, so they could winter with the Edisons. Like Seminole Lodge, Mangoes is furnished as it appeared in the 1920s.

You must visit the homes via guided tours, which depart the visitor center every few minutes.

OTHER DOWNTOWN ATTRACTIONS

The Georgian Revival **Burroughs Home,** 2505 1st St., at Fowler Street (☎ **941/ 332-6125**), was built on the banks of the Caloosahatchee River in 1901 by cattleman John Murphy and later sold to the Burroughs family. You must take a tour in order to visit the premises; they are given on the hour Tuesday to Friday from 11am to 3pm. Admission is $3 for adults, $1 for children 6 to 12, free for children 5 and under. Park free in the Sheraton Harbor Place garage across the street.

Housed in the restored Spanish-style depot served by the Atlantic Coast Line from 1924 to 1971, the **Fort Myers Historical Museum,** 2300 Peck St., at Jackson Street (☎ **941/332-5955**), features exhibits depicting Fort Myers's history from the ancient Calusa peoples and the Spanish conquistadors to the first settlers. A replica of an 1800s "Cracker" home stands outside, as does the Esperanza, the longest and one of the last of the plush Pullman private cars. World War II buffs can see the remains of a P-39 Aircobra, which helps explain the town's role in training fighter pilots back then. Admission is $4 for adults, $2 for children 11 and under. Open Tuesday to Saturday from 9am to 4pm.

Rather than have the kids go stir crazy on a rainy day, head for the **Imaginarium,** 2000 Cranford Ave., at Martin Luther King Jr. Boulevard (☎ **941/337-3332**), an entertaining, hands-on museum in the old city water plant. A host of toylike exhibits explains such basic scientific principles as gravity and the weather. There are nature shows in the theater every hour on the half hour. Admission is $6 for adults, $5.50 for seniors, $3 for children 3 to 12. Open Tuesday to Saturday from 10am to 5pm. Closed Thanksgiving and Christmas.

A NEARBY HISTORICAL ATTRACTION

Koreshan State Historic Site. U.S. 41 at Corkscrew Rd. (15 miles south of downtown Fort Myers). ☎ **941/992-0311**. Admission $3.25 per vehicle, $1 pedestrians or bikers. Park daily 8am–sunset; settlement buildings daily 8am–5pm. From I-75, take Exit 19 and go 2 miles west to U.S. 41.

The Koreshan Unity Movement (pronounced Kor-*esh*-en), a sect led by Chicagoan Cyrus Reed Teed, established a self-sufficient settlement on these 300 acres on the narrow Estero River in 1894. They believed that humans lived *inside* the earth and— ahead of their time—that women should have equal rights. You can visit their garden and several of their buildings, plus view photos from their archives. Nature and canoe trails wind downriver to Mound Key, an islet made of the shells discarded by the Calusa Indians (see "Canoeing & Kayaking" under "Enjoying the Outdoors," below). There's also a picnic and camping area (see "Where to Stay," below).

PARKS & NATURE PRESERVES

One of the easiest and most informative ways to see Southwest Florida's abundant wildlife is on a "swamp buggy" ride with ✪ **Babcock Wilderness Adventures,** on

Fla. 31 about 11 miles northeast of Fort Myers (☎ **800/500-5583** for reservations, or 941/338-6367 for information). Experienced naturalists lead 90-minute tours through the Babcock Ranch, the largest contiguous cattle operation east of the Mississippi River and home to countless birds and wildlife as well as domesticated bison and quarter horses. Alligators scurry from a bridge or lie motionless in the dark-brown waters of the mysterious Telegraph Swamp when the buggies pass overhead. Visitors dismount to visit an enclosure where southern cougars stand in for their close cousins, the rare Florida panthers (which are tan, not black).

Unlike most wildlife tours in the region, this one covers five different ecosystems, from open prairie to cypress swamp. A replica of an Old Florida house built by the crew making the Sean Connery movie *Just Cause* serves as a small museum. A restaurant serves lunch (alligator bites are on the menu). Admission is $17.95 for adults, $9.95 for children 3 to 12. The tours usually leave on the hour between 9am and 3pm from November to April, from 9am to noon from May through October. Reservations are required, so call ahead.

AN OLD-FASHIONED TRAIN RIDE

The **Seminole Gulf Railway** (☎ 941/275-8487), the original railroad that ran between Fort Myers and Naples, today chugs as far south as Bonita Springs on dinner excursions and sightseeing trips, and there's an occasional twilight and murder mystery run. Call for the schedules, which vary from season to season. Reservations are required for the dinner trip. The trains depart Fort Myers from the Metro Mall Station, a small blue building on the western edge of the Metro Mall parking lot on Colonial Boulevard at Metro Parkway. The Bonita Springs station is on Old U.S. 41 at Pennsylvania Avenue.

SHOPPING

An institution for more than 50 years, **The Shell Factory,** 5 miles north of the Caloosahatchee River bridge on U.S. 41 (☎ **941/995-2141**), carries one of the world's largest collections of shells, corals, sponges, and fossils. Entire sections are devoted to shell jewelry and shell lamps. Many items here cost under $10, some under $1. Open daily from 10am to 6pm.

Bargain hunters can browse more than 800 booths carrying antiques, crafts, fashions, and produce at **Fleamasters,** 4135 Dr. Martin Luther King Jr. Blvd. (Fla. 82), 1½ miles west of 1-75 (☎ **941/334-7001**). There are snack bars and entertainment, too. Open on Friday, Saturday, and Sunday from 8am to 4pm. You'll find even more old stuff at **AMTEL Fleamarket Mall,** in the old Metro Mall shopping complex at the corner of Metro Parkway and Colonial Boulevard (☎ **941/939-3132**), where stalls are open Wednesday to Sunday from 9am to 5pm.

Anchored by Saks Fifth Avenue and Jacobson's, the Spanish-style **Bell Tower Shops,** Tamiami Trail (U.S. 41) at Daniels Parkway (☎ **941/489-1221**), is Fort Myers's upscale mall. Open Monday to Wednesday from 10am to 7pm, Thursday to Saturday from 10am to 9pm, and Sunday from noon to 5pm. You'll find most of the familiar national stores at **Edison Mall,** Cleveland Avenue (U.S. 41) at Winkler Avenue (☎ **941/939-5464**), including JC Penney, Sears, Dillards, and a two-part Burdine's. Open Monday to Saturday from 10am to 9pm, Sunday from 11:30am to 5:30pm.

Outlet shoppers will find a large Levi's store among other major-brand shops at the **Sanibel Factory Stores,** on the way to the beaches at the junction of Summerlin Road and McGregor Boulevard (☎ **888/SHOP-333** or 941/454-1616). Open Monday to Saturday from 10am to 9pm, Sunday from 11am to 6pm.

ENJOYING THE OUTDOORS

CANOEING & KAYAKING   The area's slow-moving rivers and quiet, island-speckled inland waters offer fine canoe and kayak ventures; you'll visit birds and manatees along the way. Two popular local venues are the winding waterways around Pine Island west of town and the Estero River south of Fort Myers. The Estero River route is an official Florida canoe trail and leads 3½ miles from U.S. 41 to Estero Bay, which is itself a state aquatic preserve (see "Enjoying the Outdoors" in section 2). Near the mouth of the river lies **Mound Key State Archeological Site,** one of the largest Calusa shell middens. Scholars believe that this mostly artificial island dates back some 2,000 years and was the capital of the Calusa chief who ruled all of South Florida when the Spanish arrived. There's no park ranger on the key, but signs explain its history.

Estero River Outfitters, at the Estero River bridge on U.S. 41 (☎ 941/992-4050), rents canoes for $22.50 to $27.50 a day, and kayaks from $17.50 to $27.50. Open daily 7am to 6pm. Nearby, **Koreshan State Historic Site,** half a mile south of the bridge at the intersection of U.S. 41 and Corkscrew Road (☎ 941/992-0311), rents canoes for $3 an hour, $15 per day (see "A Nearby Historical Attraction," above).

Based in Matlacha on Pine Island, the **Gulf Coast Kayak Company** (☎ 941/283-1125 or 941/283-6213) has guided nature, manatee-watching, and sunset trips, plus overnight and longer expeditions to North Captiva and Cayo Costa. Call for reservations and schedules.

CRUISES   J.C. Boat Cruises (☎ 941/334-7474) presents a variety of year-round cruises on the Caloosahatchee River and its tributaries, including lunch and dinner voyages on the sternwheeler *Captain J.P.* The 3-hour Everglades Jungle Cruise is a good way to observe the area's wildlife, with lots of manatees to be seen from November to April. A full-day cruise goes all the way up the Caloosahatchee to Lake Okeechobee and back. The ticket office is at the downtown Fort Myers City Yacht Basin, Edwards Drive at Lee Street, opposite the chamber of commerce. Prices range from $14 to $74. Schedules change and advance reservations are strongly recommended.

Another way to see manatees and other wildlife is with **Fort Myers Manatee and Eco Tours** (☎ 941/693-1434), based at the Coastal Marine Mart on Fla. 80 just east of I-75. Cruises usually depart at 10am, noon, and 2 and 4pm, but call ahead for reservations. Fares are $12.75 for adults, $6.75 for children under 12.

The *Tropic Star* (☎ 941/283-0015) leaves the Four Winds Marina on Pine Island daily at 9:30am for Cayo Costa and Cabbage Key. Fares are $20 for adults, $12 for children 3 to 12. See "Nearby Island Hopping" in section 3, on Sanibel and Captiva islands, for information about Cayo Costa and Cabbage Key.

The sleek, 100-foot-long yacht *Sanibel Harbour Princess* (☎ 941/644-2128) goes on dinner cruises from its base at Sanibel Harbour Resort & Spa (see "Where to Stay," below). Prices range from $25 to $35 per person, depending on the season, and include a glass of champagne and buffet dinner nightly and entertainment on weekends. There's a Sunday brunch cruise during winter. Call for reservations and departure times.

GOLF & TENNIS   For an excellent rundown of Southwest Florida golf courses, pick up a free copy of *Golfer's Guide,* available at the visitor information centers and many hotel lobbies. See "The Active Vacation Planner," in chapter 2, for information about subscribing or ordering the current edition. And don't forget that you can call **Tee Times USA** (☎ 800/374-8633 or 888/465-3356) and book starting times at Florida courses.

Although it looks like an exclusive private enclave, the **Fort Myers Country Club,** McGregor Boulevard at Hill Avenue (☎ **941/936-2457**), actually is a municipal course. Designed in 1917 by Donald Ross, it's flat and uninteresting by today's standards, but it's right in town. **Smitty's,** a steak and seafood restaurant, now occupies the fine old clubhouse. The city's other municipal course is the more challenging **Eastwood Golf Club,** on Ortiz Avenue between Colonial and Dr. Martin Luther King Jr. boulevards in the eastern suburbs (☎ **941/275-4848**). Greens fees at both range from about $30 in summer to $55 during winter. Nonresidents must book tee times at least 24 hours in advance.

Other area courses open to the public include the Tom Fazio–designed **Gateway Golf & Country Club,** on Daniels Parkway east of the airport (☎ **941/561-1010**); the two nationally acclaimed **Pelican's Nest** courses in Bonita Springs (☎ **941/947-4600**); **Coral Oaks Golf Club** in Cape Coral (☎ **941/283-4800**); **Alden Pines Country Club** on Pine Island (☎ **941/283-2179**); **San Carolos Golf Club** in South Fort Myers (☎ **941/267-3131**); **Bonita Springs Golf & Country Club** in Bonita Springs (☎ **941/992-2800**); and **El Rio Golf Club** (☎ **941/995-2204**) and **Riverbend Golf Club** (☎ **941/543-2200**), both in North Fort Myers.

Tennis buffs can play at the **Fort Myers Racquet Club,** 4900 Deleon St. (☎ **941/278-7277**), which has eight lighted courts. **Sanibel Harbour Resort & Spa** is well known for its excellent tennis programs for both juniors and adults (see "Where to Stay," below).

WATCHING THE BOYS OF SPRING

While many Major League Baseball teams have jumped around Florida for their **spring training,** the Boston Red Sox and the Minnesota Twins have worked out in Fort Myers for years. The **Boston Red Sox** play at the 6,500-seat City of Palms Park, at Edison Avenue and Broadway (☎ **941/334-4700**). The **Minnesota Twins** work out at the 7,500-seat Lee County Sports Complex, on Six Mile Cypress Parkway between Daniels and Metro parkways (☎ **800/338-9467** or 941/768-4270).

Fort Myers is about an hour's drive south of Charlotte County Stadium (☎ **941/625-9500**), where the **Texas Rangers** hold their spring training. To get there, take I-75 north to Exit 32, then west to the end of Toledo Blade Boulevard. Turn right there onto Fla. 776. The stadium is on the left.

WHERE TO STAY

As in the rest of southern Florida, room rates here are highest, and reservations essential, during winter, from mid-December to April. Even hotels and motels removed from the beach charge premium rates then. If you can't get a room at the properties mentioned below, the **Lee Island Coast Visitor and Convention Bureau** operates a free reservation service (☎ **800/733-7935**) covering many more accommodations in Fort Myers, Fort Myers Beach, and Sanibel and Captiva islands.

Don't be misled by our categories, which are determined by high, winter-season rates. During the off-season they drop by as much as 50% or more. All hotel bills in Southwest Florida are subject to a 9% tax.

Fort Myers has almost every chain motel along Cleveland Avenue (U.S. 41), in all price ranges. Many business travelers stay at the **Holiday Inn Central,** 2431 Cleveland Ave. (☎ **800/998-0466** or 941/332-3232), but the location near the corner of Edison Avenue is a plus for vacationers, too; it's a 2-block walk to the Boston Red Sox training facility and a short drive to the Edison and Ford homes. There's an outdoor pool, a 24-hour Denny's restaurant, and a tavern with live entertainment. Winter rates are $129 to $139 double; off-season they drop to $59 to $85 double.

If you want more space and a kitchen, **Residence Inn by Marriott,** 2960 Colonial Blvd. (☎ **800/331-3131** or 941/936-0110; fax 941/936-4144), diagonally across the intersection from the Courtyard by Marriott (see below), has 78 units ranging from L-shaped suites to two-bedroom apartments. They cost from $139 to $179 during winter, from $79 to $99 off-season, including continental breakfast and weekday cocktail receptions. A similar choice is **Homewood Suites Hotel,** 5255 Big Pine Way (☎ **800/225-5466** or 941/275-6000; fax 941/275-6601), a more luxurious establishment at the Bell Tower Shops complex. It charges $179 to $189 in winter, $109 off-season, including breakfast and evening wine, beer, and an extensive snack buffet. Both hotels have pools, exercise rooms, and coin laundries.

On Daniels Parkway near the airport at Exit 22 off I-75 are new, completely modern versions of **Hampton Inn** (☎ **800/426-7866** or 941/768-2525), **Comfort Suites** (☎ **800/435-8234** or 941/768-0005), and **Sleep Inn** (☎ **800/358-3170** or 941/561-1117).

The only true campground here is about 15 miles south of downtown Fort Myers at **Koreshan State Historic Site,** on U.S. 41 in Estero (☎ **941/992-0311;** fax 941/992-1607), which has 60 wooded sites for tents or RVs at $16 per night during winter, $10 a night off-season (see "What to See & Do," above, for information about the historic site). Reservations are accepted up to 11 months in advance year-round.

VERY EXPENSIVE

❂ **Sanibel Harbour Resort & Spa.** 17260 Harbour Pointe Rd., Fort Myers, FL 33908. ☎ **800/767-7777** or 941/466-4000. Fax 941/466-2150. www.sanibel-resort.com. 240 units, 80 2-bedroom condo apts. A/C MINIBAR TV TEL. Winter $270–$325 double; $335 suite; $320–$599 condo apt. Off-season $130–$225 double; $240 suite; $169–$449 condo apt. Packages available. AE, DC, DISC, MC, V. Valet parking $8; free self-parking. Take the last exit off Summerlin Rd. before the Sanibel Causeway toll plaza.

This secluded, sports-oriented resort overlooks San Carlos Bay and Sanibel Island from Punta Rassa, next to the Sanibel Causeway (a complimentary shuttle takes guests to the island three times a day). A waterside cupola-topped pavilion evokes the turn-of-the-century resort that once stood on this point, but the 11-story hotel is modern and luxurious throughout. All rooms and most of the condo apartments have wonderful water and island views from their balconies, including spectacular sunsets over Sanibel. This large hostelry hosts many conventions and groups, although active couples make up a sizable portion of the clientele. Tennis fans take note: The resort includes a 5,000-seat stadium that has hosted Davis Cup matches in the past.

Dining/Diversions: The intimate Chez Le Bear leads the food outlets here, with the casual Promenade providing calorie-conscious fare for the pumping-iron set. Lounges have entertainment during the winter season, and there's a sports bar.

Amenities: Concierge, room service (5am to midnight), laundry, children's activity program. There's a state-of-the-art, 40,000-square-foot fitness center with spa, massage, and facials. Other sporting facilities include bay-side indoor and outdoor swimming pools with hot tubs and bars; 13 lighted tennis courts; jogging, fitness, and kayak trails; a marina with boat and water-sports equipment rentals and day and sunset cruises. Except for sunset cruises, only guests can use the facilities here, and they pay extra for most activities.

EXPENSIVE

Sheraton Harbor Place. 2500 Edwards Dr. (at Fowler St.), Fort Myers, FL 33901. ☎ **800/ 833-1620** or 941/337-0300. Fax 941/337-1530. 416 units. A/C MINIBAR TV TEL. Winter $155–$165 double; $165–$185 suite. Off-season $95–$115 double; $115–$135 suite. AE, DC, DISC, MC, V.

Downtown Fort Myers's only large hotel caters primarily to conventiongoers and business travelers. Service is efficient, but don't expect personalized treatment if a large group such as the Boston Red Sox is in town (the big leaguers usually stay here during spring training). Most rooms in the 25-story tower have spectacular views, many over the Caloosahatchee River. Suites come equipped with kitchenettes and bookcaselike cabinets that divide the living and sleeping areas.

Dining/Diversions: With a river view from the second floor, La Tiers restaurant is open for breakfast, lunch, and dinner. Opening to a resortlike area with two outdoor swimming pools, the Aqua Bar is surrounded by waterfalls and flaunts Florida's largest indoor mural, depicting an undersea fantasy world. Entertainment is offered on Friday and Saturday evenings in the Marina Lounge, which overlooks the river.

Amenities: Complimentary airport, Edison/Ford homes shuttles; concierge; room service (6:30am to 10pm). Heated indoor and outdoor swimming pools, lighted tennis court, exercise room, game room, bike rentals, gift shop, Laundromat.

MODERATE

✪ **Courtyard by Marriott.** 4455 Metro Pkwy. (at the corner of Colonial Blvd.), Fort Myers, FL 33901. ☎ **800/321-2211** or 941/275-8600. Fax 941/275-7087. 149 units. A/C TV TEL. Winter $129 double. Off-season $64 double. Weekend rates available. AE, DC, DISC, MC, V.

This exceptionally comfortable hotel designed for business travelers is situated out of the major traffic, 4 miles south of downtown and 10 miles north of the beach. Surrounding a landscaped courtyard with a swimming pool, the sizable rooms all have sofas or easy chairs and rich mahogany writing tables and chests of drawers, plus extra little features like two phones and hand-basin faucets dispensing piping-hot water for tea and instant coffee (which are supplied). The marble lobby features a fireplace and dining area serving breakfast only. Other facilities include an exercise room, indoor spa pool, and guest laundry.

Holiday Inn SunSpree Resort. 2220 W. 1st St. (at Euclid Ave.), Fort Myers, FL 33901. ☎ **800/HOLIDAY** or 941/334-3434. Fax 941/334-3844. 152 units. A/C TV TEL. Winter $119–$169 double. Off-season $79–$129 double. AE, DC, DISC, MC, V.

This islandy riverside hotel is best known locally for the adjacent Shooters Waterfront Café USA, an enormously popular restaurant and bar (see "Where to Dine," below). Some of the suites are near the outdoor bar where Shooters' bands play—which can mean a bit too much entertainment for some guests' ears (others love the constant nighttime action). Rooms at the front the property, however, are far enough removed to render a quiet and convenient base from which to explore the nearby Edison and Ford Winter Estates and other downtown attractions.

The L-shaped building flanks a large courtyard with both adults' and children's pools surrounded by palms and a colorful patio. There's a fenced children's playground adjacent. Other facilities include a beauty salon with massage, an activities desk, and a small reading room off the marble-floored lobby. Shooters opens for breakfast at 7am daily, and the Oasis Restaurant is virtually across the street (see "Where to Dine," below).

INEXPENSIVE

✪ **Budgetel Inn.** 2717 Colonial Blvd., Fort Myers, FL 33907. ☎ **800/428-3438** or 941/275-3500. Fax 941/275-5426. 122 units. Winter $79–$89 double. Off-season $42–$46 double. Rates include continental breakfast. AE, DC, DISC, MC, V.

Like most members of the small but growing Budgetel Inn chain, this modern, four-story establishment offers exceptional value with large, well-equipped rooms. It's centrally situated near the Courtyard by Marriott and Residence Inn by Marriott (see above) and offers an outdoor swimming pool. Entered from exterior walkways, the comfortably furnished rooms have extras like coffeemakers, desks, and free local calls (I consider Budgetel Inns to be the poor person's Courtyard by Marriott). Complimentary juice and Danish are left at your door before dawn.

WHERE TO DINE

Some Southwest Florida restaurants adjust their hours from season to season and even from year to year, so you may want to call ahead to make sure of an establishment's business hours.

Fort Myers's main commercial strip, Cleveland Avenue (U.S. 41), has most national fast-food and family chain restaurants, especially near College Parkway. There's a branch of **Mel's Diner,** the excellent regional chain, at 4820 S. Cleveland Ave., opposite Page Field (☎ **941/275-7850**), offering inexpensive diner-style fare including breakfast served anytime.

EXPENSIVE

The Chart House. 2024 W. 1st St. (at Henley Place). ☎ **941/332-1881.** Reservations recommended. Main courses $15–$36. AE, DC, DISC, MC, V. Mon–Fri 11:30am–3:30pm and 4:30–9:30pm; Fri 11:30am–3:30pm. Sun–Thurs 4:30–10pm, Fri–Sat 4:30–11pm. SEAFOOD/BEEF.

You can't dine outdoors here, but great views are a prime draw at this riverside member of the national chain. Seafood offerings include orange-basil salmon and charcoal-broiled fresh fish and lobster. The grill also produces fine steaks, and prime rib is a house specialty. The lengthy salad bar is one of the area's best. Early birds can enjoy the fine sunsets and save $5 off the price of any main course.

✪ **Peter's La Cuisine.** 2224 Bay St. (at Bayview Court). ☎ **941/332-2228.** Reservations recommended. Main courses $25–$30; snacks in upstairs bar $6.50–$15. AE, MC, V. Mon–Fri 11:30am–2pm and 5:30–9:30pm, Sat–Sun 5:30–9:30pm. Upstairs Bar & Bistro, Mon–Fri 4pm–2am, Sat–Sun 5:30pm–2am. CONTINENTAL.

Even other restaurateurs say Bavarian-born chef Peter Schmid's elegant establishment, in downtown's second oldest building, is their favorite place to dine. Peter masterfully blends European cuisine with local seafood, fruits, and vegetables. In addition to seafood, Peter offers pheasant, veal, and steaks with continental sauces. The dining room has a refined ambience, with tuxedoed waiters providing efficient and unobtrusive service, while his casual Upstairs Bar & Bistro is lively and offers light fare—best bets are the same delightful appetizers served downstairs—and nightly entertainment (see "Fort Myers After Dark," below). Patrons up there can wander out onto a rooftop garden.

MODERATE

✪ **Sasse's.** 3651 Evans Ave. (between Carrell Rd. and Winkler Ave.). ☎ **941/278-5544.** Reservations not accepted. Main courses $8–$18. No credit cards. Tues–Fri 11:30am–1:15pm, Wed–Sat 5:30–8:15pm. CONTINENTAL/ITALIAN.

In a small shopping strip near the Fort Myers Recreation Center north of the Edison Mall, this popular little spot offers one of the area's most unusual and reasonably priced dining experiences. Aromas waft from the wood-fired oven in the open kitchen, from which come enormous slabs of pizzalike bread (served with seasoned olive oil for dipping) and the likes of log-roasted lemon chicken. The selections change daily, although you can usually count on braised lamb shank served over steamed vegetables and veal scallopini stuffed with prosciutto, roasted peppers, and mozzarella. It's all of a quality rarely found at these prices, and the portions are so huge that most patrons carry home doggie bags (there's a $5 fee to share a single dish). The storefront setting is too cramped for romantic dining, but it's fun and the food is certainly worth putting up with the din of busily working chefs and happily chatting diners.

✪ Shooters Waterfront Café USA. At Holiday Inn SunSpree Resort, 2220 W. First St. (at Euclid Ave.). ☎ **941/334-2727.** Reservations not accepted. Salads and sandwiches $6–$10; main courses $10–$16; Sun brunch $15. AE, DC, DISC, MC, V. Daily 7–10am and 11am–11pm (bar open later); Sun brunch 10am–2pm. AMERICAN.

Granted, this pub gets noisy and crowded after sunset, when it turns into Fort Myers's most popular watering hole, but the entire north wall slides open to a river-side deck, making this the most attractive spot in town for a relaxing, alfresco lunch break while seeing the sights or for watching the sun set over the Caloosahatchee. The cuisine is typically modern pub fare: a variety of pizzas, California-style pastas, grilled fish, seafood platters, steaks, and prime rib. The best bet for lunch is the reliable grouper (fried, blackened, or grilled) sandwich.

INEXPENSIVE

Basile's. In the Edison Park Shopping Center, 2215-C Winkler Ave. (between Cleveland Ave. and Fowler St., opposite Edison Mall). ☎ **941/278-4600.** Reservations recommended in winter. Pastas and main courses $8–$14; early bird specials $14 (for 2 persons). MC, V. Mon–Fri 11am–10pm, Sat noon–10pm, Sun noon–9:30pm. ITALIAN.

Transplanted New Yorker Sal Basile's small dining room has a wall-size mural of an Italian scene to set the stage for food reminiscent of Little Italy. You can order the usual run of pastas or try the veal shantella with shrimp and scallops in a delightful cream sauce. The portions are huge and are accompanied by soup, salad, and very garlicky homemade rolls. These same monstrous meals are offered for lunch at greatly reduced prices, and complete dinners for two are served on Friday, Saturday, and Sunday for $12.95. Early birds get a choice of pastas.

The adjoining **Taste of New York** (same phone) has excellent pizza to dine in or carry out.

✪ Farmers Market Restaurant. 2736 Edison Ave. (at Cranford Ave.). ☎ **941/334-1687.** Breakfast $3–$5; sandwiches $2–$6; meals $4–$8. No credit cards. Mon–Sat 6am–8pm, Sun 6am–7pm. SOUTHERN.

The retail Farmers Market next door may be tiny, but the best of the cabbage, okra, green beans, and tomatoes ends up here at this plain and simple restaurant frequented by everyone from business executives to truck drivers. The specialties of the house are smoked beef, pork barbecue, and other Southern favorites like country-fried steak, fried chicken livers and gizzards, and smoked ham hocks with a bowl of black-eyed peas. Yankees can order fried chicken, roast beef, or pork chops, and they can have hash browns instead of grits with their big breakfast.

Oasis Restaurant. In Edison-Ford Sq., 2222 McGregor Blvd. (at Euclid Ave.). ☎ **941/334-1566.** Breakfast $3–$6; sandwiches, burgers, and salads $4–$5.50. No credit cards. Mon–Fri 7am–3pm, Sat–Sun 8am–2pm. AMERICAN.

Near the Edison and Ford homes, Bonnie Grunberg and Tammie Shockey work hard to make their narrow storefront establishment appeal to young professionals who don't mind sitting elbow to elbow while recovering from a night at Shooters Waterfront Café USA (just behind this shopping center) with a "hangover" omelette—Italian sausage and vegetables under melted cheese. Breakfast fare is served all day here, and you can take advantage of a $1.99 eye-opening special weekdays from 7 to 9:30am. Lunches provide made-to-order Reubens, Monte Cristos, and Philly cheese-steak subs, plus soups and salads.

FORT MYERS AFTER DARK

For entertainment ideas and schedules, consult the daily *News-Press,* especially Friday's "Gulf Coasting" section. Also be on the lookout for *Happenings,* a tabloid-size entertainment guide which is distributed free at the visitor information offices and in some hotel lobbies.

The city's showcase performing arts venue is the $7 million **Barbara B. Mann Performing Arts Hall,** 8099 College Pkwy., at Summerlin Road (☎ **941/489-3033**), on the campus of Edison Community College. It features world-famous performers, Broadway plays, and wintertime concerts by the **Southwest Florida Symphony** (☎ **941/433-3040** for information, or 941/481-4849 for tickets).

Originally a downtown vaudeville playhouse, the 1908-vintage **Arcade Theater,** 2267 1st St. (☎ **941/332-6688**), presents a variety of performances.

Leading the bar scene, ✪ **Shooters Waterfront Café USA,** at the Holiday Inn Sun-Spree Resort, 2220 W. 1st St. (☎ **941/334-2727**), has live bands or a DJ spinning CDs almost every night at a riverside "chickee hut," a thatched-roof bar. National musicians often perform in the casual **Upstairs Bar & Bistro** above Peter's La Cuisine, 2224 Bay St. (☎ **941/332-2228**); recent guests have included Maria Muldaur, Matt "Guitar" Murphy, Debbie Davis, and Savoy Brown. See "Where to Dine," above, for more about these two establishments.

If you *must* watch your favorite team play back home, **Slugger's Sports Bar & Grill,** 16440 S. Tamiami Trail (U.S. 41), at Island Park Drive, about 12 miles south of downtown (☎ **941/489-0505**), is the largest such facility in the region, with nearly two dozen TV screens. Families are welcome, if they can stand the smoke (cigars are allowed in one corner).

2 Fort Myers Beach

13 miles S of Fort Myers, 28 miles N of Naples, 12 miles E of Sanibel Island

Often overshadowed by trendy Sanibel and Captiva islands to the north and ritzy Naples to the south, down-to-earth Fort Myers Beach on Estero Island offers just as much sun and sand, and at more moderate prices, as its affluent neighbors.

Droves of both families and young singles flock to the busy intersection of San Carlos and Estero boulevards, an area so packed with bars, beach apparel shops, restaurants, and motels that the locals call it "Times Square." The city has spiffed up Times Square lately by installing a pedestrian-only mall and improving traffic flow, and some of the establishments have been upgraded.

That Coney Island image certainly doesn't apply to the rest of Estero Island, where old-fashioned beach cottages, manicured condos, and quiet motels beckon couples and families in search of more sedate vacations. In fact, promoters of the southern end of the island say that they're not in Fort Myers Beach; they're on Estero Island. It's their way of distinguishing their part of town from congested Times Square.

The island is separated from the mainland by narrow Matanzas Pass and broad Estero Bay. While the pass is the area's largest commercial fishing port (when they say "fresh off the boat" here, they aren't kidding), the bay is an official state aquatic preserve inhabited by a host of birds as well as manatees, dolphins, and other sea life. Nature cruises go forth onto this lovely protected bay, which is dotted with islands.

A few miles south of Fort Myers Beach, a chain of pristine barrier islands includes unspoiled Lover's Key, a state park where a tractor-pulled tram runs through a mangrove forest to a lovely beach.

ESSENTIALS

GETTING THERE   From Fort Myers, take either McGregor Boulevard or Summerlin Road and turn left on San Carlos Boulevard (County Road 865). From I-75 and the airport, follow Daniels Parkway (which becomes Cypress Lake Drive after it crosses U.S. 41) due west. Turn left on Summerlin Road, then left again on San Carlos Boulevard. From Naples, take either I-75 or U.S. 41 north to Bonita Springs, then go west on Bonita Beach Road (County Road 865), which turns north into Estero Boulevard through Fort Myers Beach.

See section 1, "Fort Myers," for information about Southwest Florida International Airport, car-rental firms, Amtrak's trains, and Greyhound/Trailways bus service to the area.

VISITOR INFORMATION   The **Fort Myers Beach Chamber of Commerce,** 17200 San Carlos Blvd., Fort Myers Beach, FL 33931 (☎ **800/782-9283** or 941/454-7500; fax 941/454-7910; www.coconet.com/fmbeach), provides free information, sells a detailed street map for $1, and operates a visitor welcome center on the mainland portion of San Carlos Boulevard just south of Summerlin Road. Open Monday to Friday from 8am to 6pm, Saturday from 10am to 6pm, and Sunday from 11am to 5pm.

Over at the beach, the **Tourist Information Center** on Estero Boulevard at Chapel Street (☎ **941/463-3178**) is operated by Hussey Real Estate, but it's a good source for maps and brochures as well as reservations at hotels, motels, condos, and cottages. It's open Monday to Friday from 10am to 6pm, Saturday and Sunday from 10am to 4pm.

GETTING AROUND   An alternative to heavy wintertime traffic and limited parking is the **Beach Connection Trolley,** which during winter operates daily from 8am to 8pm between Summerlin Square Shopping Center, at Summerlin Road and San Carlos Boulevard on the mainland, and Bonita Beach. The route takes it along the full length of Estero Boulevard, including Lover's Key. During the off-season it runs from Bowditch Regional Park at the north end of Estero Boulevard south to Lover's Key. It costs 25¢ per ride. Ask your hotel staff or call **LeeTran** (☎ **941/275-8726**) for schedules.

During the winter LeeTran also operates a Monday-to-Saturday beach shuttle from the parking lots at the Summerlin Square Shopping Center, Summerlin Road at San Carlos Boulevard; the Sanibel Factory Outlets, Summerlin Road at McGregor Boulevard; the McGregor Point Shopping Center, Gladiolus Drive at McGregor Boulevard; and the Main Street Park 'n' Ride Lot on San Carlos Island. The Main Street–Bowditch Park section also runs on Sunday. The shuttle fare is $1.

For a cab, call **Local Motion Taxi** (☎ **941/463-4111**).

There are no bike paths per se here, although many folks ride along the paved shoulders of Estero Boulevard. A variety of rental bikes, scooters, and in-line skates are available at **Fun Rentals,** 1901 Estero Blvd. at Ohio Avenue (☎ **941/463-8844**), and **Scooters, Inc.,** 1698 Estero Blvd. at Avenue E (☎ **941/463-1007**). Both charge about $20 a day for scooters, from $6 an hour to $14 a day for bikes.

HITTING THE BEACH

A prime attraction for beachgoers is the gorgeous ✪ **Lover's Key–Carl E. Johnson State Recreation Area,** 8700 Estero Blvd. (☎ **941/463-4588**), on the totally preserved Lover's Key, south of Estero Island. Although the highway runs down the center of the island, access to this unspoiled beach from the parking lot is restricted to footpaths or a tractor-pulled tram through a bird-filled forest of mangroves and casuarinas.

The beach itself is known for its multitude of shells. There are bathhouses with outdoor showers, a snack shop, and canoe and kayak rentals at the parking lot. The park is open daily from 8am to 5pm. Admission is $4 per vehicle with two to eight occupants, $2 for vehicles with a single occupant, and $1 for pedestrians and bicyclists. No alcohol is allowed, nor are pets permitted on the beach or in the water (you must keep them on a leash elsewhere in the park).

On Estero Island, **Lynn Hall Memorial Park** features a fishing pier and beach right in the middle of Times Square. It has changing rooms, rest rooms, and one of the few public parking lots in the area; the meter costs 75¢ per hour, but keep it fed—there's a $32 fine if your time runs out! At the island's north end, **Bowditch Regional Park** has picnic tables, cold-water showers, and changing rooms. It has parking only for drivers with disabled permits, but it's the turnaround point for the Beach Connection Trolley.

Several beach locations are hotbeds of parasailing, WaveRunners, sailboats, and other beach activities. **Times Square,** at the intersection of San Carlos and Estero boulevards, and the **Best Western Beach Resort,** about a quarter-mile north, are popular spots on Estero's busy north end. Another hotbed is on the beach in front of **Anthony's on the Gulf** restaurant and the **Junkanoo Beach Bar** in the middle beach area (see "Where to Dine," below). Down south, activities are centered around the **Holiday Inn** and the **Outrigger Beach Resort** (see "Where to Stay," below).

ENJOYING THE OUTDOORS

BOATING & BOAT RENTALS   Powerboats are available from the **Mid Island Marina** (☎ 941/765-4371), the **Fort Myers Beach Marina** (☎ 941/463-9552), the **Fish Tale Marina** (☎ 941/463-3600), the **Palm Grove Marina** (☎ 941/463-7333), and the **Summer Winds Marina** (☎ 941/454-6333). **Dockside Boat Rentals** (☎ 941/765-4433) rents them at the Best Western Pink Shell Resort on Estero Island's northern end.

CRUISES   Two of the best environmental tours in this area are with ✪ **Calusa Coast Outfitters,** 7225 Estero Blvd., at the Fish Tale Marina behind Villa Santini shopping center (☎ **941/463-4448**). Guests who go with Arden Arrington, a director of the Southwest Florida Historical Society, can listen through hydrophones as dolphins "speak" to each other, or they can go on a guided walk on historic Mound Key, the old Calusa Indian shell island at the mouth of the Estero River. Arden's 3-hour dolphin tours depart Tuesday and Thursday at 2pm and cost $28.50 for adults, $25 for seniors, $14 for kids under 13. The Mound Key trips depart Tuesday and Thursday at 10am (they involve considerable hiking at Mound Key and are not recommended for children or adults with health problems). They cost $28.50 for adults. Reservations are required for all trips, so call ahead.

Another way to see the dolphins up close is on a WaveRunner tour with **Holiday Water Sports,** which operates on the beach in front of the Best Western Pink Shell (☎ **941/765-4386**) and the Best Western Beach Resort (☎ **941/463-6778**), both north of Times Square. They don't do these exciting excursions all the time, so call for details.

Much easier nature excursions are on the *Island Queen* (☎ 941/765-4433), a pontoon boat that operates out of the Best Western Pink Shell Beach Resort marina on the north end of the island (see "Where to Stay," below). It usually goes on 1½-hour nature cruises Monday, Wednesday, and Friday afternoons. Prices are $12.50 for adults, $7 for children. The *Island Queen* also has bay fishing trips Monday, Wednesday, and Friday mornings ($25 adults, $22.50 children) and shelling trips on Thursday ($25 adults, $12 children). Reservations are recommended.

A similar pontoon boat, the *Pelican Queen,* operates from Mid Island Marina, 4765 Estero Blvd. (☎ **941/765-4354**). It has sightseeing nature cruises from 10am to 1pm Monday to Saturday, with adults paying $14, children $8.

For sailing enthusiasts, the 72-foot topsail schooner *Island Rover* (☎ **941/ 691-7777**) has morning family cruises, afternoon sunbathing excursions, sunset sails, and moonlight cruises on the gulf from its base under the Sky Bridge on Estero Island. Prices are $15 for adults, $10 for children on the day sails; $25 per person for the sunset and moonlight trips. Soft drinks, beer, wine, and champagne are available on board. The schedule changes by season, so call ahead for information and reservations. The *Island Rover* also is available for "boat-and-breakfast" cruises during the winter months, with rates starting at $149 double.

FISHING   Anglers can surf-cast, throw their lines off the pier at Times Square, or venture offshore on a number of charter fishing boats that dock at marinas under both ends of the Skyway Bridge. Agents have booths there to take reservations even when the boats are out.

No reservations are required on "party boats" that take groups out from December to April. The *Black Whale III* (☎ **941/765-5550**) and the *Island Lady* (☎ **941/ 936-7470**) are docked at Fisherman's Wharf, virtually under the San Carlos Island end of the Skyway Bridge. The *Miss Point Lookout III* (☎ **941/765-7786**) is based at the Palm Grove Marina, on Main Street on San Carlos Island. The *Great Getaway* and *Great Getaway II* (☎ **941/466-3600**) sail from the Getaway Marina on San Carlos Boulevard about half a mile north of the bridge. They all depart between 8 and 9:30am, charge between $25 and $40 per person, depending on the length of the voyage, and have air-conditioned lounges with bars.

GOLF & TENNIS   Before heading to the more challenging mainland courses, duffers can tune their game at the par-61 **Bay Beach Golf Club,** 7401 Estero Blvd. (☎ **941/463-2064**). It's open to the public daily from 7:30am to 5pm. Bay Beach Golf Club also has tennis courts available.

SCUBA DIVING & SNORKELING   Scuba diving is available at **Seahorse Scuba,** 17849 San Carlos Blvd. (☎ **941/454-3111**). Two-tank dives cost $55. Groups of four snorkelers can go on their own excursions for $25 each, including equipment. The company also offers dive packages including bed-and-breakfast accommodations.

WHERE TO STAY

The hostelries recommended below are removed from the crowds of Times Square, but three chain motels offer comfortable accommodations right in the center of the action: **Ramada Inn** (☎ **800/544-4592** or 941/463-6158), **Days Inn** (☎ **800/ 544-4592** or 941/463-9759), and **Howard Johnson's Motel** (☎ **800/544-4592** or 941/463-9231). The midrise **Best Western Beach Resort** (☎ **800/336-4045** or 941/ 463-6000) is a quarter mile north, just far enough to escape the noise but still have a lively beach.

Fort Myers Beach has a multitude of condominiums and cottages that offer good value, especially for families or groups who would like to have a kitchen and other comforts of home. The Best Western Pink Shell Resort (see below) has a selection of luxurious condos and some of the most charming cottages.

Among several "condo hotels" here, **Pointe Estero Island Resort,** 6640 Estero Blvd., Fort Myers Beach, FL 33931 (☎ **800/237-5141** or 941/765-1155; fax 941/ 765-0657), a 16-story luxury tower facing the beach, has 60 spacious apartments with Jacuzzi bathtubs and screened balconies with gorgeous gulf or bay views. Rates range from $215 to $365 a day during winter, from $125 to $285 off-season. The same company also handles the less-expensive, bay-side **Santa Maria,** 7317 Estero Blvd., Fort Myers Beach, FL 33931 (☎ **800/765-6701** or 941/765-6700; fax 941/ 765-6909), and the **Grand View Resort,** 8701 Estero Blvd., Fort Myers Beach, FL 33931 (☎ **800/723-4944** or 941/765-4422; fax 941/765-4499), a 14-story high-rise on Lover's Key with its own palm-fringed beach and wonderful gulf, island, and bay views from balcony suites.

A number of agents offer weekly or monthly rentals, including **Hussey Real Estate** (☎ **941/463-3178;** fax 941/463-5434), which operates the "Tourist Information Center" on Estero Boulevard (see "Essentials," above), and **Bluebill Properties** (☎ **800/237-2010** or 941/463-1141), which represents properties throughout Southwest Florida. The chamber of commerce (see "Essentials," above) publishes a complete list of accommodations and rental agents.

For information about rate seasons, see "Where to Stay" in section 1.

For campers, the somewhat cramped **Red Coconut RV Resort,** 3001 Estero Blvd. (☎ **941/463-7200;** fax 941/463-2609), has sites for RVs and tents on both the gulf side of the road and right on the beach. They cost $36 to $49 a night during winter, $24.50 to $44 off-season.

○ Best Western Pink Shell Beach Resort. 275 Estero Blvd., Fort Myers Beach, FL 33931. ☎ **800/554-5454** or 941/463-6161. Fax 941/481-4947. www.southseas.com. 208 units. A/C TV TEL. Winter $185–$259 double; $239–$395 condo or cottage. Off-season $119–$155 double; $135–$289 condo or cottage. Packages and weekly rates available. AE, DC, DISC, MC, V.

Not to be confused with the nearby Best Western Beach Resort, this popular, family-oriented establishment is quietly situated near Estero's north end; it fronts both the gulf and Matanzas Pass. It has hotel rooms, suites, one- and two-bedroom apartments, and beach cottages. Making up for a lack of luxury with lots of 1950s-style charm, the cottages are heavily booked during the winter months, so reserve early. The so-called villas here actually are spacious and luxurious apartments in one of two midrise, gulf-front buildings with lovely views of Sanibel Island from their screened balconies. The second midrise holds the hotel rooms and standard efficiencies, the least expensive units here.

The gulf beach side of the property has water-sports equipment to rent, three heated swimming pools, a kiddie pool, and a chickee bar serving libation and sporting entertainment at sunset. Sailboats and nature and sightseeing cruises pick up guests at the bay-side marina, which rents boats. Facilities also include a coin laundry, store for buying victuals, lighted tennis courts, and rental bikes. Every unit has cooking facilities, but the Hungry Pelican Café, on a deck overlooking the channel, serves breakfast, lunch, and dinner.

Holiday Inn. 6890 Estero Blvd., Fort Myers Beach, FL 33931. ☎ **800/465-4329** or 941/463-5711. Fax 941/463-7038. 105 units. A/C TV TEL. Winter $179–$209 double. Off-season $89–$139 double. AE, DISC, MC, V.

Built by the shifting sands, the slowly emerging Little Estero Island (actually a peninsula) has left the surf a considerable distance from this modern, two-story motel, the center of beach activity on Estero's south end. Guests need not walk far to a courtyard swimming pool, tiki bar, and grill serving lunches and snacks. Beachfront suites are the choice accommodation here. Otherwise, you're better off paying a little more for a room facing the central courtyard rather than one looking out on the parking lots. The shops and restaurants of Villa Santini Plaza are a short walk away. With many European guests, staff here is multilingual.

Dining/Diversions: The dining room serves breakfast, lunch, and dinner and has entertainment Wednesday to Sunday.

Amenities: Room service (7am to 9pm), laundry, free morning newspaper. Outdoor pool, two lighted tennis courts, WaveRunners and parasailing, shuffleboard courts, coin laundry, gift shop.

Island House Motel. 701 Estero Blvd., Fort Myers Beach, FL 33931. ☎ **941/463-9282.** Fax 941/463-2080. 5 units. A/C TV TEL. Winter $99 efficiency. Off-season $49 efficiency. Weekly rates available. MC, V.

Sitting on stilts in the Old Florida fashion, but with modern furnishings, Ken and Sylvia Lachapelle's clapboard-sided establishment enjoys a quiet location directly across the boulevard from the Best Western Beach Resort and within walking distance of busy Times Square. Four of their units have screened porches; all have kitchens and ceiling fans. Ken and Sylvia maintain an open-air lounge with a small library beneath one of the units. They also have a small pool and sundeck area, a guest laundry, beach chairs, and they provide free local calls. Book as early as possible for February and March.

✪ **Outrigger Beach Resort.** 6200 Estero Blvd. (P.O. Box 271), Fort Myers Beach, FL 33931. ☎ **800/749-3131** or 941/463-3131. Fax 941/463-6577. www.outriggerfmb.com. E-mail: rooms@outriggerfmb.com. 144 units. A/C TV TEL. Winter $105–$195 double. Off-season $80–$135 double. DISC, MC, V.

The same friendly owners have maintained this clean, pleasant gulf-side motel since 1965. Their "garden efficiencies" in the original building have the feel of small cottages, with excellent ventilation through both front- and rear windows and doors opening to backyard decks. Other buildings here are two-story blocks containing motel-style rooms and efficiencies. The latter have window-style air-conditioning units but also sport front and rear jalousie windows to let in natural breezes. While some rooms have views of the parking lot, most face a courtyard with a swimming pool, a large wooden deck for sunning, and a friendly beachside tiki bar that dispenses libations until 8pm and is one of the best places here for a sunset cocktail. The Deckside Café serves inexpensive breakfasts and is open for sandwiches and snacks until 8pm. There's a coin laundry on the premises.

Palm Terrace Apartments. 3333 Estero Blvd., Fort Myers Beach, FL 33931. ☎ **800/320-5783** or 941/765-5783. Fax 941/765-5783. 9 units. Winter $82–$125 apt. Off-season $48–$80 apt. Weekly rates available. AE, DISC, MC, V.

Many European guests stay in these comfortable, well-maintained apartments about midway down the beach. The smaller, less-expensive units are on the ground level, with sliding glass doors opening to a grassy yard, but even they have cooking facilities including microwave ovens. Most units here are upstairs, with screened porches or decks overlooking a courtyard with a heated swimming pool. There's beach access across Estero Boulevard, and Anthony's on the Gulf and the Junkanoo Beach Bar are 3 short blocks away.

Sandpiper Gulf Resort. 5550 Estero Blvd., Fort Myers Beach, FL 33931. ☎ **941/463-5721.** Fax 941/463-5721, ext. 299. 63 units. A/C TV TEL. Winter $115–$145 suite for two. Off-season $69–$89 suite for two. DISC, MC, V.

The units at this clean gulf-side motel all have living and sleeping areas, full kitchens, convertible sofas, and sundecks overlooking either the gulf or a courtyard with a heated swimming pool and hot tub. Steps lead from the bedecked pool directly to the beach. Some suites are in two- or three-story buildings arranged in a U with the flattened ends right on the beach; others are in the Sandpiper II, a palm-fronted high-rise with its own heated pool next door. All suites are identical, but those facing directly on the beach are more expensive. Facilities include a coin laundry and gift shop. Restaurants are nearby.

WHERE TO DINE

The busy area around Times Square has fast-food joints to augment several local restaurants catering to the beach crowds. The pick is the **Beach Pierside Grill,** directly on the beach at the foot of Lynn Hall Memorial Pier (☎ 941/765-7800), a lively pub which bears the bright blond wood trim and vivid fabric colors reminiscent of establishments in Miami's South Beach. It all opens onto a large beachside patio with dining at umbrella tables, outstanding sunsets, and live bands playing at night. The reasonably priced fare is a catchall of conch fritters, shrimp and fish baskets, burgers, and seafood main courses. They take reservations—a plus in this busy area. Food is served daily from 11am to 11pm, and the bar stays open 'til past midnight daily during summer, on weekends off-season.

Although it was closed and awaiting new owners during my recent visit, you may want to check out the **Gulf Shore Restaurant,** on the beach at 1270 Estero Blvd. (☎ 941/463-9951). Home of the Crescent Beach Casino back in the 1920s, this old clapboard building offers splendid views of the gulf and beach. The adjacent Cottage Bar was expected to resume its role as the most infamous watering hole on the beach.

You'll find a row of national chain family restaurants at the Summerlin Square shopping center, on the mainland at San Carlos Boulevard and Summerlin Road. The beach trolley runs to Summerlin Square during the winter.

MODERATE

✪ **Anthony's on the Gulf.** 3040 Estero Blvd., on the beach at Donora Blvd. ☎ **941/ 463-2600.** Reservations not accepted. Pasta $9–$13; main courses $13–19; burgers and sandwiches $5–$7. AE, DISC, MC, V. Daily 11:30am–11pm (Sun–Thurs 11:30am–10pm off-season). ITALIAN.

Right on the beach and above the constant party in the Junkanoo Beach Bar downstairs (see "Fort Myers Beach After Dark," below), this establishment has large windows with gulf views and the appropriately named Sunset Terrace, one of the better places on the island for a day-ending cocktail or an alfresco lunch or dinner. Inside, a casual, unpretentious tropical ambience is enhanced by an old-fashioned, pole-driven ceiling fan reaching the full length of the dining room. This setting more than makes up for a somewhat less-than-inspired menu offering traditional Italian pizzas and pastas, and main courses of veal, chicken, and seafood. Sandwiches and burgers are available at all hours here.

If Italian isn't your forte, the **Beach Light Grill,** on the other side of the Junkanoo Beach Bar (☎ 941/463-6139), offers the same beachside gulf view to go with moderately priced Florida- and Caribbean-accented cuisine.

✪ **Channel Mark.** 19001 San Carlos Blvd. (at the north end of San Carlos Island). ☎ **941/ 463-9127.** Reservations not accepted. Main courses $12–$25; sandwiches $6–$7. AE, DC, DISC, MC, V. Sun–Thurs 11am–10pm, Fri–Sat 11am–11pm. SEAFOOD.

Nestled by the "Little Bridge" leading onto San Carlos Island's northern end, every table here looks out on a maze of channel markers on Hurricane Bay. A dock with palms growing through it makes this a relaxing place for a waterside lunch. The atmosphere changes dramatically at night, with ceiling fans, potted plants, rattan chairs, well-spaced tables, and soft, indirect lighting creating a relaxed tropical ambience ideal for kindling romance. Congenial owners Mike McGuigan and Andy Welsh greet each guest and put a creative spin on their seafood dishes, such as a rich concoction of snapper smothered in a roasted macadamia-nut sauce and topped with fresh strawberry butter. Even their fried items are more innovative than your usual fare:

Their renowned, delicately seasoned crab cakes are lightly breaded with cornflakes and almonds. Calorie counters can opt for shrimp or mahimahi perfectly grilled over mesquite. The adjacent lounge offers the same menu and has live entertainment on weekends.

Italian Fisherman. In Villa Santini Plaza, 7205 Estero Blvd. ☎ **941/463-5544.** Reservations not accepted. Main courses $9–$18; pasta $7–$12; pizza $10.50–$21. Early bird specials $8. AE, DC, DISC, MC, V. Sun–Thurs 4–9pm; Fri–Sat 4–9:30pm; early bird specials daily 4–6pm. ITALIAN/SEAFOOD.

Within walking distance of the Holiday Inn and other south-end accommodations, this split-level storefront establishment offers good food at reasonable prices. Lamps suspended from the ceiling add a touch of elegance, spotlighting the black booths and cafe chairs. Locals come here for the traditional Italian specialties, such as a heaping mound of shrimps and scallops surrounded by mussels and clams, all under a fradiavolo sauce (a spicy version of marinara sauce) rich in sweet plum tomatoes. Early bird specials feature smaller portions of the regular main courses plus soup, vegetables, and bread. You can order pizza at the adjoining **Coconuts Lounge & Eatery,** a popular local sports pub that is open daily from 3pm to midnight.

Loggerheads. In Villa Santini Plaza, 7205 Estero Blvd. ☎ **941/463-4644.** Reservations recommended on weekends. Sandwiches and burgers $5–$8; main courses $10–$15. AE, DISC, MC, V. Winter daily 8am–midnight. Off-season daily 11am–11pm. SEAFOOD/AMERICAN.

The motto "The Local's Nest" accurately describes this friendly storefront restaurant, where charter boat captains congregate around a big square bar on one side of the knotty-pine-accented dining room. The menu offers a wide range of appetizers, big salads, sandwiches, burgers, and main course options from both land and sea. Most of the main courses feature heavy cream sauces over pasta (the house specialty is scallops, spinach, artichokes, tomatoes, and bacon in a horseradish-tinged cream sauce), but you can order traditionally fried, grilled, broiled, or blackened seafood.

✪ **Matanzas Inn Restaurant.** At Matanzas Marina, 416 Crescent St. (under the Skyway Bridge on Estero Island). ☎ **941/463-3838.** Reservations not accepted. Main courses $13–$18; sandwiches and light fare $6–$9. AE, DC, DISC, MC, V. Daily 11am–10pm. Closed Thanksgiving and Christmas. SEAFOOD.

Although it's in the busy Times Square tourist district, this casual, friendly, and consistent restaurant is popular with local residents who appreciate seafood fresh off the boats docking at Matanzas Marina. Dining is on a dock next to the marina or in a dark-paneled room hung with ceiling fans. The menu highlights fried, broiled, blackened, or charcoal-grilled seafood. A light-fare menu offers shrimp salad, fish sandwiches, and hamburgers.

✪ **Papa Mondo Risorante Italiano.** 1821 Estero Blvd., at Ohio Ave. ☎ **941/765-9660.** Reservations recommended. Main courses $10–$16; fixed-price menu $19. AE, MC, V. Daily noon–10pm. Closed New Years Day, Christmas, Easter. NORTHERN ITALIAN.

Brothers-in-law Andrea Mazzonetto (he's the chef) and Pasquale Riso hail from Italy, and the fare they present in their attractive dining room—or out on their roadside patio—is the real thing. They make everything from scratch—you can watch them producing pasta at a big machine behind a big picture window. The homemade pasta shows up in the likes of *stracci bianchi e neri ai frutti di mare,* an excellent combination of white and black pasta sautéed with fresh seafood and shaved zucchini in a white wine sauce. Ask your server to explain each evening's three pasta and three meat offerings (a special fixed-price menu features a sampling of all six).

INEXPENSIVE

Greco's Italian Deli. In Villa Santini Plaza, 7205 Estero Blvd. ☎ **941/463-5634.** Subs and sandwiches $4–$5; pizzas $12–$15; ready-to-cook meals $6–$8. No credit cards. Winter Mon–Sat 8am–6pm. Off-season Mon–Sat 8am–5pm. ITALIAN.

Wonderful aromas of baking pizzas, calzones, cannolis, breads, and cookies have been wafting from Greco's since 1958. Order at the counter over a chiller packed with fresh deli meats, Italian sausage, and cheeses, then devour your goodies at tables inside, out on the covered walkway, or take them to the beach for a picnic. You can also take "heat-and-eat" meals of spaghetti, lasagna, eggplant parmigiana, manicotti, and ravioli to your hotel or condo oven. Shelves are loaded with Italian wines, pastas, butter cookies, and anisette toast.

Strawberrie Corner Café & Ice Cream Parlor. 6035 Estero Blvd. ☎ **941/463-1155.** Menu items $4–$6. No credit cards. Daily 11am–9:30pm. Closed Sept. DELI.

"Your Willpower Ends Here" warns a sign on the front door of this bright ice-cream parlor and deli on Estero Boulevard's only sharp curve, known as Strawberry Corner. Strawberry-print wallpaper, strawberry dolls, and photos of strawberries provide the decor, and strawberry shortcake is the house specialty. In addition, the menu offers terrific homemade soups, seafood salads, and made-to-order deli sandwiches. Each white table here is adorned with colorful fresh flowers.

FORT MYERS AFTER DARK

The area around Times Square is always active, on weekends off-season and every day during winter. In the very heart of Times Square at the foot of Lynn Hall Memorial Pier, the **Beach Pierside Grill,** 1000 Estero Blvd. (☎ **941/765-7800**), has live entertainment on its beachside patio (and happy hours Monday to Friday from 3 to 6pm featuring $1 draft beers). Facing due west, **Jimmy's Beach Bar,** in the Days Inn at 1130 Estero Blvd. (☎ **941/463-9759**), has live music nightly for the "best sunsets on the island" (actually you can say that of all the beachside establishments here).

Away from the maddening crowds, the ✪ **Junkanoo Beach Bar,** under Anthony's on the Gulf, 3040 Estero Blvd. (☎ **941/463-2600**), attracts a more affluent crowd for its Bohemian-style parties that run from 11:30am to 1:30am daily. Live bands specialize in reggae and other island music. The menu offers inexpensive subs, sandwiches, burgers, and pizzas, and a concessionaire rents beach cabanas and water-sports toys, making it a good place for a lively day at the beach.

Locals in the know head for **The Beached Whale,** 1249 Estero Blvd. (☎ **941/463-5505**), and **The Reef,** 2601 Estero Blvd. (☎ **941/463-8414**), two pubs that consistently have the best bands and the least tourists.

On the more couples- and family-oriented south end of Estero Island, the **Holiday Inn,** 6890 Estero Blvd. (☎ **941/463-5711**), has live music for dancing Wednesday to Saturday and a deejay on Sunday from 9pm to 1am.

On Sunday afternoons, revelers jam the docks for the famous outdoor reggae parties at **The Bridge Waterfront Restaurant,** 708 Fisherman's Wharf (☎ **941/765-0050**), which is under the Sky Bridge on San Carlos Island.

3 Sanibel & Captiva Islands

14 miles W of Fort Myers, 40 miles N of Naples

Sanibel and Captiva are unique in Florida. Here you will find none of the neon signs, amusement parks, and high-rise condos that clutter most beach resorts in the state.

Indeed, Sanibel's main drag, Periwinkle Way, runs under a canopy of whispery pines and gnarled oaks so thick they almost obscure the small signs for chic shops and restaurants. This wooded ambience is the work of local voters, who have saved their trees and tropical foliage, limited the size and appearance of signs, and permit no building higher than the tallest palm and no WaveRunner or other noisy beach toy within 300 yards of their gorgeous, shell-strewn beaches. I've been to Sanibel many times, but it was only recently that I saw an aerial photo of the island and realized its southern shore is lined with hotels and condominiums. The foliage disguises the buildings that well.

Furthermore, more than half of the two islands is preserved in its natural state as wildlife refuges. Here you can ride, walk, bike, canoe, or kayak through the J. N. (Ding) Darling National Wildlife Refuge, one of Florida's best.

Legend says that Ponce de León named the larger of these two barrier islands "San Ybel," after Queen Isabella of Spain. Another legend claims Captiva's name comes from the infamous pirate José Gaspar's keeping captured women here. The modern era dates from 1892, when a few farmers settled on the islands. One of them, Clarence Chadwick, started an unsuccessful key lime and copra plantation on Captiva; many of his towering coconut palms still stand, adding to that skinny island's tropical luster.

Concluding that their terrific fishing grounds could be more profitable than their sandy soil, local residents soon switched from farming to fishing camps. Affluent anglers flocked to the islands, first by private boat and then by ferry. When the Sanibel Causeway connected the islands to the mainland in 1963, the public at large began discovering their world-famous shelling beaches, wildlife, and aesthetic beauty.

ESSENTIALS

GETTING THERE   From I-75 and the airport, follow Daniels Parkway due west, turn left on Summerlin Road (County Road 869), and proceed to the Sanibel Causeway ($3 per car toll going to the island, free coming back). From Fort Myers, take McGregor Boulevard or Summerlin Road, which merge, to the Sanibel Causeway.

See "Getting There," in section 1 of this chapter, for information about air, train, and bus service. The Amoco station at 1015 Periwinkle Way, at Causeway Road, is the Sanibel agent for **Enterprise Rent-a-Car** (☎ **800/325-8007** or 941/395-3880).

VISITOR INFORMATION   The **Sanibel-Captiva Islands Chamber of Commerce,** 1159 Causeway Rd., Sanibel Island, FL 33957 (☎ **941/472-1080;** fax 941/472-1070; www.sanibel-captiva.org; e-mail: island@sanibel-capitva.org), maintains a visitor center on Causeway Road as you drive onto Sanibel from Fort Myers. The chamber gives away an *Island Guide* (in English, German, and Spanish) and sells a detailed street map for $2 ($3 by mail). Other books are for sale, including comprehensive shelling guides and a helpful collection of menus from the islands' restaurants. There are phones for making hotel and condo reservations. Open Monday to Saturday from 9am to 7pm, Sunday from 10am to 5pm.

GETTING AROUND   Neither Sanibel nor Capitva has public transportation. **No parking** is permitted on any street or road on Sanibel. Free beach parking is available on the Sanibel Causeway. Other municipal lots are either reserved for local residents or have a 75¢ hourly fee. Accordingly, many residents and visitors get around by bicycle (see "More Ways to Enjoy the Outdoors," below).

If you need a cab, call **Sanibel Taxi** (☎ **941/472-4160**).

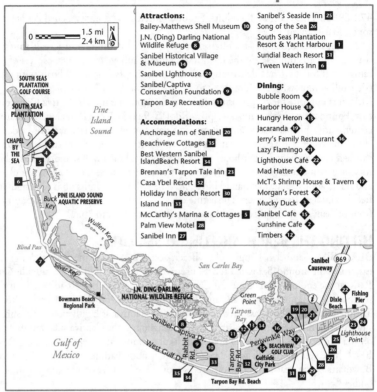

Attractions:
Bailey-Matthews Shell Museum ⑩
J.N. (Ding) Darling National Wildlife Refuge ⑧
Sanibel Historical Village & Museum ⑭
Sanibel Lighthouse ㉔
Sanibel/Captiva Conservation Foundation ⑨
Tarpon Bay Recreation ⑪

Sanibel's Seaside Inn ㉕
Song of the Sea ㉖
South Seas Plantation Resort & Yacht Harbour ①
Sundial Beach Resort ㉛
'Tween Waters Inn ⑥

Accommodations:
Anchorage Inn of Sanibel ⑳
Beachview Cottages ㉟
Best Western Sanibel IslandBeach Resort ㉞
Brennan's Tarpon Tale Inn ㉓
Casa Ybel Resort ㉜
Holiday Inn Beach Resort ㉚
Island Inn ㉝
McCarthy's Marina & Cottages ⑤
Palm View Motel ㉘
Sanibel Inn ㉗

Dining:
Bubble Room ④
Harbor House ⑱
Hungry Heron ⑬
Jacaranda ⑲
Jerry's Family Restaurant ⑯
Lazy Flamingo ㉑
Lighthouse Cafe ㉒
Mad Hatter ⑦
McT's Shrimp House & Tavern ⑰
Morgan's Forest ㉙
Mucky Duck ③
Sanibel Cafe ⑮
Sunshine Cafe ②
Timbers ⑫

PARKS & NATURE PRESERVES

Named for the *Des Moines Register* cartoonist who was a frequent visitor here and who started the federal Duck Stamp program, the ✪ **J. N. (Ding) Darling National Wildlife Refuge,** on Sanibel-Captiva Road (☎ 941/472-1100), is home to alligators, raccoons, otters, and hundreds of species of birds. Occupying more than half of Sanibel Island, this 6,000-plus acres of mangrove swamps, winding waterways, and uplands has a 2-mile trail and a 5-mile, one-way **Wildlife Drive.** The visitor center shows brief videos about the refuge's inhabitants every half hour and sells a map keyed to numbered stops along the Wildlife Drive for $1. The best times for viewing the wildlife are early morning, late afternoon, and at low tide (tables are posted at the visitor center and are available at the chamber of commerce). Mosquitoes and "no-see-ums" (tiny, biting sand flies) are especially prevalent at dawn and dusk, so bring repellent.

Admission to the visitor center is free. The Wildlife Drive costs $4 per vehicle, $1 for hikers and bicyclists (free to holders of current federal Duck Stamps and National Park Service access passports). The visitor center is open from November to April, Saturday to Thursday from 9am to 5pm; off-season, Saturday to Thursday from 9am to 4pm. The center is open on federal holidays from January through May, closed on holidays the rest of the year. The Wildlife Drive is open all year, Saturday to Thursday from 1 hour after sunrise to 1 hour before sunset (that is, it's closed on Friday).

If you want a naturalist to explain what you're seeing, take a 2-hour narrated **tram tour** given by **Tarpon Bay Recreation,** at the north end of Tarpon Bay Road (☎ 941/

472-8900). These cost $8 for adults, $4 for children 12 and under. Schedules are seasonal, so call ahead.

Tarpon Bay Recreation also offers a variety of guided **canoe and kayak tours** in season, with an emphasis on the historical, cultural, and environmental aspects of the refuge (call for the schedule). It also rents canoes, kayaks, and small boats with electric trolling motors (see "More Ways to Enjoy the Outdoors," below).

Almost opposite the refuge visitor center, the nonprofit **Sanibel/Captiva Conservation Foundation,** 3333 Sanibel–Captiva Rd. (☎ 941/472-2329), maintains a nature center, native plant nursery, and 4½ miles of nature trails on 1,100 acres of wetlands along the Sanibel River. You can learn more about the islands' unusual ecosystems through environmental workshops, guided trail walks, beach walks, and a natural-history boat cruise (call for schedules). Various items are for sale, including native plants and publications about the islands' birds and other wildlife. Admission is $3 for adults, free for children 16 and under. The nature center is open in winter Monday to Saturday from 8:30am to 4pm, off-season Monday to Friday 8:30am to 3pm.

HITTING THE BEACH: SHELLING & SEA LIFE

BEACHES Sanibel has four public beach-access areas with metered parking: the eastern point around **Sanibel Lighthouse,** which has a fishing pier; **Gulfside City Park,** at the end of Algiers Lane, off Casa Ybel Road; **Tarpon Bay Road Beach,** at the south end of Tarpon Bay Road; and **Bowman's Beach,** off Sanibel-Captiva Road. **Turner Beach,** at Blind Pass between Sanibel and Captiva, is highly popular at sunset since it faces due west; there's a small free parking lot on the Captiva side, but parking on the Sanibel side is limited to holders of local permits. All except Tarpon Bay Road Beach have rest rooms. *Be forewarned:* Although nude bathing is illegal, the end of Bowman's Beach near Blind Pass often sees more than its share of bare straight and gay bodies.

Another popular beach on Captiva is at the end of Andy Rosse Lane in front of the Mucky Duck Restaurant. It's the one place here where you can rent motorized watersports equipment (see "More Ways to Enjoy the Outdoors," below).

SHELLING Sanibel and Captiva are famous for their seashells, and local residents and visitors alike can be seen in the "Sanibel stoop" or the "Captiva crouch" while searching for some 200 species. February to April, or after any storm, are the best times of the year to look for whelks, olives, scallops, sand dollars, conch, and many other varieties. Low tide is the best time of day. The shells can be sharp, so wear Aqua Socks or old running shoes whenever you go walking on the beach.

With so many residents and visitors scouring Sanibel, you may have better luck on the adjacent shoals and nearby islands, such as Upper Captiva and Cayo Costa (see "Nearby Island Hopping," below). **Captiva Cruises** (☎ 941/472-5300) has shelling trips from the South Seas Plantation Resort & Yacht Harbour on Captiva daily at 9am and 1pm. They cost $35 for adults, $17.50 for children.

At least 15 charter-boat skippers also offer to take guests on shelling expeditions to these less-explored areas. Their half-day rates are about $180 for up to six people, so get up a group to go. Several operate from the **'Tween Waters Inn Marina** (☎ 941/472-5161) on Captiva, including **Capt. Mike Fuery** (☎ 941/472-1015, or 941/994-7195 on his boat). Others are based at **Jenson's Twin Palms Marina,** on Captiva (☎ 941/472-5800), and at the **Sanibel Marina,** on North Yachtsman Drive, off Periwinkle Way east of Causeway Boulevard (☎ 941/472-2723). They all distribute brochures at the chamber of commerce visitor center (see "Essentials," above) and are listed in the free tourist publications found there.

Caution: Florida law prohibits taking live shells from the beaches, and federal regulations prevent them from being removed from the J. N. (Ding) Darling National Wildlife Refuge.

Before you start stooping, visit the impressive **Baily-Mathews Shell Museum,** 3075 Sanibel-Captiva Road (☎ **941/395-2233**), the only museum in the United States devoted solely to saltwater, freshwater, and land shells (yes, snails are included). Shells from as far away as South Africa surround a 6-foot globe in the middle of the main exhibit hall, thus showing their geographic origins. A spinning wheel case identifies shells likely to wash up on Sanibel. Other exhibits are devoted to shells in tribal art, fossil shells found in Florida, medicinal qualities of various mollusks, the endangered Florida tree snail, and "sailor's Valentines"—shell craft made by natives of Barbados for sailors to bring home to their loved ones. The upstairs library attracts serious malacologists. The museum is open Tuesday to Sunday from 10am to 4pm; admission is $5 adults, $3 children 8 to 16, free for children under 8.

MORE WAYS TO ENJOY THE OUTDOORS

BICYCLING, WALKING, JOGGING & IN-LINE SKATING   Paved bicycle paths follow alongside most major roads, including the entire length of Periwinkle Way and along Sanibel-Captiva Road to Blind Pass, making Sanibel a paradise for cyclists, walkers, joggers, and in-line skaters. And you can walk or bike the 5-mile, one-way nature trail through the J.N. (Ding) Darling National Wildlife Refuge.

The chamber of commerce visitor center has bike maps, as do Sanibel's rental firms: **Finnimore's Cycle Shop,** 2353 Periwinkle Way (☎ **941/472-5577**); **The Bike Rental** 2330 Palm Ridge Rd. (☎ **941/472-2241**); **Island Moped,** 1470 Periwinkle Way (☎ **941/472-5248**); and **Tarpon Bay Recreation,** at the north end of Tarpon Bay Road (☎ **941/472-8900**). On Captiva, **Jim's Bike & Skate Rentals** on Andy Rosse Lane (☎ **941/472-1296**) rents bikes and beach equipment. Bike rates range from $5 per hour to $15 a day for basic models. Both Finnimore's and Jim's rent in-line skates.

There are no bike paths on Captiva, where trees alongside the narrow roads can make for dangerous riding.

BOATING & FISHING   On Sanibel, rental boats and charter-fishing excursions are available from **The Boat House** at the Sanibel Marina, on North Yachtsman Drive (☎ **941/472-2531**), off Periwinkle Way east of Causeway Road. **Tarpon Bay Recreation,** at the north end of Tarpon Bay Road (☎ **941/472-8900**), rents boats with electric trolling motors and tackle for fishing.

On Captiva, check with **Sweet Water Rentals** at the 'Tween Waters Inn Marina (☎ **941/472-6376**), **Jenson's Twin Palms Marina** (☎ **941/472-5800**), and **McCarthy's Marina** (☎ **941/472-5200**), all on Captiva Road. Rental boats cost about $125 for half a day, $200 for a full day; that's about twice the price you'll pay elsewhere in Southwest Florida, including Naples.

Many **charter-fishing captains** are docked at these marinas. Half-day rates are about $200 for up to four people. The skippers leave free brochures at the chamber of commerce visitor center (see "Essentials," above), and they're listed in the free tourist publications found there.

CANOEING & KAYAKING   As noted under "Parks & Nature Preserves," above, **Tarpon Bay Recreation** (☎ **941/472-8900**) has guided canoe and kayak trips in the J. N. (Ding) Darling National Wildlife Refuge. Do-it-yourselfers can rent canoes and kayaks here. They cost $20 for the first 2 hours, $5 for each additional hour. On Captiva, the **'Tween Waters Inn Marina** (☎ **941/472-5161**) rents canoes and kayaks, as does **WildSide Adventures,** based at McCarthy's Marina (☎ **941/935-2925**).

Naturalist, avid environmentalist, and former Sanibel mayor **Mark "Bird" Westall** (☎ **941/472-5218;** fax 941/472-5128) takes visitors on guided canoe trips through the wildlife refuge and on the Sanibel River. His excursions are timed for low tide and cost $35 for adults, $15 for children under 18. He will tailor shorter trips to accommodate children or anyone else not up to 2½ to 3 hours in a canoe. On Captiva, naturalist **Brian Houston** leads kayaking trips from 'Twin Waters Inn Marina, but make your reservations at Tarpon Bay Recreation on Sanibel (☎ **941/472-8900**). Brian charges $35 per person for his morning and midday trips, $25 for a shorter version leaving at 4pm. Reservations are essential with both Bird and Brian.

GOLF & TENNIS   Golfers may view a gallery of wild animals while playing the 5,600-yard, par-70, 18-hole course at the **Dunes Golf and Tennis Club,** 949 Sandcastle Rd., Sanibel (☎ **941/472-2535**), whose back nine runs across a wildlife preserve. Call a day in advance for seasonal greens fees and a tee time. The Dunes also has seven tennis courts. The **South Seas Plantation Resort & Yacht Harbour** has tennis courts and a 9-hole golf course, but they're for guests only.

SAILING   If you want to learn how to sail, noted yachties Steve and Doris Colgate have a branch of their **Offshore Sailing School** at the South Seas Plantation Resort & Yacht Harbour (☎ **941/472-5111**, ext. 7141). Also based on Captiva, two sailboats take guests out on the waters of Pine Island Sound: Mike McMillan's *Adventure* (☎ **941/472-7532** or 941/472-4386) and Mic Gurley's *New Moon* (☎ **941/ 395-1782**). Reservations are required.

WATER SPORTS   Sanibel may prohibit motorized water-sports equipment on its beaches, but Captiva doesn't. **Yolo Watersports** (☎ **941/472-9656**) offers parasailing and WaveRunner rentals on the beach in front of the Mucky Duck Restaurant, at the gulf end of Andy Rosse Lane on Captiva.

Both scuba divers and snorkelers can go along with trips offered by the **Redfish Dive Center** (☎ **941/472-3483**), the **Pieces of Eight Dive Center** (☎ **941/ 472-9424**), and **Captiva Dive** (☎ **941/395-2000**). All rent equipment and teach diving.

MORE TO SEE & DO

The **Sanibel Historical Village & Museum,** 950 Dunlop Rd. (☎ **941/472-4648**), includes the pioneer-vintage Rutland home and the 1926 versions of Bailey's General Store (complete with Red Crown gasoline pumps), the post office, and Miss Charlotta's Tea Room. Displays highlight the islands' prehistoric Calusa tribal era, old photos from pioneer days, turn-of-the-century clothing, and a variety of memorabilia. Special exhibits feature quilts in January, valentines and old lace in February, and antique toys, dollhouses, and 200 teddy bears in December. Open Wednesday to Saturday from 10am to 4pm (and Sunday from 1 to 4pm between mid-December and Easter); closed mid-August to mid-October. Admission is by $2 donation.

At the east end of Periwinkle Way, the **Sanibel Lighthouse** has marked the entrance to San Carlos Bay since 1884. The light keepers used to live in the cottages at the base of the 94-foot tower. The now-automatic lighthouse isn't open to visitors, but the grounds and beach are.

In addition to its island trips (see "Nearby Island Hopping," below), **Captiva Cruises** (☎ **941/472-5300**) goes out daily on dolphin-watching and sunset cruises from the South Seas Plantation Resort & Yacht Harbour on Captiva. These cost $17.50 for adults, $10 for children. Reservations are required.

SHOPPING

If you have no luck scouring the beaches for shells, several Sanibel shops sell thousands of them. **Sanibel Sea Shell Industries,** 905 Fitzhugh St. (☎ **941/472-1603**), has one of the largest collections, with more than 10,000 shells in stock. **She Sells Sea Shells** has two locations: 1157 Periwinkle Way near Causeway Road (☎ **941/472-6991**) and 2422 Periwinkle Way near the island's center (☎ **941/472-8080**). Others include **Neptune's Treasures Shell Shop,** in the Tree Tops Center, 1101 Periwinkle Way opposite the Dairy Queen (☎ **941/472-3132**), which also has a good collection of fossils.

You can burn up a rainy day and lots of credit at Sanibel's numerous upscale boutiques carrying expensive jewelry and apparel. Many are in **Periwinkle Place, Tahitian Gardens,** and **The Village,** the main shopping centers along Periwinkle Way. In The Village, **Toys Ahoy!** (☎ **941/472-4800**) carries fascinating toys, games, and stuffed animals. In Tahitian Gardens, the **Audubon Nature Store** (☎ **941/395-2020**) carries gifts and books with a wildlife theme, and **The Chesire Cat** (☎ **941/472-3545**) offers nature toys and other unique items for kids.

More than a dozen Sanibel galleries feature original works of art; pick up a gallery guide at the chamber of commerce visitor center (see "Essentials," above). On Captiva, the tree-houselike **Jungle Drums,** on Andy Rosse Lane (☎ **941/395-2266**), has the area's most unique collection of wildlife art.

Founded in 1899, **Bailey's General Store** is still going strong at the corner of Periwinkle Way and Tarpon Bay Road (☎ **941/472-1516**), with a supermarket, deli, salad bar, hardware store, beach shop, shoe repair, and Western Union all under one roof.

WHERE TO STAY

While modern resorts may try to re-create a South Seas island setting, there are still many Old Florida–style cottages on the two islands that really do look like they belong on Bora Bora. Some also represent good value if you can do without modern luxuries. The 32 pink clapboard structures at **Beachview Cottages,** 3325 W. Gulf Dr. (near Rabbit Road), Sanibel Island, FL 33957 (☎ **800/860-0532** or 941/472-1202; fax 941/472-4720), flank a narrow, unpaved lane running from the road to the beach and lined with coconut palms and colorful hibiscus. Winter rates here are $125 to $230 a day, but book well in advance because this clean, well-managed property is popular. Off-season, they go for $90 to $160 a day. Also, see the introduction to Captiva Island accommodations, below, for **McCarthy's Marina & Cottages.**

Sanibel also has many condominium resorts; in fact, some accommodations recommended below are condo complexes operated as hotels. **1-800-SANIBEL** is a reservations service that will book you into most properties here, including condos and cottages (☎ **800/726-4235**). The largest rental agents are **Priscilla Murphy Realty,** 1177 Causeway Blvd. (P.O. Box 5), Sanibel Island, FL 33957 (☎ **800/237-6008** or 941/472-4883; fax 941/472-8995), and **VIP Vacation Rentals,** 1509 Periwinkle Way, Sanibel Island, FL 33957 (☎ **800/237-7526** or 941/472-1613; fax 941/481-8477). The chamber of commerce's *Island Guide* lists others (see "Essentials," above).

Only two chain hotels are present here. **Best Western Sanibel Island Beach Resort,** 3287 W. Gulf Dr. (near Rabbit Road), Sanibel Island, FL 33957 (☎ **800/554-5454** or 941/472-1700, www.southseas.com), has 45 spacious rooms, efficiencies, and apartments whose screened balconies face either the beach or a lawn festooned with palms, pink hibiscus, orange trees, a swimming pool, tennis courts, and white Adirondack chairs for lounging. Bicycles and beach equipment are complimentary. There's no restaurant on the premises, but you can dine at other nearby establishments. Winter rates range from $200 to $370 in a unit for two. Off-season, they cost $145 to $250.

The **Holiday Inn Beach Resort,** 1231 Middle Gulf Dr. (at the end of Donax Street), Sanibel Island, FL 33957 (☎ **800/HOLIDAY** or 941/472-4123), is on the beach, but its rooms don't have balconies or patios. It has a tennis court, bike rentals, a gift shop, a children's playground and activities program with an environmental emphasis, and Morgan's Forest restaurant (see "Where to Dine," below). Rates range from $195 to $240 in winter, from $119 to $150 off-season.

If you can't get into one of those, try the **West Wind Inn,** 3345 W. Gulf Dr. (☎ **800/824-0476** or 941/472-1541; fax 941/472-8134), and the **Snook Motel,** 3033 W. Gulf Dr. (☎ **800/741-6166** or 941/472-1345; fax 941/472-2148), two very comfortable, on-the-beach establishments near the Best Western Sanibel Beach Resort. The West Wind Inn has a restaurant on the premises.

In general, Sanibel and Captiva room and condo rates are highest during the shelling season, February to April. January is usually somewhat less expensive. But note that most rates fall drastically during the off-season, making these otherwise expensive islands much more affordable. Since most properties on the islands are geared to 1-week vacations, you can also save by purchasing a package deal if you're staying for 7 nights or longer.

The islands' sole campground, the **Periwinkle Trailer Park,** 1119 Periwinkle Way, Sanibel Island (☎ **941/472-1433**), is so popular it doesn't even advertise. No other camping is permitted on either Sanibel or Captiva.

Sanibel Island
Very Expensive

✪ **Casa Ybel Resort.** 2255 W. Gulf Dr., Sanibel Island, FL 33957. ☎ **800/276-4753** or 941/472-3145. Fax 941/472-2109. 114 units. A/C TV TEL. Winter $375 1-bedroom suite; $430 2-bedroom suite. Off-season $195–$230 1-bedroom suite; $235–$270 2-bedroom suite. Packages and weekly rates available. AE, DISC, MC, V.

On the historic site of Sanibel's first beachfront resort, the Thistle Lodge, the present-day Casa Ybel's turn-of-the-century central building houses a restaurant of that name, where both guests and nonguests can enjoy wonderful cuisine and magnificent gulf views. In four-story gray buildings on the beautifully landscaped grounds, the spacious one- and two-bedroom suites are bright, with tropical rattan furniture, pastel carpeting, ceramic-tile floors, and screened porches facing the gulf. Reflecting Thistle Lodge, the swimming pool here is one of Florida's most picturesque.

Amenities: Concierge, adult and children's activities program. Whirlpool; six tennis courts with resident pro; water-sports center with sailboats, Windsurfers, and beach equipment for rent; rental bikes; children's pool and playground; golf privileges at the Dunes Golf and Tennis Club; coin laundry.

Sanibel Inn. 937 E. Gulf Dr., Sanibel Island, FL 33957. ☎ **800/554-5454** or 941/472-3181. Fax 941/472-5234. 98 units. A/C TV TEL. Winter $265–$395 condo apt. Off-season $140–$270 condo apt. Packages available. AE, DC, DISC, MC, V.

A back-to-nature theme prevails at this beachside inn, in both the room decor and the grounds planted with native Florida foliage specifically designed to attract butterflies and hummingbirds. The attractively furnished condos come complete with refrigerators, microwave ovens, VCRs, and coffeemakers. The condo apartments are some of Sanibel's most luxurious.

Dining: The Portofino Restaurant offers breakfasts to guests and northern Italian dinners to all comers. Poolside cafe open for lunch.

Amenities: Nature-oriented children's activities program, laundry. Swimming pool in tropically landscaped area with boardwalk leading to the beach, two tennis courts with professionals available, bike and water-sports equipment rentals, gift shop; golfers can play at the Dunes Golf and Tennis Club.

Sanibel's Seaside Inn. 541 E. Gulf Dr., Sanibel Island, FL 33957. ☎ **800/554-5454** or 941/472-1400. Fax 941/472-6518. www.southseas.com. 32 units. A/C TV TEL. Winter $190–$350. Off-season $150–$200. Rates include continental breakfast. Packages available. AE, DC, DISC, MC, V.

This comfortable and friendly Key West–style establishment enjoys a tranquil location near the island's southeastern tip. All units have open-air balconies or porches. The studios have wet bars, refrigerators, microwave ovens, and coffeemakers, and all units have VCRs. The duplex, 1960s-style cottages are spacious, brightly furnished one-bedroom units, but the choice here are the beachfront efficiencies, whose screened porches face the gulf.

Amenities: Complimentary continental breakfast baskets delivered the previous afternoon. The swimming pool and suntanning patio are next to the beach. Barbecue grills, shuffleboard, guest laundry, complimentary bikes. Golfers can play at the Dunes Golf and Tennis Club.

Song of the Sea. 863 E. Gulf Dr., Sanibel Island, FL 33957. ☎ **800/231-1045** or 941/472-2220. Fax 941/472-8569. 30 units. www.southseas.com. A/C TV TEL. Winter $305–$350 double. Off-season $170–$215 double. Rates include continental breakfast. Packages available. AE, DC, DISC, MC, V.

Popular with Europeans, the rooms at this motel-like inn are warmly furnished and decorated in the continental fashion, including down pillows and comforters, duvet covers, and Thomasville pine armoires to conceal the TVs and VCRs. All units have kitchenettes, sliding glass doors opening to screened porches, dinette tables with wing chairs, and ceiling fans. The apartments have bedrooms barely large enough to hold their queen-size beds. A pathway leads next door to the Sanibel Inn (see above), where guests can use the facilities and dine at Portofino Restaurant.

Dining: An extensive continental breakfast is served in the public building and eaten at umbrella tables on a brick patio.

Amenities: Guests receive complimentary video movies, beach umbrellas, and bicycle use. Heated swimming pool, outdoor whirlpool, shell-cleaning shack, library, bikes, coin laundry; tennis privileges at the Dunes Golf and Tennis Club.

✪ Sundial Beach Resort. 1451 Middle Gulf Dr., Sanibel Island, FL 33957. ☎ **800/237-4184** or 941/472-4151. Fax 941/472-8892. www.southseas.com. 270 units. A/C TV TEL. Winter $275–$575 condo apt. Off-season $145–$325 condo apt. Packages available. AE, DC, DISC, MC, V.

The largest resort on Sanibel, this popular family-oriented condominium complex stars an enormous, palm-studded, beachside pool and bar area. The one-, two-, and three-bedroom condominiums are housed in two- and three-story buildings (as high as they get on Sanibel) and have screened balconies overlooking the beach or tropically landscaped gardens. The condos are individually owned, so the decor varies but is always tasteful. VCRs and movies can be rented.

Dining/Diversions: There are several dining options here, including the award-winning Windows on the Water dining room, which offers glorious gulf views at breakfast, lunch, and dinner (reservations not accepted). Master chefs put on a show as they prepare delicious steak, chicken, and seafood dishes right by your table in Noopie's Japanese Seafood & Steakhouse; dinner reservations are required (☎ 941/ 395-6014). The Deli offers piled-high sandwiches, snacks, pizza, and picnic foods from early morning to 11pm. Crocodial's Patio Bar and Grille offers sandwiches, hamburgers, and salads poolside. The relaxing lobby lounge is popular at sunset, and a dance band plays Top 40 hits from 7 to 11pm.

Amenities: Concierge, laundry, baby-sitting, recreation program for kids (including tours of a small ecology center with a touch tank), grocery-shopping service (stocks condos before arrival), daily adult activities program, complimentary marine biology program, in-room massage. 12 tennis courts with pro, 5 swimming pools, jogging trail, games area, bike and boat rentals, fitness center, coin laundry, business center; golfers can play at the Dunes Golf and Tennis Club.

Moderate

Brennan's Tarpon Tale Inn. 367 Periwinkle Way, Sanibel Island, FL 33957. ☎ 941/ 472-0939. Fax 941/472-6202. www.tarpontale.com. E-mail: brennan@tarpontale.com. 5 units. A/C TV. Winter $109–$169. Off-season $69–$139. Rates include continental breakfast. DISC, MC, V.

Self-described "reformed journalists" Terry and Carlene Brennan preside over this low-slung gray building in the "Old Sanibel" neighborhood, the island's first settlement where the ferries from Fort Myers used to dock near the lighthouse. White walls and tile floors make their comfortable units bright, while French doors lead to gardens dense with seagrape, palm, and ficus trees, which provide privacy for a large outdoor hot tub. Three of their five units have separate bedrooms, while two other "deluxe studios" actually are two-bedroom suites. All have kitchens, and the Brennans deliver continental breakfast makings the night before. Newspapers, bicycles, and beach chairs and umbrellas (the gulf is about 150 yards away) are complimentary, and there's a social hour for guests twice a week. The rooms don't have phones (guests can hook their laptop computer modems into a jack in the common room), but they do have TVs and VCRs, and there's a video-rental store next door. Guests can use a coin laundry.

Island Inn. 3111 W. Gulf Dr., Sanibel Island, FL 33957. ☎ 800/851-5088 or 941/ 472-1651. Fax 941/472-0051. 56 units. A/C TV TEL. Winter (including breakfast and dinner) $170–$280 double. Off-season (no meals) $95–$215 double. AE, DISC, MC, V.

It's difficult to get accommodations here during the peak winter season, but it's worth trying, for this classic beach resort has been in business for more than 100 years. Its original central building houses a bright, genteel dining room, a spacious lounge, and a library brightly furnished with old-style bentwood and wicker sofas and chairs. This is the kind of place where guests dress for dinner—jackets and ties recommended for men during the winter season—and seating is assigned (some guests have had the same table for years).

This main building looks out over a sandy, South Pacific–like yard to the gulf. Although neither charming in an Old Florida sense nor luxurious by today's standards, the cottages and motel rooms (with or without kitchens) are modern and comfortable and have screened porches or balconies. There's a small swimming pool, a tennis court, and a croquet area.

Inexpensive

Anchorage Inn of Sanibel. 1245 Periwinkle Way, Sanibel Island, FL 33957. ☎ 941/ 395-9688. 9 units, 3 cottages. A/C TV. Winter $89 double; $150 cottage. Off-season $59 double; $99 cottage. AE, DISC, MC, V.

This modest establishment is well maintained by the owners of the Holiday Inn Beach Resort (guests here can use the beach and play tennis there). Standard rooms, efficiencies, and two-room units are in low-slung buildings with broad common porches facing a central courtyard with small pool. Although these units would rent for half these rates elsewhere, they are clean and a good value for Sanibel. The three cottages are A-frame contraptions with spiral staircases to a second-story sleeping loft.

✪ **Palm View Motel.** 706 Donax St., Sanibel Island, FL 33957. ☎ **941/472-1606.** Fax 941/472-6733. 8 units. A/C TV. Winter $80 double; $100–$150 efficiency and apts. Off-season $45 double; $55–$90 efficiency and apts. MC, V.

In a quiet residential area less than a block from the Holiday Inn Beach Resort, Werner and Edelgard Papke's little motel is the jewel of Sanibel's few inexpensive accommodations. Originally from Germany, the Papkes have lived on the premises since 1979, keeping their grounds groomed and their units clean and very well maintained. The traditional furnishings are from the 1970s but are nonetheless comfortable. The best choices here are the spacious, well-ventilated one- and two-bedroom apartments. All units except two motel rooms have kitchens; these two rooms interconnect and are often rented together.

CAPTIVA ISLAND

As on Sanibel, cottages offer some of the best values on Captiva. Strongly reminiscent of the genuine South Pacific is **McCarthy's Marina & Cottages,** 15041 Captiva Dr. (P.O. Box 580), Captiva Island, FL 33924 (☎ **941/472-5200;** fax 941/472-6405), where four simple houses sit in a bay-side palm and orange grove. The popular beach at the end of Andy Rosse Lane is just a block away. McCarthy's cottages range from $130 to $165 a day during winter, $85 to $115 a day off-season.

✪ **South Seas Plantation Resort & Yacht Harbour.** P.O. Box 194, Captiva Island, FL 33924. ☎ **800/554-5454** or 941/472-5111. Fax 941/481-4947. www.southseas.com. 600 units. A/C TV TEL. Winter $180 double; to $880 apt, cottage, town house, or private home. Off-season $130–$165 double; to $620 apt, cottage, town house, or private home. $8 per person per day gratuity added to all bills in lieu of tipping. Packages available. AE, DC, DISC, MC, V.

Formerly Clarence Chadwick's 330-acre copra plantation, this exclusive establishment is the premier property on these two islands. It's one of the best choices in southern Florida for serious tennis buffs (18 courts with pro), and its gulf-side golf course is one of the most picturesque nine-holers anywhere. The resort occupies all of Captiva's northern third, making it ideal if you want to step from your luxury villa or condo right onto 2½ miles of gorgeous beach. There's no central focus here, for this really is a sprawling real estate development. There are no high-rise buildings, but an assortment of luxury homes and condos are so spread out along the shore that a free trolley shuttles back and forth through the mangrove forests that separate them. The great variety of accommodations include luxury villas with private pools and their own tennis courts (many are occupied exclusively by their owners; watch for famous folks wandering about). With three bedrooms or more, some units are ideal for families or couples who want to share the cost of a vacation. The least expensive (and least inspired) units are the "Harbourside" hotel rooms at the yacht basin and marina near the island's northern tip, the jumping-off point for Captiva Cruises and Steve and Doris Colgate's Offshore Sailing School.

The resort's no-cash, charge-to-your-room policy prevents gate-crashers from dining or playing here.

Dining: Set in the plantation workers' waterside commissary, the upscale King's Crown serves gourmet-quality seafood dinners in a romantic setting. Cap'n Al's Dockside Grill is a pleasant spot for alfresco breakfasts, lunches, and dinners while waiting to see the resident manatees surfacing in the yacht harbor.

Amenities: Concierge, room service (until 11pm), laundry, grocery-shopping service that stocks condos before arrival, baby-sitting and activities program for children and teenagers. 18 tennis courts (7 lighted), nine-hole golf course, 2 marinas (1 with sailing school), 18 swimming pools (many with bars), water-sports center (arranges for parasailing, windsurfing, boat rentals, scuba diving, and more), rental bikes, boutique, nature center; golfers can also play at the Dunes Golf and Tennis Club. Outside the main gate, Chadwick's Shopping Center includes high-fashion boutiques, jewelry stores, and gift shops, all open to the public.

✪ **'Tween Waters Inn.** P.O. Box 249, Captiva Island, FL 33924. ☎ **800/223-5865** or 941/472-5161. Fax 941/472-0249. 106 units. A/C TV TEL. Winter $185–$475. Off-season $110–$350. Packages available. DISC, MC, V.

Wedged between the gulf beach and the bay on the narrowest part of Captiva, this venerable establishment was the regular haunt of cartoonist J. N. (Ding) Darling. Anne Morrow Lindbergh also spent a winter here, writing *A Gift from the Sea.* Just as Darling preserved the islands' wildlife, the 'Tween Waters has saved the cottages he stayed in. Situated in a sandy palm grove, these pink shiplap buildings capture Old Florida with simple white furniture and terrazzo floors. Some face the gulf; others, the bay. The hotel rooms and apartments are in two modern buildings (a third is expected to be open in 1998) on stilts with screened balconies facing the gulf or bay.

Dining/Diversions: The Canoe Club is a bargain, with inexpensive salads, sandwiches, burgers, and pizzas; it has a bay-side deck for lunches. The Old Captiva House restaurant appears very much as it did in Ding Darling's days (his cartoons adorn the walls) and offers reasonably priced breakfasts, lunches, and seafood dinners during winter (only breakfast and dinner off-season). The popular Crow's Nest Lounge has live entertainment and provides snacks and light evening meals from 9pm to 1am.

Amenities: Charter captains dock at the full-service marina (see "Hitting the Beach: Shelling & Sea Life" and "More Ways to Enjoy the Outdoors," above). Canoes, bikes, and beach cabanas can be rented. Very large swimming pool complex, complete with wood decking and a bar, adjacent to three lighted tennis courts. Fitness center.

WHERE TO DINE

Some restaurants here close or take long vacations during the off-season, so it's wise to call ahead if you're on the islands between May and November.

SANIBEL ISLAND

The lively **Cheeburger Cheeburger,** 2413 Periwinkle Way, at Palm Ridge Road (☎ 941/472-6111), has Sanibel's biggest and best burgers.

Much of the "help" on this affluent island dines at **Jerry's Family Restaurant,** 1700 Periwinkle Way at Casa Ybel Road (☎ 941/472-9300), which offers wholesome and inexpensive diner fare (ingredients come fresh from the adjacent Jerry's Supermarket). Both the restaurant and supermarket are open daily from 6am to 11pm. Breakfast is served from 6am to 4pm, and you can usually get a table quickly here (which can't be said of Sanibel's other popular breakfast spots).

Also, you'll find very reasonably priced pub fare at Sanibel's lively sports bars, such as the **Lazy Flamingo I** (see below) and the **Sanibel Grill,** 703 Tarpon Bay Rd., near Palm Ridge Road (☎ 941/472-3128), which actually serves as the bar for the

Timbers, the fine seafood restaurant next door (see below). They all have reduced price beer and munchies during televised football games.

For picnics at Sanibel's beaches or on a canoe, **Isabella's Italian Food & Deli,** 1523 Periwinkle Way, at Fitzhugh Street (☎ **941/472-0044**), has subs, pastas, and the island's best pizza, all by carryout or delivery only (toy car collectors note the more than 400 die-cast models on display). The deli and bakery in **Bailey's General Store,** at Periwinkle Way and Tarpon Bay Road (☎ **941/472-1516**), carries a gourmet selection of breads, cheeses, and meats. **Huxter's Deli and Market,** 1203 Periwinkle Way, east of Donax Street (☎ **941/472-6988**), has sandwich fixings and "beach box" lunches to go.

Expensive

✪ **Mad Hatter.** 6467 Sanibel-Captiva Rd., at Blind Pass. ☎ **941/472-0033.** Reservations suggested. Main courses $18–$29. AE, DISC, MC, V. Mid-Dec to Apr Tues–Sat 11:30am–2pm, daily 5–9:30pm. May to mid-Dec Mon–Sat 5–9:30pm. INNOVATIVE/NEW AMERICAN.

Brian and Jayne Baker's popular gulf-front restaurant has only 12 tables, but each has a glorious water view that's perfect at sunset. And the food, a fantasy of New American cuisines, based on California, the Southwest, and the South, with some exotic accents, is worthy of the view. The menu changes frequently, with no dish repeated (so as not to bore their loyal local following). One recent offering was a delicious mixture of angel-hair pasta, grilled marinated shrimp, tomatoes, capers, wild mushrooms, and green olives accompanied by fresh avocado and a vegetable crepe topped with a tomato-mole sauce. Whatever they serve, you'll enjoy.

Moderate

✪ **Harbor House.** 1244 Periwinkle Way (near Donax St.). ☎ **941/472-1242.** Reservations not required. Main courses $10–$19; early bird specials $9. AE, MC, V. Nov–May daily 11:30am–2pm and 5–9:30pm. June–Oct daily 5–9:30pm. AMERICAN.

Dating from 1948, this family owned establishment is Sanibel's oldest seafood restaurant, and a warm, Old Florida atmosphere prevails under the beamed ceiling of its paneled dining room. The seafood selections are down-home as well, with shrimp, scallops, and freshly caught fish either broiled, fried, blackened, or bronzed (not quite blackened in order to preserve the seafood's natural flavor). Stone crab claws and Florida lobster are offered during their seasons. The early bird specials are a bargain. Made with limes from the family's own trees, the key lime pie here is an award-winner.

Jacaranda. 1223 Periwinkle Way (east of Donax St.). ☎ **941/472-1771.** Reservations recommended. Main courses $15–$22. AE, DC, DISC, MC, V. Daily 5–10pm. Lounge daily 4pm–12:30am. Closed Christmas. SEAFOOD/PASTA.

Named for the purple-flowered jacaranda tree, this friendly and casual restaurant features a raw bar and lounge in a screened patio. Recipient of several dining awards, it's best known for expertly prepared fish and seafood, which the chef will bake, sauté, or blacken. A favorite pasta dish is linguine and a dozen littleneck clams tossed in a piquant red or white clam sauce. For dessert, the gooey turtle pie—ice cream, caramel, fudge sauce, chopped nuts, and whipped cream—will send you away stuffed. With live music nightly, the Patio Lounge attracts an affluent middle-age and seniors crowd.

✪ **McT's Shrimp House & Tavern.** 1523 Periwinkle Way (at Fitzhugh St.). ☎ **941/472-3161.** Reservations not accepted. Main courses $13–$20; early bird specials $9. AE, DC, DISC, MC, V. Shrimp House daily 4:45–10pm; McT's Tavern daily 4pm–12:30am. SEAFOOD.

Shrimp reigns at this casual, Old Florida–style establishment, where you'll see a line outside at 4:15pm waiting for the early bird specials served to the first 100 persons in the door. Everyone else gets to view the daily catch displayed in a chiller case, including the night's shrimp ready for the chef to prepare in one of at least a dozen ways, from steamed to fried in a coconut and almonds batter. There's also grouper and swordfish, plus steaks and chicken for the land-minded, but stick to the shrimp here (see below for Timbers, which does a much better job cooking fish). With a pinball machine and a huge sports TV in the rear of the building, McT's Tavern offers an extensive choice of appetizers and light dinners.

Morgan's Forest. 1231 Middle Gulf Dr., at the Holiday Inn Beach Resort. ☎ **941/ 472-3351.** Reservations not accepted. Main courses $13–$23. AE, DC, DISC, MC, V. Mon–Sat 7–11am and 5–10pm, Sun 7am–noon and 5–10pm. SEAFOOD.

The kids will love dining in this miniature jungle patterned after the Rainforest Cafés elsewhere. Almost hidden among all the foliage are mechanical but lifelike moving jaguars, monkeys, birds, and a huge python entangled in vines above the bar. Squawking bird sounds, strobe-lightning bolts followed by claps of thunder, and an occasional faux fog rolling across the floor add to the Amazonian ambience. The owners of Fort Myers Beach's excellent Channel Mark are in charge here, which means that your taste buds will be as entertained as your eyes and ears. Their fine crab cakes are the pick of a menu otherwise accented with South- and Central American seasonings. Order the shrimp Belize only if you're ready for a thick cream sauce and blazing hot Cajun spices. Obviously there's a children's menu.

✪ **Timbers.** 703 Tarpon Bay Rd. (at Palm Ridge Rd.). ☎ **941/472-3128.** Reservations not accepted. Main courses $13–$23; early birds get $2.50 off regular price. AE, MC, V. Winter daily 4:30–10pm. Off-season daily 5–10pm. SEAFOOD/STEAK.

This casual, upstairs restaurant, with bamboo railings, oversized canvas umbrellas, and paintings of tropical scenes through faux windows, consistently has the freshest fish available. You can view the catch in the fish market out front and have the chef charcoal-grill or blacken it to order. The steaks are aged and cut on the premises. You can order a drink from the adjoining Sanibel Grill sports bar and wait for a table outside on the shopping center's porch.

Inexpensive

✪ **Hungry Heron.** In Palm Ridge Place, 2330 Palm Ridge Rd. (at Periwinkle Way). ☎ **941/ 395-2300.** Reservations not accepted but call for preferred seating. Main courses $8–$15; sandwiches, burgers, snacks $4.50–$9; weekend breakfast buffet $6. AE, DISC, MC, V. Winter Mon–Fri 11am–10pm, Sat–Sun 7:30–11:30am (buffet) and 7:30–10pm. Off-season daily 11am–9pm. AMERICAN.

Ted and Jim Iannelli's tropically decorated eatery is Sanibel's most popular family restaurant. There's something for everyone on their huge, tabloid-size menu—from hot and cold appetizers and overstuffed "seawiches" to pasta and steamed shellfish. And if the 250 regular items aren't enough, there's a list of nightly specials. Seafood, steaks, and stir-fries from a sizzling skillet are popular with local residents, who bring the kids here for fun and a children's menu. Cartoons run all the time, and a magician circulates among the tables from 5 to 9pm every day except Tuesday. An all-you-can-eat breakfast buffet on Saturday and Sunday in winter is an excellent value.

The Lazy Flamingo I. 1036 Periwinkle Way, near Causeway Blvd. ☎ **941/472-6939.** Reservations not accepted. Sandwiches and snacks $5–$9; main courses $11–$15. AE, DC, DISC, MC, V. Daily 11:30am–1am. SEAFOOD/PUB FARE.

T-shirts and shorts or jeans are the dress code at this very casual sports pub that always seems packed by the young and young-at-heart, who flock here for reasonably priced food, a wide choice of beers iced down in a huge box behind the bar, and sports TVs. Some of that beer is used to steam shrimp and a finger-stinging collection of oysters, clams, and spices known as "The Pot." It also serves conch fritters, conch chowder, and conch salad. The flamingo-pink menu also has an array of sandwiches, burgers, fish platters, and very spicy "Dead Parrot Wings." Fillet your own catch, and the chef will cook it to order for $6. Happy hour prices prevail whenever football games are on the TVs.

A sister institution, the **Lazy Flamingo II,** 6520 Pine Ave., at Sanibel-Captiva Rd. one-quarter of a mile south of Blind Pass (☎ **941/472-5353**), has the same menu and hours.

Lighthouse Café. In Seahorse Shops, 362 Periwinkle Way (at Buttonwood Ave., east of Causeway Rd.). ☎ **941/472-0303.** Reservations not accepted but call ahead for preferred seating. Breakfast $3–$6; main courses $8–$14. MC, V. Daily 7am–3pm and 5–9pm. Closed for dinner mid-Apr to mid-Dec. AMERICAN.

Decorated with photos and drawings of lighthouses, this casual storefront establishment appropriately near the Sanibel Lighthouse dishes up breakfast omelettes that are meals in themselves, especially the ocean frittata containing delicately seasoned scallops, crabmeat, shrimp, broccoli, fresh mushrooms, and crowned by an artichoke heart and creamy Alfredo sauce. Seafood Benedict is another unusual offering. There's also an interesting sandwich menu. Reasonably priced dinners are served during winter only.

✪ **Sanibel Café.** In the Tahitian Gardens Shops, 2007 Periwinkle Way. ☎ **941/472-5323.** Call ahead for preferred seating. Breakfast $3–$9; salads and burgers $4–$9; main courses $6–$9.50. MC, V. Daily 7am–8pm. AMERICAN.

Seashells are the theme at Lynda and Ken Boyce's pleasant cafe whose tables are museum-like glass cases containing delicate fossilized specimens from the Miocene and Pliocene epochs. Fresh-squeezed orange and grapefruit juice, Danish Havarti omelettes, and homemade muffins and biscuits highlight the breakfast menu (eggs Benedict and fruit-filled waffles are served until closing), while lunch features specialty sandwiches; shrimp, Greek, and chicken-and-grape salads made with a very light, fat-free dressing; and a limited list of main courses such as grilled or blackened chicken breast. Lynda and Ken even serve a sugar-free pancake syrup, but you can fatten up on Lynda's homemade red raspberry jam, apple or cherry crisps, and terrific key lime pie.

CAPTIVA ISLAND

You can't miss the **Green Flash,** 15183 Captiva Rd. (☎ **941/472-3337**), which sits at the infamous "curve" where Captiva Road takes a sharp turn to the north. You won't see the green flash as the sun sets here, for this modern establishment looks eastward across Pine Island Sound. On the other hand, it makes for a nice view at lunch, and seeing the full moon turn the sound into glistening silver is worth having at least a late-evening drink here. The menu features continental-style seafood and other American fare.

Just outside South Seas Plantation & Yacht Harbour, **Chadwick's Restaurant & Lounge** (☎ **941/472-1511,** ext. 5181) is noted in these parts for its all-you-can-eat theme buffets at lunch Monday to Saturday ($9.50 per person) and at dinner nightly ($21 adults, $11 for kids 4 to 20, free for children under 4). There's also an extensive and free happy hour munchie buffet daily from 4:30 to 7:30pm.

Big deli sandwiches and picnic fare are available at the **Captiva Island Store,** Captiva Road at Andy Rosse Lane (☎ **941/472-2374**), and **C. W.'s Market and Deli,** at the entrance to the South Seas Plantation Resort & Yacht Harbour (☎ **941/ 472-5111**). The beach is a block from these stores.

✪ **The Bubble Room.** 15001 Captiva Rd. (at Andy Rosse Lane). ☎ **941/472-5558.** Reservations not accepted. Main courses $14–$27; lunch $6–$12. AE, DC, DISC, MC, V. Daily 11:30am–2:30pm and 5:30–10pm. Closed Christmas. STEAK/SEAFOOD.

The gaudy bubble-gum pink, yellow, purple, and green exterior of this amusing restaurant is only a prelude to the 1930s, 1940s, and 1950s Hollywood motif inside. The dining rooms are adorned with a collection of puppets, statues of great movie stars, toy trains, thousands of movie stills, and antique jukeboxes that play big band–era tunes. The menu carries on the cinematic theme: prime ribs Weismuller, Eddie Fisherman fillet of fresh grouper, and Henny Young-One boneless breast of young chicken. Both adults and children (who can dine for $7 at dinner, $3.50 at lunch) are attracted to this expensive but fun establishment, where the portions are huge. For lighter appetites, the "Tiny Bubble" sampler includes a salad, choice of appetizer, and a large slice of key lime pie.

✪ **Mucky Duck.** Andy Rosse Lane (on the gulf). ☎ **941/472-3434.** Reservations not accepted. Lunch $5–$10; dinner main courses $12–$18. AE, DISC, MC, V. Mon–Sat 11:30am–2:30pm and 5–9:30pm. SEAFOOD/PUB FARE.

A Captiva institution since 1976, this lively, British-style pub is the one place here where you can dine right by the beach. If you don't get a real seat with this great view, the humorous staff will gladly roll a fake window over to appease you. The menu offers a selection of fresh seafood items, plus English fish-and-chips, steak-and-sausage pie, and a ploughman's lunch. There's a children's menu and a vegetarian platter. No smoking is allowed inside. You can't make a reservation, but you can order drinks from the bar and bide your wait at beachside picnic tables out front (come early for sunset).

✪ **Sunshine Cafe.** In Captiva Village Square, Captiva Rd. at Laika Lane. ☎ **941/472-6200.** Reservations recommended. Small platters $6–$9; large platters $19–$22; sandwiches $7–$7.50. AE, DISC, MC, V. Daily 11:30am–4pm and 5–9:30pm. ECLECTIC.

This friendly, open-kitchen cafe has only 10 tables—five inside, five on the shopping center's porch—but the food is worth the close quarters. Everything except the bread is prepared on the premises. Specialties are charcoal-grilled steak and shrimp, spicy chicken breast, po-boy sandwiches, and fresh nightly pastas, but delicious daily specials usually feature fresh fish. The portions are large here, so the "small platters," such as black beans and rice, actually make a substantial meal at a reduced price. Various desserts are offered daily; the apple crisp is a winner. Anything on the menu can be ordered to carry out.

SANIBEL & CAPTIVA ISLANDS AFTER DARK

You won't find glitzy nightclubs on these family-oriented islands, but night owls have some fun places to roost at the resorts and restaurants mentioned above. Here's a brief recap:

ON SANIBEL The Sundial Beach and Tennis Resort's **Lobby Lounge,** 1451 Middle Gulf Dr. (☎ **941/472-4151**), features entertainers during dinner, then live bands for dancing from 9pm on. The **Patio Lounge,** in the Jacaranda, 1223 Periwinkle Way (☎ **941/472-1771**), attracts an affluent crowd of middle-agers and seniors to its live music every evening. **McT's Tavern,** 1523 Periwinkle Way (☎ **941/472-3161**), has darts, video games, and a large-screen TV for sports fans. **Legends Bar & Grille,** at Tarwinkle's Seafood Restaurant, 2447 Periwinkle Way, at Tarpon Bay Road (☎ **941/472-1366**); the **Sanibel Grill,** 703 Tarpon Bay Rd. (☎ **941/472-4453**); and the two **Lazy Flamingo** branches (see "Where to Dine," above) are other popular sports bars.

Cheeseburgers on Cabbage Key

You never know who's going to get off a boat at 100-acre Cabbage Key and walk unannounced into the funky ✪ **Cabbage Key Inn,** a rustic house built in 1938 by the son and daughter-in-law of mystery novelist Mary Roberts Rinehart. Ernest Hemingway liked to hang out here in the early days, and novelist John D. MacDonald was a frequent guest 30 years later. Today you could find yourself rubbing elbows at the bar with the likes of Walter Cronkite, Ted Koppel, Sean Connery, or Julia Roberts. Singer and avid yachtie Jimmy Buffett likes Cabbage Key so much that it inspired his hit song "Cheeseburger in Paradise."

A path leads from the tiny marina across a lawn dotted with coconut palms to this white clapboard house that sits atop an ancient Calusa shell mound. Guests dine in the comfort of two screened porches and seek libations in the Rineharts' library-turned-bar, its pine-paneled walls now plastered with dollar bills left by visitors. The straight-back chairs and painted wooden tables are showing their age, but that's part of Cabbage Key's laid-back, don't-give-a-hoot charm.

In addition to the famous thick, juicy cheeseburgers so loved by Jimmy Buffett, the house specialties are fresh broiled fish and shrimp steamed in beer. Lunches range from $4 to $9; dinners are $16 to $20.

For overnight or longer, the Cabbage Key Inn has six rooms and six cottages, all with original 1920s furnishings, private baths, and air conditioners. Four of the cottages have kitchens, and one room reputedly has its own ghost. Rates are $65 single or double for rooms, $145 to $200 for cottages. Reserve well in advance for major holidays and during the tarpon season from February to May. For information or reservations, contact **Cabbage Key Inn,** P.O. Box 200, Pineland, FL 33945 (☎ **941/283-2278;** fax 941/283-1384).

You can get to Cabbage Key from Pine Island near Fort Myers via the inn's own launch, which leaves daily from the Mattson Marine marina, or on the *Tropic Star* (☎ **941/283-0015**), which departs the Four Winds Marina daily at 9:30am. The *Tropic Star* charges $20 for adults, $12 for children. Captiva Cruises (☎ **941/472-5300**) goes there daily from Captiva Island, charging $27.50 per adult, $15 for children.

From December to April, professional actors perform Broadway dramas and comedies Monday to Saturday at 8pm in Sanibel's state-of-the-art, 150-seat **Pirate Playhouse,** 2200 Periwinkle Way (☎ **941/472-0006**). Call for the schedule and ticket prices.

Originally a one-room school built in 1896 and later housing the Pirate Playhouse before its new facility was constructed across the road, the **Old Schoolhouse Theater,** 1905 Periwinkle Way (☎ **941/472-6862**), complements its neighbor by offering Broadway musicals and revues from December to April. From May to November, the Off Beach Players perform comedies and mystery plays for all ages. Call for the current schedule and prices.

For laughs, the **Sanibel Island Comedy Club,** 975 Rabbit Rd., at Sanibel-Captiva Road next to Loco's Steakhouse and Cantina (☎ **941/472-8833**), attracts national comedians by offering them a working vacation here (call for schedule).

ON CAPTIVA   The **Crow's Nest Lounge,** in the 'Tween Waters Inn, on Captiva Road (☎ **941/472-5161**), is Captiva's top nightspot for dancing. **Chadwick's Lounge,** at the entrance to the South Seas Plantation Resort & Yacht Harbour (☎ **941/472-5111**), has a large dance floor and music from 9pm on.

NEARBY ISLAND HOPPING

Sanibel and Captiva are jumping-off points for island-hopping boat trips to barrier islands and keys teeming with ancient legends and Robinson Crusoe–style beaches. You don't have to get completely lost out there, however, for several islets have comfortable inns and restaurants. The trip across shallow Pine Island Sound is itself a sightseeing adventure, with playful dolphins surfing on the boats' wakes and a variety of cormorants, egrets, frigate birds, and (in winter) rare white pelicans flying above or lounging on sandbars between meals.

Captiva Cruises (☎ 941/472-5300) has daily trips from the South Seas Plantation Resort & Yacht Harbour on Captiva. The *Lady Chadwick* goes to Cabbage Key (see box) and Useppa Island, where passengers disembark for lunch. The *Island Lady* goes to Boca Grande (see section 4) by way of Cayo Costa State Park. These day trips cost $27.50 per adult, $15 for children to Cabbage Key or Useppa; $35 for adults, $17.50 for children to Boca Grande or Cayo Costa. They usually leave at 10:30am. Reservations are required.

From Pine Island off Fort Myers, you can take the *Tropic Star* (☎ 941/283-0015) to both Cabbage Key and Cayo Costa (see "Cruises" in section 1).

CAYO COSTA   You can't get any more deserted than at ✪ **Cayo Costa State Park** (pronounced *Kay*-oh *Cos*-tah), which occupies a 2,132-acre, completely unspoiled barrier island with miles of white-sand beaches, pine forests, mangrove swamps, oak-palm hammocks, and grasslands. Other than natural wildlife, the only permanent residents here are three park rangers.

Day-trippers can bring their own supplies and use a picnic area with pavilions. A tram carries visitors from the sound-side dock to the gulf beach (50¢ round-trip fare). The state maintains 12 very basic cabins and a primitive campground on the northern end of the island near Johnson Shoals, where the shelling is spectacular. Cabins cost $20 a day, and campsites are $13 a day all year. There's running water on the island but no electricity.

The park is open daily from 8am to sundown. There's a $2 per person honor-system admission fee for day visitors. Overnight slips at the dock cost $13 a day. For more information or cabin reservations, contact **Cayo Costa State Park**, P.O. Box 1150, Boca Grande, FL 33921 (☎ 941/964-0375). Office hours are Monday to Friday from 8am to 5pm.

UPPER (NORTH) CAPTIVA   Cut off by a pass from Captiva, its northern barrier island sibling is occupied by the **North Captiva Island Club**, P.O. Box 1000, Pineland, FL 33945 (☎ 800/576-7343 or 941/395-1001; fax 941/472-5836), an upscale resort. Despite the development, however, about 750 of the island's 1,000 acres are included in a state preserve. The club rents accommodations ranging from efficiencies to luxury homes. There's scheduled water taxi service from **Jenson's Twin Palms Marina** on Captiva (☎ 941/472-5800), or you can get here from Matson Marine on Pine Island with **Island Charters** (☎ 800/340-33321 or 941/283-1113). Both charge $25 per person round-trip,

✪ **USEPPA ISLAND**   Lying near Cabbage Key, Useppa was a refuge of Pres. Theodore Roosevelt and his tarpon-loving industrialist friends at the turn of the century. New York advertising magnate Barron G. Collier bought the island in 1906 and built a lovely wooden home overlooking Pine Island Sound. His mansion is now the **Collier Inn**, where day-trippers and overnight guests can partake of lunches and seafood dinners in a country-club ambience. They also can visit the **Useppa Museum**, which explains the island's history and displays 4,000-year-old Calusa artifacts. Admission is by $2 donation.

The Collier Inn is the centerpiece of the **Useppa Island Club,** an exclusive development with more than 100 luxury homes, all of the clapboard-sided, tin-roofed style of Old Florida. For information, rates (all on the modified American plan), and reservations, contact **Collier Inn & Cottages,** P.O. Box 640, Bokeelia, FL 33922 (☎ **941/ 283-1061;** fax 941/283-0290).

4 Boca Grande

63 miles NW of Fort Myers, 105 miles NW of Naples, 50 miles SE of Sarasota

After he lost to Bill Clinton back in 1992, George Bush and wife Barbara licked their wounds at Boca Grande (pronounced *Grand*). They chose well, for this charming village on Gasparilla Island is definitely a president's kind of place. Legend says that the infamous pirate José Gaspar lived in style on this 7-mile-long barrier island. So did the du Pont family, which founded Boca Grande in the 1880s. They were followed by the Astors, Morgans, Vanderbilts, and other moneyed clans, who still turn the island into a Florida version of Nantucket during their winter "social season."

In addition to the warm weather, the lure was some of the world's best tarpon fishing. Descendants of the watermen who were here first—and who guided the rich and famous—still work their 1920s-vintage marinas and live on streets named Dam-If-I-Know, Dam-If-I-Care, and Dam-If-I-Will. You can see their modest homes with backyards full of old sheds, boats, and fishnets, but high hedges hide the "beach-fronter" mansions around 29th Street.

ESSENTIALS

GETTING THERE   From the north on I-75, take Exit 32 in Charlotte County, then head west to the end of Toledo Blade Boulevard. Turn right there onto Fla. 776, then left on Fla. 771 to Placida and the Boca Grande Causeway ($3.20 toll to the island, free coming back). From the south on I-75, take Exit 31 and go south on Kings Highway (Fla. 769), then an immediate left on Veterans Boulevard (Fla. 776) and left on Fla. 771 to the Boca Grande Causeway. It's about 1½ hours from Fort Myers.

Captiva Cruises (☎ **941/472-5300**) has daily trips from the South Seas Plantation Resort & Yacht Harbour on Captiva to Boca Grande (see "Nearby Island Hopping" in section 3). The fare is $35 adults, $17.50 children.

VISITOR INFORMATION   Contact the **Boca Grande Chamber of Commerce,** 5800 Gasparilla Rd. (P.O. Box 704), Boca Grande, FL 33921 (☎ **941/964-0568;** fax 941/964-0620; www.charlotte-online.com/bocagrande; e-mail: bgcc@ewol.com). The office is in the Courtyard Shops, on the left as you drive onto the island. You can also find information in a rack in the Theater Mall on Park Avenue in the heart of town.

GETTING AROUND   **Boca Grande Taxi & Limousine** (☎ **800/771-7433** or 941/964-0455) will take you around in style, but many visitors choose to see this town on foot, or by bicycle or golf cart rented from **Island Bike 'n' Beach,** 333 Park Ave. (☎ **941/964-0711**). Bikes range from $6 an hour to $18 a day. The company also rents baby strollers, beach chairs and umbrellas, boogie boards, tennis racquets, and other items. Now a paved, 7-mile-long **bike path,** the bed of the old Charlotte Harbor and Northern Railroad runs by the depot on its way from the island's south end all the way north to the causeway.

EXPLORING THE TOWN

The pink-brick **Railroad Depot,** at the corner of Park Avenue and 4th Street, has been restored to its turn-of-the-century grandeur when it was Boca Grande's lifeline to the world. It now houses a cluster of upscale boutiques and the Loose Caboose Restaurant and Ice Cream Parlor, where Katherine Hepburn once satiated her sweet tooth (see "Where to Dine," below).

You can stand on the railway platform and see numerous high-end **boutiques** and **art galleries** along 4th Street and Railroad and Park avenues. Across the street, **Fugate's** has been selling everything from rain slickers to wedding gowns since 1916.

Banyan Street (actually 2nd Street) is canopied with tangled banyan trees and is one of the prettiest places for a stroll. Nearby, **St. Andrew's Episcopal Church** and the **First Baptist Church,** both at Gilchrist and 4th streets, and the **United Methodist Church,** at Gilchrist and 3rd streets, all date from the town's early years.

The **Johann Fust Community Library,** at Gasparilla Road and 10th Street (☎ **941/964-2488**), contains 12,000 volumes and the extraordinary **Du Pont Shell Collection,** all gathered by Henry Francis du Pont during nearly 50 years of combing the island's beaches. The library has a lovely interior garden and outdoor reading room. Open December to April, Monday to Friday from 10am to noon and 4 to 6pm; the rest of the year, Monday to Friday from 4 to 6pm.

At the south end of the island, the **Boca Grande Lighthouse** began marking the pass into Charlotte Harbor in 1890 (the steel tower on Gulf Boulevard served as the light from 1966 to 1986, when the old building was restored). **Gasparilla Island State Recreation Area** around the lighthouse is open daily from 8am to sunset.

ENJOYING THE OUTDOORS

By far the biggest event here is the chamber of commerce–sponsored **World's Richest Tarpon Tournament,** usually the second week in July, when anglers try to reel in $100,000. Charter fishing is available through **Boca Grande Charter Booking Services,** located at **Miller's Marina** on Harbor Drive (☎ **941/964-2232**). You can rent boats at **Whidden's Marina** (☎ **941/964-2878**) also on Harbor Drive. The **Boca Grande Pass Marina** (☎ **941/964-0607**), on the south end of the island at the old phosphate port (now an oil transshipment facility), also is a base for charter fishing boats. Miller's Marina (☎ **941/964-2283**) has backwater nature tours and parasailing during the winter season.

Beach access is limited by the expensive homes along the gulf, but there's a **public beach** just south of town on Gulf Boulevard. **Gasparilla Island State Recreation Area** has a small beach park just south of the village and a lovely strip of sand on the island's south end. The area is open daily from 8am to sunset. Admission is $2 per vehicle.

Also near the south end, **Sun Chaser Watersports,** on the beach at South Beach restaurant (☎ **941/769-2142**), rents ocean kayaks and Windsurfers.

Boca Grande Ferry Service (☎ **941/964-1100** or 941/964-0607) takes passengers out to Cayo Costa, Cabbage Key, and other islands. It departs at 10:30am daily from the Boca Grande Pass Marina on the island's south end. Fares are $16 to $20, depending on the destination. Reservations are required. See "Nearby Island Hopping" in section 3 of this chapter, on Sanibel and Captiva Islands, for information about Cayo Costa and Cabbage Key.

WHERE TO STAY

The only way to stay on the beach here is to rent a condo or a house. One example is **Sundown Colony,** a group of 28 spacious, two-story, two-bedroom/two-bath town homes right on the beach a mile south of town. Rates range from $945 to $1,800 a week, depending on the season. It's one of several rental properties managed by **Boca Grande Real Estate,** P.O. Box 686, Boca Grande, FL 33921 (☎ **800/881-2622** or 941/964-0338; fax 941/964-2301).

✪ **Gasparilla Inn & Cottages.** 500 Palm Ave. (P.O. Box 1088), Boca Grande, FL 33921. ☎ **941/964-2201.** Fax 941/964-2733. 150 units. A/C TV TEL. Winter $350–$525 double. Off-season $228 double. Rates include all meals. No credit cards. Closed June–Oct.

Opened in 1912, this architectural beauty with stately columns, Southern-style verandas, and handsome wood floors is still the winter home for affluent socialites. So exclusive is this enclave of the well-to-do that it doesn't even advertise (nor does the staff readily answer questions from guidebook writers, for that matter). So many of its regulars return from one social season to the next that it's difficult to get a room or cottage from mid-January to April. The rooms here are in the original inn, and old-fashioned but updated cottages are scattered around the grounds.

Dining: Unless you have the good fortune (literally) to stay here, forget the high-ceilinged, aristocratic dining room in which guests dress for dinner. You can have a meal in the more modern and much more relaxed Pink Elephant Restaurant, nearby at 5th Street and Bayou Avenue (☎ **941/964-0100**).

Amenities: Behind the inn, guests can play tennis on private courts or golf on an excellent 18-hole course along the shores of Charlotte Harbor. At the beach, they can play with water-sports equipment at their own private club.

Innlet on the Waterfront. 12th St. (at E. Railroad Ave.; P.O. Box 248), Boca Grande, FL 33921. ☎ **941/964-2294.** Fax 941/964-0382. 32 units. A/C TV TEL. Winter $95–$135 double. Off-season $85–$115 double. MC, V.

This motel has a large veranda across the back, from which guests can view Boca Grande Bayou, the creeklike waterway forming the town's eastern boundary. The efficiencies, opening to the veranda and equipped with kitchens, are more expensive than the standard motel units. There's a swimming pool and marina on the premises, but no restaurant.

WHERE TO DINE

For picnic fixings, go to the village's sole grocery, **Hudson's,** on Park Avenue between 4th and 5th streets opposite the Railroad Depot (☎ **941/964-2570**). It's open Monday to Saturday from 8am to 5:30pm.

✪ **Jam's Italian Restaurant.** Railroad Ave. at 5th St. ☎ **941/964-2002.** Pizzas $5–$14; pastas $5.50–$10; sandwiches $3–$6. AE, MC, V. Mon–Thurs 11am–9pm, Fri–Sat 11am–10pm, Sun noon–9pm. ITALIAN.

Although President Bush usually hobnobbed at the Gasparilla Inn when he was here, he did join his White House staffers once at their hangout in this pleasant Italian restaurant, whose motto is "More food for less lira." Neither the food nor the value has changed since they scarfed down tons of excellent pizza and pasta while watching ball games on three TVs. Jam's even has a White House plaque to prove the staffers were here.

Loose Caboose. Park Rd. at 3rd St., in the Railroad Depot. ☎ **941/964-0440.** Reservations not accepted. Salads and sandwiches $3.50–$10; main courses $6.50–$14. MC, V. Winter daily 9am–9pm. Off-season daily 9am–6pm. Closed Thanksgiving and Christmas. AMERICAN.

Everyone from actress Katherine Hepburn down to local bank clerks who can't afford to live on the island flock here for good yet inexpensive fare. You can dine inside the old Railroad Depot or outside under its soaring brick arches. Tops here are warm Oriental salads and sandwiches composed with Black Forest ham and brie, but you can order a variety of fare from nachos to baskets of fried oysters or shrimp. A limited dinner menu is offered during the winter season.

Loons on a Limb. 3rd St. at Railway Ave. ☎ **941/964-0155.** Reservations recommended for dinner. Breakfast $4.50–$8; main courses $11–$20. No credit cards. Winter daily 7:30–11:30am and 6–9pm. Off-season daily 7:30–11:30am. Closed Aug, Thanksgiving, and Christmas. SEAFOOD/THAI/CREOLE.

Owned and operated by Boca Grande natives, "The Loon" is famous for both eggs Benedict and grits, which speaks reams about this town's split personality. It's one of the few places on the island serving breakfast. Talented chef Michael Perlov usually prepares a chalkboard dinner menu from October to May, featuring seafood prepared in Creole and Thai fashions. Photos and paintings of wild birds share the tongue-in-groove walls with a stuffed deer's head.

✪ **South Beach.** 777 Gulf Blvd. (south end of island). ☎ **941/964-0765.** Reservations recommended. Main courses $12–$22. AE, DISC, MC, V. Daily 11am–10pm. Bar open until 2am. SEAFOOD.

The only place on Gasparilla where you can dine or have a sunset cocktail by the gulf, this casual establishment has a covered patio with plastic chairs and tables right by the white sand. Patrons also have a view of the beach through the window walls of the dining room, whose solid walls bear a jungly mural and works by local artists. The regular menu features the usual assortment of shrimp, grouper, and broiled mahimahi, but the specials such as stone crab claws or pompano are your best bets. Wednesday usually is all-you-can-eat shrimp night ($19), while Friday offers a stuffing of fish ($17). Bands make music on the patio on weekends during the winter season.

✪ **PJ's Seagrille.** Park Ave. and 4th St. ☎ **941/964-0806.** Reservations recommended. Main courses $15–$21. MC, V. Mon–Sat 11:30am–2:30pm and 5:30–9:30pm, Sun 11am–2:30pm (brunch) and 5:30–9:30pm. Closed Aug–Sept. FLORIDA/CARIBBEAN.

Chef Jimmy Turner's Gasparilla crab cakes and seafood pasta head the playbill at this 1928 movie theater turned into a minimall and fine restaurant. Nightly specials include a variety of other fresh-off-the-boat seafood, plus steaks grilled over an open flame and lamb osso buco. Dine inside or on a screened porch.

5 Naples

42 miles S of Fort Myers, 106 miles W of Miami, 185 miles S of Tampa

Because its wealthy residents are accustomed to the very best, Naples is easily Southwest Florida's most sophisticated city. Indeed, its boutiques and galleries would upstage those in Palm Beach or Beverly Hills. And yet Naples has an easygoing friendliness to all comers, who can find some surprisingly affordable places to stay within easy reach of its long, magnificent beach and pricey resorts.

Naples began in 1886, when a group of 12 Kentuckians and Ohioans bought 8,700 acres, laid out a town, and started selling lots. They built a pier and the 16-room Naples Hotel, whose first guest was Pres. Grover Cleveland's sister Rose. She and other notables soon built a line of beach homes known as "Millionaires' Row." Known today as Olde Naples and carefully protected by its modern residents, their original settlement still retains the air of that time a century ago.

Even the newer sections of Naples have their charm, thanks to Ohio manufacturer Henry B. Watkins Sr. In 1946, Watkins and his partners bought the old hotel and all the town's undeveloped land and laid out the Naples Plan, which created the environmentally conscious city you see today. While strict zoning laws preserve the old part of town, the Naples Plan blends development with the natural environment along the town's 10 miles of beachfront.

ESSENTIALS

GETTING THERE   From Miami, U.S. 41 (the Tamiami Trail) leads through the Everglades to Naples. A faster route from Miami and Fort Lauderdale is via I-75 ("Alligator Alley"), which will also bring you south from Tampa and Fort Myers. From I-75, take Immokalee Road (Exit 17) for Vanderbilt Beach, Pine Ridge Road (Exit 16) for the Pelican Bay area north of downtown, or Davis Boulevard (Exit 15) for downtown.

Most visitors arrive at the **Southwest Florida International Airport,** 35 miles north of Naples (see "Getting There" under "Essentials," in section 1, on Fort Myers). **Naples Municipal Airport,** on North Road off Airport-Pulling Road (☎ **941/643-6875**), is served by **American Eagle** (☎ **800/433-7300**) and **US Airways Express** (☎ **800/428-4322**). Taxis await all flights outside the small terminal building.

VISITOR INFORMATION   The **Naples Area Chamber of Commerce** maintains a visitor center at 895 5th Ave. South (at U.S. 41), Naples, FL 34102 (☎ **941/262-6141;** fax 941/262-8374; www.naples-online.com), which has a host of free information and phones for making hotel reservations. It sells a detailed street map for $2. By mail, they will send a complete Naples vacation packet for $7 ($12 to Canada, $25 outside North America) and the street map for $3. The visitor center is open Monday to Friday from 9am to 5pm, Saturday and Sunday from 10am to 3pm.

You can get on-the-street information at **kiosks** in the Marketplace at Tin City on U.S. 41 at the Gordon River Bridge, and on 3rd Street South at 12 Avenue South in Olde Naples.

GETTING AROUND   The **Naples Trolley** (☎ **941/262-7300**) clangs around 25 stops between the Marketplace at Tin City in Olde Naples and Vanderbilt Beach on Monday to Saturday from 8:30am to 5:15pm and on Sunday from 10:15am to 5:15pm. Daily fares are $12 for adults, $5 for children 3 to 12, free for children under 3, with free reboarding. You can buy tickets from the driver or at the Naples Trolley Depot and Welcome Center, 1010 6th Ave. S. (two blocks west of Tin City), and at the chamber of commerce visitor center. Schedules are available in brochure racks in the lobbies of most hotels and motels.

Call **Yellow Cab** (☎ **941/262-1312**), **Maxi Taxi** (☎ **941/262-8977**), or **Naples Taxi** (☎ **941/775-0505**). Fares are $1.75 for the first tenth of a mile, 30¢ for each two-tenths of a mile thereafter.

The Naples Area Chamber of Commerce (see above) distributes an area bicycle route map. Rent a bike from **The Bike Route,** 655 N. Tamiami Trail (☎ **941/262-8373**). For scooters, call **Good Times Rental,** 1947 Davis Blvd. (☎ **941/775-7529**).

HITTING THE BEACH

Access to Olde Naples's gorgeous white-sand beach is at the gulf end of each avenue, although parking in the neighborhood can be precious. Try the metered lots on 12th Avenue South near the **Naples Pier,** the town's most popular beaching spot. Families gather on the beach north of the pier, while local teens congregate on the south side. There's a food concessionaire on the pier.

Also popular with families, lovely **Lowdermilk Park,** on Millionaire's Row at Gulf Shore Boulevard and North Banyan Boulevard, has a pavilion, rest rooms, showers, a refreshment counter, professional-quality volleyball courts (the area's best players practice here), a duck pond, and picnic tables. There's metered parking, so bring quarters. A few blocks farther north is another metered parking lot with beach access beside the Naples Beach Hotel & Golf Resort, 851 Gulf Shore Blvd. N., at Golf Drive.

Nature lovers head to the Pelican Bay development north of the historic district and the popular ✪ **Clam Pass County Park** (☎ **941/353-0404**). A free tram takes you along a 3,000-foot boardwalk winding through mangrove swamps and across a back bay to a beach of fine white sand. It's a strange sight, what with high-rise condos standing beyond the mangrove-bordered backwaters, but this actually is a miniature wilderness. Some 6 miles of canoe and kayak trails—with multitudes of birds and an occasional alligator—run from Clam Pass into the winding streams. The beach pavilion here has a snack bar, rest rooms (foot showers only), picnic tables, and beach equipment rentals, including one- and two-person kayaks and 12-foot canoes. Entry is from a metered parking lot beside the Registry Resort at the end of Seagate Drive. There's a $3 per vehicle parking fee. You can push, but not ride, bicycles on the boardwalk.

At **Vanderbilt Beach,** about 4 miles north of Olde Naples, the **Delnor-Wiggins State Recreation Area,** at the west end of Bluebill Avenue–111th Avenue North (☎ **941/597-6196**), has been listed among America's top 10 stretches of sand by "Dr. Beach." It has bathhouses, a boat ramp, and the area's best picnic facilities. Fishing from the beach is excellent here. The area is open daily from 8am to sunset. Admission is $2 per vehicle with one occupant, $4 for vehicles with two to eight occupants, $1 for pedestrians and bikers.

OTHER OUTDOOR ACTIVITIES

BOATING & BOAT RENTALS   Powerboat rentals are available from **Club Nautico,** at the Boat Haven Marina, 1484 E. Tamiami Trail (☎ **941/774-0100**), on the east bank of the Gordon River behind Kelly's Fish House; the **Port-O-Call Marina,** 550 Port of Call Way (☎ **941/774-0479**); the **Parkshore Marina,** 4310 Gulf Shore Blvd. N. (☎ **941/434-6964**), in the Village Shops at Venetian Bay; the **Brookside Marina,** 2023 Davis Blvd. (☎ **941/774-9100**); and the **Cove Marina,** 860 12th Ave. S. (☎ **941/263-7250**), at the City Docks.

Sailing enthusiasts can line up a charter with **Sailboats Unlimited,** at the City Docks on 12th Avenue South (☎ **941/262-0139**).

CRUISES   The Gordon River and Naples Bay from the U.S. 41 bridge on 5th Avenue South to the gulf are prime territory for sightseeing, dolphin watching, and sunset cruises. The double-decked *Double Sunshine* (☎ **941/263-4949**) sallies forth onto the river and bay daily from Tin City, where it has a ticket office. The 1½-hour cruises usually leave at 10am, noon, 2pm, and an hour before sunset. They cost $15 per adult, $10 for children under 12.

The *Sweet Liberty* (☎ **941/793-3525**), a 53-foot sailing catamaran, makes morning shelling cruises to Keewaydin Island, a private wildlife sanctuary south of Olde Naples. The vessel then spends the afternoon sightseeing and the evening on sunset cruises on Naples Bay before docking at Boat Haven Marina on the east side of the Gordon River Bridge. Shelling cruises cost $25 for adults, $10 for children; sightseeing and sunset cruises cost $20 for adults, $10 for children.

For a good deal more luxury, the 83-foot *Naples Princess* (☎ **800/728-2970** or 941/649-2275) has narrated breakfast, lunch, and sunset dinner cruises from Olde Naples Seaport, 10th Avenue South at 10th Street South. These usually leave at 9am, noon, and sunset. With extensive continental breakfast and sandwich lunch buffets, the two daytime cruises are excellent values at $20 and $25 per person. Call for schedule and prices of sunset cruises.

FISHING   The locals like to fish from the **Naples Pier** (see "Exploring the Town," below). The pier has tables on which to clean your catch, but watch out for the ever-present pelicans, which are master thieves. You can buy tackle and bait from the local marinas (see "Boating & Boat Rentals," above).

The least expensive way for singles, couples, and small families to fish without paying for an entire boat is on the 34-foot *Lady Brett* (☎ **941/263-4949**), which makes two daily trips from Tin City for $45 per person. Rod, reel, bait, and fishing license are included, but bring your own drinks and lunch. A number of charter boats are based at the marinas mentioned under "Boating & Boat Rentals," above; call or visit them for booking information and prices.

GOLF Most of Naples' excellent golf courses are private clubs, but the area also has a few of America's best public golf courses, including the ✪ **Lely Flamingo Island Club** and the **Lely Mustang Golf Club,** both on U.S. 41 between Naples and Marco Island (☎ **800/388-GOLF** or 941/793-2223). The Lely Flamingo course was designed by Robert Trent Jones Sr., and its hourglass fairways and fingerlike bunkers present many challenges. Designed by Lee Trevino, the new Lely Mustang course is more forgiving but still fun. Former PGA Tour player Paul Trittler has his golf school at these courses. You'll pay a price here in winter, when 18-hole fees are about $135 at Lely Flamingo and $148 at Lely Mustang, including cart and range balls, but they drop progressively after Easter to about $40 and $48, respectively, in the muggy summer months.

Boyne South, on U.S. 41 between Fla. 931 and Fla. 92 (☎ **941/732-5108**), is another winner, with lots of wildlife inhabiting its many lakes (a 16-foot alligator reportedly resides near the 17th hole). There's a driving range, practice facility, and restaurant, and instruction is available. Wintertime fees are $70, but in the off-season they drop to $35 or less. Tee times are taken up to 4 days in advance.

Another local favorite is the player-friendly **Hibiscus Golf Club,** one-half mile east of U.S. 41 off Rattlesnake Hammock Road in East Naples (☎ **941/774-0088**). There's a pro shop and a teaching professional on hand. Fees are about $70 in winter, cart included, dropping to about $25 in summer.

In Olde Naples, nonguests can sign up to play at **Naples Beach Hotel & Golf Club** (see "Where to Stay," below).

In Golden Gate, west of I-75, the **Quality Inn Golf & Country Club,** 4100 Golden Gate Pkwy. (☎ **800/228-5151** or 941/455-1010), has an 18-hole course and 153 rooms, suites, and efficiencies.

SCUBA DIVING The **Under Seas Dive Academy,** 998 6th Ave. S., in Olde Naples (☎ **941/262-0707**), takes divers into the gulf, teaches diver-certification courses, and rents water-sports equipment. So does Kevin Sweeney's **SCUBA-d-ventures,** 971 Creech Rd., at Tamiami Trail (☎ **941/434-7477**).

TENNIS In Olde Naples, the city's **Cambier Park Tennis Center,** 755 8th Ave. S., at 9th Street South (☎ **941/434-4694**), offers 12 lighted clay courts. It's one of the few public tennis facilities anywhere to match those found at luxury resorts. Play costs $6 for 90 minutes. It's open Monday to Friday from 8am to 10pm, Saturday and Sunday from 8am to 5pm. Book with the pro in the middle of the courts. There's an adjacent children's playground.

Nonguests can play at the **Naples Beach Hotel & Golf Club,** 851 Gulf Shore Blvd. N. (☎ **941/261-2222**), for $9.50 an hour, but call ahead to reserve court time.

Dedicated buffs can play to their hearts' content on the 11 clay and 5 hard courts at **World Tennis Center Resort & Club,** 4800 Airport-Pulling Rd., at Pine Ridge Road (☎ **800/292-6663** or 941/263-1900; fax 941/649-7855), but you must stay in one of the 72 two-bedroom condominiums here to use them. There's a restaurant, swimming pool, and sauna on the premises.

WATER SPORTS **Good Times Rental,** 1947 Davis Blvd. (☎ **941/775-7529**), rents WaveRunners, windsurfers, skim boards, canoes, snorkeling gear, rafts, and other beach equipment. Hobie Cats and Windsurfers can also be rented on the beach at the **Naples Beach Hotel & Golf Club,** 851 Gulf Shore Blvd. N. (☎ 941/261-2222), and at **Clam Pass County Park,** at the end of Seagate Drive (☎ 941/353-0404). See "Hitting the Beach," above, for more about Clam Pass County Park.

EXPLORING THE TOWN

During the winter you can take evening horse-drawn carriage rides around Olde Naples with the **Naples Horse & Carriage Co.** (☎ 941/649-1210). Prices begin at $30 per person for a 30-minute ride. The carriages can hold up to four adults.

❂ OLDE NAPLES

Its history may only go back to 1886, but the beach skirting **Olde Naples** still has the charm of that Victorian era. The heart of the district lies below 5th Avenue South (that's where U.S. 41 takes a 45° turn). The town docks are on the bay side, the glorious beach along the gulf. Laid out on a grid, the tree-lined streets run between many houses, some dating from the town's beginning, and along Millionaires' Row between Gulf Shore Boulevard and the beach. With these gorgeous homes virtually hidden in the palms and casuarinas, the Naples Beach seems a century removed from the high-rise condos found farther north.

The **Naples Pier,** at the gulf end of 12th Avenue South, is a focal point of the neighborhood. Built in 1888 to let steamers land potential real-estate customers, the original 600-foot-long, T-shaped structure was destroyed by hurricanes and damaged by fire. Local residents have rebuilt it because they like strolling its length to catch fantastic gulf sunsets—and to get a glimpse of Millionaire's Row from the gulf side. The pier is now a state historic site. It's open 24 hours a day, but parking in the nearby lots is restricted between 11pm and 7am.

Nearby, **Palm Cottage,** 137 12th Ave. S., between 1st Street and Gordon Drive (☎ 941/261-8164), was built in 1885 by one of Naples's founders, *Louisville Courier-Journal* publisher Walter Haldeman, as a winter retreat for his chief editorial writer. After World War II, its socialite owners hosted many galas attended by Hollywood stars such as Hedy Lamarr, Gary Cooper, and Robert Montgomery. One of the few remaining Southwest Florida houses built of tabbie mortar (made by burning shells), Palm Cottage today is the home of the Naples Historical Society, which maintains it as a museum filled with authentic furniture, paintings, photographs, and other memorabilia. Tours are given during winter, Monday to Friday from 1 to 4pm. Adult admission is by $5 donation; free for children.

Near the Gordon River Bridge on 5th Avenue South, the old corrugated waterfront warehouses are now a shopping-and-dining complex known as the **Marketplace at Tin City,** which tourists throng to and local residents assiduously avoid during the winter months.

MUSEUMS & ZOOS

Caribbean Gardens. 1590 Goodlette-Frank Rd. (at Fleischman Blvd.). ☎ 941/262-5409. Admission $13.95 adults, $8.95 children 4–15, free for children 3 and under. Daily 9:30am–5:30pm (last admission at 4:30pm). Closed Easter, Thanksgiving, and Christmas.

A family favorite formerly known as "Jungle Larry's," for noted animal trainer and owner Larry Tetzlaff, this zoo features a variety of animals and birds, including a fascinating community of primates living free on their own island. You can see them on a safari through the spectacular tropical gardens. Many visitors are captivated by the Big Cat Show, in which lions and tigers are put through their paces by Larry's son, David Tetzlaff, himself a talented trainer. Big Cat show times vary, so call for the schedule. You can also see three of the world's 40 golden tigers here. For kids, there's a Petting Farm, elephant rides, and a playground. The Canyon Cafe serves snacks, and there are picnic facilities on the premises.

☼ Teddy Bear Museum. 2511 Pine Ridge Rd. (at Airport-Pulling Rd.). ☎ **800/681-2327** or 941/598-2711. Admission $6 adults, $4 seniors, $2 children 4–12, free for children under 4. Winter Mon and Wed–Sat 10am–5pm, Sun 1–5pm. Off-season Wed–Sat 10am–5pm, Sun 1–5pm. Closed New Year's Day, July 4, Thanksgiving, and Christmas.

Another family favorite, this entertaining museum contains 3,000-plus examples of stuffed teddy bears from around the world. They're cleverly displayed descending from the rafters in hot-air balloons, attending board meetings, sipping afternoon tea, celebrating a wedding, even doing bear things like hibernating. There's a gift shop where you can buy your own bears.

PARKS & NATURE PRESERVES

You don't have to go far east of Naples to reach the magnificent Everglades, much of it protected by Everglades National Park and Big Cypress National Preserve. See chapter 7 for full details on activities in and near the national park. Other nearby nature preserves are described in section 6 of this chapter, on Marco Island.

One of the largest private preserves is the **☼ Corkscrew Swamp Sanctuary** (☎ **941/348-9151**), 16 miles northeast of Naples off Immokalee Road (County Road 846). Maintained by the National Audubon Society, this 11,000-acre wilderness is home to countless wood storks that nest high in the cypress trees from November to April. Wading birds also are best seen in winter, when the swamp is likely to be dry (they don't nest when water levels are high). The birds congregate around pools near a boardwalk that leads 2 miles through the largest bald cypress forest with some of the oldest trees in the country. Ferns and orchids also flourish. Admission is $6.50 for adults, $5 for full-time college students, $3 for children 6 to 18, and free for children 5 and under. The sanctuary is open December to April, daily from 7am to 5pm; May to November, daily from 8am to 5pm. To reach the sanctuary, take Exit 17 off I-75 and go east on Immokalee Road (County Road 846).

About a 30-minute drive away, the **Corkscrew Marsh Trail System,** on Corkscrew Road south of Fla. 82, consists of a 5-mile loop through mostly pine forests managed jointly by the Corkscrew Regional Ecosystem Watershed Trust and the South Florida Water Management District. Only hikers are allowed to use these trails, which are free but have no drinking water or rest rooms.

You can also experience Southwest Florida's abundant natural life without leaving town at **The Conservancy's Naples Nature Center,** 14th Avenue North, east of Goodlette-Frank Road (☎ 941/262-0304), one of two preserves operated by The Conservancy of Southwest Florida (see the Briggs Nature Center in section 6). There are nature trails, an aviary with bald eagles and other birds, and electric boat rides through a mangrove forest to observe wildlife (you can also rent canoes and kayaks and see it by yourself). A nature store carries interesting gift items. The trails and boat rides are free. Admission is $5 for adults, $2 for children 3 to 12, free for children under 3. Canoe and kayak rentals are $13 for 2 hours, $5 for each additional hour. The center is open year-round Monday to Saturday from 9am to 4:30pm, and also on Sunday from 1 to 5pm from January through March.

SHOPPING

Two blocks of **3rd Street South,** at Broad Avenue, are the Rodeo Drive of Naples. This glitzy collection of jewelers, clothiers, and art galleries may be too rich for many wallets, but the window shopping here is unmatched. Be sure to pick up a free brochure, which lists the merchants and has a map of the area, from the chamber of commerce visitors center (see "Essentials," above).

Nearby, the **5th Avenue South** shopping area, between 3rd and 9th streets south, is longer and a bit less chic, with stockbrokerages and real-estate offices thrown into the mix of boutiques and antique dealers. Both areas have several bistros and other dining spots. Also in Olde Naples, the **Old Marine Marketplace at Tin City,** 1200 5th Ave. S., at the Gordon River, has 50 boutiques selling everything from souvenirs to avant-garde resort wear and imported statuary. There are more boutiques in the **Dockside Boardwalk,** ½ block west on 6th Avenue South.

Even the malls in Naples have their charms. The **Village at Venetian Bay,** 4200 Gulf Shore Blvd., at Park Shore Drive, evokes images of its Italian namesake, with 50 canal-side shops featuring high-fashion men's and women's clothiers and fine-art galleries. Ornate Mediterranean architecture and a tropical waterfall highlight the open-air **Waterside Shops at Pelican Bay,** Seagate Drive at North Tamiami Trail (U.S. 41), where the anchor stores are Saks Fifth Avenue and Jacobson's. There's a huge Barnes & Noble bookstore across Seagate Drive.

Coastland Center, on North Tamiami Trail (U.S. 41) between Fleischman Boulevard and Golden Gate Parkway, is the regular mall here, but it's a monster (you'll walk nearly a mile from end to end). Burdine's, Dillards, and JC Penney anchor most of the familiar national chains.

Discount shoppers can head to **Coral Isle Factory Outlets,** on Fla. 951 about a mile south of U.S. 41 on the way to Marco Island, although it's smaller and less promising than the Sanibel Factory Outlets in Fort Myers (see "Shopping," in section 1). You'll find the usual clothiers here, plus outlets for Villeroy & Fosh, Mikasa, and Coach Leathers.

WHERE TO STAY

While Naples has some of the most expensive resorts in the region, it also has some surprisingly reasonable rates, particularly at several older but very well maintained "apartment hotels" in the historic district within a few blocks of the beach. The **Olde Naples Inn & Suites** is one of the best (see listing under "Inexpensive," below). Others include the **Beachcomber Club,** 290 5th Ave. S. (☎ 800/634-1311 or 941/262-8112); **Flamingo Apartment Motel,** 383 6th Ave. S. (☎ 941/261-7017; fax 941/261-7769); **Mahalo Apartment Motel,** 441 8th Ave. S. (☎ 941/261-6332; fax 941/263-0182); **Neptune Apartment Hotel,** 651 3rd Ave. S. (☎ 941/262-6126; fax 941/263-6126); **Suntide Apartment Motel,** 649 10th Ave. S. (☎ 941/261-8131); and **Tropical Apartments,** 745 4th Ave. S. (☎ 941/262-1011). They are very popular from mid-December to mid-April, when many guests stay a month or more, so book as early as possible.

Most Naples establishments offer weekly and monthly rates during winter, especially the town's many condominium complexes, including the Park Shore Resort (see below). One of the biggest condo-rental agents here is **Bluebill Properties,** 26201 Hickory Blvd., Bonita Springs, FL 33923 (☎ 800/237-2010 or 941/597-1102; fax 941/597-7175).

Even the national chain motels in Naples tend to be of higher quality and better value than their counterparts elsewhere in Southwest Florida. Within walking distance of the historic district, the **Comfort Inn on the Bay,** 1221 5th Ave. S. (☎ 800/228-5150 or 941/649-5800), enjoys a picturesque setting on Naples Bay. Known for its poolside tiki bar, the **Howard Johnson Resort Lodge,** 221 9th St. S. (☎ 800/654-2000 or 941/262-6181), is also within walking distance of Olde Naples.

Also note that **The Registry Resort,** 475 Seagate Dr., Naples, FL 34103 (☎ **800/ 247-9810** or 941/597-3232; fax 941/597-3147), will have another name by the time you visit. Along with the Ritz-Carlton Naples (see below), this sports-minded luxury establishment has been consistently rated as one of America's finest beach resorts, although like the Ritz-Carlton it's not directly on the beach but on the eastern edge of Clam Pass County Park (guests have to ride the tram like everyone else). Dining here has been at least on a par with the Ritz-Carlton, with the magnificent Lafite dining room offering some of the city's finest French cuisine nightly during winter, on Friday and Saturday evening off-season. Sports buffs come here for a full-service spa and a tennis center with 15 courts.

VERY EXPENSIVE

Edgewater Beach Hotel. 1901 Gulf Shore Blvd. N., Naples, FL 34102. ☎ **800/821-0196** or 941/262-6511. Fax 941/262-1234. 126 suites. A/C TV TEL. Winter $260–$580. Off-season $140–$375. AE, DC, DISC, MC, V.

Situated near the northern end of Millionaires' Row, this all-suite resort attracts both couples and families, but although more elegant, the ambience here is not as relaxed as at the Naples Beach Hotel & Golf Club (see below), its chief Olde Naples rival. The Edgewater doesn't have its own golf course and tennis courts, but the front desk will arrange golf, tennis, sightseeing tours, fishing excursions, and other activities. Two pastel-pink original buildings and a newer seven-story tower form a courtyard that opens to the beach. Tastefully decorated, the oversize suites have Mexican tile floors and kitchens with microwaves and coffeemakers. The balconies are adorned with white grillwork railings.

Dining/Diversions: For guests only, the sixth-floor Club at the Edgewater offers romantic candlelight dinners and great gulf views (it's suggested that men wear jackets and ties). In winter, there's live piano music in the lobby lounge. Breakfast and lunch are served in a courtyard-level cafe, while a poolside bar serves lunch.

Amenities: Concierge, laundry. Heated courtyard swimming pool; rental of watersports equipment, cabanas, chairs, and umbrellas; boutique; access to a nearby golf course and tennis courts.

✪ **Naples Beach Hotel & Golf Club.** 851 Gulf Shore Blvd., Naples, FL 33940. ☎ **800/ 237-7600** or 941/261-2222. Fax 941/261-7380. 315 units. A/C TV TEL. Winter $205–$315 double; $280–$435 suite. Off-season $95–$170 double; $140–$240 suite. Packages available. AE, DC, DISC, MC, V.

Although Henry B. Watkins Sr. bought the Naples Hotel along with the town's undeveloped land in 1946, he soon replaced that turn-of-the-century building with this charming establishment, still owned and operated by his family. The beachside setting on Millionaires' Row in Olde Naples couldn't be better for carrying on the hallowed, friendly, and relaxed Old Florida ambience Watkins installed a half century ago. The least-expensive units here, in fact, are in the Old Florida Wing, a two-story relic from 1948, but recently spiffed up during a $10 million overhaul. The old wing's comfortable rooms and suites open to long, railing-enclosed porches with views across a manicured lawn to the gulf. Other accommodations here are more modern and spacious, but all have lots of bright colors and old-style accents (the recent addition of sliding wooden louvers in the place of drapes has added a tropical touch to the deluxe units). Most suites have private balconies that look out on the beach, the gulf, and lush gardens that contain more than 4,000 orchids.

Dining/Diversions: Since the resort predates the strict historic district zoning laws, it has Olde Naples's only two restaurants and bars directly on the beach. HB's on the

Gulf is a casual spot for an al fresco, beachside lunch or dinner. Wedged between the beach and an Olympic-size pool, the Sunset Beach Bar is one of the region's most famous beachside open-air, thatch-roofed chickee bars and is always crammed as the sun sets over the gulf. It's especially active on Sunday afternoon during the winter season, when live bands perform. Inside the main building but facing the gulf, the semicircular Everglades Dining Room emphasizes traditional Florida cuisine, offers an excellent breakfast buffet to guests and nonguests alike (a genuine all-you-can-eat bargain at $7 a head for continental, $9.50 for hot foods), and has live entertainment and dancing Tuesday to Saturday night in winter. Off the lobby, the Seminole Store offers inexpensive pastries, pizzas, salads, and sandwiches in addition to a wide range of Florida products. Complimentary afternoon tea is served in the lobby lounge.

Amenities: Concierge, turndown, complimentary newspaper, laundry, activities desk, supervised children's program with its own playroom. 18-hole par-72 championship golf course, six tennis courts, Olympic-size swimming pool, sailboat and other water-sports equipment rentals at the beach, gift shop, beauty salon.

✪ Ritz-Carlton Naples. 280 Vanderbilt Beach Rd., Naples, FL 34108. ☎ **800/241-3333** or 941/598-3300. Fax 941/598-6690. 463 units. A/C TV TEL. Winter $425–$695 double; from $850 suite. Off-season $200–$425 double; from $575 suite. AE, DC, DISC, MC, V.

This opulent 14-story Mediterranean-style hotel at Vanderbilt Beach, 4 miles north of Olde Naples, is a favorite of affluent guests who like standard Ritz-Carlton amenities such as imported marble floors, antique art, Oriental rugs, Waterford crystal chandeliers, and British-style afternoon tea. All guest rooms overlook the gulf, but not all have balconies. The very rich book suites on the top-level Ritz-Carlton Club floor, where the rates are just as high as the rooms, but note that the cost of a standard room drops by half during the summer months. The staff starts fawning over you as soon as you pull up the royal palm-lined driveway, and they don't stop until you depart.

Guests can relax in high-backed rockers on the verandas or unwind by the heated swimming pool set in a landscaped terrace, but they must walk through a narrow mangrove forest to reach the beach. This stretch of sand is part of a public park, but the hotel has staff out there to answer phones, deliver drinks and snacks, and rent cabanas, boats, and other toys (only towels, chairs, and ice water are complimentary).

Dining/Diversions: Reminiscent of a British private club, the wood-paneled Grill Room is notable for some of Naples's finest and most expensive cuisine at dinner. The Dining Room is almost as good but more moderately priced. A casual cafe by the pool serves breakfast, lunch, and dinner. Live music entertains guests by the pool during the afternoon, and bands play for dancing in the Club each evening.

Amenities: Heated swimming pool with Jacuzzi, six lighted tennis courts, fitness center with spa treatments, golf privileges at nearby private clubs.

EXPENSIVE

Park Shore Resort. 600 Neapolitan Way, Naples, FL 34103. ☎ **800/548-2077** or 941/263-2222. Fax 941/262-0946. 156 units. A/C TV TEL. Winter $204–$224 condo. Off-season $91–$154 condo. AE, DC, DISC, MC, V.

A good bet if you want a kitchen and more space than a hotel room, these attractive one- and two-bedroom condos surround an artificial lagoon with waterfalls cascading on its own island. Guests can walk across a bridge to the artificial island, where they can swim in the heated pool, order from the bar, and barbecue.

Dining: The Island Club restaurant serves lunch, dinner, and Sunday brunch, and there are plenty of other restaurants nearby.

Amenities: Children's activities program, daily maid service, complimentary shuttle to the beach daily at 11am and 2:30pm. Tennis, racquetball, volleyball, basketball, and shuffleboard courts; whirlpool; laundry room.

Vanderbilt Inn on the Gulf. 11000 Gulf Shore Dr., Naples, FL 34108. ☎ **800/643-8654** or 941/597-3151. Fax 941/597-3099. 163 units. A/C TV TEL. Winter $180–$295 double. Off-season $95–$160 double. (Highest rates for beachfront units.) Weekly rates available. AE, DC, DISC, MC, V.

Cheerful tropical decor in the accommodations and public areas sets the tempo for a casual, fun vacation at this motel. It's located 4 miles north of Olde Naples on Vanderbilt Beach, where guests can go parasailing and rent boats and water-sports equipment. About half the rooms face a beachside courtyard with a kidney-shaped, heated swimming pool surrounded by a brick terrace and tropical grounds. The other rooms face the exterior parking lots. Although the rooms are entered from exterior walkways, their big windows are darkly tinted to provide privacy. All rooms have refrigerators, and 16 also have cooking facilities.

Dining/Diversions: A thatch-roofed Chickee Bar and Restaurant serves alfresco lunches and dinners and draws a crowd for sunset happy hour Monday to Friday from 4:30 to 8:30 and on Saturday and Sunday when bands play from 3:30 to 7:30pm. Also popular for lunch, the Seabreeze Lounge turns lively on Saturday night when its band cranks up. The Jasmine Court serves breakfast and romantic candlelit dinners (early bird specials from 5 to 7pm, and guests 12 and under dine free when accompanied by adults).

Amenities: Concierge; limited room service; baby-sitting. Outdoor heated pool, kid's pool, bicycle rentals, coin laundry.

MODERATE

Inn by the Sea. 287 11th Ave. S., Naples, FL 34102. ☎ **941/649-4124.** 5 units. A/C. Winter $149–$189 double. Off-season $94–$114 double. Rates include continental breakfast. AE, DISC, MC, V. Children 13 and under not accepted.

Listed in the National Register of Historic Places, this bed-and-breakfast 2 blocks from the beach in the heart of Olde Naples was built in 1937 as a boardinghouse by Alice Bowling, one of Naples's first schoolteachers and a grocer and entrepreneur to boot. Owned and operated by Peggy Cormier, the Federal-style house still has much of its original pine floors, matching pine or cypress woodwork, and exterior pinkish galvanized shingles. Comfy wicker furniture and ceiling fans add to the Old Florida ambience. Two of the five rooms have separate sitting areas. Bikes are provided, and guests are served oranges from the backyard tree.

Inn of Naples. 4055 N. Tamiami Trail (U.S. 41), Naples, FL 34103. ☎ and fax **800/237-8858** or 941/649-5500. 100 units. A/C MINIBAR TV TEL. Winter $138–$176 double; $176–$275 suite. Off-season $69–$126 double; $126–$176 suite. Rates include continental breakfast. AE, DC, DISC, MC, V.

Many business travelers who can't afford the Ritz-Carlton like to stay at this comfortable, semielegant establishment near Park Shore Drive and Pelican Bay. The five-story Spanish-style building with red-tile roof and arches contains guest rooms and suites furnished with oak and pine furniture. All are equipped with easy chairs or love seats, writing desks, two telephones, VCRs, refrigerators as well as minibars, and spacious baths with separate dressing areas. Each unit also has a balcony, although some are postage-stamp size and close to noisy external air-conditioning units. The inn's presidential suite is a 1,200-square-foot apartment called the Grand Mizner.

There's an exercise room for burning off the calories ingested at an Italian restaurant that serves lunch and dinner, either indoors or in a screened patio next to a heated, terra-cotta-lined swimming pool and whirlpool, both surrounded by colorful bougainvillea and other tropical foliage.

INEXPENSIVE

Lighthouse Inn Motel. 9140 Gulf Shore Dr. North, Naples, FL 34108. ☎ **941/597-3345.** Fax 941/597-5541. 15 units. A/C TV. Winter $90 double; $95 efficiency; $105 apt. Off-season $40 double; $49 efficiency; $59 apt. MC, V.

A relic from decades gone by, Judy and Buzz Dugan's spotlessly clean, two-story motel sits across the street from other more expensive properties on Vanderbilt Beach and within walking distance of the Ritz-Carlton Naples. The efficiencies and apartments are simple, with freshly painted cinder-block walls and small kitchens. The one kitchenless room has a small fridge and coffeemaker. Most guests take advantage of weekly and monthly rates in winter, when it's heavily booked. Buzz's Lighthouse Café next door is a pleasant place for an inexpensive, dockside breakfast, lunch, or dinner.

✪ **Olde Naples Inn & Suites.** 801 3rd St. S., Naples, FL 34102. ☎ **800/637-6036** or 941/262-5194. Fax 941/262-4876. www.bestof.net/naples/hotels/oldenaples inn. 60 units. A/C TV TEL. Winter $99–$179 double. Off-season $55–$92 double. Rates include continental breakfast. AE, DC, DISC, MC, V.

In the heart of Olde Naples, this dated but extraordinarily well maintained apartment hotel is just 2 blocks from the beach and 4 blocks from the 3rd Street South shopping area (which more than makes up for the lack of an on-site restaurant). Its eclectic combination of rooms, efficiencies, and one- and two-bedroom suites are in three buildings occupying about 60% of a city block, but the tropical landscaping makes it seem smaller. Some of the bath and kitchen fixtures apparently date from the 1950s, but otherwise the units are comfortably furnished, immaculately maintained, and breezy. There are two heated swimming pools, laundry facilities, and off-street parking.

Stoney's Courtyard Inn. 2630 N. Tamiami Trial (U.S. 41), Naples, FL 34103. ☎ **800/432-3870** or 941/261-3870. Fax 941/261-4932. 76 units. A/C TV TEL. Winter $90–$105 double; $125 suite. Off-season $45–$60 double; $70–$105 suite. Rates include continental breakfast. AE, DISC, MC, V.

If you can't get into one of the apartment hotels, this pleasant, locally owned motel is the next best bargain in town. It does indeed have a courtyard, with tropical foliage and a genuine thatch pavilion next to a heated swimming pool. The rooms facing this scene are worth an additional $5 per night over those on the parking lot side. All open to external walkways, and most are of standard motel configuration, with two double beds, a spacious dressing area with an open closet, an armoire for the cable TV, and a combination bath. Restaurants are nearby on U.S. 41.

✪ **Tides Inn of Naples.** 1801 Gulf Shore Blvd. N., Naples, FL 34102. ☎ **800/438-8763** or 941/262-6196. Fax 941/262-3055. 35 units. A/C TV TEL. Winter $105–$235 double. Off-season $65–$130 double. AE, MC, V.

There's a very good reason why this immaculate two-story motel stays heavily booked during the winter months: It's right on the beach, just one door removed from the Edgewater Beach Hotel, and on the edge of Millionaires' Row and Olde Naples. Comfortable suites and efficiencies, all tropically furnished and decorated, have screened balconies or patios angled to face the beach across a courtyard with coconut palms and heated swimming pool. (Motel rooms have no balcony or patio and overlook the parking lot.) In winter, the suites and efficiencies must be reserved for at least a month; otherwise, ask for a room and pray for a cancellation. It's certainly worth a try, for you can't stay anywhere else on a Naples beach for these rates.

WHERE TO DINE

Many first-time visitors opt to have a lunch or dinner at the Marketplace at Tin City, on the Gordon River at 5th Avenue South, where the **Riverwalk Fish & Ale House** (☎ 941/262-2734) and **Merriman's Wharf** (☎ 941/261-1811) specialize in moderately priced seafood and steaks.

You'll find budget-priced fast-food and family-style restaurants along U.S. 41, including a branch of **Mel's Diner**, 3650 Tamiami Trail North (☎ 941/643-9898).

Naples's beaches are ideal for picnics. In Olde Naples, you can get freshly baked breads and pastries, prepacked gourmet sandwiches, and fruit plates at **Tony's Off Third**, 1300 3rd St. S. (☎ 941/262-7999). It's also a fine place for coffee while window-shopping on 3rd Avenue South. The **Pelicatessen,** in the Waterside Shops at Pelican Bay, Seagate Drive at North Tamiami Trail (☎ 941/597-3003), offers imported cheeses, freshly sliced meats, unusual salads, and shelves of gourmet items. Buy there and take it to Clam Pass County Park, at the end of Seagate Drive.

VERY EXPENSIVE

✪ Sign of the Vine. 980 Solana Rd. (off N. Tamiami Trail, behind DeVoe Cadillac). ☎ **941/ 261-6745.** Reservations required. Main courses $30–$40. AE. Oct–May Mon–Sat 6–10pm; Aug–Sept Fri–Sat 6–10pm. Closed June–July. INTERNATIONAL.

Ever since owners/chefs Nancy and John Christiansen converted this gracious, old-fashioned house in 1985, their gourmet restaurant has been the kind of place Neapolitans go for special celebrations when price comes second to fine cuisine and romantic ambience. Flickering candlelight, a fireplace, fresh flowers, antique dinnerware, and hand-lettered menus are perfect for such occasions. The Christiansens offer a creative international menu, including Jack's lobster hash with mushrooms and artichokes in a sassy Pernod-cream sauce accompanied by vegetable baklava. All dinners come with homemade country cheese, relish cart, salad with Nancy's own dressing, home-baked French bread, Ohio tomato pudding, corn soufflé with sweet onion cream, hot popovers with tangerine and lime butter, and fresh orange-and-ginger sorbet. Nancy specializes in grandmother-style desserts like warm bread pudding with a whisky/brown-sugar sauce.

MODERATE

Bay-side: A Seafood Grill and Bar. In the Village on Venetian Bay, 4270 Gulf Shore Blvd. N. (at Park Shore Dr.). ☎ **941/649-5552.** Reservations accepted upstairs only. Downstairs sandwiches, pasta, and light meals $7.50–$15; upstairs main courses $15–$21.50. AE, DC, DISC, MC, V. Winter downstairs daily 2–11pm; upstairs daily 11:30am–2pm and 5:30–10pm. Off-season downstairs daily 2–10pm; upstairs daily 11:30am–2pm and 6–9:30pm. SEAFOOD.

This two-level restaurant in the southern half of the Village on Venetian Bay makes for a nice shopping-break lunch or a relaxed dinner with a gorgeous water view. Upstairs is more expensive and formal, with an outdoor patio and continental gourmet cuisine featuring seafood with a Mediterranean flair. The casual, moderately priced downstairs dining area specializes in pastas, sandwiches, and salads. Both have sinfully delicious desserts. Entertainment is featured in the downstairs bar, nightly during the winter season and on weekends the rest of the year. There's valet parking after 5:30pm.

✪ Bistro 821. 821 5th Ave. S. (between 8th and 9th sts. S.). ☎ **941/261-5821.** Reservations recommended. Main courses $10–$23. AE, DC, MC, V. Sun–Thurs 5–10pm; Fri–Sat 5–10:30pm. MEDITERRANEAN.

One of several chic bistros near the eastern end of the 5th Avenue South shopping strip, this popular, noisy bistro began the trend toward Mediterranean restaurants here (see Terra, below). A bench covered in bright print fabric runs down one side of this storefront to a bar and open kitchen in the rear. Although the quarters are too close for private conversations, small spotlights hanging from the ceiling romantically illuminate each table. The house specialty is rotisserie chicken, and a daily risotto leads a menu featuring penne pasta in a vodka sauce, and a seasonal vegetable plate with herb couscous. There's sidewalk dining here, too.

Michelbob's Rib Capital of Florida. 371 Airport-Pulling Rd. (at Progress Ave.). ☎ **941/ 643-7427.** Reservations not accepted. Sandwiches $3.50–$6.50; platters $8–$19. AE, DC, MC, V. Winter Mon–Thurs 11am–9pm, Fri–Sat 11am–10pm, Sun 8am–1:30pm (brunch) and 1:30–9pm. Off-season Mon–Sat 11am–9pm, Sun 8:30am–1:30pm (brunch) and 1:30–9pm. BARBECUE.

The name says it all about this barnlike establishment, winner of more than 20 national and international cook-offs for the best ribs and barbecue sauces. The big specialty is baby back ribs, imported from Denmark (where the hogs are reputedly tulip-fed). Sliced pork or beef platters and sandwiches are also offered but don't match the ribs. There's a children's menu and an extensive Sunday brunch buffet. The smoke aroma comes from the barbecue pit, not from cigarettes or cigars, since no smoking is permitted.

Terra. 1300 3rd St. S. (actually on 13th Ave. S.). ☎ **941/262-5550.** Reservations recommended. Pizzas and sandwiches $6.50–$12.50; main courses $10.50–$27. AE, DC, DISC, MC, V. Daily 11:30am–10pm (bar until 11:30pm). MEDITERRANEAN.

This elegant yet casual restaurant in the heart of the 3rd Street South shopping district has muted lighting, a few antiques and paintings, and green-and-black woven rattan chairs at oak tables inlaid with terra-cotta tiles. A pianist lends romance as you enjoy Mediterranean dishes such as lamb shank osso buco, tasty wild mushroom lasagna, a risotto of the day, and personal-size pizzas. Italian panini sandwiches, including a lamb shank version accompanied by ratatouille, are served at both lunch and dinner, so you don't necessarily have to spend a fortune here.

Tommy Bahama's Tropical Café. 1220 3rd St. S. (at 12th Ave. S.). ☎ **941/643-6889.** Sandwiches $6–$9; main courses $12–$22. AE, DC, MC, V. Daily 11am–10pm. CARIBBEAN.

You walk through a thatch gateway into this lively, island-style pub—an incongruous sight in the middle of the staid 3rd Street South shopping enclave. Diners gather on a large front patio under shade trees or inside, where a large back-wall mural creates a Polynesian scene. There's an open kitchen and serving bar on one side of the dining room, a real bar dispensing drinks on the other. In between, round-backed cane chairs and classic ceiling fans add to the exotic mood. Although the Caribbean cuisine doesn't quite live up to the ambience, you'll have too much fun here to care if it's not gourmet. If a meal doesn't appeal, a blackened red-snapper sandwich is served at all hours. The restaurant is an offshoot of Tommy Bahama's tropical clothing store next door.

INEXPENSIVE

✪ **Dock at Crayton Cove.** 12th Ave. S. (at the City Dock in Olde Naples). ☎ **941/ 263-9940.** Reservations not accepted. Main courses $13–$19; sandwiches $5–$10.50. AE, DISC, MC, V. Mon–Sat 11:30am–1am, Sun noon–midnight. SEAFOOD.

Located right on the City Dock, this lively pub is the best place in town for an open-air meal or a cool drink while watching the boats go back and forth across Naples Bay. The chow emphasizes well-prepared local seafood, from hearty chowders by the mug to grilled swordfish, with Jamaican-style jerk shrimp thrown in for spice. On the light side, there's grilled seafood Caesar salad and a good selection of sandwiches, hot dogs, and other pub-style fare, plus a raw bar which is open daily from 3 to 6pm. Unlike its sister establishment, the tourist-frequented Riverwalk Fish House at Tin City, "The Dock" is highly popular with local residents, who regularly socialize at the bar during happy hours daily from 4 to 7pm and from 9pm to midnight. If you're here on the second Saturday in May, the "Great Dock Canoe Race" draws thousands of onlookers.

✪ **First Watch.** In Gulf Shore Square, 1400 Gulf Shore Blvd. (at Banyan Rd.). ☎ **941/ 434-0005.** Most items $3.50–$6.50. AE, DISC, MC, V. Daily 7am–2:30pm. AMERICAN.

Just like its sibling in Sarasota, this corner shop with big louvered shutters to temper the morning sun is one of Naples's favorite spots for breakfast, late brunch, or a midday meal. This is anything but a diner, however. Instead you get classical music and widely spaced tables topped with pitchers of lemon-tinged ice water. A young staff provides quick and friendly service. The menu leans heavily on healthy selections, but you can get your cholesterol from a sizzling skillet of fried eggs served over layers of potatoes, vegetables, and melted cheese. Lunch features large salads, sandwiches, and quesadillas. In addition to the dining room, there's additional seating in the shopping center's courtyard.

Old Naples Pub. 255 13th Ave. S. (between 3rd and 4th sts. S., behind Thalheimer's Jewelers). ☎ **941/649-8200.** Salads, sandwiches, and burgers $5–$9; main courses $13. Mon–Sat 11am–11pm, bar open until midnight; Sun noon–10pm, bar open until 11pm. AMERICAN.

You would never guess that the person sitting next to you at the bar is very, very rich, so relaxed is this small, somewhat cramped pub in the middle of the 3rd Street South shops. Diners fortunately find more room at tables on the shopping center's patio. Inside, the pine-paneled walls are hung with trophy fish, a dart board, and old newspaper clippings about Naples. The menu features very good pub fare, including homemade soups, nachos, red beans and rice, burgers, and sandwiches ranging from charcoal-grilled bratwurst to fried grouper. Only two main courses are offered: platters with either New York strip steak or grilled tuna. You can catch live entertainment here Monday to Saturday evenings and jazz on Sunday from 5 to 8pm.

✪ **Silver Spoon Café.** In the Waterside Shops at Pelican Bay, 5395 N. Tamiami Trail (at Seagate Dr.). ☎ **941/591-2123.** Reservations not accepted, but call ahead for preferred seating. Main courses $8.50–$14; pizza and pasta $7–$10; soups, salads, and sandwiches $6–$8.50. AE, DC, DISC, MC, V. Sun–Thurs 11am–10pm, Fri–Sat 11am–11pm. AMERICAN/ITALIAN.

Befitting the swanky Waterside Shops complex, this chic bistro flaunts sophisticated black-and-white high-tech decor and has large window walls overlooking the mall action. Thick sandwiches are served with either french fries, spicy pecan rice, or black beans. The tomato-dill soup and the gourmet pizzas and pasta dishes are popular, especially with the after-theater crowds from the nearby Philharmonic Center for the Arts, and the less-expensive main courses such as orange Dijon chicken are both tasty and excellent value. Matron shoppers love to do lunch here, so come early or be prepared for a wait.

NAPLES AFTER DARK

For entertainment ideas, check the *Naples Daily News,* especially the "Neapolitan" section in Friday's edition.

Much of Naples's nightlife centers on the hotels and restaurants mentioned above. The beachside "chickee hut" bar at the **Naples Beach Hotel & Golf Club** (☎ 941/ 261-2222) is always popular and has live entertainment many nights and is *the* place to go on Sunday afternoon and early evening. So is the beachside bar at the **Vander-**

bilt Inn on the Gulf (☎ 941/597-3151). If it hasn't changed it name or character, the Club Zanzibar in the **Registry Resort** (☎ 941/597-3232) has deejay music for listening and dancing. Among the restaurants, the **Bay-side: A Seafood Grill & Bar** (☎ 941/649-5552) has pianists or jazz musicians. Since their schedules vary by season, it's always best to call ahead.

The **Olde Naples Pub,** 255 13th Ave. S. (☎ 941/649-8200), in the 3rd Street South shopping area, has a pianist Monday to Saturday evening and jazz in the court-yard on Sunday from 5 to 8pm. See "Where to Dine," above.

The **Old Marine Marketplace at Tin City,** the restored waterfront warehouses on 5th Avenue South on the west side of the Gordon River, comes alive during the winter when visitors flock to its shops and the **Riverwalk Fish & Ale House** (☎ 941/262-2734), which has live entertainment during the season.

The impressive **Philharmonic Center for the Arts,** 5833 Pelican Bay Blvd., at West Boulevard (☎ 941/597-1900), is the home of the Naples Philharmonic, but its year-round schedule is filled with cultural events such as performances by the Bolshoi Ballet, concerts by celebrated artists and internationally known orchestras, and Broadway plays and shows aimed at children and families. Call "The Phil" for a copy of its seasonal calendar.

6 Marco Island

15 miles SE of Naples, 53 miles S of Fort Myers, 100 miles W of Miami

Capt. William Collier would hardly recognize Marco Island if he were to come back from the grave today. No relation to Collier County founder Barron Collier, the captain settled his family on the north end of this largest of Florida's Ten Thousand Islands back in 1871. He traded pelts with the Native Americans, caught and smoked fish to sell to Key West and Cuba, and charged fishermen and other guests $2 a day for a room in his home. By 1896, he was doing such a roaring tourist business that he built a proper inn.

His Old Marco Inn still stands (it's now a fine restaurant), along with a few other turn-of-the-century buildings. But Captain Collier would be shocked to come across the high-rise bridge to the island and see it now sliced by human-made canals and virtually covered by resorts, condos, shops, restaurants, and winter homes. These are the products of an extensive real-estate development begun in 1965, which means that Marco lacks any of the charm found in Naples and on Sanibel and Capitva islands. Much of the sales effort here was aimed at the northeastern states, so the island smacks more of New York and Massachusetts rather than the laid-back Midwestern style of its neighbors.

Marco's year-round population of some 10,000 swells to more than 30,000 during the winter season. Most of this multitude are retirees coming south for the winter, families on vacation, and groups convening at the island's three big resort hotels. While here, they enjoy Marco's crescent-shaped beach, the nearby waterways running through a maze of small islands, excellent boating and fishing, and the island's proximity to thousands of acres of wildlife preserves.

ESSENTIALS

GETTING THERE　From either I-75 or U.S. 41, take Fla. 951 south directly to Marco Island.

See the Fort Myers and Naples sections, earlier in this chapter, for information about the **Southwest Florida International Airport** and the **Naples Municipal**

Airport, respectively, and about Amtrak's train service and Greyhound/Trailways buses to those cities.

VISITOR INFORMATION   The **Marco Island Area Chamber of Commerce,** 1102 N. Collier Blvd., Marco Island, FL 34145 (☎ **800/788-6272** or 941/ 394-7549; fax 941/394-3061; www.marco-island-florida.com/chamber; e-mail: chamber@)marco-island-florida.com), provides free information about the island. There's a message board and phone outside for making hotel reservations even when the office is closed. The chamber is open Monday to Friday from 9am to 4pm and Saturday from 10am to 3pm during winter.

GETTING AROUND   Starting and ending at the Marriott resort, **Marco Island Trolley Tours** (☎ **941/394-1600**) makes four complete loops around the island from 10am to 3:15pm on Monday to Saturday. The conductors sell tickets and render an informative narration about the island's history. Daily fare is $10 for adults, $4 for children 11 and under, with free reboarding.

For a cab, call **A-Action Taxi** (☎ **941/394-4400**), **Classic Taxi** (☎ **941/ 394-1888**), or **A-Ok Taxi** (☎ **941/394-1113**).

Depending on the type, rental bicycles cost $10 to $20 a day at **Beach Sports,** 571 S. Collier Blvd. (☎ **941/642-4282**), opposite the Hilton, and at **Scootertown,** 842 Bald Eagle Dr. (☎ **941/394-8400**), north of North Collier Boulevard near Old Marco. Scooters cost $45 a day.

HITTING THE BEACH & OTHER OUTDOOR ACTIVITIES

BEACHES   The sugar-white Crescent Beach curves for 3½ miles down the entire western shore of Marco Island. Its southern 2 miles are fronted by an unending row of high-rise condos and hotels, but the northern 1½ miles are preserved in **Tigertail Public Beach** (☎ **941/642-8414**). A sandbar offshore here creates a shallow lagoon safe for swimming and perfect for learning to windsurf. There are rest rooms, cold-water outdoor showers, a children's playground, and volleyball nets. Tigertail Beach Rentals gives windsurfing lessons, conducts pontoon-boat nature and shelling tours, and rents cabanas, chairs, umbrellas, sailboats, Windsurfers, kayaks, water tricycles, and other toys. A display illustrates the shells you'll find on the beach. **Todd's at Tigertail** (☎ **941/394-8828**) has a fully screened patio where it serves inexpensive hot dogs, sandwiches, salads, and other snacks daily from 10am to 4pm. The park is at the end of Hernando Drive. It's open daily from dawn to dusk. There's no admission charge to the beach, but parking in the lot costs $3 per vehicle.

The beaches in front of the Marriott, Hilton, and Radisson resorts have parasailing, windsurfing, and other water-sports activities, all for a fee. In addition, **Beach Sports,** 571 S. Collier Blvd. (☎ **941/642-4282**), opposite the Hilton, rents Windsurfers, snorkeling gear, skim boards, fishing gear, tennis racquets, and a wide range of other equipment, including beach baby strollers. Beach Sports also has a scuba-dive operation charging $60 to $80 per dive, depending on depth, and teaching novice to advance courses.

If you're not staying at the big resorts, Collier County maintains a $3 per vehicle parking lot and access to the developed beach on the southern end of the island, on Swallow Avenue at South Collier Boulevard.

OUTDOOR ACTIVITIES   A single source of information and the easiest way to book backcountry fishing, shelling, sightseeing, and sunset excursions through the beautiful inland waterways is through **Sea Excursions** (☎ **941/642-6400**). Per person prices are about $20 for sightseeing, $25 for shelling, $35 for fishing, and $25 for sunset cruises. Reservations are required.

Or you can arrange it yourself at **Factory Bay Marina,** on North Bald Eagle Drive (☎ **941/642-6717**), the island's major center for boating, fishing, and cruising. Here you can rent powerboats, take airboat rides, and charter fishing boats with captains. A half day of deep sea fishing on the party boat *Marco Cat* costs $45 for adults, $35 for children under 12, including license, bait, and tackle. You can go on 1½ airboat tours through the Ten Thousand Islands on the *Marco Eagle* or the *Marco Flyer* for $20 adults, $10 children under 12. The pontoon boat *Curve Ball* has 2-hour shelling excursions to remote beaches for $25 adults, $18 for children 8 to 16, $12 for kids under 8. It also runs sunset cruises. Call the marina for schedules and reservations.

Pier 81 Marina, also on Bald Eagle Drive (☎ **941/642-7881**), is home base to the *Rosie* (☎ **941/394-7673**), an old-fashioned, 105-foot-long paddlewheeler that has year-round sightseeing, lunch buffet, and dinner cruises. Call for its prices and seasonal schedule.

Naples' Lely and Boyne South golf courses are a short drive away (see "Other Outdoor Activities," in section 5, above). The closest public courses are the **Marco Shores Golf Club,** 1450 Mainsail Dr. (☎ **941/394-2581**), and **Marriott's Golf Club at Marco** (☎ **941/353-7061**), both in the marshlands off Fla. 951 north of the island. A sign at the Marriott's course ominously warns: PLEASE DON'T DISTURB THE ALLI-GATORS. Fees range from about $115 in winter down to $75 in summer.

Tennis courts are at the **Marco Island YMCA** (☎ **941/394-3144**) and the **Collier County Racquet Club** (☎ **941/394-5454**), both on San Marco Road, and at the **Tommie Barfield Elementary School,** Trinidad Avenue and Kirkwood Street (☎ **941/394-2611**).

PARKS & NATURE PRESERVES

Many species of birds inhabit ✪ **Collier Seminole State Park,** 20200 E. Tamiami Trail, Naples, FL 34114 (☎ **941/394-3397**), an inviting, 6,423-acre preserve on the edge of Big Cypress Swamp, 12 miles east of Marco Island on U.S. 41 just east of Fla. 92. Given to the state by Barron Collier, it offers fishing, boating, picnicking, canoeing over a 13-mile loop with a primitive campsite, observing nature along 6 miles of hiking trails (open during dry periods) and a 1-mile nature walk, and regular tent and RV camping (see "Where to Stay," below). A "walking" dredge used to build the Tamiami Trail in the 1920s sits just inside the park entrance. Housed in a replica of a Seminole Wars–era log fort, an interpretive center has information about the park, and there are ranger-led programs from December to April. Narrated boat tours wander through the winding waterways daily from 9:30am to 3:30pm. Canoes can be rented, but the park has only four camping sites along the canoe trails. Admission to the park is $3.25 per vehicle, $1 for pedestrians and bikers. The boat tours cost $8.50 for adults, $5.50 for children 6 to 12, free for children 5 and under. Canoes rent for $3 per hour, $15 a day. The park is open daily from 8am to sundown.

Operated by The Conservancy and part of the Rookery Bay National Estuarine Research Reserve, the ✪ **Briggs Nature Center,** on Shell Island Road, off Fla. 951 between U.S. 41 and Marco Island (☎ **941/775-8569**), has a half-mile boardwalk through a pristine example of Florida's disappearing scrub lands, home to the threatened scrub jays and gopher tortoises. Rangers lead a variety of nature excursions (call for the seasonal schedule), and there's a self-guided canoe trail and canoes for rent during winter ($13 for the first 2 hours, $5 for each additional hour). During winter, the *Sea Queen* has three nature cruises daily on the bay ($20 per person). The center is open Monday to Friday from 9am to 4:30pm year-round, Saturday from 9am to 4:30pm October to May, and Sunday from 1 to 5pm January to March. The interpretive center and a butterfly garden (27 varieties) are free. Admission to the boardwalk is

$3 for adults, $1 for children 3 to 12, free for children under 3. For more information, contact **The Conservancy of Southwest Florida,** 1450 Merrihue Dr., Naples, FL 34102 (☎ **941/262-0304;** fax 941/262-0672).

WHERE TO STAY

There are no chain hotels on Marco Island other than the large Marriott, Hilton, and Radisson properties listed below, which stand in a row along Cresent Beach on the island's southwestern corner. On the other hand, Marco is loaded with condominium resorts. The **Paramount Suite Hotel,** 901 S. Collier Blvd., Marco Island, FL 34145 (☎ **800/323-8860** or 941/394-8860; fax 941/394-3040), on the inland side of the boulevard but near the big resorts, has 47 one- and two-bedroom units. Daily rates range from $145 to $186 in winter, $109 to $159 off-season. On the beach, **The Surf Club,** 540 S. Collier Blvd., Marco Island, FL 34145 (☎ **800/449-2837** or 941/642-5800; fax 941/642-7245), has 44 apartments ranging from $275 to $300 in winter, $165 to $225 off-season. Rental agents representing house and condo owners include **Century 21 First Southern Trust** (☎ **800/255-9487** or 941/394-7658; fax 941/394-0004; e-mail: cent21sst@aol.com) and **Marco Beach Rentals** (☎ **800/423-7809** or 941/642-5400).

As elsewhere in South Florida, the high season here is from mid-December to mid-April. Rates drop precipitously in the off-season.

There's no campground in the developed part of Marco Island. **Collier Seminole State Park,** 20200 E. Tamiami Trail, Naples, FL 34114 (☎ **941/394-3397;** fax 941/394-5113), 12 miles east via Fla. 92, has 130 tent and RV sites laid out in circles and shaded by palms and live oaks. It has hot showers and a screened, open-air lounge. From December through April, sites cost $16 with electricity, $14 without. Off-season rates are $10.75 with electricity, $8.50 without. Reservations are accepted up to 11 months in advance. No pets are allowed in the campground.

✪ **Boat House Motel.** 1180 Edington Place, Marco Island, FL 34148. ☎ **941/642-2400.** Fax 941/642-2435. www.theboathousemotel.com. 25 units. A/C TV TEL. Winter $75–$149 double; $125–$200 apt or cottage. Off-season $55–$75 double; $75–$135 apt or cottage. MC, V.

One of the best bargains in these parts, this comfortable little motel sits beside the Marco River in Old Marco, on the island's northern end. The rooms are in a two-story, lime-green-and-white building ending at a wooden dock. Here there's a small heated swimming pool with lounge furniture, picnic tables, and barbecue grills. Two rooms on the end have their own decks, and all open to tiny courtyards. Bright paint, ceiling fans, and louvered doors add a tropical ambience throughout. The one-bedroom condos next door open to a riverside dock, upon which is built a two-bedroom cottage named "The Gazebo," whose peaked roof is supported by umbrella-like spokes from a central pole. Facilities include a guest laundry, small library, and bicycle rentals. Olde Marco restaurants are a short stroll away.

Marco Island Hilton Beach Resort. 560 S. Collier Blvd., Marco Island, FL 34145. ☎ **800/443-4550** or 941/394-5000. Fax 941/394-8410. 298 units. A/C MINIBAR TV TEL. Winter $239–$329 suite. Off-season $119–$179 suite. Packages available. AE, DC, DISC, MC, V.

This 11-story tower overlooks the gulf, a courtyard with a multiangled swimming pool wrapped around four coconut palms, and a shingle-roofed public building noted for its large cage with colorful parrots. A boardwalk leads to the beach, where a stand rents water-sports equipment. The suites all have curved balconies angled to give water views, wet bars, refrigerators, and coffee/tea-making facilities, while one-bedroom units have cooking facilities.

Dining/Diversions: One kitchen here serves two outlets: the elegant Sandcastles for dinner and the adjacent Paradise Café for casual indoor/outdoor breakfasts, lunches, and dinners. The Beach Club by the pool serves lunches, snacks, and drinks. Sandcastles Lounge has a piano bar with nightly entertainment.

Amenities: Concierge, room service, activities desk, baby-sitting, children's program, valet parking, laundry. Swimming pool, whirlpool spa, water-sports rentals, three lighted tennis courts, fitness center (with saunas, steam rooms, and massage therapy), gift shop, conference facilities.

✪ **Marco Island Marriott Resort & Golf Club.** 400 S. Collier Blvd., Marco Island, FL 34145. ☎ **800/438-4373** or 941/394-2511. Fax 941/642-2628. 786 units. A/C TV TEL. Winter $290–$350 double; from $459 suite. Off-season $129–$199 double; from $259 suite. Packages available. AE, DC, DISC, MC, V.

Often cited as one of the nation's top large resorts (it's the biggest on Florida's Gulf Coast), this deluxe establishment has two nine-story towers and two A-frame public wings forming two beachfront courtyards with swimming pools, bars, and water-sports centers. Luxuriously furnished and decorated, the spacious accommodations range from hotel rooms to two-bedroom suites. All have balconies or patios with indirect views of the gulf. Popular with couples and families as well as groups, it's the only North American resort to have won the National Parenting Center's seal of approval.

Dining/Diversions: Six restaurants offer a variety of cuisines to suit many tastes and pocketbooks, from near-gourmet northern Italian to carryout pizza. The Lobby Lounge features piano music and views of the gulf.

Amenities: Concierge, valet parking, room service, activities desk, laundry, baby-sitting, award-winning children's activities program. Golfers can play the resort's 18-hole championship golf course (on the mainland). On the premises are swimming pools, a miniature golf course, lighted tennis courts and pro shop, a health club, a game room, boat and water-sports rental, a shopping mall with chic boutiques, a beauty salon, and conference facilities.

Radisson Suite Beach Resort. 600 S. Collier Blvd., Marco Island, FL 34145. ☎ **800/992-0651** or 941/394-4100. Fax 941/394-0262. 269 units. A/C TV TEL. Winter $239 double; $269–$469 suite. Off-season $109 double; $139–$239 suite. Packages available. AE, DC, DISC, MC, V.

This 11-story family-oriented resort seems like a motel with an abundance of growth hormone, since entry to the rooms and suites is from outside walkways with bright-blue railings, rather than from interior hallways. Although it lacks the quality of the Marriott and Hilton resorts, the two-bedroom suites here do *directly* face the gulf, which the competition's don't. Most of the 55 hotel rooms, however, look out on the Hilton next door. The building partially encloses a landscaped courtyard with a swimming pool, from which a boardwalk leads to the beach where guests can rent umbrellas, cabanas, and water-sports equipment. The rooms have microwave ovens and coffeemakers, and the one- and two-bedroom apartments have fully equipped kitchens and dining areas (some have two baths). All units have screened balconies.

Dining/Diversions: Dining outlets here are designed to keep families fed. An indoor dining room serves moderately priced breakfasts, lunches, and dinners, while Bluebeard's Beach Club Grill offers inexpensive lunches, early dinners, snacks, and drinks by the pool. A Pizza Hut Express is on the premises, and a small store provides limited groceries, wine, and beer. There's also a poolside bar for cocktails.

Amenities: Concierge, activities desk, laundry, children's program. Heated swimming pool; whirlpool; exercise room; recreation center with programs for adults and children; shop with groceries; tennis, basketball, and volleyball courts.

WHERE TO DINE

For inexpensive fare, head for the Town Center Mall, at the corner of North Collier Boulevard and Bald Eagle Drive, where you'll find two good choices: **Susie's Diner** (☎ 941/642-6633) is popular with the locals for breakfasts and especially for Susie's inexpensive full-meal lunch specials. She's open Monday to Saturday from 6:30am to 2:30pm and Sunday from 6:30am to 1pm (for breakfast only). **Breakfast Plus** (☎ 941/642-6900) has eye-openers ranging from bacon and eggs to kippers to latkes. It's open daily from 7am to 2:30pm.

The island's popular sports bars also offer inexpensive pub fare to go with their multitudinous TVs. Most popular is **Rookie's Bar & Grill,** in Mission de San Marco Plaza at the corner of South Collier Boulevard and Winterberry Drive (☎ 941/394-6400). Others are the **Crazy Flamingo,** in the Town Center Mall, North Collier Boulevard at Bald Eagle Drive (☎ 941/642-9600); and the **Sand Bar,** on Bald Eagle Drive north of North Collier Boulevard (☎ 941/642-3625).

Cafe de Marco. 244 Palm St., Old Marco. ☎ **941/394-6262.** Reservations recommended. Main courses $16–$21. Minimum charge $13 per adult (except early bird specials, $11), $4.50 per child. AE, MC, V. Winter daily 5–10pm. Off-season Mon–Sat 5–10pm. SEAFOOD.

This homelike establishment at the Marco Village shops was originally constructed as housing for maids at the Olde Marco Inn next door. The chef specializes in excellent treatments of fresh seafood, from mesquite-grilled swordfish to his own luscious creation of seafood and vegetables combined in a lobster sauce and served over linguine. The early bird specials here are a very good value.

Little Bar & Restaurant. Harbor Place (County Rd. 892), Goodland. ☎ **941/394-5663.** Reservations recommended for dinner. Main courses $13–$17; early bird specials $8–$10. DISC, MC, V. Daily 11:30am–10pm (bar until 2am); early bird specials 5–6pm. Closed Aug. SEAFOOD.

This very casual waterfront establishment is located in the heart of Goodland, an Old Florida fishing village on the eastern edge of Marco Island, some 7 miles (and at least 30 years) removed from the heavily developed western end of the island. One dining room here actually was the interior of the *Star of the Everglades,* a boat that took Presidents Truman and Eisenhower around and appeared in the Burl Ives movie *Winds Across the Everglades.* Other rooms possess antique bits and pieces from various buildings in the Chicago area, including an old pipe organ. A screened porch beside Goodland's fishing boat harbor is this area's most popular spot for lunches featuring seafood and other sandwiches. Daily specials from a nightly chalkboard might include Everglades frogs' legs.

Kahuna Restaurant. 1035 N. Collier Blvd., in Town Center. ☎ **941/394-4300.** Reservations not accepted. Sandwiches and burgers $3–$7; main courses $6–$11. MC, V. Daily 11am–9pm. AMERICAN.

Advertising itself as the "Island's Family Restaurant," Kahuna certainly is the least expensive choice here for dinner. The decor is plain and simple, with a mix of coral-colored booths and round tables under black ceiling fans. The burgers are some of Marco's best (there's a condiment bar with a variety of fixings). Main courses include several fried seafood selections, sautéed crab cakes, and charcoal-grilled tuna, but your best bet should be a nightly special such as salmon in a light dill sauce. Don't expect gourmet dining here, but the quality is fine for the price.

✪ **Kretch's.** 527 Bald Eagle Dr. (south of N. Collier Blvd.). ☎ **941/394-3433.** Reservations recommended in winter. Main courses $13–$23. DC, MC, V. Mon–Fri 11am–3pm and 5–9pm, Sat–Sun 5–9pm. Closed Mon off-season and Easter, July 4, Thanksgiving, and Christmas. SEAFOOD/CONTINENTAL.

Noted pastry chef Bruce Kretschmer has created a sinfully rich seafood strudel by combining shrimp, crab, scallops, cheeses, cream, and broccoli in a flaky Bavarian pastry and serving it all under a lobster sauce. Cholesterol counters can choose from broiled or charcoal-grilled fish, shrimp, Florida lobster tail, steaks, or lamb chops. Bruce's popular "Mexican Friday" lunches feature delicious tacos and other inexpensive, south-of-the-border selections. Sunday is home-cooking night during winter, with chicken and dumplings, Yankee pot roast, and braised lamb shanks.

✪ **Olde Marco Inn.** 100 Palm St., Old Marco. ☎ **941/394-3131.** Reservations recommended. Main courses $13–$25. AE, DC, DISC, MC, V. Daily 5:30–10pm. INTERNATIONAL.

Built by Capt. William Collier in 1883 and fully restored to Victorian elegance by its present-day owner Marion Blomeier, this large clapboard building has several dining rooms, a ballroom, and a pleasant veranda, all richly furnished (the huge crystal chandelier dominating the ballroom belonged to the late band leader Guy Lombardo). Seafood, beef, chops, and poultry are prepared with an international flair appropriate to Mrs. Blomeier's continental birth. Relax before or after dinner in the popular piano bar.

Snook Inn. 1215 Bald Eagle Dr. (at Palm St.), Old Marco. ☎ **941/394-3313.** Reservations not accepted. Main courses $11–$19; sandwiches $8–$10. AE, DC, DISC, MC, V. Daily 11am–10pm. SEAFOOD.

The choice seats at this Old Florida establishment are in an enclosed dock right beside the scenic Marco River. Although seafood is the specialty, tasty steaks, chicken, burgers, and sandwiches are among the choices. The dockside Chickee Bar is a fun place, especially during sunset happy hour Monday to Friday from 4 to 6pm. The bar really rocks when live entertainment is featured during the winter season. Call for free shuttle service from anywhere on Marco Island.

MARCO ISLAND AFTER DARK

It's not after dark, but one of the biggest parties in Florida takes place every Sunday afternoon at ✪ **Stan's Idle Hour Seafood Restaurant,** on County Rd. 892 in Goodland (☎ **941/394-3041**), where owner Stan Gober—an Ernest Hemingway lookalike—plays host and fires up the barbecue grills; bands crank up country music for dancing the "Buzzard Lope;" and men compete to see who has the best legs. Stan's Goodland Mullet Festival, always the weekend before the Super Bowl, is the mother of all parties.

Over on the developed part of the island, everyone turns out for outdoor entertainment at the **Mission San Marco Plaza** shopping center, South Collier Boulevard at Winterberry Drive, every Tuesday night year-round.

The lounges in the **Marriott and Hilton resorts** (see "Where to Stay," above) provide pianists every evening. The **Olde Marco Inn** and the **Snook Inn** have live entertainment nightly during the winter season (see "Where to Dine," above). The schedules vary by season, so call ahead.

One of the most lively local spots is **La Casita Mexican Restaurant,** in the Shops of Marco, San Marco Road at Barfield Drive (☎ **941/642-7600**), where owners Frankie Ray and Maryellen play a variety of Mexican, Irish, popular, and traditional music Monday to Saturday. On Sunday, 1950s and 1960s dance music is highlighted.

Another choice is **Alan's Hideaway Piano Bar,** 23 Front St. (☎ **941/642-0770**), where owner Alan Bogdan plays.

The Tampa Bay Area 11

by Bill Goodwin

Many families visiting Orlando's theme parks eventually drive an hour west on I-4 to another major kiddie attraction, Busch Gardens Tampa Bay. But this area shouldn't be a mere side trip from Disney World, for Florida's central west coast is an exciting destination unto itself.

At the head of the bay, the city of Tampa is the commercial center of Florida's west coast—the country's eleventh busiest seaport and a center of banking, high-tech manufacturing, and cigar making (half a billion drugstore stogies a year). Downtown Tampa may roll up its sidewalks after dark, but you can come here during the day to see the sea life at the Florida Aquarium and stroll through the Henry B. Plant Museum, housed in an ornate, Moorish-style hotel built a century ago to lure tourists to Tampa. A trolley will take you on a short ride to Ybor City, the historic Cuban enclave which is now an exciting entertainment and dining venue. And out in the suburbs, Busch Gardens may be best known for its scintillating rides, but it's also one of the world's largest zoos.

Two bridges and a causeway will whisk you westward across the bay to the Pinellas Peninsula, one of Florida's most densely packed urban areas. Over here on the bay front, lovely downtown St. Petersburg is famous for wintering seniors, a shopping and dining complex built way out on a pier, and the world's largest collection of Salvador Dalí's surrealist paintings.

Keep driving west and you'll come to a line of barrier islands where St. Pete Beach, Treasure Island, Clearwater Beach, and other gulf-side communities boast 28 miles of sunshine, surf, and white sand. Yes, they're lined with resorts and condos of every description and price, but parks on each end preserve two of the nation's finest beaches.

Drive north up the coast, and you'll go back in time at the old Greek sponge enclave of Tarpon Springs, one of Florida's most attractive small towns, and at Weeki Wachee Springs, a tourist attraction where "mermaids" have been entertaining underwater for half a century.

Heading south, the Sunshine Skyway will take you soaring 175 feet above the bay to Bradenton, Sarasota, and another chain of barrier islands. One of Florida's cultural centers, affluent Sarasota is the gateway to St. Armands and Longboat keys, two playgrounds of the rich and famous, and to Lido and Siesta keys, attractive to families of more modest means. Even more reasonably priced is Anna Maria Island, off the riverfront town of Bradenton. You might say the bridge from Longboat to Anna Maria goes from one price range to another.

Tampa & St. Petersburg

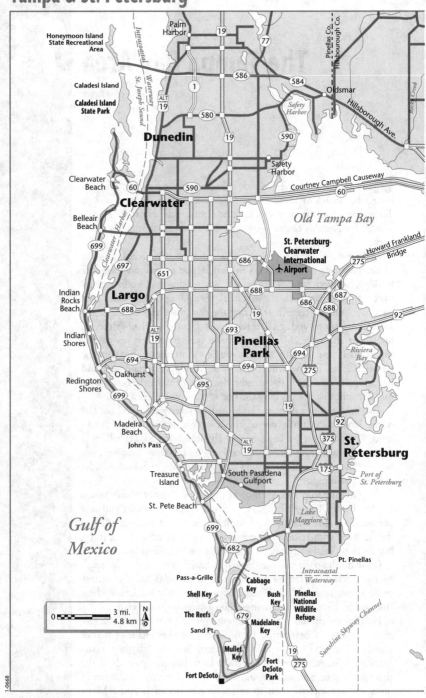

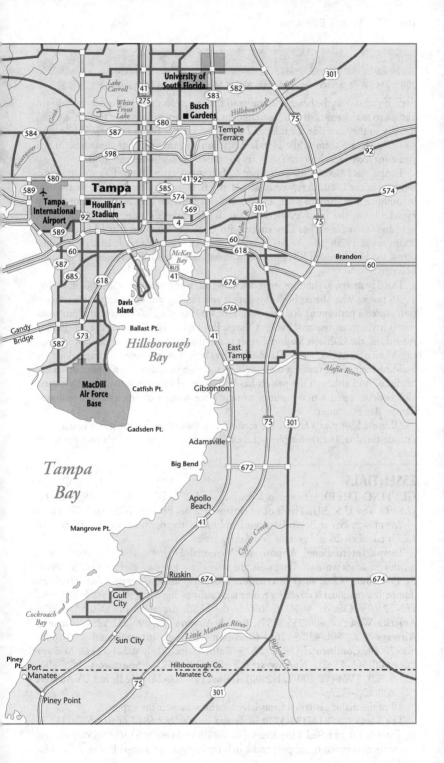

1 Tampa

200 miles SW of Jacksonville, 254 miles NW of Miami, 63 miles N of Sarasota

Even if you stay at the beaches 20 miles to the west, you should consider driving into Tampa to see its sights. If you have children in tow, they will *demand* that you go into the city so they can ride the rides and see the animals at Busch Gardens. While here, you can educate them at the Florida Aquarium and the city's fine museums. And if you don't have kids, historic Ybor City has the bay area's liveliest nightlife.

Tampa was a sleepy little port when Cuban immigrants founded Ybor City's cigar industry in the 1880s. A few years later Henry B. Plant put Tampa on the tourist map by building a railroad to town and the bulbous minarets over his garish Tampa Bay Hotel. During the Spanish American War, Teddy Roosevelt trained his Rough Riders here and walked the Ybor City streets with Cuban revolutionary José Marti. A land boom in the 1920s gave the city its charming, Victorian-style Hyde Park suburb, just across the Hillsborough River from downtown, now a gentrified redoubt of the baby boomers.

The downtown skyline we see today, however, is the product of a 1980s and early 1990s boom, when banks built skyscrapers and the city put up an expansive convention center, a performing arts center, and the Ice Palace, a 20,000-seat bay-front arena that is home to professional hockey's Tampa Bay Lightning. Alongside the new Florida Aquarium, the Garrison Seaport Center is a major home port for cruise ships bound for Mexico and Caribbean. Baseball's New York Yankees helped things along by building their spring training complex here, including a scaled-down replica of Yankee Stadium. And although the project has been plagued by controversy, the city fathers also hope to build a new stadium to satisfy the owners of pro football's resurgent Tampa Bay Buccaneers.

All this adds up to a fast-paced, modern city on the go. Tampa isn't a beach vacation destination, but there's plenty here to keep both adults and kids busy for a few days.

ESSENTIALS

GETTING THERE   Tampa is accessible via I-275, I-75, I-4, U.S. 19, U.S. 41, U.S. 92, and U.S. 301. The Busch Gardens area lies between I-75 and I-275 north of downtown; exit at Busch Boulevard and follow the signs. Downtown is south of I-275; take Exit 26 and go south on Ashley Street.

Tampa International Airport, off Memorial Highway and Fla. 60, 5 miles northwest of downtown Tampa, is the major air gateway to this area, although **St. Petersburg–Clearwater International Airport** has limited service (see section 2). Tampa International is served by most major airlines, including **Air Canada** (☎ 800/ 268-7240 in Canada, 800/776-3000 in the U.S.), **American** (☎ 800/433-7300), **America West** (☎ 800/235-9292), **British Airways** (☎ 800/247-9297), **Cayman Airways** (☎ 800/422-9626), **Canadian Airlines International** (☎ 800/ 426-7000), **Continental** (☎ 800/525-0280), **Delta** (☎ 800/221-1212), **Midway** (☎ 800/446-4392), **Northwest** (☎ 800/225-2525), **Southwest** (☎ 800/ 435-9792), **TWA** (☎ 800/221-2000), **United** (☎ 800/241-6522), and **US Airways** (☎ 800/428-4322).

All of the major car-rental firms have booths at or near the airport.

The Limo (☎ **813/396-3730** in Tampa or 800/282-6817 or 813/572-1111 in St. Petersburg) and **Red Line Limo** (☎ **800/359-5466** or 813/535-3391) operate van services between the airport and hotels throughout the Tampa Bay area. Fares for one person vary considerably depending on where you're going (some hotels have special rates). One passenger will pay at least $6 to Tampa's West Shore area or downtown Tampa, $13 to Busch Gardens or Clearwater Beach, and $17 to downtown St. Petersburg. **Taxis** are plentiful at the airport; the ride to downtown Tampa takes about 15 minutes and costs $11 to $14. In addition, the **Hillsborough Area Regional Transit Authority/HARTline** (☎ 813/254-HART) operates service between the airport and downtown on its local no. 31 bus from 6am and 8:15pm. Look for the HARTline bus sign outside each airline terminal; the fare is $1.15 (exact change required).

Amtrak trains arrive downtown at the **Tampa Amtrak Station,** 601 Nebraska Ave. N. (☎ 800/USA-RAIL).

VISITOR INFORMATION Contact the **Tampa/Hillsborough Convention and Visitors Association (THCVA),** 400 N. Tampa St., Tampa, FL 33602-4706 (☎ 800/44-TAMPA or 813/223-2752; fax 813/229-6616; www.thcva.com) for advance information. Once you're downtown, head to the THCVA's visitors information center at the corner of Ashley and Madison streets. It's open Monday to Saturday from 9am to 5pm.

Near Busch Gardens, the **Tampa Bay Visitor Information Center,** 3601 E. Busch Blvd., at N. Ednam Place (☎ 813/985-3601), is a privately owned operation (see Swiss Chalet Tours under "Organized Tours," below), but it offers free brochures about attractions in Tampa and sells discounted tickets to many attractions. You may be able to both save about $2 a head and avoid waiting in long Busch Gardens ticket lines by buying here, and the staff gives expert advice about how to get the most out of your visit.

CITY LAYOUT Other than business travelers and sports fans, most visitors to Tampa head 7 miles north of downtown to the suburban area around **Busch Gardens Tampa Bay,** the city's major attraction. The main drag here is Busch Boulevard, which passes the park entrance as it runs east-west between I-75 and I-275. It's a busy commercial strip where you'll find dozens of restaurants and hotels.

Tampa's compact **downtown** area is primarily a daytime business and financial hub. Here you'll find the Florida Aquarium and the Garrison Seaport Center. The grid streets are all one way except for pedestrians-only Franklin Street. From the southern tip of Franklin, you can ride the people mover, an elevated tram that automatically shuttles over to **Harbour Island** (see "Getting Around," below). Across the narrow Garrison Channel from downtown, Harbour Island is a struggling urban development project whose spaces for restaurants and shops stand vacant.

When the downtown sidewalks roll up at 5pm, **Ybor City** comes alive. Centered along 7th Avenue East on the northeastern edge of downtown, Ybor is Tampa's lively Latin Quarter, settled for more than 100 years by Cuban immigrants. Today it's home to hot new restaurants, clubs, arts and crafts shops, and hand-rolled cigars.

Just across the Hillsborough River from downtown, **Hyde Park** is the city's oldest and once again its poshest residential neighborhood, complete with the upscale shops and trendy restaurants of **Old Hyde Park Village.** This Victorian neighborhood is on the National Register of Historic Districts. **Bayshore Boulevard** runs from Hyde Park south along the shores of Hillsborough Bay; with a view across the water to the downtown skyline, it's the most beautiful part of Tampa, a gorgeous route for driving, biking, or in-line skating.

Kennedy Boulevard is the main drag from downtown to the **West Shore** area, lying near the bay west of Hyde Park and south of Tampa International Airport. Westshore is a suburban commercial and financial hub, with office buildings, business-oriented hotels, and a shopping mall.

GETTING AROUND   Like most other Florida destinations, it's virtually impossible to see Tampa's major sights and enjoy the best restaurants without a car. Nevertheless, the **Tampa-Ybor Trolley** connects downtown, Harbour Island, the Florida Aquarium, the Garrison Seaport Center, and Ybor City daily from 9am to 4pm, with additional service between downtown and the aquarium daily from 7:30 to 9am and from 4 to 5:30pm. The fare is 25¢ per person. Get a route map at the visitor information center (see above), or call HARTline at ☎ **813/224-4278** for information. The 18 stops are marked with green and orange signs.

There's little reason to go to Harbour Island unless you're staying there, but the **Harbour Island People Mover,** an automated tram on elevated tracks, runs between the third level of the Fort Brooke Parking Garage, on Whiting Street at Franklin Street, and Harbour Island continuously Monday to Saturday from 7am to midnight and Sunday from 8am to midnight (there's a shuttle bus off-hours). The fare is 25¢ each way.

The **Hillsborough Area Regional Transit/HARTline** (☎ **813/254-HART**) provides regularly scheduled bus service between downtown Tampa and the suburbs. Fares are $1.15 for local rides, $1.50 for express routes; correct change is required. Pick up a route map at the visitor information center (see above).

Taxis in Tampa don't normally cruise the streets for fares, but they do line up at public loading places, such as hotels, the performing arts center, and bus and train depots. If you need a taxi, call **Tampa Bay Cab** (☎ **813/251-5555**), **Yellow Cab** (☎ **813/253-0121**), or **United Cab** (☎ **813/253-2424**). Fares are 95¢ at flag fall plus $1.50 for each mile.

EXPLORING THE THEME & ANIMAL PARKS

Adventure Island. 10001 McKinley Dr. (between Busch Blvd. and Bougainvillea Ave.). ☎ **813/987-5600.** Admission $22.95 adults, $20.95 children 3–9, plus tax. Free for children 2 and under. Note: Prices keep increasing, so expect to pay slightly more. Seasonal passes available. Mid-Feb to Labor Day daily 10am–5pm; Sept–Oct Fri–Sun 10am–5pm (extended hours in summer and on holidays). Closed Nov to mid-Feb. Take Exit 33 off I-275, go east on Busch Blvd. for 2 miles, turn left onto McKinley Dr. (N. 40th St.), and entry is on right.

If the summer heat gets to you before one of Tampa's famous thunderstorms brings late-afternoon relief, you can take a waterlogged break at this 36-acre outdoor water theme park near Busch Gardens Tampa Bay (see below). In fact, you can frolic here even during the cooler days of spring and fall, when the water is heated. The Key West Rapids, Tampa Typhoon, Gulf Scream, and other exciting water rides will drench the teens, while other calmer rides are geared for kids. There are places to picnic and sunbathe, a games arcade, a volleyball complex, and an outdoor cafe. If you forget to bring your own, a surf shop sells bathing suits, towels, and suntan lotion.

✪ **Busch Gardens Tampa Bay.** 3000 E. Busch Blvd. (at McKinley Dr./N. 40th St.). ☎ **813/987-5283.** Admission $37.95 adults, $31.95 children 3 to 9, plus tax. Free for children 2 and under. Note: Prices keep increasing, so expect to pay slightly more. Seasonal passes available. Parking $4 cars, $3 motorbikes, $5 campers and trailers. Take I-275 north of downtown to Busch Blvd. (Exit 33), and go east 2 miles. From I-75, take Exit 54 and follow Fowler Ave. and the signs west.

Although its thrill rides, live entertainment, shops, restaurants, and games get most of the ink, this venerable theme park (it predates Disney World) ranks among the top zoos in the country. This is a great place for the kids to see in person all those wild beasts they've watched on the Discovery Channel. The animals—several thousand of them—live in naturalistic environments and help carry out an overall "Dark Continent" of Africa theme.

The park is divided into several areas, each with its own theme, animals, live enter-tainment, thrill rides, kiddie attractions, dining, and shopping. A monorail train will take you from one to another. A Skyride cable car soars over the park, offering a bird's-eye view of the beasts (but not much else).

Allow at least a day here, and arrive early—but try not to come when it's raining, since some rides may not operate and you won't get a rain check for admission on another day. You can avoid waiting in long lines, and save a few dollars, by buying your tickets in advance at the **Tampa Bay Visitor Information Center** (see "Essen-tials," above). Bring comfortable shoes, and remember, you can get wet on some of the rides, so wear appropriate clothing. You can exchange foreign currency in the park, and interpreters are available.

As soon as you're through the turnstiles, pick up a copy of a park map and the day's activity schedule, which tells what's showing and when at the park's 14 entertainment venues. Then take a few minutes to carefully plan your time.

Just past the main gate you'll come to **Morocco,** a walled city with exotic architec-ture, craft demonstrations, a sultan's tent with snake charmers, and an exhibit fea-turing alligators and turtles. The Moroccan Palace Theater features "Hollywood Live on Ice," which many families consider to be the park's best entertainment. Here you can also attend "American Jukebox," a song and dance show, in the Marrakesh Theater, or a live TV show in the Tangiers Theater.

After watching the snake charmers in Morocco, walk eastward to the main Skyride and monorail station and **Crown Colony,** home of a team of Anheuser-Busch's big-footed Clydesdale horses, the park's hospitality center, and Questor, a flight-simulator adventure ride.

From here, take the monorail train to **Egypt,** which mirrors that country's culture and history, including a replica of King Tutankhamen's tomb. Adults and older kids can ride Montu, the tallest and longest inverted roller coaster in the world with seven upside-down loops, one of them barely missing a crocodile pit. Youngsters can dig for their own ancient treasures in a sand area. Everyone can join comedian Martin Short, who plays a shady Egyptian tour guide in Akbar's Adventure Tours, a wacky simulator that transports one and all across Egypt via camel, biplane, and mine car.

From Egypt, walk under the monorail and out onto the **Serengeti Plain,** where glass walls separate you from lions, hippos, crocodiles, hyenas, meerkats, and vultures among more than 500 African animals roaming freely on an 80-acre natural grassy veldt.

After you've seen them close-up, get back on the monorail and ride across the plain and around the park to **Nairobi,** where you can see gorillas and chimpanzees in the Myombe Reserve, replicating their natural tropical habitat. Nairobi also has a baby animal nursery, a petting zoo, turtle and reptile displays, an elephant exhibit, and Noc-turnal Mountain, a simulated environment that allows you to observe animals that are active in the dark.

From Nairobi, walk into **Timbuktu,** evoking an ancient desert trading center with African craftspeople at work. Here you'll find several rides, including a train for kids, one through a sandstorm, another on swinging boats, and Scorpion, a 360° roller coaster. Plan to have lunch here at Das Festhaus, a 1,000-seat, air-conditioned German festival hall featuring a lively musical show (be sure to arrive at least 15 min-utes before show time). The kids will enjoy the Dolphin Theater, with performing porpoises, otters, and sea lions.

After lunch, head to **The Congo,** highlighted by rare white Bengal tigers living on Claw Island. The Congo also is home to Kumba, the largest and fastest roller coaster in the southeastern United States, and the Python, which twists and turns for 1,200

Tampa Attractions

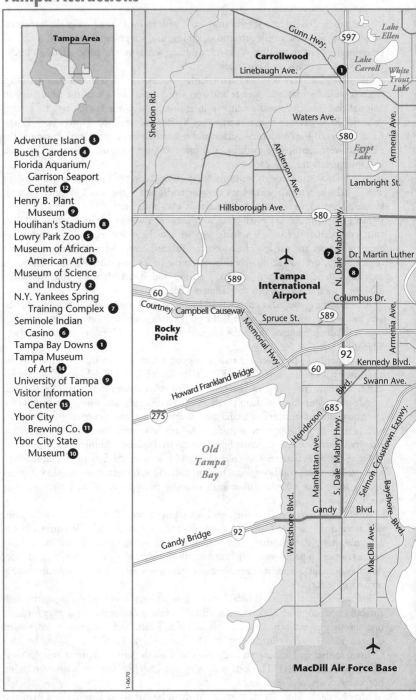

Adventure Island **3**
Busch Gardens **4**
Florida Aquarium/
  Garrison Seaport
  Center **12**
Henry B. Plant
  Museum **9**
Houlihan's Stadium **8**
Lowry Park Zoo **5**
Museum of African-
  American Art **13**
Museum of Science
  and Industry **2**
N.Y. Yankees Spring
  Training Complex **7**
Seminole Indian
  Casino **6**
Tampa Bay Downs **1**
Tampa Museum
  of Art **14**
University of Tampa **9**
Visitor Information
  Center **15**
Ybor City
  Brewing Co. **11**
Ybor City State
  Museum **10**

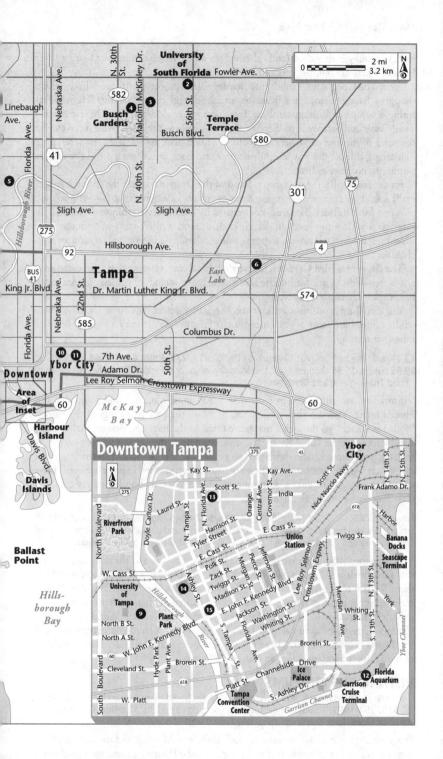

feet. You will get drenched (and refreshed on a hot day) by riding the Congo River Rapids. There are bumper cars and kiddie rides here, too.

From The Congo, walk south into **Stanleyville,** a prototype African village, with a shopping bazaar, orangutans living on an island, and the Stanleyville Theater, featuring a troupe of Russian acrobats. Two more water rides are here: the Tanganyika Tidal Wave and Stanley Falls. Serving ribs and chicken, the Stanleyville Smokehouse has some of the best chow here. This also is a good place to board the monorail for a sightseeing ride all the way around the park and back, since you'll avoid the crowds waiting to board elsewhere.

From Stanleyville, the next stop is **Land of the Dragons,** where the younger set can easily spend an entire day enjoying a variety of play elements in a fairy-tale setting, plus just-for-kids rides. The area is dominated by Dumphrey, a whimsical dragon who interacts with visitors and guides children around a three-story tree house with winding stairways, tall towers, stepping stones, illuminated water geysers, and an echo chamber.

The last stop is **Bird Gardens,** the park's original core, offering rich foliage, lagoons, and a free-flight aviary for hundreds of exotic birds, including golden and American bald eagles. Catch the Bird Show here.

You can finish your visit back at the hospitality center in Crown Colony, where adults can imbibe some of Anheuser-Busch's famous beers (there's a limit of two free mugs per seating).

✪ **Florida Aquarium.** 701 Channelside Dr. ☎ **813/273-4000.** Admission $10.95 adults, $9.95 seniors, $5.95 children 3–12, free for children under 3. Parking $3. Daily 9:30am–5pm. Closed Thanksgiving and Christmas.

Visitors here are introduced to more than 5,300 aquatic animals and plants that call Florida home. Various exhibits allow you to follow the pristine springs of the Florida Wetlands Gallery, go through a mangrove forest in the Bays and Beaches Gallery, and stand amazed at the Coral Reefs. The most impressive display is a 43-foot-wide, 14-foot-tall panoramic window with schools of fish and lots of sharks and stingrays. You can watch a diver twice a day. There's a half-million-dollar "Explore a Shore" playground to educate the kids, a deep water exhibit, and a tank housing moray eels. The Cafe Ray serves snacks and light meals.

Lowry Park Zoo. 7530 North Blvd. ☎ **813/932-0245.** Admission $7.50 adults, $6.50 seniors, $4.95 children 3–11, free for children 2 and under. Daily 9:30am–5pm. Closed Thanksgiving and Christmas. Take I-275 to Sligh Ave. (Exit 31) and follow the signs.

Watching the 2,000-pound manatees, the komodo dragons, and the red pandas makes this a worthwhile excursion after the kids have seen the plains of Africa at Busch Gardens. With lots of greenery, bubbling brooks, and cascading waterfalls, this 24-acre zoo displays animals in settings similar to their natural habitats. Other major exhibits include a Florida wildlife display, an Asian Domain, a Primate World, an Aquatic Center, a free-flight aviary with a birds of prey show, a children's petting zoo and hands-on Discovery Center, and an endangered species carrousel ride. There are plenty of food outlets here, including an on-site McDonald's.

VISITING THE MUSEUMS

Henry B. Plant Museum. 401 W. Kennedy Blvd. (between Hyde Park and Magnolia aves.). ☎ **813/254-1891.** Admission free; suggested donation $3 adults, $1 children 12 and under. Tues–Sat 10am–4pm, Sun noon–4pm. Take Fla. 60 west of downtown.

You can't miss the 13 silver minarets and distinctive Moorish architecture, modeled after the Alhambra in Spain, that make this National Historic Landmark a focal point of the Tampa skyline. Originally built in 1891 as the 511-room Tampa Bay Hotel by railroad tycoon Henry B. Plant, it's filled with art and furnishings from Europe and the Orient. Other exhibits focus on the history of the original railroad resort, Florida's early tourist industry, and the hotel's role as a staging point for Teddy Roosevelt's Rough Riders during the Spanish American War.

✪ **Museum of African-American Art.** 1308 N. Marion St. (entry and parking lot face N. Florida Ave. between Scott and Laurel sts.), downtown. ☎ **813/272-2466.** Admission $3 adults, $2 seniors and children grades K–12. Tues–Fri 10am–4:30pm, Sat 10am–5pm. Take Exit 26 off I-275.

Recently renovated to the tune of $200,000, the museum is touted as the first of its kind in Florida and one of four in the United States. It's the home of the Barnett-Aden collection, considered the state's foremost collection of African American art. More than 80 artists are represented in the display, which includes sculptures and paintings that depict the history, culture, and lifestyle of African Americans from the 1800s to the present, with special emphasis on the works of artists active during the Harlem Renaissance.

✪ **Museum of Science and Industry (MOSI).** 4801 E. Fowler Ave. (at N. 50th St.). ☎ **813/987-6300.** www.tampatrib.com/mosi. Admission $11 adults; $9 seniors, college students with identification, and children 13–18; $7 children 2–12; free for children under 2. MOSIMAX tickets $6 adults; $5 seniors, college students, and children 3–18; $4 kids 2–12. Combination tickets available. Free parking. Daily 9am–5pm or later. From downtown, take I-275 north, then Fowler Ave. east 2 miles to museum on right.

A great place to take the kids on a rainy day, MOSI is the largest science center in the Southeast and has more than 450 interactive exhibits. Guests can step into the Gulf Hurricane and experience gale-force winds, defy the laws of gravity in the unique *Challenger* space experience, or cruise the mysterious world of microbes in LifeLab. The Amazing You allows visitors to explore the body, Our Florida focuses on environmental factors, and Our Place in the Universe introduces them to space, flight, and beyond. You can also watch stunning movies in MOSIMAX, Florida's first IMAX dome theater.

Tampa Museum of Art. 600 N. Ashley St. (at Twiggs St.), downtown. ☎ **813/274-8130.** Admission $5 adults, $4 seniors and students with identification, $3 children 6–18, free for children 5 and under, by donation for everyone Wed 5–9pm and Sat 10am–noon. Mon–Tues and Thurs–Sat 10am–5pm, Wed 10am–9pm, Sun 1–5pm. Take I-275 to Exit 25 (Ashley St.).

Located on the east bank of the Hillsborough River next to the round NationsBank building (locals facetiously call it the "Beer Can") and just south of the Tampa Bay Performing Arts Center, this fine-arts complex offers eight galleries with changing exhibits ranging from classical antiquities to contemporary Florida art. There's also a 7-acre riverfront park and sculpture garden. Museum tours are offered on Wednesday and Saturday at 1pm and on Sunday at 2pm.

YBOR CITY

A few short years ago the part of Tampa northeast of downtown was known simply as the Latin Quarter, the historic district famous for cigars and Columbia, the largest Spanish restaurant in the world (see "Where to Dine," below). It takes its present name from Don Vicente Martinez Ybor ("*Ee*-bore," a Spanish cigar maker who arrived here in 1886 via Cuba and Key West. Soon his and other Tampa factories were producing more than 300,000 hand-rolled stogies a day.

It may not be the cigar capital of the world anymore, but Ybor is the happening part of Tampa, a cross between New Orleans's Bourbon Street, Washington's Georgetown, and New York's SoHo. By day, you can stroll past the art galleries, boutiques, and trendy new restaurants and cafes that line 7th Avenue East. At night, when good food and great music dominate the scene, streets will be bustling until 4am. Unique shops offer a wide assortment of goodies, from silk boxer shorts to unique tattoos. Dozens of outstanding nightclubs and dance clubs have waiting lines out the door. Live-music offerings run the gamut from jazz and blues to indie rock. There are lots of police around in the wee hours, but be as cautious here as you would exploring any big city at night.

✪ **Ybor City Walking Tours** are an ideal way to check out the highlights of this historic district. Free 1½-hour tours are sponsored by the Ybor City State Museum (see below) and are led by enthusiastic local volunteers. Tours start at the information desk in Ybor Square shopping center, on 13th Street between 8th and 9th avenues, and cover over three dozen points of interest before ending at the Ybor City State Museum. January to April the tours depart on Tuesday, Thursday, and Saturday at 11am; May to December, only on Thursday and Saturday.

Cigar smokers will enjoy a stroll through the **Ybor City State Museum,** 1818 9th Ave., between 18th and 19th streets (☎ **813/247-6323**), housed in the former Fer- lita Bakery (1896–1973). You can take a self-guided tour around the museum to see a collection of cigar labels, cigar memorabilia, and works by local artisans. Admission is $2 per person, including a 30-minute guided tour of **La Casita,** a renovated cigar worker's cottage adjacent to the museum; it's furnished as it was at the turn of the cen- tury. The museum is open Tuesday to Saturday from 9am to noon and 1 to 5pm (La Casita, from 10am to 3pm).

Another interesting stop here is the **Ybor City Brewing Company,** 2205 N. 20th St., facing Palm Avenue (☎ **813/242-9222**). Housed in a 100-year-old, three-story former cigar factory, this microbrewery produces Ybor Gold and other brews, none with preservatives. Admission of $2 per person includes a tour of the brewery and taste of the end result. Open Tuesday to Saturday from 11am to 3pm.

ORGANIZED TOURS

Swiss Chalet Tours, 3601 E. Busch Blvd. (☎ **813/985-3601**), opposite Busch Gar- dens in the privately run Tampa Bay Visitor Information Center (see "Essentials," above), operates guided bus tours of Tampa, Ybor City, and environs. The 4-hour half- day tours are given daily; they cost $35 for adults and $25 for children. The 8-hour full-day tours are given on Tuesday and Friday, and cost $60 for adults and $50 for children. Reservations are required at least 24 hours in advance; passengers are picked up at major hotels and various other points in the Tampa/St. Petersburg area. Tours can also be booked to Sarasota, Bradenton, and other regional destinations.

OUTDOOR ACTIVITIES & SPECTATOR SPORTS

Tampa Outdoor Adventures (☎ **800/44-TAMPA,** ext. 6, or 813/223-2752) is a one-stop source of information and reservations for a variety of recreational activities in the Tampa area, from ballooning to yachting. In addition, try these contacts directly:

BIKING, IN-LINE SKATING & JOGGING   Bayshore Boulevard, a 7-mile prom- enade, is famous for its sidewalk right on the shores of Hillsborough Bay. Reputed to be the world's longest continuous sidewalk, it's a favorite for runners, joggers, walkers, and in-line skaters. The route goes from the western edge of downtown in a southward direction, passing stately old homes of Hyde Park, a few high-rise condos, retirement communities, and houses of worship, ending at Ballast Point Park. The view from the promenade across the bay to the downtown skyline is unmatched here (Bayshore Boulevard also is great for a drive).

Rent bicycles and in-line skates at **Blades & Bikes,** in a pink-and-blue shop at 201-A W. Platt St., at South Parker Street (☎ 813/251-0780), a block west of the northern end of Bayshore Boulevard. Prices for both bikes and blades range from $8 for 1 hour to $20 for all day. Hours are Monday to Friday from 10am to 7pm, Saturday from 9am to 7pm, and Sunday from 10am to 5pm.

CANOEING   You can paddle downstream along a 20-mile stretch of the Hillsborough River amid 16,000 acres of rural lands in Wilderness Park, the largest regional park in Hillsborough County. **Canoe Escape,** 9335 E. Fowler Ave. (☎ 813/986-2067), rents canoes for $13 per person or $26 per craft. The company also has 2- to 6-hour guided trips. Open Monday to Friday from 9am to 5pm and Saturday and Sunday from 8am to 6pm.

FISHING   There's good freshwater fishing for trout in **Lake Thonotosassa,** east of the city, or for bass along the **Hillsborough River.** Pier fishing on Hillsborough Bay is also available from **Ballast Point Park,** 5300 Interbay Blvd. (☎ 813/831-9585). Ballast Point Park is at the southern end of Bayshore Boulevard and has a terrific view back across the bay to downtown.

   Light Tackle Fishing Expeditions (☎ 813/963-1930) offers sportfishing trips for tarpon, redfish, cobia, trout, and snook. Prices start at $50 per person.

GOLF   Tampa has three municipal golf courses where you can play for $26 to $34, a relative pittance when compared to the privately owned courses here and elsewhere in Florida. The **Babe Zaharias Municipal Golf Course,** 11412 Forest Hills Dr., north of Lowry Park (☎ 813/631-4374), is an 18-hole, par-70 course with a pro shop, putting greens, and a driving range. It's the shortest of the municipal courses, but small greens and narrow fairways present ample challenges. Water presents obstacles on 12 of the 18 holes at **Rocky Point Municipal Golf Course,** 4151 Dana Shores Dr. (☎ 813/673-4316), located between the airport and the bay. It's a par-71 course with a pro shop, practice range, and putting greens. On the Hillsborough River in north Tampa, the **Rogers Park Municipal Golf Course,** 7910 N. 30th St. (☎ 813/673-4396), is an 18-hole, par-72 championship course with a lighted driving and practice range. They all are open daily from 7am to dusk, and lessons and club rentals are available.

   Another inexpensive place to play is the **University of South Florida Golf Course,** Fletcher Avenue and 46th Street (☎ 813/632-6893), just north of the USF campus. This 18-hole, par-71 course is nicknamed "The Claw" because of its challenging layout. It offers lessons and club rentals. Greens fees range from about $19 to $25, or $25 to $35 with a cart, depending on the season and time of day. It's open daily from 7am to dusk.

   Other courses open to the public include the **Hall of Fame Golf Club,** just south of the airport at 2222 N. Westshore Blvd. (☎ 813/876-4913), an 18-hole, par-72 affair with a driving range; **Persimmon Hill Golf Club,** 5109 Hamey Rd. (☎ 813/623-6962); **Silver Dollar Trap & Golf Club,** 17000 Patterson Rd., Odessa (☎ 813/920-3884); and **Westchase Golf Club,** 1307 Radcliff Dr. (☎ 813/854-2331).

   You can book starting times and get information about these and the area's other courses by calling **Tee Times USA** (☎ 800/374-8633).

   If you want to do some serious work on your game, the **Arnold Palmer Golf Academy World Headquarters** is at the renowned Saddlebrook Resort, 5700 Saddlebrook Way, Wesley Chapel, 12 miles north of Tampa (☎ 800/729-8383 or 813/973-1111). There are 2-, 3-, and 5-day programs available for adults and juniors ranging from $248 to $320 per person per night, double occupancy, including accommodations, breakfast, daily instruction, 18 holes of golf daily, cart and greens fees, and nightly club storage and cleaning. You have to stay at the resort or enroll in the golf program to play at Saddlebrook. See "Where to Stay," below, for more information about the resort.

SPECTATOR SPORTS National Football League fans can catch the improving **Tampa Bay Buccaneers** at Houlihan's Stadium, 4201 N. Dale Mabry Hwy., at Dr. Martin Luther King Jr. Boulevard (☎ 813/872-BUCS). Their season runs from September through December, and tickets range from $20 to $30.

You can also watch two of the nation's better college football teams in the **Outback Bowl** on New Year's Day (☎ 813/874-BOWL).

The Arena Football League's **Tampa Bay Storm** play in the 20,000-seat ICE PALACE, downtown between the Tampa Convention Center and the Florida Aquarium, from May through July (☎ 813/276-7300). Tickets cost $12 to $18.

The National Hockey League's **Tampa Bay Lightning** also play in the ICE PALACE, beginning every October (☎ 813/229-8800). Tickets range from $17.50 to $75.

New York Yankees fans can watch the Boys in Blue during baseball spring training from mid-February through March at Legends Field, opposite Houlihan's Stadium (☎ 813/875-7753). A scaled-down replica of Yankee Stadium, it's the largest spring-training facility in Florida, with a 10,000-seat capacity. Tickets range from $6 to $10. The club's minor league team, the **Tampa Yankees** (same phone), plays at Legends Field from April to September. Tickets are $3 for adults, $2 for kids.

The only oval thoroughbred race course on Florida's west coast, ✪ **Tampa Bay Downs,** 11225 Racetrack Rd., Oldsmar (☎ 800/200-4434 in Florida, or 813/855-4401), is the home of the Tampa Bay Derby. Races are held from December to May, and the track presents simulcasts year-round. Call for post times. Admission is $1.50 to the grandstand, $3 to the clubhouse. Parking costs $1.

Professional players volley the lethal *pelota* at the **Tampa Jai-Alai Fronton,** 5125 S. Dale Mabry Hwy., near Gandy Boulevard (☎ 813/831-1411). Admission is $1 to $4 and parking is $1 or free. It's open year-round, with games Monday to Saturday beginning at 6:45pm, and matinees on Monday, Wednesday, Friday, and Saturday beginning at noon.

TENNIS The **City of Tampa Tennis Complex,** at the Hillsborough Community College, 3901 Tampa Bay Blvd. (☎ 813/348-1173), across from Houlihan's Stadium, is the largest public complex in Tampa, with 16 hard courts and 12 clay courts. It also has four racquetball courts, a pro shop, locker rooms, showers, and lessons. Reservations are recommended. Prices range from $2.50 to $5 per person per hour. It's open Monday to Thursday from 8am to 9pm, Friday from 8am to 7pm, and Saturday and Sunday from 8am to 6pm.

On the water and overlooking Harbour Island, the **Sandra W. Freedman Tennis Complex,** in Marjorie Park, 59 Columbia Dr., Davis Island (☎ 813/259-1664), has eight clay courts. Reservations are required. The price is $5 per person per hour, and it's open Monday to Friday from 8am to 9pm and Saturday and Sunday from 8am to 6pm.

Beginners to highly skilled players can sharpen their games at the **Phil Green Tennis Program,** located at the Saddlebrook Resort, 5700 Saddlebrook Way, Wesley Chapel (☎ 800/729-8383 or 813/973-1111). Packages start at $372 person for 2 days, or $816 person for 6 days, double occupancy, including tennis instruction, unlimited playing time, video analysis, agility exercises, fitness center, and accommodations at the Saddlebrook Resort for 5 days and 6 nights. You must be a member or a guest to play here (see "Where to Stay," below).

SHOPPING

Hyde Park and Ybor City are two areas of Tampa worth some window shopping, perhaps sandwiched around lunch at one of their fine restaurants (see "Where to Dine," below).

✪ **Old Hyde Park Village,** 1507 W. Swann Ave., at South Dakoka Avenue (☎ 813/251-3500), is a terrific alternative to cookie-cutter suburban malls. Walk around little shops in the sunshine and check out Hyde Park, one of the city's oldest and most historic neighborhoods at the same time. The cluster of 50 upscale shops and boutiques is set in a village layout. The selection includes Williams-Sonoma, Pottery Barn, Banana Republic, Brooks Brothers, Crabtree & Evelyn, Godiva Chocolatier, Laura Ashley, Polo Ralph Lauren, and Talbots, to name a few. There's a free parking garage on South Oregon Avenue behind Jacobson's department store. The shops are open Monday to Wednesday and Saturday from 10am to 6pm, Thursday and Friday from 10am to 9pm, and Sunday from noon to 5pm.

Ybor City, along East 7th Avenue East between 14th and 22nd streets, has several shops worth browsing. **Adam's Ybor City Hats,** 1621 E. 7th Ave. East(☎ 813/229-2850), has a mind-boggling inventory of more than 18,000 hats of every description. **La France,** 1612 E. 7th Ave. (☎ 813/248-1381), has racks upon racks of vintage clothing and funky costumes. Named after the Irish monk who became the patron saint of gardeners, **St. Fiacre's Herb Shop,** 1807 N. 16th St. (☎ 813/248-1234), stocks a wide array of fresh herbs, herbal products, fragrances, exotic teas, T-shirts, herbal gift baskets, and books.

Cigar aficionados can stock up at **El Sol,** 1728 E. 7th Ave. (☎ 813/247-5554), the city's oldest cigar store, and at **Metropolitan Cigars & Wine,** 2014 E. 7th Ave. (☎ 813/248-3304).

You can watch an artisan rolling stogies at **Tampa Rico Cigar Co.,** one of the shops in **Ybor Square,** 1901 13th St., at 8th Avenue (☎ 813/247-4497), a shopping complex listed on the National Register of Historic Places. The three brick buildings date from 1886 and once comprised the largest cigar factory in the world. Today it's primarily notable for several small shops selling an amazing variety of collectibles.

The main mall in the city is **West Shore Plaza,** on Kennedy Boulevard where it turns into Memorial Highway (Fla. 60). Burdines, JC Penney, and Dillards are the anchors. **University Mall** is nearest Busch Gardens, on Fowler Avenue just east of I-275. Burdines, Dillards, JC Penney, and Sears are the biggies both there and at **Brandon TownCenter,** at I-4 and Fla. 60 in the eastern suburb of Brandon, where most stores have unusually large amounts of floor space and, hence, more merchandise from which to choose.

If you want to stock up on fresh Florida fruits and vegetables, head to **Whaley's Markets,** 533 S. Howard Ave., at DeLeon, northwest of Hyde Park (☎ 813/254-2904). This purveyor of gourmet foods has a terrific selection of marmalades and other local foods, including picnic items and deli sandwiches. They'll ship your citrus home. Open Monday to Saturday from 7am to 9pm and Sunday from 7am to 8pm.

WHERE TO STAY

I've organized the accommodations listings below into two geographic areas: near Busch Gardens and downtown. If you're going to Busch Gardens, Adventure Island, Lowry Park Zoo, and the Museum of Science and Industry (MOSI), the motels near Busch Gardens are much more convenient than those downtown, about 7 miles to the south. The downtown hotels are geared to business travelers, but staying there will put you near the Florida Aquarium, the Museum of African-American Art, the Tampa

Tampa Accommodations & Dining

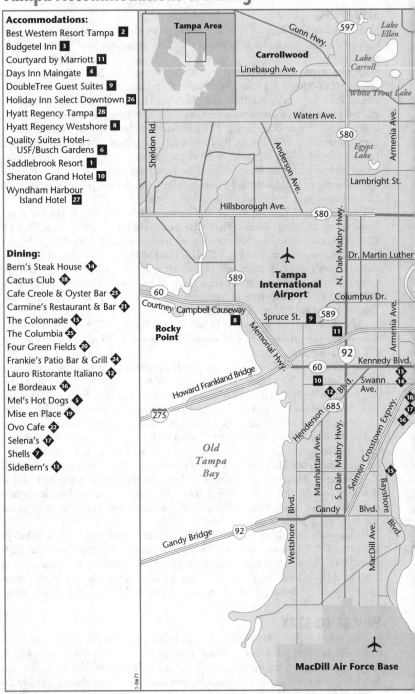

Accommodations:

Best Western Resort Tampa **2**
Budgetel Inn **3**
Courtyard by Marriott **11**
Days Inn Maingate **4**
DoubleTree Guest Suites **9**
Holiday Inn Select Downtown **26**
Hyatt Regency Tampa **28**
Hyatt Regency Westshore **8**
Quality Suites Hotel–
 USF/Busch Gardens **6**
Saddlebrook Resort **1**
Sheraton Grand Hotel **10**
Wyndham Harbour
 Island Hotel **27**

Dining:

Bern's Steak House **14**
Cactus Club **18**
Cafe Creole & Oyster Bar **23**
Carmine's Restaurant & Bar **21**
The Colonnade **15**
The Columbia **25**
Four Green Fields **20**
Frankie's Patio Bar & Grill **24**
Lauro Ristorante Italiano **12**
Le Bordeaux **16**
Mel's Hot Dogs **5**
Mise en Place **19**
Ovo Cafe **22**
Selena's **17**
Shells **7**
SideBern's **13**

372

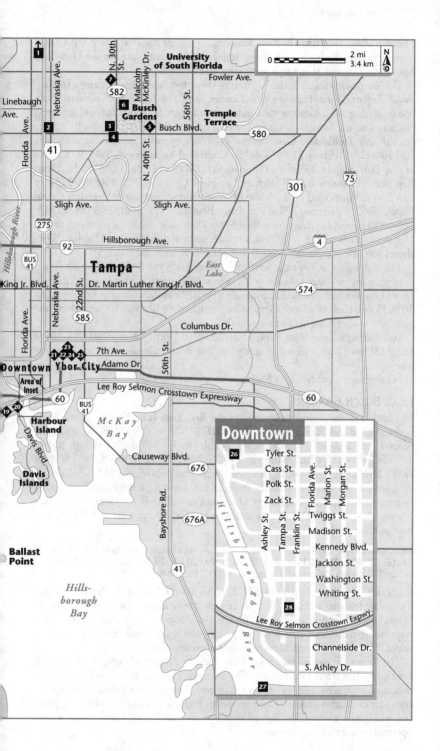

Museum of Art, the Henry B. Plant Museum, the Tampa Bay Performing Arts Center, scenic Bayshore Boulevard, the dining and shopping opportunities in the Hyde Park historic district, and Ybor City's restaurants and nightlife.

The Westshore area, near the bay west of downtown and south of Tampa International Airport, is another commercial center, with a wide range of national chain hotels catering to business travelers and conventioneers. It's convenient to Houlihan's Stadium and the New York Yankees' spring training complex. Here you'll find the Spanish-style **Doubletree Guest Suites,** 4400 W. Cypress St., at Manhattan Avenue (☎ **800/222-TREE** or 813/873-8675); **Courtyard by Marriott,** 3805 W. Cypress St., at Dale Mabrey Highway (☎ **800/321-2211** or 813/874-0555); the **Hyatt Regency Westshore,** 6200 Courtney Campbell Causeway (☎ **800/233-1234** or 813/874-1234), nestled on a 35-acre bay-side nature preserve; the **Sheraton Grand Hotel,** 4860 W. Kennedy Blvd., at Shore Boulevard (☎ **800/325-3535** or 813/286-4400), across the street from West Shore Plaza mall and home to one of former Miami Dolphins Coach Don Shula's steak houses; and the **Tampa Marriott Westshore,** 1001 N. Westshore Blvd. (☎ **800/228-9290** or 813/287-2555).

The high season in Tampa generally runs from January to April, but you won't find as large an increase here as at the beach resorts. Most hotels offer discounted package rates in the summer and weekend specials all year, dropping their rates by as much as 50%. Hotels often combine tickets to major attractions like Busch Gardens in their packages, so always ask about special deals.

Hillsborough River State Park, 15402 U.S. 301 North, Thonotosassa, FL 33592 (☎ **813/986-1020**), offers 118 campsites year-round, plus fishing, canoeing, and boating.

Hillsborough County adds 12% tax to your hotel room bill.

NEAR BUSCH GARDENS

In addition to the listings below, there's the **Red Roof Inn,** 2307 E. Busch Blvd., between 22nd and 26th streets (☎ **800/THE-ROOF** or 813/932-0073), a pleasant property on landscaped grounds where doubles go for $69 double in high season, $45 off-season. **Days Inn Maingate,** 2901 E. Busch Blvd., at 30th Street (☎ **800/ DAYS-INN** or 813/933-6471), charging $64 per double in winter, $42 to $52 double off-season, is less appealing than the Budgetel Inn across the street (see below), but it's convenient for families on a budget since you can walk to Busch Gardens from here (there're also two more Days Inns within a short drive of Busch Gardens). Both motels have outdoor pools.

Best Western Resort Tampa at Busch Gardens. 820 E. Busch Blvd. (at I-275), Tampa, FL 33612. ☎ **800/288-4011** or 813/933-4011. Fax 813/932-1784. 255 units. A/C TV TEL. Winter $99 double. Off-season $59 double. AE, DC, DISC, MC, V.

Right at the Busch Boulevard exit off I-275, this motel is fine for families on a budget. The lobby leads to an enclosed skylit atrium-style courtyard with fountains, streetlights, benches, a pool, and tropical foliage. Guest rooms in this wing open to walkways facing the indoor atrium or the parking lots. Newer units are in a four-story annex. They all have standard furnishings and coffeemakers.

The Palm Grill Restaurant off the lobby features a variety of dishes, while the Bull Pen Sports Bar offers pub fare and libation until 11pm nightly. Services include a concierge desk, secretarial services, valet laundry, limited room service, and courtesy transport to Busch Gardens. There are indoor and outdoor heated swimming pools, two whirlpools, a sauna, four lighted tennis courts, exercise and game rooms, a coin-operated laundry, and a gift shop.

Budgetel Inn. 9202 N. 30th St. (at Busch Blvd.), Tampa, FL 33612. ☎ **800/428-3438** or 813/930-6900. Fax 813/930-0563. 150 units. A/C TV TEL. Winter $77 double. Off-season $57 double. Rates include continental breakfast. AE, DC, DISC, MC, V.

Fake banana trees and a parrot cage welcome guests to the terra-cotta-floored lobby of this comfortable and convenient member of a fine chain of budget-conscious motels. All rooms are spacious and have ceiling fans, bright wood furniture with tropical trim, desks, phones with long cords, and coffeemakers (a bag with Danish pastries or a blueberry muffin and juice is hung on your doorknob before dawn). Rooms with king beds also have recliners. Outside, a courtyard with an unheated swimming pool has plenty of space for sunning. There's a game room and coin laundry, and local telephone calls are free. There's no restaurant on the premises, but plenty are nearby.

✪ **Quality Suites Hotel—USF Near Busch Gardens.** 3001 University Center Dr., Tampa, FL 33612. ☎ **800/786-7446** or 813/971-8930. Fax 813/971-8935. 150 units. A/C TV TEL. Winter $99–$159 suite for 2. Off-season $89–$139 suite for 2. Rates include full breakfast buffet and evening cocktail reception. AE, DC, DISC, MC, V.

Actually on North 30th Street, between Busch Boulevard and Fletcher Avenue, this hacienda-style all-suite hotel sits about a mile from the Busch Gardens entrance and is the pick of the hotels in this area. The complex encloses a lushly tropical courtyard surrounding a heated pool, hot tub, covered games area, and outdoor seating for Ruzik's Roost, a beach-bar type grill serving a complimentary breakfast buffet plus lunch and dinner (it can get noisy on this end of the courtyard, so ask for a suite away from the action). Opening to this pleasant vista, each suite has two TVs, and a separate bedroom with built-in armoire and well-lit mirrored vanity area. Living/dining rooms have a sofa bed, La-Z-Boy recliner, wet bar, coffeemaker, microwave, and stereo/VCR unit. Facilities also include a 24-hour gift shop/food store, VCR rentals, whirlpool, meeting rooms, and coin-operated laundry.

DOWNTOWN TAMPA

Holiday Inn Select Downtown. 111 W. Fortune St. (at Ashley St.), Tampa, FL 33602. ☎ **800/513-8940** or 813/223-1351. Fax 813/221-2000. 312 units. A/C TV TEL. Winter $105–$150 double. Off-season $89–$125 double. AE, DC, DISC, MC, V. Take Ashley St. (Exit 25) off I-275, turn right at bottom of ramp to hotel.

This modern 14-story hotel is adjacent to the Tampa Bay Performing Arts Center and within walking distance of the Tampa Museum of Art. The guest rooms are spacious, with dark-wood furnishings, full-length wall mirrors, coffeemakers, irons and boards. Most rooms on the upper floors have views of the Hillsborough River, and rooms on the 11th floor come equipped with microwave ovens and refrigerators. The lobby level offers three dining choices: a restaurant for moderately priced meals, one for light fare, and a lounge for drinks and occasional live music. There's limited room service, airport courtesy shuttle, an outdoor heated swimming pool, whirlpool, fitness room, gift shop, and both laundry service and a coin-operated Laundromat.

✪ **Hyatt Regency Tampa.** 2 Tampa City Center (corner of E. Jackson St.), Tampa, FL 33602. ☎ **800/233-1234** or 813/225-1234. Fax 813/273-0234. 518 units. A/C TV TEL. Winter $194–$210. Off-season $145–$160 double. Weekend packages available off-season. AE, DC, DISC, MC, V. Valet parking $7.

In the center of the downtown business district, it's not surprising that this Hyatt caters primarily to the corporate crowd. It's just off the Franklin Street pedestrian mall and a short walk from the Harbour Island People Mover. The Hyatt signature eight-story atrium lobby has a cascading waterfall and lots of foliage. Many units on the upper floors have bay or river views.

Dining/Diversions: Creative American cuisine is featured at City Center Cafe. Light lunches are offered at Deli Express. For libations with piano music, try Saltwaters Lounge (there's not much else going on downtown after dark).

Amenities: Concierge, 24-hour room service, valet laundry, airport courtesy shuttle. Outdoor heated swimming pool, whirlpool, health club.

✪ **Wyndham Harbour Island Hotel.** 725 S. Harbour Island Blvd., Harbour Island, Tampa, FL 33602. ☎ **800/WYNDHAM** or 813/229-5000. Fax 813/229-5322. 299 units. A/C MINIBAR TV TEL. Winter $139–$219 double. Off-season $99–$169 double. AE, DC, DISC, MC, V.

With the shops closed, there's not much action on this little island, but you'll enjoy quiet elegance at this 12-story luxury property. It has great views of the surrounding channels that link the Hillsborough River and the bay. The bedrooms, all with views of the water, are furnished in dark woods and floral fabrics, and each has a well-lit marble-trimmed bathroom, executive desk, and work area, plus in-room conveniences such as a coffeemaker, iron, and ironing board.

Dining/Diversions: Watch the yachts drift by as you dine at the Harbourview Room, or enjoy your favorite drink in the Bar, a clubby room with equally good views. Snacks and drinks are available during the day at the Pool Bar.

Amenities: Concierge, room service, secretarial services, notary public, evening turndown, valet laundry, courtesy airport shuttle. Outdoor heated swimming pool and deck, newsstand/gift shop, guest privileges at the Harbour Island Athletic Club.

A NEARBY RESORT

✪ **Saddlebrook Resort.** 5700 Saddlebrook Way, Wesley Chapel, FL 33543. ☎ **800/729-8383** or 813/973-1111. Fax 813/973-4504. 800 units. A/C TV TEL. Winter $215–$360 double. Off-season $180–$325 double. AE, DC, DISC, MC, V. Head 1 mile east of I-75 off Fla. 54 (Exit 58).

Set on 480 acres of natural countryside, this internationally renowned golf and tennis resort is off the beaten path (30 minutes north of Tampa International Airport) but worth the trip. Join pros such as Pete Sampras at the Phil Green Tennis Program, or perfect your swing at the Arnold Palmer Golf Academy (see "Outdoor Activities & Spectator Sports," above).

Dining/Diversions: The casual but elegant Cypress Restaurant consistently wins accolades. It's famous for grand holiday buffets and popular Friday-night seafood buffets. Enjoy indoor or outdoor dining at Terrace on the Green, overlooking the Cypress Lagoon and the 18th green. The Little Club offers an American menu and the popular TD's sports bar/tavern. The Poolside Cafe is great for dining in your bathing suit alfresco.

Amenities: Concierge, room service, baby-sitting, children's activities program, airport courtesy shuttle. Two 18-hole championship golf courses, 45 tennis courts, 270-foot-long half-million-gallon superpool, whirlpool, 7,000-square-foot luxury spa, fitness center, basketball and volleyball courts, softball field.

WHERE TO DINE

As with the hotels, I have organized the restaurants below by geographic area: near Busch Gardens, in or near Hyde Park (just across the Hillsborough River from downtown), and in Ybor City (on the northeastern edge of downtown).

NEAR BUSCH GARDENS

You'll find the national fast-food and family restaurants east of I-275 on Busch Boulevard and along Fletcher Avenue near University Mall.

✪ **Mel's Hot Dogs.** 4136 E. Busch Blvd., at 42nd St. ☎ **813/985-8000.** Main courses $3–$6.50. No credit cards. Daily 11am–9pm. AMERICAN.

Catering to everyone from businesspeople on a lunch break to hungry families craving inexpensive all-beef hot dogs, this red-and-white cottage offers everything from "bagel-dogs" and corn dogs to a bacon/cheddar Reuben. All choices are served on a poppy seed bun and most come with french fries and a choice of coleslaw or baked beans. Even the decor is dedicated to wieners: The walls and windows are lined with hot-dog memorabilia. And just in case hot-dog mania hasn't won you over, there are a few alternative choices (sausages, chicken breast, and beef and veggie burgers).

Shells. 11010 N. 30th St. (between Busch Blvd. and Fowler Ave.). ☎ **813/977-8456.** Reservations not accepted. Main courses $6–$17. AE, DISC, MC, V. Mon–Thurs 11:30am–10pm, Fri–Sat 11:30am–11pm, Sun noon–10pm. SEAFOOD.

You'll see Shells restaurants in many parts of Florida, and with good reason, for this casual, award-winning chain consistently provides excellent value, especially if you have a family to feed. They all have the same menu and prices and are particularly known for their spicy Jack Daniel's buffalo shrimp and scallop appetizers. Main courses range from the usual fried seafood platters to pastas and charcoal-grilled shrimp, fish, steaks, and chicken. I counted 21 tender, bite-size shrimp in a light, garlic-tinged cream sauce and served over linguine—a bargain for $9.50. Another 30 of them were perfectly charcoal-grilled on a skewer and served with saffron rice and steamed vegetables for $11. There's also a children's menu.

HYDE PARK
Expensive
Bern's Steak House. 1208 S. Howard Ave. (at Marjory Ave.). ☎ **813/251-2421.** Reservations required. Main courses $19–$35. AE, DC, DISC, MC, V. Daily 5–11pm. Closed Christmas. AMERICAN.

The exterior of this famous steak house looks like a factory built almost under the Lee Roy Selmon Crosstown Expressway. Inside, however, you'll find eight ornate dining rooms with themes like Rhône, Burgundy, and Irish Rebellion. They set an appropriately dark atmosphere for meat lovers, for here you order and pay for charcoal-grilled steaks (beef or buffalo) according to the thickness and weight. They come with onion soup, salad, baked potato, garlic toast, onion rings, and vegetables grown in Bern's own organic garden. The phone book–size wine list offers more than 7,000 selections.

The big surprise here is the dessert quarters upstairs, where 50 romantic booths paneled in aged California redwood can privately seat from 2 to 12 guests. Each of these little chambers is equipped with a phone for placing your order and a closed-circuit TV for watching and listening to a resident pianist. The dessert menu offers almost 100 delicious selections, plus some 1,400 after-dinner drinks. It's possible to reserve a booth for dessert only, but preference is given to those who dine. You can get some of the same sweet things nearby at SideBern's (see below).

Le Bordeaux. 1502 S. Howard Ave. (2 blocks north of Bayshore Blvd.). ☎ **813/254-4387.** Reservations accepted only for parties of 6 or more. Main courses $15–$28. AE, DC, MC, V. Mon–Thurs 6–10pm, Fri–Sat 5:30–11pm, Sun 5:30–9:30pm. TRADITIONAL FRENCH.

This bistro's authentic French fare is some of the region's best, but keep a reign on your credit card—everything's sold à la carte, so you can ring up a hefty bill quickly. French-born chef/owner Gordon Davis offers seating in a living room–style main dining room of this converted house expanded to include a plant-filled conservatory. His menu changes daily, but you can count on homemade pâtés and pastries, and the specials often include salmon en croûte, pot au feu, veal with wild mushrooms, and fillet of beef au Roquefort. Part of the establishment is the Left Bank Jazz Bistro, with live entertainment.

Moderate

⭘ **Lauro Ristorante Italiano.** 3915 Henderson Blvd. (2 blocks west of Dale Mabry Hwy., between Watrous and Neptune aves.). ☎ **813/281-2100.** Reservations recommended. Main courses $10–$25. AE, DC, DISC, MC, V. Mon–Fri 11:30am–2pm and 5:30–10pm, Sat 5:30–11pm. ITALIAN.

Known for extraordinary sauces and pastas, chef/owner Lauro Medeglia is a native Italian who cooks his home fare with love. Though his restaurant is off the beaten track, it's worth the detour. Classical decor and soft music have made it one of Tampa's favorite places to "pop the question," and smartly attired waiters render efficient yet friendly and unobtrusive service. Try the caprese, putanesca, gnocchi, or agnolotti.

⭘ **Mise en Place.** In Grand Central Place, 442 W. Kennedy Blvd. (at S. Magnolia Ave., opposite the University of Tampa). ☎ **813/254-5373.** Reservations accepted only for parties of 6 or more. Main courses $13–$21. AE, DC, DISC, MC, V. Mon–Fri 11am–3pm, Tues–Thurs 5:30–10pm, Fri–Sat and 5:30–11pm. INTERNATIONAL.

Look around at all those happy, stylish people soaking up the trendy ambience, and you'll know why chef Marty Blitz and his wife, Marianne, are the culinary darlings of Tampa. They continue to present the freshest of ingredients, with a creative international menu that changes daily. Main courses often include such choices as roast duck with Jamaica wild-strawberry sauce, grilled swordfish with three-melon mint salsa, or Ethiopian lentil stew served with steamed *injera* bread. There's valet parking at the rear of the building on Grand Central Place.

After dinner you can wander next door into **442,** an upscale bar with live jazz and blues.

Selena's. In Old Hyde Park shopping complex, 1623 Snow Ave. (south of Swan St.). ☎ **813/251-2116.** Reservations recommended. Main courses $10–$18. AE, MC, V. Mon–Thurs 11am–10pm, Fri–Sat 11am–11pm, Sun 11am–9pm. LOUISIANA.

This charming restaurant seems straight out of New Orleans. Sit in the plant-filled Patio Room, the eclectic Queen Anne Room, or watch the world go by at the outdoor cafe. Local seafoods, especially grouper and shrimp, top the menu at dinner, with many of the dishes served Louisiana style (to exercise your taste buds, try the rustic crab cakes with Cajun spices or the "voodoo" shrimp Creole). The vegetarian broccoli, cauliflower, and mushrooms over linguine has justifiably won awards. Other choices include pastas, chicken, steaks, and apricot-glazed quail. At night, jazz sounds enliven the proceedings, as musical groups perform in the upstairs lounge.

Inexpensive

Cactus Club. In Old Hyde Park shopping complex, 1601 Snow Ave. (south of Swan St.). ☎ **813/251-4089.** Reservations not accepted. Main courses $6.50–15. AE, DC, MC, V. Mon–Thurs 11am–11pm, Fri–Sat 11am–midnight, Sun 11am–10:30pm. AMERICAN SOUTHWEST.

Watch all the shoppers go by at Old Hyde Park from this fun and casual cafe with a Southwestern accent. Dine inside or outside on tacos, enchiladas, chili, sizzling fajitas, hickory-smoked baby back ribs, Jamaican jerk chicken, guacamole/green-chile burgers, fajitas, quesadillas, sandwiches, smoked chicken salad, and more. It's always packed at lunchtime—get here early.

The Colonnade. 3401 Bayshore Blvd. (at W. Julia St.). ☎ **813/839-7558.** Reservations accepted only for large parties. Main courses $8–$18. AE, DC, DISC, MC, V. Sun–Thurs 11am–10pm, Fri–Sat 11am–11pm. AMERICAN/SEAFOOD.

Locals have been flocking to this rough-hewn, shiplap place since 1935, primarily for the great view of Hillsborough Bay across Bayshore Boulevard. The food is a bit on the Red Lobsterish side, but get here early or wait for a window table; the vista is worth it. Fresh seafood is the specialty: grouper prepared seven ways, crab-stuffed flounder, Maryland-style crab cakes, even wild Florida alligator as an appetizer. Prime rib, steaks, and chicken are also available.

Four Green Fields. 205 W. Platt St. (between Parker St. and Plant Ave.). ☎ **813/254-4444.** Reservations accepted. Sandwiches $6; main courses $8.50–$14. AE, MC, V. Mon–Sat 11am–2am, Sun noon–2am. IRISH/AMERICAN.

This thatched-roof pub may be surrounded by palm trees instead of potato fields, but it still offers the ambience and tastes of Ireland just across the bridge from the downtown convention center. Staffed by genuine Irish immigrants, the large room with a square bar in the center smells of Irish ale. The Gaelic stew is predictably bland, but the salads and sandwiches are passable. The crowd usually is young, especially for live Irish music on Thursday, Friday, and Saturday nights.

SideBern's. 2208 W. Morrison Ave. (at S. Howard St.) ☎ **813/258-2233.** Reservations not accepted. Sandwiches and salads $4–$7.50; desserts $4–$5.50. AE, DC, DISC, MC, V. Sun and Tues–Thurs 6–11pm, Fri–Sat 6pm–1am. SANDWICHES/SALADS/DESSERTS.

The owners of Bern's Steakhouse (see above) opened this informal outlet to accommodate everyone who wanted to partake of their gourmet goodies but couldn't fit into the dessert rooms at the main restaurant. Their most popular desserts are offered at this sophisticated bistro, whose cathedral ceiling covers an open kitchen (wonderful aromas) and cherry-wood tables and chairs. Banana cheesecake is a consistent winner, as is the chocolate pâté served with Curaçao, raspberry, or rum sauce. Sandwiches are served on a choice of regular wheat, foccaccia, or roasted garlic potato bread. Tops among these features a tender, perfectly charcoal-grilled tenderloin steak accompanied by baked-potato salad, lettuce, tomato, a huge slice of onion, and shaved cucumber salad—a meal in itself. Top-notch coffees are roasted on the premises.

YBOR CITY
Moderate
✪ **Cafe Creole and Oyster Bar.** 1330 9th Ave. (at Avenida de Republica de Cuba/14th St.). ☎ **813/247-6283.** Reservations not accepted but call for preferred seating. Main courses $9–$17. AE, DC, DISC, MC, V. Mon–Thurs 11:30am–10pm, Fri 11:30am–11:30pm, Sat 5–11:30pm. CREOLE/CAJUN.

Resembling a turn-of-the-century railway station, this brick building dates from 1896 and was originally known as El Pasaje, the home of the Cherokee Club, a gentlemen's hotel and private club with a casino and a decor rich in stained-glass windows, wrought-iron balconies, Spanish murals, and marble bathrooms. Specialties include exceptionally prepared Louisiana crab cakes, oysters, blackened grouper, and jambalaya. If you're new to cuisine to the bayou, try the Creole sampler. Dine inside or out.

✪ **Columbia.** 2117 E. 7th Ave. (between 21st and 22nd sts). ☎ **813/248-4961.** Reservations recommended. Main courses $12–$23. AE, DC, DISC, MC, V. Mon–Thurs 11am–10pm, Fri–Sat 11am–11pm, Sun noon–9pm. SPANISH.

Dating from 1905, this hand-painted tile building occupies an entire city block in the heart of Ybor City. Tourists flock here to soak up the ambience and so do the locals because it's so much fun to clap along during fire-belching floor shows in the main dining room. You can't help coming back time after time for the famous Spanish bean soup and original "1905" salad. The paella à la valenciana is outstanding, with more than a dozen ingredients from gulf grouper and gulf pink shrimp to calamari, mussels, clams, chicken, and pork. The decor throughout is graced with hand-painted tiles, wrought-iron chandeliers, dark woods, rich red fabrics, and stained-glass windows. You can breathe your own fumes in the Cigar Bar.

✪ **Frankie's Patio Bar & Grill.** 1905 E. 7th Ave. (between 19th and 20th sts.). ☎ **813/249-3337.** Reservations accepted only for large parties. Main courses $8–$14; sandwiches $4.25–$6.50. AE, MC, V. Mon–Tues 11am–3pm, Wed–Thurs 11am–1am, Fri–Sat 11am–3am. INTERNATIONAL.

Known mostly as a venue for outstanding musical acts, this Ybor City attraction is also fun at lunch and dinner. With exposed industrial pipes, the large three-story restaurant stands out from the usual Spanish-themed, 19th-century architecture of Ybor City. There's seating indoors, on a large outdoor patio, or on an open-air balcony overlooking the action on the street. It's a fun atmosphere, and the food blends Cuban, American, Creole, and Italian influences. Live jazz, blues, reggae, and rock add to the atmosphere Wednesday to Saturday.

Ovo Cafe. 1901 E. 7th Ave. (at 19th St.). ☎ **813/248-6979.** Reservations not accepted. Main courses $8–$15. AE, MC, V. Mon–Tues 11am–4pm, Wed–Sat 11am–2am, Sun 11am–10pm. INTERNATIONAL.

This cafe, popular with the business set by day and the club crowd at night, is Tampa's answer to SoHo. You'll find a blend of good food, eclectic art, and pleasing surroundings. Locals love the "ménage à trois" omelettes at breakfast. The fresh Ovo's chicken feta salad is a great lunch choice. An eclectic menu includes pierogies, smoked tuna sandwiches, and shrimp bisque soup. The big surprise is finding Dom Perignon on the menu, as well as root-beer floats made with Absolut vodka.

Inexpensive

✪ **Carmine's Restaurant & Bar.** 1802 E. 7th Ave. East (at 18th St) ☎ **813/248-3834.** Reservations not accepted. Sandwiches $4–$7; main courses $5–$16 (most $7–$8). No credit cards. Mon–Tues 9am–10pm, Wed–Thurs 9am–midnight, Fri–Sat 9am–3am, Sun 9am–6pm. CUBAN/ITALIAN/AMERICAN.

Bright blue poles hold up an ancient pressed-tin ceiling above this noisy corner cafe, one of Ybor's most popular hangouts. A great variety of patrons gather at a stainless steel–topped bar or sit at an eclectic collection of chairs and tables that appear to have been gathered at a long series of yard sales. For lunch or dinner, you can order a genuine Cuban sandwich—smoked ham, roast pork, Genoa salami, Swiss cheese, pickles, salad dressing, mustard, lettuce, and tomato on a crispy, submarine roll. There's a vegetarian version, too, and the combination half sandwich and bowl of Spanish soup made with sausages, potatoes, and garbanzo beans makes a hearty meal for just $4. Main courses are led by Cuban-style roast pork, thin-cut pork chops with mushroom sauce, spaghetti with a blue crab tomato sauce, and a few seafood and chicken platters.

TAMPA AFTER DARK

The Tampa/Hillsborough Arts Council maintains an **Artsline** (☎ 813/229-ARTS), a 24-hour information service providing the latest on current and upcoming cultural events. Racks in many restaurants and bars have copies of *Weekly Planet, Focus,* and *Accent on Tampa Bay,* three free publications detailing what's going on in the entire bay area. And you can check the "Baylife" and "Friday Extra" sections of the *Tampa Tribune* and the Friday "Weekend" section of the *St. Petersburg Times.* The visitor center usually has copies of the week's newspaper sections (see "Essentials," above). And be on the lookout for the slick bimonthly magazine *Event Guide Tampa Bay,* which gives a rundown on what's going on.

THE CLUB & MUSIC SCENE   Ybor City is Tampa's favorite nighttime venue by far. All you have to do is stroll along 7th Avenue East between 15th and 20th streets to find a club or bar to your liking. The avenue is packed with people of every possible age and description on Friday and Saturday from 9pm to 3am, but you'll also find something going on from Tuesday to Thursday and even on Sunday. You don't need addresses or phone numbers; your ears will guide you along 7th Avenue East.

Starting at 15th Street and heading east, you'll come first to **The Masquerade,** with retro and old wave bands on Friday to Sunday. The body-pierced 20-something crowd gets primed at **Club Hedo** and **Cherry's** before dancing at **The Rubb** across the avenue. Between 16th and 17th streets, the **Blue Shark** features the blues (and refuses to sell alcoholic beverages to anyone who appears to be intoxicated).

Between 17th and 18th streets, you'll smell the cigar smoke coming from the sidewalk tables of the **Green Iguana Bar & Grill,** a refined establishment frequented by young professionals. The **Irish Pub** is just that, while **Fat Tuesday** has a large dance floor and long bar. Between 18th and 19th streets, you'll see **Harpo's** and **The Polyester Patio,** which don't extract a cover charge. Keep going across 19th Street to **The Beach Club,** the kind of noisy joint that advertises "no panties" on Thursday. Upstairs over Bubba's is one of Ybor's best clubs, **Blues Ship Café on Top,** which features live blues, jazz, and reggae. And last but not least is the warehouselike ✪ **Frankie's Patio Bar & Grill,** known for its reasonably priced food as well as its outstanding musical acts (see "Where to Dine," above). Across the avenue, country meets city at **Spurs in Ybor,** a country-and-western joint.

Lastly, comedy-lovers can get their laughs at **Key West on 7th,** between 20th and 21st streets.

Although not in the heart of Ybor's bar scene, the ✪ **Jazz Cellar,** on 9th Avenue East between 13th Street and Avenida de Republica de Cuba (14th Street), features contemporary jazz, rhythm and blues, and just plain blues. This basement establishment is on the north side of Ybor Square. Call ☎ **813/248-1862** for reservations.

Elsewhere in town, you can lose your life savings playing bingo, poker, and the video slot machines at the **Seminole Indian Casino,** 5223 N. Orient Rd., at Hillsborough Road east of the city (☎ **800/282-7016** or 813/621-1302). It's open 24 hours every day of the year.

THE PERFORMING ARTS   With a prime downtown location on 9 acres along the east bank of the Hillsborough River, the huge **Tampa Bay Performing Arts Center,** 1010 N. MacInnes Pl. (☎ **800/955-1045** or 813/229-STAR), is the largest performing-arts venue south of the Kennedy Center in Washington, D.C. Accordingly, this four-theater complex is the focal point of Tampa's performing arts scene, presenting a wide range of Broadway plays, classical and pop concerts, operas, cabarets, improv, and special events.

A sightseeing attraction in its own right, the restored ✪ **Tampa Theatre,** 711 Franklin St. (☎ **813/223-8981**), dates from 1926 and is on the National Register of Historic Places. It presents a varied program of classic, foreign, and alternative films, as well as concerts and special events.

The 74,301-seat **Houlihan's Stadium,** 4201 N. Dale Mabry Hwy. (☎ **813/673-4300**), is frequently the site of headliner concerts. The **USF Sun Dome,** 4202 E. Fowler Ave. (☎ **813/974-3111**), on the University of South Florida campus, hosts major concerts by touring pop stars, rock bands, jazz groups, and other contemporary artists.

2 St. Petersburg

20 miles SW of Tampa, 289 miles NW of Miami, 84 miles SW of Orlando

On the western shore of the bay, St. Petersburg stands in contrast to Tampa, much like San Francisco compares to Oakland in California. While Tampa is the area's business, industrial, and shipping center, St. Petersburg was conceived and built almost a century ago primarily for tourists and wintering snowbirds. Here you'll find one of the most picturesque and pleasant downtowns of any city in Florida, with a waterfront promenade and the famous, pyramid-shaped Pier offering great views across the bay, plus quality museums, interesting shops, and fine restaurants.

Away from downtown, the city pretty much consists of strip malls dividing residential neighborhoods, but plan at least to have a look around the charming bay-front area. If you don't do anything else, go out on The Pier and take a pleasant stroll along Bayshore Drive.

All is not completely happy in this urban paradise, however, for St. Petersburg was rocked by riots after a white police officer shot and killed a black motorist in late 1996. Although all was calm at press time, you should avoid the area south of I-175 and east of I-275.

ESSENTIALS

GETTING THERE   To reach downtown from Tampa, take I-275 or the Gandy Causeway (U.S. 92) across the bay, then I-275 south to I-375 east to the waterfront. From Sarasota and Bradenton, take I-275 north across the towering Sunshine Skyway ($2 toll) to I-175 or I-375 east. From points north, take congested U.S. 19 straight to downtown.

Tampa International Airport, approximately 16 miles northeast of St. Petersburg, is the prime gateway for the area (see "Getting There" in section 1, above). **St. Petersburg–Clearwater International Airport,** on Roosevelt Boulevard (Fla. 686) about 10 miles north of downtown St. Petersburg (☎ **727/535-7600**), primarily handles charter flights, although limited regular service is provided by two commuter carriers, **American Trans Air** (☎ **800/225-2995**) and **SunJet** (☎ **800/478-6538**). Incidentally, St. Petersburg–Clearwater International was the birthplace of commercial aviation, since the world's first scheduled carrier, the St. Petersburg–Tampa Airboat Line, took off from there in 1914.

All major car-rental firms are represented at the airports.

The Limo (☎ **800/282-6817** or 727/572-1111) and **Red Line Limo** (☎ **800/359-5466** or 727/535-3391) offer 24-hour van service between both Tampa International or St. Petersburg–Clearwater airports and any St. Petersburg area destination or hotel. The flat-rate, one-way fare is about $13 from the Tampa airport and $11.50 from the St. Petersburg–Clearwater airport to any St. Pete or gulf beach destination. **Yellow Cab Taxis** (☎ **727/821-7777**) line up outside baggage-claim areas. Average fare from the Tampa airport to St. Petersburg or any of the gulf beaches is about $25 to $35 per taxi (one or more passengers). The fare from the St. Petersburg–Clearwater airport is approximately $15 to $20.

Amtrak (☎ **800/USA-RAIL** for reservations) has rail service to Tampa (see "Getting There," in section 1).

VISITOR INFORMATION   For advance information about both St. Petersburg and the beaches, contact the **St. Petersburg/Clearwater Area Convention & Visitors Bureau,** 14450 46th St. N., Clearwater, FL 34622 (☎ **800/345-6710,** or

Downtown St. Petersburg

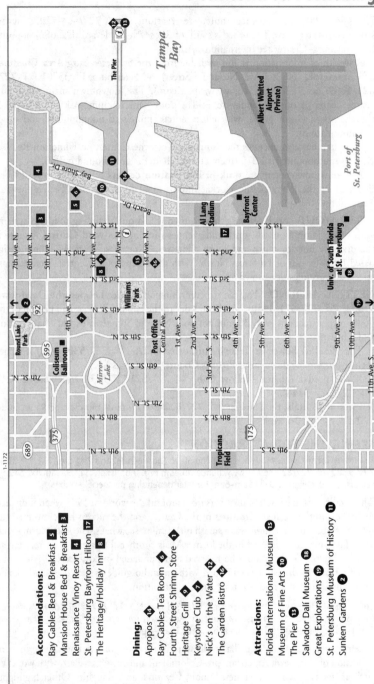

Accommodations:
Bay Gables Bed & Breakfast **5**
Mansion House Bed & Breakfast **3**
Renaissance Vinoy Resort **4**
St. Petersburg Bayfront Hilton **17**
The Heritage/Holiday Inn **8**

Dining:
Apropos **14**
Bay Gables Tea Room **6**
Fourth Street Shrimp Store **1**
Heritage Grill **9**
Keystone Club **7**
Nick's on the Water **12**
The Garden Bistro **16**

Attractions:
Florida International Museum **15**
Museum of Fine Arts **10**
The Pier **13**
Salvador Dalí Museum **18**
Great Explorations **19**
St. Petersburg Museum of History **11**
Sunken Gardens **2**

1-1172

383

727/464-7200 for advance hotel reservations; fax 727/464-7222; www.
stpete-clearwater.com). The office is south of Roosevelt Boulevard (Fla. 686) opposite
St. Petersburg–Clearwater International Airport.

A wealth of information is also available from the **St. Petersburg Area Chamber
of Commerce,** 100 2nd Ave. N. (at 1st Street), St. Petersburg, FL 33701 (☎ 727/
821-4069; fax 727/895-6326; www.stpete.com). This downtown main office and
visitor center is open Monday to Friday from 8am to 5pm. Ask for a copy of
the chamber's visitor guide, which lists hotels, motels, condominiums, and other
accommodations.

The chamber also operates the **Suncoast Welcome Center,** on Ulmerton Road at
Exit 18 southbound off I-275 (there's no exit here for northbound traffic).

Also downtown, there are **walk-in information centers** on the first level of The
Pier and in the lobby of the Florida International Museum (see "Seeing the Top
Attractions," below).

CITY LAYOUT   St. Petersburg's **downtown** is laid out according to a grid system,
with streets running north-south and avenues running east-west. **Central Avenue** is
the dividing line for north and south addresses. "Northeast" avenues—those designated NE—lie east of 1st Street North. With the exception of Central Avenue, most
streets and avenues downtown are one way.

GETTING AROUND   You can see everything on the free **Looper: the Downtown
Trolley** (☎ 727/571-3440), which runs out to the end of The Pier and past all of the
downtown attractions every 30 minutes from 11am to 5pm daily except Thanksgiving
and Christmas.

The **Pinellas Suncoast Transit Authority/PSTA** (☎ 727/530-9911) operates
regular bus service throughout Pinellas County. The fare is $1.

If you need a cab, call **Yellow Cab** (☎ 727/821-7777) or **Independent Cab**
(☎ 727/327-3444).

Pierside Rentals, on The Pier (☎ 727/822-8697), rents bicycles for $5 an hour,
$20 a day, or $50 a week.

SEEING THE TOP ATTRACTIONS

Florida International Museum. 100 2nd St. N. (between 1st and 2nd aves. N.). ☎ **800/
777-9882** or 727/822-3693. www.floridamuseum.org. Admission $13.95 adults, $12.95
seniors, $5.95 children. Daily 9am–6pm (or later depending on special exhibits).

This facility attracted 600,000 visitors from around the world in 1995 when it opened
its first exhibition, called "Treasures of the Czars," and the success has continued (its
recent exhibit on the *Titanic* was a smash hit). Call to see what's scheduled during your
visit. The museum is housed in the former Maas Brothers Department Store, long an
area landmark. Tickets should be reserved and purchased in advance to be sure of a
specific time. Each visitor is equipped with an audio guide as part of the admission
price; allow at least 2 hours to tour a major exhibition.

Museum of Fine Arts. 255 Beach Dr. NE (at 3rd Ave. N.). ☎ **727/896-2667.** Admission
Mon–Sat $6 adults, $5 seniors, $2 students. Admission free on Sun. Tues–Sat 10am–5pm,
Sun 1–5pm; winter, third Thurs of each month 10am–9pm.

Resembling a Mediterranean villa on the waterfront, this museum houses a permanent
collection of European, American, pre-Colombian, and Far Eastern art, with works by
such artists as Fragonard, Monet, Renoir, Cézanne, and Gauguin. Other highlights
include period rooms with antiques and historical furnishings, plus a gallery of
Steuben crystal, a new decorative-arts gallery, and world-class rotating exhibits.

The Pier. 800 2nd Ave. NE. ☎ **727/821-6164.** www.stpete-pier.com. Free admission to all the public areas and decks; donations welcome at the aquarium. Valet parking $5, self-parking $3. Pier Mon–Sat 10am–9pm, Sun 11am–6pm. Aquarium Mon–Sat 10am–8pm, Sun noon–6pm. Restaurant hours vary.

Walk or ride out on The Pier and enjoy this festive waterfront dining and shopping complex overlooking Tampa Bay. Originally built as a railroad pier in 1889, today it's capped by a spaceshiplike inverted pyramid offering five levels of shops and restaurants, plus an aquarium, tourist information desk, observation deck, catwalks for fishing, boat docks, a small bay-side beach, miniature golf, boat and water-sports rentals, sightseeing boats, and a food court. You can rent boats and go on cruises from here (see "Outdoor Activities & Spectators Sports," below), and from November to April climb aboard the *H.M.S. Bounty,* a replica of the famous vessel built in 1960 for the Marlon Brando version of *Mutiny on the Bounty* (30-minute tours of the ship cost $5 for adults, $4 for seniors, and $3 for kids 5 to 17; call ☎ **727/896-5668** for more information). A free trolley service operates between The Pier and the parking lots on shore.

✪ **Salvador Dalí Museum.** 1000 3rd St. S. (near 11th Ave. S.). ☎ **727/823-3767.** Admission $8 adults, $7 seniors, $4 students, free for children 9 and under. Mon–Wed 9:30am–5:30pm, Thurs 9:30am–8pm, Fri–Sat 9:30am–5:30pm, Sun noon–5pm. Closed Thanksgiving and Christmas.

Located on Tampa Bay south of The Pier, this starkly modern museum houses the world's largest collection of works by the renowned Spanish surrealist. Valued at over $150 million, it includes 94 oil paintings, more than 100 watercolors and drawings, and 1,300 graphics, plus posters, photos, sculptures, objets d'art, and a 5,000-volume library on Dalí and surrealism. There also are special exhibits of works by other famous artists.

MORE ATTRACTIONS

Great Explorations: The Hands On Museum. 1120 4th St. S. (at 11th Ave. S.). ☎ **727/821-8885.** Admission $5, free for children 2 and under. Mon–Sat 10am–5pm, Sun noon–5pm.

With a variety of hands-on exhibits, this museum is great for a rainy day or for kids who've overdosed on the sun and need to cool off indoors. They can explore a long, dark tunnel; measure their strength, flexibility, and fitness; paint a work of art with sunlight; and play a melody with a sweep of the hand.

St. Petersburg Museum of History. 335 2nd Ave. NE. ☎ **727/894-1052.** Admission $4 adults, $3.50 seniors, $1.50 children 7–17, free for children 6 and under. Mon–Sat 10am–5pm, Sun 1–5pm.

Located at the foot of The Pier, this museum features a permanent interactive exhibition chronicling St. Petersburg's history, ranging from prehistoric artifacts to documents, clothing, and photographs. There are also computer stations where you can "flip through the past." Walk-through exhibits include a replica of the Benoist airboat, which made the world's first scheduled commercial flight from St. Petersburg in 1914.

Sunken Gardens. 1825 4th St. N. (between 18th and 19th aves. NE). ☎ **727/896-3186.** Admission $14 adults, $8 children 3–11, free for children 2 and under. Daily 9:30am–5pm.

One of the city's oldest attractions, this 7-acre tropical garden park dating back to 1935 is a holdover from Florida's early tourist days. It contains a vast array of 5,000 plants, flowers, and trees, and there are bird and alligator shows.

OUTDOOR ACTIVITIES & SPECTATOR SPORTS

You can get up-to-the-minute recorded information about the city's sports and recreational activities by calling the **Leisure Line** (☎ 727/893-7500).

BIKING   With miles of flat terrain, the St. Petersburg area is ideal for bikers, in-line skaters, and hikers. The **Pinellas Trail** is especially good, since it follows an abandoned railroad bed 47 miles from St. Petersburg north to Tarpon Springs. The St. Pete trailhead is on 34th Street South (U.S. 19) between 8th and Fairfield avenues south. It's packed on the weekends. Free strip maps of the trail are available at the St. Petersburg Area Chamber of Commerce (see "Visitor Information," above).

It's a long way from the trailhead, but you can rent bikes from **Pierside Rentals** on The Pier (see "Getting Around," above, and "Boat Rentals," below).

BOAT RENTALS   On The Pier, **Pierside Rentals** (☎ 727/363-0000) rents Wave-Runners and jet boats. Prices for WaveRunners begin at $45 for an hour; for jet boats, from $55 per hour. Open daily from 9am to dusk.

CRUISES   The *Caribbean Queen* (☎ 727/895-BOAT) departs from The Pier and offers 1-hour sightseeing and dolphin-watching cruises around Tampa Bay. Sailings are daily at 1, 3, and 5pm; they cost $10 for adults, $8 for seniors and juniors 12 to 17, $5 for children 3 to 11, and free for children 2 and under.

GOLF   One of the nation's top 50 municipal courses, the ✪ **Mangrove Bay Golf Course,** 875 62nd Ave. NE (☎ 727/893-7797), hugs the inlets of Old Tampa Bay and offers 18-hole, par-72 play. Facilities include a driving range; lessons and golf-club rental are also available. Fees are about $22, $32 including a cart in winter, slightly lower off-season. Open daily from 6:30am to 6pm.

The city also operates the challenging, par-3 **Twin Brooks Golf Course,** 3800 22nd Ave. S. (☎ 727/893-7445).

In Largo, the **Bardmoor Golf Club,** 7919 Bardmoor Blvd. (☎ 727/397-0483), is often the venue for major tournaments. Lakes punctuate 17 of the 18 holes on this par-72 championship course. Lessons and rental clubs are available, as is a Tom Fazio–designed practice range. Call the clubhouse for seasonal greens fees. Open daily from 7am to dusk.

Adjacent to the St. Petersburg–Clearwater airport, the **Airco Flite Golf Course,** 3650 Roosevelt Blvd., Clearwater (☎ 727/573-4653), is a championship 18-hole, par-72 course with a driving range. Golf-club rentals are also available. Greens fees including cart range from $25 to $35 in winter, about $20 off-season. Open daily from 7am to 6pm.

Call **Tee Times USA** (☎ 800/374-8633) to reserve times at these and other area courses.

If you want to take up golf or sharpen your game, TV "Golf Doctor" Joe Quinzi hosts his **Quinzi Golf Academy** (☎ 727/725-1999) at the Safety Harbor Resort and Spa (see "Where to Stay," below). His school offers personalized instructions and clinics for up to six players.

SAILING   The **Annapolis Sailing School,** 6800 Sunshine Skyway Lane S. (☎ 800/638-9192 or 727/867-8102), almost at the foot of the Sunshine Skyway bridge, can teach you to sail or perfect your sailing skills. Various courses are offered at this branch of the famous Maryland-based school, lasting 2, 5, or 8 days. Prices range from $250 to $2,215 per person, depending on season and length of course.

The school is based at the **Holiday Inn SunSpree Resort,** 6800 Sunshine Skyway Lane S., St. Petersburg, FL 33711 (☎ 800/227-8045 or 727/867-1151), a recently renovated motel where doubles range from $89 to $159 in winter, $69 to $129 off-season.

SPECTATOR SPORTS   St. Petersburg has always been a baseball town, and **Tropicana Field,** a 45,000-seat domed stadium alongside I-175 between 9th and 16th streets south, is the home of the **Tampa Bay Devil Rays,** the area's expansion team which began American League play 1998. The season runs from April through September. Call ☎ 727/898-RAYS for schedule and ticket information. The Devil Rays move outdoors to Al Lang Stadium, on 2nd Avenue South at 1st Street South (☎ 727/822-3384), for their spring training games from mid-February through March. Tickets to the spring games range from $3 to $12.

The **Philadelphia Phillies** play their spring-training season at Jack Russell Stadium, 800 Phillies Dr., in nearby Clearwater (☎ 727/442-8496). Admission is $8 to $9. Their minor league **Clearwater Phillies** play in the stadium from April to September. Grant Field, 373 Douglas Ave. in Dunedin (☎ 727/733-0429), is the winter home of the **Toronto Blue Jays.**

SHOPPING

The Pier, at the end of 2nd Avenue NE (☎ 727/821-6164), houses more than a dozen boutiques and craft shops, but nearby Beach Drive, running along the waterfront, is one of the most fashionable downtown strolling and shopping venues. Here you'll find the **Glass Canvas Gallery,** at 4th Avenue NE (☎ 727/821-6767), featuring a dazzling array of glass sculpture, tableware, art, and craft items by 250 local, national, and international artists. Also at 4th Avenue NE, **P. Buckley Moss** (☎ 727/894-2899), a museum-grade store carrying the works of the individualistic artist best known for her portrayal of the Amish and the Mennonites. The works include paintings, graphics, figurines, and collector dolls. **Red Cloud,** between 1st and 2nd avenues (☎ 727/821-5824), is an oasis for Native American crafts, from jewelry and headdresses to sculpture and art.

Central Avenue is another shopping area, featuring the **Gas Plant Antique Arcade,** between 12th and 13th streets (☎ 727/895-0368), the largest antique mall on Florida's west coast, with over 100 dealers displaying their wares. The **Florida Craftsmen Gallery,** at 5th Street (☎ 727/821-7391), is a showcase for the works of more than 150 Florida artisans and craftspeople: jewelry, ceramics, woodwork, fiber works, glassware, paper creations, and metalwork. And **Haslam's,** between 20th and 21st streets west (☎ 727/822-8616), claims to be Florida's largest bookstore, with more than 300,000 new and used volumes.

In the suburbs, outlet shoppers can browse Corning Revere, Linens 'N Things, BonWorth, Dress Barn, Van Heusen, Bugle Boy, L'eggs, Bass Shoes, T.J. Maxx, and more at the air-conditioned **Bay Area Outlet Mall,** at the intersection of U.S. 19 and East Bay Drive (☎ 727/535-2337), west of St. Petersburg-Clearwater International Airport.

WHERE TO STAY

Ask the **St. Petersburg Area Chamber of Commerce** (see "Essentials," above) for a copy of its visitor guide, which lists a wide range of hotels, motels, condominiums, and other accommodations. In addition, the St. Petersburg/Clearwater Convention & Visitors Bureau has a free **reservations service** (☎ 800/345-6710).

You'll find plenty of chain motels along U.S. 19.

With regard to prices, the high season is from January to April. The hotel tax rate in Pinellas County is 11%.

VERY EXPENSIVE

✪ **Renaissance Vinoy Resort.** 501 5th Ave. NE (at Beach Dr.), St. Petersburg, FL 33701.
☎ **800/HOTELS-1** or 727/894-1000. Fax 727/822-2785. 360 units. A/C MINIBAR TV TEL.
Winter $265–$365 double. Off-season $145–$235 double. AE, DC, DISC, MC, V. Valet parking
$12; self-parking $8.

Built as the Vinoy Park in 1925 during Florida's heyday of grand hotels, this elegant
Spanish-style establishment reopened in 1992 after a total and meticulous $93 million
restoration that has made it more luxurious than ever. Dominating the northern part
of downtown, it overlooks Tampa Bay and is within walking distance of The Pier,
Central Avenue, museums, and other attractions. All the guest rooms, many of which
enjoy lovely views of the bay front, are designed to offer the utmost in comfort and
include three phones, an additional TV in the bathroom, hair dryer, bath scales, and
more; some units in the new wing also have whirlpools and private patios/balconies.

Dining/Diversions: Marchand's Grille, an elegant room overlooking the bay, specializes in steaks, seafood, and chops. The Terrace Room is the main dining room for
breakfast, lunch, and dinner. Casual lunches and dinners are available at the indoor-
outdoor Alfresco, near the pool deck, and at the Clubhouse at the golf course on Snell
Isle. There are also two bar/lounges.

Amenities: Concierge, 24-hour room service, laundry service, tour desk, child care,
complimentary coffee and newspaper with wake-up call. Two swimming pools (connected by a roaring waterfall), 14-court tennis complex (9 lighted), 18-hole private
championship golf course on nearby Snell Isle, private 74-slip marina, two croquet
courts, fitness center (with sauna, steam room, spa, massage, and exercise equipment),
access to two bay-side beaches, shuttle service to gulf beaches, hair salon, gift shop.

MODERATE

Mansion House Bed & Breakfast. 105 5th Ave. NE (at 1st St. N.), St. Petersburg, FL 33701.
☎ **800/274-7520** or 727/821-9391. Fax 727/821-9391 (same as phone). www.mansion-
bandb.com. 6 units (all with bathroom). A/C. Winter $110–$150 double. Off-season
$95–$130 double. Rates include full breakfast. AE, MC, V.

This two-story, shingle-and-stucco house was built in 1904 by a local doctor and
extensively renovated in 1991. Sporting a faux fireplace adorned with hand-painted
tiles, the comfortable living room opens to a sunroom, off which a small screened
porch provides mosquito-free lounging and the only place where guests can smoke
here. There's another front parlor upstairs with a TV. Tall, old-fashioned windows let
lots of light into the attractive guest rooms. The "Pembrooke" room actually is upstairs
over the carriage house; it has its own refrigerator, phone, TV, and four-poster bed
with mosquito net. In an unusual architectural twist, the "Harlech" room has a toilet
and hand basin in one converted closet, a shower in another. Proprietors Rob and
Rosie Ray serve a full breakfast in two formal dining rooms and keep fruit bowls and
snacks available at all hours. There's a whirlpool bath in its own screened hut in the
backyard.

St. Petersburg Bayfront Hilton. 333 1st St. S. (between 3rd and 4th aves. S., opposite
Al Lang Field), St. Petersburg, FL 33701. ☎ **800/HILTONS** or 727/894-5000. Fax 727/
823-4797. 333 units. A/C TV TEL. Winter $159 double. Off-season $119 double. Packages
available. AE, DC, MC, V.

This 15-story convention hotel has a spacious lobby with a rich decor of marble,
crystal, tile, antiques, artwork, and potted trees and plants. The bedrooms are furnished with traditional dark woods, floral fabrics, a king-size bed or two double beds,
and an executive desk; many have views of the bay. Cafe 333 is a full-service restaurant specializing in continental cuisine, while the First Street Deli provides light fare.

Brandi's Lobby Bar has piano entertainment. Facilities include an outdoor heated swimming pool, whirlpool, health club with a sauna, and gift shop.

INEXPENSIVE

Bay Gables Bed & Breakfast. 136 4th Ave. NE (between Beach Dr. and 1st St. N), St. Petersburg, FL 33701. ☎ **800/822-8803** or 727/822-8855. Fax 727/824-7223. 9 units. A/C. $85–$135 double. Rates include continental breakfast. MC, V.

You can walk to The Pier from this charming B&B, which was built in the 1930s. It overlooks a flower-filled garden with a gazebo and faces a fanciful Victorian-style house whose first floor is a tearoom/restaurant (see "Where to Dine," below). The guest rooms have been furnished with ceiling fans and Victorian pieces, including some canopy beds. All units have bathrooms with claw-foot tubs and modern showers; half of the rooms have a porch, while the rest have a separate sitting room and kitchenette. Continental breakfast is served in the common room, on the garden deck, or in the gazebo. This is a professionally managed operation; the owners don't live on the premises.

✪ **Heritage/Holiday Inn.** 234 3rd Ave. N. (between 2nd and 3rd sts.), St. Petersburg, FL 33701. ☎ **800/283-7829** or 727/822-4814. Fax 727/823-1644. 71 units. A/C TV TEL. Winter $86–$107 double. Off-season $58–$74 double. Rates include continental breakfast. AE, DC, DISC, MC, V.

No ordinary Holiday Inn, the Heritage dates from the early 1920s and is the closest thing to a Southern mansion you'll find in the heart of downtown. With a sweeping veranda, French doors, and tropical courtyard, it attracts an eclectic clientele, from young families to seniors. The furnishings include period antiques. There's a heated swimming pool and a whirlpool in a small tropical courtyard between the main building and the Heritage Grill next door, one of the area's most popular restaurants (see "Where to Dine," below).

A NEARBY SPA

✪ **Safety Harbor Resort and Spa.** 105 N. Bayshore Dr., Safety Harbor, FL 34695. ☎ **800/BEST-SPA** or 727/726-1161. Fax 727/726-4268. www.southseas.com. 192 units. Winter $159–179 double. Off-season $109–$145 double. Packages from $134 per person double occupancy. AE, DC, DISC, MC, V.

Sanibel Island's excellent South Seas Resorts Company recently took over this tranquil, waterfront retreat on Old Tampa Bay and gave it a much-needed face-lift and upgrading. The full-service spa offers pampering from massages to hydrotherapy and a full menu of fitness classes from boxing to yoga. The resort sits on 22 waterfront acres in the sleepy town of Safety Harbor, north of St. Petersburg. Guests have been enjoying the curative mineral waters for more than 50 years and the water-fitness programs receive acclaim every year. This is also a good place to work on your game at the Quinzi Golf Academy (see "Outdoor Activities & Spectator Sports," above).

Dining: Nutritious menus emphasizing American fusion cuisine use lots of Florida ingredients in both the Spa Dining Room and the resort's Cafe, which is open to the public for lunch and dinner.

Amenities: Concierge, limited room service, laundry, valet parking. Clarins Skin Institute, spa salon, fitness center, Phil Green Tennis Academy, natural mineral springs.

WHERE TO DINE

Don't overlook the food court at **The Pier,** where the inexpensive chow is accompanied by a very rich, but quite free, view of the bay. Among the stalls, **Alessi Deli** is a good bet for salads, pastries, and coffee. Upstairs there's a branch of Tampa's famous **Columbia Restaurant** (see "Where to Dine" in section 1, above).

MODERATE

Apropos. 300 2nd Ave. NE (at Bayshore Dr.). ☎ **727/823-8934.** Reservations accepted only for dinner. Breakfast $3.50–$6; lunch $5–$9; dinner main courses $9–$16. DC, MC, V. Tues–Sat 7:30–10:30am and 11am–3pm; Thurs–Sun 6–10pm (Sun brunch 8:30am–2pm). AMERICAN.

Sitting at the foot of The Pier, Apropros is a fine place to breakfast before your tour of downtown, perhaps with a brie and bacon omelette, or a seasonal fruit plate, or just plain eggs. At lunch, the view through the masts in the adjacent marina sets the scene for the likes of shrimp and artichoke salad with a sherry mayonnaise dressing. And at dinner, you can choose from a blackboard offering the chef 's nightly nouveau cuisine selections. You'll find as many locals here as tourists.

Bay Gables Tea Room & Garden. 136 4th Ave. NE (between Beach Dr. and 1st St. N.). ☎ **727/822-0044.** Reservations recommended for lunch, required for afternoon tea. Main courses $6–$12 plus 18% service charge. MC, V. Mon–Sat 11am–2pm, afternoon tea at 3pm; Sun brunch 10am–2pm. AMERICAN.

Set in the beautifully restored 1910 Victorian Bay Gables Bed & Breakfast (see "Where to Stay," above), replete with Old Florida antiques and frilly trimmings, this spot less than 2 blocks from the bay-front caters mostly to the midday shopping crowd. Meals are served on heirloom china and silver in the cozy atmosphere of three small rooms and a tiny porch upstairs or on a wraparound ground-floor veranda. The menu is simple but freshly prepared, featuring salads, quiches, soups, and finger sandwiches.

Garden Bistro. 217 Central Ave. ☎ **727/896-3800.** Reservations recommended for dinner. Main courses $10–$16. AE, MC, V. Daily noon–2pm and 5–2am. MEDITERRANEAN.

A popular hot spot with those in the know, this lively restaurant combines European ambience with Moroccan cuisine. Choice seats are under huge shade trees in the garden, screened from the street by a trellis fence. Inside, the decor blends the American Southwest with the Mediterranean, with arches, a 19th-century tiled floor, modern local art, and lots of flowers and plants. The creative menu features couscous, a daily tajin (a traditional Moroccan stew), pastas such as wild mushrooms with strips of roast duck, and smoked salmon in a light cream sauce. On Friday and Saturday, live jazz adds to the ambience from 9pm to 1am.

Heritage Grill. 256 2nd St. N. (at 3rd Ave. N.). ☎ **727/823-6382.** Reservations recommended. Main courses $17–$20. AE, DC, DISC, MC, V. Mon–Fri 11:30am–2pm and 5:30–10pm, Sat 5:30–10pm. AMERICAN.

Next door to the Heritage/Holiday Inn (see "Where to Stay," above), this 1920s-vintage house has been transformed into a restaurant-cum-modern art gallery, with the walls displaying for-sale works by local artists. The colorful place mats are hand painted once a week, and even the waiters are part of the art scene—their tuxedo shirts also are hand-painted. For something old, look behind the bar as you enter: The ornate mahogany liquor and wine cabinet reportedly came from the Mississippi home of Confederate Pres. Jefferson Davis. When you're ready to dine, the menu offers dishes like sautéed macadamia nut-crusted chicken breast stuffed with prosciutto and sun-dried tomatoes and New Zealand lamb chops with a roasted garlic and rosemary demiglaze.

Keystone Club. 320 4th St. N. (between 3rd and 4th aves. N.). ☎ **727/822-6600.** Reservations recommended. Main courses $11–$23; early bird specials $7.50–$12. AE, DC, DISC, MC, V. Mon–Fri 11am–2:30pm and 5–10pm, Sat 4–10pm, Sun 4–9pm. Early bird specials winter only, Mon–Fri 4:30–5:30pm, Sat–Sun 4–5:30pm. STEAKS/PRIME RIB.

Resembling an exclusive men's club, this cozy restaurant's forest-green walls accented by dark wood and etched glass create an atmosphere that's reminiscent of a Manhattan-style chophouse. But women are also welcome to partake of the beef, which is king here. Specialties include roast prime rib, New York strip steak, and filet mignon. Seafood also makes an appearance, with fresh lobster and grouper at market price. During winter, "sunset" early bird specials include lunch-size portions, a beverage, and dessert.

INEXPENSIVE

✪ **Fourth Street Shrimp Store.** 1006 4th St. N. (at 10th Ave. N.). ☎ **727/822-0325.** Reservations not accepted. Sandwiches $2.50–$6; main courses $4–$12. MC, V. Sun–Thurs 11am–9pm, Fri–Sat 11am–10pm. SEAFOOD.

If you're anywhere in the area, don't miss at least driving by to see the colorful, cartoonlike mural on the outside of this eclectic establishment just north of downtown. On first impression it looks like graffiti, but it's actually a gigantic drawing of people eating. Inside, it gets even better, with paraphernalia and murals on two walls making the dining room seem like a warehouse with windows looking out on an early-19th-century seaport (one painted sailor permanently peers in to see what you're eating). You'll pass a seafood market counter when you enter, from which comes the fresh namesake shrimp, the star here. You can also pick from grouper, clam strips, catfish, or oysters fried, broiled, or steamed, all served in heaping portions. This is the best and certainly the most interesting bargain in town.

Nick's on the Water. On The Pier, east end of 2nd Ave. NE. ☎ **727/898-5800.** Reservations recommended for dinner. Main courses $8–$18. AE, DC, MC, V. Sun–Thurs 11:30am–10pm, Fri–Sat 11:30am–11pm. ITALIAN/SEAFOOD.

Located on the main level of The Pier, this informal restaurant offers expansive views of downtown St. Petersburg and the bay-front marina. The menu features a variety of Italian choices, including Nick's tortellini, but the specialty of the house is wood-fired fish, meats, and pizza. The veal dishes also are a big hit, especially the française, with sautéed medallions.

ST. PETERSBURG AFTER DARK

Good sources of nightlife information are the Friday "Weekend" section of the *St. Petersburg Times,* the "Baylife" and "Friday Extra" sections of the *Tampa Tribune,* and the *Weekly Planet,* a tabloid available at the visitor information offices and in many hotel and restaurant lobbies. The bimonthly magazine *Event Guide Tampa Bay* gives a rundown on what's going on.

THE CLUB & MUSIC SCENE   A historic attraction as well as an entertainment venue, the Moorish-style **Coliseum Ballroom,** 535 4th Ave. N. (☎ 727/892-5202), has been hosting dancing, big bands, boxing, and other events since 1924 (it even made an appearance in the 1985 movie *Cocoon*). An acquaintance of mine said it's fun to watch the town's many seniors doing the jitterbug just like it was 1945 again! Call for the schedule and prices.

A much younger set heads to the casual, downtown **Big Catch,** 9 1st St. NE (☎ 727/821-6444), featuring live and danceable rock and Top 40 hits, as well as darts, pool, and hoops. North of downtown, the **Ringside Cafe,** 2742 4th St. N. (☎ 727/894-8465), in a renovated boxing gymnasium, is an informal neighborhood cafe with a decided sports motif. The music focuses on jazz and blues (and sometimes reggae).

PERFORMING ARTS VENUES   **Tropicana Field,** 1 Stadium Dr. (☎ 727/ 825-3100), has a capacity of 50,000 for major concerts, but also hosts a variety of smaller events when the Devil Rays aren't playing baseball.

The **Bayfront Center,** 400 1st St. S. (☎ **727/892-5767,** or 727/892-5700 for recorded information), houses the 8,100-seat Bayfront Arena and the 2,000-seat Mahaffey Theater. The schedule includes a variety of concerts, Broadway shows, big bands, ice shows, and circus performances.

3 The St. Pete & Clearwater Beaches

If you're looking for sun and sand, you'll find plenty of both on the 28 miles of slim barrier islands that skirt the gulf shore of the Pinellas Peninsula. With some one million visitors coming here every year, don't be surprised if you have lots of company. But you'll also discover quieter neighborhoods geared to families, and this area has some of the nation's finest beaches, which are protected from development by parks and nature preserves.

At the southern end of the strip, St. Pete Beach is the granddaddy of the area's resorts. In fact, visitors started coming here nearly a century ago, and they haven't quit. Today St. Pete Beach is heavily developed and often overcrowded during the winter season. If you like high-rises and mile-a-minute action, St. Pete Beach is for you. But even here, Pass-a-Grille, on the island's southern end, is a quiet residential enclave with eclectic shops and a fine public beach.

A more gentle lifestyle begins just to the north on 3½-mile-long Treasure Island. From there, you cross famous John's Pass to Sand Key, a 12-mile island occupied by primarily residential Madeira Beach, Redington Beach, North Redington Beach, Redington Shores, Indian Shores, Indian Rocks Beach, and Belleair Beach. Finally the road crosses a soaring bridge to Clearwater Beach, whose silky sands attract active families and couples.

If you like your great outdoors unfettered by development, the jewels here are Fort Desoto Park, down below St. Pete Beach at the mouth of Tampa Bay, and Caladesi Island State Park, north of Clearwater Beach. They are consistently rated among America's top beaches. And Sand Key Park, looking at Clearwater Beach from the southern shores of Little Pass, is one of Florida's finest local beach parks.

ESSENTIALS

GETTING THERE   To reach St. Pete Beach and Treasure Island from I-275, take Exit 4 and follow the Pinellas Bayway (Fla. 682) west (50¢ toll). For Indian Rocks Beach, take Exit 18 and follow Ulmerton Road due west to the gulf. For the Redington beaches, take Exit 15 and follow Gandy and Park boulevards (Fla. 694) due west (Park Boulevard also is known as 74th Avenue North). For Clearwater Beach, take the Courtney Campbell Causeway (Fla. 60) west from Tampa; the causeway becomes Gulf-to-Bay Boulevard (also Fla. 60), which leads straight west into Clearwater.

See "Getting There" in sections 1 and 2 for information about flights to, and transportation from, Tampa International and St. Petersburg–Clearwater International airports.

VISITOR INFORMATION   See "Visitor Information" in section 2 for the St. Petersburg/Clearwater Area Convention & Visitors Bureau and the St. Petersburg Area Chamber of Commerce. You can get information specific to the beaches from the **Gulf Beaches of Tampa Bay Chamber of Commerce,** 6990 Gulf Blvd. (at 70th Avenue), St. Pete Beach, FL 33706 (☎ **800/944-1847** or 727/360-6957; fax

St. Pete & Clearwater Beaches

Accommodations:
Beach Haven **17**
Belleview Biltmore
    Resort & Spa **1**
Best Western Sea
    Stone Resort **28**
Captain's Quarters Inn **9**
Clearwater Beach Hotel **22**
Colonial Gateway Inn **10**
Days Inn Island
    Beach Resort **12**
Don CeSar Beach
    Resort and Spa **18**
Great Heron Inn **4**
Island's End Resort **20**
Palm Pavilion Inn **21**
Pelican—East & West **2**
Radisson Sandpiper
    Beach Resort **14**
Radisson Suite Resort
    on Sand Key **30**
Sheraton Sand Key
    Resort **29**
Sun West Beach Motel **27**
TradeWinds Resort **16**

Dining:
Bob Heilman's
    Beachcomber **24**
Bubby's Bistro
    & Wine Bar **25**
Crabby Bill's **15**
Frenchy's Cafe **23**
Guppy's **3**
Hurricane **19**
Internet Outpost **11**
Lobster Pot **6**
Omi's Bavarian Inn **8**
Seafood & Sunsets
    at Julie's **26**
Scandia **5**
Skidder's **13**
The Wine Cellar **7**

727/360-2233). The main office is open Monday to Friday from 9am to 5pm. The chamber also has welcome centers at 501 150th Ave. in Maderia Beach (☎ 727/391-7373); at 105 5th Ave. in Indian Rocks Beach (☎ 727/595-4575); and at 152 108th Ave. in Treasure Island (☎ 727/367-4529).

For advance information about Clearwater Beach, contact the **Greater Clearwater Chamber of Commerce,** 128 N. Osceola Ave. (P.O. Box 2457), Clearwater, FL 34615 (☎ **727/461-0011**).

CITY LAYOUT   These barrier islands are barely wide enough to accommodate **Gulf Boulevard,** the main drag that runs all the way from St. Pete Beach north to the top of Sand Key. Once you cross Little Pass into Clearwater Beach, **Gulfview Boulevard** and **Mandalay Avenue** become the central north-south arteries.

Street addresses are geared to the short, numbered avenues crossing the main drags; they increase as you go north from 1st Avenue in Pass-a-Grille to 200th Avenue in Indian Rocks Beach, where the numbering begins all over again with another 1st Avenue. The Pinellas Byway comes onto St. Pete Beach at 34th Avenue, so turn right and head north on Gulf Boulevard to reach street addresses above 3400; turn left, or south, for lower numbers. Street numbers in Clearwater Beach start at Little Pass and increase as you go north.

GETTING AROUND   **BATS City Transit** (☎ **727/367-3086**) offers bus service along the St. Pete Beach strip. The fare is $1.

Treasure Island Transit System (☎ **727/547-4575**) runs buses along the Treasure Island strip. The fare is $1.

The **Jolley Trolley** (☎ **727/445-1200**), operated in conjunction with the City of Clearwater, provides service in the Clearwater Beach area, from downtown to the beaches as far south as Sand Key. It also goes to the Belleview Biltmore Resort & Spa (see "Where to Stay," below). The ride costs 25¢.

Along the beach, the major cab company is **BATS Taxi** (☎ **727/367-3702**).

Water Taxis operate along the bay side of the islands Tuesday to Sunday from 11am to 1am (☎ **727/323-8294**). It's best to call for reservations. Rides cost $5 per person one way, or you can buy an all-day pass for $15 per person.

You can rent bicycles and scooters in St. Pete Beach from **Beach Cyclist Sports Center,** 7517 Blind Pass Rd. (☎ **727/367-5001**), and **Cycle & Scooter Services,** 7116-A Gulf Blvd. In Clearwater Beach, contact **Transportation Station,** 652 Gulfview Blvd. (☎ **727/443-3188**). See "Outdoor Activities," below, for more information.

HITTING THE BEACH

This entire stretch of coast is one long beach, but since hotels, condominiums, and private homes occupy much of it, you may want to sun and swim at one of the area's public parks. The very best are described below, but there's also the fine **Pass-a-Grille Public Beach,** on the southern end of St. Pete Beach, where you can watch the boats going in and out of Pass-a-Grille Channel. This and all other Pinellas County public beaches have metered parking lots, so bring a supply of quarters.

Clearwater Public Beach has beach volleyball, water-sports rentals, lifeguards, rest rooms, showers, and concessions. The swimming is excellent, and there's a children's playground and a pier for fishing. Gated municipal parking lots here cost $1 per hour or $7 a day. The lots are right across the street from Clearwater Beach Marina, a prime base for boating, cruises, and other waterborne activities (see "Outdoor Activities," below).

✪ **CALADESI ISLAND STATE PARK**   Occupying a 3½-mile island north of Clearwater Beach, **Caladesi Island State Park** boasts a lovely, relatively secluded beach with fine soft sand edged in sea grass and palmettos. Dolphins cavort in the waters offshore. In the park itself, there's a nature trail, and you might see one of the rattlesnakes, black racers, raccoons, armadillos, or rabbits that live here. A concession stand, ranger station, and bathhouses (with rest rooms and showers) are available. Caladesi Island is accessible only by ferry from **Honeymoon Island State Recreation Area**, which is connected by Causeway Boulevard to Dunedin, north of Clearwater. (Honeymoon Island isn't great for swimming, but it has its own rugged beauty and a fascinating nature trail.) You'll first have to pay the admission to Honeymoon Island: $4 per vehicle with two to eight occupants, $2 per single-occupant vehicle, $1 for pedestrians and bicyclists. Beginning daily at 10am, the ferry departs Honeymoon Island every hour on winter weekdays, every 30 minutes on summer weekdays, and every 30 minutes on weekends year-round. Rides cost $6 for adults and $3.50 for kids. The two parks are open daily from 8am to sunset. The two islands are administered by **Gulf Islands Geopark,** no. 1 Causeway Blvd., Dunedin, FL 34698 (☎ **727/469-5942**).

✪ **FORT DESOTO PARK**   South of St. Pete Beach at the very mouth of Tampa Bay, this group of five connected barrier islands has been set aside by Pinellas County as a 900-acre bird, animal, and plant sanctuary. Besides the stunning white-sugar sand beach (where you can watch the manatees and dolphins play offshore), there's a Spanish American War–era fort, great fishing from piers, a large playground for kids, and 4 miles of trails winding through the park for in-line skaters, bicyclists, and joggers.

Sitting on an island by themselves, the park's 230 campsites all have water and electricity hookups, but they usually are sold out, especially on weekends. Sites cost $18.76 a night. To make reservations, you must appear *in person* and pay for your site no more than 30 days in advance at the campground office, at 631 Chestnut St. in Clearwater, or at 150 5th St. North in downtown St. Petersburg. You must camp here at least 2 nights, but you can stay no more than 14 nights. The park is open from 8am to dusk, although campers and persons fishing from the piers can stay later. Admission is free. To get here, take the Pinellas Byway (50¢ toll) east from St. Pete Beach and follow Fla. 679 (35¢ toll) and the signs south to the park. For more information, contact the park at 3500 Pinellas Bayway, Tierra Verde, FL 33715 (☎ **727/866-2662**).

SAND KEY PARK   This fine county park on the northern tip of Sand Key facing Clearwater Beach sports a wide beach and gentle surf and is relatively off the beaten path in this commercial area. It's great to get out of the hotel for a morning walk or jog here. Open 8am to dark. Admission is free, but the parking lot has meters. For more information, call ☎ **727/464-3347.**

OUTDOOR ACTIVITIES

BICYCLING & IN-LINE SKATING   With miles of flat terrain and paved roads, the beach area is ideal for bikers and in-line skaters, and the 47-mile-long Pinellas Trail runs close by on the mainland (see "Outdoor Activities & Spectator Sports," in section 2, above). In St. Pete Beach, you can rent bicycles, skates, and scooters from **Beach Cyclist Sports Center,** 7517 Blind Pass Rd. (☎ **727/367-5001**), and **Cycle & Scooter Services,** 7116-A Gulf Blvd. In Clearwater Beach, contact **Transportation Station,** 652 Gulfview Blvd. (☎ **727/443-3188**). Bikes at all three range from about $5 per hour to $20 a day; scooters, about $13 a hour to $40 per day.

BOATING, FISHING & OTHER WATER SPORTS   You can indulge in parasailing, boating, deep-sea fishing, wave running, sightseeing, dolphin watching, waterskiing, and just about any other waterborne diversion your heart could desire here. All you have to do is head to one of two beach locations: **Hubbard's Marina,** at John's Pass Village and Boardwalk (☎ 727/393-1947), in Madeira Beach on the southern tip of Sand Key; or **Clearwater Beach Marina,** at Coronado Drive and Causeway Boulevard (☎ 800/772-4479 or 727/461-3133), which is at the beach end of the causeway leading to downtown Clearwater. Agents in booths there will give you the schedules and prices, answer any questions you have, and make reservations if necessary. Go in the early morning to set up today's activities, or in the afternoon to book tomorrow's.

CRUISES   The **Shell Key Shuttle,** Merry Pier, 801 Pass-a-Grille Way in southern St. Pete Beach (☎ 727/360-1348), uses a 57-passenger catamaran to shuttle out to Shell Island, one of Florida's last completely undeveloped barrier islands. It's great for bird-watchers, who could spot a remarkable 88 different species, including some of North America's rarest shorebirds. Boats leave daily at 10am, noon, and 2pm, plus 4pm in summer. Prices are $10 for adults, $5 for children 12 and under. The ride takes 15 minutes, and you can return on any shuttle you wish. Departing Hubbard's Marina at John's Pass Village and Boardwalk in Madeira Beach, **Shell Island Adventure** (☎ 727/399-9633) has a 5-hour daily trip to the island, including a barbecue lunch for $27 adults, $15 for kids, and you can rent beach chairs, umbrellas, snorkeling gear, and other equipment once you get there.

   Captain Memo's Pirate Cruise, at Clearwater Beach Marina (☎ 727/446-2587), sails the *Pirate's Ransom,* an authentic reproduction of a pirate ship, on 2-hour daytime "pirate cruises" as well as sunset and evening champagne cruises. Cruises operate year-round, daily at 10am and 2, 4:30, and 7pm. For adults, daytime or sunset cruises cost $27; evening cruises, $30; both daytime and evening cruises cost $20 for seniors and juniors 13 to 17, $17 for children 2 to 12, free for children under 2.

   Two paddle-wheel riverboats operate here: The ***Show Queen*** has lunch, sunset dinner, and Sunday brunch cruises from Clearwater Beach Marina (☎ 727/461-3113). The *Starlite Princess* does likewise from 3400 Pasadena Ave. S. (☎ 727/462-2628), at the eastern side of the Corey Causeway linking St. Pete Beach to the mainland. Call for schedules and prices.

ATTRACTIONS ON LAND

Clearwater Marine Aquarium. 249 Windward Passage, Clearwater. ☎ **727/447-0980.** Admission $6.75 adults, $4.25 children 3–11, free for children 2 and under. Mon–Fri 9am–5pm, Sat 9am–4pm, Sun 11am–4pm. The aquarium is off the causeway between Clearwater and Clearwater Beach; follow the signs.

This little jewel of an aquarium on Clearwater Harbor is very low key and friendly; it's dedicated to the rescue and rehabilitation of marine mammals and sea turtles. Exhibits include dolphins, otters, sea turtles, sharks, stingrays, mangroves, and sea grass.

✪ **John's Pass Village and Boardwalk.** 12901 Gulf Blvd. (at John's Pass), Madeira Beach. ☎ **800/944-1847** or 727/397-1511. Free admission. Shops and activities daily 9am–6pm or later.

Casual and charming, this Old Florida fishing village on John's Pass consists of a string of simple wooden structures topped by tin roofs and connected by a 1,000-foot boardwalk. Most of the buildings have been converted into shops, art galleries, restaurants, and saloons. The focal point is the boardwalk and marina, where many water sports are available for visitors (see "Outdoor Activities," above).

✪ **Suncoast Seabird Sanctuary.** 18328 Gulf Blvd., Indian Shores. ☎ **727/391-6211.** Free admission, donations welcome. Daily 9am–dusk. Free tours Wed and Sun 2pm.

At any one time there are usually more than 500 sea and land birds living at the sanctuary, from cormorants, white herons, and birds of prey to the ubiquitous brown pelican. The nation's largest wild-bird hospital, dedicated to the rescue, repair, recuperation, and release of sick and injured wild birds, is also here.

The Tampa Bay Holocaust Memorial and Educational Research Center. 55 5th St. S., at Duhme Rd. (113th St. N.), Madeira Beach. ☎ **727/821-8261.** Admission by $6 donation adults, $5 seniors. Mon–Fri 10am–4pm, Sun noon–4pm.

Situated on the mainland grounds of the Jewish Community Center of Pinellas County, this thought-provoking museum has exhibits about the Holocaust, including a boxcar used to transport human cargo to the Auschwitz death camp in Poland. Its main focus, however, is to promote tolerance and understanding in the present. It was founded by Walter P. Loebenberg, a local businessman who escaped Nazi Germany in 1939 and fought with the U.S. Army in World War II.

SHOPPING

In addition to being a sightseeing attraction here, **John's Pass Village and Boardwalk,** on John's Pass in Madeira Beach, just north of Treasure Island (☎ 727/391-7373), is the key shopping venue on the beaches. The houses of this old fishermen's village have been converted into more than 60 shops selling everything from antiques and beachwear to every souvenir you can imagine. There are also several art galleries, including the **Bronze Lady,** featuring the world's collection of works by the late comedian-artist Red Skelton, best known for his numerous clown paintings. The shops here are open daily from 9am to 6pm or later.

If you're in the market for some one-of-a-kind hand-hammered jewelry, try **Evander Preston Contemporary Jewelry,** 106 8th Ave., Pass-a-Grille (☎ 727/367-7894), a unique gallery/workshop housed in a 75-year-old building in Pass-a-Grille's small business district. Open Monday to Saturday from 10am to 5:30pm.

Among the shops in St. Pete Beach's Corey Landings Area, the town's original business strip along 75th Street east of Gulf Boulevard, **The Shell Store** (☎ 727/360-0586) specializes in corals and shells, with an on-premises minimuseum illustrating how they live and grow. There's a good selection of shell home decorations, shell hobbyist supplies, shell art, planters, and jewelry. Open Monday to Saturday from 9:30am to 5pm.

On the mainland in Clearwater, the ✪ **Senior Citizen Craft Center Gift Shop,** 940 Court St. (☎ 727/442-4266), is one of the area's most unique gift shops—an outlet for the work of some 400 local senior citizens. You'll find knitwear, crochet work, woodwork, stained glass, clocks, scrimshaw, jewelry, pottery, tile work, ceramics, and hand-painted clothing. It's off the beaten tourist track but well worth a visit. Open Monday to Friday from 10am to 4pm, but it's staffed by volunteers, so call ahead.

WHERE TO STAY

St. Pete Beach has national chain hotels and motels of every name and description along Gulf Boulevard. For even more choices, the **St. Petersburg Area Chamber of Commerce** lists a wide range of hotels, motels, condominiums, and other accommodations in its annual visitor guide (see "Essentials" in section 2). You can also use the St. Petersburg/Clearwater Convention & Visitors Bureau's free **reservations service** (☎ 800/345-6710).

As is the case throughout Florida, there are at least as many rental condominiums here as there are hotel rooms. Many of them are in high-rise buildings right on the beach. Among several local rental agents, **Excell Vacation Condos,** 14955 Gulf Blvd.,

Madeira Beach, FL 33708 (☎ **800/733-4004** or 727/391-5512; fax 727/393-8885; www.islandtime.com/vacation), and **JC Resort Management,** 17200 Gulf Blvd., North Redington Beach, FL 33708 (☎ **800/535-7776** or 727/397-0441; fax 727/397-8894; www.jcresort.com), have many from which to choose.

With regard to prices, high season runs from January to April. Ask about special discounted packages in the summer. Any time of year, though, it's wise to make reservations early. The hotel tax in Pinellas County is 11%.

I have organized accommodations geographically, starting with the congested St. Pete Beach area on the south end of the strip, then the mostly residential Indian Rocks Beach area, then the relatively quiet but still busy Clearwater Beach at the north.

ST. PETE BEACH AREA
Very Expensive
✪ **Don CeSar Beach Resort and Spa.** 3400 Gulf Blvd. (at 34th Ave./Pinellas Byway), St. Pete Beach, FL 33706. ☎ **800/282-1116,** 800/637-7200, or 727/360-1881. Fax 727/367-3609. www.media.don-cesar.com. 345 units. A/C MINIBAR TV TEL. Winter $275–$350 double; $340–$745 suite. Off-season $175–$300 double; $230–670 suite. AE, DC, MC, V. Valet parking $10, free self-parking.

Dating from 1928 and listed on the National Register of Historic Places, this Moorish-style "Pink Palace" tropical getaway is so romantic you may bump into six or seven honeymooning couples in one weekend. Sitting majestically on 7½ acres of beachfront, the landmark sports a lobby of classic high windows and archways, crystal chandeliers, marble floors, and original artworks. Most rooms have high ceilings and offer views of the gulf or Boca Ciega Bay. In addition to the 275 rooms under the minarets of the original building, the resort has 70 luxury condos in The Don CeSar Beach House, a midrise building several blocks to the north (there's complimentary transportation between the two). The service is good, although the front desk can get a bit overwhelmed when groups are checking in.

Dining/Diversions: The pricey but intimate Maritana Grille can't be beat for fresh gourmet seafood and caviar, if your budget can afford a serious splurge. Other outlets include the King Charles Restaurant (offering a sumptuous Sunday brunch), the Sea Porch Cafe for indoor or outdoor dining by the pool and beach, the Lobby Bar, two beachside bars, and an ice-cream parlor.

Amenities: Concierge, 24-hour room service, valet parking, laundry, newspaper delivery, in-room massage, business services, complimentary coffee in lobby, baby-sitting, children's program. Beach, two outdoor heated swimming pools, whirlpool, exercise room, sauna, steam room, volleyball, gift shops, rentals for water-sports equipment, hairdresser, shopping arcade with upscale jewelers and men's and women's resort wear.

Expensive
Radisson Sandpiper Beach Resort. 6000 Gulf Blvd. (at 60th Ave.), St. Pete Beach, FL 33706. ☎ **800/333-3333,** 727/562-1222, or 727/360-5551. Fax 727/562-1222. 159 units. A/C TV TEL. Winter $149–$197 double; $227–$267 suite. Off-season $115–$147 double; $157–$199 suite. AE, DC, DISC, MC, V.

Right on the beach, this employee-owned sister of the TradeWinds (see below) has a well-landscaped, tropical courtyard separating its two six-story wings, both set back from the main road. Decorated with light woods, pastel tones, and touches of rattan, most units here have coffeemakers, toasters, small refrigerators, dishwashers, and wet bars. Suites also have a living area with sofa bed.

Dining: Piper's Patio is a casual cafe with indoor/outdoor seating and the Sand Bar offers frozen drinks, snacks, and fine sunsets by the pool. There's a Chili Peppers Mexican restaurant on the premises.

Amenities: Concierge, room service, valet laundry, newspaper delivery, in-room massage, baby-sitting. Beachfront heated swimming pool, another heated swimming pool in its own greenhouse, two air-conditioned sports courts (for racquetball, handball, and squash), exercise room, volleyball, shuffleboard, game room, gift shop/general store.

✪ **TradeWinds Resort.** 5500 Gulf Blvd. (at 55th Ave.), St. Pete Beach, FL 33706. ☎ **800/237-0707** or 727/367-6461. Fax 727/360-3848. 377 units. A/C TV TEL. Winter $195–$221 double. Off-season $135–$180 double. Discount packages available in summer and fall. AE, DC, DISC, MC, V. Valet parking $3–$6; free self-parking.

Don't be dismayed by the outward appearance of this six- and seven-story, concrete-and-steel monstrosity, for underneath and beside it runs a maze of brick walkways, patios, and lily ponds connected by a quarter mile of streams. It all gives surprising charm to this employee-owned hotel. The guest units, which look out on the gulf or the 18 acres of grounds, have up-to-date kitchens or kitchenettes, contemporary furnishings, and private balconies. The children's program and summer packages are a big hit with families from around the world, attracting lots of Europeans.

Dining/Diversions: The top spot for lunch or dinner is the Palm Court, with an Italian-bistro atmosphere; for dinner, there's also Bermudas, a casual family spot. Other food outlets include the Fountain Square Deli, Pizza Hut, and Tropic Treats. Bars include Reflections piano lounge; B.R. Cuda's, with live entertainment and dancing; and the Flying Bridge, a Florida cracker-house-style beachside bar floating on one of the lily ponds.

Amenities: With the employees having a stake in the profits as well as the tips, you should get good service here. Room service, valet parking, laundry, baby-sitting, children's program. Four heated swimming pools, whirlpools, sauna, fitness center, four tennis courts, racquetball, croquet, water-sports rentals, gas grills, guest laundry, video-game room, gift shops, full-service hair salon with massage and tanning.

Moderate

Colonial Gateway Inn. 6300 Gulf Blvd. (at 63rd Ave.), St. Pete Beach, FL 33706. ☎ **800/237-8918** or 727/367-2711. Fax 727/367-7068. 200 units. A/C TV TEL. Winter $97–$123 double. Off-season $73–$115 double. Efficiencies $10 more. AE, DC, DISC, MC, V.

On the beachfront, this U-shaped complex of one- and two-story units is a favorite with families. The rooms, most of which face the pool and a central landscaped courtyard, are contemporary, with light woods and beach tones. About half the units are efficiencies with kitchenettes.

On the premises is a branch of the very good Shells seafood restaurant (see "Where to Dine," in section 1). Bambooz Lounge and the Swigwam beach bar offer light refreshments. Facilities include an outdoor heated swimming pool with an expansive concrete deck, a kiddie pool, shuffleboard, and a game room. The water-sports shack here offers parasailing equipment rentals and also services the Days Inn Island Beach Resort next door (see below).

Days Inn Island Beach Resort. 6200 Gulf Blvd. (at 62nd Ave.), St. Pete Beach, FL 33706. ☎ **800/544-4222** or 727/367-1902. Fax 727/367-4422. 102 units. A/C TV TEL. Winter $118–$148 double. Off-season $78–$108 double. AE, DC, DISC, MC, V.

Two long, gray buildings flank a courtyard with heated swimming pool at this beachside property popular with young families. Furnished in dark woods and rich tones, most of the guest rooms have picture-window views of the courtyard. All units have refrigerators and coffeemakers, and about half have kitchenettes. Inside the building, Players Bar & Grille has sports TVs, pizzas, pub fare, and free hot snacks from noon to 7pm daily. Outside, Jimmy B.'s beach bar is a fine place for a sunset cocktail (happy hour runs from noon to 7:30pm) and evening entertainment, including beachside bonfires on Saturdays in winter. Facilities include two outdoor heated swimming pools, volleyball, horseshoes, shuffleboard, and a game room.

Inexpensive

✪ **Beach Haven.** 4980 Gulf Blvd. (at 50th Ave.), St. Pete Beach, FL 33706. ☎ **727/ 367-8642.** Fax 727/360-8202. 18 units. A/C TV TEL. Winter $75–$125 double. Off-season $50–$108 double. MC, V.

Nestled on the beach between two high-rise condos, these low-slung, pink-with-white-trim structures look from the outside like the early 1950s motel they once were. But Jone and Millard Gamble (they also own the charming Island's End Resort, below) have replaced the innards and installed bright tile floors, vertical blinds, pastel tropical furniture, and many modern amenities, including TVs, VCRs, refrigerators, and coffeemakers. Five of the original quarters remain as motel rooms (with shower-only bathrooms), but the Gambles linked the others to make 12 one-bedroom and one two-bedroom units. The top choice is the one-bedroom unit with sliding glass doors opening to a deck shaded by a sprawling Brazilian pepper tree. There's an outdoor heated pool surrounded by a white picket fence, plus a sunning deck with lounge furniture by the beach. You don't get maid service on Sunday or holidays, and the rooms and baths are 1950s smallish, but every unit here is bright, airy, and comfortable. Complimentary coffee and tea are served to all guests 2 days a week, and guests can use barbecue grills and a coin laundry. This is the heart of the hotel district, so lots of restaurants are just steps away.

Captain's Quarters Inn. 10035 Gulf Blvd. (between 100th and 101st aves.), Treasure Island, FL 33706. ☎ **800/526-9547** or 727/360-1659. Fax 727/363-3074. 8 units, 1 cottage. A/C TV TEL. Winter $70–$100 double. Off-season $55–$75 double. Weekly rates available. MC, V.

This nautically themed property is a real find, offering well-kept accommodations on the gulf at inland rates. All but one of the units sit on 100 yards of beach, an ideal vantage point for sunset-watching. Six units are efficiencies (two of them on the beach) with minikitchens including microwave oven, coffeemaker, and wet bar or sink. There's also a bay-side cottage with separate bedroom and a full kitchen. Facilities include an outdoor solar-heated freshwater swimming pool, a sundeck, guest barbecues, and a library. Small pets are accepted.

✪ **Island's End Resort.** 1 Pass-a-Grille Way (at 1st Ave.), St. Pete Beach, FL 33706. ☎ **727/ 360-5023.** Fax 727/367-7890. 6 units. A/C TV TEL. Dec 15 to June 1 $82–$175 cottage. Off-season $61–$175 cottage. Weekly rates available. MC, V.

A wonderful respite from the madding crowd, and a great bargain to boot, this little all-cottage hideaway sits right on the southern tip of St. Pete Beach, smack-dab on Pass-a-Grille, where the Gulf of Mexico meets Tampa Bay. You can step from the six contemporary cottages right onto the beach. And since the island curves sharply here, nothing blocks your view of the emerald bay. If you prefer to swim directly in the gulf or grab a brilliant sunset, the Pass-a-Grille public beach is virtually next door. Linked to each other by boardwalks, the comfortable one- or three-bedroom cottages have dining areas, living rooms, VCRs, and kitchens; the one three-bedroom unit also has its own private pool. Facilities include a fishing dock, patios, decks, barbecues, and hammocks. Owners Jone and Millard Gamble are no fools: They live at this shady, idyllic setting.

INDIAN ROCKS BEACH AREA

Great Heron Inn. 68 Gulf Blvd. (south of 1st Ave.), Indian Rocks Beach, FL 33785. ☎ **727/595-2589.** Fax 727/596-7309. 16 units. A/C TV TEL. Winter $85–$88 double. Off-season $59–$63 double. Weekly and monthly rates available. DISC, MC, V. Hotel is 4 blocks south of Fla. 688.

Formerly known as Alpaugh's Gulf Beach Apartments but now owned and operated by transplanted Michiganders Ralph and Teena Hickerson, this family oriented motel sits at the narrowest section of Indian Rocks Beach, facing the gulf on one side and its own Intracoastal Waterway dock on the other. The buildings flank a central courtyard with a heated pool. The rooms offer modern furnishings, and each unit has a full kitchen and dining area. Facilities include coin-operated laundry, and picnic tables. There's a boat dock across the boulevard.

✪ Pelican—East & West. 108 21st Ave. (at Gulf Blvd.), Indian Rocks Beach, FL 33785. ☎ **727/595-9741.** 8 units. A/C TV. Winter $50–$75 double. Off-season $40–$60 double. Weekly rates available. MC, V.

"PDIP" (Perfect Day in Paradise) is the motto at Mike and Carol McGlaughlin's motel complex, which offers a choice of two settings. Their lowest rates are at Pelican East, in a residential setting 500 feet from the beach, where four suites each have a bedroom and a separate kitchen. You'll pay more at Pelican West, but it's directly on the beachfront. The four beachside apartments each have a living room, bedroom, kitchen, patio, and unbeatable views of the gulf. You don't get phones in your rooms here or a swimming pool to splash around in, but it's clean and modern in all other respects.

CLEARWATER BEACH

Expensive

✪ Radisson Suite Resort on Sand Key. 1201 Gulf Blvd., Clearwater Beach, FL 33767. ☎ **800/333-3333** or 727/596-1100. Fax 727/595-4292. 220 units. A/C MINIBAR TV TEL. Winter $179–$279 suite. Off-season $135–$219 suite. AE, DC, DISC, MC, V. From Clearwater Beach, go south across Clearwater Pass Bridge; hotel is on left.

You'll see the beauty of Sand Key from the suites in this boomerang-shaped, 10-story hotel overlooking Clearwater Bay. The gulf is just beyond the Sheraton Sand Key Resort across the street, and beautiful Sand Key Park is a few steps away. The whole family will enjoy exploring the adjacent boardwalk with 25 shops and restaurants. Each suite has a bedroom with a balcony offering water views, as well as a complete living room with a sofa bed, wet bar, entertainment unit, coffeemaker, and microwave oven.

Dining/Diversions: The Harbor Grille offers fresh seafood, steaks, and grand bay views. The Harbor Lounge has live entertainment, while Kokomo's serves light fare and tropical drinks.

Amenities: Room service, laundry, free trolley to the beach, year-round children's activities program at "Lisa's Klubhouse," free valet parking, masseuse. Bay-side outdoor heated swimming pool with waterfall, sundeck, sauna, exercise room, guest laundry, waterfront boardwalk with a variety of shops and restaurants.

Moderate

Best Western Sea Stone Resort. 445 Hamden Dr. (at Coronado Dr.), Clearwater Beach, FL 33767. ☎ **800/444-1919,** 800/528-1234, or 727/441-1722. Fax 727/449-1580. 108 units. A/C TV TEL. Winter $103–$201 double. Off-season $72–$140 double. AE, DC, DISC, MC, V.

Located just across the street from the beach in Clearwater's busy south end, the Sea Stone Suites is a six-story building of classic Key West–style architecture containing 43 one-bedroom suites, each with a kitchenette and a living room. Their living room windows look across external walkways to the harbor. A few steps away, the older five-story Gulfview Wing offers 65 bedrooms. The furnishings are bright and airy, with pastel tones, light woods, and sea scenes on the walls. The on-site Marker 5 Restaurant serves breakfast only. There's valet laundry service, newspaper delivery, and complimentary coffee in the lobby. Facilities include a heated outdoor swimming pool, whirlpool, boat dock, coin-operated laundry, and meeting rooms.

✪ **Clearwater Beach Hotel.** 500 Mandalay Ave. (at Belmont St.), Clearwater Beach, FL 33767. ☎ **800/292-2295** or 727/441-2425. Fax 727/449-2083. 157 units. A/C TV TEL. Winter $105–$185 double. Off-season $98–$118 double. AE, DC, MC, V.

Besides the great beach location, you'll enjoy easy access to many nearby shops and restaurants from this Old Florida–style hotel. It's been owned and operated by the same family for more than 40 years and attracts an older clientele. Directly on the gulf, the complex consists of a six-story main building and two- and three-story wings. Rooms and rates vary according to location—bay view or gulf view, poolside or beachfront. Some rooms have balconies. The dining room is romantic at sunset and offers great views of the gulf, while the nautically themed lounge has entertainment nightly. A bar provides snacks and libations beside an outdoor heated swimming pool. There's valet laundry and parking, and limited room service.

Palm Pavilion Inn. 18 Bay Esplanade (at Mandalay Ave.), Clearwater Beach, FL 33767. ☎ **800/433-PALM** or 727/446-6777. 28 units. A/C TV TEL. Winter $82–$117 double. Off-season $56–$81 double. AE, DISC, MC, V.

Just north of the tourist area, this quiet beachfront spot is removed from the bustle yet within easy walking distance of all the action. The three-story art deco building is artfully trimmed in pink and blue. The lobby area and guest rooms, also art deco in design, feature rounded light-wood and rattan furnishings, bright sea-toned fabrics, photographs from the 1920s to 1950s era, and vertical blinds. Rooms in the front of the house face the gulf, while those in back face the bay. Four efficiencies have kitchenettes. Facilities include a rooftop sundeck, beach access, heated swimming pool, complimentary coffee, and beach chair and umbrella rentals. By the beach, the Palm Pavillion Grill & Bar is a fine place to catch the sunset and some live entertainment Tuesday to Sunday nights during winter, on weekends off-season. Lighted tennis courts and an athletic center are across the street.

Sheraton Sand Key Resort. 1160 Gulf Blvd., Clearwater Beach, FL 33767. ☎ **800/325-3535** or 727/595-1611. Fax 727/596-8488. 390 units. A/C TV TEL. Winter $170–$200 double. Off-season $130–$170 double. AE, DC, DISC, MC, V. From Clearwater Beach, go south across Clearwater Pass Bridge; hotel is on right.

Away from the honky-tonk of Clearwater, this hotel on 10 acres right next door to Sand Key Park is a big favorite with water-sports enthusiasts. It also gets lots of European guests year-round, which explains why the room rates don't drop much during the off-season. The guest rooms here all have coffeemakers, hair dryers, and a balcony or patio with views of the gulf or the bay.

Dining: Rusty's Restaurant serves breakfast and dinner; for lighter fare, try the Island Café, the Sundeck, or Fast Johnny's Poolside Snack Bar. The Snack Store is open 24 hours.

Amenities: Limited room service, newspaper delivery, in-room massage, valet parking and laundry, baby-sitting, children's program (summer only). Beachside outdoor heated swimming pool, fitness center, whirlpool, three lighted tennis courts, beach volleyball, newsstand, game room, children's pool, playground, water-sports rentals, 24-hour general store.

Inexpensive

✪ **Sun West Beach Motel.** 409 Hamden Dr. (at Bayside Dr.), Clearwater Beach, FL 33767. ☎ **727/442-5008.** Fax 727/461-1395. www.clearwaterbeach.com/SUNWEST/sunwest. E-mail: sunwest@mail.gte.net. 14 units. A/C TV TEL. $40–$61 double; $48–$79 efficiency. MC, V.

Overlooking the bay and yet only a 2-block walk from the beach, this well-maintained one-story motel has a heated pool, fishing/boating dock, sundeck, shuffleboard court, and guest laundry. All units, which face either the bay, the pool, or the sundeck, have contemporary resort-style furnishings. The four motel rooms have small refrigerators, and the 10 efficiencies have kitchens.

A HISTORIC HOTEL ON THE MAINLAND

Belleview Biltmore Resort & Spa. 25 Belleview Blvd. (P.O. Box 2317), Clearwater, FL 33757. ☎ **800/237-8947** or 727/442-6171. Fax 727/441-4173 or 727/443-6361. 240 units. A/C MINIBAR TV TEL. Winter $190–$210 double; $260–$450 suite. Off-season $150–$190 double; $220–$430 suite. AE, DC, DISC, MC, V. Resort is 1 mile south of downtown on Belleview Rd., off Alt. U.S. 19.

The Gulf Coast's oldest operating luxury tourist hotel, this gabled clapboard structure was built in 1896 by Henry B. Plant as the Hotel Belleview to attract customers to his Orange Belt Railroad. On a bluff overlooking the bay, it's the largest occupied wooden structure in the world. Today it attracts mostly groups and serious golfers (guests can play at the adjoining Belleview Biltmore Country Club, an 18-hole par-72 championship course), but there's no denying its Victorian charm and old-fashioned ambience—once you get past the out-of-place, glass-and-steel foyer added by more recent owners. The creaky hallways lead to several shops and a museum explaining the hotel's history. Large, high-ceilinged guest rooms are decorated in Queen Anne style, with dark-wood period furniture.

Dining/Diversions: The informal indoor/outdoor Terrace Café provides breakfast, lunch, or dinner. There's also a pub in the basement, a lounge, and a poolside bar.

Amenities: Room service, dry cleaning and valet laundry, nightly turndown on request, currency exchange, baby-sitting. Four red-clay tennis courts; indoor and outdoor heated swimming pools (one with a waterfall); whirlpool; spa with sauna, Swiss showers, workout gym; jogging and walking trails; bicycle rentals; yacht charters; gift shops; newsstand; golf privileges at the country club.

WHERE TO DINE

St. Pete Beach and Clearwater Beach both have a wide selection of national chain fast-food and family restaurants along their main drags.

As with the accommodations above, I have grouped the restaurants by geographic area: St. Pete Beach, including Pass-a-Grille; Indian Rocks Beach, including Madeira Beach, Redington Beach, North Redington Beach, Redington Shores, and Indian Shores; and finally, Clearwater Beach.

ST. PETE BEACH AREA

✪ **Crabby Bill's.** 5100 Gulf Blvd. (at 51st Ave.), St. Pete Beach. ☎ **727/360-8858.** Reservations not accepted. Sandwiches $4–$6; main courses $6–$18. AE, MC, V. Mon–Thurs 11am–10pm, Fri–Sat 11am–11pm, Sun noon–10pm. SEAFOOD.

The least expensive gulf-side dining here, this member of a small local chain sits right on the beach in the heart of the hotel district. It's a great place to bring the kids, especially after 5:30pm Tuesday, when they eat free and are entertained by games and contests. There's a small al fresco area off one of the two bars here, but big glass windows enclose the large dining room. They offer fine water views from picnic tables equipped with rolls of paper towels and buckets of saltine crackers, the better to eat the Alaskan, snow, golden, and stone crabs that are the big draws here. The crustaceans fall into the moderate price category, but most other main courses, such as fried clam strips or a combo broiled fish platter, are inexpensive. The creamy smoked fish spread is a delicious appetizer, and you'll get enough to whet the appetites of at least two persons for just $4.

Internet Outpost Cafe. 7400 Gulf Blvd. (at Corey Ave./75th Ave.), St. Pete Beach. ☎ **727/360-7806.** Reservations not accepted. Coffee and pastries $1–$2; sandwiches $5. AE, MC, V. Mon 6–10pm, Tues–Thurs 10am–10pm, Fri–Sat 10am–midnight, Sun 11am–6pm. PASTRIES/SANDWICHES.

If you left your laptop at home and can't stand not getting your e-mail or surfing the Net any longer, head for this cozy coffee emporium with nine computer terminals, all with fast connections to the Internet ($2 for 15 minutes access time). You can also lounge on the sofas and wing chairs while sipping your caffeine, kill a rainy afternoon playing chess, or listen to live music on Friday and Saturday evenings. In addition to coffees, teas, and pastries, the fare includes freshly made chicken salad, as well as Cuban, spicy turkey, and other sandwiches.

Hurricane. 807 Gulf Way (at 9th Ave.), Pass-a-Grille. ☎ **727/360-9558.** Reservations not accepted. Salads and sandwiches $2.50–$9; main courses $7–$17. MC, V. Daily 8am–1am (breakfast Mon–Fri 8–11am, Sat–Sun 8am–noon). SEAFOOD.

A longtime institution across the street from Pass-a-Grille Public Beach, this 3-level gray Victorian building with white gingerbread trim is a great place to toast the sunset, especially on the rooftop. It's more beach bar than fine restaurant, but the grouper sandwiches are a big hit, and there's always fresh fish to be broiled or fried and shrimp and crab to be steamed. You can dine inside the knotty-pine paneled dining room or on the sidewalk terrace, where bathers from across Gulf Way are welcome (there's a walk-up bar for beach libation). The joint jumps at night when one level turns into a virtual dance hall.

Skidder's Restaurant. 5799 Gulf Blvd. (at 60th Ave.), St. Pete Beach. ☎ **727/360-1029.** Reservations not accepted. Breakfast $3–$6; sandwiches and burgers $3–$7; pizza $5.50–$15; main courses $8–$15. AE, DC, DISC, MC, V. Daily 7am–9pm. ITALIAN/GREEK/AMERICAN.

A local favorite, this inexpensive family restaurant in the hotel district offers a full range of breakfast fare plus pizzas (available to eat here or carry out), burgers and sandwiches, big salads, gyro and souvlaki platters, and Italian-style veal and chicken dishes (sautéed in wine with artichokes is a house specialty). Divided by cut-glass panels, the dining room has ceiling fans rotating over gray tables and booths.

INDIAN ROCKS BEACH AREA

You'll find a bay-front edition of **Shells,** the fine and inexpensive local seafood chain, opposite the Lobster Pot on Gulf Boulevard at 178th Avenue in Redington Shores (☎ **813/393-8990**). See "Where to Dine," in section 1, for more information about Shells' menu and prices, which are the same at all branches.

✪ **Guppy's.** 1701 Gulf Blvd. (at 17th Ave.), Indian Rocks Beach. ☎ **813/593-2032.** Reservations not accepted. Sandwiches $5–$7; main courses $9–$20. AE, DC, DISC, MC, V. Sun–Thurs 11:30am–10:30pm; Fri–Sat 11:30am–11:30pm. SEAFOOD.

Locals love this small bar and grill across from Indian Rocks Public Beach because they know they'll always get terrific chow (it's associated with the excellent Lobster Pot, mentioned below). You won't soon forget the salmon coated with potatoes and lightly fried to brown, then baked with a creamy leek and garlic sauce; it's fattening, yes, but also a bargain at $9. Another good choice is lightly cooked tuna (only slightly more done than sushi) finished with a peppercorn sauce. The atmosphere is casual beach friendly, with a fun bar in the rear. Scotty's famous upside-down apple-walnut pie topped with ice cream will require a little extra work on the weights tomorrow. You can dine outside on a patio beside the main road.

✪ **Lobster Pot.** 17814 Gulf Blvd. (at 178th Ave.), Redington Shores. ☎ **727/391-8592.** www.beachdirectory.com. Reservations recommended. Main courses $14.50–$29.50. AE, DC, MC, V. Mon–Thurs 4:30–10pm, Fri–Sat 4:30–11pm, Sun 4–10pm. SEAFOOD.

Step into this weathered-looking restaurant near the beach and owner Eugen Fuhrmann will tell you to get ready to experience the finest seafood in the area. The prices are high, but the variety of lobster dishes is amazing. The lobster américaine is flambéed in brandy with garlic, and the bouillabaisse is as authentic as any you'd find in the south of France. In addition to lobster, there's a wide selection of grouper, snapper, salmon, swordfish, shrimp, scallops, crab, and Dover sole, prepared simply or with elaborate sauces. There's no ordinary children's menu here: It features half a main lobster and a petite filet mignon.

Omi's Bavarian Inn. 14701 Gulf Blvd. (at 147th Ave.), Madeira Beach. ☎ **727/393-9654.** Reservations recommended. Main courses $7–$15. AE, DISC, MC, V. Daily 3–9:30pm. GERMAN.

This little restaurant is a small patch of Germany on the gulf, featuring schnitzels, sauerbraten, schweinebraten (roast pork), chicken paprikash, beef goulash, Bavarian bratwurst, and stuffed peppers. Seafood and steak are also on the menu.

Scandia. 19829 Gulf Blvd. (between 198th and 199th aves.), Indian Shores. ☎ **727/ 595-5525.** Reservations recommended. Main courses $7–$21. DISC, MC, V. Tues–Sat 11:30am–9pm, Sun noon–8pm. Closed Sept. SCANDINAVIAN.

Unique in decor and menu in these parts, this chalet-style restaurant in the northern fringes of Indian Shores brings a touch of Hans Christian Andersen to the beach strip. The menu offers Scandinavian favorites, from smoked salmon and pickled herring to roast pork, sausages, schnitzels, and Danish lobster tails. There are also a few international dishes such as curried chicken, North Sea flounder, Canadian scallops, Boston scrod, and shrimp and grouper from gulf waters.

✪ **Wine Cellar.** 17307 Gulf Blvd. (at 173rd Ave.), North Redington Beach. ☎ **727/ 393-3491.** Reservations recommended. Main courses $13–$30. AE, DC, MC, V. Tues–Sat 4:30–11pm, Sun 4–11pm. CONTINENTAL.

Every evening during the high season and on weekends all year, the cars pack the parking lot at this restaurant, which is highly popular with locals and visitors alike. You'll find an assortment of divided dining rooms, and the cuisine offers the best of Europe and the States. Start off with caviar, move on to a fresh North Carolina rainbow trout or chateaubriand, and top it all off with chocolate velvet torte. There's jazz in the lounge on Thursday, Friday, and Saturday evenings and Dixieland jazz on Sunday, and you'll often find noisy private parties going on.

CLEARWATER BEACH

✪ **Bob Heilman's Beachcomber.** 447 Mandalay Ave. (at Papaya St.). ☎ **727/442-4144.** Reservations recommended. Main courses $12–$24. AE, DC, DISC, MC, V. Mon–Sat 11:30am– 11pm, Sun noon–10pm. AMERICAN.

In a restaurant row opposite the beach, this nautically attired establishment has been popular for more than 45 years. It's a classy bistro, with a pianist adding to an elegant but relaxed ambience. The menu presents a variety of fresh seafood, beef, veal, and lamb selections. The "back-to-the-farm" fried chicken—from an original 1910 Heilman family recipe—is incredible.

Bubby's Bistro & Wine Bar. 447 Mandalay Ave. (at Papaya St., behind Bob Heilman's Beachcomber). ☎ **727/446-9463.** Reservations not accepted. Sandwiches and pizzas $6–$12; main courses $10–$17. AE, DC, DISC, MC, V. Daily 5pm–midnight. AMERICAN.

Bob and Sherri Heilman opened this dark, very urban bistro behind their popular restaurant in 1993, and it's been a local hit ever since. The wine-cellar theme is amply justified by the real thing: a walk-in closet with several thousand bottles kept at a constant 55°F. Walk through and pick your vintage, then listen to jazz while you dine inside at tall, bar-height tables or outside on a covered patio. The chef specializes in gourmet pizzas on homemade focaccia crust (as a tasty appetizer), plus charcoal-grilled veal chops, filet mignon, fresh fish, and monstrous pork chops with caramelized Granny Smith apples and a Mount Vernon mustard sauce. Everything's served à la carte here, so watch your credit card. On the other hand, there's an affordable sandwich menu featuring the likes of bronzed grouper and chicken with a spicy Jack cheese.

Frenchy's Cafe. 41 Baymont St. ☎ **727/446-3607.** Reservations not accepted. Main courses $5–$15. AE, MC, V. Mon–Thurs 11:30am–11pm, Fri–Sat 11:30am–midnight, Sun noon–11pm. SEAFOOD.

Always popular with locals and visitors in the know, this casual cafe makes the best grouper sandwiches in the area and has all the awards to prove it. They're fresh, thick, juicy, and always delicious. The atmosphere is pure Florida casual style, and there's always a wait.

For more casual fare directly on the beach, **Frenchy's Rockaway Grill,** at 7 Rockaway St. (☎ **727/446-4844**), has a wonderful outdoor setting.

✪ **Seafood & Sunsets at Julie's.** 351 S. Gulfview Blvd. (at 5th St.), Clearwater Beach. ☎ **727/441-2548.** Reservations recommended. Main courses $8–$15. AE, MC, V. Daily 11am–10pm. SEAFOOD.

A Key West–style tradition takes over Julie Nichols' place at dusk as both locals and visitors gather to toast the sunset over the beach across the street. The best seats are in the tiny upstairs dining room. Check out the seafood menu featuring mahimahi charcoal-broiled with sour cream, fresh Florida grouper, and Mike Macy's stuffed flounder.

THE BEACHES AFTER DARK

If you haven't already found it during your sightseeing and shopping excursions, the restored fishing community of **John's Pass Village and Boardwalk,** on Gulf Boulevard at John's Pass in Madeira Beach, has plenty of restaurants, bars, and shops to keep you occupied after the sun sets. Elsewhere, the nightlife scene at the beach revolves around rocking bars that pump out the music until 2am.

Down south in Pass-a-Grille, there's the popular, always lively lounge in **Hurricane,** on Gulf Way at 9th Avenue opposite the public beach (see "Where to Dine," above).

On Treasure Island, **Beach Nutts,** on West Gulf Boulevard at 96th Ave. (☎ 727/367-7427), is perched atop a stilt foundation like a wooden beach cottage on the Gulf of Mexico. The music ranges from Top 40 to reggae and rock. **Manhattans,** Gulf Boulevard at 116th Avenue (☎ 727/363-1500), offers a variety of live music, from country to contemporary and classic rock. Up on the northern tip of Treasure Island, **Gators on the Pass** (☎ 727/367-8951) claims to have the world's longest waterfront bar, with a huge deck overlooking the waters of John's Pass. The complex also includes a no-smoking sports bar and a three-story tower with a top-level observation deck for panoramic views of the Gulf of Mexico. There's live music, from acoustic and blues to rock, most nights.

In Clearwater Beach, the **Palm Pavilion Grill & Bar,** on the beach at 18 Bay Esplanade (☎ 727/446-6777), has live music Tuesday through Sunday nights during winter, on weekends off-season. Nearby, **Frenchy's Rockaway Grill,** at 7 Rockaway St. (☎ 727/446-4844), is another popular hangout.

If you're into laughs, **Coconuts Comedy Club,** at the Howard Johnson motel, Gulf Boulevard at 61st Avenue in St. Pete Beach (☎ 727/360-5653), has an ever-changing program of live stand-up funny men and women. Call for the schedule, performers, and prices.

For a more highbrow evening, go to the Clearwater mainland and the 2,200-seat **Ruth Eckerd Hall,** 1111 McMullen-Booth Rd. (☎ 727/791-7400), which hosts a varied program of Broadway shows, ballet, drama, symphonic works, popular music, jazz, and country music.

4 Tarpon Springs

30 miles N of St. Petersburg, 23 miles W of Tampa, 13 miles N of Clearwater

One of Florida's most fascinating small towns, Tarpon Springs calls itself the "Sponge Capital of the World." That's because Greek immigrants from the Dodecanese Islands settled here in the late 19th century to harvest sponges, which grew in abundance off-shore. By the 1930s, Tarpon Springs was producing more sponges than any other place in the world. A blight ruined the business in the 1940s, but the descendants of those early immigrants stayed on. Today they comprise about a third of the population, making Tarpon Springs a center of transplanted Greek culture.

Although sponges still arrive at the historic Sponge Docks on Dodecanese Boulevard, the town's mainstays today are commercial fishing and tourism. With a lively, carnival-like atmosphere, the docks are a great place to spend an afternoon or early evening, poking your head into shops selling sponges and other souvenirs while Greek music comes from the dozen or so family restaurants purveying authentic Aegean cuisine. You can also venture offshore from here, for booths on the docks hawk sightseeing and fishing cruises.

Just south of the docks, restored Victorian homes facing the winding creek known as Spring Bayou make this one of the most picturesque towns in the state.

ESSENTIALS

GETTING THERE   From Tampa or St. Petersburg, take U.S. 19 north and turn left on Tarpon Avenue (County Road 582). From Clearwater Beach, take Alt. U.S. 19 north through Dunedin. The center of the historic downtown district is at the intersection of Pinellas Avenue (Alt. U.S. 19) and Tarpon Avenue. To reach the Sponge Docks, go 10 blocks north on Pinellas Avenue and turn left at Pappas' Restaurant onto Dodecanese Boulevard.

VISITOR INFORMATION   The **Tarpon Springs Chamber of Commerce** (☎ 727/937-6109) has an information office on Dodecanese Boulevard at the Spong Docks. Open Tuesday to Saturday from 10:30am to 4:30pm, Sunday from 11am to 5pm.

EXPLORING THE TOWN

Two areas are worth visiting here. You'll first come to the **Tarpon Springs Downtown Historic District,** with its turn-of-the-century commercial buildings along Tarpon Avenue and Pinellas Avenue (Alt. U.S. 19). The **Tarpon Springs Cultural Center,** on

Pinellas Avenue a block south of Tarpon Avenue, explains the town's history and has visitor information. On Tarpon Avenue west of Pinellas Avenue, you'll come to the Victorian homes overlooking **Spring Bayou.** This creekside area makes for a delightfully picturesque stroll.

The carnival-like **Sponge Docks** line Dodecanese Boulevard, which is peppered with shops, restaurants, and fishing- and sightseeing boats pulling at their mooring lines along the riverside boardwalk. Poke your head into the old rickety warehouse which is now home to the **Spongeorama** (☎ 727/943-9509), a dusty museum dedicated to sponges and sponge divers. You can buy a wide variety of sponges here (they'll ship them home) and watch a 30-minute video about sponge diving several times a day. Admission is free. The Spongeorama is open daily from 10am to 5pm. In the **Coral Sea Aquarium,** at the western end of the boulevard (☎ 727/938-5378), a scuba diver feeds sharks at 11:30am and 1, 2:30, and 4pm. The aquarium is open daily from 10am to 5pm. Admission is $4 adults, $3.25 seniors, $2 for children 3 to 11, free for kids under 3.

You also can **cruise** down the Anclote River to watch sponge divers at work, go fishing on a party boat, or perhaps have lunch or dinner afloat. Booths along the docks sell tickets for a variety of these excursions. Make your reservations as soon as you get here, then go sightseeing ashore while you wait for the next boat to shove off.

Bikers, in-line skaters, hikers, and joggers can come right through downtown on the **Pinellas Trail,** which runs along Safford Avenue and crosses Tarpon Avenue 2 blocks east of Pinellas Avenue (see "Outdoor Activities & Spectator Sports" in section 2, above).

WHERE TO STAY

In addition to the establishments listed below, there are national chain motels on busy U.S. 19, including the **Holiday Inn Hotel & Suites,** 38724 U.S. 19 North (☎ **800/HOLIDAY** or 727/934-5781); **Days Inn Tarpon Springs,** 40050 U.S. 19 (☎ **800/DAYS-INN** or 727/934-0859); and the **Best Western Tahitian Resort,** 2337 U.S. 19 North in Holiday (☎ **800/931-0333** or 727/937-4121).

Spring Bayou Inn. 32 W. Tarpon Ave., Tarpon Springs, FL 34688. ☎ **727/938-9333.** Fax same as phone. 5 units (3 with bathroom). Winter $60–$110 double. Off-season $54–$99 double. Weekly rates available. No credit cards. House is in the block west of Pinellas Ave. (Alt. U.S. 19).

Built around the turn of the century, this historic district bed-and-breakfast is virtually across Pinellas Avenue from downtown and within a mile of the Sponge Docks. The large, comfortable home reflects an elegance of the past without giving up modern-day conveniences. Enjoy a complimentary cup of tea or glass of wine in the afternoon and complimentary breakfast in the morning. The best room has a king-size bed, sitting area, private bath, and balcony.

✪ **The Westin Innisbrook Resort.** 36750 U.S. 19 (P.O. Box 1088), Tarpon Springs, FL 34688. ☎ **800/456-2000** or 727/942-2000. Fax 727/942-5577. 1,000 units. Winter $195–$370 double. Off-season $135–$360 double. Golf packages available. AE, DC, DISC, MC, V.

Golf Digest, Golf magazine, and others pick this as one of the country's best places to play (provided you stay here, of course). The 1,000-acre resort has 90 holes on championship courses that are more like the rolling links of the Carolinas than the usually flat courses found in Florida. Each December, the most famous course, the Copperhead, hosts the JC Penny Classic, a major stop on the PGA circuit. Innisbrook has the largest resort-owned and -operated golf school in North America, and the Nick

Mermaids & Manatees

Drive north of Clearwater for an hour on congested U.S. 19, and you'll come to one of Florida's original tourist attractions, the famous ✪ **Weeki Wachee Spring** (☎ **800/678-9335** or 352/596-2062). "Mermaids" have been putting on acrobatic swimming shows behind 4-inch-thick windows here every day since 1947. It's a sight to see them doing their dances in waters that come from one of America's most prolific freshwater springs, which pours some 170 million gallons of 72°F water a day into the river. The show combines elements of Hans Christian Andersen's fairy tales with the real story of Pocahontas. Admission is $16.95 for adults, $12.95 for children 3 to 10, plus tax. Kids under 3 get in free. The springs are open daily from 9am to 4pm in winter, to 5pm the rest of the year.

There's more than mermaids at Weeki Wachee Spring, for you can take a Wilderness River Cruise across the Weeki Wachee River, visit the Animal Forest Petting Zoo, take in the live Exotic Birds of Prey show, and send the kids on flume and bumper-boat rides at **Buccaneer Bay** water park (☎ **352/596-2062**). Buccaneer Bay is open from March to Labor Day, daily from 10am to 5pm. Admission is $11.95 for adults, $9.95 for kids 3 to 10.

If you decide to stay overnight here, there's a **Holiday Inn** across U.S. 19 from the springs (☎ **800/678-9335** or 352/596-2062).

From Weeki Wachee, travel 21 miles north to the ✪ **Homosassa State Wildlife Park,** on U.S. 19 in Homosassa Springs (☎ **352/628-5343**). The highlight here is a floating observatory where visitors can "walk" underwater and watch manatees in a rehabilitation facility, as well as thousands of fresh- and salt-water fish. You'll also see deer, bears, bobcats, otters, egrets, and flamingos along unspoiled nature trails. The park is open daily from 9am to 5:30pm. Admission is $7.95 for adults and $4.95 for children 3 to 12, which includes a 30-minute narrated boat ride.

About 7 miles north of Homosassa Springs, some 300 manatees spend the winter in Crystal River, and you can swim, snorkel, or scuba with them in the warm-water natural spring of Kings Bay. **American Pro Diving Center,** 821 S.E. Hwy. 19, Crystal River, FL 34429 (☎ **800/291-DIVE** or 352/563-0041), offers daily dive and snorkel tours. Early mornings are the best time to see the manatees, so try to take the 7am departure. The trips range from $21.50 to $50 per person. Call for the schedule and reservations.

You can stay in Crystal River at hotels that have their own dive shops and marinas, such as the 142-room **Plantation Inn and Golf Resort,** at 9301 W. Ft. Island Trail (☎ **800/632-6262** or 352/795-4211), or the 100-room **Best Western Crystal River Resort,** at 614 NW U.S. 19 (☎ **800/435-4409** or 352/795-3171).

During mid-February you can enjoy the Crystal River Chamber's **Florida Manatee Festival,** with a seafood festival, golf tournament, art show, concerts, and manatee displays.

For more information about the area, contact the **Nature Coast Chamber at Crystal River,** 28 NW Hwy. 19, Crystal River, FL 34425 (☎ **352/795-3149;** fax 352/795-4260). The chamber's visitor center is open Monday to Thursday from 8:30am to 5pm, Friday from 8:30am to 4pm.

Bollettieri Tennis Academy here boasts 11 clay and 4 Laykold courts. There's even a children's program to take care of the kids. The spacious quarters actually are privately owned homes and apartments spread all over the premises, so there are no focal points here except the building where you check in and the golf and tennis clubhouses.

WHERE TO DINE

Your Tarpon Springs experience will be incomplete without taking a Greek meal here. In addition to Hellas Restaurant & Bakery listed below, you'll find about a dozen other family owned restaurants along the lively Sponge Docks, all of them clean, inviting, and serving authentic, inexpensive Greek fare.

If you're shopping or sightseeing downtown, or biking on the Pinellas Trail as it runs along Safford Avenue, you can stop into **Yours Truly Gourmet Café,** 150 Tarpon Ave. (☎ 727/934-1770), a bistro-style restaurant with a winding wrought-iron staircase lending a quaint Bourbon Street feel. Dinner-size salads and New American–style seafood are the specialties here (check out the famous french-fried shrimp with cherry sauce).

✪ **Hellas Restaurant & Bakery.** Sponge Docks, 785 Dodecanese Blvd. ☎ **727/ 943-2400.** Reservations not accepted. Sandwiches and salads $4–$6; main courses $7–$14. AE, DISC, MC, V. Daily 11am–10pm. GREEK.

The lovely hand-painted tile tables on the street-side patio here make fine spots from which to watch the action on the Sponge Docks while sampling authentic Aegean cuisine. If you like feta cheese, you'll enjoy the pungent Greek-style shrimp or scallops. If not, opt for the perfectly panfried grouper or any of the Aegean standbys: moussaka, pastisio, dolmades, or one of the largest gyro sandwiches in town. The bakery supplies baklava, galactombouriko (egg custard), and other desserts from the old country. With Greek cuisine, Greek music, and a Greek-looking (if not Greek-accented) waiter, it's easy to imagine yourself quayside on Mykonos.

Pappas' Restaurant. Sponge Docks, 10 Dodecanese Blvd. (at Pinellas Ave./Alt. U.S. 19). ☎ 727/937-5101. Reservations not accepted. Main courses $8.50–$26. AE, MC, V. Sun–Thurs 11:30am–10:30pm, Fri–Sat 11:30am–11:30pm. SEAFOOD.

Although it offers a few Greek-style salads and main courses, Pappas is famous statewide for its fresh American-style seafood—shrimp, grouper, red snapper, and even stone crab claws in season—most of it right off the boat. The family run restaurant has been operating on the banks of the Anclote River since 1925 when it was founded by Louis Pappamichaelopoulus of Sparta, Greece. You get nice river views from the tall windows of this modern building. Downstairs, you can poke through several shops, including one selling hand-rolled cigars.

5 Sarasota

52 miles S of Tampa, 150 miles SW of Orlando, 225 miles NW of Miami

Far enough away from Tampa Bay to have an identity very much its own, Sarasota is one of Florida's cultural centers. In fact, many retirees spend their winters here because there's so much to keep them entertained and stimulated, including the very fine Asolo Center for the Performing Arts and the Van Wezel Performing Arts Hall. Like affluent Naples down in Southwest Florida, it also has an extensive array of first-class resorts, restaurants, and upscale boutiques.

Sarasota is also known for the series of long, narrow barrier islands lying just off-shore: **St. Armands Key,** with one of Florida's ritziest shopping districts; **Siesta Key,** a quiet and mostly residential enclave popular with artisans and writers; **Lido Key,** with a string of affordable hotels attractive to family vacationers; and **Longboat**

Sarasota & Bradenton

Tampa Bay

Sunshine Skyway

Fort DeSoto

Fort DeSoto Park

679

Edgemont Channel

Egmont Key State Park

Southwest Channel

275

19

Gillette

Tamiami Trail

75

41

683

Terra Ceia

19

Rubonia

41

Parrish

75

301

Anna Maria

DeSoto National Monument

683

Memphis

Ellenton

Holmes Beach

Manatee River

Manatee Ave.

Palmetto

70

Anna Maria Island

64

Arcadia Rd.

64

Bradenton

789

Cortez

Samoset

Bradenton Beach

684

Oneco

Longbeach

Bayshore Gardens

70

41

301

70

Longboat Key

Tallevast

Braden River

Whitfield Estates

Sarasota-Bradenton Airport

789

MANATEE CO.

University Parkway

SARASOTA CO.

Mote Marine Aquarium

Sarasota

75

St. Armands Key

780

Fruitville

780

Lido Key

773

Gulf of Mexico

Siesta Key

758

41

Bee Ridge Road

Bee Ridge

Gulf Gate

72

Crescent

789

Vamo

Casey Key

Osprey

41

681

Cow Pen Slough

Laurel

Nokomis

Venice

0   3 mi.
    4.8 km

N

1-1083

411

Key, one of Florida's wealthiest islands that stretches north to Bradenton. Together, 35 miles of gloriously white beaches fringe these keys.

Legend has it that Sarasota was named after the explorer Hernando de Soto's daughter, Sara (hence, Sara-sota). In more recent times, the town's most famous resident was circus legend John Ringling, who came here in the 1920s, built a palatial bay-front mansion known as Ca'd'Zan, acquired extensive real estate holdings, erected a magnificent museum to house his world-class collection of baroque paintings, and built the causeway out to St. Armands and Lido keys.

ESSENTIALS

GETTING THERE To reach downtown, St. Armands Key, Lido Key, and Longboat Key, take Exit 39 off I-75 and follow Fruitville Road (Fla. 780) west. To reach southern Sarasota and Siesta Key, take Exit 38 and follow Bee Ridge Road (Fla. 758) west. U.S. 41 runs north-south through downtown.

Sarasota-Bradenton International Airport (☎ 941/359-2770) is located north of downtown off University Parkway between U.S. 41 and U.S. 301. Airlines serving the airport include **American Eagle** (☎ 800/433-7300), **America Trans Air** (☎ 800/225-2995), **Canadian Airlines International** (☎ 800/426-7000), **Continental** (☎ 800/525-0280), **Delta** (☎ 800/221-1212), **Northwest/KLM** (☎ 800/225-2525), **TWA** (☎ 800/221-2000), and **US Airways** (☎ 800/428-4322).

The major car-rental companies have booths at the airport.

Diplomat Taxi (☎ 941/355-5155) has a monopoly on service from the airport to hotels in Sarasota and Bradenton. Look for the cabs at the west end of the terminal outside baggage claim. The fare is about $9 to downtown Sarasota, $10 to $15 to St. Armands and Lido keys, $14 to $21 to Siesta Key, and $14 to $35 to Longboat Key.

Amtrak has bus connections to its Tampa station (☎ 800/USA-RAIL).

VISITOR INFORMATION Contact the **Sarasota Convention and Visitors Bureau,** 655 N. Tamiami Trail (U.S. 41), Sarasota, FL 34236 (☎ 800/522-9799 or 941/957-1877; fax 941/951-2956; www.sarasota/online.com). The bureau and its helpful visitor center are in a blue pagoda-shaped building on Tamiami Trail (U.S. 41) at 6th Street. They're open Monday to Saturday from 9am to 5pm.

For specific information about Siesta Key, contact the **Siesta Key Chamber of Commerce,** 5100-B Ocean Blvd., Sarasota, FL 34242 (☎ 941/349-3800; fax 941/349-9699), and ask for a copy of its biennial visitor guide.

CITY LAYOUT The **downtown** area on the mainland hugs Sarasota Bay, the modern urban skyline edged by picturesque marinas, landscaped drives, and historic Spanish-style buildings. From downtown proper, the **John Ringling Causeway** leads west across the bay to the famous **St. Armands Circle** shopping and restaurant district. From there, a short bridge leads due west to **Lido Key** and its family-oriented beach. **Benjamin Franklin Drive** is Lido's main drag along the gulf. From St. Armands Circle, **John Ringling Parkway** (Fla. 789) goes north across a bridge to **Longboat Key,** where it continues as **Gulf of Mexico Drive** for 12 miles into Manatee County and Bradenton. South of downtown, both the **Siesta Drive Causeway** and the **Stickney Point Bridge** link the city to Siesta Key. Siesta's main drag is **Midnight Pass Road,** running the length of the island.

GETTING AROUND A private company, **Trolley Systems of America** (☎ 800/787-6554 or 941/346-3115), provides regular service from downtown to the beaches and along the keys Tuesday to Saturday from 9:30am to 6pm. The Siesta Key Trolley runs from downtown out to Siesta Key. The Anna Maria Trolley runs from downtown to Lido and Longboat keys north as far as Anna Maria Island, with pickups in

Bradenton twice a day (see section 6 for information about Bradenton and Anna Maria Island). The fare is $5 regardless of how far you go, free for kids under 3. Call for the exact schedule and to make reservations.

Sarasota County Area Transit (SCAT) (☎ **941/316-1234**) provides regularly scheduled bus service Monday to Saturday from about 7am to 6pm. The Sarasota Convention and Visitor Bureau distributes route maps (see "Visitor Information," above). Route number 4 runs between downtown and St. Armands and Lido Keys; number 18, downtown and Longboat Key; and number 11, downtown and Siesta Key. The standard fare is 50¢; exact change is required. The main downtown transfer station is at 1st Street and Lemon Avenue.

Taxi companies include **Diplomat Taxi** (☎ **941/355-5155**), **Green Cab Taxi** (☎ **941/922-6666**), and **Yellow Cab of Sarasota** (☎ **941/955-3341**).

HITTING THE BEACH

Much of the area's 35 miles of beaches are occupied by hotels and condominium complexes, but there are excellent public beaches here. After you've driven the length of Longboat Key and admired the luxurious homes and condos blocking access to the beach, take a right off St. Armands Circle onto Lido Key and **North Lido Beach.** Unfortunately recent storms have robbed most of the sand here, but the south end of the island is occupied by **South Lido Beach Park,** with plenty of shade making it a good spot for picnics and walks.

Sarasota's most popular beach is **Siesta Key Public Beach,** with a picnic area, 700-car parking lot, and crowds of families. More secluded and quiet is **Turtle Beach,** at Siesta Key's south end. It has shelters, boat ramps, picnic tables, and volleyball nets.

OUTDOOR ACTIVITIES & SPECTATOR SPORTS

BICYCLING & IN-LINE SKATING   You can bike and skate from downtown to Lido and Longboat keys, since paved walkways/bike paths run alongside the John Ringling Causeway and then up Longboat. Narrow streets make Siesta Key less appealing. You can rent bikes and blades at **Sarasota Bicycle Center,** 4084 Bee Ridge Rd. just east of downtown (☎ **941/377-4505**), and at **Siesta Sports Rentals,** 6551 Midnight Pass Rd. on Siesta Key (☎ **941/346-1797**). **C.B.'s Saltwater Outfitters,** 1249 Stickney Point Rd., at the Siesta Key side of the Stickney Point Bridge (☎ **941/349-4400**), rents bicycles.

BOAT RENTALS   **All Watersports,** in the Boatyard Shopping Village, on the mainland end of Stickney Point Bridge (☎ **941/921-2754**), rents personal watercraft such as WaveRunners, jet boats, and jet-skis, as well as speedboats, runabouts, and bowriders. At the island end of the bridge, **C.B.'s Saltwater Outfitters,** 1249 Stickney Point Rd. (☎ **941/349-4400**), and **Siesta Key Boat Rentals,** 1265 Old Stickney Point Rd. (☎ **941/349-8880**), both rent runabouts, pontoon boats, and other craft. Bait and tackle are available at the marinas.

CRUISES   From October to May, you can head over to Marina Jack's Marina, U.S. 41 at Island Park Circle for 2-hour sightseeing and sunset cruises around Sarasota's waterways aboard the 65-foot, two-deck *Le Barge* (☎ **941/366-6116**). The cruises run Tuesday to Sunday, with the sightseeing cruise ($16 per person) leaving at 2pm. The sunset cruises ($15 adults, $5 for kids under 13) change with the time of sunset. Snacks and libation are available for an extra charge. Call for reservations.

FISHING   Charter fishing boats dock at most marinas here. The **Flying Fish Fleet,** downtown at Marina Jack's Marina, U.S. 41 at Island Park Circle (☎ **941/366-3373**), offers party boat charter-fishing excursions, with bait and tackle furnished. Prices for half-day trips are $28; all-day voyages are $40. Seniors and children pay less. Call for the schedule. You can also charter a 39-foot custom sportfishing boat; 4-hour trips cost about $300.

GOLF   The **Bobby Jones Golf Complex,** 1000 Circus Blvd. (☎ 941/365-GOLF), is Sarasota's only municipal facility, but it has two 18-hole championship layouts—the American (par 71) and British (par 72) courses—and the 9-hole Gillespie executive course (par 30). Tee times are assigned 3 days in advance. Greens fees range from $25 to $31, including cart rental.

You can also tune your game at the public **Village Green Golf Club,** 3500 Pembroke Dr., near Bee Ridge and Beneva roads (☎ 941/925-2755), whose executive-length 18 holes can be parred in 58.

The semiprivate **Rolling Green Golf Club,** 4501 Tuttle Ave. (☎ 941/355-6620), is an 18-hole, par-72 course. Facilities include a driving range, rental clubs, and lessons. Tee times are assigned 2 days in advance. Prices, including cart, are about $40 in winter, $25 off-season.

Also semiprivate, the **Sarasota Golf Club,** 7820 N. Leewynn Dr. (☎ 941/371-2431), is an 18-hole, par-72 course. Facilities include a driving range, lessons, club rentals, restaurant, lounge, and golf shop. Fees, including carts, are about $42 in winter, $25 off-season.

If you have reciprocal privileges, **University Park Country Club,** west of I-75 on University Parkway (☎ 813/359-9999), is Sarasota's only nationally ranked course.

SAILING   The 41-foot, 12-passenger sailboat *Enterprise,* docked at Marina Jack's Marina, U.S. 41 at Island Park Circle (☎ 941/951-1833), cruises the waters of both Sarasota Bay and the Gulf of Mexico. Half-day cruises cost $35; the sunset cruise, $20. Departure times vary, and reservations are required.

Based on Siesta Key, **Siesta Sailing** (☎ 888/539-7245 or 941/346-7245) has half-day, full-day, and 2-day cruises on three boats, ranging from $50 to $225 per person, respectively. Reservations are essential.

If you'd like more room on deck for sunning, **Fat Cat Cruises** (☎ 941/362-7564) has 2-hour catamaran cruises in the bay waters off Siesta and Lido keys. Call for reservations and prices.

SPECTATOR SPORTS   **Ed Smith Stadium,** 2700 12th St., at Tuttle Avenue (☎ 941/954-4101 or 941/954-7699), is the winter home of the **Cincinnati Reds,** who hold spring training here in February and March. East of downtown, the stadium seats 7,500 fans. Admission is $5 to $10.

The **Sarasota Polo Club,** 8201 Polo Club Lane, Sarasota (☎ 941/359-0000), midway between Sarasota and Bradenton, is the site of weekly polo matches from November through March, on Sunday afternoons. Call for the schedule of matches and admission fees.

TENNIS   The **Colony Beach & Tennis Resort,** one of the country's finest playing-and-practicing facilities (see "Where to Stay," below), is the big draw here for tennis players who can afford it.

The rest of us can play at **Payne Park Tennis Center,** 2050 Adams Lane (☎ 941/364-4605), a downtown public facility with nine Har-Tru tennis courts, available for play on a first-come, first-served basis. The price is $4.50 per person per hour. It's open daily from 8am to 9pm.

WATER SPORTS   The downtown center for jet-skiing, wave running, sailing, and other water-sports activities is **O'Leary's,** in the Island Park Marina, U.S. 41 and Island Park Circle (☎ 941/953-7505). It's open daily from 8am to 8pm.

On Siesta Key, **Sweet Water Kayaks,** 5263 Ocean Blvd., Suite 7 (☎ **941/ 346-1179**), rents fully equipped single and double sea kayaks for use in the gulf bays and Intracoastal Waterway. One-person models go for $35 for 2 hours or $60 a day per day, while tandems cost $50 for 2 hours or $60 a day. They also teach 2-hour beginners sea kayaking courses for $45 per person. Open daily from 10am to 6pm.

Also on Siesta Key, **Siesta Sports Rentals,** 6551 Midnight Pass Rd. (☎ **813/ 346-1797**), rents kayaks and sailboats, plus beach chairs and umbrellas.

You can soar above the bay with **Siesta Parasail,** based at CB's Saltwater Outfitters at the western end of the Stickney Point Bridge (☎ **941/349-1900**).

EXPLORING THE AREA
MUSEUMS & ART GALLERIES

Cars & Music of Yesterday Museum. 5500 N. Tamiami Trail (at University Pkwy). ☎ **941/ 355-6228.** Admission $9 adults, $5 children 6–12, free for children under 6. Daily 9am–6pm. Take U.S. 41 north of downtown; museum is 2 blocks west of the airport.

View more than 80 classic and antique autos, from Rolls-Royces and Pierce Arrows to the four cars used personally by circus czar John Ringling. In addition, there are more than 1,200 antique music boxes, from tiny music boxes to a huge 30-foot Belgian organ. Check out the Penny Arcade with antique games, and grab a cone at the ice-cream and sandwich shop.

✪ **Ringling Museums.** Bayshore Rd. at N. Tamiami Trail (U.S. 41). ☎ **941/359-5700,** or 941/351-1660 for recorded information. Admission $9 adults, $8 seniors, free for children 12 and under. Daily 10am–5:30pm. From downtown, take U.S. 41 north to University Pkwy. and follow signs to museum.

This is a huge 60-acre site—showman John Ringling collected art on a grand scale. The **John and Mable Ringling Museum of Art,** housed in a pink Italian Renaissance villa, is filled with more than 500 years of European and American art, including one of the world's most important collections of grand 17th-century baroque paintings. The old master collection also includes five world-renowned tapestry cartoons by Peter Paul Rubens and his studio. The museum houses collections of decorative arts and traveling exhibits. The Ringlings' 30-room winter residence **Ca'd'Zan** (House of John), built in 1925 and modeled after a Venetian palace, is on display and filled with personal mementos. The grounds also include **Circus Galleries,** a building devoted to circus memorabilia including parade wagons, calliopes, costumes, and colorful posters; and the historic **Asolo Theater,** a 19th-century Italian court playhouse; plus a classical courtyard, rose garden, restaurant, and shops.

Sarasota Visual Art Center. 707 N. Tamiami Trail (at 6th St.). ☎ **941/365-2032.** Free admission. Mon–Fri 10am–4pm, Sat–Sun 1–4pm.

Sarasota is home to more than 40 art galleries and exhibition spaces, all open to the public year-round. A convenient artistic starting point is this downtown community art center, next to the Sarasota Convention and Visitors Bureau. It contains three galleries and a small sculpture garden, presenting the area's largest display of art by national and local artists, from paintings and pottery to sculpture, cartoons, jewelry, and enamelware. There are also art demonstrations and special events.

PARKS, NATURE PRESERVES & GARDENS

The peaceful ✪ **Marie Selby Botanical Gardens,** South Palm Avenue, at U.S. 41 (☎ **941/366-5731;** www.selby.org), on the bay just south of downtown, is said to be the only botanical garden in the world specializing in the preservation, study, and research of epiphytic plants ("air plants"), such as orchids, pineapples, and ferns. It's home to more than 20,000 exotic plants, including more than 6,000 orchids, as well as a bamboo pavilion, butterfly and hummingbird garden, medicinal plant garden, waterfall garden, cactus and succulent garden, fernery, hibiscus garden, palm grove, two tropical food gardens, and a native shore-plant community. Admission is $8 for adults, $4 for children 6 to 11, free for children 5 and under accompanied by an adult. Open daily from 10am to 5pm.

Between downtown and the airport, the 10-acre **Sarasota Jungle Gardens,** 37–01 Bayshore Rd. (☎ **941/355-5305**), features lush tropical vegetation, cool jungle trails, tropical plants, exotic waterfowl, and reptiles in natural habitats. In addition, there are bird shows, reptile shows, a petting zoo, and a shell and butterfly museum. Admission is $9 for adults, $8 seniors, $5 for children 4 to 12, free for children 3 and under. Open daily from 9am to 5pm except Christmas. From downtown, take U.S. 41 north to Myrtle Street, turn left, and go two blocks.

On City Island, at the southern end of Longboat Key, kids love the ✪ **Mote Marine Aquarium,** 1600 Thompson Pkwy. (☎ **800/691-MOTE** or 941/388-4441) because they get to touch cool stuff like a stingray (minus the stinger, of course) and watch sharks in the shark tank. Part of the noted Mote Marine Laboratory complex, this facility focuses on the marine life of the Sarasota area and nearby gulf waters, including a manatee exhibit. The kids won't believe all the sea horse babies that come from the dad's pouch (one of Mother Nature's strange-but-true surprises). There are also many research-in-progress exhibits, and you can go on 1-hour, 45-minute environmental tours abroad a boat named the *Explorer* daily or on tropical sunset cruises daily (call ahead for times, reservations, and prices). Admission is $8 for adults, $6 for children 4 to 17, free for children 3 and under. Open daily from 10am to 5pm. From St. Armands Circle, go north toward Longboat Key; the aquarium is at the foot of the Lido-Longboat bridge.

On the aquarium grounds, **Pelican Man's Bird Sanctuary,** 1708 Thompson Pkwy. (☎ **941/388-4444**), is a sanctuary and rehabilitation center where more than 5,000 injured birds and other wildlife are treated each year. The sanctuary is home to about 30 species of birds. There's a gift shop with many bird-oriented items for sale. Admission is free, but donations are encouraged. Open daily from 10am to 5pm. From St. Armands Circle go north toward Longboat Key and follow the signs.

In the country, the **Myakka River State Park,** on Fla. 72 about 9 miles east of I-75, is one of Florida's largest, covering more than 35,000 acres of wetlands, prairies, and dense woodlands along the Myakka River. It's an outstanding wildlife sanctuary and breeding ground, home to hundreds of species of plants and animals, including alligators. Get an overview of the entire park via a 1-hour tram tour (during the winter) or a 1-hour airboat ride (year-round). Admission is $1 per person or $4 per car with two to eight occupants. **Myakka Wildlife & Nature Tours** (☎ **941/365-0100**) has nature excursions through the park by boat and tram. These cost $7 for adults, $3 for children 12 and under. Call for the schedules, which change seasonally. The park is open daily from 8am to sunset. For more information, contact the headquarters at 13207 S.R. 72, Sarasota, FL 34241 (☎ **941/361-6511**).

Near Myakka, you can see the famous **Lippizzan Stallions** do their dancing show at the Ottomar Herrmann training grounds, on Singletary Road (☎ **941/322-1501**). They perform at 3pm Thursday and Friday, at 10am Saturday from January to March. Call for ticket prices.

SHOPPING

Visitors come from all over the world to shop at ✪ **St. Armands Circle,** on St. Armands Key just inside Lido Key. Wander around this outdoor circle of more than

150 international boutiques, gift shops, galleries, restaurants, and nightspots, all surrounded by lush landscaping, patios, and antiques. Pick up a map at the Sarasota Convention and Visitors Bureau (see "Essentials," above). Many shops here are comparable to those in Palm Beach and on Naples's Third Avenue South, so check your credit-card limits—or resort to some great window shopping. I love to browse through **Global Navigator** (☎ **813/388-4515**), a travel equipment and apparel shop that reminds me of Banana Republic when it carried really unique items.

On Longboat Key, **Avenue of the Flowers** off Gulf of Mexico Drive is another good place to overmax your cards.

Downtown, the **Burns Court** and **Herald Square** historic districts, centered on Pineapple Avenue south of Ringling Boulevard, have a trove of upscale boutiques and art galleries worth exploring. Nearby, **Main Street** is more pedestrian, but it boasts a few art galleries and the **Main Bookshop** (☎ **941/366-7653**), the city's largest and most interesting bookstore for browsers and shoppers alike (open daily from 9am to 11pm). You can pick from the freshest of Florida's fruits and vegetables at the downtown **farmer's market,** from 7am to noon on Saturday on Lemon Avenue between Main and 1st streets.

Sarasota Square Mall, 8201 S. Tamiami Trail, at Beneva Road (☎ **941/922-9600**), south of downtown, is the area's largest enclosed mall. **Sarasota Outlet Mall,** on University Parkway just west of I-75 (☎ **941/359-2050**), has about 40 of the better known factory stores.

WHERE TO STAY

In addition to the chain hotels listed below, you'll find the **Comfort Inn** (☎ **800/228-5150** or 941/355-7091), **Days Inn Airport** (☎ **800/329-7466** or 941/355-9271), and **Hampton Inn** (☎ **800/336-9335** or 941/351-7734) standing side by side on Tamiami Trail (U.S. 41) between 47th Street and Mecca Drive, just south of the airport and near the Ringling Museums and the Asolo Center for the Performing Arts. All are of recent vintage and thoroughly modern. Also on U.S. 41 north between downtown and the airport, the local **Knights Inn** (☎ **800/843-5644** or 941/355-8867) and **Super 8 Motel** (☎ **800/800-8000** or 941/355-9326) were recently renovated and offer clean, comfortable, and inexpensive motel rooms. A new **Courtyard by Marriott** (☎ **800/321-2211** or 941/355-3337) and a **Sleep Inn** (☎ **800/627-5447** or 941/359-8558) are nearby on University Parkway opposite the airport.

With the beaches here virtually lined with condominiums, it's not surprising that the Resort at Longboat Key Club, the Colony Beach & Tennis Resort, and the Crescent View Beach Club (see below) actually are all condo projects operated as hotels. A good starting point in finding other options is the annual visitors guide published by the Sarasota Convention and Visitors Bureau (see "Essentials," above). It lists and briefly describes all the projects as well as the real estate agents who represent individual owners who rent their properties out. Among the agencies requiring stays of less than a month are **Argus Property Management,** 1200 Siesta Bayside, Sarasota, FL 34242 (☎ **800/237-2252** or 941/346-3499; fax 941/349-6156; www.argusmgmt. com); **Longboat Accommodations,** 4030 Gulf of Mexico Dr., Longboat Key, FL 34228 (☎ **800/237-9505** or 941/383-9505; fax 941/383-1830; www.longboatkey. com); and **Michael Saunders & Company,** 100 S. Washington Blvd., Sarasota, FL 34236 (☎ **800/881-2222** or 941/951-6668; www.michaelsaunders.com).

The hotels below are organized by geographic region: on the mainland, on Lido Key, on Longboat Key, and on Siesta Key. Some of the Longboat Key hotels mentioned below actually are in Manatee County, about halfway between Bradenton and downtown Sarasota.

With regard to prices, the high season here is from January to April. The best bargains are found May to September. Rates are usually higher along the beaches at all times, so bargain hunters should stick to the downtown area and commute to the beach. The hotel tax here is 9%.

ON THE MAINLAND

Best Western Midtown. 1425 S. Tamiami Trail (U.S. 41, at Prospect St.), Sarasota, FL 34239. ☎ **800/722-8227,** 800/528-1234, or 941/955-9841. Fax 941/954-8948. 100 units. A/C TV TEL. Winter $96–$106 double. Off-season $66–$82 double. Rates include continental breakfast. AE, DC, DISC, MC, V.

Location is the buzzword here, for this modern L-shaped two- and three-story hotel is 2 miles in either direction from the main causeways leading to the keys. Although positioned next to the Midtown Plaza shopping center, it's set back from the busy main road. Tropical palms and plantings surround a heated outdoor swimming pool and sundeck. Guests can graze a buffet-style breakfast, and there's a guest laundry. The rooms are modern and cheery, with light woods and Florida pastel tones. Some of them have kitchenettes.

Hyatt Sarasota. 1000 Blvd. of the Arts, Sarasota, FL 34236. ☎ **800/233-1234** or 941/953-1234. Fax 941/952-1987. 297 units. A/C TV TEL. Winter $199–$210 double. Off-season $109–$159 double. AE, DC, DISC, MC, V.

Located beside Sarasota Bay and boasting its own marina, this 10-story tower is the downtown area's centerpiece hotel. Attracting business travelers and groups, it sits adjacent to the Civic Center, the Van Wezel Performing Arts Hall, and the Sarasota Garden Club and is within walking distance of downtown shops and restaurants. The contemporary bedrooms have balconies overlooking the marina or bay; they have coffeemakers and hair dryers.

Dining/Diversions: The main dining room, Scalini, features northern Italian cuisine. The Boathouse offers casual fare and water views of the marina, while Tropics Lounge provides libations.

Amenities: Concierge, room service, valet parking and laundry, newspaper delivery, airport shuttle ($3 per person), baby-sitting. Heated outdoor swimming pool, patio, health club, marina.

Wellesley Inn & Suites. 1803 N. Tamiami Trail (U.S. 41, at 18th St.), Sarasota, FL 34234. ☎ **800/444-8888** or 941/366-5128. Fax 941/953-4322. 106 units. A/C TV TEL. Winter $110 double; $140 suite. Off-season $44 double; $60–$70 suite. Rates include continental breakfast. AE, DC, DISC, MC, V.

The closest chain motel to downtown, this four-story hotel with an impressive portico overlooks a marina and boatyard, but you won't have a balcony from which to enjoy the view. The bedrooms are spacious, with light woods, pastel tones, and coffeemakers. Suites have microwave ovens and refrigerators, which you can request for the rooms. There's laundry service, an outdoor heated swimming pool, and complimentary airport shuttle.

LIDO KEY

✪ **Half Moon Beach Club.** 2050 Ben Franklin Dr. (at Taft Dr.), Sarasota, FL 34236. ☎ **800/358-3245** or 941/388-3694. Fax 941/388-1938. 85 units. A/C MINIBAR TV TEL. Winter $115–$225 double. Off-season $85–$159 double. AE, DC, DISC, MC, V.

Near the south end of Lido, this two-story art deco–style hotel is right on the beach and less than half a block from South Lido Beach Park. The front of the building forms a circle around a small but very attractive courtyard with a heated pool and sunning area. From there, guests take a hallway through a motel-style block of rooms to the beach, where they can rent cabanas and order libation to be delivered from the bar inside. The spacious guest rooms are furnished with light woods, refrigerators, and coffeemakers, and some have kitchenettes with microwave ovens. Facilities include Seagrapes, an indoor/outdoor restaurant; an outdoor heated swimming pool; volleyball; a gulf-front sundeck; a coin laundry; and bike and video rentals. Complimentary newspapers are delivered to the rooms each morning.

Holiday Inn Lido Beach. 233 Ben Franklin Dr. (at Thoreau Dr.), Sarasota, FL 34236. ☎ **800/HOLIDAY** or 941/388-3941. Fax 941/388-4321. 140 units. A/C TV TEL. Winter $175–$219 double. Off-season $119–$179 double. AE, DC, MC, V.

Conveniently located at the north end of Lido, this modern seven-story hotel is within walking distance of St. Armands Circle. Unfortunately, the beach across the street has been heavily eroded by recent storms, losing much of the sand that once covered the rocks here. The bedrooms have balconies that face the gulf or the bay and are furnished with light woods, pastel fabrics, coffeemakers, and hair dryers.

Dining: The rooftop restaurant and lounge offers panoramic views of the Gulf of Mexico. Other outlets include a lobby lounge and a casual pool bar.

Amenities: Room service, valet laundry, baby-sitting, newspaper delivery. Outdoor heated swimming pool with gulf view, coin laundry, bicycle rentals, water-sports equipment.

LONGBOAT KEY

✪ **Colony Beach & Tennis Resort.** 1620 Gulf of Mexico Dr., Longboat Key, FL 34228. ☎ **800/4-COLONY** or 941/383-6464. Fax 941/383-7549. 235 units. Winter $300–$450 suite. Off-season $190–$350 suite. Packages available. AE, DISC, MC, V.

Sitting 3 miles north of St. Armands Circle, this beachside facility is consistently rated one of the nation's finest tennis resorts. Luxurious one- and two-bedroom villa suites, complete with living rooms, dining areas, fully equipped kitchenettes, and sun balconies, are built around 21 courts, two of them lighted for night play. A staff of 10 professionals conducts highly acclaimed programs for adults and children. The beachside Colony Restaurant and swimming pool date from 1952 when this was a beach club. Next door are three private gulf-side cottages right on the superb beach; they are the most expensive accommodations here. The villa suites date from 1974 but were extensively renovated and modernized in 1997.

Dining/Diversions: The Colony Restaurant offers continental cuisine for lunch and dinner (jackets requested for men at dinner). Sharing the old building, the informal Dining Room provides breakfast, lunch, and dinner. The poolside Colony Patio & Bar has casual dining. The lavish Sunday brunch here is popular with locals as well as out-of-towners. The Colony Lounge has nightly entertainment.

Amenities: Concierge, laundry and dry cleaning, baby-sitting, valet parking, courtesy limo, outstanding year-round supervised children's programs for ages 3 to 12. Health spa, complimentary tennis, beachfront swimming pool, fitness center, golf, deep-sea fishing, water sports, aerobic classes, bicycle rental, boutiques, beauty salon.

Holiday Inn Hotel & Suites. 4949 Gulf of Mexico Dr., Longboat Key, FL 34228. ☎ **800/ HOLIDAY** or 941/383-3771. Fax 941/838-7871. 146 units. A/C TV TEL. Winter $189–$259 double; $229–$329 suite. Off-season $129–$229 double; $159–$299 suite. AE, DC, DISC, MC, V.

In Manatee County about halfway up Longboat Key, 8 miles north of St. Armands Circle, this family oriented beachside motel recently underwent a multimillion-dollar renovation and upgrading. An indoor courtyard with a swimming pool, whirlpool, games area, and restaurants by Pizza Hut, Nathan's Famous, Mrs. Fields Cookies, and

Seattle's Best Coffee makes this a good respite on rainy days or during a cool snap. The contemporary rooms and suites have patios or balconies, with the choice units facing the beach.

Dining: In addition to the fast-food outlets, there's a restaurant-pub and a beachside snack bar.

Amenities: Concierge, limited room service, laundry. Indoor and outdoor pools and whirlpools, four lighted tennis courts, exercise room with sauna, gift shops, guest laundry, bicycle rental, water sports.

✪ **Longboat Key Hilton Beach Resort.** 4711 Gulf of Mexico Dr., Longboat Key, FL 34228. ☎ **800/282-3046** or 941/383-2451. Fax 941/383-7979. 102 units. A/C MINIBAR TV TEL. Winter $195–$295 double; $275–$375 suite. Off-season $140–$200 double; $225–$315 suite. Packages available. AE, DC, MC, V.

Also in Manatee County, 7½ miles north of St. Armands Circle, this five-story concrete building is surrounded by lush foliage and gardens. A much more charming gray wooden structure to one side holds all of the public facilities and more than makes up for the blandness of the rooms' building. The bar and pool area here are pleasant areas for relaxing lunches or sunset cocktails. The bedrooms are furnished in a tropical style. All have coffeemakers and hair dryers, and most have a patio or narrow balcony. A few gulf-front rooms are the most expensive.

Dining: The main restaurant offers great views of the gulf to accompany a seafood menu, while the poolside bar serves lunch and beverages.

Amenities: Room service, valet laundry, free shuttle to St. Armands Key for shopping. Heated outdoor swimming pool, private beach, bicycle and water-sports equipment rentals, one tennis court, shuffleboard.

Resort at Longboat Key Club. 301 Gulf of Mexico Dr. (P.O. Box 15000), Longboat Key, FL 34228. ☎ **800/237-8821** or 941/383-8821. Fax 941/383-0359. www.longboatkeyclub. com. 232 units. Winter $315–$515 suite. Off-season $155–$315 suite. Packages available off-season. AE, DISC, MC, V.

Part of a real estate development on 410 acres at the southern end of Longboat Key, this award-winning condo resort pampers the country-club set with upscale restaurants and a variety of recreational activities in a lush tropical setting. The suites, with private balconies overlooking the Gulf of Mexico, a lagoon, or golf course fairways, are luxurious. All have custom-designed furnishings and tropical fabrics. All but 20 units have full kitchens.

Dining/Diversions: Orchid's Restaurant has the feel of an elegant supper club, serving continental cuisine in a romantic setting, while the adjacent Orchid's Lounge offers casual dining and live entertainment. Barefoots Bar & Grille offers relaxed poolside dining. Overlooking the Islandside Golf Course, Island House Restaurant is famous for its champagne brunch, while Spike 'n Tees serves breakfast and lunch in an outdoor setting. At Harborside Marina, the Dining Room offers nightly theme buffets, while breakfast, lunch, and dinner are served at The Grille.

Amenities: Concierge, room service (7am to midnight), valet laundry, baby-sitting, supervised children's activities (in summer), in-room massage, newspaper delivery. Two golf courses (45 holes), golf school, two tennis centers (38 courts), 500 feet of beach with water sports, exercise track, steam rooms, jogging paths, nature trails, swimming pool, whirlpool, bicycle rentals, tour desk, boutiques.

SIESTA KEY

✪ **Best Western Siesta Beach Resort.** 5311 Ocean Blvd. (at Calle Miramar), Sarasota, FL 34242. ☎ **800/223-5786** or 941/349-3211. Fax 941/349-7915. 53 units. A/C TV TEL.

Winter $120 double; $159–$220 suite. Off-season $59 double; $85–$120 suite. Weekly rates available. AE, DC, DISC, MC, V.

In Siesta Village on the northern end of the key, this older but very well maintained motel has two buildings across the street from each other. It offers standard hotel rooms and one- and two-bedroom suites, all decorated in pastel tones with light woods. The suites have kitchenettes. Facilities include a heated swimming pool, whirlpool, and guest laundry. Public beach access is across the street, and Siesta Key Public Beach is about half a mile away.

Crescent View Beach Club. 6512 Midnight Pass Rd. (at Old Stickney Point Rd.), Sarasota, FL 34242. ☎ **800/344-7171** or 941/349-2000. Fax 941/349-9748. 26 units. A/C TV TEL. Winter $190–$350 efficiency or suite for 2. Off-season $120–$260 efficiency or suite for 2. AE, DISC, MC, V.

Located in the business district where Stickney Point Bridge comes onto Siesta Key in its midsection, this four-story establishment offers one- and two-bedroom condo suites facing the beach and gulf as well as efficiencies overlooking the pool or garden. All units are decorated in tropical tones with rattan furnishings; each has a living/dining area and a balcony. The smaller units have kitchenettes with microwave ovens and coffeemakers; the condo suites have completely outfitted kitchens with dishwashers. There's a guest laundry on the premises.

Gulf Sun Motel. 6722 Midnight Pass Rd. (at Sarasota Circle), Sarasota, FL 34242. ☎ **800/ 653-6753** or 941/349-2442. Fax 941/349-7141. 17 units. A/C TV TEL. Winter $90 double; $115–$125 efficiency. Off-season $50 double; $65–$75 efficiency. DISC, MC, V.

Also in Siesta Key's midsection business district, this one-story, 1960s motel with red Spanish tile roof is clean and within a 2-block walk of Crescent Beach. The bedrooms have standard furnishings with queen-size beds and refrigerators. All but two units here are efficiencies with kitchens. A swimming pool is set in the motel's roadside lawn.

✪ Turtle Beach Resort. 9049 Midnight Pass Rd., Sarasota, FL 34242. ☎ **941/349-4554.** Fax 941/918-0203. 5 units. A/C TV TEL. Winter $1,200–$1,700 per week cottage. Off-season $125–$200 per day cottage. AE, DC, DISC, MC, V.

On Siesta Key's south end near Turtle Beach, this intimate little bay-side charmer began life years ago as a traditional Old Florida fishing camp. In the early 1990s, owners Gail and Dave Rubinfeld renovated the small clapboard cottages and turned them into this comfortable inn. With an eye to romance, they gave each cozy unit a patio with its own whirlpool shielded from view by a high wooden fence.

The cottages are done in Victorian, Southwest, Key West, country French, or traditional American country cottage decor. The living room of the American country model sits, docklike, right on the bay (it's justifiably the honeymoon cottage), and the Southwest model looks across the bay-side pool to the water. There's no restaurant on the grounds, but Ophelia's on the Bay seafood restaurant next door was once the old fishing camp's dining room, and two units have kitchens (all have microwave ovens and coffeemakers). The complex is tightly packed, but heavy tropical foliage provides privacy. Guests can use fishing poles and paddleboats. No smoking is allowed inside, but the Rubinfelds do take pets (10% extra charge). Winter rentals are by the week, but you might be able to get a few nights if there's a vacancy.

WHERE TO DINE

The restaurants below are organized geographically: on the mainland, on St. Armands Key (next to Lido Key), and on Siesta Key. You can also drive up to the north end of

Longboat Key to Moore's Stone Crab, which is just across the bridge on Bradenton Beach (see "Where to Dine," in section 6, below).

The Tamiami Trail (U.S. 41) has most of the national chain fast-food and family restaurants, especially in the area around Sarasota Square Mall south of downtown.

ON THE MAINLAND
Moderate

Bijou Cafe. 1287 1st St. (at Pineapple Ave.). ☎ **941/366-8111.** Reservations recommended. Main courses $17–$23. AE, DC, MC, V. Mon–Thurs 11:30am–2pm and 5–9:30pm, Fri 11:30am–2pm and 5–10:30pm, Sat 5–10:30pm, Sun 5–9:30pm. Closed Sun June–Dec. INTERNATIONAL.

Locals always recommend the award-winning cuisine at this charming cafe in the heart of the theater district. Menu highlights include the likes of prime veal Louisville (with crushed pecans and bourbon-pear sauce), sautéed red snapper, and New Orleans crab cakes. Watching your weight? You may request a "fit and trim" menu. The outstanding wine list has been recognized by *Wine Spectator* magazine.

Cafe of the Arts. 5230 N. Tamiami Trail (near University Pkwy.). ☎ **941/351-4304.** Reservations recommended for dinner. Main courses $11–$20. AE, DISC, MC, V. Mon–Fri 11am–3pm and 5–9pm, Sat 9am–3pm and 5–9pm, –Sun 9am–3pm and 5–9pm. FRENCH.

Warm and soothing hospitality with a European flair welcomes you to Alain Taulere's cafe-bakery-wine bar. Across from the Ringling museum complex, this gathering place offers an artsy ambience with photos of entertainers and scenes of Europe on the walls. Dinner dishes range from heart-healthy vegetable platters to rack of lamb dijonnais. Don't leave until you sample the chocolate eclair or strawberry mousse. Breakfast is served Saturday and Sunday.

Coasters Marina Bar & Restaurant. In Sarasota Boat Yard Shopping Village, 1500 Stickney Point Rd. (east end of Stickney Point Rd. Bridge). ☎ **941/923-4848.** Reservations recommended. Main courses $13–$17. AE, DC, DISC, MC, V. Sun–Thurs 11:30am–10pm, Fri–Sat 11:30am–10:30pm (bar to 1:30am). SEAFOOD.

On the bay in a quaint, New England–style shopping complex and marina, this casual restaurant offers great water views and fresh seafood selections like grouper, snapper, swordfish, and mahimahi. The indoor brasserie-style dining room leads to an outdoor sundeck and waterfront patio. There's a children's menu and entertainment Thursday to Saturday during winter.

Marina Jack. In Island Park, Bayfront at Central Ave. ☎ **941/365-4232.** Reservations recommended. Main courses $9–$22. MC, V. Dining room daily noon–3pm and 5–10pm; lounge daily noon–10pm. SEAFOOD/CONTINENTAL.

Be sure to make reservations before you go to this longtime favorite. It has spectacular water vistas and a carefree "on vacation" attitude. Overlooking the waterfront with a wraparound 270° view of Sarasota Bay and Siesta and Lido keys, this restaurant is synonymous with seafood. The menu offers fresh native fish such as grouper, red snapper, swordfish, tuna, and dolphin, prepared charcoal-grilled, pan-seared, blackened, or sautéed. In addition, there are half a dozen shrimp selections, crab-stuffed roughy, and Caribbean lobster, as well as steaks, chicken, and pastas. The dining room closes daily from 3 to 5pm, but the Deep Six Lounge continues serving a snack menu.

If you prefer to dine on the bay rather than beside it, the paddle-wheel sightseeing boat *Marina Jack II* (☎ 941/366-9255) offers dinner cruises from October to August. Call for information and reservations.

✪ **Michael's on East.** 1212 East Ave. S. (between Bahia and Prospect sts.). ☎ **941/ 366-0007.** Reservations recommended. Main courses $14.50–$26. AE, DC, MC, V. Winter

Mon–Fri 11:30am–2pm, daily 5:30–10pm. Off-season Mon–Fri 11:30am–2pm, Mon–Sat 6–10pm. CREATIVE INTERNATIONAL.

At the rear of the Midtown Plaza shopping center on U.S. 41 south of downtown, this chic art-deco bistro is one of the top places here for fine dining. Huge cut-glass walls create three intimate dining areas, one with a black marble bar for pre- or after-dinner drinks. Prepared with fresh ingredients and a creative flair, the offerings here will tempt your taste buds. A heart of palm salad with mangoes, stone crab meat, and a brazil nut dressing is an exciting starter. From there, you can progress to spicy Louisiana-style crab cakes, seared Chilean sea bass with a roasted garlic and lemon sauce, or perhaps duckling served with a Bartlett pear relish.

Nick's on the Water. In Sarasota Quay, Tamiami Trail at Fruitville Rd. ☎ **941/954-3839.** Reservations recommended. Main courses $10–$18. AE, DISC, MC, V. Winter Sun–Thurs 11:30am–10pm, Fri–Sat 11:30am–11pm. Off-season Sun–Thurs 11:30am–9pm, Fri–Sat 11:30am–10pm ITALIAN/SEAFOOD.

In the Sarasota Quay waterfront dining, shopping, and entertainment complex a block north of the John Ringling Causeway, this indoor/outdoor spot is really two restaurants. One is a terrace overlooking the marina; the other, an indoor wine bar with a winery ambience. The menu offers pizzas and pastas as well as such traditional Italian dishes as veal or chicken prepared parmigiana, marsala, or française style, and shrimp scampi or fradiavolo. There are sports TVs in the bar and live entertainment Thursday to Saturday nights.

Inexpensive
First Watch. 1395 Main St. (at Central and Pineapple aves.). Reservations not accepted. Breakfast $3–$6; sandwiches and salads, $4–$6.50. AE, DISC, MC, V. Daily 7am–2:30pm. AMERICAN.

Like its sister establishment in Naples (see section 5 in chapter 10), this bright dining room with natural wood Windsor chairs at oak-trimmed tables is *the* downtown place for breakfast or lunch (it's usually packed on weekend mornings, so be prepared to wait). Traditional breakfast offerings range widely, from bacon and eggs and omelettes to a skillet layered with eggs and vegetables. There are several healthy choices, too, such as oatmeal cooked with cinnamon and apples. Lunch adds sandwiches on fresh bread and creative salads, including a tasty white-meat chicken version with raisins and crunchy water chestnuts.

Patrick's. 1400 Main St. (at Pineapple and Central aves.). ☎ **941/952-1170.** Reservations not accepted. Sandwiches and burgers $5.50–$7; main courses $11–$15. AE, MC, V. Daily 11am–midnight (Sun brunch 11am–3pm). AMERICAN.

With a semicircular facade, this informal, polished-oak and brass-rail brasserie offers wide-windowed views of downtown's main intersection. The decor also boasts hanging plants and ceiling fans, plus a unique collection of sports memorabilia. The menu offers a range of pub fare: steaks and chops, burgers, seafood, pastas, salads, sandwiches, and omelettes; plus veal piccata, francese, or marsala; broiled salmon with dill-hollandaise sauce; and sesame chicken.

○ Yoder's. 3434 Bahia Vista St. (west of Bahia Rd.). ☎ **941/955-7771.** Reservations not accepted. Breakfast $2–$6; sandwiches and burgers $3–$6; main courses $6.50–$12. No credit cards. Mon–Sat 6am–8pm. AMISH/AMERICAN.

It's worth driving about 3 miles east of downtown to check out this good-value, award-winning eatery operated by an Amish family (both Sarasota and Bradenton have sizable Amish communities). Evoking the Pennsylvania Dutch country, the simple dining room displays handcrafts, photos, and paintings celebrating the Amish way.

The menu emphasizes plain, made-from-scratch cooking such as home-style meat loaf, baked and southern fried chicken, country-smoked ham, and fried fillet of flounder. Burgers, salads, soups, and sandwiches are also available. Leave room for traditional shoo-fly pie. There's neither alcohol nor smoking here. They don't take credit cards, but there's an ATM machine near the entrance.

ST. ARMANDS KEY
Expensive
✪ **Cafe l'Europe.** 431 St. Armands Circle (at John Ringling Blvd.). ☎ **941/388-4415.** Reservations recommended. Main courses $18–$26. Pretheater dinner, $55 per couple. AE, DC, MC, V. Daily 11am–4pm and 5–10pm (pretheater dinner, daily 5–6:15pm). CONTINENTAL.

As its name implies, a European atmosphere prevails at this consistently excellent restaurant, with a decor of brick walls and arches, dark woods, brass fixtures, pink linens, and hanging plants. The menu offers selections ranging from bouillabaisse Marseilles (with lobster, snapper, shrimp, and clams) to veal and portobello napoleon with fresh tomato, garlic, and herb sauce over bow-tie pasta. A fine value, the fixed-price, pretheater dinner includes a bottle of wine.

Moderate
Charley's Crab. 420 St. Armands Circle (between John Ringling Blvd. and Blvd. of the Presidents). ☎ **941/388-3964.** Reservations recommended. Main courses $13.50–$20; dinner sandwiches $7–$10.50. AE, MC, V. Mon–Thurs 11:30am–10pm, Fri–Sat 11:30am–10:30pm, Sun noon–10pm. SEAFOOD.

A favorite for people-watching, Charley's is popular not just for crab cakes and crab fettuccine (with mushrooms and basil in a shrimp sauce) but for a full range of seafood dishes. Alfresco diners fill sidewalk tables early at lunch and dinner as shoppers stroll past. A pianist adds to the lively outdoor atmosphere. Large windows in the comfortable indoor dining room give a great view of the passing parade as well.

Columbia. St. Armands Circle (between John Ringling Blvd. and John Ringling Pkwy.). ☎ **941/388-3987.** Reservations recommended. Main courses $14–$22. Early bird specials $10–$14. AE, DC, DISC, MC, V. Mon–Sat 11am–11pm, Sun noon–10pm. Early bird specials daily 4–6pm. SPANISH.

Like the original Columbia in Tampa's Ybor City (see "Where to Dine," in section 1), this one is a culinary tour de force of Spanish specialties. You can dine outside or inside, where old-world decor combines graciousness with New World efficiency and impeccable service. If you can't decide what to order, try the paella valenciana prepared with grouper, shrimp, calamari, mussels, clams, chicken, and lean pork. All main dishes include Cuban bread and rice or potato. The early bird specials are good values for pretheater dining. The Patio Lounge is one of the liveliest spots here for evening entertainment from Thursday to Sunday.

Hemingway's. 325 John Ringling Blvd. (½ block off St. Armands Circle). ☎ **941/388-3948.** Reservations recommended. Main courses $12–$22; dinner sandwiches $8–$12. AE, DC, DISC, MC, V. Sun–Thurs 11:30am–10pm, Fri–Sat 11:30am–11pm. FLORIDIAN/CARIBBEAN.

For a casual spot with an eclectic "Floribbean" menu and a large bar with a friendly, laid-back Key West ambience, take the elevator or climb the winding stairs to this above-the-mob second-floor hideaway. Hemingway's is charming and comfortable in the best Old Florida tradition. The decor features a mix of green floral booths and tables with rattan chairs. You might start with gator bits or conch fritters, then choose from an evenly distributed mix of seafood, barbecued ribs, and other meats. Mariner's shrimp is a healthy winner: they're perfectly charcoal grilled, basted with a light teriyaki sauce, and served over rice with fresh asparagus and baby carrots.

Inexpensive

The Buttery. 470 John Ringling Blvd. (1 block off St. Armand's Circle). ☎ **941/388-1523.** Reservations not accepted. Breakfast $4–$8; sandwiches $5.50–$6.50; main courses $8–$10 at dinner. AE, DISC, MC, V. Daily 6:30am–11pm. AMERICAN/DINER.

On the John Ringling Boulevard spoke of St. Armands Circle, this plain, informal diner is the only inexpensive place to eat in this affluent area. It offers standard breakfast and lunch choices as well as mesquite-grilled breast of chicken, Jamaican jerk chicken, fish-and-chips, grilled grouper, and an 8-ounce rib eye steak at dinner. You can order breakfast anytime.

SIESTA KEY

Turtles. 8875 Midnight Pass Rd. (at Turtle Beach Rd.). ☎ **941/346-2207.** Reservations not accepted. Salads and sandwiches $6–$9; main courses $9–$15; early bird specials $8. AE, DC, DISC, MC, V. Winter daily 11:30am–11pm. Off-season daily 11:30am–9:30pm. Early bird specials daily 4–6pm. AMERICAN.

With tropical overtones and breathtaking water vistas across from Turtle Beach, this informal restaurant on Little Sarasota Bay has tables both indoors and on an outside deck at which to try dishes such as snapper New Orleans, Florida-style blue crab cakes, or steak under a Jack Daniels whiskey sauce. There's a selection of pastas and platters to devour. The early bird specials include a medium-sized fish portion.

SARASOTA AFTER DARK

The cultural capital of Florida's west coast, Sarasota is home to a host of performing arts, especially during the winter season. To get the latest update on what's happening any time of year, call the city's 24-hour **Artsline** (☎ **941/365-ARTS**).

THE PERFORMING ARTS   Designated as the State Theater of Florida in 1965, the ✪ **Asolo Center for the Performing Arts,** 5555 N. Tamiami Trail (U.S. 41), at the Ringling museum complex (☎ **941/351-8000**), is home to the Asolo Theatre Company and the Conservatory for Professional Actor Training. The main stage, the 487-seat Harold E. and Ethel M. Mertz Theatre, is an attraction in itself—the former Dumfermline Opera House, originally constructed in Scotland in 1900 and transferred piece by piece to Sarasota in 1987. In 1994–95 the 161-seat Asolo Conservatory Theatre was added as a smaller venue for experimental and alternative offerings. The season runs from December to mid-June for the main stage and from November to May for the smaller theater. Ticket prices range from $5 to $39.

Free guided tours of the center are offered Wednesday to Saturday from 10 to 11:30am, except from June to August and during technical rehearsals between plays; call for tour times.

Downtown, the lavender, seashell-shaped **Van Wezel Performing Arts Hall,** 777 N. Tamiami Trail (U.S. 41), at 9th Street (☎ **941/953-3366**), is visible for miles on the bay-front skyline. It offers excellent visual and acoustic conditions, with year-round programs ranging from symphony and jazz concerts, opera, musical comedy, and choral productions to ballet and international productions. It's the home of the Florida West Coast Symphony, the Jazz Club of Sarasota, the Sarasota Ballet of Florida, and the Sarasota Concert Band.

Downtown Sarasota's theater district is home to the **Florida Studio Theatre,** 1241 N. Palm Ave., at Cocoanut Avenue (☎ **941/366-9796**), which has contemporary performances from December to August, including a New Play Festival in May. **The Opera House,** 61 N. Pineapple Ave., between Main and 1st streets

(☎ 941/953-7030), hosts the Sarasota Opera in February and March, while the Sarasota Ballet and other companies take the stage the rest of the year. Next door to The Opera House, the **Golden Apple Dinner Theatre,** 25 N. Pineapple Ave. (☎ 941/366-5454), presents cocktails, dinner, and a professional Broadway-style show year-round. The professional, nonequity **Theatre Works,** 1247 1st St., at Cocoanut Ave. (☎ 941/952-9170), presents musical revues and other works all year.

THE CLUB & MUSIC SCENE   You can find plenty of music to dance to at **Sarasota Quay,** the downtown waterfront dining-shopping-entertainment complex on Tamiami Trail (U.S. 41) a block north of John Ringling Causeway. Just walk around this brick building and your ears will take you to the action. The laser sound-and-light crowd gathers at **In Extremis** (☎ 941/954-2008), where a high-energy deejay spins Top 40 tunes. **Downunder Jazz Bar** (☎ 941/951-2467) offers contemporary jazz. Michael's Seafood Grill turns into **Anthony's After Dark** rocking disco at 10:30pm. And the Vineyard at **Nick's on the Water** restaurant offers live entertainment on weekends and sports TV all week.

Over on St. Armands Circle, the Patio Lounge in the Columbia Restaurant (☎ 941/388-3987) is one of the liveliest spots along the beach strip, featuring live, high-energy dance music on Tuesday to Sunday evenings.

You laughing types can get yours at **Coconuts Comedy Club,** 8440 N. Tamiami Trail (U.S. 41), north of downtown (☎ 941/351-8225). Open Thursday to Saturday nights.

6 Bradenton & Anna Maria Island

26 miles S of St. Petersburg, 41 miles SW of Tampa, 15 miles N of Sarasota

Visitors often overlook Bradenton as they speed south on their way to Sarasota and beyond. But if you stop, you'll thoroughly enjoy this pleasant town on the Manatee River, and especially **Anna Maria Island,** northernmost in the chain of barrier islands stretching from Tampa Bay to Sarasota. Anna Maria claims 7½ miles of white-sand beaches—but no glitzy resorts, just a lot of casual island getaways. The island's communities—Bradenton Beach, Holmes Beach, and Anna Maria—are popular with family vacationers and seniors, offering a variety of public beaches, fishing piers, bungalows, and low-rise motels. You can have a very relaxing beach vacation here without the high-rises, bustle, and out-of-sight prices found elsewhere.

Bradenton and Manatee County also own the northern half of Longboat Key, connected by bridge to Anna Maria Island. Most of the Longboat resorts are closer to Sarasota than to Bradenton, so I have included them in section 5 of this chapter. On the northern tip of Longboat, the little fishing village of Longbeach was established in 1885 and still has some remnants of Old Florida.

Although mainland Bradenton has been touched by urban sprawl in recent years, the town maintains links with the past through its historic Old Main Street, many Spanish-style buildings, and historic parks and sites. Compared to affluent Sarasota, its southern neighbor, Bradenton is a working-class community synonymous with the sweet aroma of fresh oranges. As the home of Tropicana, this city of 40,000 people is a major producer of orange juice and citrus products.

ESSENTIALS

GETTING THERE   From Tampa, take I-75 south. From St. Petersburg, go south across the Sunshine Skyway on I-275, then follow U.S. 19 and U.S. 41 south. The easiest way from I-75 into downtown Bradenton is to take Exit 43 and follow U.S. 301 south across the Manatee River.

Bradenton shares **Sarasota-Bradenton International Airport** with Sarasota (see "Essentials," in section 5, above). **Diplomat Taxi** (☎ **941/355-5155**) charges about $20 to downtown Bradenton, $30 to Bradenton Beach, and $35 to Anna Maria Island.

VISITOR INFORMATION　For a packet of information about Bradenton, Anna Maria Island, and surrounding Manatee County, contact the **Greater Bradenton Area Convention and Visitors Bureau,** P.O. Box 1000, Bradenton, FL 34206 (☎ **800/ 4-MANATEE** or 941/729-9177; fax 941/729-1820; www.floridaislandbeaches.org).

For maps, brochures, and specific information, call or drop by the **Manatee County Tourist Information Center,** on U.S. 301 just west of Exit 43 off I-75 (☎ **941/729-7040**). Open daily except holidays from 8:30am to 5:30pm, it has a volunteer staff on hand to answer your questions.

CITY LAYOUT　Bradenton is laid out in a grid. The east-west line of demarcation is **14th Street (U.S. 41),** which runs north-south through town. All **streets** are numbered and run north-south; they're designated as "east" or "west" of U.S. 41. Also numbered, **avenues** run east-west, ascending numerically from the Manatee River. Like the streets, avenues are also labeled as "east" or "west" of U.S. 41.

The basic core of **downtown** hugs the Manatee River near 12th Street. Originally known as Main Street, 12th Street (or "Old Main Street") today contains a row of historic old buildings leading to the Manatee River and a waterfront pier.

Seven miles due west of downtown, narrow **Anna Maria Island** has three beach communities: **Anna Maria,** to the north, **Holmes Beach** in the center, and **Bradenton Beach** to the south. **Gulf Drive** is the main north-south drag through all three towns.

Two major arteries lead due west to Anna Maria Island. **Manatee Avenue** (Fla. 64) is the northern route, running from downtown straight to Holmes Beach and Anna Maria. **Cortez Road/44th Avenue West** (Fla. 684) goes through the southern suburbs to Bradenton Beach; it passes through the old fishing community of **Cortez,** now a busy cruise and dining spot, just before crossing a bridge to Anna Maria Island.

From Anna Maria's southern tip, a bridge crosses over to **Longboat Key** and another old fishing village, **Longbeach.** From there, **Gulf of Mexico Drive** leads 12 miles south to St. Armands Key in Sarasota (see section 5).

GETTING AROUND　Based in Sarasota (see section 5, above), **Trolley Systems of America** (☎ **800/787-6554** or 941/346-3115) provides service along Anna Maria Island Tuesday to Saturday, with pickups in Bradenton twice a day. The fare is $5, free for kids under 3. Call for the exact schedules and to make reservations.

Manatee County Area Transit, known locally as **Manatee CAT** (☎ **941/ 749-7116**), operates scheduled public bus service throughout the area. The basic fare is $1, with exact change required. Route number 5 goes out Cortez Avenue to Anna Maria Island. From downtown, take route number 4 to Blake Hospital and transfer there to route number 5.

Taxi companies in Bradenton include **Bruce's Taxi** (☎ **941/755-6070**), **Checker Cab** (☎ **941/751-3181**), and **Yellow Cab** (☎ **941/748-4800**).

HITTING THE BEACH

There are four public beaches on Anna Maria Island, all with rest rooms, picnic areas, lifeguards, and free parking. The largest and best is **Coquina Beach,** which occupies the southern mile of the island below Bradenton Beach. It has both gulf and bay sides, is sheltered by whispering Australian pines, and has large parking lots. **Cortez Beach** is in Bradenton Beach, just north of Coquina Beach. In the island's center, **Manatee**

County Public Beach is at Gulf Drive. **Holmes Beach** is at the west end of Manatee Avenue (Fla. 64). **Anna Maria Bayfront Park** is on Bay Boulevard at the northwest end of the island, fronting both the bay and the Gulf of Mexico.

OUTDOOR ACTIVITIES & SPECTATOR SPORTS

BIKING & IN-LINE SKATING   The flat terrain makes for good in-line skating and fine if not challenging bike riding. **Native Rentals,** 5302 Marina Dr. in Holmes Beach (☎ 941/778-7757), rents both, with bikes starting at $3 an hour or $9 per day, skates for $4 an hour or $15 a day. The office is behind the BP service station on Gulf Drive in the Holmes Beach business district. Open Monday to Saturday from 7am to 7pm, Sunday from 9am to 5pm.

BOATING & FISHING   When Florida's ban on net fishing devastated its traditional business, the village of Cortez on the east side of the Cortez Bridge aimed for another catch: tourist dollars. Here you can rent boats, go deep-sea fishing, and take a sightseeing cruise on the bay, all provided by the **Cortez Fleet,** 4330 127th St. W. (☎ 941/794-1223). The rental part of the business has ski and pontoon boats, Wave-Runners, and other equipment, ranging in price from $45 an hour for WaveRunners to $155 for a day's use of a pontoon boat. Party boat deep-sea fishing voyages range from 4 hours to 9 hours, with prices starting at $25 for adults, $22 for seniors, and $12.50 for children. Call for the schedules, which can change from day to day.

On Anna Maria Island, you can rent boats from **Bradenton Beach Marina,** 402 Church Ave. (☎ 941/778-2288); **Captain's Marina,** 5501 Marina Dr., Holmes Beach (☎ 941/778-1977); and **Five O'Clock Marina,** 412 Pine Ave., Anna Maria (☎ 941/778-5577). On northern Longboat Key, **Cannons Marina,** 6040 Gulf of Mexico Dr. (☎ 941/383-1311), also rents boats. Several deep-sea fishing charter boats are based at these marinas.

You also can fish from **Anna Maria City Pier,** on the north end of Anna Maria Island, and at the **Bradenton Beach City Pier,** at Cortez Road. Both are free of charge.

CRUISES   The *Miss Cortez XI* (☎ 941/794-1223), operated by the Cortez Fleet (see "Boating & Fishing," above), makes sightseeing cruises to **Egmont Key State Park,** on historic Egmont Key 3 miles off the northern end of Anna Maria Island at the mouth of Tampa Bay. This uninhabited island is the site of a lighthouse, of now-crumbling Fort Dade (built in 1900 during the Spanish American War but abandoned long ago), and of threatened gopher tortoises. Sea turtles come ashore here to nest. You can go snorkeling and shelling here, so bring your swim suit and gear. This cruise costs $14 for adults, $8 for children 14 and under. Call for the schedules and reservations, which are recommended.

You can also get to Egmont Key on a 30-foot sloop-rigged sailboat with **Spice Sailing Charters** (☎ 941/778-3240), based at the Galati Yacht Basin on Bay Boulevard on northern Anna Maria Island. The company also has sunset cruises. Call for schedule, prices, and reservations, which are required.

That paddlewheeler you see going up and down the bay is the ***Seafood Shack Showboat,*** operated by the Seafood Shack restaurant, 4110 127th St. W., in Cortez (☎ 800/299-5048 or 941/794-5048). It has afternoon and sunset cruises to Sarasota Bay, Tampa Bay, and as far away as the Sunshine Skyway. Prices range from $11.22 to $14.95 for adults, $10.28 to $14.02 for seniors, and $4.67 to $5.61 for children 4 to 11. The *Showboat* goes to a different destination each day, so call for the schedule.

Open-air, eight-passenger craft are operated by **Manatee Airboat Tours,** Perico Harbour Marina, Manatee Avenue (U.S. 64) (☎ 941/730-1011). The ride lasts

55 minutes, with departures year-round. Rides cost $12 for adults, $10 for children. Call for schedule and reservations.

You can also skim across the bays with **Sun Hovercraft Rides,** 12507 Cortez Rd., Cortez (☎ **941/792-1290**). They run from Tuesday to Sunday. Call for times, prices, and reservations.

GOLF   The city and county operate several municipal courses where you can play without breaking your budget.

Locals say they prefer the county's 18-hole, par 72 **Buffalo Creek Golf Course,** on the north side of the river at 8100 Erie Road in Palmetto (☎ **941/776-2611**). At well over 7,000 yards, it's the longest in the area, and lots of water and alligators will keep you entertained. Wintertime greens fees are about $34 with cart, $24 without. They drop to about $18 and $16, respectively, during summer.

You'll pay the same at **Manatee County Golf Course,** 5290 66th St. W. (☎ **941/792-6773**), an 18-hole, par-72 course on the southern rim of the city. Both county courses require that tee times be set up at least 2 days in advance.

Also open to the public, the city's **River Run Golf Links,** 1801 27th St. E. (☎ **941/747-6331**), set beside the Braden River, is an 18-hole, par-70 course with lots of water in its layout. Winter fees here are about $26 with cart, $17 walking. They're about $16 riding, $8 walking in summer. A 2-day advance notice is required for tee times here, too.

Other courses include the **Palma Sola Golf Club,** 3807 75th St. W. (☎ **941/792-7476**), just north of Fla. 684 and east of Palma Sola Bay, with an 18-hole, par-72 course and the same 2-day advance booking requirement.

Situated just off U.S. 41, the **Heather Hills Golf Club,** 101 Cortez Rd. W. (☎ **941/755-8888**), operates an 18-hole, par-61 executive course on a first-come, first-served basis. There's a driving range and clubs can be rented. It's open daily from 6:30am until dark.

Bradenton also is home to the well-known **David Leadbetter Golf Academy,** 1414 69th Ave. (at U.S. 41) (☎ **800/424-3542** or 941/739-2483), a part of the Nick Bollettieri Sports Academy (see "Tennis," below). Presided over by one of golf's leading instructors, this facility offers practice tee instruction, video analysis, and scoring strategy, as well as general tuition. Prices start at $150.

SPECTATOR SPORTS   The **Pittsburgh Pirates** do their February-through-March spring training at 6,562-seat **McKechnie Field,** 9th Street West and 17th Avenue West (☎ **941/748-4610**), south of downtown. Admission ranges from $5.50 to $8.50.

TENNIS   The **Nick Bollettieri Sports Academy,** 5500 34th St. W. (☎ **800/872-6425** or 941/755-1000), is one of the world's largest tennis-training facilities, with more than 70 championship courts and a pro shop. It's open year-round, and reservations are required for all activities. One-day instructional programs cost $163 for adults, $155 for juniors age 8 to 18. Overnight packages start at $285 for adults, $185 for juniors. The academy also has training courses in soccer, baseball, and football.

The municipal **Walton Racquet Center,** 5502 33rd Ave. Dr. W. (☎ **941/742-5973**), has eight clay and eight hard tennis courts plus eight racquetball courts. It's open Monday to Thursday from 7am to 9:30pm, on Friday from 7:30am to 5:45pm, and on Saturday and Sunday from 7am to 1pm. Prices are $2.50 per person for 1½ hours on the hard courts, $4.50 on the clay courts, and $3 for racquetball.

EXPLORING THE AREA

On weekends, you can see the sights of rural Manatee County northwest of Bradenton on a 1¼-hour narrated sightseeing tour aboard a 1950s diesel-engine train operated by the **Florida Gulf Coast Railroad**, 83rd Street East, off U.S. 301 in Parrish (☎ **941/ 722-4272**). The schedule and fares are seasonal, so call before driving out here.

Art League of Manatee County. 209 9th St. W. (Business U.S. 41, at 3rd Ave. W.). ☎ **941/746-2862.** Free admission. Mon–Fri 9am–4:30pm.

Bradenton's downtown cultural hub, this gallery offers an ever-changing program of art exhibits, shows, courses, workshops, and craft demonstrations.

✪ **DeSoto National Memorial.** DeSoto Memorial Hwy. (north end of 75th St. W.). ☎ **941/792-0458.** Free admission. Daily 9am–5pm. Take Manatee Ave. (Fla. 64) west to 75th St. W. and turn right; follow the road to its end and the entrance to the park.

Nestled on the Manatee River west of downtown, this park re-creates the look and atmosphere of when Spanish explorer Hernando de Soto landed here in 1539. It includes a restoration of de Soto's original campsite and a scenic half-mile nature trail that circles a mangrove jungle and leads to the ruins of one of the first settlements of the area. From December to March, park employees dress in 16th-century costumes and portray the way the early settlers lived, including demonstrations of cooking and musket firing.

Gamble Plantation. 3708 Patten Ave., Ellenton. ☎ **941/723-4536.** Free admission. Tours $3 adults, $1.50 children 6–12, free for children under 6. Thurs–Mon 9am–5pm; guided tours given at 9:30 and 10:30am, and 1, 2, 3, and 4pm. Take U.S. 301 north of downtown to Ellenton; the site is on the left at the juncture of U.S. 301 and Ellenton-Gillette Rd. (Fla. 683).

Situated northeast of downtown Bradenton, this is the oldest structure on the southwestern coast of Florida, and a fine example of an antebellum plantation home. Built over a 6-year period in the late 1840s by Maj. Robert Gamble, it was constructed primarily of "tabby mortar" (a mixture of oyster shells, sand, molasses, and water), with 10 rooms, verandas on three sides, 18 exterior columns, and 8 fireplaces. It's maintained as a state historic site and includes a fine collection of 19th-century furnishings. Entrance to the house is by tour only, although the grounds may be explored on your own.

Manatee Village Historical Park. 6th Ave. E. and 15th St. E. ☎ **941/749-7165.** Free admission; donations welcome. Mon–Fri 9am–4:30pm, Sun 1:30–4:30pm. Call for Sat hours. Closed Sun July–Aug. From downtown, go east on 6th Ave. E. through a merger with Manatee Ave., then right on 15th St. E.

A tree-shaded park with a courtyard of hand-laid bricks, this national historic site features restored buildings from the city of Bradenton and the surrounding county. It contains the Manatee County Court House, dating from 1860 and the oldest structure of its kind still standing on the south Florida mainland; a Methodist church built in 1887; a typical "Cracker Gothic" house built in 1912; and the Wiggins General Store, dating from 1903 and full of local memorabilia from swamp root and grub dust to louse powder, as well as antique furnishings and an art gallery.

✪ **South Florida Museum, Bishop Planetarium, and Parker Manatee Aquarium.** 201 10th St. W. (on the riverfront, at Barcarrota Blvd.). ☎ **941/746-4131.** Admission $6 adults, $5 seniors, $3.50 children 5–12, free for children 4 and under. Jan–Apr and July Mon–Sat 10am–5pm, Sun noon–5pm. May–June and Aug–Dec Tues–Sat 10am–5pm, Sun noon–6pm. From U.S. 41, take Manatee Ave. west to 10th St. W. and turn right.

The star at this downtown complex is "Snooty," the oldest manatee born in captivity (1948) and Manatee County's official mascot. Snooty and a friend acquired in 1998 live in the Parker Manatee Aquarium. The South Florida Museum tells the story of Florida's history, from prehistoric times to the present, including a Native American collection with life-size dioramas and a Spanish courtyard containing replicas of 16th-century buildings. The Bishop Planetarium features a 50-foot hemispherical dome that arcs above a seating area, for laser light and educational star shows.

SHOPPING

For discount shopping, the focal point of the Bradenton area is the **Gulf Coast Factory Shops,** on U.S. 301 at exit 43 off I-75 in Ellenton (☎ **941/723-1150**), about a 15-minute drive northeast of downtown (turn left at the first stoplight east of I-75). This Spanish-style, coral stucco outdoor center has more than 100 factory and outlet stores, including a Saks Off Fifth Avenue (I found mostly leftovers from the main stores), Coach Leather, Liz Claiborne, Bass Shoes, Corning Revere, Jockey, Levi's, Nike, Ann Taylor, Donna Karan, Jones New York, Geoffrey Beene, Van Heusen, Maidenform, Royal Doulton, Sony, and Bose. Shops are open Monday to Saturday from 10am to 9pm and Sunday from 11am to 6pm.

WHERE TO STAY

The Bradenton Area Convention and Visitors Bureau (see "Essentials," above) operates a free **reservation service** (☎ **800/4-MANATEE**), and its annual visitor guide lists all of Manatee County's accommodations, including condominium complexes. **A Paradise Rental Management,** 5201 Gulf Dr., Holmes Beach, FL 34217 (☎ **800/237-2252** or 941/778-4800; fax 941/778-7090; www.manatee-online.com/aparadise), represents a number of condo complexes with weekly rates ranging from $500 off-season to $1,950 a week during winter.

Except for those near I-75 east of the city, Bradenton has few national chain motels. On the other hand, those on U.S. 41 and University Parkway near the Sarasota-Bradenton International Airport are about halfway between downtown and Sarasota. On Longboat Key, the Hilton and Holiday Inn are equally convenient to Anna Maria Island and Bradenton. See "Where to Stay," in section 5, for details about nearby Sarasota accommodations. The high season here is January to April. Hotel tax is 9% in Manatee County.

ON THE MAINLAND

Five Oaks Bed and Breakfast Inn. 1102 Riverside Dr. (at 11th Ave. W.), Palmetto, FL 34221. ☎ **941/723-1236.** 4 units. A/C TEL. Year-round $75–$110 double. Rates include breakfast. AE, MC, V. Go north across the river on 9th St. W. (Business U.S. 41), take first left on Riverside Dr., and go 3 blocks to house on right.

Known for its full Southern-style breakfast, this Victorian inn sits on the north shore of the Manatee River directly opposite downtown, surrounded by palm trees, oaks, and gardens overlooking the water. Guests enjoy use of a parlor with a fireplace, and an enclosed wraparound solarium/sunporch or formal dining room filled with wicker and rattan furnishings. Those in search of total quiet will enjoy it here, since kids are not welcome, and the rooms don't have televisions.

✪ **Holiday Inn Riverfront.** 100 Riverfront Dr. W. (at 3rd St. W.), Bradenton, FL 34205. ☎ **800/HOLIDAY** or 941/747-3727. Fax 941/746-4289. 153 units. A/C TV TEL. Winter $119–$139 double. Off-season $89–$109 double. Golf packages available. AE, DC, DISC, MC, V. From U.S. 41, go west on Manatee Ave. (Fla. 64) and turn right on 3rd St. W. to hotel on left.

This five-story Spanish hacienda–style structure overlooking the Manatee River is Bradenton's prime commercial hotel. The highlight is a remarkable riverside landscaped courtyard with fountains and tropical trees. Inside, the public areas reflect an Iberian ambience, with dark wood trim, tile floors, and high-beamed ceilings. The bedrooms are contemporary, with standard hotel furnishings augmented by coffeemakers, irons and boards, and hair dryers. Those above the ground floor have balconies and views of the river or the courtyard. Facilities include a Spanish-themed restaurant, a nautical-style lounge, heated outdoor swimming pool, exercise room, and gift shop. There's laundry and room service and weekday complimentary newspaper delivery.

⊙ **Park Inn Club and Breakfast.** 4450 47th St. W. (at 44th Ave./Cortez Rd.), Bradenton, FL 34210. ☎ **800/437-PARK** or 941/795-4633. Fax 941/795-0808. 130 units. A/C TV TEL. Winter $109–$139 double. Off-season $79–$109 double. Rates include continental breakfast and evening cocktails. Golf packages available. AE, DC, DISC, MC, V. From I-75, take Exit 41 and follow Fla. 70 west 6½ miles, turn right on U.S. 41 north, left on 44th Ave. W. (Fla. 684) to 47th St. W., and hotel is on left.

Families will find this busy Cortez Road/44th Avenue location to be convenient, for there are ample chain restaurants and a multiscreen cinema in the adjacent shopping centers. And you can't get lost driving to Bradenton Beach, a straight-line, 6-mile trip west on Cortez Road. The three-story contemporary building is wrapped around a central courtyard with a patio and swimming pool. The guest rooms are spacious, and the suites have whirlpools. All bathrooms here have hair dryers, phones, and TV speakers. Facilities include a courtyard pool and a lounge in which guests are served breakfast and complimentary cocktails each evening. Guests get free use of Gold's Gym next door.

ANNA MARIA ISLAND

Anna Maria's lone chain motel is the moderately priced **Econo Lodge Surfside**, 2502 Gulf Dr. N. (at 25th St. N.), Bradenton Beach, FL 34217 (☎ **800/55-ECONO** or 941/778-6671; fax 941/778-0360). Recently remodeled, this beachfront facility has 18 suites and 36 spacious rooms in its main three-story building, plus 18 rooms in another one-story building on the beach and 5 more across the street (the least expensive).

⊙ **Catalina Beach Resort.** 1325 Gulf Dr. N. (at 14th St. N.), Bradenton Beach, FL 34217. ☎ **941/778-6611.** Fax 941/778-6748. 35 units. A/C TV TEL. Winter $81 double; $112–$184 suite. Off-season $49–$57 double; $69–$125 suite. Weekly rates available. AE, DC, DISC, MC, V.

In a shady spot across Gulf Drive from the beach, 10 short blocks north of the Cortez Bridge, this two-story Spanish-style motel offers exceptional value. Its well-kept rooms have modern furnishings and bright Florida colors. Most units are one- and two-bedroom suites with kitchenettes. Facilities include a restaurant, outdoor solar-heated swimming pool, barbecue grills, shuffleboard courts, guest laundry, fishing and boating dock, and water-sports rentals.

⊙ **Harrington House.** 5626 Gulf Dr. (at 55th St.), Holmes Beach, FL 34217. ☎ **941/778-5444.** Fax 941/778-0527. www.harhousebb.com. 12 units. A/C TV. Winter $149–$225 double. Off-season $109–$225 double. MC, V.

Flowers will be everywhere and a private beach awaiting when you arrive at this bed-and-breakfast, the best romantic lovers' getaway hereabouts. In a tree-shaded setting on the beach overlooking the Gulf of Mexico, this three-story clapboard house was built in 1925 and exudes an Old Florida ambience. The eight bedrooms are individually decorated with antique, wicker, or rattan furnishings. Some units have four-poster or brass beds, and the higher-priced rooms have French doors leading to balconies overlooking the gulf. In addition to the bedrooms in the main house, four rooms are available in the adjacent Beach House, a remodeled 1920s captain's home updated. All guests enjoy use of the high-ceilinged living room with fireplace, an outdoor pool, patio, and complimentary use of bicycles, kayaks, and other sports equipment.

WHERE TO DINE
ON THE MAINLAND

✪ **Miller's Dutch Kitchen.** 3401 14th St. W. (U.S. 41, at 34th Ave. W.). ☎ **941/ 746-8253.** Reservations not accepted. Sandwiches $2.50–$5; main courses $6.25–$13. MC, V. Mon–Sat 11am–8pm. Closed Christmas. AMERICAN.

There's a charming treat waiting inside this modern, nondescript brick building among the auto dealers on busy U.S. 41, for its Pennsylvania Dutch country dining room is surrounded by a balcony, around whose edge chugs a model train. Over the balcony railing you'll see quilts and other handcrafts, all products of Bradenton's Amish community and all very much for sale. Although plain, the food here is as fresh as it gets. The regular American items such as fried shrimp, stuffed flounder, and barbecued pork ribs are augmented by daily Amish specialties such as cabbage rolls and Dutch casserole (noodles, peas, cheese, potatoes, beef, mushrooms, and chicken soup with croutons). Leave room for dessert: You can choose from 30 types of homemade pies. No smoking and no alcohol here.

Twin Dolphin Marina Grill. On The Pier, 1200 1st Ave. W. (north end of 12th St. W.). ☎ **941/748-8087.** Reservations recommended on weekends. Main courses $12–$32. AE, DC, DISC, MC, V. Sun–Thurs 11:30am–10pm, Fri–Sat 11:30am–11pm. FLORIBBEAN.

With commanding views of the Manatee River, this restaurant is *the* place to dine downtown. It's housed in a stately Spanish-style landmark building at the foot of 12th Street (Old Main Street) on Memorial Pier. The menu offers the day's fresh catch either grilled, broiled, blackened, bronzed, or jerked Jamaican-style. Florida lobster tails are served fried in a light tempura sauce, or you can opt for crab cakes, shrimp Provençal, or sushi-quality yellowfin tuna glazed with a teriyaki sauce. Lighter fare is available outside at **Flipper's Dockside Patio Grill,** a tropical-style bar by the river.

ANNA MARIA ISLAND
Expensive

✪ **Beach Bistro.** 6600 Gulf Dr. N. (at 66th St.), Holmes Beach. ☎ **941/778-6444.** Reservations recommended. Main courses $19–$29. AE, DC, DISC, MC, V. Daily 5:30–10pm. INTERNATIONAL.

Winner of a Golden Spoon award as one of Florida's 20 best restaurants, this small, 12-table culinary oasis is Anna Maria Island's top place for fine dining. It sits right beside the beach, offering wide-windowed views of the gulf waters. A romantic ambience and overall elegance is enhanced by crisp linens, sparkling crystal, and fresh flowers on every table. Check out the nightly specials, such as Bistro bouillabaisse made with premium fish, shrimp, scallops, and squid. Regular offerings include grouper Picasso finished with fresh fruits and berries.

Moderate

The Beachhouse. 200 Gulf Dr. N. (at Cortez Rd.), Bradenton Beach. ☎ **941/779-2222.** Reservations not accepted on patio, but call for preferred seating inside. Sandwiches $6.50–$9; main courses $10–$19. AE, DC, DISC, MC, V. Daily 11:30am–10:30pm. AMERICAN.

This large, lively place sits right on Bradenton Beach with a huge open deck and a covered pavilion facing out to the gulf. Even inside, wide windows let in the view. Owned by Ed Chiles, son of the current Florida governor, the Beachhouse offers daily fresh fish specials, including the signature beechnut grouper (with nutty crust in citrus-butter sauce). There's also a good variety of fare, including seafood salads and pastas, crab cakes, fish-and-chips, and broiled steaks. Local musicians play out on the patio most afternoons and evenings.

Rotten Ralph's. 902 S. Bay Blvd., Anna Maria. ☎ **941/778-3953.** Reservations not accepted. Sandwiches and burgers $4–$8; main courses $11–$17. DC, DISC, MC, V. Daily 11am–9pm. From Gulf Dr., turn toward the bay on Pine Ave., then right at a dead end to the end of Bay Blvd. SEAFOOD.

On the north end of the island overlooking Bimini Bay, this casual Old Florida–style restaurant has both indoor and outdoor seating. The menu offers many seafood choices from scallops and shrimp to crab cakes, snow crab, oysters, and grouper. Other choices include Danish baby back ribs and Anna Maria chicken (marinated and grilled with a honey-mustard sauce).

✪ **Sandbar.** 100 Spring Ave. (east of Gulf Dr.), Anna Maria. ☎ **941/778-0444.** Reservations not accepted on deck; call for preferred seating in the main restaurant. Snacks $6–$9; main courses $12–$18. AE, DC, DISC, MC, V. Dining room daily 11:30am–3pm and 4–10pm; deck daily 11:30am–10pm. SEAFOOD.

Sitting on the site of the former Pavilion, built in 1913 when people from Tampa and St. Pete took the ferry here, this popular restaurant is perched right on the beach overlooking the gulf. The air-conditioned, knotty-pine dining room offers several preparations of seafood (stuffed grouper, crab cakes over a roasted pepper sauce, fried shrimp) as well as landlubber's steaks and chicken. But the real action here is under the umbrellas on the lively beachside deck, where a menu of sandwiches, salads, and a few platters are served all day and night. Live music makes a party on the deck Monday to Friday nights and on Saturday and Sunday from 1 to 10pm. The inside bar is one of the few I've seen in Florida with no sports TVs.

Seafood Shack. 4110 127th St. W. (east end of Cortez Bridge), Cortez. ☎ **941/794-1235.** Reservations not accepted. Main courses $10–$24. AE, DISC, MC, V. Sun–Thurs 11:30am–9pm, Fri–Sat 11:30am–10pm. Cross Cortez Bridge (Fla. 684) and take first left. SEAFOOD.

A tradition since 1972, this large, informal seafood restaurant sits on the Cortez village waterfront, on the mainland but close enough to Anna Maria Island to be a popular beach dining spot. The menu offers many different seafood combinations and at least six different shrimp dishes (from scampi to stuffed), but the "Shack specialty" is sautéed frogs' legs. Downstairs, the publike **Marina Grill** offers snacks, burgers, fried seafood baskets, and main courses for less than $10.

The cruising paddlewheeler *Seafood Shack Showboat* is docked beside the restaurant (see "Outdoor Activities & Spectator Sports," above). Cruise tickets get you dinner discounts in the restaurant.

Inexpensive

✪ **Gulf Drive Café.** 900 Gulf Dr. N. (at 9th St.), Bradenton Beach. ☎ **941/778-1919.** Reservations not accepted. Breakfast $2.25–$5.25; sandwiches and burgers $4–$5.25; main courses $6–$11. DISC, MC, V. Daily 7am–9:30pm. SEAFOOD.

Locals flock to this bright gulf-side cafe for the best bargains on the beach. With big windows, bentwood cafe chairs with colorful cushions, and lots of hanging plants and ceiling fans, the coral and green dining room opens to a beachside patio with tables shaded by a trellis. The breakfast fare is led by sweet Belgian waffles, which are available all day. You can also order salads, sandwiches, and burgers anytime here, with quiche du jour, Mediterranean seafood pasta, and regular seafood platters joining the show at 4pm.

LONGBOAT KEY

✪ **Moore's Stone Crab.** 800 Broadway (at Bayside Dr). ☎ **941/383-1748.** Reservations not accepted. Sandwiches and salads $6–$10; main courses $10–$22. DISC, MC, V. Winter daily 11:30am–9:30pm. Off-season Mon–Fri 5–10pm, Sat–Sun 11:30am–10pm. SEAFOOD.

In Longbeach, the old fishing village on the north end of Longboat Key, this popular bay-front restaurant began in 1967 as an offshoot of a family seafood business established 40 years earlier. From the outside, in fact, it still looks a little like a packing house, but the view of the bay dotted with mangrove islands makes a fine complement to stone crabs fresh from the family's own traps from October to March. Otherwise, the menu offers every imaginable seafood, most of it fried or broiled. Sandwiches and salads are served all day.

BRADENTON AFTER DARK

Locals and visitors alike head south to neighboring Sarasota for their culture (see "Sarasota After Dark," in section 5). Meantime, the action here is at beach restaurants and pubs.

Live bands lend a party atmosphere to the gulf-side deck at the **Sandbar** restaurant every night and from 1pm on weekends (see "Where to Dine," above). The elegant **Cafe Robar,** at the corner of Gulf Drive and Pine Avenue in Anna Maria (☎ **941/778-6969**), offers piano music and a sing-along bar on Tuesday to Sunday evenings. **D. Coy Ducks Bar & Grille,** in the Island Shopping Center at Marina Drive and 54th Street in Holmes Beach (☎ **941/778-5888**), has a varied program of live Dixieland bands, jazz pianists, and guitarists.

12

Walt Disney World & Orlando

by Mary Meehan

More than 30 years ago, while flying over 43 square miles of scrub brush and swampland just south of a sleepy Southern town, Walt Disney saw what he needed to create a whole new world. Orlando, where the biggest tourist draw before 1972 had been a downtown fountain, would never be the same. Today, as the millennium approaches, it seems at least one full-scale theme park opens every year, and visitors have never had more options. (The fact that the Orlando International Airport is undergoing a billion-dollar expansion should clue you in to how busy this place is.)

With so many tourist attractions vying for your time and money, advance planning is a must. Walt's world now claims four distinct parks, two entertainment districts, enough hotels to fill a small city, and several smaller attractions including water parks and putt-putt courses.

Universal Studios Florida is rapidly expanding, adding a nighttime entertainment destination, CityWalk, in 1998. A second park, Islands of Adventure, is scheduled to open in 1999. Universal, The Sequel, showcases stomach-churning thrill rides and many attractions with Baby Boomer appeal, like Cat in the Hat and Spider Man. The one-two punch of both parks could give The Mouse some serious competition.

Sea World is also growing, although at a slower pace. A major renovation in 1997 updated its 1970s look, and Sea World has also added its most expansive attraction yet, a roller coaster called Journey to Atlantis.

And as if that weren't enough competition, after years of cowering to the Mouse, Universal and other non-Disney attractions are banding together to offer special packages and discounts. These "Flex Passes" offer visitors the choice of several parks for one flat price and is a direct assault on Disney's multiday pass system.

Of course, Disney is going about its ever-expanding business. It has entered the cruise business and opened yet another theme park, Animal Kingdom, in 1998.

Coming to Orlando, it's easy to get overwhelmed by the urge to do everything and then some. But, to borrow a phrase from my New York in-laws: Fugedaboudit. As your guide, I can promise you that a 2-week stay isn't long enough to hit everything. But don't panic—I've done it all so you won't have to. Every inch of every park, every restaurant,

The Orlando/Walt Disney World Area

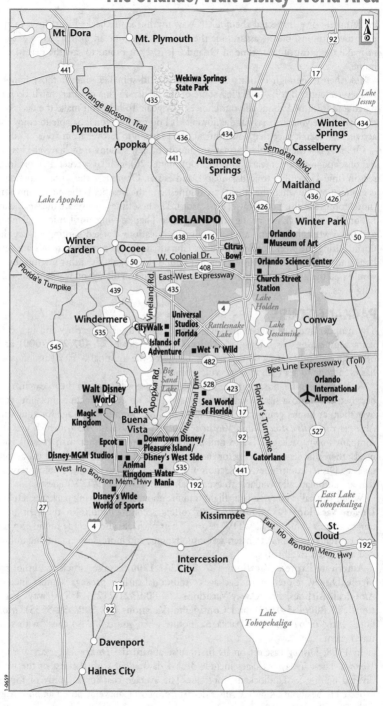

every hotel—I've inspected them all. (Okay, my husband checked out those theme park men's rooms, but he assures me they're fine.) I provide an insider's view of how to make the most of your time in Orlando. It is, I am proud to say, the place I call home.

Yes, there're enough options to make your head spin like one of those famous Disney tea cups. But by following some of the advice in this chapter, you'll be prepared and informed about all your choices. My goal? To help you make the decisions that will make your trip easy and enjoyable. If I do my job, you'll be able to enjoy the activities at such a pace that you won't need a vacation to recover from your vacation.

Orlando is a theme-park destination, and its busiest seasons are whenever kids are out of school—summer (early June to about August 20), holiday weekends, Christmas season (mid-December to mid-January), and Easter. Obviously, the whole experience is more enjoyable when the crowds are thinnest and the weather is the most temperate (hotel rooms are also priced lower off-season). The best times to visit are the week after Labor Day until Thanksgiving, the week after Thanksgiving until mid-December, and the 6 weeks before and after school spring vacations. Packed parking lots are the norm during the weeks before and after Christmas. In the summer, crowds are very large and weather is oppressively hot and humid. I probably shouldn't say this, but I would pull the kids out of school for a few days around an off-season weekend to avoid long lines.

PACKAGE TOURS

The number and diversity of package tours to Orlando is staggering, and in recent years competition has intensified. **Universal City Travel** (☎ 407/224-7000) now offers special "other attraction" packages, including the multipark "Flex Pass." Disney has even gone to sea with its own cruise ship.

As always, significant savings are available for those willing to do the research. Your best bet: Stop into a sizable travel agency and pick up every brochure in sight. Pore over them at home, comparing offerings to find the optimum package for your trip. Also get the *Walt Disney World Vacations Guide* (☎ 407/934-7639), which lists the company's own packages. Try to find a package that meets rather than exceeds your needs; there's no sense in paying for elements you won't use. Also, read over the advantages to Disney resort guests in section 3; some packages list as selling points services that are automatically available to every Walt Disney World (WDW) guest.

When you call to reserve your flight, inquire about money-saving packages. **Delta's Dream Vacations** (☎ 800/872-7786) offers accommodations in different price ranges at your choice of all WDW resorts. Their packages also include round-trip airfare, car rental or airport transfer, accommodations, and more, some including unlimited admission to all parks.

American Express Vacations (☎ 800/241-1700) is also officially authorized to use Disney resorts in its packages. Additional airline package sources include **American Airlines' Fly AAway Vacations** (☎ 800/321-2121), **US Airways Vacations** (☎ 800/455-0123), and **Continental Vacations** (☎ 800/634-5555). Most hotels listed below also offer packages; inquire when you call. Also check with your travel agent.

In 1998, Disney cast off on its first cruise aboard the *Disney Magic* and *Disney Wonder*. These 7-day packages include 3 or 4 days afloat with the rest of the week divided among its landlocked properties. The average cost for a family of four is expected to be about $4,500. Cruises depart from Port Canaveral, about an hour from Orlando. For information, or to receive a brochure outlining the packages, call ☎ 407/566-3500.

Since 1996, Universal Studios has offered its own packages through **Universal City Travel Company** (☎ 800/224-3838). These packages highlight Universal and offer special VIP access to the park and rides and discounts to other parks. Universal City Travel also offers trips that include stays at beach hotels before or after the theme park trips. These excursions are billed as "an alternative resort experience."

1 Orientation

ARRIVING

BY PLANE THE MAJOR AIRLINES Delta (☎ 800/221-1212) has the most flights into Orlando International Airport: more than 27%. It offers service from 200 cities and has a Fantastic Flyer program for kids. **Delta Express** offers direct service from 14 cities and also has the Fantastic Flyer program for kids. Other carriers include **Air Jamaica** (☎ 800/523-5585), **America West** (☎ 800/235-9292), **American** (☎ 800/433-7300), **American Trans Air** (☎ 800/293-6194), **British Airways** (☎ 800/247-9297), **Canadian Airlines,** (☎ 800/426-3838), **Continental** (☎ 800/231-0856), **Midway** (☎ 800/446-4392), **Northwest** (☎ 800/225-2525), **SunJet** (☎ 800/478-6738), **Southwest** (☎ 800/435-9792), **Transbrasil** (☎ 800/872-3153), **TWA** (☎ 800/221-2000), **United** (☎ 800/241-6522), **US Airways** (☎ 800/428-4322), and **Virgin Atlantic** (☎ 800/862-8621).

Orlando International Airport, which is undergoing a billion-dollar expansion, is thoroughly user-friendly, with centrally located information kiosks (see "Visitor Information," below). All major car-rental companies are located at or near the airport.

The airport is 25 miles from Walt Disney World. **Mears Transportation Group** (☎ 407/423-5566) shuttle vans ply the route from the airport (board outside baggage claim) to all Disney resorts and official hotels as well as most other area hostelries. Their vehicles operate around the clock, departing every 15 to 25 minutes in either direction. Rates vary with your destination. The round-trip cost for adults is $21 between the airport and downtown Orlando or International Drive, $25 for Walt Disney World/Lake Buena Vista or Kissimmee/U.S. 192. Children 4 to 11 are charged $14 and $17, respectively; children 3 and under ride free.

BY CAR Orlando is 436 miles from Atlanta and 230 miles from Miami.

From points north, take I-75 south to the Florida Turnpike to I-4, which runs right through the city. If you're taking I-95 south, you'll intersect with I-4 near Daytona Beach.

American Automobile Association (AAA) (☎ 800/336-4357) and some other automobile club members can call local offices for maps and optimum driving directions.

BY TRAIN Amtrak trains (☎ 800/872-7245) pull into stations at 1400 Sligh Blvd., between Columbia and Miller streets in downtown Orlando (about 23 miles from Walt Disney World), and 111 Dakin Ave., at Thurman Street in Kissimmee (about 15 miles from Walt Disney World). There is also a stop in Winter Park, about 10 miles north of Orlando, at 150 W. Morse Blvd., and in Sanford, about 23 miles northeast of Orlando. The Sanford station, located at 600 Persimmon Ave., is also the end terminal for the Auto Train.

Amtrak's Auto Train offers the convenience of having a car in Florida without having to drive it there. The Auto Train begins in Lorton, Virginia—about a 4-hour drive from New York, 2 hours from Philadelphia—and ends up at Sanford, Florida, about 23 miles northeast of Orlando. Once again, reserve early for the lowest fares. The Auto Train departs Lorton and Sanford at 4:30pm daily, arriving at its destination at 9am the next morning. *Note:* You have to arrive 1 or 2 hours before departure time so they can board your car. Call ☎ **800/872-7245** for details.

To inquire about Amtrak's money-saving packages, including hotel accommodations (some at WDW resorts), car rentals, tours, and so on, with your train fare, call ☎ **800/321-8684.**

VISITOR INFORMATION

Contact the **Orlando/Orange County Convention & Visitors Bureau,** 8723 International Dr., Suite 101, Orlando, FL 32819 (☎ **407/363-5871**). They can answer all your questions and will send you maps, brochures (including the informative *Official Visitors Guide,* the *Official Attractions Guide,* the *Official Accommodations Guide,* and the *African-American Visitors Guide*), and the "Magicard," good for discounts of 10% to 50% on accommodations, attractions, car rentals, and more. Discount tickets to attractions other than Disney parks are sold on the premises, and the multilingual staff can also make dining reservations and hotel referrals. The bureau is open daily, except Christmas, from 8am to 8pm.

For general information about Walt Disney World and a copy of the informative *Walt Disney World Vacations,* write or call the Walt Disney World Co., Box 10000, Lake Buena Vista, FL 32830-1000 (☎ **407/934-7639**). You can get information about Universal Studios by writing Guest Services, 1000 Universal Studios Plaza, 32819-7610.

If you're driving, you can stop at the Disney/AAA Travel Center in Ocala, Florida, at the intersection of I-75 (exit 68) and Fla. 200, about 90 miles north of Orlando (☎ **904/854-0770**). Here you can purchase tickets and Mickey ears, get help planning your park itinerary, and make hotel reservations. Hours are 9am to 6pm; until 7pm June through August.

Also contact the **Kissimmee–St. Cloud Convention & Visitors Bureau,** 1925 E. Irlo Bronson Memorial Hwy. (P.O. Box 422007), Kissimmee, FL 34742-2007 (☎ **800/327-9159** or 407/847-5000). They'll send maps, brochures, discount coupon books, and the *Kissimmee–St. Cloud Vacation Guide,* which details the area's accommodations and attractions. The state of Florida also instituted a toll-free number in 1998 (☎ **888-7-FLA-USA** [735-2872], over which you can request a visitors guide for the state, including Orlando, in English, Spanish, German, and Portuguese.

ONLINE RESOURCES

The state information Web site is **www.flausa.com**. Visit Walt Disney World's own Web site at **www.disneyworld.com**, which has extensive, entertaining, and regularly updated information, including a live-action look from video cameras perched throughout the various parks. (This is mostly long-distance shots of tourists walking about, but is still a chance to see those blue Orlando skies and dream ahead to vacation time.) You can see pictures of various attractions by clicking on the individual parks and check out every resort by going to *resorts & spas* (not resort reservations).

For information about Universal Studios Florida and Sea World, visit **www.usf.com** and **www.seaworld.com**, respectively. Both sites offer maps and a basic description of rides, shows, and ticket information. The city newspaper, the *Orlando Sentinel,* also produces Orlando Sentinel Online at **www.oso@aol.com**. Once there, click into "Theme Park Central" for a variety of information and updates on what is going on at local attractions. The Orlando/Orange County Convention & Visitors Bureau also offers a Web site a **www.goflorida.com**.

CITY LAYOUT

Orlando's major artery is I-4, which runs diagonally across the state from Tampa to Daytona Beach. Exits from I-4 take you to Walt Disney World, Sea World, International Drive, U.S. 192, Kissimmee, Lake Buena Vista, Church Street Station, downtown Orlando, and Winter Park. The **Florida Turnpike** crosses I-4 and links up with I-75 to the north. **U.S. 192,** a major east-west artery, stretches from Kissimmee (along a major motel strip) to **U.S. 27,** crossing I-4 near the Walt Disney World entrance road. Farther north, a toll road called the **Bee Line Expressway** (Fla. 528) goes east from I-4 past Orlando International Airport to Cape Canaveral.

Walt Disney World property is bounded roughly by I-4 and Fla. 535 to the east (the latter also north), World Drive (the entrance road) to the west, and U.S. 192 to the south. Epcot Center Drive (Fla. 536, the south end of International Drive) and Buena Vista Drive cut across the complex in a more-or-less east-west direction; the two roads cross at Bonnet Creek Parkway. Excellent highways and explicit signs make it very easy to find your way around.

Note: The Disney parks are actually much closer to Kissimmee than to downtown Orlando.

NEIGHBORHOODS IN BRIEF

Walt Disney World (WDW)   A city unto itself, WDW sprawls over more than 26,000 acres containing theme parks, resorts, hotels, shops, restaurants, and recreational facilities galore.

Lake Buena Vista   This area centers on a hotel village/marketplace owned and operated by Walt Disney World on the eastern edge of Disney property. However, while Disney owns all the real estate, many of the hotels, and some shops and restaurants here, are independently owned. Lake Buena Vista is a charming area of manicured lawns and verdant thoroughfares with traffic islands shaded by towering oak trees. The lovely scenery can be hard to see over the tour buses, however. This is a very busy part of town so expect long waits at restaurants during peak season. (The RainForest Cafe, for example, can have waits up to 4 hours!)

Celebration   Imagine living in a Disney world? Disney tries to re-create its squeaky-clean, completely controlled magic in this town, the first residential area ever to receive the special Disney touch. Located on 4,900 acres in northwest Osceola County, Celebration will eventually have about 8,000 residents living in Disney-designed homes and attending a Disney-run school. The homes go for around $256,000, and at least two have reportedly sold for as much as $900,000. Celebration's downtown, designed mostly for tourist trade, is architecturally interesting and features some first-rate shops and restaurants.

Kissimmee   South of the Disney parks, Kissimmee centers on U.S. 192/Irlo Bronson Memorial Highway—a somewhat tacky strip, as archetypal of American cities as Main Street. U.S. 192 is lined with budget motels, lesser attractions like Gatorland, and every fast-food restaurant you can name. Kissimmee is still, in many ways, true to its cowboy routes, and there are some wide open spaces to explore if you are in the mood for a ride in the country.

International Drive (Fla. 536)   Can you say *tourist mecca?* This area extends 7 to 10 miles north of the Disney parks between Fla. 535 and the Florida Turnpike. From bungee jumping to ice-skating and dozens of theme restaurants and T-shirt shops, this is *the* tourist strip in Central Florida. It contains numerous hotels, restaurants, shopping centers, and the Orange County Convention Center, and it offers easy access to Sea World and Universal Studios. The place is already packed but, somehow, developers manage year after year to find space for just one more attraction. *Note:* Locally, this road is always referred to as I-Drive.

Downtown Orlando   No, Downtown Disney is not *really* Downtown, the heart of the city's business and entertainment districts. To get there you have to travel on I-4 East, reaching a burgeoning Sunbelt metropolis 17 miles northeast of Walt Disney World. It includes the entertainment/shopping complex Church Street Station and the Orlando Science Center, a recently completed multimillion-dollar complex, which is the largest in the Southeast. Hundreds of clubs, shops, and restaurants are located in the heart of the city, one of the fastest-growing in the country. Dozens of antique shops line "Antique Row" on Orange Avenue near Lake Ivanhoe. The free downtown bus system, called Lymmo, makes it easy to park in one place and travel throughout downtown, including the Orlando Arena and Bob Carr Centre for the Performing Arts. Both City Hall and the courthouse offer art exhibits reflecting the diverse work of Florida artists.

Winter Park   Just north of downtown Orlando, Winter Park is the place many of central Florida's old-money families call home. As the name implies, it began as a haven for Yankees traveling away from the cold. Today, it's home to Park Avenue, a collection of upscale shops and restaurants along an original cobblestone street that is frequented by the local ladies who lunch. With the main attractions being shopping, dining, and several small museums, Winter Park is definitely a grown-up diversion.

2 Getting Around

BY CAR   Though you can get to and around Walt Disney World and other major attractions without a car, it's always handy to have one, especially if you want to see attractions beyond Disney. All major car-rental companies are represented in Orlando and maintain desks at the airport. I was quoted the lowest rates by **Value Rent-A-Car** (☎ **800/GO-VALUE**), which also offered excellent service and 24-hour pickup and return. Other companies include **Alamo** (☎ **800/327-9633**), **Avis** (☎ **800/331-1212**), **Budget** (☎ **800/527-0700**), **Dollar** (☎ **800/800-4000**), **Hertz** (☎ **800/654-3131**), and **Thrifty** (☎ **800/367-2277**).

BY BUS   Disney has its own internal transportation system that allows people staying at Walt Disney World (WDW) resorts to move easily throughout the property. This is supposed to be exclusively for Disney guests, although I've never seen anyone check for a hotel key before you board. Within WDW you can also travel via monorail, ferry, and/or water taxi to all three parks from 2 hours before opening until 2 hours after closing; you can also ride to Disney Village Marketplace, Typhoon Lagoon, Pleasure Island, Fort Wilderness, and other Disney resorts. During peak seasons, be prepared to stand on crowded buses.

Disney hostelries offer transportation to other area attractions as well, though it's not complimentary. Almost all area hotels and motels also offer transportation to Walt Disney World and other attractions, but it can be pricey.

Mears Transportation Group (☎ **407/423-5566**) operates buses to all major attractions, including Cypress Gardens, the Kennedy Space Center, Universal Studios Florida, Sea World, Busch Gardens (in Tampa), and Church Street Station, among others. Call for details.

BY TAXI   Taxis line up in front of major hotels, and at smaller hostelries the front desk will be happy to call you a cab. Or call **Yellow Cab** (☎ **407/699-9999**). The charge is $2.75 for the first mile, $1.50 per mile thereafter.

FAST FACTS: Walt Disney World & Orlando

Baby-Sitters   Most Orlando hotels offer baby-sitting services. If yours doesn't, call **KinderCare** (☎ **407/827-5444**); 24-hour advance notice is required.

Convention Center   The **Orange County Convention Center** is located at 9800 International Dr. (☎ **407/345-9800**).

Doctors and Dentists   Tourists have encountered ill-trained doctors making calls in hotels. You can get a reputable referral from **Ask-A-Nurse,** a free service operated by a local hospital chain. In Kissimmee call ☎ **407/ 870-1700;** in Orlando call ☎ **407/ 897-1700.** There are basic first-aid centers in all the major parks.

Emergencies   Dial ☎ **911** to contact the police or fire department or to call an ambulance.

Hospitals   Sand Lake Hospital, 9400 Turkey Lake Rd., is about 2 miles south of Sand Lake Road (☎ **407/351-8550**). From the WDW area, take I-4 east to Exit 29, turn left at the exit onto Sand Lake Road, and make a left onto Turkey Lake Road. The hospital is 2 miles up on your right. Walk-in medical clinics are available, with a visit usually costing under $50. Prescriptions are extra. **CentraCare,** operated by a locally run Florida Hospital, is a reputable medical facility with more than a dozen locations throughout the Orlando area. For information, and the nearest location, call ☎ **407/660-8118.** In recent years, several freestanding medical clinics have popped up, especially in the Kissimmee area. My advice: Stick with CentraCare whenever possible.

Kennels   All the major theme parks offer animal-boarding facilities at reasonable fees. At Walt Disney World, there are kennels at Fort Wilderness, Epcot, the Magic Kingdom, and Disney-MGM Studios.

Lost Children   Every theme park has a designated spot for parents to meet up with lost children. Find out where it is when you enter any park. Point out the uniformed park personnel in each park and instruct your children to ask people dressed in that uniform for help. Young children should have name tags.

Pharmacies (Late-Night)   Walgreens Drug Store, 1003 W. Vine St. (U.S. 192), just east of Bermuda Avenue (☎ **407/847-5252**), operates a 24-hour pharmacy. They can deliver to hotels for a charge ($10 from 7am to 5pm, $15 at all other times). There is an **Eckherd's Drug Store** at 7324 International Dr. (☎ **407/345-0491**) open 24-hours a day. There is also a 24-hour Eckherd's store at 1306 Bermuda Ave. (☎ 407/847-5174).

Taxes   The hotel tax is 11% in Orlando and Kissimmee; that rate includes a state sales tax (6%) that's charged on all goods except most grocery store items and medicines.

Tourist Information   See "Orientation," earlier in this chapter.

Weather   Call ☎ **407/851-7510** for a weather recording from the National Weather Service.

3   Accommodations

Reserve as far in advance as possible—the minute you've decided on the dates of your trip. The year-round sunshine, combined with the huge number of annual conventions and international visitors in Orlando virtually eliminates the concept of high and low seasons. That being said, the lowest rates are generally available in fall from September to Thanksgiving and again during January and February. The highest are during the Christmas holidays and the summer months.

Consider the cost of parking or shuttle buses to and from Disney and other theme parks when making your hotel choice—it can add up to quite a bit. Also remember to factor in the 11% hotel tax.

THE PERKS OF STAYING WITH MICKEY

There are 15 Disney-owned properties (hotels, resorts, villas, wilderness homes, and campsites) and nine privately owned "official hotels," all adjacent to the Walt Disney World complex. Due to high demand, especially during summer, you often have to take what you can get. Finding a room is a little like the game of "Go Fish"—you lay down your card and hope to find a match. Keep in mind there are often reasonably priced accommodations at some of the more expensive resorts (it doesn't hurt to ask whether that $294 room at the Grand Floridian is available). So, consider your priorities. The more expensive properties are closer to the theme parks. You may want to consider staying a short distance away and renting a car.

In addition to their proximity to the parks, there are a number of advantages to staying at a Disney hostelry or official hotel. At all Disney resorts and official hotels these include:

- Unlimited complimentary transportation via bus, monorail, ferry, and/or water taxi to/from all three parks from 2 hours before opening until 2 hours after closing. Unlimited complimentary transport is also provided to/from Disney Village Marketplace, Typhoon Lagoon, Pleasure Island, Fort Wilderness, and other Disney resorts. Three hostelries—the Polynesian, Contemporary, and Grand Floridian—are stops on the monorail. This free transport can save a lot of money. It also means that you're guaranteed admission to all parks, even during peak times when the parking lots sometimes fill up.
- Free parking at WDW parking lots (other visitors pay $6 a day).
- Reduced-price children's menus in almost all restaurants, and character breakfasts and/or dinners at most resorts.
- A guest-services desk where you can purchase tickets to all WDW theme parks and attractions and obtain general information.
- Use of—and in some cases, complimentary transport to—the five Disney-owned golf courses and preferred tee times (these can be booked up to 30 days in advance).
- Access to most recreational facilities at other Disney resorts.
- Service by the Mears airport shuttle.

Additional perks at Disney-owned hotels, resorts, villas, and campgrounds (but not at "official" hotels) charge privileges throughout Walt Disney World; offer early admission to Epcot and Disney-MGM on specific days; and allow restaurant and show reservations (including Epcot restaurants) to be made through the hotel.

WALT DISNEY WORLD CENTRAL RESERVATIONS OFFICE   To reserve a room at Disney hotels, resorts, and villas; official hotels; and Fort Wilderness homes and campsites, contact **Central Reservations Operations (CRO),** P.O. Box 10100, Lake Buena Vista, FL 32830-0100 (☎ **407/W-DISNEY** (934-7639), open Monday to Friday from 8am to 10pm and Saturday and Sunday from 9am to 6pm. Have your dates and credit card ready when you call.

The CRO can also give you information about various park ticket options and make dinner, show and character breakfast reservations when you book your room.

When you call, be sure to inquire about their numerous package plans, which include meals, tickets, recreation, and other features. Be sure to ask if any special discounts are being offered at the time of your trip. All WDW properties offer some disabled/accessible accommodations and special no-smoking rooms. You can check out the various resorts at **www.disneyworld.com** (click on *resorts & spas*). In all WDW resorts, children under 17 stay free in their parents room.

DISNEY RESORTS
VERY EXPENSIVE

✪ **Disney's Beach Club Resort.** 1800 Epcot Resorts Blvd. (off Buena Vista Dr.; P.O. Box 10000), Lake Buena Vista, FL 32830-0100. ☎ **407/W-DISNEY** (934-7639) or 407/934-8000. Fax 407/354-1866. 597 units. A/C MINIBAR TV TEL. $260–$450 double; $415–$1,085 suite. Rates vary depending on view and season. AE, MC, V. Free self- and valet parking.

From its palm-fringed entranceway and manicured gardens to its plush, sun-dappled lobby, the Beach Club resembles a luxurious Victorian Cape Cod resort. The big draw here, especially for families, is Stormalong Bay, a vast free-form swimming pool/water park that sprawls over 3 acres between the Yacht Club and Beach Club and flows into a lake; it includes a 150-foot serpentine water slide. So posh is the Beach Club—and so extensive are its sports facilities—that you might consider it for an upscale resort vacation even without the draw of the Disney parks nearby. In a similar category are its sister properties, the Yacht Club and the Grand Floridian (see below). The charming rooms, some with balconies, are furnished in bleached woods and equipped with ceiling fans, extra phones in the bathroom, and safes.

Dining/Diversions: The very elegant Ariel's is open for seafood dinners nightly. Ideal for family dining is the Cape May Café, serving character breakfasts and authentic New England clambake buffet dinners. Other facilities here serve drinks, wine by the glass, light fare, and ice cream.

Amenities: 24-hour room service, baby-sitting, guest-services desk, complimentary daily newspaper, boat transport to MGM theme park. Large outdoor swimming pool, whirlpool, quarter-mile sand beach, boat rental, fishing, two tennis courts, state-of-the-art health club, volleyball/croquet/bocci courts, 2-mile jogging trail, coin-op washers/dryers, unisex hair salon, shops, business center, video-game arcade, Sandcastle Club (a counselor-supervised children's activity center).

✪ **Disney's BoardWalk.** 2101 N. Epcot Resorts Blvd. (off Buena Vista Dr.; P.O. Box 10000), Lake Buena Vista, FL 32830-1000. ☎ **407/W-DISNEY** (934-7639) or 407/939-5100 (407/939-6200 for villas). Fax 407/354-1866. 378 units, 532 villas. A/C TV TEL. $249–$450 double; $415–$1,200 suite; $210–$780 villa. Rates vary depending on view and season. Children 17 and under stay free in parents' room. AE, MC, V. Free self- and valet parking.

The BoardWalk—occupying 45 acres along the shores of Lake Crescent—takes its theme from the plush mid-Atlantic Victorian seaside resorts of the 1920s and 1930s. A large deck with rocking chairs overlooks a village green and the lake beyond, and the stunning 70-foot lobby has a working fireplace. With shingled rooftops surrounding private courtyards and New England–style flower gardens, the property connects to a quarter-mile boardwalk complete with shops, restaurants, and street performers. There's plenty to do here once the sun goes down, making it a good choice for singles and couples without children. The B&B-style accommodations are just gorgeous and

Walt Disney World Attractions & Accommodations

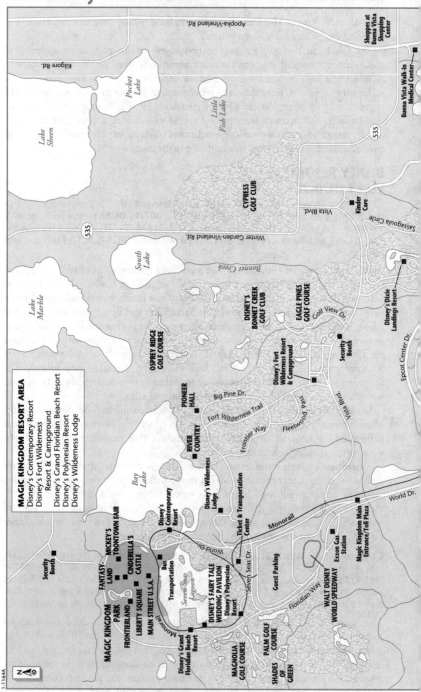

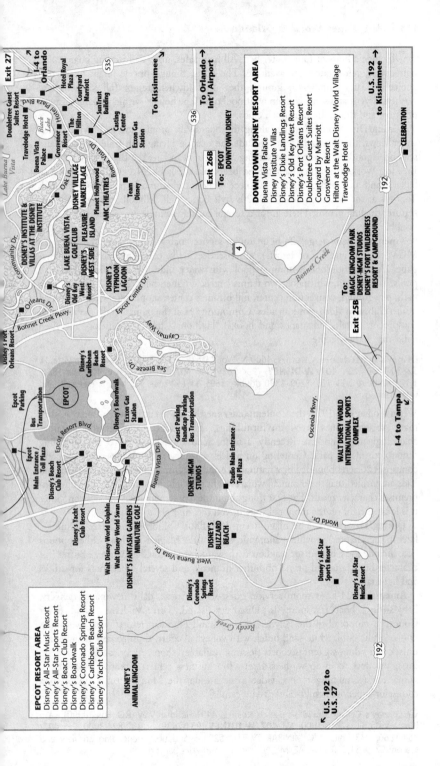

EPCOT RESORT AREA

Disney's All-Star Music Resort
Disney's All-Star Sports Resort
Disney's Beach Club Resort
Disney's Boardwalk
Disney's Coronado Springs Resort
Disney's Caribbean Beach Resort
Disney's Yacht Club Resort

DISNEY'S
ANIMAL KINGDOM

DISNEY'S
CORONADO
Springs
Resort

DISNEY'S
BLIZZARD BEACH

West Buena Vista Dr.

Disney's All-Star
Sports Resort

Disney's All-Star
Music Resort

Reedy Creek

U.S. 192 to
U.S. 27

192

Walt Disney World Dolphin
Walt Disney World Swan
DISNEY'S FANTASIA GARDENS
MINIATURE GOLF

Disney's Yacht
Club Resort

Disney's Beach
Club Resort

Epcot
Main Entrance /
Toll Plaza

Epcot
Entrance /
Toll Plaza

Bus
Transportation

Epcot
Parking

EPCOT

Epcot Resort Blvd.

Disney's
Boardwalk

Exxon Gas
Station

Disney's Caribbean
Beach Resort

Sea Breeze Dr.

Cayman Way

Guest Parking
Handicap Parking
Bus Transportation

DISNEY-MGM
STUDIOS

Studio Main Entrance /
Toll Plaza

Buena Vista Dr.

World Dr.

Osceola Pkwy.

WALT DISNEY WORLD
INTERNATIONAL SPORTS
COMPLEX

I-4 to Tampa

Exit 25B

To:
MAGIC KINGDOM PARK
DISNEY-MGM STUDIOS
DISNEY'S FORT WILDERNESS
RESORT & CAMPGROUND

Bonnet Creek

4

536

Exit 26B

To: EPCOT
DOWNTOWN DISNEY

DOWNTOWN DISNEY RESORT AREA

Buena Vista Palace
Disney Institute Villas
Disney's Dixie Landings Resort
Disney's Old Key West Resort
Disney's Port Orleans Resort
Doubletree Guest Suites Resort
Courtyard by Marriott
Grosvenor Resort
Hilton at the Walt Disney World Village
Travelodge Hotel

U.S. 192
to Kissimmee

192

CELEBRATION

Disney's Port
Orleans Resort

Bonnet Creek Pkwy.

Orleans Dr.

Community Dr.

Lake Buena
Vista

Black
Lake

DISNEY'S INSTITUTE &
VILLAS AT THE DISNEY
INSTITUTE

Oak Ln.

DISNEY VILLAGE
MARKETPLACE

LAKE BUENA VISTA
GOLF CLUB

DISNEY'S
WEST SIDE

PLEASURE
ISLAND

AMC THEATRES

Planet Hollywood

Team
Disney

DISNEY'S
TYPHOON
LAGOON

Disney's Old Key
West Resort

Epcot Center Dr.

Buena Vista Dr.

Exxon Gas
Station

Casting
Center

SunTrust
Building

The Hilton

Buena Vista Palace

Grosvenor
Resort

Travelodge Hotel

Doubletree Guest
Suites Resort

Hotel Royal
Plaza

Courtyard
Marriott

Hotel Plaza Blvd.

535

I-4 to
Orlando

Exit 27

To Kissimmee

To Orlando
Int'l Airport

447

may include a brass or four-poster bed. All have safes, irons and ironing boards, and hair dryers; refrigerators are available. The villas, though pricey, might be a good choice for large families or groups; they offer kitchenettes or full kitchens and washers/dryers, and some contain whirlpool tubs. The hotel is within walking distance of Epcot and the Yacht and Beach clubs.

Dining/Diversions: Situated along the boardwalk promenade to provide scenic water views, the dining facilities include the upscale Flying Fish Café for steak and seafood; Spoodle's, a casual spot serving Mediterranean fare; the Big River Grille and Brewing Works (featuring handcrafted beers and ales); ESPN Club, a sports bar; a bakery; and an espresso shop. A 10-piece orchestra plays music from 1940 through Top 40s at the Atlantic Dance, a 1920s-style dance hall. Jellyrolls, a sing-along bar, features dueling pianos. There are also several cocktail lounges and a carousel-themed pool bar.

Amenities: Concierge, 24-hour room service, baby-sitting, boat transport (to MGM, Epcot, and Epcot resorts), guest-services desk, complimentary daily newspaper. A large outdoor swimming pool with water slide, two additional secluded pools, kiddie pool, whirlpool, two tennis courts, croquet, bike rental, 2-mile jogging path, playground, convention center, full business center, shops, extensively equipped health club, two video-game arcades, Community Hall (for games, crafts, recreational equipment rentals, videotapes and books), Harbour Club (a counselor-supervised child-care activity center).

Disney's Contemporary Resort. 4600 N. World Dr. (P.O. Box 10000), Lake Buena Vista, FL 32830-1000. ☎ **407/W-DISNEY** (934-7639) or 407/824-1000. Fax 407/354-1866. 1,121 units. A/C TV TEL. $209–$390 double; $695–$1,150 suite. AE, MC, V. Free self- and valet parking.

When it opened in 1971, the Contemporary's aesthetic was cutting-edge. Today its dramatic angular planes, free-form furnishings, and abstract paintings appear rather charmingly retro-modern. Recently, a major renovation has spruced up the fading centerpiece of the park. Centering on a sleek 15-story A-frame tower, the property comprises 26 acres bounded by a natural lake and the Disney-made Seven Seas Lagoon. Kids are thrilled that the monorail whizzes right through the hotel; they also enjoy on-premises character meals. The best thing about the Contemporary is the location. Since it is located right on the monorail system, you can zip right to the parks.

Dining/Diversions: The magnificent 15th-floor California Grill (see "Dining," later in this chapter) provides panoramic vistas of the Magic Kingdom. Other options here include the Concourse Steakhouse, the garden-themed Chef Mickey's Buffet (for character breakfasts and prime rib buffet dinners), and several other spots for drinks and light fare.

Amenities: 24-hour room service, guest-services desk, daily newspaper delivery, baby-sitting, boat transport (to Discovery Island, Fort Wilderness, and River Country), monorail to the Polynesian and Grand Floridian resorts. Two swimming pools, kiddie pool, white-sand beach with volleyball court, shuffleboard, boat rental, unisex hair salon, six tennis courts (lessons available), shops, American Express desk, car-rental desk, coin-op washers/dryers, full business center, extensive health club, sauna/massage/tanning rooms, video-game arcade, the Mouseketeer Clubhouse (a counselor-supervised child-care/activity center).

✪ **Disney's Grand Floridian Beach Resort.** 4401 Floridian Way (P.O. Box 10000), Lake Buena Vista, FL 32830-1000. ☎ **407/W-DISNEY** (934-7639) or 407/824-3000. Fax 407/354-1866. 933 units. A/C MINIBAR TV TEL. $294–545 double, depending on view and season; $729–$1,580 suite. AE, MC, V. Free self- and valet parking.

The world renowned Grand Floridian is truly magnificent from the moment you step into its opulent five-story lobby (complete with a Chinese Chippendale aviary) under triple-domed stained-glass skylights. Here, a pianist entertains during afternoon tea, and an orchestra plays big-band music every evening. This could be a romantic choice for couples—even honeymooners (there's a wedding pavilion here, by the way). If you're into fitness, you'll appreciate the first-rate health club. The sunny rooms—with private balconies or verandas overlooking formal gardens, the pool, or a 200-acre lagoon—have two-poster beds made up with lovely floral-chintz spreads. In-room amenities include safes and ceiling fans; in the bath you'll find an extra phone, hair dryer, and terry robe. The great location offers quick access to parks and boating and water activities.

Dining/Diversions: Victoria & Albert's, Orlando's finest restaurant, is described in section 4. The lovely Grand Floridian Café, overlooking formal gardens, features Southern specialties. The exposition-themed 1900 Park Fare is the setting for character breakfasts and dinners. Flagler's offers northern Italian fare. At the gazebo-like Narcoossee's, grilled meats and seafood are prepared in an exhibition kitchen. Intimate and very Victorian, Mizner's Lounge features an international selection of ports, brandies, and appetizers. The Garden View Lounge, off the lobby, is the setting for elegant afternoon teas. Other options include the Gasparilla Grill (open 24 hours) and a pool bar.

Amenities: On-premises monorail, boat transport to Magic Kingdom, 24-hour room service, nightly turndown, baby-sitting, free trolley transport around the hotel grounds, shoe shine, massage, guest-services desk, complimentary daily newspaper. Large outdoor swimming pool with poolside changing area, kiddie pool, whirlpool, two tennis courts, boat rental, waterskiing, croquet, volleyball, playground, jogging trails, fishing excursions, white-sand beach, unisex hair salon, coin-op washers/dryers, shops, car-rental desk, state-of-the-art spa, video-game arcade, organized children's activities in summer and peak seasons, the Mouseketeer Clubhouse (a counselor-supervised child-care activity center).

Disney's Old Key West Resort. 1510 N. Cove Rd. (off Community Dr.; P.O. Box 10000), Lake Buena Vista, FL 32830-1000. ☎ **407/W-DISNEY** (934-7639) or 407/827-7700. Fax 407/354-1866. 709 units. A/C TV TEL. $195–$215 deluxe room; $224–$885 villa. Rates vary depend-ing on high and low seasons and 1-, 2-, and 3-bedroom villas. AE, MC, V. Free parking.

An understated theme (at least by Disney standards) makes the Old Key West a good choice for those seeking a quieter environment. Architecturally mirroring Key West at the turn of the century, this is a "vacation ownership" (time-share) property that rents accommodations when they're not in use by the owners. The 156-acre complex is beautifully landscaped: Tree-lined brick walkways are edged by white picket fences, palms sway softly in the breeze, shorebirds swoop lazily over lagoons, and the air is scented with honeysuckle. Most accommodations are gorgeous homes away from home with living rooms (equipped with large-screen TVs and VCRs, smaller sets and extra phones in the bedroom), fully equipped kitchens, furnished patios (offering water, woodland, or fairway views; the property overlooks the Buena Vista Golf Course), and laundry rooms. Many units contain whirlpool tubs in the master suite, and the Grand Villas have stereo systems.

Dining/Diversions: The Key West–themed Olivia's Cafe, overlooking a canal, serves all meals. There are a few other spots for drinks and light fare.

Amenities: Guest-services desk, ferry service to Disney Village Marketplace and Pleasure Island, free bus transport around the grounds, food shopping. Two tennis courts, basketball court, white-sand play area, four swimming pools, whirlpool, kiddie pool, bicycle rental, boat rental, playground, extensive health club, sauna, shuffle-board, horseshoes, volleyball, complimentary use of washers/dryers, general store, video-game arcade, video library. The Community Hall, a recreation center, shows Disney movies nightly and offers various activities.

Disney's Polynesian Resort. 1600 Seven Seas Dr. (P.O. Box 10000), Lake Buena Vista, FL 32830-1000. ☎ **407/W-DISNEY** (934-7639) or 407/824-2000. Fax 407/354-1866. 853 units. A/C TV TEL. $275–$395 double, depending on view and season; $335–$395 concierge-floor double; $415–$1,200 suite. Additional person $15 extra. AE, MC, V. Free self- and valet parking.

Just below the Magic Kingdom, the 25-acre Polynesian Resort is fronted by lush trop-ical foliage, waterfalls, and koi ponds. Inside, its skylit lobby is a virtual rain forest of tropical plantings—gorgeous by day, but rather depressingly lit for evenings. A private white-sand beach—dotted with canvas cabanas, hammocks, and large swings—looks out on a 200-acre lagoon; waterfalls, grottoes, and a water slide enhance an immense swimming pool. The large, beautiful rooms, most with balconies or patios, have canopied beds, bamboo and rattan furnishings, and walls hung with Gauguin prints. This is a great choice if you're traveling with kids, who will enjoy the Polynesian theme and kid-friendly eateries.

Dining/Diversions: 'Ohana (see "Dining," later in this chapter) is the setting for character breakfasts and all-you-can-eat island dinners featuring open-pit rock-grilled specialties. Luau Cove hosts Mickey's Tropical Luau and the Polynesian Luau Dinner Show. There are several other restaurants and bars, including a 24-hour ice-cream parlor.

Amenities: Room service, baby-sitting, on-premises monorail, boat transport (to the Magic Kingdom and the Grand Floridian Beach Resort, guest-services desk, com-plimentary daily newspaper. Two swimming pools, kiddie pool, boat rental, water-skiing, volleyball, playground, 1½-mile jogging trail, fishing excursions, coin-op washers/dryers, shops, video-game arcade, the Neverland Club (a counselor-supervised evening activity center for children).

✪ Disney's Wilderness Lodge. 901 West Timberline Dr. (on the southwest shore of Bay Lake just east of the Magic Kingdom; P.O. Box 10000), Lake Buena Vista, FL 32830-1000. ☎ **407/W-DISNEY** (934-7639) or 407/824-3200. Fax 407/354-1866. 728 units. A/C TV TEL. $165–$245 double, depending on view and season; $280–$315 junior suite; $540–$665 suite. Extra person $15. AE, MC, V. Free self- and valet parking.

The geyser out back, bubbling creek, mammoth stone hearth in the lobby, and bunk beds for the kids are just a few reasons this is one of my favorite WDW resorts. The main dining room, which has a sweeping view of 340-acre Bay Lake, might even inspire some romance. Reminiscent of rustic turn-of-the-century national park lodges, this 56-acre resort is surrounded by towering oak and pine forests. Wilderness Lodge has the advantage of feeling removed from the rest of WDW but, it should be noted, is one of the more difficult places to access via the WDW transportation system. The 5-minute geyser shows take place in the meadow periodically throughout the day, and nightly electric water pageants can be viewed from the shores of Bay Lake. The sandy lakefront beach and immense serpentine swimming pool make up for the modestly sized rooms.

The guest rooms—with patios or balconies overlooking the lake, woodlands, or meadow scenery—are furnished in Mission style and adorned with tribal friezes and landscape paintings of the Northwest.

Dining: The stunning lodgelike Artist Point, overlooking Bay Lake, is adorned with murals based on the works of Rocky Mountain School painters such as Albert Bierstadt; the menu highlights steak, seafood, and game specialties.

Amenities: Immense swimming pool (see above), kiddie pool with water slide, lake-front beach, spa pools, boat rental, bicycle rental, 2-mile jogging/bike trail, video-game arcade, gift shop, Cub's Den (a counselor-supervised activity center for children 4 to 12). Room service; guest-services desk; baby-sitting; in-room safes; boat transport to the Magic Kingdom and Contemporary Resort; bus transport to MGM, Epcot, and other park areas.

✪ **Disney's Yacht Club Resort.** 1700 Epcot Resorts Blvd. (off Buena Vista Dr.; P.O. Box 10000), Lake Buena Vista, FL 32830-1000. ☎ **407/W-DISNEY** (934-7639) or 407/ 934-7000. Fax 407/354-1866. 642 units. A/C MINIBAR TV TEL. $260–$445 double, depending on view and season; $415–$1,085 concierge-level double. AE, MC, V. Extra person $15. Free self- and valet parking.

Though first-time visitors to Orlando—who generally spend all their time in the parks—don't require extensive recreational facilities, return visitors will appreciate the extensive sports and entertainment options here. This stunning resort shares a 25-acre lake, facilities, and gorgeous landscaping with the adjacent Beach Club (described above). Its main five-story oyster-gray clapboard building is evocative of a turn-of-the-century New England yacht club. The nautical theme carries over to the very inviting rooms, decorated in snappy blue and white, with brass sconces, ship lights, and vintage maps on the walls. French doors open onto porches or balconies. The fifth floor is a concierge level, which will especially appeal to business travelers.

Dining/Diversions: The plush Yachtsman Steakhouse grills select cuts of steak, chops, and fresh seafood over oak and hickory. The Yacht Club Galley, a comfortable family restaurant, serves American regional fare. The Crew's Cup Lounge airs sporting events and features international beers. And the cozy Ale and Compass Lounge, a lobby bar with a working fireplace, proffers specialty coffees and cocktails.

Amenities: 24-hour room service, baby-sitting, guest-services desk, complimentary daily newspaper, in-room safes, boat transport to the MGM theme park, tram and boat transport to Epcot. Yacht Club facilities are identical to those of Disney's Beach Club Resort (see above).

MODERATE

✪ **Disney's Caribbean Beach Resort.** 900 Cayman Way (off Buena Vista Dr.; P.O. Box 10000), Lake Buena Vista, FL 32830-1000. ☎ **407/W-DISNEY** (934-7639) or 407/ 934-3400. Fax 407/354-1866. 2,112 units. A/C MINIBAR TV TEL. $119–$154 double. Children 16 and under stay free in parents' room. AE, MC, V. Free parking.

Though the facilities here aren't as extensive as those at some other Disney resorts, the Caribbean Beach offers especially good value for families. It occupies 200 lush, palm-fringed tropical acres, with accommodations in five distinct Caribbean "villages" grouped around a large, duck-filled lake. The main swimming pool here replicates a Spanish-style Caribbean fort, complete with water slide, kiddie pool, and whirlpool. There are other pools as well as lakefront white-sand beaches in each village. A 1.4-mile promenade, popular for jogging, encircles the lake. An arched wooden bridge leads to Parrot Cay Island where there's a short nature trail, an aviary of tropical birds, and a picnic area. The rooms are charming, with oak furnishings and chintz bedspreads. All rooms have verandas, many of them overlooking the lake.

Dining: Facilities include a festive food court, the nautically themed Captain's Tavern for American fare, and a pool bar.

Amenities: Room service (pizza only), coffee-makers, refrigerators (available for $5 a day), guest-services desk, baby-sitting, complimentary shuttle around the grounds. Seven swimming pools, video-game arcade, shops, boat rental, bicycle rental, coin-op washers/dryers, playgrounds.

Disney's Dixie Landings Resort. 1251 Dixie Dr. (off Bonnet Creek Pkwy.; P.O. Box 10000), Lake Buena Vista, FL 32830-1000. ☎ **407/W-DISNEY** (934-7639) or 407/934-6000. Fax 407/934-5777. 2,048 units. A/C TV TEL. $119–$154 room for up to 4. AE, MC, V. Free parking.

Low rates, extensive child-oriented facilities, and a food court make the Dixie Landings popular with families. Nestled on the banks of the "mighty Sassagoula River" and dotted with bayous, it shares its 325-acre site with the Port Orleans Resort (described below). It includes Ol' Man Island, a woodsy 3½-acre recreation area containing an immense swimming pool with waterfalls cascading from a broken bridge and a water slide, a playground, children's wading pool, whirlpool, and fishin' hole (rent bait and poles and angle for catfish and bass). The accommodations areas, themed after the Louisiana countryside, are divided into "parishes," with rooms housed in stately colonnaded plantation homes or rural Cajun-style dwellings fronted by brick courtyards.

Dining/Diversions: Boatwright's Dining Hall, housed in a replica of an 1800s boat-building factory, serves American/Cajun fare at breakfast and dinner. The Cotton Co-op lounge airs Monday-night football games and offers entertainment (singers and comedians) Tuesday to Saturday nights. A food court and pool bar round out the facilities.

Amenities: Six large swimming pools (one with a water slide), 1.7-mile riverfront jogging/biking path, Fulton's General Store, room service (pizza only), guest-services desk, baby-sitting, boat transport (to Port Orleans, Village Marketplace, and Pleasure Island), coin-op washers/dryers, video-game arcade, car-rental desk, bicycle and boat rental.

✪ **Disney's Port Orleans Resort.** 2201 Orleans Dr. (off Bonnet Creek Pkwy.; P.O. Box 10000), Lake Buena Vista, FL 32830-1000. ☎ **407/W-DISNEY** (934-7639) or 407/934-5000. Fax 407/934-5353. 1,008 units. A/C TV TEL. $95–$129 room for up to 4. AE, MC, V. Free parking.

This beautiful resort, themed after turn-of-the-century New Orleans, shares a site on the banks of the Sassagoula with Dixie Landings, described above. Its identical room rates and comparable facilities make it, too, a good bet for families. The midsize rooms with small bathrooms are housed in pastel buildings with shuttered windows and lacy wrought-iron balconies; they're fronted by lovely flower gardens opening onto fountained courtyards. Cherrywood furnishings, swagged draperies, and walls hung with botanical prints and family photographs make for pretty room interiors. The landscaping throughout the property is especially nice, with stately oaks, formal boxwood hedges, azaleas, and fragrant jasmine.

Dining/Diversions: Bonfamille's Café is open for breakfast and dinner, the latter featuring Creole specialties. Scat Cat's Club, a cocktail lounge off the lobby, airs Monday-night football and features family-oriented live entertainment. A food court and pool bar round out the facilities.

Amenities: Room service (pizza only), guest-services desk, baby-sitting, boat transport (to Dixie Landings, Village Marketplace, and Pleasure Island). The larger-than-Olympic-size Doubloon Lagoon swimming pool is surmounted by an enormous water slide. Whirlpool, kiddie pool, coin-op washers/dryers, video-game arcade, bicycle rental, car-rental service, boat rental, 1.7-mile riverfront jogging path, shops.

INEXPENSIVE

Disney's All-Star Music Resort. 1801 W. Buena Vista Dr. (at World Dr. and Osceola Pkwy.; P.O. Box 10000), Lake Buena Vista, FL 32830-1000. ☎ **407/W-DISNEY** (934-7639) or 407/939-6000. Fax 407/354-1866. 1,920 units. A/C TV TEL. $74–$89 double. Children 17 and under stay free in parents' room. AE, MC, V. Free parking.

Though the unbeatable combination of rock-bottom rates and extensive facilities at Disney's All-Star Music and Sports resorts (see below) is very attractive to families, there is one caveat—the rooms are small (a mere 260 square feet). They're ideal for single adults or couples traveling with one child; larger families had best be into togetherness. Set amid pristine pine forests, this Disney hostelry is part of a 246-acre complex that also includes the adjacent All-Star Sports Resort (see below). Its 10 buildings are musically themed around country, jazz, rock, calypso, and Broadway show tunes. The calypso building, for instance, has a palm-fringed roof frieze and balconies adorned with tropical birds and musical notes, while a convoy of 18-wheelers travels around the country building, which is adorned with fiddles and banjos. Oversize icons in the public areas—such as three-story cowboy boots and walk-through jukebox—are lit by neon and fiber optics at night. The attractive rooms have musically themed bedspreads, paintings, and wallpaper borders.

Dining: There's a cheerful food court with an adjoining bar.

Amenities: Room service (pizza only), baby-sitting, guest-services desk, in-room safes. Two vast swimming pools, kiddie pool, playground, coin-op washers/dryers, large retail shop, car-rental desk, video-game arcade.

Disney's All-Star Sports Resort. 1701 W. Buena Vista Dr. (at World Dr. and Osceola Pkwy.; P.O. Box 10000), Lake Buena Vista, FL 32830-1000. ☎ **407/W-DISNEY** (934-7639) or 407/939-5000. Fax 407/354-1866. 1,920 units. A/C TV TEL. $74–$89 double. Children 17 and under stay free in parents' room. AE, MC, V. Free parking.

Adjacent to and sharing facilities with the above-described All-Star Music Resort, this 82-acre hostelry is elaborately sports themed. The rooms are housed in buildings designed around football, baseball, basketball, tennis, and surfing motifs. For instance, the turquoise surf buildings have waves along their rooflines, surfboards mounted on the exterior walls, and pink fish swimming along the balcony railings. The immense public-area icons include tennis ball–can stairways and four-story football helmets and whistles. The cheerful rooms feature sports-action-motif bedspreads, paintings, and wallpaper borders; in-room safes are included. As noted above, however, the rooms here are small.

Dining: There's a brightly decorated food court with an adjoining bar.

Amenities: Room service (pizza only), baby-sitting, guest-services desk. Two vast outdoor swimming pools (one surfing themed with two 38-foot shark fins, the other shaped like a baseball diamond with an "outfield" sundeck), kiddie pool, playground, coin-op washers/dryers, shops, car-rental service, video-game arcade.

A DISNEY CAMPGROUND/WILDERNESS HOMES

Disney's Fort Wilderness Resort and Campground. 3520 N. Fort Wilderness Trail (P.O. Box 10000), Lake Buena Vista, FL 32830-1000. ☎ **407/W-DISNEY** (934-7639) or 407/824-2900. Fax 407/354-1866. 784 campsites, 408 wilderness homes. A/C TV TEL (homes only). $35–$54 campsite (depending on season, location, number of people, size, and extent of hookup); $180–$215 wilderness home. AE, MC, V. Free self-parking.

This woodsy 780-acre camping resort—shaded by towering pines and cypress trees and crossed by fish-filled streams, lakes, and canals—is ideal for family vacations. Though it's a tad less central than other Disney hotels, its abundance of on-premises facilities more than compensates. Secluded campsites offer 110/220-volt outlets, barbecue grills, picnic tables, and children's play areas. There are also wilderness homes—rustic one-bedroom cabins with piney interiors that accommodate up to six people. These have cozy living rooms with Murphy beds, fully equipped eat-in kitchens, picnic tables, and barbecue grills. Guests here enjoy extensive recreational facilities ranging from a riding stable to a nightly campfire program hosted by Chip 'n' Dale.

Dining/Diversions: The rustic log-beamed Trails End offers buffet meals, and the cozy Crockett's Tavern features Texas fare. During summer, guests enjoy a dazzling electrical water pageant from the beach, nightly at 9:45pm. And the rambunctious *Hoop-Dee-Doo Musical Revue* takes place in Pioneer Hall nightly (details in section 15).

Amenities: Guest-services desk, baby-sitting, boat transport (to Discovery Island, the Magic Kingdom, and the Contemporary Resort). Comfort station in each campground area (with rest rooms, private showers, ice machines, phones, and laundry rooms), two large swimming pools, white-sand beach, horseback riding (trail rides), petting farm, pony rides, fishing, three sand volleyball courts, ballfields, tetherball, shuffleboard, bike rentals, boat rental, 1½-mile nature trail, 2.3-mile jogging path, two tennis courts, two 18-hole championship golf courses, shops, kennel, two video-game arcades.

LAKE BUENA VISTA/OFFICIAL HOTELS

These hostelries, designated "official" Walt Disney World hotels, are located on and around Hotel Plaza Boulevard, and guests at these hotels enjoy many privileges (see above). The location is a big advantage—close to the Disney parks and within walking distance of Disney Village Marketplace and Crossroads shops and restaurants, as well as Pleasure Island nightlife.

One difference between "official" hotels and actual Disney resorts is that the former (with the exception of the Swan and Dolphin) generally have less relentless themes; decide for yourself if that's a plus or a minus. *Note:* You can also make reservations for all of the below-listed properties through Central Reservations Operations at ☎ **407/ W-DISNEY** (934-7639); see above for details.

EXPENSIVE

✪ **Buena Vista Palace Resort & Spa.** 1900 Buena Vista Dr. (just north of Hotel Plaza Blvd.; P.O. Box 22206), Lake Buena Vista, FL 32830. ☎ **800/327-2990** or 407/827-2727. Fax 407/ 827-6034. www.bvp-resort.com. 1,014 units. A/C MINIBAR TV TEL. $129–$294 double; $229–$529 1-, 2-bedroom suite. Rates depend on view and season. Children 17 and under stay free in parents' room. AE, CB, DC, DISC, MC, V. Valet parking $7; free self-parking.

Complete room renovations in fall 1997 added a new luster to this already luxurious 27-acre resort. The perks here are the European-style spa and extensive boating and recreational facilities. The spacious accommodations, most with lake-view balconies or patios, are appealingly decorated and equipped with Spectravision, safes, bedroom and bath phones, and ceiling fans. There are also luxurious one- and two-bedroom suites with living and dining rooms and a 10th-floor concierge level. For those with sensitive systems, or a Howard Hughes–type bent for cleanliness, there are 65 ecofriendly rooms featuring nonallergenic pillows and blankets and nondyed tissue, towels, and linens, filtered water, and extra air-cleaning systems.

Dining/Diversions: Arthur's 27 (perched on the 27th floor) offers haute cuisine and panoramic park views, as well as live jazz, piano-bar entertainment, and dancing in an adjoining lounge. In the Outback Restaurant, complete with a three-story indoor waterfall, an Australian storyteller entertains during dinner; steak and seafood are featured. Character breakfasts take place in the Watercress Cafe. Other venues include pool and snack bars, a pastry shop, and the Laughing Kookaburra Good Time Bar, which offers a selection of 99 beers and hosts happy-hour buffets and live bands for dancing nightly.

Amenities: Free shuttle serving WDW, two large swimming pools, whirlpool, kiddie pool, three tennis courts, boat rental, 2- and 3-mile jogging paths, sand volleyball court, bike rental, playground, car-rental desk, 24-hour room service, baby-sitting, guest-services desk, complimentary newspaper for crown-level guests, full business center, shops, coin-op washers/dryers, video-game arcade, counselor-supervised child-care program. The spa offers massage, herbal wraps, a fully equipped health club.

Hilton at Walt Disney World Village. 1751 Hotel Plaza Blvd. (just east of Buena Vista Dr.), Lake Buena Vista, FL 32830. ☎ **800/782-4414** or 407/827-4000. Fax 407/827-3890. 814 units. A/C MINIBAR TV TEL. $235–$285 double; $275–$345 double in the Tower. Rates depend on season. All children stay free in parents' room. Inquire about weekend rates. AE, CB, DC, DISC, JCB, MC, V. Valet parking $8; free self-parking.

Location. Location. Location. The Hilton is close to the theme parks but, better yet for adults, just across the street from the clubs, restaurants, and shops of Downtown Disney and Disney Village Marketplace. From the ample rooms to the palm-fringed circular driveway leading up to an imposing waterfall and fountain, this place delivers traditional Hilton panache and sophistication. Twenty-three beautifully landscaped acres include two heated swimming pools. Remember, though, being in the heart of everything can be a headache during peak seasons because of extremely heavy street traffic. Another plus is the 48 handicapped-accessible rooms.

Dining/Diversions: Choices include Finn's Grill, a Key West–themed steak and seafood restaurant; Benihana Japanese Steakhouse (for teppanyaki dining and nightly entertainment, including karaoke); and a cheerful coffee shop. John T's Plantation Bar offers dancing nightly. Kids love the Old Fashioned Soda Shoppe for pizzas, burgers, and ice-cream sundaes, plus there is a breakfast featuring Disney characters.

Amenities: 24-hour room service, concierge (sells tickets and arranges transport to all other nearby attractions/airport), baby-sitting. Two very large swimming pools, whirlpool, children's spray pool, boat rental, car-rental desk, unisex beauty salon, business center, fully equipped health club, sauna, shops, coin-op washers/dryers, video-game arcade, Vacation Station Kids Hotel (a counselor-supervised child-care center).

MODERATE

✪ **Courtyard by Marriott.** 1805 Hotel Plaza Blvd. (between Lake Buena Vista Dr. and Apopka-Vineland Rd./Fla. 535), Lake Buena Vista, FL 32830. ☎ **800/223-9930** or 407/828-8888. Fax 407/827-4623. www.marriott.com. 323 units. A/C TV TEL. $110–$169 double, depending on view and season. AE, CB, DC, DISC, JCB, MC, V. From I-4, exit 27 to Walt Disney World Village. Turn left on Hotel Plaza Blvd.; it's on the left. Free parking.

The Courtyard is a moderately priced link in the Marriott chain, with lower prices achieved via limited services, but don't envision a Spartan, no-frills atmosphere. This property was recently renovated to the tune of $4.5 million, and it's looking great. The attractive, standard-sized rooms, most with balconies, have in-room safes and pay-movie options. Kids will love the in-room Nintendo systems.

Dining/Diversions: A full-service restaurant serves American fare at all meals and provides room service. There's also a lobby cocktail lounge, a poolside bar (in season), and an on-premises deli featuring pizza and frozen yogurt.

Amenities: Free transportation to WDW parks and attractions. The guest-services desk sells tickets and arranges transport to all nearby attractions; in-room coffeemakers, refrigerators on request. Two outdoor swimming pools, a whirlpool, a kiddie pool, boat rental at nearby Disney Village Marina, a playground, car-rental desk, an exercise room, shops, coin-op washers/dryers, and a video-game arcade.

Doubletree Guest Suites. 2305 Hotel Plaza Blvd. (just west of Apopka-Vineland Rd./Fla. 535), Lake Buena Vista, FL 32830. ☎ **800/222-8733** or 407/934-1000. Fax 407/934-1011. 229 units. A/C TV TEL. $149–$263 1-bedroom suite for up to 6; $375–$1,015 2-bedroom suite. Rates depend on view and season. Children 17 and under stay free in parents' room. AE, CB, DC, DISC, JCB, MC, V. From I-4, Exit 27, to Disney Village Marketplace. Left on Hotel Plaza Blvd. Free parking.

Entered via a cheerful skylit atrium lobby with an aviary of tropical birds and theme-park murals, this seven-story all-suite hotel is a great choice for families. Children have their own check-in desk where they receive a free gift. The large one-bedroom suites, which sleep up to six, are delightfully decorated and include full living rooms, dining areas, and separate bedrooms.

Dining/Diversions: The festive Streamers serves buffet and à la carte breakfasts and dinners featuring American fare with Southwestern specialties. A bar lounge adjoins, as does a theater where kids can watch Disney movies while Mom and Dad linger over coffee. Another bar serves the pool.

Amenities: Free shuttles to WDW parks. Room service, baby-sitting, guest-services desk (sells tickets and arranges transport to all nearby attractions), in-room refrigerators, microwaves, coffeemakers, wet bar, pay movies. Large swimming pool, whirlpool, kiddie pool with fountain, two tennis courts, jogging path, volleyball, playground, car-rental desk, exercise room, shops (including a grocery), coin-op washers/dryers, video-game arcade, boat rental at nearby Disney Village Marina.

Grosvenor Resort. 1850 Hotel Plaza Blvd. (just east of Buena Vista Dr.), Lake Buena Vista, FL 32830. ☎ **800/624-4109** or 407/828-4444. Fax 407/828-8192. 626 units. A/C TV TEL. $99–$175 room for up to 4 people, depending on view and season. AE, CB, DC, DISC, JCB, MC, V. Valet parking $5; free self-parking.

In the moderately priced category, this is a comfortable choice with a British colonial theme and a few unique entertainment options. Occupying 13 lushly landscaped lakeside acres, it centers on a 19-story peach stucco building fronted by towering palms. The rooms are nicely decorated in an attractive resort motif and are equipped with VCRs (tapes can be rented), coffeemakers, safes, and minibars (stocked on request); refrigerators can be rented.

Dining/Diversions: The Baskervilles Restaurant, with a Sherlock Holmes museum on the premises, hosts Saturday-night mystery dinner-theater and buffet breakfasts and dinners, some with Disney characters. Also here: a 24-hour food court, a pool bar, and a lounge where sporting events are aired on a large-screen TV.

Amenities: Free shuttle to WDW parks and attractions, guest-services desk, (sells tickets and arranges transport to all nearby attractions), doctor on call, room service, baby-sitting, free daily newspaper. Two swimming pools, whirlpool, kiddie pool, exercise room, two tennis courts, boat rental, playground, lawn games, car-rental desk, coin-op washers/dryers, shops, video-game arcade.

Travelodge Hotel. 2000 Hotel Plaza Blvd. (between Buena Vista Dr. and Apopka-Vineland Rd./Fla. 535), Lake Buena Vista, FL 32830. ☎ **800/348-3765** or 407/828-2424. Fax 407/828-8933. www.travelodge.com. 325 units. A/C MINIBAR TV TEL. $179–$1,103 room for up to 4 people, depending on room size and season. Inquire about packages. AE, CB, DC, DISC, JCB, M, V. Free parking.

This 12-acre lakefront hotel is spiffy and immaculate, with more upscale rooms and public areas than you might expect at a Travelodge. The rates are also higher than the Travelodge norm, but represent good value for your money. The reason: This is the company's flagship hotel. Designed to resemble a Barbados plantation manor house, it has a Caribbean-resort ambience, enhanced by tropical foliage and bright floral-print fabrics. The rooms are particularly inviting, with light bleached-wood furnishings and lovely framed botanical prints and floral friezes. Furnished balconies overlook Lake Buena Vista.

Dining/Diversions: Traders, with a wall of windows facing a wooded area, is open for breakfast and steak and seafood dinners. On the 18th floor, Toppers offers magnificent views of Lake Buena Vista, as well as dancing, music videos, pool tables, and dartboards; it's a great vantage point for watching the nightly laser shows and fireworks. There's also a cocktail bar and a casual self-service eatery.

Amenities: Room service, baby-sitting, guest-services desk (sells tickets and arranges transport to all nearby attractions), free newspaper weekdays, Spectravision movies, Nintendo, coffeemakers, safes, hair dryers, and free local phone calls. Large swimming pool, kiddie pool, boat rental, playground, car-rental desk, coin-op washers/dryers, shops, video-game arcade.

OTHER LAKE BUENA VISTA AREA HOTELS

All of these hotels are within a few minutes' drive of WDW parks. In addition to the listings below, there's a **Comfort Inn** at 8442 Palm Pkwy., Lake Buena Vista, FL 32863 (☎ **800/999-7300** or 407/239-7300), charging only $39 to $69 for up to four people in a room.

VERY EXPENSIVE

✪ **Hyatt Regency Grand Cypress Resort.** One North Jacardanda (off S.R. 535), Orlando, FL 32836. ☎ **800/233-1234** or 407/239-1234; 800/835-7377 or 407/239-4700 for villas. Fax 407/239-3800, or 407/239-7219 for villas. 750 units, 146 villas. A/C MINIBAR TV TEL. $185–$310 room for up to 5; $305–$410 Regency Club double; $190–$1,400 villa. AE, CB, DC, DISC, JCB, MC, V. Valet parking $9; free self-parking. I-4 exit 27, right on County Road 535, left at second traffic light onto S.R. 535. Two lights on right.

Although only a mile from WDW, this 1,500-acre retreat ablaze with bougainvillea and hibiscus seems half a world away. A romantic getaway, an award winning golf course, a top-notch equestrian center, and a major renovation in 1997 put this resort in a class by itself. The spacious rooms are a welcome respite from the crowded parks. Topping the list of outstanding facilities is a half-acre swimming pool spanned by a rope bridge and flowing through rock grottoes (with 12 waterfalls and two steep water slides). Relax on the white-sand beach, play on 12-tennis courts, or tee off on a Jack Nicklaus–designed golf course.

The deluxe accommodations with wicker furnishings evoke the Southern luxury of a bygone era. Two floors comprise the Regency Club, a concierge level. And especially lavish are the Mediterranean-style Villas of Grand Cypress, all with patios, kitchens, living rooms, and dining rooms; some have working fireplaces and whirlpool baths.

Dining/Diversions: Casual yet elegant, Hemingway's serves Florida seafood for lunch and dinner. The lodgelike Black Swan, overlooking the golf course, features haute American/continental dinners. Similar fare is offered at the plush La Coquina, where a harpist entertains at dinner and the Sunday brunches are exquisite. Other venues include the White Horse Saloon, for prime rib dinners and country music; Trellises, a bar/lounge where a jazz ensemble entertains evenings; the lovely lake-view Cascade, serving American fare at all meals, plus Japanese breakfasts; and several poolside and snack bars.

Amenities: Free transportation around grounds and to all major attractions, 24-hour room service, baby-sitting, concierge (sells tickets to WDW parks and other nearby attractions), free transportation around the grounds, hourly shuttle between the hotel and all WDW parks (round-trip fare $6 per day), Mears airport shuttle.

Golf and tennis instruction and pro shops (the golf school here has been called one of the finest in the country), 45-acre Audubon nature walk, 4.7-mile jogging path, racquetball/volleyball/shuffleboard courts, playground, car-rental desk, unisex beauty salon, full business center, state-of-the-art health club, shops, helicopter landing pad, video-game arcade, counselor-supervised child-care center/Camp Hyatt activity center.

EXPENSIVE

✪ **Marriott's Orlando World Center.** 8701 World Center Dr. (on Fla. 536 between I-4 and Fla. 535), Orlando, FL 32821. ☎ **800/621-0638** or 407/239-4200. Fax 407/238-8777. www.marriott.com. 1,599 units. A/C MINIBAR TV TEL. $152–$259 room for up to 5 people (range reflects season); $265–$2,400 suite. AE, CB, DC, DISC, JCB, MC, V. Valet parking $8; free self-parking.

Providing the only viable competition for the above-mentioned Hyatt, this sprawling 230-acre multifacility resort, just 2 miles from WDW parks, is a top convention venue that also offers recreational facilities for the tourist. These include three swimming pools (one larger than Olympic size with slides and waterfalls), eight tennis courts, and an 18-hole/par-71 Joe Lee–designed championship golf course. A grand palm-lined driveway, flanked by rolling golf greens, leads to the main building—a massive 27-story tower fronted by flower beds and fountains.

It houses spacious guest rooms cheerfully decorated in pastel hues with bamboo and rattan furnishings. All have patios or balconies, extensive pay-movie options, irons and ironing boards, safes, and hair dryers. Step outside the tower and you'll find magnificently landscaped grounds, punctuated by rock gardens, shaded groves of pines and magnolias, and cascading waterfalls; swans and ducks inhabit over a dozen lakes and lagoons spanned by arched bridges.

Dining/Diversions: The luxurious Tuscany, Marriott's premier restaurant, offers northern Italian haute cuisine dinners. The Mikado Japanese Steak House is a serene setting for classic teppanyaki dinners. JW's Steakhouse serves breakfasts and lunches on a screened balcony and cozy dinners in a rustic pine interior. Allie's American Grille is a rather elegant family restaurant. And several smaller eateries and bars include the plush Pagoda Lounge for nightly piano-bar entertainment and Champion's, a first-rate sports bar.

Amenities: Concierge, 24-hour room service, baby-sitting, shoe shine, complimentary newspaper weekdays, 1-hour film developing, Mears transportation/sightseeing desk (sells tickets to all nearby attractions, including WDW parks; also provides transport, by reservation, to WDW, other attractions, and the airport; the round-trip fare to WDW parks is $5 per day, free for children 11 and under); golf and tennis pro shops and instruction, 18-hole miniature golf course, two volleyball courts, four whirlpools, large kiddie pool, car-rental desk, unisex beauty salon, extensive business center, state-of-the-art health club, coin-op washers/dryers, shops, video-game arcade, Lollipop Lounge (a counselor-supervised child-care/activities center). Inquire as well about organized children's activities—games, movies, nature walks, and more.

✪ **Residence Inn by Marriott.** 8800 Meadow Creek Dr. (just off Fla. 535 between Fla. 536 and I-4), Orlando, FL 32821. ☎ **800/331-3131** or 407/239-7700. Fax 407/239-7605. 688 units. A/C TV TEL. $149–$219 suite. Rates vary depending on season. Rates include full breakfast. AE, CB, DC, DISC, JCB, MC, V. Free parking.

This delightful all-suite hostelry occupies 50 acres, alternating wooded grounds with neatly manicured lawns, duck-filled ponds, fountains, and flower beds. Guests, up to four in a single suite and up to six in a double, enjoy a serene environment offering the seclusion and safety of a private community. They can also avail themselves of the extensive facilities at the adjoining Marriott's Orlando World Center (see details above) with room-charge privileges. The tastefully decorated accommodations—with fully equipped eat-in kitchens, private balconies or patios, and large living rooms—are equipped with Spectravision, VCRs (tapes are available for rental), two phones, ceiling fans, and safes. The two-bedroom units have two baths.

Dining: A full breakfast is available in the gatehouse each morning, there's a Pizza Hut on the premises, and local restaurants deliver food.

Amenities: Guest-services desk (sells tickets and provides transport to all nearby theme parks and attractions; round-trip to WDW parks is $8), baby-sitting, complimentary daily newspaper, next-day film developing, free food-shopping service, Mears airport shuttle. Three large swimming pools, two whirlpools, sports court (basketball, badminton, volleyball, paddle tennis, shuffleboard), tennis court, playground, coin-op washers/dryers, shops, two video-game arcades.

Summerfield Suites Lake Buena Vista. 8751 Suiteside Dr. (off Apopka-Vineland Rd./ S.R. 535), Lake Buena Vista, FL 32836. ☎ **800/833-4353** or 407/238-0777. Fax 407/238-0777. 150 units. A/C TV TEL. $169–$209 1-bedroom suite for up to 4; $199–$249 2-bedroom suite for up to 8. Range reflects season. Rates include continental breakfast. AE, CB, DC, DISC, MC, V. Free parking.

This all-suite property, offering free transport to and from the nearby Disney parks, is an excellent choice for families. Known for its friendliness and immaculate accommodations. The spacious suites—in buildings surrounding a palm-fringed brick courtyard with umbrella tables, fountains, and gazebos—have fully equipped eat-in kitchens, comfortable living rooms, and a bath for each bedroom. Amenities include bedroom and kitchen phones (with two lines), TVs in each bedroom and the living room (with pay-movie options), VCRs (movies can be rented), and irons and ironing boards.

Dining: Guests enjoy continental breakfast in the pleasant dining room or at umbrella tables in the courtyard; omelettes and waffles may be purchased. An on-premises lobby deli (which sells light fare and liquor) also serves the pool area. Many local restaurants deliver to the hotel.

Amenities: Guest-services desk (sells tickets to WDW parks and other nearby attractions, many of them discounted), shuttle to airport and nearby attractions ($35), free daily newspaper, complimentary grocery shopping, baby-sitting. Large swimming pool, whirlpool, kiddie pool, car-rental desk, full business services, exercise room, coin-op washers/dryers, shops, video-game arcade.

MODERATE

✪ **Holiday Inn Sunspree Resort Lake Buena Vista.** 13351 S.R. 535 (between S.R. 536 and I-4), Lake Buena Vista, FL 32821. ☎ **800/FON-MAXX** or 407/239-4500. Fax 407/239-7713. www.kidsuite.com. E-mail: Max@kidsuite.com. 507 units. A/C TV TEL. $77–$169 room for up to 4 people, depending on season. AE, CB, DC, DISC, JCB, MC, V. Free parking.

Less than a mile from WDW, this family-friendly hotel combines a chain's affordable dependability while catering to children in a big way. Kids "check in" at their own pint-size desk, receive a free fun bag containing a video-game token coupon, a lollipop, and a small gift, and get a personal welcome from animated raccoon mascots, Max and Maxine. Camp Holiday activities—magic shows, clowns, sing-alongs, arts and crafts, and much more—are available at a minimal charge for kids 2 to 12. Parents can even arrange (by reservation) for Max to come tuck a child into bed. The pretty, family-sized rooms have kitchenettes with refrigerators, microwave ovens, and coffeemakers. And if you're renting a second room for the children, "kidsuites" here—themed as igloos, space capsules, Noah's Ark, and so on—sleep up to three.

Dining/Diversions: Maxine's serves all meals, including steak and seafood dinners. Max's CyberArcade offers a video games, other family diversions, and airs sports on a large-screen TV. Kids 12 and under eat all meals free, either in a hotel restaurant with their parents or in Kid's Kottage, a cheerful facility where movies and cartoons are shown, and dinner includes a make-your-own-sundae bar.

Amenities: Free shuttle service to WDW parks, fee for shuttles to other parks. Room service, guest-services desk (sells tickets to all nearby attractions. Large swimming pool, two whirlpools, kiddie pool, playground, fitness center, coin-op washers/dryers, shops, video-game arcade, VCRs (tapes can be rented), hair dryers, safes, Camp Holiday (a counselor-supervised child-care/activity center for children 2 to 12).

Note: The **Holiday Inn Hotel & Suites,** 5678 West Irlo Bronson Hwy., Kissimmee, FL 34746 (☎ **800/FON-KIDS** or 407/396-4488) offers similar services.

ON U.S. 192/KISSIMMEE

This very American stretch of highway dotted with fast-food eateries isn't exactly scenic, but it does contain many inexpensive hotels and motels within 1 to 8 miles of Walt Disney World parks. Almost all provide, or can arrange, for shuttle service to WDW and other attractions (the cost usually runs from $10 to $14 per person). There are large, about 20 feet tall, markers along the side of the road. Aptly tagged with the word *Marker* and a number, they are a new effort to help tourists find their way along this stretch of road.

Note: U.S. 17-92 is W. Irlo Bronson Memorial Highway and eventually turns into Vine Street.

MODERATE

Comfort Inn Maingate. 7571 W. Irlo Bronson Memorial Hwy. (U.S. 192), between Reedy Creek Blvd. and Sherbeth Rd. or markers 15 and 16. ☎ **800/221-2222** or 407/396-7500. 225 units. A/C TV TEL. $69–$199 double. AE, DC, DISC, MC, V.

The Comfort Inn is located just 6 miles from WDW parks and 7 miles from Universal Studios. Interiors are recently refurbished and include refrigerators, microwaves, and sleep sofas. The rooms aren't huge, but they are large enough for a family to be comfortable.

INEXPENSIVE

In addition to the listings below, there are scores of other inexpensive but perfectly serviceable motels within a few miles of the WDW parks. All have swimming pools and arrange for transportation to and from for a fee. Many sell tickets to attractions, but it's a good idea to stick to ordering tickets through the parks themselves.

Days Inn. 4104 and 4125 W. Irlo Bronson Memorial Hwy. (U.S. 192, at Hoagland Blvd. N. or markers 15 and 16), Kissimmee, FL 34741. ☎ **800/647-0010**, 800/DAYS-INN, or 407/846-4714. Fax 407/932-2699. 220 units. A/C TV TEL. $39–$59 room for up to 4, depending on season; $37–$63 efficiency; $55–$75 Jacuzzi room (for 1 or 2 people). Rates include continental breakfast. Rates may be higher during major events. AE, CB, DC, DISC, MC, V. Free parking.

Offering good value for your hotel dollar, these two Days Inns—on either side of U.S. 192—share facilities, including two swimming pools, coin-op washers and dryers, and a video-game arcade. Several restaurants (which deliver food), a large shopping mall with a 12-theater movie house, and a supermarket are within walking distance.

The rooms at both locations are clean and attractive standard motel units. The best bets are the efficiency units with fully equipped kitchenettes at no. 4104. On the other hand, at no. 4125 you can ask for a room with a large Jacuzzi, a refrigerator, and a microwave oven. All accommodations offer pay-movie options and in-room safes, and both locations serve free coffee, juice, and doughnuts in their lobbies each morning. Guest services at no. 4104 sells tickets (many of them discounted) and arranges transport to all nearby attractions, including WDW parks. A big plus: Round-trip transport to WDW parks is free. Airport transfers can be arranged.

Howard Johnson Express Inn. 4836 W. Irlo Bronson Hwy. (between markers 11 and 12). ☎ **800/952-5464** or 407/396-4762) Fax 407/396-4866. 131 units. A/C TV TEL. $39.95–$66 doubles and suite. Take 1-4 to Exit 25A, 3.5 miles on right. Free parking.

As a lakefront property, this is one of the more scenic Kissimmee offerings. You can have picnics by the lake or rent jet-skis for about $60 an hour. The pink-and-blue buildings contain clean, comfortable rooms, and some of the suites contain in-room Jacuzzis, microwave ovens, and refrigerators. There is a large heated swimming pool and a video game room. There's a free shuttle to the WDW parks, and transportation to other attractions can be arranged for a fee.

✪ **Larson's Lodge Main Gate.** 6075 W. Irlo Bronson Memorial Hwy. (U.S. 192, just east of I-4 between markers 8 and 9 across from the old-fashioned water tower marking the entrance to Celebration), Kissimmee, FL 34747. ☎ **800/327-9074** or 407/396-6100. Fax 407/396-6965. 128 units. A/C TV TEL. $59–$79 double, depending on season. All units have microwave and refrigerator. Children under 18 stay free in parents' room. Inquire about packages. AE, CB, DC, DISC, MC, V. Free parking.

With a water park (Watermania) next door, a playground, poolside picnic tables, barbecue grills, and an on-site Shoney's restaurant, Larson's Lodge is a good choice for families. Accommodations are equipped with refrigerators, microwave ovens, and safes, and there are efficiency units with fully equipped kitchenettes. There's a supermarket just a few minutes away by car.

The guest-services desk can arrange transport to nearby attractions and the airport. Round-trip to WDW parks is $10. On-premises facilities include a large heated swimming pool and whirlpool, shops, coin-op washers/dryers, and a video-game arcade. Guests enjoy a free newspaper and coffee in the lobby each morning. Pets are permitted.

Quality Inn on Lake Cecile. 4944 W. Irlo Bronson Memorial Hwy. (between Markers 5 and 6) , Kissimmee, FL 34746. ☎ **800/228-1828** or 407/396-4455. 200 units. A/C TV TEL. $59–$79 double. Rates include extended continental breakfast. AE, CB, DC, DISC, JCB, MC, V. Free parking.

Located on the banks of beautiful Lake Cecile, the lakefront property gives this hotel an edge over the competition. You can rent jet-skis or water skis. There is a food court and scheduled transportation to the WDW parks. Rooms are small, but clean and comfortable; ideal for young singles or young couples looking for a bargain.

Super 8 Motel. 1815 W. Vine St. (U.S. 192), between Bermuda and Thacker aves. (the markers stop before they reach downtown Kissimmee). ☎ **800/325-4348** or 407/847-6121. A/C TV TEL. $29.95–$59.95 double depending on season. Rates include continental breakfast. AE, DISC, MC, V.

Formerly the Colonial Motor Lodge, this facility was completely renovated in 1997 and includes basic rooms with laundry facilities, and cable TV. There are suites that sleep six along with standard motel rooms and two-bedroom apartments featuring fully equipped kitchens.

Other national chains represented along this strip of highway include **Ramada Inn,** 5150 W. Irlo Bronson Memorial Hwy. (U.S. 192), ☎ **800/544-5712** or 407/396-1212. (This property accepts pets and is adjacent to a 1950s-style Hollywood Diner.) And **Motel 6,** at 7455 W. Irlo Bronson Hwy., (☎ **800/466-8356** or 407/394-6422).

INTERNATIONAL DRIVE

The hotels and resorts listed here are 7 to 10 miles north of the Walt Disney World parks (a quick freeway trip) and close to Universal Studios Florida and Sea World. Though you won't get away from rambunctious kids anywhere in this town, International Drive hotels do tend to be more adult oriented.

VERY EXPENSIVE

✪ **Peabody Orlando.** 9801 International Dr. (between the Bee Line Expwy. and Sand Lake Rd.), Orlando, FL 32819. ☎ **800/PEABODY** (732-3639) or 407/352-4000. Fax 407/351-0073. www.peabody-orlando.com. 891 units. A/C MINIBAR TV TEL. $240–$300 room for up to 3 people; $450–$1,350 suite. Children 17 and under stay free in parents' room. Inquire about packages and holiday/summer discounts and senior rate for those over 50. AE, CB, DC, DISC, JCB, MC, V. Valet parking $7; free self-parking.

This hotel is famous for the resident ducks that make their daily march through the lobby, accompanied by the music of John Philip Sousa. There may be a little disarray here until 2000 as a second 700-room tower is under construction, but the addition may translate into better deals. The ambience will surely survive the jackhammers. The hallmark of the Peabody is an ambience of sophistication not found elsewhere in Orlando, and this aura extends to its top-rated restaurants.

The luxurious rooms have handsome bamboo and bleached-wood furnishings, two phones, Spectravision and laser-disc movie setups (there's a vast video library), and, in the bathroom, cosmetic lights, fine European toiletries, a hair dryer, and a small TV. The concierge-level Peabody Club occupies the top three floors. Seniors should note the over-50 rate above, compensation for wrinkles indeed.

Dining/Diversions: Dux, the Peabody's elegant signature restaurant, and the casual 24-hour B-Line Diner are detailed in "Dining," later in this chapter. Capriccio, for sophisticated Italian fare, is open for dinner and champagne Sunday brunches. Combos play jazz, blues, and show tunes in the atrium Lobby Bar nightly. The lobby is the setting for exquisite afternoon English teas on weekdays. Sporting events are aired in the cozy duck-themed Mallards Lounge. And alfresco jazz concerts take place on the fourth-floor recreation level in the spring and fall.

Amenities: Concierge (7am to 11pm), 24-hour room service, baby-sitting, nightly bed turndown on request, free daily newspaper, transport between the hotel and all WDW parks throughout the day (unlimited daily round-trips cost $6), Mears transportation/sightseeing desk (sells tickets to all nearby attractions, including WDW parks and dinner shows; also provides transport, by reservation, to attractions and the airport). Olympic-length swimming pool, outdoor whirlpool, kiddie pool, four tennis courts, 7-mile jogging path, car-rental desk, Delta Airlines desk, full-service unisex salon, business center, state-of-the-art health club, shops, video-game arcade; golf privileges at four nearby courses.

EXPENSIVE

Summerfield Suite. 8480 International Dr. (between the Bee Line Expwy. and Sand Lake Rd.), Orlando, FL 32819. ☎ **800/833-4353** or 407/352-2400. Fax 407/238-0778. 146 units. A/C TV TEL. $159–$199 1-bedroom suite for up to 4; $179–$239 2-bedroom suite for up to 8. Range reflects room size and season. Rates include continental breakfast. AE, CB, DC, DISC, MC, V. Free parking.

This delightful hotel—with potted palms on open-air balconies creating a welcoming resort ambience—is built around a nicely landscaped central courtyard. Like its sibling property in Lake Buena Vista, it's notably friendly and well run. The spacious, neat-as-a-pin suites, very attractively decorated, contain fully equipped eat-in kitchens, comfortable living rooms, and large dressing areas. All offer irons and ironing boards, phones in each bedroom and kitchen, and satellite TVs (with pay-movie options) in each bedroom and living room (the latter with a VCR; movie rentals are available).

Dining: An extensive continental buffet breakfast is served in a charming dining room (waffles and omelettes can be purchased), and the cozy lobby bar is a popular gathering place in the evenings. Local restaurants deliver food to the premises.

Amenities: Concierge/tour desk (sells tickets to WDW parks and other nearby attractions), daily newspaper delivery, transport between the hotel and all WDW parks (round-trip fare is $7), shuttle available to the airport and nearby attractions, complimentary grocery shopping. Nice-size swimming pool, whirlpool, kiddie pool, car-rental desk, business services, exercise room, coin-op washers/dryers, 24-hour shop, video-game arcade.

MODERATE

Orlando Marriott. 8001 International Dr. (at Sand Lake Rd.), Orlando, FL 32819. ☎ **800/421-8001** or 407/351-2420. Fax 407/351-5611. www.marriott.com. 1,078 units. A/C TV TEL. $99–$300 double. Children 17 and under stay free in parents' room. AE, DC, DISC, MC, V. Free self-parking.

The grounds at this verdant 48-acre hotel—varying neatly manicured lawns and flower beds with fern gullies, lush tropical foliage, and serene lagoons—offer a feeling of plush resort seclusion that's all the more appealing because you're actually in the heart of a busy area, near a number of great restaurants. And the rates are very reasonable in light of the facilities you'll enjoy here. The accommodations, housed in pale-pink stucco bilevel villas, are attractively decorated in resort mode; half have balconies or patios, and about a fifth contain full kitchens. All offer pay-movie stations and safes; many are also equipped with hair dryers, electric shoe-shine machines, irons and ironing boards.

Dining: The tropical Grove specializes in steaks, prime rib, and seafood. The Chelsea Cafe serves American fare at all meals. A club called Illusions features a deejay spinning Top 40 tunes, as well as blackjack, a pool table, and darts. Fast food is available, plus a cozy lobby bar and several poolside bars.

Amenities: Room service, baby-sitting, guest-services desk (sells tickets, many of them discounted, and arranges transportation to/from WDW parks and all other nearby attractions), 24-hour free tram service around the property, Mears airport shuttle. Round-trip fare to WDW parks is $8.

Residence Inn by Marriott. 7975 Canada Ave. (just off Sand Lake Rd. a block east of International Dr.), Orlando, FL 32819. ☎ **800/227-3978** or 407/345-0117. Fax 407/352-2689. www.marriott.com. 176 units. A/C TV TEL. $135–$189 for up to 8. Rates include extended continental breakfast. AE, DC, DISC, MC, V. Free parking.

Marriott's Residence Inns were designed to offer home-away-from-home comfort for traveling businesspeople, but the concept also works well for families. The accommodations buildings are surrounded by well-tended lawns, shrubbery, and beds of geraniums, and the handsomely decorated suites offer full eat-in kitchens and comfortable living-room areas. All but studio doubles have wood-burning fireplaces, and two-bedroom penthouses (great for families) have full baths upstairs and down. Amenities include irons, ironing boards, and safes.

Dining: The comfortably furnished gatehouse is the setting for an extended continental breakfast daily, and complimentary beer, wine, and hors d'oeuvres Monday to Thursday from 5:30 to 7pm. Local restaurants deliver food (there are menus in each room).

Amenities: Guest-services desk (sells tickets—most of them discounted—and provides transport to all nearby theme parks and attractions), complimentary daily newspaper, free food-shopping service (microwave dinners are sold in the lobby), Mears airport shuttle. Free shuttle to WDW parks. Three swimming pools (one quite large), two kiddie pools, whirlpool, four tennis courts, basketball court, sand volleyball court, playground, business center, exercise room, 1.4-mile jogging trail, coin-op washers/dryers, food/sundries shop, picnic tables, barbecue grills, car-rental desk, unisex hair salon, two video-game arcades, free use of nearby health club.

BEYOND THE PARKS: ORLANDO & WINTER PARK

ORLANDO

The Courtyard at Lake Lucerne. 211 N. Lucerne Circle E., Orlando, FL 32801. ☎ **800/ 444-5289** or 407/648-5188. Fax 407/246-1368. 24 units. A/C TV TEL. $69 double; $96–$165 suites. Rates include continental breakfast. AE, DC, MC, V. Free self-parking. Take Orange Ave. south, immediately following City Hall (domed building with fountains and glass sculpture) turn left onto Anderson. After two lights, at Delaney Ave., turn right. Take first right onto Lucerne Circle N. (Be aware of one-way streets.) Follow brown, "historic inn" signs.

Orlando literally grew around this B&B which now stands incongruously amid a tangle of interstate ramps. Each unit in the three distinct buildings (Phillips, Norment-Perry, Wellborn) that make up the property was designed by a different artist or decorator. With wide porches and ceiling fans, the I.W. Phillips House (1916) creates an antebellum splendor that never actually flourished this far south.

Suites at the Phillips overlook a shared courtyard insulated from the urban hum by old-growth trees. A fountain's gentle trickle is the only sound you'll hear while strolling the brick walkways. The solitude isn't as complete in the front rooms of Norment-Perry. Traffic sounds there are minimal, but audible.

Since opening in 1986, the Courtyard has served mostly business VIPs and locals on weekend getaways. With few amenities, it's a place for simple, private pleasures.

Downtown's most famous entertainment district, Church Street Station, is less than 6 blocks north. Since the Courtyard is undergoing an expansion as this book goes to press, more rooms should be available soon.

Amenities: The staff fulfills most duties of a hotel concierge. Nightly turndown, coffee and refreshments in lobby, complimentary chilled wine with check-in. Suites in the Wellborn include minikitchens with refrigerators, microwaves, and coffeemakers. The Courtyard's two honeymoon suites have double whirlpool tubs. Others have claw-foot tubs and sunrooms. The single room has a basic shower and closet-sized toilet.

The Harley of Orlando. 151 E. Washington St., Orlando, FL 32801. ☎ **800/321-2323** or 407/841-3220. Fax 407/849-1839. 264 units. A/C TV TEL. $95–$150 double. AE, MC, V. Free self-parking. Take I-4 to the Anderson St. exit. Turn left on Rosalind. The hotel entrance is located on the left, directly across from the entrance to Lake Eola Park.

Just 15 minutes from the Orlando International Airport and about 25 minutes from the attractions, the Harley of Orlando is an urban alternative to the Disney resorts. Request a balcony room so you can overlook Lake Eola Park, one of the most beautiful spots in the city. The carpet in this five-story structure is a little threadbare in places, but the rooms, done in dark colors, are comfortable and clean.

Dining/Diversions: The Cafe on the Park Restaurant does a competent job on standards such as prime rib. The Sunday brunch, which is buffet-style, is well worth the price. The Monkey Bar Lounge, done up in gilded chrome and leather, isn't the hippest place in town, but the drinks pack a punch and you don't have to drive to get home. The Church Street Station entertainment complex and the nightclubs and restaurants of downtown are just a short walk away. (Or catch a ride on the free city bus, Lymmo, which picks up passengers just up the block.)

Amenities: Room service, no-smoking rooms, complimentary morning paper (Monday through Friday), free parking, pool, sundeck.

Radisson Place Hotel Orlando. 60 S. Ivanhoe Blvd., Orlando, FL 32804. ☎ **800/ 333-3333** or 407/425-4455. Fax 407/425-7440. 367 units. A/C TV TEL. $104–$129 double. AE, DISC, MC, V. Take I-4 to Princeton St. (Exit 43). Turn right at the bottom of the ramp. Turn left on Orange Ave. Go through the light, bearing to the right around the landscaping and the miniature Statue of Liberty; the hotel is on the left.

The 15-story Radisson Place Hotel, built in 1985, is really geared more toward the business traveler than the family crowd, but located right off I-4, just blocks from downtown and 15 minutes from the airport, it's also a good bet for families. However, this place has a relatively stuffy air, with all that gleaming brass, marble, and oversized ferns. The rooms are tastefully appointed with solid-color bedspreads and carpets. The views of downtown Orlando from the upper floors are impressive, and the suites are a cut above what you will find for the price elsewhere. It is located just across from Lake Ivanhoe, which has a series of exercise stations and a well-lit path for walking or jogging. There is even a small park for the kids less than a mile away. There are some rooms on the premises designed to accommodate the physically challenged.

Dining: 'Lando Sam's Restaurant offers American cuisine in a casual, colorful setting with a piano player tinkling the ivories on a dark-wood baby grand. The decor is heavy on the shiny brass and ferns. The food isn't anything you wouldn't expect at any run-of-the-mill hotel eatery. The same goes for 'Lando Sam's Lounge. There are daily breakfast and luncheon buffets in the restaurant that are, if nothing else, solid values for the price. Your best bet, however: Ask for a list of restaurants in nearby downtown; there are a few choice eateries within walking distance (if under a mile or so is walking distance). Try Brian's, just down the street, a non-retro diner with great breakfast food and coffee.

Amenities: Concierge, room service (including late-night room service), minibars, valet parking, transportation desk to arrange for taxi or limo service, attraction ticket information available. (Also, right next door is the Greater Orlando Chamber of Commerce, which has plenty of brochures on area attractions in the lobby.) Outdoor swimming pool, Jacuzzi, sundeck, two outdoor tennis courts, well-equipped health club, boutique.

Twin Towers and Convention Center. 5780 Major Blvd., Orlando, FL 32819. ☎ **800/ 327-2110** or 407/351-1000. Fax 407/363-0106. 761 units. A/C TV TEL. Summer $119–145 double depending on the season; $375–$900 suite year-round. AE, DC, DISC, MC, V. Located directly across from the main gate of Universal Studios. Free parking.

From your balcony you can watch the palms waving at Universal's entrance and the bungee jumpers in the parking lot next door waving on their way down. Built in the 1970s as a convention hotel, the property underwent a makeover in the 1980s as owners realized families would be flocking to Universal right across the street. The location is convenient without being amid the congestion of International Drive, and you're just minutes from WDW without being engulfed by the Mouse and the associated higher prices. The hotel still attracts a lot of convention business, but those facilities are in a building separate from the rooms. Aside from occasionally being trapped in the elevator with a herd of human Elk, you'll hardly notice. Just a side note: That red building on the property that looks like an old-fashioned schoolhouse is just that—the Little Red School House, a public school run in cooperation with the local school district for the children of Twin Towers employees.

Dining/Diversions: The Palm Court Restaurant serves three meals a day, and the Everglades Lounge has frequent entertainment and a big-screen TV. Although Palm

Court does an adequate job, there are plenty of other dining options nearby. Most, like the Hard Rock Cafe, are comparable in price but more interesting. The lounge acts are best left alone, but the big-screen TV offers a great respite for sports fans who need a break from quality time with the family.

Amenities: Room service, baby-sitting, children's program, laundry. Deli, pool, whirlpool, sauna, exercise room, playground, game room.

WINTER PARK

Best Western Mount Vernon Inn. 110 S. Orlando Ave., Winter Park, FL 32789 ☎ **407/647-1166.** Fax 407/647-8011. 147 units. A/C TV TEL. $78–$88 double; manager special Mar–Christmas, $51.50 double. AE, MC, V. Free self-parking. The Inn is located on U.S. Rte. 17–92 between Fairbanks Ave. and Lee Rd., across from Houston's steak house.

This is one of the best bargains in town, a place where old-money families know their guests will get comfortable accommodations at a reasonable price (look for lots of late-model Caddies in the parking lot). There are some nice views available overlooking the pool, and about a block away across the street is a city park the kiddies will love. But, overall, there is nothing too fancy about the Mount Vernon. It is, however, centrally located between the beaches and the theme parks and very close to downtown Winter Park and downtown Orlando.

Dining/Diversions: The Red Fox Lounge features nightly entertainment that's generally along the lines of a guy with a hair weave and a synthesizer. Unless that sounds really hip to you, it's better to venture to downtown Winter Park or Orlando for entertainment.

The Coach Dining room is open for breakfast and lunch from 6:30am to 2pm. The food is plentiful and filling, but this is a place you eat to be sated, not necessarily satisfied. There are many fine restaurants nearby. One tip: If you make reservations significantly in advance, save yourself a late-night check-in headache by calling before you leave home to make sure you are still on the books.

Amenities: There is a pool, but from there you're pretty much on your own. What do you expect for $78?

✪ **Langford Resort Hotel.** 300 E. New England Ave. (at Interlachen Ave.), Winter Park, FL 32789. ☎ **407/644-3400.** Fax 407/628-1952. 220 units. A/C TV TEL. $75–$115 double; $200 suite. Children 17 and under stay free in parents' room. Rooms with kitchenettes $10 extra. AE, DC, MC, V. Free self-parking. I-4 West through downtown Orlando to Winter Park. Take Fairbanks exit, 69. Go east 2 miles to Park Ave. Turn left. Go 2 blocks. Turn right on New England. Two blocks on right.

In pre-Disney days, Winter Park was one of central Florida's most-visited resorts, and the Langford was the place to stay. Vaughn Monroe entertained in the lounge, and the guest roster listed people like Eleanor Roosevelt, Mamie Eisenhower, Lillian Gish, Vincent Price, and Dina Merrill. Ronald and Nancy Reagan celebrated their 25th wedding anniversary here. Stars and just-plain-folk alike came to gawk at the "jungle" and other theme rooms as well as the poolside bathrooms with their wacky paintings of mermaids and mermen.

Today, while kitschy but no longer glamorous, this friendly, family-run resort offers extensive facilities at very reasonable rates. The midsize rooms show the wear of the years, but the lobby and hallways have recently been renovated. An on-site spa offers a full range of treatments: sauna, steam, massage (shiatsu, Swedish, and deep athletic), body wraps, seaweed wraps, salt glows, facials, manicures, pedicures, and beauty packages. The hotel's central location, on a lovely street shaded by tall oaks draped with Spanish moss, is another plus. Room decor varies and it is notably eclectic. Many rooms have balconies and/or fully equipped kitchenettes with two-burner stoves and small refrigerators. The little ones will love the kiddie pool and the small video-game arcade.

4 Dining

Since most visitors spend the majority of their time in the Walt Disney World area, I've focused on the best choices throughout that vast enchanted empire. Also listed are a few worthwhile choices beyond the realm.

Almost every mid- and low-priced restaurant offers a children's menu and usually provides some kind of kids' activity (mazes, coloring, paper dolls) as well. The downside of restaurants that cater to kids is that they're noisy. If that will ruin your appetite, remember this rule: The higher the prices, the fewer the children. If you're looking for a quiet meal, head for restaurants on International Drive, Downtown Disney, or downtown Orlando.

See also the listings for dinner shows in section 15 of this chapter.

HOW TO ARRANGE PRIORITY SEATING AT WALT DISNEY WORLD RESTAURANTS

Priority seating at Walt Disney World restaurants means you get the next available table but does not reserve a table specifically for you. That means you may still have a bit of a wait, even with a reservation. Without priority seating you may not be able to get a table at all, especially during special events or peak season. You can arrange priority seating up to 60 days in advance at almost all full-service Magic Kingdom, Epcot, Disney-MGM Studios, Animal Kingdom resort, and Disney Village restaurants—as well as character meals and shows throughout the complex—by calling ☎ **407/ WDW-DINE** (939-3463). Nighttime shows can actually be booked as far in advance as you wish. Exceptions to this format are noted in the listings below.

Since this priority-seating phone number was instituted in 1994, it has become much more difficult to obtain a table by just showing up. So, I strongly advise you to avoid disappointment by calling ahead. However, if you don't reserve in advance, you can take your chances reserving in the parks themselves:

Epcot: Make reservations at the WorldKey interactive terminals at Guest Relations in Innoventions East, at Worldkey Information Service Satellites located on the main concourse to World Showcase and at Germany in World Showcase, or at the restaurants themselves.

Magic Kingdom: Reserve at the restaurants themselves.

Disney-MGM Studios: Make reservations at the Hollywood Junction Station on Sunset Boulevard or at the restaurants themselves.

Animal Kingdom: Call ☎ **407/WDW-DINE** (939-3463).

TIPS ON WALT DISNEY WORLD RESTAURANTS

- A pocket-sized guide produced by American Express, appropriately titled *Guidebook,* offers invaluable assistance in picking a restaurant. There are also pocket-sized guides to individual restaurants displayed in the lobbies of some hotels.
- All park restaurants have no-smoking interiors; you can smoke only on patios and terraces.
- All sit-down restaurants in Walt Disney World take American Express, Master-Card, Visa, and the Disney Card. The Disney Card enables WDW resort guests to charge items at WDW restaurants and shops to their rooms.
- Guests at Disney resorts and "official" hostelries can make restaurant reservations through the guest-services or concierge desks.

WALT DISNEY WORLD

The following listings encompass restaurants in the Magic Kingdom, Epcot, Disney-MGM Studios, Disney Village, and Animal Kingdom.

Note: Alcohol is not served in the Magic Kingdom, though it's available in the other Disney parks.

EPCOT

An ethnic meal at one of the World Showcase pavilions is a traditional part of the Epcot experience, but many are a bit pricey for the value. Families on a budget will probably opt to eat at the outdoor cafes near each pavilion. Check the Guidemap you receive upon entering the park for details.

All the sit-down restaurants are expensive, except for the moderately priced Le Cellier Steakhouse in Canada, the Biergarten in Germany, and Akershus in Norway.

World Showcase

These restaurants are arranged geographically, beginning at the Canada pavilion and proceeding counterclockwise around the World Showcase Lagoon.

CANADA This is a good choice for families. Located in the Victorian Hotel du Canada, **Le Cellier Steakhouse** has a castlelike ambience, offering seating in tapestried chairs under vaulted stone arches. You won't need reservations here—it's a self-service buffet. Regional dishes include Cheddar-cheese soup, carved pemeal bacon (a pork loin with a light cornmeal crust), French-Canadian tourtière, maple-syrup pie, and Canadian beers. Meals run about $10 per person.

UNITED KINGDOM The Tudor-beamed **Rose & Crown,** entered via a cozy pub with a pungent aroma of ale, is evocative of Victorian England. The outdoor seating overlooking the lagoon is a good place to check out IllumiNations. The menu features traditional items—smoked salmon with Stilton cheese, prime rib, Yorkshire pudding, sherry trifle. Wash it all down with a pint of Irish lager beer, Bass ale, or Guinness stout. Lunch entrees are $9 to $15; dinner is $10 to $30. Traditional afternoon tea is served daily at 3:30pm; the cost is $9.95. Another option here is bar fare (sausage rolls, Cornish pasties, a Stilton cheese and fruit plate), all under $4.50. If the pub is too crowded, as it can be in peak season, grab some tasty fish-and-chips sold from the outdoor cart.

FRANCE **Chefs de France** is under the auspices of a world-famous culinary triumvirate—Paul Bocuse, Roger Vergé, and Gaston LeNôtre. Its art nouveau/fin-de-siècle interior is agleam with mirrors and brass candelabra chandeliers. I recommend the seafood cream soup with crab dumplings (as featured by Vergé at Moulin de Mougins). Entree selections at dinner include a superb broiled salmon in sorrel-cream sauce à la façon de Bocuse (it's served with ratatouille and new potatoes) and Vergé's sautéed beef tenderloin with raisins and brandy sauce. And among desserts, LeNôtre's soufflé Grand-Marnier is the standout. The distinguished chefs also composed the restaurant's wine list. Entrees range from $21 to $40 per person.

The ✪ **Bistro de Paris,** upstairs from Chefs de France and serving dinner only, offers similar fare in a more serene country-French setting. Highlights here include grilled beef tenderloins with mushrooms and seafood casserole served with garlic sauce. There's also a fine selection of French wines, and the crème brûlée is unbeatable. Prices range from $21 to $40 per person.

Lighter meals of traditional cafe fare are available throughout the day at **Au Petit Café,** a sidewalk bistro adjacent to Chefs de France on an awninged terrace overlooking the lagoon. No reservations are required. Entrees are usually under $10.

MOROCCO   The palatial ✪ **Restaurant Marrakesh** features exquisitely carved archways, hand-set mosaic tile work, and a beamed ceiling painted with Moorish motifs. Belly dancers perform while you dine on lamb couscous, braised tagine of chicken or shish kebab. The Moroccan diffa (traditional feast), which lets you sample a variety of dishes, is recommended. This exotic restaurant perhaps best captures the international-experience spirit of Epcot. A meal will cost $21 to $40 per person; the Moroccan diffa is $29.95 for two at lunch, $53.90 for two at dinner.

JAPAN   The **Mitsukoshi Restaurant** centers on a teppanyaki steak house where you'll sit at a grill table while white-hatted chefs rapidly dice, slice, stir-fry, and propel cooked food onto your plate. It's a real treat to watch the cleaver-wielding chef preparing your food. Since you share a table with strangers, teppanyaki makes for a convivial dining experience. An elaborate dinner for two (of which an abbreviated version is available at lunch) includes a shrimp appetizer, salad, soup, grilled fresh vegetables with udon noodles, succulent morsels of grilled beef tenderloin and lobster, steamed rice, choice of dessert (perhaps chestnut cake), and green tea. And even à la carte entrees include plenty of extras. Lunch will run between $10 and $20 per person; the complete meal described above costs $39.50 for two at lunch, $59.90 for two at dinner.

Adjoining the teppanyaki rooms is a U-shaped **tempura counter** where you can also order some sushi and sashimi items. Meals will cost between $10 and $20 for lunch and $21 to $40 for dinner. No reservations are required for counter seating.

For me, the gem of this complex is the peaceful, plant-filled **cocktail lounge** with large windows overlooking the lagoon—a very pleasant setting for appetizers and sake. Menu items are $3.95 to $8.25, and no reservations are required. A window seat here is another great venue to view IllumiNations.

Finally, housed in a replica of the 16th-century Katsura Imperial Villa in Kyoto is **Yakitori House,** a bamboo-roofed cafeteria serving Japanese snack-fare items, all under $7, and full children's meals for under $5. The umbrella tables on a terrace overlooking a rock waterfall are a nice touch.

ITALY   Patterned after Alfredo De Lelio's celebrated establishment in Rome, **L'Originale Alfredo di Roma Ristorante** suggests a seaside Roman palazzo with beautiful trompe l'oeil frescoes. The theatricality of an exhibition kitchen, charming Italian waiters, and exuberant strolling musicians create a festive ambience. If you want a quieter setting, ask for a seat on the veranda. De Lelio invented fettuccine Alfredo—and it remains an excellent entree choice here. And there's a sublime tiramisu for dessert. A special vegetarian menu is available, and the list of Italian wines is extensive. Meals will cost between $10 and $20 for lunch, $21 to $40 for dinner. Inquire about the early bird special when making reservations.

GERMANY   Lit by street lamps, the **Biergarten** simulates a Bavarian village courtyard at Oktoberfest with autumnal trees, a working water wheel, and geranium-filled flower boxes adorning Tudor-style houses. Entertainment might be an oompah band or a strolling accordionist, and guests are encouraged to dance and sing along. All-you-can-eat buffet meals featuring traditional fare (sauerbraten, spaetzle with gravy, sauerkraut with salads) are offered at lunch and dinner. Beverages and desserts are extra. The lunch buffet is $10.95 for adults, $5.50 for children 3 to 11; dinner is $15.75 for adults, $6.99 for children.

At **Sommerfest,** a cafeteria with indoor seating and courtyard tables overlooking a fountain, you can purchase bratwurst sandwiches with sauerkraut, goulash soup, and desserts such as apple strudel. All items are under $5.

CHINA One of the most attractive of the World Showcase restaurants, ✪ **Nine Dragons,** with windows overlooking the lagoon, has intricately carved rosewood paneling and furnishings and a beautiful dragon-motif ceiling. Begin your meal here with a selection of dim sum. Entrees highlight dishes from four regions of China. You can order Chinese or California wines with your meal, but I especially love the fresh melon juice, either nonalcoholic or mixed with rum or vodka. Meals cost between $8.50 to $18.50 at lunch (most are under $15), $10.50 to $23.75 at dinner.

Or you can opt for egg rolls, pork fried rice, or stir-fried chicken and vegetables served over noodles at the open-air **Lotus Blossom Café,** a pleasant and inexpensive self-service eatery.

NORWAY **Akershus** re-creates a 14th-century castle fortress that stands in Oslo's harbor. Its pristine white stone interior, with Gothic stone archways creating intimate dining niches, is softly lit by gas lamps, candelabra chandeliers, and flickering sconces. The meal is an immense smorgasbord of traditional dishes—smoked pork with honey mustard, strips of venison in cream sauce, gravlax in mustard sauce, an array of Norwegian breads and cheeses, and much more. Norwegian beer and aquavit complement a list of French and California wines. The lunch buffet costs $11.95 for adults, $5.25 for children 4 to 9, free for children 3 and under; the dinner buffet is $18.95 for adults, $7.950 for children. There are also nonsmorgasbord children's meals for $4.75.

Another facility in this pavilion, the **Kringla Bakeri og Kafe,** offers covered outdoor seating and inexpensive light fare—open-face sandwiches, cheese and fruit platters, waffles sprinkled with powdered sugar, and fresh-baked Norwegian pastries. No reservations are required.

MEXICO The setting for the ✪ **San Angel Inn** is a hacienda courtyard amid dense jungle foliage in the shadow of a crumbling Yucatán pyramid. It's nighttime: The tables are candlelit (even at lunch) and the lighting is very low. The Popocatepetl volcano erupts in the distance, spewing molten lava, and you can hear the sounds of faraway birds. Thunder, lightning, and swiftly moving clouds add a dramatic note, but the overall ambience is soothing and, importantly, cool. Order an appetizer of queso fundido (melted cheese with Mexican pork sausage, served with homemade corn or flour tortillas), and follow it with an entree of filete ranchero (grilled tenderloin of beef served over corn tortillas with sauce ranchero, poblano pepper strips, Monterey Jack cheese, onions, and refried beans). Combination platters are also an option at both meals. They also offer a vegetarian menu, and the margaritas here are as good as they get. Meals cost $10 to $20 per person.

The **Cantina de San Angel,** a cafeteria with outdoor seating at umbrella tables overlooking the lagoon, offers affordable tacos, burritos, and combination plates, along with frozen margaritas; a complete children's meal is under $5.

Future World
At the Living Seas pavilion, dine "under the sea" at the enchanting ✪ **Coral Reef,** where all seating rings a 5.6-million-gallon coral-reef aquarium inhabited by more than 4,000 denizens of the deep. Strains of Debussy's *La Mer* and Handel's *Water Music* playing softly in the background help set the tone. Tiered seating, much of it in semicircular booths, ensures everyone a good view. The menu features (what else?) seafood—creamy lobster bisque, sautéed mahimahi in lemon-caper butter, and shrimp satay served atop red-pepper pasta. There are also steak and chicken dishes. For dessert, choose the white-chocolate-mousse cake topped with Mickey ears. Meals cost between $21 and $40 per person.

THE MAGIC KINGDOM

There are dozens of fast-food eateries throughout the Magic Kingdom. In addition to the places below, I also recommended the Diamond Horseshoe Saloon Revue in Frontierland, which combines a light meal with a 30- to 45-minute Western-themed musical revue (see section 6).

LIBERTY SQUARE   The **Liberty Tree Tavern** replicates an 18th-century pub, with low-beamed ceilings and a vast brick fireplace hung with copper pots. Main courses range from New England pot roast with mashed potatoes and vegetables to a traditional roast turkey dinner with all the trimmings, and there's apple crisp topped with vanilla ice cream for dessert. I prefer the food here to King Stefan's (below), and this restaurant is also more likely to be able to seat large parties. Open from 11am to 3pm and 4pm until park closing. See details about character dinners below.

In the mood for a light but satisfying meal? I'm partial to the baked- and sweet-potato cart in Liberty Square and the adjacent fruit stand. The turkey legs in Frontierland, although not exactly light, are tasty, easy to eat, and filling.

CINDERELLA'S CASTLE   **King Stefan's Banquet Hall** has an imposing Gothic interior with leaded-glass windows and heraldic banners suspended from a vaulted ceiling. The sturdy oak tables are candlelit. The dainty damsel herself probably never dined on hearty cuts of steak and prime rib, but you may as well indulge in a caloric splurge. For an appetizer, I recommend the almond-breaded Brie served with wild-lingonberry relish. Cinderella often greets guests in the downstairs entrance hall. Lunch will cost between $10 and $20 per person, dinner $21 to $40 per person. King Stefan's also hosts daily character breakfasts; see details below.

MAIN STREET   Inspired by the Disney movie *Lady and the Tramp,* **Tony's Town Square Restaurant** is Victorian plush. The walls are hung with original cels from the movie. There's additional seating in a sunny plant-filled solarium. Tony's opens early for breakfast (you can eat here while waiting for the other lands to open). The rest of the day the fare is Italian—antipasto, pastas, calzones, subs, and salads—while at dinner your options range from garlicky sautéed shrimp and vegetables over linguine in a light cream sauce to a 12-ounce strip steak/sautéed lobster combination. Breakfast items cost under $10, lunch, $10 to $20, and dinner $20 to $40.

DISNEY-MGM STUDIOS

There are more than a dozen eateries in this park, with names like the Studio Commissary and Starring Rolls Bakery. The four listed below, my favorites, are all sit-down restaurants requiring reservations. You'll find the best food is at the Derby.

The **Hollywood Brown Derby,** modeled after the famed Los Angeles celebrity haunt where Louella Parsons and Hedda Hopper held court, mirrors its defunct West Coast counterpart with interior palm trees, and mahogany-wainscoted walls hung with more than 1,500 caricatures from Barbara Stanwyck to Rin Tin Tin). The Derby's signature dish is the Cobb salad, invented by owner Bob Cobb in the 1930s. You might try the champagne-flavored oyster-Brie soup, followed by baked grouper meunière served atop pasta, and a dessert of grapefruit cake with vanilla icing (another house specialty). Lunch ranges from $10 to $20 per person; dinner, $21 to $40.

The **Sci-Fi Dine-In Theater Restaurant** replicates a 1950s Hollywood drive-in movie theater. Diners sit in flashy convertible cars under a twinkling starlit sky, while friendly servers bring complimentary popcorn. The video plays, (just like TV at home) with newsreels, cartoons, horror movie clips, and coming attractions. Try a Towering Terror (barbecued pork ribs with veggies and fries) and Plucked from Deepest Space (a grilled chicken sandwich with Cajun rémoulade sauce and fries). Finish up with the Cheesecake That Ate New York. Your bill is presented as a speeding ticket. Meals cost between $10 and $20 for lunch, $21 to $40 for dinner.

The **50s Prime Time Cafe** places diners in a time warp/sitcom psychodrama. The eating areas look like homey 1950s kitchens, wherein black-and-white TV sets air clips of shows like *My Little Margie* and *Topper*. The service staff greets diners like family ("Hi Sis, I'll go tell Mom you're home!") and may threaten you with no dessert if you don't eat your veggies or report you to Mom for resting your elbows on the table. The food—meat loaf with mashed potatoes, Granny's pot roast, Dad's chili, and such—isn't all that great, but the place is fun anyway. Desserts include banana splits and S'mores. Between $10 and $20 for lunch, $21 to $40 for dinner.

Toy Story Pizza Planet, located in the Muppet's Courtyard, offers what the name implies along with salads, espresso, and cappuccino. The food is not exactly gourmet, but meals are under $10 per person and kids of all ages love the many games and diversions. This is a boisterous family eatery.

ANIMAL KINGDOM

The **RainForest Cafe** here, just like the one in Disney Village Marketplace, is a huge draw for sit-down dining. Other options include **Tuskers House** in Africa, which serves Rotisserie, grilled and fried chicken, and salads. The **Restaurantorsaurus** (yep, you guessed it, this one is in DinoLand U.S.A.) serves hamburgers, hot dogs, and authentic McDonald's french fries and Chicken McNuggets. The meals at both restaurants will run between $10 and $20 per person.

DISNEY RESORTS
VERY EXPENSIVE

✪ **Victoria & Albert's.** In Disney's Grand Floridian Beach Resort, 4401 Floridian Way. ☎ **407/WDW-DINE** (939-3463). Reservations required. Jackets required for men. $80 per person fixed price; $25 additional for the Royal Wine Pairing. AE, MC, V. Daily seatings at 6–6:45pm and 9–9:45pm. Free self- and validated valet parking. AMERICAN REGIONAL.

It's not often that I'd describe a dining experience as flawless, but Victoria & Albert's, the World's (Walt Disney World, that is) most elite restaurant, won me over. Its intimate dining room is plush; diners sink into leather-upholstered Louis XIII–style chairs at exquisitely appointed tables. A maid and butler provide deft and gracious service, and a harpist plays softly while you dine.

Dinner, a seven-course affair, changes nightly. It might include hors d'oeuvres of Florida lobster tail or vermouth-poached jumbo sea scallops served in a crisp rice-noodle basket. Entrees include delicacies such as a fan of juicy sautéed Peking duck breast with wild rice and crabapple chutney. A salad of esoteric greens in an orange-sherry vinaigrette clears the palate for the next course—English Stilton served with pine-nut bread, port wine, and a pear poached in burgundy, cognac, and cinnamon sugar. The conclusion: a sumptuous hazelnut and Frangelico soufflé, followed by coffee and chocolate truffles. There is, of course, an extensive wine list. I suggest that you opt for the Royal Wine Pairing, which offers an appropriate wine with each course.

EXPENSIVE

✪ **Ariel's.** At Disney's Grand Floridian Beach Resort, 1800 Epcot Resorts Blvd. ☎ **407/ WDW-DINE** (939-3463). Main courses $17.95–$24. AE, MC, V. Daily 6–10pm. Free valet and self-parking. SEAFOOD.

Named for the *Little Mermaid* character, this exquisite restaurant overlooks Storm-along Bay. Its tables are elegantly appointed with fish- and seashell-motif china, a prismed 2,000-gallon coral-reef tank is filled with tropical fish, and whimsical fish mobiles and glass bubbles dangle from a vaulted ceiling. For your appetizer, consider the scrumptious New England silver-dollar crab cakes served with spicy tartar sauce. I also recommend the traditional paella and Maine lobster sautéed with shiitake mushrooms served atop tricolor pasta with lemon-butter sauce. There are a few nonseafood items, as well as an extensive wine list.

✪ **California Grill.** At Disney's Contemporary Resort, 4600 N. World Dr. ☎ **407/WDW-DINE** (939-3463) or 407/824-1576. Main courses $14.75–$27.50. AE, MC, V. Daily 5:30–10pm. CALIFORNIA.

High above the Magic Kingdom (on the resort's 15th floor), this stunning restaurant offers scenic views of the park and lagoon below. A zigzaggy Wolfgang Puckish interior incorporates art deco elements, but the central focus is a dramatic exhibition kitchen with a wood-burning oven and rotisserie.

The menu changes seasonally, but the sushi sampler always makes for a good beginning here, as does ravioli filled with goat cheese, shiitake mushrooms, and sun-dried tomatoes. The whole-wheat-crusted pizzas might comprise a light entree. Heartier choices include braised lamb shank (with wild-chanterelle risotto and orange-nuanced bread topping) or grilled pork tenderloin served atop polenta with crimini mushrooms and a garnish of crispy fried sage. For dessert, it's hard to surpass the butterscotch crème brûlée with almond biscotti. If you like a close-up view of chefs at work, ask to sit at the kitchen counter. There's a good selection of California wines to complement your meal.

✪ **Hemingway's.** In the Hyatt Regency Grand Cypress, 1 Grand Cypress Blvd. (off Fla. 535). ☎ **407/239-1234.** Reservations recommended. Main courses $7.50–$19.75 at lunch, $20–$28 at dinner. AE, CB, DC, DISC, JCB, MC, V. Tues–Sat 11:30am–2:30pm; daily 6–10:30pm. Free self- and validated valet parking. SEAFOOD.

Fronted by a waterfall cascading into stone-bedded streams, Hemingway's evokes Key West's famous denizen, with photographs of "Papa" and his fishing and hunting trophies adorning the walls. This casually elegant (and generally child-free) restaurant is ideal for romantic dinners. Weather permitting, you can sit on a screened wooden deck near the waterfall.

Ask not for whom the bell tolls, but rather for an appetizer of deep-fried baby squid and grilled eggplant in garlicky herb-seasoned tomato coulis. For dinner you might try the golden brown beer-battered coconut shrimp served with roasted potatoes, al dente vegetables, and orange marmalade-horseradish sauce. Also recommended are the deliciously light, moist crab cakes; ask for Cajun tartar sauce to top them. For dessert, key lime pie appropriately reaches its apogee here. The lunch menu offers similar fare, along with paella, sandwiches, and salads. In the adjoining Hurricane Lounge—a congenial setting with a beautiful oak bar—specialties include a variety of island rums and the Papa Doble, a potent tropical rum and fruit libation invented by Hemingway himself (legend has it he once drank 16 of them in one sitting!).

MODERATE

✪ **Cape May Café.** At Disney's Grand Floridian Beach Resort, 1800 Epcot Resorts Blvd. ☎ **407/WDW-DINE** (939-3463). Dinner $19.95 adults, $9.50 children 3–11; character breakfast, $14.95 adults, $8.50 children. AE, MC, V. Daily 5:30–9:30pm. Free valet and self-parking. CLAMBAKE BUFFET.

A hearty 19th-century-style New England clambake is featured here nightly. Sand sculptures and furled striped beach umbrellas create the ambience of an upscale seaside resort. Aromatic New England chowder, steamed clams and mussels, corn on the cob, chicken, lobster, and red-skin potatoes are cooked up in a crackling rockweed steamer pit that serves as the restaurant's centerpiece. And these traditional clambake offerings are supplemented by dozens of salads, hot dishes (barbecued pork ribs, smoked sausage, pastas), and a wide array of oven-fresh breads and desserts. There's a full bar.

'Ohana. At Disney's Polynesian Resort, 1600 Seven Seas Dr. ☎ **407/WDW-DINE** (939-3463). Buffet $20.95 adults, $8.95 children 3–11, free for children 3 and under. AE, MC, V. Daily 5–10pm. Transportation to WDW resorts. Free parking. PACIFIC RIM.

You'll be welcomed here with warm island hospitality by a server who'll address you as "cousin." The setting is South Seas exotic, with thatched roofing and tapa-cloth tenting overhead, carved Polynesian columns, and an open kitchen centering on a wood-burning 18-foot fire-pit grill. There's lots going on at all times. The blowing of a conch shell summons a storyteller, coconut races take place down the central aisle, couples get up and dance to island music, and people celebrating birthdays participate in hula-hoop contests as everyone sings "Happy Birthday" to them in Hawaiian. Kids especially love all the hoopla, so if you're looking for an intimate venue, this isn't it.

Soon after you're seated, a lazy Susan arrives laden with steamed dumplings in soy-sesame oil, napa cabbage slaw with honey mustard, black-bean and corn relish, and several tangy sauces. The courses tend to arrive in rapid succession, so ask your waiter to slow the pace if it's too fast. The feast includes salad; fresh-baked herbed focaccia; grilled chicken, smoky pork sausage, marinated turkey breast, mesquite-seasoned beef, teriyaki ribs, and jumbo shrimp; stir-fry noodles and vegetables; fresh pineapple with caramel sauce; soft drinks; and coffee. The passion-fruit crème brûlée is extra but worth it. A full bar offers tropical drinks, including nonalcoholic ones for kids.

WALT DISNEY WORLD VILLAGE MARKETPLACE/ PLEASURE ISLAND

Disney's Village Marketplace is located on Pleasure Island, Disney's West Side, about 2½ miles from Epcot, off Buena Vista Drive. The Marketplace is a collection of cedar-shingled shops and restaurants overlooking a scenic lagoon. Pleasure Island, a complex of nightclubs and shops, adjoins. The West Side, which opened in 1997, is a collection of upscale shops and restaurants and a movie theater. *Note:* You don't have to pay the entrance fee to Pleasure Island to dine at its restaurants. There is no entrance fee to the West Side.

VERY EXPENSIVE

Fulton's Crab House. Aboard the riverboat docked at Pleasure Island. ☎ **407/934-BOAT** (2628). Reservations recommended, especially during peak season. Main courses lunch, $8.95–$15.95; dinner, 4.95–$50. AE, MC, V. Daily 4pm–midnight. SEAFOOD/STEAKS

Fulton's operates aboard a replica of a 19th-century Mississippi riverboat that's permanently moored on the shores of Lake Buena Vista. An interior decorated with nautical artifacts reflects the seafood menu. There is a deck for outdoor dining and children's menu. The casual Stone Crab Lounge serves light fare from 11:30am to 2am.

Start with the Florida stone crab claws with mustard sauce and lime or sample the oyster bar. For a main course, try the tuna fillet, grilled and served with lemon grass dipping sauce. A hearty eater may want to try the steak and lobster dinner, served with asparagus and a tangy house steak sauce. For a tart taste of Florida, try the key lime cheesecake for dessert. This place boasts one of the area's better wine lists. A character breakfast, 8:30am and 10am daily is $12.95 for adults, $7.95 for children and features Mickey, Minnie, Pluto and Goofy.

Moderate

Fireworks Factory. 1630 Lake Buena Vista Dr., Pleasure Island. ☎ **407/934-8989.** Reservations recommended. Main courses $13.95–$25. AE, MC, V. Daily 11:30am–11:30pm (dinner served from 4pm, light fare and drinks served until 2am). Valet parking $5; free self-parking. AMERICAN REGIONAL.

This exuberant corrugated-tin warehouse has big red pipes overhead and exposed brick or tin walls hung with neon signs and advertisements for fireworks. This is a good choice for family dining, because the portions are generous and kids are encouraged to color on the paper table toppers.

During either lunch or dinner, start off with an appetizer sampler (spicy chicken wings, shrimp quesadillas, and apple-wood-smoked baby back ribs). Dinner entrees range from Cajun shrimp pasta to oak-roasted salmon served with roasted tomato/corn relish and angel-hair sweet potatoes. Another good choice is the mesquite-smoked barbecued beef sandwich. For dessert, I recommend the giant Toll House cookie served warm and topped with vanilla ice cream and hot fudge. They also offer more than 45 varieties of domestic and imported beer, ale, and stout.

Planet Hollywood. Pleasure Island. ☎ **407/827-7827.** Reservations not accepted. Main courses $7.50–$18.95. AE, DC, MC, V. Daily 11am–2am. AMERICAN.

Planet Hollywood was born in 1994 with a lavish opening-night party hosted by Schwarzenegger, Stallone, Willis, and Moore. The excitement they generated has started to dim and the once hours-long lines have thinned. A fiber-optic ceiling creates a planetarium effect, and a veritable show-business museum displays more than 300 items ranging from Peter O'Toole's *Lawrence of Arabia* costume to the front end of the bus from the movie *Speed* (it's suspended from the ceiling!). Previews of soon-to-be-released movies and video montages from films and TV are aired while you dine.

The big surprise amid all the special effects is that the food is actually good. You can opt to nosh on appetizers—hickory-smoked buffalo wings, pot stickers, or nachos. There are also burgers, sandwiches, salads, pizzas, pastas, and platters of grilled steak, ribs, or pork chops. The desserts are worth saving room for. Lines can get long during special events and peak season.

Portobello Yacht Club. Pleasure Island. ☎ **407/934-8888.** Reservations strongly recommended. Main courses lunch $7.95–$8.95, dinner $14.95–$29.95; pizzas $6.95–$8.95. AE, MC, V. Daily 11:30am–midnight (dinner served from 4pm). Valet parking $5; free self-parking. NORTHERN ITALIAN.

Occupying a gabled Bermuda-style house and having undergone extensive recent renovations, Yacht Club is casual, with an interior suggesting luxury cruise ship. From the lively mahogany-paneled bar, you can watch oak-fired pizzas being prepared in an exhibition kitchen. Multipaned windows overlook Lake Buena Vista, as do the tables on the covered patios.

The pizzas, with crisply thin crusts and toppings such as quattro formaggi (four cheeses) with sun-dried tomatoes, are a tasty deal for lunch or dinner. For the evening meal try Costoletta Di MaiAle, marinated roasted pork loin with fennel, carrots, and roasted garlic whipped potatoes. Also try the Spaghettini Alla Portobello with Alaskan crab and other seafood in a light sauce of olive oil, wine, and herbs. For dessert, I recommend the crema bruccioto (white-chocolate custard with a caramelized sugar glaze). The Portobello also has quite an extensive wine list.

✪ **RainForest Cafe.** Disney Village Marketplace; look for the smoking volcano. ☎ **407/827-8500.** Reservations accepted on-site. Main courses $5.50–$17.95. AE, DISC, MC, V. Sun–Thurs 10:30am–11pm; Fri–Sat 10:30am–midnight. CALIFORNIA.

First piece of advice: Don't arrive starving. Waits of 4 hours aren't unheard of, so plan on making your reservations and then exploring the rest of the Village. (Lines may shorten as a second RainForest is added near Animal Kingdom, but don't count on it.) With its lush, dark interiors, calls of the wild, and unique animal-style bar stools, you feel far removed from the rush of the parks. Kids especially love the jungle setting—This is, after all, one place where monkey business is encouraged. The food is pretty good, too. Try unusual delicacies like Rasta Pasta, bow-tie noodles mixed with spinach, roasted red peppers, broccoli, and Parmesan cheese—the whole dish smothered in a garlic-pesto cream sauce. There is an extensive menu, including a reduced-price menu for children. Top off your meal with coconut bread pudding with dried apricots; the lavish garnish of whipped cream, toasted coconut, and chocolate shavings is almost as good as the dessert itself. There's a good selection of beer and wine. *Note:* The tables are very close together, so those with physical disabilities may find it difficult to maneuver.

DISNEY'S WEST SIDE

Bongo Cuban Cafe. Disney's West Side. ☎ **407/828-0999.** Reservations not accepted. Priority seating for parties of 7 or more. Main courses $8.95–$24.95. Daily 11am–2am. AE, DISC, DC, V, MC. CUBAN.

Created by Cuban American singer Gloria Estefan and her husband, Emilio, the cafe is Disney's version of old Havana. There are leopard spotted chairs and mosaic bar stools shaped like bongo drums. A Desi Arnez look-alike might even show up to sing a few tunes. The upbeat salsa music makes this a noisy location, so seek out the patio or the upstairs lounge for some privacy and quiet. A Cuban sandwich, thinly toasted bread with ham and cheese, is prepared right here. (Kids also might like it.) Start with the thick, slightly spicy, black bean soup and try a dinner of arroz con pollo (chicken with rice). Coffee lovers will love the thick, dark Cuban coffee.

House of Blues. Disney's West Side, under the old-fashioned water tower. ☎ **407/934-2583.** Reservations not accepted (except for Gospel Brunch). $13.95–$18.95. AE, DISC, MC, V. MISSISSIPPI DELTA.

This place offers hearty potions of down-home food served in atmosphere literally shaking with rock 'n' roll. The music in the nightclub next door is as much of a draw as the food—it's incredibly packed on days of big concerts. Funky, colorful folk art covers the rustic walls from floor to ceiling. There's a nice view of the bay from tables on the back patio. But let's not forget the food. The spicy jambalaya and gumbo are good bets, and the baby back ribs with garlic mashed potatoes and turnip greens are literally finger-lickin' good. Try the bread pudding for dessert. There's a children's menu offering staples like grilled cheese and burgers. The Sunday Gospel Brunch, $23.99 for adults and $11.99 for children 4 to 12, features foot-stomping music and an awe-inspiring array of Southern fare such as cheese grits and sausage. Foreign visitors might especially enjoy this cultural immersion. Make your reservations early because this tends to sell out.

Wolfgang Puck's Cafe. Disney's West Side. ☎ **407/WDW-DINE** (939-3463). Reservations recommended. $8.95–$18.95. AE, V, MC. Daily 11am–midnight. CALIFORNIA CUISINE.

Avant-garde chef Wolfgang Puck has brought his West Coast creations to the heart of Florida. You can eat gourmet pizza, with a thin crisp crust and exotic toppings, on an outdoor patio or dine inside. An appetizer of vegetable spring rolls or a sampling from the sushi bar should be followed by the fresh grilled chicken or the Chinois chicken salad.

❁ CITYWALK

Universal's answer to Pleasure Island and Disney's West Side, CityWalk is scheduled to open in fall 1998. The restaurants were not yet open at press time, but here's what to expect. This 12-acre entertainment complex could easily be renamed theme-restaurant heaven. Not only is it home to the world's largest Hard Rock Cafe—the grande dame of all theme restaurants—but also the NASCAR Cafe, the Motown Cafe, and Marvel Mania, a theme send-up to villains and superheroes. CityWalk also contains a hearty dose of Cajun spice with Pat O'Brien's, a re-creation of the joint in New Orleans, and Emeril's of New Orleans, featuring the Creole-based cuisine of chef Emeril Lagasse. If that's not enough to keep you busy, there is the Down Beat Jazz Hall of Fame, a tribute to reggae mon Bob Marley, and a 5,000-seat Cineplex Odeon Megaplex.

BEYOND DISNEY: INTERNATIONAL DRIVE

There are some top-notch restaurants along International Drive, located about a 10-minute drive from Walt Disney World parks.

VERY EXPENSIVE

❁ **Dux.** In the Peabody Orlando, 9801 International Dr. ☎ **407/345-4550.** Reservations recommended. Main courses $19–$45.95. AE, CB, DC, DISC, JCB, MC, V. Mon–Thurs 6–10pm, Fri–Sat 6–11pm. Closed Sun. Free self- and validated valet parking. INTERNATIONAL.

Named for the hotel's signature ducks that parade ceremoniously into the lobby each morning to Sousa's *King Cotton* march, this is one of Central Florida's most highly acclaimed restaurants. Its textured gold walls are hung with watercolors representing 72 ducks! The tables are exquisitely appointed, and a lavish dessert display table with a floral centerpiece serves as a visual focus.

The internationally nuanced menu changes seasonally. At a recent dinner I started off with an appetizer of pot stickers stuffed with portobello mushrooms, scallions, and creamed goat cheese. The entree was grilled Florida black grouper marinated in West Indian spices, served with a plantain-yam mash and tropical chutney. And dessert was a hazelnut-meringue napoleon topped with homemade Frangelico ice cream and a dusting of Brazilian cocoa. Dux has an extensive, award-winning wine list.

MODERATE

B-Line Diner. In the Peabody Orlando, 9801 International Dr. ☎ **407/345-4460.** Reservations not accepted. Main courses $5.95–$29. AE, CB, DC, DISC, JCB, MC, V. Daily 24 hours. Free self- and validated valet parking. AMERICAN.

This popular local eatery is of the nouvelle art deco diner genre—an idealized version of America's ubiquitous roadside joints. A high-gloss peach-and-gray interior gleams with chrome edging that adorns everything from a cove ceiling to peach Formica tables, and gorgeous flower arrangements add upscale panache. A jukebox plays oldies tunes.

The seasonally varying menu offers sophisticated versions of diner food such as honey-ginger buffalo wings, a grilled pork chop with hazelnut wild rice and sun-dried cherry sauce, or a ham and cheese sandwich on baguette. Other items, such as a falafel sandwich on pita bread with mint-yogurt sauce, bear no relation to traditional diner fare. Portions are hearty. A glass display case here is filled with scrumptious fresh-baked desserts, and they also offer ice-cream sundaes. There's a full bar.

❁ **Cafe Tu Tu Tango.** 8625 International Dr. (just west of the Mercado). ☎ **407/248-2222.** Reservations accepted. Tapas (tasting portions) $3–$7.95. AE, DISC, MC, V. Sun–Thurs 11:30am–11pm, Fri–Sat 11:30am–1am. INTERNATIONAL TAPAS.

Though you might question the need for yet another theme experience outside the parks, this restaurant is a welcome respite from Orlando's predictable chain gang. For one thing, there's the ongoing performance-art experience taking place while you dine: One evening, an elegantly dressed couple might tango past your table. Another time, a belly dancer might perform or a magician might demonstrate a few tricks tableside. In addition, there is a studio area in which artists are always creating pottery, paintings, and jewelry.

Tu Tu's colorful ambience is a lot of fun, but the real draw here is the food. The larger your party, the more dishes you can sample; two full plates will sate most appetites. My favorites include Cajun egg rolls (filled with blackened chicken, corn, and Cheddar and goat cheese, served with chunky tomato salsa and Creole mustard) and pepper-crusted seared-tuna sashimi with crispy rice noodles and cold spinach in a sesame-soy vinaigrette. International wines can be ordered by the glass or bottle. There are great desserts here, too, such as creamy almond/amaretto flan and rich guava cheesecake with strawberry sauce.

✪ **Ming Court.** 9188 International Dr. (between Sand Lake Rd. and the Bee Line Expwy.). ☎ **407/351-9988.** Reservations recommended. Dim sum items mostly $1.95–$2.50; main courses $12.50–$19.95. AE, CB, DC, DISC, JCB, MC, V. Daily 11am–2:30pm and 4:30pm–midnight. Free self-parking. CHINESE REGIONAL.

This is sophisticated Chinese cuisine that can hold its own against what you'd find in New York or California. Ming Court is fronted by a serpentine "cloud wall" crowned by engraved sea-green Chinese tiles (it's a celestial symbol; you dine above the clouds here, like the gods). Its candlelit interior is stunningly decorated in soft earth tones. The glass-walled terrace rooms overlook lotus ponds filled with koi. A musician plays classical Chinese music on a zheng (a long zither) at dinner.

The menu offers diverse specialties from throughout China. Begin by ordering a variety of appetizers such as wok-charred Mandarin pot stickers or crispy wontons stuffed with vegetables and cream cheese. Entrees will open up new culinary vistas to even the most sophisticated diners. Lightly battered deep-fried chicken breast is served with a delicate lemon-tangerine sauce. The Szechuan charcoal-grilled filet mignon is topped with a toasted onion/garlic/chile sauce and served with stir-fried julienne vegetables. And crispy stir-fried jumbo Szechuan shrimp are enhanced by a light fresh tomato sauce. At lunch, you can order dim sum. There's an extensive wine list.

INEXPENSIVE

✪ **Bahama Breeze.** 8849 International Dr., Orlando. ☎ **407/248-2499.** Reservations not accepted. Main courses $6.95–$14.95; sandwiches and salads $5.95–$6.95. AE, MC, V. Sun–Thurs 4pm–1am, Fri–Sat 4pm–2am. CARIBBEAN

Traditional Caribbean foods are used to create unusual items such as moist and tasty "fish in a bag"—strips of mahimahi in a parchment pillow flavored with carrots, sweet peppers, mushrooms, celery, and spices. Also try the paella, a rice dish brimming with shrimp, fish, mussels, chicken, and chunks of sausage. The coconut curry chicken is also worth a try—sautéed chunks of chicken sprinkled with fresh coconut. For dessert try the piña colada bread pudding, a cube of custard bread in a sweet coconut sauce, or the tart key lime pie. Created by Orlando-based Darden Restaurants, the same folks who brought you Red Lobster and Olive Garden, this Bahama Breeze is essentially a test kitchen for what may soon be a national chain. Unlike Darden's other creations, which serve solid but not necessarily savory offerings, Bahama Breeze is a unique dining experience that challenges the taste buds. You can even watch your entrees being prepared in the open kitchen. The drink menu includes more than 50 beers, and the expected collection of fruity, pseudo-exotic drinks such as the Very Berry Daiquiri. Happy-hour prices are featured round-the-clock.

IN KISSIMMEE

There is a system of markers by the side of the road along Irlo Bronson Highway, U.S. Hwy. 17-92.

✪ **Medieval Times.** 4510 W. Irlo Bronson Memorial Hwy. (between markers 14 and 15 or on U.S. Hwy. 192, 11 miles east of the main Disney entrance, next to Super Wal-Mart), Kissimmee. ☎ **800/229-8300** or 407/239-0214. Reservations recommended. $37.95 adults, $22.95 children 3–12. AE, DISC, MC, V. Show daily 8pm. Free parking.

Jim Carrey fans know that the *Cable Guy* went to the California branch of Medieval Times to duel with his hapless friend. A long-time favorite for Orlando visitors, the Kissimmee-based show is billed as "dinner and tournament." It lives up to that billing, with jousting contests, armored clashes, and 80 Andalusian stallions that perform with military precision. It's all staged for the 1,000 "special guests" of the castle, who come to the dark, cavernous space to eat off of heavy pewter plates while watching the tournament contestants tumble about before them. The menu includes a wine cocktail, fresh vegetable soup, whole roasted chicken, spareribs, herb basted potato, and dessert. The price includes dinner, beverages, and the show. The castle is air-conditioned and accessible to travelers with disabilities. It's a popular spot, so reservations are suggested.

DINING WITH DISNEY CHARACTERS

Especially for the 10-and-under set, it's a thrill to dine in a restaurant where costumed Disney characters show up to greet the customers, sign autographs, pose in family photos, and interact with little kids. Make reservations as far in advance as possible for these very popular meals. The **breakfast** prices are all around $15 for adults and $8 for children; at **dinner** $20 for adults, $9 for children 3 to 11, free for children 2 and under. Prices vary from location to location, but you will often have to take what is available, especially if you don't make reservations far in advance. It's best to make reservations when you book your hotel. Call ☎ **407/WDW-DINE** (939-3463). AE, MC, V.

Note: On selected days, Disney resort guests can arrive earlier at some of the below-listed character breakfasts.

✪ **Artist Point.** At Disney's Wilderness Lodge, 901 Timberline Dr. Breakfast with Pocahontas and friends. Daily 7:30–11am.

In a rustic lodgelike dining room with a beamed ceiling supported by tree-trunk beams and large windows providing scenic lake views, Pocahontas and friends host all-you-can-eat buffet breakfasts.

Cape May Café. At Disney's Grand Floridian Beach Resort, 1800 Epcot Resorts Blvd. Daily 7:30–11am.

The Cape May Café, a delightful New England–themed dining room, serves lavish buffet character breakfasts with Admiral Goofy and his crew as hosts, including Chip 'n' Dale and Pluto (exact characters may vary).

Chef Mickey's. At Disney's Contemporary Resort, 4600 N. World Dr. Daily 7:30–11:30am and 5–9:30pm.

The whimsical Chef Mickey's is the setting for buffet character breakfasts and dinners. Chef Mickey's ✪ **prime rib buffet dinner,** complete with a varying cast of characters, includes a make-your-own-sundae bar.

✪ Garden Grill. In The Land pavilion at Epcot. Daily 8:30–11:30am, 11:30am–3:30pm, and 3:30–8pm.

This is a revolving restaurant with seating in comfortable semicircular booths. As you dine, your table travels past desert, prairie, farmland, and rain-forest environments. There's a "momma's-in-the-kitchen" theme here: You'll be given a straw hat upon entering, and the just-folks service staff speaks in country lingo. The hearty family-style meals are hosted by Mickey, Minnie, and Chip 'n' Dale. Extensive American breakfasts and lunches are offered; dinners include several entrees (roast chicken, farm-raised fish, and hickory-smoked steak), smashed potatoes, vegetables, squaw bread and biscuits, salad, beverage, and dessert.

King Stefan's Banquet Hall. In Cinderella's Castle in the Magic Kingdom. Daily 8–10am.

This Gothic castle, the focal point of the park, serves up character breakfast buffets daily. Hosts vary, but Cinderella always puts in an appearance. This is one of the most popular character meals in the park, so reserve far in advance. It's a great way to start your day in the Magic Kingdom.

✪ Liberty Tree Tavern. In Liberty Square in the Magic Kingdom. Daily 4pm to park closing.

This Williamsburg-like 18th-century pub offers character dinners hosted by Mickey, Goofy, Pluto, Chip 'n' Dale, and Tigger (some or all of them). Meals, served family style, consist of salad, roast chicken, marinated flank steak, trail sausages, homemade mashed potatoes, rice pilaf, vegetables, and a dessert of warm apple crisp with vanilla ice cream.

✪ Luau Cove. At Disney's Polynesian Resort, 1600 Seven Seas Dr. Daily 7:30–10:30am; dinner at 4:30pm.

Luau Cove, an exotic open-air facility, is the setting for an island-themed character show called Mickey's Tropical Luau. It's an abbreviated version of the Polynesian Luau Dinner Show described later in this chapter in section 15, featuring Polynesian dancers along with Mickey, Minnie, Pluto, and Goofy. Your set-price meal includes honey-roasted chicken, vegetables, glazed cinnamon bread, and an ice-cream sundae. Guests are presented with shell leis upon entering.

The Polynesian also hosts Minnie's Menehune Character Breakfast in the Polynesian-themed 'Ohana (described above). Traditional breakfast foods are prepared on an 18-foot fire pit and served family style. Minnie, Goofy, and Chip 'n' Dale appear, and there are children's parades with Polynesian musical instruments.

✪ 1900 Park Fare. At Disney's Grand Floridian Beach Resort, 4001 Grand Floridian Way. Daily 7:30am–11:30am and 5:30–9pm.

This exquisitely elegant Disney resort hosts character meals in the festive exposition-themed 1900 Park Fare. Big Bertha—a French band organ that plays pipes, drums, bells, cymbals, castanets, and xylophone—provides music. Mary Poppins, Winnie the Pooh, Goofy, Pluto, Chip 'n' Dale, and Minnie Mouse appear at the elaborate buffet breakfasts. Mickey and Minnie appear at nightly buffets which feature prime rib, stuffed pork loin, fresh fish, and more.

Soundstage Restaurant. At Disney-MGM Studios, adjacent to the Magic of Disney Animation. Daily 8:30–10:30am and 11:30am–3:30pm.

A vast buffet meal is set out in this warehouse-motif restaurant decorated with movie props and posters, and selected characters from the movies *Aladdin* and *Pocahontas* sign autographs as favorite tunes from both Disney hits play in the background.

Watercress Café. At the Buena Vista Palace, 1900 Buena Vista Dr. ☎ **407/827-2727.** Reservations not accepted. Sun 8–10:30am.

The plant-filled Watercress Café, with large windows overlooking Lake Buena Vista, is the setting for Sunday-morning character breakfasts featuring Minnie, Goofy, and Pluto. Both à la carte and buffet meals are offered. Since reservations are not accepted, arrive early to avoid a wait.

5 Tips for Visiting Walt Disney World Attractions

Walt Disney World encompasses the Magic Kingdom; the new Animal Kingdom; Epcot; Disney-MGM Studios; Pleasure Island; the Walt Disney Village Marketplace, Disney's West Side, a lakeside enclave of shops and restaurants; three water parks (Typhoon Lagoon, River Country, and Blizzard Beach); and Discovery Island, a nature preserve and aviary. Pleasure Island, the Marketplace, and the West Side are also referred to as Downtown Disney. For the purposes of this chapter, I've limited the number of attractions to include only the Magic Kingdom, Epcot, Disney-MGM, and Animal Kingdom.

TIPS FOR PLANNING YOUR TRIP

Planning is essential. Unless you're staying for considerably more than a week, you can't possibly experience all the rides, shows, and attractions here, not to mention the vast array of recreational facilities. You'll only wear yourself to a frazzle trying—it's better to follow a relaxed itinerary, including leisurely meals and recreational activities, than to make a demanding job out of trying to see everything.

Read the *Vacation Guide* and the detailed descriptions in this book. It's a good idea to make a daily itinerary, putting your activities in some kind of sensible geographical sequence so you're not zigzagging all over the place. Familiarize yourself in advance with the layout of each park. Schedule in sit-down shows, recreational activities (a boat ride or swim late in the afternoon can be wonderfully refreshing), and at least one unhurried meal. Make sure to have an agreed-upon meeting place should the family get separated. My suggested itineraries are given below.

INFORMATION   Call or write the **Walt Disney World Co.,** P.O. Box 10000, Lake Buena Vista, FL 32830-1000 (☎ **407/934-7639**), for a copy of *Walt Disney World Vacations,* an invaluable planning aid. Once you've arrived in town, guest-services and concierge desks in all area hotels—especially the Disney properties and "official" hotels—have **up-to-the-minute information** about what's going on in the parks. If your hotel doesn't have this information, call ☎ **407/824-4321.**

There are also **information locations** in each park—at City Hall in the Magic Kingdom, at Innoventions East near the WorldKey terminals in Epcot, and at the Guest Services Building in Disney-MGM Studios.

BUY TICKETS IN ADVANCE   You can purchase 4- or 5-day passes (see details below) before your trip by calling **Ticket Mail Order** (☎ **407/824-6750**). You can also order tickets online at **www.disneyworld.com**. Allow 21 days for processing your request, and include a $2 postage-and-handling charge. Of course, you can always purchase tickets at any of the parks, but why stand in an avoidable line? *Note:* One-day tickets can be purchased only at the park entrances.

ARRIVE EARLY   Always arrive at the parks a good 30 to 45 minutes before opening time, thus avoiding a traffic jam entering the park and a long line at the gate. Early arrival also lets you experience one or two major attractions before big lines form. In high season the parking lots sometimes fill up, and you may even have to wait to get in. The longest lines in all parks are between 11am and 4pm.

PARKING Parking (free to guests at WDW resorts) costs $6 per day no matter how many parks you visit. *Be sure to note your parking location before leaving your car.* Write it down if necessary. There are special lots for travelers with disabilities at each park (call ☎ 407/824-4321 for details). Don't worry about parking far from the entrance gates; there is a constant tram service.

WHEN YOU ARRIVE IN THE PARKS Upon entering any of the major Disney parks, you'll be given an **entertainment schedule** and a comprehensive park **guide map,** which contains a map of the park and lists all attractions, shops, shows, and restaurants. If you lose the map, ask at the cash register at one of the many shops. They usually have a few extra copies.

If you've formulated an itinerary before arrival, you already know the major shows (check show schedules for additional ideas) you'll want to see during the day and what arrangements you need to make. If you haven't done this, use your early arrival time, while waiting for the park to open, to figure out which shows to attend, and, where necessary, make reservations for them as soon as the gates swing open.

LEAVING THE PARKS If you leave any of the parks and plan to return later in the day, be sure to get your hand stamped when exiting. You will also need your paper pass if you are park hopping.

BEST DAYS TO VISIT The busiest days at the Magic Kingdom and Epcot are Monday through Wednesday; at Disney-MGM Studios, they're Thursday and Friday. Surprisingly, weekends are the least busy at all parks. Sunday is generally a slow day. In peak seasons, especially, arrange your visits accordingly.

OPERATING HOURS Hours of operation vary somewhat throughout the year:

The **Magic Kingdom, Animal Kingdom,** and **Disney-MGM Studios** are generally open from 9am to 7pm, with extended hours, sometimes as late as midnight, during major holidays and the summer months.

Epcot is generally open from 9am to 9pm, with Future World open from 9am to 9pm and World Showcase from 11am to 9pm—once again with extended holiday hours.

✪ **Typhoon Lagoon** and **Blizzard Beach** are open from 10am to 5pm most of the year (with extended hours during some holidays) and 9am to 8pm in summer.

River Country and **Discovery Island** are open from 10am to 5pm most of the year (with extended hours during some holidays) and 10am to 7pm in summer.

Note: Epcot and MGM sometimes open a half hour or more before the posted time. Keep in mind, too, that Disney resort guests enjoy early admission to all three major parks on designated days.

TICKETS There are several ticket options, but most people get the best value from 4- and 5-day passes. All passes offer unlimited use of the WDW transportation system. The prices quoted-include sales tax, and they are, of course, subject to change. If you are staying for a few days, it makes sense to get a pass.

Unless you are a WDW veteran who has a very specific agenda, you'll get the most for your money by sticking with the **Four-Day Value Pass,** which allows access to one park a day, over the **Five Day Park Hopper Pass** or **All-in-One Pass** (6 days), which allow access to multiple parks on any given day. (The price of a Value Pass, plus two single day admission tickets is also less than the All-in-One Pass.)

What you are paying for is the ability to travel among the different parks. But, in truth, doing this means you spend a chunk of your day on a monorail or in line, so make the most of one park at a time, especially if you are traveling with children.

Adult prices are paid by anyone over 10 years of age. **Children's rates** are for ages 3 to 9. **Children 2 and under** are admitted free.

A **1-day, one-park ticket for the Magic Kingdom, Epcot, or Disney-MGM Studios** is $42.00 for adults, $34.00 for children.

A **1-day ticket to Typhoon Lagoon or Blizzard Beach** is $25.95 for adults, $20.50 for children.

A **1-day ticket to River Country** is $15.95 for adults, $12.50 for children.

A **1-day ticket to Pleasure Island** is $18.95. Since this is primarily an 18 and over entertainment complex, there is no special pricing for children.

The **4-Day Value Pass** provides admission for 4 days to one major park per day. Adults pay $149.00; children, $119.00.

The **5-Day Park-Hopper Pass** provides unlimited admission to the Magic Kingdom, Epcot, and Disney-MGM Studios on any 5 days; you can visit any combination of parks on any given day. It also includes admission to Typhoon Lagoon, River Country, Blizzard Beach, Discovery Island, and Pleasure Island for a period of 7 days beginning the first date stamped. Adults pay $189.00; children, $151.00.

The **All-in-One Hopper Pass** (6 days) is $249.00 for adults, $199.00 for children.

If you're staying at any Walt Disney World resort or "official" hotel, you're also eligible for a money-saving **Be Our Guest Pass** priced according to length of stay. It also offers special perks.

If you plan on visiting Walt Disney World more than once during the year, inquire about a money-saving annual pass ($299.00 for adults, $250.00 for children).

BEHIND THE SCENES:
SPECIAL TOURS IN WALT DISNEY WORLD

In addition to the greenhouse tour described below in Epcot's The Land pavilion, the Disney parks offer a number of walking tours and learning programs. Call ☎ **407/WDW-TOUR** (939-8687) for more information. These tours include:

* The **Hidden Treasures of World Showcase** focuses on the architecture and entertainment offerings of Epcot's international pavilions; The East explores Mexico, Norway, China, Germany, and Italy; and the American Adventure and West visits Canada, the United Kingdom, France, Morocco, Japan, and the United States; $25 per person (in addition to park admission). The 6-hour Hidden Treasures tour takes you to all 11 international pavilions and includes lunch at Restaurant Marrakesh in Morocco; $65 per person; theme park admission is not required.
* **Gardens of the World,** a 3-hour tour of the extraordinary landscaping at Epcot, is led by a Disney horticulturist; the cost is $25 per person.
* The 4-hour **Keys to the Kingdom** orientation provides a glimpse into the high-tech operational systems behind the magic of the Magic Kingdom; it costs $45 per person (in addition to park admission). There are also learning programs (☎ **407/363-6000**) on subjects ranging from animation to international cultures. Call for details.

SUGGESTED ITINERARIES

You won't see all the attractions at any of the parks in a single day. Read through the descriptions, decide which are musts for you, and try to get to them. My favorite rides and attractions are starred. It's more fun to keep a relaxed pace than to race around like a maniac trying to do it all.

A Day in the Magic Kingdom

Get to the park well before opening time, tickets in hand. When the gates open, make a dash for Extra "TERROR"estrial Alien Encounter in Tomorrowland, which, as the newest major attraction, will have very long lines later in the day.

Then, hightail it to Frontierland and ride Splash Mountain—there's hardly any shade for those waiting in line at this attraction, so you don't want to do it in the afternoon. Afterward, it should still be early enough to beat the lines at one more major attractions—head over to Adventureland and do Pirates of the Caribbean.

Then, relax and take it slow. Complete whatever else interests you in Adventureland. Then walk over to Frontierland and enjoy the attractions there until lunch. Have lunch while taking in the 12:15 or 1:30pm show at the Diamond Horseshoe Saloon Revue (they don't take reservations, so arrive early).

After lunch, continue visiting Frontierland attractions as you please, or proceed to the Hall of Presidents and the Haunted Mansion in Liberty Square. By 2:30pm (earlier in peak seasons), you should snag a seat on the curb in Liberty Square along the parade route. After the parade, continue around the park taking in Fantasyland and Tomorrowland attractions. (If you really want to beat the lines, skip the parade and breeze through the minimal lines in the rest of the park.)

If you have little kids (age 8 and under) in your party, start your day instead by taking the WDW Railroad from Main Street to Mickey's Toontown Fair to meet the characters. Work your way through Fantasyland until lunch, once again at the Diamond Horseshoe. After lunch, visit the Country Bear Jamboree in Frontierland and proceed to Adventureland for the Jungle Cruise, Swiss Family Treehouse, and Tropical Serenade. Once again, stop in good time to get parade seats (in Frontierland). Little kids need to sit right up front to see everything. That's a long enough day for most young children, and your best plan is to go back to your hotel for a nap or swim. If, however, you wish to continue, return to Frontierland and/or Fantasyland for the rides you didn't complete earlier.

If You Can Spend Only 1 Day at Epcot

Epcot really requires at least 2 days, so this is a highlight tour. As above, arrive early, tickets in hand. If you haven't already made lunch reservations in advance by calling ☎ **407/WDW-DINE** (939-3463), make your first stop at the WorldKey terminals in Innoventions East. I suggest a 1pm lunch at the San Angel Inn Restaurant in Mexico. If you don't like Mexican food, move up one pavilion to Norway and reserve for the buffet at Akershus. You can make dinner reservations at the same time. Plan dinner for about 7pm, which will allow you time to eat and find a good viewing spot for IllumiNations (usually at 9pm, but check your schedule).

Spend no more than an hour exploring Innoventions. Then move on to the Universe of Energy show. Continue to the Wonders of Life pavilion where must-sees include Body Wars, Cranium Command, Test Track, and The Making of Me.

And if time allows—it will depend on line waits at attractions—take in the show at Horizons before heading into World Showcase for lunch in Mexico. At lunch, check your show schedule and decide which shows to incorporate into your day.

Then walk around the lagoon, visiting highlight attractions: *Wonders of China,* the American Adventure, *Impressions de France,* and *O Canada!,* allowing yourself some time for browsing and shopping. After dinner, stay on for IllumiNations.

A Word About Epcot Dining: Sit-down meals at World Showcase pavilions and the Living Seas are a pleasant but pricey part of the Epcot experience. There are plenty of less-expensive eateries throughout the park, including ethnic ones with cafe seating in many World Showcase pavilions. And since these don't require reservations, you're not tied down to specific mealtimes. See your *Epcot Guidemap* for details.

If You Can Spend 2 Days at Epcot

Ignore the 1-day itinerary above, but do begin your day by making all necessary restaurant reservations—once again for lunch in Mexico or Norway at about 1pm. Make reservations for your second day at the same time.

Skip Innoventions East for now and work your way thoroughly through the Universe of Energy, Wonders of Life, Horizons, and World of Motion pavilions, keeping your lunch reservation time in mind. After lunch, walk clockwise around the lagoon, visiting each foreign pavilion and taking in as many shows as you like (consult your show schedule and try to keep pace as well as possible). Leave IllumiNations for your second day's visit.

Begin your second day exploring Innoventions East, and proceed counterclockwise, taking in Spaceship Earth, Innoventions West, the Living Seas (its Coral Reef restaurant is a good choice for lunch), and all the other pavilions on the west side of the park. Cap your Epcot visit with IllumiNations.

A Day at Disney-MGM Studios Theme Park

Since show times change frequently here, it's impossible to really give you a workable itinerary. Upon entering the park, if you haven't already made dining arrangements, stop at the Hollywood Brown Derby and make lunch reservations. Or, you may want to conserve touring time by having a light lunch at a casual eatery and saving the Derby for a relaxing dinner.

Make a beeline for the *Twilight Zone Tower of Terror*. While you're waiting in line, plan the rest of your schedule, being sure to include these not-to-be-missed attractions: *Indiana Jones Epic Stunt Spectacular, Star Tours, Jim Henson's Muppet Vision 4-D*. If you have kids 10 or under in your party, visit the back of the park where there are exhibits and shows tied to whatever is the company's newest release. Get in line 30 minutes before at the Backlot Theater for these shows. Also be sure to be early for Indiana Jones; the shows often fill up. And all kids love the parade; snag a good seat on the parade route 30 minutes ahead of time as well.

Time for more? See the Beauty and the Beast Show and Voyage of the Little Mermaid. Ride the Great Movie Ride and Star Tours, and take time to take in Superstar Television, Inside the Magic, and the Backstage Studio Tour. In peak seasons, stick around for the fireworks.

6 The Magic Kingdom

Centered around Cinderella Castle, the Magic Kingdom occupies about 100 acres, with 45 major attractions and numerous restaurants and shops through its seven "lands." From the parking lot, you'll have to take a short monorail or ferry ride to the Magic Kingdom entrance. During peak attendance times, arrive at the Magic Kingdom an hour prior to opening time to avoid long lines at these conveyances.

Upon entering the park, consult your *Magic Kingdom Guidemap* to get your bearings. It details every shop, restaurant, and attraction in every land. Also consult your entertainment schedule to see what's on for the day.

If you have questions, most park employees are very knowledgeable, and City Hall, on your left as you enter, is both an information center and, along with Mickey's Toontown Fair, a likely place to meet up with costumed characters. There's a stroller-rental shop just after the turnstiles to your right, and the Kodak Camera Center, near Town

The Magic Kingdom

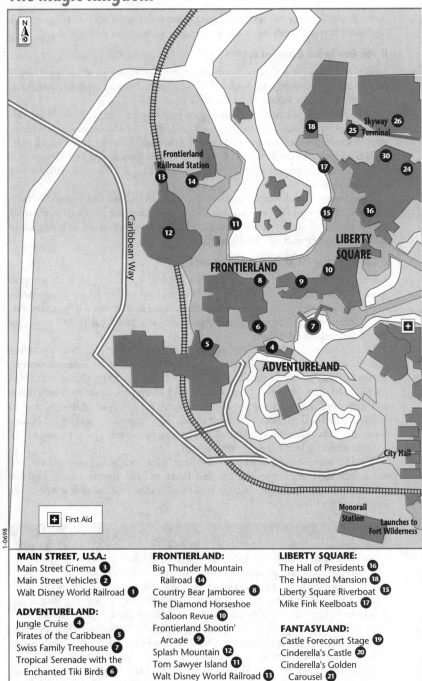

N

Frontierland
Railroad Station

Caribbean Way

FRONTIERLAND

**LIBERTY
SQUARE**

Skyway
Terminal

ADVENTURELAND

City Hall

First Aid

Monorail
Station

Launches to
Fort Wilderness

1-0698

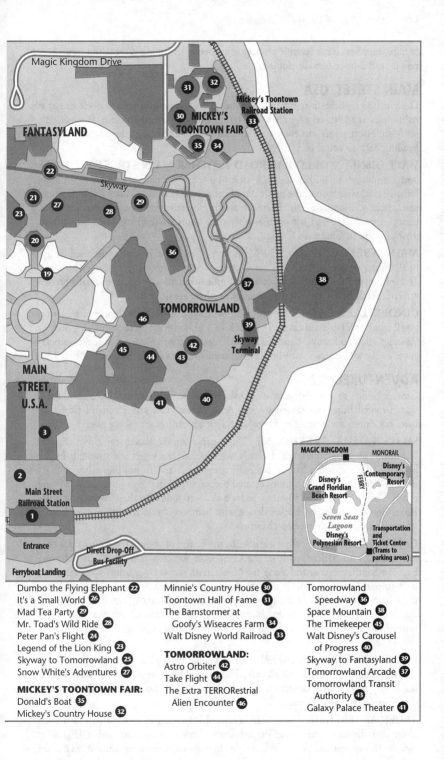

Magic Kingdom Drive

FANTASYLAND

Skyway

MICKEY'S
TOONTOWN FAIR

Mickey's Toontown
Railroad Station

TOMORROWLAND

Skyway
Terminal

MAIN
STREET,
U.S.A.

Main Street
Railroad Station

Entrance

Direct Drop-Off
Bus Facility

Ferryboat Landing

MAGIC KINGDOM   MONORAIL

Disney's
Grand Floridian
Beach Resort

Disney's
Contemporary
Resort

FERRY

Seven Seas
Lagoon

Disney's
Polynesian Resort

Transportation
and
Ticket Center
(Trams to
parking areas)

Dumbo the Flying Elephant 22
It's a Small World 26
Mad Tea Party 29
Mr. Toad's Wild Ride 28
Peter Pan's Flight 24
Legend of the Lion King 23
Skyway to Tomorrowland 25
Snow White's Adventures 27

MICKEY'S TOONTOWN FAIR:
Donald's Boat 35
Mickey's Country House 32

Minnie's Country House 30
Toontown Hall of Fame 31
The Barnstormer at
  Goofy's Wiseacres Farm 34
Walt Disney World Railroad 33

TOMORROWLAND:
Astro Orbiter 42
Take Flight 44
The Extra TERRORestrial
  Alien Encounter 46

Tomorrowland
  Speedway 36
Space Mountain 38
The Timekeeper 45
Walt Disney's Carousel
  of Progress 40
Skyway to Fantasyland 39
Tomorrowland Arcade 37
Tomorrowland Transit
  Authority 43
Galaxy Palace Theater 41

487

Square, supplies all conceivable photographic needs, including camera and camcorder rentals and 2-hour film developing.

MAIN STREET, USA

Designed to replicate a typical turn-of-the-century American street (albeit one that culminates in a 13th-century castle), this is the gateway to the Kingdom. Don't dawdle on Main Street when you enter the park; leave it for the end of the day when you're heading back to your hotel.

WALT DISNEY WORLD RAILROAD & OTHER MAIN STREET VEHICLES
You can board an authentic 1928 steam-powered railroad here for a 15-minute journey clockwise around the perimeter of the park. There are stations in Frontierland and Mickey's Toontown Fair. There are also horse-drawn trolleys, horseless carriages, jitneys, omnibuses, and fire engines plying the short route along Main Street from Town Square to Cinderella Castle.

MAIN STREET CINEMA   The Main Street Cinema is an air-conditioned hexagonal theater where vintage black-and-white Disney cartoons (including *Steamboat Willie* from 1928, in which Mickey and Minnie debuted) are aired continually on two screens. You'll have to watch these standing—there are no seats.

CINDERELLA'S CASTLE   At the end of Main Street, in the center of the park, you'll come to a fairyland castle, 185 feet high and housing a restaurant (King Stefan's Banquet Hall) and shops. Cinderella herself, dressed for the ball, often makes appearances in the lobby area. Don't linger here; there's really not much to see.

ADVENTURELAND

Cross a bridge to your left and stroll into an exotic jungle of lush tropical foliage, thatch-roofed huts, and carved totems. Amid dense vines and stands of palm and bamboo, drums are beating and swashbuckling adventures are taking place.

SWISS FAMILY TREEHOUSE   This attraction is based on Swiss Family Robinson, about a shipwrecked family who created an ingenious dwelling in the branches of a sprawling banyan tree. Using materials and furnishings salvaged from their downed ship, the Robinsons created bedrooms, a kitchen, a library, and a living room. Visitors ascend the 50-foot tree for a close-up look into these rooms. Note the Rube Goldberg rope-and-bucket device with bamboo chutes that dips water from a stream and carries it to treetop chambers.

✪ **JUNGLE CRUISE**   What a cruise! In the course of about 10 minutes your boat sails through an African veldt in the Congo, an Amazon rain forest, the Mekong River in Southeast Asia, and along the Nile. Lavish scenery, cascading waterfalls, and lush foliage (most of it real) include dozens of audio-animatronic birds and animals—elephants, zebras, lions, giraffes, crocodiles, tigers, even fluttering butterflies. But the adventures aren't all on shore. Passengers are menaced by everything from water-spouting elephants to fierce warriors who attack with spears. Disney at its cheesy best.

PIRATES OF THE CARIBBEAN   You'll proceed through a long grottolike passage to board a boat into a pitch-black cave. There, amid fiery explosions and a redundant sea shanty, are a ragtag collection of yo-ho-hoing mates. Loud explosions can make this scary for young children.

TROPICAL SERENADE   In a large hexagonal Polynesian-style dwelling, 250 tropical birds, chanting totem poles, and singing flowers whistle, tweet, and warble. Highlights include a thunderstorm in the dark, a light show over the fountain, and, of course, the famous "in the tiki, tiki, tiki, tiki, tiki room" song. You'll find yourself singing it all day. This is a must for young children.

FRONTIERLAND

From Adventureland, step into the wild and woolly past of the American frontier, where rough-and-tumble architecture runs to log cabins and rustic saloons, and the landscape is Southwestern scrubby with mesquite, saguaro cactus, yucca, and prickly pear. Across the river is Tom Sawyer Island, reachable via log rafts.

✪ **SPLASH MOUNTAIN**   Themed after *Song of the South,* the first part of Splash Mountain takes you on a leisurely journey in a hollowed-out log craft along the canals of a flooded mountain. With its audio-animatronics and constant theme song, this portion of Splash Mountain is basically "It's a Small World" set in the backwoods. At 9 minutes, it's the longest of the Disney thrill rides. It all culminates in a breathtaking five-story splashdown from mountaintop to briar-filled pond at 40 miles per hour. There is no way to avoid getting wet.

✪ **BIG THUNDER MOUNTAIN RAILROAD**   This mining disaster–themed roller coaster derives its thrills from hairpin turns and descents in the dark. It's situated in a 200-foot-high red stone mountain with 2,780 feet of track winding through windswept canyons and bat-filled caves. You'll board a runaway train that careens through the ribs of a dinosaur, under a thundering waterfall, past spewing geysers and bubbling mud pots, and over a bottomless volcanic pool. Riders are threatened by flash floods, earthquakes, rickety bridges, and avalanches. This ride is especially fun after dark.

DIAMOND HORSESHOE SALOON REVUE & MEDICINE SHOW   Here's an opportunity to sit down in air-conditioned comfort and enjoy a rousing Western revue. The "theater" is a re-creation of a turn-of-the-century saloon. Marshall John Charles sings and banters with the audience, Jingles the Piano Man plays honky-tonk tunes, there's a magic act, and dance-hall girls do a spirited cancan—all with lots of humor and audience participation. There are seven shows daily; plan on going around lunch so you can eat during the show. The menu features deli or peanut butter and jelly sandwiches served with chips.

COUNTRY BEAR JAMBOREE   I've always loved the Country Bear Jamboree, a 15-minute show featuring a troupe of fiddlin', banjo-strummin', harmonica-playin' audio-animatronic bears belting out rollicking country tunes and crooning plaintive love songs. A special holiday show plays throughout the Christmas season each year.

FRONTIERLAND SHOOTIN' ARCADE   Combining state-of-the-art electronics with a traditional shooting-gallery format, this vast arcade presents an array of 97 targets (slow-moving ore cars, buzzards, grave-diggers) in a three-dimensional 1850s gold-mining-town scenario. To keep the Western ambience authentic, newfangled electronic firing mechanisms loaded with infrared bullets are concealed in genuine Hawkins 54-caliber buffalo rifles. When you hit a target, elaborate sound and motion gags are set off. You get 25 shots for 50¢.

LIBERTY SQUARE

Serving as a transitional area between Frontierland and Fantasyland, Liberty Square evokes 18th-century America with Georgian architecture and Colonial Williamsburg–type shops. You might encounter a fife-and-drum corps marching along Liberty Square's cobblestone streets.

THE HALL OF PRESIDENTS   In this redbrick colonial hall, all American presidents—from George Washington to Bill Clinton (who recorded the voice for his character)—are represented by audio-animatronic figures. They dramatize important events in the nation's history, from the signing of the Constitution through the space age. The show begins with a film, projected on a 180° screen, about the importance of the Constitution. Maya Angelou narrates.

✪ **THE HAUNTED MANSION**   Its eerie ambience enhanced by inky darkness, spooky music, and mysterious screams and rappings, this mansion is replete with bizarre scenes and objects: a ghostly banquet and ball, a graveyard band, a suit of armor that comes alive, luminous spiders, a talking head in a crystal ball, weird flying objects, and much more. At the end of the ride, a ghost joins you in your car. The experience is more amusing than terrifying, so you can take small children inside.

BOAT RIDES   A steam-powered sternwheeler called the *Liberty Belle* and two Mike Fink keel boats (the *Bertha Mae* and the *Gullywhumper*) depart (the latter summers and holidays only) from Liberty Square for scenic cruises along the Rivers of America. Both ply the identical route and make a restful interlude for foot-weary park goers.

FANTASYLAND

The attractions in this happy "land"—based on such Disney film classics as *Snow White* and *Peter Pan*—are especially popular with young visitors. If your kids are 8 or under, you might want to make it your first stop in the Magic Kingdom.

LEGEND OF THE LION KING   This stage spectacular based on Disney's blockbuster motion-picture musical combines animation, movie footage, sophisticated puppetry, and high-tech special effects.

SNOW WHITE'S ADVENTURES   Until recently, there was no Snow White at this attraction, which concentrated mostly on the cackling, toothless evil queen and left small children screaming in terror. It has been toned down now, with Snow White appearing in a number of pleasant scenes—at the castle courtyard wishing well, in the dwarfs' cottage, receiving the prince's kiss that breaks the witch's spell, and riding off with the prince to live "happily ever after." Even so, this could be scary for kids 6 and under.

MAD TEA PARTY   This is a traditional amusement park ride à la Disney with an *Alice in Wonderland* theme. Riders sit in oversized pink teacups on saucers that careen around a circular platform. Believe it or not, this can be a pretty wild ride or a tame one—it depends on how much you spin, a factor under your control via a wheel in the cup.

MR. TOAD'S WILD RIDE   Riders navigate a series of dark rooms, hurtling into solid objects (a fireplace, a bookcase, a haystack) and through barn doors into a coop of squawking chickens. They're menaced by falling suits of armor, snorting bulls, and an oncoming locomotive in a pitch-black tunnel, and are sent to jail (for car theft), to hell (complete with pitchfork-wielding demons), and through a fiery volcano.

CINDERELLA'S GOLDEN CAROUSEL   It's a beauty, built by Italian woodcarvers in the Victorian tradition in 1917 and refurbished by Disney artists who added scenes from the Cinderella story. The band organ plays such Disney classics as "When You Wish Upon a Star."

DUMBO, THE FLYING ELEPHANT   This is a very tame kiddie ride in which the cars—baby elephants (Dumbos)—go around and around in a circle gently rising and dipping. But it's very exciting for wee ones.

IT'S A SMALL WORLD   You know the song—and if you don't, you will. It plays continually as you sail "around the world" through vast rooms designed to represent different countries. They're inhabited by appropriately costumed audio-animatronic dolls and animals, all singing in tiny voices. This cast of thousands includes Chinese acrobats, Russian dancers, Indian snake charmers, Arabs on magic carpets, African drummers, a Venetian gondolier, and Australian koalas. Cute. Very cute.

PETER PAN'S FLIGHT   Riding in Captain Hook's ship, passengers careen through dark passages while experiencing the story of *Peter Pan.* The adventure begins in the Darlings' nursery and includes a flight over nighttime London to Never-Never Land, where riders encounter mermaids, Indians, a ticking crocodile, the lost boys, Tinker-bell, Hook, Smee, and the rest. It's fun.

SKYWAY   Its entrance close to Peter Pan's Flight, the Skyway is an aerial tramway to Tomorrowland, which makes continuous round-trips throughout the day.

MICKEY'S TOONTOWN FAIR
Head off those cries of "where's Mickey?" by taking the kids to this 2-acre replacement for Mickey's Starland that was unveiled during the 25th anniversary celebration in 1996. Toontown Fair offers kids a chance to meet their favorite Disney characters including Mickey, Minnie, Donald Duck, and Goofy. Set in a whimsical collection of candy-striped tents harking back to those turn-of-the-century county fairs, highlights include the Toontown Hall of Fame, animated shorts hosted by the stars, and both Mickey's and Minnie's country houses. Everything is brightly colored and kid-friendly in the best Disney tradition; there is even a kid-sized roller coaster. Toontown Fair has its own stop on the WDW Railroad.

TOMORROWLAND
In 1994, the Disney people decided that Tomorrowland (originally designed in the 1970s) was beginning to look like "Yesterdayland." It has now been revamped to reflect the future as a galactic, science fiction–inspired community inhabited by humans, aliens, and robots. A vast state-of-the-art video-game arcade has also been added.

❂ **EXTRA "TERROR"ESTRIAL ALIEN ENCOUNTER**   Director George Lucas contributed his space-age vision to this major new Tomorrowland attraction. The action begins at the Interplanetary Convention Center where a mysterious corporation called X-S Tech, a company from a distant planet, is marketing an interplanetary "tele-transporter" to Earthlings. In order to demonstrate it, X-S technicians try to teleport their sinister corporation head, Chairman Clench, to Earth. But the machine mal-functions, sending him to a distant planet instead and inadvertently teleporting a fear-some man-eating extraterrestrial to Earth. Dark and truly scary, it is not your typical thrill ride. Lots of high-tech effects, from the alien's breath on your neck to a mist of alien slime. May not be suitable for young children.

THE TIMEKEEPER   This Jules Verne/H.G. Wells–inspired multimedia presenta-tion combines Circle-Vision and IMAX footage with audio-animatronics. It's hosted by Timekeeper, a mad scientist robot, and his assistant, 9-EYE, a flying female camera-headed droid and time machine test pilot. In an unpredictable jet-speed escapade, the audience hears Mozart as a young prodigy playing his music to French royalty, visits medieval battlefields in Scotland, watches Leonardo at work, and floats in a hot-air balloon above Moscow's Red Square.

❂ **SPACE MOUNTAIN**   Space Mountain entertains visitors on its long lines with space-age music, exhibits, and meteorites, shooting stars, and space debris whizzing about overhead. These "illusioneering" effects, enhanced by appropriate audio, con-tinue during the ride itself, which is a cosmic roller coaster in the inky starlit blackness of outer space. Your rocket climbs high into the universe before racing through a serpentine complex of aerial galaxies, making thrilling hairpin turns and rapid plunges. (Though it feels as though you're going at breakneck speed, your car actually never goes faster than 28 miles per hour.) Nab the front seat of the train for the best ride.

TAKE FLIGHT   A breezy look through the story of flight. High-tech special effects and 70mm live-action film footage add dramatic 3-D–style verisimilitude. Guests travel from a futuristic airport up a hillside to witness a flying circus, parachutists, stunt flyers, wing walkers, crop dusters, and aerial acrobats. The action moves on to the ocean-hopping age of commercial flight, and finally your vehicle is pulled into a giant jet engine and sent into outer space at a simulated speed of 300 miles per hour.

WALT DISNEY'S CAROUSEL OF PROGRESS   This 22-minute show in a revolving theater features an audio-animatronic family in various tableaux demonstrating a century of development (beginning in 1900) in electric gadgetry and contraptions from Victrolas to virtual reality.

SKYWAY   Its Tomorrowland entrance just west of Space Mountain, this aerial tramway to Fantasyland makes continuous round-trips throughout the day.

TOMORROWLAND TRANSIT AUTHORITY   A futuristic means of transportation, these small five-car trains have no engines. They work by electromagnets, emit no pollution, and use little power. Narrated by a computer guide named Horack I, TTA offers an overhead look at Tomorrowland, including a pretty good preview of Space Mountain. If you're only in the Magic Kingdom for a day, this can be skipped.

TOMORROWLAND SPEEDWAY   This is a great thrill for kids (including teens still waiting to get their driver's license) who get to put the pedal to the metal, steer, and vroom down a speedway in an actual gas-powered sports car. Maximum speed on the 4-minute drive around the track is about 7 miles per hour, and kids have to be 4 feet 4 inches tall to drive alone.

ASTRO ORBITER   This is a tame, typical amusement-park ride. The "rockets" are on arms attached to "the center of the galaxy," and they move up and down while orbiting spinning planets.

PARADES, FIREWORKS & MORE

You'll get an *Entertainment Show Schedule* when you enter the park, which lists all kinds of special goings-on for the day. These include concerts (everything from steel drums to barbershop quartets), encounters with Disney characters, holiday events, and the three major happenings listed below.

✪ **THE 3 O'CLOCK PARADE: *"REMEMBER THE MAGIC"***   You haven't really seen a parade until you've seen one at Walt Disney World. This spectacular daily event kicks off at 3pm year-round on Main Street and meanders through Liberty Square and Frontierland. The route is outlined on your *Entertainment Show Schedule.*

The only problem: Even during slow seasons, you have to snag a seat along the curb a good 30 minutes before it begins—earlier during peak travel times. (That's a long time to sit on a hard curb.)

But the parade is worth a little discomfort. In addition to Mickey and all his Disney pals—everyone from Minnie to Winnie (the Pooh)—there are elaborate floats, stunning costumes, special effects, and a captivating cavalcade of dancers, singers, and other talented performers. Great music, too.

✪ **SPECTROMAGIC**   Along a darkened parade route (the same one as above), 72,000 watts of dazzling high-tech lighting effects (including holography) create a glowing array of pixies and peacocks, sea horses and winged horses, flower gardens and fountains. Roger Rabbit is the eccentric conductor of an orchestra producing a rainbow of musical notes that waft magically into the night air. There are dancing ostriches from Fantasia, whirling electric butterflies, bejeweled coaches, luminescent ElectroMen atop spinning whirlyballs, and, of course, Mickey, surrounded by a sparkling confetti of light. And the music and choreography are on a par with the technology.

Once again, very early arrival is essential to get a seat on the curb. SpectroMagic takes place nightly in summer, on selected nights during Christmas and Easter vacation times, and during other special celebrations. Consult your *Entertainment Show Schedule* for details.

✪ **FIREWORKS**   Like SpectroMagic, Fantasy in the Sky Fireworks, immediately preceded by Tinker Bell's magical flight from Cinderella Castle, take place nightly in summer, on selected nights during Christmas and Easter vacation times, and during other special celebrations. Consult your *Entertainment Show Schedule* for details. Suggested viewing areas are Liberty Square, Frontierland, and Mickey's Toontown Fair.

7 Epcot

Ever growing, Epcot today occupies 260 acres so stunningly landscaped as to be worth visiting for botanical beauty alone. There are two major sections, Future World and World Showcase.

Epcot is huge, and walking around it can be exhausting (some say Epcot's acronym stands for "Every Person Comes Out Tired"). Don't try to do it all in 1 day. Conserve energy by taking launches across the lagoon from the edge of Future World to Germany or Morocco. There are also double-decker buses circling the World Showcase Promenade and making stops at Norway, Italy, France, and Canada.

Unlike the Magic Kingdom, Epcot's parking lot is right at the gate. If you don't get them in the parking lot or at the gate, stop by the Innoventions East information center when you come in to pick up an *Epcot Guidemap* and *Entertainment Schedule,* and, if you so desire, make reservations for lunch or dinner. Many Epcot restaurants are described in the "Dining" section, earlier in this chapter.

Strollers can be rented to your left at the Future World entrance plaza and in World Showcase at the International Gateway between the United Kingdom and France.

FUTURE WORLD

The northern section of Epcot (where you enter the park) comprises Future World, centered on a giant geosphere known as Spaceship Earth. Future World's 10 themed areas, sponsored by major corporations, focus on discovery, scientific achievements, and tomorrow's technologies in areas running the gamut from energy to undersea exploration.

✪ **SPACESHIP EARTH**   This massive, silvery geosphere symbolizes Epcot, so it is a must-do. But long lines can be avoided by saving it until later in the day when you can, more than likely, simply walk right in. Inside, a show takes visitors on a 15-minute journey through the history of communications. You board time-machine vehicles to the distant past, where an audio-animatronic Cro-Magnon shaman recounts the story of a hunt while others record it on cave walls. You advance thousands of years to ancient Egypt, where hieroglyphics adorn temple walls and writing is recorded on papyrus scrolls. You'll progress through the Phoenician and Greek alphabets, the Gutenburg printing press, and the Renaissance. Technologies develop at a rapid pace, through the telegraph, telephone, radio, movies, and TV, and from there it's a short step to the age of electronic communications. You're catapulted into outer space to see "Spaceship Earth" from a new perspective, returning for a finale that places the audience amid interactive global networks. High-tech special effects, animated sets, and laser beams make this quite an exciting experience.

At the end of this journey through time, AT&T invites guests to sample an interactive computer-video wonderland that includes a motion-simulator ride through the company's electronic network. This exhibit complements Innoventions, detailed below.

INNOVENTIONS   The pair of crescent-shaped buildings to your right and left just beyond Spaceship Earth house a constantly evolving 100,000-square-foot exhibit that showcases cutting-edge technologies and future products. Leading manufacturers sponsor ever-changing exhibit areas here. You'll get a chance to preview virtual reality, check out electric cars, experience interactive television, and try out more than 200 new computer programs and games. Kids will be thrilled to preview new Sega video games. It is a chance to feel, hear, and see the future, hands-on.

The **virtual reality offerings**—from swimming with sharks at the Vivid Group pod to a walking tour of St. Peter's Basilica by ENEL—are the latest high-tech wonders and a chance to experience what you have been reading about in science magazines.

There are several show areas: You can be interviewed by Jay Leno on TV; Sky Cyberguy takes you on a tour of the future of wireless communication; The Honeywell's Home Automation at the House of Innoventions Tour visits the computer-controlled abode of the future. The computer literate will find this a fascinating place to play, but the technologically challenged will find it less rewarding.

The two-story **Discovery Center,** located to the right of Innoventions, includes an information resource area where guests can get answers to all their questions about Epcot and Walt Disney World attractions. The Discovery Center also houses several shops including Field Trips, which features educational products and software.

✪ THE LIVING SEAS   This pavilion contains the world's sixth "ocean," a 5.7-million-gallon saltwater aquarium (complete with a coral reef) inhabited by more than 4,000 sea creatures including sharks, barracudas, parrot fish, rays, and dolphins among them. A 2½-minute multimedia preshow about today's ocean technology is followed by a 7-minute film demonstrating the formation of the earth and seas as a means to support life.

After the film, visitors enter hydrolators for a rapid descent to the ocean floor. Upon arrival, they board Seacabs that wind around a 400-foot-long tunnel to enjoy stunning close-up views of ocean denizens in a natural coral-reef habitat. The ride concludes in the Seabase Concourse, which is the visitor center of **Seabase Alpha,** a prototype ocean-research facility of the future. Here, informational modules focus on practical resources grown in controllable undersea environments, marine mammals, the study of oceanography from space, and life in a coral-reef community. You can step into a diver's JIM Suit and use controls to complete diving tasks, and expand your knowledge of oceanography via interactive computers.

Note: Via a program called **Epcot DiveQuest,** certified divers can participate in a program that includes a 30- to 40-minute scuba dive in the Living Seas aquarium; for details, call ☎ **407/WDW-TOUR.**

THE LAND   This largest of Future World's pavilions highlights humankind's relation to food and nature.

Living with the Land: A 13-minute boat ride takes you through three ecological environments (a rain forest, an African desert, and windswept American plains), each populated by appropriate audio-animatronic denizens. New farming methods and

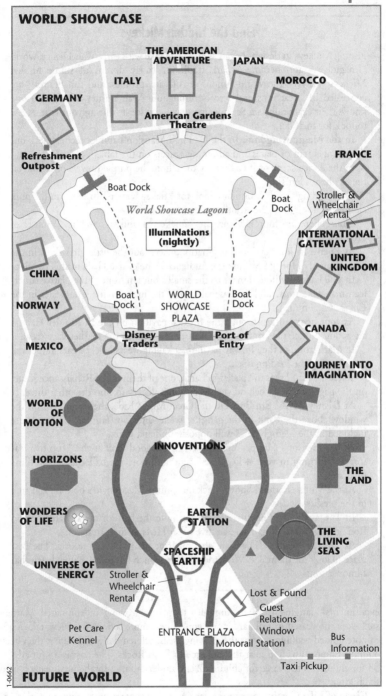

Epcot

WORLD SHOWCASE

THE AMERICAN ADVENTURE

JAPAN

ITALY

MOROCCO

GERMANY

American Gardens Theatre

Refreshment Outpost

FRANCE

Boat Dock

World Showcase Lagoon

Boat Dock

IllumiNations (nightly)

Stroller & Wheelchair Rental

INTERNATIONAL GATEWAY

UNITED KINGDOM

CHINA

NORWAY

Boat Dock

WORLD SHOWCASE PLAZA

Boat Dock

CANADA

MEXICO

Disney Traders

Port of Entry

JOURNEY INTO IMAGINATION

WORLD OF MOTION

INNOVENTIONS

HORIZONS

THE LAND

WONDERS OF LIFE

EARTH STATION

THE LIVING SEAS

UNIVERSE OF ENERGY

SPACESHIP EARTH

Stroller & Wheelchair Rental

Lost & Found

Guest Relations Window

Pet Care Kennel

ENTRANCE PLAZA

Monorail Station

Bus Information

Taxi Pickup

1-0662

FUTURE WORLD

Find the Hidden Mickeys

Hiding Mickeys in designs began as an inside joke with early Walt Disney World "Imagineers" and became a park tradition. Today dozens of subtle hidden Mickeys (HMs)—the world-famous set of ears, profiles, and full figures—are concealed in attractions and resorts throughout Walt Disney World. No one knows their exact number. See how many you can locate during your visit. A few to look for include:

In the Magic Kingdom: In the Haunted Mansion banquet scene, check out the arrangement of plates and adjoining saucers on the table.

In the Africa scene of It's a Small World, note the purple flowers on a vine on the elephant's left side.

While riding Splash Mountain, look for Mickey lying on his back in the pink clouds to the right of the steamboat.

Hint: There are four HMs in the Timekeeper and five in the Carousel of Progress.

At Epcot: In Journey into Imagination, check out the little girl's dress in the lobby film of "Honey I Shrunk the Audience," one of five HMs in this pavilion.

In The Land pavilion, don't miss the small stones in front of the Native American man on a horse and the baseball cap of the man driving a harvester in the *Circle of Life* film.

As your boat cruises through the Mexico pavilion on the El Rio del Tiempo attraction, notice the arrangement of three clay pots in the marketplace scene.

In Maelstrom, in the Norway pavilion, a Viking wears Mickey ears in the wall mural facing the loading dock.

There are four HMs in Spaceship Earth, one of them in the Renaissance scene, on the page of a book behind the sleeping monk. Try to find the other three.

At Disney-MGM Studios: On the Great Movie Ride, there's an HM on the window above the bank in the gangster scene, and four familiar characters are included in the hieroglyphics wall opposite Indiana Jones.

At Jim Henson's Muppet Vision 4-D, take a good look at the "Top five reasons for turning in your 4-D glasses" sign, and note the balloons in the film's final scene.

At the Monster Sound Show, check out Jimmy Macdonald's bolo tie and ring in the preshow video.

In The Twilight Zone Tower of Terror, note the bell for the elevator behind Rod Serling in the film. There are five other HMs in this attraction.

At Disney Resorts: There are also HMs at many Disney resorts. The best place to look for them is at Wilderness Lodge, which has more than a dozen that I know about.

experiments—ranging from hydroponics to plants growing in simulated Martian soil!—are showcased in real gardens. If you'd like a more serious overview, take a 45-minute guided walking tour of the growing areas, offered daily. Sign up at the Green Thumb Emporium shop near the entrance to Food Rocks. The cost is $5 for adults, $3 for children 3 to 9, free for children 2 and under. It's not, by the way, really geared to children.

Circle of Life: Combining spectacular live-action footage with animation, this 15-minute, 70mm motion picture based on *The Lion King* is a cautionary environmental tale.

Food Rocks: Audio-animatronic rock performers deliver an entertaining message about nutrition here.

✪ **JOURNEY INTO IMAGINATION**   In this terrific pavilion, even the fountains are magical, with arching streams of water that leap into the air like glass rods. Its major attractions are:

Honey I Shrunk the Audience: This 3-D attraction is based on the Disney hit *Honey I Shrunk the Kids* films. The audience, after being menaced by hundreds of mice and a 3-D cat, is shrunk and given a good shaking by a gigantic 5-year-old. Dramatic 3-D action is enhanced by vibrating seats and creepy tactile effects. Finally, everyone returns to proper size—everyone but the family dog, which creates the final, not altogether pleasant, special effect (I won't reveal it).

Journey into Imagination Ride: Visitors board moving cars for a 14-minute ride. After a simulated flight across the nighttime sky, you enter the "Imaginarium," where whimsical tableaux featuring audio-animatronic characters explore creativity in the fine arts, performing arts, literature, science, and technology. The ride culminates at Image Works.

Image Works: Here you'll find dozens of hands-on electronic devices and interactive computers. You can activate musical instruments by stepping on hexagons of colored light, participate in a TV drama, draw patterns with laser beams, and conduct an electronic philharmonic orchestra.

TEST TRACK   Called a mix of General Motors engineering and Disney imagineering, the newest Epcot attraction has guests in the driver's seat to experience the rigors of automobile testing. During a preshow (essentially a GM commercial) guests will learn how the company works to promote automotive safety, reliability, and performance. Then they'll board full-scale six-passenger test cars and travel on what appears to be an actual roadway, accelerating on long straight-aways, hugging hairpin turns, climbing steep hills, and braking abruptly—often in less-than-perfect road conditions. The ride will culminate with a terrifying high-speed outdoor run along the track's steeply banked "speed loop" that extends far beyond the pavilion facility. Cars will go at a top speed of 65 miles per hour. This was formerly World of Motion.

HORIZONS   This futuristic pavilion presents an unending series of new horizons. You board gondolas for a 15-minute journey into the next millennium. The first tableau honors visionaries of past centuries (like Jules Verne) and looks at outdated visions of the future and classic sci-fi movies. You'll ascend to an area where an IMAX film projected on two 80-foot-high screens presents a kaleidoscope of brilliant micro- and macroimages—growing crystals, colonies in space, a space shuttle launching, DNA molecules, and a computer chip. Then you'll travel to 21st-century cityscapes, desert farms, floating cities under the ocean's surface, and outer space colonies populated by audio-animatronic denizens. For the return to 20th-century earth, you can select one of three futuristic transportation systems: a personal spacecraft, a desert Hovercraft, or a minisubmarine.

✪ **WONDERS OF LIFE**   Housed in a vast geodesic dome fronted by a 75-foot replica of a DNA molecule, this pavilion offers some of Future World's most engaging shows and attractions, including the following:

The Making of Me: This captivating 15-minute motion picture starring Martin Short combines live action with animation and spectacular in-utero photography to create the sweetest introduction imaginable to the facts of life. Don't miss it, but expect some questions from young children.

Body Wars: You're miniaturized to the size of a single cell for a medical rescue mission inside the immune system of a human body. Your mission: save a miniaturized immunologist who has been accidentally swept into the bloodstream. This motion-simulator ride takes you on a wild journey through gale-force winds (in the lungs) and pounding heart chambers.

Cranium Command: In this hilarious multimedia attraction, Buzzy, an audio-animatronic brain-pilot-in-training, is charged with the seemingly impossible task of controlling the brain of a typical 12-year-old boy. The boy's body parts are played by Charles Grodin, Jon Lovitz, Bob Goldthwait, Kevin Nealon and Dana Carvey (as Hans and Franz), and George Wendt. It's another must-see attraction.

There are large areas filled with fitness-related shows, exhibits, and participatory activities, including a film called *Goofy About Health;* Coach's Corner, where your tennis, golf, or baseball swing is analyzed by experts; and the Sensory Funhouse, where you can test your perceptions. Both grown-ups and kids will enjoy playing here in air-conditioned comfort. Try working out on a video-enhanced exercise bike, get a computer-generated evaluation of your health habits, and take a video voyage to investigate the effects of drugs on your heart. There's much, much more. You could easily spend hours here.

UNIVERSE OF ENERGY This 32-minute ride-through attraction—with visitors seated in solar-powered "traveling theater" cars—aims to better our understanding of America's energy problems. Recently refurbished, it's called **Ellen's Energy Adventure** and features comedian and television star Ellen DeGeneres as an energy expert tutored to be a *Jeopardy!* contestant by Bill Nye, the Science Guy. On a massive screen in Theater I, an animated motion picture depicts the earth's molten beginnings, its cooling process, and the formation of fossil fuels. You'll move from Theater I to travel back 275 million years into an eerie storm-wracked landscape of the Mesozoic era, a time of violent geological activity. Here, you'll be menaced by giant audio-animatronic dragonflies, pterodactyls, dinosaurs, earthquakes, and streams of molten lava before entering a steam-filled tunnel deep through the bowels of the volcano to emerge back in the 20th century in Theater II. In this new setting, which looks like a NASA Mission Control room, a 70mm film projected on a massive 210-foot wraparound screen depicts the challenges of the world's increasing energy demands and the emerging technologies that will help meet them. Your moving seats now return to Theater I where swirling special effects herald a film about how energy impacts our lives. It all ends on an upbeat note, with a vision of an energy-abundant future and Ellen as a new *Jeopardy!* champion.

WORLD SHOWCASE

Surrounding a 40-acre lagoon at the park's southern end is World Showcase, a permanent community of 11 miniaturized nations, all with indigenous landmark architecture, landscaping, background music, restaurants, and shops. The cultural facets of each nation are explored in art exhibits, dance performances, innovative rides, films, and attractions. Employees in each pavilion are natives of the country represented.

✪ **CANADA** Our neighbors to the north are represented by diverse architecture ranging from a mansard-roofed replica of Ottawa's Château Laurier (here called the Hôtel du Canada) to a rustic stone building modeled after a famous landmark near Niagara Falls. A Native American village signifies the culture of the Northwest, while the Canadian wilderness is reflected by a steep mountain (a Canadian Rocky), a waterfall cascading into a white-water stream, and a "forest" of evergreens, stately cedars, maples, and birch trees. Don't miss the stunning floral displays inspired by the Butchart Gardens in Victoria, British Columbia. The pavilion's highlight attraction is *O Canada!,* a dazzling 18-minute, 360° Circle-Vision film that reveals Canada's scenic splendor. Canada pavilion shops carry everything from soapstone carvings and snow-shoes to rabbit-skin caps and heavy knitted sweaters—and, of course, maple syrup.

UNITED KINGDOM Centered on Brittania Square—a formal London-style park, complete with copper-roofed gazebo bandstand and a statue of the Bard—the U.K. pavilion evokes Merry Olde England. Four centuries of architecture are repre-sented along quaint cobblestone streets, troubadours and minstrels entertain in front of a traditional British pub, and a formal garden replicates the landscaping of 16th-and 17th-century palaces. High Street and Tudor Lane shops display a broad sampling of British merchandise, including toy soldiers, Paddington bears, Scottish tartans, and shortbreads. A tea shop occupies a replica of Anne Hathaway's thatch-roofed 16th-century cottage in Stratford-upon-Avon.

✪ FRANCE This pavilion is entered via a replica of the beautiful cast-iron Pont des Arts footbridge over the Seine. It leads to a park inspired by Seurat's painting *A Sunday Afternoon on the Island of La Grande Jatte*. A one-tenth replica of the Eiffel Tower looms above the *grands boulevards*. The highlight attraction is **Impressions de France.** Shown in a palatial (mercifully sit-down) theater à la Fontainebleau, this 18-minute film is a scenic journey through diverse French landscapes projected on a vast 200° wraparound screen. Emporia in the covered shopping arcade have interiors ranging from a turn-of-the-century bibliothèque to a French château. Merchandise includes French art prints, cookbooks, wines (there's a tasting counter), fancy French food-stuffs, Limoges boxes, Madeline and Babar books and dolls, perfumes, and original letters of famous Frenchmen ranging from Jean Cocteau to Napoléon. Another mar-ketplace revives the defunct Les Halles, where Parisians used to sip onion soup in the wee hours. The heavenly aroma of a boulangerie penetrates the atmosphere, and mimes, jugglers, and strolling chanteurs entertain.

MOROCCO This exotic pavilion is heralded by a replica of the Koutoubia Minaret, the prayer tower of a 12th-century mosque in Marrakesh. The Medina (old city), entered via a replica of an arched gateway in Fez, leads to Fez House (a traditional Moroccan home) and the narrow winding streets of the *souk,* a bustling marketplace where all manner of authentic handcrafted merchandise—pottery, Berber and Rabat carpets, ornate silver boxes, straw baskets, and prayer rugs—is on display. There are weaving demonstrations in the *souk* throughout the day. The Medina's rectangular courtyard centers on a replica of the ornately tiled Najjarine Fountain in Fez, the set-ting for musical entertainment. The pavilion's Royal Gallery contains an ever-changing exhibit of Moroccan art, and the Center of Tourism offers a continuous three-screen slide show.

JAPAN Heralded by a flaming-red *torii* (gate of honor) on the banks of the lagoon, and the graceful blue-roofed Goju No To pagoda (inspired by a shrine built at Nara in A.D. 700), this pavilion focuses on Japan's ancient culture. In a traditional Japanese garden, trees and flowering shrubs frame a contemplative setting of pebbled footpaths, rustic bridges, waterfalls, exquisite rock landscaping, and a pond of golden koi. The **Yakitori House** is based on the renowned 16th-century Katsura Imperial Villa in Kyoto, considered by many to be the crowning achievement of Japanese architecture. Exhibits ranging from 18th-century Bunraki puppets to samurai armor take place in the moated White Heron Castle, a replica of the Shirasagi-Jo, a 17th-century fortress overlooking the city of Himeji. And the **Mitsukoshi Department Store** (Japan's answer to Macy's) is housed in a replica of the Shishinden (Hall of Ceremonies) of the Gosho Imperial Palace built in Kyoto in A.D. 794. It sells lacquerware, kimonos, kites, fans, dolls, samurai swords, bonsai trees, Japanese foods, and even modern electronics.

In the courtyard, artisans demonstrate the ancient arts of *anesaiku* (shaping brown rice candy into dragons, unicorns, and dolphins), *sumi-e* (calligraphy), and *origami* (paper folding). Be sure to include a show of traditional Japanese music and dance at this pavilion in your schedule. It's one of the best in the World Showcase.

✪ AMERICAN ADVENTURE   Housed in a vast Georgian-style structure, the American Adventure is a 29-minute dramatization of U.S. history using a 72-foot rear-projection screen, rousing music, and a large cast of lifelike audio-animatronic figures, including narrators Mark Twain and Ben Franklin. The "adventure" begins with the voyage of the *Mayflower* and encompasses major historic events. You view Jefferson writing the Declaration of Independence, the expansion of the frontier, Mathew Brady photographing a family about to be divided by the Civil War, the stock market crash of 1929, the attack on Pearl Harbor, and the Eagle heading toward the moon. While waiting for the show to begin, you'll be entertained by the Voices of Liberty Singers performing American folk songs in the Main Hall. A shop called Heritage Manor Gifts sells signed presidential photographs, needlepoint samplers, quilts, Davy Crockett hats, books on American history, classic political campaign buttons, and vintage newspapers.

ITALY   One of the prettiest World Showcase pavilions, Italy lures visitors over an arched stone footbridge to a replica of the Venetian Doge's Palace. Other architectural highlights include the 83-foot campanile (bell tower) of St. Mark's Square, Venetian bridges, and a central piazza enclosing a version of Bernini's Neptune Fountain. A garden wall suggests a backdrop of provincial countryside, and Mediterranean citrus, olive trees, cypress, and pine frame a formal garden. Gondolas are moored on the lagoon. Shops here carry Perugina chocolates, kitchenware, cameo and filigree jewelry, Murano and Venetian glass, alabaster figurines, and inlaid wooden music boxes. A troupe of street actors performs a contemporary version of 16th-century commedia dell'arte in the piazza.

GERMANY   Enclosed by towered castle walls, this festive pavilion is centered on a cobblestone *platz* (plaza) with pots of colorful flowers girding a fountain statue of St. George and the Dragon. An adjacent clock tower is embellished with whimsical glockenspiel figures that herald each hour with quaint melodies. The pavilion's outdoor biergarten—where it's Oktoberfest all year long—was inspired by medieval Rothenberg. Shops here carry cuckoo clocks, cowbells, Alpine hats, German wines (there's a tasting counter), toys (including an extensive selection of beautiful German dolls and teddy bears), and books. An artisan demonstrates the molding and painting of Hummel figures; another paints exquisite detailed scenes on eggs.

✪ CHINA   Bounded by a serpentine wall that snakes around its outer perimeter, the China pavilion is entered via a vast ceremonial gate inspired by the Temple of Heaven in Beijing. Passing through the gate, you'll see a half-size replica of this ornate red-and-gold circular temple, built in 1420 during the Ming Dynasty. Gardens simulate those in Suzhou, with miniature waterfalls, fragrant lotus ponds, groves of bamboo, and weeping mulberry trees. The highlight attraction here is ***Wonders of China,*** a 20-minute, 360° Circle-Vision film that explores 6,000 years of dynastic and Communist rule and the breathtaking diversity of the Chinese landscape. Adjacent to the theater, an art gallery houses changing exhibits of Chinese art. A bustling marketplace offers an array of merchandise including silk robes, jade figures, cloisonné vases, dolls, fans, and wind chimes. Artisans here demonstrate calligraphy.

NORWAY   Centered on a picturesque cobblestone courtyard, this pavilion evokes ancient Norway. A *stavekirke* (stave church), styled after the 13th-century Gol Church of Hallingdal, houses changing exhibits. A replica of Oslo's 14th-century Akershus

Castle, next to a cascading woodland waterfall, is the setting for the pavilion's featured restaurant. Other buildings simulate the red-roofed cottages of Bergen and the timber-sided farm buildings of the Nordic woodlands. There's a two-part attraction here. **Maelstrom,** a boat ride in a dragon-headed Viking vessel, traverses Norway's fjords and mythical forests to the music of *Peer Gynt*—an exciting journey during which you'll be menaced by polar bears prowling the shore and trolls that cast a spell on the boat. The watercraft crashes through a narrow gorge and spins into the North Sea where a violent storm is in progress. But the storm abates, and passengers disembark safely in a 10th-century Viking village to view the 70mm film ***Norway,*** which documents a thousand years of history. Shops feature hand-knit wool hats and sweaters, toys (there's a Lego table where kids can play while you shop), wood carvings, Scandinavian foods, pewter ware, and jewelry.

MEXICO   You'll hear the music of marimba and mariachi bands as you approach the festive showcase of Mexico, fronted by a towering Mayan pyramid modeled on the Aztec Temple of Quetzalcoatl (God of Life). Upon entering the pavilion, you'll find yourself in a museum of pre-Colombian art and artifacts. Down a ramp is a small lagoon, the setting for **El Rio del Tiempo,** where visitors board boats for 8-minute cruises through Mexico's past and present. Shops in and around the Plaza de Los Amigos (a "moonlit" Mexican *mercado*) display an array of leather goods, baskets, sombreros, piñatas, pottery, jewelry, serapes, colorful papier-mâché birds, and blown-glass objects (an artisan gives demonstrations). La Casa de Vacaciones, sponsored by the Mexican Tourist Office, provides travel information.

SHOWS & SPECTACULARS

As at the Magic Kingdom, check your show schedule upon entering the park and plan ahead for one or more of the below-listed performances.

WORLD SHOWCASE PAVILION SHOWS   These international entertainments make up an important part of the Epcot experience. There are Chinese lion dancers and acrobats, German oompah bands, Caledonian bagpipers, Italian "living statues" and stilt walkers, colonial fife-and-drum groups, Moroccan belly dancers, and much more. Don't miss the Voices of Liberty Singers at American Adventure and the traditional music and dance displays in Japan.

✪ ILLUMINATIONS   A backdrop of classical music by international composers, high-tech lighting effects, darting laser beams, fireworks, and rainbow-lit dancing fountains combine to create this awesome 16½-minute Epcot spectacular, presented nightly. Each nation is highlighted in turn—colorful kites fly over Japan, the giant Rockies loom over Canada, a gingerbread house rises in Germany, and so on. Don't miss it! Find a seat around the lagoon about a half hour before show time.

RHYTHMS OF THE WORLD   Varied international cultural performances take place at the America Gardens Theater in World Showcase.

8 Disney-MGM Studios

Disney-MGM Studios offers exciting movie and TV-themed shows and behind-the-scenes "reel-life" adventures. Its main streets include Hollywood Boulevard and Sunset Boulevard, with art deco movie sets evocative of Hollywood's glamorous golden age. There's also a New York street lined with Gotham landmarks (the Empire State, Flatiron, and Chrysler buildings) and typical New York characters including peddlers hawking knock-off watches. More important, this is a working movie and TV studio, where shows are in production even as you tour the premises.

A Fairy-Tale Wedding

Fly down the aisle on Aladdin's magic carpet? Drive into the sunset in a glass coach pulled by six white horses? Have Mickey and Minnie greet guests at the reception? Take the plunge, literally and figuratively, on the Twilight Zone Tower of Terror?

If you've always dreamed of meeting Prince Charming, then having a fairy-tale wedding, the folks at Disney are happy to oblige—for a price. Recognizing that Disney World is a popular honeymoon destination, Disney in 1995 cut out the middleman and officially went into the wedding business. The first step was to build a multimillion-dollar, nondenominational chapel in the middle of Seven Seas Lagoon. The next was to let the world know Disney's wedding chapel was open for business. The first nuptials were televised live on the Lifetime cable channel. (With construction still in progress, the bride and groom wore white hard hats.) About 1,700 were married that first year, and now thousands of couples mix matrimony with Disney magic at the pavilion, which resembles a Victorian summer house.

An intimate gathering for two is about $2,000. The *average* Disney wedding costs $19,000 and is attended by 100 people (prince not included). People from as far away as the Netherlands have traveled to Orlando to celebrate their lifetime commitment. One couple had every guest wear Mickey Mouse ears to the ceremony. Another exchanged Donald and Daisy caps instead of wedding rings. A third walked out of the church to *"Zip-a-dee-doo-dah,"* and one blushing bride topped her veil with Mickey's famous ears. And those are just the examples Disney is willing to promote.

Certainly, there have been wackier nuptials—considering that wedding-bound couples are limited only by their imagination and their money. From rented coachmen to topiaries in the shape of Pluto, Disney serves up whichever Disney reference or character the couple desires, even if it is "Goofy."

Arrive at the park early, tickets in hand. Unlike the Magic Kingdom and Epcot, MGM's 110 acres of attractions can pretty much be seen in 1 day. The parking lot is right at the gate, although trams do run. Pay attention to your parking location, which is not as distinctly marked as in the Magic Kingdom.

If you don't get a *Disney-MGM Studios Guidemap* and *Entertainment Show Schedule* when you enter the park, you can pick them up at **Guest Services** (MGM's information center). First thing to do is check show times and work out an entertainment schedule based on highlight attractions and geographical proximity. My favorite MGM restaurants are described in the "Dining" section of this chapter. **Strollers** can be rented at Oscar's Super Service inside the main entrance. Note the "Character Spotlight" on the back of the guidemap. This will tell you the time and location that Disney characters will appear and be available for autographs.

✪ **THE TWILIGHT ZONE TOWER OF TERROR**　A thrilling journey to another dimension! Legend has it that during a violent storm on Halloween night 1939, lightning struck the Hollywood Tower Hotel, causing an entire wing—along with an elevator full of people—to disappear. Rod Serling is about to introduce you to those who disappeared as you become the star in a special episode of *The Twilight Zone*. After various spooky adventures, the ride ends in a dramatic climax: a terrifying 13-story fitful, free-fall plunge into *The Twilight Zone!* The best thrill ride at Disney with a "preshow" so authentic that maintenance crews kept fixing leaking pipes designed to drip as part of the ambience.

THE MAGIC OF DISNEY ANIMATION   You'll see Disney characters come alive at the stroke of a brush or pencil as you tour actual glass-walled animation studios and watch artists at work. The tour also includes entertaining video talks by animators and a grand finale of magical moments from Disney classics. Try to visit this popular attraction early in the morning—long lines form later in the day.

DISNEY-MGM STUDIO BACKLOT TOUR   This 25-minute tram tour takes you behind the scenes for a close-up look at the vehicles, props, costumes, sets, and special effects used in your favorite movies and TV shows. You'll see real costumers stitching away in wardrobe, the house facade of television's *The Golden Girls,* and even carpenters building sets. Most of the sets are pretty dated or from short-lived shows you've probably never seen. Things pick up considerably once the tram ventures into **Catastrophe Canyon,** where an earthquake causes canyon walls to rumble and riders are threatened by a raging fire, massive explosions, torrents of rain, and flash floods! Then you're taken behind the scenes to see how filmmakers use special effects to create such disasters. After the tram tour, visit **Studio Showcase,** a changing walk-through display of sets and props from popular and classic movies.

✪ **BACKSTAGE PASS TO *101 DALMATIANS***   Have a "De Vil" of a good time spotting Cruella and the other stars of Disney's live-action remake of the animated classic. The stark, eerie sets from Cruella's movie are among the top attractions during this short tour. Wizzer, the most fluid of the canine actors, is featured in a film about the life of a four-pawed star. Taking a cue from Universal, where you Ride the Movies, the special-effects show allows one lucky—usually tall and male—spectator to ride in the movies by re-creating Jeff Daniels' runaway bike scene. Real Dalmatians are also on display, but don't call PETA yet. The pups pull only 2-hour shifts and are treated better, one employee grumbled, than most of the two-legged "cast" members.

Note: This exhibit changes as Disney unveils its latest release. Other "Making of" shows are usually added as movies come out. Check your park schedule for information.

✪ **VOYAGE OF *THE LITTLE MERMAID***   Hazy light, creating an underwater effect in the reef-walled theater, helps set the mood for this charming musical spectacular based on the Disney feature film. The show combines live performers with more than 100 puppets, movie clips, and innovative special effects. It all has a happy ending, as most of the young audience knows it will—they've seen the movie.

✪ **THEATER OF THE STARS**   This 1,500-seat covered amphitheater is currently presenting a live Broadway-style production of *Beauty and the Beast,* based on the Disney movie version. Sets and costumes are lavish, production numbers spectacular. Arrive early to get a good seat. Also catch the *Hunchback of Notre Dame* stage show at the nearby theater.

Note: Disney often changes shows to tie in with recent movies. Some other Disney release may be highlighted during this show by the time you visit.

✪ **JIM HENSON'S MUPPET VISION 3-D**   Disney has slightly revamped this longtime favorite. The film still stars Kermit and Miss Piggy and combines Jim Henson's puppets with Disney audio-animatronics and special-effects wizardry, 70mm film, and cutting-edge 3-D technology. The coming-at-you action includes flying Muppets, cream pies, cannonballs, fiber-optic fireworks, bubble showers, even an actual spray of water. Statler and Waldorf critique the action (which includes numerous mishaps and disasters) from a mezzanine balcony. Kids in the first row interact with the characters. In the preshow area, guests view a hilarious Muppet video on overhead monitors and see an array of Muppet movie props.

STAR TOURS   A wild galactic journey based on the *Star Wars* trilogy (George Lucas collaborated on its conception), this action-packed adventure uses dramatic film footage and flight-simulator technology to transform the theater into a vehicle careening through space. The spaceship lurches out of control, and passengers experience sudden drops, violent crashes, and oncoming laser blasts. The harrowing ride ends safely, and you exit into a *Star Wars* merchandise shop. A good thrill, with generally short lines.

✪ THE GREAT MOVIE RIDE   Film footage and audio-animatronic replicas of movie stars take you on a nostalgic journey through some of the most famous scenes in movie history. The action is enhanced by dramatic special effects, and your tram is always hijacked en route by outlaws or gangsters. The setting for this attraction is a full-scale reproduction of Hollywood's famous Mann's Chinese Theatre, complete with hand- and footprints of the stars out front.

✪ ABC SOUND STUDIO ONE SATURDAY MORNING   Scream. Wave your hands. Making a little noise is likely to help get you from the audience onto the stage where you will then take part in creating the sound effects to go along with the video. The real stars are the tourists trying to make it all happen like the professionals. Volunteer. You're on vacation. You'll *probably* never see these people again. If you can't muster the gumption to go on stage, the postshow, Soundworks, provides the opportunity for a little joyful noise on interactive computers and away from the crowd.

SUPERSTAR TELEVISION   This 30-minute show takes guests through a broadcast day that spans TV history. During the preshow, "casting directors" choose volunteers from the audience to reenact 15 famous television scenes (arrive early if you want to snag a role and *wave that hand!*). The broadcast day begins with a 1955 black-and-white *Today* show featuring Dave Garroway and continues through *Late Night with David Letterman,* including scenes from a classic *I Love Lucy* episode (the candy factory), *General Hospital, Bonanza, Gilligan's Island, Cheers,* and *The Golden Girls,* among others. Real footage is mixed with live action, and though occasionally a star is born, there's plenty of fun watching amateur actors freeze up, flub lines, and otherwise deviate from the script.

GOOSEBUMPS HORRORLAND FRIGHT SHOW   Shows throughout the day from 9:30am to 4pm Monday through Saturday bring the scary characters from the R.L. Stine book series to life.

✪ INDIANA JONES EPIC STUNT SPECTACULAR   Visitors get an inside look at the world of movie stunts in this dramatic 30-minute show, which re-creates major scenes from the Indiana Jones series. The show opens on an elaborate Mayan temple backdrop. Indiana Jones crashes dramatically onto the set via a rope, and, as he searches with a torch for the golden idol, he encounters booby traps, fire and steam, and spears popping up from the ground before being chased by a rolling boulder! The set is dismantled to reveal a colorful Cairo marketplace where a sword fight ensues, and the action includes jumps from high places, virtuoso bullwhip maneuvers, lots of gunfire, and a truck bursting into flames. An explosive finale takes place in a desert scenario. Throughout, you'll get to see how elaborate stunts are pulled off and wonder how close the actors really do come to peril. (Here it is— another chance to be part of the fun. Arrive early and sit near the stage for your shot at short-lived stardom. Go ahead, you're running out of chances—*and this time you get to wear a turban.*)

PARADES, SHOWS, FIREWORKS & MORE   Disney plugs its soon-to-be classic Hercules in this parade. It features all of the movie's adorable cast and songs from the soundtrack that you and your children will, undoubtedly, soon have memorized. The parade takes place daily; check your entertainment schedule for route and times.

The ✪ **Sorcery in the Sky** fireworks show is presented nightly during summer and peak seasons. Check your entertainment schedule to see if it's on.

The **Visiting Celebrity** program features frequent appearances by stars such as Betty White, Burt Reynolds, Joan Collins, Leonard Nimoy, and Billy Dee Williams. They visit attractions, record their handprints in front of the Chinese Theater, and appear at question-and-answer sessions with park guests. Check your entertainment schedule to see if it's happening during your visit.

A movie set replica serves as a playground in the *Honey, I Shrunk the Kids* **Movie Set Adventure.** Outside props include 30-foot blades of grass, giant Legos, and a sliding pond made from an immense film reel.

Centering on a gleaming 14½-foot bronze Emmy, the **Academy of Television Arts & Sciences Hall of Fame Plaza,** adjacent to SuperStar Television, honors TV legends. Bronze sculptures of Carol Burnett, Sid Caesar, Red Skelton, Milton Berle, and other television luminaries are displayed.

9 Animal Kingdom

Disney's fourth major park combines animals, elaborate landscapes, and rides to create yet another reason not to venture outside of Disney World. Michael Eisner says it's the next best thing to going to Africa, and it is interesting to see how Disney integrates the wonders of nature with the magic of make-believe, but don't cancel that safari vacation.

Open since spring 1998, Animal Kingdom is divided into five "regions": The Oasis, a main entryway; Safari Village, a shopping area/entertainment area; Dinoland U.S.A., focusing on issues of extinction; Camp Minnie-Mickey, the equivalent of ToonTown in the Magic Kingdom; and Africa, the main animal viewing area, which is dedicated to African wildlife.

The park covers more than 500 acres, nearly twice the size of Epcot. At the heart of it all is a 14-story "Tree of Life," an intricately carved free-form representation of animals hand-crafted by Disney artists. This impressive landmark is nearly as tall and as imposing as the silver golf-ball dome, also known as Spaceship Earth, that has come to best symbolize Epcot. The "Asia" section of the park is expected to open late in 1999.

THE OASIS

Basically the garden entrance to the park, the painstakingly designed landscaped sets with streams, grottoes, and waterfalls, sets the tone for the rest of the park.

SAFARI VILLAGE

Like Cinderella's Castle in the Magic Kingdom and the silver, golf-ball dome in Epcot, the 14-story Tree of Life located here is the park's central landmark. It is an intricately carved free-form representation of animals hand-crafted by Disney artists. Teams of artists worked for months creating the various sculptures, and it is worth a leisurely stroll. One of the creators says he expects it to become one of the most photographed works of art in the world.

IT'S TOUGH TO BE A BUG!   The creepy (crawly) special effects of this tour of a bug's life will keep you on the edge of your seat. Fun for the family but not for the arachnaphobic. Located inside the Tree of Life in a 430-seat theater.

DISCOVERY RIVER BOATS   Rolling along the river may be just the thing to give adults an overview of what they are going to see. This is a leisurely tour of the many attractions and gives you a good idea of what you put at the top of your list. Children, however, may find it hard to keep still if they have just entered the park, so you may want to save this for later in the day when your feet need a rest.

THE GARDEN PATH   A leisurely stroll (are you detecting a theme here?) through the root system of The Tree of Life. This soft landscape is filled with otters, flamingos, tamarinds, lemurs, tortoises, and colorful ducks, storks, cranes, and cockatoos.

DINOLAND U.S.A.

Enter by passing under "Olden Gate Bridge," a 40-foot tall Brachiosaurus reassembled from excavated fossils and you will find a world filled with a series of wooden cabins and national-park-like structures that give the land a nostalgic '50s and '60s look.

JOURNEY INTO JUNGLE BOOK   He's still the King of the Swingers, so come and relive the adventures of Mowgli, the man-child abandoned as a baby and raised by wolves. When Mowgli's life is threatened by a fierce Bengal tiger, a wise and caring panther attempts to guide the boy back to the "man-village" where he rightfully belongs.

COUNTDOWN TO EXTINCTION   This ride is along the same lines as *Star Wars* and *Body Wars*, with stationary seating that bobs and weaves in front of a special effects screen. This has got nothing on *Back to the Future*, but it is a bit of a thrill. One minute you're entering the Dino Institute to study creatures that roamed the earth long ago. The next you're hurtling back 65 million years to rescue the last dinosaur from extinction. Along the way you dip and soar avoiding asteroids and snarling dinos while speeding toward a happy ending.

CRETACEOUS TRAIL   Wander back in time as you stroll down a path filled with living plants and animal species that have survived since the age of the dinosaur. You'll encounter a Chinese alligator, Florida soft-shelled turtle, and red-legged seriama. Along the way, you'll discover the evolution of a dig site.

THE BONEYARD   Kids love the chance to slip, slither, slide, and crawl through this giant playground and dig site. Discover the remains of triceratops, T-rex, and other vanished giants. You can even dig up the bones of a woolly mammoth in the dig site.

CONSERVATION STATION   This offers a behind-the-scenes look at how Disney cares for animals inside the park. It includes the **Affection Section,** where you can cuddle with some friendly animals, explore their private habitats, and learn how they are cared for and fed. Check out Eco Heroes, interactive videos that connect you to endangered animal information, world-famous biologists and conservationists, and Song of the Rainforest, surrounding you with the sounds of the endangered wildlife of that deep jungle. But, unless you are into doing a little research on your vacation, skip Eco Web, a computer link to conservation organizations worldwide.

CAMP MINNIE-MICKEY

Join your favorite Disney characters "on vacation" in Camp Minnie-Mickey, an entire land that re-creates a kid-friendly Adirondack resort.

COLORS OF THE WIND   Pocahontas and Grandmother Willow and some new creatures from the forest perform in a stage show at Grandmother Willow's Grove, a cozy 350-seat theater.

FESTIVAL OF *THE LION KING* Arrive early for this popular attraction that regularly draws enough people to fill the 1,000-seat pavilion. Based loosely on the animated movie, this stage show combines the pageantry of a parade with a tribal celebration. In an interesting switch, the audience is seated in the center of the theater as the action moves around them.

CHARACTER GREETING PAVILIONS This is a must for people traveling with children. A variety of Disney characters greet you, from Winnie the Pooh to Timon and Baloo. Mickey, in recognition of the his star status, can be found in his own pavilion.

AFRICA

Enter through the town of Harambe, a realistic representation of an African coastal village poised on the edge of the 21st century. Whitewashed structures built of coral stone and thatched with reed by craftsmen brought over from Africa surround a central marketplace rich with local wares and colors.

GORILLA FALLS EXPLORATION TRAIL There are no visible barriers between you and the animals as you watch a troop of African gorillas emerging from the reeds. Bathed in lush jungle foliage, this entire area is filled with exotic East African animals that range from toothy reptiles to brightly colored birds. Don't forget to visit the underwater hippo-viewing area and a savanna overlook.

KILIMANJARO SAFARIS This is one of the few "rides" in the park. Visitors board a safari vehicle to explore 100 lush acres of savanna, forest, rivers, and rocky hills, all graced with hundreds of free roaming animals. There are some surprises as your bush pilot tries to escape a band of poachers.

10 Other Walt Disney World Attractions

✪ TYPHOON LAGOON

Located off Lake Buena Vista Drive, halfway between Walt Disney World Village and Disney-MGM Studios, this is the ultimate in water theme parks. Its fantasy setting is a palm-fringed tropical island village of ramshackle tin-roofed structures, strewn with wreckage left by a legendary "great typhoon." A storm-stranded fishing boat dangles precariously atop the 95-foot-high Mount Mayday, the steep setting for several major park attractions. Every half hour the boat's smokestack erupts, shooting a 50-foot geyser of water into the air.

In summer, arrive no later than 9am to avoid long lines; the park is often filled to capacity by 10am and closed to later arrivals. Beach towels and lockers can be obtained for a minimal fee, and all beach accessories can be purchased at Singapore Sal's. Light fare is available at two restaurants, and there are picnic tables. Guests are not permitted to bring their own floatation devices into the park.

The major attraction, of course, is **Typhoon Lagoon,** a large and lovely blue lagoon, the size of two football fields and surrounded by white sandy beach. It's the park's main swimming area; young children can wade in the lagoon's peaceful bay or cove.

Hop onto a raft or inner tube and meander along the lazy 2,100-foot Castaway Creek. Circling the lagoon, **Castaway Creek** tumbles through a misty rain forest and past caves and secluded grottoes. There are exits along the route where you can leave the creek; if you do the whole thing, it takes about a half hour. There's also a variety of water slides and three white-water rides (Keelhaul Falls has the most winding spiral route, Mayday Falls the steepest drops and fastest water, while the slightly tamer Gangplank Falls uses large tubes so the whole family can ride together).

Guests are given free snorkel equipment (and instruction) for a 15-minute swim through **Shark Reef,** a 362,000-gallon simulated coral-reef tank populated by about 4,000 colorful denizens of the deep. If you don't want to get in the water, you can observe the fish via portholes in a walk-through area.

Many of the above-mentioned attractions require guests to be at least 4 feet tall. But the **Ketchakiddie Creek** section of the park is a kiddie area exclusively for those under 4 feet. An innovative water playground, it has bubbling fountains to frolic in, small water slides, a pint-sized white-water tubing adventure, spouting whales and squirting seals, rubbery crocodiles to climb on, grottoes to explore, and waterfalls to loll under.

✪ BLIZZARD BEACH

Blizzard Beach is Disney's newest, and zaniest, water park—a 66-acre "ski resort" in the midst of a tropical lagoon. The park centers on a 90-foot snowcapped mountain (Mt. Gushmore), which swimmers ascend via chairlifts, and the on-premises restaurant resembles a ski lodge.

It's located on World Drive, just north of the All-Star Sports and Music resorts. Arrive at or before park opening to avoid long lines and to be sure you get in. Beach towels and lockers are available for a small charge, and you can buy beach accessories at the Beach Haus.

Mt. Gushmore attractions include **Summit Plummet,** which starts 120 feet up and makes a 55-mile-per-hour plunge straight down to a splash landing at the base of the mountain, and the **Slush Gusher,** another Mt. Gushmore speed slide (a bit tamer than the above) that travels along a snowbanked mountain gully. **Teamboat Springs** is the world's longest white-water raft ride, with six-passenger rafts twisting down a 1,200-foot series of rushing waterfalls; and other water slides, flumes, an inner-tube run, and a chairlift complete the fun.

A nice-sized sandy beach below Mt. Gushmore offers **Tike's Peak,** a scaled-down kiddie version of Mt. Gushmore attractions; **Melt-Away-Bay,** a 1-acre free-form wave pool fed by melting-snow waterfalls; **Cross Country Creek,** where inner tubers can float in a lazy circle around the entire park; and **Ski Patrol Training Camp,** which is designed for preteens and features a rope swing, a T-bar drop over water, slides, and a challenging ice-floe walk along slippery floating icebergs.

RIVER COUNTRY

One of the many recreational facilities at the Fort Wilderness Resort campground, this miniature water park is themed after Tom Sawyer's swimming hole. Kids can scramble over artificial boulders that double as diving platforms over a 330,000-gallon clearwater pool. Two 16-foot water slides also provide access to the pool. Attractions on the adjacent Bay Lake, which is equipped with ropes and ships' booms for climbing, include a pair of flumes—one 260 feet long, the other, 100 feet—that corkscrew through **Whoop-N-Holler Hollow; White Water Rapids,** which carries inner tubers along a winding 230-foot creek with a series of chutes and pools; and the **Ol' Wading Pool,** a smaller version of the swimming hole designed for young children. There are poolside and beachside areas for sunning and picnicking, plus a 350-yard boardwalk nature trail. Beach towels and lockers can be obtained for a minimal fee. Light fare is available at Pop's Place.

To get here, take a launch from the dock near the entrance to the Magic Kingdom or a bus from its Transportation and Ticket Center.

FANTASIA GARDENS

In an ever-growing effort to remove all reasons to leave Disney property, 1996 saw the addition of this 18-hole miniature golf course based on the characters of the classic Disney animated film *Fantasia*. Hippos dance, broomsticks leap, and magic abounds, but it's still up to you to sink that hole in one.

11 Universal Studios Florida & Islands of Adventure

✪ UNIVERSAL STUDIOS FLORIDA

Universal Studios Florida, 1000 Universal Studios Plaza (☎ **407/363-8000; www.usf.com**), bills itself as the "No. 1 Movie Studio and Theme Park in the World." It is a working motion-picture and television production studio, although most of the production goes on inside at the Nickelodeon sound stages. But remember cable's *The Swamp Thing* or the short-lived *SeaQuest*? Those television series were shot on the property. Occasionally visitors will come upon an actual working shoot. But every day you will amble amid reel history in the form of some 40 actual sets displayed along "Hollywood Boulevard" and "Rodeo Drive." On hand to greet visitors are Hanna-Barbera characters (Yogi Bear, Scooby Doo, Fred Flintstone, and others) and a talented group of actors representing Universal stars from Harpo Marx to the Blues Brothers.

A 1-day ticket costs $44.52 for ages 10 and over, $36.04 for children 3 to 9; a 2-day ticket is $63.33 for ages 10 and over, $52.73 for children 3 to 9; an annual pass (admission for a full year) is $79.50 for ages 10 and over, $63.60 for children 3 to 9; children 2 and under enter free. Parking costs $6 per vehicle, $7 for RVs and trailers.

The park is open 365 days a year from 9am; closing hours vary seasonally, so call before you go. To get there, take I-4 east, making a left on Sand Lake Road, then a right onto Turkey Lake Road, and follow the signs.

MAJOR ATTRACTIONS

Rides and attractions use cutting-edge technology, such as OMNIMAX 70mm film projected on seven-story screens, to create terrific special effects. While waiting in line, you'll be entertained by excellent preshows, better even than those at *that other theme park*. Universal, as a whole, takes itself less seriously than the Mouse That Roared, and the atmosphere is peppered by subtle reminders that in the competitive 1990s it is *not* a small world after all.

CITYWALK   The 12-acre entertainment complex could easily be renamed theme-restaurant heaven. Not only is it home to the world's largest **Hard Rock Cafe**—the grande dame of all theme restaurants—but also the **NASCAR Cafe,** the **Motown Cafe,** and **Marvel Mania,** a theme send-up of villains and superheroes. CityWalk, which opened in 1998, also contains a hearty dose of Cajun spice with **Pat O'Brien's,** a re-creation of the joint in New Orleans, and **Emeril's of New Orleans,** featuring the Creole-based cuisine of chef Emeril Lagasse. If that's not enough to keep you busy, there is the **Down Beat Jazz Hall of Fame,** a tribute to reggae mon Bob Marley, and a 5,000-seat **Cineplex Odeon Megaplex.**

Finally, celebrity hounds may catch a live taping involving one of their favorite stars at the E! Entertainment Television Production Center.

A DAY IN THE PARK WITH BARNEY   Set in a parklike theater-in-the-round, this musical show, starring the popular purple one, Baby Bop, and BJ, uses song, dance, and interactive play to deliver an environmental message. For young children, this could be the highlight of the day.

TERMINATOR 2: 3-D BATTLE ACROSS TIME   He's back, at least in Orlando. This is billed as "the quintessential sight and sound experience for the 21st century!" James Cameron, the director of *T2* (and the more recent smash *Titanic*), has overseen this production. It features the Big Man, Ahrrnaald, himself, along with other original cast members, and combines 70mm 3-D film (using three 23-by-50-foot screens) with live stage action and thrilling technical effects.

JAWS   You didn't *really* think it was safe to go back into the water, did you? As your boat heads out to the open seas, an ominous dorsal fin appears on the horizon. What follows is a series of terrifying attacks from a 3-ton, 32-foot-long great white shark that tries to sink its teeth into passengers. And there's more trouble ahead. The boat is surrounded by a 30-foot wall of flame from burning fuel that let's you truly feel the heat. I won't tell you how it ends, but let's just say, blackened shark, anyone? (The effects are more startling after dark.)

E.T. ADVENTURE   You'll be given a passport to E.T.'s home, which needs his healing powers to rejuvenate it. You'll soar with E.T. on a mission to save his ailing planet, through the forest and into space, aboard a star-bound bicycle, all to the accompaniment of that familiar movie theme music. A cool wooded forest serves as one of the most pleasant waits for any ride in Central Florida, and the ride is worth the wait.

✪ **BACK TO THE FUTURE**   You'll blast through the space-time continuum, plummet into volcanic tunnels ablaze with molten lava, collide with Ice Age glaciers, thunder through caves and canyons, and be swallowed by a dinosaur in this spectacular multisensory adventure. You twist, you turn, you dip and dive and feel like you are really flying. Stick to seats in the back of the car to avoid ruining the illusion by glimpsing your neighbors careening hydraulically in the next bay.

✪ **KONGFRONTATION**   It's the last thing the Big Apple needs—King Kong is back! As you stand in line in a replica of a grungy, graffiti-scarred New York subway station, CBS newsman Roland Smith reports on Kong's terrifying rampage. Everyone must evacuate to Roosevelt Island, so it's all aboard the tram. Cars collide and hydrants explode below, police helicopters hover overhead putting you directly in the line of fire, the tram malfunctions, and, of course, you encounter Kong—32 feet tall and 13,000 pounds. He emits banana breath in your face and menaces passengers, dangling the tram over the East River. A great thrill, or just another day in New York.

✪ **EARTHQUAKE, THE BIG ONE**   You board a BART train in San Francisco for a peaceful subway ride, but just as you pull into the Embarcadero station there's an earthquake—the big one, 8.3 on the Richter scale! As you sit helplessly trapped, vast slabs of concrete collapse around you, a propane truck bursts into flames, a runaway train comes hurtling at you, and the station floods (60,000 gallons of water cascade down the steps).

TWISTER   Visitors from the twister-prone Midwest may find this re-creation a little too close to the real thing. An ominous funnel cloud, 5 stories tall, is created by 2 million cubic feet of air per minute. The freight-train fills the theater, and cars, signs, and trucks fly about as the audience watches just 20 feet away. The windy version of Earthquake.

NICKELODEON STUDIOS TOUR   You'll tour the soundstages where Nick shows are produced, view concept pilots, visit the kitchen where gak and green slime are made, play typical show games, and try out new Sega video games. There's lots of audience participation, and one volunteer will get slimed.

WILD, WILD, WILD WEST SHOW   Stunt people demonstrate falls from three-story balconies, gun and whip fights, dynamite explosions, and other oater staples. This is a well-performed, lively show that is especially popular with foreign visitors with celluloid visions of the American west. Kids, do not try this at home.

BEETLEJUICE GRAVEYARD REVUE   Dracula, Wolfman, the Phantom of the Opera, Frankenstein and his bride, and Beetlejuice put on a funky, and very funny, rock musical with pyrotechnic special effects and MTV-style choreography. Loud and lively enough to scare some small children.

THE FUNTASTIC WORLD OF HANNA-BARBERA   This motion-simulator ride takes guests careening through the universe in a spaceship piloted by Yogi Bear to rescue Elroy Jetson. Before this wild ride, you'll learn about how cartoons are created. After it, in an interactive area, you can experiment with animation sound effects—boing! plop! splash!—color in your own cartoons. This is a great place for kids of all ages to take some time and play.

ADDITIONAL ATTRACTIONS

Other park attractions include the **Gory, Gruesome & Grotesque Horror Makeup Show** for a behind-the-scenes look at the transformation scenes from movies like *The Fly* and *The Exorcist;* **a tribute to Lucille Ball,** America's queen of comedy; **Fievel's Playland,** an innovative Western-themed playground based on the Spielberg movie *An American Tail; Hercules & Xena, Wizards of The Screen,* which puts you on the set with the buff gladiators as the audience battles to make the sound effects match the videos; and **Alfred Hitchcock's 3-D Theatre,** a tribute to the master of suspense in which Tony Perkins narrates a reenactment of the famous shower scene from *Psycho,* and *The Birds,* as if it weren't scary enough, becomes an in-your-face 3-D movie.

Descendants of Lassie, Benji, Mr. Ed, and other animal superstars perform their famous pet tricks in the **Animal Actors Show.** During **Screen Test Home Video Adventure,** a director, crew, and team of "cinemagicians" put visitors on the screen in an exciting video production. And **Dynamite Nights Stuntacular,** a nightly show, combines death-defying stunts with a breathtaking display of fireworks.

More than 25 shops in the park sell everything from Lucy collectibles to Bates Motel towels, and restaurants run the gamut from Mel's Drive-In (of *American Graffiti* fame) to the Hard Rock Cafe to Schwab's.

ISLANDS OF ADVENTURE

Universal's second park is scheduled to open in 1999 with a vibrantly colored, cleverly themed collection of fast, fun rides for kids of all ages. With Steven Spielberg on board as creative consultant, Islands of Adventure will contain some of the most thrilling and technologically advanced rides and attractions ever made, as well as the world's most beloved characters. Divided into four areas, Seuss Landing, Toon Lagoon, Lost Continent, and Jurassic Park, this park offers the biggest concentration of thrill rides and coasters of any park in the area. Park hours and ticket prices had not been released at press time but should be similar to Universal Studios Florida (see above). For information online, check out www.usf.com.

SEUSS LANDING

This 10-acre island is the only place in the world where Dr. Suess's world-famous characters and children's books are brought to life.

CAT IN THE HAT   Six-passenger couches travel through 18 show scenes past Thing 1, Thing 2. The highlight is a revolving 24-foot tunnel that alters your perceptions and leaves your head spinning.

ONE FISH, TWO FISH, RED FISH, BLUE FISH   The point here is to avoid getting sprayed as you guide your fish through the ride taking directions from a Seussian rhyme. Of course, if the kids are driving, bring a raincoat. Special adaptations are available for guests with disabilities to enjoy the fire from their chair.

CARO-SEUSS-EL   Go in and out, up and down on one of seven characters from the world of Seuss, including the elephant-birds from *Horton Hatches an Egg*.

SYLVESTER MCMONKEY MCBEAN'S VERY UNUSUAL DRIVING MACHINES   The name is almost as long as the ride, but children will love steering along the elevated track through Seuss Landing.

IF I RAN THE ZOO   An interactive playland for kids of all ages, this includes everything from flying water snakes to a chance to tickle the toes of a Seussian animal. A nice place to let the kids burn off some excited energy.

Marvel Super Hero Island

Thrill junkies will love the twisting, turning, and stomach-churning rides based on characters from Marvel Comics.

THE SPIDER-MAN ADVENTURE   Combines moving rides with 3-D action and special effects taking guests on a tour of the Daily Bugle where Peter Parker suddenly encounters evil villains and becomes Spider-Man. The high-tech ride, similar to Back to the Future, includes a simulated 400-foot drop that feels an awful lot like the real thing.

INCREDIBLE HULK COASTER   Blasting from zero to 40 miles per hour in 2 seconds, you'll spin upside down 100 feet from the ground. Coaster lovers love this 2-minute, 15-second ride that includes seven roll-overs and two deep drops.

DR. DOOM'S FEARFALL   You are in for a rush as you drop, with feet dangling, down one of two, 200-foot steel towers. It's similar to Tower of Terror at Disney, but with the added thrill of hanging free.

Toon Lagoon

More than 150 life-sized sculpted cartoon images let you know you have entered this section dedicated to your favorites from the Sunday funnies.

DUDLEY DO-RIGHT'S RIPSAW FALLS   This water ride, touted as the first flume ride to send riders plummeting below the water's surface, takes you around a 400,000-gallon lagoon, culminating in a 75-foot drop at 50 miles per hour. Once again you will get wet. Very wet.

POPEYE & BLUTO'S BILGE RAT BARGES   Whirling 12-person rafts bump and churn their way through a white-water ride encountering some scary creatures along the way, including the twirling octopus boat wash. *Note:* You can get completely soaked.

COMIC STRIP LANE   Beetle Bailey, Hagar the Horrible, and Dagwood and Blondie are highlighted in this lively jaunt through some of the best-loved comic strips of all time.

Jurassic Park

Okay, stay with me here. This is the theme park creation based on a movie featuring a theme park creation that might become a movie. Yes, all the basics from Stephen Spielberg's wildly successful movies, and some of the high-tech wizardry, are incorporated in a lushly landscaped tropical locale.

JURASSIC PARK RIVER ADVENTURE   Come face to face with the living, breathing inhabitants of Jurassic Park. Five-story dinosaurs come within inches of the ride where Tyrannosaurus Rex decides you look like a tasty morsel. To escape you take an 85-foot plunge straight down the longest, fastest, steepest water descent ever built.

TRICERATOPS ENCOUNTER Pet a "living" dinosaur and learn from the trainers about the care and feeding of the 24-foot long, 10-foot-high triceratops. The creature's responses to touch include realistic blinks and muscle flinches.

DISCOVERY CENTER Within the celebrated gates of Jurassic Park's Visitors Center, guests will find a variety of entertaining and educational opportunities. Mostly a good place to play in the air-conditioning with a lot of stuff kids of all ages can touch and enjoy.

PTERANODON FLYERS Get a bird's-eye view of the Jurassic Park compound while soaring on the backs of these gentle flying dinosaurs.

CAMP JURASSIC This interactive play area offers everything from lava pits with undiscovered dinosaur bones to a rain forest. Watch out for the dangerous spitters.

Lost Continent

Although they've mixed their millennia here—ancient Greek gods with medieval forests—Universal has done a great job creating a foreboding mood in this newest section of the park.

ESCAPE FROM THE LOST CITY Similar to the Earthquake attraction in the other Universal park, this ride exposes you to torrents of waters and blasts of heat and fire. The idea is that parkgoers are trapped in the midst of a battle between Poseidon, the god of water, and Zeus, who hurls fire. It's more interesting than frightening, but it still offers a thrill.

DUELING DRAGONS This coaster ride holds you suspended with your legs dangling freely beneath you, like you're sitting on a jet-propelled swing. Be warned—it's not for the faint of heart. The intertwined tracks add an extra element of excitement as you zip through at 60 miles per hour. At times, riders of the dueling coasters are just 12 inches apart. I recommend the very first seat for a truly thrilling ride.

THE 8TH VOYAGE OF SINBAD This stunt show explores the next voyage of the mythical traveler and relies heavily on pyrotechnics for its thrill factor. May be too intense for younger children.

12 Sea World

This popular 200-plus-acre marine-life park, at 7007 Sea World Dr. (☎ **407/ 351-3600,** www.seaworld.com), explores the mysteries of the deep in a format that combines entertainment with wildlife-conservation awareness. Bell-bottoms and Marcia Brady prints may be the current rage in fashion, but Sea World of Florida certainly made the right decision updating its dated 1970s look.

A 55-foot lighthouse topped with a rotating white light in the middle of a harbor decorated with the a painting of Shamu anchors the nautically themed renovation. To get to the beacon, visitors will walk underneath a sea of blue and aquamarine "metal waves" and cross wooden bridges nestled amid a rocky shore complete with lapping water and splashing waves.

The upgrades of the ticket booths, turnstiles, guest relations window, tram stop, and a new gift shop make this a world to see. A second phase is in the works, so visitors may encounter some dust.

But it is worth visiting this beautifully landscaped park, centering on a 17-acre lagoon that includes flamingo and pelican ponds and a lush tropical rain forest. Shamu, a killer whale, is the star of the park, along with his expanding family, including several baby whales. The pace is much more laid-back than either Universal or Disney and is a good way to end a long week of trudging through the other parks. Be sure to budget some extra money to buy smelt to feed the animals—the close encounters offered at many wading and feeding pools are more than half the fun. Sea World can't compete with the high-tech wonders abounding elsewhere, but where else can you discover that a stingray feels like crushed velvet or learn the song of a seal?

A 1-day ticket costs $44.52 for ages 10 and over, $36.04 for children 3 to 9; children 2 and under enter free. Parking costs $6 per vehicle, $7 for RVs and trailers.

The park is open 365 days a year from 9am to 7pm, later during summer and holidays when there are additional shows at night. Call before you go. To get there, take I-4 to the Bee Line Expressway (Fla. 528) and follow the signs.

MAJOR ATTRACTIONS

✪ **WILD ARCTIC**   Enveloping guests in the beauty, exhilaration, and danger of a polar expedition, Wild Arctic combines a high-definition adventure film with flight-simulator technology to evoke breathtaking Arctic panoramas. After a hazardous flight over the frozen north, visitors emerge at a remote research base—home to four polar bears (including star residents and polar twins Klondike and Snow), seals, walruses, and white beluga whales.

✪ **JOURNEY TO ATLANTIS**   This is the park's first true thrill ride. Taking a cue from Disney Imagineerers, Sea World has created a story line to go with the ride—something about Greek fishermen and ancient Sirens in a battle over good and evil. (A "media horde" is somehow involved.) But what really matters is the promise of "two of the steepest, wettest, fastest drops to be found in any theme park."

The bottom line is a wild ride down with 60-foot drops and the promise of "luge-like curves." Journey to Atlantis breaks from Sea World's "edutainment" formula that seemed to stress equal measures of learning and fun. No hidden lessons here, it's just a splashy thrill.

✪ **MERMAIDS, MYTHS & MONSTERS**   This nighttime multimedia spectacular is a must-see, featuring fireworks and hologram-like imagery against a towering 60-foot screen of illuminated water. King Neptune rises majestically from the deep, as do terrifying sea serpents, storm-tossed ships, and frolicking mermaids. Not quite the Disney fireworks, but an interesting show worth waiting for.

TERRORS OF THE DEEP   This exhibit houses 220 specimens of venomous and otherwise scary sea creatures in a tropical-reef habitat. Immense acrylic tunnels provide close encounters with slithery eels, three dozen sharks, barracudas, lionfish, and poisonous pufferfish. A theatrical presentation focusing on sharks puts across the message that pollution and uncontrolled commercial fishing make humankind the ultimate "terror of the deep."

✪ **MANATEES: THE LAST GENERATION?**   Today the Florida manatee is in danger of extinction, with as few as 2,000 remaining. Underwater viewing stations, innovative cinema techniques, and interactive displays combine to create an exciting format for teaching visitors about the manatee and its fragile ecosystem. Also on display here are hundreds of other native fish as well as alligators, turtles, and shorebirds.

✪ **KEY WEST AT SEA WORLD**   It's not quite the way Ernest Hemingway saw it, but this 5-acre paved paradise dotted with palms, hibiscus, and bougainvillea is set in a Caribbean village offering island cuisine, street vendors, and entertainers. The attraction comprises three naturalistic animal habitats: Stingray Lagoon, where visitors enjoy hands-on encounters with harmless southern diamond and cownose rays;

Dolphin Cove, a massive habitat for bottlenose dolphins set up for visitor interaction; and Sea Turtle Point, home to threatened and endangered species such as green, loggerhead, and hawksbill sea turtles. Shortly after opening, dolphins showed their intelligence by realizing how easy humans are to tease. They'd routinely swim just out of arms' reach but discovered that there are advantages to coming in a little closer—namely smelt.

KEY WEST DOLPHIN FEST   At the Whale and Dolphin Stadium, a partially covered stadium, whales and Atlantic bottlenose dolphins perform flips and high jumps, swim at high speeds, twirl, swim on their backs, and give rides to trainers—all to the accompaniment of calypso music. The tricks are impressive, but go before the show-stopping behemoth, Shamu, puts these little mammals to shame.

BAYWATCH NIGHTS   Actors and stunt drivers re-create some of the high-powered drama of the most popular syndicated television show in the world. Sorry, no Pamela Anderson (or is it still Lee?) look-alikes.

WINDOW TO THE SEA   A multimedia presentation takes visitors behind the scenes at Sea World and explores a variety of marine subjects. These include an ocean dive in search of the rare six-gilled shark, a killer whale giving birth, babies born at Sea World (dolphins, penguins, walruses), dolphin anatomy, and underwater geology.

SHAMU: WORLD FOCUS   Sea World trainers develop close relationships with killer whales, and in this partly covered open-air stadium, they direct performances that are extensions of natural cetacean behaviors—twirling, waving tails and fins, rotating while swimming, and splashing the audience. Splash zones are clearly marked, sit in the upper tiers if you don't want to get soaked. The evening show here, called "Shamu: Night Magic," uses rock music and special lighting effects. There is no reason to attend both shows, unless you really like whales. The tricks are much the same. I'd opt for the evening show, taking advantage of shorter lines as others flock to the stadium in the afternoon. If you do decide on the afternoon show, arrive at least 30 minutes early. The stadium does fill up.

Shamu: Close Up!, an adjoining exhibit, lets you get close up to killer whales and talk to trainers; don't miss the underwater viewing area here and a chance to see a mother whale with her offspring. Talk about a big baby!

✪ PENGUIN ENCOUNTER   This display of hundreds of penguins and alcids (including adorable babies) native to the Antarctic and Arctic regions also serves as a living laboratory for protecting and preserving polar life. On a moving walkway, you'll view six different penguin species congregating on rocks, nesting, and swimming underwater. There's an additional area for puffins and murres (flying Arctic cousins of penguins).

HOTEL CLYDE & SEAMORE   Two sea lions, along with a cast of otters and walruses, appear in this fishy *Fawlty Towers* comedy with a conservation theme.

SWIM WITH THE DOLPHINS   For a fee, you can also take a **DIP:** Dolphin Interactive Program.

Sea World has expanded this program that allows eight people a chance to frolic with some of friends of Flipper. You pay $125 for roughly 20 minutes of hand-to-fin contact. The rest of the time is spent learning about how to interact with the dolphin and wrestling your body in and out of those tricky wet suits. (As you'll quickly learn, there is no graceful way.)

Beginning in October 1998, there will be both an 8am and a 10:30am session. Make your reservations, accepted only through fax or mail, at least 6 weeks in advance.

Children under 13 cannot participate, but can observe for $39.95 if they accompany a paid participant (that rule applies to all observers). The cost of a DIP includes admission to the park (annual pass holders pay less). And, interestingly enough, you don't have to be able to swim. For information, call ☎ **407/363-2380.**

The park's other attractions include **Pacific Point Preserve,** a 2½-acre naturalistic setting that duplicates the rocky northern Pacific Coast home of California sea lions and harbor and fur seals; **Tropical Reef,** a tide pool of touchables, such as sea anemones, starfish, sea cucumbers, and sea urchins; plus a 160,000-gallon artificial **coral-reef aquarium,** home to 1,000 brightly hued tropical fish displayed in 17 vignettes of undersea life; and **Shamu's Happy Harbor,** an innovative 3-acre play area that has a four-story net tower with a 35-foot crow's-nest lookout, water cannons, remote-controlled vehicles, and a water maze, one of the most extensive play areas at any park. Bring extra clothes for the tots.

A **Hawaiian dance troupe** entertains in an outdoor facility at Hawaiian Village; if you care to join in, grass skirts and leis are available. You can ascend 400 feet to the top of the **Sea World Sky Tower** for a revolving 360° panorama of the park and beyond (there's an extra charge of $3 per person for this activity). And at the 5.5-acre **Anheuser-Busch Hospitality Center** you can try free samples of Anheuser-Busch beers and snacks and stroll through the stables to watch the famous Budweiser Clydesdale horses being groomed (Anheuser-Busch owns Sea World).

The **Aloha! Polynesian Luau Dinner and Show,** a musical revue featuring South Seas food, song, and fire dancing, takes place nightly at 6:30pm. Park admission is not required. The cost is $35.95 for adults, $25.95 for children 8 to 12, $15.95 for children 3 to 7, and free for children 2 and under. Reservations are required (☎ **800/ 227-8048** or 407/363-2559).

Visitors can take 90-minute behind-the-scenes **tours** of the park's breeding, research, and training facilities and/or attend a 45-minute presentation about Sea World's animal behavior and training techniques. The cost for either tour is $5.95 for ages 10 and over, $4.95 for children 3 to 9, and free for children 2 and under.

13 More Area Attractions

KISSIMMEE

Kissimmee's sights are about a 10- to 15-minute drive from the Walt Disney World area.

✪ **Gatorland.** 14501 S. Orange Blossom Trail (U.S. 441, between Osceola Pkwy. and Hunter's Creek Blvd.). ☎ **407/855-5496.** Admission $14.79 adults, $9.49 children 10–12, $6.78, children 3–9. Free for one child 3–9 with each paying adult. Daily 8am–6pm. Free parking.

Founded in 1949 with a handful of alligators living in huts and pens, Gatorland today features thousands of alligators and crocodiles on a 70-acre spread. Breeding pens, nurseries, and rearing ponds are situated throughout the park, which also displays monkeys, snakes, deer, goats, birds, sheep, Florida lake turtles, a Galápagos tortoise, and a bear. A 2,000-foot boardwalk winds through a cypress swamp and a 10-acre breeding marsh with an observation tower. Or you can take the free Gatorland Express Train around the park. Educational shows are scheduled throughout the day. An open-air restaurant, shop, and picnic facilities are on the premises. Plan to spend a couple of hours.

Splendid China. Formosa Gardens Blvd., off W. Irlo Bronson Memorial Hwy. (U.S. 192, between Entry Point Blvd./Sherbeth Rd. and Black Lake Rd.). ☎ **407/396-7111.** Admission $26.99 adults, $16.99 children 5–12, free for children 4 and under. Daily from 9:30am; closing hours vary seasonally (call ahead). Free parking.

This 76-acre outdoor attraction features more than 60 miniaturized replicas of China's most noted manufactured and natural wonders, spanning 5,000 years of history and culture. Park highlights include a half-mile-long copy of the 4,200-mile Great Wall, the Forbidden City's 9,999-room Imperial Palace, Tibet's sacred Potala Palace, the massive Leshan Buddha, carved out of a mountainside between A.D. 713 and A.D. 803, the Stone Forest of Yunan, and the Mongolian mausoleum of Genghis Khan. Live shows (acrobats, martial-arts demonstrations, storytelling, dance, puppetry, and more) take place throughout the day; check your entertainment schedule. There's recorded commentary at each attraction.

Free trams circle the park, stopping at major attractions for pickup and drop-off. The 2-hour guided walking tours, departing several times a day, cost $5.35 per person (children 11 and under are free), and 1-hour golf-cart tours ($45 per six-person cart including guide) depart every half hour. This attraction can be explored in several hours.

INTERNATIONAL DRIVE

Like Kissimmee's attractions, these are about a 10- to 15-minute drive from the Disney area.

Ripley's Believe It or Not! Museum. 8201 International Dr. (1½ blocks south of Sand Lake Rd.). ☎ **407/345-0501.** Admission $10.55 adults, $7.37 children 4–12, free for children 3 and under. Daily 10am–midnight.

It's always fun to peruse a Ripley collection of oddities, curiosities, and fascinating artifacts from faraway places. Among the hundreds of items and mannequins on display here are a 1,069-pound man, a five-legged cow, a mosaic of the Mona Lisa created from 1,426 pieces of toast, torture devices from the Spanish Inquisition, a Tibetan flute made from human bones, a shrunken head, and Ubangi women with wooden plates in their lips. A baby boom among workers in 1995 was attributed to a fertility idol displayed at the museum and increased traffic from other women hoping for similar luck. Your visit shouldn't take more than an hour.

Wet 'n Wild. 6200 International Dr. (at Republic Dr.). ☎ **800/992-WILD** or 407/351-WILD. Admission $23.95 adults, $18.95 children 3–9, free for children 2 and under. Open daily; hours vary seasonally (call before you go). Free parking. Take I-4 east to Exit 30A and follow the signs.

When temperatures soar, head for this 25-acre water park and cool off by jumping waves, careening down steep flumes, and running rapids. Among the highlights: **Fuji Flyer** (a six-story toboggan ride along 450 feet of banked curves); **The Surge** (one of the longest, fastest multipassenger tube rides in the Southeast); **Bomb Bay** (enter a bomblike casing 76 feet in the air for a speedy vertical flight straight down to a target pool); **Black Hole** (step into a spaceship and board a two-person raft for a 30-second, 500-foot, twisting, turning, reentry through total darkness propelled by a 1,000-gallon-a-minute blast of water!); **Raging Rapids,** a simulated white-water tubing adventure with a waterfall plunge; and **Lazy River,** a leisurely float trip. There are additional flumes, a vast wave pool, a large and innovative children's water playground, a sunbathing area, and a picnic area.

Food concessions are located throughout the park, lockers and towels can be rented, and you can purchase beach accessories at the gift shop. It's easy to spend the whole day here, so remember your sunscreen.

ORLANDO

All the following Orlando attractions are in close proximity to each other, making for a pleasant day's excursion. Loch Haven Park is about 35 minutes by car from the

Disney area. You can probably also incorporate some Winter Park sights into the same day.

✪ **Orlando Science Center.** 777 E. Princeton St. (between Orange and Mills aves.), in Loch Haven Park. ☎ **407/896-7151.** Basic admission $8 adults, $6.50 children 3–11, free for children 2 and under. Additional charges for CineDome movies and planetarium shows. Mon–Thurs 9am–5pm, Fri and Sat 9am–9pm, Sun noon–5pm. Closed Thanksgiving and Christmas. Take I-4 east to Exit 43 (Princeton St.). It is the building with the large, shiny silver dome.

A $44 million expansion completed in 1997 made the Orlando Science Center the largest center of its kind in the southeastern United States. The exhibits are state of the art and geared toward encouraging kids to have fun while learning. This is the kind of museum where kids are encouraged to touch. The CineDome projects images onto an eight-story domed screen with a powerful audio system generating more than 28,000 watts of sound. Families can easily spend half a day touring the 10 exhibit halls.

✪ **Harry P. Leu Gardens.** 1920 N. Forest Ave. (between Nebraska St. and Corrine Dr.). ☎ **407/246-2620.** Admission $3 adults, $1 children 6–16, free for children 5 and under. Gardens daily 9am–5pm; Leu House tours Sun–Mon 1–3:30pm, Tues–Sat 10am–3:30pm. Closed Christmas. Take I-4 east to Exit 43 (Princeton St.), follow Princeton St. east, make a right on Mills Ave., turn left on Virginia Dr., and look for the gardens on your left.

At this delightful 50-acre botanical garden on the shores of Lake Rowena, meandering paths lead through forests of giant camphors, moss-draped oaks, palms, cycads, and camellias. Exquisite formal rose gardens display 75 varieties. Free 20-minute tours of the Leu House, built in 1888, take place on the hour and half hour. The house is a veritable decorative arts museum filled with Victorian, Empire, and Chippendale pieces. It takes about 2 hours to see the house and gardens.

Orange County Historical Museum. 812 E. Rollins St. (between Orange and Mills aves.), in Loch Haven Park. ☎ **407/897-6350.** Admission $2 adults, $1.50 seniors 65 and over, $1 children 6–12, free for children 5 and under; Mon admission by donation. Mon–Sat 9am–5pm, Sun noon–5pm. Closed New Year's Day, Martin Luther King, Jr., Day, Memorial Day, July 4, Labor Day, Thanksgiving, and Christmas. Take I-4 east to Exit 43 (Princeton St.) and follow the signs to Loch Haven Park.

This museum focuses on Central Florida history, beginning with prehistoric cultures that existed here 12,000 years ago. Other exhibits include displays of Seminole pottery and clothing, items from a pioneer kitchen, artifacts from an 1892 courthouse, a chronicle of the citrus industry, and re-creations of a turn-of-the-century country store, a Victorian parlor, and the old *Orlando Sentinel* composing room. Also on the premises is Fire Station No. 3, a restored 1926 firehouse.

Orlando Museum of Art. 2416 N. Mills Ave. (off U.S. 17/92), in Loch Haven Park. ☎ **407/896-4231.** Admission $4 adults, $2 children 4–11, free for children 3 and under. Museum Tues–Sat 9am–5pm, Sun noon–5pm; Art Encounter Tues–Fri and Sun noon–5pm, Sat 10am–5pm. Closed New Year's Day, Memorial Day, July 4, Labor Day, Thanksgiving, and Christmas. Free parking. Take I-4 east to Exit 43 (Princeton St.) and follow the signs to Loch Haven Park.

Also undergoing a multimillion-dollar expansion, the museum displays its permanent collection of 19th- and 20th-century American art, pre-Colombian art, and African art on a rotating basis. These holdings are augmented by long-term loans focusing on Mayan archaeology and arts of the African sub-Saharan region. "Art Encounter" is an interactive hands-on area for children. At this writing, a 31,000-square-foot expansion is underway, which will allow for major exhibitions.

WINTER PARK

This lakeside town is a lovely place to spend an afternoon. Visit the Morse Museum, cruise the lakes, and browse in the posh boutiques that line Park Avenue.

To get to Winter Park from Orlando (about a 5-mile drive), continue east on I-4 to Fairbanks Avenue (Exit 45), turn right, and proceed about a mile, making a left on Park Avenue.

✪ **Charles Hosmer Morse Museum of American Art.** 445 Park Ave. (between Canton and Cole aves.). ☎ **407/645-5311.** Admission $3 adults, $1 students of any age. Tues–Sat 9:30am–4pm, Sun 1–4pm. Closed New Year's Day, Memorial Day, July 4, Labor Day, Thanksgiving, and Christmas.

This gem of a museum was founded by Hugh and Jeannette McKean in 1942 to display their art collection, which includes 40 magnificent, vibrant colored windows and 21 paintings by Louis Comfort Tiffany. In addition, there are non-Tiffany windows ranging from creations by Frank Lloyd Wright to 15th- and 16th-century German masters; leaded lamps by Tiffany and Emile Gallè; paintings by John Singer Sargent, Maxfield Parrish, and others; jewelry designed by Tiffany, Lalique, and Fabergé; photographic works by Tiffany and other 19th-century artists; and art nouveau furnishings.

Scenic Boat Tour. On the lake at the eastern end of Morse Blvd. ☎ **407/644-4056.** Admission $6 adults, $3 children 2–11, free for children under 2. Weather permitting, tours depart daily, every hour on the hour 10am–4pm. Closed Christmas.

For over half a century tourists have been boarding pontoons at this location for leisurely hour-long cruises on Winter Park's beautiful chain of natural lakes. The ride traverses area lakes, winding through canals built by loggers at the turn of the century and tree-shaded fern gullies lined with bamboo and lush tropical foliage. You'll view magnificent lakeside mansions, pristine beaches, cypress swamps, and dozens of marsh birds—possibly even an American bald eagle. The captain regales passengers with local lore. It's a delightful, laid-back trip.

14 Outdoor Activities & Spectator Sports

OUTDOOR ACTIVITIES

The **Walt Disney World (WDW) recreational facilities** (☎ 407/824-4321) listed below are all open to the public, no matter where you're staying. Call for further information about WDW recreational facilities.

BIKING Bike rentals (single- and multispeed bikes for adults, tandems, and children's bikes) are available from the **Bike Barn** (☎ 407/824-2742) at Fort Wilderness Resort and Campground. Rates are $5 per hour, $12 per day, $18 overnight. Both Fort Wilderness and Disney's Village Resort offer good bike trails.

BOATING At the **Walt Disney World Village Marketplace Marina** (☎ 407/828-2204) you can rent Water Sprites, canopy boats, and 20-foot pontoon boats.

The **Bike Barn** at Fort Wilderness (☎ 407/824-2742) also rents canoes and paddleboats ($6 per half hour, $10 per hour).

FISHING Fishing excursions on Lake Buena Vista, mainly for largemouth bass, can be arranged up to 14 days in advance by calling ☎ 407/824-2621. No license is required. The fee is $137.50 for up to five people for 2 hours, and rates include gear and guide.

You can also rent cane poles and rods and reels at the Bike Barn (☎ 407/824-2742) to fish in Fort Wilderness canals. No license is required.

GOLF Like most of Florida, Orlando is a golfer's paradise, with 123 courses within a 45-minute drive of downtown. Courses are designed by Arnold Palmer, Jack Nicklaus, Tom Fazio, Pete Dye, Robert Trent Jones, and other major players.

Consider calling **Golfpac** (☎ **800/327-0878** or 407/260-2288), an organization that packages golf vacations (with accommodations and other features) and pre-arranges tee times at over 40 Orlando-area courses. The further in advance you call (I'm talking months here), the better your options.

The most famous local courses include the legendary ✪ **Arnold Palmer's Bay Hill Club,** 9000 Bay Hill Blvd. (☎ **800/523-5999** or 407/876-2429), site of the Bay Hill Invitational. Its 18th hole, nicknamed the Devil's Bathtub, is supposed to be the toughest par-4 on the tour.

✪ **Walt Disney World Resorts** (☎ **407/824-2270**) offer 99 holes of golf; they operate five championship 18-hole, par-72 golf courses and one 9-hole, par-36 walking course. All are open to the general public and offer pro shops, equipment rentals, and instruction. For tee times and information, call up to 7 days in advance (up to 30 days for Disney resort and "official-hotel" guests). The most famous hazard is a sand trap on the Magnolia Course's sixth hole in the shape of Mickey Mouse. Call ☎ **407/W-DISNEY** (934-7639) for information about golf packages.

Also notable are two beautifully landscaped facilities: the award-winning 45-hole, par-72 Jack Nicklaus–designed course at the **Villas of Grand Cypress** (☎ **800/835-7377** or 407/239-4700) and the 18-hole, par-71 Joe Lee–designed championship course at the **Marriott Orlando World Center** (☎ **800/621-0638** or 407/239-4200).

The **Falcon's Fire Golf Club,** 3200 Seralago Blvd., in Kissimmee (☎ **407/239-5445**), a challenging Ree Jones course, has 136 bunkers and water on 10 holes.

South of Kissimmee, in Haines City, is the **Grenelefe Golf & Tennis Resort** (☎ **800/237-9549** or 941/422-7511), with three championship courses. It's the home of the Wally Armstrong Golf School, and annually hosts U.S. Seniors Open and U.S. Women's Open qualifiers.

HAYRIDES The hay wagon departs from Pioneer Hall at Fort Wilderness nightly at 7 and 9:30pm for hour-long old-fashioned hayrides with singing, jokes, and games. The cost is $6 for adults, $4 for children 3 to 10, free for children 2 and under; children under 12 must be accompanied by an adult. No reservations—it's first-come, first-served.

HORSEBACK RIDING Disney's Fort Wilderness Resort and Campground offers 45-minute scenic guided-tour **trail rides** (☎ **407/824-2832**) daily, with four to six rides per day. The cost is $17 per person. Children must be at least 9 years old. Call for information and reservations up to 5 days in advance.

TENNIS There are 17 lighted tennis courts located throughout the Disney properties. Most are free and available on a first-come, first-served basis. If you're willing to pay for court time, courts can be reserved up to several months in advance at the **Contemporary** (☎ **407/824-3578**) or the **Grand Floridian** (☎ **407/824-2435**). Both charge $12 per hour; you can also reserve lesson times with resident pros. There's a large pro shop at the Contemporary where equipment can be rented.

SPECTATOR SPORTS

Disney's Wide World of Sports, at Walt Disney World (☎ **407/363-6600**), is a massive complex offering everything from basketball to gymnastics and soccer. It's also the spring training site of the Atlanta Braves and training site of the Harlem Globetrotters. Ticket prices vary.

The Orlando Centroplex administers six public sports and entertainment facilities in the downtown area. These include three major sporting arenas: the Florida Citrus Bowl, the Orlando Arena, and Tinker Field.

The **Florida Citrus Bowl,** 1 Citrus Bowl Place, at West Church and Tampa streets (☎ **407/896-2442** for information, or 407/839-3900 to charge tickets), seats 70,000 people for major sporting events including the annual CompUSA Florida Citrus Bowl game, college football games, and NFL preseason games. Parking is $5. Take I-4 east to the East-West Expressway and head west to U.S. 441, make a left on Church Street, and follow the signs.

The **Orlando Magic** play at the **Orlando Arena,** 600 W. Amelia St., between I-4 and Parramore Avenue (☎ **407/849-2020** for information, or 407/839-3900 to charge tickets). Tickets to Magic games (about $13 to $50) usually have to be acquired far in advance. There are generally about 1,000 tickets available for sale before each game. Single tickets are often available when the Magic goes against low-profile NBA competitions, such as the Timberwolves. Parking at the arena costs $5 (for up-to-the-minute parking information, tune your car radio to 1620 AM). Take I-4 east to Amelia Avenue, turn left at the traffic light at the bottom of the off-ramp, and follow the signs. Call to find out about other sporting events when you're in town. Orlando is also home to several other professional teams, including the **Predators,** an arena football team, and the **Solar Bears,** an ice hockey team.

Spring training for the **Houston Astros** begins in late February, with exhibition games through March or early April at the **Osceola County Stadium,** 1000 Bill Beck Blvd., in Kissimmee (☎ **407/933-2520**). Tickets are $6, $8, and $10. Call for details and tickets.

The **Bay Hill Invitational Golf Tournament** is held in mid-March at Arnold Palmer's Bay Hill Club, 9000 Bay Hill Blvd. (☎ **407/876-2888** for details). And another stop on the PGA tour is October's **Walt Disney World Oldsmobile Golf Classic** (☎ **407/824-4321**). Daily ticket prices range from $8 to $15. Call for details.

15 Walt Disney World & Orlando After Dark

My hat's off to those of you who, after a long day of traipsing around amusement parks, still have the energy to venture out at night in search of entertainment. That being said, you will find plenty to do. And this being kids' world, many evening shows inside the parks are geared to families. There is adult entertainment at Pleasure Island, CityWalk, and in downtown Orlando at Church Street Station and the many bars and restaurants that normally cater to locals.

Check the **"Calendar"** section of Friday's *Orlando Sentinel* for up-to-the-minute details on local clubs, visiting performers, concerts, and events. Also check out the *Orlando Sentinel Online* at **www.oso.aol.com**. It has hundreds of listings. The *Orlando Weekly* is a free magazine circulated through boxes in Central Florida and highlighting more offbeat and, often, up-to-date performers and performances.

Tickets to many performances are handled by **Ticketmaster** (☎ **407/839-3900** to charge tickets).

WALT DISNEY WORLD DINNER SHOWS

Other nighttime park options include SpectroMagic, fireworks, and IllumiNations (see sections 6 to 9 in this chapter for details).

Hoop-Dee-Doo Musical Revue. Disney's Fort Wilderness Resort and Campground, 3520 N. Fort Wilderness Trail. ☎ **407/WDW-DINE** (939-3463). Reservations required. Admission $37 adults, $19.50 children 3–11; taxes and gratuities extra. Show times daily at 5, 7:15, and 9:30pm. Free parking.

Fort Wilderness's rustic log-beamed Pioneer Hall is the setting for this 2-hour down-home musical revue. It's a high-energy show, with 1890s costumes, corny vaudeville jokes, rousing songs, and lots of good-natured audience participation. During the show, you'll chow down on an all-you-can-eat barbecue dinner including a big slab of strawberry shortcake for dessert. Beverages are included. If you catch an early show, stick around for the Electrical Water Pageant at 9:45pm, which can be viewed from the Fort Wilderness Beach.

Polynesian Luau Dinner Show. At Disney's Polynesian Resort, 1600 Seven Seas Dr. ☎ **407/WDW-DINE** (939-3463). Reservations required. Admission $38 adults, $19.50 children 3–11, free for children 2 and under; taxes and gratuities extra. Show times daily at 6:45 and 9:30pm. Free valet and self-parking.

This delightful 2-hour dinner show features a colorfully costumed cast of entertainers from New Zealand, Tahiti, Hawaii, and Samoa performing authentic hula, warrior, ceremonial, love, and fire dances on a flower-bedecked stage. There's even a Hawaiian/Polynesian fashion show. It all takes place in a heated open-air theater (dress for the weather). The meal, served family style, includes a big platter of fresh island fruits, half a barbecued chicken, vegetables, cinnamon bread, beverages, and a tropical ice-cream sundae. There's also a 4:30pm version daily (see Luau Cove listing in "Dining with Disney Characters" in section 4 of this chapter).

ENTERTAINMENT COMPLEXES: PLEASURE ISLAND, CHURCH STREET STATION, CITYWALK & DISNEY'S WEST SIDE

✪ **Pleasure Island.** In Walt Disney World, adjacent to Walt Disney World Village. ☎ **407/934-7781.** Free before 7pm, $19.03 after 7pm (admission included in the 5-Day World-Hopper Pass). Clubs daily 7pm–2am; shops daily 11am–2am. Valet parking $5; free self-parking.

This Walt Disney World theme park is a 6-acre complex of nightclubs, restaurants, shops, and movie theaters; for a single admission price, you can enjoy a night of club-hopping until the wee hours. The park is designed to suggest an abandoned waterfront industrial district with clubs in "converted" ramshackle lofts, factories, and warehouses, but the streets are festive with brightly colored lights and balloons. You'll be given a map and show schedule when you enter the park; take a look at it and plan your evening around shows that interest you. You can feel perfectly secure sending your teenage kids here for the evening, though they must be 18 to get in unless accompanied by a parent or legal guardian.

The on-premises clubs come and go. At this writing they include the following. **Island Jazz** is a big barnlike club featuring contemporary and traditional live jazz. **Mannequins Dance Palace** is a high-energy dance club with a large rotating dance floor and a deejay playing contemporary tunes at an ear-splitting decibel level (you must be 21 to get in). The **Neon Armadillo Music Saloon** features live country bands nightly; dancers whirl around the floor doing the Texas two-step or cotton-eyed Joe (lessons are given Sunday from 7 to 8pm). Sometimes name stars come in and take the stage.

The most unusual of Pleasure Island's clubs (and my personal favorite) is the **Adventurers Club,** chock-full of artifacts ranging from early aviation photos to shrunken heads. In the eerie Mask Room, more than 100 masks move their eyes, jeer, and make odd pronouncements. Improvisational comedy shows take place throughout the evening in the main salon, and there are diverse 20-minute cabaret shows in the library. You could easily hang out here all night sipping potent tropical drinks in the library and at the bar.

The **Comedy Warehouse,** another of my favorites, has a rustic interior with tiered seating. A very talented troupe performs improvisational comedy based on audience suggestions. There are five shows a night, and bar drinks are available. Arrive early.

Live bands play classic rock at the **Rock & Roll Beach Club.** There are bars on all three floors. The first level contains the dance floor; the second and third levels offer air hockey, pool tables, basketball machines, pinball, video games, darts, and a pizza and beer stand. There's also **8 Trax,** a 1970s-style club with about 50 TV monitors airing shows and videos over the dance floor. A deejay plays disco music, and guests can play Twister.

In addition, live bands, including occasional big-name groups, play the **West End Plaza** outdoor stage and the **Hub Stage;** check your schedule for show times. You can star in your own music video at **SuperStar Studios.** There are carnival games, a video-game arcade, a Velcro wall, and an Orbitron (originally developed for NASA, it lets you experience weightlessness). And every night features a midnight **New Year's Eve celebration** with fireworks and confetti. **Shops and eateries** are found throughout the park, including **Planet Hollywood** (see "Dining," earlier in this chapter).

Disney keeps its expansion plans very secret. But word has it that Pleasure Island will soon double in size to compete with Universal's E-Zone. Rumored additions include the 1,500-seat Dan Aykroyd–conceived **House of Blues;** an expanded 24-screen movie complex; a **Wolfgang Puck's Cafe,** serving his uniquely California cuisine; **Lario's,** a restaurant created by Miami's favorite Home Girl, Gloria Estefan, featuring Latin American entertainment; a performing arts theater; and more. A lushly tropical **RainForest Cafe** has already opened in the Disney Village Marketplace, replete with indoor waterfalls, thunder, lightning, and tropical birds.

✪ **Church Street Station.** 129 W. Church St. (off I-4 between Garland and Orange aves.), in downtown Orlando. ☎ **407/422-2434.** Free before 5pm, $16.95 after 5pm; always free to restaurants, the Exchange Shopping Emporium, and the Midway game area. Clubs daily until 2am; shops daily until 11pm. Valet parking $6 at Church St. and Garland Ave.; several parking lots are nearby (call for specifics). Take I-4 east to Exit 38 (Anderson St.), stay in the left lane, and follow the blue signs. Most hotels offer transportation to and from Church St.

Though not part of Walt Disney World, Church Street Station in downtown Orlando operates on a principle similar to Pleasure Island. Occupying a cobblestone city block lined with turn-of-the-century buildings, it, too, is a shopping/dining/nightclub complex offering an evening of diverse entertainment for a single admission price. There are 20 live shows nightly; consult your show schedule upon entering.

Stunning interiors are the rule here. It's worth coming by just to check out the magnificent woodwork, stained glass, and thousands of authentic antiques. The shopping is pretty good, also.

Highlights include **Rosie O'Grady's Good Time Emporium,** an 1890s antique-filled saloon, where Dixieland bands, banjo players, singing waiters, and cancan dancers entertain nightly. Light fare is available. Adjoining Rosie's, **Apple Annie's Courtyard** evokes a Victorian tropical garden. Patrons sip potent tropical drinks while listening to folk and bluegrass music.

The plush interior of **Lili Marlene's Aviator's Pub & Restaurant** is embellished with World War I memorabilia, stained-glass transoms, and accoutrements from an 1850 Rothschild town house in Paris. The menu features premium aged steaks, prime rib, and fresh seafood. The whimsical **Phineas Phogg's Balloon Works,** with hot-air balloons and airplanes over the dance floor, is a high-energy club playing loud, pulsating music. Every Wednesday from 6:30 to 7:30pm beers cost just 5¢ here. No one under 21 is admitted.

The stunning trilevel **Cheyenne Saloon and Opera House** is constructed of golden oak lumber from a century-old Ohio barn. Quality Western art is displayed throughout, including many oil paintings and 11 Remington sculptures. Balcony seating, in restored church pews, overlooks the stage, the setting for entertainment ranging from country bands to clogging exhibitions.

The **Orchid Garden Ballroom,** with ornate white wrought-iron arches and Victorian lighting fixtures suspended from an elaborate oak-paneled ceiling, is the setting for an oldies dance club. A DJ plays rock 'n' roll classics interspersed with live bands. As the evening progresses, so do the musical decades. Brick columns, oak paneling, and a gorgeous antique oak-and-mahogany bar characterize **Crackers Oyster Bar,** a cozy late-1800s-style dining room that features fresh Florida seafood and more than 50 imported beers.

In addition, the 87,000-square-foot Exchange houses the carnival-like **Commander Ragtime's Midway of Fun, Food and Games** (including an enormous video-game arcade), a food court, and more than 50 specialty shops. You can rent a **horse-drawn carriage** out front for a drive around the downtown area and Lake Eola. And **hot-air balloon flights** can be arranged (☎ **407/841-8787**).

MAJOR CONCERT HALLS & AUDITORIUMS

Three large entertainment facilities, administered by the Orlando Centroplex, host most big-name performers playing the Orlando area.

The **Florida Citrus Bowl,** 1610 W. Church St., at Tampa Street (☎ **407/ 849-2020** for information, or 407/839-3900 to charge tickets), with 70,000 seats, is the largest. This is the setting for major rock concerts and headliners. To reach the Citrus Bowl, take I-4 east to the East-West Expressway and head west to U.S. 441; make a left on Church Street, and follow the signs. Parking is $5.

The 17,500-seat **Orlando Arena** at 600 W. Amelia St., between I-4 and Parramore Avenue (☎ **407/849-2020** for information, or 407/839-3900 to charge tickets), also hosts major performers in addition to an array of family-oriented entertainment such as ice-skating and the circus every January. To reach the arena, take I-4 east to Amelia Avenue, turn left at the traffic light at the bottom of the off-ramp, and follow the signs. Parking is $5.

The area's major cultural venue is the **Bob Carr Performing Arts Centre,** 401 W. Livingston St., between I-4 and Parramore Avenue (☎ **407/849-2020** for information, or 407/839-3900 to charge tickets). Concert prices vary with performers; ballet tickets are $15 to $35; opera tickets, $12 to $45; the Broadway Series, $24.50 to $46.50. This 2,500-seat facility is home to the **Orlando Opera Company** and the **Southern Ballet Theater,** both of which have October-to-May seasons. The **Orlando Broadway Series** (September to May) features original-cast Broadway shows. Also featured at the Bob Carr are concerts and comedy shows. To get here, take I-4 east to Amelia Avenue, turn left at the traffic light at the bottom of the off-ramp, and follow the signs. Parking is $5.

16 A Side Trip to Cypress Gardens

Founded in 1936, ✪ **Cypress Gardens** came into being as a 16-acre public garden along the banks of Lake Eloise, with cypress-wood-block pathways and thousands of tropical and subtropical plants. It's located on Fla. 540 at Cypress Gardens Boulevard

(40 miles southwest of Walt Disney World), in Winter Haven (☎ **800/282-2123** or 941/324-2111).

Today it has grown to more than 200 acres, with ponds and lagoons, waterfalls, classic Italian fountains, topiary, bronze sculptures, manicured lawns, and ancient cypress trees shrouded in Spanish moss. All this forms a backdrop to ever-changing floral displays of 8,000 varieties of plants from more than 90 countries. Southern belles in Scarlett O'Hara costumes stroll the grounds or sit on benches under parasols in idyllic tree-shaded nooks.

In the late winter and early spring, more than 20 varieties of bougainvillea, 40 of azalea, and hundreds of kinds of roses burst into bloom. Crape myrtles, magnolias, and gardenias perfume the late-spring air, while brilliant birds of paradise, hibiscus, and jasmine brighten the summer landscape. And in winter the golden rain trees, floss silk trees, and camellias of autumn give way to millions of colorful chrysanthemums and red, white, and pink poinsettias.

Strolling the grounds is, of course, the main attraction (there are more than 2 miles of winding botanical paths, and half the park's acreage is devoted to floral displays), but this being Central Florida, it's not the only one. Several shows are scheduled throughout the day (check your schedule upon entering the park). The world-famous **Greatest American Ski Team** performs on Lake Eloise in a show augmented by an awesome hang-gliding display. The breathtaking **ice-skating show** is the Russian answer to America's Ice Capades. **Varietè Internationale** features specialty acts from all over the world. An enchanting exhibit called **Wings of Wonder** surrounds visitors with more than 1,000 brightly colored free-flying butterflies in a 5,500-square-foot Victorian-style glass conservatory. **Electric boats** navigate a maze of lushly landscaped canals in the original botanical gardens area. You can ascend 153 feet to the **Island in the Sky** for a panoramic vista of the gardens and a beautiful chain of Central Florida lakes. **Carousel Cove,** with eight kiddie rides and arcade games, centers on an ornate turn-of-the-century-style carousel. It adjoins another kid pleaser, **Cypress Junction,** an elaborately landscaped model railroad that travels over 1,100 feet of track with up to 20 trains moving at one time. **Cypress Roots,** a museum of park memorabilia, displays photographs of famous visitors (Elvis on water skis, Tiny Tim tiptoeing through the roses) and airs ongoing showings of *Easy to Love* starring Esther Williams (it was filmed here). Wind up your visit with a relaxing 30-minute narrated **pontoon cruise** on scenic Lake Eloise, past virgin forest, bulrushes, and beautiful shoreline homes (there's a $4 per person charge).

You'll find both restaurants and a picnic area on the premises. Admission is $29.50 for ages 10 and over, $19.50 for children 3 to 9, free for children 2 and under, $24.50 for seniors. It's open daily from 9:30am to 5:30pm, with extended hours during peak seasons. To get there, take I-4 West to U.S. 27 south, and proceed west to S.R. 540; parking is free.

13

Northwest Florida: The Panhandle

by Bill Goodwin

If you like beaches, you'll love Florida's northwestern Panhandle. Thanks to quartz washed down from the Appalachian Mountains, the beaches here along the Gulf of Mexico consist of dazzlingly white sand that is so talcumlike it actually squeaks when you walk across it. And walk across it you can, for some 100 miles of these incomparable sands are protected in state parks and the gorgeous Gulf Islands National Seashore.

Pensacola, Fort Walton Beach, Destin, and Panama City Beach have long been summertime beach meccas for families, couples, and singles from the adjoining states of Georgia and Alabama—a geographic proximity that lends this area the languid charm of the Deep South. Indeed, Southern specialties like turnip greens and cheese grits appear frequently on menus here.

But there's more here than beaches and Southern charm. Offshore, you'll find abundant marine life growing over the Gulf's natural sand-bar system, which makes for good snorkeling and scuba diving. Championship catches of grouper, amberjack, snapper, mackerel, cobia, sailfish, wahoo, tuna, and blue marlin have made Destin one of the world's fishing capitals. In the interior near Pensacola, the Blackwater, Shoal, and Yellow rivers teem with bass, bream, catfish, and largemouth bass, and also offer some of Florida's best canoeing and kayaking adventures.

The area also is steeped in history. Rivaling St. Augustine as Florida's oldest town, picturesque Pensacola carefully preserves a heritage derived from Spanish, French, English, and American conquest. Famous for its oysters, Apalachicola saw the invention of the air conditioner, a moment of great historical note in Florida. And Tallahassee, seat of state government since 1824, has a host of 19th-century buildings and homes, including the Old State Capitol.

EXPLORING NORTHWEST FLORIDA BY CAR

Both I-10 and U.S. 98 link Tallahassee and Pensacola, some 200 miles apart. The fastest route is I-10, but all you'll see is a huge pine forest divided by two strips of concrete. Plan to take U.S. 98, a scenic excursion in itself. This highway is particularly beautiful as it literally skirts the bay east of Apalachicola and the Gulf west of Port St. Joe. There's another lovely stretch along skinny Okaloosa Island and across the high-rise bridge between Fort Walton Beach and Destin. From the bridge you'll see the brilliant color of the Gulf and immediately understand why they call this the Emerald Coast.

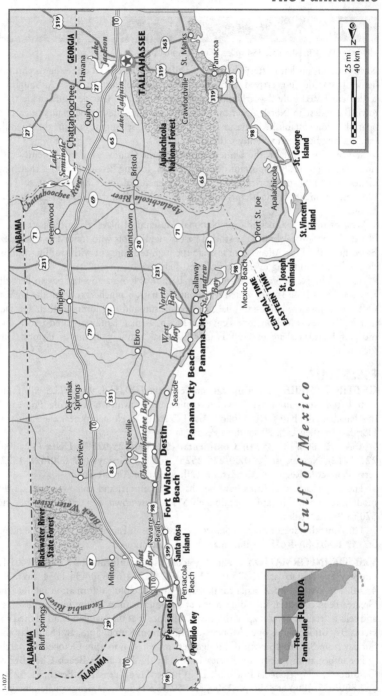

The Panhandle

Gulf of Mexico

527

1 Pensacola

191 miles W of Tallahassee, 354 miles W of Jacksonville

Native Americans left pottery shards and artifacts in the coastal dunes here centuries before Tristan de Luna arrived with a band of Spanish colonists in 1559. Although his settlement lasted only 2 years, modern Pensacolans claim that de Luna made their town the oldest in North America. Pensacola actually dates its permanence from a Spanish colony established here in 1698, however, so St. Augustine wins this friendly feud, having been permanently settled in 1565.

France, Great Britain, the United States, and the Confederacy subsequently captured this strategically important deep-water port, leaving Pensacola with a charming blend of Old Spanish brickwork, colonial French balconies reminiscent of New Orleans, and magnificent Victorian mansions built by British and American lumber barons.

West of town, the magnificent National Museum of Naval Aviation at the U.S. Naval Air Station celebrates the storied past of naval pilots who trained at Pensacola. Based here, the Blue Angels demonstrate the high-tech present with thrilling exhibitions of precision flying in the navy's fastest fighters.

Also on the Naval Station, historic Fort Barrancas looks across the bay to Perdido Key and Santa Rosa Island, which reach out like narrow pinchers to form the harbor. Out there, powdery white-sand beaches beckon sun-and-surf lovers to their spectacular gulf shores, which include Pensacola Beach, a small family-oriented resort, and most of Florida's share of Gulf Islands National Seashore, home of historic Fort Pickens.

ESSENTIALS

GETTING THERE From the east or west, take I-10, U.S. 90, or U.S. 98. From I-10, Exit 4 puts you on I-110, which terminates in downtown Pensacola. From I-65 in Alabama, take Exit 69 and follow Ala. 113 south to Flomaton near the Alabama-Florida line, then U.S. 29 south to Pensacola.

ASA (☎ 800/282-3424), **Continental** (☎ 800/525-0280), **Delta** (☎ 800/221-1212), **Northwest** (☎ 800/225-2525), and **US Airways** (☎ 800/428-4322) serve **Pensacola Regional Airport,** on 12th Avenue at Airport Road.

The major car-rental firms have booths at the airport, and taxis wait outside the modern terminal. Fares are approximately $11 to downtown, $15 to Gulf Breeze, and $20 to Pensacola Beach.

The **Amtrak** transcontinental *Sunset Limited* stops in Pensacola at 980 E. Heinberg St. (☎ 800/USA-RAIL for information and reservations).

VISITOR INFORMATION The **Pensacola Visitor Information Center,** 1401 E. Gregory St., Pensacola, FL 32501 (☎ 800/874-1234 or 850/434-1234; fax 850/432-8211; www.visitpensacola.com), gives away helpful information about the Greater Pensacola area, including maps of self-guided tours of the historic districts, and sells a detailed street map of the area. The office is at the mainland end of the Pensacola Bay Bridge and is open Monday to Friday from 8am to 5pm, and Saturday and Sunday from 8am to 4pm April through September, 9am to 4pm October to March.

For information specific to the beach, contact the **Pensacola Beach Chamber of Commerce,** 735 Pensacola Beach Blvd. (P.O. Box 1174), Pensacola Beach, FL 32561 (☎ 800/635-4803 or 850/932-1500; fax 850/932-1551; www.pensacolabeach.com). The chamber's offices and visitor center are on the right-hand side as you drive onto Santa Rosa Island across the Bob Sikes Bridge. They're open daily from 9am to 5pm.

Pensacola

GETTING AROUND   To see the historic sights in town, park at the Pensacola visitor center (see above) and take the **Five Flags Trolley** (☎ 850/436-9383). The one-way East Bay (Blue) Line runs Monday to Friday from 9am to 4pm between the visitor center and downtown. The Palafox (Red) Line runs Monday to Friday from 7am to 6pm north-south along Palafox Street between the waterfront and North Hill Preservation District. Both pass through Historic Pensacola Village. The 25¢ fare includes a transfer between the two lines. The visitor center has free route maps.

Escambia County Area Transit System (ECAT) runs **buses** around town Monday to Saturday from 6am to 6pm. The base fare is $1. Call ☎ **850/463-9383,** ext. 611, for schedules. The ECAT buses don't go to Gulf Breeze or the beach, but a free **Island Trolley** operates along the full length of Pensacola Beach from May to September on Friday, Saturday, and Sunday from 10am to 3am. One route runs parallel to the beach on Via de Luna and Fort Pickens Road. A second runs along Pensacola Beach Boulevard from the Bob Sikes Bridge to the Via de Luna/Fort Pickens Road intersection.

If you need a cab, call **Airport Express Taxi** (☎ 850/572-5555), **Crosstown Cab** (☎ 850/456-TAXI), **Pensacola Red & Gold Taxi** (☎ 850/505-0025), or **Yellow Cab** (☎ 850/433-3333).

TIME Pensacola is in the **central time zone,** 1 hour behind Miami, Orlando, and Tallahassee.

HITTING THE BEACH

Stretching eastward 47 miles, from the entrance to Pensacola Bay to Fort Walton Beach, skinny **Santa Rosa Island** is home to the resorts, condominiums, cottages, restaurants, and shops of **Pensacola Beach,** the area's prime vacation spot. This relatively small and low-key resort began life a century ago as the site of a beach pavilion, or "casino" as such facilities were called back then, and the heart of town—at the intersection of Pensacola Beach Boulevard, Via de Luna, and Fort Pickens Road—is still known as **Casino Beach.** At the base of the town's water tank, this lively area sports restaurants, snack bars, a games arcade for kids, a minigolf course, public rest rooms, walk-up beach bars with live bands blaring away, an indoor sports bar, and an outdoor concert pavilion with summertime entertainment. And the shops, restaurants, and bars of **Quietwater Boardwalk** are just across the road on the bay side of the island. If you want an active beach vacation, it's all here in one compact zone.

One reason Pensacola Beach is so small is that most of Santa Rosa Island is included in the ✪ **Gulf Islands National Seashore.** Jumping from island to island from Mississippi to Florida, this magnificent preserve includes mile after mile of undeveloped white-sand beach and rolling dunes covered with sea grass and sea oats. Established in 1971, the national seashore is a protected environment for more than 280 species of birds. Visitors enjoy swimming, boating, fishing, scuba diving, camping, and ranger-guided fort tours and nature hikes.

✪ **Fort Pickens,** built in the 1830s to team with Fort Barrancas in guarding Pensacola's harbor entrance, stands silent guard in the dunes at the western end of Santa Rosa. This huge brick structure saw combat during the Civil War, but it's famous today as the prison home of Apache medicine man Geronimo from 1886 to 1888. A small museum features displays about Geronimo, coastal defenses, and the seashore's ecology. The fort and museum are open April to October daily from 9:30am to 5pm; November to March daily from 8:30am to 4pm. Both are closed on Christmas.

Seven-day admission permits to the Fort Pickens area are $6 per vehicle, $3 per pedestrian or bicyclist, free for holders of National Park Service passports. For more information, contact the **Gulf Islands National Seashore** at 1801 Gulf Breeze Pkwy., Gulf Breeze, FL 32561 (☎ 850/934-2600).

NATURE PRESERVES & ZOOS

A former federal tree plantation, the Gulf Islands National Seashore's 1,378-acre **Naval Live Oaks Area,** on U.S. 98 a mile east of Gulf Breeze (☎ 850/934-2600), is a place of primitive beauty. Nature trails lead through the oaks and pines to picnic areas and a beach; pick up a map at the headquarters building, which has a small museum and a gorgeous view through the pines to Santa Rosa Sound. Picnic areas and trails are open from 8am to sunset all year except Christmas. The visitor center is open April to October, daily from 8:30am to 5pm; November to March, daily from 8:30am to 4:30pm. Admission is free.

The Zoo, on U.S. 98 about 10 miles east of Gulf Breeze, 15 miles east of Pensacola (☎ 850/932-2229), has more than 700 exotic animals—including white tigers, rhinos, and gorillas—on 50 acres of landscaped habitats. Japanese gardens, elephant shows, a giraffe feeding tower, and a petting farm make for a fun visit. A Safari Line train chugs through a 30-acre wildlife preserve with free-ranging herds. Admission is $9.75 adults, $8.75 seniors, $5.75 children 3 to 11, free for children 2 and under. Open during summer daily from 9am to 5pm; off-season daily from 9am to 4pm. It's also open from 6 to 9pm from the day after Thanksgiving until January 4 for a holiday lights festival, when proceeds go to charity. Closed Thanksgiving and Christmas days.

OUTDOOR PURSUITS

CANOEING & KAYAKING   Less than 20 miles northeast of Pensacola via U.S. 90, the little town of Milton is the official "Canoe Capital of Florida" (by an act of the state legislature, no less). It's a well-earned title, for the nearby Blackwater River, Cold-water River, Sweetwater Creek, and Juniper Creek are all perfect for canoeing, kayaking, tubing, rafting, and paddleboating.

The Blackwater is considered one of the world's purest sand-bottom rivers. It has remained a primordial, backwoods beauty, thanks in large part to Florida's largest state forest (183,000 acres of oak, pine, and juniper) and ✪ **Blackwater River State Park,** 7720 Deaton Bridge Rd., Holt, FL 32564 (☎ 850/953-5363), where you can closely observe plant life and wildlife along nature trails. The park has facilities for fishing, picnicking, and camping. Admission is $2 per day per vehicle with up to eight occupants. Campsites cost $8 per night ($10 with electricity), and discounts for stays of 7 days or longer are available.

Adventures Unlimited, Rte. 6, Box 283, Milton (☎ **800/239-6864** or 850/ 623-9197), is a year-round resort with canoeing, kayaking, rafting, camping, a high-and low-challenge course, and paddleboating expeditions in the state park and sur-rounding rivers. Special arrangements are made for novices. Canoes rent from $13 per person, kayaks from $17, and inner tubes for $9. The company also has 14 cottages on the Coldwater River ranging from $39 to $109 a night. Campsites cost $15 a night.

Blackwater Canoe Rental, 10274 Pond Rd., Milton (☎ **800/967-6789** or 850/623-0235), also rents canoes, kayaks, floats, tubes, and camping equipment. It has day trips by canoe, kayak, or inner tubes ranging from $9 to $19 per person and overnight excursions ranging from $19 to $28 per person. Tents, sleeping bags, and coolers are available for rent.

FISHING   Red snapper, grouper, mackerel, tuna, and billfish are abundant in these waters. Anglers congregate along the **Pensacola Bay Bridge Fishing Pier** (it's on the old bridge). The **Bob Sikes Bridge Fishing Pier** also is on the old bridge.

Fishing charter services are offered by **Scuba Shack/Charter Boat *Wet Dream,*** 719 S. Palafox St., in Pensacola (☎ 850/433-4319); *Hooligan* **Charters** (☎ 850/ 968-1898) and *Rocky Top* **Charters** (☎ 850/432-7536), both at Pitt Slip Marina off East Main Street in Pensacola; and *Lo-Baby* **Charters,** 38 High-point Dr., in Gulf Breeze (☎ 850/934-5285). At Pensacola Beach, choose from *Chulamar* (☎ 850/ 434-6977), *Lively One* (☎ 850/932-5071), *Boss Lady* (☎ 850/932-0305 or 850/ 477-4033), *Entertainer* (☎ 850/932-0305), *Exodus* (☎ 850/626-2545 or 850/ 932-0305), and *Lady Kady* (☎ 850/932-2065 or 850/932-0305). Expect to pay between $300 and $750 for one to four passengers, depending on length of trip. You may be able to save by driving to Destin, where party boats charge less per person (see "Outdoor Activities" in section 2, below). Sightseeing and evening cruises here go for about $50 per person.

GOLF   The Pensacola area has its share of Northwest Florida's numerous champi-onship golf courses. Look for free copies of *Gulf Coast Tee Time,* an annual directory describing all of them, at the visitor information offices and in many hotel lobbies (see

"The Active Vacation Planner" in chapter 2 for information about ordering copies). Reasonably priced golf packages can be arranged through many local hotels and motels.

Among this region's best courses is **Marcus Pointe,** on Marcus Pointe Boulevard off North W Street (☎ **800/362-7287** or 850/484-9770), which has hosted the Nike Tour, the American Amateur Classic, and the Pensacola Open. *Golf Digest* magazine has described this wide-ranging, 18-hole course as a "great value," and it is: Greens fees with cart are about $40 to $49, depending on the season.

The Moors, on Avalon Boulevard north of I-10 (☎ **800/727-1010** or 850/ 995-4653), also has greeted the Nike Tour and is home to the Emerald Coast Classic, a PGA seniors event. Pot bunkers here make you think you're playing in Scotland. Greens fees here are about $30 without cart. The Moors also has a lodge with eight luxury rooms.

Others worth considering are **Scenic Hills,** on U.S. 90 northwest of town (☎ **850/476-9611**), whose rolling fairways are unique for this mostly flat area; the 36-hole **Tiger Point,** 1255 Country Club Rd. east of Gulf Breeze by Santa Rosa Sound (☎ **850/932-1330**), overlooking the water (the fifth-hole green of the East Course actually sits all by itself on an island); **Hidden Creek,** 3070 PGA Blvd., in Navarre between Gulf Breeze and Fort Walton Beach (☎ **850/939-4604**); **Creekside Golf Course,** 2355 W. Michigan Ave. (☎ **850/944-7969**); and **Osceola Municipal Golf Course,** 300 Tonawanda, off Mobile Highway (☎ **850/456-2761**).

In addition, the **Perdido Bay Golf Resort,** 1 Doug Ford Dr., near Perdido Key (☎ **800/874-5355** or 850/492-1223), has accommodations available for visiting golfers. It was home of the PGA Pensacola Open from 1978 to 1987.

WATER SPORTS　Visibility in the waters around Pensacola can range from 30 to 50 feet inshore to 100 feet 25 miles offshore. Although the bottom is sandy and it's too far north for coral, the battleship USS *Massachusetts,* submerged in 30 feet of water 3 miles offshore, is one of some 35 artificial reefs where you can spot loggerhead turtles and other creatures.

Scuba Shack, 711 S. Palafox St. (☎ **850/433-4319**), is Pensacola's oldest dive shop, offering sales, rentals, classes, and diving and fishing charters on the *Wet Dream,* moored behind the office. **Dive Pros,** 7203 U.S. 98 West (☎ **850/456-8845**), with a branch in Gulf Breeze (☎ **850/934-8845**), offers rentals, all levels of instruction, and diving excursions. The *Chulamar* at Pensacola Beach (☎ **850/434-6977**) and the *Lo-Baby,* in Gulf Breeze (☎ **850/934-5285**), both make arrangements for diving excursions.

Kirk Newkirk's **Key Sailing Center,** 500 Quietwater Beach Rd., on the Quietwater Beach Boardwalk (☎ **850/932-5550**), rents Hobie Cats, pontoon boats, WaveRunners, jet-skis, and windsurfing boards. So does **Bonifay Water Sports** next door (☎ **850/932-0633**) and **Radical Rides,** 444 Pensacola Beach Blvd., near the Bob Sikes Bridge (☎ **850/934-9743**).

EXPLORING HISTORIC PENSACOLA

Civil War Soldiers Museum. 108 S. Palafox St. (south of Romana St.). ☎ **850/469-1900.** Admission $5 adults, $2 children 6–12, free for children 5 and under. Mon–Sat 10am–4:30pm. Closed New Year's Day, Thanksgiving, and Christmas.

Founded by Dr. Norman Haines Jr., a local physician who grew up discovering Civil War relics in Sharpsburg, Maryland, this storefront museum in the heart of the Palafox Street business district emphasizes how ordinary soldiers lived during that bloody conflict. The doctor's collection of military medical equipment and treatment methods is especially informative. A 23-minute video tells of Pensacola's role during the Civil War. The museum's bookstore carries more than 600 titles about the war.

✪ **Historic Pensacola Village.** 205 E. Zaragossa St. (east of Tarragona St.). ☎ **850/ 444-8905.** Admission $6 adults, $5 seniors, $2.50 children 4–16, free for children 3 and under. Tues–Sat 10am–4pm. Guided tours Mon–Sat 11am and 1pm. Closed state holidays.

Bounded by Government, Taragona, Adams, and Alcanz streets, this original part of Pensacola resembles a shady English colonial town—albeit with Spanish street names—complete with town green and **Christ Church,** built in 1823 and resembling Bruton Parrish in Williamsburg, Virginia. It has some of Florida's oldest homes (now owned and preserved by the state), along with charming boutiques and interesting restaurants. During summer, costumed characters go about their daily chores and demonstrate old crafts, and University of Florida archaeologists unearth the old Spanish commanding officer's compound at Zaragossa and Tarragona streets. Among the landmarks to visit are the **Museum of Industry,** the **Museum of Commerce,** the French Creole–style **Charles Lavalle House,** the elegant **Victorian Dorr House,** the French Colonial–Creole **Quina House,** and **St. Michael's Cemetery** (land was deeded by the king of Spain).

Another fascinating site is the **Julee Cottage Black History Museum,** 204 Zaragossa St. Built around 1790, this small house was owned by Julee Panton, a freed slave who ran her own business, invested in real estate, and loaned money to slaves so they could buy their freedom. Today the museum recalls her life and deeds, as well as the achievements of other African Americans with Pensacola associations.

Across Taragona Street, the **Pensacola City of Five Flags Exhibit,** in the J. Earle Bowden Building, 120 E. Church St., traces the city's history from Spanish colonial times to the present. Of special interest is the archaeological section, where you can see one of the oldest coins ever found in North America, minted between 1471 and 1474.

Start your tour by buying tickets at **Tivoli House,** 205 E. Zaragossa St., just east of Tarragona Street, where you can get free maps and brochures and purchase audio driving tapes of the city's three historic districts for $5. Admission to the village includes the T. T. Wentworth Jr. Florida State Museum (see below), where you also can buy tickets.

Adjacent to the village, Pensacola's **Vietnam Memorial,** on Bayfront Parkway at 9th Avenue, is known as the "Wall South," since it is a three-quarters-size replica of the national Vietnam Veterans Memorial in Washington, D.C. Look for the Huey helicopter atop the wall.

✪ **National Museum of Naval Aviation.** Radford Blvd., U.S. Naval Air Station. ☎ **850/ 452-3604.** Free admission. IMAX movies $4.50 adults, $4 seniors and children under 13. Daily 9am–5pm; guided tours daily at 9:30am, 11am, 1pm, and 2:30pm; IMAX films on the hour daily 10am–4pm. Closed New Year's Day, Thanksgiving, and Christmas.

The U.S. Navy and Marine Corps have trained at the sprawling U.S. Naval Air Station since they began flying airplanes early in this century. Celebrating their heroics, this truly remarkable museum has more than 100 aircraft dating from the 1920s to the space age. There's even a torpedo bomber flown by former Pres. George Bush during World War II. Both children and adults can sit at the controls of a jet trainer. You can almost feel the tug of gravity while watching the Blue Angels and other naval aviators soaring about the skies in *The Magic of Flight,* a stunning IMAX film shown on a screen six times the size of the average cinema.

Fort Barrancas (☎ **850/934-2600**) also is definitely worth a visit while you're at the naval station. On Taylor Road near the museum, this imposing brick structure overlooks the deep-water pass into Pensacola Bay. The Spanish built the water battery in 1797. Linked to the battery by a tunnel, the incredibly intricate brickwork of the upper section was constructed by American troops between 1839 and 1844. Entry is by a drawbridge across a dry moat, and an interior scarp gallery goes all the way around the inside of the fort. Meticulously restored and operated by the National Park Service as part of Gulf Islands National Seashore, it's open from April to October, daily from 9:30am to 5pm; November through March, Wednesday to Sunday from 10:30am to 4pm. Guided tour schedules change from season to season, so call for the latest information. Admission is free.

The **Pensacola Lighthouse,** opposite the museum entrance on Radford Boulevard, has guided ships to the harbor entrance since 1825. The lighthouse is not open to the public, but you can drive right up to it. The nearby **Lighthouse Point Restaurant** (☎ **850/452-3251**) offers bountiful, all-you-can-eat luncheon buffets and magnificent bay views for just $5.50 per person; it's open Monday to Friday from 10:30am to 2pm, and reservations are not required.

The Naval Station is southwest of downtown Pensacola. Enter either at the Main Gate at the south end of Navy Boulevard (Fla. 295) or at the Back Gate on Blue Angel Parkway (Fla. 173). No passes are required.

Pensacola Museum of Art. 407 S. Jefferson St. (at Main Street). ☎ **850/432-6247.** Admission free on Tues; other days, $2 adults, $1 active-duty military and students, free for kids under 6. Tues–Fri 10am–5pm, Sat 10am–4pm, Sun 1–4pm.

Housed in what was the city jail from 1906 to 1954, this museum showcases permanent art and sculpture collections as well as art on loan, from tribal art to classic European pieces to avant-garde modern works.

T. T. Wentworth Jr. Florida State Museum. 330 S. Jefferson St. (at Church St.). ☎ **850/444-8586.** Admission $6 adults, $5 seniors and military, $2.50 children 4–16, children 3 and under free (includes Historic Pensacola Village). Tues–Sat 10am–4pm.

The classic yellow brick building houses exhibits of western Florida's history and has a special hands-on Discovery Museum for children on the third floor.

HISTORIC DISTRICTS

In addition to Historic Pensacola Village in the Seville Historic District (see above), the city has two other preservation areas worth a stroll. The Pensacola Visitor Information Center provides free walking-tour maps, and you can buy an audiotape driving tour for $5 at Tivoli House in Historic Pensacola Village (see above).

PALAFOX HISTORIC DISTRICT   Running up Palafox Street from the water to Wright Street, the Palafox Historic District is also the downtown business district. Beautiful Spanish Renaissance- and Mediterranean-style buildings stand from the early days, including the ornate Saenger Theatre. In 1821 Gen. Andrew Jackson formally accepted Florida into the United States during a ceremony in Plaza Ferdinand VII, now a National Historic Landmark. His statue commemorates the event.

The Palafox district is home to the **Pensacola Museum of Art,** in the old city jail, and the **T. T. Wentworth Jr. Florida State Museum** (see "Exploring Historic Pensacola," above).

NORTH HILL PRESERVATION DISTRICT   Another entry in the National Register of Historic Places, the North Hill Preservation District covers the 50 square blocks north of the Palafox Historic District bounded by Wright, Blount, Palafox, and Reus streets. Descendants of Spanish nobility, timber barons, British merchants, French Creoles, buccaneers, and Civil War soldiers still live in some of the more than

500 homes. They are not open to the public, but are a bonanza for anyone interested in architecture. In 1863 Union troops erected a fort in Lee Square, at Palafox and Gadsden streets. It later was dedicated to the Confederacy, complete with a 50-foot-high obelisk and sculpture based on John Elder's painting *After Appomattox.*

SHOPPING

Sightseeing and shopping can be combined in Pensacola's Palafox and Seville historic districts, where many shops are housed in renovated centuries-old buildings. The **Quayside Art Gallery,** on Plaza Ferdinand at the corner of Zaragossa and Jefferson streets (☎ **850/438-2363**), is the largest cooperative gallery in the Southeast. More than 100 artists display their works here, and the friendly staff will direct you to other nearby galleries.

North T Street between West Cervantes Street and West Fairfield Drive has so many antique dealers and small flea markets that it's known as **Antique Alley.** Others have booths in the **Ninth Avenue Antique Mall,** 380 N. 9th Ave. between Gregory and Strong streets (☎ **850/438-3961**). Get a complete list of local antique dealers from the Pensacola Visitor Information Center (see "Essentials," above).

Browsers will enjoy poking through the 400 dealer spaces covering 45 acres at the **Flea Market,** on U.S. 98, opposite the zoo about 10 miles east of Gulf Breeze (☎ **850/934-1971**). It's open on Saturday and Sunday from 9am to 5pm. Admission is free.

WHERE TO STAY

The high season at all of the Northwest Florida beaches runs from Easter to Labor Day, and hotel or motel reservations are essential during this time. Room rates are highest during school vacation from mid-May to mid-August, and premiums are charged at Easter, Memorial Day, July 4, and Labor Day. There's another high-priced peak in March, when thousands of raucous college students invade during spring break. Economical times to visit are April (except Easter) and September—the weather's warm, most establishments are open, and room rates are significantly lower than during summer. The least expensive rates come during winter, but many attractions and some restaurants may be closed then.

The Pensacola Visitor Information Center (see "Essentials," above) publishes a complete list of rental condominiums and cottages. Among the leading rental agents are **Gulf Coast Accommodations,** 400 Quietwater Beach Rd., Box 12, Pensacola Beach, FL 32561 (☎ **800/239-4334** or 850/932-9788; fax 850/932-3449; www.innisfree.com/gca); **JME Management,** 22A Via de Luna, Pensacola Beach, FL 32562 (☎ **800/554-3695** or 850/932-0775; fax 850/932-0787); and **Tristan Realty,** P.O. Box 1611, Gulf Breeze, FL 32562 (☎ **800/445-9931** or 850/932-7363; fax 850/932-8361; www.pcola.com/tristan/).

For camping, the **Fort Pickens Area** of Gulf Islands National Seashore (☎ **800/365-2267** for reservations, or 850/934-2621 for recorded information) has 200 sites (135 with electricity) in a pine forest about 7 miles west of Pensacola Beach on the bay side of Santa Rosa Island. Nature trails lead from the camp through Blackbird Marsh and to the beach. A small store sells provisions. Sites cost $15 a night without power, $20 a night with it. Golden Age and Golden Access cardholders get a 50% discount. You can make reservations up to 5 months in advance.

Escambia County adds 11.5% to all hotel and campground bills.

The accommodations listed below are arranged by geographic area: downtown Pensacola and Pensacola Beach.

PENSACOLA

The University Mall complex at I-10 and Davis Highway, about 5 miles north of downtown, has a host of chain motels, including **Residence Inn by Marriott** (☎ 800/331-3131 or 850/479-1000), in which all rooms and apartments have kitchens and fireplaces, and **Fairfield Inn by Marriott,** 7325 N. Davis Hwy. (☎ 800/331-3131 or 850/484-8001). The recently renovated **Motel 6-North** (☎ 800/466-8356 or 850/476-5386) is within walking distance on the north side of I-10. There's an ample supply of inexpensive restaurants on Plantation Road and in the adjacent mall.

New World Landing. 600 S. Palafox St. (at Pine St.), Pensacola, FL 32501. ☎ **850/ 432-4111.** Fax 850/432-6836. 15 units. A/C TV TEL. $85 double; $130 suite. AE, DC, MC, V.

Near the scenic bay and in the historic district, this urban version of a comfortable country inn is enhanced by flower gardens and fountains. From the colonial-style lobby, a grand staircase leads to high-ceilinged and spacious rooms artistically decorated with antiques. The rooms depict aspects of Pensacola's rich history: four flaunt Spanish decor, four are trés chic French style, four portray Early Americana, and four focus on Olde England.

The adjoining New World Landing Restaurant and pub recalls the city's colorful historic past, honoring Spain with a Barcelona Room, spotlighting French history in a Marseilles Room, and giving tribute to the city itself in the Pensacola Room. Fresh seafood in wine or butter sauce is a specialty, but the menu also features excellent steaks, prime rib of beef, veal, and more. Lunch is served Monday to Friday; dinner, Tuesday to Saturday.

Pensacola Grand Hotel. 200 E. Gregory St. (at Alcanz St.), Pensacola, FL 32501. ☎ **800/ 348-3336** or 850/433-3336. Fax 850/432-7572. 212 units. A/C TV TEL. $90–$100 double; $204–$408 suite. Weekend rates available. AE, DC, DISC, MC, V.

Opposite the Civic Center in the Seville Historic District near the southern end of I-110, this unique hotel has turned the historic L&N Railroad Depot into a grand lobby with bar, restaurants, lounges, meeting rooms, and a cozy library. You'll see such turn-of-the-century accoutrements as an ornate railroad clock, original oak stair rails, imported marble, ceramic mosaic tile floors, and old-fashioned carved furniture. The plush L&N Lobby Bar and the 1912 Restaurant capture this railroad ambience. A two-story glass Galleria links the depot to a modern 15-story tower, whose rooms and suites are popular with business travelers and groups. Facilities include a fitness center and outdoor pool.

Seville Inn. 223 E. Garden St. (between Alcanz and Manresa sts.), Pensacola, FL 32501. ☎ **800/277-7275** or 850/433-8331. Fax 850/432-6849. 120 units. A/C TV TEL. Summer $69–$79 double; winter $39–$44 double. Rates include continental breakfast. AE, DC, MC, V.

This dated but clean two-story motel is conveniently located at the edge of the Seville Historic District, across the street from the Civic Center, and about 4 blocks from the Saenger Theatre. An outdoor swimming pool is open during the warm months. Guests receive complimentary local phone calls, and passes to the Pensacola Greyhound track and Seville Quarter entertainment complex (see "Pensacola After Dark," below).

PENSACOLA BEACH

If you don't need a room right on the beach and don't mind hunting for a parking spot once you get there during the summer, you can save by staying on U.S. 98 in Gulf Breeze, a short ride across the Bob Sykes Bridge to Pensacola Beach. The pick here is the **Holiday Inn-Bay Beach,** 51 Gulf Breeze Pkwy. (☎ **800/HOLIDAY** or 850/932-2214; fax 904/932-0932), which sits on a small beach with a grand view of Pensacola across the bay. There's a pool in a grassy bay-side courtyard, plus the very good Bon Appetit Cafe. Double rooms range from $70 to $100 during summer, $60 to $80 off-season. For basic accommodations, try the **Gulf Coast Inn Motel,** 843 Gulf Breeze Pkwy. (☎ **850/932-2222**), an older but clean establishment where doubles cost $38 to $48 in summer, $30 to $40 off-season.

Moderate

Best Western Pensacola Beach. 16 Via de Luna Dr., Pensacola Beach, FL 32561. ☎ **800/934-3301** or 850/934-3300. Fax 850/934-9780. 122 units. A/C TV TEL. Summer $119–$139 double. Off-season $59–$109 double. Rates include continental breakfast. Golf packages available. AE, DC, DISC, MC, V.

On the Gulf front, this casual hotel is notable for bright, clean, and extra-spacious accommodations, complete with refrigerators, coffeemakers, microwaves, and wet bars. Outside corridors lead to all rooms. Although none has its own balcony or patio, units facing the beach have great views; the less-expensive "inland" rooms don't. Two swimming pools, the Cabana Bar, and a children's playground are on the beach. Chan's Market Café (see "Where to Dine," below) sits in the parking lot.

Clarion Suites Resort & Convention Center. 20 Via de Luna Dr., Pensacola Beach, FL 32561. ☎ **800/874-5303** or 850/932-4300. Fax 850/934-9112. 86 units. A/C TV TEL. Summer $110–$161 up to 4 persons. Off-season $67–$123 up to 4 persons. Rates include continental breakfast. AE, DC, DISC, MC, V.

Built to resemble a village of cottages, this tin-roofed, pastel-sided beachfront resort offers one-bedroom suites that can accommodate four people. The attractively decorated accommodations include a living room with a dining area, bathroom (39 bilevel loft suites have 1½ baths), kitchen, and private entrance. The living rooms and bedrooms each have their own TVs and telephones. There's no restaurant, but complimentary continental breakfast is served daily in the lobby, and eateries are within walking distance. Facilities include a swimming pool, fitness center, children's play area, beach pavilion, coin laundry, and conference rooms.

Comfort Inn Pensacola Beach. 40 Fort Pickens Rd., Pensacola Beach, FL 32561. ☎ **800/934-5470** or 850/934-5400. Fax 850/932-7210. 99 units. A/C TV TEL. Summer $109–$129. Off-season $59–$89. Rates include continental breakfast. AE, DC, DISC, MC, V.

On the bay side of Fort Pickens Road opposite Casino Beach and the Quietwater Boardwalk, this four-story motel has medium-size rooms with bright furniture, spreads, and drapes. They all open to external walkways, thereby eliminating balconies and reducing views and privacy. Armoires hide the televisions and provide closets. There's a pool and exercise room here. Breakfast is served in a room off the lobby.

The Dunes. 333 Fort Pickens Rd., Pensacola Beach, FL 32561. ☎ **800/83-DUNES** or 850/932-3536. Fax 850/932-7088. 76 units. A/C TV TEL. Summer $115–$145 double; $230–$275 suite. Off-season $70–$90 double; $195–$245 suite. Packages available. AE, DISC, MC, V.

This eight-story tower has spacious rooms, all with balconies with gorgeous gulf or bay vistas. They come equipped with coffeemakers and hair dryers, and the penthouse suites have their own Jacuzzis. The small but pleasant Gulf Front Cafe serves breakfast, lunch, and dinner. The kids can participate in the supervised children's program from May to Labor Day. The hotel will even take care of the kids so Mom and Dad can take Saturday night off. Facilities also include a heated swimming pool, jogging trail, bike path, and volleyball area. There's an undeveloped dune preserve next door.

Hampton Inn Pensacola Beach. 2 Via de Luna, Pensacola Beach, FL 32561. ☎ **800/ 320-8108** or 850/932-6800. Fax 850/932-6833. 181 units. A/C TV TEL. Summer $99–$139 double. Off-season $65–$109 double. Rates include continental breakfast. AE, DC, DISC, MC, V.

Opened in 1995, this pastel, four-story hotel sits right by the Gulf next to Casino Beach. The bright lobby opens to a wooden sundeck with beachside swimming pools on either side (one is heated). Half the oversize rooms have balconies overlooking the Gulf; these are more expensive than rooms on the bay side, which have nice views but no outside sitting areas. Each unit is equipped with a refrigerator, microwave oven, and wet bar. There's no restaurant on the premises, but Chan's Gulfside Café and Surfside Saloon is next door. Guests have their own coin laundry. Local calls are free to guests, and the TVs carry HBO.

Holiday Inn Pensacola Beach. 165 Fort Pickens Rd., Pensacola Beach, FL 32561. ☎ **800/ 465-4329** or 850/932-5361. Fax 850/932-7121. 150 units. A/C TV TEL. Summer $105–$130 double. Off-season $65–$110 double. Senior citizen discounts. AE, DC, DISC, MC, V.

This nine-story establishment boasts terrific views from its brightly furnished upper-floor rooms and Penthouse Lounge. It's one of the oldest hotels in the area, which means the rooms aren't as large as at other new properties, such as the Hampton Inn; there's adequate space for a king-size bed, but rooms with two double beds are relatively cramped. They all have private balconies, however, with the most expensive rooms facing directly onto the Gulf. The Penthouse Lounge serves dinners and has summertime entertainment. Facilities include a lobby bar looking out to a beachside heated swimming pool.

Inexpensive

✪ **Five Flags Inn.** 299 Fort Pickens Rd., Pensacola Beach, FL 32561. ☎ **850/932-3586.** Fax 850/934-0257. 49 units. A/C TV TEL. Summer $85 double. Off-season $49–$69 double. Packages available. AE, DISC, MC, V.

This friendly motel between the Holiday Inn and The Dunes looks like a jail from the road, but don't be fooled. Big picture windows look out to the swimming pool and gorgeous white-sand beach, which comes right up to the property. Although the accommodations are small, the rates are a bargain for well-furnished, gulf-front rooms.

WHERE TO DINE
PENSACOLA

Housed in the 1879-vintage Moreno Cottage, **Mr. P's Sandwich Shop,** 221 E. Zaragossa St., opposite Old Christ Church (☎ 850/433-0294), is a good place to stop for inexpensive soups, salads, quiches, and sandwiches while touring Historic Pensacola Village. Open Monday to Saturday from 11am to 2pm.

Other low-priced options here include two branches of **Barnhill's Country Buffet,** one on North Davis Highway and Olive Road north of I-10 (☎ 850/477-5465), and a second on U.S. 98 at Oriole Drive 3 miles east of Gulf Breeze (☎ 850/932-0403). Both offer a cornucopia of fried chicken and fish, baked ham, roast beef, a tasty pot roast, boiled cabbage and collard greens, old-fashioned 'Nilla Wafer banana pudding, and other Southern fare. Adults pay $5.59 a head at lunch, while kids 12 and under are charged 40¢ times their age. At dinner, the prices jump to $7 and 45¢. Both Barnhill's are open Sunday to Thursday from 10:45am to 8pm, Friday and Saturday from 10:45am to 8:30pm (to 8:30 and 9pm, respectively, in summer). MasterCard and Visa cards are accepted.

✪ **Hopkins' Boarding House.** 900 N. Spring St. (at Strong St.). ☎ **850/438-3979.** Reservations not accepted. Breakfast $3.50; full meals $7. No credit cards. Tues–Sun 7–9:30am, 11:15am–2pm, and 5:15–7:30pm; Sun noon–2pm. SOUTHERN.

There's a delicious peek into the past when you dine at this Victorian boardinghouse in the heart of the North Hill Preservation District. Outside, ancient trees shade a wraparound porch with old-fashioned rocking chairs in which to await the next available place at the large dining tables inside. You could be seated next to the mayor or a mechanic, for everyone in town dines here, and everyone eats family style. Platters are piled high with seasonal Southern-style vegetables from nearby farms. Tuesday is famous as Fried Chicken Day, and you're likely to be served fried fish on Friday. Every Yankee should sample the piping-hot grits accompanying each bountiful breakfast. In true boardinghouse fashion, guests bus their own dishes and pay the one price when they're finished eating.

✪ **Jamie's.** 424 E. Zaragossa St. (between Alcanz and Florida Blanca). ☎ **850/434-2911.** Reservations recommended at both lunch and dinner. Main courses $18–$23. AE, DISC, MC, V. Mon 6–10pm, Tues–Sat 11:30am–2:30pm and 6–10pm. CONTINENTAL/AMERICAN.

Occupying a restored Victorian home in Historic Pensacola Village, the town's classiest and most romantic restaurant enhances the dining experience with glowing fireplaces, soft candlelight, gleaming antiques, and subdued background music. The menu changes regularly to include such creative dishes as veal Oscar with a Cajun-spiced hollandaise sauce giving it a distinct Louisiana twist. The menu includes Jamie's recommended wines for each course.

Marina Oyster Barn. 505 Bayou Blvd. (on Bayou Texar). ☎ **850/433-0511.** Reservations not accepted. Sandwiches $2.50–$5.50; main courses $5.50–$12; lunch specials $3.75–$5.50. AE, DISC, MC, V. Tues–Sat 11am–9pm (lunch specials 11am–2pm). Go east on Cervantes St. across the Bayou Texar Bridge, then left at the stoplight on Perry Ave., and left again to the end of Strong St. SEAFOOD.

Exuding the ambience of the quickly vanishing Old Florida fish camps, this plain but clean restaurant at the Johnson-Rooks Marina has been a favorite with seafood lovers since 1969, for both its view and its down-home-style seafood. Served raw, steamed, fried, or Rockefeller, freshly shucked oysters are the main feature; but the seafood salad here is first-rate, and the fish, shrimp, and oysters are breaded with cornmeal in true Southern fashion. The daily luncheon specials give you a light meal at a bargain price.

McGuire's Irish Pub & Brewery. 600 E. Gregory St. (between 11th and 12th aves.). ☎ **850/433-6789.** Reservations not accepted. Snacks, burgers, and sandwiches $7.50–$8; meals $13–$25. AE, DC, DISC, MC, V. Mon–Sat 11am–2am, Sun 11am–3pm (brunch) and 3pm–1am. AMERICAN/IRISH.

Every day is St. Patrick's Day here, with corned beef and cabbage, Irish stew, and such hybrids as an scampi o'fettucini (shrimp in Alfredo sauce). Super-size hamburgers, tender steak, grilled fish, beer-batter shrimp, barbecued and prime ribs, hearty bean soup, and salads are also on the menu. You can watch the house beer being brewed in copper kettles and dine in a cellarlike room with 8,000 bottles of wine on display. You can leave an autographed dollar bill; more than 125,000 of them line the bar's walls and ceilings (famous folks' bucks are framed near the entrance). Live music is offered most nights.

Skopelos on the Bay. 670 Scenic Hwy. (U.S. 90 east, at E. Cervantes St.). ☎ **850/432-6565.** Reservations recommended. Main courses $13–$19. AE, DISC, MC, V. Tues–Sat 5–10:30pm. SEAFOOD/STEAKS/GREEK.

Perched on a bluff overlooking the bay, Skopelos is famous hereabouts for its great views and creative seafood dishes, such as the scampi Cervantes, a sautéed fillet of scampi topped with crabmeat. Other seafood selections range from broiled scallops to Mediterranean-style grouper prepared with a sauce of tomato and roasted eggplant. The menu also features charcoal-grilled steaks and chicken and roast leg of lamb. Befitting the owner's Greek heritage, roast lamb is served with moussaka, dolmades, titopita, and spanakopita.

PENSACOLA BEACH

Chan's Gulfside Café & Surfside Saloon. 2½ Via de Luna (at Fort Pickens Rd.). ☎ **850/ 932-3525.** Reservations recommended upstairs, not accepted downstairs. Upstairs main courses $17–$23. Downstairs, sandwiches and burgers $6–$9, main courses $10–$18. AE, DC, DISC, MC, V. Upstairs Sun–Thurs 5:30–10pm, Fri–Sat 5:30–11pm. Downstairs daily 11am–2am (to 11pm off-season). SEAFOOD.

Offering Pensacola Beach's only gulf-front dining, this modern complex on Casino Beach offers two lively dining choices. The upstairs Florida Room is more formal yet still relaxed, with blond wood and widely spaced tables enjoying terrific views of the beach and gulf. Cuisine here features mesquite-fired tuna, grouper, and shrimp, plus the likes of coconut shrimp, triggerfish with Rockefeller spinach, and grouper Lyonnaise. The downstairs pub is completely informal, with a long bar where fans can sample an extensive collection of beers from microbreweries while watching their favorite teams on several TVs. Although not of the same quality, many of the same wood-grilled items are offered down here, along with pub-style fare such as pastas, salads, burgers, sandwiches, pastas, and baskets full of fried seafood or chicken. The pub opens to a beachside patio, which has outdoor dining and live entertainment during summer.

✪ **Chan's Market Café.** 16 Via de Luna. ☎ **850/932-8454.** Breakfast/lunch/snacks $3–$7; dinner $4–$7. AE, DISC, MC, V. Daily 7am–9pm. AMERICAN.

The aroma of cappuccino and pastries in the oven permeates this pleasant little cafe and bakery, which shares quarters with a liquor store in the parking lot of the Best Western Pensacola Beach. It's the best place on the beach for a breakfast of freshly baked croissants or bagels. Lunches and dinners feature economical ($4 to $7) white-plate specials of such favorites as meat loaf, rotisserie chicken, pot roast, and grilled fish, all served with a choice of Southern-style veggies. Or you can order a heaping sandwich made with one of Chan's large, flaky croissants.

Flounder's Chowder and Ale House. 800 Quietwater Beach Rd. (at Via de Luna and Fort Pickens Rd.). ☎ **850/932-2003.** Reservations not accepted. Main courses $15–$18; burgers and sandwiches $7–$8. AE, DC, DISC, MC, V. Mon–Sat 11am–2am (to 11pm in winter), Sun 11am–2pm (brunch) and 2pm–2am (to 11pm in winter). SEAFOOD.

From Cajun to Florentine, you can order flounder in many different preparations at this publike establishment, whose decor features stained-glass windows from an old New York convent and confessional-booth walls from a New Orleans church. Bookshelves give a cozy, studious feel to one dining room, but Flounder's lively atmosphere is more accurately captured by the glass walls of another dining area; these face a popular beachside bar where patrons boogie to live reggae bands during the summer season (see "Pensacola After Dark," below). Burgers, salads, and sandwiches are offered all day, and there's a children's menu. A glass of champagne accompanies a sumptuous bay-side Sunday brunch.

Jubilee Restaurant & Entertainment Complex. 400 Quietwater Beach Rd. (Via de Luna at Fort Pickens Rd.), on Quietwater Beach Boardwalk. ☎ **850/934-3108.** Reservations not required. Topside main courses $16–$22. Beachside Café sandwiches and salads $6–$8, main courses $10–$17. AE, DC, DISC, MC, V. Beachside Café Mon–Sat 11am–11pm, Sun 10am–11pm; Topside daily 6–10pm (Sun brunch 9am–2pm). SEAFOOD/CAJUN/AMERICAN.

At this beachside restaurant complex, complete with Capt'n Fun's Beach Bar, most dining is very casual, even in the elegant, near-gourmet Topside Restaurant. Up there, where you'll get a bird's-eye view of the sound, the chef excels in the preparation of local fish and shellfish, especially with Louisiana flavors. There's a larger difference in quality than price downstairs in the pub-style Beachside Café, opening to a sound-side dock and offering a varied menu of fish, pastas, sandwiches, salads, and barbecue pork, shrimp, and oysters. The J-Sweet Coffee & Dessert Room has homemade sweets and gourmet coffees. On summer evenings there are live bands for dancing under the stars and indoor entertainment year-round.

PENSACOLA AFTER DARK

THE CLUB & BAR SCENE   Pensacola's downtown entertainment center is at ✪ **Seville Quarter,** 130 E. Government St., at Jefferson Street (☎ 850/434-6211), in the Seville Historic District. This restored antique brick complex with New Orleans–style wrought-iron balconies is actually a collection of pubs and restaurants whose names capture the ambience: Rosie O'Grady's Goodtime Emporium, Lili Marlene's Aviator's Pub, Apple Annie's Courtyard, End o' the Alley Bar, Phineas Phogg's Balloon Works (a dance hall, not a balloon shop), and Fast Eddie's Billiard Parlor (which has electronic games for kids, too). The pubs all serve up libations, food, and live entertainment from Dixieland jazz to country and western. Get a monthly calendar at the information booth next to Rosie O'Grady's. Open daily from 11am to 2am.

Every night is party time at **McGuire's Irish Pub & Brewery,** 600 E. Gregory St. (☎ 850/433-6789), the city's popular Irish pub, brewery, and eatery (see "Where to Dine," above). Irish bands appear nightly during summer, on Saturday and Sunday the rest of the year. For live laughs, the **Coconuts Comedy Club,** in the Holiday Inn, University Mall, 7200 Plantation Rd. (☎ 850/484-NUTS), features comedians from Thursday to Saturday. Doors open at 7:30pm, with the first performance usually at 8:30pm. Cover charge is $4 on Thursday, $6 on Friday and Saturday.

Nightlife at the beach centers around **Quietwater Boardwalk,** Via de Luna at Fort Pickens Road (no phone), a shopping/dining complex on Santa Rosa Sound. Jubilee's Beachside Café and Entertainment Complex heads the list. The Sun Ray Taco Shop offers live bands nightly during the summer, on weekends off-season, and a no-name sports bar keeps the TVs going. With the lively Flounder's Beach and Reggae Bar just a few steps away, it's easy to barhop until you find a band and crowd to your liking. Across Via de Luna at Casino Beach, **The Dock** (☎ 850/934-3316) and **Chan's Gulfside Saloon** next door (☎ 850/932-3525) both have beachside live bands nightly during summer, on weekends off-season. You can catch all the games here at **Sidelines Sports Bar & Restaurant** (☎ 850/934-3660). See "Where to Dine," above, for details about Chan's, Jubilee's, and Flounder's.

Over on Perdido Key, about 15 miles west of downtown Pensacola, the ✪ **Flora-Bama Lounge,** on Fla. 292 at the Florida–Alabama line (☎ 850/492-0611), is almost a shrine to country music. This slapped-together gulf-side pub is famous for its special jam sessions from noon until way past midnight on Saturday and Sunday. Flora-Bama is the prime sponsor and a key venue for the Frank Brown International Songwriters' Festival during the first week of November. If you've never attended an Interstate Mullet Toss, catch the fun here during the last weekend of April. The raw oyster bar is popular all the time. Take in the great gulf views from the Deck Bar. It's open daily from 8:30am to 2:30am.

THE PERFORMING ARTS   Pensacola has a surprisingly sophisticated array of entertainment choices for such a relatively small city. For a schedule of upcoming events, get a copy of *Vision,* a bimonthly newsletter published by the Arts Council of Northwest Florida, P.O. Box 731, Pensacola, FL 32594 (☎ **850/432-9906**). Also pick up *Sneak Preview,* a calendar of events at the Pensacola Civic Center and the Saenger Theater. Both publications are available at the Pensacola Visitor Information Center (see "Essentials," above). Tickets for all major performances can be purchased by phone from **Ticketmaster** (☎ **800/488-5252** or 850/433-6311).

The highlight venue here is the ornate **Saenger Theater,** 118 S. Palafox St., near Romano Street (☎ **850/444-7686**), a painstakingly restored masterpiece of Spanish baroque architecture. The variety of presentations includes the local opera company and symphony orchestra, Broadway musicals, and touring performers. The 10,000-seat **Pensacola Civic Center,** 201 E. Gregory St., at Alcanz Street (☎ **850/433-6311**), hosts a variety of entertainment. Call ahead for the current schedule.

2 Fort Walton Beach & Destin

40 miles E of Pensacola, 160 miles W of Tallahassee

At the outbreak of the Civil War in 1861, a small Confederate contingent set up camp on Santa Rosa Sound to guard the eastern approaches to Pensacola. The Rebels beat a hasty retreat when Yankee troops shelled their position from Okaloosa Island, but the name they gave their little outpost has remained to this day: Fort Walton.

Back then the only settlement in these parts was Destin, a tiny fishing village east of Fort Walton and separated from it by East Pass, which lets broad, beautiful Choctowhatchee Bay flow into the Gulf of Mexico. And even though the U.S. government established sprawling Eglin Air Force Base here in the 1930s, Fort Walton had just 90 residents as late as 1940.

But then came World War II, and Eglin grew into a major U.S. Army Air Corps training base. When Okaloosa Island became popular with Alabamians and Georgians after the war, Fort Walton officially added "Beach" to its name. Although summertime tourism dominates Okaloosa Island, mainland Fort Walton Beach still relies on the U.S. Air Force for its year-round living.

On a picturesque harbor and world famous for its fishing, Destin stands in contrast to its friendly, down-to-earth neighbor. No longer a sleepy village, Destin today is Northwest Florida's fastest growing vacation destination. It has multitudes of high-rise condominiums, the huge Sandestin luxury resort, several excellent golf courses, and some of Northwest Florida's best restaurants and lively nightspots. By and large, it attracts a generally more affluent crowd than does its more down-to-earth neighbor.

To the east of Destin, development in the beaches of southern Walton County has been slower and more controlled, with cottages nestled among sand dunes and sea oats. Walton County is home both to charming DeFuniak Springs and the village of Seaside. While DeFuniak Springs is a genuine Victorian town nestled around an inland lake, Seaside was built on a lovely stretch of beach in the 1980s—but with Victorian architecture that makes it look a century older. Seaside's gulf-side honeymoon cottages make for one of Florida's most romantic retreats, and the village has interesting shops and art galleries, delightful restaurants, a stamp-size post office, and a resident population of artists, writers, and other creative folks, who permit no cars in their pleasant little enclave.

ESSENTIALS

GETTING THERE   From east or west, take I-10 or U.S. 98. For Fort Walton Beach, exit I-10 at Crestview and follow Fla. 85 south for 24 miles. For Destin and the beaches of southern Walton County, exit I-10 at DeFuniak Springs and follow U.S. 331 south to Santa Rosa Beach. You can avoid the beach traffic between there and Destin by leaving U.S. 331 at Freeport and taking Fla. 20 west to Villa Tasso, then Fla. 293 across the Mid Bay Bridge ($2 toll). From the north, take U.S. 331 south through Alabama.

Flights arriving at and departing from **Okaloosa County Air Terminal** actually use the field at Eglin Air Force Base. The terminal is on Fla. 85 north of Fort Walton Beach and is served by **American Eagle** (☎ **800/433-7300**), **Delta Connection/ASA** (☎ **800/221-1212**), **Northwest/KLM** (☎ **800/225-2525**), and **US Airways Express** (☎ **800/428-4322**). The major car-rental firms are here, or you can take a taxi or limousine that's waiting outside the modern terminal. Fares are based on a zone system: to Fort Walton Beach, $10 to $14; to Destin, $20 to $22; and to Sandestin, $28 to $30.

The *Sunset Limited* transcontinental service on **Amtrak** (☎ **800/USA-RAIL**) stops at Crestview, 26 miles north of Fort Walton Beach.

VISITOR INFORMATION   For advance information about both Fort Walton Beach and Destin, contact the **Emerald Coast Convention and Visitors Bureau,** P.O. Box 609, Fort Walton Beach, FL 32549 (☎ **800/322-3319** or 850/651-7131; fax 850/651-7149; www.destin-fwb.com). The bureau shares quarters with the **Okaloosa County Visitors Welcome Center** in a tin-roofed, beachside building on Miracle Strip Parkway (U.S. 98) on Okaloosa Island at the eastern edge of Fort Walton Beach. Stop there for brochures, maps, and other information, especially the *Insider,* a free tabloid with an excellent listing of restaurants and attractions. The welcome center is open during summer daily from 8am to 5pm. Off-season hours are Monday to Friday from 8am to 5pm, Saturday and Sunday from 10am to 4pm.

The **Destin Area Chamber of Commerce,** P.O. Box 8, Destin, FL 32541 (☎ **850/837-6241;** fax 850/654-5612; www.destinfl.com/chamber), gives away brochures and sells maps of the area. The chamber has resided at 1021 U.S. 98 East, opposite the Holiday Inn in Destin, but it expects to move in 1999, so call for the new location. Open Monday to Friday from 9am to 5pm all year.

For information about the beaches of South Walton, contact the **South Walton Tourist Development Council,** P.O. Box 1248, Santa Rosa Beach, FL 32459 (☎ **800/822-6877** or 850/267-1216; fax 850/267-3943; www.beachesofsouthwalton.com). Its **visitor center** is at the intersection of U.S. 98 and U.S. 331 in Santa Rosa Beach (☎ **850/267-3511**). Open daily 8:30am to 4:30pm, later in summer.

GETTING AROUND   For a cab in Fort Walton Beach, call **Charter Taxis** (☎ **850/863-5466**), **Crosstown Taxi** (☎ **850/244-7303**), **JC's Cab** (☎ **850/865-0578**), **Veterans Cab Co.** (☎ **850/243-1403**), **Yellow Cab** (☎ **850/244-3600**), or **Checker Cab** (☎ **850/244-4491**). In Destin, call **Destin Taxi** (☎ **850/654-5700**). Fares are based on a zone system rather than meters, with a $3 minimum. Trips within Fort Walton Beach or Destin should range from $3 to $5.

STREET ADDRESSES   Don't worry if you're confused by the street addresses here, for even many local residents don't fully comprehend the post office's naming and numbering system. This is especially true of addresses along U.S. 98, which runs east-west through the area.

In Fort Walton Beach, U.S. 98 is known as the "Miracle Strip Parkway," with "southwest" and "southeast" addresses on the mainland and "east" addresses on Okaloosa Island.

In Destin, U.S. 98 is officially known as "Hwy. 98 East" from the Destin Bridge to Airport Road, and street numbers get progressively higher as you head east from the bridge. The post office calls U.S. 98 the "Emerald Coast Parkway" east of Airport Road, although locals still say a place is on "98 East." To add to the confusion, "Old Hwy. 98 East" is a short spur from Airport Road to the western side of Henderson Beach State Recreation Area, and "Scenic Hwy. 98 East" runs along the beach from the eastern side of Henderson Beach to Sandestin.

In south Walton County, U.S. 98 is known as the Emerald Coast Parkway, but the street numbering system changes completely once you pass the county line.

In other words, call and ask for directions if you're not sure how to find an establishment here.

TIME   The area is in the central time zone, an hour behind Miami, Orlando, and Tallahassee.

HITTING THE BEACH

FORT WALTON BEACH   Do your loafing on the white sands of **Okaloosa Island,** joined to the mainland by the high-rise Brooks Bridge over Santa Rosa Sound. Most resort hotels and amusement parks are grouped around the Gulfarium on U.S. 98 east of the bridge. Here you'll find **The Boardwalk,** a collection of tin-roofed beachside buildings between the Gulfarium and the Ramada Inn, has a games arcade for the kids, the Soggy Dollar Saloon for adults, and covered picnic areas, a summertime snack bar, and Harpoon Hanna's restaurant (see "Where to Dine," below). Just to the east, you can use the free facilities at **Beasley Park,** home of the Okaloosa County Visitor Welcome Center.

Across U.S. 98, the **Okaloosa Area, Gulf Islands National Seashore** has picnic areas and sailboats for rent on Choctawhatchee Bay, plus access to the Gulf. Admission to this part of the national seashore is free.

DESTIN   The 208-acre ✪ **Henderson Beach State Recreation Area,** east of Destin Harbor on U.S. 98, allows easy access to swimming, sunning, surf fishing, picnicking, and seabird-watching. There are rest rooms, outdoor showers, and surf chairs for disabled persons. The area is open daily from 8am to sunset. Admission is $2 per vehicle, $1 for pedestrians and cyclists. Several good restaurants are just outside the park's western boundary. Campsites will be opened here somewhere in 1999. For more information, contact the area at 1700 Emerald Coast Pkwy., Destin, FL 32541 (☎ **850/837-7550**).

The **James W. Lee Park,** Destin and Sandestin on Scenic Hwy. 98, has a long white-sand beach overlooked by covered picnic tables, an ice-cream parlor, and **The Crab Trap Restaurant** (☎ **850/654-2822**), whose moderately priced snacks and seafood make it a fine spot for lunch with a view or dinner with a sunset.

SOUTHERN WALTON COUNTY   Sporting perhaps the finest stretch of white sand on the Gulf, ✪ **Grayton Beach State Recreation Area,** on County Road 30A, also has 356 acres of pine forests surrounding scenic Western Lake. There's a boat ramp and campground with electric hookups on the lake (see "Where to Stay," below). Get a self-guided-tour leaflet for the nature trail at the main gate. It's open daily from 8am to sunset. Admission is $3.25 per vehicle with up to 8 occupants, $1 per pedestrian or bicyclist. For more information, contact the area at 357 Main Park Rd., Santa Rosa Beach, FL 32459 (☎ **850/231-4210**).

Seaside has free public parking along County Road 30A and is a good spot for a day at the beach, a stroll or bike ride around the quaint village, and a tasty meal at one of its restaurants.

OUTDOOR PURSUITS

BOATING & BOAT RENTALS   Powerboat lovers can get their thrills during the summer season on the *Sea Blaster* (☎ 850/837-1136 or 850/664-7872), one of the world's largest speedboats. It roars out every 2 hours from 11am to 5pm from AJ's Seafood & Oyster Bar on Destin Harbor. Rides cost $12 for adults, $7 for children 12 and under.

Pontoon boats are highly popular for use on the back bays and on Sunday-afternoon floating parties in East Pass. Several companies rent them, including **Best Boat Rentals** (☎ 850/664-7872) on Okaloosa Island in Fort Walton Beach and **Adventure Pontoon Rentals** (☎ 850/837-3041), **B&J Boat Rentals** (☎ 850/243-4488), and **Premier Powerboat Rentals** (☎ 850/837-7755), all on Destin Harbor. Expect to pay about $70 for a half day, $120 for all day. Premier Powerboat Rentals also has speedboats for rent, ranging from $120 for a half day to $190 for all day.

Hobie Cats, WaveRunners, jet boats, jet-skis, and fishing craft rentals are available from many marinas, as well as from several beachfront resorts. **Paradise Water Sports** (☎ 850/664-7872) rents equipment and offers parasailing rides at seven locations along U.S. 98, and **Boogies** (☎ 850/654-4497) is at the east end of the Destin Bridge.

CRUISES   The *Emerald Magic* (☎ 850/837-1293) and the *Southern Star* (☎ 850/837-7741) have daily dolphin and sunset cruises from June through August, by arrangement the rest of the year. The *Emerald Magic* is operated by Moody's, on U.S. 98 at Destin Harbor (see "Fishing," below), while the *Southern Star* docks in Destin at the Harbor Walk Marina, behind the Lucky Snapper Restaurant. Expect to pay about $15 for adults, $12 for seniors, and $5 for children, depending on the cruise.

If you want to learn to sail, **Sailing South** (☎ 850/837-7245), on U.S. 98 at Destin Harbor, teaches 2-day basic courses for $220 per person. It also charters 24-foot boats to qualified sailors, and it has a 72-foot schooner available for crewed charters. If you can't sail and don't want to learn, you can go out on the 54-foot schooners *Nathaniel Bowditch* (☎ 850/650-8787), *Flying Eagle* (☎ 850/837-4986 or 850/837-3700), or *Blackbeard* (☎ 850/837-2793), all of which have afternoon and sunset trips for about $25 per person.

On Okaloosa Island, **Leeside Bareboat Sailing,** at the Leeside Motel, 1352 U.S. 98 east (☎ 850/244-5454), rents 25- and 30-foot Catalina sloops bareboat (you do the skippering) at prices ranging from $95 per half day to $450 for 3 days.

FISHING   Billing itself as the "World's Luckiest Fishing Village," Destin has Florida's largest charter-boat fleet, with more than 140 vessels based at the marinas lining the north shore of Destin Harbor, on U.S. 98 east of the Destin Bridge. Arranging a trip is as easy as walking along the Destin Harbor waterfront, where you will find the booking booths of several agents, such as **Pelican Charters** (☎ 850/837-2343), **Harbor Cove Charters** (☎ 850/837-2222), and **Fishermen's Charter Service** (☎ 850/654-4665). They all can arrange for you to fish until your heart's content. Rates for private charters range from about $360 to $900 per boat, depending on length of voyage.

A less-expensive way to try your luck is on a larger group-oriented party boat such as those operated by **Moody's,** at 194 U.S. 98 east on Destin Harbor (☎ 850/837-1293). Moody's charges $30 per person for its morning runs (the best fishing) and $25 for afternoon trips. Children 8 to 12 and nonfishing sightseers are charged half price. Other party boats are the *Emmanuel* (☎ 850/837-6313), the *Lady Even-thia* (☎ 850/837-6212), and three craft operated by **Capt. Duke's Boat Service** (☎ 850/837-6152), all based at **Destin Harbor.**

You don't have to go to sea to fish from the catwalk of the 3,000-foot **Destin Bridge** over East Pass. The marinas and bait shops at Destin Harbor can provide gear, bait, information, and a fishing license.

GOLF   The area takes great pride in having more than 250 holes of golf. For advance information on all area courses, contact the **Emerald Coast Golf Association,** P.O. Box 304, Destin, FL 32540 (☎ 850/654-7086). Also look for *Gulf Coast Tee Time,* the free annual directory published in Pensacola (see "Golf" under "Outdoor Pursuits" in section 1, above). And be sure to inquire if your choice of accommodations here offers golf packages, which can represent significant savings.

On the mainland, nonresidents are welcome to play at the city-owned **Fort Walton Beach Golf Club,** on Lewis Turner Boulevard (County Road 189) north of town (☎ 850/862-3314 or 850/862-0933). The club has two 18-hole courses—**the Pines** (☎ 850/833-9529) and **the Oaks** (☎ 850/833-9530)—plus a pro shop. Greens fees at both courses are about $26.50 year-round, including a cart.

In Destin, scenic **Indian Bayou Golf and Country Club,** off Airport Road (☎ 850/837-6191), has three 9-hole courses with large greens and wide fairways. They look easy, but watch out for water hazards and strategically placed hidden bunkers! Fees with a cart range from $45 to 45, including cart.

In southern Walton County, **The Resort at Sandestin** on U.S. 98 East (☎ 850/267-8211 for tee times), is the largest facility here (see "Where to Stay," below). Its 63 holes are spread over three outstanding championship courses: Baytowne, Burnt Pine, and Links. The Baytowne and Links courses overlook Choctawhatchee Bay. Fees for 18 holes are about $66 from mid-February through October, about $48 the rest of the year.

Scenery is on display at **Emerald Bay Golf Club,** 2 miles east of the Mid-Bay Bridge on U.S. 98 (☎ 850/837-5197). Some of the 27 championship holes here run along Choctawahatchee Bay, so water adds both beauty and challenges to the other-wise wide and forgiving fairways. Greens fees range between $60 and $75, with cart.

In southern Walton County, the semi-private **Santa Rosa Golf & Beach Club,** off County Road 30A in Dune Allen Beach (☎ 850/267-2229 or 850/654-7888), offers a challenging 18-hole course through tall pines looking out to vistas of the Gulf. The club has a pro shop, beachside restaurant, lounge, and tennis courts. The **Seascape Resort & Conference Center,** 100 Seascape Dr. (☎ 850/837-9181), off County Road 30A, features a Joe Lee–designed 18-hole course winding through woods and around lakes, with a premium placed on accuracy rather than power. The center also has tennis courts, accommodations, restaurant, bar, and pro shop.

In Niceville, a 20-minute drive north via the Mid Bay Bridge, nonguests may play golf (four 9-hole courses) or tennis (21 courts) at the **Bluewater Bay Resort** (☎ 850/897-3613), which also has condos for rent.

Call ahead for reservations and current fees at all these clubs.

SCUBA DIVING & OTHER WATER SPORTS   At least a dozen dive shops are located along the beaches. Considered one of the best, **Scuba Tech Diving Charters** has two locations in Destin: at 301 U.S. 98 East in Destin (☎ 850/837-2822) and at 10004 U.S. 98 East (☎ 850/837-1933), about a half mile west of the Sandestin Beach Resort. Reef or wreck dives start at $45 to $85, depending on length. Open-water courses cost about $225; resort courses, $75. **Fantasea,** at the foot of the Destin

Bridge, 1 U.S. 98 east (☎ **800/326-2732** or 850/837-6943), and the **Aquanaut Scuba Center,** 24 U.S. 98 east (☎ **850/837-0359**), are other local operators.

The three diving operators and *Kokomo* **Snorkeling Adventures,** 500 U.S. 98 East in Destin (☎ **850/837-9029**), all take snorkelers on excursions into the Gulf of Mexico and Choctawhatchee Bay for $20 per person, including gear.

TENNIS   **The Resort at Sandestin,** U.S. 98 East (☎ **850/837-2121**), has 16 courts open to the public, including hard, clay, and grass. *Tennis* magazine rated it one of the nation's top 50 tennis resorts and the only ranked resort with natural grass courts.

EXPLORING THE AREA

Gulfarium. 1010 Miracle Strip Pkwy. (U.S. 98) on Okaloosa Island. ☎ **850/244-5169.** Admission $15 adults, $13 seniors, $10.70 children 4–11, free for children 3 and under. Daily 9am through last show; shows daily at 10am, noon, 2pm, and 4pm; additional shows at 6 and 8pm in summer.

One of the nation's original marine parks features ongoing shows with dolphins, California sea lions, Peruvian penguins, loggerhead turtles, dolphins, sharks, sting rays, moray eels, and alligators. There are fascinating exhibits, including the Living Sea, with special windows that provide viewing of undersea life. During one of the shows, a scuba diver explains the sea life while swimming among them. A gift shop offers an extensive collection of marine-oriented souvenirs.

Indian Temple Mound and Museum. 139 Miracle Strip Pkwy., on the mainland. ☎ **850/ 833-9595.** Park free; museum $2 adults, $1 children 6–17, free for children 5 and under. Park daily dawn–dusk. Museum Oct–May Mon–Fri 11am–4pm, Sat 9am–4pm; June–Sept Mon–Sat 9am–5pm (summer hours may vary, so call ahead).

This ceremonial mound, one of the largest ever discovered, dates from A.D. 1200. The museum, located next to it, showcases ceramic artifacts from southeastern Native American tribes. The largest such collection, it contains more than 6,000 items. Exhibits depict the lifestyles of the four tribes that lived in the Choctawhatchee Bay region for 10,000 years.

✪ **U.S. Air Force Armament Museum.** At Eglin Air Force Base, Eglin Pkwy. (Fla. 85), 5 miles north of downtown. ☎ **850/882-4062.** Free admission. Daily 9:30am–4:30pm. Closed New Year's Day, Thanksgiving, and Christmas.

Located on the world's largest air force base (more than 700 square miles), this fascinating museum traces military developments from World War II through the Korean and Vietnam wars to the Persian Gulf War. On display are 28 reconnaissance, fighter, and bomber planes, including the SR-71 Blackbird spy plane. Also exhibited are war films, photographs, rockets, bombs, and missiles. The base itself is home to the world's largest environmental test chamber, in the McKinley Climatic Laboratory, and to the 33rd Tactical Fighter Wing, the "Top Guns" of Desert Storm. World War II's historic Doolittle's Tokyo Raiders trained here.

✪ **Eden State Gardens.** County Rd. 395, Point Washington. ☎ **850/231-4214.** Grounds and gardens $2 per vehicle; mansion tours $1.50 adults, 50¢ children 12 and under. Gardens and grounds daily 8am–5pm; mansion tours on the hour Thurs–Mon 9am–4pm.

Evoking images from *Gone With the Wind,* the magnificent 1895 Greek Revival–style Wesley Mansion has been lovingly restored and richly furnished. It stands overlooking scenic Choctawhatchee Bay and is surrounded by immense moss-draped oak trees and the Eden Gardens, resplendent with camellias, azaleas, and other typical Southern flowers. Picnicking is allowed on the plantation grounds. The gardens and mansion are north of Seagrove Beach in southern Walton County.

The Round Town

Noted for its well-preserved Victorian homes encircling a round, 60-foot-deep lake, **DeFuniak Springs** makes for an interesting sightseeing excursion from the beaches. Founded in 1882 when the L&N Railroad built a station at the lake, the little town (pop. 5,100) came to prominence a few years later when the Chautauqua Society of New York decided to make its winter home here. Built of clapboard in 1909, the impressively domed and columned **Chautauqua Auditorium** still overlooks the lake, as does the tiny building that houses Florida's oldest library, built in 1886. In addition to its books, the library holds a fascinating collection of medieval weapons and armor.

The town is still a hotbed of cultural activities, highlighted by the annual **Chautauqua Festival,** usually in late April, featuring sports activities, arts and crafts, and fireworks. On the first weekend in December, townsfolk are joined by visitors from all over to don period costumes at the annual Victorian Ball, which is accompanied by a homes tour earlier in the day.

Chautauqua Vineyards, at I-10 and U.S. 331 (☎ 850/892-5887), has free tours and tastings on Monday to Saturday from 9am to 4:30pm and on Sunday from noon to 4:30pm. The office is beside the Comfort Inn.

To get there from the beaches, take U.S. 331 north to I-10. Look for the "Historic District" sign about 2 miles north of the interstate and turn right on Live Oak Avenue to Circle Drive, which circles the lake. Main Street, the old train station, and the town's business district lie on the lake's north shore.

The **Walton County Chamber of Commerce,** in the Chautauqua Auditorium on the lakeshore (P.O. Box 29), DeFuniak Springs, FL 32433 (☎ 850/892-3191; fax 850/892-9688), has maps and booklets for self-guided tours and a list of local shops and antique dealers. The staff will know when the Chautauqua Festival, Victorian Ball, and other events are scheduled. The office is open Monday to Friday from 8am to 5pm.

Dressed in Victorian finery, **Dianne Pickett** (☎ 850/892-4300) leads guided tours of the town. Book at least a day in advance.

SHOPPING

The major shopping attractions here are two well-stocked manufacturers' outlet malls. By far the best is ✪ **Silver Sands Factory Stores,** on U.S. 98 between Destin and Sandestin. One of the largest outlet malls in Florida, this one has the upscale likes of Anne Klein, Donna Karan, J. Crew, Jones New York, Brooks Brothers, Hartman Luggage, Coach leathers, Bose electronics, and so many more you'll have to drive from one end to the other to spot your favorite brands. There's even a food court with a branch of Harbor Docks Restaurant (see "Where to Dine," below). On the Fort Walton Beach mainland, you'll find a limited selection of factory stores on U.S. 98 in the **Brooks Bridge 98 Center,** at the northern end of the Brooks Bridge, and at **Bayview 98 Center,** about 1 mile to the west.

Over at the Sandestin Beach Resort on U.S. 98, you can window-shop in **The Market at Sandestin,** where 28 shops purvey expensive clothing, gifts, and Godiva chocolates.

WHERE TO STAY

The area has a vast supply of condos and cottages for rent. One good-value example is Venus Condos, listed below. The tourist information offices (see "Essentials," above) will provide lists of others for rent. The largest rental agent is **Abbott Realty Services,** 3500 Emerald Coast Pkwy., Destin, FL 32541 (☎ **800/336-4853** or 850/837-4853; fax 850/654-2937; www.abbott-resorts.com). It publishes a magazine-size annual brochure picturing and describing its many accommodations throughout the area.

For campers, **Grayton Beach State Recreation Area,** 357 Main Park Rd., Santa Rosa Beach (☎ **850/231-4210**), which actually is on County Road 30A, offers hookups for RVs as well as primitive sites in a beautiful 356-acre setting. Campfire interpretive programs are available to campers (call for the current schedule). Sites cost $14 from March to September, $8 from October to February. You can reserve sites up to 11 months in advance by contacting the park.

Camping on the Gulf Holiday Travel Park, 10005 W. Emerald Coast Pkwy. (U.S. 98), Destin (☎ **850/837-6334**), just west of the Sandestin Beach Resort, is the area's largest and oldest campground and the only one with sites directly on the beach. During summer, campsites cost $50 on the beach, $30 inland; off-season, they go for $28 and $23, respectively. Reserve your summertime site well in advance.

State and local governments add 9% to all hotel and campground bills.

FORT WALTON BEACH

Among the chain motels here, the moderately priced **Rodeway Inn,** 866 Santa Rosa Blvd. (☎ **800/458-8552** or 850/243-3114), and **Days Inn & Suites Gulfside Resort,** 573 Santa Rosa Blvd. (☎ **800/DAYS-INN** or 850/244-8686), are right on Okaloosa Island's beach.

Four Points Sheraton. 1325 E. Miracle Strip Pkwy. (U.S. 98), Fort Walton Beach, FL 32548. ☎ **800/874-8104** or 850/243-8116. Fax 850/244-3064. 229 units. A/C TV TEL. Summer $99–$150 double. Off-season $60–$115 double. Rates include full breakfast. AE, DC, DISC, MC, V.

This beachfront resort sports very spacious rooms decorated with vivid, tropical colors. The older wings here surround a lush tropical courtyard with a South Pacific–style bar adjacent to a heated swimming pool and whirlpool. A cutout in the new, seven-story gulf-side building covers a second swimming pool and allows access to the beach. Rooms have refrigerators, microwave ovens, and coffeemakers, and some also have kitchenettes. Dining is in the Plantation Grill dining room and in Dempsey's Grill and Bar, which, along with the beach bar, provides entertainment during summer. There's an exercise room and coin laundry.

Marina Motel. 1345 E. Miracle Strip Pkwy (U.S. 98), Fort Walton Beach, FL 32548. ☎ **800/ 237-7021** or 850/244-1129. Fax 850/243-6063. 38 units. A/C TV TEL. Summer $58–$66 double; $95 apt. Off-season $39–$56 double; $60–$75 apt. AE, DC, DISC, MC, V.

This family operated motel may be rather pedestrian-looking, but it makes up for a lack of charm with clean, comfortable rooms and a location directly across U.S. 98 from the magnificent public beach at Beasley Park. A low-slung, brick-fronted motel block holds most of the rooms. Other units are in two-story stucco structures near a marina whose 560-foot pier is home to charter-fishing boats. Two one-bedroom apartments at the end of the complex overlook the marina and bay. All units here have refrigerators and microwaves; 16 have full kitchens. If traffic is too busy to cross U.S. 98 to the beach, you can sun at the motel's little bay-side beach or take a dip in its roadside pool. There's also a guest laundry.

Radisson Beach Resort. 1110 Santa Rosa Blvd. (at U.S. 98), Fort Walton Beach, FL 32548. ☎ **800/732-4853** or 850/243-9181. Fax 850/664-7652. 188 units. A/C TV TEL. Summer $125–$160 double. Off-season $70–$145 double. Packages available. AE, DC, DISC, MC, V.

A glass-enclosed elevator climbs up through a soaring, lean-to atrium lobby to rooms with spectacular gulf views from a six-story building at this resort (which until a recent upgrading was the Holiday Inn Fort Walton Beach). Less-expensive rooms are in two-story buildings flanking a courtyard surrounding a pool and open on one end to the beach. A lobby cafe serves breakfast, lunch, and dinner, and an atrium bar has nightly entertainment during summer. Facilities here include three outdoor pools (one under a glass roof), a children's playground, a beach bar and barbecue area, two lighted tennis courts, exercise room, gift shop, and convention center.

✪ **Ramada Plaza Beach Resort.** 1500 E. Miracle Strip Pkwy. (U.S. 98), Fort Walton Beach, FL 32548. ☎ **800/874-8962** or 850/243-9161. Fax 850/243-2391. www.ramadafwb.com. 353 units. A/C TV TEL. Summer $110–$150 double; $235–$300 suite. Off-season $65–$85 double; $135–$160 suite. AE, DC, DISC, MC, V.

Considered Fort Walton Beach's prime hotel, this big resort with a gaudy, Vegas-style gold facade boasts one of the most beautiful swimming pool/patio areas anywhere, with waterfalls cascading over lofty rocks and a romantic grotto bar, all surrounded by thick tropical foliage. Unfortunately all this is cut off from the beach by a six-story block of hotel rooms. The tastefully furnished rooms in this building have gulf or courtyard views, but the less-expensive units in a two-story structure next door overlook a parking lot.

On-site dining options include the casual Pelican's Roost, which features seafood favorites year-round, and a barbecue shack near the pool. The family oriented Lobster House serves moderately priced seafood in summer. The Boardwalk beach pavilion and restaurants are next door (see "Where to Dine," below). For entertainment, there's dancing in Bubble's Lounge. Facilities here include three swimming pools (one indoors), a children's pool, a health spa, three whirlpools, and a gift shop.

✪ **Venus Condos.** 885 Santa Rosa Blvd., Fort Walton Beach, FL 32548. ☎ **800/476-1885** or 850/243-0885. Fax 850/664-5221. 45 units. A/C TV TEL. Summer $105–$170 apt. Off-season $50–$125 apt. Weekly and monthly rates available. DISC, MC, V.

Offering considerably more space than a hotel would at these rates, this pleasant, three-story enclave on western Okaloosa Island is immaculately maintained. Each of the one-, two-, and three-bedroom units has a long living-dining-kitchen room, with a rear door leading to a balcony or patio. Facilities include a guest laundry and a grassy courtyard with palm trees, swimming pool, and large barbecue pit. A lighted tennis court destroyed by Hurricane Opal should be rebuilt by the time you arrive. The beach is a short walk across the dunes.

DESTIN

Until 1997, the local **Motel 6,** 405 U.S. 98 East (☎ **800/466-8356** or 850/ 837-0007; fax 850/837-5325), sitting across the highway from the harbor, was a Comfort Inn. Then the Motel 6 chain bought it and renovated the rooms, which in this case means they removed rather than added some amenities. Nevertheless, the units were spiffed up, and they are generally larger than at many other members of this cut-rate chain. There's an outdoor swimming pool on premises. Room rates are $56 double in summer, about $44 off-season.

Expensive

✪ **Henderson Park Inn.** 2700 Scenic Hwy. 98 East (P.O. Box 30), Destin, FL 32540. ☎ **800/336-4853** or 850/837-4853. Fax 850/654-0405. 35 units. A/C TV TEL. Summer $180–$279 double. Off-season $114–$223 double. Rates include buffet breakfast. Packages and weekly rates available. AE, DISC, MC, V.

At the end of Old U.S. 98 on the undeveloped eastern edge of the Henderson Beach State Recreation Area, this shingle-sided, Cape Hatteras–style bed-and-breakfast is a romantic, get-away-from-it-all escape without screaming kids (no children are accepted). Individually decorated in a Victorian theme, the rooms have high ceilings, fireplaces, Queen Anne furniture, and gulf views from private balconies. Some have canopy beds. The main building (15 rooms are in a separate shingle-sided structure next door) sports a beachside veranda complete with old-fashioned rocking chairs to sit and admire the glorious sunsets.

Dining: All rates include daily Southern-style buffet breakfast and beer and wine at the nightly before-dinner social hour in The Veranda Restaurant, which opens to the wraparound porch of the main building. Reservations are recommended for The Veranda's gourmet-style dinners.

Amenities: Heated swimming pool, beachside sundeck, complimentary beach umbrellas and chairs, beach gazebo, nightly turndown.

Moderate

Best Western SummerPlace Inn. 14047 Emerald Coast Pkwy. (U.S. 98, at Airport Rd.), Destin, FL 33541. ☎ **800/BEACH-99** or 850/650-8003. Fax 850/650-8004. 72 units. A/C TV TEL. Summer $120–$170. Off-season $60–$100. Rates include continental breakfast and local telephone calls. AE, DC, DISC, MC, V.

Across U.S. 98 from the Hampton Inn Destin (see below), this four-story, Spanish-motif building opened in 1997, offering innlike rooms and suites decorated with wildlife prints. All units have refrigerators and coffeemakers, and a few suites have Jacuzzis in their living rooms. Gulf-side units have balconies; those facing the bay do not. Doors open from an indoor pool, whirlpool, and exercise equipment to an out-door pool. Amenities include a coin laundry, small business center, a video games arcade. A complimentary shuttle runs to the beach—handy, since otherwise you'd have to negotiate your way across busy U.S. 98 to reach the Gulf. There are three restaurants next door, and those on Old Hwy. 98 East are a short walk away.

Hampton Inn Destin. 1625 Hwy. 98 East (at Old Hwy. 98 and Airport Rd.), Destin, FL 32541. ☎ **800/HAMPTON** or 850/654-2677. Fax 850/654-0745. 104 units. A/C TV TEL. Summer $135–$150 double; $160–$180 suite. Off-season $59–$79 double; $85–$110 suite. Rates include continental breakfast. AE, DC, DISC, MC, V.

This pink, two-story building sits at the junction of the new and old U.S. 98s, about 100 yards west of Henderson Beach State Recreation Area (see "Hitting the Beach," above) and near a covey of restaurants just outside the recreation area and another bunch of them across U.S. 98. There's beach access through a line of condos sitting across the old highway, which means you don't have to fight the traffic on U.S. 98 to reach the Gulf. External corridors lead to the standard motel-style rooms and suites with two rooms and kitchenettes. A gazebo-like sitting area offers shade next to a heated outdoor pool.

Holiday Inn of Destin. 1020 Hwy. 98 East (P.O. Box 577), Destin, FL 32541. ☎ **800/HOLIDAY** or 850/837-6181. Fax 850/837-1523. 233 units. A/C TV TEL. Summer $130–$165 double. Off-season $75–$105 double. Packages available. AE, DC, DISC, MC, V.

Most of the nicely furnished rooms in this gulf-front resort are in a round high-rise building. Get one facing south or east because a tall condo next door blocks southwest-facing units from enjoying the spectacular gulf views. The rooms in an older, four-story building are more spacious than those in the tower. Some of these older units open to an enclosed "Holidome," a fountained lobby sporting a comfort-able mezzanine lounge with indoor pool, billiard, Ping-Pong, and Foosball tables. The tropically attired Destin Cafe in the lobby serves breakfast, lunch, and dinner. Children can play in their own pool or in a video-game arcade (there's a summertime activities program for them). Adults can use a whirlpool, sauna, and exercise room, or spend money at the gift shop.

SOUTHERN WALTON COUNTY

If you want to stay near The Resort at Sandestin (see below) without paying its prices, there's a modern **Sleep Inn** a mile west at 5000 Emerald Coast Pkwy./U.S. 98 (☎ **800/627-5337** or 850/654-7022).

A Highlands House Bed & Breakfast. 4193 W. County Rd. 30A (P.O. Box 1189), Santa Rosa Beach, FL 32459. ☎ **850/267-0110.** Fax 850/267-3602. 7 units (all with bathroom). A/C. Mar–Nov $70–$135 double. Dec–Feb $70–$135 double. Rates include full breakfast. Extra person $20. Children 10 and under stay free in parents' room. DISC, MC, V.

Beautifully situated in Dune Allen Beach, this B&B was built by innkeepers Joan and Ray Robins in the style of luxurious 18th-century plantation homes in the South Carolina Low Country, where they once lived. Although the house isn't directly on the beach, a path leads along a streambed to the sands. The Robinses furnished their dream inn with four-poster rice beds, comfy wingback chairs, and antique accoutrements. The most expensive rooms have French doors that open to an extra-wide porch with wicker furniture and a view of the Gulf. One unit has a fireplace; another, a whirlpool tub. The less-expensive models are in an old but modernized house to the rear of the main building. The delicious breakfasts often include brandy-battered French toast heaped with strawberries and cream.

✪ **The Resort at Sandestin.** 9300 Hwy. 98 W., Destin, FL 32541. ☎ **800/277-0800** or 850/267-8000 in the U.S., or 800/933-7846 in Canada. Fax 850/267-8222. 175 units, 400 condo apts. Summer $145–$215 double; $195–$676 condo apt. Off-season $75–$185 double; $90–$475 condo apt. Packages available. Rates include health club, bicycle, boogie board, canoe, and kayak use, 1 hour tennis daily, discounts on other amenities. AE, DC, DISC, MC, V.

One of Florida's best sports-oriented resorts, this luxurious real estate development sprawls over 2,300 acres complete with a spectacular beach 5 miles west of Destin. An array of handsomely decorated accommodations overlooks the Gulf or Choctawhatchee Bay, the golf fairways, lagoons, or a nature preserve. The hotel rooms are in the Inn at Sandestin, on the bay. All the other accommodations—junior suites, condominium apartments, villas, and three-bedroom penthouses—are spread over the property and come complete with kitchen, living room, and patio or balcony. Most amenities are a short walk or bike or tram ride away, and a tunnel runs under U.S. 98 to connect Sandestin's gulf and bay areas.

Dining: The Sunset Bay Café offers breakfast, lunch, and dinner by the bay, but the dining delight here is the romantic **Elephant Walk** (☎ 850/267-4800), located on the Gulf. There's a story here: In 1890 a tea planter in Ceylon named John Whiley tried to prevent damage to his trees by building a huge home across an elephant herd's path to the river. When the thirsty stampede reduced his house to ruins, Whiley vowed never to return. He roamed for 30 years, buying treasures in all four corners of the world. Then he discovered Northwest Florida and settled here. His eclectic purchases are displayed in this lovely building designed to evoke his Ceylon mansion. The candlelit dining room features entirely different, gourmet-quality choices for dinner each evening.

Amenities: Free shuttle tram around the resort; arrangements for deep-sea fishing and other outside activities; summer children's program for ages 3 to 13; rental bikes, boats, and water-sports equipment; fishing and charter boats based at Baytowne

Marina; fully equipped sports spa and health center; 9 swimming pools; 3 wading pools; children's playground; conference center; 63 holes of championship golf; Golf Learning Center with Tom Stickney; outstanding Bayside Tennis Center with clinic and hard, Rubico, and grass courts.

✪ **Sandestin Beach Hilton Golf & Tennis Resort.** 4000 Sandestin Blvd. S., Destin, FL 32541. ☎ **800/445-8667** or 850/267-9500. Fax 850/267-3076. 598 suites. A/C TV TEL. Summer $210–$320 suite. Off-season $110–$295 suite. Golf and tennis packages available. AE, DC, DISC, MC, V.

Consisting of adjacent 15- and 7-story towers, this all-suites, family-oriented beach-side resort is nicely situated on the grounds of The Resort at Sandestin (see above) and shares its golf and tennis facilities. The spacious suites here feature a special area for children's bunk beds. Another family convenience is a dressing room with a second sink outside the bathroom. Other room amenities include plenty of closet space, a wet bar, in-room refreshment center, refrigerator, and small hot plate. Balconies look out to splendid gulf views.

Dining/Diversions: On-premises dining includes Seagrapes for fine dining and the moderately priced Sandcastles Restaurant and Lounge in the lobby. The elegant Elephant Walk (see The Resort at Sandestin, above) is next door. In the summer the Beach Club Grill is enjoyably casual, and the Ice Cream Shop features sweet treats.

Amenities: Concierge, 24-hour room service, baby-sitting, summer programs for children and teenagers, two outdoor swimming pools (one heated), heated indoor pool with whirlpool and sauna, guest laundry, gift shop, video rentals.

✪ SEASIDE

If you decide to rent a home or romantic honeymoon cottage in this quaint village, contact the **Seaside Cottage Rental Agency,** P.O. Box 4730, Seaside, FL 32459 (☎ **850/231-1320** or 800/277-8696; fax 850/231-2219; www.seasidefl.com). It has some 240 cottages in its rental inventory, from one- to six bedrooms. The beachside honeymoon cottages are a favorite getaway for newlyweds or anyone else looking for a romantic escape.

✪ **Josephine's French Country Inn at Seaside.** County Rd. 30A (P.O. Box 4767), Seaside, FL 32459. ☎ **800/848-1840** or 850/231-1940. Fax 850/231-2446. www. josephinesfl.com. 9 units. A/C TV TEL. $130–$215 double. Rates include gourmet breakfast. Weekly rates available. AE, MC, V.

With its six large Tuscan columns reminiscent of an elegant Virginia mansion, Josephine's is an elegant country inn, with mahogany four-poster beds, lace comforters, rich furnishings, and marble bathtubs. Most guest rooms also have fireplaces. Conveniences like wet bars, microwaves, coffeemakers, and small refrigerators are neatly incorporated into the design so they don't conflict with the nostalgic charm. Sumptuous breakfasts are served either in-room (beside the fireplace or on your private veranda) or in the gracious dining room. The Guest House offers four suites, two with gulf views. Each has a fireplace, kitchen, and full bath. No smoking or pets are allowed inside. Guests can use the house bicycles for free.

With rich mahogany furniture and a wealth of period accoutrements, the dining room here is one of the region's finest places for a gourmet romantic dinner. Glowing with candlelight, this intimate room seats only 22 people. Josephine's Maryland-style crab cakes are consistently delicious.

Seaside Motor Court. County Rd. 30A (P.O. Box 4730), Seaside, FL 32459. ☎ **800/ 277-8696** or 850/231-1320. Fax 850/231-2219. www.seasidefl.com. 6 units. A/C TV TEL. $125–$250 double. AE, DC, DISC, MC, V.

Reminiscent of the one-story motels of the 1940s, this establishment in the center of things has standard rooms furnished with tasteful decor. Although they lack the usual porches and furbelows of Seaside's architecture, the motel rooms are perfect for an overnight stay. The more expensive units have refrigerators, coffeemakers, and a separate bedroom.

WHERE TO DINE

Except for the strip on Okaloosa Island, a plethora of national fast-food and family chain restaurants line U.S. 98.

FORT WALTON BEACH
Moderate

✪ **Caffè Italia.** 189 Brooks St., on the mainland in the block west of Brooks Bridge. ☎ **850/664-0035.** Reservations recommended in winter. Pizza and pasta $5.50–$13; main courses $13–$16. AE, DC, DISC, MC, V. Tues–Sun 11am–10pm. Closed Thanksgiving and Christmas. NORTHERN ITALIAN.

Nada Eckhardt is from Croatia, but she met her American husband, Jim, while working at a restaurant named Caffè Italia in northern Italy. The Eckhardts duplicated that establishment in this 1925 Sears & Roebuck mail-order house tucked away on the waterfront. You can dine on the patio with a view of the sound through sprawling live oak trees (one table is set romantically under its own gazebo), or inside, where Nada has installed floral tablecloths and photos from the old country. Her menu is limited to excellent pizzas, pasta dishes such as tortellini with mushrooms and peas in Alfredo sauce, northern Italian risotto with either asparagus or smoked salmon, and meat and seafood dishes to fit the season. Don't expect to make a full meal by ordering only a pasta here, for meals are served in the authentic Italian fashion, with a small portion of pasta preceding the seafood or meat course. On the other hand, you can quickly fill up on the seasoned, pizza-dough breadsticks served with olive oil for dipping. The cappuccino here is absolutely first-rate, as are the genuine Italian desserts.

Harpoon Hanna's at the Boardwalk. 1450 E. Miracle Strip Pkwy. ☎ **850/243-5500.** Reservations accepted. Sandwiches and burgers $6–$9; main courses $9–$17. AE, DISC, MC, V. Summer daily 11am–11pm; off-season, Mon–Sat 11am–9pm, Sun noon–9pm. SEAFOOD.

Don't expect fine cuisine here, but this is the one place in Fort Walton Beach where you can have lunch or dinner right beside the beach. Part of the Boardwalk complex and built to look like an old-fashioned beach pavilion, it has big windows that swing up to let in gulf breezes. A deck is used for alfresco dining in good weather, and the outdoor Ship's Deck Bar is a great spot to catch a sunset. The menu features such items as coconut shrimp and blackened, fried, broiled, sautéed, or grilled fish. There's a children's menu. The restaurant's snack menu is available next door at the Soggy Dollar Saloon, which has live entertainment during the summer.

Pandora's Restaurant & Lounge. 1120B Santa Rosa Blvd. ☎ **850/244-8669.** Reservations recommended after 4pm. Main courses $11–$20. AE, DC, DISC, MC, V. Sun–Thurs 5–10pm, Fri–Sat 5–10:30pm. STEAKS/PRIME RIB/SEAFOOD.

The front part of this unusual restaurant is a beached yacht now housing the main-deck lounge. Below is a beamed-ceilinged dining room aglow with lights from copper chandeliers. Several varieties of freshly caught fish are among the seafood choices here, but steaks and prime rib keep the locals coming back for more. The tender beef is cut on the premises and grilled to perfection. The delicious breads and pies are home-made. Live entertainment and dancing are an added attraction in the lounge.

There's another Pandora's in Grayton Beach at the corner of Fla. 283 and County Road 30A (☎ 850/231-4102).

✪ **Staff's Seafood Restaurant.** 24 SW Miracle Strip Pkwy. (U.S. 98), on the mainland. ☎ **850/243-3526.** Reservations not necessary. Main courses $12–$27. AE, DISC, MC, V. Summer daily 5–11pm. Off-season Mon–Thurs 5–9:30pm, Fri–Sat 5–10pm. SEAFOOD/ STEAKS.

Considered the first Emerald Coast restaurant, Staff's started as a hotel in 1913 and moved to this barnlike building in 1931. Among the display of memorabilia are an old-fashioned phonograph lamp and a 1914 cash register. All main courses are served with heaping baskets of hot, home-baked wheat bread from a secret 70-year-old recipe. One of the most popular main dishes is the "seafood skillet," sizzling with broiled grouper, shrimp, scallops, and crabmeat drenched in butter and sprinkled with cheese. Its tangy seafood gumbo also has gained fame for this casual, historic restaurant. In addition to the bread, main courses are accompanied by salad and dessert.

Inexpensive

Two good inexpensive choices are on the mainland a few minutes drive from the beach. One is **Barnhill's Country Buffet,** 431 Mary Ester Cutoff, opposite Santa Rosa Mall (☎ **850/243-1103**), a member of the chain I described in Pensacola (see "Where to Dine" in section 1). It has the same hours and prices as the Pensacola branches.

For the best barbecue in these parts, head to **Mary's Kitchen,** 575-D N. Beal Pkwy., in the small shopping center at the corner of Mary Esther Cutoff (☎ **850/ 863-1141**). Beef and pork are slowly smoked in a brick pit that sits in the middle of the dining room here. Ask for the sauce on the side, then apply as much or as little as suits your taste. Sandwiches cost $2 to $5, while barbecue platters go for $5.50 to $6.50. Open Monday to Friday from 11am to 8pm. No credit cards.

✪ **Magnolia Grill.** In Brooks Bridge 98 Center, 255 SE Miracle Strip Pkwy. (U.S. 98), on the mainland at the north end of Brooks Bridge. ☎ **850/302-0266.** Reservations accepted. Sandwiches and salads $3–$6.25. Main courses $8–$14. AE, MC, V. Mon–Sat 11am–9pm. SEAFOOD/CAJUN/ITALIAN.

Don't think this is just another shopping center restaurant, for the Magnolia Grill is the province of Tom Rice, an accomplished local chef who honed his skills at several other establishments before opening his own here in 1996. Upon first impression, the decor resembles a diner with an old-fashioned ice-cream parlor, but look again. Tom and his wife, Peggy, scoured every attic in town for an amazing collection of 1940s to 1960s memorabilia. Every table has an old radio or portable typewriter, and the walls sport a collection of photos that show Fort Walton Beach a half century ago. You may not notice, but the divider down the center of the room actually is the art deco sign salvaged from Eloise Shop, once an elegant ladies' clothier here. Tom also has resurrected some favorite old local recipes, including a scintillating asparagus mold served under a horseradish sauce, and J.S.'s Famous Warm Cuban Sandwich. Otherwise, his seafood, Cajun, and Italian fare shows the fine touch he has developed over the years.

DESTIN

If you didn't catch a fish to be grilled at Fisherman's Wharf (see below), you buy one to brag about from **Sexton's Seafood,** 602 Hwy. 98 East opposite Destin Harbor (☎ **805/837-3040**). It's the best market here.

Moderate

AJ's Seafood & Oyster Bar. 116 Hwy. 98 East, Destin Harbor. ☎ **850/837-1913.** Reservations not accepted. Main courses $12–$19; sandwiches and salads $5.50–$8. AE, DISC, MC, V. Summer daily 11am–midnight (bar until 2am). Off-season daily 11am–10pm. SEAFOOD.

Jimmy Buffet tunes set the tone at this fun, tiki-topped establishment on the picturesque Destin Harbor docks, where fishing boats unload their daily catches right into the kitchen. Obviously, the best items here are grilled or fried fish, but raw or steamed Apalachicola oysters also lead the bill of fare. You can sample a bit of everything with a "run of the kitchen" seafood patter. AJ's is most famous for its topside Club Bimimi, featuring reggae music and limbo contests every summer evening (you may want to have dinner elsewhere if you're not in the partying mood). At lunch, picnic tables on the covered dock make a fine venue with a view across the harbor to the Gulf.

✪ **Back Porch.** 1740 Old Hwy. 98 East. ☎ **850/837-2022.** Reservations not accepted. Main courses $11–$18; sandwiches, burgers, and pastas $6.50–$8. AE, DC, DISC, MC, V. Summer daily 11am–11pm. Off-season daily 11am–10pm. From U.S. 98, turn toward the beach at the Hampton Inn. SEAFOOD.

A cedar-shingled seafood shack whose long porch offers glorious beach and gulf views, this popular, casual restaurant originated charcoal-grilled amberjack, which you'll now see on menus throughout Florida. Other fish and seafood, as well as chicken and juicy hamburgers, also come from the coals. Monthly specials feature crab, lobster, and seasonal fish. Come early, order a rum-laden Key Lime Freeze, and enjoy the sunset. The Back Porch sits with a number of other restaurants (see below for Scampi's and June's Dunes) near the western boundary of the Henderson Beach State Recreation Area.

Fisherman's Wharf. 210D Hwy. 98 E., Destin Harbor. ☎ **850/654-4766.** Reservations not accepted. Sandwiches and burgers $6.50–$9; main courses $14–19; cook-your-catch $8. AE, DC, DISC, MC, V. Summer daily 11am–11pm (deck bar open later). Off-season daily 11am–9pm. SEAFOOD.

Have that fish you caught filleted, bring it here, and the chef will charcoal grill it at this atmospheric restaurant next to the charter fleet marina. If you had no luck, and didn't stop by Sexton's Seafood on the way here to buy a few fillets (see above), you can select from the restaurant's fresh-off-the-boat catch for grilling, broiling, frying, or blackening. Charcoal grilling is the house specialty—my triggerfish fillet was white and flaky but still moist. All main courses come with a trip to a central salad bar and rice pilaf, baked potato, or roasted vegetables. Although this building dates from 1996, it evokes an Old Florida fish camp, with rough-hewed wood walls and double-hung windows looking out to a large harborside deck, a venue during the summer season for two libation bars, an oyster bar, and live music.

Harbor Docks. 538 U.S. 98 E., Destin Harbor. ☎ **850/837-2506.** Reservations not accepted. Main courses $14–$20; burgers and sandwiches $8.50–$10. AE, DC, DISC, MC, V. Daily 4:30am–10:30am and 11am–11pm. Closed for breakfast Thanksgiving–Feb 14. SEAFOOD/SUSHI.

The harbor views are spectacular from indoors or outdoors at this casual, somewhat rustic establishment whose splendid hand-carved wood-and-marble bar dates from 1890. Specialties include a sautéed daily catch served with artichoke hearts. Appetizers on the dinner menu might feature smoked yellowfin tuna with mustard sauce and shrimp nachos, and sushi is offered daily from 5:30 to 10pm. Hearty fishermen's breakfasts are cooked by the owners of the Silver Sands, a popular local haunt that burned down. At night, frequent live entertainment keeps the action going on the outdoor deck.

✪ **Marina Cafe.** 404 Hwy. 98 E., Destin Harbor. ☎ **850/837-7960.** Reservations recommended. Main courses $16–$23; pizza and pasta $8–$17. AE, DC, DISC, MC, V. Daily 5–10pm. Closed Jan. ITALIAN/NEW AMERICAN.

Destin's finest restaurant provides a classy atmosphere with soft candlelight, subdued music, and formally attired waiters. The outdoor balconied deck overlooks Destin Harbor and is the setting for drinks and appetizers. Inside, window walls provide the same view. The creative chef prepares pizzas and pastas with a special flair, with an emphasis on light, spicy fare. Menu highlights include a fettuccine combined with andouille sausage, shrimp, crawfish tails, and a piquant tomato-cream sauce.

McGuire's Irish Pub & Brewery. 33 Hwy. 98 E., Destin Harbor (in Harborwalk Center near Destin Bridge). ☎ **850/650-0000.** Reservations not accepted. Snacks, burgers, and sandwiches $7.50–$8; meals $13–$25. AE, DC, DISC, MC, V. Mon–Sat 11am–2am, Sun 11am–1am (brunch 11am–3pm). AMERICAN/IRISH.

Like Pensacola's original McGuire's (see "Where to Dine" in section 1, above), this younger sibling sports thousands of dollar bills stuck on the ceilings and walls, plus Notre Dame University football schedules, a prominent logo of the Boston Celtics pro basketball team, and much other memorabilia recalling Irish American lore. This is Destin's most popular hangout, and many patrons congregate at the big oak bar in the center of the dining room, especially when live entertainment starts nightly at 9pm. If you're here to dine, you can opt for a table on either side of the bar or up on a rooftop deck. Dining here is almost secondary to the see-and-be-seen scene, but you can order corned beef and cabbage, Irish stew, scampi o'fettucini (shrimp in Alfredo sauce), big salads, super-size hamburgers, steaks, and various seafood offerings.

Inexpensive

✪ **Callahan's Island Restaurant & Deli.** 950 Gulf Shore Dr. (2 blocks south of U.S. 98). ☎ **850/837-6328.** Main courses $6–$14; sandwiches and burgers $3.50–$6. DISC, MC, V. Summer Mon–Thurs 10am–9pm, Fri 10am–10pm, Sat 8:30am–9pm. Off-season Mon–Thurs 8:30am–9pm, Fri 10am–9pm, Sat 8am–10:30am. STEAKS/DELI.

The best place in the area for picnic fare, this family operated deli offers burgers, excellent Rubens and other made-to-order sandwiches, pastas, and nightly specials such as charcoal-grilled chicken, grilled pork chops, and teriyaki-style stir-fry. A long refrigerator case across the rear holds a variety of top-grade cheeses, deli meats, steaks, and chops (choose your own cut, and the chef will charcoal grill it to order). Tables and booths are set up garden fashion, adding an outdoorsy ambience to this pleasant storefront establishment. Locals like to do lunch here. Breakfast is served only on Saturday morning.

Donut Hole. 635 U.S. 98 E., Destin. ☎ **850/837-8824.** Reservations not accepted. Breakfast $3.50–$7; sandwiches, salads, burgers $3.50–$5.50; meals $6.75. No credit cards. Summer daily 24 hours. Off-season daily 6am–10pm. Daily specials year-round 11am–8pm. Closed 2 weeks in Dec. SOUTHERN/AMERICAN.

Having spent his early career as a traveling salesman based in Texas, owner Bill Chandler designed this very popular establishment to be "the restaurant I couldn't find when I was on the road." Available around the clock during summer, his breakfasts highlight freshly baked doughnuts and other pastries. Daily special meals feature Southern favorites such as meat loaf, country-style steak, crispy fried chicken, salmon patties, and chicken and dumplings, all cooked on the premises using fresh vegetables and other top-quality ingredients.

There's a Donut Hole II Café and Bakery (☎ 850/267-3239) on U.S. 98 East in southern Walton County 2½ miles east of the Sandestin Beach Resort. It's known more for its bakery than for meals. Open daily from 6am to 7pm.

Harry T's Boat House. 320 U.S. 98 East, Destin Harbor. ☎ **850/654-4800.** Reservations not accepted. Main courses $6.50–$17; sandwiches and burgers $7–$9.50. AE, MC, V.

Summer Mon–Sat 11am–2am, Sun 10am–2am. Off-season Mon–Sat 11am–11pm, Sun 10am–11pm. Sun brunch year-round 10am–2pm. AMERICAN.

The family of trapeze artist "Flying Harry T" Baben opened this lively, fun restaurant on the ground floor of Destin Harbor's tallest building to honor his memory. Standing guard is a stuffed Stretch, Harry's beloved giraffe. Other decor features circus memorabilia and relics from the luxury cruise ship *Thracia*, which sank off the Emerald Coast in 1927; Harry T was presented with the ship's salvaged furnishings and fixtures for personally leading the heroic rescue of its 2,000 passengers.

The tabloid-style menu offers a wide range of such taste-tempters as chimichangas, Cajun-style burgers, blackened grouper sandwich, and buffalo wings. Kids eat for 99¢ until 7pm. Both the dining room and the downstairs lounge (with live entertainment Friday and Saturday nights) enjoy harbor views.

✪ **June's Dunes.** 1780 Old Hwy. 98 E. ☎ **850/654-0455.** Breakfast $2–$4; sandwiches and burgers $2–$4. No credit cards. Daily 5:30am–2pm. Closed Thanksgiving week. AMERICAN.

Locals love to eat at the rustic picnic tables of this red wooden structure, where June Decker has served beachside breakfasts and lunches since 1951. June's menu is chalked on a board over the counter of her screened-in kitchen. Give her your order and pick up your food when she calls your name. Breakfasts include waffles, French toast, fruit plates, and biscuits with sausage gravy. Lunches feature sandwiches, burgers (for $2, believe it or not), and German and Polish sausages with sauerkraut. June's little establishment is just west of the Henderson Beach State Recreation Area. Windows along three walls let in gulf breezes and lovely beach views.

✪ **Scampi's.** 1741 Old Hwy. 98 E. ☎ **850/837-7686.** Reservations not accepted. Main courses $8–$14; seafood buffet $15 adults, $7 children 8–12, $4 children 4–7, free for children under 4. AE, DC, DISC, MC, V. Daily 4:30–9:30pm. Closed mid-Oct to mid-Feb. SEAFOOD.

Constructed from the historic pilings of the old Destin Bridge, this two-level restaurant is especially popular for the bountiful seafood buffet. An entire baked fish is the star of this veritable groaning board. For starters, the regular menu has just-shucked oysters, and a steaming hot bowl of piquant seafood gumbo is almost a meal in itself. Just about any piscine preference will be satisfied in this casual, friendly restaurant. The lengthy bar and cocktail lounge are a local rendezvous. This place lies near the Back Porch, reviewed above.

SOUTHERN WALTON COUNTY

Buster's Oyster Bar and Seafood Restaurant. 125 Poinciana Blvd., in Delchamps Plaza, U.S. 98 at Scenic Hwy. 98. ☎ **850/837-4399.** Reservations not accepted. Main courses $10–$14; sandwiches and burgers $5.50–$7. AE, DC, DISC, MC, V. Summer daily 11am–11pm. Off-season daily 11am–10pm. SEAFOOD.

Shingles, plants, and wood make this local favorite seem not at all like a shopping-center restaurant, 1 mile west of The Resort at Sandestin. Buster claims that more than five million oysters have been shucked here, and with good reason, since they go for $1.59 a dozen during his daily 5 to 6pm happy hour. Buster also likes to add something outrageous to his tabloid-style menu, such as "a toasted sea spider sandwich" (soft-shell crab). Fried, broiled, steamed, or blacked fish and seafood dinners are prepared to order. Kids have their own menu.

Chan's Market Café. 5494 U.S. 98 E., in the Market at The Resort at Sandestin. ☎ **850/837-1334.** Reservations not accepted. Breakfast $3–$7; sandwiches and salads $3.50–$7; meals $5–$8. DISC, MC, V. Mar–Labor Day, daily 7am–9pm; Labor Day–Feb, daily 7am–6pm. AMERICAN.

The inexpensive prices and good food at this red-and-black-accented cafe draw scores of families vacationing at The Resort at Sandestin. A wide array of offerings include freshly baked croissants and bagels at breakfast or deli sandwiches at lunch, charcoal-grilled chicken and burgers, and meals featuring amberjack or yellowfin tuna grilled over coals. During the off-season, "white-plate" specials of meat loaf, chicken Parmesan, and roast turkey with dressing are good values at $4 to $6. Seating is both indoors and, in good weather, outside on a shaded veranda beside a pond filled with lily pads. An outdoor oyster bar is open from March to Labor Day.

✪ **Criolla's.** 170 E. County Rd. 30A, ¼ mile east of County Rd. 283, Grayton Beach. ☎ **850/267-1267.** Reservations recommended. Main courses $15–$25. DISC, MC, V. Apr–Sept Mon–Sat 6–10pm; Feb–Mar and Oct–Nov Tues–Sat 6–9:30pm. Closed Dec–Jan. LOUISIANA CREOLE/CARIBBEAN.

One of Florida's finest restaurants, this charming establishment derives its name from the archaic word *criollo*, signifying persons of pure Spanish descent born in the New World. The attractive decor, combining New Orleans with the Caribbean, features potted palms, whirling ceiling fans, and tropical island paintings. Seasonal menus carry out the theme, always offering Creole and Caribbean selections. Many fish dishes carry the wonderful aroma of smoke from a wood-fired grill. An "Island Hopper" menu offers gourmet appetizers, main courses, and homemade sweets at fixed prices.

✪ **Lake Place Restaurant.** 5960 County Rd. 30A, Dune Allen Beach. ☎ **850/267-2871.** Reservations required in summer, recommended off-season. Main courses $17–$27. AE, DISC, MC. V. Tues–Sat 5:30–9pm. SEAFOOD.

Owners Richard and Evalee Grenamyer scour the markets each morning for fresh fish, which they serve at this rustic plank building on the shores of picturesque Lake Allen. You can order the daily catch crispy fried, sautéed with white wine and roasted garlic sauce, or herb crusted with jumbo crabmeat and butter sauce. If the day's species don't appeal, fresh salmon is prepared on a seasoned cedar plank. There are steaks, lamb and pork chops, and free-range chicken for landlubbers. An excellent wine list changes daily to complement each evening's special dishes.

SEASIDE

✪ **Bud and Alley's.** County Rd. 30A, in the beachside shops. ☎ **850/231-5900.** Reservations recommended. Sandwiches $8; main courses $16–$27.50. MC, V. Summer Wed–Mon 11:30am–3pm and 6–9:30pm. Off-season Wed–Mon 11:30–3pm and 5:30–9pm. Closed January. SEAFOOD/STEAKS/MEDITERRANEAN.

Seaside's first restaurant is still number one to its steady patrons. The freshest of seafoods can be selected from seasonal menus featuring an innovative selection of Basque, Italian, Louisianan, and Floridian dishes prepared by owners and accomplished chefs Scott Witcoski and Dave Raushkolb. You can dine indoors or outdoors, on the screened porch, or under an open-air gazebo where you hear the waves splashing against the white sands. Opening at 3pm except during winter, a roof deck offers a variety of tapas as appetizers or light meals. Jazz is usually in the spotlight on weekends. On New Year's Eve, everyone in town and from miles around celebrates at Bud and Alley's. Call ahead to see if a noted guest chef is cooking or a special wine-tasting dinner is scheduled (there's an extensive list here). No smoking.

Shades. Town Sq. and Markets. ☎ **850/231-1950.** Reservations not accepted. Main courses $14–$17; sandwiches and burgers $5–$9. AE, DISC, MC, V. Summer daily 8–10am and 11am–10pm. Off-season daily 8–10am and 11am–9pm. AMERICAN.

In another life this was a rustic house built in the early 1900s in the small town of Chattahoochee. It was moved to Seaside's Town Square some 70 years later and reborn as this quaint restaurant, which doubles as Seaside's community pub. Stacked-high sandwiches, hot wings, and hamburgers are popular for lunch. At dinner, the bountiful fried seafood platter is a big favorite. Dine inside or on the porch in warm weather.

FORT WALTON BEACH & DESTIN AFTER DARK

Most resorts spotlight live entertainment during the summer season, including the Radisson Beach Resort and the Ramada Beach Resort in Fort Walton Beach, and the Sandestin Hilton and The Resort at Sandestin in southern Walton County (see "Where to Stay," above). It's a good idea to inquire ahead to make sure what's scheduled, especially during the slow season from October through February.

FORT WALTON BEACH   Country music and dancing fans will find a home at the **Seagull,** on Miracle Strip Parkway (U.S. 98) opposite the Gulfarium (☎ 850/243-3413). The generations of air force pilots who have hung out here call it the "Dirty Gull." Its main rival for the country set is the **High Tide Oyster Bar,** at Okaloosa Island off the Brooks Bridge (☎ 850/244-2624). Over at the Boardwalk on U.S. 98 East, the **Soggy Dollar Saloon** (☎ 850/243-5500) has live music on weekends.

The young beach set is attracted to rock and reggae in Shanty Town, on the east side of Brooks Bridge, where **Hoser's,** 1225 Santa Rosa Blvd. (☎ 850/664-6113), is the liveliest pub (its name mirrors a fire-fighting motif).

DESTIN   Twenty-somethings are attracted to the dance club, rowdy saloon, Jimmy Buffet–style reggae bar, and sports TV and billiards parlor all under one roof at the acclaimed **Nightown,** 140 Palmetto St. (☎ 850/837-6448), near the harbor on the inland side of U.S. 98 East. One admission of $3 to $7 covers it all. Not far away, the **Fish Heads** pub, at 414 U.S. 98 East (☎ 850/837-4848), features the "Big Red Snapper," a lethal mixture of rum and vodka. Nearby, **Hogs Breath Destin,** 541 Hwy. 98 East (☎ 850/837-5991), is another lively pub with bands playing beach music.

Several Destin restaurants offer entertainment nightly during summer, on weekends off-season. The dockside **AJ's Club Bimini,** 116 U.S. 98 East (☎ 850/837-1913), has live reggae under a big thatch-roofed deck. A somewhat older, if not more sober, crowd gathers for entertainment at the big harborside deck at **Fisherman's Wharf,** on U.S. 98 East (☎ 850/654-4766); at **The Deck,** on U.S. 98 East at the Harbor Docks restaurant, overlooking the harbor (☎ 850/837-2506); at **Harry T's Boat House** (☎ 850/654-6555), also on the harbor; and for Irish tunes nightly year-round at **McGuire's Irish Pub & Brewery** (☎ 850/650-0000), in the Harborwalk Shops on U.S. 98 just east of the Destin Bridge. See "Where to Dine," above, for details about the restaurants. The **Grande Isle Sky Bar,** above Grazti Italian Restaurant, 1771 Old Hwy. 98 (☎ 850/837-7475), draws the after-dinner crowd from the Back Porch and Scampi's restaurants, both adjacent.

Out toward Sandestin, **Fudrucker's Beachside Bar & Grill,** 20001 Hwy. 98 East (☎ 850/654-4200), opposite the Henderson Beach State Recreation Area, offers double the fun with two summertime stages, one on the bay-side deck, the other in the Down Under Bar. There's another Fudrucker's at 108 Santa Rosa Blvd. on Okaloosa Island in Fort Walton Beach (☎ 850/243-3833).

3 Panama City Beach

100 miles E of Pensacola, 100 miles SW of Tallahassee

Ask O. J. Simpson what the Panhandle's main attraction is, and he'll probably tell you Panama City Beach. This was, after all, the first place outside Southern California he visited after he was acquitted of murder. Simpson still had some money when he came here to see his then-girlfriend's family and to play a little golf.

He was one of an increasing number of upscale visitors who are changing the image of this 22-mile stretch of gorgeous white sand. Panama City Beach has long been known as the "Redneck Riviera," since it's a summertime mecca for millions of low- and moderate-income vacationers from nearby southern states. It still has a seemingly unending strip of bars, amusement parks, and old-fashioned motels. But this lively and crowded destination now also has luxury resorts and condominiums to go along with its great beaches, golf courses, fishing, boating, and fresh seafood.

Panama City Beach is also the most seasonal resort in Northwest Florida, as many restaurants, attractions, and even some hotels close between October and spring break in March. On the other hand, spring break is a big deal here; MTV even sets up shop in Panama City Beach for its annual beach-party broadcasts.

ESSENTIALS

GETTING THERE   Interstate 10 runs east–west, 45 miles to the north. From I-10, take U.S. 231 south to Panama City, or Fla. 77 south to the beach. U.S. 98, the Gulf-hugging east–west artery, runs through both Panama City Beach and nearby Panama City.

ASA (☎ 800/292-3424), **Delta Connection** (☎ 800/221-1212), **Northwest Airlink** (☎ 800/225-2525), and **US Airways Express** (☎ 800/428-4322) fly into Panama City/Bay County International Airport, on Airport Road, north of St. Andrews Boulevard, in Panama City.

The major car-rental firms have booths at the airport. You can take a taxi to your hotel (see "Getting Around," below). Taxi fares from the airport to the beach range from about $12 to $25.

The *Sunset Limited* transcontinental service on **Amtrak** (☎ 800/USA-RAIL) stops at Chipley, 45 miles north of Panama City.

VISITOR INFORMATION   For advance information, contact the **Panama City Beach Convention & Visitors Bureau,** P.O. Box 9473, Panama City Beach, FL 32407 (☎ 800/PC-BEACH or 850/233-6503; www.travelfile.com/get?pcbeach). It operates the **James I. Lark Sr. Visitors Information Center,** on the beach at 12015 Front Beach Rd. opposite the Miracle Strip Amusement Park.

You can buy detailed maps at **Alvin's Island Tropical Department Store,** across the street from the visitor center.

GETTING AROUND   Call **AAA Taxi** (☎ 850/785-0533), **Yellow Cab** (☎ 850/763-4691), or **Deluxe Coach Service** (☎ 800/763-0211 or 850/763-0211). Fares are based on a zone system rather than on meters. Local fares in Panama City Beach will range from $4.50 to $9.

TIME   The Panama City area is in the central time zone, 1 hour behind Miami, Orlando, and Tallahassee.

HITTING THE BEACH

A nearly unbroken strand of fine white sand fronts all the 22 miles of Panama City Beach, but the highlight for many here is ✪ **St. Andrews State Recreation Area,** 4607 State Park Lane, at the east end of the beach (☎ 850/233-5140). With more than 1,000 acres of dazzling white sand and dunes, this preserved wilderness demonstrates what the area looked like before motels and condominiums lined the beach. Lacy, golden sea oats sway in the refreshing gulf breezes, and fragrant rosemary grows wild. Picnic areas are on both the gulf beach and Grand Lagoon. Rest rooms and open-air showers are available for beachgoers. For anglers, there are jetties and a boat ramp. A nature trail reveals wading birds and perhaps an alligator or two. And drive carefully here, for the area is home to foxes, coyotes, and a herd of deer. Overnight camping is permitted (see "Where to Stay," below). On display is a historic turpentine still formerly used by lumbermen to make turpentine and rosin, both important for caulking the old wooden ships. Admission is $4 per car with two to eight occupants, $2 for single-occupant vehicles, and $1 for pedestrians and cyclists. The area is open daily from 8am to sunset.

A few hundred yards across an inlet from St. Andrews State Recreation Area sits pristine ✪ **Shell Island,** a 7½-mile-long, 1-mile-wide barrier island. This uninhabited natural preserve is great for shelling and also fun for swimming, suntanning, or just relaxing. Visitors can bring chairs, beach gear, coolers, food, and beverages. The island is accessible only by boat. A **ferry shuttle** (☎ 850/233-5140) runs from April to October between St. Andrews State Recreation Area and the island every 30 minutes: daily from 9am to 5pm in summer, weekends from 10am to 3pm in spring and fall. Fares are $7.50 for adults, $5.50 for children 11 and under, plus admission fees to the state recreation area (see above). A special snorkel package costs $16.95, including shuttle ride and equipment, and a 3-hour "ecosnorkel" tour for $24.95 departs twice daily.

Several cruise boats go to Shell Island. The glass-bottom *Capt. Anderson III* cruises there from Capt. Anderson's Marina, 5500 N. Lagoon Dr., at Thomas Drive (☎ 850/234-3435). The *Island Queen* paddle wheeler departs from the pier at Marriott's Bay Point Resort Village, 4200 Marriott Dr., off Jan Cooley Road (☎ 850/234-3307), ext. 1816). The *Island Star* and *Island Runner* (☎ 850/235-2809) both leave from Hathaway Marina, on U.S. 98 at the west end of Hathaway Bridge. All of these boats charge about $10 for adults, $5 for children. The *Miss Ashely* (☎ 850/785-4878) has all-day shelling, swimming, and snorkeling trips for about $18 adults, $7.50 for children, including food and soft drinks.

The more adventurous can take the 2½-hour tours offered by **Shell Island Wave Runner Tours** (☎ 850/785-4878), at the east end of Hathaway Bridge. The trips cost about $70 for single boats, $80 for doubles. Reservations are required, so call ahead. Or you can paddle over to the island with **Shell Island Kayaks,** based at St. Andrews State Recreation Area (☎ 850/235-4004). Full-day rentals are $35 for a single, $45 for a tandem.

The *Glass Bottom Boat* (☎ 850/234-8944) stops at Shell Island as part of its "sea school" trips from Treasure Island Marina, 3605 Thomas Dr. at Grand Lagoon (see "Cruises," under "Outdoor Activities," below).

OUTDOOR PURSUITS

BOATING   A variety of rental boats are available at the marinas near the Thomas Drive bridge over Grand Lagoon. These include the **Capt. Davis Queen Fleet,** based at Capt. Anderson's Marina, 5500 N. Lagoon Dr. (☎ 800/874-2415, or 850/234-3435 from nearby states); the **Panama City Boat Yard,** 5323 N. Lagoon Dr. (☎ 850/234-3386); the **Passport Marina,** 5325 N. Lagoon Dr. (☎ 850/234-5609); the **Port Lagoon Yacht Basin,** 5201 N. Lagoon Dr. (☎ 850/234-0142); the **Pirates Cove Marina,** 3901 Thomas Dr. (☎ 850/234-3839); and the **Treasure Island Marina,** 3605 Thomas Dr. (☎ 850/234-6533).

You can put to gulf under sail with **Bombay Sailing Charters** (☎ 850/234-7794), which charges $25 per person for half-day trips, $20 for sunset or moonlight cruises. **Port to Port Sailing Charters** (☎ 850/230-0830) rents Sunfish and regular sailboats, with or without captain.

Many resorts and hotels provide beach toys for their guests' use. WaveRunners, jet boats, inflatables, and other equipment can be rented from **Panama City Beach Sports** (☎ 850/234-0067), **Raging Rentals** (☎ 850/234-6775), and **Lagoon Rentals** (☎ 850/234-7245).

CRUISES   One of the most comprehensive outings here is aboard the *Glass Bottom Boat*, based at Treasure Island Marina, 3605 Thomas Dr., at Grand Lagoon (☎ 850/234-8944). Its 3-hour, narrated "sea school" cruise includes underwater viewing, dolphin-watching, bird-feeding, and a 1-hour stop for swimming at Shell Island. Along the way, the crew picks up and rebaits a crab trap and explains the creatures brought up in a shrimp net. The boat has a snack bar and air-conditioned cabin. The trips cost about $14 for adults and $8 for children. This same company operates a **Super Shelling Safari,** on which guests are taken to the eastern end of Shell Island to scavenge in the shallow water for shells (wear your bathing suit). Call for cruise times, exact prices, and reservations.

The **Capt. Davis Queen Fleet,** based at Capt. Anderson's Marina, 5500 N. Lagoon Dr. (☎ 800/874-2415 from neighboring states, or 850/234-3435 in Florida), has daily sightseeing trips, nature cruises, dolphin-watching and bird-feeding excursions, and dinner-dance cruises during the summer season. So do the *Island Star* and *Island Runner* (☎ 850/235-2809), both at the Hathaway Marina on U.S. 98 at the west end of Hathaway Bridge. The 32-foot *AquaStar* (☎ 850/230-2800) has dolphin-watching cruises to the shallow waters off Shell Island, where larger boats can't go.

FISHING   You can cast your line from the concrete **Dan Russell Municipal Pier,** which unlike other piers in the area, withstood Hurricane Opal in 1995.

A relatively inexpensive way for novices to try their luck fishing is with **Capt. Anderson's Deep Sea Fishing,** at Capt. Anderson's Marina on Thomas Drive at Grand Lagoon (☎ 800/874-2415 or 850/234-5940). The captain's party-boat trips last from 5 to 12 hours, with prices ranging from about $30 to $50 per person, including bait and tackle. Observers can go along for half price.

More expensive are the charter-fishing boats that depart daily from March to November from the marinas mentioned in "Boating," above.

GOLF   Thirty-six holes of championship golf are offered at ✪ **Marriott's Bay Point Resort Village,** 4200 Marriott Dr., off Jan Cooley Road (☎ 850/234-3307), where the Bruce Devlin–designed Lagoon Legends and the Club Meadows courses offer 36 holes of championship play—Lagoon Legends is rated as one of the country's most difficult. Both have clubhouses, putting greens, driving ranges, clinics, and private instruction. Greens fees with cart range from about $50 in summer to $80 in winter, depending on day of the week. See "Where to Stay," below.

The **Edgewater Beach Resort,** 11212 U.S. 98A (☎ 850/235-4044), also has a 9-hole resort course.

O. J. Simpson made the rounds at **The Hombre,** 120 Coyote Pass, 3 miles west of the Hathaway Bridge off Panama City Beach Parkway/U.S. 98 (☎ 850/234-3573). This par-72 championship course is home to the Nike Panama City Beach Classic. Fifteen of its 18 holes have water hazards (the unforgiving 7th hole sits on an island). Greens fees are about $65 in summer, $60 in winter, including cart.

The championship course at the semiprivate **Holiday Golf Club,** 100 Fairway Blvd. (☎ 850/234-1800), sports lake-line fairways and elevated greens. Greens fees with cart are about $45 in summer, $35 in winter. You can play at night here on a lighted 9-hole, par-29 executive course.

The least expensive place to play here is the flat and forgiving **Signal Hill,** 9516 N. Thomas Dr. (☎ **850/234-3218**), where you'll pay about $20 to walk 18 holes in summer, $13 in winter. Add about $10 per person for a cart.

SCUBA DIVING & SNORKELING   Although the area is too far north for extensive coral formations, more than 50 artificial reefs and shipwrecks in the Gulf waters off Panama City attract a wide variety of sea life. Local operators include **Hydrospace Dive Shop,** 6422 W. Hwy. 98 (☎ **850/234-3036**); the **Panama City Dive Center,** 4823 Thomas Dr. (☎ **850/235-3390**); **Emerald Coast Divers,** 5121 Thomas Dr. (☎ **800/945-DIVE** or 850/233-3355), **West End Dive Center,** 17320 Panama City Beach Pkwy. (☎ **850/235-7873**), and **Pete's Scuba Center,** 9007 Front Beach Rd. (☎ **800/401-DIVE** or 850/230-8006). These companies lead dives, teach courses, and take snorkelers to the grass flats off Shell Island.

EXPLORING THE AREA

Gulf World. 15412 Front Beach Rd. (at Hill Ave.), Panama City Beach. ☎ **850/234-5271.** Admission $16 adults, $9.55 children 5–12, free for children 4 and under. Summer daily 9am–7pm. Off-season Tues–Sun 9am–7pm. Closed Thanksgiving and 3 days at Christmas.

This landscaped tropical garden and marine showcase features shows with talented dolphins, sea lions, penguins, and more. Not to be upstaged, parrots perform daily, too. Sea turtles, alligators, and other critters also call Gulf World home. Scuba demonstrations, shark feedings, and underwater shows keep the crowds entertained.

Museum of Man in the Sea. 17314 Panama City Beach Pkwy. (at Heather Dr., west of Fla. 79), Panama City Beach. ☎ **850/235-4101.** Admission $5 adults, $2.50 children 6–16, free for children 5 and under. Daily 9am–5pm. Closed New Year's Day, Thanksgiving, and Christmas.

Owned by the Institute of Diving, this unusual museum exhibits relics from the first days of scuba diving, historical displays of the underwater world dating from 1500, and treasures recovered from sunken ships, including Spanish treasure galleons. Hands-on exhibits include experiments on water and air pressure, light refraction, and why diving bells work. Both kids and adults can climb through a submarine, see live sea animals in a pool, and look out of a diving helmet. Videos and aquariums explain the sea life found in St. Andrew Bay.

✪ **ZooWorld Zoological & Botanical Park.** 9008 Front Beach Rd. (near Moylan Dr.), Panama City Beach. ☎ **850/230-1243.** Admission $8.95 adults, $7.95 seniors, $6.50 children 3–11, free for children under 3. Daily 9am–sunset. Closed Christmas.

The largest captive alligator in Florida ("Mr. Bubba") lives in a re-created pine forest habitat at this educational and entertaining zoo, an active participant in the Species Survival Plan, which helps protect endangered species with specific breeding and housing programs. Other guests here include rare and endangered animals as well as orangutans and other primates, big cats, more reptiles, and other creatures. Also included are a walk-through aviary, a bat exhibit, and a petting zoo.

AMUSEMENT PARKS

An exciting, 105-foot-high roller coaster is just one of the 30 rides at the **Miracle Strip Amusement Park,** 12000 Front Beach Rd., at Alf Coleman Road (☎ **850/ 234-5810**). Little ones will love the traditional carousel. The 9 acres of fun include nonstop live entertainment and tons of junk food. Hours and prices change from year to year, so call for the latest. It's closed from Labor Day to mid-March.

Adjoining the amusement park, the **Shipwreck Island Water Park** (☎ **850/ 234-0368**) offers a variety of water-related fun, including the 1,600-foot winding

Lazy River for tubing and a daring 35-m.p.h. Speed Slide. The Tad Pole Hole is exclusively for young kids. Lounge chairs, umbrellas, and inner tubes are free, and lifeguards are on duty. Admission is less than $20. Open June to mid-August; call for hours.

SHOPPING

An attraction in itself is the main branch of **Alvin's Island Tropical Department Store,** 12010 Front Beach Rd. (☎ **850/234-3048**), opposite the James I. Lark Sr. Visitors Information Center. It not only sells a wide range of beach gear and apparel; it has cages containing colorful parrots, tanks with small sharks, and an enclosure with alligators. The sharks are fed at 11am daily; the gators get theirs at 4pm (the older ones are too lethargic to eat during the cool winter months).

The **African Curio Shoppe,** 8730 Thomas Dr., at Joan Road (☎ **800/235-1351** or 850/235-1288), is another fascinating place to browse for stuffed animal heads and wood carvings, soapstone sculptures, leather bags, and other handcrafts from Africa. Open daily 9:30am to 9:30pm in summer, Wednesday to Saturday 9am to 6pm off-season.

WHERE TO STAY

There are literally scores of motels along the beach here, ranging from small mom-and-pop operations to sizable members of national chains. The annual guide distributed by the Panama City Beach Convention & Visitors Bureau has a complete list (see "Essentials," above). Among the beachside chain motels, you'll find the **Best Western Casa Loma** (☎ 800/528-1234 or 850/234-1100), the **Days Inn Beach** (☎ **800/329-7466** or 850/233-3333), and the **Ramada Inn Beach & Convention Center** (☎ **800/228-3344** or 850/234-1700). The somewhat less expensive **Best Western Del Coronado** (☎ **800/528-1234** or 850/234-1600) is open from March to September.

Panama City Beach also abounds with condominium complexes, such as the Edgewater Beach Resort listed below. Although it's not on the beach, the **Inn at St. Thomas Square,** 8730 Thomas Dr., Panama City Beach, FL 32408 (☎ **800/ 874-8600** or 850/234-0349; fax 850/235-8104), has charm and enjoys a quiet location. The complex consists of some units above the small St. Thomas Square shopping center, at Thomas Drive and Joan Road, but highly preferable are the Spanish-style, town-house-looking apartments set along the skinny upper arm of Grand Lagoon. There's a pool and tennis court on the premises. Rates range from $85 for efficiencies to $165 for three-bedroom apartments in summer. Off-season they go for $55 to $99, respectively. The complex is managed by Basic Management Inc., which also has some beachfront units to rent, obviously at higher rates.

Among the many other agencies offering condominium apartments are **St. Andrew Bay Resort Management,** 726 Thomas Dr., Panama City Beach, FL 32408 (☎ **800/ 621-2462** or 850/235-4075; fax 850/233-2833; www.sabre1.net); and **Condo World,** 8815A Thomas Dr. (P.O. Box 9456), Panama City Beach, FL 32408 (☎ **800/ 232-6636** or 850/234-5564; fax 850/233-6725; www.condoworld-pcb-fla.com).

This area has two of the Panhandle's finest campgrounds, both with sites right beside the water. ☺ **St. Andrews State Recreation Area,** 4607 State Park Lane, Panama City Beach (☎ **850/233-5140**), one of this area's major attractions (see "Hitting the Beach," above), has RV and tent sites beautifully situated in a pine forest right on the shores of Grand Lagoon. Rates from March to September are $17 to $19 for waterfront sites, $15 to $17 for others. They drop to $8 to $12 from October to February. Reservations are required, up to 11 months in advance. No pets are allowed.

You can bring your pet, but not your tent, to **Magnolia Beach RV Park,** 7800 Magnolia Beach Rd., Panama City Beach (☎ **850/235-1581**), with great views of Panama City from an idyllic setting under magnolias and moss-draped oaks on the shores of St. Andrew Bay. Rates are $20 to $24 a night in summer, $16 to $19 off-season. The park is 2 miles from Marriott's Bay Point Resort Village. Take Magnolia Beach Road off Thomas Drive and go straight to the camp.

Bay County adds 3.5% tax to all hotel and campground bills, bringing the total add-on tax to 9.5%.

MODERATE

Edgewater Beach Resort. 11212 Front Beach Rd. (P.O. Box 9850), Panama City Beach, FL 32407. ☎ **800/874-8686** or 850/235-4044. Fax 850/233-7599. 510 units. Summer $105–$358 condo. Off-season $57–$144 condo. Weekly rates and maid service available. DC, DISC, MC, V.

One of the Panhandle's largest condominium resorts, this sports-oriented facility enjoys a beautiful beachfront location and 110 tropically landscaped acres. Units in five gulf-side towers enjoy commanding views of the emerald Gulf and gorgeous sunsets from their private balconies. A pedestrian overpass leads across Front Beach Road to low-rise apartments and town homes fringing ponds and the fairways of the resort's own 9-hole golf course. A daytime shuttle runs around the resort to three swimming pools, whirlpools, 12 tennis courts (6 lighted), and the 18-hole Hombre Golf Club a quarter mile north.

Food outlets here serve all three meals, and the Shoppes at Edgewater restaurants are across the road.

Holiday Inn SunSpree Resort. 11127 Front Beach Rd., Panama City Beach, FL 32407. ☎ **800/633-0266** or 850/234-1111. Fax 850/235-0888. 342 units. A/C TV TEL. Summer $149–$259 double. Off-season $59–$129 double. Weekly and monthly rates available. AE, DC, DISC, MC, V.

One building removed from the Edgewater Beach Resort and across the road from the Shoppes at Edgewater, this 15-story hotel is designed in an arch, with all rooms having balconies looking directly down on a foot-shaped swimming pool and wooden sundeck beside the beach. The hotel has won architectural awards for its dramatic lobby with a waterfall and the Fountain of Wishes (coins go to charity). The attractive, spacious guest rooms feature full-size ice-making refrigerators, microwave ovens, and two spacious vanity areas with their own lavatory sinks.

There's a poolside grill for lunches, while the lobby restaurant under a skylight dome features good breakfasts, lunches, and dinners at moderate prices. There's a Pizza Hut outlet for carryout pies. The lively Starlight Lounge serves drinks until late and usually offers entertainment during the peak summer season. The lobby bar has sports TVs, and there's poolside entertainment during summer evenings. Facilities include a swimming pool, sundeck, whirlpool, exercise and game rooms, gift shop, and children's playground.

✪ **Marriott's Bay Point Resort Village.** 4200 Marriott Dr., Panama City Beach, FL 32408. ☎ **800/874-7105** or 850/234-3307. Fax 850/233-1308. 355 units. A/C TV TEL. Summer $119–$169 double. Off-season $99–$129 double. Packages available. AE, DC, DISC, MC, V. From Thomas Dr., take Magnolia Beach Rd. and follow the signs for 3 miles.

Not only is this luxurious vacation miniworld ranked among the nation's top 25 golf and tennis resorts, it's an extraordinarily good value for Florida. Although guests pay extra for most activities, its room rates are among the top steals in the state. That's because the property is not beside the Gulf; instead, it's the centerpiece of a real estate development sprawling over 1,100 landscaped acres on a peninsula bordered by St. Andrew Bay and Grand Lagoon. Situated beside the lagoon, the luxurious, vivid-coral stucco hotel is surrounded by gardens, palm trees, oaks, and magnolias. From the glamorous three-story lobby, window walls look out to scenic water views and four swimming pools (one in its own glass-enclosed building). Furnished in dark woods, the Marriottesque rooms are spacious and luxurious.

You won't go hungry here, for the Bay View Restaurant in the hotel serves break-fast, lunch, and dinner featuring moderately price buffets. Outlets in the Lagoon Legends pro shop next door serve breakfast, snacks, and light meals at lunch. Snacks and libations also are proffered from March to October on the long pier in front of the hotel, where day-long beach parties go on during summer. Sports fans will find TVs going nonstop in the English-style bar off the lobby.

The highlights for duffers are the Lagoon Legends and the Club Meadows golf courses (see "Outdoor Pursuits," above). The Bay Point Tennis Center has 12 clay courts (4 lighted), a tennis shop, clinics, and lessons. Water sports here are at Grand Lagoon beach, reached by the hotel's long pier, where both guests and nonguests can rent WaveRunners and boats, and go waterskiing and parasailing during the season. The *Island Queen* paddle wheeler departs the pier for sunset cruises and excursions to Shell Island. Guests can burn off the calories at two health clubs and excess money at the Bay Town Shops, which have a deli and dry cleaner. Over at the marina, the Bay Point Billfish Invitational in July is one of the world's richest. Rent a bike or scooter at the front desk to get around this widespread resort.

INEXPENSIVE

Flamingo Motel. 15525 Front Beach Rd., Panama City Beach, FL 32413. ☎ **800/ 828-0400** or 850/234-2232. 67 units. A/C TV TEL. Summer $66–$119. Off-season $32–$74. AE, DISC, MC, V.

Evoking Key West, this well-maintained, family-owned motel takes great pride in its gorgeous tropical garden surrounding a heated swimming pool and a large sundeck overlooking the Gulf. The brightly decorated rooms have either full kitchens or refrig-erators and microwave ovens. They can sleep two to six people, some in separate bed-rooms. Kitchenette rooms in a two-story motel block across the road are less appealing but will accommodate six to eight. Budget-conscious families can opt for the low-priced rooms, accommodating two to four. Some units have shower-only baths. The Dan Russell fishing pier is only half a mile away, Gulf World is within walking dis-tance, and Shuckums Oyster Pub & Seafood Grill is across the road, (see "Exploring the Area," above, and "Where to Dine," below). Forget spending spring break here unless you're a family or a couple.

Next door, the midrise **Flamingo Towers** was due to open in 1998, with 49 junior suites, all sporting balconies facing the Gulf. The complex will have its own pool and hot tub.

Georgian Terrace. 14415 Front Beach Rd., Panama City Beach, FL 32413. ☎ **850/ 234-2144** or 850/234-8413. 28 units. A/C TV TEL. Summer $69–$109 double. Off-season $43–$89 double. AE, DISC, MC, V.

Right on the beach, Karen Grant's two-level motel offers clean, quiet, and cozy apart-ments. Opening to the beach, cheerfully decorated, and lined with knotty pine, they all have full kitchens separated by room dividers. The homey decor is extended to each unit's private enclosed sunporch. A greenhouse-enclosed heated pool area with lush tropical plantings and attractive lounge chairs makes this place a good pick off-season. There's a rare stretch of undeveloped beach almost next door.

Sunset Inn. 8109 Surf Dr., Panama City Beach, FL 32408. ☎ and fax **850/234-7370.** 62 units. A/C TV TEL. Summer $55–$155 double. Off-season $35–$110 double. Weekly and monthly rates available. AE, DISC, MC, V.

This very well maintained establishment off Thomas Drive near the east end of the beach is right on the Gulf but away from the crowds. The beachside units accommodate families in one- and two-bedroom apartments with kitchens, while across the street stands an older block of efficiencies and a new building with tropically furnished one- and two-bedroom condos (the most expensive units here). The inn sports a large heated swimming pool and a spacious sundeck with steps leading down to the beach.

WHERE TO DINE

Except for fast-food joints, there aren't many national chain family restaurants in Panama City Beach (you'll find those along 15th and 23rd streets over in Panama City). There is one local chain worth a meal: the **Montego Bay Seafood Houses,** which offer a wide range of munchies, sandwiches, burgers, and seafood main courses, most in the inexpensive category. Branches are at the "curve" on Thomas Drive (☎ 850/234-8687); at the intersection of Thomas Drive and Middle and Front Beach roads (☎ 850/236-3585); and in the Shoppes at Edgewater, Front Beach Drive at Beckrich Road (☎ 850/233-6033).

Pay attention to the restaurant hours here, for some places are closed during the winter months.

MODERATE

Boar's Head Restaurant. 17290 Front Beach Rd. (just west of Fla. 79). ☎ **850/234-6628.** Reservations accepted. Main courses $14–$21.50. AE, DC, DISC, MC, V. Summer daily 4:30–10pm. Off-season Sun–Thurs 4:30–9pm, Fri–Sat 4:30–10pm. STEAKS/SEAFOOD.

An institution here since 1978, this shingle-roofed establishment appears from the road to be a South Seas resort. Inside, its impressive beamed ceiling, stone walls, and fireplaces create a warm, almost English tavern atmosphere suitable to the house specialties: tender, marbled prime rib of beef and perfectly cooked steaks. Beef eaters don't have the Boar's Head to themselves, however, for the coals are also used to give a charred flavor to shrimp and tuna. Other cooking styles are offered too, including a combination of lobster, shrimp, and scallops in a cream sauce over angel-hair pasta. And venison, quail, and other game find their way here during winter. An extensive wine list has won awards, and a cozy tavern to one side has live music, usually Wednesday to Saturday evenings.

✪ **Canopies.** 4423 W. Hwy. 98, Panama City (1 mile east of Hathaway Bridge on U.S. 98). ☎ **850/872-8444.** Reservations recommended. Main courses $14–$25. Early bird specials $10. AE, DISC, MC, V. Daily 5–10pm. Early bird specials daily 5–6pm. Closed Thanksgiving and Christmas. SEAFOOD/STEAKS.

This area's most elegant restaurant and purveyor of its finest cuisine occupies a 1910-vintage gray clapboard house with a magnificent view of St. Andrew Bay. Dining is on an enclosed veranda, but the dark, cozy bar in the old living room invites before- or after-dinner drinks. The menu changes every week or two, but consistent favorites are a creamy she-crab soup under a flaky croissant dome; grilled tuna, salmon, or grouper with a trio of sauces; sautéed grouper with lump crabmeat in a sherry-butter sauce; and sushi-quality yellowfin tuna in a sherry-soy sauce and served over a haystack of leaks. Landlubbers can partake of award-winning beef, veal, lamb, pork, and game dishes. White chocolate mousse is among several gourmet dessert and coffee creations to top off these delicious meals.

Capt. Anderson's Restaurant. 5551 N. Lagoon Dr. (at Thomas Dr.). ☎ **850/234-2225.** Reservations not accepted. Main courses $10–$35. AE, DC, DISC, MC, V. Mon–Sat 4–10pm (or later, depending on crowds). Closed Nov–Jan. SEAFOOD.

Overlooking Grand Lagoon, this famous restaurant attracts early diners who come to watch the fishing fleet unload the catch of the day at the busy marina. It's so popular, in fact, that you may have to wait 2 hours for a table during the peak summer months, either in the air-conditioned lounge or admiring the views from the open-air top deck. The Captain's menu is noted for grilled local fish, crabmeat-stuffed jumbo shrimp, and a heaped-high seafood platter. A Greek salad accompanies dinner. If this is your first time at Panama City Beach, don't miss the local atmosphere at Capt. Anderson's.

✪ **Hamilton's Seafood Restaurant & Lounge.** 5711 N. Lagoon Dr. (at Thomas Dr.). ☎ **850/234-1255.** Reservations not accepted. Main courses $13–$18. AE, DISC, MC, V. Sun–Thurs 4–10pm, Fri–Sat 4–11pm. Closed 1 day a week off-season (call ahead). SEAFOOD.

Proprietor Steve Stevens continues in the tradition of his noted Biloxi, Mississippi, restaurateur father. The attractive blond-wood and knotty-pine restaurant lies on Grand Lagoon. The baked oysters Hamilton appetizer—a rich combination of oysters, shrimp, and crabmeat—almost left me too full for a main course. Several other dishes are unique to Hamilton's, such as spicy snapper étouffée and a Greek-accented shrimp Cristo. Mesquite-grilled fish and steaks are also house specialties, and vegetarians can order a coal-fired vegetable kebab served over angel-hair pasta. A Lagoon Saloon makes the wait for a table go by quickly, and you can choose from an extensive selection of well-chosen California and French wines.

✪ **Marina Grill.** 6426 U.S. 98 west (at the west end of Hathaway Bridge). ☎ **850/ 233-0008.** Reservations not accepted. Main courses $13–$17. AE, DISC, MC, V. Sun–Thurs 11am–10pm, Fri–Sat 11am–11pm. LOUISIANA/SEAFOOD.

Ships' lanterns, knotty pine, and big windows looking to the boats moored in Hathaway Landing Marina give this spot an appropriately nautical ambience, perfect for enjoying the area's best New Orleans–style seafood and Cajun dishes. Some items, such as jambalaya pasta with shrimp and andouille sausage, will be familiar to anyone who has been to New Orleans, but other dishes are more creative. One example is the fried grouper brochette, which should be attacked only if you have a hearty appetite and a slim waistline. Doesn't sound that unusual? But wait. These morsels of grouper, green pepper, and onion are first dashed with Cajun spices, battered, and fried together, then served smothered with a rich garlic-butter sauce containing fresh diced tomatoes and green onions. Although the grouper taste gets totally lost in all this, it's an absolutely terrific concoction. Grilled and sautéed local seafood is also available. The big thatch roof of Hathaway's Landing waterside pub is next door.

INEXPENSIVE

✪ **Billy's Steamed Seafood Restaurant.** 3000 Thomas Dr. (between Grand Lagoon and Magnolia Beach Rd.). ☎ **850/235-2349.** Reservations not accepted. Sandwiches $2.50–$5; seafood $6.50–$18. AE, MC, V. Summer Sun–Thurs 11am–9:30pm, Fri–Sat 11am–10pm. Off-season daily 11am–9pm. Closed Nov–Feb. SEAFOOD.

More a lively raw bar than a restaurant, Billy and Eloise Poole's casual spot is famous for serving the best crabs in town. These are hard-shell blue crabs prepared Maryland style: steamed with lots of spicy Old Bay Seasoning. Unlike the crab houses in Baltimore, however, Billy and Eloise remove the top shell, clean out the "mustard" (intestines), and cut the crabs in two for you: All you have to do is "pick" the meat. The staff will demonstrate how to do that. Other steamed morsels include shrimp (also with spicy seasoning), oysters, crabs, and lobster served with corn on the cob and garlic bread. Order anything from the briny deep here, but pass over other items. If you're in town during the off-season, check to see if the Pooles have an all-you-can-eat crab feast scheduled.

Cajun Inn. In The Shoppes at Edgewater, 477 Beckrich Rd., at Front Beach Rd. ☎ **850/ 235-9987.** Reservations not accepted. Main courses $8–$15; sandwiches $4–$6. AE, DC, DISC, MC, V. Daily 11am–10pm. LOUISIANA CAJUN.

Almost hidden away in the "elbow" of The Shoppes at Edgewater, next to a multi-screen cinema, this cozy, family owned restaurant with high-backed wooden booths and Mardi Gras decor brings the Big Easy to the Gulf. Offerings include jambalaya, seafood étouffée, peppered shrimp or crayfish, and Cajun-style blackened fish. Po-boys (overstuffed hoagie sandwiches of fried oysters or fried shrimp) are a lunchtime specialty. You won't get gourmet New Orleans cuisine at these prices, but your tongue will have plenty of spice to savor. Dine inside, or outside on the shopping center walkway.

✪ **Shuckums Oyster Pub & Seafood Grill.** 15614 Front Beach Rd. (at Powell Adams Dr.). ☎ **850/235-3214.** Reservations not accepted. Main courses $11–$14; burgers and sandwiches $6–$10. DISC, MC, V. Summer daily 11am–2am. Off-season Sun–Thurs 11am–9pm, Sat–Sun 11am–midnight. SEAFOOD.

"We shuck 'em, you suck 'em" is the motto of this noisy, lively, and smoky pub, which became famous when comedian Martin Short tried unsuccessfully to shuck oysters here during the making of an MTV spring-break special. The original bar is virtually papered over with dollar bills signed by old and young patrons who have been flocking here since 1967. The obvious specialty is fresh Apalachicola oysters, served raw, steamed, or baked with a variety of toppings. Otherwise, the menu consists of pub fare and mediocre seafood main courses.

SPECIAL DINING EXPERIENCES

You've got to see the **Treasure Ship,** at Treasure Island Marina, 3605 S. Thomas Dr., at Grand Lagoon (☎ **850/234-8881**), to believe it. This amazing 2 acres of ship space claims to be the world's largest land-based Spanish galleon, a replica of the three-masted sailing ships that carried loot from the New World to Spain in the 16th and 17th centuries. You can get anything from an ice-cream cone to peel-it-yourself shrimp to a sophisticated dinner in various dining rooms and eateries. The restaurants and bars open daily at 4:30pm; closed from October through December.

Lady Anderson **dinner-dance cruises** are a romantic evening escape; they're available from March through October. Boarding is at Capt. Anderson's Marina, 5550 N. Lagoon Dr. (☎ **850/234-5940**), at 6:30pm Monday to Saturday, with the cruises lasting from 7 to 10pm. Buffet dinners are featured, followed by live music for dancing. Tickets cost $32.50 for adults, $20 for children 11 and under (tips included). This triple-decker fun boat is so popular that reservations must be made well in advance.

PANAMA CITY & PANAMA CITY BEACH AFTER DARK

The Breakers, 12627 Front Beach Rd. (☎ **850/234-6060**), is the area's premier supper club, with unsurpassed gulf views and music for dining and dancing. Open daily at 4pm during summer, Monday to Saturday during the off-season. The beachfront **Harpoon Harry's Waterfront Cafe** is part of the same complex.

Romantic lounges with both live entertainment and dancing are at the **Treasure Ship,** 3605 S. Thomas Dr. (☎ **850/234-8881**), and the **Boar's Head,** 17290 Front Beach Rd. (☎ **850/234-6628**). See "Where to Dine," above, for more information.

✪ **Hathaway's Landing,** on U.S. 98 at the west end of the Hathaway Bridge (☎ **850/230-0409**), has one of the largest thatch pavilions in Florida, under which live entertainment takes place nightly and on Saturday and Sunday afternoons from March to September. The emphasis is on Jimmy Buffet–style music, reggae, and some country and western. Away from the beach, it draws lots of customers over 30 years old.

The 20-something crowd likes to boogie all night at beach clubs such as **Schooners,** 5121 Gulf Dr. (☎ **850/235-9074**), where every table has a gulf view; **Spinnaker's,** on the beach at 8795 Thomas Dr. (☎ **850/234-7882**); and **Club La Vella,** one of Florida's largest nightclubs (it's a bikini contest kind of place), also on the beach at 8813 Thomas Dr. (☎ **850/234-3866**). They often stay open until 4am in summer while their bands play on. **Pineapple Willie's Lounge,** beachside at 9900 S. Thomas Dr. (☎ **850/235-0928**), is open from 11am until 2am, serving very good ribs (basted with Jack Daniels whisky) and spotlighting live entertainment during summer, a host of sports TV all year.

THE PERFORMING ARTS   The Rader family and a cast of 20 perform year-round in the ✪ **Ocean Opry Show,** 8400 Front Beach Rd., Panama City Beach (☎ **850/234-5464**), the area's answer to the Grand Ole Opry. Popcorn, hot dogs, and soft drinks are sold at the theater. There's a show every night at 8pm during the summer, less frequently off-season. Admission is $18 for adults, $9 for children ($20 to $30 when stars like Roy Clarke, George Jones, and Glen Campbell are in town). The box office opens at 9am Monday to Saturday, and reservations are recommended.

Across the Hathaway Bridge, downtown Panama City has a lively arts scene, with several galleries in its small downtown area and the **Martin Theater,** Harrison Avenue at 4th Street (☎ **850/736-8080**), a grand cinema that has been renovated and converted to host dramas and musicals staged by the Martin Ensemble (an excellent local repertory company) and performances by touring artists. Also on the downtown waterfront at the end of Harrison Avenue, the **Marina Civic Center** (☎ **850/763-4696**) hosts a variety of performances by nationally known troupes and artists throughout the year. Call for a schedule and ticket prices.

4 Apalachicola

65 miles E of Panama City, 80 miles W of Tallahassee

Sometimes called Florida's Last Frontier, Apalachicola makes a fascinating day trip from Panama City Beach or Tallahassee for many visitors, as well as a destination in its own right. The long, gorgeous beaches here are among the nation's best, and the bays and estuaries—justifiably famous for Apalachichola oysters—are great for fishing and boating. And if you love nature, the area also is rich in wildlife preserves.

The charming little town of Apalachicola (pop. 2,600) was a major seaport during autumns from 1827 to 1861, when plantations in Alabama and Georgia shipped tons of cotton down the Apalachicola River to the Gulf. The town had a racetrack, an opera house, and a civic center that hosted balls, socials, and gambling. The population shrank during the mosquito-infested summer months, however, when yellow fever and malaria epidemics struck. It was during one of these outbreaks that Dr. John Gorrie of Apalachicola tried to develop a method of cooling his patients' rooms. In doing so, he invented the forerunner of the air conditioner, a device that made Florida tourism possible and life a whole lot more bearable for locals.

Apalachicola has traditionally made its living primarily from the Gulf and the lagoonlike bay that lies behind a chain of offshore barrier islands. Today Apalachicola

produces the bulk of Florida's oyster crop, and shrimping and fishing are major industries. The town also has been discovered by a number of urban expatriates, who have
moved here, restored old homes, and opened interesting antique and gift shops. (Do
you know of any other town this size where you can buy Crabtree & Evelyn products?)
They'll be glad to see you.

ESSENTIALS

GETTING THERE   Apalachicola is about 65 miles east of Panama City via U.S.
98, and about 80 miles west of Tallahassee via U.S. 319 and U.S. 98. From I-10, take
Exit 21 at Marianna, then follow Fla. 71 south to Port St. Joe, and U.S. 98 east to
Apalachicola.

VISITOR INFORMATION   The **Apalachicola Bay Chamber of Commerce,**
99 Market St., Apalachicola, FL 32320 (☎ **850/653-9419;** fax 850/653-8219;
www.homtown.com/apalachicola; E-mail chamber1@supernet.net), supplies information about the area from its office on Market Street (U.S. 98) between Avenue D and
Avenue E. The chamber is open Monday to Friday from 9:30am to 4pm, Saturday
from 10am to 3pm.

TIME   The town is in the **eastern time zone,** like Orlando, Miami, and Tallahassee
(it's 1 hour ahead of Panama City Beach and the rest of the Panhandle). Many shops
are closed on Wednesday afternoon, when Apalachicolans go fishing.

BEACHES, PARKS & WILDLIFE REFUGES

Countless terns, snowy plover, black skimmers, and other birds nest along the dunes
and 9 miles of beaches (which some experts consider to be among America's best) at
✪ **St. George Island State Park,** on the island's eastern end (☎ **850/927-2111**).
The wildlife can be viewed from a hiking trail and observation platform. The park has
picnic areas, rest rooms, showers, a boat launch, and a campground with electric
hookups. Entry to the park costs $2 for a vehicle with one occupant, $4 for vehicles
with up to 8 occupants, and $1 for pedestrians and bicyclists.

  The beaches are even longer at ✪ **St. Joseph Peninsula State Park,** at the end of
County Road 30E, about 26 miles west of Apalachicola (☎ **850/227-1327**). The
peninsula is populated by cottages and a few shops around Cape San Blas, but beyond
the park entrance it's totally preserved. Facilities include picnic areas, a marina with a
boat ramp, campgrounds with electricity, and eight remote cabins. Entry fees are
$3.25 per vehicle with up to eight occupants, $1 for pedestrians and bicyclists.

  Both state parks are open daily from 8am to sunset.

  There are no facilities whatsoever at the **St. Vincent National Wildlife Refuge**
(☎ **850/653-8808**), southwest of Apalachicola. This 12,358-acre barrier island has
been left in its natural state by the U.S. Fish and Wildlife Service, but visitors are welcome to walk through its pine forests, marshlands, ponds, dunes, and beaches. In
addition to native species like the bald eagle and alligators, the island is home to a
small herd of sambar deer from Southeast Asia. Red wolves are bred here for reintro-
duction to other wildlife areas. Access is by boat only, usually from Indian Pass, 21
miles west of Apalachicola via U.S. 98 and County Roads 30A and 30B. The chamber
of commerce (see "Essentials," above) will arrange to have a boat captain take you over,
and some cruise operators go there (see "Cruises," below). The refuge headquarters, at
the north end of Market Street in town, has exhibits of wetland flora and fauna. It's
open Monday to Friday from 8am to 4:30pm. The rangers conduct managed hunts
for deer and wild hogs from November to January.

The huge **Apalachicola National Forest** begins a few miles northeast of town. It has a host of facilities, including canoeing and mountain-bike trails. See section 5 of this chapter, on Tallahassee, for details.

OUTDOOR ACTIVITIES

CRUISES   Jeanni McMillan of ✪ **Jeanni's Journeys** (☎ **850/927-3259**) takes guests on narrated nature cruises to the barrier islands and on canoe and kayak trips in the creeks and streams of the Apalachicola River basin. She also has night hikes with blue crab netting, shelling excursions, and fishing and scalloping trips, plus excursions tailored exclusively for children. Prices range from $30 to $75 per person. Reservations are required, so call her to find out what she's offering when you'll be in town. Jeannie also rents canoes, kayaks, sailboats, and sailboards.

Other cruise operators to contact are **Eco Ventures** (☎ **850/653-2593**), which goes out in the motorized, covered-deck *Osprey* Tuesday to Saturday from 5 to 7pm, earlier in winter; **Capt. Tom's Adventures in Paradise** (☎ **850/653-8463**), offering a variety of barrier island trip and backwater canoeing; and **Captain Tony Charters** (☎ **850/653-3560**), which has sightseeing trips and excursions to St. Vincent Island. Contact them in advance for schedules and reservations.

The *Governor Stone,* an 1877-vintage Gulf Coast schooner, makes cruises on Apalachicola Bay each day during the summer months, less frequently off-season. This fine old craft has seen duty as a cargo freighter, oyster buyer, sponge boat, and U.S. Merchant Marine training vessel. It departs from the Rainbow Inn dock on Water Street, but book in advance at the Maritime Museum at 268 Water St., north of Avenue F (☎ **850/653-8700** for schedule and reservations); reservations are recommended. The cruises cost $20 for adults, $10 for children 12 and under.

FISHING   Fishing is excellent in these waters, where trout, redfish, flounder, tarpon, shark, drum, and others abound. The chamber of commerce (see "Essentials," above) can help arrange charters on the local boats, many of which dock at the Rainbow Inn on Water Street. For guides, contact **Professional Guide Service** (☎ **850/670-8834**) or **Boss Guide Services** (☎ **850/653-8139**).

EXPLORING THE TOWN

Start your visit by picking up a map and a self-guided tour brochure from the chamber of commerce (see "Essentials," above), and then stroll around Apalachicola's waterfront, business district, and Victorian-era homes.

Along Water Street, several tin warehouses evoke the town's seafaring days of the late 1800s, as does the 1840s-era **Sponge Exchange** at Commerce Street and Avenue E. A highlight of the residential area, centered around Gorrie Square at Avenue D and 6th Street, is the Greek Revival–style **Trinity Episcopal Church,** built in New York and shipped here in 1837. At the water end of 6th Street, Battery Park has a children's playground. A number of excellent art galleries and gift shops are grouped on Market Street, Avenue D, and Commerce Street.

The showpiece at the ✪ **John Gorrie State Museum,** Avenue D at 6th Street (☎ **850/653-9347**), is a display replica of Doctor Gorrie's cooling machine, a prototype of today's air conditioner. Open Thursday to Monday from 9am to 5pm. Closed New Year's Day, Thanksgiving, and Christmas. Admission is $1, free for children 6 and under.

There's a small **Maritime Museum** at 268 Water St., north of Avenue F. It's usually open Tuesday to Saturday from 1 to 4pm. Admission is free.

It's only open Saturdays from 1 to 4pm, but the **Raney House Museum,** on Market Street, at Avenue F (no phone), shows what life was like when Apalachicola was a booming cotton port. The stately house was built in 1838, and the Apalachicola Area Historical Society has furnished it with 19th-century pieces. Admission is by $2 donation.

The **Estuarine Walk,** at the north end of Market Street on the grounds of the Apalachicola National Estuarine Research Reserve (☎ 850/653-8063), contains aquariums full of fish and turtles and displays of various other estuarine life. Open Monday to Friday from 8am to 5pm. Admission is free.

WHERE TO STAY

Outside the state park, the dunes of St. George Island are virtually lined with beach cottages and a few condominiums. These are available on a weekly or monthly basis. Among the rental agents are **Anchor Realty & Mortgage Co.,** 212 Franklin Blvd., St. George Island, FL 32328 (☎ 800/824-0416 or 850/927-2625; www.fla-beach.com); **Gulf Coast Vacation Rentals,** 45 E. 1st St. (HCR Box 90), St. George Island, FL 32328 (☎ 800/367-1680 or 850/927-2596); and **Sun Coast Vacation Property Management,** HCR Box 2, St. George Island, FL 32328 (☎ 800/341-2021 or 850/927-2282).

At **St. George Island State Park,** summertime camping fees are $14.84 per night for a campsite with electricity, $12.72 without, including tax. Off-season they go for $10.60 and $8.48, respectively. Primitive camping (take everything with you, including water) costs $3 a night per adult, $2 for children. For more information, contact the park at 1900 E. Gulf Beach Dr., St. George Island, FL 32328 (☎ 850/927-2111).

Campsites at **St. Joseph Peninsula State Park** cost $15 a night from March 1 to October 31, $8 a night the rest of the year. Cabins rent for $70 a night during summer, $55 a night off-season, with minimum stays of 5 nights during summer, 2 nights off-season. You can contact the park at 8899 Cape San Blas Rd., Port St. Joe, FL 32456 (☎ 850/227-1327).

✪ **Coombs House Inn.** 80 6th St., Apalachicola, FL 32320. ☎ 850/653-9199. Fax 850/653-2785. 18 units. A/C TV TEL. $89–$129 double. Rates include continental breakfast. AE, MC, V.

This large house in the historic district was built in 1905 by a lumber baron, and it shows: Polished black cypress paneling lines the entire central hallway and grand parlor. The house had gone to seed by the early 1990s, when noted interior designer Lynn Wilson bought it and completely restored it, furnishing it throughout with Victorian reproductions. Each of the 10 rooms in the main house is tastefully decorated; outstanding is the Coombs Suite, with bay windows, sofa, four-poster bed, and its own whirlpool. Less grand but still impressive are eight rooms in another restored Victorian (the "Annex") half a block away. One of these rooms has a whirlpool tub and bidet. One room in each house is equipped for disabled guests. A major truck route, U.S. 98, runs along the north side of both houses; request a south room to escape the periodic road noise. Guests can use the house bikes for free.

✪ **Gibson Inn.** 51 Ave. C, Apalachicola, FL 32320. ☎ 850/653-2191. Fax 850/653-3521. 30 units. A/C TV TEL. $65–$80 double; $75–$115 suite. AE, MC, V.

Built in 1907 as a seaman's hotel and gorgeously restored in 1985, this cupola-topped inn is such a brilliant example of Victorian architecture that it's listed on the National Register of Historic Inns. No two guest rooms are alike (some still have the original sinks in the sleeping area), but all are richly furnished with period reproductions. Nonguests are welcome to wander upstairs and peek into unoccupied rooms (whose doors are left open). Room and dining reservations are advised, especially on weekends, and rooms should be booked well in advance in summer—and as much as 5 years ahead for the seafood festival in November. Grab a drink from the bar and relax in one of the high-back rockers on the old-fashioned veranda. The dining room serves excellent seafood and is open to all comers, so don't expect this to be private like a bed-and-breakfast; instead, you'll find yourself in a reborn, absolutely charming turn-of-the-century hotel.

Magnolia Hall Guest House. 177 5th St., Apalachicola, FL 32320. ☎ **850/653-2431.** 2 units. A/C TV. $150 double first night, $100 double each additional night. Rates include full breakfast. MC, V.

Annegret and Douglas Gaidry have restored this two-story merchant's mansion to more than its 1838 splendor. It sits on a hill, giving the two huge upstairs guest rooms a view of the bay. The house has 12-foot ceilings and 11-foot windows, meaning that guests can step through their windows onto a wraparound porch, where the Gaidrys serve mint juleps while you rock away the late afternoon. Annegret also delivers morning coffee to the rooms and serves a full breakfast in the formal dining room. Many furnishings here are antiques, some dating from 1838 (one of the four-poster beds was in the house when the Gaidrys bought it). They have installed modern baths, one of which has a spa tub, and walk-in closets stocked with robes. Guests can also swim in the pool and roam 4 acres of lovely Southern-style gardens.

Rainbow Inn. 123 Water St., Apalachicola, FL 32320. ☎ **850/653-8139.** Fax 850/653-2018. 27 units. A/C TV TEL. Summer $69–$129 double. Off-season $59–$109 double. AE, DC, DISC, MC, V.

This two-story motel's rough-hewn exterior timbers make it look like one of the neighboring waterfront warehouses. And there's absolutely nothing fancy here, except views of Apalachicola Bay from the rooms. Those on the second floor have their own balconies with views. All are furnished with bright fabrics and have light paneled walls. The most expensive unit is a suite with kitchen and Jacuzzi. Caroline's Restaurant serves breakfast, lunch, and seafood dinners, and the Roseate Spoonbill Cocktail Lounge, over the restaurant, is a popular local watering hole with a grand view and music on an outdoor deck on weekends.

WHERE TO DINE

Townsfolk still plop down on the round stools at the marble-topped counter to order Coca-Colas and milk shakes at the **Old Time Soda Fountain & Luncheonette,** 93 Market St. (☎ 850/653-2006). This 1950s relic was once the town drugstore. It's open Monday to Saturday from 10am to 5pm.

Local sweet tooths also find satisfaction at **Delores Sweet Shoppe,** 29 Ave. E, at Commerce St. (☎ 850/653-9081), where Delores Roux's cookies, brownies, cakes, and key lime pies are famous hereabouts. She also serves sandwiches and chili for lunch. Open Monday to Friday from 9am to 5pm.

Apalachicola Seafood Grill & Steakhouse. 100 Market St. (at Ave. E/U.S. 98). ☎ **904/653-9510.** Reservations recommended in summer. Salads and sandwiches $6–$7; main courses $8–$15. AE, DISC, MC, V. Mon–Sat 11:30am–9pm. SEAFOOD/STEAKS.

With cafe curtains bedecking its storefront windows, this establishment from the outside looks like the typical small-town diner it once was, but this sophisticated restaurant offers Apalachicola-style gumbo and oyster stew; sautéed smoked oysters; meal-size salads and sandwiches; and charcoal-grilled grouper, yellowfin tuna, and salmon. The "basic meals" for $10 or less feature southern-style fried oysters, fish, scallops, and shrimp accompanied by potatoes and daily vegetable.

⊙ The Boss Oyster. 125 Water St. ☎ **850/653-9364.** Reservations not accepted. Main courses $10–$23; sandwiches $6–$8. AE, DC, DISC, MC, V. Sun–Thurs noon–9pm, Fri–Sat 2–10pm. SEAFOOD.

You've probably heard about the aphrodisiac properties of Apalachicola oysters. Well, this rustic, dockside eatery is a good place to see if it's true. The bivalves are served raw, steamed, or under a dozen toppings ranging from capers to crabmeat. They'll even steam three dozen of them and let you do the shucking. Steamed crabs and shrimp and fried seafood platters also are offered, as are delicious po-boy sandwiches with fried oysters or shrimp. Dine inside or at picnic tables on a screened dockside porch. Everyone in town eats here, from bankers to watermen.

⊙ Chef Eddie's Magnolia Grill. Ave. E (U.S. 98; at 11th St.). ☎ **850/653-8000.** Reservations recommended. Main courses $12–$24. MC, V. Mon–Sat 6–10pm. Closed 2½ weeks starting weekend after Thanksgiving. SEAFOOD/SOUTHERN.

One of the top places to dine in Northwest Florida, Boston-bred owner/chef Eddie Cass's pleasant restaurant occupies a small bungalow built in the 1880s and still in possession of the original black cypress paneling in its central hallway. Eddie has turned the old living room into the dining quarters, where he offers nightly specials emphasizing fresh local seafood and New Orleans–style sauces. He received more than 2,000 orders for his spicy seafood gumbo at a recent Florida Seafood Festival, and you will long remember his snapper or mahimahi Pontchartrain, with cream and artichoke hearts. Eddie and his wife, Bettye, do not allow smoking inside the house.

5 Tallahassee

163 miles W of Jacksonville, 191 miles E of Pensacola, 250 miles NW of Orlando

Tallahassee was selected as Florida's capital in 1823 because it was halfway between St. Augustine and Pensacola, then the state's major cities. That location puts it almost in Georgia; in fact, Tallahassee has more in common with Macon than with Miami. There's more Old South ambience here than anywhere else you're likely to visit in Florida. You'll find lovingly restored antebellum mansions, towering pine and sprawling live oak trees, richly scented magnolia blossoms, and colorful springtime azaleas. Tradition and history are important here, and you can visit many lovingly restored 19th-century homes and buildings, including the 1845 Old Capitol.

That's not to say you won't find the modern era in this extraordinarily pleasant small city, beginning with the New Capitol Building towering 22 stories over downtown. And usually sleepy Tallahassee takes on a very lively persona when the legislature is in session and when the powerful football teams of Florida State University and Florida A&M University take to the gridiron.

You'll think you're in an enormous forest, since local residents need permits to cut down trees. Majestic, moss-draped live oaks form virtual tunnels along Tallahassee's five official Canopy Roads, which are lined with historic plantations, ancient Native American settlement sites and mounds, gorgeous gardens, quiet parks with picnic areas, and beautiful lakes and streams.

Given its mild climate, state parks, federal forests, and wildlife refuges, the Tallahassee area is a popular destination for outdoor activities: boating and canoeing, golf and tennis, biking and hiking. The nearby Apalachicola National Forest is a virtual gold mine of outdoor recreational pursuits. If you're more inclined to give your credit cards a workout, the nearby town of Havana is Florida's antiquing capital.

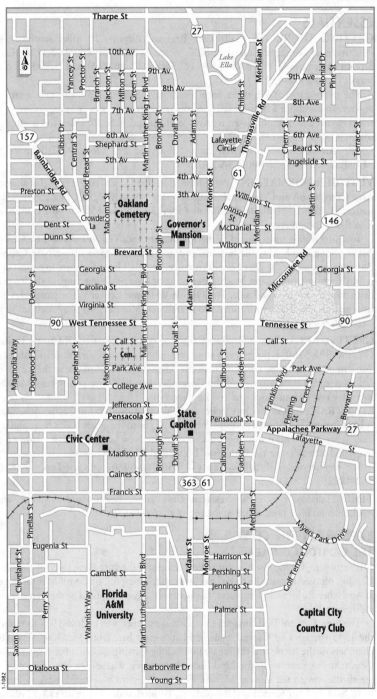

ESSENTIALS

GETTING THERE   The Tallahassee Regional Airport, 10 miles southwest of downtown on Southeast Capital Circle, is served by **ASA** (☎ **800/282-3424**), **Gulf Stream International** (☎ **800/992-8532**), **Delta** (☎ **800/221-1212**), and **US Airways** (☎ **800/428-4322**).

The major car-rental agencies have booths at the airport. You can take a taxi to downtown for about $10 to $15. There was no shuttle bus service at press time.

From east and west, highway access is via I-10 and U.S. 90. From the north and south, it's U.S. 27 and U.S. 319.

The **Amtrak** transcontinental train Sunset Limited stops in Tallahassee at 918½ Railroad Ave. (☎ **800/USA-RAIL**).

VISITOR INFORMATION   For information in advance, contact the **Tallahassee Area Convention and Visitors Bureau,** 200 W. College Ave. (P.O. Box 1369), Tallahassee, FL 32302 (☎ **800/628-2866** or 850/413-9200; fax 850/487-4621; www.co. leon.fl.us/cvb/homepage).

Your first stop in town should be the **Tallahassee Area Visitor Information Center** (same phone numbers as the bureau), in the West Plaza foyer of the New Capitol Building, just inside the Duval Street entrance. The staff here dispenses free street and public transportation maps, brochures, and pamphlets outlining tours of the historic districts and the Canopy Roads. The **Florida Welcome Center** in the same foyer has information about the entire state. Both are open Monday to Friday 8am to 5pm, weekends 9am to 3pm.

GETTING AROUND   Built like an old-time streetcar, the free **Old Town Trolley** (☎ **850/891-5200**) is the best way to see the sights of historic downtown Tallahassee. You can get on or off at any point between Adams Street Commons, at the corner of Jefferson and Adams streets, and the Governor's Mansion. The trolley runs Monday to Friday every 10 minutes between 7am and 6pm.

TALTRAN provides city **bus** service from its downtown terminal at Tennessee and Adams streets (☎ **850/891-5200**). The fare is $1. Both the ticket booth there and the Tallahassee Area Visitor Information Center in the New Capitol Building have route maps and schedules for the Old Town Trolley and TALTRAN buses.

For taxi service, call **Yellow Cab** (☎ **850/580-8080**) or **City Taxi** (☎ **850/ 562-4222**).

TIME   Tallahassee is in the **eastern time zone,** like Orlando, Miami, and Apalachicola. It's 1 hour ahead of the rest of the Panhandle.

EXPLORING THE CITY
THE CAPITOL COMPLEX

After stopping by the visitor information center on the first-floor foyer of the New Capitol, proceed to tour the rest of Florida's capitol complex, on South Monroe Street at Apalachee Parkway. It dominates the downtown area and should be the start of your sightseeing here.

The **New Capitol Building,** a $43 million skyscraper, was built in 1977 to replace the 1845-vintage Old Capitol. State legislators meet here from March to May. The chambers of the house and the senate have public viewing galleries. For a spectacular view, take the elevators to the 22nd-floor **observatory,** where on a clear day you can see all the way to the Gulf of Mexico. The New Capitol is open Monday to Friday from 8am to 5pm (closed major holidays). **Guided tours** (☎ **850/413-9200**) are scheduled on the hour, Monday to Friday from 9 to 11am and 1 to 3pm, and on Saturday, Sunday, and holidays from 9am to 3pm.

Directly in front of the skyscraper is the strikingly white ✪ **Old Capitol** (☎ 850/ 487-1902). With its majestic dome, this "Pearl of Capitol Hill" has been restored to its original beauty. An eight-room exhibit portrays Florida's political history. Turn-of-the-century furnishings, cotton gins, and other artifacts are also of interest. The Old Capitol is open Monday to Friday from 9am to 4:30pm, Saturday from 10am to 4:30pm, and Sunday and holidays from noon to 4:30pm. Admission is free to both the old and the new capitols.

Facing the Old Capitol across Monroe Street are the twin granite towers of the **Vietnam Veterans Memorial,** honoring Florida's Vietnam vets.

The Old Town Trolley will take you to the lovely Georgian-style **Governor's Mansion,** north of the capitol at Adams and Brevard streets (☎ 850/488-4661). Enhanced by a portico patterned after Andrew Jackson's columned antebellum home, the Hermitage, and surrounded by giant magnolia trees and landscaped lawns, the mansion is furnished with 18th- and 19th-century antiques and such collectibles as the hollowware from the battleship USS *Florida.* Tours are given when the legislature is in session from March to May. Call for a schedule and reservations.

Adjacent to the Governor's Mansion, **The Grove** was home to Ellen Call Long, known as "The Tallahassee Girl," the first child born after Tallahassee was settled.

HISTORIC DISTRICTS

While modern buildings have made inroads in downtown, Tallahassee makes an ongoing effort to preserve many of its historic homes and buildings. Many of them are concentrated in three historic districts within an easy walk north of the capitol complex. The information center in the New Capitol (see "Essentials," above) distributes free walking-tour brochures covering the three areas. Taken together, they're about 4 miles long and should take half a day. Most interesting is the Park Avenue District, 3 blocks north of the capitol, which you can see in about 1 hour.

Tours of Tallahassee (☎ 850/513-1230) has 2-hour walking tours around the capitol complex and nearby historic districts Monday to Saturday at 10am, 1pm, and 3pm. These cost $6 for adults, $4 for children 5 and up. The company also has van tours of the area, which cost $20 for adults, $20 for children, free for children under 5. Call ahead for van tour schedules and reservations.

ADAMS STREET COMMONS This 1-block winding brick and landscaped area along Adams Street begins on the north side of the capitol complex. It retains an old-fashioned town-square atmosphere. Restored buildings include the Governor's Club, a 1900s Masonic lodge, and Gallie's Hall, where Florida's first five African American college students received their Florida A&M University diplomas in 1892. Restaurants, shops, and Gallie Alley are also here. Adams Street crosses Park Avenue 3 blocks north of the capitol.

PARK AVENUE HISTORIC DISTRICT The 7 blocks of Park Avenue between Martin Luther King Jr. Boulevard and North Meridien Street are a lovely promenade of beautiful trees, gardens, and outstanding old mansions. This broad avenue with a shady median strip lined with moss-bearded live oaks was originally named 200 Foot Street and then McCarty Street, but was renamed Park Avenue to satisfy a snobbish Anglophile society matron who didn't want an Irish name imprinted on her son's wedding invitations.

Several Park Avenue historic homes are open to the public, including the **Knott House Museum,** at Calhoun Street (see "Museums & Art Galleries," below). **The Columns,** at Duval Street, was built in the 1830s and is the city's oldest surviving building (it's home of the Tallahassee Chamber of Commerce). **The First Presbyterian**

Church, at Adams Street, built in 1838, is the city's oldest church and has been an important African American historic site since slaves were welcome to worship here without their masters' consent. **The Walker Library,** between Monroe and Calhoun streets, was one of Florida's first libraries, dating from 1903 (it's home to Springtime Tallahassee, which sponsors the city's top special event). Just north of Park Avenue on Gadsden Street, the **Meginnis-Monroe House** contains the Lemoyne Art Gallery (see "Museums & Art Galleries," below).

At Martin Luther King Jr. Boulevard, the adjacent **Old City Cemetery** and **Episcopal Cemetery** contain the graves of Prince Achille Murat, Napoleon's nephew, and Princess Catherine Murat, his wife and George Washington's grand-niece. Also buried here are two governors and numerous Confederate and Union soldiers who died at the Battle of Natural Bridge during the Civil War. The cemeteries are important to African American history since a number of slaves and the first black Florida A&M graduates are interred here. The visitor information center in the New Capitol has a cemetery walking-tour brochure.

CALHOUN STREET HISTORIC DISTRICT   Affectionately called "Gold Dust Street" in the old days, the 3 blocks of Calhoun Street between Tennessee and Georgia streets, and running east on Virginia Street to Leon High School, sport elaborate homes built by prominent citizens between 1830 and 1880. A highlight here is the **Brokaw-McDougall House,** in front of Leon High School at the eastern end of Virginia Street, which was built in 1856.

MUSEUMS & ART GALLERIES

Black Archives Research Center and Museum. On the Florida A&M University campus, at Martin Luther King Jr. Blvd. and Gamble St. ☎ **850/561-2603.** Free admission. Mon–Fri 9am–4pm. Closed major holidays. Parking lot next to building.

Housed in the columned library built by Andrew Carnegie in 1908, this fascinating research center and museum displays one of the nation's most extensive collections of African American artifacts as well as such treasures as a 500-piece Ethiopian cross collection. The archives contain one of the world's largest collections on African American history. Visitors here can listen to tapes of gospel music and of elderly people reminiscing about the past. Florida Agricultural and Mechanical University (FAMU) was founded in 1887, primarily as a black institution. Today it's acclaimed for its business, engineering, and pharmacy schools.

The Florida A&M University Art Gallery. In Foster-Tanner Art Building, between Osceola and Gamble sts., off Martin Luther King Jr. Blvd. ☎ **850/599-3161.** Free admission. Mon–Sat 9am–5pm.

The focus in this gallery is on works by African American artists, with a wide variety of paintings, sculptures, and more. Exhibits change five times between September and May with local, national, and international artists in the limelight.

Florida State University Museum of Fine Arts. 250 Fine Arts Building, at Copeland and Call sts., on the FSU campus. ☎ **850/644-6836.** Free admission. Sept–Apr Mon–Fri 10am–4pm, Sat–Sun 1–4pm; May–July Mon–Fri 10am–4pm. Closed Aug.

A permanent art collection here features 16th-century Dutch paintings, 20th-century American paintings, Japanese prints, pre-Colombian artifacts, and much more. Touring exhibits are displayed every few weeks.

Knott House Museum ("The House That Rhymes"). 301 E. Park Ave. (at Calhoun St.). ☎ **850/922-2459.** Free admission (donations encouraged). Wed–Fri 1–4pm, Sat 10am–4pm.

Adorned by a columned portico, this stately 1843 mansion is furnished with Victorian elegance and boasts the nation's largest collection of 19th-century gilt-framed mirrors. The most unusual feature is the eccentric rhymes written by Mrs. Knott and attached by satin ribbons to tables, chairs, and lamps. Her poems comment upon 19th-century women's issues, plus the social, economic, and political events of the era. The house is in the Park Avenue Historic District and is listed in the National Register of Historic Places. It's preserved as it looked in 1928, when the Knott family left it and all of its contents to the city. The museum gift shop carries Victorian greeting cards, paper dolls, tin toy replicas, reprints of historic newspapers, and other nostalgic items.

Lemoyne Art Gallery. 125 N. Gadsden St. (between Park Ave. and Call St.). ☎ **850/ 222-8800.** Free admission except $1 during Christmas season. Tues–Sat 10am–5pm, Sun 2–5pm. Closed New Year's Day, last 2 weeks in July, Thanksgiving, Christmas Day.

This restored 1852 antebellum home is listed on the National Register of Historic Places and is a lovely setting for fine art. Known as the **Meginnis-Monroe House,** the gallery itself is named in honor of Jacques LeMoyne, a member of a French expedition to Florida in 1564. Commissioned to depict the natives' dwellings and map the sea coast, LeMoyne was the first European artist known to have visited North America. Exhibits here include permanent displays by local artists, traveling exhibits, sculpture, pottery, and photography—everything from the traditional to the avant-garde. The gardens, with an old-fashioned gazebo, are spectacular during the Christmas holiday season. Programs of classical music are combined with visual arts during the year; check in advance for the current schedule.

Museum of Florida History. In the R.A. Gray Building, 500 S. Bronough St. (at Pensacola St.). ☎ **850/488-1484.** Free admission. Mon–Fri 9am–4:30pm, Sat 10am–4:30pm, Sun and holidays noon–4:30pm. Closed Thanksgiving and Christmas.

An 11-foot-tall mastodon greets you at the official state history museum, which takes you back 12,000 years to the first Native Americans to live in Florida (mastodons were very much alive back then). Ancient artifacts from Native American tribes are exhibited, plus such relics from Florida's past as 16th- and 17th-century sunken Spanish galleon treasures and a reconstructed steamboat. Inquire about guided tours and special exhibits. There's an interesting museum gift shop.

ARCHAEOLOGICAL SITES

de Soto Historical Site. 1022 de Soto Park Dr. (off Lafayette St.). ☎ **850/922-6007.** Free admission. Grounds daily 8am–5pm (mansion closed to the public).

During the winter of 1539, Spanish conquistador Hernando de Soto, his troops, and friars, set up an encampment here before continuing their ill-fated search for gold. It's believed the friars celebrated the first Christmas mass in North America. An archaeologist searching for Spanish mission ruins discovered the de Soto encampment site in 1986. Rare copper coins, armor fragments, and a preserved pig's jaw have been unearthed. Former Gov. John Martin had no idea de Soto had camped here when he built his English hunting lodge–style mansion at the site in the 1930s. A colorful living-history time trail with exhibits and speakers is presented in January. Call for the date and program schedule.

Lake Jackson Mounds State Archaeological Site. 3600 Indian Mounds Rd. (off N. Monroe St., north of I-10). ☎ **850/922-6007.** Free admission. Daily 8am–sunset.

Artifacts discovered on this 18-acre excavation have revealed that native tribes settled on the shores of Lake Jackson (still one of the nation's best bass-fishing spots) centuries ago. A ceremonial complex flourished here around A.D. 1200, which includes six earth temple mounds and a burial mound. Part of the village and plaza area and two of the largest mounds are within the state site. The largest mound is 36 feet high with a base that measures 278 by 312 feet.

Mission San Luís. 2020 Mission Rd. (between W. Tennessee and Tharpe sts.). ☎ **850/ 487-3711.** Free admission. Mon–Fri 9am–4:30pm, Sat 10am–4:30pm, Sun noon–4:30pm. Closed Thanksgiving and Christmas. From downtown, take Tennessee St. (U.S. 90) west, turn right on White Dr., then right on Mission Rd. to the entrance.

A Spanish Franciscan mission named San Luís was set up in 1656 on this hilltop, already a principal village of the Apalachee Indians. From then until 1704 it served as the capital of a chain of Spanish missions in Northwest Florida. The mission complex included a tribal council house, a Franciscan church, a Spanish fort, and residential areas. Although there are no visible remains from this period, the first of two 17th-century reconstructions was completed in 1996. Interpretive displays are located across the 60-acre site and inside the visitor center. Call for information about archaeological excavations and living-history programs.

TRAVELING THE CANOPY ROADS

Graced by canopies of live oaks draped with Spanish moss, St. Augustine, Miccousukee, Meridian, Old Bainbridge, and Centerville roads are the five official Canopy Roads leading out of Tallahassee. Driving is slow on these winding, two-lane country roads (the locals only reluctantly are turning some limited sections of them into four-lane highways), some of them canopied for as much as 20 miles. Take along a picnic lunch, since there are few places to eat along these tranquil byways.

The visitor information center in the New Capitol provides a useful driving guide map of the Canopy Roads and Leon County's country lanes (see "Essentials," above).

If you have time for only one, take **Old Bainbridge Road,** which leads to the Lake Jackson Mounds State Archaeological Site in the northwest suburbs and on to Havana, Florida's antiquing capital 12 miles north of Tallahassee (see "Shopping," below).

PARKS & NATURE PRESERVES

In 1923 New York financier Alfred B. Maclay and his wife, Louise, began planting the floral wonderland of **Maclay State Gardens,** which surrounded their winter home on Lake Hall, 3540 Thomasville Rd. (U.S. 319), north of I-10 (☎ 850/487-4556). After her husband's death in 1944, Louise Maclay continued his dream of an ornamental garden to delight the public. In 1953 the land was bequeathed to the state of Florida. The more than 300 acres of flowers feature at least 200 varieties; 28 acres are devoted exclusively to azaleas and camellias. The beautifully restored home contains a camellia information center, and the surrounding park offers nature trails, canoe rentals, boating, picnicking, swimming, and fishing. The high blooming season is January to April, with the peak about mid-March. Admission to the park is $3.25 per vehicle with up to eight passengers, $1 for pedestrians and cyclists. Admission to the gardens during the blooming season from January to April is $3 for adults, $1.50 for children 11 and under; the gardens are free from May to December. The park and gardens are open daily from 8am to sunset. The Maclay House is open from January to April only, daily from 9am to 5pm.

Beyond the house and gardens, the state park also includes Lake Overstreet, around which wind 5½ miles of hiking, biking, and horseback riding trails, making this a major venue for those outdoor activities.

SHOPPING

Antique hounds flock to the little village of ✪ **Havana,** 12 miles northwest of I-10 on U.S. 27. Havana used to make its living from shade tobacco, and when that industry went into decline in the 1960s, the town went with it. Things turned around 20 years later, however, when Havana began opening art galleries and antique, hand-craft, and collectible shops. Today these are housed in lovingly restored, turn-of-the-century brick buildings along Havana's commercial streets. Just drive into town on Main Street (U.S. 27), turn left on 7th Avenue, find a parking place, and start browsing. You'll have plenty of company on weekends. After shopping, stick around and have a humongous steak at the nearby Nicholson Farmhouse (see "Where to Dine," below).

Bradley's Country Store, about 8 miles north of I-10 on Centerville Road (☎ 850/893-1647), sells more than 80,000 pounds of homemade sausage per year, both over the counter and from mail orders. You can also buy coarse-ground grits, country-milled cornmeal, hogshead cheese, liver pudding, cracklings, and specially cured hams. On the National Register of Historic Places, the friendly store is also a sightseeing attraction with self-guided tours. Open Monday to Friday from 9am to 6pm, Saturday from 9am to 5pm.

OUTDOOR ACTIVITIES & SPECTATOR SPORTS

BIKING & IN-LINE SKATING   The 16-mile **Tallahassee–St. Marks Historic Railroad State Trail** is the city's most popular bike route. Constructed with the financial assistance of wealthy Panhandle cotton-plantation owners and merchants, this was Florida's oldest railroad, functioning from 1837 to 1984. Cotton and other products were transported to St. Marks (see "Side Trips from Tallahassee," below) for shipment to other cities. In recent years the tracks were removed and 16 miles of the historic trail were improved for joggers, hikers, bicyclists, and horseback riders. A paved parking lot is at the north entrance, on Woodville Highway (Fla. 363) just south of Southeast Capital Circle.

Rental bikes and in-line skates are available at the north entrance from **About Bikes** (☎ 850/656-0001). Bike-rental rates are $9 for 2 hours, $16 for 4 hours, $35 for 24 hours, and various rates for families and groups. Guide maps and refreshments are also on hand. The shop is open April through October, Monday to Friday from 2 to 8pm, Saturday and Sunday from 9am to 5pm. Hours from November through March are Monday to Friday from noon to 6pm, Saturday and Sunday from 9am to 5pm.

The **Apalachicola National Forest** also has extensive biking trails (see "Side Trips from Tallahassee," below), and there are 5½ miles of trails at **Maclay State Gardens** (see "Parks & Nature Preserves," above).

GOLF   Play golf at outstanding Hilaman Park, 2737 Blair Stone Rd., where the ✪ **Hilaman Park Municipal Golf Course** features 18 holes (par-72), a driving range, racquetball, squash courts, and a swimming pool. Rental equipment is at the club, and there's a restaurant, too (☎ 850/891-3935 for information and fees). Compared to most courses in Florida, greens fees are a steal: $25 on weekdays, $30 on weekends, including cart (they're just $12.36 and $17.04, respectively, if you walk). The park also includes the **Jake Gaither Municipal Golf Course,** at Bragg and Pasco streets (☎ 850/891-3942), with a 9-hole, par-35 fairway and a pro shop. The Gaither course was recently renovated, so call for fees.

The leading golf course is at the **Killearn Country Club and Inn** (☎ 800/476-4101 or 850/893-2186), which once hosted the Sprint Classic. Moss-draped oaks enhance the beautiful 27-hole championship course, which is for members and hotel guests only (see "Where to Stay," below).

SPECTATOR SPORTS   Tallahassee succumbs to football frenzy whenever the perennially powerful Seminoles of **Florida State University** take to the gridiron. Hollywood star Burt Reynolds, who played defensive back for the 'Noles in 1957, can easily get tickets; the rest of us should call ☎ **850/644-1830** well in advance. Even when the Seminoles play on the road, everything except Tallahassee's many sport bars comes to a stop while fans watch the games on TV.

The **Florida A&M University** Rattlers are cheered on by the school's high-stepping, world-famous Marching 100 Band. Call ☎ **850/599-3230** for FAMU schedules and tickets.

Both FSU and FAMU have seasonal basketball, baseball, tennis, and track schedules. Call the numbers above for information.

Ice-hockey fans can watch the **Tallahassee Tiger Sharks** compete in the East Coast Hockey League from October to March. Games are played in the Tallahassee-Leon County Civic Center, 505 W. Pensacola St. (☎ **800/322-3602,** or 850/222-0400 for schedules and ticket information).

WHERE TO STAY

There is no high or low season here, but every hotel and motel for miles around is completely booked during FSU and FAMU football weekends from September to November, and again at graduation in May. Reserve well in advance or you may have to stay 60 miles or more from the city. For the schedules, call FSU or FAMU (see "Spectator Sports," above).

Except for the special weekends, rates at Tallahassee's hotels and motels are less than you'll pay at the beaches. Accordingly, the inexpensive establishments here offer much better quality accommodations than you'll find for the same price at the resort areas.

Most hotels are concentrated in three areas: downtown Tallahassee, north of downtown along North Monroe Street at Exit 29 off I-10, and along Apalachee Parkway east of downtown.

North Monroe Street at I-10 has most of the national chain motels catering to the highway traffic. On Apalachee Parkway east of the Capitol, the choices are **Best Western Pride Inn & Suites** (☎ **800/827-7390** or 850/656-6312), **Days Inn** (☎ **800/235-2525** or 850/224-2181), **La Quinta Inn** (☎ **800/531-5900** or 850/878-5099), **Motel 6** (☎ **800/466-8356** or 850/87-6171), and **Ramada Inn** (☎ **800/721-9890** or 850/877-3171).

Tax on all hotel and campground bills is 10% in Leon County.

MODERATE

✪ **Courtyard by Marriott.** 1018 Apalachee Pkwy., Tallahassee, FL 32301. ☎ **800/321-2211** or 850/222-8822. Fax 850/561-0354. 154 units. A/C TV TEL. Sun–Thurs $104 double; Fri–Sat. $59 double. AE, DC, DISC, MC, V.

Just a mile east of the Old Capitol, this comfortable member of the business traveler-oriented chain encloses a landscaped courtyard with a swimming pool and gazebo. About half the rooms face the courtyard; the others face parking lots. They are a bit cramped for families but ideal for singles and couples. All have sofas or easy chairs and rich mahogany writing tables and chests of drawers, plus features like two phones with modem ports, voice mail, and hand-basin faucets dispensing piping-hot water for tea and instant coffee (which are supplied). Other facilities include an exercise room and indoor spa pool. The marble-floored lobby features a lounge with fireplace and a dining area open for a breakfast buffet only. An Olive Garden, Bennigan's, and several other restaurants are within walking distance or a short drive away. The Parkway Shopping Center is also across the road.

DoubleTree Hotel. 101 S. Adams St., Tallahassee, FL 32301. ☎ **800/222-TREE** or 850/224-5000. Fax 850/513-9516. 251 units. A/C TV TEL. $79–$129 double; $175–$300 suite. AE, DC, DISC, MC, V.

Until recently the Holiday Inn Capitol Plaza, this 16-story hotel is one of the tallest buildings in town. Just 2 blocks from the Capitol Building at Park Avenue, it's usually booked solid during legislative sessions from March through May. Politicians and lobbyists, who love the spacious guest rooms, have power lunches at Jacob's on the Plaza, the hotel's Southern-accented restaurant. Amenities include room service, an exercise room, golf privileges, same-day laundry service, and complimentary airport transportation. There's an outdoor swimming pool, a gift shop, parking garage, and convention facilities.

✪ **Governors Inn.** 209 S. Adams St., Tallahassee, FL 32301. ☎ **800/342-7717** in Florida, or 850/681-6855. Fax 850/222-3105. 40 units. A/C TV TEL. $119–$129 double; $139–$219 suite. Rates include continental breakfast and evening cocktails. AE, DC, DISC, MC, V.

Just half a block from the Old Capitol, this elegant, richly furnished hotel was once a livery stable on historic Adams Commons. Part of the building's original architecture has been preserved, including the impressive beams. The guest rooms are distinctive, with four-poster beds, black-oak writing desks, rock-maple armoires, and antique accoutrements. The suites, each one named for a Florida governor, are sumptuous, some with whirlpool bath or loft bedroom with wood-burning fireplace. Among the amenities are comfy robes.

Complimentary continental breakfast and afternoon cocktails are presented in the pine-paneled Florida Room. Services include valet parking, nightly turndown, newspapers delivered daily to rooms, same-day laundry service, shoe shine, room service, airport transportation, and health club privileges.

✪ **Radisson Hotel.** 415 N. Monroe St. (at Virginia St.), Tallahassee, FL 32301. ☎ **800/333-3333** or 850/224-6000 (latter also is fax). 116 units. A/C TV TEL. $106 double; $150–$197 suite. AE, DC, DISC, MC, V.

About half a mile north of the Capitol, this seven-story establishment is Tallahassee's second most elegant hotel (behind the Governor's Inn), with an innlike lobby with reproduction antiques and cheerfully decorated guest rooms. The master suites come equipped with whirlpool baths, wet bars, concierge, and turndown services. There's a fitness facility with a sauna, and the hotel provides business services and complimentary airport transportation. The pleasant Plantation Dining Room is open daily for breakfast, lunch, and dinner.

INEXPENSIVE

Cabot Lodge North. 2735 N. Monroe St., Tallahassee, FL 32303. ☎ **800/223-1964** or 850/386-8880. Fax 850/386-4254. 160 units. A/C TV TEL. $66–$78 double. Rates include continental breakfast and evening reception. AE, DC, DISC, MC, V.

A clapboard plantation-style house with a tin roof and a partially screened wraparound porch provides Southern country charm to distinguish this friendly motel from its nearby competitors. Guests can sit and relax in straight-back rockers on the porch or on comfy sofas and easy chairs by a fireplace in the living room. Although the guest rooms in the two-story motel buildings out back don't hold up their end of the atmosphere factor, they're still quite satisfactory at these rates, and they give quick access to the outdoor swimming pool. Guests can graze at a continental breakfast buffet, drink coffee all day, and partake in free evening cocktails.

Killearn Country Club and Inn. 100 Tyron Circle, Tallahassee, FL 32308. ☎ **800/ 476-4101** or 850/893-2186. Fax 850/893-8267. 39 units. A/C TV TEL. $80 double. Golf packages available. AE, DISC, MC, V.

Located in upscale Killearn Estates between Thomasville and Centerville roads north of I-10, this country club is home to Tallahassee's leading 18-hole golf course, which house guests can play for $30 Monday to Friday, $40 on weekends, making this one of the region's best golf-resort bargains. The rooms and suites have sitting areas and dressing rooms; some have wet bars, and some open to central living rooms (which lobbyists turn into hospitality areas to influence legislators from March to May). Each unit is individually decorated and has a balcony overlooking the woodland-bordered golf course. The club also offers eight tennis courts, plus racquetball and handball courts. The swimming pool is Olympic size, and there's an exercise facility and miles of surrounding roads for jogging. Moderate prices prevail in the classy, beamed-ceilinged Oak View restaurant.

✪ **Quality Inn & Suites.** 2020 Apalachee Pkwy., Tallahassee, FL 32301. ☎ **800/228-5151** or 850/877-4437. Fax 850/878-9964. 100 units. A/C TV TEL. $62–$81 double; $67–$72 suite. Rates include continental breakfast. AE, DC, DISC, MC, V.

In contrast to every Quality Inn I've ever seen, there's real charm here. In fact, an almost English country inn atmosphere prevails in the classy, marble-lined lobby and spacious guest rooms, which are furnished with sofas, reclining wing chairs, two doubles or a king-size bed, desks, and coffeemakers. Complimentary continental breakfasts are served in a ground-level lounge with views of the inn's swimming pool. Guests can partake in a free work-night wine bar. There's a pool on the premises, and guests receive passes to the nearby YMCA. Several fast-food and family-style restaurants are within a short walk.

Riedel House Bed & Breakfast. 1412 Fairway Dr., Tallahassee, FL 32301. ☎ **850/ 222-8569.** 3 units (all with bathroom). A/C. $75 double (higher on special weekends). Rates include breakfast. No credit cards.

Surrounded by majestic live oaks, pines, magnolias, and flowers, this white-brick, Federal-style, two-story home was built in 1937 for the Cary D. Landis family (he was a former Florida attorney general). The present owner and innkeeper is talented artist and art teacher Carolyn Riedel. A spiral staircase leads from the beautiful foyer to her art gallery and spacious guest rooms, each adorned with period furniture and antiques. Carolyn serves an extensive continental breakfast in the dining room overlooking terraced gardens. Located in the prestigious Capitol Country Club area, the Riedel House is within walking distance of public tennis courts and the club's golf course.

WHERE TO DINE

Numerous budget-priced fast-food and family chain restaurants lie along Apalachee Parkway and North Monroe Street.

MODERATE

Anthony's. 1950 Thomasville Rd., at Bradford Rd. in the Betton Place Shops. ☎ **850/ 224-1447.** Reservations recommended. Main courses $11–$15. AE, MC, V. Mon–Sat 5:30–10pm, Sun 5:30–9pm. ITALIAN.

Locals come to see and be seen at Dick Anthony's elegantly relaxed trattoria. Among his specialties are pesce Venezia, spinach fettuccine tossed in a cream sauce with scallops, crabmeat, and fish. Chicken piccata and chicken San Marino are also favorites, and

Dick's thick, juicy steaks are always popular with beef eaters. A wall-size wine cupboard features choices from Italy and the United States by the bottle or glass. Espresso pie leads the dessert menu.

✪ **Chez Pierre.** 1215 Thomasville Rd. (at 6th Ave.) ☎ **850/222-0936.** Reservations recommended. Lunch $5.50–$11; main courses $12–$22. AE, DC, MC, V. Mon–Sat 11am–2:30pm and 5:30–10pm. FRENCH.

You become an instant Francophile in Florida at this chic restaurant in a beautifully restored 1920s brick home a few blocks north of the intersection of North Monroe Street and Thomasville Road. French-born chef Eric Favier and his American wife and partner, Karen Cooley, offer traditional French cuisine either inside the house—the walls are adorned with changing works by local artists—or outside on a large deck nearly shaded by live oaks draped with Spanish moss. Eric offers daily specials to take advantage of fresh produce, but his constant winners are chicken crepes, a version of provincial ratatouille, half a roasted chicken with a different sauce each day, Bretagne-style fresh mussels, and crab cakes with a luscious mustard sauce. French table wines are moderately priced, and California house wines are also served. Live music accompanies dining Thursday to Saturday nights, and you can take a horse-drawn carriage ride Friday and Saturday evenings. No smoking except on the front porch, where stogies and brandy can be enjoyed while lounging in wicker chairs. Book as early as possible for Bastille Day (July 14), which sees a humongous party here.

Silver Slipper. 531 Scotty's Lane (1 block south of the Tallahassee Mall behind Scotty's Hardware). ☎ **850/386-9366.** Reservations recommended. Main courses $11–$29. AE, DC, DISC, MC, V. Mon–Sat 5–11pm. STEAK/SEAFOOD.

Established in 1938, the oldest family-operated restaurant in Florida has served thick, tender, juicy Black Angus steaks to every president from Kennedy to Bush (they got a Christmas card from Clinton). From the award-winning menu you can also select seafood dishes, lamb, and veal. Although steaks and tender prime rib draw the crowds, a dozen bacon-wrapped big shrimp or bits of Black Angus beef are the culinary stars here. Featuring live entertainment on Tuesday to Saturday, the cocktail lounge is a favorite haunt of politicians and lobbyists. It's open until midnight on Monday to Thursday, until 2am on Friday and Saturday. Private, curtained booths are available in the dining room.

The Wharf. 4141 Apalachee Pkwy. (2 miles east of Capital Circle). ☎ **850/656-2332.** Reservations not accepted. Main courses $9–$24 (most $11–$16). AE, DC, DISC, MC, V. Sun–Thurs 4–9pm, Fri–Sat 4–10pm. SEAFOOD.

With or without children, local residents drive out in droves to this rough-hewn establishment evoking the ambience of an Old Florida fishing camp. The basic fried, broiled, or blackened dinners here are in the old-time tradition too, with flounder or the day's fresh catch served with their heads off but their bones left very much intact. Accompanied by a salad or coleslaw, potatoes or cheese grits, these filling main courses are a bargain at $9. If you don't feel up to dissecting your catch, you can choose shrimp or scallops for a few dollars more. The menu also offers shrimp Creole, seafood au gratin, and a selection of seafood pastas. Several dining rooms—most divided by skinny aquariums built into the walls—make The Wharf seem smaller and more intimate than a 400-seat restaurant. Sweet tooths are satisfied by homemade desserts such as an anything-but-ordinary bread pudding. There's also a kid's menu here. Mom and Dad's Italian Restaurant (see below) is next door and is a bit easier to see from Apalachee Parkway.

INEXPENSIVE

✪ **Bahn Thai.** 1319 S. Monroe St. (near Oakland Ave.). ☎ **850/224-4765.** Reservations accepted. Main courses $5.75–$15. Lunch buffet $5.25. DISC, MC, V. Mon–Thurs 11am–2:30pm and 5–10pm, Fri 11am–2:30pm and 5–10:30pm, Sat 5–10:30pm. THAI/CANTONESE.

Lamoi (Sue) Snyder and progeny have been serving the spicy cuisine of her native Thailand at this storefront since 1979. In deference to local Southerners, who may never have sampled anything spicier than cheese grits, much of her menu is devoted to mild Cantonese-style Chinese dishes. More adventurous diners flock here to order such authentic tongue-burners as yon voon-sen, a combination of shrimp, chicken, bean threads, onions, lemongrass, ground peanuts, and the obligatory chili peppers. Sue's specialty, however, is her deliciously sweet, ginger-hinted version of Penang curry. You can ask her to turn down the heat in her other Thai dishes. Come at lunch and sample it all from the all-you-can-eat buffet, a real bargain.

Barnacle Bill's Seafood Restaurant. 1830 N. Monroe St. (north of Tharpe St.). ☎ **850/385-8734.** Reservations not accepted. Main courses $8–$17 (most $9); sandwiches and salads $5–$8. AE, MC, V. Daily 11am–11pm. SEAFOOD.

There's always plenty of action at this noisy, very casual spot, with sports TVs over an enormous tile-topped raw bar in the middle of the room. Freshly shucked Apalachicola oysters are the feature at the bar, but the menu offers a mélange of seafood to please the palates of the singles, couples, and families who flock here. The cooking is simple (often done by FSU students working part-time jobs), but the ingredients are the freshest available. The young staff is accomplished at charcoal grilling mahimahi, tuna, amberjack, and grouper. Skillet dishes combine shrimp, oysters, or scallops with vegetables and kielbasa sausage, but order one only if you like the strong smoked flavor of kielbasa. For a smoked sensation you definitely will enjoy, try the mahimahi and amberjack cured on the premises. Carbohydrate lovers can order a half pound of their favorite seafood served with Alfredo or scampi sauce over linguine. During summer, guests can sit at outdoor tables under a lean-to tent. Bands play in the Half Shell Lounge every weekend.

Food Glorious Food. 1950 Thomasville Rd., at Bradford Rd. in the Betton Place Shops. ☎ **850/224-9974.** Reservations not required. Most items $6.25–$12.50. AE, DISC, MC, V. Mon–Sat 11am–8pm. AMERICAN/INTERNATIONAL.

Very unusual and very healthy sandwiches, salads, and pastas have made this deli/cafe the talk of the town. Items displayed in a cold case change daily and could include such mouth-waterers as Mexican lasagna, a tasty dish of layered baked polenta with piquantly spiced chicken, tomato-chile sauce, and a topping of Monterey Jack cheese. There's always gazpacho, salad, a daily quiche, and plenty of tempting pastries and cookies. You can get it to go or dine at a few tables inside or, in good weather, on the outside courtyard.

Mom and Dad's Italian Restaurant. 4175 Apalachee Pkwy. (2 miles east of Capital Circle). ☎ **850/877-4518.** Reservations not accepted. Main courses $7.50–$16. AE, DC, DISC, MC, V. Tues–Thurs 5–10pm, Fri–Sat 5–11pm. ITALIAN.

Diane Violante and Gary McLean have been making their own pastas and baking Italian breads at this popular, aroma-filled trattoria since 1963. Diane is a native of Abruzzo, Italy, so her specialty is "spaghetti à la Bruzzi"—a casserole of vermicelli, sautéed mushrooms, and tomato meat sauce topped with mozzarella and Parmesan cheeses. Diane, Gary, and their son, Gene, ensure that all plates are piled high, making the drive out here well worth the time.

NEARBY DINING

✪ **Nicholson Farmhouse.** Fla. 12, 3½ miles west of Havana. ☎ **850/539-5931.** Reservations recommended. Main courses $10–$25. AE, DISC, MC, V. Tues–Sat 4–10pm. STEAKS.

This quaint cottage was built in 1828 by Dr. Malcolm Nicholson and is now on the National Register of Historic Places. Longing for a place where he could order a 32-ounce steak, the doctor's great-great-grandson, Paul Nicholson, turned the old house into a restaurant in 1988. His casual, very informal operation has been so successful that he has added two turn-of-the-century farmhouses and made extra dining space of the smokehouse and other outbuildings. At least an inch thick and aged on the premises, Paul's tender steaks are charcoal-grilled to perfection. Grilled chicken breasts, boneless pork chops, shrimp, and fish are also offered. Each table gets a bowl of boiled peanuts as munchies. There's a children's menu. Nonalcoholic beverages are served, and you may bring your own wine or spirits. Guests can take mule-drawn wagon rides around the farm Thursday to Saturday. This is the most popular weekend dining spot in the area, so make reservations well in advance for FSU football and graduation weekends.

TALLAHASSEE AFTER DARK

Check the "Limelight" section of Friday's *Tallahassee Democrat* for what's playing.

As a college town, Tallahassee has numerous pubs and nightclubs with live dance music, not to mention a multitude of sports bars. A good place to pick up copies of the *Break* and other entertainment tabloids with news about what's going on is **Barnacle Bill's Seafood Emporium,** which is also one of several restaurants featuring entertainment. Others include **Chez Pierre** and the **Silver Slipper** (see "Where to Dine," above).

For laughs, Dooley's Down Under pub becomes the **Comedy Zone,** a weekend comedy club in the Ramada Inn, 2900 N. Monroe St., at I-10 (☎ **850/386-1027**). Call for schedule and reservations.

The major performing-arts venue is the **Tallahassee-Leon County Civic Center,** 505 W. Pensacola St. (☎ **800/322-3602** or 850/222-0400), which features a Broadway series, concerts, and sporting events including FSU collegiate basketball and Tiger Sharks pro hockey. Special concerts are presented by the **Tallahassee Symphony Orchestra** at FSU Ruby Diamond Auditorium, College Avenue and Copeland Street (☎ **850/224-0462**). The **FSU Mainstage/School of Theatre,** Fine Arts Building, Call and Copeland streets (☎ **850/644-6500**), presents excellent productions from classic dramas to comedies.

SIDE TRIPS FROM TALLAHASSEE

The following excursions generally are on the way to Apalachicola, so if you're headed that way, plan to make a detour or two.

WAKULLA SPRINGS

The world's largest and deepest freshwater spring is 15 miles south of Tallahassee in the 2,860-acre ✪ **Edward Ball Wakulla Springs State Park** (☎ **850/922-3632**). Edward Ball, a financier who administered the DuPont estate, turned the springs into a preservation area. Divers have mapped an underwater cave system extending more than 6,000 feet back from the spring's mouth. Wakulla has been known to dispense an amazing 14,325 gallons of water per second at certain times. Mastodon bones, including those of Herman, now in Tallahassee's Museum of Florida History, were found in the caves. The 1930s Tarzan movies starring Johnny Weissmuller were filmed here.

A free orientation movie is offered at the park's theater. You can hike or bike along the nature trails, and swimming is allowed, but only in designated areas. It's important to observe swimming rules since alligators are present. Glass-bottom-boat sightseeing and wildlife-observation tours are offered daily: from 9:45am to 5pm during daylight saving time, 9:15am to 4:30pm the rest of the year. They cost $4.50 for adults, half price for children.

Entrance fees to the park are $3.25 per vehicle with up to eight passengers, $1 for pedestrians and bicyclists. The park is open daily from 8am to dusk.

The park entrance is just east of the junction of Fla. 61 and Fla. 267.

Where to Stay & Dine

Wakulla Springs Lodge. 550 Wakulla Springs Dr., Wakulla Springs, FL 32305. ☎ **850/ 224-5950.** Fax 850/561-7251. 28 units. A/C TV TEL. $65–$90 double; from $250 suite. MC, V.

On the grounds of Edward Ball Wakulla Springs State Park, the lodge is distinctive for its magnificent Spanish architecture and ornate old-world furnishings, such as rare Spanish tiles, black-granite tables, marble floors, and ceiling beams painted with Florida scenes by a German artist (supposedly Kaiser Wilhelm's court painter). The high-ceilinged guest rooms are simple by today's standards but are beautifully furnished and have marble bathrooms.

You don't have to be a lodge guest to dine in the lovely Ball Room, enhanced by an immense fireplace and arched windows looking onto the springs. Very reasonably priced meals feature Southern cuisine. The coffee shop provides snacks and light meals (there's a 60-foot-long marble drugstore-style counter for old-fashioned ice-cream sodas).

THE ST. MARKS AREA

Rich history lives in the area around the little village of **St. Marks,** 18 miles south of the capital at the end of both Fla. 363 and the Tallahassee–St. Marks Historic Railroad State Trail (see "Outdoor Activities," above).

After marching overland from Tampa Bay in 1528, the Spanish conquistador Panfilo de Narvaez and 300 men arrived at this strategic point at the confluence of the St. Marks and Wakulla rivers near the Gulf of Mexico. Since their only avenue back to Spain was by sea, they built and launched the first ships made by Europeans in the New World. Some 11 years later, Hernando de Soto and his 600 men arrived here after following Narvaez's route from Tampa. They marked the harbor entrance by hanging banners in the trees, then moved inland. Two wooden forts were built here, one in 1679 and one in 1718, and a stone version was begun in 1739. The fort shifted among Spanish, British, and Native American hands until Gen. Andrew Jackson took it away from the Spanish in 1819.

Parts of the old Spanish bastion wall and Confederate earthworks built during the Civil War are in the **San Marcos de Apalache State Historic Site,** reached by turning right at the end of Fla. 363 in St. Marks and following the paved road. A museum built on the foundation of the old marine hospital holds exhibits and artifacts covering the area's history. The site is open Thursday to Monday from 9am to 5pm; closed New Year's Day, Thanksgiving, and Christmas. Admission to the site is free; admission to the museum costs $1, free for children 6 and under. For more information, contact the site at P.O. Box 27, St. Marks, FL 32355 (☎ **850/925-6216**).

De Soto's men marked the harbor entrance in what is now the ✪ **St. Marks Lighthouse and National Wildlife Refuge,** P.O. Box 68, St. Marks, FL 32355 (☎ **850/ 925-6121**). Operated by the U.S. Fish and Wildlife Service, this 65,000-acre preserve occupies much of the coast from the Aucilla River east of St. Marks to the Ochlock-onee River west of Panacea, and is home to more species of birds than anyplace else in Florida except the Everglades. The visitor center is off U.S. 98 about 2 miles east of St. Marks (turn south at Newport on Lighthouse Road [County Road 59]). Stop there for self-guided-tour maps of the roads and hiking trails through the preserve. Built of limestone blocks 4 feet thick at the base, the 80-foot-tall St. Marks Lighthouse has marked the harbor entrance since 1842. The nearby beach is a popular crabbing spot.

Admission to the refuge is $4 per vehicle. The refuge is open daily from sunrise to sunset; the visitor center, Monday to Friday from 8am to 4:15pm and Saturday and Sunday from 10am to 5pm (closed all federal holidays). Contact the refuge for information about seasonal tours and hunting.

In 1865, during the final weeks of the Civil War, Federal troops landed at the light-house and launched a surprise attack on Tallahassee. The Confederates quickly assembled an impromptu army of wounded soldiers, old men, and boys as young as 14. This ragtag bunch fought the Federal regulars for 5 days at what is now the **Natural Bridge State Historic Site.** Surprisingly, the old men and boys won. As a result, Tallahassee remained the only Confederate state capital east of the Mississippi never to fall into Yankee hands. The historic site is on County Road 2192, 6 miles east of Woodville on the St. Marks River, halfway between Tallahassee and St. Marks. Follow the signs from Fla. 363 and go to the end of the pavement. It's open daily from 8am to sunset and admission is free. For more information, contact the San Marcos de Apalache State Historic Site (see above).

APALACHICOLA NATIONAL FOREST

The largest of Florida's three national forests, this huge preserve encompasses 600,000 acres stretching from Tallahassee's outskirts southward to the Gulf Coast and westward some 70 miles to the Apalachicola River. Included are a variety of woodlands, rivers, streams, lakes, and caves populated by a host of wildlife. There are picnic facilities with sheltered tables and grills, canoe and mountain-bike trails, campgrounds with tent and RV sites, and a number of other facilities, some of them especially designed for visitors with disabilities.

The **Leon Sinks Area** is closest to Tallahassee, 5½ miles south of Southeast Capital Circle on U.S. 319 near the Leon-Wakulla County line. Nature trails and boardwalks lead from one sinkhole (a lake formed when water erodes the underlying limestone) to another. The trails are open daily from 8am to 8pm.

A necessary stop before heading into this wilderness is the **Wakulla Area Ranger Station,** Rte. 6, Box 7860, Crawfordville, FL 32327 (☎ **850/926-3561**), which provides information about the forest and its facilities and sells topographical and canoe trail maps. The station is on U.S. 319 about 20 miles south of Tallahassee and 5 miles north of Crawfordville. It's open Monday to Thursday from 8am to 5pm and Friday from 8am to 4pm.

14

Northeast Florida

by Bill Goodwin

Known as the "First Coast," Northeast Florida traces its history from 1513, when Juan Ponce de León happened upon these sandy shores. In 1565 the Spanish established a colony at St. Augustine, making it the country's oldest permanent settlement. (No, it wasn't Jamestown in 1607 or the Pilgrims at Plymouth Rock in 1620.)

If they were to come back to life today, those early colonists would feel right at home in St. Augustine, where the streets of the restored Old City look like they did in Spanish times. For us modern mortals, St. Augustine offers a rich look back to when the settlers struggled to establish a life in a new and unfamiliar world.

But they would surely be astonished at what they would see elsewhere in Northeast Florida.

To the south, their eyes would pop open with disbelief at Cape Canaveral, where rockets blast off at the Kennedy Space Center. Nearby in Cocoa Beach, they would see another of our peculiar curiosities: surfers. And in Daytona Beach, they would hear the deafening roar of the stock cars and motorbikes that make this beach town the "World Center of Racing."

Heading north along the coast, they would come to the rich folks' haven of Ponte Vedra Beach, where golf definitely takes precedence over manual labor. And they would marvel at sprawling Jacksonville, Florida's largest metropolis and a thriving example of what we call the New South.

Up on the Georgia border, they'd cross a bridge to Amelia Island, where exclusive resorts take full advantage of 13 miles of beautiful beaches. Amelia's Victorian-era town, Fernandina Beach, would seem modern to them; to us, it's a quaint and historic retreat.

1 Cocoa Beach, Cape Canaveral & the Kennedy Space Center

46 miles SE of Orlando, 186 miles N of Miami, 65 miles S of Daytona

Known as "The Space Coast" after its most famous occupant, the NASA space program, the area around Cape Canaveral was once a sleepy place where city dwellers escaped the crowds from the exploding urban centers of Miami and Jacksonville. Now, the region has grown to accommodate its own crowds, especially hordes of tourists who come to visit the Kennedy Space Center and enjoy 72 miles of beaches, plus fishing, surfing, golfing, and tennis.

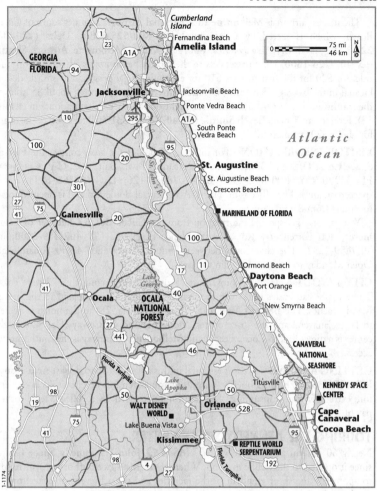

I Dream of Jeannie fans will recognize this as the home of television's most famous astronaut, Maj. Anthony Nelson, who lived with his bottle-dwelling Jeannie in Cocoa Beach.

Thanks to NASA, this also is a prime destination for nature lovers. The space agency originally took over much more land that it has needed to launch rockets. Rather than sell off the unused portions, it turned them over to the Cape Canaveral National Seashore and the Merritt Island National Wildlife Refuge, which have preserved them in their pristine natural states.

ESSENTIALS

GETTING THERE   Most people who visit the space center stay in nearby Cocoa Beach; dozens of beachfront hotels and restaurants make it a convenient home base. If you're driving from north or south, take I-95 to Fla. 520 east (the Merritt Island Causeway). You'll cross the Indian River and Banana River before hitting Fla. A1A, the north-south artery running along the Atlantic Ocean and connecting the beach towns from Sebastian Inlet to Port Canaveral.

The nearest airport is **Melbourne International Airport,** 22 miles south of Cocoa Beach, which is served by **Continental** (☎ 800/525-0280), **Delta** (☎ 800/221-1212), and **US Airways** (☎ 800/428-4322). **Melbourne Airport Shuttle** (☎ 407/724-1600) takes passengers to the Cocoa Beach hotels, about a 45-minute ride, for $20 for the first person, $10 for each additional person. The shuttle desk is located in the baggage claim area. **Orlando International Airport,** about 35 miles to the southwest, is a larger hub with more flight options (see "Orientation," in chapter 12). From there, **Cocoa Beach Shuttle** (☎ 407/784-3831) will take you to the beach for about $20 per person.

VISITOR INFORMATION   For information about the area, contact the **Florida Space Coast Office of Tourism,** 8810 Astronaut Blvd., Suite 102, Cape Canaveral, FL 32920 (☎ **800/872-1969** or 407/868-1126; fax 407/868-1193; www.spacecoast.com). The office is on Fla. A1A at Central Boulevard and is open Monday to Friday from 8am to 5pm.

You can also get specific information from the **Cocoa Beach Chamber of Commerce,** 400 Fortenberry Rd., Merritt Island, FL 32952 (☎ **407/459-2200;** fax 407/459-2232). The chamber is between Plumosa Street and Merritt Square Mall. Open Monday to Friday from 9am to 5pm.

CITY LAYOUT   Fla. A1A joins nearly a dozen towns along this 72-mile coast. Three major causeways lead from the mainland across Merritt Island to the barrier island beaches: The **Bennett Memorial Causeway** (Fla. 528) to the north is nearest to Port Canaveral and the space center; **Merritt Island Causeway** (Fla. 520) in the center is a direct link to Cocoa Beach; and **Melbourne Causeway** is the southernmost access.

GETTING AROUND   A car is essential in this area. The **Space Coast Area Transit** (☎ 407/633-1878) does operate buses, but routes tend to be circuitous and therefore extremely time-consuming. The fare for riders aged 18 to 60 is $1. All others pay 50¢.

TOURING THE KENNEDY SPACE CENTER

Nearly 60 million people have visited NASA's ✪ **John F. Kennedy Space Center** since it opened to the public in 1963. Whether you're a space buff or not, you're sure to appreciate the sheer grandeur of the facilities and the achievement of technology displayed here. Astronauts departed Earth at this site in 1969 en route to the most famous "small step" in history—man's first voyage to the moon.

All visitors must stop at the privately operated **Kennedy Space Center Visitor Center,** on NASA Parkway ½ mile west of Fla. 3 (☎ **407/452-2121;** www.kscvisitor.com). You can get here from Titusville on the mainland via the NASA Parkway Causeway (Fla. 405), or from Cape Canaveral and Cocoa Beach via Fla. 3. All other space center roads are closed to the public. From Orlando, take the Bee Line Expressway (Fla. 528) east, and where the road divides, go left on Fla. 407, make a right on Fla. 405, and follow the signs. Parking is free.

The center is open from 9am to dusk every day except Christmas and some launch days, but arrive early and pick up a schedule of events and a map to help plan your day. The offerings can be confusing, but a knowledgeable and helpful staff is on duty to answer questions and give advice. You'll need at least a full day to see and do everything.

The best way to get an overview of the area, and the only way to see actual working facilities, is by taking a **bus tour.** Two main tours are offered; each departs the visitor center every 15 minutes starting at 9:45am, with the last tour leaving late in the

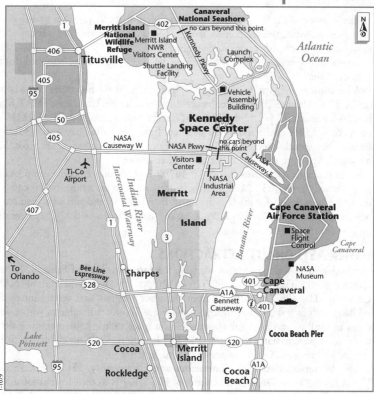

afternoon (call for details). The tours will take at least 2 hours, depending on how interested you are in hanging out at the stops along the way. Buses run continuously, so you can reboard as you wish.

The better of the two is the **Kennedy Space Center Tour,** which visits facilities now in use, including the Complex 39 Space Shuttle launch pads and the massive Vehicle Assembly Building where shuttles are prepared for launch. The tour includes the impressive Apollo/Saturn V Center, a $37 million, 100,000-square-foot exhibit that includes the most powerful rocket ever launched by the United States, the 363-foot-tall Saturn V. Videos, artifacts, photos, and interactive exhibits bring the history of the Apollo program to life.

The **Cape Canaveral Tour** is more historical and stops at the Cape Canaveral Air Station, where America's first satellites and astronauts were launched into space. Other stops include the launch pads currently used for unmanned launches, the original site of Mission Control, and the Air Force Space Museum.

For the same price as the longer tours, you can take the **Saturn Express Tour.** This scenic 15-minute drive to the new Apollo/Saturn V Center (described above) is a worthwhile abbreviated trip if you are short of time or have no patience for lengthy bus tours.

Back at the visitor center, rockets, interactive exhibits, and IMAX movies will both inform you and keep you entertained. Not to be missed, the 3-D IMAX movie *L-5: First City in Space* depicts future life among the stars. Two other IMAX films are also shown on the 5½-story-high screens every day: the 37-minute *Dream Is Alive,* giving an insider's view of the Space Shuttle program with in-flight footage shot by astronauts on various missions, and *Destiny in Space*, a Leonard Nimoy–narrated odyssey of the universe with exterior shots of shuttle flights.

Several dining venues in the visitors center will keep you fed and refreshed during your day here.

Admission to the visitors center is free, but tickets for the **bus tours** cost $10 for adults, $7 for children 3 to 11, free for children 2 and under. The regular **IMAX films** cost $6 for adults, $4 for children 3 to 11, free for children under 3. The 3-D IMAX movie costs $7 for adults and $5 for children. If you have a full day here, a **Mission Pass** is a better deal. It includes a bus tour and any two IMAX movies. These cost $23 for adults, $16 for kids 3 to 11, free for children under 3.

If you'd like to **see a launch,** call ☎ **407/867-4636** for a schedule of upcoming take-offs and ☎ **407/452-2121** for ticket information. At press time, tickets cost $10 to see the launch, $15 for the launch and an IMAX movie, and you were required to buy them in person at the visitors center up to 5 days before a launch. They were sold on a first-come, first-served basis.

OTHER ASTRONAUT ATTRACTIONS

In addition to honoring our space voyagers, the **Astronaut Hall of Fame,** 6225 Vectorspace Blvd., Titusville (☎ **407/269-6100**), at the mainland end of NASA Causeway (Fla. 405), has artifacts from the space program and several interactive exhibits, such as a flight simulator and a G Force Trainer that subjects you to four times the pull of gravity. A full-size replica of a space shuttle holds a theater with a multimedia presentation. Admission is $13.95 for adults, $9.95 for children 6 to 12, free for kids under 6. Open daily from 9am to 5pm.

The **Astronaut Memorial Planetarium and Observatory,** 1519 Clearlake Rd., Cocoa Beach (☎ **407/634-3732**), south of Fla. 528, has its own International Hall of Space Explorers, but its big attractions are sound and light shows in the planetarium. The building is open Tuesday, Friday, and Saturday from 6:30 to 9pm on a regular basis, but call for the show schedule. Admission to the building is free; shows cost $4 for adults, $3 for seniors and students, and $2 for kids 12 and under.

BEACHES & WILDLIFE REFUGES

To the north of the Kennedy Space Center, ✪ **Canaveral National Seashore** is a protected 13-mile stretch of barrier island beach backed by cabbage palms, sea grapes, palmettos, marshes, and Mosquito Lagoon. This is a great area for watching herons, egrets, ibis, willets, sanderlings, turnstones, terns, and other birds, and giant sea turtles nest here from May to August. You might also glimpse dolphins and manatees in Mosquito Lagoon. Canoeists can paddle along a marked trail through the marshes of Shipyard Island, and you can go backcountry camping here from November through April (permits required).

The southern access gate and ranger station is east of Titusville on Fla. 402, just east of Fla. 3. A paved road leads from there to undeveloped ✪ **Playalinda Beach,** one of Florida's most beautiful. It's now officially illegal, but nude sunbathing has long been a tradition here (at least for those willing to walk a few miles to the more deserted areas). The main visitor center is at **Apollo Beach,** at the north end of the island, via Fla. A1A south from New Smyrna Beach. Admission fees are $5 per motor vehicle, $1 for pedestrians or bicyclists. For more information, contact the seashore at 308 Julia St., Titusville, FL 32796 (☎ **407/267-1110**).

Its neighbor to the south and west is the 140,000-acre **Merritt Island National Wildlife Refuge,** home to hundreds of species of shorebirds, waterfowl, reptiles, alligators, and mammals, many of them endangered. Stop and pick up a map and other information at the visitors center, on Fla. 402 about 4 miles east of Titusville (it's on the way to Playalinda Beach). You can see some of nature's creatures from the 6-mile-long Black Point Wildlife Drive, or you can hike one of three nature trails through the hammocks and marshes. The visitors center is open Monday to Friday from 8:30am to 4:30pm, Saturday and Sunday from 9am to 5pm (closed Sunday from May through October). Admission is free. For more information, contact the refuge at P.O. Box 6504, Titusville, FL 32782 (☎ **407/861-0667**).

Other beach areas here include **Port Canaveral Beach,** which boasts bike paths, campsites, wide beaches, parks, and dozens of shops and restaurants.

The beach at ✪ **Cocoa Beach Pier,** on Meade Avenue east of Fla. A1A (☎ **407/783-7549**), is also a popular spot, especially for surfers. Appearing rustic and slapped-together, the pier was built in 1962 and shortly thereafter became the East Coast's surfing capital. It has 842 feet of fishing, shopping, and food and drinks overlooking a wide, sandy beach (see "Where to Dine," below).

OUTDOOR PURSUITS

CRUISES   **Port Canaveral** is where a handful of the major Caribbean-bound cruise ships depart, including the *Disney Magic* and *Disney Wonder.* You can go on day trips under sail with **Tradewinds Sail Charters,** at the Port Canaveral Seaport (☎ **888/635-1895** or 407/635-1898; fax 407/456-5770; www.yourlink.net/tradewinds). Many cruises are offered, from a 2-hour port excursion ($35 per person) to weekend getaways to Daytona Beach ($275 per person) to a week-long cruise to the Bahamas ($500 per person).

ECOTOURS   Call **Funday Discovery Tours** (☎ **407/725-0796**) to arrange back-country kayaking, airboat rides, horseback tours, and bird-watching expeditions. Prices range from $39 to $69 for adults, $19 to $49 for children 6 to 12.

FISHING   Whether you choose freshwater, shore, or deep-sea fishing, Brevard County has endless opportunities to cast a line. **Mosquito Lagoon** and **Eddy Creek** to the north are where you'll find trout and redfish. The **Indian River** and **Banana River** also yield trout and redfish as well as snook, ladyfish, and black drum. Bass fishers enjoy a region in the west called **Farm 13/Stick Marsh** with more than 20,000 acres of freshwater angling. Head to Port Canaveral for offshore catches like snapper and grouper. Many beachside accommodations arrange fishing charters and the port is lined with charter boats. For private outings, call **Dominics Guide Service** (☎ **800/BASS-909** or 407/242-892), one of the oldest licensed guides in the area.

You can go deep-sea fishing on the *Miss Cape Canaveral,* an 85-foot party boat docked at 670 Glen Cheek Dr., on the south dock in Port Canaveral (☎ **407/783-5274** or 407/648-2211 in Orlando). The day-long voyages leave daily at 8am and cost $55 per person, including breakfast, lunch, unlimited beer and soft drinks, gear, bait, and license.

GOLF   You can read about Northeast Florida's best courses in the free *Golfer's Guide,* available at the tourist information offices and in many hotel lobbies. See "The Active Vacation Planner," in chapter 2, for information about ordering copies.

In Cocoa Beach, the municipal **Cocoa Beach Country Club,** 500 Tom Warringer Blvd. (☎ **407/868-3351**), has 27 holes of championship golf and 10 lighted tennis courts set on acres of natural woodland, rivers, and lakes. Greens fees are about $38 in winter, dropping to about $32 in summer, including cart.

On Merritt Island south of the Kennedy Space Center, **The Savannahs at Sykes Creek,** 3915 Savannahs Trial (☎ **407/455-1377**), has 18 holes over 6,636 yards bordered by hardwood forests, lakes, and savannahs inhabited by a host of wildlife. You'll have to hit over a lake to reach the seventh hole. Fees with cart are $35 in winter, less in summer.

The best nearby course is the Gary Player–designed **Baytree National Golf Club,** 8010 N. Wickham Rd., ½ mile east of I-95 in Melbourne (☎ **407/259-9060**). Challenging marshy holes are flanked by towering palms. This par-72 course has 7,043 yards with a unique red-shale waste area. Fees are $85 in winter, dropping to about $50 in summer, including cart.

In Melbourne Beach, the expanded executive course at **Spessard Holland Golf Club,** 2374 Oak St. (☎ **407/952-4530**), lies between the Atlantic and the bays, making it one of the area's most scenic. The par-67 course covers 5,130 yards, with six holes of no more than 191 yards presenting opportunities for holes-in-one. Winter fees here are $32 with cart, less in summer.

SURFING   Rip through some totally awesome waves at the **Cocoa Beach Pier** area or down south at the **Sebastian Inlet.** Get outfitted at Ron Jon Surf Shop (see "Shopping," below). Or, call ✪ **Cocoa Beach Surfing School,** 301 N. Atlantic Ave., at Desperados Restaurant (☎ **407/452-0854**). They offer equipment and lessons for beginners or pros at area beaches. Be sure to bring along a towel, flip-flops, sunscreen, and a lot of nerve.

SPECTATOR SPORTS   The Boys of Spring here take the form of Miami's **Florida Marlins,** who play their spring training baseball games from mid-February through March at the Space Coast Stadium, 5800 Stadium Pkwy., off I-95 Exit 73 in Melbourne (☎ **407/633-9200**). Tickets range from $5 to $12.

SHOPPING

If you haven't already been lured by the hundreds of billboards along the highway beckoning you to the 24-hour surf shop, once you drive through Cocoa Beach, you'll definitely notice the glaringly original building that houses the **Ron Jon Surf Shop,** at 4151 N. Atlantic Ave. (☎ **407/799-8888**), set beside Fla. A1A a block from the beach. It's a Hollywood version of art deco gone wild with tropical colors, lights, and towering sand sculptures of famous sports heroes. Inside you'll find souvenirs of every description and everything you need to make you look like a surfer. The shop also rents beach bikes, boogie boards, surfboards, scuba diving gear, and in-line skates by the hour, day, or week, and they teach scuba lessons. They even have a cafe (more like a fast-food burger joint).

The **Merritt Square Mall,** at 777 E. Merritt Island Causeway, has more than 100 stores, including Florida's own department store, Burdine's, and many specialty shops as well as a 12-screen movie theater.

Bargain hunters can dig through the wares of hundreds of merchants at **Frontenac Flea Market,** open Friday through Sunday from 8am until 4pm. It's located at 5605 U.S. 1 midway between Cocoa and Titusville.

WHERE TO STAY

If you want to combine your space center visit with some beaching, your best bet is to locate in Cocoa Beach, about a half-hour drive south.

The area has a plethora of rental condominiums and cottages. **King Rentals Inc.,** 320 N. Atlantic Ave., Cocoa Beach, FL 32930 (☎ **888/295-0934** or 407/784-5046; www.kingrentals.com), has a wide selection in its inventory.

Given the proximity of Orlando and the generally warm weather all year, there is little if any seasonal fluctuation in room rates here.

You'll pay a 4% hotel tax on top of the Florida sales tax here.

COCOA BEACH

Cocoa Beach Hilton. 1550 N. Atlantic Ave., Cocoa Beach, FL 32931. ☎ **800/526-2609** or 407/799-0003. Fax 407/799-0344. 298 units. A/C TV TEL. Winter $129–$149 double; from $300 suite. Off-season $119–$129 double; from $200 suite. AE, DC, DISC, MC, V. Free parking.

True, there isn't much competition, but a recent upgrading has made this Hilton more upscale than the other chains represented here. No doubt you will run into a crew of name-tagged conventioneers, since it's especially popular with large groups. Rooms are a decent size, most have at least some view of the ocean, and all have coffeemakers, irons and boards, and hair dryers. The best part is that you're right on the beach and can rent water and sports equipment. Other diversions include a game room, weight room, and a modestly sized outdoor heated pool surrounded by a sundeck. An ocean-side restaurant and bar serves food and drinks, and room service is available until 10pm. Laundry, dry cleaning, and complimentary weekday newspaper delivery are convenient extras.

Comfort Inn & Suite Resort. 3901 N. Atlantic Ave. (Fla. A1A, at Brevard Lane), Cocoa Beach, FL 32931. ☎ **800/247-2221** or 407/783-2221. Fax 407/783-0461. 144 units. A/C TV TEL. $55–$87 double; $61–$135 suite. AE, DC, DISC, MC, V.

Half a block from the beach and a block from the congestion around Ron Jon Surf Shop (see "Shopping," above), this resort was born in the 1960s as a one-story motel enclosing a courtyard, which today sports a pool, whirlpool, bar with snacks, and volleyball and shuffleboard courts. Long since updated, the older rooms are medium-size and have doors opening to the courtyard and to the surrounding parking lots. Those in the south wing have cathedral ceilings, which lend an almost cottagelike ambience. Newer one-bedroom suites are in their own midrise building at the beach end of the courtyard. The resort has a lounge but no restaurant (fast-food outlets sit across Atlantic Avenue).

Econo Lodge. 1275 N. Atlantic Ave. (Fla. A1A, at Holiday Lane), Cocoa Beach, FL 32931. ☎ **800/553-2666** or 407/783-2252. Fax 407/783-4485. 128 units. A/C TV TEL. $39–$75 double. AE, DC, DISC, MC, V. Pets accepted.

Across the avenue from the Holiday Inn Cocoa Beach (see below), this Econo Lodge is more charming than most members of this budget-priced chain. About half of its spacious rooms face a tropical courtyard with an L-shaped swimming pool whose bottom displays the names of the seven original astronauts. A poolside tiki hut serves libation and other refreshments, and there's a Chinese restaurant on the premises. Some units have kitchenettes.

Holiday Inn Cocoa Beach. 1300 N. Atlantic Ave. (Fla. A1A, at Holiday Lane), Cocoa Beach, FL 32931. ☎ **800/226-6587** or 407/783-2271. Fax 407/783-8878. 515 units. A/C TV TEL. $69–$99 double. AE, DC, DISC, MC, V.

Set on 30 beachside acres, this sprawling complex offers a wide variety of hotel rooms, efficiencies, and cottagelike villas in several buildings flanking a central courtyard with tropical foliage and eight tennis courts. A large heated pool sits to one side, and guests can use sports equipment at the beach. Dining outlets include Willard's Restaurant, specializing in buffets, and the Oceanside Cafe by the beach. There's a volleyball court, whirlpool, concierge desk, beauty salon, coin-op laundry, and gift shop. A convention center draws groups here.

CAPE CANAVERAL

Radisson Resort at the Port. 8701 Astronaut Blvd. (Fla. A1A, at Central Blvd.), Cape Canaveral, FL 32920. ☎ **800/333-3333** or 407/784-0000. Fax 407/784-3737. 200 units. A/C TV TEL. $119 double. AE, DC, DISC, MC, V. Free parking.

Although it's not on the beach, this resort complex is the closest major hotel to Port Canaveral, making it a handy base if you're visiting the space center or waiting to board one of the cruise ships based here. If you don't feel like driving a mile to the beach, relax at the lushly landscaped deck area where there's an outdoor heated pool (with a waterfall cascading over fake rocks) and a separate kids' pool. A large health club, whirlpool, and night-lit tennis courts are also on the premises. The hotel caters to a business crowd, which means lots of convenient services and facilities such as room service, laundry and dry cleaning, baby-sitting, express checkout, courtesy van to Port Canaveral, a conference desk, car-rental desk, and beauty salon.

WHERE TO DINE

On the **Cocoa Beach Pier,** at the beach end of Meade Avenue, the view down the coast overwhelms the seafood offerings at **The Pier House Restaurant** (☎ **407/ 783-7549**), a favorite haunt of astronauts on break (open daily from 5 to 10pm). So is the adjacent **Marlins Good Times Bar & Grill** (same phone), where inexpensive pub fare is offered daily from 11am until the last patron crawls home. Even if you don't dine on the pier, the outdoor, tin-roofed **Mai Tiki Bar** is a fine place to have a drink while watching the surfers or a sunset.

Cocoa Beach has more fast-food chains than you could ask for along Fla. A1A and Fla. 520, a profusion of bars serving bar snacks, Chinese restaurants, and barbecue joints. The best dining choices here, however, are on Cocoa Beach about 3 miles south of the Fla. 520 causeway, to wit:

Bernard's Surf. 2 South Atlantic Ave. (at Minuteman Causeway Rd.), Cocoa Beach. ☎ **407/ 783-2401.** Main courses $15–$25. Early bird specials (4–6:30pm) $8–$11. AE, DC, DISC, MC, V. Mon–Sat 11am–11pm, Sun 5–10pm. SEAFOOD/STEAKS.

This Florida institution has been serving standard steak and seafood fare in a large and elegant setting since 1948. Photos on the wall testify to the claim that many astronauts come here to celebrate their landings. House specials like the filet mignon served with sautéed mushrooms and bérnaise sauce are your best bets. Grilled swordfish and other fish are always good choices, too. A warm loaf of fresh bread is irresistible served with roasted whole garlic.

✪ **The Mango Tree.** 118 N. Atlantic Ave. (Fla. A1A, between N. 1st and N. 2nd sts.), Cocoa Beach. ☎ **407/799-0513.** Reservations recommended. Main courses $13–$29. AE, MC, V. Tues–Sun 6–9pm. CONTINENTAL.

Gourmet seafood, pastas, and chicken are served in a plantation-home atmosphere with elegant furnishings in this stucco house, now the finest dining venue here. A waterfall splashing into a Japanese koi pond provides a pleasing backdrop out in the lush tropical gardens. The chef does his daily spin on fresh tuna fillets, but you can chose from roast Long Island duckling, tournedos with peppercorn mushroom sauce, and other excellent offerings drawing their inspiration from the continent.

Rusty's Seafood & Oyster Bar. 2 S. Atlantic Ave. (Fla. A1A, at Minuteman Causeway Rd.), Cocoa Beach. ☎ **407/783-2401.** Reservations not accepted. Sandwiches and salads $3–$8; main courses $5–$15. AE, DC, DISC, MC, V. Daily 11am–2am. SEAFOOD/PUB FARE.

Adjacent to and part of Bernard's Surf (see above), this lively sports bar with indoor and outdoor seating offers inexpensive chow ranging from very spicy seafood gumbo to a pot of seafood that will give two normal persons their fill of steamed oysters, clams, shrimp, crab legs, potatoes, and corn on the cob. Daily happy hours from 3 to 6pm see oysters (raw or steamed) and spicy Buffalo wings go for 25¢ each.

THE SPACE COAST AFTER DARK

For a rundown of current performances and exhibits, call the **Brevard Cultural Alliance's Arts Line** (☎ 407/690-6819). For live music, walk out on the **Cocoa Beach Pier,** on Meade Avenue at the beach, where **Marlins Good Times Bar & Grill** (☎ 407/783-7549) has bands on weekends, more often during the winter season, and the al fresco **Mai Tiki Bar** is a great place to hang out over a cold beer.

2 Daytona Beach

54 miles NE of Orlando, 251 miles N of Miami, 78 miles S of Jacksonville

Daytona Beach is a town with many personalities. It is at once the "World's Most Famous Beach," the "World Center of Racing," and a mecca for spring break. It has been a destination for racing enthusiasts since the days when cars were called horseless carriages and raced on the hard-packed sand beach. One thing is for sure: Daytonans still love their cars. Recent debate over the environmental impact of unrestricted driving on the beach caused an uproar from citizens who couldn't imagine it any other way. As it worked out, they can still drive on the sand, but not in areas where sea turtles are nesting.

Today, hundreds of thousands of race enthusiasts come to the home of the National Association for Stock Car Auto Racing (NASCAR) for the Daytona 500, the Pepsi 400, and other races throughout the year. The Speedway is home to Daytona USA, a state-of-the-art motor-sports entertainment attraction worth a visit even by non-racing fans.

Daytona Beach Shores even provides a drive-in church where a dedicated following flocks to hear Sunday morning sermons from speakers hooked to their car windows.

But you don't have to be a car aficionado to enjoy Daytona. It has 23 miles of sandy beach, an active nightlife, surprisingly good museums, and good shopping options. Be sure to check the "Florida Calendar of Events" in chapter 2 to know when the town belongs to college students during spring break, hundreds of thousands of leather-clad motorcycle buffs during Bike Week, or racing enthusiasts for big competitions. Don't bother trying to find a hotel room, drive the highways, or enjoy a peaceful vacation at those times. You won't be able to.

ESSENTIALS

GETTING THERE   If you're driving from north or south, take I-95 and head east on International Speedway Boulevard (U.S. 92). From Tampa or Orlando, take I-4 east and follow the Daytona Beach signs to I-95 north to U.S. 92. From northwestern Florida, take I-10 east to I-95 south to U.S. 92.

Continental (☎ 800/525-0280) and **Delta** (☎ 800/221-1212) fly into **Daytona Beach International Airport,** 4 miles inland from the beach near the speedway.

All major car-rental agencies operate from the airport. But why not rent a Harley? This is Daytona, after all. Call **American Road Collection** (☎ 888-RENT-HD3 or 904/238-1999). Rates start at about $100 a day, twice that amount during biker events.

Call **Yellow Cab Co.** (☎ 904/255-5555). The ride from the airport to most beach hotels runs between $10 and $15.

Daytona-Orlando Transit Service (DOTS) (☎ 800/231-1965 or 904/257-5411) provides van transportation to or from Orlando International Airport. The fare is $26 for adults one way, $46 round-trip; children 11 and under are charged half. The service brings passengers to the company's terminal at 1598 N. Nova Rd., at 11th Street (LPGA Boulevard), or, for an additional fee, to beach hotels.

VISITOR INFORMATION The **Daytona Beach Area Convention & Visitors Bureau,** 126 E. Orange Ave. (P.O. Box 910), Daytona Beach, FL 32115 (☎ **800/854-1234** or 904/255-0415; fax 904/255-5478; www.daytonabeach-tourism.com), can help you with information on attractions, accommodations, dining, and events. The office is on the mainland just west of the Memorial Bridge. The information area of the lobby is open daily from 9am to 7pm; office hours are Monday to Friday from 9am to 5pm. The bureau also maintains a branch at Daytona USA, 1801 W. International Speedway Blvd.

CITY LAYOUT The Halifax River flows north to south through the middle of the city, separating the mainland from the beaches, which sit along a skinny, barrier island–like peninsula. From north to south, the **Seabreeze, Main Street, Charlton Blank** (International Speedway Blvd./U.S. 92), and **Memorial bridges** lead from downtown Daytona over to the beach. **Atlantic Avenue (Fla. A1A)** runs north-to-south along the beach through the towns of Ormond Beach, Daytona Beach, and Daytona Beach Shores. Fla. A1A returns to the mainland at Port Orange, but Atlantic Avenue continues south to Ponce Inlet, where it dead-ends.

On the mainland, **Ridgewood Avenue (U.S. 1)** runs inland paralleling the west side of the Halifax River, and I-95 vaguely parallels the river still farther west. **International Speedway Boulevard (U.S. 92)** is the main east-west artery from I-95 to downtown and the beach.

GETTING AROUND Although it's primarily a driver's town, VOLTRAN, Volusia County's public transit system (☎ **904/761-7700**), runs a **trolley** along Atlantic Avenue on the beach, Monday to Saturday from noon to midnight. Fares are 75¢ for adults, 35¢ for seniors and children 6–17, free for kids under 6 riding with an adult. VOLTRAN also runs **buses** throughout downtown and the beaches Monday through Saturday until 7:30pm and on Sunday until 7pm.

A VISIT TO THE WORLD CENTER OF RACING

Opened in 1959 with the first Daytona 500, the 480-acre ✪ **Daytona International Speedway complex,** at 1801 W. International Speedway Blvd. (U.S. 92 at Bill France Boulevard; P.O. Box 2801), Daytona Beach, FL 32120-2801 (☎ **904/253-RACE** for tickets, or 904/254-2700 for information), is certainly the keynote of the city's fame. It presents about nine weekends of major racing events annually, featuring stock cars, sports cars, motorcycles, and go-carts, and is also used for automobile testing. Its grandstands seat over 120,000.

Big events sell out months in advance (tickets to the Daytona 500 in February are gone as early as a year ahead of time), so get your tickets and reserve your accommodations well before your trip.

To learn more about racing, head for the **World Center of Racing Visitors' Center** at the east end of the Speedway and NASCAR office complex. Open daily from 9am to 5pm, the center is also the departure site for entertaining 25-minute guided tram tours of the facility. Admission is $5, free for children 6 and under. Tours depart daily every 30 minutes between 9:30am and 4pm, except during races and special events.

On the Speedway grounds, the phenomenally popular 50,000-square-foot ✪ **Daytona USA** (☎ **904/947-6800**) is a state-of-the-art interactive motor-sports entertainment attraction presenting the history, color, and excitement of stock-car, go-cart, and motorcycle racing in Daytona. Bring your video camera. There are lots of colorful photo-ops here. Visitors can participate in a pit stop on a NASCAR Winston Cup stock car, see the actual winning Daytona 500 car still covered in track dust, talk via video with favorite competitors, and play radio or television announcer by calling the

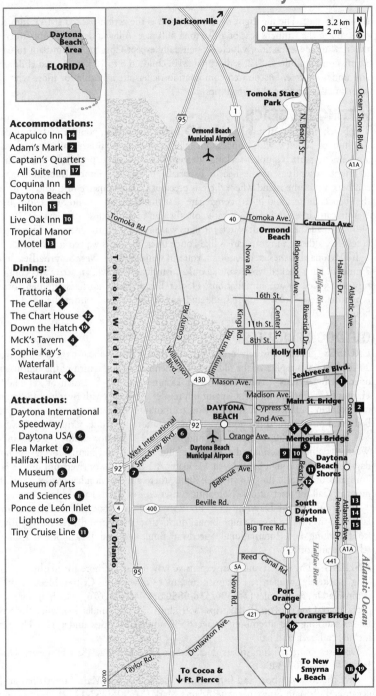

Accommodations:
Acapulco Inn 14
Adam's Mark 2
Captain's Quarters
   All Suite Inn 17
Coquina Inn 9
Daytona Beach
   Hilton 15
Live Oak Inn 10
Tropical Manor
   Motel 13

Dining:
Anna's Italian
   Trattoria 1
The Cellar 3
The Chart House 12
Down the Hatch 19
McK's Tavern 4
Sophie Kay's
   Waterfall
   Restaurant 16

Attractions:
Daytona International
   Speedway/
   Daytona USA 6
Flea Market 7
Halifax Historical
   Museum 5
Museum of Arts
   and Sciences 8
Ponce de León Inlet
   Lighthouse 18
Tiny Cruise Line 11

finish of a race. The highlight of the attraction is the action-packed IMAX film that puts you in the winner's seat of a Daytona 500 race. Allow at least 3½ hours to enjoy this new theme attraction, which is open daily except Christmas from 9am to 6pm. Admission for adults is $12, seniors pay $10, children 6 to 12 pay $6, and children 5 and under are free. Discounted combination tickets are available for those who also want to take the tour of the facilities.

HITTING THE BEACH

The beach near the **Adam's Mark** and ✪ **Main Street Pier,** popular with families, is the hub of activity, with concessions, the city's famous **Boardwalk,** and a small amusement park. Couples seeking greater privacy usually prefer the northern or southern extremities of the beach. Especially peaceful is **Ponce Inlet** at the very southern tip of the island where there is precious little commerce or traffic to disturb the silence. Surfers and bikers congregate near the **Main Street** and **Sun Glow piers.**

You can drive and park directly on the sand along most of Daytona Beach's 500-foot-wide beaches, but watch for signs warning of sea turtles nesting. There's a $5 access fee, although in some areas like Ponce Inlet, the fee is waived in winter.

If Daytona's beaches aren't enough, you can venture south. **New Smyrna Beach** has 7 miles of hard-packed white sand, a quiet historic downtown, an active arts community, and excellent accommodations. **Flagler Beach** to the north is another pristine beach for those looking for solitude and natural beauty away from the condos and hotels.

OUTDOOR PURSUITS

CRUISES Take a leisurely cruise on the Halifax River aboard the 14-passenger, 25-foot *Fancy,* a replica of the old fantail launches used at the turn of the century. It's operated by **A Tiny Cruise Line River Excursions,** 425 S. Beach St., at Halifax Harbor (☎ **904/226-2343**). Captain Jim regales passengers with river lore and points out dolphins, manatees, herons, diving cormorants, pelicans, egrets, osprey, oyster beds, and other natural phenomena during the morning cruise. Cruises are $8.75 to $14 for adults, $5.50 to $7.50 for children 4 to 12, free for children 3 and under. Weather permitting, cruises depart year-round (with a brief hiatus during the holidays), Monday through Saturday at 11:30am. A 1-hour tour of riverfront homes is at 2pm and of historic downtown at 3:30pm; there are no Monday cruises in winter months. Call for reservations. Romantic sunset cruises are also available.

Water Wheels of Daytona (☎ **407/255-2400**) uses one vehicle for combined land-and-river tours: It's an amphibious "duck" that crawls into the river at the Riverfront Parking Lot, International Speedway Boulevard and Beach Street. Call for schedule and prices.

FISHING The easiest and least expensive way to fish offshore for marlin, sailfish, king mackerel, grouper, red snapper, and more is with the **Critter Fleet,** 4950 S. Peninsula Dr., Ponce Inlet (☎ **800/338-0850** or 904/767-7676), which operates two party boats. One goes on all-day trips ($50 adults, $30 kids under 12), while the other makes morning and afternoon voyages ($30 adults, $20 kids under 12). The fares include rod, reel, and bait.

Deep-sea charter fishing boats dock at **Sea Love Marina,** 4884 Front St., Ponce Inlet (☎ **904/767-3406**).

Save the cost of a boat and fish with the locals from the **Main Street Pier,** at the ocean end of Main Street near the Adam's Mark (☎ **904/253-1212**). Admission to the pier is $1 for adults, 50¢ for kids. Bait and fishing gear are available, and no license is required.

GOLF   There are more than a dozen excellent courses within 25 minutes of the beach, and most hotels can arrange starting times for you. **Golf Daytona Beach,** 126 E. Orange Ave., Daytona Beach, FL 32114 (☎ **800/881-7065** or 904/239-7065; fax 904/239-0064; www.golf-daytona.com), publishes an annual brochure describing the major courses. It's available at the tourist information offices (see "Essentials," above).

Daytona's best known course is the ✪ **LPGA International,** 300 Championship Dr. (☎ **904/274-5742**), one of the nation's top-rated links for women golfers. Designed by Rees Jones, the 7,088-yard, 18-hole course boasts five sets of tees and a number of challenging holes. A second 18-hole course designed by Lloyd Clifton is due to be on line by 1999. Just down the street from the Ladies Professional Golf Association headquarters, this center for professional and amateur women golfers has workshops and teaching programs, and the pro shop carries a great selection of ladies' equipment and clothing. Greens fees with a cart are usually about $75, less in summer.

Another Lloyd Clifton–designed course, the centrally located 18-hole, par-72 **Indigo Lakes Golf Course,** 2620 W. International Speedway Blvd. (☎ **904/ 254-3607**), has flat fairways and large bunkered Bermuda greens. Fees here are about $55 in winter, including a cart, less in summer.

The semiprivate South Course at **Pelican Bay Country Club,** 550 Sea Duck Dr. (☎ **904/788-6494**), is one of the area's favorites, with fast greens to test your putting skills. With-cart fees are $40 in winter, less in summer (no walking allowed). The North Course here is for members only.

The city's prime municipal course is the **Daytona Beach Country Club,** 600 Wilder Blvd. (☎ **904/258-3119**), which has 36 holes. Winter fees here are $18 to walk, $26.50 to share a cart. They drop $3 in summer.

HORSEBACK RIDING   **Shenandoah Stables,** 1759 Tomoka Farms Rd., off U.S. 92 (☎ **904/257-1444**), offers daily trail rides and lessons. Call for prices and schedules.

WATER SPORTS   For jet-ski rentals, contact **Daytona High Performance—MBI,** 925 Sickler Dr., at the Seabreeze Bridge (☎ **904/257-5276**). Additional water-sports equipment, as well as bicycles, beach buggies, and mopeds, can be rented along the beach in front of major hotels. A good place to look is in front of the **Adam's Mark,** on the beach at 100 N. Atlantic Ave.

MUSEUMS

✪ **Halifax Historical Museum.** 252 S. Beach St. (just north of Orange Ave.). ☎ **904/ 255-6976.** Admission $3 adults, $1 children 11 and under; free for everyone Sat. Tues–Sat 10am–4pm.

This local history museum is housed in a former bank and is worth seeing just for the 1912 neoclassical architectural details. A mural of Old Florida wildlife graces one wall, the stained-glass ceiling reflects the sunlight, and across the room, an old gold metal teller's window still stands. Its eclectic collection includes Native American artifacts, more than 10,000 historic photographs, possessions of past residents (such as a ball gown worn at Lincoln's inauguration), and, of course, model cars.

Mark Martin's Klassix Auto Museum. 2909 W. International Speedway Blvd., at Tomoka Farms Rd., just west of I-95. ☎ **904/252-3800.** Admission $8.50 adults, $4.25 children 7–12, free for children under 7. Daily 9am–6pm.

This museum showcases Corvettes—a model from every year since 1953. Also on display are collector cars (including cars from the movie *Days of Thunder*) and historic Daytona vehicles from all motor sports. A 1950s-style soda shop and gift shop are on the premises.

Museum of Arts and Sciences. 1040 Museum Blvd. (off Nova Rd./Fla. 5A). ☎ **904/ 255-0285.** Museum $4 adults, $1 children and students with ID, free for children 5 and under; planetarium shows $2. Tues–Fri 9am–4pm, Sat–Sun noon–5pm. Take International Speedway Blvd. west, make a left on Nova Rd. (Fla. 5A), and look for a sign on your right.

Most impressive in this eclectic collection are the Cuban works—mostly paintings acquired in 1956, when Cuban dictator Fulgencio Batista donated his private collection to the city. One highlight is a portrait of Eva ("Evita") Perón, said to be the only existing painting completed while she was alive. Other exhibits include *Masterworks of American Art,* a gallery dedicated to the prehistory of Florida, and *Africa: Life and Ritual.*

Ponce de León Inlet Lighthouse & Museum. 4931 S. Peninsula Dr., Ponce Inlet. ☎ **904/ 761-1821.** Admission $4 adults, $1 children 11 and under. May–Aug daily 10am–8pm; Sept–Apr daily 10am–4pm (last admission an hour before closing). Follow Atlantic Ave. south, make a right on Beach St., and follow the signs.

If you are in the area, this 175-foot lighthouse—the second tallest in the United States—is worth a quick stop. Built in the 1880s, and restored in the 1970s, this brick-and-granite sentinel's beacon is visible for 16 nautical miles. The head lighthouse keeper's cottage now houses a museum of exhibits of maritime artifacts. The first-assistant keeper's house is furnished to reflect turn-of-the-century occupancy. A concise 12-minute video details the structure's history. Outside, you can walk around the tugboat *F.D. Russell,* now sitting high-and-dry in the sand.

SHOPPING

Daytona Beach's main riverside drag, Beach Street, is one of the few areas in town where people actually stroll. The street is wide and inviting, with decorative wrought-iron archways and fancy brickwork overlooking the Halifax River.

Today, between Bay Street and Orange Avenue, Beach Street offers more than a dozen antique shops, a magic shop, an excellent historical museum (see "Museums," above), several good cafes, and the world famous ✪ **Dunn Toys & Hobbies** (see box below), which has an antiques mall upstairs.

Cycle fans should stop at the **Harley Davidson Store**, 290 Beach St., at Dr. Mary McLeod Bethune Boulevard, a 20,000 square-foot retail store and new diner serving breakfast and lunch (☎ **904/253-2453**). It's one of the largest dealerships in the country. In addition to hundreds of gleaming new and used Hogs, you'll find as much fringy leather as you've ever seen in one place.

The **Daytona Flea Market,** on Tomoka Farms Road at the junction of I-95 and U.S. 92, a mile west of the Speedway (☎ **904/252-1999**), is huge, with 1,000 covered outdoor booths plus 100 antique vendors in an air-conditioned building. It's open year-round Friday through Sunday from 8am to 5pm. Admission and parking are free.

WHERE TO STAY

Room rates here are highest from the day after Christmas all the way to Labor Day, and they skyrocket during major events at the Speedway, during bikers' gatherings, and whenever college students are on break (see "Florida Calendar of Events," in chapter 2). Daytona Beach hotels fill to the bursting point during these periods, and even if you can find a room, there's often a minimum-stay requirement.

In addition to the listings below, there are dozens of hotels and motels along Atlantic Avenue, many of them family owned and operated. The Daytona Beach Area Convention & Visitors Bureau (see "Essentials," above), distributes a list of Superior

Toys to Enjoy: A "Dunn" Deal

Since 1905, the Dunns have been selling toys in downtown Daytona. Back then they owned a hardware store with a small toy department upstairs. Now this 18,000 square-foot emporium, **Dunn Toys & Hobbies,** 166 S. Beach St. (☎ **904/253-3644**), carries one of the country's largest selection of toys, games, art supplies, puzzles, model kits, costumes, collectibles, and other diversions for kids of all ages.

In fact, one of the store's most illustrious visitors was President Clinton, who stopped by during his 1996 campaign. "Yeah, it was incredible," said Wes Dunn, the store's fifth-generation Dunn owner. "I was really honored."

You can buy one of the "Radar Frogs" (a motion-sensitive toy that ribbits when you walk by) like the one Clinton brought back to the White House. The store is still adorned with photos of the historic visit. The president even ate a strawberry ice-cream cone from the store's old-fashioned soda fountain/coffee shop—where, by the way, you can get incredibly cheap sandwiches, bagels, hot dogs, soups, salads, and pastries. They serve a great soup and sandwich or salad combo for $3. The homemade chicken salad, with fresh apple chunks and all white meat, is fantastic.

But, perhaps the best offerings at Dunn's are the family activities. On Friday night, the tiny storefront cafe is packed to capacity with families enjoying sing-alongs, puppet shows, or theater performances with a simple kid-centric dinner like macaroni and cheese or pizza, and, of course, dessert. The cost is minimal: $5 for adults and $3 for kids under 12. It fills up early, so call for reservations. Wednesday at 3pm is the gathering spot for stay-at-home moms and dads who come out with the children for free puppet performances, storytelling, and crafts.

Of course, while you're there you won't be able to help buying some souvenirs to take home, and you can browse through **Dunn's Antique Mall,** on the second floor.

The store and cafe is open Monday through Saturday from 9am until 6pm. Friday night, they're open until 8pm.

Small Lodgings. None of these properties has more than 75 rooms, and all have been inspected for cleanliness, quality, comfort, privacy, and safety.

Among the other chain motels here, one of the better options is the **Days Inn,** 1909 S. Atlantic Ave., at Flamingo Ave., in Daytona Beach (☎ **800/224-5056** or 904/255-4492), a nine-story beachfront hotel with a swimming pool/kiddie pool and a sundeck overlooking the beach. The **Ramada Inn Surfside,** 3125 S. Atlantic Ave. (☎ **800/255-3838** or 904/788-1000), also boasts a prime beachfront location. Families will appreciate its efficiency units with fully equipped eat-in kitchens and, in summer, free children's activities. Facilities include a large swimming pool, oceanfront picnic tables, and more. All rooms at these two properties have ocean views and balconies. In addition, there are three oceanfront **Howard Johnsons** to choose from (☎ **800/446-4656**).

In addition to the 6% state sales tax, Daytona levies a 4% tax on hotel bills.

AT THE BEACHES

✪ **Acapulco Inn.** 2505 S. Atlantic Ave. (between Dundee Rd. and Seaspray St.), Daytona Beach, FL 32118. ☎ **800/874-7420,** 800/245-3580, or 904/761-2210. Fax 904/253-9935 or 904/761-2216. 133 units. A/C TV TEL. $50–$100 double; $54–$124 efficiency. Monthly rates and packages available. AE, DC, DISC, MC, V.

This Mayan-themed, midrise hotel is one of five beachfront hostelries managed by Oceans Eleven Resorts (the first toll-free and fax numbers given above go to Oceans Eleven's central reservations desk) and is a great choice for families. It's especially popular with Canadian snowbirds, who return year after year for the warm hospitality, clean ocean-view rooms with balconies, and organized activities like Bingo, bridge, and mah-jongg. All of the 42 hotel rooms have small refrigerators, and 91 efficiencies have fully equipped eat-in kitchens.

A large dining room overlooks the ocean, serving American fare at breakfast and lunch; a comfortable lounge adjoins. Facilities include a heated oceanfront swimming pool, two whirlpools, a kiddie pool, a picnic area, a coin-op laundry, and a video-game room. An on-staff PGA pro helps guests plan golf vacations and will arrange lessons and tee times.

Adam's Mark Daytona Beach Resort. 100 N. Atlantic Ave. (between Earl St. and Auditorium Blvd.), Daytona Beach, FL 32118. ☎ **800/872-9269** or 904/254-8200. Fax 904/253-0275. 413 units. A/C MINIBAR TV TEL. $99–$179 double; $159–$400 suite. AE, DC, DISC, MC, V. Valet parking $8; free self-parking in lot across the street.

This is Daytona's most central beachfront hotel, and one of its most luxurious, designed so that every room has an ocean view. Although the lobby and common areas are more elegantly detailed, guest rooms are not as spacious or well laid out as the less-expensive and quieter Hilton farther south (see below). It's right at the band shell, and, in season, its beach and boardwalk concessions offer parasailing, bicycle rentals, motorized four-wheelers, surfboards, boogie boards, cabanas, and umbrellas.

Dining/Diversions: The hotel's premier dining room features steak and seafood dinners. Another facility, with picture windows overlooking the beach and umbrella tables outside, serves all meals. There's also a complex of small beachfront restaurants and bars with outdoor cafe seating. The sophisticated Clocktower Lounge offers a piano bar or other live music nightly.

Amenities: Concierge, room service, dry cleaning and laundry, self-service Laundromat, free newspapers in executive-level rooms, baby-sitting, secretarial services, express checkout, indoor/outdoor heated swimming pool and kiddie pool, beach, health club, 2 whirlpools, steam and sauna, bicycle rental, children's center, business center, conference rooms, sundeck, water-sports equipment, sand volleyball court, playground, gift shops.

Captain's Quarters All Suite Inn. 3711 S. Atlantic Ave. (½ mile south of the Dunlawton Ave.), Daytona Beach, FL 32127. ☎ **800/332-3119** or 904/767-3119. Fax 904/767-0883. 27 units. A/C TV TEL. $85–$100 double; $140–$165 oceanfront penthouse suite. Lower rates available for extended stays. AE, DISC, MC, V.

A great choice down on the quiet southern part of Daytona Beach, this five-story beachfront inn has spacious suites, all with ocean or river views and large living/dining-room areas, balconies, and fully equipped kitchens. The country-look bedrooms have French doors that open onto balconies or patios with wooden rockers. Each is equipped with two cable TVs and VCRs (movies can be rented). The penthouse suite has a fireplace, a spa tub, and a big picture window overlooking the ocean. On-premises facilities include a heated swimming pool, a sundeck with love-seat swings and barbecue grills, and coin-op washer/dryers. The restaurant, which has an outdoor deck overlooking the ocean, is open for breakfast and lunch except on Tuesday. Newspapers are complimentary.

✪ **Daytona Beach Hilton Oceanfront Resort.** 2637 S. Atlantic Ave. (between Florida Shores Blvd. and Richard's Lane), Daytona Beach, FL 32118. ☎ **800/525-7350** or 904/767-7350. Fax 904/760-3651. 218 units. A/C TV TEL. $89–$150 river-view double; $124–$189 oceanfront double; from $250 suite. AE, DC, DISC, MC, V.

The best hotel choice here, the Hilton welcomes guests in an elegant terra-cotta-tiled lobby with comfortable seating areas, a fountain, and potted palms. The large guest rooms here are grouped in pairs and can be joined to form a suite; one of each pair has a balcony, the other does not. All have ocean and/or river views and major convenient extras like safes, coffeemakers, irons, full-size ironing boards, hair dryers, and small refrigerators. The hotel also has a small fitness room, unisex hair salon, and gift shop. Daily newspapers are complimentary. Kids appreciate the video-game room with pool table and the kiddie pool on the beautiful oceanfront sundeck where you can often see seagulls drinking from the large heated pool. A surprisingly good lobby restaurant, one of Daytona's most beautiful, serves all meals; patio dining is an option. A comfy bar/lounge with game tables adjoins; it's the setting for nightly entertainment. In summer, reggae bands play near the poolside bar.

Tropical Manor Motel. 2237 S. Atlantic Ave. (at Bonner Ave.), Daytona Beach, FL. ☎ **800/253-4920** or 904/252-4920. 71 units. A/C TV TEL. Winter $33–$43 double; $34–$100 efficiency/suite; $95–$135 3-bedroom suite. High-season $52–$63 double; $54–$127 efficiency/suite; $165–$237 3-bedroom suite. AE, DC, DISC, MC, V.

This Caribbean-tinted beachfront motel wins points for its unique and colorful murals, pleasant staff/owners, and meticulous upkeep. Located square in the middle of Daytona's nicest beach, these funky accommodations also offer sundecks, umbrella-covered tables, lounge areas, a large heated pool, water slide, shuffleboard court, cookout area, heated kiddie pool, and two gazebos—all surrounded by lush tropical foliage. The rooms are not large or particularly fancy, but many come with cable TV, kitchens, and ocean views. Especially good for families are the two- and three-bedroom suites.

BED-AND-BREAKFASTS ON THE MAINLAND

✪ **Coquina Inn.** 544 S. Palmetto Ave. (at Cedar St.), Daytona Beach, FL 32114. ☎ **800/805-7533** or 904/254-4969. Fax 904/254-4969. 4 units. A/C TV. $80–$110 double ($175–$200 double during special events). Rates include full breakfast. AE, MC, V. Free parking. No children under 11 accepted.

This charming coquina and cream-stucco house was built in 1912 in the Old Daytona historic section, just south of the Beach Street business district. It sits on a tranquil shady street half a block west of the Halifax River, about a 5-minute drive to the beaches. Innkeepers Joe Witek and Craig Heidel serve breakfast on fine china in their crystal-chandeliered dining room, and complimentary tea and sherry are available in the parlor throughout the day. A sitting room outfitted in a mishmash of antiques is a tranquil spot to enjoy the fireplace and a selection of books and magazines. Each of the guest rooms is decorated differently. In the sunny Hibiscus Room, French doors lead to a private plant-filled balcony (with Jacuzzi) overlooking an ancient live oak draped with Spanish moss. It and the next-door Jasmine Room (it has a fireplace) can be combined to create a two-bedroom/two-bath suite. All rooms have cable TVs. Beach cruiser bikes are available at no charge. New in 1997 were two octagonal wooden decks, one with a large whirlpool under a Victorian gazebo, and a gift shop. There is no smoking inside.

Live Oak Inn. 444-448 S. Beach St. (at Loomis Ave.), Daytona Beach, FL 32114. ☎ **888/881-4664** or 904/252-4667. Fax 904/239-0068. 12 units. A/C TV TEL. $80–$150 double.

Rates include extended continental breakfast. AE, MC, V. Free parking. No children 9 and under accepted.

Facing the river and occupying two adjoining restored 19th-century houses with a front lawn enclosed by a white picket fence, this B&B is surrounded by centuries-old live oaks. An inviting front porch with white wicker rocking chairs faces the street and a marina beyond. The guest rooms—seven with private sun porches or balconies—are delightfully decorated, with area rugs strewn on polished oak floors and wood-bladed fans whirring slowly overhead. Yours might be furnished with an Eastlake bed, or perhaps you'll get a Victorian sleigh bed with a patchwork quilt and a private plant-filled sun porch furnished with Adirondack chairs. The rooms look out on the Halifax Harbor Marina or a garden, and all are equipped with remote-control cable TVs, VCRs, and Victorian soaking tubs or Jacuzzis. Breakfast is served on an enclosed porch with lace-curtained windows. No smoking is permitted in the house.

WHERE TO DINE

Perhaps as a concession to the spring-break crowd, Daytona Beach has a profusion of fast-food places that line the major thoroughfares, especially along International Speedway Boulevard, near the racetrack. You'll find many old and new restaurants on and around Beach Street. An old favorite is the little diner inside Dunn's Toy Store (see box, above). Also check out the Main Street Pier, where a casual oceanfront restaurant serves burgers and chicken wings and lots of beer.

AT THE BEACHES

✪ **Anna's Italian Trattoria.** 304 Seabreeze Blvd. (at Peninsula Dr.). ☎ **904/239-9624.** Reservations recommended. Main courses $9–$17. AE, DISC, MC, V. Mon–Sat 5–10pm. ITALIAN.

The Triani family lends a warm, friendly air to this simple yet comfortable trattoria. Many of the pastas are homemade, but a star here is risotto alla Anna, an Italian version of Spanish paella. Portions are hearty; main courses come with soup or salad and a side dish of angel-hair pasta or a vegetable. There's a good selection of Italian wines to complement your meal. Everything is cooked to order, so allow plenty of time. Free parking is available in a lot on Seabreeze Boulevard across Peninsula Drive.

Down the Hatch. 4894 Front St., Ponce Inlet. ☎ **904/761-4831.** Reservations not accepted; call ahead for priority seating. Breakfast $2–$5; main courses $8–$15; early bird menu (served 11:30am–5pm) $5–$7. Kids' menu. AE, MC, V. Daily 7am–10pm. Take Atlantic Ave. south, make a right on Beach St., and follow the signs. SEAFOOD.

Occupying a half-century-old fish camp on the Halifax River, Down the Hatch serves up fresh fish and seafood (note its shrimp boat docked outside). You can start your day here with a bagel or a country-style breakfast while taking in the scenic views of boats and shorebirds through the big picture windows—you might even see dolphins frolicking. At night, arrive early to catch the sunset over the river, and also to beat the crowd at this very popular place. In summer, light fare is served outside on an awninged wooden deck. Portions are large.

Sophie Kay's Waterfall Restaurant. 3516 S. Atlantic Ave. (at Raymond Ave.). ☎ **904/756-4444.** Reservations recommended. Main courses $7–$24; early bird menu served 4–6:30pm, $8–$10. AE, DC, DISC, MC, V. Mon–Thurs 4–10pm, Fri–Sat 4–11pm, Sun noon–10pm. (Bar serves light fare, Sun–Thurs until midnight, Fri–Sat until 1am.) CONTINENTAL.

Longtime Daytona restaurateur, cookbook author, and local television personality Sophie Kay has created a faux-tropical atmosphere with romantic details like a rock waterfall that cascades into a goldfish pond, full-size palm trees, candles, and soft piano music. Oysters Rockefeller (bubbling with cheese) or shrimp scampi make excellent starters. Sophie's chef has a great hand with pasta, and the primavera linguine in delicate white-wine sauce is perfection. Also very good is the baked seafood served en papillote in a creamy lobster béchamel sauce. Many people come here for filet mignon, roast prime rib au jus with creamy horseradish sauce, or surf-and-turf combinations. For dessert, don't pass up Sophie's delicious twice-baked cheesecake on a buttery graham-cracker crust. After dinner, adjourn to the piano bar for cocktails.

ON THE MAINLAND

The Cellar. 220 Magnolia Ave. (between Palmetto and Ridgewood aves.). ☎ **904/ 258-0011.** Reservations accepted only for large parties. Soups, salads, sandwiches $6–$7. AE, DC, DISC, MC, V. Mon–Fri 11am–3pm. AMERICAN.

An excellent place for lunch while you're touring downtown, this tea room occupies the basement of a Victorian home (listed in the National Register of Historic Places) built in 1907 for Pres. Warren G. Harding. It couldn't be more charming, with low ceilings, fresh flowers on every table, and backlit stained-glass windows. In the warm months there's outdoor seating at umbrella tables on a covered garden patio. A small but varied menu includes soups, salads, sandwiches, fresh seafood, chicken, and pastas.

✪ **The Chart House.** 1100 Marina Point Dr. (off Beach St. south of business district). ☎ **904/255-9022.** Reservations recommended. Main courses $16–$25. AE, DC, DISC, MC, V. Sun–Thurs 5–9:30pm; Fri–Sat 5–10:30pm. SEAFOOD/STEAKS/PRIME RIB.

This member of the upscale chain offers some of the area's finest dining. The setting is stunning—under a soaring teepee roof and with big windows looking out to water views on three sides. The menu is led by gargantuan cuts of tender prime rib, but the daily fresh catch dishes and perfectly grilled steaks also draw the locals for special-occasion dinners. Caviar stars on the bountiful salad bar.

McK's Tavern. 218 S. Beach St. (between Magnolia St. and Ivy Lane). ☎ **904/238-3321.** Reservations not accepted. Main courses $8–$14, salads and sandwiches $4–$7. AE, MC, V. Mon–Sat 11am–3am, Sun 4pm–3am. IRISH/AMERICAN.

Especially worth knowing about because it serves food until three in the morning, this upscale Irish tavern has a highly eclectic menu. The pub fare includes vegetarian burritos and a few main courses of steaks, chicken, and "Mumzy's" meat loaf. Club sandwiches and burgers round out the large and reasonably priced selection. The food is not exceptional, but it's perfectly acceptable, especially once you've had a few Bass ales. The service is sometimes rushed, but usually pleasant.

DAYTONA BEACH AFTER DARK

THE PERFORMING ARTS   Check the Friday edition of the Daytona Beach *News-Journal* for weekly listings of upcoming events, or call the **Peabody Auditorium,** 600 Auditorium Blvd., between Noble Street and Wild Olive Avenue (☎ **904/ 255-1314**), the city's major venue for high-brow performances.

They may look like them, but that's not Elvis Presley, Elton John, or Dolly Parton making music at **Legends in Concert,** in the Coliseum Theater, 176 N. Beach St. on the downtown waterfront (☎ **904/258-1500**). No, these are look-alikes doing very close imitations of a host of music's big names. The curtain rises on this Las Vegas–style revue Tuesday to Thursday at 8pm, Friday and Saturday at 6 and 9pm, and Sunday at 6pm, with matinees Tuesday, Wednesday, and Sunday at 2pm. Tickets are $19.95 adults, $16.95 seniors, and $9.95 for kids under 15, plus tax. Not all of the "stars" appear at once, so call to see who'll be on stage.

New Smyrna Beach: An Artist's Escape

Just 10 minutes south of Daytona, the little town of New Smyrna Beach couldn't be more laid-back than its neighbor. Instead of being a mecca for racers and bikers, it attracts some of the world's most acclaimed artists.

Only 19½ square miles, New Smyrna Beach was founded in 1767 by a Scottish physician, Andrew Turnbull, who named it after his wife's Greek/Turkish hometown, Smyrna. Once brimming with farms and mills, these days, about the most exciting thing that happens here is the perennial shuffleboard championships among the town's older occupants, who make up more than a third of its 17,500 or so residents.

The town's true calling, however, is as a retreat where artists come to work and escape from the world. Now more than 2 decades old, the generic-sounding **Atlantic Center for the Arts,** 1414 Art Center Ave. (☎ **904/427-6975**), sits on 67 acres of lush canopied waterfront, down a long dirt road just past a stretch of biker bars on U.S. 1 north of the New Smyrna Beach Airport. Pulitzer Prize–winning director and playwright Edward Albee, choreographer Trisha Brown, and visual artist Robert Rauschenberg are among the noted celebrities who have come here to create. A small gallery showing works by some of the artists-in-residence is open to the public Monday through Friday from 9am to 5pm, Saturday from 10am to 2pm. In town, **Harris House,** at 214 S. Riverside Dr., at Douglas St. (☎ **904/423-1753**), offers exceptional exhibits in its tiny Old Florida-style house by the scenic Indian River.

Farther east, a 13-mile stretch of beach is as wide and hard-packed as Daytona's—but minus the bikers, spring breakers, and tourist throngs. Only half a dozen hotels and two B&Bs host guests in this Old Florida town, though dozens of oceanfront condominiums offer very affordable rates for overnight visitors. For details, contact the **East Volusia Chamber of Commerce,** 115 Canal St., New Smyrna Beach, FL 32168 (☎ **800/541-9621** or 904/428-2449; fax 904/423-3512). The chamber's visitors center is open Monday to Friday from 9am to 5pm, to 3pm on Saturday. Even if you don't choose to stay here, it is worth an afternoon to stroll the historic downtown area, stop at a gallery, or drive along the beach without fear of hitting a traffic jam.

You might just see a real country music star at the **Daytona Opry,** 2400 Ridgewood Ave., South Daytona (☎ **904/756-6779**), whose shows usually are Monday to Saturday at 7pm, with a matinee Sunday at 2pm (but call to make sure). Tickets are $17.95 adults, $10.95 kids under 12.

Under the city auspices, the **Oceanfront Bandshell** (☎ **904/258-3169**), on the boardwalk next to the Adam's Mark Hotel, hosts a series of free big-band concerts at the band shell every Sunday night from early June to Labor Day. It's also the scene of raucous spring-break concerts.

THE CLUB & BAR SCENE   In addition to the following, the piano bar at **Sophie Kay's Waterfall Restaurant** (see "Where to Dine," above) and the sophisticated **Clocktower Lounge** at the Adam's Mark (see "Where to Stay," above) are worth a visit. Especially during biker festivities, Main Street is a happening area where dozens of bars and restaurants catering to the leather set are in full swing.

A popular beachfront bar for more than 40 years, **Ocean Deck,** 127 S. Ocean Ave., next to the Mayan Inn (☎ **904/253-5224**), is packed with a mix of locals and tourists, young and old, who come for live music and cheap drinks. Often reggae or ska bands will play after 9:30pm. Park across Ocean Avenue at the beach and surf shop, Reggae Republic (under the same ownership).

A typical spring-break party spot, **Razzles,** 611 Seabreeze Blvd., between Grandview and South Atlantic avenues (☎ 904/257-6236), plays Top 40 tunes and highenergy music until 3am nightly. There's plenty to keep you occupied if you're not dancing—10 pool tables, a blackjack table, air hockey, electronic darts, pinball, and video games. The crowd is young, 18 and up, and the scene is wild.

3 St. Augustine: America's First City

105 miles NE of Orlando, 302 miles N of Miami, 39 miles S of Jacksonville

With its 17th-century fort, horse-drawn carriages clip-clopping along narrow streets, old city gates, and reconstructed 18th-century Spanish Quarter, St. Augustine seems more like a picturesque European village than a modern American city. This is an exceptionally charming town, complete with palm-lined ocean beaches, excellent restaurants, an active nightlife, and shopping bargains—but its primary lure is historic.

This is, after all, the oldest permanent European settlement in the United States. The Spaniard Juan Ponce de León, who later undertook a Quixotic quest for the Fountain of Youth, sighted this coast in 1513, landed somewhere between present-day Jacksonville and Cape Canaveral, and named it "La Florida." Spain concentrated its efforts on Florida's west coast until 1562, when a group of French Huguenots settled near the mouth of the St. Johns River, near present-day Jacksonville. Three years later, a Spanish force under Pedro Menéndez de Avilés arrived on the scene, wiped out the Huguenot men (de Avilés spared their women and children), and established a settlement on the harbor he named "St. Augustín."

The colony survived attacks by pirates, Indians, and the British over the next 2 centuries. The Treaty of Paris ending the French and Indian War ceded the town to Britain in 1763, but the British gave it back 20 years later. The United States took control when it acquired Florida from Spain in 1821.

Notwithstanding today's tourist attraction here, Ponce de León never did find his elusive Fountain of Youth.

ESSENTIALS

GETTING THERE   St. Augustine is about equidistant (a 1-hour drive) from airports in Jacksonville and Daytona Beach.

If you're coming from north or south, take I-95 to a St. Augustine exit to U.S. 1 (Exits 92 to 95 are for St. Augustine; ask when you reserve accommodations which is closest). From Orlando and points southwest, take I-10 to I-95 south to U.S. 1.

VISITOR INFORMATION   Before you go, contact the **St. Johns County Visitors and Convention Bureau,** 88 Riberia St., Suite 250, St. Augustine, FL 32084 (☎ **800/OLD-CITY** or 904/829-1711, fax 904/829-6149; www.oldcity.com), and request the *Visitor's Guide,* detailing attractions, events, restaurants, accommodations, shopping, and more.

You Web browsers can also go to the advertiser-supported **www.staugustine.com**.

Upon arrival, stop first at the **St. Augustine Visitor Information Center,** 10 Castillo Dr., at San Marco Avenue opposite the Castillo de San Marcos National Monument (☎ **904/825-1000**). There are numerous ways to see the city, depending on your interest and time, and this is the best place to make your plans. And you can park all day in the visitor center lots for $3. You can view a free visitor information video, pick up brochures, and obtain tickets for sightseeing trains and trolleys, which include discount admissions to the attractions (see "Getting Around," below). The center is open daily from 8:30am to 7:30pm from Memorial Day to Labor Day, until 6:30pm from April to Memorial Day and the day after Labor Day to the end of October, and until 5:30pm from November to March. It and most area attractions are closed on Christmas.

In the historic district, there's a small **information kiosk** on St. George St. at Cathedral Place. It's open daily from 9am to 5pm except Christmas.

Over on St. Augustine Beach, there's a walk-in visitors information center at the **St. Johns County Fishing Pier,** 350 A1A Beach Blvd., St. Augustine Beach, FL 32084 (☎ **904/471-1596**). It's open daily from 8:30am to 5pm.

CITY LAYOUT   St. Augustine is a small town bounded to the west by U.S. 1, to the east (along the coast of the Intracoastal Waterway and Matanzas Bay) by Avenida Menendez. The North Bridge leads to Fla. A1A north and Vilano Beach; the beautiful Bridge of Lions connects to Fla. A1A south and St. Augustine Beach. Fla. 16, on the north side of town, provides access to I-95. The heart of town is still the original plaza, laid out in the 16th century, bounded east and west by Charlotte and St. George streets, north and south by Cathedral Place and King Street. The old Spanish Quarter is farther north on St. George Street, between Cuna and Orange streets just south of the visitor information center.

GETTING AROUND   There are a number of **parking** lots in the historic district, though they're sometimes crowded and difficult to find. Your best bet is to park at the visitor information center ($3 a day) and to walk from there or take a trolley or train. Otherwise, you'll have to carry a pocketful of quarters to feed the meters in the other lots.

Sightseeing trolleys, trains, and horse-drawn carriages are the easiest way to get around. The trolleys and trains follow 7-mile routes, stopping at the visitors center and at or near most attractions. You can busy tickets at the visitors center or from the drivers.

St. Augustine Historical Tours (☎ **800/397-4071** or 904/829-3800) operates the green-and-white, open-air trolleys between 8:30am and 5pm daily (last trolley departs at 4:30pm). You can park your car at the headquarters (the Old Jail and Florida Heritage Museum), which are also stops on the tour. There are 25 stops, including Sebastian Winery, one of the few vintners in Florida. For the price of your ticket you can get off at any stop, visit the attractions, and step aboard the next vehicle that comes along. Several trolleys make a continuous circuit along the route throughout the day; you won't ever have to wait more than 15 or 20 minutes. If you don't get off at any attractions, it takes about 1½ hours to complete the tour.

St. Augustine Sightseeing Trains (☎ **800/226-6545** or 904/829-6545) is almost identical to the company above, but takes a different route and makes 20 stops leaving out the Old Jail and Florida Heritage Museum. Rumor has it that an old feud keeps the owner from promoting his competitor across the street. Its vehicles are red-and-blue open-air trains.

Both companies charge $12 for adults, $5 for children 6 to 12, free for children 5 and under.

You may also want to see the sights from the back of a horse-drawn carriage. **Colee's Carriage Tours** (☎ **904/829-2818**) has been showing people around town since 1877. The carriages line up at the bay front, just south of the fort. Slow-paced, entertainingly narrated 1-hour rides past major landmarks and attractions are offered from

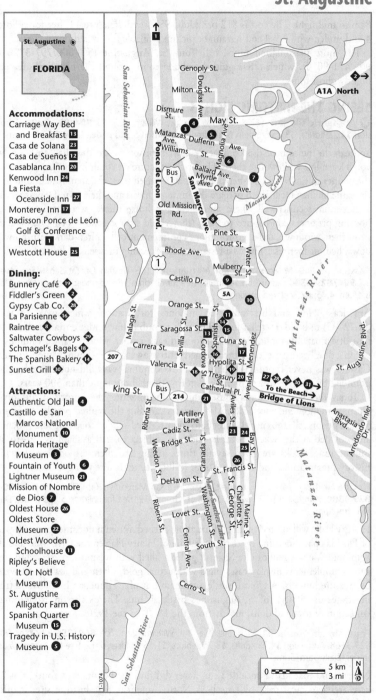

St. Augustine

Accommodations:
Carriage Way Bed
  and Breakfast **13**
Casa de Solana **23**
Casa de Sueños **12**
Casablanca Inn **20**
Kenwood Inn **24**
La Fiesta
  Oceanside Inn **27**
Monterey Inn **17**
Radisson Ponce de León
  Golf & Conference
  Resort **1**
Westcott House **25**

Dining:
Bunnery Café **19**
Fiddler's Green **2**
Gypsy Cab Co. **28**
La Parisienne **16**
Raintree **8**
Saltwater Cowboys **29**
Schmagel's Bagels **18**
The Spanish Bakery **14**
Sunset Grill **30**

Attractions:
Authentic Old Jail **4**
Castillo de San
  Marcos National
  Monument **10**
Florida Heritage
  Museum **3**
Fountain of Youth **6**
Lightner Museum **21**
Mission of Nombre
  de Dios **7**
Oldest House **26**
Oldest Store
  Museum **22**
Oldest Wooden
  Schoolhouse **11**
Ripley's Believe
  It Or Not!
  Museum **9**
St. Augustine
  Alligator Farm **31**
Spanish Quarter
  Museum **15**
Tragedy in U.S. History
  Museum **5**

8am to midnight. The cost is $12 per adult, $5 for children 5 to 11, free for children 4 and under, with hotel and restaurant pickup available for an additional charge.

For more personalized tours, call **Tour St. Augustine** (☎ **800/797-3778** or 904/471-9010), which offers guided walking tours around the historical area and nightly ghost tours.

SEEING THE HISTORIC SIGHTS

✪ **Authentic Old Jail.** 167 San Marco Ave. (at Williams St.). ☎ **904/829-3800.** Admission $4.25 adults, $3.25 children 6–12, free for children 5 and under. Daily 8:30am–5pm.

You can do the tour of this compact Victorian prison in less than half an hour, but you'll learn lots while you're there. The brick structure was built in 1890, and it served the county until 1953. The sheriff and his wife raised their children upstairs and used the same kitchen facilities to prepare the inmates' meals and their own. Downstairs are a maximum-security cell where murderers and horse thieves were confined; a cell housing prisoners condemned to hang (they could see the gallows being constructed from their window); and a grim solitary-confinement cell—pitch-dark with no windows, bed, or mattress. There's a restaurant here serving inexpensive lunch fare.

Castillo de San Marcos National Monument. 1 E. Castillo Dr. (at San Marco Ave.). ☎ **904/829-6506.** Admission $4 adults, free for children 16 and under with an adult. Daily 8:45am–4:45pm. Metered parking.

America's oldest and best-preserved masonry fortification, which took 23 years (1672–95) to build, is stellar in design, with a double drawbridge entrance over a 40-foot dry moat. Diamond-shaped bastions in each corner, which enabled cannons to set up a deadly crossfire, contained domed sentry towers. The seemingly indestructible Castillo was never captured in battle, and its coquina walls did not crumble when pounded by enemy artillery or violent storms throughout more than 300 years.

Today the old storerooms house exhibits documenting the history of the fort, a national monument since 1924. Also, visitors can tour the vaulted powder magazine, a dank prison cell, the chapel, and guard rooms. A self-guided tour map and brochure are provided at the ticket booth. In addition, subject to staff availability, 20- to 30-minute ranger talks are given several times a day, and there are occasional living-history presentations and cannon firings (call for times before you go).

Florida Heritage Museum. In the Old Jail, 167 San Marco Ave. (at Williams St.). ☎ **904/829-3800.** Admission $4.25 adults, $3.25 children 6–12, free for children 5 and under. Daily 8:30am–5pm.

History buffs will appreciate the information-packed museum documenting 400 years of Florida's past, focusing on the colorful life of Henry Flagler, the Civil War, and the Seminole Wars. A replica of a Spanish galleon filled with weapons, pottery, and treasures complements display cases filled with actual gold, silver, and jewelry recovered by treasure hunters. A typical wattle-and-daub hut of a Timucuan in a forest setting illustrates the lifestyle of St. Augustine's first residents. There's also an extraordinary collection of toys and dolls, mostly from the 1870s to the 1920s.

Fountain of Youth. 11 Magnolia Ave. (at Williams St.). ☎ **800/356-8222** or 904/829-3168. Admission $4.75 adults, $3.75 seniors, $1.75 children 6–12, free for children 5 and under. Daily 9am–5pm.

Never mind that Juan Ponce de León never did find the Fountain of Youth, this 25-acre archaeological park bills itself as North America's first historic site. It offers hokey 45-minute guided tours beginning with a planetarium show about 16th-century celestial navigation, during which the audience experiences a hurricane at sea.

The famed fountain itself is located in the Springhouse along with a coquina stone cross believed to date from Ponce de León's ostensible visit in 1513. Visitors get to sample the sulfury and not very tasty spring water from a paper cup. Please let us know if it works!

✪ Lightner Museum. 75 King St. (at Granada St.). ☎ **904/824-2874.** Admission $6 adults, $2 college students with ID and children 12–18, free for children 11 and under. Daily 9am–5pm.

Henry Flagler's opulent Spanish Renaissance–style Alcazar Hotel, built in 1889, closed during the Depression and stayed vacant until Chicago publishing magnate Otto C. Lightner bought the building in 1948 to house his vast collection of Victoriana. The building is an attraction in itself and makes a gorgeous museum, centering on an open palm courtyard with an arched stone bridge spanning a fish pond. The first floor houses a Victorian village, with shop fronts representing emporia selling period wares. A Victorian Science and Industry Room displays shells, rocks, minerals, and Native American artifacts in beautiful turn-of-the-century cases. Other exhibits include stuffed birds, an Egyptian mummy, steam engine models, and amazing examples of Victorian glassblowing. And a room of automated musical instruments is best seen during the daily concerts of period music at 11am and 2pm.

Mission of Nombre de Dios. San Marco Ave. and Old Mission Rd. ☎ **904/824-2809.** Free admission; donations appreciated. Daily 7am–6pm.

This serene setting overlooking the Intracoastal Waterway is believed to be the site of the first permanent mission in the United States, founded in 1565. The mission is a popular destination of religious pilgrimages. Whatever your beliefs, it's a beautiful tree-shaded spot, ideal for quiet meditation.

✪ The Oldest House. 14 St. Francis St. (at Charlotte St.). ☎ **904/824-2872.** Admission $5 adults, $4.50 seniors 55 and over, $3 students, free for children 6 and under; $12 families. Daily 9am–5pm; tours depart on the hour and half hour (last tour at 4:30pm).

Archaeological surveys indicate that a dwelling stood on this site as early as the beginning of the 17th century. What you see today, called the Gonzáles-Alvarez House (for two of its prominent owners), evolved from a two-room coquina dwelling built between 1702 and 1727. The rooms are furnished to evoke various historical eras.

Admission also entitles you to explore the adjacent **Manucy Museum of St. Augustine History,** where artifacts, maps, and photographs document the town's history from its origins through the Flagler era.

The Oldest Store Museum. 4 Artillery Lane (between St. George and Aviles sts. behind Trinity Episcopal Church). ☎ **904/829-9729.** Admission $5 adults, $1.50 children 6–12, free for children 5 and under. Mon–Sat 9am–5pm, Sun noon–5pm (in summer, Sun 10am–5pm).

The C&F Hamblen General Store was St. Augustine's one-stop shopping center from 1835 to 1960, and the museum on its premises today replicates the emporium at the turn of the century. On display are over 100,000 items sold here in that era, many of them gleaned from the store's attic. They include high-button shoes, butter churns, spinning wheels, 1890s bathing suits, barrels of dill pickles (you can purchase one), and medicines that were 90% alcohol. Some 19th-century brand-name products shown here are still available today, among them Hershey's chocolate, Coca-Cola, Ivory soap, and Campbell's soups. It all makes for fascinating browsing.

The Oldest Wooden Schoolhouse in the U.S.A. 14 St. George St. (between Orange and Cuna sts.). ☎ **800/428-0222** or 904/824-0192. Admission $2 adults, $1.50 for seniors 55 and over, $1 children 6–12, free for children 5 and under. Daily 9am–5pm.

This red-cedar and cypress structure, held together by wooden pegs and handmade nails, is more than 2 centuries old, with hand-wrought beams still intact. The classroom is re-created today using animated pupils and teacher, complete with a dunce and a below-stairs "dungeon" for unruly children. The last class was held here in 1864. You can park in the pay lot on the corner of Orange Street and Avenida Menendez.

✪ **Spanish Quarter Village.** Entrance at 33 St. George St. (between Cuna and Orange sts.). ☎ **904/825-6830.** Admission to all exhibit buildings $5 adults, $4.50 seniors, $2.50 students 6–18, free for children 5 and under; $10 per family. Daily 9am–5pm.

This 2-block area south of the City Gate is St. Augustine's most comprehensive historic section, where the city's colonial architecture and landscape have been re-created. Interpreters in 18th-century attire are on hand to help you envision the life of early inhabitants. Candlelight tours are offered at dusk on weekends during spring. About 90% of the buildings in the area are reconstructions, with houses named for prominent occupants. The Spanish Colonial–style **Florencia House** serves as the museum entrance and store.

The St. Augustine Lighthouse and Museum. 81 Lighthouse Ave. (off Fla. A1A east of the Bridge of Lions). ☎ **904/829-0745.** Admission to lighthouse and museum $4 adults, $3 seniors, $2 children 7–11, free for kids under 7. Museum only $2.50 adults, $1.75 seniors, free for kids under 12. Museum daily 9am–5pm. Lighthouse daily 9:30am–4:30pm.

This 165-foot tall structure was built in 1875 to replace the old Spanish lighthouse which had stood at the inlet since 1565. Sitting in a shady grove of live oaks, the lightkeeper's Victorian cottage was destroyed by fire in 1970 but meticulously reconstructed by the local Junior League. It now houses a museum explaining the history of both the lighthouse and the area. You should be in reasonable physical condition to climb the 219 steps to the top of the lighthouse, where you can see 19 nautical miles on a clear day. Children must be 7 years old and at least 4 feet tall to make the ascent.

OTHER ENTERTAINING ATTRACTIONS

3-D World. 28 San Marco Ave. (at Castillo Dr.). ☎ **904/824-1220.** Admission $9 per person. Daily 10am–10pm.

Put on your Polaroid glasses and take a 3-D underwater plunge in The Bahamas at one of two movie theaters here. The second screen shows *Escape from Capt. Nemo,* an action adventure. One of the other of the 45-minute productions begins every 15- to 20 minutes. It's a good place to park the kids when they tire of walking through old buildings.

Ripley's Believe It or Not! Museum. 19 San Marco Ave. (at Castillo Dr.). ☎ **800/584-2956** or 904/824-1606. www.ripleys.com. Admission $8.50 adults, $5.50 seniors, $7 teens 13–18, $4.50 children 5–12, free for children 4 and under. Daily 9am–10pm. Free parking.

Housed in a converted 1887 Moorish Revival residence—complete with battlements, massive chimneys, and rose windows—this immense display comprises hundreds of oddities collected by Robert Ripley and enhanced by later additions. Like the Ripley's in a dozen other U.S. cities, the exhibits run a wide gamut, from a Haitian voodoo doll owned by Papa Doc Duvalier to letters carved on a pencil with a chain saw by Ray "Wild Mountain Man" Murphy. This retro freak show is augmented by videos, photos, and film including footage of amazing people tricks, like the man who made a habit of banging nails into wood planks with his hands and pulling them out with his teeth. If you don't mind your kids being exposed to this kind of bizzaro, Ripley's is a good place to take them for all or part of an evening.

⊗ **St. Augustine Alligator Farm and Zoological Park.** 999 Anastasia Blvd. (Fla. A1A), at Old Quarry Rd. ☎ **904/824-3337.** Admission $10.95 adults, $9.95 seniors 65 and over, $6.95 children 3–10, free for children under 3. June–Labor Day, daily 9am–6pm; Labor Day–May, daily 9am–5pm. Free parking.

You can't leave Florida without seeing at least one real live gator, and there are more than 1,000 of them on display at this century-old attraction. In fact, it houses the world's most complete collection of crocodilians, a category that includes alligators, crocodiles, caiman, and gavial. Other creatures living here include geckos, prehensile-tailed skinks, lizards, snakes, tortoises, spider monkeys, and exotic birds. There are ponds filled with a variety of ducks, geese, and swans, as well as a petting zoo with pygmy goats, potbellied pigs, miniature horses, mouflon sheep, and deer. Entertaining (and educational) 20-minute alligator and reptile shows take place hourly throughout the day, and spring through fall you can often see narrated feedings. If you're into this kind of thing, allow at least 2 hours to tour the extensive and well-maintained facilities.

NEARBY PORPOISE SHOWS

Marineland of Florida. 9507 Ocean Shore Blvd. (Fla. A1A), Marineland (18 miles south of St. Augustine). ☎ **904/471-1111.** Admission $14.95 adults, $9.95 for children 13–18, $7.95 children 3–12, free for children 2 and under. Daily 9am–5:30pm.

If you haven't seen porpoises jumping out of a big tank elsewhere in Florida, you can at this beachfront marine life park on the Atlantic Ocean. This is the first park to successfully maintain the animals in an oceanarium. Today Marineland features porpoise shows in a vast saltwater oceanarium as well as displays of other marine animals. A second oceanarium is home to marine specimens representing more than 125 species; the 35,000-gallon Wonders of the Spring aquarium holds native Florida species.

HITTING THE BEACH

There are several places to find sand and sea, but the 1,800-acre **Anastasia State Recreation Area,** on Anastasia Boulevard (Fla. A1A) across the Bridge of Lions and just past the Alligator Farm, has 4 miles of sandy beach bordered by picturesque dunes, as well as a lagoon flanked by tidal marshes. Also available are shaded picnic areas with grills, rest rooms, windsurfing, sailing and canoeing (on a saltwater lagoon), a nature trail, and saltwater fishing (for bluefish, pompano, and whiting from the surf; sea trout, redfish, and flounder—a license is required for out-of-state residents). In summer, you can rent chairs, beach umbrellas, and surfboards. There's good bird watching here too, especially in spring and fall; pick up a brochure at the entrance. Admission is $3.25 per vehicle and $1 for bicyclists and pedestrians. The day-use area is open daily from 8am to sunset.

Anastasia is one of Florida's most popular state facilities for **camping,** with its 139 wooded sites in high demand all year. They have picnic tables, grills, and electricity and rent for $14 to $18 a night. Campsite reservations are required: make them up to 11 months in advance by writing or calling **Anastasia State Recreation Area,** 1340A A1A South, St. Augustine, FL 32084 (☎ **904/461-2033**).

To reach **St. Augustine Beach,** take the Bridge of Lions to Fla. A1A and proceed south past the Alligator Farm to Dondanville Road, where you can park right on the beach.

North of town, you can reach **Vilano Beach** by taking the Vilano Bridge and making a left on Fla. A1A; there's a parking lot at Surfside Ramp (on your right shortly after your turn onto A1A). You can park on the beach at Vilano too, but beware of soft sand. A few miles farther north along Fla. A1A, you'll come to a parking area with covered picnic tables and grills. It's a popular beach for fishing, but the surf is too rough for swimming.

All St. Augustine beaches charge a fee of $3 per car at official access points from Memorial Day to Labor Day; the rest of the year you can park free, but there are no lifeguards on duty and no toilet facilities on the beach.

FISHING, CRUISES & OTHER OUTDOOR PURSUITS

For additional outdoor options, contact the St. Johns County Visitors and Convention Bureau (see "Essentials," above) and ask them to send you a copy of its *Outdoor Recreation Guide.*

CRUISES   The Usina family has been running **St. Augustine Scenic Cruises** (☎ **800/542-8316** or 904/824-1806) on Matanzas Bay since the turn of the century. They offer 75-minute narrated tours aboard open-air sightseeing boats departing from the Municipal Marina just south of the Bridge of Lions. You can sometimes spot dolphins, brown pelicans, cormorants, and kingfishers. Snacks, soft drinks, beer, and wine are sold on board. Weather permitting, departures normally are at 11am and 1, 2:45, and 4:30pm daily except Christmas, with an additional tour at 6:15pm from April 1 to May 21 and Labor Day to October 15; May 22 to Labor Day there are two additional tours, at 6:45 and 8:30pm. Call ahead—schedules can change. Fares are $9.50 adults, $8 seniors, $6.50 juniors ages 13 to 18, $4.50 children 4 to 12, free for children under 4. If you're driving, allow extra time to find a parking space on the street.

FISHING   See **Anastasia State Recreation Area** under "Hitting the Beach," above, for information about surf casting. You can also cast your line off **St. Johns County Fishing Pier,** on the north end of St. Augustine Beach (☎ **904/461-0119**). The pier is open 24 hours daily and has a bait shop with rental equipment that is open from 6am to 10pm. Admission to the pier is $2 adults, $1 children.

For full-, half-day, and overnight **deep-sea fishing** excursions (for snapper, grouper, porgy, amberjack, sea bass, and other species), contact the **Sea Love Marina,** 250 Vilano Rd. (Fla. A1A north), at the eastern end of the Vilano Beach Bridge (☎ **904/824-3328**). Full-day trips on the party boat *Sea Love II* cost $45; half-day trips, $30. No license is required, and rod, reel, bait, and tackle are supplied. Bring you own food and drink.

GOLF   The PGA Tour's world headquarters and the area's best golf resorts are in Ponte Vedra about a half-hour's drive north on Fla. A1A, closer to Jacksonville than St. Augustine (see "Where to Stay," in section 4, below, for details). There are only a few courses in St. Augustine, including those at the **Radissons Ponce de León Resort** (see "Where to Stay," below) and the **St. Augustine Shores Golf Club,** 707 Shores Blvd., off U.S. 1 (☎ **904/794-4653**). The latter is a par-70 course featuring 18 holes, lots of water, a lighted driving range and putting green, and a restaurant and lounge. Greens fees are $25.50 to $29.50, including cart, less in the summer months.

SAILING   You can rent sailboats, go on a variety of cruises, or learn to sail with **St. Augustine Sailing,** 3076 Harbor Dr. (☎ **800/683-7245** or 904/829-0648). Call for details, prices, and reservations.

WATER SPORTS   Jet-skis and surfing and windsurfing equipment can be rented at **Surf Station,** 1020 Anastasia Blvd. (Fla. A1A), a block south of the Alligator Farm (☎ **904/471-9463**); **Raging Water Sports,** at the Conch House Marina Resort, 57 Comares Ave. (☎ **904/829-5001**), which is off Anastasia Ave. (Fla. A1A) halfway between the Bridge of Lions and the Alligator Farm; and **Watersports of St. Augustine,**

at Sea Love Marina, 250 Vilano Rd. (Fla. A1A north), at the eastern end of the Vilano Beach Bridge (☎ **904/823-8963**).

SHOPPING

The winding streets of the historic district are home to dozens of **antiques stores** and **art galleries** stocked full of original paintings, sculptures, bric-a-brac, fine furnishings, china, and other treasures. Brick-lined **Aviles Street,** 1 block from the river, has an especially good mix of shops for browsing, as does **St. George Street** south of the visitor center. The **Alcazar Court at the Lightner Museum** has a good selection of antiques shops (see "Seeing the Historic Sights," above). The visitor center has complete lists of art galleries and antique shops, the latter published by **The Antique Dealers Association of St. Augustine,** 60 Cuna St., St. Augustine, FL 32084 (no phone).

Chocoholics will find their version of heaven at **Whetstone Chocolates,** 2 Coke Rd. (Fla. 312), between U.S. 1 and the Mickler O'Connell Bridge (☎ **904/825-1700**). Free tours of the store and factory usually take place Monday to Saturday from 10am to 5:30pm, but call to make sure of the factory's schedule.

The biggest shopping draw here is the **St. Augustine Outlet Mall,** on Fla. 16 about ¼ mile west of I-95 at Exit 95 (☎ **904/825-1555**), about a 10-minute drive from downtown. Among the 95-plus stores are outlets by Laura Ashley, Sunglass Hut, Levi's, Adolfo II, Mikasa, Brooks Brothers, Coach, and more than a dozen shoe manufacturers. It's open until 9pm Monday through Saturday, 6pm on Sunday.

WHERE TO STAY

If you're going to be here for a week or longer, consider ✪ **Villas on the Bay,** 105 Marine St., between San Salvador and St. Francis streets. (☎ **904/826-0575;** fax 904/826-1892; www.thevillas.com), whose nine one- and two-bedroom suites occupy a building that served as a Civil War military hospital. The spacious suites are furnished with antiques and Victoriana and have private balconies sporting spectacular bay views, rocking chairs, and/or hammocks. Most also have double Jacuzzi tubs. Rates range from $550 to $750 a week. Out at the beach, the **Ocean Gallery,** 4600 Fla. A1A South, between Dondonville Road and Trade Winds Lane (☎ **800/940-6665** or 904/471-6663; fax 904/471-5994), has about 200 condo apartments in its rental inventory. The complex is set on 44 attractively landscaped acres with gardens, lakes, and lagoons. They range from $375 to $985 a week, depending on size, season, and view.

Almost all accommodations increase prices on weekends when the town is most crowded with visitors. St. Johns County charges a 9% tax on hotel bills.

The best **camping** here is at Anastasia State Recreation Area (see "Hitting the Beach," above), but reserve your site as early as possible.

IN ST. AUGUSTINE

St. Augustine is known for its many colorful and popular bed-and-breakfasts in restored historic homes. Most neither take young children nor allow smoking inside the house. Check before booking. All the B&Bs listed below are within walking distance of the historic district, or right in it. They all provide free parking.

There are plenty of moderate and inexpensive motels and hotels here, including several along Ponce de Léon Boulevard (U.S. 1) at or near the Fla. 16 intersection north of the historic district. The pick is the **Quality Inn Alhambra,** 2700 Ponce de León Blvd., at Fla. 16 (☎ **800/223-4153** or 904/824-2883), a well-run family owned property with large, attractively decorated rooms, some with Jacuzzis. There's a large swimming pool and whirlpool. Rooms range from $59 to $125 double. Among the budget-priced motels, the **Super 8,** 3552 N. Ponce de León Blvd., between Rambla and Fairbanks streets (☎ **800/800-8000** or 904/824-6399), has attractively landscaped grounds with a palm-fringed lawn surrounding a swimming pool. The upstairs units with peaked beamed ceilings are especially appealing. Doubles range from $35 to $43.

Closer to the historic district, the two-story stucco **Comfort Inn,** 1111 Ponce de León Blvd., at Old Mission Road (☎ **800/575-5288** or 904/824-5554), has large suites with double-sink dressing rooms and parlor areas with extra TVs and pull-out sofas, making them ideal for families. Doubles range from $42 to $99, depending on size and time of year.

Carriage Way Bed and Breakfast. 70 Cuna St. (between Cordova and Spanish sts.), St. Augustine, FL 32084. ☎ **800/908-9832** or 904/829-2467. Fax 904/826-1461. 9 units. A/C TEL. $69–$130 double. Rates include full breakfast. AE, DISC, MC, V.

Occupying an 1883 Victorian wood-frame house fronted by roses and hibiscus, the Carriage Way is like coming to an old friend's house. It is not fancy or formal, but is comfortable and well worn. Rooms are furnished with simple antique reproductions, including many four-poster beds. One room even retains its original fireplace. A console TV, books, magazines, and games are provided in a homey parlor. The energetic and hospitable owners/hosts Bill and Diane Johnson, who live on the premises, offer many extras: old one-speed bicycles, decanters of red wine and sherry on a buffet table in the hallway, and a refrigerator stocked with beer and soft drinks.

Casa de Solana. 21 Aviles St. (at Cadiz St.), St. Augustine, FL 32084. ☎ **904/824-3555.** Fax 904/824-3316. 4 units. A/C TV. $125–$145 double. Rates include full breakfast. AE, DISC, MC, V.

Built in 1763 on a narrow cobbled street, this charming colonial house is the seventh oldest in the city. In the mid-1800s, its coquina-stone exterior was covered over with the pale-pink stucco you see today. The house also sports a lovely walled garden planted with jasmine and trumpet vines. The rooms are nicely decorated with an eclectic mix of antique pieces. Yours might have a four-poster, brass, art deco, or mahogany bed. A welcoming decanter of sherry awaits your arrival in the room. Three suites have full living rooms (the fourth has a small parlor), and one has a balcony. Hostess Faye McMurry's homemade breakfasts always include delicious fresh-baked muffins. There's a baby grand in the dining room, scene of occasional impromptu nighttime sing-alongs.

Casa de Sueños. 20 Cordova St. (at Saragossa St.), St. Augustine, FL 32084. ☎ **800/ 824-0804** or 904/824-0887. Fax 800/735-7534 or 904/825-0074. www.oldcity.com/suenos. E-mail: suenos@aug.com. 6 units. A/C TV TEL. $95–$165 double; $145–$185 suite. Rates include full breakfast. AE, DISC, MC, V.

Casa de Sueños offers small and thoughtfully decorated rooms in a turn-of-the-century house that was later transformed into the Mediterranean style you see today. When innkeepers Sandy and Ray Tool renovated the space in 1993, they updated with made-to-look-like antiques and many modern conveniences, including some whirlpools, dimmer switches on the lights, ceiling fans, hand-held shower attachments, and Touch-Tone phones with modem jacks. In the downstairs parlor you'll find a CD/cassette/record player, TV, VCR, books, magazines, games, and a small refrigerator stocked with beer and soft drinks. A fax and copy machine are available, too.

Besides your hosts and fellow guests, you'll meet Spice, an endearing Golden Lab that likes attention, and Holly, a folksy guitarist who entertains on weekend social hours and on Sunday morning. If you are into this kind of campy thing, you'll love the very popular Casa de Sueños. Breakfasts are superb here, and huge. When it is offered, the strawberry-covered French toast is especially delicious. You'll always appreciate fresh-baked breads, muffins, or biscuits. Services include nightly turndown with a chocolate and complimentary daily newspapers.

✪ **Casablanca Inn on the Bay.** 24 Avenida Menendez (between Hypolita and Treasury sts.), St. Augustine, FL 32084. ☎ **800/826-2626** or 904/829-0928. Fax 904/826-1892. 19 units. A/C. $89–$199 double. Rates include full breakfast. AE, DISC, MC, V.

This 1914 Mediterranean-style white stucco house faces the bay, although only a few of the rooms actually offer views. The most stunning are the two second-floor suites whose bay-front balconies have generously sized hammocks and private porches. The furnishings—a mix of turn-of-the-century American oak, European, and Victorian pieces—are of a higher quality than those at many other inns. Unique touches in each room might include glass figurines, oil paintings, or rare books. One modern convenience is a cassette player with a small selection of classical tapes. This may be appreciated, especially if you are on a ground-floor room that unfortunately suffers from the noise of the street and next-door bar and grill.

Guests can use the microwave and refrigerator in the kitchen and help themselves to complimentary beer, wine, soft drinks, chocolates, and fresh-baked cookies at all hours; hors d'oeuvres are served every afternoon; and weekend visitors get free champagne. Breakfast can be enjoyed alfresco on the porch or in a glass-enclosed conservatory. Ask to use the house bicycles to tour the city.

✪ **Kenwood Inn.** 38 Marine St. (at Bridge St.), St. Augustine, FL 32084. ☎ **904/824-2116.** Fax 904/824-1689. 14 units. A/C. $85–$115 double; $150 3-room suite for 1 or 2. Rates include continental breakfast. Extra person $10. DISC, MC, V.

Somewhere between a B&B and a cozy inn, the Kenwood is one of Old Town's best accommodations. This Victorian wood-frame house with graceful verandas has served as a boardinghouse or inn since the late 19th century. Rooms are larger and more private than most other accommodations in converted single-family homes. Everything from the carpeting to the linens to the china is first-class. It's unusual also because of its relatively large outdoor space, which includes an outdoor swimming pool, a lushly landscaped sundeck, and a secluded garden courtyard (complete with a fish pond and neat flower bed under a sprawling pecan tree). Complimentary sherry, tea, and coffee are offered throughout the day.

Monterey Inn. 16 Avenida Menendez (between Cuna and Hypolita sts.), St. Augustine, FL 32084. ☎ **904/824-4482.** Fax 904/829-8854. 59 units. A/C TV TEL. Winter Sun–Thurs, $32–$69 double. Fri–Sat $49–$150 double. AE, DISC, MC, V.

For the price, you can't find a better choice this close to the attractions and nightlife of Old Town, and you couldn't ask for a more well-kept though modest place to spend the night. Three generations of the Six family have run this simple two-story motel overlooking the Matanzas Bay. With renovations constantly in the works, you'll find the 1960s building and grounds always clean and functional. Rooms are not especially spacious but they are comfortable. A small swimming pool, pleasant staff, and free coffee each morning are just some of the extras at this super-affordable and convenient spot.

✪ **Radisson Ponce de León Golf & Conference Resort.** 4000 U.S. Hwy. 1 north, St. Augustine, FL 32095. ☎ **800/333-3333** or 904/824-2821. Fax 904/824-8254. 193 units. A/C TV TEL. $99–$149 double; $119–$159 minisuite. Golf, family, and other packages available. AE, DC, DISC, MC, V. Free parking.

Located just a 5-minute drive from historic Old Town, this 400-acre resort has been a St. Augustine tradition since Henry Flagler built it in 1916. Pres. Warren G. Harding came here in 1921 to relax before his inauguration. In addition to the impressive Donald Ross–designed par-72 course, the resort features an 18-hole putting green next to the large outdoor swimming pool. Also on the grounds, amidst the palms, magnolias, and centuries-old live oaks and clumps of sawgrass, are six night-lit tennis courts, a sand volleyball court, shuffleboard, croquet, boccie, basketball, and horseshoes.

Many of the rooms and suites feature furnished patios or balconies overlooking the golf course, and coffeemakers. The minisuites, ideal for families, have small sitting rooms separated from sleeping areas by trellises.

A golf-side restaurant serves continental meals. On weekend evenings you can join conferences unwinding in the lounge for live piano entertainment in a cozy bar overlooking the greens.

Westcott House. 146 Avenida Menendez (between Bridge and Francis sts.), St. Augustine, FL 32084. ☎ **904/824-4301.** Fax 904/824-4301. 9 units. A/C TV TEL. Sun–Thurs $95–$175 double; Fri–Sat $150–$175 double. Rates include continental breakfast. AE, DISC, MC, V. Parking is on the street or free in a nearby lot.

Overlooking Matanzas Bay on the edge of historic Old Town, this two-story, wood-frame house offers rare opportunities for an uncluttered view from the porch, second-story veranda, and a shady courtyard. The rooms—some with bay windows and/or working fireplaces—are exquisitely furnished and immaculate; everything here just gleams! Yours might have authentic Victorian furnishings and a brass bed made up with a white quilt and lace dust ruffle, with extras like hair dryers and terry bathrobes. Complimentary fresh fruit and brandy are available all day in the parlor of one of the town's most well-kept inns.

AT THE BEACHES

St. Augustine Beach has its share of chain motels, all on A1A Beach Boulevard (Fla. A1A). They include the **Best Western Ocean Inn** (☎ **800/528-1234** or 904/ 471-8010); **Days Inn Beach** (☎ **800/DAYS-INN** or 904/461-4774); **Econo Lodge** (☎ **800/446-6900** or 904/471-2330); **Hampton Inn** (☎ **800/426-7866**); **Holiday Inn Beachside** (☎ **800/626-7263** or 904/471-2555), with a popular tiki bar; **Howard Johnson Resort Hotel** (☎ **800/752-4037** or 904/471-2575); and **Ramada Limited** (☎ **800/2-RAMADA** or 904/471-1440).

La Fiesta Oceanside Inn. 810 A1A Beach Blvd. (Fla. A1A), St. Augustine Beach, FL 32084. ☎ **800/852-6390** or 904/471-2220. Fax 904/471-0186. 36 units. A/C TV TEL. $49–$159 double. DISC, MC, V.

Housed in two-story tan stucco buildings with Spanish-style terra-cotta roofs, La Fiesta is attractive from the road. Inside, the generic Formica and wood-outfitted rooms are average chain motel-like, but a new block under construction at press time should add suites with more charm. The location couldn't be better, since you are directly on the beach and close to the best dining and drinking spots. Some rooms have wet bars, small refrigerators, double-size tubs, and king-size beds. A cafe serves breakfast daily. Other facilities include coin-op washer/dryers, a boardwalk over the dunes, a children's playground, a swimming pool, an 18-hole beachfront miniature golf course, and a picnic area with a barbecue grill.

WHERE TO DINE

In a town as heavily touristed as St. Augustine, there are, of course, a fair number of "tourist trap" restaurants. But on the whole, the food in St. Augustine, even at the popular eateries, is fairly priced and of good quality. For good late-night bites, see A1A Ale Works and Ann O'Malley's in "St. Augustine After Dark," below.

IN ST. AUGUSTINE

Bunnery Café. 35 Hypolita St. (east of St. George St.). ☎ **904/829-6166.** Reservations not accepted. Everything under $4. No credit cards. Daily 9am–5:30pm. BAKERY.

Alluring aromas waft from the Bunnery, a bakery and cafe in the heart of the historic district. It's lovely to come here for breakfast. Or arrive weary from a day of sight-seeing, plop yourself into a chair on the arcaded terra-cotta patio, and indulge in a fresh-baked cinnamon roll, pecan sticky bun, or strawberry and cream-cheese croissant accompanied by a big cup of cappuccino.

✪ **Gypsy Cab Co.** 828 Anastasia Blvd. (Fla. A1A, at Ingram St., east of Bridge of Lions). ☎ **904/824-8244.** Reservations not accepted. Main courses $9–$17; sandwiches and salads $5–$7. AE, DC, DISC, MC, V. Mon and Wed–Thurs 11am–10pm; Tues 4:30–10pm; Fri–Sat 11am–11pm, Sun 10:30am–10pm. NEW AMERICAN.

Billing itself as a temple of "urban cuisine," this high-energy establishment with bright and art-filled dining rooms offers the likes of Shrimp Buena Vista, a concoction featuring gulf shrimp, linguine, Canadian bacon, green peas, and onions in a white-wine sauce. It was delicious. Salads and sandwiches are also excellent. Since the menu changes daily, it is tough to give recommendations, although the black-bean soup, which is a constant, is worth a try if you want something hearty. Park free behind the building, not in Trader Jack's lot next door.

✪ **La Parisienne.** 60 Hypolita St. (between Spanish and Cordova sts.). ☎ **904/829-0055.** Reservations recommended. Main courses $9–$24. AE, DISC, MC, V. Thurs–Tues 11am–3pm; Thurs–Sun 5–9pm. TRADITIONAL FRENCH.

La Parisienne will remind you of Paris. The lovely dining room has a rough-hewn beamed pine ceiling, lace-curtained windows, and ladderback chairs. Begin with escargot in a garlic cream sauce, then go on to a classic steak au poivre and roast rack of lamb coated with Dijon mustard and fresh garlic. The lunch menu offers traditional bistro fare, such as quiche Lorraine, croque monsieur, and salad niçoise. At afternoon tea, you might enjoy oven-fresh chocolate eclairs, praline ganaches, or fruit tarts.

✪ **Raintree.** 102 San Marco Ave. (at Bernard St.). ☎ **904/824-7211.** Reservations recommended. Main courses $12–$20; early dinner selections (served 5–6pm except holidays and special events) $9–$13; full children's dinners $7. AE, MC, V. Sun–Fri 5–9:30pm, Sat 5–10pm. Courtesy car provides transportation from/to downtown hotels. CONTINENTAL/AMERICAN.

Occupying an 1879 Victorian house, this is one of St. Augustine's most romantic yet casual restaurants. Bamboo furnishings, dozens of plants and ficus trees, and an awning create an indoor-garden setting, and cut-crystal lamps cast a soft glow. When the weather is warm, you might opt for after-dinner drinks or a selection of coffees and desserts on the open-air porch, balcony, or lushly planted brick patio. To start, you might try veal-stuffed mushrooms or a blue-crab cake with a spicy horseradish sauce. Duck and lamb dishes are tasty and served with light but delicious fruit-based condiments. More serious main courses include fresh fish (perhaps grouper with sautéed mushrooms in a white-wine/Dijon-mustard cream sauce), beef Wellington, and filet mignon béarnaise. An extensive dessert and coffee cart tempts with a variety of hot crepes and an exemplary crème brûlée. The list of more than 300 vintages has won *Wine Spectator* awards.

Schmagel's Bagels. 69 Hypolita St. (at Cordova St.). ☎ **904/824-4444.** Bagels and sandwiches $4–$5. No credit cards. Mon–Sat 7:30am–3pm, Sun 8:30am–2pm. BAGEL SANDWICHES.

Yes, bagels have made it to St. Augustine, and Schmagel's makes them almost like the real plump New York ones. They come in 12 varieties—everything from cinnamon-raisin to blueberry. A variety of toppings ranges from traditional cream cheese and lox to a BLT. For breakfast you can also get bacon and eggs, homemade soups, and fresh-baked fruit muffins.

The Spanish Bakery. 42½ St. George St. (between Cuna and Orange sts.). ☎ **904/471-3046.** Reservations not accepted. Lunch specials $3; cookies and rolls 40¢–50¢ each. No credit cards. Daily 9:30am–3pm. Closed Thanksgiving and Christmas. COLONIAL.

Occupying a reconstructed 17th-century kitchen building, this little family-operated establishment bakes almond, lemon, and cinnamon cookies using recipes from the Spanish colonial period, when a lack of refrigeration limited the use of milk and eggs. A couple of these crunchy morsels, eaten at the picnic tables outside, make a fine snack while you're touring the historic district. Or you can have lunch here, choosing from daily specials such as spicy Spanish-style chili over rice served with soup, a small loaf of freshly baked bread, and a drink.

AT THE BEACHES

✪ **Fiddler's Green.** 2750 Anahma Dr. (at Ferrell Rd.), Vilano Beach. ☎ **904/824-8897.** Reservations recommended Sun–Fri, not accepted Sat. Main courses $9–$17. AE, CB, DC, DISC, MC, V. Sun–Thurs 5–9pm, Fri–Sat 5–10pm. Closed Mon Nov–Dec. Take Fla. A1A north across the Vilano Bridge and bear right to Vilano Beach. FLORIDIAN/SEAFOOD.

Situated right on the Atlantic, the shiplike Fiddler's Green is appropriately entered via a kind of gangplank. Inside, rustic elegance is achieved with two blazing coquina stone fireplaces and a profusion of hanging plants. Start your meal with crunchy-peppery conch fritters (ask for tarragon tartar and pepper sauce with them) or a platter of oysters "Rockefiddler" with oven-browned Cheddar topping. For a main course I like fish Matanzas—fresh catch of the day (perhaps red snapper) pan-blackened with a mélange of spices and served with drawn butter.

Salt Water Cowboy's. 299 Dondanville Rd. (off Fla. A1A), St. Augustine Beach. ☎ **904/471-2332.** Reservations not accepted, so arrive early to avoid a wait. Main courses $9–$15. AE, DC, DISC, MC, V. Jan–Oct daily 5–10pm. Nov–Dec Sun–Thurs 5–9pm, Fri–Sat 5–10pm. Follow A1A Beach Blvd. south; just past the restaurant's billboard make a right onto Dondanville Rd. at the traffic light. SEAFOOD/BARBECUE.

Arrive early for dinner at Salt Water Cowboy's—not only to beat the crowd but also to enjoy a spectacular view of the sun setting over a saltwater marsh. Designed to resemble a turn-of-the-century fish camp, this rambling restaurant has a rustic candlelit interior and a mix of dining areas ranging from intimate booths to an outdoor plant-filled deck shaded by live oaks and lit by tiki torches. Order up a half dozen oysters or perhaps some 'gator bits while you peruse the menu. For openers, there's a very rich and creamy chowder with big chunks of clam, potato, and celery. A main course of fork-tender baby back ribs is a great choice. Another winner: oysters, scallops, or shrimp fried in light cornmeal batter.

Sunset Grille. 421 A1A Beach Blvd. (Fla. A1A at 15th St.), St. Augustine Beach. ☎ **904/471-5555.** Reservations not accepted. Main courses $8–$16. DISC, MC, V. Mon–Fri 11am–10pm (limited late-night menu served until midnight), Sat–Sun 7am–10pm. AMERICAN.

This casual Key West–style sports bar is a kick-back kind of place with half a dozen TVs and a mixture of music blaring from loud speakers. You can escape the noise in a small dining room to the rear, but what's the point? The action take precedence over the food here. Sunday afternoon a live band plays oldies and the place is mobbed. At lunch or dinner you can dine on sandwiches, burritos, or burgers. A more substantial dinner might consist of blackened chicken or grilled fresh fish or shrimp, with most main courses priced under $10. The windows latch up and have stools outside so the beach crowd (the ocean is across the street) can eat and drink in bathing attire.

ST. AUGUSTINE AFTER DARK

Especially on weekends, the Old Town is full of strollers and partiers making the rounds to the dozens of active bars, clubs, and restaurants. For up-to-date details on what's happening in town, check the local daily, the *St. Augustine Record,* or the more irreverent *Folio Weekly.*

Ann O'Malley's, 23 Orange St., near the Old City Gate, (☎ **904/825-4040**), is the quintessential Irish pub open every day and night until 1am. Besides the selection of ales, stouts, and drafts, this is one of the only spots in town to grab a late-night bite. Granted, the deli-meat sandwiches and salads are nothing to write home about, but they're fresh and cheap.

The best-looking crowd in town can be found at the **A1A Ale Works,** 1 King St., at Avenida Menendez (☎ **904/829-2977**). Twenty-something hipsters and middle-age partiers mingle at this handsome, New Orleans–style microbrewery and restaurant. Thursday through Saturday nights downstairs, you'll find live music, often in the form of an acoustic guitarist and singer performing light rock and R&B tunes on a crowded window-front stage.

Popular with locals, **Mill Top Tavern,** 19½ St. George St., at the Fort (☎ **904/ 829-2329**), is a warm and rustic tavern housed in a 19th-century mill building (the waterwheel is still outside). Weather permitting, it's an open-air space. There's music every day from 1pm until 1am.

One of St. Augustine's most famous nighttime hangouts is **Scarlett O'Hara's** at 70 Hypolita St., at Cordova Street (☎ **904/824-6535**). A catacomb of cozy rooms with working fireplaces in a rambling 19th-century wood-frame house is the setting for live rock, jazz, and R&B bands nightly from 9:30pm. And though there's no dance floor, people get up and dance wherever. Sporting events are aired on a large-screen TV in a tropically themed oyster bar. Park in a lot across Cordova Street.

If you're looking for a real bikers' hangout, **Trade Winds Tropical Lounge** at 124 Charlotte St., between Cathedral Place and Treasury Street (☎ **904/829-9336**), is the place. It often features live local bands playing a mix of Southern rock, oldies, folk, country, and blues.

Out at St. Augustine Beach, a casual and happening beach club, **Cafe Iguana,** 321 A1A Beach Blvd. (☎ **904/471-7797**), hosts retro music, semifunny comedians, and a sloppy dance scene Tuesday through Saturday nights. Several nights will find local live music and various contests. Especially popular is Friday's Happy Hour from 4:30 to 8pm and Wednesday's ladies' night.

Also at the beach is **Panama Hattie's Saloon,** 361 A1A Beach Blvd. (☎ **904/ 471-2255**), a funky and very popular beach bar with a rustic interior housing bars and dance floors on two levels. The older crowd hangs downstairs where on Friday and Saturday nights there are oldies bands while upstairs on the beach deck a deejay plays Top 40 tunes.

4 Jacksonville

36 miles S of Georgia, 134 miles NE of Orlando, 340 miles N of Miami

Once infamous for its smelly paper mills, the sprawling metropolis of "Jax" is now one of the insurance and banking capitals of the South and home to many Fortune 500 companies. Accordingly, its tourism facilities cater to the business travelers who make up more than 70% of the city's visitors. The result is a downtown that is a vibrant center of activity on weekdays, but virtually deserted in the evenings and weekends.

Development is rampant throughout Duval County, with hotels, restaurants, attractions, and clubs rapidly springing up, especially in suburban areas near the interstate highways. Nevertheless, there are shady older neighborhoods to explore, 20 miles of Atlantic Ocean beaches upon which to sun and swim, many championship golf courses to play, and an abundance of beautiful and historic national and state parks to roam.

Although it claims to be the capital of Florida's historic "First Coast," Jacksonville dates its beginnings from an early 1800s settlement named Cowford, because cattle crossed the St. Johns River here. Cowford changed its name to Jacksonville in 1822 to honor Gen. Andrew Jackson, the provisional governor who forced Spain to cede Florida to the United States 2 years earlier.

ESSENTIALS

GETTING THERE   I-95 and I-10 intersect in downtown Jacksonville. I-295 bypasses the city to the west.

Air South (☎ 800/247-7688), **AirTran** (☎ 800/AIR-TRAN), **American** (☎ 800/433-7300), **Continental** (☎ 800/525-0280), **Delta** (☎ 800/221-1212), **Northwest** (☎ 800/225-2525), **Midway** (☎ 800/446-4392), **Southwest** (☎ 800/ 435-9792), **TWA** (☎ 800/221-2000), **United** (☎ 800/241-6522), and **US Airways** (☎ 800/428-4322) fly into **Jacksonville International Airport** on the city's north side, about 12 miles from downtown. The **First Coast Information Booth,** on the lower level by the baggage area (☎ 904/741-4902), is open daily from 9am to 10pm. **Gator City Taxi** (☎ 904/741-0008) provides transportation to and from the airport. Fares are about $20 to downtown, $40 to $45 to beach hotels, $55 to $65 to the St. Augustine area.

There's an **Amtrak** station in Jacksonville at 3570 Clifford Lane, off U.S. 1, just north of 45th Street (☎ 800/USA-RAIL).

VISITOR INFORMATION   Contact the **Jacksonville and the Beaches Convention & Visitors Bureau,** 3 Independent Dr., Jacksonville, FL 32202 (☎ 800/ 733-2668 or 904/798-9148; fax 904/789-9103; e-mail: jaxflcvb@jax-inter.net), for maps, brochures, calendars, and advice. In the Chamber of Commerce Building across Water Street from Jacksonville Landing, the office is open Monday to Friday from 8am to 5pm.

CITY LAYOUT   Jacksonville is intersected by the wide and winding St. Johns River, so getting around often involves crossing a bridge or two. The **Main Street Bridge** carries U.S. 1 and U.S. 92 across the St. Johns River in the heart of downtown; it has a footpath, so you can walk across it between Jacksonville Landing and the Southbank Riverwalk (see "Exploring the Area," below). From downtown, the main arteries to the beaches are **Atlantic Boulevard** (Fla. 10) and **Beach Boulevard** (U.S. 92). The freeway-grade **J. Turner Butler Boulevard** (Fla. 202) runs from the southern suburbs to Ponte Vedra Beach. North of the river, **Heckscher Drive** (Fla. 105) is the main east-west artery. Over on the beaches, **Third Street/Fla. A1A** runs north-south between Neptune Beach and Ponte Vedra Beach. The **St. Johns River Ferry** (☎ 904/ 241-9969) shuttles vehicles across the river at Mayport daily from 6:20am to 10:15pm. It shortens the trip between the Jacksonville beaches and Amelia Island, but call before driving out here to make sure it's running. One-way fare is $2.50 per vehicle.

GETTING AROUND   You're better off having a car if you want to explore this vast area. You can hail a **taxi** downtown if you spot one, although it is usually best to call

Gator City Taxi (☎ 904/355-8294) for a pickup. Fares are $1.25 when the meter drops, and 25¢ for each ⅛ mile thereafter. The **Jacksonville Transportation Authority** (☎ 904/630-3100) provides local **bus service** 7 days a week, with most buses running between 4:30am and 12:30am. The fare is 60¢ for adults, free for seniors and children shorter than 42 inches accompanied by an adult. A bus to the beach costs $1.10 each way.

EXPLORING THE AREA

Anheuser-Busch Brewery. 111 Busch Dr. ☎ 904/751-8118. Free admission. Mon–Sat 9am–4pm. Guided tours depart on the hour. Take I-95 north to Busch Dr. (exit 125), go east to brewery on left.

If you're into beer, you may appreciate the free and informative 30-minute tour of these monstrous and pungent-smelling facilities where Budweiser, Bud Light, Michelob, Busch, and O'Doul's are brewed. The best part is the conclusion of the tour, when you can quaff two free glasses of beer (or soft drinks) in the hospitality center. Bring a sweater, since you'll pass through 45° chambers where stainless-steel vaults hold the fermenting ale. You can take the guided tour, show yourself around, or head straight to the bar and extensive gift shop. Call ahead to see if the Anheuser-Busch Clydesdale horses are visiting.

✪ **Cummer Museum of Art & Gardens.** 829 Riverside Ave. (between Post and Fisk sts.). ☎ 904/356-6857. Admission $5 adults; $3 seniors over 65, students, and military; $1 children under 5; free for everyone Tues after 4pm. Tues and Thurs 10am–9pm, Wed and Fri–Sat 10am–5pm, Sun 2–5pm.

Built on the grounds of a private Tudor mansion, this modestly sized but outstanding museum is worth a visit for anyone who appreciates the visual arts. The permanent collection encompasses works from 2000 B.C. to the present. It's especially rich in American impressionist paintings and includes an impressive collection of 18th-century porcelain and 18th- and early-19th-century Japanese Netsuke ivory carvings. Don't miss the stunning Italian and English gardens set on the scenic St. Johns River.

Jacksonville Landing. 2 Independent Dr. (between Main and Pearl sts.), on the St. Johns River. ☎ 904/353-1188. Free admission. Mon–Thurs 10am–8pm, Sat 10am–9pm, Sun noon–5:30pm; bars and restaurants may be open later. Parking $4.80 maximum daily charge. From I-95, take Exit 107 downtown to Main St., go over the Blue Bridge, turn left at Bay St., then go 2 blocks and make a left on Laura St., which dead-ends at the Landing. Parking lot is on east side of complex.

This 6-acre dining/shopping/entertainment complex on the waterfront has more than 65 shops, including some of the mall regulars. Diners can choose from about half a dozen full-service restaurants plus a food court with indoor and outdoor seating overlooking the river. Also on the premises are a couple of bars and a small maritime museum. The Landing is the scene of numerous special events ranging from arts festivals to baseball-card shows. From March to the end of December there are free outdoor rock, blues, country, and jazz concerts every Friday and Saturday night. Call to find out what's going on at the Landing during your stay.

✪ **Jacksonville Zoo.** 8605 Zoo Rd. ☎ 904/757-4462 or 904/757-4463. Admission $6.50 adults, $4.50 seniors 65 and over, $4 children 3–12, free for children 2 and under; shows are free. Daily 9am–5pm (Memorial Day through Labor Day Fri–Sat until 8pm). Take I-95 north to Hecksher Dr. (Exit 124A) and follow the signs.

In the midst of a 10-year expansion plan, the Jacksonville Zoo is well on its way to becoming one of the country's best. The main exhibits are centered around an extensive and growing collection of African wildlife including lions, impalas, ostriches, rhinos, elephants, antelopes, Nile crocodiles, cheetah, Kirk's dik-diks, monkeys, and South African crested porcupines. You'll enter the 73-acre park through the authentic thatched roof built in 1995 by 24 Zulu craftsmen. Whether you go on foot or by tram, allow at least 2 hours to tour this vast and lush zoo, just south of the airport. When you arrive, ask about current animal shows and special events. Strollers and wheelchairs are available for rent.

Southbank Riverwalk. On the south bank of the St. Johns River, flanking Main Street Bridge between San Marco Blvd. and Ferry St. ☎ **904/396-4900.** Take I-95 north to the Prudential Dr. exit, make a right, and follow the signs.

This 1.2-mile wooden zigzag boardwalk bordering the St. Johns River is filled with joggers, tourists, and folks sitting on benches watching the riverboats and shorebirds. The downtown skyline across the river is reflected on the water. The **Friendship Fountain,** at the west end, is, at 200 feet in diameter, the nation's largest self-contained fountain; it's especially beautiful at night when illuminated by 265 colored lights. Farther along, you'll pass military memorials, and the **Museum of Science & History of Jacksonville,** at Museum Circle and San Marco Boulevard (☎ **904/ 396-7062**), an interactive children's museum focusing on science and the history of northeast Florida (admission $6 adults, $4 kids 3 to 12). The Riverwalk is the scene of seafood fests, parties, parades, and arts and crafts festivals. Food vendors, picnic tables, and restaurants line the route.

THE TIMUCUAN ECOLOGICAL & HISTORIC PRESERVE: A NEW BREED OF NATIONAL PARK

Named after the native people who inhabited Central and North Florida some 1,000 years before European settlers arrived, the **Timucuan Ecological and Historic Preserve** offers visitors an opportunity to explore untouched wilderness, historical buildings, and informative exhibits on the area's natural history. This 46,000-acre preserve is not your average national park. Besides the enormous size, it's unusual in that it hasn't been hacked off from the rest of the community and drawn within arbitrary boundaries. The result is a vast, intriguing system of sites joined by rural roads alongside tumble-down fish camps, trailer parks, strip malls, condominiums, and stately old homes.

South of the River

The prime attractions are on the south bank of the St. Johns River between downtown and the beaches. Your starting point here is the ✪ **Fort Caroline National Memorial,** on Ft. Caroline Road (☎ **904/641-7155**), which serves park headquarters. This was the site of the 16th-century French Huguenot settlement that was wiped out by the Spanish who landed at St. Augustine. This two-thirds-size replica shows you what the original was like. You can see archaeological artifacts and two very well produced half-hour videos highlighting the area. The fort and all other park facilities are open daily from 9am to 5pm except Christmas. Admission is free.

The fort sits at the northwestern edge of the 600-acre **Theodore Roosevelt Area,** a beautiful wood- and marshland rich in history and undisturbed since the Civil War. On a 2-mile hike along a centuries-old park trail, you'll see a wide variety of birds, wildflowers, and maritime hammock forest. Bring binoculars if you have them, since such birds as the endangered wood stork, great and snowy egrets, ospreys, hawks, and painted buntings make their home here in spring and summer. On the ground, you might catch sight of a gray fox or furry raccoon. You may also want to bring a blanket and picnic basket to spread out under the ancient oak trees that shade the banks of the

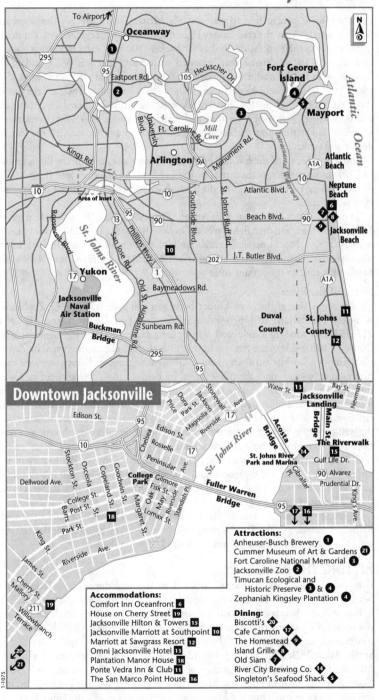

Jacksonville

To Airport
Oceanway
295
95 Eastport Rd.
105 Heckscher Dr.
Fort George Island
University Blvd.
Ft. Caroline Rd.
Mill Cove
Mayport
Kings Rd.
Arlington 9A
Monument Rd.
Atlantic Beach
A1A
10
Area of Inset
13
95
90
Southside Blvd.
St. Johns Bluff Rd.
Atlantic Blvd.
Neptune Beach
Beach Blvd. 90
Jacksonville Beach
St. Johns River
San Jose Rd.
Phillips Hwy.
10
202 J.T. Butler Blvd.
Yukon
Old St. Augustine Rd.
1
Baymeadows Rd.
A1A
Jacksonville Naval Air Station
Buckman Bridge
Sunbeam Rd.
Duval County
St. Johns County
11
12
295
95
Roosevelt Blvd.

Downtown Jacksonville

Edison St.
Stonewall
Dora Park St.
Jackson
Price
Magnolia
Riverside
17 Ave.
Water St.
Bay St.
Jacksonville Landing
13
10
Edison St.
Chelsea
Rosselle
Peninsular
17 Ave.
Acosta Bridge
Main St. Bridge
The Riverwalk
Stockton St.
Osceola St.
Copeland St.
Goodwin St.
College Park
Gilmore
Fisk St.
May
Oak
Riverside
Margaret St.
Lomax St.
Standish Pl.
St. Johns River
St. Johns River Park and Marina
14
15
Gulf Life Dr.
Dellwood Ave.
College St.
Post St.
Barrs St.
Park St.
18
Riverside Ave.
Fuller Warren Bridge
95
Gibraltar Pl.
90 Alvarez
Prudential Dr.
King St.
James St.
Cherry St.
Mallory
17 16
211
Willowbranch Terrace
19
20
21

Attractions:
Anheuser-Busch Brewery ❶
Cummer Museum of Art & Gardens ㉑
Fort Caroline National Memorial ❸
Jacksonville Zoo ❷
Timucan Ecological and
    Historic Preserve ❸ & ❹
Zephaniah Kingsley Plantation ❹

Dining:
Biscotti's ⑳
Cafe Carmon ⑰
The Homestead ⑨
Island Grille ⑧
Old Siam ⑦
River City Brewing Co. ⑭
Singleton's Seafood Shack ❺

Accommodations:
Comfort Inn Oceanfront ⑥
House on Cherry Street ⑲
Jacksonville Hilton & Towers ⑮
Jacksonville Marriott at Southpoint ⑩
Marriott at Sawgrass Resort ⑫
Omni Jacksonville Hotel ⑬
Plantation Manor House ⑱
Ponte Vedra Inn & Club ⑪
The San Marco Point House ⑯

1-1075

St. Johns River, where recreational and commercial boats still ply the wide and winding waters. After the trail crosses Hammock Creek, you're in ancient Timucuan country, where their ancestors lived as far back as 500 B.C. Farther along is the site of a cabin in the wilderness that belonged to reclusive brothers Willie and Saxon Browne, who lived without the modern conveniences of indoor plumbing or electricity until the last brother's death in 1960. If you're here on a weekend, take the 1½ -hour guided tours of the fort and Theodore Roosevelt Area, offered every Saturday and Sunday at 1pm (when weather and staffing permit); park rangers provide a wealth of fascinating information about history, flora, and fauna. Call the fort for details and schedules.

About ½ mile east of the fort is the **Ribault Monument** on St. Johns Bluff, erected in 1924 to commemorate the arrival in 1562 of French Huguenot Jean Ribault, who died defending Fort Caroline from the Spanish. It's worth a stop just for the dramatic view of the area.

To get here from downtown, take Atlantic Boulevard (Fla. 10) east, make a left on Monument Road, and turn right on Fort Caroline Road; the Theodore Roosevelt Area is entered from Mt. Pleasant Road, about 1 mile southeast of the fort; look for an inconspicuous sign on your left that says TRAILHEAD PARKING, and follow the narrow dirt road to the parking lot.

North of the River

On the north side of the river, history buffs also will appreciate the ✪ **Zephaniah Kingsley Plantation,** at 11676 Palmetto Ave. on Fort George Island (☎ **904/ 251-3537**). A winding 3-mile road runs under a canopy of trees with dense tropical foliage on either side to the remains of this 19th-century plantation owned by Zephaniah Kingsley, a white man who held some seemingly contradictory views on race. Although he owned more than 200 slaves, he believed that "the coloured race were superior to us, physically and morally." He married a Senegalese woman—one of his former slaves—and ultimately moved his family to Haiti in 1837 to escape what he called the "spirit of intolerant injustice" at home. The National Park Service maintains the well-preserved two-story residence, kitchen house, barn/carriage house, and remnants of 23 slave cabins built of "tabby mortar"—oyster shell and sand. A self-guided tour is the best way to see it all; clear and informative signs tell the history of this former citrus, cotton, and sugarcane farm, and of the workers who built it. Allot about an hour. A well-stocked book and gift shop will keep you even longer. Rangers sometimes offer interpretive programs.

To get here from I-95, take Heckscher Drive (Fla. 105) east and follow the signs. From Fort Caroline, take Fla. 9A north over the St. Johns River to Hecksher Drive east. The plantation is about 12 miles east of Fla. 9A, on the left.

HITTING THE BEACH

Fish, swim, snorkel, sail, sunbathe, or stroll on the sand dunes along Jacksonville's beaches—they're just a 20- to 30-minute drive from downtown via Atlantic, Beach, or J. Turner Butler boulevards. At 4th Avenue North you'll find free beach parking and rest rooms. ✪ **Jacksonville Beach** is probably the liveliest of the bunch, with beach concessions, rental shops, and a fishing pier. This is also the most popular local surfing beach. **Atlantic Beach,** farther north, has great nightlife and restaurants along the Atlantic. To the south, the ritzy enclave of **Ponte Vedra Beach** is actually in St. Johns County (St. Augustine), but it's so much closer to Jacksonville that I've included it in this chapter. Here you'll find the Marriott at Sawgrass Resort and the Ponte Vedra Inn & Club, both with outstanding golf courses (see "Where to Stay," below).

OUTDOOR ACTIVITIES & SPECTATOR SPORTS

BIKES, BALLOONS, BOATS & SKY-DIVING   A one-stop outfitter for all kinds of outdoor fun is **Outdoor Adventures** (☎ 904/393-9030), offering kayaking and canoeing, ballooning, bicycle trips, and other outdoor adventures, both day trips and longer camping trips. Call for schedules, prices, and reservations. If you want to learn to skydive, **Blue Sky Adventures** (☎ 904/272-4864) offers parachute training.

FISHING/CRUISING   You can go **fishing** for whiting, mackerel, flounder, blue-fish, catfish, and more off the **Jacksonville Beach Fishing Pier,** just south of Beach Boulevard at 6th Avenue (☎ 904/246-6001). No license is required, and rods, reels, and bait can be rented on the premises. The pier is open daily: from 6am to 11pm Memorial Day to Labor Day, until 9pm the rest of the year. It costs $4 for adults to fish the pier, $2 for children 8 and under and seniors over 60.

Another option is to fish for red snapper, grouper, sea bass, small sharks, amberjack, and more, 15 to 30 miles offshore in the Atlantic Ocean aboard the *King Neptune,* a 65-foot air-conditioned deep-sea fishing boat. It departs at 8am daily from 4378 Ocean St., a half mile south of the Mayport Ferry (☎ 904/246-7575). The price is $40 per person, including all bait and tackle. You don't need a license, but reservations are required. The boat usually returns by 5pm.

GOLF   Golfers will be glad to know that Jacksonville offers a great variety of public golf courses, many of which are ranked among the top in the country. Of course the most famous course is the TPC course at the Marriott Sawgrass, in Ponte Vedra, located in the next county and open only to resort guests (see "Where to Stay," below). Top courses open to the public include the semiprivate **Cimarrone,** at 2690 Cimar-rone Blvd. (☎ 904/287-2000), a fast and watery course with affordable greens fees ranging from $30 to $50; and the public **Golf Club of Jacksonville,** at 10440 Tour-nament Lane (☎ 904/779-0800), which is managed by the PGA Tour. It's a great bargain, with rates ranging from $28 to $39.

On your way out to the beach, the semiprivate **Windsor Parke Golf Club,** at 4747 Hodges Blvd., at J. Turner Butler Boulevard (☎ 904/223-GOLF), is one of the most challenging and scenic courses in Jacksonville. Designed by Arthur Hill, the 6,740 yards of green are surrounded by towering pines and lots of water. After it opened in 1991, *Golf Digest* rated it the best new course in the Southeast. Fees are usu-ally less than $45 and include a cart, even on the weekends. Nonmembers should call 4 or 5 days in advance for tee times.

Due to open in 1998, the **World Golf Village,** on 240 acres in St. Johns County, off I-95 and Golf Parkway (☎ 904/273-3350), brings together the biggest golf orga-nizations, professionals, and duffers from around the world. The centerpiece is the **World Golf Hall of Fame,** a 75,000-square-foot museum paying tribute to golf's finest.

For a review of other options in Northeast Florida, call ☎ 800/555-0807 to request a copy of *Florida Golf Vacations.* And be on the lookout for the free *Golfer's Guide* in the visitor centers and hotel lobbies (see "The Active Vacation Planner," in chapter 2, for information about ordering copies).

HORSEBACK RIDING   For a scenic ride along the sand and dunes, call **Sawgrass Stables,** 23900 Marsh Landing Pkwy., off Fla. A1A in Ponte Vedra Beach (☎ 904/ 285-3791). Rates start at $35 for a supervised ride. Lessons are also available.

SPECTATOR SPORTS   The 73,000-seat **Alltel Municipal Stadium,** 1 Stadium Place, at East Duval and Haines streets (☎ 904/630-3901 for information, or 904/353-3309 to charge tickets) hosts the annual Florida-Georgia football game every

October, other college football games September to December, motor-sports events, and the National Football League's **Jacksonville Jaguars** (☎ **904/633-6000** for ticket information). One of the stadium's biggest draws is the **Toyota Gator Bowl,** usually on New Year's Day (see "Florida Calendar of Events," in chapter 2).

Adjacent to the stadium, and under the same auspices, is the 10,600-seat **Jacksonville Veterans Memorial Coliseum,** 1145 E. Adams St. (☎ **904/630-3900** for information, or 904/353-3309 to charge tickets), home of the **Jacksonville Lizards** East Coast Hockey team, and a venue for NHL exhibition games, Division I college basketball games, ice-skating exhibitions, wrestling matches, and various family shows.

Jax has yet to get a big league baseball team, but you can see the **Jacksonville Suns,** a Detroit Tigers affiliate, play their Class AA minor league games from April to early September at Wolfson Park, 1201 E. Duval St. (☎ **904/358-2842**). Tickets range from $4 to $7.

TENNIS As home to the International Association of Tennis Professionals, Jacksonville also abounds in high-quality tennis courts, including the notable facilities at the Ponte Vedra Beach and Amelia Island resorts (see "Where to Stay," below, and in section 5). In the city, **Southside Park,** 1541 Hendricks Ave., off Atlantic Boulevard (☎ **904/399-1761**), has six city-run Har-Tru courts for daytime play and six asphalt-base courts lit for night play. There's no charge to play. There are additional city courts (14 clay, two Har-Tru, and a practice wall, all lit for night play) at **Boone Park,** 3730 Park St., just east of Roosevelt Boulevard (☎ **904/384-8687**). There's a small charge here. Both locations are open daily year-round and offer lessons from resident tennis pros. Call for hours, and make reservations a day or two in advance.

WATER & ENTERTAINMENT PARK **Adventure Landing,** 1944 Beach Blvd., at 20th Street. Jacksonville Beach (☎ **904/246-4386**), is a pirate theme park with all kinds of fun activities for kids and adults. A giant water park, open March through September, is a great way to cool off. Or, you can try your hand in the huge arcade with video games, laser tag, virtual reality machines, and carnival-style games. Outside you can ride the go-carts or bumper boats, play miniature golf, and take some swings in the batting cages. Admission to the water park is about $16 for adults, $13 for children under 48 inches, free for children 3 and under. There are separate charges for activities.

SHOPPING & BROWSING

Jacksonville has shopping opportunities galore, including Jacksonville Landing (see "Exploring the Area," above); an upscale mall, **The Avenues Mall,** south of town at 10300 Southside Blvd.; as well as a number of flea markets, including the **Beach Boulevard Flea and Farmer's Market,** on Beach Boulevard (Fla. 90) (☎ **904/645-5961**). More than 600 vendors show up daily, from 9am to 5pm, to sell their wares in a partially covered facility.

The **San Marco Square** shopping district, at San Marco and Atlantic boulevards south of downtown, is a quaint shopping district in the middle of a stunning residential area. Shops in meticulously refashioned Mediterranean revival buildings sell antiques and home furnishings as well as clothing, books, and records.

Another worthwhile neighborhood to explore is the **Avondale/Riverside** historic district southwest of downtown along St. Johns Avenue between Talbot Avenue and Boone Park, on the north bank of the river. More than 60 boutiques, antique stores, art galleries, shoe stores, and cafes line the wide, tree-lined avenue.

Nearby, the younger set hangs out at **Five Points,** on Park Street where used record stores, vintage clothiers, coffee shops, smoke shops, and funky art galleries stay open late.

Like St. Augustine, Jacksonville is a mecca for chocoholics, particularly **Peterbrooke Chocolatier Production Center,** 1470 San Marco Blvd., in the San Marco Square neighborhood (☎ **904/398-4812**). If you've never tried chocolate-covered popcorn or pretzels, this is the place. Open Monday to Friday from 10am to 5pm.

WHERE TO STAY

I've arranged the accommodations listed below geographically, in and around downtown first, followed by the beach scene. The suburbs have dozens more to choose from, especially along I-95. Many are clustered south of downtown in the **Southpoint** (Exit 101, J. Turner Butler Boulevard/Fla. 202) and **Baymeadows** (Exit 101, Baymeadows Road/Fla. 152) suburban areas. These locales have a multitude of chain restaurants, and you can hop on the highways and zoom to the beach or downtown—although you aren't really at either one if you stay out here. Tops is the **Jacksonville Marriott at Southpoint,** 4670 Salisbury Rd. (☎ **800/228-9290** or 904/296-2222), among the area's best all-around hotels. Also here are a comfortable and inexpensive **Budgetel Inn**, 3199 Hartley Rd. (☎ **800/428-3488** or 904/268-9999); a recently enlarged and renovated **Embassy Suites** at 9300 Baymeadows Rd., east of I-95 (☎ **800/362-2779** or 904/731-3555); and a **Motel 6,** at 8285 Dix Ellis Trail (☎ **800/4-MOTEL-6** or 904/731-8400).

For a complete list of lodgings, contact the Jacksonville and the Beaches Convention & Visitors Bureau (see "Essentials," above).

Note that rates in the downtown hotels are higher midweek when rooms are in demand by business travelers. Beach accommodations are somewhat less expensive in the cold months from December through March.

IN JACKSONVILLE

The House on Cherry Street. 1844 Cherry St. (on the St. Johns River), Jacksonville, FL 32205. ☎ **904/384-1999.** Fax 904/384-5013. 4 units (all with bathroom). A/C TV. $79–$99 double. Rates include continental breakfast. AE, MC, V.

This colonial-style wood-frame house, nestled in a tree-shaded cul-de-sac on the St. Johns River, is ideal for a romantic B&B vacation (no small children are accepted). French doors open to a delightful screened-in back porch furnished with rocking chairs; it overlooks an expanse of tree-shaded lawn (where guests play croquet) leading to the river. You might select the Rose or Duck rooms, both with canopied four-poster beds and river views. Ducks are rather a theme here, with hundreds of antique decoys on display. All accommodations offer adjacent sitting rooms, ceiling fans, and are supplied with fresh flowers, books, and magazines. Complimentary wine and hot and cold hors d'oeuvres are presented daily at 6pm on the patio or in the dining room. An upstairs refrigerator is stocked with free soft drinks and beer, and there are bicycles for guest use. Genial owners/hosts Carol and Merrill Anderson keep a gentle pet greyhound, formerly a racing dog, named Streak, but don't bring your own pet. No smoking is permitted.

Jacksonville Hilton & Towers. 1201 Riverplace Blvd. (at Main St. on Southbank Riverwalk), Jacksonville, FL 32207. ☎ **800/HILTONS** or 904/393-8800. Fax 904/398-5570. 310 units. A/C TV TEL. $89–$149 double; $114–$174 suite. AE, DC, DISC, MC, V. Valet parking $5; free self-parking.

Once known as the Jacksonville Hotel, this 10-story Hilton opened in 1997 after extensive renovation. Featured is the Elvis Room, where "the King" purportedly stayed half a dozen times between 1955 and 1976. It and the other units have dark wood furniture, two phones with data ports, irons and boards, hair dryers, and balconies overlooking the river. A branch of Ruth's Chris Steakhouse offers expensive but extraordinarily tender beef, while a lobby cafe with open kitchen feeds the rest of us. There's an outdoor pool and an exercise room for keeping fit.

Omni Jacksonville Hotel. 245 Water St. (across from Jacksonville Landing between Pearl and Hogan sts.), Jacksonville, FL 32202. ☎ **800/THE-OMNI** or 904/355-OMNI. Fax 904/791-4809. 354 units. A/C MINIBAR TV TEL. $79–$199 double; $300–$500 suite. AE, DC, DISC, MC, V. Valet parking $8; self-parking $6.

Jacksonville's best downtown digs is directly across the street from Jacksonville Landing and caters primarily to a corporate clientele who fill the gleaming marble lobby and meeting facilities during the week. The spacious guest rooms, thoroughly renovated in 1995, have blond-wood furnishings, plenty of lighting, and all the practical necessities you could ask for, including a reasonably priced minibar, a writing desk, two phones with voice mail and data ports), hair dryers, a fully prepped coffeemaker, large closets, and an iron and ironing board. Dining options in the hotel include a reasonably priced room serving continental cuisine as well as an extensive room service menu until 11pm. Sports-minded guests will appreciate the jogging and walking maps provided in each room, the outdoor swimming pool, and the well-equipped but closet-sized exercise room.

✪ Plantation Manor Inn. 1630 Copeland St. (between Oak and Park sts.), Jacksonville, FL 32204. ☎ **904/384-4630.** Fax 904/387-0960. 9 units. A/C TV TEL. $95–$150 double. Rates include full breakfast. AE, DC, MC, V.

The setting for many weddings and special events, this three-story plantation-style home in the historic Riverside district is just 10 minutes from downtown. Its homey interior, outfitted with a mix of thrift-store antiques, features glossy pine floors and gorgeous cypress paneling, wainscoting, and carved moldings. Breakfast, including fresh-baked muffins and breads, is served in a lovely dining room with a working fireplace. When the sun is shining, take the morning meal on an enclosed brick patio, a delightful setting with ivy-covered walls, flower beds, and garden furnishings under the shade of a massive oak tree. The patio also contains a lap pool and whirlpool spa. On the second floor you can enjoy a big wraparound porch with seating amid potted geraniums, hibiscus, and bougainvillea.

The San Marco Point House. 1709 River Rd. (between Riviera and Laverne sts.), Jacksonville, FL 32207. ☎ **904/396-1448.** Fax 904/396-7760. E-mail: sanmarcopt@aol.com. 5 units (all with bathroom). A/C TV TEL. $75–$100 double. Rates include full breakfast. AE, MC, V.

Within hailing distance of trendy restaurants in the San Marco Square neighborhood and ½ block from a promenade along the river, this Sears Craftsman bungalow was built in 1921. Downstairs has two sitting rooms, one with a fireplace, the other with French doors opening to a side patio. But wait until you see the African lion skin, snarling head and all, lying on the floor of the small lounge at the top of the stairs. No, neither Owner Todd Kemp nor innkeeper Linda Olsvasky are big-game hunters; it and the other stuffed trophies in this Hemingwayesque room were purchased at estate sales. The guest rooms in the house are adorned with an eclectic mix of furnishings, including some antiques, and all have little sitting alcoves backed by bay windows. More private is the one room in a small cottage in the backyard.

AT THE BEACHES

A dozen modest hotels line Jacksonville Beach's 1st Street, along the Atlantic Ocean, including a **Holiday Inn Sunspree** (☎ **800/HOLIDAY** or 904/249-9071), where all rooms come with refrigerators, microwaves, and coffee pots; **Days Inn Oceanfront**

Resort (☎ **800/321-2037** or 904/249-7924); and **Ramada Resort** (☎ **800/ 2-RAMADA** or 904/241-5333).

Comfort Inn Oceanfront. 1515 N. 1st St. (two blocks east of Fla. A1A), Jacksonville Beach, FL 32250. ☎ **800/654-8776** or 904/241-2311. Fax 904/249-3830. 180 units. A/C TV TEL. $79–$129 double; $140–$175 suite. Rates include continental breakfast. AE, DC, DISC, MC, V.

One of the best-priced options on the beachfront, this Comfort Inn offers rooms with balconies or screened patios. Microwave and/or refrigerator units are available for an extra charge. An especially good deal here is a honeymoon suite with whirlpool tub and living-room area. Continental breakfast and light fare are served in a small pool-side dining room. An oceanfront lounge features live music for dancing on weekend nights from April to Labor Day. There's a large pool with rock waterfalls and a palm-fringed sundeck, secluded grotto whirlpool, small fitness room, gift/sundries shop, and multicourt sand volleyball park.

Sea Horse Oceanfront Inn. 120 Atlantic Blvd. (between Ocean Blvd. and the beach), Neptune Beach, FL 32266. ☎ **800/881-2330** or 904/246-2175. Fax 904/246-4256. 38 units. A/C TV TEL. $69–$109 double; $175–$250 penthouse suite for up to 6. AE, DC, DISC, MC, V.

All the rooms at this well-run beachfront property offer ocean views from balconies or patios. Families will appreciate the six units here with fully equipped kitchenettes, not to mention a nice-size oceanfront pool, volleyball, shuffleboard, picnic tables, and a barbecue grill. And young couples will enjoy proximity to some of Jacksonville's top nightspots. If you have a large family or group, consider the vast and lovely third-floor penthouse—it has a big living room and dining area, a full kitchen, a separate bedroom as well as sofa beds, and a huge balcony furnished with a dining table and chaises longues. A coffee shop adjoins the motel, and many other restaurants are within easy walking distance, as is a launderette.

AT PONTE VEDRA BEACH

✪ **Marriott at Sawgrass Resort.** 1000 TPC Blvd. (off Fla. A1A between U.S. 210 and J. Turner Butler Blvd.), Ponte Vedra Beach, FL 32082. ☎ **800/457-GOLF**, 800/228-9290, or 904/285-7777. Fax 904/285-0906. 508 units (including 160 condos). A/C MINIBAR TV TEL. $115–$225 double; $210–600 suites and condos. Golf packages available. AE, DC, DISC, MC, V. Valet parking $8; free self-parking.

The nation's second-largest golf resort, this duffer's paradise is virtually surrounded by 99 holes, including the TPC-Stadium Course, home of the annual Players Championship every March. In fact, it has appeared on every critic's "best-of" list since it was built by Pete Dye in 1980.

Redecorated in 1997, the guest rooms in the main building have two phones, hair dryers, irons and boards, and coffeemakers. Best for families are the one- and two-bedroom villas on or near a golf course. They offer fully equipped kitchens, living rooms, and large furnished patios or balconies. Especially luxurious are the one- to three-bedroom beachfront villas, which sport huge kitchens, living rooms with working fireplaces, full dining rooms, and large screened wooden decks.

Dining/Diversions: The resort's gourmet dining room serves steaks and seafood. The Cabana Club restaurant, a 10-minute drive from the resort, has simple beach food and light snacks downstairs and nouvelle cuisine upstairs; an outdoor patio and an adjoining lounge feature nightly music and dancing.

Amenities: Concierge, room service, dry cleaning and laundry service, baby-sitting, secretarial services, express checkout, valet parking, complimentary shuttle to/from the beach and golf courses, newspaper delivery, nightly turndown on request, airport transfer available, rental VCRs, 2 swimming pools (one Olympic size), kiddie pool, use of 2½-mile private beach and pool at the nearby Cabana Club, 2 first-rate health clubs, whirlpool, sauna, bicycle rental, 5 championship golf courses, golf/tennis pro shop and teaching pros/clinics, 4 driving ranges, 6 putting greens, children's program offering daily activities for ages 3 to 12, recreation room, playground. There's also a teen program, business center, conference rooms, self-service Laundromat, 8 tennis courts, sports-equipment rentals (windsurfing boards, bicycles, fishing poles), lagoons stocked for fishing, nature and biking trails, horseback riding, an extensive complex of boutiques and specialty shops for sporting equipment, gifts, and resort wear.

✪ **Ponte Vedra Inn & Club.** 200 Ponte Vedra Blvd. (off Fla. A1A), Ponte Vedra Beach, FL 32082. ☎ **800/234-7842** or 904/285-1111. Fax 904/285-2111. 222 units. A/C MINIBAR TV TEL. $140–$380 suite. Golf packages available. AE, DC, DISC, MC, V.

This luxurious 300-acre private country club and spa is the perfect place to pamper yourself. The Ponte Vedra Inn is ultra-elegant from the moment you drive up to its manicured front lawn, which doubles as a putting green. The property has a private sand beach and boardwalk. Inside, a charming lobby adjoins the lodgelike Great Lounge, with overstuffed sofas and armchairs and massive fireplaces at either end.

The spacious rooms, all with furnished patios or balconies, are individually decorated; some have four-poster or sleigh beds. In-room amenities include wet bars, coffeemakers, safes, and ceiling fans. You'll find a hair dryer, scale, luxury bath products, and plush terry robe in the bath, a cosmetic mirror and double sink in your large dressing room. Microwave ovens and small refrigerators are available on request.

A gorgeous on-premises spa offers ocean-view massage rooms, hair-salon services, herbal and seaweed wraps, facials, hydrotherapy, fitness training, waxing, manicures, pedicures, nutrition consultations, and much more. Treat yourself to a "day of beauty."

Dining/Diversions: Breakfast is served in a formal dining room. Steak and seafood highlight the menu at the more casual dinner-only restaurant. A golf club restaurant, with an adjoining bar, overlooks the greens and a lagoon. Another elegant dining room, with tiered ocean-view seating, features American/continental lunches and dinners; a pianist entertains at dinner, and there's dancing on Friday and Saturday nights to a live trio in the adjoining lounge.

Amenities: Concierge, 24-hour room service, nightly turndown, shoe shine, complimentary newspaper each morning, dry cleaning and laundry services, twice-daily maid service, baby-sitting, express checkout, valet parking, courtesy car or limo, 3 outdoor swimming pools (one Olympic size), kiddie pool, oceanfront whirlpool, 2 championship 36-hole golf courses, 15 tennis courts (7 lighted), golf/tennis pro shops and instruction, upscale shops, florist, water-sports equipment rental, bicycle rental, children's programs, steam, sauna, extensive 10,000-square-foot health club, sand volleyball court, business center, secretarial services, conference center, self-service Laundromat, library, beauty salon.

WHERE TO DINE

Once a town where any dish other than Southern fried chicken or catfish was considered exotic, Jacksonville's dining scene is evolving into culinary diversity. The convention and visitors bureau's annual guide (see "Essentials," above) contains a complete list of restaurants, which now includes a handful of sushi bars, one or two authentic Mexican eateries, a few Jewish delis, and some Cuban diners. The area even has half a dozen Thai restaurants, such as Old Siam, listed below.

IN JACKSONVILLE

Don't forget that **Jacksonville Landing** on the downtown riverfront has several full-service restaurants and an inexpensive food court with outdoor seating (see "Exploring the Area," above).

✪ Biscotti's. 3556 St. Johns Ave. (between Talbot and Ingleside aves. in the Avondale section). ☎ **904/387-2060.** Sandwiches and salads $5–$7; pastas and pizzas $7–$10; nightly fish special from $12. AE, DC, DISC, MC, V. Tues–Thurs 7am–10pm, Fri 7am–midnight, Sat 8am–midnight, Sun 8am–3pm. CALIFORNIA/ECLECTIC.

This brick-walled little neighborhood gem might have come out of New York's East Village, San Francisco's downtown, or Washington's Georgetown. A young and hip wait staff is pleasant and well informed. Daily specials, like pan-seared salmon or pork loin, are always fresh and beautifully presented. The huge and inventive salads are especially good: Try the Oriental version with chicken breast, orange slices, roasted peppers, and creamy sesame dressing. Pizzas, too, are served with wonderfully exotic and delicious toppings—ever try guacamole and black beans on your slice? On warm days choose a seat outside for great people-watching.

✪ Cafe Carmon. 1986 San Marco Blvd. (between Carlo St. and Naldo Ave.). ☎ **904/399-4488.** Reservations not accepted. Sandwiches $7–$8.50; main courses $7–$15. AE, DC, DISC, MC, V. Mon–Thurs 11am–11pm, Fri–Sat 11am–midnight, Sun 11am–9pm. FLORIDA CAFE.

A short drive from the Southbank Riverwalk, this comfy and casual restaurant is located in the heart of the San Marco Square shopping and dining district. In the daytime it's a mecca for shoppers and professionals; most nights the place is jammed with an after-theater crowd dropping in for cappuccinos and delectable desserts. The inside is sparsely decorated in black-and-white tile; the brick patio out front offers cafe seating. At lunch or dinner, you can order delicious salads, such as sautéed goat cheese with sun-dried tomatoes, toasted hazelnuts, cilantro, and mixed greens in a tangy vinaigrette. Generous-sized dinner options include a grilled, sautéed, or blackened fresh catch (often grouper) prepared Provençal, in beurre blanc sauce, or with pineapple salsa. Great lunch fare here, too.

River City Brewing Company. 835 Museum Circle (on Southbank Riverwalk). ☎ **904/398-2299.** Reservations only for parties of 8 or more. Main courses $14–$24; Sun brunch buffet $16 adults, $13 seniors, $8 children 3–12. AE, DC, DISC, MC, V. Mon–Thurs 11am–3pm and 5–10pm, Fri–Sat 11am–3pm and 5–11pm, Sun 10:30am–2:30pm and 5–10pm. Lounges and terrace open for light fare Sun–Tues until midnight, Wed–Sat until 2am. CALIFORNIA/LOUISIANA.

Occupying a prime location on the south bank of the St. Johns River, this gorgeous restaurant and microbrewery is an excellent choice for lunch or dinner. Its glass walls provide most tables with dramatic waterfront and skyline views. Or for an even better vantage point, sit outside on the enormous covered deck. Some weekends you'll hear live bands performing on the riverside stage.

Some guests find the home brews to be bitter, but all rave about the super pastas, steaks, and seafood. Appetizers, too, are excellent. The crab cakes are delicately sautéed and served with a mix of baby greens and a tangy mango salsa. Pot stickers filled with morsels of shrimp and vegetables are also sautéed and seasoned with an Asian flair. For a main course, try the Cajun chicken linguine with mushrooms and ham in a spicy cream sauce.

Sunday brunch brings incredible buffets with fresh fruits and vegetables, bagels with smoked salmon and cream cheese, French toast, dozens of salads, and a carving station with honey-baked ham and prime rib. There is also a selection of decadent desserts.

AT THE BEACHES

✪ **The Homestead.** 1712 Beach Blvd. (next to Adventure Landing, between 15th and 19th sts.), Jacksonville Beach. ☎ **904/249-5240.** Reservations only for large parties. Full dinners $7–$14. AE, DISC, MC, V. Mon–Fri 11am–4pm, daily 4:30pm–midnight. SOUTHERN.

This Jacksonville institution is usually packed with regulars waiting for a table in this log-cabinlike restaurant that has been serving big eaters since 1947. There's a good reason for the greasy atmosphere, for the big draw here is Southern fried chicken served in a skillet with homemade buttermilk biscuits and fresh honey, coleslaw, black-eyed peas, rice and gravy, creamed peas, and a choice of daily vegetables. Other favorites, like the saucer-sized chicken dumpling, is served with thick gravy and all the fixings. The narrow 50-foot-long copper-topped bar is a popular hangout for the local beach drinkers and the major nighttime haunt of celebrity golfers during Tournament Players Club championship games.

✪ **Island Grille.** 981 N. 1st St. (at 9th Ave.), Jacksonville Beach. ☎ **904/241-1881.** Reservations recommended. Main courses $14–$17; main-course salads $9–$11. AE, DC, DISC, MC, V. Mar–Oct daily 11:30am–10pm. Nov–Feb Mon–Tues 4:30–10pm, Wed–Thurs 11:30am–10pm, Fri–Sat 11:30am–11pm, Sun 11:30am–10pm. (Bar open to 1:30am.) "FLORIBBEAN"/CONTINENTAL.

One of the area's most popular dining venues, especially in summer when the beach crowd vies for seats on the huge oceanfront deck, the Island Grille serves a varied menu with lots of innovative seafood as well as basic offerings like shrimp scampi, New York strip steak, pasta primavera, and even burgers. The many salads including one topped with tuna tataki are delicious and large. The appetizers here are so good you might just graze; they range from Bahamian conch fritters served with spicy pink rémoulade to escargots served in mushroom caps. You can enjoy good live music Wednesday through Saturday evenings.

Old Siam. 1716 N. Third St. (Fla. A1A, in Holiday Plaza shopping center, between 16th and 17th aves. N.), Jacksonville Beach. ☎ **904/247-7763.** Reservations only for parties of 6 or more. Main courses $8–$16. AE, MC, V. Mon–Tues 5–10pm, Wed–Fri 11:30am–2:30pm and 5–10pm, Fri–Sat 5–11pm; Sun 5–9:30pm. THAI.

The best of the area's Thai restaurants, Pam Souvannasoth's trendy little enclave serves fine cuisine from his homeland and a good selection of wines to match its spicy yet subtle flavors. Pam's signature dish is his seafood special: shrimp, sea scallops, mussels, squid, and crab claws in a red chile sauce accented with sweet basil. The chiles in his "number 3" spice level (out of 6) touched my tongue but did not overwhelm the other seasonings. Standard favorites like Pad Thai are light and perfectly balanced with sweet and slightly sour fish sauce.

✪ **Singleton's Seafood Shack.** 4728 Ocean St. (Fla. A1A, at St. Johns River Ferry landing), Mayport. ☎ **904/246-4442.** Full dinners $9–$13; sandwiches and salads $2–$6. DISC, MC, V. Sun–Thurs 10am–9pm, Fri–Sat 10am–10pm. SEAFOOD.

Capt. Ray Singleton has been serving fresh catches from this wooden shack since 1969. Locals swear this is the best fish camp in Jacksonville; a taste of any of the fresh catches like the blackened mahimahi or Cajun shrimp will confirm it. Unlike most other rustic fish houses in Florida's northeast that tend to overbatter and overfry everything that comes into the kitchen, Singleton's offers a variety of preparations for every imaginable kind of seafood. Of course, the fried standbys like conch fritters, shrimp, clam strips, and calamari are available, too. Along with your entree, try the grouper or cobia with mushroom and wine sauce—your Styrofoam plate will come stacked with a choice of side items like black beans and rice, coleslaw, fries, and hush puppies. You can also choose from a selection of chicken. Just off the waterside patio, check out the captain's model boat "museum," a wood shop filled with his finely carved ships.

JACKSONVILLE AFTER DARK

"Where do you take a date in Jacksonville?" goes an old local joke. The answer: "St. Augustine." Those who lament the lack of a nightlife remember when there really wasn't much to do after dusk unless you drove down to the Old City. These days, options beyond leaving town or lounging at the hotel bar are increasing. In addition to the spots recommended below, check listings in the weekend section of Friday's *Florida-Times Union,* or *FOLIOWEEKLY,* the free local alternative paper, available at restaurants, hotels, and all over town.

THE BAR SCENE   You will find several libation options downtown at **Jacksonville Landing** (see "Exploring the Area," above), including a lively waterfront **Hooters** (☎ 904/356-5400), plus free outdoor rock, blues, country, and jazz concerts every Friday and Saturday night except during winter. The downtown post-teen crowd hangs at **Moto Lounge,** 214 W. Adams St. (☎ **904/355-6686**), where local and regional bands perform.

In the Avondale neighborhood, **Partners,** 3585 St. Johns Ave. at Ingleside Avenue. (☎ **904/387-3585**), has a mellow piano-bar ambience, innovative American food, and live jazz Wednesday to Saturday nights, making it a local favorite.

In the southern suburbs, an older crowd gathers at **T-Birds,** 9039 Southside Blvd. between Baymeadows Road and Phillips Highway (☎ **904/363-3399**), where a deejay spins dance music and good-time rock 'n' roll Tuesday to Saturday until 2am. Occasionally, former headliners you haven't heard from in years appear, such as the Little River Band, Starship, Kansas, and ELO. Also big here is happy hour, featuring a lavish complimentary buffet and drink specials from 5 to 7:30pm weeknights.

Out at Neptune Beach, one of the more popular spots is **Ragtime Tavern and Taproom,** 207 Atlantic Blvd. (☎ **904/241-7877**). This beach bar and restaurant features local groups playing live jazz and blues Thursday to Sunday nights. Weekends, especially, the place is really jumping and the crowd is young, but it's lively rather than rowdy. Ragtime brews its own beer. It's open nightly until at least 12:30am. Across the street is the **Sun Dog Diner,** at 207 Atlantic Blvd. (☎ **904/241-8221**), with nightly acoustic music and decent diner food.

The favorite pub in Jacksonville Beach, **Sloppy Joe's,** 200 N. 1st St. (☎ **904/ 270-1767**), is an off-shoot of the Key West institution.

THE PERFORMING ARTS   With the 73,000-seat **Alltell Stadium,** at East Duval and Haines streets (☎ **904/630-3900**), the 10,600-seat **Jacksonville Veterans Memorial Coliseum,** 1145 E. Adams St. (☎ **904/630-3900** for information or 904/353-3309 to charge tickets), and the 3,200-seat **Florida Times Union Center for the Performing Arts,** 300 Water St., between Hogan and Pearl streets (☎ **904/ 630-3900**), Jacksonville has plenty of seats for concerts, touring Broadway shows, dance companies, and big-name performers. Check the local papers mentioned above for current offerings, or call the *Times-Union's* automated information service for up-to-date schedules (☎ **904/355-1500,** ext. 7450).

5 Amelia Island

32 miles NE of Jacksonville, 192 miles NE of Orlando, 372 miles N of Miami

Exclusive and beautiful Amelia Island is a charming getaway about a 45-minute drive northeast of downtown Jacksonville. Right near the Georgia border, this barrier island has 13 beautiful miles of beach and offers world-class tennis and golfing at two of Florida's most luxurious resorts. Yes, it has two paper mills and a small seaport, but the island's bay-side town of ✪ **Fernandina Beach** also boasts a 50-block area of gorgeous Victorian and Queen Anne homes listed in the National Register of Historic Places.

The town's Victorian district dates from the late 19th century, when the island's timber, phosphate, and naval stores industries boomed. The 1970s and '80s saw another economic explosion, as real estate developers built condos, cottages, and the two big resorts which now dominate the southern end of the island. In recent years, Fernandina Beach has seen another big boom, this time in bed-and-breakfastestablishments.

ESSENTIALS

GETTING THERE   The island is served by **Jacksonville International Airport** (see "Essentials," in section 4, above). The scenic drive here from downtown Jacksonville is via Heckscher Drive (Fla. 105) and Fla. A1A; from the beaches, via Fla. A1A north and the St. John's River Ferry. The fast, four-lane way is via I-95 north and the Buccaneer Trail (Fla. A1A) east.

VISITOR INFORMATION   For advance information, contact the **Amelia Island–Fernandina Beach–Yulee Chamber of Commerce,** 102 Centre St. (P.O. Box 472), Fernandina Beach, FL 32035 (☎ **800/2-AMELIA** or 904/261-3248; fax 904/261-6997; www.goflorida.com/amelia-island). The chamber's visitor information center, in the old train station at the bay end of Centre Street, is open Monday to Friday from 9am to 5pm.

GETTING AROUND   There's no public transportation on this 13-mile-long island, so you'll need a vehicle. The **Old Towne Carriage Company** (☎ **904/ 277-1555**) offers narrated, horse-drawn carriage tours of Fernandina Beach's historic district, leaving from the waterfront on Centre Street. They close for 2 months during the winter when the horses are put out to pasture. Rides cost $15 for adults, $7.50 for kids under 13.

HITTING THE BEACH

Wrapping around the island's northern end and backed by rolling dunes, the exquisite white-sand beach at ✪ **Fort Clinch State Park** is one of the area's most beautiful and is filled with shells and driftwood. Also, the best part is that the coast curves here, which gives the feeling of being in a private cove. The park entrance is on Atlantic Avenue, just west of Fletcher Avenue; wooden boardwalks lead from the parking area to the sands. At the western end of the beach, a jetty and a pier jutting into Cumberland South are popular with anglers. Entrance fees are $3.25 per vehicle with up to 8 occupants, $1 for pedestrians and bicyclists. There are 62 campsites available at $20.62 per night with electricity, $18.53 without. You can reserve a site up to 11 months in advance (a very good idea in summer) by contacting the park at 2601 Atlantic Ave., Fernandina Beach, FL 32034 (☎ **904/277-7274**).

Main Beach, on North Fletcher Avenue (Fla. A1A) and Trout Street, is the center of activity, with good swimming, rest rooms, picnic shelters, showers, a food concession, a playground, and more. There's lots of free parking, and this area is popular with families.

Pets on leashes are allowed on all the island's public beaches.

OUTDOOR PURSUITS

BOATING, FISHING, SAILING & KAYAKING   The **Amelia Island Charter Boat Association** (☎ **904/261-2870**) can help arrange deep-sea fishing charters, party-boat excursions, sailing trips, sightseeing cruises, and more.

Voyager Adventures, based at Fernandia Harbor Marina, 3977 1st Ave. (☎ **904/ 321-1244;** fax 904/321-2505), has several cruises aboard the *Voyager,* a 100-foot replica of a 19th-century gaff-rigged packet schooner. A prime destination is Cumberland Island, across the sound in Georgia (remember when John F. Kennedy Jr. was married over there without a single paparazzi present?). Also based at the marina, **Windward Sailing School** (☎ 904/261-9125) will teach you to skipper your boat. Call these companies for details, prices, and reservations.

Kayak Amelia (☎ 904/321-0697; www.kayakamelia.com) has learning and advanced-level trips on the back bays. Half-day trips cost $50 per person; sunset paddles on Friday, $25 per person.

GOLF & TENNIS If you're not staying in a resort with golf and tennis facilities, try the 27-hole **Fernandina Municipal Golf Course** (☎ 904/277-7370) and the two tennis courts at the municipal park in Fernandina Beach at Atlantic Avenue and 11th Street.

HORSEBACK RIDING **Seahorse Stables,** 7500 Fla. A1A (☎ 904/261-4878), is open daily and can arrange horseback riding on the beach at the south end of the island for $35. Reservations are required.

SCENIC CRUISES Departing from the city marina on Front Street in Fernandina Beach, the sleek *Good Times Too* (☎ 904/277-8482) goes cruising on the inland waterways hereabouts. Call for schedule and prices.

SCUBA DIVING **Aqua Explorers Dive Center,** 2856 Sadler Rd. (☎ 904/ 261-5989), open Monday to Saturday from 10am to 6pm, teaches certification courses, arranges charters, and sells and rents equipment.

SHOPPING

Stroll down **Centre Street** in downtown Fernandina Beach, with its vintage storefronts and charming boutiques. Quality antiques, consignment shops, and bookstores line the wide boulevard ending at the marina. On the south end of the island, **Palmetto Walk,** under a canopy of live oaks, is another good shopping bet. The chamber of commerce has complete lists and descriptions of the island's many up-scale stores (see "Essentials," above).

WHERE TO STAY

I don't know for sure, but there may be more bed-and-breakfast inns in Fernandina Beach alone than in the entire rest of Florida. Indeed, more than two dozen of the town's charming Victorian and Queen Anne houses have been restored and turned into B&Bs, and apparently they all stay busy, especially on weekends. Industry veteran David Caples, who holds seminars nationwide for wannabe innkeepers, is based here at the Elizabeth Pointe Lodge (see below). For a complete list, contact the chamber of commerce (see "Essentials," above), or check out the Web site of the **Amelia Island Bed & Breakfast Association** at www.ameliaislandinns.com (the association does not have an address or phone number).

Also, a number of agencies will book vacation properties ranging from affordable cottages to magnificent mansions. Contact **Amelia Island Lodging Systems,** 584 S. Fletcher Ave., Fernandina Beach, FL 32034 (☎ 800/872-8531 or 904/261-4148; fax 904/261-9200), which even has a lighthouse for rent. Or try **Amelia Island Resort Rentals,** 5012 First Coast Hwy. (P.O. Box 6159), Amelia Island, FL 32035 (☎ 800/ 874-8679 or 904/261-9444; fax 904/261-9479; www.amelia.com).

The island has two chain motels: a **Hampton Inn** (☎ 800/HAMPTON or 904/321-1111) and a **Shoney's Inn** (☎ 800/222-2222 or 904/277-2300), both on Sadler Road a block from the beach.

Your best **camping** option here is Fort Clinch State Park (see "Hitting the Beach," above).

✪ **Amelia Island Plantation.** 3000 First Coast Hwy., Amelia Island, FL 32034. ☎ **800/ 874-6878** or 904/261-6161. Fax 904/277-5159. 680 units (including 430 villas). A/C TV TEL. $140–$262 double; $163–$610 villa. Highest rates mid-Mar to April. Packages available. AE, DISC, MC, V.

This huge real estate development occupies 1,250 lush beachfront acres that encompass manicured emerald golf greens as well as a breathtaking coastal wilderness of marshes and lagoons. Towering oaks form a leafy canopy over the grounds, which are home to herons, egrets, sea turtles, deer, and other wildlife.

Guests choose this rustically elegant resort for its natural beauty and its outstanding sports offerings. Most notable are the two consistently top-rated championship golf courses open to resort guests; they comprise 54 holes (designed by Pete Dye and Tom Fazio) bordering the ocean, swamps, marshes, and woodlands. The Long Point course, a breathtakingly beautiful 18-holer, has two par-3s in a row bordering the ocean.

The plantation's 27 tennis courts (ranked among the nation's top 50 by *Tennis* magazine) are the setting for many professional tournaments, including the annual Bausch & Lomb Championships. The fitness center is state of the art, and there are 21 swimming pools dotting the complex.

There are 250 spacious upscale rooms in a beachfront hotel, but most of the accommodations here are one- to three-bedroom privately owned homes that are rented out most of the year. All but a few have balconies or patios. Each is uniquely decorated with an eclectic mix of high-end furnishings. All offer fully equipped kitchens, living and dining areas, washer/dryers, hair dryers, and safes (VCRs can be rented).

Dining: The plantation's signature dining room, with stunning ocean and golf-course views, offers exceptional continental dining. There's dancing and entertainment in an adjoining lounge with an awninged terrace. A less-formal grill overlooking woodlands specializes in fresh seafood. Other facilities include a sports-themed ocean-front restaurant and bar and a golf-course snack shop and restaurant.

Amenities: Concierge, room service, tram transport around the property, shuttle to/from downtown Fernandina, nightly turndown on request, baby-sitting and kid's activities program, golf and tennis pro shops, resident tennis and golf pros/clinics, health and fitness center (including racquetball, indoor/outdoor lap pool, steam, sauna, whirlpool, massage, spa treatments, and more), unisex hair salon, 7 miles of bike and hiking trails, deep-sea and other fishing, bicycle rental, year-round counselor-supervised youth program for ages 3 through teens, horseback riding, sailing, basketball court, three children's playgrounds, boat and beach rentals in season, clothing boutiques, convenience store, snack shops, and gift store.

✪ **Beachside Motel Inn.** 3172 S. Fletcher Ave. (Fla. A1A, south of Simmons Rd.), Fernandina Beach, FL 32034. ☎ **904/261-4236.** Fax 904/261-8336. 20 units. A/C TV TEL. $65–$103 double; $79–$139 efficiency. Weekly discounts available. AE, MC, V.

The only motel beside the beach here, this inexpensive property is clean and well maintained by resident owners Jerry and Joy Knight. The white and blue 2-story 1970s stucco building sits on a beautiful stretch of public but uncluttered beach. The rooms, many with ocean views, are spacious and furnished with standard motel furnishings. Many long-term visitors return each season to stay in the efficiencies with fully equipped kitchens. An outdoor pool is surrounded by lounge chairs and a spacious deck overlooking the ocean. The hotel is convenient to lots of sports activities and good restaurants (The Surf Restaurant and its outdoor pub is directly across the road). Room rates include free coffee each morning and a selection of store-bought breakfast rolls, doughnuts, and pastries.

Elizabeth Pointe Lodge. 98 S. Fletcher Dr. (just south of Atlantic Ave.), Fernandina Beach, FL 32034. ☎ **800/772-3359** or 904/277-4851. Fax 904/277-6500. 24 units, 1 cottage. A/C TV TEL. $125–$195 double; $215 cottage. Rates include buffet breakfast and evening social hour. Packages available. AE, DISC, MC, V.

Sitting right on the beach, this three-story, Nantucket-style shingle-sided building's Victorian appearance belies the fact that it was built in 1991 by B&B guru David Caples. Big-paned windows look out from the comfy lounge (with library and fireplace) and dining room to an expansive front porch and the surf beyond. Antiques and reproductions, handmade quilts, and other touches lend the 20 rooms in the main building a turn-of-the-century cottage ambience. They all have oversize bathtubs (some with Jacuzzi jets), robes, irons, and ironing boards. Four other rooms are in the Harris Lodge next door, and there's the two-bedroom, two-bathroom Mills Cottage for rent. The main house's dining room provides breakfast, a light-fare lunch and dinner menu, and 24-hour room service.

✪ Fairbanks House. 227 South 7th St. (between Beech and Cedar sts.), Fernandina Beach, Amelia Island, FL 32034. ☎ **800/261-4838** or 904-277-0500. Fax 904/277-3103. 9 units, 3 detached cottages. A/C TV TEL. $125–$225 double; $175 cottage. Rates include full breakfast. AE, DISC, MC, V.

With all the amenities and almost as much privacy as a first-class hotel in a superbly refurbished 1885 Italianate home, the Fairbanks House is a top B&B choice for those looking to be pampered. Many rooms and all the cottages offer private entrances for guests who prefer not to walk through the main house. Room no. 3, in the back of the house on the main floor, is one of the finest rooms, with a private entrance, a large sitting room, a plush king-size bed, period antiques, porcelain, oil paintings, and fresh flowers. Occupying the entire top floor, the two-bedroom Tower Suite has plenty of room to spread out, plus 360° views and its own Jacuzzi. Note that Fairbanks is the only B&B on the island with a pool. No smoking indoors.

✪ Ritz-Carlton Amelia Island. 4750 Amelia Island Pkwy., Amelia Island, FL 32034. ☎ **800/241-3333** or 904/277-1100. Fax 904/261-9064. 449 units. A/C MINIBAR TV TEL. $129–$339 double; $289–$449 suite. Golf and tennis packages available. AE, DC, DISC, MC, V. Valet parking $9; free self-parking.

Opened in 1991 on 13 acres of stunning beachfront, this stand-out member of the world-renowned chain offers glitzier and grander accommodations than its older neighbor, the Amelia Island Plantation. Its public areas are adorned with millions of dollars worth of museum-quality art and furnishings. The dining rooms proffer award-winning cuisine, and the staff provides flawless Ritz-style service. Extensive recreational facilities include 9 tennis courts and a beautiful and challenging 18-hole championship golf course.

The exquisite guest rooms—all oceanfront or ocean view, with balconies or patios—are furnished in handsome mahogany pieces. You'll find VCRs, safes, hair dryers, scales, cosmetic mirrors, and extra phones in the magnificent marble bathrooms. Concierge-level guests enjoy a stunning lounge with a working fireplace.

Dining: The Ritz-Carlton offers three main dining venues. Overlooking the ocean, The Grill is one of the best restaurants in the state. The plush lobby lounge is the setting for traditional afternoon teas on weekends; it has a working fireplace with floor-to-ceiling beachfront windows as well as outdoor patio seating. A cafe serves regional American fare at all meals and features healthful macrobiotic fare as well. Also, a gourmet take-out shop sells the oft-requested Ritz dressings, condiments, and sauces in addition to salads, sandwiches, and decadent desserts.

Amenities: Concierge, 24-hour room service, nightly turndown, dry cleaning and laundry services, free daily newspaper, twice-daily maid service, baby-sitting/nannies, secretarial services, express checkout, outdoor pool on a palm-fringed island between the beach and beautiful manicured lawns, heated indoor pool, fitness center, personal trainers by advance reservation, whirlpool, sauna, spa treatments, bicycle rental, 18-hole golf course, resident golf and tennis pros, golf lessons and swing seminars, counselor-supervised program for children 3 to 17, children's playground, business center, conference rooms, 9 night-lit tennis courts, golf and tennis pro shops, beauty salon, boutiques, jet-ski, sailboat, kayak, and beach rentals (umbrellas, cabanas, chaise longues) in summer.

WHERE TO DINE

In addition to Shakespeare's Kitchen (see below), you'll find several restaurants, pubs, and snack shops along Centre Street, between the bay and 8th Street (Fla. A1A), in Fernandina Beach's old town.

✪ **Beech Street Grill.** 801 Beech St. (at 8th St./Fla. A1A), Fernandina Beach. ☎ **904/277-3662.** Reservations strongly suggested. Main courses $17–$25; pastas $12–$17. AE, DC, DISC, MC, V. Daily 6–10pm. REGIONAL NEW AMERICAN.

Surpassed only by The Grill in the Ritz-Carlton as the island's best restaurant, the Beech Street Grill pleases all palates with a large menu of fish, chicken, and meat choices including seasonal game like roasted venison loin in a black currant sauce with sweet potato and onion hash. Nightly fish specialties are always exceptional, but be sure to ask the price, since some can be higher than printed menu options. A Parmesan-encrusted grouper with a tropical fruit salsa is superb. When available, seared tuna is always perfect, too. The dense and tasty crab cakes or the chewy steamed dumplings are great choices for starters, as is the huge mixed green salad with mustard-basil vinaigrette and toasted pecans and blue cheese. Housed in a century-old landmark home and a newer addition adjacent to the original building, three dining rooms offer large tables in a lively atmosphere. Attentive and knowledgeable waiters serve the showy plates with efficiency and grace.

Cafe Atlantis. 22 S. 4th St. (½ block south of Centre St.). ☎ **904/277-0042.** Reservations suggested. Main courses $17–$22. AE, DC, DISC, MC, V. Daily 5:30–9:30pm. ECLECTIC/NEW WORLD.

Chef/owner Brian Batsel, who left a cooking position at the Ritz-Carlton and who earlier broke in his Southwestern cuisine spurs at the notable Red Sage in Washington, D.C., expands his range here to include Asian-inspired salads, Caribbean pork and chicken dishes, Spanish seafood stews, and local seafood specialties to create a thoroughly exciting menu. Offered on a bitter chilly January night, the black-bean soup with cilantro and a cream garnish was rich and tasty, if a little tame. Ask for hot sauce; you'll get the real thing, a bright orange scotch bonnet pepper puree with a real kick.

✪ **Shakespeare's Kitchen.** Upstairs at 316 Centre St. (between 3rd and 4th sts. ☎ **904/277-2076.** Sandwiches and salads $6–$8; dinner main courses $10–$13. DISC, MC, V. Mon–Sat 8–10:30am and 11:30am–3pm, Thurs–Sat 6–10pm, Sun 10am–2pm. SANDWICHES/SALADS.

A tiny and sunny dining room hidden on the second floor of a store on Centre Street, Linda Harter's seedsy-weedsy spot provides hearty and healthful breakfasts, homemade sandwiches like roasted bell peppers and goat cheese on rustic white bread, and salads such as blackened chicken and pasta. Linda serves her sandwiches with a side such as pasta salad with fresh herbs and field greens, making for a substantial portion. Dinner sees a few main courses added to the mix, usually pastas. You can wash it down with a glass of perfumed Hawaiian iced tea. A loyal following of young professionals and shoppers chows down at the small antique tables inside or at wrought-iron versions out on a rooftop deck.

AMELIA ISLAND AFTER DARK

This romantic island goes to bed early. If you tire of the lounges in the island's resorts, check out the **Palace Saloon,** 117 Centre St., at 2nd St. (☎ **904/261-6320**). It claims to be Florida's oldest watering hole (open since 1878). Complete with a pressed-tin ceiling and a mahogany bar, it once hosted the Carnegies and the du Ponts; now, a lively bar and an adjacent pool bar and stage area are often packed. Some nights you'll find live local blues or rock.

Index

Page numbers in italics refer to maps.

FROMMER'S® COMPLETE TRAVEL GUIDES

(Comprehensive guides with selections in all price ranges—from deluxe to budget)

Alaska
Amsterdam
Arizona
Atlanta
Australia
Austria
Bahamas
Barcelona, Madrid & Seville
Belgium, Holland &
  Luxembourg
Bermuda
Boston
Budapest & the Best of
  Hungary
California
Canada
Cancún, Cozumel & the
  Yucatán
Cape Cod, Nantucket &
  Martha's Vineyard
Caribbean
Caribbean Cruises &
  Ports of Call
Caribbean Ports of Call
Carolinas & Georgia
Chicago
China
Colorado
Costa Rica
Denver, Boulder &
  Colorado Springs
England
Europe
Florida

France
Germany
Greece
Hawaii
Hong Kong
Honolulu, Waikiki & Oahu
Ireland
Israel
Italy
Jamaica & Barbados
Japan
Las Vegas
London
Los Angeles
Maryland & Delaware
Maui
Mexico
Miami & the Keys
Montana & Wyoming
Montréal & Québec City
Munich & the Bavarian Alps
Nashville & Memphis
Nepal
New England
New Mexico
New Orleans
New York City
Nova Scotia, New
  Brunswick &
  Prince Edward Island
Oregon
Paris
Philadelphia & the Amish
  Country

Portugal
Prague & the Best of the
  Czech Republic
Provence & the Riviera
Puerto Rico
Rome
San Antonio & Austin
San Diego
San Francisco
Santa Fe, Taos &
  Albuquerque
Scandinavia
Scotland
Seattle & Portland
Singapore & Malaysia
South Pacific
Spain
Switzerland
Thailand
Tokyo
Toronto
Tuscany & Umbria
USA
Utah
Vancouver & Victoria
Vermont, New Hampshire &
  Maine
Vienna & the Danube Valley
Virgin Islands
Virginia
Walt Disney World &
  Orlando
Washington, D.C.
Washington State

FROMMER'S® DOLLAR-A-DAY GUIDES

(The ultimate guides to comfortable low-cost travel)

Australia from $50 a Day
California from $60 a Day
Caribbean from $60 a Day
England from $60 a Day
Europe from $50 a Day
Florida from $60 a Day
Greece from $50 a Day
Hawaii from $60 a Day
Ireland from $50 a Day

Israel from $45 a Day
Italy from $50 a Day
London from $70 a Day
New York from $75 a Day
New Zealand from $50 a Day
Paris from $70 a Day
San Francisco from $60 a Day
Washington, D.C., from
  $60 a Day

FROMMER'S® MEMORABLE WALKS

Chicago
London

New York
Paris

San Francisco

FROMMER'S® PORTABLE GUIDES

Acapulco, Ixtapa/ Zihuatenejo	Dublin	Puerto Vallarta, Manzanillo & Guadalajara
Bahamas	Las Vegas	San Francisco
California Wine Country	London	Sydney
	Maine Coast	Tampa Bay & St. Petersburg
Charleston & Savannah	New Orleans	Venice
Chicago	New York City	Washington, D.C.
	Paris	

FROMMER'S® NATIONAL PARK GUIDES

Grand Canyon	Yosemite & Sequoia/
National Parks of the American West	Kings Canyon
Yellowstone & Grand Teton	Zion & Bryce Canyon

THE COMPLETE IDIOT'S TRAVEL GUIDES
(The ultimate user-friendly trip planners)

Cruise Vacations	Las Vegas	New York City
Planning Your Trip to Europe	Mexico's Beach Resorts	San Francisco
Hawaii	New Orleans	Walt Disney World

SPECIAL-INTEREST TITLES

The Civil War Trust's Official Guide to the Civil War Discovery Trail	Outside Magazine's Adventure Guide to the Pacific Northwest
Frommer's Caribbean Hideaways	Outside Magazine's Guide to Family Vacations
Israel Past & Present	Places Rated Almanac
New York City with Kids	Retirement Places Rated
New York Times Weekends	Washington, D.C., with Kids
Outside Magazine's Adventure Guide to New England	Wonderful Weekends from Boston
	Wonderful Weekends from New York City
Outside Magazine's Adventure Guide to Northern California	Wonderful Weekends from San Francisco
	Wonderful Weekends from Los Angeles

THE UNOFFICIAL GUIDES®
(Get the unbiased truth from these candid, value-conscious guides)

Atlanta	Florida with Kids	Miami & the Keys	Skiing in the West
Branson, Missouri	The Great Smoky	Mini-Mickey	Walt Disney World
Chicago	& Blue Ridge	New Orleans	Walt Disney World
Cruises	Mountains	New York City	Companion
Disneyland	Las Vegas	San Francisco	Washington, D.C.

FROMMER'S® IRREVERENT GUIDES
(Wickedly honest guides for sophisticated travelers)

Amsterdam	London	New Orleans	San Francisco
Boston	Manhattan	Paris	Walt Disney World
Chicago			Washington, D.C.

FROMMER'S® DRIVING TOURS

America	Florida	Ireland	Scotland
Britain	France	Italy	Spain
California	Germany	New England	Western Europe

WHEREVER YOU TRAVEL, *ℋ*ELP IS NEVER FAR AWAY.

From planning your trip to providing travel assistance along the way, American Express® Travel Service Offices are always there to help you do more.

Florida

American Express Travel Service
32 Miracle Mile
Coral Gables
305/446-3381

American Express Travel Service
330 Biscayne Boulevard
Miami
305/358-7350

American Express Travel Service
3312-14 N.E. 32nd Street
Fort Lauderdale
954/565-9481

American Express Travel Service
2 West Church Street, Suite 1
Orlando
407/843-0004

American Express Travel Service
9908 Baymeadows Road
Jacksonville
904/642-1701

American Express Travel Service
1390 Main Street
Sarasota
941/365-2520

American Express Travel Service
Epcot Center
Walt Disney World Resort
Lake Buena Vista
407/827-7500

American Express Travel Service
One Tampa City Center
Tampa
813/273-0310

Travel

http://www.americanexpress.com/travel

American Express Travel Service Offices are located throughout Florida. For the office nearest you, call 1-800-AXP-3429.